AN INTRODUCTION TO POLICING

EIGHTH EDITION

AN INTRODUCTION TO POLICING

EIGHTH EDITION

John S. Dempsey

Captain, New York City Police Department (Retired)
Professor Emeritus of Criminal Justice,
Suffolk Community College
Mentor in Criminal Justice and Public Administration,
SUNY-Empire State College

Linda S. Forst

Captain, Boca Raton Police Department (Retired)
Professor of Criminal Justice, Shoreline Community College

CENGAGE
Learning®

Australia • Brazil • Mexico • Singapore • United Kingdom • United States

An Introduction to Policing, 8ᵗʰ Edition
John S. Dempsey, Linda S. Forst

Product Director: Marta Lee-Perriard

Product Manager: Carolyn Henderson-Meier

Content Developer: Margaux Cameron

Media Developer: Jessica Alderman

Product Assistant: Stephen Lagos

Marketing Manager: Kara Kindstrom

Content Project Manager: Rita Jaramillo

Art Director: PMG, Brenda Carmichael

Manufacturing Planner: Judy Inouye

Production Service: Integra, Alverne Bell

Photo Researcher: Hemalatha Dhanapal

Text Researcher: Pinky Subi

Copy Editor: Nina Taylor

Text and Cover Designer: Lumina Datamatics

Compositor: Integra Software Services Pvt. Ltd.

Cover image credit: justasc/Shutterstock

© 2016, 2014 Cengage Learning

WCN: 01-100-101

ALL RIGHTS RESERVED. No part of this work covered by the copyright herein may be reproduced, transmitted, stored, or used in any form or by any means graphic, electronic, or mechanical, including but not limited to photocopying, recording, scanning, digitizing, taping, Web distribution, information networks, or information storage and retrieval systems, except as permitted under Section 107 or 108 of the 1976 United States Copyright Act, without the prior written permission of the publisher.

For product information and technology assistance, contact us at
Cengage Learning Customer & Sales Support, 1-800-354-9706.

For permission to use material from this text or product,
submit all requests online at **www.cengage.com/permissions**.
Further permissions questions can be e-mailed to
permissionrequest@cengage.com

Library of Congress Control Number: 2014939369

Student Edition:
ISBN-13: 978-1-285-86273-6

Loose-leaf Edition:
ISBN-13: 978-1-305-63340-7

Cengage Learning
20 Channel Center Street
Boston, MA 02210
USA

Cengage Learning is a leading provider of customized learning solutions with office locations around the globe, including Singapore, the United Kingdom, Australia, Mexico, Brazil, and Japan. Locate your local office at **www.cengage.com/global**.

Cengage Learning products are represented in Canada by Nelson Education, Ltd.

To learn more about Cengage Learning Solutions, visit **www.cengage.com**.

Purchase any of our products at your local college store or at our preferred online store **www.cengagebrain.com**.

Printed in the United States of America
Print Number: 03   Print Year: 2016

DEDICATION

To my family: Marianne, John, Donna, Cathy, Diane, Danny, Nikki, Erin, and John, and in memory of Anne Marie (1970–2002); also, in memory of James J. Fyfe and Patrick J. Ryan. —J.S.D.

This book is dedicated to my late husband, Captain James E. Duke, Jr. (pictured below), and our beautiful daughters, Brynn and Juleigh, as well as my new son-in-law, Taylor. —L.S.F.

HONORING THE MEMORY AND CELEBRATING THE LIFE OF JOHN S. DEMPSEY (JACK)

Jack Dempsey, senior author of *An Introduction to Policing, Introduction to Investigations, Introduction to Private Security*, and *POLICE* died on Sunday, August 3, 2014, in New York at the age of 68. Jack was a member of the New York Police Department from 1964 to 1988, rising through the ranks of police officer, sergeant, lieutenant, and captain. He received his BA from John Jay College of Criminal Justice, his Masters in criminal justice from Long Island University, and his Masters in public administration from Harvard University, John F. Kennedy School of Government.

Upon his retirement from law enforcement, Jack dedicated his time and efforts to teaching and mentoring students at Suffolk Community College and State University of New York, Empire College and across the country. He was awarded the prestigious "Who Made a Difference Award" from Suffolk Community College for his dedication to his students.

Jack's commitment to professional law enforcement was visible in everything he did. It is impossible to know just how many students and police officers he influenced and educated as his books are widely read across the nation. Jack had a magnetic personality and a lot of charisma, making it easy for him to share his beliefs in ethical and professional law enforcement as well as his unending desire to serve his community and students in any way that he could.

He was also devoted to his family and was so happy to spend time relaxing with his wife, children, and grandchildren. He always had pictures to show, stories to tell and we all knew he was the "Grand Dude." He was well known for his infectious laugh, sense of humor, and New York accent!

Law enforcement is more professional, police officers are safer, and society has benefited due to Jack's efforts. For those of us lucky enough to know him personally, he impacted our lives tremendously and we will be forever grateful for his friendship, kindness, generosity, support, and mentoring. Jack's legacy will live on for generations.

Linda Forst

BRIEF CONTENTS

PART I

Police History and Organization

1 Police History | 2
2 Organizing Public Security in the United States | 39
3 Organizing the Police Department | 71

PART II

The Personal Side of Policing

4 Becoming a Police Officer | 104
5 The Police Role and Police Discretion | 133
6 Police Culture, Personality, and Stress | 161
7 Minorities in Policing | 193
8 Police Ethics and Police Deviance | 226

PART III

Police Operations

9 Patrol Operations | 260
10 Investigations | 298
11 Police and Their Clients | 328
12 Community Policing | 363
13 Police and the Law | 394

PART IV

Critical Issues in Policing

14 Computers, Technology, and Criminalistics in Policing | 458
15 Homeland Security | 525

CONTENTS

About the Authors | xvii
Preface | xix

PART I
Police History and Organization | 1

CHAPTER 1

Police History | 2

Early Police | 3

English Policing: Our Heritage | 4

  Early History | 4

  Seventeenth-Century Policing:
    Thief-Takers | 5

  Henry Fielding and the Bow Street
    Runners | 6

  Peel's Police: The Metropolitan Police
    for London | 6

American Policing:
The Colonial Experience | 9

  The North: The Watch | 9

  The South: Slave Patrols and Codes | 9

American Policing: Eighteenth and
Nineteenth Centuries | 10

  The Urban Experience | 10

  The Southern Experience | 15

  The Frontier Experience | 15

American Policing: Twentieth and
Twenty-First Centuries | 17

  Policing from 1900 to 1960 | 17

  Policing in the 1960s and 1970s | 20

  Policing in the 1980s and 1990s | 26

  Policing in the 2000s | 29

CHAPTER 2

Organizing Public Security in the United States | 39

The U.S. Public Security Industry | 40

Local Law Enforcement | 42

  Metropolitan Law Enforcement | 43

  County Law Enforcement | 45

  Rural and Small-Town Law Enforcement | 46

  Indian Country and Tribal Law Enforcement | 48

  Campus Law Enforcement | 49

  Local Law Enforcement and Illegal Immigration | 50

Law Enforcement in the Era of Reduced
Budgets | 51

State Law Enforcement | 55

Federal Law Enforcement | 56

  Department of Justice | 56

  Department of the Treasury | 61

  Department of Homeland Security | 62

  Department of the Interior | 62

  Department of Defense | 63

  U.S. Postal Service | 63

  Other Federal Enforcement Agencies | 63

  Joint Federal and Local Task Force Approach
    to Law Enforcement | 66

International Police | 66

CHAPTER 3

Organizing the Police Department | 71

Organizing the Department:
Managerial Concepts | 72

Division of Labor | 72

Managerial Definitions | 72

Managers, Supervisors... or Leaders? | 74

Ethical Leadership | 75

Traditional Organizational Model and Structure | 75

Chain of Command | 78

Span of Control | 82

Delegation of Responsibility and Authority | 82

Unity of Command | 82

Rules, Regulations, and Discipline | 82

Alternative Organizational Models and Structures | 82

Organizing by Personnel | 84

The Civil Service System | 84

Sworn and Nonsworn (Civilian) Personnel | 85

Rank Structure | 86

Other Personnel | 89

Lateral Transfers | 91

Police Unions | 91

Organizing by Area | 93

Beats | 93

Precincts/Districts/Stations | 93

Organizing by Time | 95

The Three-Tour System | 95

Tour Length: 8 Hours, 10 Hours, or 12 Hours | 95

Tour Conditions | 96

Steady (Fixed) Tours | 97

Organizing by Function or Purpose | 97

Line and Staff (Support) Functions | 97

Police Department Units | 98

PART II

The Personal Side of Policing | 103

CHAPTER 4

Becoming a Police Officer | 104

Finding Information on Jobs in Policing | 106

Standards in Police Selection | 107

Physical Requirements | 107

Smoking | 107

Age Requirements | 108

Education Requirements | 108

Prior Drug Use | 110

Criminal Record Restrictions | 111

The Recruitment Process | 111

The Job Analysis | 113

The Selection Process | 114

Characteristics of Good Police Officers | 115

Written Examination | 116

Physical Agility Test | 117

Polygraph Examination | 118

Oral Interview | 118

Background Investigation | 120

Psychological Appraisal | 120

Medical Examination | 121

The Police Training Process | 121

Recruit Training | 122

The Police Academy | 122

Field Training | 123

Probationary Period | 127

Firearms Training | 128

In-Service, Management, and Specialized Training | 128

CHAPTER 5

The Police Role and Police Discretion | 133

The Police Role | 134
  Crime-Fighting Role | 134
  Order-Maintenance Role | 136

Ambiguity of the Police Role | 136
  The Police Role in the Aftermath of 9/11 | 137

Goals and Objectives of Policing | 140
  Primary Goals and Objectives | 140
  Secondary Goals and Objectives | 140

Police Operational Styles | 140

Police Discretion | 142
  What Is Discretion? | 143
  How Is Discretion Exercised? | 144
  Why Is Discretion Exercised? | 144
  What Factors Influence Discretion? | 144
  How Can Discretion Be Controlled? | 147
  CALEA Standards | 148

Police Shootings and the Use of Deadly Force | 149
  Police Use of Force | 150
  Number of Citizens Shot by the Police | 151
  Do Police Discriminate with Their Trigger Fingers? | 151
  Departure from the "Fleeing Felon" Rule | 152
  Firearms Training | 154
  Less-than-Lethal Force | 155

CHAPTER 6

Police Culture, Personality, and Stress | 161

The Police Culture or Subculture | 162
  The Blue Wall of Silence | 164

The Police Personality | 165
  What Is the Police Personality? | 165
  Is the Police Personality Innate or Learned? | 166

  Police Cynicism | 167
  The *Dirty Harry* Problem | 167

Police Stress | 168
  What Is Stress? | 169
  Nature of Stress in Policing | 169
  Factors Causing Stress in Policing | 171
  Effects of Stress on Police Officers | 174
  Stress and Police Families | 176
  Police Departments Dealing with Stress | 176

Police Suicide | 178

Police Danger | 181
  Officers Killed in the Line of Duty | 181
  Officers Assaulted in the Line of Duty | 183
  Police and Contagious Diseases | 183

CHAPTER 7

Minorities in Policing | 193

Discrimination in Policing | 194
  Discrimination Against Women | 194
  Discrimination Against African Americans | 196

How Did Women and Minorities Strive for Equality? | 197
  The Civil Rights Act of 1964 | 198
  The Omnibus Crime Control and Safe Streets Act of 1968 | 198
  The Equal Employment Opportunity Act of 1972 | 199
  The Civil Rights Act of 1991 | 199
  Federal Courts and Job Discrimination | 199
  Affirmative Action Programs | 200

White Male Backlash | 201

Minorities Proving Themselves on the Job | 203
  Academic Studies | 203

Minorities in Policing Today | 208
  Female Representation | 208
  African American Representation | 210
  Hispanic Representation | 211
  Asian Representation | 212

Muslim Representation | 213

Gay and Lesbian Representation | 213

Challenges Persist for Minorities in Policing | 215

Challenges for Women | 215

Challenges for African Americans | 220

Challenges for Other Minorities | 221

CHAPTER 8

Police Ethics and Police Deviance | 226

Ethics and the Police | 227

The Dilemma of Law Versus Order | 229

Review of the Police | 229

Police Corruption | 231

Corruption Makes Good Books and Films | 231

Examples of Police Corruption | 232

Reasons for Police Corruption | 233

Types and Forms of Corruption | 234

Noble Cause Corruption | 235

Effects of Police Corruption | 236

Other Police Misconduct | 238

Drug-Related Misconduct | 238

Sleeping on Duty | 238

Police Deception | 238

Sex-Related Misconduct | 239

Domestic Violence in Police Families | 241

Biased-Based Policing | 243

Police Brutality | 246

Responses to Police Corruption | 247

Investigations | 247

Discipline and Termination | 248

Preventive Administrative Actions | 248

Citizen Oversight | 250

Police Civil and Criminal Liability | 251

State Liability | 252

Federal Liability | 252

Reasons for Suing Police Officers | 253

Effects of Lawsuits on Police Departments and Officers | 254

The Emotional Toll of Police Lawsuits | 254

PART III

Police Operations | 259

CHAPTER 9

Patrol Operations | 260

Traditional Methods of Police Work | 261

Police Patrol Operations | 261

Activities of the Patrol Officer | 262

The Legacy of O. W. Wilson | 262

Evaluating the Effectiveness of Police Work | 262

Random Routine Patrol: The Kansas City Study | 263

Rapid Response to Citizens' 911 Calls | 264

Academic Studies of the Police Patrol Function | 265

From the Foot Beat to the Patrol Car | 266

One-Officer Versus Two-Officer Patrol Cars | 268

Return to Foot Patrol | 269

Patrol Innovations: Working Smarter | 270

Evidence-Based Policing | 270

Predictive Policing | 270

Smart Policing | 271

Personnel Deployment | 272

Directing Patrol Efforts | 272

Differential Response to Calls for Service and the 911 System | 273

Reverse 911 | 274

Smart911 | 275

Allocation of Resources | 275

Personnel | 275

Vehicles | 276

Alternative Strategies | 277

Tactical Operations | 277

Specialized Policing Responses to Individuals with Mental Illness | 279

Decoy Vehicles | 281

Alternative Vehicle Deployment | 282

Police Traffic Operations | 284

Video Camera Traffic Enforcement | 286

The Challenge of Distracted Drivers | 286

Efforts Against Drunk Drivers and Impaired Drivers | 287

Fighting Aggressive Driving | 288

Police Automobile Pursuits | 289

Other Police Operational Units | 291

SWAT Teams and Police Paramilitary Units | 292

K-9 Units | 293

CHAPTER 10

Investigations | 298

Retroactive Investigation of Past Crimes by Detectives | 299

Detective Operations | 300

The Investigative Process | 300

What Detectives Do | 301

The Detective Mystique | 302

Alternatives to Retroactive Investigation of Past Crimes by Detectives | 303

Improved Investigation of Past Crimes | 304

Managing Criminal Investigations (MCI) | 304

Mentoring and Training | 305

Crime Analysis and Information Management | 305

Crime Analysis | 305

Information Management | 306

Multiagency Investigative Task Forces | 307

Repeat Offender Programs (ROPs) | 309

Internet Registries | 312

Global Positioning System (GPS) Technology, Smartphones, and Social Media | 313

Surveillance Cameras | 314

Cold-Case Squads | 315

Proactive Tactics | 316

Decoy Operations | 316

Stakeout Operations | 317

Sting Operations | 318

Cybercrime Investigations | 320

Undercover Operations | 320

Police Undercover Investigations | 321

Federal Undercover Investigations | 321

Drug Undercover Investigations | 321

Entrapment | 323

CHAPTER 11

Police and Their Clients | 328

The Need for Proper Police–Community Relationships | 329

Human Relations, Public Relations, Community Relations | 330

Public Opinion and the Police | 333

Police and Minority Communities | 334

Multiculturalism | 334

African Americans | 335

Hispanic Americans | 335

Asian Americans | 336

Native Americans | 336

Arab Americans and Muslims | 337

Jews | 338

Women | 338

Gays and Lesbians | 339

New Immigrants | 339

Police and Special Populations | 341

The Physically Challenged | 341

The Aging Population | 342

Young People | 343

Crime Victims | 347

Victims of Domestic Violence | 348

The Mentally Ill | 350

The Homeless | 351

Community Crime Prevention Programs | 352

Neighborhood Watch Programs | 352

National Night Out | 353

Citizen Patrols | 353

Citizen Volunteer Programs | 353

Home Security Surveys and Operation Identification | 355

Police Storefront Stations or Ministations | 355

Crime Stoppers | 355

Mass Media Campaigns | 355

Chaplain Programs | 357

Citizen Police Academies | 357

Other Police-Sponsored Crime Prevention Programs | 358

Police and Business Cooperation | 358

CHAPTER 12

Community Policing | 363

Corporate Strategies for Policing | 364

The Philosophy of Community Policing and Problem-Solving Policing | 365

Community Policing | 367

Problem-Solving Policing | 370

Successful Examples of Community-Oriented Policing | 372

Community Policing Today | 373

Resident Officer Programs: The Ultimate in Community Policing? | 376

The Federal Government and Community Policing | 379

The Crime Bill | 379

Office of Community Oriented Policing Services (COPS) | 379

Some Accomplishments of Community Policing | 382

The Debate Continues on Community Policing | 383

Homeland Security and the Future of Community Policing | 388

CHAPTER 13

Police and the Law | 394

Crime in the United States | 395

The Judicial Process | 395

How Do We Measure Crime? | 396

How Much Crime Occurs in the United States? | 397

Arrests in the United States | 398

Crime and Punishment | 398

The Police and the U.S. Constitution | 399

The Bill of Rights and the Fourteenth Amendment | 402

The Role of the Supreme Court in Regulating the Police | 403

The Exclusionary Rule | 403

The Police and Arrest | 407

Probable Cause | 408

Reasonable and Deadly Force in Making Arrests | 410

Police Traffic Stops | 411

The Police and Search and Seizure | 414

Canine Sniffs | 416

The Warrant Requirement and the Search Warrant | 417

Exceptions to the Warrant Requirement | 421

The Police and Custodial Interrogation | 432

The Path to *Miranda* | 432

The *Miranda* Ruling | 434

The Erosion of *Miranda* | 435

The *Dickerson* Ruling and Beyond | 441

Police and Surreptitious Recording of Suspects' Conversations | 445

Police Eyewitness Identification Procedures | 446

Lineups, Showups, and Photo Arrays | 446

Other Identification Procedures | 448

PART IV
Critical Issues in Policing | 457

CHAPTER 14

Computers, Technology, and Criminalistics in Policing | 458

Computer Technology in Policing | 459
  Computer-Aided Dispatch (CAD) | 460
  Automated Databases | 463
  Automated Crime Analysis
    (Crime Mapping) | 464
  Computer-Aided Investigation (Computer-Aided
    Case Management) | 465
  Computer-Assisted Instruction | 467
  Administrative Uses of Computers | 467
  Computer Networks and the Internet | 469
  Mobile Technology | 469

Fingerprint Technology | 472
  Basic Categories of Fingerprints | 473
  Automated Fingerprint Identification
    Systems | 475
  Automated Palm Print Technology | 478

Less-than-Lethal Weapons | 478
  Chemical Irritant Sprays | 479
  The Taser and Other Stun Devices | 479
  Safety and Effectiveness of Less-than-Lethal
    Weapons | 479

Surveillance Technology | 482
  Surveillance Vans | 482
  Vehicle Tracking Systems | 483
  Night Vision Devices | 483
  Global Positioning Systems | 484
  Surveillance Aircraft | 484
  Electronic Video Surveillance | 485
  Cell Phone Monitoring | 487

Advanced Photographic Techniques | 488
  Digital Photography | 488
  Aerial Photography | 488
  Mug Shot Imaging | 488
  Age-Progression Photographs | 489
  Composite Sketches | 489

Modern Forensics or Criminalistics | 490
  The *CSI* Effect | 492
  The Modern Crime Lab | 493
  Crime Lab Accreditation | 497
  Computer/Digital Forensics | 498

DNA Profiling | 501
  The Science of DNA | 502
  The History of DNA in U.S. Courts | 504
  Current Technology | 506
  DNA Databases | 506
  Other Current DNA Issues | 507

Biometric Identification | 509

Videotaping | 511

Robotics | 511

Concerns About Technology and
Civil Liberties | 512

CHAPTER 15

Homeland Security | 525

Homeland Security | 526

Terrorism | 527
  International Terrorism | 528
  Domestic Terrorism | 532

Methods of Investigating Terrorism | 537
  Proactive Methods | 537
  Reactive Methods | 537

Post-9/11 Response to Terrorism and
Homeland Defense | 540
  9/11 Commission's Review of Efforts for Homeland
    Security | 541

Federal Law Enforcement Efforts for Homeland Security | 543

Department of Homeland Security (DHS) | 543

Federal Bureau of Investigation (FBI) | 545

Secure Communities: DHS and FBI | 546

Office of the Director of National Intelligence (ODNI) | 547

Other Federal Agencies | 547

State and Local Law Enforcement Efforts for Homeland Security | 549

Security Versus Civil Liberties | 557

Glossary | 569

Index | 581

JOHN S. DEMPSEY was a member of the New York City Police Department (NYPD) from 1964 to 1988. He served in the ranks of police officer, detective, sergeant, lieutenant, and captain. His primary assignments were patrol and investigations. He received seven citations from the department for meritorious and excellent police duty. After retiring from the NYPD, Mr. Dempsey served until 2003 as Professor of Criminal Justice at Suffolk County Community College on Eastern Long Island where he won the college's prestigious "Who Made a Difference Award" for his teaching and work with students. In 2005, he was designated Professor Emeritus by the college. Mr. Dempsey also serves as a mentor at the State University of New York, Empire College, where he teaches criminal justice and public administration courses and mentors ranking members of law enforcement and criminal justice agencies.

In addition to this book, Mr. Dempsey is the author of *Introduction to Investigations*, Second Edition (Thomson Wadsworth, 2003), *POLICE2* (Delmar/Cengage Learning, 2013), and *Introduction to Private Security*, Second Edition (Wadsworth/Cengage Learning, 2011).

Mr. Dempsey holds A.A. and B.A. degrees in behavioral science from the City University of New York, John Jay College of Criminal Justice; a master's degree in criminal justice from Long Island University; and a master's degree in public administration from Harvard University, the John F. Kennedy School of Government. He is a member of the Academy of Criminal Justice Sciences (ACJS), the International Association of Chiefs of Police, ASIS International, the Northeastern Association of Criminal Justice Sciences (NEACJS), and the Criminal Justice Educators Association of New York State. His latest academic distinctions were the Outstanding Contributor Award from the ACJS Community College Section in 2004 and the Fellows Award from the NEACJS in 2005.

Mr. Dempsey is married and has four children and four grandchildren.

LINDA S. FORST is a retired police captain from the Boca Raton (Florida) Police Services Department. She joined the department in 1977 and served as a patrol officer, investigator, sergeant, lieutenant, and captain. She spent most of her career in patrol but also worked in investigations, professional standards, training, hiring, and support services. She was the first female field training officer, sergeant, lieutenant, and captain in the department. She has extensive training in accident investigation, domestic violence, sexual violence, community policing, and police management, and she served on the board of directors of the local battered women's shelter for many years. Together with a state representative, she contributed to the development of Florida's stalking law and amended the sexual battery statute to better serve the community. She received numerous commendations during her career, including Boca Raton's Citizen of the Year in 1994, and brought home many gold medals from the state and International Police Olympics while representing Boca Raton.

Ms. Forst earned her B.A. in criminal justice, M.Ed. in community college education, and Ed.D. in adult education from Florida Atlantic University. Her dissertation was on acquaintance rape prevention programs. She is a graduate of University of Louisville's Sex Crime Investigation School and Northwestern University's School of Police Staff and Command. Ms. Forst is the author of numerous publications in magazines, journals, and newspapers, and presents regularly at conferences and to community groups. She is the author of *The Aging of America: A Handbook for Police Officers* (Charles C. Thomas, 2000) and *POLICE* (Delmar/Cengage, 2011). Ms. Forst is a member of Academy of Criminal Justice Sciences, the Washington Association of Sheriffs and Police Chiefs, the International Association of Chiefs of Police, the International Association of Women Police, and the National Association of Women Law Enforcement Executives. She has instructed for Northwestern's School of Police Staff and Command as well as Palm Beach Community College and Florida Atlantic University. Currently she is a professor of criminal justice at Shoreline Community College in Seattle, Washington.

Ms. Forst is the mother of two daughters.

About the Contributor

STEVEN B. CARTER is a retired police sergeant from the Modesto (California) Police Department. He joined the department in 1985 as a Police Reserve and served as a police officer, detective, patrol sergeant, training sergeant, administrative services sergeant, and acting watch commander. While a patrol officer, he hosted a weekly live television show (*CrimeLine*) on the local cable station and was the recipient of a "Telly Award" for a segment on domestic violence. As a detective, he was assigned to economic crimes and burglary, and was a member of the homicide crime scene team, acting as crime scene manager. He has presented before the California State Assembly Central Valley Legislative Law Summit on computer crimes and law enforcement response. As administrative sergeant he supervised background investigations, and as training sergeant he proposed and implemented a departmental five-year training plan and started the "Leadership in Police Organizations" program. He is a graduate of the Los Angeles Police Department's West Point Leadership Program and is a California POST Master Instructor. He retired in 2007.

Mr. Carter earned a B.A. from Simpson College and is a consultant and subject matter expert with Steven Carter & Associates in Modesto, California. He is a member of the Academy of Criminal Justice Sciences and an associate member of the International Association of Chiefs of Police. He has served as a Peer Review Panel member for the Edward Byrne Grant Funding Program through the Department of Justice and is currently on the City of Modesto Planning Commission. He has authored several Cengage textbook supplements and is the author of *Instructor's Resource Manual with Test Bank* for *Introduction to Private Security* by John S. Dempsey.

Mr. Carter is married and has three daughters and six grandchildren.

An Introduction to Policing, Eighth Edition, is an introductory text for college students who are interested in learning who the police are, what they do, and how they do it. The policing profession is a noble one, and we sincerely hope this text teaches those preparing to enter law enforcement how to continue in this great tradition.

This book provides a general overview of policing in our society so that students can understand why and how policing is performed. It is, above all, a text for students. It will show you the jobs available in policing, how you can go about getting them, what skills you will need, and what you will do when you get those jobs. In addition, we try to give you an idea, a sense, and a flavor of policing. We want you to get a clear look at policing, not only for your academic interest but, more importantly, to help you determine if policing is what you want to do with the rest of your life.

An Introduction to Policing explores the subject matter from the perspective of two individuals who have devoted their lives to active police work and education. We wrote this new edition, in part, out of a desire to combine the practical experience gained from a collective 44 years on the job in the field of policing with the equally valuable insights gained from our years of formal education and teaching.

Changes to the Eighth Edition

In response to student and reviewer feedback, this edition provides the latest in academic and practitioner research as well as the latest applications, statistics, court cases, information on careers, and criminalistic and technological advances. As always, coauthor Linda Forst continues to lend additional geographic and gender perspective to the text.

The Eighth Edition continues to reflect the increasing emphasis on policing and homeland security, and we have added or strengthened topics such as community policing; self-defense and "stand your ground" laws; the new IACP Women's Leadership Institute; social media campaigns; cybercrime; the law enforcement partnership with the Special Olympics; police response to the mentally ill; budget issues and police academy funding; female, homosexual, and minority officers in the profession; drug investigations in light of emerging medical and recreational marijuana legislation; recognizing and responding to elder abuse; and more. This edition has seven new Guest Lectures by experts in the field on topics such as the Sandy Hook Elementary School shootings, the Wisconsin State Capitol protests, human trafficking, technology in child pornography investigations, and emerging new philosophies in the police academy. In addition to fully updated statistics, cases, and studies, the following updates have been made within chapters:

Chapter 2

- NEW Guest Lecture: "A Sound Base and Broad Mind Lead to Endless Successes and Countless Opportunities"
- NEW discussion of cooperation between law enforcement agencies in security efforts
- NEW On the Job: "Working Together Toward a Common Goal"
- Updated information on Operation Fast and Furious

Chapter 3

- NEW Table: Taylor's Four Scientific Management Principles
- NEW section: Lateral Transfers
- NEW topic: Fraternal Order of Police
- Updated explanation of team leadership principles

Chapter 4

- NEW Guest Lecture: "From Warriors to Guardians"
- Updated information about eligibility and education requirements for police applicants
- NEW information about recruiting through school-based programs

Chapter 5

- NEW Guest Lecture: "Trafficking Investigations Can Involve Expanding Police Roles"
- NEW topic: broken windows theory
- NEW coverage of workforce approaches for small departments
- NEW and updated discussion of race-based police discretion
- NEW and expanded topics: stop-and-frisk, drug and alcohol impairment, and domestic violence
- Updated discussion of use-of-force standards

Chapter 6

- NEW section: Post-Traumatic Stress Disorder
- NEW Table: Signs and Symptoms of Post-Traumatic Stress Disorder
- Expanded coverage of police suicide

Chapter 7

- NEW Guest Lecture: "No Prince Charming"
- Updated information on affirmative action Supreme Court rulings
- NEW and updated information on department statistics, recruiting efforts, leadership opportunities and examples, and other resources for minorities in policing

Chapter 8

- NEW information on sexual misconduct research and recommended policies from the IACP and racial profiling
- NEW topic: mediation meetings
- NEW topic: "uniform cams"
- Updated coverage of lawsuits against police departments

Chapter 9

- NEW section: Predictive Policing
- NEW section: Smart Policing
- NEW section: Smart911
- NEW section: Specialized Policing Responses to Individuals with Mental Illness
- NEW section: The Challenge of Distracted Drivers
- NEW topic: states' legalization of recreational marijuana
- NEW topic: motorcycle swarms
- NEW topic: swatting
- NEW You Are There!: "RADAR at the King County Sheriff's Office"

Chapter 10

- NEW Guest Lecture: "The Sandy Hook Elementary School Shooting Investigation and Response"
- NEW section: Surveillance Cameras
- NEW section: Cybercrime Investigations
- NEW topic: social media use in investigations, specifically the 2013 Boston Marathon bombing
- NEW topic: National Institute of Justice grant program "Solving Cold Cases with DNA"
- NEW topic: prescription drug fraud
- NEW discussion of multiagency investigative task forces in human trafficking

Chapter 11

- NEW You Are There!: "Law Enforcement and Special Olympics"
- NEW and updated information on domestic violence, including smartphone and social media use
- NEW coverage of mass media campaigns, specifically the 2013 Boston Marathon bombing

Chapter 12

- NEW topic: Detroit Mini-Station Program
- Updated coverage of the Elgin, Illinois, police department community outreach programs
- Updated information on the IACP Community Policing Awards

Chapter 13

- NEW Guest Lecture: "A View from the Interior: Policing the Protests at the Wisconsin State Capitol"

- NEW You Are There!: "The Castle Doctrine in 'Stand Your Ground' Laws"
- NEW You Are There!: "*Texas v. Cobb* (2001)"
- NEW You Are There!: "*Missouri v. Seibert* (2004)"
- NEW topic: canine sniff case law in *Florida v. Harris* (2013)
- NEW topic: NYPD stop-and-frisk encounters
- NEW topic: search consent in *Fernandez v. California* (2014)
- NEW topic: Americans with Disability Act in *Seremeth v. Frederick County et al.* (2012)
- NEW topic: medical procedures in *Missouri v. McNeely* (2013)

Chapter 14

- NEW Guest Lecture: "The Evolution of Technology and Child Pornography Investigations"
- NEW section: Cell Phone Monitoring
- NEW section: Drones
- NEW section: Identity Theft
- NEW coverage of cybercrime, including new key terms *phishing, Trojan horse,* and *spyware*
- Updated discussion of DNA collection

Chapter 15

- NEW topic and key term: terrorist watchlist
- Updated coverage of sovereign citizens
- Updated information on the National Security Council staff
- Updated coverage of the DHS
- Updated coverage of Secure Communities
- Updated information on agency training in homeland security, specifically small and mid-sized local agencies

Pedagogical Features

Within each chapter, we have included the following pedagogical elements:

- NEW *Learning Objectives* serve as chapter road maps to orient students to the primary knowledge goals of each chapter.
- *Chapter Introductions* preview the material to be covered in the chapter.

- *Chapter Summaries* reinforce the major topics discussed in the chapter and help students check their learning.
- *Review Exercises* are projects that require students to apply their knowledge to hypothetical situations much like those they might encounter in actual police work. These exercises can be assigned as final written or oral exercises or serve as the basis for lively class debates.
- *Web Exercises* ask students to research police topics on the Internet.
- *Definitions of Key Terms* appear on the same page on which each key term is first used, and in the full glossary at the end of the book.

Boxed Features

To further heighten the book's relevancy for students, we have included the following boxed features in all chapters:

- *You Are There!* These boxes take students back to the past to review the fact pattern in a particular court case or to learn the details about a significant event or series of events in history. They are intended to give the students a sense of actually being at the scene of a police event.
- *On the Job* These features recount personal experiences from our own police careers. They are intended to provide a reality-based perspective on policing, including the human side of policing.
- *Guest Lectures* These essays from well-respected veterans of law enforcement and higher education offer practitioner-based insights into crucial law enforcement issues and challenges.

Ancillaries

A number of supplements are provided by Cengage Learning to help instructors use *An Introduction to Policing* in their courses and to aid students in preparing for exams. Supplements are available to qualified adopters. Please consult your local sales representative for details.

To access additional course materials, please visit **www.cengagebrain.com**. At the CengageBrain.com home page, search for the ISBN of your title (from the back cover of your book), using the search box at the top of the page. This will take you to the product page where these resources can be found.

CENGAGE **brain**

To get access, visit CengageBrain.com.

For the Instructor

- **MindTap Criminal Justice** MindTap from Cengage Learning represents a new approach to a highly personalized, online learning platform. A fully online learning solution, MindTap combines all of a student's learning tools—readings, multimedia, activities, and assessments into a singular Learning Path that guides the student through the curriculum. Instructors personalize the experience by customizing the presentation of these learning tools for their students, allowing instructors to seamlessly introduce their own content into the Learning Path via "apps" that integrate into the MindTap platform. Additionally, MindTap provides interoperability with major Learning Management Systems (LMS) via support for open industry standards and fosters partnerships with third-party educational application providers to provide a highly collaborative, engaging, and personalized learning experience.

- **Online Instructor's Resource Manual** Revised to reflect new content in the eighth edition, the manual includes learning objectives, key terms, a detailed chapter outline, a chapter summary, lesson plans, discussion topics, student activities, "What If" scenarios, media tools, and a sample syllabus. The learning objectives are correlated with the discussion topics, student activities, and media tools.

- **Online Test Bank** The expanded test bank includes 30 percent more questions than the prior edition. Each chapter of the test bank contains questions in multiple-choice, true/false, completion, essay, and new critical thinking formats, with a full answer key. The test bank is coded to the learning objectives that appear in the main text, and includes the section in the main text where the answers can be found. Finally, each question in the test bank has been carefully reviewed by experienced criminal justice instructors for quality, accuracy, and content coverage so instructors can be sure they are working with an assessment and grading resource of the highest caliber.

- **Cengage Learning Testing Powered by Cognero** This assessment software is a flexible, online system that allows you to import, edit, and manipulate test bank content from the *An Introduction to Policing* test bank or elsewhere, including your own favorite test questions; create multiple test versions in an instant; and deliver tests from your LMS, your classroom, or wherever you want.

- **PowerPoint® Lectures** Helping you make your lectures more engaging while effectively reaching your visually oriented students, these handy Microsoft PowerPoint® slides outline the chapters of the main text in a classroom-ready presentation. The PowerPoint® slides are updated to reflect the content and organization of the new edition of the text, are tagged by chapter learning objective, and feature some additional examples and real-world cases for application and discussion.

For the Student

- **MindTap Criminal Justice** MindTap from Cengage Learning represents a new approach to a highly personalized, online learning platform. A fully online learning solution, MindTap combines all of a student's learning tools—readings, multimedia, activities, and assessments into a singular Learning Path that guides the student through the curriculum. Instructors personalize the experience by customizing the presentation of these learning tools for their students, allowing instructors to seamlessly introduce their own content into the Learning Path via "apps" that integrate into the MindTap platform. Additionally, MindTap provides interoperability with major Learning Management Systems (LMS) via support for open industry standards and fosters partnerships with third-party educational application providers to provide a highly collaborative, engaging, and personalized learning experience.

Acknowledgments

So many people have helped us make the successful transition from the world of being street cops to the world of academia and so many more helped in the publication of this book. It is impossible to mention them all, but there would be no *An Introduction to Policing*, Eighth Edition, without them.

Both authors would like to sincerely thank product manager Carolyn Henderson-Meier for her faith, patience, and constant assistance in this project, and associate content developer Margaux Cameron for her intelligent and insightful assistance in all stages of the development of this book. Also, we applaud the intelligent and excellent copyediting of Nina Taylor and the super production efforts of Alverne Bell of Integra, as well as photo researcher Hemalatha Dhanapal and text researcher Pinky Subi. To the many students who came to our offices or classes wanting to know about the material we have put into this text, you were the inspiration for this work. This book is for you. To the great men and women we worked with in our police departments, the heart of this book comes from you.

The authors would also like to thank all the professors across the country, particularly those former women and men in blue who have made that transition from the streets to the classrooms, for their adoptions of the first seven editions and their kind words and sage advice. They inspired us to prepare this eighth edition. We would especially like to thank the reviewers of this edition, who provided outstanding and detailed feedback: Chris McFarlin, Tri-County Technical College; and Stacey Hervey, Community College of Denver. Their names appear along with those of the reviewers of previous editions in the list that follows this preface, as a special tribute to all who have helped us refine the book over the years.

John Dempsey would like to offer special tribute to his former partners in the NYPD, the late Jimmy Fyfe and Pat Ryan, who continually served as his academic and intellectual stimulation. Through their careers and academic achievements, both served as an inspiration to generations of New York City cops, and they will surely be missed in academia and policing. Anything I have achieved in scholarship I owe to Jim and Pat. Also, I would like to mention Dave Owens and thank him for his friendship and leadership in our professional associations, as well as the members of the Great Uncaught, my speaking partners across the country: Lorenzo Boyd, Jim Burnett, Pat Faiella, Tom Lenahan, Jim Ruiz, Donna Stuccio, and Ed Thibault. It is always an honor and privilege to be in your gracious company. Also, to my partner, Linda Forst, for adding so much to this book.

Again, as always to my family: Marianne, my love and best friend; my children, John, Donna, and Cathy; my daughter-in-law, Diane; and in memory of Anne Marie, my special hero—your love and patience has sustained me over the years. Finally, to Danny and Nikki Dempsey and Erin and John Gleeson, my grandchildren: Who loves you more than the Grand Dude?

Linda Forst would like to thank many people who led her down the path to a challenging and fulfilling career in law enforcement. My late father, Calvin, taught me to have a great respect for the police and regularly "backed up" officers in our small town of Ardsley, New York, where he owned a chicken take-out restaurant. My mother, Betty, gave me her unwavering support despite her concerns for my safety in my chosen career. I'm indebted to the late former Chief of the Boca Raton Police Department (and later Sheriff of Palm Beach County) Charles McCutcheon who had faith in my abilities and gave me my start in law enforcement when not many chiefs were supporting women in the profession. He was a leading police professional in the push for education and innovation in police work. I'd also like to thank Dr. Bill Bopp, my first criminal justice professor, who welcomed me in his class at Florida Atlantic University when I showed up on a whim. He opened up a whole new world to me and served as a role model and mentor for many years. I hope that I may have the impact on students that he had on me. I am eternally grateful to my late husband, Jim Duke, who supported and encouraged females in law enforcement long before it was politically correct and who was always there for me as I confronted various challenges while rising through the ranks. I also thank attorney Michael Salnick, the best criminal defense attorney in Palm Beach County, for his part in making me a better investigator, as well as for his friendship and support over the years. I continue to be indebted to former Washington State Patrol Captains Steve Seibert and Tom Robbins (Chief of Wenatchee PD) for their support and assistance since we first met at Northwestern University's School of Police Staff and Command in 1989.

I thank Jack Dempsey for his confidence in me and his unending support as well as his big heart. I am also blessed with loving and supportive daughters, Brynn and Juleigh, who were understanding of the demands placed on my time. My blessings recently expanded with the addition of a new son-in-law, Taylor, and I am comforted to know that both of my daughters have this great man in their lives. They are all an endless source of pride and joy.

I also want to thank the generous practitioners who agreed to share their "stories" throughout the book in an effort to assist students' understanding of the police field: Lorenzo Boyd, Michelle Bennett, David Swim, Jeff Magers, Claudia Leyva, Adolfo Gonzales, Charles Johnson, John Lovick, and Jim Nielsen. For this latest edition, I am additionally grateful to Jeff Wickett, Susan Riseling, Sue Rahr, Brian Lewis, Ruth Roy, Michael Kehoe, Tim Luckie, Rex Caldwell, and Scott Strathy, who generously and openly shared their knowledge with our readers. A special thanks also to Sergeant Cesar Fazz and Officer Eric Cazares of the Yuma, Arizona, Police Department for their time and insights into law enforcement in the Southwest.

We both would like to offer a special tribute to all the heroes of September 11, 2001, who rushed in so that others could get out. You are truly symbols of the great public servants who work in emergency services in our nation.

Jack Dempsey
Linda Forst

Reviewers of *An Introduction to Policing*

Thomas F. Adams, Del Mar College

Frank Alberico, Joliet Junior College

Douglas Armstrong, McNeese State University

Dan Baker, University of South Carolina

Elaine Bartgis, University of Central Oklahoma

Michael Blankenship, Memphis State University

Max L. Bromley, University of South Florida–St. Petersburg

Joseph Bunch, Rockville Community College

Paul Clark, Community College of Philadelphia

Frank Cornacchione, Pensacola Junior College

Steve Ellwanger, East Tennessee State University

George R. Franks, Jr., Stephen F. Austin State University

Alvin Fuchsman, Northern Virginia Community College

Edmund Grosskopf, Indiana State University

Joseph Hanrahan, Westfield State University

John Harlan, Stephen F. Austin State University

Pamela Hart, Iowa Western Community College

Stacey Hervey, Community College of Denver

Patrick Hopkins, Harrisburg Area Community College

Charles Kelly, Jr., Southeastern Louisiana University

Ken R. Kerley, University of Alabama at Birmingham

Gary Keveles, University of Wisconsin–Superior

Julius Koefoed, Jr., Kirkwood Community College

James Lauria, Pittsburgh Technical Institute

Tom Lenahan, Herkimer County Community College

Walter Lewis, St. Louis Community College at Merrimac

David Mackey, St. Anselm College

Anthony Markert, Western Connecticut State University

Chris McFarlin, Tri-County Technical College

Michael E. Meyer, University of North Dakota

Kenneth Mullen, Appalachian State University

Willard M. Oliver, Sam Houston State University

Hugh O'Rourke, Westchester Community College

Leslie K. Palmer, Rasmussen College–Online

Gregory Petrakis, University of Missouri–Kansas City

Charles Purgavie, Ocean County Community College

Chester Quarles, University of Mississippi

Elizabeth Quinn, Fayetteville State University

Jayne Rich, Atlantic Community College

John Sargent, Jr., Kent State University

Mahendra Singh, Grambling State University

William Sposa, Bergen Community College

David Streater, Catawba Valley Community College

Christine L. Stymus, Bryant & Stratton College

Sam Swaim, Indian Hills Community College

R. Alan, Thompson, Old Dominion University

Gary Tucker, Sinclair Community College

Roger Turner, Shelby State University

Arvind Verma, Indiana University

William Vizzard, California State University–Sacramento

Thomas Washburn, Centennial Law and Justice Program

Harrison Watts, Washburn University

Police History and Organization

Mikael Karlsson/Alamy

CHAPTER 1
Police History

CHAPTER 2
Organizing Public Security in the United States

CHAPTER 3
Organizing the Police Department

Police History

Library of Congress Prints and Photograph Division

LEARNING OBJECTIVES

- Explain the primary means of ensuring personal safety prior to the establishment of formal, organized police departments.

- Discuss the influence of the English police experience on American policing.

- Characterize the regional differences in American policing prior to the 20th century.

- Describe how the turbulent times of the 1960s and 1970s influenced American policing.

- Identify at least four events or people instrumental in the development of 20th-century American policing, and describe their influence.

OUTLINE

Early Police

English Policing: Our Heritage
Early History
Seventeenth-Century Policing: Thief-Takers
Henry Fielding and the Bow Street Runners
Peel's Police: The Metropolitan Police for London

American Policing: The Colonial Experience
The North: The Watch
The South: Slave Patrols and Codes

American Policing: Eighteenth and Nineteenth Centuries
The Urban Experience
The Southern Experience
The Frontier Experience

American Policing: Twentieth and Twenty-First Centuries
Policing from 1900 to 1960
Policing in the 1960s and 1970s
Policing in the 1980s and 1990s
Policing in the 2000s

INTRODUCTION

The word *police* comes from the Latin word *politia*, which means "civil administration." *Politia* goes back to the Greek word *polis*, "city." Etymologically, therefore, the police can be seen as those involved in the administration of a city. *Politia* became the French word *police*. The English adopted it and at first continued to use it to mean "civil administration."[1] The specific application of *police* to the administration of public order emerged in France in the early 18th century. The English word took on this meaning as well with the formation of the Marine Police, a force established in 1798 to protect merchandise in the port of London.

The reference to the police as a "civil authority" is very important. The police represent the civil power of government, as opposed to the military power of government. We use the military in times of war. The members of the military, by necessity, are trained to kill and destroy, which is appropriate in war. But do we want to use military forces to govern or patrol our cities and towns? We, the authors of this textbook, do not think so. Imagine that you and some of your classmates are having a party. The party gets a bit loud, and your neighbors call 911. Instead of a police car, an armored personnel carrier and tanks arrive at the party, and twenty soldiers come out pointing M16 assault rifles at you. This may seem like a silly example, but think about it: Surely we need a civil police, not the military, in our neighborhoods.

This chapter will discuss early forms of policing and what some believe was the direct predecessor of the American police—the English police. Policing in the United States began with the colonies, including the watch and ward in the North and the slave patrols in the South, which some scholars believe could have been the first actual modern American police patrol organizations. A summary of the 18th- and 19th-century experience will focus on the urban, southern, and frontier experiences. The chapter will then turn to modern times—20th- and 21st-century policing—and discuss the American police from 1900 to 1960, the turbulent decades of the 1960s and 1970s, and more recent changes in the 1980s and 1990s. It will end with a discussion of policing since the onset of the new millennium, emphasizing the dramatic, unprecedented changes in police organization and operations brought about by the terrorist attacks of September 11, 2001.

Early Police

Policing—maintaining order and dealing with lawbreakers—was always a private matter in early societies.[2] Citizens were responsible for protecting themselves and maintaining an orderly community. Uniformed, organized police departments as we think of them today were rare. Actually, as we will see in this chapter, modern-style police departments didn't appear until the 14th century in France and the 19th century in England.

The first people we would consider law enforcement professionals were unpaid magistrates (judges), who were appointed by the citizens of Athens starting around the sixth century BCE. The magistrates adjudicated cases, but private citizens arrested offenders and punished them. The Romans began electing magistrates around the third century BCE and also created the first specialized investigative unit, called *questors*, or "trackers of murder," around the fifth century BCE. In most societies, people in towns would group together and form a watch, particularly at night, at the town borders or gates to ensure that outsiders did not attack the town.

Around the first century BCE, the Roman emperor Augustus picked special, highly qualified members of the military to form the **Praetorian Guard**, which could be considered the first police officers. Their job was to protect the palace and the emperor. Augustus also established both the Praefectus Urbi (Urban Cohort), which used executive and judicial power to protect the city, and the Vigiles of Rome. The **Vigiles** began as firefighters and were eventually also given law enforcement responsibilities, patrolling Rome's streets day and night. The Vigiles could be considered the first civil police force designed

Praetorian Guard Select group of highly qualified members of the military established by the Roman emperor Augustus to protect him and his palace.

Vigiles Early Roman firefighters who also patrolled Rome's streets to protect citizens.

to protect citizens. They were quite brutal, and our words *vigilance* and *vigilante* come from them.[3]

Also in Rome in the first century CE, public officials called lictors were appointed to serve as bodyguards for the magistrates. The lictors would bring criminals before the magistrates upon their orders and carry out the magistrates' determined punishments, including the death penalty. The lictors' symbol of authority was the fasces, a bundle of rods tied by a red thong around an ax, which represented their absolute authority over life and limb.

During the twelfth and thirteenth centuries, kings on the European continent began to assume responsibility for the administration of the law. They began to appoint officials for that purpose to replace the watch and other private forms of defense. In the 13th century in Paris, Louis IX appointed a provost, who was assigned to enforce the law and supervise the night watch. The provost was assisted by investigating commissioners and sergeants. In 1356, France created a mounted military patrol, the Maréchausée, to maintain peace on the highways. The Maréchausée evolved into the Gendarmerie Nationale, which today polices the areas outside France's major cities.

By the 18th century, both Paris and Munich had armed, professional police that were credited with keeping the cities safe and orderly.

English Policing: Our Heritage

The American system of law and criminal justice was borrowed from the English police experience, which is colorful and closely related to the development of English society.[4]

----

mutual pledge A form of community self-protection developed by King Alfred the Great in the latter part of the ninth century in England.

constable An official assigned to keep the peace in the mutual pledge system in England.

shire-reeve Early English official placed in charge of shires (counties) as part of the system of mutual pledge; evolved into the modern concept of the sheriff.

hue and cry A method developed in early England for citizens to summon assistance from fellow members of the community.

watch and ward A rudimentary form of policing, designed to protect against crime, disturbances, and fire. All men were required to serve on it.

Early History

Sir Robert Peel is generally credited with establishing the first English police department, the London Metropolitan Police, in 1829. However, the first references to an English criminal justice or law enforcement system appeared some 1,000 years earlier, in the latter part of the ninth century, when England's king, Alfred the Great, was preparing his kingdom for an impending Danish invasion. Part of King Alfred's strategy against the Danes was maintaining stability in his own country and providing a method for people in villages to protect one another. To achieve this stability, King Alfred established a system of **mutual pledge** (a form of societal control where citizens grouped together to protect each other), which organized the responsibility for the security of the country into several levels. At the lowest level were *tithings,* 10 families who grouped together to protect one another and to assume responsibility for the acts of the group's members. At the next level, 10 tithings (100 families) were grouped together into a *hundred.* The hundred was under the charge of a **constable**, who might be considered the first form of English police officer and was responsible for dealing with more serious breaches of the law. Groups of hundreds within a specific geographic area were combined to form *shires* (the equivalent of today's county). The shires were put under the control of the king and were governed by a **shire-reeve**, or sheriff. For the most part, though, people were supposed to police their own communities through the mutual pledge system. If trouble occurred, a citizen was expected to raise the **hue and cry** (yell for help), and other citizens were expected to come to assistance.

Over the centuries, as formal governments were established, a primitive formal criminal justice system evolved in England. In 1285 CE, the Statute of Winchester established a rudimentary criminal justice system in which most of the responsibility for law enforcement remained with the people themselves. The statute formally established (1) the watch and ward, (2) the hue and cry, (3) the parish constable, and (4) the requirement that all males keep weapons in their homes for use in maintaining the public peace.

The **watch and ward** required all men in a given town to serve on the night watch. The watch, therefore, can be seen as the most rudimentary form of metropolitan policing. The watch was designed to protect against crime, disturbances, and fire. Watchmen had three major duties:

- Patrolling the streets from dusk until dawn to ensure that all local people were indoors and quiet and that no strangers were roaming about
- Performing duties such as lighting street lamps, clearing garbage from streets, and putting out fires
- Enforcing the criminal law

If it became necessary for a watchman to pronounce the hue and cry, all citizens would then be required to leave their homes and assist the watch; not to do so was a crime under the Statue of Winchester. The statute also established the office of parish constable, who was responsible for organizing and supervising the watch. The parish constable was, in effect, the primary urban law enforcement agent in England.

In the early 14th century, with the rise of powerful centralized governments and the decline of regional ones, we see the beginnings of a more formal system of criminal justice, with a separation of powers and a hierarchical system of authority.

Seventeenth-Century Policing: Thief-Takers

In 17th-century England, law enforcement was still seen as the duty of all the people in a community, even though more and more officials were being charged with enforcing the law and keeping the peace. We can now see the beginnings of a tremendously fragmented and inept criminal justice system. The next criminal justice positions to be created were magistrates and beadles. Magistrates assisted the justices of the peace by presiding in courts, ordering arrests, calling witnesses, and examining prisoners. Beadles were assistants to the constables and walked the streets removing vagrants. The impact of the magistrates, constables, and beadles was minimal, and the people in those positions were mostly corrupt.

The 17th-century English policing system also used a form of individual, private police. Called **thief-takers**, these private citizens had no official status and were paid by the king for every criminal they arrested—similar to the bounty hunter of the American West. The major role of the thief-takers was to combat highway robbery committed by highwaymen, whose heroes were the likes of such legendary outlaws as Robin Hood and Little John. By the 17th century, highwaymen had made traveling through the English countryside so dangerous that no coach or traveler was safe. In 1693, an act of Parliament established a monetary reward for the capture of any road agent, or armed robber. A thief-taker was paid upon the conviction of the highwayman and also received the highwayman's horse, arms, money, and property.

The thief-taker system was later extended to cover offenses other than highway robbery, and soon a sliding scale of rewards was established. Arresting a burglar or footpad (street robber), for example, was worth the same as catching a highwayman, but catching a sheep stealer or a deserter from the army brought a much smaller reward. In some areas, homeowners joined together and offered supplementary rewards for the apprehension of a highwayman or footpad in their area. In addition, whenever there was a serious crime wave, Parliament awarded special rewards for thief-takers to arrest particular felons.

Often criminals would agree to become thief-takers and catch other criminals to receive a pardon from the king for their own crimes. Thus, many thief-takers were themselves criminals. Thief-taking was not always rewarding, because the thief-taker was not paid if the highwayman was not convicted. The job also could be dangerous because the thief-taker had to fear the revenge of the highwayman and his relatives and associates. Many thief-takers would seduce young people into committing crimes and then have other thief-takers arrest the youths during the offenses. The two thief-takers would then split the fee. Others framed innocent parties by planting stolen goods on their persons or in their homes. Although some real criminals were apprehended by thief-takers, the system generally created more crime than it suppressed.

thief-takers Private English citizens with no official status who were paid by the king for every criminal they arrested. They were similar to the bounty hunter of the American West.

Henry Fielding and the Bow Street Runners

Henry Fielding, the 18th-century novelist best known for writing *Tom Jones*, may also be credited with laying the foundation for the first modern police force. In 1748, during the heyday of English highwaymen, Fielding was appointed magistrate in Westminster, a city near central London. He moved into a house on Bow Street, which also became his office. In an attempt to decrease the high number of burglaries, street and highway robberies, and other thefts, Fielding and his half-brother, Sir John Fielding, established relationships with local pawnbrokers. The Fieldings provided lists and descriptions of recently stolen property and asked the pawnbrokers to notify them should such property be brought into pawnshops. They then placed the following ad in the London and Westminster newspapers: "All persons who shall for the future suffer by robber, burglars, etc., are desired immediately to bring or send the best description they can of such robbers, etc., with the time and place and circumstances of the fact, to Henry Fielding Esq., at his house in Bow Street."[5]

The Fieldings' actions brought about what we can call the first official crime reports. They were able to gain the cooperation of the high constable of Holborn and several other public-spirited constables. Together they created a small investigative unit, which they called the Bow Street Runners. The runners were private citizens who were not paid by public funds but who were permitted to accept thief-taker rewards.

Eventually, the government rewarded the Fieldings' efforts, and their Bow Street Runners were publicly financed. In 1763, John Fielding was given public funds to establish a civilian horse patrol of eight men to combat robbers and footpads on the London streets. The patrol proved successful but was disbanded after only nine months because of a lack of government support.

Londoners debated whether to have a professional police department. Although certainly enough crime, vice, theft, and disorder occurred to justify forming a civil police force, most people did not want a formal, professional police department for two major reasons. Many felt that a police force would threaten their tradition of freedom. Additionally, the English had considerable faith in the merits of private enterprise, and they disliked spending public money.

Despite the widespread public fear of establishing a civil police force, a small, permanent foot patrol financed by public funds was established in London in 1770. In 1789, a London magistrate, Patrick Colquhoun, lobbied for the creation of a large, organized police force for greater London, but his ideas were rejected after much government and public debate. In 1798, Colquhoun was able to establish the small, publicly funded Marine Police, patterned after the Fieldings' Bow Street Runners, to patrol the Thames. Some consider Colquhoun's force the first civil police department in England.

In 1804, a new horse patrol was established for central London. It included two inspectors and 52 men who wore uniforms of red vests and blue jackets and trousers, making them England's first uniformed civil police department. As the problems of London in the late eighteenth and early nineteenth centuries increased (due to the Industrial Revolution, massive migration to London, poverty, public disorder, vice, and crime), the people and Parliament finally agreed that London needed a large, organized, civil police department.

Peel's Police: The Metropolitan Police for London

In 1828, Sir Robert Peel, England's home secretary, basing his ideas on those of Colquhoun, drafted the first police bill, the Act for Improving the Police in and near the Metropolis (the Metropolitan Police Act). Parliament passed the act in 1829. It established the first large-scale, uniformed, organized, paid, civil police force in London. More than one thousand men were hired. Although a civil rather than a military force, it was structured along military lines, with officers wearing distinctive uniforms. The first London Metropolitan Police wore three-quarter-length royal blue coats, white trousers, and top hats. They were armed with truncheons, the equivalent of today's police baton. The police were commanded by two magistrates, later called commissioners.

London's first police commissioners were Colonel Charles Rowan, a career military officer, and Richard Mayne, a lawyer. Peel, Rowan, and Mayne believed that mutual respect between the police and citizens would be crucial to the success of the new force. As a result, the early "bobbies" (called that in honor of their founder) were chosen for their ability to reflect and inspire the highest personal ideals among young men in early 19th-century England. The control of the new police was delegated to the home secretary, a member of the democratically elected government. Thus, the police as we know them today were, from their very beginning, ultimately responsible to the public.

Peel has become known as the founder of modern policing; however, it must be noted that he was never a member of a police department. His link to policing comes from his influence in getting the police bill passed. The early London police were guided by **Peel's Nine Principles**, as described by the New Westminster Police Service:

1. The basic mission for which the police exist is to prevent crime and disorder.

2. The ability of the police to perform their duties is dependent upon public approval of police actions.

3. Police must secure the willing cooperation of the public in voluntary observance of the law to be able to secure and maintain the respect of the public.

4. The degree of cooperation of the public that can be secured diminishes proportionately to the necessity of the use of physical force.

5. Police seek and preserve public favour not by catering to public opinion but by constantly demonstrating absolute impartial service to the law.

6. Police use physical force to the extent necessary to secure observance of the law or to restore order only when the exercise of persuasion, advice, and warning is found to be insufficient.

7. Police, at all times, should maintain a relationship with the public that gives reality to the historic tradition that the police are the public and the public are the police, the police being only members of the public who are paid to give full-time attention to duties which are incumbent on every citizen in the interests of community welfare and existence.

8. Police should always direct their action strictly towards their functions and never appear to usurp the powers of the judiciary.

9. The test of police efficiency is the absence of crime and disorder, not the visible evidence of police action in dealing with it.[6]

Peel's principles were concerned with the preventive role of the police and positive relationships and cooperation between the police and the community it served. Consider the similarity between Peel's principles and the concepts of *community policing* that have influenced policing during the past few decades. See Chapter 12 for a complete discussion of community policing.

As a result of the formation of the new police force, the patchwork of private law enforcement systems in use at the time was abolished. Many believe that the English model of policing eventually became the model for the United States.

The Metropolitan Police was organized around the **beat system**, in which officers were assigned to relatively small permanent posts and were expected to become familiar with them and the people residing there, thereby making the officer a part of neighborhood life. This system differed from the patrols of the Paris police, which consisted of periodic roving surveillance of areas. Paris police patrols were never assigned to the same area on successive nights, thus not encouraging a close familiarity between the police and the public.

....

Peel's Nine Principles Basic guidelines created by Sir Robert Peel for the London Metropolitan Police in 1829.

beat system System of policing created by Sir Robert Peel for the London Metropolitan Police in 1829 in which officers were assigned to relatively small permanent posts.

The main job of the new police was suppressing mob disorder, winning support from the public, and developing a disciplined force. The development of a professional and disciplined force was difficult, as Thomas Reppetto tells us:

> On September 29, 1829, the force held a muster of its first 1,000 recruits. It was a rainy day, and some of the men broke out very un-military umbrellas, while others, carrying on the quite military habit of hard drinking, showed up intoxicated. The umbrella problem was eliminated by an order issued that day, but drinking was not so easily handled. In the first eight years, 5,000 members of the force had to be dismissed and 6,000 resigned. After four years only 15 percent of the 3,400 original recruits were left.[7]

Rowan, a former army colonel and a veteran of the Battle of Waterloo, was responsible for the efforts to instill military discipline on the new police department.

Unfortunately, the new police were not immediately well received. Some elements of the population saw the police as an occupying army, and open battles occurred between the police and citizens. The tide of sentiment turned in favor of the police, however, when an officer was viciously killed in the Cold Bath Fields riot of 1833. At the murder trial, the jury returned a not guilty verdict, inspiring a groundswell of public support for the much-maligned police. Eventually, Peel's system became so popular that all English cities adopted his idea of a civil police department.

In an interesting recent article in the *British Journal of Criminology*, Lucia Zedner explores the similarities between law enforcement in England before the creation of the London Metropolitan Police and policing today in our post-9/11 world. As evidence of similarities, she points to the generalized insecurity and mounting demands for protection common both then and now. She also writes that today's trend toward community participation in protective efforts reflects patterns of enlisting individuals and community organizations in voluntary activities of self-protection in the pre-Peel era, before Peel's government-sponsored police concept. Zedner points out that today we use private security companies to police neighborhoods, businesses, and commercial areas, a practice similar to that in the 18th century. She concludes, "Although the state can no longer claim a monopoly over policing [today], it must retain responsibility for protecting the public interest in policing measures and the maintenance of civil rights in the context of security measures being used."[8]

YOU ARE THERE

Sir Robert Peel: The Founder of Modern Policing

Sir Robert Peel is one of the most important persons in 19th-century British history. He dominated Parliament throughout the period of 1830 to 1850. He became a Member of Parliament (MP) in 1809 at the age of 21, after his father bought him a seat, and he became undersecretary of war and the colonies in 1810.

In 1812, Peel was appointed as Chief Secretary for Ireland. In that post, he attempted to end corruption in Irish government by trying to stop the practice of selling public offices and the dismissal of civil servants for their political views. Eventually, he became seen as one of the leading opponents to Catholic Emancipation. In 1814, he established a military-type "peace preservation" force in Ireland that eventually evolved into the Royal Irish Constabulary (RIC). In 1818, he resigned his post in Dublin and returned to London.

Peel was Home Secretary from 1822 to 1827. Distressed over the problems of law and order in London, he persuaded the House of Commons to pass the Metropolitan Police Act in 1829. The first Metropolitan Police patrols went onto the streets on September 29, 1829.

Peel was prime minister twice, from 1834 to 1835 and from 1841 to 1846. He died in 1850 as the result of injuries he sustained in a fall from his horse while riding up Constitution Hill in London. Many have called him among the most important statesmen in the history of England. Because of Peel's connection with the creation of both the modern Irish and English police, the Irish police were known as "peelers" and the English police as "bobbies," thus magnifying Peel's role in the development of modern policing.

Source: Thomas A. Reppetto, *The Blue Parade* (New York: Free Press, 1978), pp. 16–22.

American Policing: The Colonial Experience

The North: The Watch

The American colonists did not have an easy life.[9] They were constantly at risk from foreign enemies, Native Americans, and their fellow colonists. Their only protection was self-defense and, sometimes, the military or militia. By the 17th century, the northern colonies started to institute a civil law enforcement system that closely replicated the English model. The county sheriff was the most important law enforcement official; in addition, he collected taxes, supervised elections, and had much to do with the legal process. Sheriffs were not paid a salary but, much like the English thief-taker, were paid fees for each arrest they made. Sheriffs did not patrol but stayed in their offices.

In cities, the town marshal was the chief law enforcement official, aided by constables (called *schouts* in the Dutch settlements) and night watchmen. Night watch was sometimes performed by the military. The city of Boston created the first colonial night watch in 1631 and created the position of constable three years later. In 1658, eight paid watchmen replaced a patrol of citizen volunteers in the Dutch city of Nieuw Amsterdam. The British inherited this police system in 1664 when they took over the city and renamed it New York. By the mid-1700s, the New York night watch was described as "a parcel of idle, drinking, vigilant snorers, who never quell'd any nocturnal tumult in their lives; but would perhaps, be as ready to joining in a burglary as any thief in Christendom."[10]

The South: Slave Patrols and Codes

Protection against crime and criminals in the southern American colonies was mainly the responsibility of the individual citizen, as it had been in early England.[11] There was little law and order as we understand it now. When immediate action was needed, people generally took matters into their own hands, which led to an American tradition of vigilantism and lynching.

Many police historians and scholars indicate that the **slave patrols** of the American South were the precursor to the modern American system of policing. These patrols were a formal system of social control, particularly in rural areas, to maintain the institution of slavery by enforcing restrictive laws against slaves. Slave patrols were prominent in many of the early colonies as a means of apprehending runaway slaves and protecting the white population from slave insurrections or crimes committed by slaves. Policing experts actually conclude that the patrol function and concept were first accepted as a police practice by slave patrols in the South.[12]

Police historian Sam Walker wrote, "In some respects, the slave patrols were the first modern forces in this country."[13] M. P. Roth, in his *Crime and Punishment: A History of the Criminal Justice System*, writes that "the evolution of the southern slave patrols in the early 1700s marked the first real advances in American policing."[14] As early as the 1660s, Maryland and Virginia developed slave codes, which defined the black slave and his or her family as pieces of property who were indentured to their masters for life and forbidden to engage in many activities that whites engaged in. Slave masters were given the legal authority to control their property—slaves—through physical discipline and punishment.[15]

The slave codes were enforced by developing southern police departments to directly support slavery and the existing economic system of the South. These codes were adopted by colonial and, later, state legislatures. Slave patrols became the police mechanism to support the southern economic system of slavery. Slave codes were designed to ensure the economic survival of southern society—the use of slave labor to produce goods. Slaves were valuable property, and the codes were meant to prevent them from running away or engaging in insurrection. Simply put, these early slave codes were intended to preserve the social order in which whites dominated and subjugated blacks.

The southern slave codes mandated that slaves had no rights as citizens because they were considered property. Even the U.S. Supreme Court, in its infamous **Dred Scott decision**, *Dred Scott v. Sandford* (1857), held that Dred Scott, a black slave, could not sue in court for his freedom because he was not a citizen, but a piece of property.[16]

Researcher Sally E. Hadden, in her book *Slave Patrols: Law and Violence in Virginia and the*

---

slave patrols Police-type organizations created in the American South during colonial times to control slaves and support the southern economic system of slavery.

Dred Scott decision Infamous U.S. Supreme Court decision of 1857 ruling that slaves had no rights as citizens because they were considered to be property.

Carolinas, reported that the first slave patrols were authorized in South Carolina to protect white families from slaves. Members of the slave patrols (free white men and some women) could enter, without permission, any homes of blacks or whites suspected of harboring slaves who were violating the law. The colonial assembly in South Carolina developed specific rules, guidelines, and duties for the slave patrols, which were in effect until the Civil War.[17]

Slave patrols became commonplace by the early 18th century and were often combined with local militia and police duties. These patrols varied in size but generally were small. Each well-armed patrol, operating on horseback, was generally required to inspect each plantation within its district at least once a month and to seize any contraband possessed by slaves. North Carolina's slave patrol system was developed in the 1700s under the local justice of the peace, and the patrols were required to visit each plantation in their districts every two weeks. They were allowed to flog or whip any slave caught in a minor violation of the slave codes. Tennessee's slave patrol system began in 1753 and was administered through county courts, which required the patrollers to inspect all plantations within the county four times a year. Kentucky used its slave patrol system as a traditional police mechanism. It patrolled for runaway slaves, highwaymen (robbers), and other threats to the peace. In some Kentucky counties, the patrol worked 24 hours a day, seven days a week.

American Policing: Eighteenth and Nineteenth Centuries

Historically, American policing attempted to control crime and disorder in urban and frontier environments. Although the urban and frontier experiences differed in many ways, both could be classified as brutal and corrupt.

The Urban Experience

During the 18th century, the most common form of American law enforcement was the system of constables in the daytime and the watch at night. Crime, street riots, and drunkenness were very common, and law enforcement personnel were incompetent in handling the situation. From 1790 to 1845, New York

City's population rose from 33,000 to 370,000 people, most of which were new immigrants. With the increased population and poverty, crime dramatically increased. An 1840 New York newspaper reported,

> Destructive rascality stalks at large in our streets and public places, at all times of day and night, with none to make it afraid; mobs assemble deliberately.... In a word, lawless violence and fury have full dominion over us.[18]

In 1842, a special citizens' committee of New Yorkers wrote,

> The property of the citizen is pilfered, almost before his eyes. Dwellings and warehouses are entered with an ease and apparent coolness and carelessness of detention which shows that none are safe. Thronged as our city is, men are robbed in the street. Thousands that are arrested go unpunished, and the defenseless and the beautiful are ravished and murdered in the daytime, and no trace of the criminals is found.[19]

EARLY POLICE DEPARTMENTS The tremendous migration to large American cities and the poverty and discrimination these new residents encountered led to enormous social problems, including crime and disorder. In response, many large cities began to create formal police departments using the Peelian model.

The first organized American police department in the North was created in Boston in 1838. It consisted of only eight members and worked at first only in the daytime; in 1851, they also assumed the night watch. In 1853, the office of police chief was created, and, in 1854, police stations were constructed. The force was not fully uniformed until 1859, when members were required to wear blue jackets and white hats. In addition to police duties, they were charged with maintaining public health until 1853.

In 1844, the New York state legislature authorized communities to organize police forces and gave special funds to cities to provide 24-hour police protection. In New York City, under the leadership of Mayor William F. Havermeyer, a London-style police department was created on May 23, 1845. The first New York police officers were issued copper stars to wear on their hats and jackets but were not allowed to wear full uniforms until 1853. In fact, the first New York cops did not want to wear even their copper stars because doing so made them targets for the city's ruffians. The New York City police were also in charge of street sweeping until 1881.

Philadelphia started its police department in 1854. By the outbreak of the Civil War, Chicago, New Orleans, Cincinnati, Baltimore, Newark, and a number of other large cities had their own police departments. The new police departments replaced the night watch system. As a result, constables and sheriffs were relieved of much of their patrol and investigative duties. However, they performed other duties in the fledgling criminal justice system, such as serving court orders and managing jails.

POLITICS IN AMERICAN POLICING Nineteenth-century American policing was dominated by local politicians and was notorious for brutality, corruption, and ineptness: "In addition to the pervasive brutality and corruption, the police did little to effectively prevent crime or provide public services. . . . Officers were primarily tools of local politicians; they were not impartial and professional public servants."[20] In his book *Low Life: Lures and Snares of Old New York*, Luc Sante writes, "The history of the New York police is not a particularly illustrious one, at least in the nineteenth and early twentieth centuries, as throughout the period the law enforcement agents of the city continually and recurrently demonstrated corruption, complacency, confusion, sloth, and brutality."[21]

In 1857, political differences between the Democrats, who controlled New York City, and the Republicans, who controlled New York State, caused a full-scale police war. The corrupt New York City police force, the Municipal Police, under the control of New York's mayor Fernando Wood, was replaced by the Metropolitan Police, created and controlled by Governor John A. King. Wood, however, refused to disband the Municipals. Thus, the city had two separate police departments, each under the control of one of the two enemy factions.

On June 16, 1857, the two police departments clashed at New York's City Hall. Fifty Metropolitan police arrived at City Hall with a warrant to arrest Wood. Almost 900 members of the Municipal Police attacked the Metropolitans, causing them to retreat. As the Metropolitans were retreating, the state called in the Seventh Regiment of the National Guard under the command of General Sandford. The members of the National Guard marched on City Hall and raised their weapons as if to fire at the Municipals. Eventually Wood surrendered to arrest, and no

First Urban U.S. Police Departments

Boston

1838	Boston Police Department is created, with eight officers who only work in the daytime.
1851	Boston Police Department assumes the night watch.
1853	First Boston police chief is appointed.
1854	First Boston police stations are built.
1859	Boston police officers receive first uniforms.

New York

1845	New York City Police Department is created, with officers on the job 24 hours a day, 7 days a week.
1853	New York City police are required to wear uniforms.
1857	Police "civil war" erupts at New York City Hall.

Philadelphia

1854	Philadelphia Police Department is created.

© 2016 Cengage Learning®

You Decide: Where Does the Term "Cops" Come From?

When the first members of the NYPD began to patrol in the summer of 1845, they only wore badges on their civilian clothing. The badges were eight-pointed stars (representing the first eight paid members of the old watch during Dutch times) with the seal of the city at the center and were made of stamped copper. The newspapers of the time referred to the new force as the "Star Police," but people seeing the shiny copper shields began to call them "coppers," which was later shortened to "cops." The term "constable on patrol" is also used in Britain, which may account for the use of the term "cops" in England as well.

© 2016 Cengage Learning®

GUEST LECTURE

Photo courtesy of M.S. Lakeyva

LORENZO BOYD

Dr. Lorenzo M. Boyd is a former deputy sheriff in Suffolk County, Massachusetts. He has taught at Old Dominion University and the University of North Texas. He is currently an associate professor on the faculty of Fayetteville State University in North Carolina.

COUNTY SHERIFF'S DEPARTMENTS: WORKING IN RELATIVE ANONYMITY

Although Sir Robert Peel is credited with establishing the precursor to the modern municipal police department, the office of the sheriff has origins that date back to the ninth century and England's King Alfred the Great. The office of sheriff is the oldest law enforcement office known within the common law system, and it has always been accorded great dignity and high trust.

The role of the sheriff has changed and evolved over time. Today, as in the past, the sheriff is the lead law enforcer in the county, entrusted with the maintenance of law and order and the preservation of "domestic tranquility."

Sheriffs are also responsible for a host of other criminal justice functions and related activities, including law enforcement, jail administration, inmate transportation, court services, and civil process. The responsibilities of the sheriff cover a wide range of public safety functions that vary based on jurisdiction. Sheriffs are the only elected law enforcement officials in most states. Today, for instance, sheriffs in Massachusetts are elected in each of the 14 counties, and sheriffs in Virginia are elected in each of the 95 counties and 28 major cities. The sheriff in the county that contains the state capital is called the "high sheriff" and is the ranking sheriff in the state.

In Massachusetts, the primary function of the sheriff's department is administration of the county jail and house of correction (in Massachusetts, jail is pretrial only, and the house of correction is short-term postconviction). The law enforcement function, though important, is secondary to the jail function. Because "care, custody, and control" of inmates are paramount, many sheriff's deputies function more as corrections officers than as police officers. In spite of the rich, long law enforcement history of the sheriff's department, often deputies acquiesce to a support role in dealing with municipal police departments. Long before sheriff's deputies can hone their skills on the streets of Boston, they must first serve a significant amount of time working in the county jail.

In most cities, the city police handle day-to-day police work, and the sheriff's department patrols county and rural areas that do not have a municipal police force. Sheriff's deputies handle many prisoner transport functions to and from court and jails, police raids, and "sting" operations. Sheriff's departments also employ a tactical emergency response team, similar to that of police SWAT teams. These tactical teams in the sheriff's department are referred to as Sheriff's Emergency Response Teams (SERT). Inside the jail and house of correction, the SERT team is responsible for quelling cellblock riots, hostage situations, gang rivalries, and forced cell moves.

When I was first deputized in 1988, I was under the impression that I was poised to help save the world. "Fighting crime and saving lives" was the motto that I thought I would adopt. Little did I know that I had a lot to learn about the criminal justice system in general and the sheriff's department in particular. I quickly learned to be proficient at the behind-the-scenes, less-glorious duties that make the sheriff's department so important.

shots were fired. In court, the mayor was released and the judge decided that the Metropolitan Police would be the official New York City police.

The primary job of 19th-century police was to serve as the enforcement arm of the political party in power, protect private property, and control the rapidly arriving foreign immigrants. In the late 1800s, police work was highly desirable because it paid

more than most other blue-collar jobs: The average factory worker earned $450 a year, whereas a police officer was paid on average $900.

Politics dominated police departments, and politicians determined who would be appointed a police officer and who would be promoted to higher ranks. Job security for police officers was nonexistent because when a new political party gained control

Training for sheriff's deputies includes both tactical police training and training for correctional settings. Deputies have to be able to react to situations both in the jail and on the streets at a moment's notice. In the academy, I endured 80 hours of firearms training, 60 hours of criminal law, 40 hours of constitutional law, 20 hours of patrol procedures, 10 hours of self-defense, and a host of other seemingly peripheral topics. My time in the training academy, although critical, did little to prepare me mentally for my first assignment.

Once the academy was over, I donned a pressed uniform and a freshly polished pair of military-style boots and was ready to assume my position in the criminal justice system. I then reported for duty at the Suffolk County Jail in downtown Boston and awaited my new assignment. One thing that I will never forget happened on my first day of work. When I walked into the jail for the first time, the large steel door slammed behind me with a sound that was unnerving. That sound separated freedom from incarceration.

When I reported for duty on that first day, I was given handcuffs, a set of keys, and a radio, and I was assigned to run an inmate housing unit in the county jail. The jail is divided into different inmate housing units, which are treated as separate self-contained jails. I was assigned, on my first day, to what is often called the worst unit in the jail: the homicide unit. In this unit, more than forty men were housed, each facing a trial for murder. It is in situations like these that you find out what you are really made of, mentally. It was a bit intimidating standing face-to-face with the people I had read about in the newspapers or seen on the evening news accused of having committed the most heinous of crimes. These are the people I had to interact with for eight hours a day, every day, in the jail. This is where I was sent to hone my skills, in relative anonymity. If I were good at my job, no one would ever talk about it. Only when things get out of control do the media shine a spotlight on the sheriff's department.

Every problem that occurs in municipal police departments also is present in the sheriff's department. There are power struggles, codes of silence, corruption, and intradepartmental strife. These problems are exacerbated due to the close quarters of the jail. Most of the deputies are struggling to get out of jail duty and move on to patrol, transportation, warrant-management teams, SERT teams, or other glorious assignments. Getting out of the jail onto the streets is something that both deputies and inmates strive for, sometimes with equal fervor.

Often it is the city or state police who make the big arrests in sting operations or on the streets, usually with backup from, or transportation provided by, the sheriff's department. Sheriff's deputies still tend to do the dirty work of transportation, classification, and custody when the city or state police are conducting press conferences. The sheriff's deputies have to deal with the housing, classification, control, and transportation of offenders long after the city or state police have closed their cases. Much of the work of the sheriff's department goes on behind the scenes, with little or no public accolades; nevertheless, the work of the sheriff's department continues in its professional manner, often unnoticed by the public.

In retrospect, I have asked myself again and again if my time in the sheriff's department was a positive one. Overall, I am happy with my experiences, both good and bad, because those experiences helped to mold a view of the criminal justice system. The sheriff's department operates in the best (or worst) of both worlds. Deputies get to patrol the streets as well as learn the inner workings of corrections. I think the sheriff's department is the backbone of criminal justice, even though the deputies tend to work in relative anonymity.

Source: Reprinted by permission of Dr. Lorenzo M. Boyd.

of city government, it would generally fire all police officers and hire new ones.

Regarding the influence of politics on the hiring of police officers, Walker wrote,

Ignorance, poor health, or old age was no barrier to employment. An individual with the right connections could be hired despite the most obvious lack of qualifications. Recruits received no formal training. A new officer would be handed a copy of the police manual (if one could be found) containing the local ordinances and state laws, and sent out on patrol. There he could receive on-the-job training from experienced officers who, of course, also taught the ways of graft and evasion of duty.[22]

Robert M. Fogelson wrote about the political impact of politicians on the police:

> Most patrolmen who survived for any length of time quickly . . . learned that a patrolman placed his career in jeopardy more by alienating his captain than by disobeying his chief and more by defying his wardman, who regulated vice in the precinct, than by ignoring [his sergeant].[23]

According to one researcher, "They [the police] knew who put them in office and whose support they needed to stay there. Their job was to manage their beat; often they became completely enmeshed in the crime they were expected to suppress. Corruption, brutality, and racial discrimination, although not universal, were characteristic of most big city departments."[24]

THE EARLY POLICE OFFICER'S JOB   The role of the American urban police in the eighteenth and nineteenth centuries was varied and often not limited to law enforcement. The early police performed many duties they do not have today, including cleaning streets, inspecting boilers, caring for the poor and homeless, operating emergency ambulances, and performing other social services.

In the English tradition, American police in the North were not issued firearms. However, this changed quickly in 1858, when a New York City police officer shot a fleeing felon with a personal weapon. The case was presented to a grand jury, which did not indict the officer. Police officers in New York then began to arm themselves. A similar incident in Boston led to the arming of that police force. By the early 1900s, cities commonly issued revolvers to their police officers. Officers patrolled on foot with no radios, backup, or supervision. They relied on brute force to avoid being beaten up or challenged by local toughs.

Citizens had a tremendous hatred for 19th-century police officers and saw them as political hacks. Street gangs subjected the police to frequent abuse, and suspects often had to be physically subdued before arrest. Commenting on this lack of respect by citizens, Walker notes, "A tradition of police brutality developed out of this reciprocal disrespect. Officers sought to gain with their billy clubs the deference to their authority that was not freely given."[25] Regarding this brutality, the social reformer Lincoln Steffens wrote, "He saw the police bring in and kick out their bandaged, bloody

New York City Police Museum

The New York City Police Department (NYPD) has protected the city for more than 150 years. Its period of development to its modern-day structure dates back to the 17th century. The New York City Police Museum is located at 100 Old Slip in Manhattan's financial district, within view of the Brooklyn Bridge and the Fulton Fish Market. The building was built in 1909 as the new home for the First Precinct. It was considered a model police facility when built, and chiefs of police throughout the country visited the new station house, looking to copy some of its features in their own buildings. The museum both captures the history of the NYPD and provides a present-day look at the world of law enforcement through the eyes of its officers. Its exhibits include an array of weapons, police shields, fingerprinting and forensic art stations, and the "Policing a Changed City" exhibit about the new, modern NYPD. The museum collects, preserves, and interprets objects related to the history of the NYPD and provides information about this history through exhibitions, lectures, the Internet, publications, school events, and other educational programs. It houses one of the largest collections of police memorabilia in the United States, as well as an extensive photo collection and some police records dating back to the inception of the NYPD in 1845.

Source: "New York City Police Museum," from www .nycpm.org.

prisoners, not only strikers and foreigners, but thieves too, and others of the miserable, friendless, troublesome poor."[26]

Corruption and mismanagement were rampant in 19th-century police departments. Consequently, between 1860 and 1866, the police forces of Baltimore, Chicago, Cleveland, Detroit, Kansas City, and St. Louis were placed under state control. Boston was the first city to form a detective division to investigate past crimes. However, early detectives were as corrupt as their uniformed counterparts, private thief-takers, and bounty hunters.

In the latter part of the 19th century, we begin to see some practical and technological advances in policing. The public health and social welfare responsibilities that formerly were the province of the police, including sweeping sidewalks and housing the homeless, were transferred to newly created municipal agencies. In the 1850s, precincts began to be linked to central headquarters by telegraph machines. In the 1860s, telegraph signal stations were installed, first in Chicago and then in Cincinnati. These enabled officers to check with their precincts for instructions or to call for assistance using Morse code. In 1881, the Morse code signal system was replaced by telephone call boxes in Cincinnati. A police officer could now call from his beat for a patrol wagon to transport prisoners. A red light on the top of a call box could summon officers for messages from their precinct headquarters.

The Southern Experience

As discussed earlier, slave patrols were an early form of American southern policing and perhaps the first organized police operations in the United States. Casting their doubt that Peel's London police were the major influence in creating American police departments, Wadman and Allison point out that before the widespread creation of police departments in the North, the largest law enforcement organization in the United States was Charleston's slave patrol with about 100 members in 1837. Also, the Savannah Police Department was organized in 1852, had 86 officers, and operated day and night watches. In 1850, the Mobile (Alabama) Police Department had 30 officers. During the Civil War, the Richmond (Virginia) Police Department had 11 daytime patrolmen and 72 nighttime patrolmen. However, crime increased so much in Richmond that Confederate President Jefferson Davis declared martial law in 1862.[27]

Atlanta, Georgia, was a major railroad hub and supply center for Confederate forces during the Civil War, with troops and refugees flooding into and out of the city from late 1861 through the end of the war in 1865. The Atlanta Police Department doubled in size during the war, from 14 to 28; the officers faced challenges brought by the war, as well as by maintaining the traditional social order through the slave code. The most serious crime problems in Atlanta were white rowdyism, vandalism, and theft. The Fulton County court dealt with more cases involving whites than those involving bonded slaves and black refugees. Larceny and burglary were the most popular crimes in Atlanta and often involved Confederate soldiers on post in Atlanta.

The largest obstacle facing Atlanta police leaders was finding qualified, trustworthy men to serve. Because of the lack of available recruits, the force was "made up of the poor, elderly, and the not-so-honest element."[28] Although the department never exceeded 30 men at any one time during the war, 48 policemen were found guilty of misconduct and 22 were dismissed. Charges ranged from drunkenness while on duty to extortion and illegal arrest. In 1864, the city hired a city marshal to organize patrols and assist the police, but the attempt failed.[29]

After the Civil War, from 1867 to 1877, law enforcement duties were provided by the military in the districts created from the Confederacy. In Northern-occupied southern states, U.S. marshals often called on federal troops to form a posse to enforce local laws. The army also guarded polling places and curbed the actions of the Ku Klux Klan. Once southern states regained representation in Congress, they tried to prevent such practices.

Many police departments across the South reorganized during this time to meet Reconstruction standards. However, in many cases, police officials under the prewar system simply returned to their posts, and the militia-like nature of slave patrols and volunteer companies survived the war in the newly reorganized police departments. In addition to maintaining public order, police continued to be the upholders of white supremacy in their communities.

Some police departments reluctantly hired blacks on their forces to satisfy demands brought on by Reconstruction. Montgomery, Alabama, and Vicksburg, Mississippi, hired large numbers of blacks on their police departments for a brief time, but most places, like Norfolk, Virginia, had only a token few. These black officers were taunted by whites, who often paid them no heed.[30]

The Frontier Experience[31]

Life on the American frontier was not easy. Early settlers faced tremendous problems from the weather, the terrain, Native Americans, and the criminals within their own ranks. Formal law enforcement on the frontier was rare. What little there was consisted mainly of the locally elected county sheriff and the appointed town marshal, sometimes alongside the U.S. marshal, the U.S. Army, or the state militia.

SHERIFFS AND TOWN MARSHALS The locally elected county sheriffs and the town marshals (appointed by the mayor or city council) were usually the only law enforcement officers available on the frontier. Most of the sheriff's time was spent collecting taxes and performing duties for the courts.

If a crime spree occurred or a dangerous criminal was nearby, the sheriff would call upon the *posse comitatus*, a common law descendent of the old hue and cry. (The Latin term *posse comitatus* means "the power of the county.") No man above the age of 15 could refuse to serve as a member of a legally constituted posse. The posse was often little more than a legalized form of vigilantism. Vigilantism and lynch mobs were common in the Old West because of the lack of professional law enforcement. Many famous town marshals, such as James Butler (Wild Bill) Hickok of Hays City, Kansas, and later Abilene, Kansas, and Wyatt Earp of Dodge City, Kansas, were really semi-reformed outlaws. There was little to distinguish the good guys from the bad guys in the American frontier's criminal justice system.

FEDERAL MARSHALS The Federal Judiciary Act of 1789, which created the office of the U.S. Marshal, also gave the marshals the power to call upon the militia for assistance, a power formalized under federal *posse comitatus* legislation in 1792. The members of the militia were technically members of the federal marshal's posse and aided him in performing his civil duties. In 1861, Congress passed a law empowering the president to call upon the militia or regular army to enforce the law when ordinary means were insufficient.

THE MILITARY Civilian authorities used the military in both the North and the South. Excesses by the military in enforcing the law resulted in Congress passing the Posse Comitatus Act of 1879, forbidding the use of the military to enforce civilian law except where expressly authorized by law. Some of these exceptions applied in the frontier to prevent trespassing on Native American reservations or to enforce unpopular federal decisions regarding territories such as Arizona and New Mexico. The use of the military in the Old West ended in the last quarter of the 19th century.

STATE POLICE AGENCIES Some states and territories created their own police organizations. In 1823, Stephen Austin hired a dozen bodyguards to protect fellow "Texicans" from Native Americans and bandits. Austin's hired guns were officially named the Texas Rangers upon Texas's independence in 1835. The Rangers served as a border patrol for the Republic of Texas, guarding against marauding Native Americans and Mexicans. When Texas was admitted to the Union in 1845, the Texas Rangers became the first U.S. state police agency.

Unlike present-day state police, the Texas Rangers and their counterparts, the Arizona Rangers (1901) and the New Mexico Mounted Patrol (1905), were primarily border patrols designed to combat cattle thievery and control outlaw activities on the Rio Grande. With Pennsylvania leading the way in 1905, other states outside the Southwest began to create their own state police agencies.

PRIVATE POLICE Private police were much more effective than public law enforcement agencies on the frontier. Allan Pinkerton, a native of Scotland, was a former police detective who established a detective agency in Chicago in 1850. The Pinkerton Agency first gained notoriety just before the Civil War, when it thwarted the alleged "Baltimore Plot" to assassinate president-elect Abraham Lincoln. By the 1880s, Pinkerton's National Detective Agency had offices in nearly two dozen cities. In the West, Pinkerton's customers included the U.S. Department of Justice, various railroad companies, and major land speculators. The agents arrested train robbers and notorious gangsters, including the James Gang in the 1880s and Robert Leroy Parker (Butch Cassidy) and Harry Longbaugh (the Sundance Kid) in the early 1900s. The agents also arrested John and Simeon Reno, who organized the nation's first band of professional bank robbers. Pinkerton's agents were hired in the East by mining and manufacturing companies to suppress labor organizations, such as the Molly Maguires in 1874 and 1875, as well as to suppress the Homestead Riots in Pittsburgh in 1892. The Pinkertons employed informants throughout the United States and its territories and offered cash rewards for information. They mainly protected the interests of the railroads, wealthy eastern bankers, and land speculators.

posse comitatus Common law descendent of the old hue and cry. If a crime spree occurred or a dangerous criminal was in the area, the U.S. frontier sheriff would call upon the *posse comitatus*, a Latin term meaning "the power of the county."

In competition with the Pinkerton Agency during the latter part of the 19th century was the Rocky Mountain Detective Association, which pursued and apprehended bank and train robbers, cattle thieves, murderers, and the road agents who plundered highways and mining communities throughout the Southwest and Rocky Mountain area.

Also in competition with the Pinkertons was Wells Fargo and Company, started in 1852 by Henry Wells and William G. Fargo as a banking and stock association designed to capitalize on the emerging shipping and banking opportunities in California. Wells Fargo operated as a mail-carrying service and stagecoach line out of more than a hundred offices in the western mining districts. Because the company carried millions of dollars in gold and other valuable cargo, it created a guard company to protect its shipments. The Wells Fargo private security employees were effective in preventing robberies and thefts; moreover, specially trained and equipped agents relentlessly hunted down the criminals who held up its banks and carriers.

American Policing: Twentieth and Twenty-First Centuries

The first half of the 20th century saw such dramatic negative events as the Boston police strike, National Prohibition, and the issuance of the *Wickersham Commission Report*. However, innovation and an increase in professionalism grew to characterize the American police, partly through the efforts of such early police professionals as August Vollmer, O. W. Wilson, and J. Edgar Hoover.

Policing from 1900 to 1960[32]

As we have seen, American policing historically was characterized by ineptness, corruption, and brutality. At the start of the 20th century, serious attempts were made to reform the police.

Even earlier, Theodore Roosevelt had attempted reform as part of the New York City Board of Police Commissioners between 1895 and 1897. Roosevelt raised police recruitment standards and disciplined corrupt and brutal officers. He was a colorful and proactive leader who traveled through the streets watching the actions of his police. However, despite much publicity and some superficial changes, Roosevelt's efforts failed when the corrupt Tammany Hall political machine was returned to power in 1897. Reppetto tells us, "Roosevelt was a man of dash and vigor, but his influence on the police, like his military career, was more form than substance, and things soon returned to normal."[33]

During the progressive era of American government from 1900 to 1914, attempts at reforming the police originated outside police departments from middle-class, civic-minded reformers. For the most part, however, these attempts failed.

PROFESSIONALISM An early attempt at police reform was the creation in 1893 of a professional society, the International Association of Chiefs of Police (IACP). Its first president was the Washington, D.C., chief of police, Richard Sylvester. The IACP became the leading voice of police reform during the first two decades of the 20th century by consistently calling for the creation of a civil service police and for the removal of political influence and control over the police. The IACP remains a significant force in policing today.

Eventually a federal law, the Pendleton Act, was passed in 1883 to establish a civil service system that tested, appointed, and promoted officers on a merit

A suffragette is arrested by police in 1908.

© Trinity Mirror/Mirrorpix/Alamy

system. Local governments later adopted the civil service system, and political influence slowly evaporated from police departments. Even today, however, not all U.S. police agencies are governed by civil service rules. Furthermore, despite civil service systems, politics continued to play some part in American law enforcement.

TECHNOLOGY In the 20th century, the use of technology grew phenomenally in American police departments. By 1913, the police motorcycle was being used by departments in the Northeast. The first police car was used in Akron, Ohio, in 1910, and the police wagon was first used in Cincinnati in 1912. By the 1920s, the patrol car was in widespread use. The patrol car began to change police work by allowing the police to respond quickly to crimes and enabling each officer to cover much more territory.

The widespread use of the one-way radio in the 1930s and the two-way radio in the 1940s, combined with the growing use of the patrol car, revolutionized police work. Once a call came in to police headquarters or a precinct, a police car could be dispatched almost immediately, providing rapid response to calls for service and emergencies. Although police administrators joyfully greeted this innovation, motorized patrol eventually distanced the police from the community and played a part in the serious problems in policing that arose in the 1960s.

THE BOSTON POLICE STRIKE The Boston police strike of 1919 was one of the most significant events in the history of policing, and it increased interest in police reform. While other professions were unionizing and improving their standards of living, police salaries lagged behind, and the police were becoming upset with their diminished status in society. The fraternal association of Boston police officers, the Boston Social Club, voted to become a union affiliated with the American Federation of Labor (AFL). On September 9, 1919, 70 percent of Boston's police officers—1,117 men—went on strike. Rioting and looting immediately broke out, and Governor Calvin Coolidge mobilized the state militia. Public support went against the police, and the strike was broken. All the striking officers were fired and replaced by new recruits. The strike ended police unionism for decades. Coolidge became a national hero and went on to become president of the United States. Many say that his action in firing the Boston police propelled him to the presidency.

NATIONAL PROHIBITION Another significant event in 20th-century policing, and one that stirred up another police reform movement, was the prohibition of alcohol. The **Volstead Act** (National Prohibition) was passed in 1919 and became law in 1920 as the Eighteenth Amendment to the Constitution. It forbade the sale and manufacture of alcohol, attempting to make America a dry nation. Traditional organized crime families received their impetus during this period as gangsters banded together to meet the tremendous demand of ordinary Americans for alcohol. When the Eighteenth Amendment was repealed in 1933 by the Twenty-First Amendment, the organized crime families funneled the vast amount of capital that they had received in the alcohol trade into other vice crimes, such as illegal gambling, prostitution, loan sharking, labor racketeering, and, later, drug dealing.

Local law enforcement was unable to stop the alcohol and vice operations of organized crime and became even more corrupt as many law enforcement officers cooperated with organized crime. As a result, between 1919 and 1930, 24 states formed commissions to study the crime problem and the ability of the police to deal with crime.

THE WICKERSHAM COMMISSION In 1929, President Herbert Hoover created the National Commission on Law Observance and Enforcement with George W. Wickersham as its chair. The commission was popularly known as the **Wickersham Commission** and conducted the first national study of the U.S. criminal justice system. The *Wickersham Commission Report*, issued in 1931, criticized the Volstead Act, saying it was not enforced because it was unenforceable. National Prohibition was repealed in 1933.

The commission report found that the average police commander's term of office was too short to be effective and that responsibility to politicians made the position insecure. The report indicated that there was a lack of effective, efficient, and honest patrol officers, and no efforts had been made to educate, train, or discipline officers or to fire

---

Volstead Act (National Prohibition, Eighteenth Amendment) Became law in 1920 and forbade the sale and manufacture of alcohol.

Wickersham Commission Published the first national study of the U.S. criminal justice system, in 1931.

incompetent ones. Further findings showed that police forces, even in the biggest cities, did not have adequate communication systems or equipment.

Two volumes of the *Wickersham Commission Report, Lawlessness in Law Enforcement* (volume 2) and *The Police* (volume 14), concerned themselves solely with the police. *Lawlessness in Law Enforcement* portrayed the police as inept, inefficient, racist, and brutal, and accused them of committing illegal acts. The volume concluded, "The third degree—the inflicting of pain, physical or mental, to extract confessions or statements—is extensively practiced."[34]

The *Wickersham Commission Report* blamed the shortcomings of the police on a lack of police professionalism. *The Police*, written primarily by August Vollmer, discussed methods that could be used to create a professional police force in the United States. The methods the commission advocated included increased selectivity in the recruitment of officers, better pay and benefits, and more education for police officers.

The *Wickersham Commission Report* angered citizens and started another groundswell for police reform. With the onset of the Great Depression, however, police reform became less important than economic revival, and another attempt at police reform failed.

AUGUST VOLLMER From 1905 to 1932, August Vollmer was the chief of police in Berkeley, California. Vollmer instituted many practices that started to professionalize policing in the United States. Among those practices was incorporating university training as a part of police training. Vollmer also introduced the use of intelligence, psychiatric, and neurological tests to aid in the selection of police recruits and initiated scientific crime detection and crime-solving techniques. In addition, Vollmer helped develop the School of Criminology at the University of California at Berkeley, which became the model for programs related to law and criminal justice throughout the United States. In addition to authoring the *Wickersham Commission Report*'s volume *The Police*, Vollmer trained numerous students who went on to become reform-oriented and progressive police chiefs. Vollmer can certainly be considered the father of modern American policing.

O. W. WILSON A disciple of Vollmer's, O. W. Wilson pioneered the use of advanced training for police officers when he took over and reformed the Wichita, Kansas, police department in 1928. While there, Wilson conducted the first systematic study of the effectiveness of one-officer squad cars. Despite officers' complaints about risks to their safety, his study showed that one-officer cars were more efficient, effective, and economical than two-person cars. Wilson believed that police departments should maximize patrol coverage by replacing foot patrols with one-person auto patrols. He advocated rapid response to calls for service as a key criterion by which to judge the effectiveness of police departments.

As dean of the School of Criminology at the University of California at Berkeley from 1950 to 1960 and superintendent of the Chicago police from 1960 to 1967, Wilson developed modern management and administrative techniques for policing. The core of Wilson's approach to police administration was managerial efficiency. He was the author of the first two textbooks on police management: the International City Management Association's *Municipal Police Administration* and his own text, *Police Administration*, which became the bible of policing for decades.

Almost every U.S. police department since the 1950s has been organized around the principles espoused in Wilson's books. He developed workload formulas, some of which remained unchanged for decades, based on reported crimes and calls for service on each beat.

RAYMOND BLAINE FOSDICK AND BRUCE SMITH Other early pioneers in the movement toward police professionalism were Raymond Blaine Fosdick and Bruce Smith, even though neither was a police officer. Fosdick is noted for the first scholarly research regarding the police. In 1915, he published *European Police Systems*, which examined the police structures and practices of Europe. In 1920, he published *American Police Systems* after studying the police of 72 U.S. cities.

Smith, a researcher and later manager of the Institute of Public Administration, also contributed to our early knowledge of the police. His efforts in surveying and researching police departments in approximately 50 leading American cities in 18 states led to his noteworthy 1940 book *Police Systems in the United States*; a second edition was published in 1949.

JOHN EDGAR HOOVER One cannot discuss law enforcement in the 20th-century United States without mentioning J. Edgar Hoover. In 1921, President

Warren G. Harding appointed Hoover, an attorney working for the U.S. Department of Justice, as assistant director of the Bureau of Investigation, the forerunner of the Federal Bureau of Investigation (FBI). Upon the retirement of the bureau's director in 1924, President Calvin Coolidge appointed Hoover as the director. Over the next 48 years, Hoover was reappointed as director of the FBI by each succeeding U.S. president and remained director until his death in 1972.

Under Hoover's leadership, the FBI changed from an inefficient organization into what many consider to be the world's primary law enforcement agency. Among his major contributions were the hiring of accountants and lawyers as special agents; the introduction of the FBI *Uniform Crime Reports*, which have been the leading source of crime and arrest statistics in the United States since 1930; the development of the National Crime Information Center (NCIC); the development of the FBI's Ten Most Wanted Criminals Program, otherwise known as Public Enemies; the development of the FBI Academy at Quantico, Virginia; and the popularizing of the FBI through the media as incorruptible, crime-fighting G-men.

During the past few decades, Hoover's reputation has diminished. Revelations have surfaced about his use of the media to build a myth about the FBI, his single-mindedness about Communism, and his domestic surveillance operations over prominent Americans.

KEFAUVER COMMITTEE In 1950, in response to fear about crime and the corruption of law enforcement officers, the U.S. Senate's Crime Committee, chaired by Senator Estes Kefauver, was created. The Kefauver Committee held televised public hearings that led to the discovery of a nationwide network of organized crime, a syndicate that has commonly been called the Mafia or Cosa Nostra. The hearings also revealed that many law enforcement officers nationwide were on the syndicate's payroll. The public was shocked at these tales of corruption, and another attempt at police reform began. David R. Johnson wrote about this decade:

> The 1950s marked a turning point in the history of professionalism. Following major scandals, reformers came to power across the nation. Politicians had real choices between the

traditional and new models of policing because a number of professional police reformers were available for the first time. With an enraged middle class threatening their livelihoods, the politicians opted for reform.[35]

Policing in the 1960s and 1970s

The 1960s and 1970s were times of great tension and change and probably formed the most turbulent era for policing in U.S. history. Numerous social problems permeated these decades, and the police were at the center of each one. The struggle for racial equality reached its peak, accompanied by marches, demonstrations, and riots that burned down whole neighborhoods in U.S. urban centers. The Vietnam War was reaching its height, soldiers were dying, and students across the United States were protesting the war and governmental policies. The Supreme Court decided in case after case to protect arrested persons from oppressive police practices. The police seemed to be more the targets of radical groups than the respected protectors of the people. In short, during this time of dramatic social changes in the United States, the police were not only right in the middle, but often the focus of it all.

Because of their role, the police were caught between those fighting for their civil rights and the government officials (the employers of the police) who wanted to maintain the status quo, between demonstrating students and college and city administrators. The police received much criticism during these years. Some of it was deserved, but much of it was for circumstances beyond their control.

James Q. Wilson perhaps best described the decade of the 1960s when he wrote, "It all began about 1963; that was the year, to over-dramatize a bit, that a decade began to fall apart."[36]

SUPREME COURT DECISIONS The 1960s saw the Warren Court at its peak—a U.S. Supreme Court that focused dramatically on individual rights. Police actions ranging from arrests to search and seizure to custodial interrogation were being declared unconstitutional. Chapter 13, "Police and the Law," will focus on these decisions. The Court made dramatic use of the exclusionary rule, a 1914 Supreme Court ruling that declared that evidence seized by the police in violation of the Constitution could not be used against a defendant in federal court, thus leading to the possibility that a guilty defendant could go free because of procedural errors by the police.

Many important police-related cases were decided in this era. *Mapp v. Ohio* (1961) finally, after much warning, applied the exclusionary rule to all states in the nation.[37] *Escobedo v. Illinois* (1964) defined the constitutional right to counsel at police interrogations.[38] *Miranda v. Arizona* (1966) required the police to notify a person who is in police custody and who is going to be interrogated of his or her constitutional rights.[39]

THE CIVIL RIGHTS MOVEMENT Legal segregation of the races finally ended with the landmark Supreme Court case of *Brown v. Board of Education of Topeka* (1954), which desegregated schools all over the nation.[40] However, equal treatment of the races did not occur overnight. Numerous marches and demonstrations occurred before the Civil Rights Act of 1964 was passed. Because the police are the enforcement arm of government, they were used to enforce existing laws, which in many cases meant arresting and inhibiting the freedom of those marching for equality.

In 1960, the Freedom Riders left Washington, D.C., by bus to confront segregation throughout the South. The buses and protesters were harassed, temporarily halted, and attacked by violent white mobs in Anniston and Birmingham, Alabama. The police were used to inhibit these marches for equality.

In 1962, there were mass arrests of civil rights demonstrators in Albany, Georgia. Also in 1962, James Meredith became the first African American to enroll at the University of Mississippi. President John F. Kennedy was forced to send U.S. marshals and the armed forces into Mississippi to protect Meredith against attacks by segregationists, because the local police were unable or unwilling to protect him.

The Reverend Martin Luther King, Jr., was at the forefront of the civil rights marches. In 1963, King led 25,000 demonstrators on a historic march on Washington that culminated in his "I have a dream" speech. During this speech, a defining moment of the movement, a white uniformed police officer stood behind King in a highly visible position, perhaps as a symbolic representation of the new role of the police in America's social history. Officers were to act as defenders rather than oppressors.

Also in 1963, in Birmingham, Alabama, four African American girls were killed when a bomb exploded during a church service at the 16th Street Baptist Church. King led a peaceful march against segregation in Birmingham, Alabama, while Birmingham's sheriff Bull Connor unleashed hoses and police dogs against the demonstrators. The actions of police personnel like Connor caused the police much negative press and have affected police–minority group relationships ever since.

In 1965, African Americans and other civil rights demonstrators attempted a peaceful march to Selma, Alabama. During the march, Alabama state police, under directions from state officials, stopped the marchers at the Edmund Petus Bridge in Selma, where a Boston minister was murdered and white toughs beat many others. A massive civil rights march then proceeded from Selma to Montgomery, Alabama, under the protection of the National Guard.

Police were charged with keeping the peace during the Civil Rights marches of the 1960s, like this one led by Dr. Martin Luther King Jr. This role continues to be important today as citizens gather to make their message known.

AP Images

The civil rights movement continued and succeeded partly by enrolling more minorities as voters, outlawing forms of government-sanctioned segregation, and ensuring that more minorities participated in government. Today, many of the mayors and politicians in our large cities are members of minority groups. The civil rights movement led to efforts to increase the recruitment and hiring of blacks and other minorities in our nation's police departments and other agencies of the criminal justice system.

Although the civil rights movement was necessary in the evolution of our nation, the use of the police by government officials to thwart the movement left a wound in police-community relations that still has not healed. The 1991 beating of Rodney King in Los Angeles and the 1992 jury verdict acquitting the four Los Angeles police officers who were charged in King's beating (described later) angered people across the United States. The resulting riots in Los Angeles and other cities seemed to bring the United States back to the same strained racial conditions that existed in the 1960s.

POLICE RESPONSE TO CIVIL DISOBEDIENCE

The United States has a rich history of civil disobedience. As the Declaration of Independence states: "That whenever any Form of Government becomes destructive of these ends, it is the Right of the People to alter or to abolish it, and to institute new Government, laying its foundation on such principles and organizing its powers in such form, as to them shall seem most likely to effect their Safety and Happiness." The founding fathers of our republic laid out the reasons for civil disobedience, resulting in the Revolution and eventual founding of a new nation. The civil disobedience of our recent history has loosely followed these same principles, even though they may have been manifested in entirely different ways that are unacceptable to the majority of Americans.

In early Roman society, military cohorts formed a defensive square to ward off assaults. These squares were able to move in any direction, protecting their flanks and rear, and allowing the "front" to change as needed. During the last several decades, U.S. law enforcement has used a modified version of this defensive square when addressing violent civil disobedience.

The media have played a large role in publicizing confrontations between demonstrators and the police. This publicity has brought the events of the day into the living rooms of families and has changed how the police are viewed. Because of media slant, the public sometimes views these incidents as "assaults" by the police on "innocent" demonstrators.

Furthermore, with the advent of the 24-hour news media and the availability of social media to almost everyone, news and video about police activity are now distributed on an almost minute-by-minute basis. It is not hard to find information about police activity on the Internet, often posted by citizens rather than news media. Law enforcement is incorporating the new technology into their departments; most departments now have an assigned media relations officer who is familiar with the technology. These topics will be covered in more depth in Chapter 14, "Computers, Technology, and Criminalistics in Policing."

Today, most police departments, when called to respond to some incident of civil disobedience or activity in which the public may have an interest, assign someone to make a video recording of the event from the time police become involved to when they depart. This step can provide a safeguard to departments and officers for liability purposes, and it can help answer questions from the media when departments are presented with video recordings of civil disobedience.

ANTI–VIETNAM WAR DEMONSTRATIONS

The Vietnam War was another turbulent, heart-rending experience in American history, and again the police were used in a manner that tarnished their image. There were numerous and violent confrontations between opponents of the Vietnam War and the government's representatives—the police—on college campuses and city streets.

In 1967, hundreds of thousands of people using civil disobedience tactics marched in antiwar demonstrations in New York City, San Francisco, Washington, D.C., and numerous other cities around the nation, often clashing with the police, whose job it was to enforce the law and maintain order.

At the Democratic Party presidential convention in Chicago in 1968, police–citizen violence occurred that shocked the nation and the world. With information that 10,000 protesters organized by antiwar groups, including the Youth International Party (Yippies), were coming to Chicago for the 1968 National Democratic Convention, Chicago mayor

Unrest at the University of California at Davis

In November 2011, on the campus of the University of California at Davis, police and demonstrators confronted each other. Although confrontations between the police and demonstrators at the UC Davis campus are not uncommon, what was different about this event was the absolute outrage of the media and community over what has been a fairly common police practice, the use of pepper spray.

The demonstrators in this incident, who were illegally encamped on UC Davis property, were protesting the rise in state tuition costs in California. The campus community authorities asked the police to remove the demonstrators. What was not widely reported in the media was that police had arrested several "campers" who refused to leave the premises and, after those arrests, were surrounded by demonstrators demanding the release of those arrested. In California, this kind of action is called delaying or obstructing officers in the performance of their duties. It is also a very hazardous situation for officers.

Demonstrators told the police they could leave if they released the arrested protestors. The police response was to form a defensive square within the circle of demonstrators and give orders declaring the demonstration an illegal assembly. The police then warned the demonstrators that they would be pepper-sprayed if they did not move. The demonstrators did not move, and they were pepper-sprayed. However, the news that night, as well as a video of the incident that went viral on the Internet, showed only the pepper spraying and did not discuss the officers' reasons for using the pepper spray.

In the aftermath of this incident, some officers were placed on administrative leave, and the public called for the resignation of the Chancellor of UC Davis and the firing of the UC Davis Chief of Police.

In January 2013, UC Davis agreed to pay $1 million to 36 plaintiffs in a lawsuit against the university. The officer who was the focus of the lawsuit also received $38,056 from the State of California Workers' Compensation Board for continuing internal and external stress from the incident.

As a result of the investigation, the police department at UC Davis has undergone significant reforms aimed at preventing similar incidents in the future.

© 2016 Cengage Learning®

Richard J. Daley mobilized the National Guard and the Chicago police. On August 28, the protesters attempted to force their way into the convention. Police and the National Guard chased the crowd through downtown Chicago.

There are many different viewpoints of this chaotic disturbance in the streets of Chicago. Many report that the police command structure broke down and that the police became a mob that ran through the streets and assaulted protesters, reporters, and bystanders. A study subsequent to the convention, the *Walker Report,* called the incident a police riot, but others perceived it as the police doing their job. Many stress that the Yippies and other protesters were attempting to break up a lawfully gathered assembly by illegal means.

Eight members of the Yippies were charged with conspiracy for starting the disturbances in Chicago and were dubbed the "Chicago Eight." In 1969, the Chicago Eight trial began (it was later called the Chicago Seven trial due to the severance from the trial of Bobby Seales, the cofounder of the Black Panther Party). A Students for a Democratic Society (SDS) splinter group, the Weathermen, organized the Days of Rage in Chicago, which resulted in violent rampaging in the streets and more confrontation with the police. In 1970, all of the Chicago Eight were acquitted of conspiracy charges; convictions on lesser charges were later overturned as well.

CAMPUS DISORDERS In addition to the civil rights movement of the 1960s, demonstrations, marches, and civil disobedience also took place on college campuses across the nation. These events protested a perceived lack of academic freedom, the Vietnam War, the presence of Reserve Officers' Training Corps (ROTC) units on campuses, and many other issues. Again, the police were used to enforce the law.

In 1960, the Student Nonviolent Coordinating Committee (SNCC) was organized to coordinate student civil rights protests, and, in 1961, the SDS held its first national convention in Port Huron, Michigan. These two groups had a tremendous impact on the 1960s. Teach-ins, rallies, student strikes, takeovers of campus buildings, and the burning of draft cards were some of the tactics used on the campuses. The campus protests caused college administrators to call in local police departments to maintain order. That, in turn, caused students to complain about the actions of the police, again making the police the focus of anger and attention.

In 1968, a state of civil disorder was declared in Berkeley, California, following recurring police–student confrontations. Protests, riots, and violent clashes between students and the police replaced education on many college campuses in the United States.

Probably the most widely publicized campus protest of the 1960s was the student takeover at Columbia University, in New York City, in the spring of 1968. Students employed every tactic that had been used in earlier campus protests, including teach-ins, rallies, picketing, sit-ins, a student strike, and the takeover of university buildings. As negotiations between the college administration and the student rebels broke down, the administration decided to call in the police.

In the early morning of April 30, 1968, after students had taken over many college buildings, 2,000 police officers moved onto the campus and methodically cleared five occupied buildings. The effort to clear the remaining buildings became violent. Finally, the police were able to secure all buildings by arresting 692 students. In late May, the students again took over two buildings on Columbia's campus. The administration again called the police. The Cox Commission, formed to investigate the violence that ensued at Columbia University, reported on the police action that followed:

> Hell broke loose. One hundred students locked arms behind the barricades at Amsterdam Avenue. Hundreds more crowded close to the gate. The police swiftly dismantled the obstruction. The hundred broke and ran. But 2,000 students live in dormitories facing South Field. Many of them and hundreds of other people were crowded on the campus. For most,

the character of the police action was a profound shock; neither they nor others in the Columbia community appreciated the extent of the violence which is the probable concomitant of massive police action against hundreds, if not thousands, of angry students. As police advanced, most students fled. . . . Some police first warned the students; others chased and clubbed them indiscriminately. But not all students went to their dormitories and some who fled came back out to attack the police. Bottles and bricks were hurled by students. A number of police were injured. The action grew fierce. . . . By 5:30 A.M. the campus was secured.[41]

The campus antiwar riots reached their peak in 1970. The firebombing of a University of Wisconsin ROTC building began a wave of some 500 bombings or arsons on college campuses. Students rampaged through Cambridge's Harvard Yard, two students were killed and nine wounded by police gunfire at Jackson State College in Mississippi, and four students were killed by the National Guard at a protest at Kent State University, causing many U.S. colleges and universities to close for the year. Again, clashes between the police and students caused wounds that were hard to heal.

URBAN RIOTS Major riots erupted in the ghettos of many U.S. cities during the 1960s. Most started directly following a police action. This is not to say that the police caused the riots; rather, a police action brought to the surface numerous underlying problems, which many say were the actual causes of the riots.

In the summer of 1964, an off-duty white New York City police lieutenant shot an African American youth who was threatening a building superintendent with a knife. This shooting precipitated the 1964 Harlem riot. Riots also occurred that summer in Rochester, New York; Jersey City, New Jersey; and Philadelphia. In 1965, riots occurred in Los Angeles (the Watts district), San Diego, and Chicago. In 1966, riots again occurred in Watts, as well as in Cleveland, Brooklyn, and Chicago. In 1967, major riots occurred in Boston's Roxbury section, in Newark, and in Detroit.

The riot in Detroit was responsible for 43 deaths, 2,000 injuries, and property damage estimated at more than $200 million; 7,000 people were arrested. The Watts riot was responsible for 34 deaths, more than 1,000 injuries, and the arrests of nearly 4,000 people. The Newark riot was responsible for 26 deaths and 1,500 injuries.

In 1968, riots occurred in cities all over the United States—including Baltimore, Boston, Chicago, Detroit, Kansas City, Newark, New York City, and scores of other cities—following the murder of Dr. King. The worst riot occurred in Washington, D.C., with 12 people killed, 1,200 people injured, 7,600 people arrested, and nearly $25 million in property damage. Nationwide, 55,000 federal troops and National Guard members were called out. Forty-six deaths resulted from the riots, and 21,270 people were arrested.

Again, the efforts of the police to maintain order during these massive shows of civil disobedience and violence caused wounds in police–community relations that have yet to heal. Problems between the minority communities and the police continued, as did the riots. Several radical groups, including the Black Panther Party and the Black Liberation Army, waged urban warfare against the police, resulting in many deaths among their members and the police.

CREATION OF NATIONAL COMMISSIONS In the wake of the problems of the 1960s, particularly the problems between the police and citizens, three national commissions were created. The first was the **President's Commission on Law Enforcement and Administration of Justice**, which issued a report in 1967 entitled *The Challenge of Crime in a Free Society* and a collection of task force reports covering all aspects of the criminal justice system.

The second national commission was the **National Advisory Commission on Civil Disorders (Kerner Commission)**, which released a report in 1968 that decried white racism and a rapidly polarizing society. The report stated, "Our nation is moving toward two societies, one black, one white, separate and unequal." The commission concluded, "Abrasive relationships between police and Negroes and other minority groups have been a major source of grievance, tension, and, ultimately, disorder."[42]

The third was the President's Commission on Campus Unrest. Its report, issued in 1970, called the gap between youth culture and mainstream society a threat to U.S. stability. All three commissions are mentioned often in this text.

CORRUPTION AND THE KNAPP COMMISSION The corruption that historically permeated American policing in the past has continued into the present. Approximately every 20 years, the nation's largest and most visible police department, the New York City Police Department (NYPD), has been the subject of a major scandal involving police corruption and governmental hearings: the Seabury Hearings in the 1930s, the Gross Hearings in the 1950s, and the Knapp Commission in 1970.

The Knapp Commission resulted from allegations made by New York City plainclothes police officer Frank Serpico and New York City police sergeant David Durk. Serpico was a Bronx officer (assigned to enforce antigambling laws) who was aware of widespread graft and bribes received in his unit. He took his tales of corruption to major police department officials, including the second-highest ranking officer in the department; to the city's Department of Investigation; and eventually to the mayor's office. When Serpico finally realized that no one was taking his claims seriously, he and Durk went to a *New York Times* reporter, who wrote a series of stories about corruption in the department that shocked the public. The *Times* articles forced the mayor, John Lindsey, to appoint a commission to investigate police corruption, which popularly became known as the Knapp Commission. Chapter 8, "Police Ethics and Police Deviance," will focus on the Knapp Commission and police corruption and misconduct. The revelations of the Knapp Commission regarding widespread, systemic, organized corruption in the NYPD led to sweeping changes in the department's organization, philosophy, operations, and procedures.

POLICE RESEARCH The decades of the 1960s and 1970s saw tremendous research into policing, which brought about sweeping changes in thinking about how police work is done in the United States. One of the most significant developments in modernizing and professionalizing the police was the creation of the Law Enforcement Assistance Administration (LEAA) within the U.S. Department of Justice

President's Commission on Law Enforcement and Administration of Justice Commission that issued a report in 1967 entitled *The Challenge of Crime in a Free Society*. The commission was created in the wake of the problems of the 1960s, particularly the problems between police and citizens.

National Advisory Commission on Civil Disorders (Kerner Commission) Commission created in 1968 to address the reasons for the riots of the 1960s.

through Title I of the Omnibus Crime Control and Safe Streets Act of 1968. The LEAA spent more than $60 million in its first year alone, and, between 1969 and 1980, it spent more than $8 billion to support criminal justice research, education, and training.

The LEAA required each state to create its own criminal justice planning agency, which in turn was required to establish an annual, comprehensive, statewide criminal justice plan to distribute LEAA funds throughout the state. One of LEAA's primary benefits to police officers was its Law Enforcement Education Program (LEEP), which provided funds for the college education of police officers.

An independent organization, the Police Foundation, joined LEAA as a funding source for research on innovative police projects. The most significant of these projects were the Kansas City Preventive Patrol Experiment, the Rand Corporation's study of the criminal investigation process, the Police Foundation's study of team policing, and the Newark Foot Patrol Experiment. These innovative studies began to change the way we thought about policing in the United States.

As we will see later in Chapter 9, "Patrol Operations," traditional policing involved three major strategies: (1) routine random patrol, (2) rapid response to 911 calls by citizens, and (3) retroactive investigation of past crimes by detectives. Academic research, starting in the 1960s and continuing through today, has indicated that these three strategies have not worked. This research has led police administrators to implement the innovative approaches to policing that will be discussed in Chapter 10, "Investigations."

DEVELOPMENT OF THE IDEOLOGY OF A DIVERSE DEPARTMENT Until the late 1960s, women constituted only a very small percentage of police officers in the United States, and they generally were restricted to performing only certain duties, including guarding female prisoners, juvenile work, routine clerical work, issuing parking tickets, and sometimes vice work. It was presumed that women, because of their gender and typical smaller size, were not capable of performing the same type of patrol duty as men. Black and other minority group officers also faced tremendous discrimination in policing. The national commissions discussed earlier, the Civil Rights Act of

1964, and the Equal Employment Opportunity Act of 1972 began to address the inequities of race and gender in employment. Also, the concept of affirmative action and individual and class action lawsuits began to influence police departments to address traditional employment inequities and led to more women and minority group officers being granted true representation in law enforcement. As Chapter 2, "Organizing Public Security in the United States," shows, women, blacks, and other minorities are indeed equally and fairly represented today in our police and sheriff's departments. Chapter 7, "Minorities in Policing," will address at length the history of the struggle for equality in policing.

Policing in the 1980s and 1990s

The tremendous turmoil that permeated society and policing during the decades of the 1960s and 1970s gave way to somewhat more peaceful times in the 1980s and 1990s. The police, as always, were confronted by a myriad of issues and events that severely tested their professionalism and ability. Prominent among those events were the first terrorist bombing of New York City's World Trade Center in 1993 and the bombing of the Federal Building in Oklahoma City, Oklahoma, in 1995. In these cases, police agencies from all over the nation performed numerous heroic and successful actions that saved lives and resulted in the eventual criminal prosecution of the offenders.

Some of the many positive developments of the 1980s and 1990s included the development of a computer revolution in policing involving communications, record keeping, fingerprinting, and criminal investigations; a drastic reduction in violent crime; and the birth of two major new concepts of police work, community policing and problem-solving policing. Community policing and problem-solving policing can be seen either as new approaches to policing or as a return to the policing of the past—the cop on the beat. Chapter 12, "Community Policing: The Debate Continues," covers these concepts. The computer and technology revolution in policing is covered in Chapter 14, "Computers, Technology, and Criminalistics in Policing."

Some believe that the highlight of recent developments in policing is the significant crime reductions that occurred throughout the nation in the

| History Is All Relative | ON THE JOB |

I remember when I started at the police department in 1977. I finished the police academy and went on to eight weeks of field training with a more senior officer. The department didn't have a formalized program at the time; they simply put rookie officers with more experienced officers who they felt could teach them how our department did things.

Besides my training officer, I met lots of other officers eager to share their knowledge with me on how to "really do the job." I had some "old timers" tell me about how different it was when they started with the department. "They handed me a badge and a gun and told me to go out and enforce the laws… we didn't have any of this training stuff," one told me. This was hard for me to imagine as I thought of all the information I had learned in the academy and was learning during training—not to mention the liability involved. "We never had air-conditioned cars," another told me as I cringed at the thought of driving around in the south Florida heat and humidity without the benefit of air conditioning. "There was no such thing as backup," another said. "We just broke up the fights in the projects and threw 'em in the drunk tank to sober up for a few hours." Again, the thought of detaining people for drunkenness with no real reason to deprive them of their liberty made me nervous. I chalked it up to "the old days" and smiled smugly at how far we'd come and how advanced we were now.

Now, as I teach my classes, and we talk about the "history" of law enforcement and how police officers actually relied on car radios and worked without the luxury of portable radios, and how we used .38 revolvers and were ecstatic when speed-loaders became part of our equipment, students are shocked to realize I worked that way. They are shocked to learn we used payphones as a means of communication when we didn't want to use the radio. They can't imagine life without everyone having cellphones. Their jaws really hit the desks when I talk about our early use of "cellphones." I was a lieutenant in charge of the midnight shift when we got our first portable phone. The shift commanders carried the phone in their cars for use in emergency situations where we did not want the press or others to hear our radio transmissions or we had to call "the brass" at home to brief them on situations. This "portable" phone (and I use the term loosely) was mounted in a briefcase and weighed more than 15 pounds. If a situation occurred where we were setting up at a scene, I would take the briefcase out of the car, lay it on the trunk, and screw antennas into the phone assembly. Then I hoped the bad guys couldn't hear me pushing the numbers (it sounded loud at 3:00 a.m. in the quiet streets) or see all the lights associated with the phone, and, most of all, I hoped it worked. Sometimes, I just felt it wasn't worth all the trouble to use it. If nothing else, these stories make students appreciate the ease of communications that law enforcement enjoys today.

—Linda Forst

late 20th century. In 1997, the FBI reported that serious crime had declined 3 percent, the fifth annual decrease in a row since 1992. Violent crime, including homicide, robbery, rape, and aggravated assault, dropped 7 percent from the previous year. This decrease in violent crime was the largest in 36 years. The homicide rate nationwide was the lowest it had been since 1969.[43] These crime decreases continued throughout the decade and into the 21st century.

Some criminologists attributed this decline to a number of factors, including community policing, problem-solving policing, and aggressive zero-tolerance policing. Other factors considered were increased jail and prison populations, demographic changes in the numbers of crime-prone young people, and community efforts against crime.

The explanation, however, that has gained the most popularity among law enforcement officials, politicians, and criminologists is that the reduced crime rates are the result of aggressive police tactics like those introduced in New York City by its former commissioner, William J. Bratton. Bratton completely reengineered the NYPD to make reducing crime its primary objective. The keynote behind Bratton's reengineering was a process known as CompStat.

CompStat was originally a document, referred to as the "CompStat book," which included current year-to-date statistics for criminal complaints and arrests developed from a computer file called Comparative Statistics—hence, CompStat. Central to CompStat are the semiweekly crime-strategy sessions conducted at police headquarters. At each CompStat meeting, sophisticated computer-generated maps addressing a seemingly unlimited variety of the latest crime details confront and challenge the precinct commanders. The commanders are held responsible for any increases in crime and must present innovative solutions to address their precincts' crime problems. In these sessions, crime-fighting techniques are developed for implementation. The essence of CompStat is a four-step process:

1. Timely and accurate intelligence
2. Use of effective tactics in response to that intelligence
3. Rapid deployment of personnel and resources
4. Relentless follow-up and assessment

One writer summed up the essence of NYPD's policing strategy as follows:

> The multifaceted CompStat process is perhaps best known to law enforcement insiders for its high-stress, semiweekly debriefing and brainstorming sessions at police headquarters, but it is far more. . . . CompStat is enabling the NYPD to pinpoint and analyze crime patterns almost instantly, respond in the most appropriate manner, quickly shift personnel and other resources as needed, assess the impact and viability of anti-crime strategies, identify bright, up-and-coming individuals from deep within the ranks, and transform the organization more fluidly and more effectively than one would ever expect of such a huge police agency.[44]

Another police innovation of the 1980s and 1990s was the emergence of the police paramilitary unit (PPU), which is similar, in a way, to police

SWAT units. The goal of these units is to address extremely serious violent criminal events such as hostage situations, terrorist acts, and sniper shootings. Peter B. Kraska and Victor E. Kappeler report that PPUs are equipped with an array of militaristic equipment and technology and are focused on the possibility of applying force. Kraska and Kappeler conducted a survey of 690 U.S. law enforcement agencies and found that fewer than 10 percent had PPUs in the early 1970s, but by 1995 more than 89 percent had them.[45] PPUs and SWAT teams will be discussed further in Chapter 9.

Despite all the successes of the police in the 1980s and 1990s, many of the problems of earlier decades carried over into this time. Some of the negative issues and problems confronting the police in the late 20th century were the continuing debate over misconduct by the police and the reoccurrence of riots in our communities.

The endemic corruption that has always characterized U.S. policing subsided somewhat during the 1980s and 1990s, although there were sporadic corruption scandals. The most noticeable of these included the Miami River Cops scandal of the 1980s, involving murders, extortions, and drug violations; and New York City's 77th and 32nd Precincts and "Cocaine Cops" scandals, involving drug corruption. Many other police departments throughout the nation also suffered embarrassing corruption and misconduct scandals. Chapter 8 covers this topic in detail.

In 1991, the **Rodney King incident** in Los Angeles shocked the public and may have set the police back 30 years in the progress they had made in improving relationships with the community. A citizen captured on video the police beating of Rodney King, an African American. King had taken the police on a 115-mile-per-hour chase throughout Los Angeles and, when finally stopped by the police, allegedly lunged at one of the officers. The videotape shows four Los Angeles police officers beating King, who seems to be in a prone and defenseless position on the ground, with 56 blows from nightsticks while a dozen other officers stand by and watch. Four of the officers were arrested and charged with the assault of King. They were originally acquitted in a criminal trial but were subsequently convicted in a federal trial.

With a different perspective on the Rodney King case, some have argued that the officers involved used many different types of nonlethal

---

CompStat Weekly crime strategy meetings, featuring the latest computerized crime statistics and high-stress brainstorming; developed by the New York City Police Department in the mid-1990s.

Rodney King incident The 1991 videotaped beating of an African American citizen by members of the Los Angeles Police Department.

force against King, who refused commands to stop his aggressive and threatening behavior toward the officers, instead of using deadly force. They struck him with two 50,000-volt stun-gun discharges, which did not seem to stop his erratic behavior, and used baton procedures taught at the Los Angeles Police Department (LAPD) academy. The supervising officer at the scene, Sergeant Stacey C. Koon, wrote a book about the case, *Presumed Guilty: The Tragedy of the Rodney King Affair*.[46]

The Rodney King incident was followed in 1997 with allegations that at least two police officers from New York City's 70th Precinct assaulted a Haitian American prisoner, Abner Louima, by placing a wooden stick into his rectum and then shoving the blood- and feces-covered stick into his mouth. Like the King case, this incident shocked the world. One officer was eventually convicted and imprisoned for the assault on Louima.

In 1994, a criminal trial also brought negative attention to the police. Former football star Orenthal James (O. J.) Simpson was charged by the Los Angeles police with the brutal murder of his former wife, Nicole Brown, and her friend Ronald Goldman. The trial was covered on national television and captured the attention of the world. Two hundred and fifty days and 126 witnesses later, the jury, despite overwhelming scientific evidence to the contrary, voted to acquit Simpson of all charges.

Many said the verdict was **jury nullification**; others said it was an indictment of the Los Angeles Police Department. The LAPD was accused of gross incompetence in its handling of the crime scene and forensic evidence, and one of its main witnesses, Detective Mark Fuhrman, later pled guilty to charges that he had lied while testifying in the trial.

During the 1980s and 1990s, riots again scarred our sense of domestic tranquility. The city of Miami experienced two major riots in its Overtown district in the 1980s. New York City experienced riots in the 1990s in Crown Heights and Washington Heights. Many other cities witnessed racial and civil unrest and skirmishes between the police and citizens.

Perhaps the worst riot in our nation's history occurred in 1992 following the not-guilty verdicts against the officers in the Rodney King case. The riot began in Los Angeles and spread to other parts of the country. By the second day of the riot, at least 23 people had been killed, 900 injured, and 500 arrested. Hundreds of buildings burned as the violence spread from south-central Los Angeles to other

areas. Entire inner-city blocks lay in ruin. The riot quickly spread to Atlanta, San Francisco, Madison (Wisconsin), and other cities. Fighting between African Americans and whites was reported at high schools in Maryland, Tennessee, Texas, and New York. By the end of the second day, more than 4,000 National Guard troops and 500 U.S. Marines had entered Los Angeles. Nearly a week after the riot started, calm began to appear. The final toll of the Los Angeles riot revealed that 54 people were killed; 2,383 people were injured; 5,200 buildings, mostly businesses, were destroyed by arson; and over $1 billion in property damage occurred. The riot resulted in the loss of approximately 40,000 jobs. Almost 17,000 arrests were made.

The following is a vivid newspaper description of the events during the first days of the riot:

> A gunfight broke out this afternoon between Korean merchants and a group of black men in the Korea-town section, a sharp escalation in the tensions that have divided the groups in recent months. Tall plumes of smoke rose from burning shops in the neighborhood, just north of South-Central.
>
> As fires, police sirens, and pockets of violence spread, most of the city shut down, with offices and shops closing and public transport scaling back its operations early. As the guard members were taking up positions in the badly battered South-Central area, convoys of cars carrying young men headed out into affluent West Los Angeles and Beverly Hills, shouting, brandishing hatchets, crowbars, and bottles, beating passersby, and looting shops.[47]

A special commission under the direction of William H. Webster (the former director of both the Federal Bureau of Investigation and the Central Intelligence Agency) was created to study the causes of the Los Angeles riots and issued a report that was highly critical of the LAPD.

Policing in the 2000s

As the world welcomed a new millennium, some of the same issues that influenced policing since the creation of the first organized police forces in

jury nullification A vote by jurors to either ignore the evidence in a trial or disregard the instructions of a judge to reach a verdict based on their own consciences.

the early 19th century continued to dominate the police landscape. Among these were police misconduct, corruption, and brutality. There were also many positives for the police as the crime rate decline that started to occur in the 1990s continued into the 2000s, and local, state, and federal law enforcement agencies reorganized and reengineered themselves to address the concerns of the new millennium. Numerous departments throughout the nation adopted the CompStat program. Crime in New York City, in particular, dropped to levels not seen since the 1960s.

In a 2003 report, the Police Foundation stated that the emergence of CompStat programs similar to New York City's indicated that the police had taken a lead role among criminal justice agencies in embracing and using social science to decide what problems needed solving and how to solve them. It reported that CompStat-like programs combined all of the major prescriptions offered by contemporary organizational development experts with the latest geographic information systems technology. These programs reengineered police management by using sophisticated computer maps and crime statistics to facilitate timely and targeted responses to crime problems.[48]

The Beltway Sniper Case caught the attention of the U.S. public in 2002 and engendered tremendous fear. For 23 days in October 2002, a team of snipers used a high-powered rifle to indiscriminately pick off victims in the Washington, D.C., and central Virginia regions. They shot 14 people, 10 of them fatally. The killing spree involved six homicides in one 24-hour period, followed by a series of shootings over a three-week period. The incidents and investigations spanned eight jurisdictions and involved more than 1,000 investigators. The investigators, working under the command of Police Chief Charles Moose of Montgomery County, Maryland, formed the Sniper Task Force, which involved federal, local, and state law enforcement officials. This task force had to simultaneously conduct criminal investigations of the incidents, try to prevent more from occurring, and respond to the scenes of new shootings as they occurred. "It's almost like changing the tire of a car while it's moving," said Chuck Wexler, the executive director of the Police Executive Research Forum (PERF).[49] The task force's performance set positive standards for interagency cooperation among all levels of law enforcement and positive communication with citizens. The two

snipers were apprehended on October 24, 2002, at a highway rest stop in Myersville, Maryland, based on a tip from a citizen.

Crime rates continued to decline nationwide as the police adopted or continued aggressive crime-fighting techniques. A comparison of crime over the 10-year period from 2001 to 2010 shows that violent crime decreased 13.4 percent and property crime decreased 13.0 percent. From 2009 to 2010, murder was down 4.2 percent, forcible rape down 5.0 percent, robbery down 10.0 percent, aggravated assault down 4.1 percent, property crime down 2.7 percent, larceny-theft down 2.4 percent, and motor vehicle theft down 7.4 percent.[50] Regarding the significant crime reductions since 1991, *Time* reported in 2010:

> By 1991, the murder rate in the U.S. reached a near record 9.8 per 100,000 people… Then, a breakthrough. Crime rates started falling. Apart from a few bumps and plateaus, they continued to drop through boom times and recessions, through peace and war, under Democrats and Republicans. Last year's murder rate may be the lowest since the mid-1960s, according to preliminary statistics released by the Department of Justice. The human dimension of this turn-around is extraordinary: had the rate remained unchanged, an additional 170,000 Americans would have been murdered in the years since 1992. That's more U.S. lives than were lost in combat in World War I, Korea, Vietnam and Iraq—combined. In a single year, 2008, lower crime rates meant 40,000 fewer rapes, 380,000 fewer robberies, half a million fewer aggravated assaults and 1.6 million fewer burglaries than we would have seen if rates had remained at peak levels.[51]

The academic research into policing that occurred in the 1960s and 1970s, which caused many changes in police operations, continued through the rest of the 20th century and into the twenty-first. However, in a major speech at the 2006 National Institute of Justice's (NIJ) annual conference, Los Angeles Police Chief William Bratton reflected on the tension between criminal justice practitioners and researchers by arguing that recent criminal justice research is seen by the policing community as both irrelevant to their actual work and derogatory toward police work in general. Bratton said that academics and practitioners have recently disagreed about the causes of crime and how to control it: Academics have claimed that crime is caused by a combination of different factors such as poverty, economic disparities, and racism, while most law enforcement practitioners have viewed the main cause of crime as human behavior. He challenged researchers to conduct field-relevant research that offers findings and theories that can be implemented in the field.[52] Bratton said,

> The one thing I have learned and now strongly advocate is that the police, properly resourced and directed, can control behavior to such a degree that we can change behavior. My experiences in Boston and in New York and now in Los Angeles have borne this out. I have seen nothing in the way of hard evidence to dissuade me from this simple truth.
>
> Quite simply, cops count. We are one of the most essential initiators and catalysts in the criminal justice equation. Crime may go up or down to some degree when influenced by many of the old so-called causes—which I prefer to describe as influences—but the quickest way to impact crime is with a well-led, managed, and appropriately resourced police force that embraces risk taking and not risk adversity, and a policing structure that includes accountability-focused CompStat management principles, "broken windows" quality-of-life initiatives, and problem-oriented community policing that is transparent and accessible to the public, the profession, the media, and the research community.[53]

Police corruption issues resurfaced in the 2000s. Most notably, the LAPD was involved in a major corruption scandal involving their antigang unit operating out of the department's Rampart division. Many of the unit's members were accused of framing hundreds of people, planting evidence, committing perjury, and forcing confessions through beatings. Officers were also accused of several illegal shootings. One officer who was caught stealing $1 million worth of cocaine from the police property room became an informant and cooperated with prosecutors. After this scandal came to light, hundreds of falsely obtained convictions were thrown out of court, and numerous civil lawsuits against the department ensued. The informing officer was eventually convicted and sentenced to five years in prison. Other officers were convicted and also went to prison.

The civil unrest that dominated earlier times also did not end with the new millennium. In 2001, a four-day riot occurred in Cincinnati, Ohio, after a white police officer was charged with shooting and killing an unarmed man. The American legacy of violence after sporting events and controversial police shootings continued. In October 2004, a Boston police officer fired two shots from a pepper-pellet gun in the direction of a crowd of disorderly college students surrounding Boston's Fenway Park after a Boston Red Sox game. A 21-year-old student in the crowd was struck and died from her injuries. The incident caused tremendous criticism of the Boston Police Department, and several police commanders were suspended or demoted. On July 4, 2011, a BART (Bay Area Rapid Transit) police officer shot and killed a 45-year-old man after a confrontation on a transit platform. Family members and local citizens protested the shooting, which caused days of unrest in Oakland, California. The officer involved was eventually convicted of involuntary manslaughter.

9/11 AND ITS AFTERMATH Paramount to the new issues facing the police in the 2000s were the tragic **terrorist attacks against the United States of America on September 11, 2001**. Although Chapter 15, "Homeland Security," will discuss these attacks in more detail, here we will look at some of the changes they brought in terms of policing and government, as well as public perceptions.

As the twin towers of New York City's World Trade Center's Buildings 1 and 2 were struck by planes within minutes of each other, caught on fire, and then imploded, a massive emergency response was immediate and included the New York City Police Department, the New York Fire Department, the police and rescue operations of the Port Authority of New York and New Jersey, and the city's emergency medical service. These people entered the buildings in an attempt to rescue those within them. Many of these brave rescuers were lost forever, including many members of the high command of the Fire and Port Authority departments. Medical, law enforcement, and emergency response personnel from around the world responded. Triage centers went into operation, and ordinary residents passed out bottled water to the responding emergency personnel. By the evening of September 11,

---

terrorist attacks against the United States of America on September 11, 2001 The terrorist attacks committed by al Qaeda.

Buildings 5 and 7 of the World Trade Center had also collapsed, and many buildings began to tremble and show signs of imminent collapse. The fires, smoke, and eerie ash continued blowing through the streets. Almost 3,000 innocent persons were murdered that day. Twenty-three New York City police officers, 37 Port Authority of New York and New Jersey officers, 3 New York City court officers, and more than 300 New York City firefighters paid the ultimate price to their professions that day.

Within minutes of the attacks on the World Trade Center, another plane slammed into the five-sided, five-story, concrete-walled structure of the U.S. Pentagon in northern Virginia—the headquarters and command center of the U.S. military forces. The swiftness, scale, and sophisticated coordinated operations of the terrorists, coupled with the extraordinary planning required, caused terrorism and mass murder to hit the United States on a scale not previously experienced.

Following the tragic events of 9/11, many large police departments throughout the nation started specialized antiterrorism units and trained their members in disaster control and antiterrorism duties. As one example, the New York City Police Department started a counterterrorism bureau under the command of a deputy commissioner who was a retired general with the U.S. Marine Corps. The counterterrorism bureau, containing more than 1,000 officers, consisted of a counterterrorism section and investigating units. An article in *Law Enforcement News* reported,

> In the three years since 9/11, law enforcement in America on both the local and national levels continues to be dominated and guided by the effects of the terrorist attacks. Terrorism continues to soak up both attention and resources. Some police executives have deemed it "the new normal," others talk about "terror-oriented policing."[54]

In addition to changes in policing in the wake of 9/11, a major reorganization of the federal government created the massive **Department of Homeland Security**. Chapter 2, "Organizing Public Security in the United States," and Chapter 15, "Homeland Security," will address the enormous

organizational and operational changes in federal and state law enforcement as a result of the terrorist attacks in detail. In the aftermath of 9/11, Congress passed Public Law No. 107-56, the USA Patriot Act—Uniting and Strengthening America by Providing Appropriate Tools Required to Intercept and Obstruct Terrorism. This law gives law enforcement new ability to search, seize, detain, or eavesdrop in their pursuit of possible terrorists. The law has been controversial, and many Americans believe it may threaten their civil liberties. Chapter 15 will also discuss the Patriot Act more fully.

The new antiterrorism focus of U.S. law enforcement was seen clearly as the United States went to war against Iraq in March 2003. The counterterrorism units of law enforcement agencies in the United States matched the dramatic preparations of the military forces abroad:

> As the United States waged war on Iraq, New Yorkers and others across the region are witnessing an extraordinary state of heightened security. Police officers are armed like assault troops outside prominent buildings, police boats are combing the waterfronts, and trucks are being inspected at bridges and tunnels.[55]

The NYPD's war contingency plan, Operation Atlas, has been described as the most comprehensive terrorism-prevention effort the city ever conducted. Costing at least $5 million a week in police overtime alone, it included expanded patrols on the streets—focusing on government buildings, tourist attractions, financial institutions, hotels, and houses of worship—and in the subways, on the waterways, and in the harbor. The plan strengthened checkpoints at bridges and tunnels and on the streets. There were extra patrols in Jewish neighborhoods deemed to be terrorist targets, 24-hour police coverage of Wall Street, harbor patrols to protect commuter ferries, and bomb-sniffing dogs on the Staten Island Ferry. Officers were posted outside television news outlets to prevent possible takeovers by terrorists who might want to broadcast anti-American messages.

Such precautionary measures were not limited to New York. Random car searches were reinstated at many airports throughout the nation. In Ohio, weigh stations on highways stayed open around the clock for inspections; in South Dakota, six satellite parking lots at Mount Rushmore were shut down and park rangers, brandishing shotguns, screened

---

Department of Homeland Security Federal cabinet department established in the aftermath of the terrorist attacks of September 11, 2001.

each vehicle. In San Francisco, California Highway Patrol officers, some on bikes, joined National Guard troops stationed at the Golden Gate Bridge. Washington State Troopers rode on ferries and questioned passengers, and Coast Guard cutters shadowed the boats with .50-caliber machine guns mounted on the sterns and bows.

The war efforts of 2003 also brought massive social protests like those of earlier decades. Reminiscent of the antiwar protests of the 1960s, protesters took to the streets in March 2003 in response to the U.S. invasion of Iraq. In that month, there were street marches and skirmishes with the police in New York, Chicago, Atlanta, Boston, Philadelphia, San Francisco, Washington, D.C., Madison (Wisconsin), and other cities. Again, as in the 1960s, the police seemed to be caught in the middle between officials conducting the policies of government and citizens protesting those policies.

HURRICANE KATRINA In August 2005, concerns about terrorism and protests were temporarily replaced by a natural disaster, Hurricane Katrina, which hit the Gulf Coast states of Louisiana, Mississippi, and Alabama. The extensive damage caused by Katrina led to the realization that despite the creation of the Department of Homeland Security, local, state, and federal government agencies were ill equipped to handle a major disaster. It also brought to public attention the heroic efforts of the National Guard forces, the U.S. Coast Guard, and police officers throughout the United States who aided the victims and evacuees of the tragedy. The events of Katrina, however, brought shame to some members of the New Orleans Police Department (NOPD), who were reported in the press to have abandoned duty when Katrina hit their city and to have watched looters without taking action.

As Katrina's storm surge caused catastrophic damage along the coasts of Louisiana, the levees separating the city of New Orleans from Lake Pontchartrain were breached by the storm and about 80 percent of New Orleans was flooded. Most of the residents of the affected area, primarily in the city of New Orleans and in Jefferson Parish, were forced to flee their flood-ravaged homes and neighborhoods and to abandon all their belongings. Thousands of these victims sought refuge at the New Orleans Convention Center and the huge Superdome, the football stadium used by the New Orleans Saints. The refugees were abandoned there for several days.

The problems for the criminal justice system were devastating. Police stations and courthouses were flooded, and records and files were lost to the floodwaters. Evidence from 3,000 criminal cases in New Orleans was submerged in toxic floodwaters that swamped police headquarters and the courthouse. About 6,000 prisoners in prisons and jails were evacuated due to flooding. Basic functions of government ceased during and after the storm, including most public safety record keeping. The city's 911 operators were reported to have left their phones when water began to rise around their building. Police headquarters was damaged during the flooding, and the entire police department was temporarily based at a hotel on Bourbon Street, just steps away from a group of strip clubs.

Shortly after the hurricane ended, thousands of people who had remained in the city began looting stores, particularly in the French Quarter and along the city's major commercial area, Canal Street. Drug, convenience, clothing, and jewelry stores were among the major businesses looted. Looting also occurred in other towns throughout the disaster area. One looter, who insisted that she wasn't stealing from the Winn-Dixie supermarket, was quoted as saying, "It's about survival right now. We got to feed our children. I've got eight grandchildren to feed."[56] Gunshots were frequently fired at rescue and repair workers, including police officers, firefighters, and construction and utility workers. Thousands of National Guard and federal troops were mobilized, and thousands of police officers from around the United States volunteered to travel to the area to aid in the evacuation of the remaining residents and to restore order.

Adding to the problems of Katrina for residents and rescue workers were the rancid, polluted floodwaters throughout the streets, laden with dead bodies, human waste, and sewage. Oil slicks and household chemicals floated out of the abandoned businesses and homes in the area, in addition to the remains of chemical plants and oil and gas facilities.

NOPD Superintendent Eddie Compass, who was criticized for his department's actions during Katrina, announced his retirement at the end of September 2005 and was replaced by Deputy Superintendent Warren Riley. Riley announced that he was conducting an immediate investigation of the reported misconduct by members of the department. He suspended four officers without pay and put more than a dozen others on report for alleged misbehavior after Hurricane Katrina. He also announced that he was investigating 249 officers who did not report for active duty during the storm or immediately after it. In support of his department, however, Riley said he did not know how many of his officers had actually abandoned their posts and how many simply could not get to work. It was later discovered that many officers had lost their homes to the storm or were unable to find members of their families among the chaos and destruction. Riley said,

> Those officers should not be branded quitters or cowards either. This department is not dysfunctional. The more than 2,000 men and women of this agency stand united in not letting a very small segment of members tarnish the great reputation of their department.[57]

Perhaps some of the best descriptions of the stress and the reasons for it affecting the NOPD and its officers came from former Superintendent Compass, commenting to reporters on the frustration and morale of his officers:

> If I put you out on the street and made you get into gun battles all day with no place to urinate and no place to defecate, I don't think you would be too happy either. Our vehicles can't get any gas. The water in the street is contaminated. My officers are walking around in wet shoes.... We had no food. We had no water. We ran out of ammunition. We had no vehicles. We were fighting in waist-deep water.[58]

In 2008, the New Orleans Police Department, after spending several years working out of trailers and other temporary facilities following Hurricane Katrina, moved into its newly refurbished police headquarters. The NOPD is still struggling to rebuild its ranks, which were decimated by more than 30 percent because of desertions, defections, and retirements during and after Katrina. The U.S. Census Bureau, in 2008, reported that the latest estimate of New Orleans's population is 239,000, less than half of the population before Katrina.[59] Despite the population reduction, the press reports that there is no sign of crime abating in the city.[60] Hurricane Katrina was estimated to have been responsible for more than $115 billion in damage, and the death toll of the storm has been estimated at 1,800 people, mainly from Louisiana and Mississippi. Many people remain missing.

SUMMARY

- The word *police* comes from the Latin word *politia*, which means "civil administration." Etymologically, the police can be seen as those involved in the administration of a city.

- The police represent the civil power of government, rather than the military power of government.

- The concept of preserving the peace and enforcing the law has moved from primitive forms like the watch and ward to highly organized, professional police departments. The history of policing has included brutality, corruption, incompetence, innovation, research, heroism, and professionalism.

- Around the first century BCE, special, highly qualified members of the military formed the Praetorian Guard and could be considered the first police officers. Their job was to protect the palace and the emperor.

- In 1285 CE, the Statute of Winchester established a rudimentary criminal justice system in which most of the responsibility for law enforcement remained with the people themselves. The statute formally established (1) the watch and ward, which required all men in town to serve on the night watch and was the most rudimentary form of policing; (2) the hue and cry, which required all citizens to assist the watchmen; (3) the parish constable; and (4) the requirement that all males keep weapons in their homes for use in maintaining the public peace.

- In 1828, Sir Robert Peel, England's home secretary, drafted the first police bill, the Act for Improving the Police in and near the Metropolis (the Metropolitan Police Act), which established the first large-scale, uniformed, organized, paid, civil police force in London. Thus, the police as we know them today were, from their very beginning, ultimately responsible to the public. Peel has become known as the founder of modern policing, and early police were guided by his nine principles.

- The London Metropolitan Police was organized around the "beat system," in which officers were assigned to relatively small permanent posts and were expected to become familiar with them and the people residing there. This system differed from the patrols of the Paris police, which consisted of periodic roving surveillance of areas.

- In U.S. colonial society, despite the presence of law enforcement officials, law enforcement was still mainly the responsibility of the individual citizen, as it had been in early England. There was little law and order on the colonial frontier. In the southern states, slave patrols were the dominant form of policing.

- During the 18th century, the most common form of American law enforcement in the North was the system of constables in the daytime and the watch at night.

- The first organized American police department was created in Boston in 1838, followed by New York City, Philadelphia, Chicago, New Orleans, Cincinnati, Baltimore, and Newark.

- In the 19th century, the locally elected county sheriffs and the appointed town marshals were usually the only law enforcement officers available on the American frontier. In the American South, the former slave patrols eventually evolved into formal local police departments.

- The 1960s and 1970s were probably the most turbulent era ever for policing in U.S. history. Numerous social problems permeated these decades, and the police were right in the middle of each problem.

- Academic interest in policing began in earnest in the 1960s with programs in police science, which later were expanded to include the entire criminal justice system and renamed criminal justice programs.

- Police departments have been totally revamped since the 1960s. New recruitment efforts and hiring practices have made police departments better reflect the communities they serve.

- As the world welcomed a new millennium, some of the same issues continued to dominate the police landscape: police misconduct, corruption, and brutality. There were also many positives for the police as the crime rate decline that started in the 1990s continued into the 2000s, and local, state, and federal law enforcement agencies reorganized and reengineered themselves to address the concerns of the new millennium.

- The September 11, 2001, terrorist attacks on the United States changed policing to a degree that we cannot yet imagine. The demands on the police to confront the serious crime and disorder problems they face on the streets, as well as to attempt to ameliorate all the social problems they confront there, have been increased with new duties to protect citizens from terrorist attacks.

- The disaster caused by Hurricane Katrina led to the realization that local, state, and federal government agencies, despite the creation of the Department of Homeland Security, were ill equipped to handle a major disaster.

KEY TERMS

beat system
CompStat
constable
Department of Homeland Security
Dred Scott decision
hue and cry
jury nullification
mutual pledge

National Advisory Commission on Civil Disorders (Kerner Commission)
Peel's Nine Principles
posse comitatus
Praetorian Guard
President's Commission on Law Enforcement and Administration of Justice
Rodney King incident
shire-reeve

slave patrols
terrorist attacks against the United States of America on September 11, 2001
thief-takers
Vigiles
Volstead Act (National Prohibition, Eighteenth Amendment)
watch and ward
Wickersham Commission

REVIEW EXERCISES

1. Develop a timeline for policing in the United States, listing the major developments for each era.

2. The chair of your criminal justice department has nominated you to represent the department in a 21st-century time capsule project. She asks you to contribute material to be placed in a sealed, weatherproof container that will be buried on the campus grounds. The capsule will be opened on January 1, 2114. She asks you to include at least 10 simulated, representative documents or artifacts that reflect your study of U.S. policing for the years 1900 to the present. What would you include?

3. Prepare a five- to six-page report comparing and contrasting the salient issues and developments in American policing for the time periods 1900 to 1959, 1960 to 1979, 1980 to 1999, and the 2000s.

WEB EXERCISES

1. As part of your school's "New Millennium" conference, you have been asked by your department chair to represent the criminal justice department and present a brief history of your local police department or sheriff's office. The chair asks that you gather your information from the Internet and be prepared to give a 20-minute oral presentation. If your local department's history is not on the Web, find it at an agency nearby, possibly your state police agency.

2. Use the Internet to find the latest U.S. crime statistics.

3. Use the Internet to find the latest information on police initiatives from your local police or sheriff's department.

END NOTES

1. John Ayto, *Dictionary of Word Origins* (New York: Arcade, 1990), p. 402.

2. This section on early policing is based on the following: William G. Bailey, ed., *The Encyclopedia of Police Science* (New York: Garland, 1989); John J. Fay, *The Police Dictionary and Encyclopedia* (Springfield, Ill.: Charles C. Thomas, 1988); Sanford H. Kadish, *Encyclopedia of Crime and Justice* (New York: Free Press, 1983); George Thomas Kurian, *World Encyclopedia of Police Forces and Penal Systems* (New York: Facts on File, 1989); Jay Robert Nash, *Encyclopedia of World Crime* (Wilmette, Ill.: Crime Books, 1990); Charles Reith, *The Blind Eye of History: A Study of the Origins of the Present Police Era* (London: Faber, 1912); Philip J. Stead, *The Police of Paris* (London: Staples, 1957).

3. "The words [*vigilance* and *vigilante*] come from the Latin *vigilia*, which was derived from the adjective *vigil*, meaning 'awake, alert.' Another derivative of the Latin adjective was *vigilare*, meaning 'keep watch,' which lies behind the English *reveille, surveillance,* and *vigilant.*" Ayto, *Dictionary of Word Origins,* p. 559.

4. This section on the English roots of policing is based on the following: S. G. Chapman and T. E. St. Johnston, *The Police Heritage in England and America* (East Lansing: Michigan State University, 1962); Belton Cobb, *The First Detectives* (London: Faber & Faber, 1967), p. 51; T. A. Critchley, *A History of Police in England and Wales,* 2nd ed. rev. (Montclair, N.J.: Patterson Smith, 1972); Clive Emsley, *Policing and Its Context, 1750–1870* (New York: Schocken, 1984); A. C. Germann, Frank D. Day, and Robert R. J. Gallati, *Introduction to Law Enforcement and Criminal Justice* (Springfield, Ill.: Charles C. Thomas, 1969); W. E. Hunt, *History of England* (New York: Harper & Brothers, 1938); Luke Owen Pike, *A History of Crime in England* (London: Smith, Elder, 1873–1876); Patrick Pringle, *Highwaymen* (New York: Roy, 1963); Pringle, *Hue and Cry: The Story of Henry and John Fielding and Their Bow Street Runners* (New York: Morrow, 1965); Pringle, *The Thief Takers* (London: Museum Press, 1958); Sir Leon Radiznowciz, *A History of English Criminal Law and Its Administration from 1750,* 4 vols. (London: Stevens & Sons, 1948–1968); Reith, *A New Study of Police History* (London: Oliver & Boyd, 1956); Reith, *Blind Eye of History;* Thomas Reppetto, *The Blue Parade* (New York: Free Press, 1978); Albert Rieck, *Justice and Police in England* (London: Butterworth, 1936); Robert Sheehan and Gary W. Cordner, *Introduction to Police Administration,* 2nd ed. (Cincinnati: Anderson, 1989); John J. Tobias, *Crime and Police in England, 1700–1900* (New York: St. Martin's Press, 1979).

5. Pringle, *Hue and Cry,* p. 81.

6. New Westminster Police Service, "Sir Robert Peel's Nine Principles of Policing," retrieved August 28, 2008, from www .newwestpolice.org/peel.html.

7. Reppetto, *Blue Parade,* p. 19.

8. Lucia Zedner, "Policing Before and After the Police: The Historical Antecedents of Contemporary Crime Control," *British Journal of Criminology* 46 (2006): 78–96.

9. The sections on American colonial and eighteenth- and nineteenth-century policing are based on the following: Bailey, *Encyclopedia of Police Science;* Carl Bridenbaugh, *Cities in Revolt: Urban Life in America, 1743–1776* (New York: Knopf, 1965); Bridenbaugh, *Cities in the Wilderness: Urban Life in America, 1625–1742* (New York: Capricorn, 1964); Emsley, *Policing and Its*

Context; Robert M. Fogelson, *Big City Police* (Cambridge: Harvard University Press, 1977); Roger Lane, *Policing the City, Boston 1822–1885* (Cambridge: Harvard University Press, 1967); Eric Monkkonen, *Police in Urban America: 1860–1920* (Cambridge: Harvard University Press, 1981); Reppetto, *Blue Parade*; James F. Richardson, *The New York Police: Colonial Times to 1901* (New York: Oxford University Press, 1976); Richardson, *Urban Police in the United States* (Port Washington, N.Y.: Kennikat Press, 1974); Robert C. Wadman and William Thomas Allison, *To Protect and to Serve: A History of Police in America* (Upper Saddle River, N.J.: Pearson/Prentice Hall, 2004); Samuel Walker, *A Critical History of Police Reform: The Emergence of Professionalism* (Lexington, Mass.: Lexington Books, 1977); Walker, *Popular Justice: History of American Criminal Justice* (New York: Oxford University Press, 1980).

10. Richardson, *New York Police*, p. 31.

11. The sections on the American colonial southern experience and slave patrols are based on: Sally E. Hadden, *Slave Patrols: Law and Violence in Virginia and the Carolinas* (Cambridge: Harvard University Press, 2001), pp. 19, 20, and 24; P. L. Reichel, "Southern Slave Patrols as a Transitional Police Type," *American Journal of Police* 7 (1988): 51–57; M. P. Roth, *Crime and Punishment: A History of the Criminal Justice System* (Belmont: Calif.: Thompson/Wadsworth, 2005), p. 64; K. B. Turner, David Giacopassi, and Margaret Vandiver, "Ignoring the Past: Coverage of Slavery and Slave Patrols in Criminal Justice Texts," *Journal of Criminal Justice Education* 17 (2006): 181–195; Wadman and Allison, "Policing Race and Violence in the South," in *To Protect and to Serve*, pp. 27–41; Samuel Walker, *The Police in America: An Introduction*, 2nd ed. (New York: McGraw-Hill, 1992), p. 6.

12. James A. Conser and Gregory D. Russell, *Law Enforcement in the United States* (Gaithersburg, Md.: Aspen, 2002), pp. 52, 258–259; Carl B. Klockars, *The Idea of Police* (Beverly Hills, Calif.: Sage, 1985), pp. 55–56.

13. Walker, *The Police in America*, p. 6.

14. Roth, *Crime and Punishment*, p. 64.

15. Wadman and Allison, *To Protect and to Serve*, pp. 32–33.

16. *Dred Scott v. Sandford*, 19 How. 393 (1857). For an excellent description of the *Dred Scott* case, see Fred W. Friendly and Martha J. H. Elliott, *The Constitution: That Delicate Balance* (New York: McGraw-Hill, 1984), pp. 17–22.

17. Hadden, *Slave Patrols*, pp. 185–187.

18. *Commercial Advisor*, August 20, 1840, as cited in Richardson, *New York Police*, p. 31.

19. Cited in Richardson, *New York Police*, p. 10.

20. Walker, *Popular Justice*, p. 61.

21. Luc Sante, *Low Life: Lures and Snares of Old New York* (New York: Farrar, Straus & Giroux, 1991), p. 236.

22. Walker, *Popular Justice*, p. 63.

23. Fogelson, *Big City Police*, p. 25.

24. Richard A. Staufenberger, *Progress in Policing: Essays on Change* (Cambridge, Mass.: Ballinger Publishing, 1980), pp. 8–9.

25. Walker, *Popular Justice*, p. 63.

26. Lincoln Steffens, *The Autobiography of Lincoln Steffens* (New York: Harcourt Brace Jovanovich, 1958; originally published in 1931), p. 207.

27. Wadman and Allison, "Policing Race and Violence in the South," p. 36.

28. Ibid.

29. Ibid., pp. 36–37. Also see Paul D. Lack, "Law and Disorder in Confederate Atlanta," in Eric H. Monkkonen, ed., *Crime and Justice in American History: The South*, Part 2 (Munich: K. G. Saur, 1992), pp. 249–269.

30. Wadman and Allison, "Policing Race and Violence in the South," pp. 39–40.

31. The section on the frontier experience is based on the following: James D. Horan and Howard Swiggett, *The Pinkerton Story* (New York: Putnam, 1951); Horan and Swiggett, *The Pinkertons: The Detective Dynasty That Made History* (New York: Crown, 1967); Edward Hungerford, *Wells Fargo: Advancing the American Frontier* (New York: Bonanza, 1949); David R. Johnson, *American Law Enforcement: A History* (St. Louis: Forum Press, 1981); Carolyn Lake, *Undercover for Wells Fargo* (Boston: Houghton Mifflin, 1969); Allan Pinkerton, *The Expressman and the Detective* (New York: Arno Press, 1976); Frank R. Prassel, *The Western Peace Officer: A Legacy of Law and Order* (Norman: University of Oklahoma Press, 1972); Charles A. Siringo, *A Cowboy Detective: A True Story of Twenty-Two Years with a World-Famous Detective Agency* (Lincoln: University of Nebraska Press, 1988); Bruce Smith, *Police Systems in the United States* (New York: Harper & Row, 1960); Smith, *Rural Crime Control* (New York: Columbia University Institute of Public Administration, 1933); Wadman and Allison, *To Protect and to Serve*; Walter Prescott Webb, *The Texas Rangers: A Century of Frontier Defense* (Boston: Houghton Mifflin, 1935).

32. This section on twentieth-century policing is based on the following: Jay Stuart Berman, *Police Administration and Progressive Reform: Theodore Roosevelt as Police Commissioner of New York* (New York: Greenwood Press, 1987); William J. Bopp and Donald D. Schultz, *A Short History of American Law Enforcement* (Springfield, Ill.: Charles C. Thomas, 1977); Fogelson, *Big City Police*; Richard Kluger, *Simple Justice* (New York: Vintage, 1977); Roger Lane, *Policing the City* (New York: Atheneum, 1975); Doug McAdam, *Freedom Summer* (New York: Oxford University Press, 1988); Wilbur R. Miller, *Cops and Bobbies: Police Authority in New York and London, 1830–1870* (Chicago: University of Chicago Press, 1977); Monkkonen, *Police in Urban America*; Edward P. Morgan, *The '60s Experience: Hard Lessons about Modern America* (Philadelphia: Temple University Press, 1991); Albert J. Reiss, *The Police and the Public* (New Haven: Yale University Press, 1971); Richardson, *Urban Police in the United States*; Jerome H. Skolnick, *Justice without Trial: Law Enforcement in a Democratic Society*, 2nd ed. (New York: Wiley, 1975); Jerome H. Skolnick and David H. Bayley, *The New Blue Line* (New York: Free Press, 1986); Milton Viorst, *Fire in the Streets: America in the 1960s* (New York: Simon & Schuster, 1970); Wadman and Allison, *To Protect and Serve*; Walker, *Popular Justice*; Walker, *Critical History of Police Reform*; Juan Williams, *Eyes on the Prize: America's Civil Rights Years, 1954–1965* (New York: Penguin, 1983); James Q. Wilson, *Varieties of Police Behavior: The Management of Law and Order in Eight Communities* (Cambridge: Harvard University Press, 1968).

33. Reppetto, *Blue Parade*, p. 65.

34. National Commission on Law Observance and Enforcement, *Lawlessness in Law Enforcement*, vol. 2 of the *Wickerham Report* (Washington, D.C.: U.S. Government Printing Office, 1931).

35. Johnson, *American Law Enforcement*, p. 121.

36. James Q. Wilson, *Thinking About Crime* (New York: Basic Books, 1983), p. 5.

37. *Mapp v. Ohio*, 367 U.S. 643 (1961).

38. *Escobedo v. Illinois*, 378 U.S. 478 (1964).

39. *Miranda v. Arizona*, 384 U.S. 436 (1966).

40. *Brown v. Board of Education of Topeka*, 387 U.S. 483 (1954).

41. Cox Commission, *Crisis at Columbia: Report of the Fact-Finding Commission Appointed to Investigate the Disturbances at Columbia University in April and May 1968* (New York: Vintage, 1968), pp. 181–182.

42. National Advisory Commission on Civil Disorders, *Report of the National Advisory Commission on Civil Disorders* (New York: Bantam Books, 1968), p. 299.

43. Federal Bureau of Investigation, *Uniform Crime Reports: Crime in the United States—1997* (Washington, D.C.: Federal Bureau of Investigation, 1998).

44. Peter C. Dodenhoff, "LEN Salutes Its 1996 People of the Year, the NYPD and Its CompStat Process: A Total Package of Re-engineering and Strategy-Making That Has Transformed the Nation's Largest Police Force—As It Will Law Enforcement in General," *Law Enforcement News*, December 31, 1996, pp. 1, 4.

45. Peter B. Kraska and Victor E. Kappeler, "Militarizing American Police: The Rise and Normalization of Paramilitary Units," *Social Problems* 44 (1997): 1–18.

46. Stacey C. Koon and Robert Deitz, *Presumed Guilty: The Tragedy of the Rodney King Affair* (Washington, D.C.: Regnery Gateway, 1992).

47. Seth Mydans, "23 Dead after 2d Day of Los Angeles Riot: Fires and Looting Persist Despite Curfews," *New York Times*, May 1, 1992, pp. A1, A20.

48. James J. Willis, Stephen D. Mastrofski, and David Weisburd, *CompStat in Practice: An In-Depth Analysis of Three Cities* (Washington, D.C.: Police Foundation, 2003).

49. Police Executive Research Forum, *Managing a Multijurisdictional Case: Identifying Lessons Learned from the Sniper Investigation* (Washington, D.C.: Police Executive Research Forum, 2005).

50. Federal Bureau of Investigation, *Uniform Crime Reports: Crime in the United States—2010*, Table 1A (Washington, D.C.: Federal Bureau of Investigation, 2010).

51. David Von Drehle, "Why Crime Went Away," *Time*, February 22, 2010, pp. 32–35.

52. Nancy Ritter, ed., "LAPD Chief Bratton Speaks Out: What's Wrong with Criminal Justice Research—and How to Make It Right," *National Institute of Justice Journal* 257 (2007): 28–30.

53. William Bratton, quoted in Ritter, ed., "LAPD Chief Bratton Speaks Out."

54. Marie Simonetti Rosen, "Terror-Oriented Policing's Big Shadow," *Law Enforcement News*, December 2004, p. 1.

55. Richard Perez-Pena, "A Security Blanket, but with No Guarantees," *New York Times*, March 23, 2003, pp. A1, B14.

56. Allen G. Breed, "Looting Takes Place in View of La. Police," *Washington Post*, August 30, 2005, p. 1. See also Egan, "Uprooted and Scattered Far from the Familiar," *New York Times*, September 11, 2005, pp. 1, 33; Eric Lipton, Christopher Drew, Scott Shane, and David Rhode, "Breakdowns Marked Path from Hurricane to Anarchy: In Crisis, Federal Authorities Hesitated; Local Officials Were Overwhelmed," *New York Times*, September 11, 2005, pp. 1, 28; Jere Longman, "Scouring the Neighborhoods in a Personal Appeal to Holdouts," *New York Times*, September 6, 2005, p. A22; Joseph B. Treaster and John DeSantis, "With Some Now at Breaking Point, City's Officers Tell of Pain and Pressure," *New York Times*, September 6, 2005, pp. A21, A22; Jodi Wilgoren, "Residents of a Parish Encountering Lost Dreams," *New York Times*, September 6, 2005, p. A21.

57. James Varney, "Four Officers Suspended, Acting Police Chief Says," *Nola.com*, retrieved September 30, 2005, from www.nola.com.

58. Joseph B. Treaster, "Police Quitting, Overwhelmed by Chaos," *New York Times*, September 4, 2005, p. 1.

59. Adam Nossiter, "Big Plans Are Slow to Bear Fruit in New Orleans," *New York Times*, April 1, 2008, p. A1.

60. Rick Jervis and Brad Heath, "Crime Wave Has Grip on New Orleans," *USA Today*, February 7, 2008, retrieved February 7, 2008, from www.usatoday.com.

Organizing Public Security in the United States

AP Images/Carolyn Kaster

OUTLINE

The U.S. Public Security Industry
Local Law Enforcement
 Metropolitan Law Enforcement
 County Law Enforcement
 Rural and Small-Town Law
  Enforcement
 Indian Country and Tribal Law
  Enforcement
 Campus Law Enforcement
 Local Law Enforcement and Illegal
  Immigration
**Law Enforcement in the Era of
 Reduced Budgets**

State Law Enforcement
Federal Law Enforcement
 Department of Justice
 Department of the Treasury
 Department of Homeland Security
 Department of the Interior
 Department of Defense
 U.S. Postal Service
 Other Federal Enforcement
  Agencies
 Joint Federal and Local Task Force
  Approach to Law Enforcement
International Police

LEARNING OBJECTIVES

- Describe the responsibilities, budgets, and personnel numbers for local, state, and federal law enforcement agencies, and discuss the differences between them.

- Explain the issue of sworn law enforcement employee averages and give some examples of them.

- Compare and contrast the major problems affecting metropolitan, small-town, and rural law enforcement.

- Discuss the jurisdictional confusion in Indian country and tribal law enforcement.

- Identify recent changes in law enforcement due to the economic downturn and reduced budgets.

- List some benefits of the joint task force approach to law enforcement.

INTRODUCTION

The tragic events surrounding the terrorist attacks against New York City's World Trade Center and the U.S. Pentagon on September 11, 2001, brought the issues of safety and security to the forefront for most people in the United States and, indeed, the world. The public security industry—those institutions and people who maintain order and enforce the law in the United States—was already enormous and expanding every year. Since 9/11, this growth has become even more pronounced.

The U.S. security industry spends an immense amount of money and provides jobs for millions of people. The industry operates on all governmental levels: local (villages, towns, counties, tribes, and cities), state, and federal. The public agencies are funded by income taxes, sales taxes, real estate taxes, and other taxes. Students interested in seeking a career in policing will find a vast number of various law enforcement jobs from which to choose.

This chapter will discuss the U.S. public security industry, including local, state, and federal law enforcement, as well as the international police, Interpol.

The U.S. Public Security Industry

Ensuring the safety of U.S. citizens by providing law enforcement services is an extremely complex and expensive undertaking. In 2010, the Bureau of Justice Statistics (BJS) of the U.S. Department of Justice (DOJ) reported that for the latest reporting year, local, state, and federal agencies spent approximately $260 billion on criminal justice agencies, including police, corrections, and judicial services. These agencies collectively employed about 2.4 million people, 57.5 percent at the local level, 31 percent at the state level, and 11.5 percent at the federal level. Police protection spending amounted to about $95.4 billion from the total national criminal justice budget, and local policing expenditures alone accounted for about 45 percent of the nation's entire criminal justice budget.[1]

The U.S. approach to law enforcement is unique when compared with the rest of the world. Japan and some western European countries—Denmark, Finland, Greece, and Sweden—have a single national police force.[2] The United States does not have a national police force, although many people think of the Federal Bureau of Investigation (FBI) as one. We will see later in this chapter that the FBI is an investigative agency, rather than a police agency.

Law enforcement in the United States has developed over the years based on a philosophy of **local control**, the formal and informal use of local or neighborhood forms of government to deter abhorrent behaviors. To understand how this occurred, remember that the United States was built on the fear of a large central government, as had existed in England during colonial times. The primary responsibility for police protection still falls to local governments (cities, towns, tribes, and counties). Although we have state and federal law enforcement agencies, they are minuscule in size and importance when compared to the law enforcement agencies of local government.

Because of the tremendous number of law enforcement agencies and employees in the United States and the lack of a unified system for reporting police personnel, it is very difficult to get a perfect picture of the U.S. law enforcement industry. Every few years the BJS attempts to do this as part of its Law Enforcement Management and Administrative Statistics (**LEMAS**) program.

In 2008, state and local governments in the United States operated almost 17,985 full-time law enforcement agencies. These included 12,501 local police departments (mostly municipal and county departments), 3,063 sheriff's offices, and 50 primary state police departments. (See Table 2.1.) There were also approximately 1,722 special jurisdiction law enforcement departments, including park police, transit police, college and university police,

---

local control The formal and informal use of local or neighborhood forms of government and measures to deter abhorrent behaviors.

LEMAS Statistical reports on law enforcement personnel data issued by the National Institute of Justice under its Law Enforcement Management and Administrative Statistics program.

TABLE 2.1 Employment by State and Local Law Enforcement Agencies

Type of Agency	Number of Agencies	Full-Time Employees			Part-Time Employees		
		Total	Sworn	Nonsworn	Total	Sworn	Nonsworn
Total	17,985	1,133,915	765,246	368,669	100,340	44,062	56,278
Local police	12,501	593,013	461,063	131,950	58,129	27,810	30,319
Sheriff	3,063	353,461	182,979	170,482	26,052	11,334	14,718
Primary state	50	93,148	60,772	32,376	947	54	893
Special jurisdiction	1,722	90,262	56,968	33,294	14,681	4,451	10,230
Constable/marshal	638	4,031	3,464	567	531	413	118

Source: Brian A. Reaves, *Census of State and Local Law Enforcement Agencies, 2008* (Washington, D.C.: Bureau of Justice Statistics, 2008), p. 2.

constable offices, and other specialized state and local departments.[3]

In addition to state and local law enforcement agencies and personnel, 2008 statistics regarding employment for federal law enforcement agencies indicated that the federal government employed about 120,000 full-time personnel authorized to carry firearms and make arrests.[4]

When we translate all these statistics into words, we can make some generalizations and identify trends about the U.S. law enforcement industry:

- The size and scope of the U.S. law enforcement industry are enormous.

- The U.S. law enforcement industry is tremendously diverse and fragmented.

- The U.S. law enforcement industry is predominantly local.

- There are many employment opportunities in U.S. law enforcement at the federal, state, and local levels.

The U.S. Department of Labor's Bureau of Labor Statistics reported that the employment of police and detectives is expected to increase at the same rate as the average for all occupations through the year 2016. A more security-conscious society and concern about drug-related crimes contribute to the increasing demand for police services.[5] California has the most full-time state and local law enforcement employees (126,538), followed by Texas (96,116), New York (95,105), Florida (81,312), and Illinois (52,838).[6]

Nationwide, in 2008, there were 251 full-time state and local law enforcement employees for every 100,000 residents, for a nationwide **sworn law enforcement employee average** of 2.51 law enforcement employees per 1,000 citizens. The states with the highest law enforcement averages were the District of Columbia, 7.22; Louisiana, 4.05; and New York, 3.89. The states with the lowest were Washington, 1.74; Utah, 1.75; and Oregon, 1.77.[7]

These averages involve a very imprecise science and create an especially sensitive issue for politicians, citizens, and some police officers. How many officers are enough? Jerome H. Skolnick, a law professor at New York University who has written extensively on criminal justice issues and policing, says, "There's no formula for that. Nobody knows what the precise proportions should be."[8] It is generally conceded that the size of the police department a city requires can be affected by many issues, including poverty, crime, geography, population density, and even politics.

A comparison of New York and Los Angeles provides an interesting study. New York has about 35,000 officers, a sworn law enforcement employee average of 4.2 officers for every 1,000 residents. Los Angeles, on the other hand, has a sworn law enforcement employee average of 2.37 officers for every 1,000 residents.[9] William J. Bratton, former

sworn law enforcement employee average Number of sworn law enforcement employees for each 1,000 residents.

Los Angeles police chief and former New York City police commissioner, says, "We [LAPD] are one of the smallest police departments in the country when it comes to ratio of officers to population. Boston, on a Friday night, for its 48 square miles, puts out more cars than I put out in my whole city."[10] Washington, D.C., is also an interesting example; it has an extremely high sworn law enforcement employee average of nearly 7, three times that of Los Angeles, but for decades has had among the highest rates of violent crime of any large city.

According to Franklin E. Zimring, a law professor at the University of California at Berkeley, "It is very good politics to ask for increases [in officer positions]. It is an area of municipal expenditure with more of a political halo effect than almost any other. It would be very nice if we had independent estimates of what adding a cop would do to the crime rate in other places than New York. You can't do that. The science isn't there." David M. Kennedy, the director of the Center for Crime Prevention and Control at John Jay College of Criminal Justice, agrees: "If your current operations aren't terribly effective, simply adding more officers is almost certainly not going to make a difference."[11]

The issue of sworn employee averages also affects many active officers. According to Peter C. Moskos, professor at John Jay College and a former police officer in Baltimore, "When cops don't like their job, a huge part of it is understaffing. When it's chronic, cops can't get days off, they're forced to work more overtime, and it hurts family life. An unhappy cop is a bad cop."[12]

In addition to the work done individually by local, state, and federal law enforcement agencies, these agencies also cooperate and work together to enforce the law and protect and serve the public, particularly when planning and managing security for major events.[13] At Super Bowl XLVIII in 2014, over 100 agencies were involved in the security planning and execution to ensure a safe and secure event. The lead agency at the MetLife Stadium for the event was the New Jersey State Police, and the NYPD took the lead in New York. Helicopters secured a "no-fly" zone around the stadium and F-16 jets were on alert in Atlantic City. Aaron Ford, Special Agent in Charge of the FTI's Newark Division, said, "We all have one goal: to deliver a safe and secure Super Bowl XLVIII."

Local Law Enforcement

When we use the terms *local law enforcement* or *local police*, we are talking about the vast majority of all the law enforcement employees in the United States, including metropolitan police and sheriff's offices. Metropolitan police departments are operated by cities, certain very large counties, villages, and towns, and are generally led or managed by a police commissioner or chief who is appointed by the executive of the locality. Sheriff's offices are generally operated by counties and are led or managed by a popularly elected sheriff. Officers in police departments are generally called *police officers*, whereas officers in sheriff's offices are generally termed *deputy sheriffs* or *deputies*. Prior to the 2007–2010 economic recession, jobs in these agencies increased yearly.

Police protection is primarily a local responsibility. For the latest reporting year, local governments spent 70 percent of the total police expenditures in the United States, and local police spending represented about 32 percent of the nation's total justice expenditures. Spending on local police protection remained flat between 2002 and 2007 but had increased by 170.6 percent over the previous 20 years.[14] LEMAS reported that for the latest reporting period, local police departments employed about 601,027 full-time employees, including about 463,147 sworn personnel. (See Chapter 3 of this text for an explanation of "sworn personnel.") Local departments also employed about 54,310 persons on a part-time basis, about half of whom were sworn officers.[15]

Most local law enforcement agencies are small, but the majority of local police officers are employed by larger agencies. Departments with fewer than 10 full-time officers accounted for 53 percent of all agencies, but employed just 6 percent of all officers. About 638 local police departments (5 percent) employed 100 or more full-time sworn personnel. These agencies employed 61 percent of all local police officers.[16]

Racial and ethnic minorities constitute 23.3 percent of full-time sworn personnel in local departments, and women constitute about 11.9 percent.[17] Between 2003 and 2007, the number of African American local police officers increased by 5 percent, Hispanic officers by 16 percent, officers from other ethnic minority groups by 7 percent, and female officers by 11.9 percent.[18] (See Table 2.2.)

TABLE 2.2   Gender and Race of Local Police Departments and Sheriff's Offices

Local Police Departments		Sheriff's Offices	
Total	100%	Total	100%
Total Males	88.1%	Total Males	87.1%
Total Females	11.9%	Total Females	12.9%
Total Whites	76.4%	Total Whites	81.2%
White Males	69.4%	White Males	72.0%
White Females	7.0%	White Females	9.2%
Total Black/African Americans	11.7%	Total Black/African Americans	10.0%
Black/African American Males	9.0%	Black/African American Males	7.5%
Black/African American Females	2.7%	Black/African American Females	2.5%
Total Hispanic/Latinos	9.1%	Total Hispanic/Latinos	6.9%
Hispanic/Latino Males	7.8%	Hispanic/Latino Males	6.0%
Hispanic/Latina Females	1.3%	Hispanic/Latina Females	0.9%
Total Other*	2.8%	Total Other*	1.9%
Other Males	2.5%	Other Males	1.7%
Other Females	0.3%	Other Females	0.2%

*Other category includes Asians, Native Hawaiians or other Pacific Islanders, American Indians, Alaska Natives, and any other race.

Sources: Matthew J. Hickman and Brian A. Reaves, *Local Police Departments, 2003* (Washington, D.C.: Bureau of Justice Statics, 2003), p. 7; Brian A. Reaves, *Local Police Departments, 2007* (Washington, D.C.: Bureau of Justice Statistics, 2010), p. 14; and Matthew J. Hickman and Brian A. Reaves, *Sheriffs' Offices, 2003* (Washington, D.C.: Bureau of Justice Statistics, 2006), p. 7.

Metropolitan Law Enforcement

Municipal or city governments operate the vast majority of the nearly 12,501 metropolitan police departments in the United States. The rest are operated by county, tribal, or regional jurisdictions.[19] Metropolitan police departments generally provide the duties and services we typically associate with the police. These include arresting law violators, performing routine patrol, investigating crimes, enforcing traffic laws (including parking violations), providing crowd and traffic control at parades and other public events, and issuing special licenses and permits. Some officers also perform criminal investigations or administrative, training, and technical support services.

The largest local department is the New York Police Department (NYPD), with about 36,023 sworn officers. The next largest local police department is Chicago, with nearly 13,354 sworn employees;

followed by Los Angeles, with 9,727; Philadelphia, with about 6,624; and Houston, with 5,053.[20] Approximately one of every six full-time local police officers in the United States works for these five forces.

The largest county police departments (not sheriff's offices) in the United States are the Miami-Dade County, Florida, Police Department with about 3,120 officers; the Suffolk County, New York, Police Department with more than 2,644 sworn members; the Las Vegas-Clark County, Nevada, Police Department with about 2,390 officers; the Nassau County, New York, Police Department with about 2,600 officers; and the Baltimore County, Maryland, Police Department with about 1,888 officers.[21]

Recall the earlier discussion of sworn law enforcement employee averages. Among municipal police departments in 2007, the sworn law enforcement employee average was 2.3 percent; departments serving 25,000 to 99,000 residents had the

Some Interesting Facts about Local Police Departments

- 55 percent of departments use foot patrol routinely.

- 32 percent use regular bicycle patrol.

- 91 percent participate in a 911 emergency system compared with 32 percent in 1987, and 74 percent use enhanced 911. (See Chapter 14, "Computers, Technology, and Criminalistics in Policing," for a description of 911 and enhanced 911 systems.)

- 24 percent assign full-time officers to a special unit for drug enforcement, and 35 percent assign officers to a multiagency drug task force.

- 5 percent assign officers full-time to a gang task force, and 12 percent assign officers to a multiagency gang task force.

- 16 percent maintain a written community policing plan, and 47 percent use full-time community policing officers.

- 38 percent use full-time school resource officers.

- 97 percent have a written policy on the use of deadly force, and 96 percent have a policy on the use of less than lethal force.

- 62 percent participate in emergency preparedness exercises.

- 9 percent have officers assigned to antiterrorism, and 4 percent have officers assigned full time to an antiterrorism task force.

- 61 percent use video cameras in patrol cars.

Source: Brian A. Reaves, *Local Police Departments, 2007* (Washington, D.C.: Bureau of Justice Statistics, 2010).

homelessness, unemployment, drug addiction, alcoholism, and child abuse. Since the terrorist bombings of September 11, 2001, these metropolitan departments also have had to deal increasingly with the problems of terrorism facing their cities. In addition, large municipal departments are highly visible because of their size, complexity, budgets, and innovative programs. Not only do they attempt to control crime, but municipal police also deal with significant problems to maintain public order and solve quality-of-life issues for neighborhood residents. The police handle social problems that other public and private agencies either cannot or will not handle. When there is a problem, citizens generally do not call the mayor's office—they call 911.

In many geographic areas, especially larger metropolitan areas such as New York City and Washington, D.C., metropolitan police are supplemented by special jurisdiction police agencies. In the latest reporting period, 1,733 state and local law enforcement agencies with special geographic jurisdictions or enforcement responsibilities were operating in the United States with more than 56,968 full-time sworn personnel. These agencies perform such duties as guarding government buildings and facilities; policing colleges and universities; enforcing conservation, agricultural, and parks and recreation laws; performing special criminal investigations; patrolling transportation systems and facilities; and engaging in special enforcement duties such as alcohol enforcement, gaming or racing law enforcement, business relations enforcement, or drug enforcement.[23]

The largest special jurisdiction agency in the United States, with more than 1,667 officers, is the Port Authority of New York and New Jersey Police Department (PAPD), which polices the facilities owned and operated by the bi-state Port Authority of New York and New Jersey. These facilities include the area's major airports, tunnels, bridges, and transportation systems, as well as New York's former World Trade Center. (Thirty-seven PAPD police officers were killed in the 9/11 attacks against the World Trade Center.) The next largest special jurisdiction agencies are the California Department of Parks and Recreation with about 645 sworn officers, the Florida Fish and Wildlife Conservation Commission with about 626 full-time sworn officers, the Texas Parks and Wildlife Department with about 480 sworn employees, and the Ohio Department of Natural Resources with about 394.

lowest average, 1.8 percent.[22] Big-city mayors and police chiefs are always trying to increase the number of officers in their departments.

Most academic and professional studies of policing have focused on municipal departments, because this is where the "action" is in the law enforcement world. This includes problems with crime, budgeting and funding, politics, and population changes, as well as social problems such as

County Law Enforcement

Most counties in the United States are patrolled by a sheriff's department under the leadership of an elected sheriff, although several very large counties in New York, California, Nevada, Florida, and other states have county police departments. The role of sheriff has evolved in several stages since the early English sheriff (shire-reeve). During the development of the western United States and before municipal departments were established, the sheriff often served as the sole legal authority over vast geographical areas. Today, the duties of a county sheriff's office vary according to the size and urbanization of the county. The sheriff's office may perform the duties of coroners, tax assessors, tax collectors, keepers of county jails, court attendants, and executors of criminal and civil processes, as well as law enforcement officers.

Sheriff's departments vary widely in their responsibilities within the communities they service. Some are oriented exclusively toward law enforcement, and some carry out only court-related duties. Some deal exclusively with correctional and court matters and have no law enforcement duties; others are full-service programs that perform court, correctional, and law enforcement activities.[24] To look at these differences statistically, 96 percent of sheriffs' offices are responsible for traditional law enforcement, such as responding to citizen requests for assistance, providing routine patrol services, and conducting traffic enforcement. In addition to patrol and traffic duties, about 78 percent of the offices operate one or more jails, nearly 96 percent are responsible for the serving of civil process, and 97 percent maintain court security.[25]

In the latest reporting year, sheriffs' offices had approximately 353,461 full-time employees (182,979 sworn).[26] Racial and ethnic minorities composed almost 19 percent full-time sworn personnel, up from about 13.4 percent in 1987. Women constituted about 12.1 percent, about the same as in 1987.

The largest sheriff's office in the nation is the Los Angeles County Sheriff's Department, which employs more than 9,461 full-time sworn personnel. The office provides contract patrol services to many local areas outside of their own departments. For example, Compton, California, a high-crime and gang area, has disbanded its own police department and contracted with the LA Sheriff's Department for services; as a result, it has seen a dramatic decrease in crime and an increase in police presence and citizen satisfaction. Other major sheriff's offices

YOU ARE THERE

Some Interesting Facts about Sheriffs' Offices

- 25 percent of sheriffs' offices use foot patrol routinely.

- 9 percent use regular bicycle patrol.

- 95 percent participate in a 911 emergency system compared with 28 percent in 1987, and

- 78 percent employ enhanced 911. (See Chapter 14, "Computers, Technology, and Criminalistics in Policing," for a description of 911 and enhanced 911 systems.)

- 58 percent have officers assigned full time to a special unit for drug enforcement, and nearly a quarter assign officers to a multiagency drug task force.

- 10 percent maintain a written community policing plan, and 43 percent use full-time community policing officers.

- 40 percent provide community policing training for new deputy recruits.

- 50 percent use full-time school resource officers.

- Nearly all have a written policy on pursuit driving, and about half of them restrict vehicle pursuits according to specific criteria.

- 97 percent have a written policy on the use of deadly force, and 96 percent have a policy on the use of less than lethal force.

- Nearly half have a written plan specifying actions to be taken in a terrorist attack.

- 96 percent authorize the use of chemical agents such as pepper spray, up from 52 percent in 1990.

- 67 percent use video cameras in patrol cars.

- 71 percent have written policies about racial profiling by officers.

Source: Andrea M. Burch, *Sheriffs' Offices, 2007 – Statistical Tables* (Washington, D.C.: Bureau of Justice Statistics, 2012), pp. 12, 14, 15, 18, 19.

include Cook County, Illinois, which employs 5,655 full-time sworn personnel; and Harris County, Texas, with 2,558 sworn employees.[27]

Rural and Small-Town Law Enforcement

Eighty-seven percent of police departments serve rural and small-town law enforcement, with 25 or fewer officers. Often, rural and small-town police face the same problems as large metropolitan and county police, in addition to other serious problems because of their size. The state of Wyoming, for example, has the lowest population in the United States and has vast open areas where one can drive more than 100 miles between small towns. The law enforcement officers in this state routinely face the problem of not having immediate backup. As Mike Roy, the lead instructor at the Wyoming Law Enforcement Academy, says,

> We deal with great distances out here and there is a different mentality. Every other pickup truck you stop out here has a rifle in a gun rack or a pistol in the glove box. Most of the problems we have in law enforcement center around people— where you have people you will have problems.[28]

Regarding the lack of readily available backup, Roy says, "Everyone completing our academy is instructed not to get stupid by acting alone in known volatile situations. Officers are instructed to get used to waiting for the closest help to arrive even if it's 60 miles away."[29]

Many small remote towns and villages cannot afford to hire local police officers and often rely on state troopers based in areas far away. As an example, in 2006 it took four hours for Alaska state troopers to arrive at the 200-person Eskimo village of Nunam Iqua after a man, who had spent the evening drinking home brew, choked and raped his 13-year-old stepdaughter in front of three younger children, beat his wife with a shotgun, and pistol-whipped a friend. During the attack, residents called troopers in Bethel, Alaska, 155 miles away, but because their aircraft was being serviced, the troopers had to charter a plane to get to Nunam Iqua. In 2008, it was reported that the village had hired a single public safety officer, but she had no law enforcement training and was unarmed.[30]

Alaska does have a state-funded Village Public Safety Officer (VPSO) program for small villages. The villages can hire a uniformed peace officer who receives up to 10 weeks of training from the state

troopers and carries pepper spray and a Taser, but no firearm. The turnover rate among VPSOs is as high as 40 percent because the job is stressful, with low pay and little backup. Also, many villages cannot attract good applicants because of inadequate housing, the low wages, and the high cost of living in Alaska's remote communities.[31]

Although awareness of the drug problems and dangers to police in large urban communities is widespread, many people are not aware of similar circumstances in small towns throughout America's heartland. Authorities say that locally made methamphetamine, long popular on the West Coast, has become the small-town Midwest's drug of choice, similar to the scourge that crack or rock cocaine has been to the inner city. Methamphetamine is a stimulant variously called meth, crank, ice, and speed. For years, it was made and distributed by outlaw motorcycle gangs, but today in the Midwest, meth production is a mom-and-pop operation. Medical experts say meth delivers a stronger, cheaper psychoactive kick than crack cocaine, unleashing aggression and leading to long binges that end with physical collapse.

In addition to the violence associated with meth users, their labs also prove dangerous to the police. During a lab raid in Independence, Missouri, a detective found an overhead light bulb that was filled with tiny lead pellets and gunpowder, rigged to explode when the switch was turned on. He also found pipe bombs, rattlesnakes, and toxic gases in labs.[32] The dangers of methamphetamine drug labs now require police investigators to wear hazardous material protective suits.[33]

Gangs are also becoming a problem in rural areas and small towns. Research reported by the National Youth Gang Center indicated that many small towns and rural areas are experiencing gang problems for the first time. During the period of the study, gang-problem patterns were recorded for 1,066 agencies representing rural counties and smaller cities (populations between 2,500 and 25,000). The study revealed that gangs and gang-related problems tend to emerge from larger social and economic problems in the community and are as much a consequence of these factors as a contributor. The report also stated that changing demographics in some small towns and rural areas may contribute to the emergence or escalation of gang problems and may be related to newly arrived racial or ethnic groups to an area.

The study reported that in most cases the gang problem is short-lived and dissipates quickly, since

© Mikael Karlsson/Alamy

A sheriff's deputy photographs the scene of a traffic accident. Officers in rural areas often have to handle investigations without assistance from other officers.

small towns and rural areas do not provide the necessary population base to sustain gangs, and any disruption (arrest, members dropping out) may weaken the gang.[34] The study also indicated that undue media attention and excessive use of law enforcement strategies may actually provide cohesiveness to a gang. Instead, a balanced and carefully developed collective community effort involving the following three areas can be more effective:

- Prevention programs that aim to discourage youth from developing problem behaviors and joining gangs
- Intervention programs that aim to rehabilitate delinquents and divert gang-involved youths from gangs
- Suppression activities that include law enforcement, prosecutors, and courts targeting the gangs with the most high-rate offenders

In an excellent article in the FBI *Law Enforcement Bulletin*, Supervisory Special Agent Dennis Lindsey, a senior instructor in the International Training Center, Sensitive Investigations Unit, at the DEA, and Lieutenant Sean Kelly of the Durham, New Hampshire, Police Department discuss the issues of officer stress in small-town policing. They indicate that these officers are subject to the same stress that big-town police and deputies face, and often additional types of stress due to greater difficulties in

maintaining a work–life balance.[35] Lindsey and Kelly cite a 40-year study by John M. Violanti determining that the average age of death of officers with 10 to 19 years of service was 66, while the average age of death for nonpolice was 74 years for men and 80 years for women. This research found a significantly increased risk of digestive and hematopoietic cancers among officers, as well as maladaptive behaviors such as alcohol and tobacco use, significantly high mortality risk of esophageal cancer, and cirrhosis of the liver.[36] After the dangers and rigors of a tour of duty, officers must try to "come down" and return to a normal family and social life; but small-town and rural police constantly face the inability to come down from the hypervigilant state of acting as a police officer, causing their bodies to deteriorate further and faster.[37] Lindsey and Kelly write,

Police officers who live and work in small towns almost never have an opportunity to decompress. Being well known to the residents, business owners, and others in the community, officers cannot separate on-duty and off-duty time. Essentially, small town police officers live in a fishbowl. Off-duty trips to the store frequently become job related because everyone seems to know the officers and their family vehicles. Spouses often come under close observation because residents may think "that cop" is driving past or, simply, because they are the spouse of a police officer. Taking their children to school becomes complicated when other parents wonder out loud why officers are not at work or when a school administrator asks for advice about an unruly child or parent. All of this off-duty interaction disallows decompression and contributes to stress and the deterioration of the small town police officer's body.... Or, when at a party with their spouses' friends, they must respond to questions about a police officer's conduct in an agency 3,000 miles away. An event that is supposed to be fun, that is supposed to invigorate them, and that is supposed to be enjoyable becomes another time when they must put on the shield and wear their "cop hat."[38]

Rural and small-town law enforcement agencies engage in mutual assistance programs with neighboring agencies and come to one another's aid when necessary. Limited resources, rising crime trends, and geographic barriers severely impair the ability of rural law enforcement agencies to effectively combat crimes in their communities. To ensure that they can meet the challenge of law enforcement in the 21st century, rural executives are increasingly seeking opportunities to provide more education and training for their staffs and to maximize their effectiveness through new and improved technology. This attention to the needs of rural law enforcement agencies gave birth to the National Center for Rural Law Enforcement (NCRLE), a part of the Criminal Justice Institute at the University of Arkansas in Little Rock. To assist law enforcement officials throughout the United States, the NCRLE provides management education and training courses ranging from principles of supervision to detailed courses on the legal aspects of domestic violence. The NCRLE also provides research and Internet assistance, and brings sheriffs, police chiefs, citizens, and social service agency representatives together to discuss the needs of rural communities and explore the process of creating a community coalition.[39]

Indian Country and Tribal Law Enforcement

Policing American Indians in the United States has always been contentious, especially from the tribal perspective. American Indians were first regulated by the U.S. Army and the Department of War, and then later by the Bureau of Indian Affairs and the Department of the Interior. Today the controversy over policing Indian country continues, with federal, state, and local jurisdictions attempting to intervene in tribal policing.[40] The debate has caused jurisdictional confusion, tribal discontent, and litigations in Indian country.[41] M. Wesley Clark, a senior attorney in the U.S. Drug Enforcement Administration (DEA), says, "Policing in and adjacent to land within Indian country is often a complex and, at times, confusing jurisdictional puzzle. Solving this puzzle depends on a variety of factors, including whether the crime is a felony or misdemeanor, whether the subjects and victims are Indians, and whether the crime violates tribal, state, or federal law."[42]

A report for the National Institute of Justice offered detailed information on tribal law enforcement agencies, tribal courts and services, and criminal records systems from continental American Indian jurisdictions. More than 92 percent of the 341 federally recognized American Indian tribes in the continental 48 states responded to the census. Relative to policing, the report revealed that 165 of the responding 314 tribes employed one or more full-time sworn officers with general arrest powers, with 56 percent of these also recognized to possess arrest authority by their state governments. Almost all (99 percent) of the responding tribes had cross-deputization agreements with another tribal or public agency.[43]

The governmental power to make or enforce laws in Indian country is divided among federal, state, and tribal governments. Jurisdiction in a specific incident depends on the nature of the offense, whether the offender or victim was a tribal member, and the state in which the crime occurred. Public Law 83-280 (commonly called PL 280) conferred criminal jurisdiction in Indian country to six state governments (referred to as mandatory PL 280 states)—Alaska, California, Minnesota, Nebraska, Oregon, and Wisconsin—and the federal government. It also permitted other states to acquire jurisdiction at their option. These optional PL 280 states—Arizona, Idaho, Iowa, Montana, Nevada, North Dakota, South Dakota, Utah, and Washington—assumed jurisdiction either in whole or in part over Indian country within their boundaries. In states where PL 280 does not apply, the federal government retains criminal jurisdiction for major crimes. The 1994 Crime Act expanded federal criminal jurisdiction in Indian country in such areas as guns, violent juveniles, drugs, and domestic violence.

Tribal law enforcement has inherent powers to exercise criminal jurisdiction over all members and the authority to arrest and detain non-Indians for delivery to state or federal authorities for prosecution. These tribal police powers are generally limited to the reservation. The work of tribal police is often critical to resolving criminal cases referred to state and federal agencies because tribal police usually discover the crime, interview witnesses, and investigate the circumstances involved in the crime. Often tribal police refer cases to U.S. attorneys' offices for investigation because tribal courts generally hear only misdemeanor cases.[44]

Cross-deputization agreements have been used to enhance law enforcement capabilities in areas where state and tribal lands are contiguous and intermingled. Under some agreements, federal, state, county/local, and/or tribal law enforcement officers have the power to arrest Indian and non-Indian wrongdoers whenever a violation of law occurs. States, in some cases, have recognized tribal police to have the authority to arrest tribal offenders off the reservation or detain nontribal offenders on the reservation. One study indicated that about 45 percent of the tribes with law enforcement personnel have arrest authority over tribal members off the reservation, and about 62 percent of the tribes having at least one sworn officer have arrest authority over non-Indians on tribal reservations.

In the 2008 *Tribal Census*, the largest Indian law enforcement agency was the Navajo nation in Arizona, which had 393 full-time officers with arrest powers. The next largest was the Seminole tribe of Florida—consisting of the Big Cypress, Brighton, Dania, Hollywood, and Tampa reservations—with 144 sworn officers, followed by the Salt River Police Department in Arizona with 125.[45]

Tribal police experience serious difficulties as they work to provide law enforcement services in some of the country's most remote and undeveloped areas. These tribal police officers are stretched thin over large and diverse geographical territories. In Arizona, the Hualapal nation has only one police chief and 10 commissioned officers to cover the reservation's one million acres and 2,800 residents. The Stillaguamish Tribal Police of Arlington, Washington, has only seven patrol officers to cover 650 square miles of fish and game territory, as well as a casino. Tribal police officers face severe community problems such as high unemployment and drug and substance abuse. They also lack funding to build the type of infrastructure needed to accomplish their mission of policing.[46]

In 2007, the *Denver Post* produced a series of articles on criminal justice in Indian country. It reported that Indian reservations are plagued by a systematic breakdown in the delivery of justice. Noting that the sole authority to prosecute felony crimes on reservations lies with the federal government, the report stated that U.S. attorneys and FBI investigators face huge challenges in fighting crime on reservations, as they are mistrusted and viewed as outsiders. The high levels of alcohol use among victims, suspects, and witnesses that accompany many serious crimes can make it very difficult to prove a crime. Additionally, federal law enforcement officials are burdened by competing federal priorities such as immigration and terrorism.[47]

These problems are reflected in the statistics. Between 1997 and 2006, federal prosecutors rejected nearly two-thirds of the reservation cases brought to them by FBI and Bureau of Indian Affairs investigators, more than twice the number of cases rejected for all federally prosecuted crimes. Of the nearly 5,900 aggravated assaults reported on reservations in 2006, only 558 were referred to federal prosecutors, who declined to prosecute 320 of them. Of the more than 1,000 arson complaints reported in 2006, only 24 were referred to U.S. attorneys, who declined to prosecute 18 of them. Commenting on the federal justice system, a Navajo tribal prosecutor stated, "They've created a lawless land."[48]

In 2010, the U.S. Department of Justice ordered prosecutors in 33 states to intensify efforts to fight violent crime on Indian reservations, particularly offenses against women and children. Attorney General Eric C. Holder Jr. said that 35 new assistant attorneys general and 12 other specialists from the FBI would be assigned to handle such crimes.[49]

Campus Law Enforcement

In 2008, the Bureau of Justice Statistics issued a special report on campus law enforcement. The report consisted of a survey of campus law enforcement agencies serving four-year colleges and universities with 2,500 or more students. It reported that for the 2004–2005 school year, there were a total of 750 campus law enforcement agencies: 465 for public colleges and universities and 285 for private colleges and universities. Seventy-four percent of these agencies employed sworn law enforcement officers with full arrest powers granted by a state or local government. (See Chapter 3 for an explanation of sworn versus nonsworn law enforcement officers.) Nearly all public campuses (93 percent) used sworn officers, compared to less than half (42 percent) of private campuses. Sixty-seven percent of campus law enforcement agencies used armed patrol officers. Armed officers were used at nearly 90 percent of the agencies that employed sworn officers and at about 10 percent of the agencies that used nonsworn officers.[50]

The report also indicated that 90 percent of the campus law enforcement agencies had a written emergency preparedness plan and that about 58 percent of the agencies had participated in emergency preparedness exercises during the 2004–2005 school year. Most campus law enforcement agencies had working relationships with local law enforcement and drew on their resources when needed. Nearly all campus law enforcement agencies provided 24-hour patrol services and had a three-digit emergency phone number through a 611 on-campus system or a local 911 system. Most campuses (91 percent) also had blue-light emergency campus phones to provide people on campus with direct access to campus law enforcement.[51]

Local Law Enforcement and Illegal Immigration

A controversial issue in current law enforcement is the cooperation and escalating involvement of local police with federal immigration officials in enforcing immigration laws. Immigration advocates and some local officials fear that this cooperation will further erode an already tense relationship between minority and immigrant communities and local officers entrusted with serving residents. It has become routine for some police agencies to assist immigration authorities during arrests and to call immigration officials if a criminal suspect appears to be an undocumented alien. Also, some local police have been deputized as immigration agents at the request of federal authorities under signed agreements. On the other hand, some departments generally prohibit officers from asking people they stop about their immigration status.[52]

Many police departments in cities, counties, and states have policies that restrict enforcement of federal immigration laws by local authorities. These policies, termed as "don't ask," are favored by many police chiefs when dealing with undocumented residents who have not committed crimes other than being in the country illegally. Chiefs say that these policies are an effective crime-fighting tool because they encourage illegal immigrants to report crimes without fear of deportation. They feel that the police can better fight crime by building trust with residents and encouraging them to help identify suspects and report problems. As an example, the Phoenix Police Department bars its officers from

stopping people for the sole purpose of determining immigration status. It also forbids officers to call the federal Immigration and Customs Enforcement (ICE) about people who are crime victims or witnesses or people who have committed only minor civil offenses, such as driving without a license. However, officers automatically notify ICE whenever illegal immigrants are booked into jail.[53] Those strongly opposed to illegal immigration say these policies create "sanctuary cities" for illegal immigrants, shield foreign criminals from deportation, and hamper federal efforts to combat illegal immigration and terrorism.[54]

Frustrated with ineffective immigration enforcement and often under considerable political pressure, a growing number of states, counties, and cities are requiring their law enforcement officers to help detect and deport illegal immigrants rather than just rely on federal agents. Some law enforcement agencies are training their officers to perform immigration checks themselves as part of ICE's 287(g) program. This program refers to Section 287(g) of the 1996 Immigration and Nationality Act. The 287(g) program deputizes local officers to help enforce federal immigration laws. ICE provides local officers with access to its immigration database and trains them in identifying illegal immigrants and ordering deportations with ICE's approval. ICE officials report that, under this program, local law enforcement officers have helped detect 32,000 illegal immigrants over the past three years who otherwise may have remained in the country. Approximately 55 state, county, and local law enforcement departments have taken the ICE training and more than 70 others are on the waiting list.[55] Officers undergo a five-week training course in the 287(g) program. The training includes instruction on civil rights and immigration laws, federal prohibitions on racial profiling, cross-cultural issues, and treaty obligations that require officers to notify foreign consulates about certain arrests.[56]

Some police chiefs disagree with this trend. According to Thomas Frazier, the executive director of the Major Cities Chiefs Association, a group of police chiefs from the 64 largest police departments in the United States and Canada, "Taking a patrol officer off the street to book someone who is here because of all the failures of the federal system is not a priority of big-city law enforcement."[57] In 2008, Chief Harold Hurtt of the Houston Police

Department (HPD) stated that local police do not want to be immigration officers; they want to focus on enforcing local laws. He stated that if the HPD had to enforce immigration laws, its 5-minute response time to emergency calls could possibly rise to 30 or 45 minutes.[58] Major Juan Jorge of the Harris County, Texas, Sheriff's Office agreed with Chief Hurtt, saying that local immigration enforcement could "darn near cripple" his department. He also has questioned how deputies can enforce immigration without racial profiling and how officers will determine whom to question about their citizenship. Jorge stated, "Are you going to ask everyone who looks Hispanic? Am I going to get asked every time someone sees me on the street, 'Are you legal?' "[59]

In 2007, the International Association of Chiefs of Police published a document, *Police Chiefs Guide to Immigration Issues*, to provide police chiefs with an overview of the issues surrounding immigration, both legal and illegal. It provides background information on the current resources available to law enforcement and also examines the concerns and obstacles that currently surround the debate over immigration enforcement.[60]

In 2009, the Police Foundation's report *Role of Local Police: Striking a Balance Between Immigration Enforcement and Civil Liberties* presented the findings of a Police Foundation nationwide project that examined the views of law enforcement agencies, public officials, and community stakeholders regarding the use of local law enforcement agencies in enforcing federal immigration laws under ICE's 287(g) program. The overall conclusion of the project was that the costs in lost community support for local and state police and their general public safety mission, along with increased financial costs to state and local law enforcement agencies, outweigh the benefits of the 287(g) program.[61] Furthermore, in 2010, the Department of Homeland Security's inspector general issued a special report stating that the state and local police officers who enforce federal immigration laws through ICE's 287(g) program are not adequately screened, trained, or supervised, and the civil rights of the immigrants they deal with are not consistently protected.[62]

In late April 2010, the governor of Arizona signed the nation's toughest bill on illegal immigration, making Arizona the first state to demand that immigrants carry identity documents legitimizing their presence on American soil. The law requires police officers to detain people they reasonably suspect are in the country without authorization and to verify their status with federal officials. It also makes it a state crime, a misdemeanor, to not carry immigration papers, and the law allows people to sue local governments or agencies if they believe federal or state immigration is not being enforced. A week later, the governor signed a follow-up bill to quell concerns that the measure would lead to racial profiling. The new bill states that questioning by the police regarding immigration status must follow a law enforcement officer's stopping, detaining, or arresting a person while enforcing another law. The former law required this on any "contact" between the person and the police.

The passage of these laws in Arizona led to numerous public protests across the nation. In July 2010, a federal judge issued a preliminary injunction against sections of the new law that call for police officers to check a person's immigration status while enforcing other laws. She blocked the most controversial parts of the new law in response to a legal challenge against the law by the federal government. So, the debate continues over local police enforcing the law against illegal immigration.[63]

Law Enforcement in the Era of Reduced Budgets

In 2008, the United States fell into a recession of a magnitude not seen since the Great Depression in the 1930s. Aside from the effects of this recession on the general public, local and state governments suffered dramatic losses to their financial base. These financial losses caused a dramatic reworking of priorities and reallocation of limited resources. State governments were pitted against local governments for the same financial resources.

The most significant reassessment of priorities occurred in the area of public safety. Until this time, law enforcement had been, for the most part, exempt from any reductions in budgets; they could always count on the public to raise a "hue and cry" to keep their budgets untouched. This situation changed in 2008. The public still demanded the same level of service, but at a reduced cost. The mantra of "doing more with less" held sway in many law enforcement agencies. Many line officers saw fellow officers laid

GUEST LECTURE

JEFFREY WICKETT

Jeffrey Wickett is a retired senior criminal investigator from the United States Immigration and Customs Enforcement, Homeland Security Investigations under the Department of Homeland Security, legacy U.S. Customs Investigations. He is currently employed by the World Customs Organization located in Brussels, Belgium, to manage a global security programme in which 94 nations are participating.

A SOUND BASE AND BROAD MIND LEAD TO ENDLESS SUCCESSES AND COUNTLESS OPPORTUNITIES

I knew at a very young age that I wanted to go into law enforcement, but little did I know the winding path that my career would take. I have gone from beat cop in Boca Raton, Florida, to manager of an international program in Brussels, Belgium, to reduce Improvised Explosive Device (IED) manufacture. But it's everything that happened in between that is the real story.

The story actually starts before I became a cop. I was so anxious to start on my dream career that I dual-enrolled in some college classes at Palm Beach Junior College while still attending Boca Raton High School. Unfortunately, that plan backfired when I realized I was too young to be a police officer—but I never lost my drive to become one.

When I was 21, I was hired by BRPD as a police aide (a civilian position) assigned to the Marine Unit. Having grown up in Florida in a very active outdoors family, I had accrued quite a bit of boating experience. It was a win-win situation so far as I was concerned: I was able to make a living (of sorts) doing something I loved, and I got my foot in the door of the department where I had set my sights to become a police officer.

After being on the boats for several months, a potentially tragic event occurred during my off time that gained me the attention of the chief of police and accelerated my own career. I was able to save the life of a 14-month-old girl who had fallen into a neighbor's pool. (So lesson one: Pay close attention in those mandatory CPR classes; they might actually be necessary one day.) This event brought positive public attention to the department and, as a result, I was called to the chief's office and sworn in as a police officer.

As a road cop in Boca, I preferred the higher level of activity of the evening shift. I became a Breathalyzer operator and a crime scene investigator. When the opportunity arose, I joined the Marine Unit, this time as a sworn officer. I am not going to sugarcoat those early years. Between court appearances during

prime sleep time and working a variety of off-duty details to make ends meet, sleep sometimes occurred only a few precious hours at a time. But my parents had instilled in me a strong work ethic and I was determined to do whatever was needed to proceed on my chosen career path. And I did meet my wife there: She was a dispatcher, so she said she got to tell me where to go both on duty and off, but she got paid for it at work.

I was eventually recruited by U.S. Customs into their newly created Marine Enforcement Officer (MEO) program. At the time, Customs had no requirement for a four-year college degree; experience was preferred in new hires. This changed in the early 1990s, and I decided to go back to school and finish my degree. I would advise you to try and finish school before your life has competing demands like work and family. When I went back to school, I was still working full time, and often in the Bahamas for two weeks at a time as part of a drug task force with the Bahamian government. On several occasions, my wife had to drive to the college with a tape recorder and ask another student to tape the lecture. But on the plus side, I benefited by being older and settled into a career. I was able to argue points of law with my professors because it had been my duty to enforce the laws being discussed.

During my nine years as an MEO in south Florida, I participated in the dive team, becoming a dive supervisor and then dive manager for the south Florida region. Our primary mission was to dive under ships in the Miami River checking for contraband, usually wearing a full dry suit to protect us from hazardous materials. With temperatures in the 90s, this was not as much fun as it sounds. I was also physical fitness coordinator and traveled to the renowned Cooper Clinic in Texas for training and assessment. I was on the Special Response Team (SRT) and was one of only two Customs personnel to successfully complete the grueling Miami PD SWAT training. I also had the honor and privilege to work and train with the Naval Special Warfare Development Group (DEVGRU) in both south Florida and Virginia.

In 1997, I was offered a position as special agent on a marine task force in San Diego. The task force comprised representatives from local police departments, the San Diego District Attorney's office, the California Bureau of Investigations, the

DEA, and the FBI. Here I was afforded the opportunity to work undercover, which opened up a whole new avenue of learning. I took cases from inception through the entire prosecution process. I was fortunate enough to develop cases involving drugs, the transportation of drugs, and hundreds of thousands of dollars, which in turn funded other operations for quite some time. I used confidential informants (CIs), wiretaps, and face-to-face meetings with mid-level cartel members. One case involving the transportation of drugs from South America to the United States using logistical support vessels (LSVs) was prosecuted by the U.S. Attorney's office and involved 14 defendants, each with their own defense attorney and all needing translators. That was a circus.

I was made acting supervisor for the marine task force on September 10, 2001. The next morning, I watched in horror with the rest of the world as the events of 9/11 unfolded. I was getting ready to fly out to Washington, D.C., that morning. Needless to say, that trip was canceled and the entire marine group leapt into action to take care of the logistics that needed to take place ASAP with our location on San Diego Bay, which housed the U.S. Navy Pacific Fleet. Soon thereafter, Customs Investigations was rebranded as Immigration & Customs Enforcement (ICE), Homeland Security Investigations (HSI) under the newly formed Department of Homeland Security (DHS).

In 2003, while on a naval aircraft flying from San Diego to Chicago with 1,300 pounds of marijuana as part of an undercover operation that had blossomed from a simple transport to much higher up the bad-guy chain, I received a call from the attaché in Paris, France. Up to this point in my Customs career, I had dealt with drug investigations and prosecutions and all the peripherals involved. The attaché asked if I would consider a six-month temporary assignment in the port city of Le Havre, France, in the newly created Container Security Initiative. CSI is a post-911 program in which countries all over the world agreed to have teams of American inspectors and investigators work alongside their customs folks in order to stop any Weapons of Mass Effect from gaining entry to the United States via ship containers from foreign ports. I had never met the attaché, but she was aware of some of the investigations I had done. It was quite different content, but investigative skills can be used on any type of case. With encouragement from my wife and other family members, I decided to take this opportunity to expand my horizons.

In 2005, I was fortunate enough to return to Le Havre as the permanent investigator for the CSI program. In addition to Le Havre, I also covered the port of Marseilles in the south of France. The work could get a bit tedious at times. Not all containers received physical inspections; an inspection depended on a scoring system based on factors like country of origin, shipper, receiver, commodity, and so forth. It was similar to the way my wife described dispatching: hours of sheer boredom punctuated by minutes of sheer terror.

During my time in France, I was asked to represent the attaché's office on a trip to Ghana, and later a trip to Nigeria, on some counter-terrorism issues. These were my first introductions to Africa and I immediately fell in love with the African countries and their people. They are hungry for information on how to improve their infrastructure and their lives. These experiences would open up other opportunities for me later in my career.

My wife and I loved living in the little town of Honfleur in Normandy and made lifelong friends there. We traveled as much as possible with the time off I could manage. It is much less expensive to move around in Europe when you are already there. We even chased a few stages of the Tour de France each year, which we had always dreamed of doing but never thought possible. I am putting these personal experiences in along with my career just to show another aspect of what happened because I took a chance by taking the position in France.

Toward the end of five years in France, I was asked to take a position outside of Washington, D.C., at the HSI, the investigative branch of Customs and Border Protection (CBP). This was a much larger decision than moving to France; we still had our home in San Diego and had always planned to return there. But again, I decided to try something new. And again, there was good with the bad. I dealt with offices all over the world, so there was rarely a time of day or night that my Blackberry wasn't ringing or pinging. But again, we loved living in Washington and again made lifelong friends with coworkers and neighbors. I even had the opportunity to go back to Africa a couple of times, once to teach at the International Law Enforcement Academy (ILEA) in Gaborone, Botswana, and again for a three-month temporary assignment as deputy attaché in Dakar, Senegal.

By 2011, the work was becoming mundane. I liked many aspects of it, but I missed field investigations. I had enough

(continued)

GUEST LECTURE (continued)

time in to retire and collect a pension, and I was seriously considering doing so at the end of 2012. In a casual conversation with a coworker in D.C., I found out about a position opening at the World Customs Organization in Brussels, Belgium, for programme manager for Project Global Shield. I had been involved with Project Global Shield since its inception and felt passionately about its success. The goal of the programme is to reduce the diversion and trafficking of precursor chemicals used in the manufacture of IEDs. Long story short, I am writing this from Brussels. Again, there is

good with bad in this position. Mostly the bad involves the amount of travel, usually red eyes, usually on weekends, and predominantly to Central Asia, Afghanistan, Pakistan, and other places that I never dreamed of traveling to, some that I had never even heard of. Most of my family has been forced to buy globes to find the places where I travel. The good involves the successes we have had with seizures in many countries and the many lives that have been saved, not to mention the lifelong friendships of those with whom I work.

off or furloughed from their jobs. Staffing in agencies across the United States saw reductions of 10,000 to 15,000 officers.[64]

In response to a 2010 survey by the Police Executive Research Forum (PERF), 47 percent of responding agencies indicated their budget cuts had already caused reductions in service. Eight percent no longer responded to all motor vehicle thefts, 9 percent no longer responded to burglar alarms, and 14 percent no longer responded to noninjury motor vehicle accidents.[65] These are services many in the public want to see continued and have come to expect as "basic" to police work in their communities.

Law enforcement has seen a trend toward civilianization of police services as a cost-saving measure. Many positions inside police agencies that were traditionally sworn positions have now been converted to nonsworn positions. For example, whereas police sergeants formerly supervised civilian employees in records departments, those positions have now been turned over to civilian supervisors who perform the same work at reduced cost to the agencies.

Volunteers also have become an important part of most law enforcement agencies. They provide critical police services that otherwise would be left undone or undertasked. Agencies depend upon their VIPS (Volunteers in Police Services) to provide everything from Neighborhood Watch programs to fingerprinting services, records filing, traffic control, and public outreach. These volunteers are visible in uniforms and perform traffic control duties, parking enforcement, and records functions. Some of these volunteers have prior police experience and are used as unpaid Police Reserve officers. Police Cadet and

Police Explorer programs that bring young people into the department have the added benefit of training prospective future officers for their departments.[66]

Technology has provided other cost-saving measures to police agencies. The use of technology

Reductions in Police Force from Economic Downturn

In Inkster, Michigan, 14 officers were laid off from their jobs, removing 11 officers from the streets. Inkster, which is 17 miles west of Detroit and covers an area of 6.28 square miles, faced an $8.5 million budget deficit for a town of 26,000. The state of Michigan sent a review team to the city of Inkster to review and investigate how the town would pay the budget deficit. With many communities asking for concessions from police unions that ranged from reductions in health insurance to pension and pay cuts, the Inkster police officers who were left on the force had to choose between taking a reduction in pay or facing further layoffs.

Inkster has seen their patrol force reduced from 60 officers to 40, which is about a 35 percent reduction in the force, and yet the public still expects the police department to perform its job and keep them safe. The Inkster police chief says there have been no reductions in service, but the department has been forced to reallocate resources.

© 2016 Cengage Learning®

So thank you for letting me take you with me on this walk down memory lane. I have exceeded my word limit and glossed over so much. As with life in general, when we look back, we tend to focus on the good, not the bad. I hope that this lengthy autobiography does not just seem like an old timer blowing his own horn. The point of sharing my career with you is to open your minds to possibilities. I'm just a regular Joe, but I look back at my career and think, "Wow!"

I think that education is extremely important in any career, but that foundation is critical in law enforcement. Not only is education essential through high school, college, and the academy, but part of success is keeping yourself sharp with ongoing education of some sort. Of course, life experience is equally important. I would encourage you not to just check the boxes, focused only on the next promotion. You'll miss so much along the way. Never miss an opportunity to learn something new. Don't be afraid to step outside your comfort zone. Give the job a chance; it won't let you down. A broad mind will lead to endless successes and countless opportunities.

as a force multiplier will be discussed at greater length in Chapter 14, "Computers, Technology, and Criminalistics in Policing."

State Law Enforcement

Forty-nine of the 50 U.S. states have a primary state law enforcement agency. The only state without a primary state police agency is Hawaii, although it has several law enforcement agencies with state-wide jurisdiction. (This may surprise those who are familiar with the television series *Hawaii 5-0*, which was based on the fictional Hawaiian State Police.)

In the latest reporting year, the 49 primary state law enforcement agencies had about 93,148 full-time employees and more than 60,772 full-time sworn personnel.[67] The largest state law enforcement agency is the California Highway Patrol, which has about 7,202 sworn officers, followed by the New York State Police with 4,847 sworn employees, the Pennsylvania State Police with 4,458 sworn officers, and the Texas Department of Public Safety with 3,529 sworn employees. The smallest state police agencies are the North Dakota Highway Patrol with 139 sworn employees, the South Dakota Highway Patrol with 152 sworn employees, and the Rhode Island State Police with 201 sworn personnel.[68]

Historically, state police departments were developed to deal with growing crime in nonurban areas of the country, which was attributable to the increasing mobility of Americans, the proliferation of cars, and the ease of travel. The state police agencies were formed by governors and legislators to lessen reliance on metropolitan and county police departments, which were more closely linked with politics and corruption.

At the state level, there are two distinct models of law enforcement agencies. The **centralized model of state law enforcement** combines the duties of major criminal investigations with the patrol of state highways. The centralized state police agencies generally assist local police departments in criminal investigations when requested and provide the identification, laboratory, and training functions for local departments.

The second state model, the **decentralized model of state law enforcement**, has a clear distinction between traffic enforcement on state highways and other state-level law enforcement functions. The states that use this model—many southern and midwestern as well as some western states—generally have two separate agencies, one a highway patrol and the other a state bureau of investigation. California, for example, has the California Highway Patrol and the California Division of Law Enforcement.

Although the duties of the various state-level police departments may vary considerably, the most common include highway patrol, traffic law enforcement, and the patrol of small towns.

centralized model of state law enforcement Combines the duties of major criminal investigations with the patrol of state highways.

decentralized model of state law enforcement Makes a clear distinction between traffic enforcement on state highways and other state-level law enforcement functions.

Federal Law Enforcement

Although the U.S. Constitution did not create a national police force, it did give the national government power over a limited number of crimes. Traditionally, in the United States, the creation of laws and the power to enforce them were matters for the states, which in turn gave many of their enforcement powers to local police agencies. In recent years, however, the number of crimes included in the U.S. Criminal Code has multiplied greatly, as has the number of people assigned to enforce these crimes. By the latest reporting year, about 120,000 full-time federal law enforcement employees were authorized to make arrests and carry firearms; this number did not include officers in the U.S. armed forces (Army, Navy, Air Force, Marines, and Coast Guard), federal air marshals, or Central Intelligence Agency (CIA) security protective service officers because of classified information restrictions.[69]

With the increased attention to border security and homeland defense following the terrorist attacks of 9/11, the number of federal law enforcement officers has increased daily. The total number of criminal justice system employees in the nation grew 86 percent between 1982 and the latest reported year, with federal criminal justice employees experiencing the highest increase at 168 percent. Federal expenditures increased 692 percent during that period, with an annual increase of 9.9 percent. Additionally, federal expenditures for police protection increased 708 percent for an annual percentage increase of 10 percent.[70]

For the latest reporting period, women accounted for 16 percent of federal law enforcement employees, and a third of federal officers were members of a racial or ethnic minority (17.7 percent Hispanic and 11.4 percent African American). Nationwide, there were 36 federal law enforcement officers for every 100,000 citizens. Thirty-eight percent of federal officers' duties included criminal investigation; 21 percent police response and patrol; 16 percent corrections and detention; 16 percent inspections; 5 percent court operations; and 4 percent security and protection.[71]

Four major U.S. cabinet departments administer most federal law enforcement agencies and personnel: the Department of Justice, the Department of the Treasury, the Department of Homeland Security, and the Department of the Interior. Numerous other federal agencies have law enforcement functions. Each of the agencies discussed in this section has an Internet presence, and students are urged to access these sites to obtain information regarding these agencies, their duties, and the many jobs they have available. This text pays special attention to federal law enforcement agencies because many of these agencies require a four-year college degree for appointment.

Department of Justice

The U.S. Department of Justice is the primary legal and prosecutorial arm of the U.S. government. The Department of Justice is under the control of the U.S. Attorney General and is responsible for (1) enforcing all federal laws, (2) representing the government when it is involved in a court action, and (3) conducting independent investigations through its law enforcement services. The department's Civil Rights Division prosecutes violators of federal civil rights laws, which are designed to protect citizens from discrimination on the basis of their race, creed, ethnic background, or gender. These laws apply to discrimination in education, housing, and job

A border patrol agent pats down a Mexican immigrant who is being returned to Mexico.

Photo by Gerald L. Nino/U.S. Border Patrol

opportunity. The Justice Department's Tax Division prosecutes violators of the tax laws. The Criminal Division prosecutes violators of the Federal Criminal Code for such criminal acts as bank robbery, kidnapping, mail fraud, interstate transportation of stolen vehicles, and narcotics and drug trafficking.

The Justice Department also operates the **National Institute of Justice (NIJ)** as its research arm. The National Institute of Justice maintains the **National Criminal Justice Reference Service (NCJRS)** as a national clearinghouse of criminal justice information. The NCJRS is one of the most extensive sources of information on criminal justice in the world. Created in 1972, it contains specialized information centers to provide publications and other information services to the constituencies of the U.S. Department of Justice, Office of Justice Programs (OJP) bureaus, and Office of National Drug Control Policy. Each OJP agency has established specialized information centers, and each has its own toll-free number and staff to answer questions about the agency's mission and initiatives.

The NIJ also conducts the National Crime Victimization Survey (NCVS), a twice-yearly survey of a random sample of the American public that polls citizens about their criminal victimization. Finally, the Justice Department maintains administrative control over the Federal Bureau of Investigation (FBI), the Drug Enforcement Administration (DEA), the U.S. Marshals, and the Bureau of Alcohol, Tobacco, Firearms, and Explosives (ATF).

THE FEDERAL BUREAU OF INVESTIGATION

The FBI is the best known of the federal law enforcement agencies. The FBI has more than 12,560 special agents and is the primary agency charged with the enforcement of all federal laws not falling under the purview of other federal agencies. The main headquarters of the FBI is in Washington, D.C., but it also has field offices in major American cities and abroad. The head of the FBI is known as the director and is appointed by the president of the United States, subject to confirmation by the Senate.[72]

In addition to the special agents, the FBI employs almost 18,000 support nonenforcement personnel such as intelligence specialists, language specialists, scientists, information technology specialists, and other staff who perform such duties as fingerprint examinations, computer programming, forensic or crime laboratory analysis, and administrative and clerical work.

All special agents must attend the FBI Academy, located in Quantico, Virginia. In addition to the special agents, other law enforcement officers and officers from some foreign governments attend the academy. The FBI Academy also runs the Leadership Development Institute (LDI), a one-year program to enhance the leadership skills of individuals in law enforcement command-level positions and broaden their exposure to both the domestic and international policing communities. Fellows spend six months at the academy and the remaining six months at their respective agencies or at Quantico for additional research and study.[73]

Contrary to popular opinion, the FBI is not a national police force. Rather, it is an investigative agency that may investigate acts that violate federal law. The FBI may also assist state and local law enforcement agencies and investigate state and local crimes when asked to do so by those agencies.

The FBI was created in 1908, when President Theodore Roosevelt directed the attorney general to develop an investigative unit within the Justice Department. It was first named the Bureau of Investigation; in 1935, it was renamed the Federal Bureau of Investigation. Its most prominent figure was longtime director (from 1924 to 1972) J. Edgar Hoover.

The FBI has had a colorful history. It captured the attention of the media during the Great Depression with nationwide searches and the capture of such notorious criminals as George "Machine Gun" Kelly in 1933, John Dillinger in 1934, and Charles "Pretty Boy" Floyd in 1934. Critics, however, allege that the FBI under Hoover's regime ignored white-collar crime, organized crime, and violations of the civil rights of minority groups. After Hoover's death in 1972, it was discovered that under his direction the FBI had committed many violations of citizens' constitutional rights, including spying, conducting illegal wiretaps, and burglarizing premises. These violations were mostly aimed at individuals and groups because of their political beliefs.[74] Hoover's successors reoriented the mission of the bureau and put more emphasis on the

National Institute of Justice (NIJ) The research arm of the U.S. Justice Department.

National Criminal Justice Reference Service (NCJRS) A national clearinghouse of criminal justice information maintained by the National Institute of Justice.

investigation of white-collar crime, organized crime, and political corruption.[75]

In addition to its investigative capacity, the FBI today provides many important services for law enforcement.

Identification Division

The FBI's Identification Division, created in 1924, collects and maintains a vast fingerprint file. This file is used for identification purposes by the FBI, as well as state and local police agencies.

National Crime Information Center

The National Crime Information Center (NCIC) is a tremendous computerized database of criminal information. It stores information on stolen property that has identifying information, such as serial numbers or distinctive markings. The NCIC also contains information on outstanding warrants and criminal histories. In 2005, the NCIC added an *Identity Theft File* to assist police and crime victims in investigating cases of identity theft.[76]

FBI Crime Laboratory

The FBI Crime Laboratory, created in 1932, provides investigative and analysis services for other law enforcement agencies. It is the world's largest forensic, or criminalistic (scientifically crime-related), laboratory and provides microscopic, chemical, and DNA analyses, as well as spectrography and cryptography. Skilled FBI technicians examine such evidence as hairs, fibers, blood, tire tracks, and drugs.

Uniform Crime Reports

The Uniform Crime Reports (UCR) Program produces an annual compilation that includes information on crimes reported to local police agencies, arrests, and police killed or wounded in the line of duty, along with other data. The report, titled *Crime in the United States*, is the result of a nationwide, cooperative statistical effort by the majority of the nation's city, county, and state law enforcement agencies that voluntarily report data on crimes brought to their attention by the public. Since 1930, the FBI has administered the program and issued periodic assessments of the nature and type of crime in the nation. Although the program's primary objective is to provide a reliable set of criminal statistics for use in law enforcement administration, operation, and management, over the years its data have become one of the leading social indicators for the United States. The

American public looks to the UCR for information on fluctuations in the level of crime. Criminologists, sociologists, legislators, municipal planners, the press, and students of criminal justice use the statistics for varied research and planning purposes.

The specific crimes measured by the UCR are called Part I—Index crimes. They are murder and nonnegligent manslaughter, forcible rape, robbery, aggravated assault, burglary, larceny-theft, arson, and motor vehicle theft. One of the latest additions to the UCR is the collection of hate crime statistics, mandated by the Hate Crime Statistics Act. This collection of data is being used to study crimes motivated by religious, ethnic, racial, or sexual orientation prejudice.

National Incident-Based Reporting System

In response to law enforcement's need for more flexible, in-depth data, the UCR formulated the National Incident-Based Reporting System (NIBRS), which presents comprehensive, detailed information about crime incidents to law enforcement, researchers, governmental planners, students of crime, and the general public. NIBRS is still not fully implemented throughout the United States, and the data is not pervasive enough to make broad generalizations about crime in the United States.[77]

Investigatory Activities

The FBI investigates more than 200 categories of federal crimes and also has concurrent jurisdiction with the DEA over drug offenses under the Controlled Substances Act. In 2006 it was reported that during the previous two years, FBI investigations had led to corruption convictions for more than 1,000 government employees.[78]

An August 2005 article by Special Agents Leonard G. Johns, Gerard F. Downes, and Camille D. Bibles of the FBI's Critical Incident Response Group showed how the FBI's National Center for the Analysis of Violent Crime (NCAVC) offers consultative services on cold-case serial homicides as well as several other types of cases. In this article, the authors described a series of three murders of a suspect's wives from 1978 to 1993. Information from the NCAVC led to the arrest of the subject, along with the cooperation of investigators from the U.S. Department of Interior and the National Park Service and police from Coconino and Arapahoe counties in Colorado.[79] In another article, Special Agents Eugene Rugala and James McNamara, also of the NCAVC, and George Wattendorf, a prosecutor and police officer for the Dover, New Hampshire, Police Department, discussed the assistance the NCAVC can render in stalking cases, which is an important issue because research suggests a strong connection between stalking and domestic violence—81 percent of women stalked by husbands or cohabiting partners have suffered a physical assault from that person.[80]

Traditionally the FBI focused its investigations on organized crime activities, including racketeering, corruption, and pornography; bank robbery; and white-collar crime, including embezzlement and stock and other business fraud. Today the FBI is also at the forefront of our government's efforts against domestic terrorist activity and trains special antiterrorist teams to prevent and respond to terrorist attacks. It maintains surveillance on foreign intelligence agents and investigates their activities within the United States.

Even before September 11, 2001, the federal government, realizing that both international and domestic terrorism are serious national concerns, took several law enforcement measures to deal with terrorism. However, in May 2002, following massive criticism that the FBI had failed to properly handle information that could have led to the prevention of the 9/11 attacks, Director Robert S. Mueller issued a press release outlining a complete reorganization of the FBI and creating a new strategic focus for the agency. The FBI placed the following as its three priorities: (1) protecting the United States from terrorist attack, (2) protecting the United States against foreign intelligence operations and espionage, and (3) protecting the United States against cyber-based attacks and high-technology crimes. The main organizational improvements Mueller enacted were:

- A complete restructuring of the counterterrorism activities of the bureau and a shift from a reactive to a proactive orientation
- The development of special squads to coordinate national and international investigations
- A reemphasis on the Joint Terrorism Task Forces
- Enhanced analytical capabilities with personnel and technological improvements
- A permanent shift of additional resources to counterterrorism

- The creation of a more mobile, agile, and flexible national terrorism response
- Targeted recruitment to acquire agents, analysts, translators, and others with specialized skills and backgrounds[81]

Following this new mission, the FBI implemented the Law Enforcement Online (LEO) Program, a conduit for intelligence information that forms a cornerstone for the bureau's information-sharing initiative by providing links to federal, state, local, and tribal law enforcement agencies nationwide. LEO provides communication, information, expertise, and full-time access needed by first-response public safety officers facing the initial onslaught of an emergency. The program contributes to the intelligence, investigative, and safety functions in law enforcement and has become the national communications system for all levels of the law enforcement community. Its electronic interface enables users to access it with a single log-on and provides them with a secure e-mail system. A virtual command center (VCC) runs a software program that provides the capability to maintain an awareness of evolving situations for crisis management, allowing LEO members to track, display, and disseminate information in real time about street-level and tactical activities. This system enables FBI headquarters to monitor events and resources in an affected area and to help provide federal, state, and local support to the first responders. It also serves in the investigation of crimes and terrorist threats by allowing users to obtain more comprehensive investigative information and track trends of specific crimes and multiple criminal offenses throughout the country.

The National Alert System (NAS), introduced in 2003, can deliver secure message boxes containing law enforcement–sensitive information to 20,000 online members within five minutes and simultaneously transmit them to all members' LEO e-mail accounts. An alert message contains a short synopsis and directs the recipient to additional information posted on a secure LEO site. The NAS can send up to 160,000 notifications to pagers, cell phones, and other wireless devices to advise users of the alert. The VCC and NAS features of LEO have been called "a one-stop shop" for the law enforcement community for FBI intelligence information, providing a central hub for information sharing to support investigative programs.

In 2003 the FBI created Field Intelligence Groups (FIGs) in all of its 56 field offices. These groups work closely with the Joint Terrorism Task Forces, various field office squads, and other agency components to provide valuable service to law enforcement personnel at the state and local levels by sharing intelligence gathered about transnational terrorism. The FIGs also produce and disseminate intelligence pertaining to cyber, counterintelligence, and criminal programs.[82]

See Chapter 15, "Homeland Security," for a full description of the FBI's new role in counterterrorism and homeland security.

DRUG ENFORCEMENT ADMINISTRATION The Drug Enforcement Administration (DEA) is at the vanguard of the nation's "war on drugs" by engaging in drug interdiction, conducting surveillance operations, infiltrating drug rings, and arresting major narcotics violators. The agency also tracks illicit drug traffic; registers manufacturers, distributors, and dispensers of pharmaceutical drugs and controlled substances; tracks the movement of chemicals used in the manufacture of illegal drugs; and leads the nation's marijuana eradication program. Recent legislation in various states and court decisions have changed the outlook of marijuana and will be discussed further in Chapter 9.[83]

U.S. MARSHALS SERVICE The U.S. Marshals Service performs many functions. Its primary functions are the transportation of federal prisoners between prisons and courts and the security of federal court facilities. The marshals also protect witnesses at federal trials, apprehend federal fugitives, execute federal warrants, operate the federal Witness Security Program (popularly known as witness protection), and are in charge of the federal government's asset seizure and forfeiture programs, handling the seizure and disposal of property resulting from criminal activity. In its effort to track down fugitives, the U.S. Marshals Service uses combined task forces of federal, state, and local law enforcement officers.

walking The practice of having weapons move across the border illegally.

straw buyers People with no criminal record who purchase guns for criminals or illegal immigrants who cannot legally buy them.

BUREAU OF ALCOHOL, TOBACCO, FIREARMS, AND EXPLOSIVES The Bureau of Alcohol, Tobacco, Firearms, and Explosives (ATF) is the nation's primary agency for enforcing federal laws relating to alcohol, tobacco, firearms, and explosives violations. The ATF enforces laws pertaining to the manufacture, sale, and possession of firearms and explosives; attempts to suppress illegal traffic in tobacco and alcohol products; collects taxes; and regulates industry trade practices regarding these items. As the nation's primary agency for tracing weapons and explosives, the ATF also assists other domestic and international law enforcement agencies. It traces weapons through its records of manufacturers and dealers in firearms. In addition, the ATF investigates cases of arson and bombing at federal buildings or other institutions that receive federal funds, and it investigates arson-for-profit schemes.

OPERATION FAST AND FURIOUS On the night of December 14, 2010, U.S. Border Patrol Agent Brian Terry was gunned down during a firefight on the border with five illegal immigrants. The agents were under orders to use "less lethal" beanbag ammunition; the illegal immigrants had no such orders. This unfortunate and regrettable death of an agent, who was planning to fly to Michigan with his family at the end of his shift, brought the ATF program known as "Operation Fast and Furious" to the attention of the public for the first time.

Operation Fast and Furious was first conceived in Washington, D.C., in October 2009 as a result of the frustration of seeing guns bought in the United States **walking** across the border to Mexico. By November 2009, a new strategy was proposed and put in place: Let the guns be purchased, and follow them to their eventual end. The guns would flow through the weapons trafficking network and provide a lead to the upper echelons of the network. The hope was that the operation would take down the drug cartels. Under the rules in force at ATF at the time, the program was allowed. It had the legal approval of the U.S. Attorney in Phoenix and was funded through the Department of Justice.

From the beginning, agents were concerned about the tremendous adverse risks this operation carried, even though allowing guns to be purchased intentionally and watching **straw buyers** move them on a route to Mexico carried rewards as well. They hated seeing guns move through the process and into the hands of the Sinaloa drug cartel. No one in the law enforcement community wants to see weapons of such destructive power loose in criminal hands. Also, every time agents who were watching the purchases move called their supervisors, they were denied permission to make an arrest.

The decision was made not to tell the government of Mexico or the U.S. Embassy officials in Mexico, even though the stated reason for the program was to follow the weapons and eventually take down the traffickers who were in Mexico. When the U.S. Embassy cabled Washington to complain about the large numbers of guns coming across the border, they were told, in effect, not to interfere with an ongoing investigation.

In January 2011, the U.S. Attorney in Phoenix announced a 53-count indictment involving 20 suspects. The indictment alleged that hundreds of weapons were bought and exported illegally to Mexico. During the operation, more than 2,020 guns were bought by "straw purchasers." Of those guns, 227 were recovered in Mexico; 363, including the one that killed Agent Terry, were recovered in the United States.

While this indictment was being announced, the U.S. House of Representatives was conducting investigations into the operation. Thousands of documents were subpoenaed, and testimony was taken from dozens of witnesses, including U.S. Attorney General Holder. The U.S Senate voted on an amendment to prevent the Justice Department from conducting any future gun-tracking operations.

In September 2012, an internal Justice Department investigation conducted by the inspector general faulted the agency for misguided strategies, errors in judgment, and management failures during the Arizona gun-trafficking probe: "The inspector general said … senior department officials knew or should have known that ATF had in many instances allowed straw purchasers to buy firearms knowing that someone else would transport them to Mexico."[84]

Department of the Treasury

The Department of the Treasury has administrative control over the Internal Revenue Service's Criminal Investigation Division and several important offices related to the financial aspects of crime, drug trafficking, and terrorism.

YOU ARE THERE **Lawsuit Resulting from Operation Fast and Furious**

After the slaying of U.S. Border Patrol Agent Brian Terry during Operation Fast and Furious, Attorney General Holder stated that he regretted the death of Agent Terry, but called it "unfair" to believe that the operation was the direct cause. The Terry family, however, has filed a "notice of claim," stating that they intend to sue the ATF and the Justice Department for $25 million.

Agent Terry's family, in a statement released through their lawyer, decried the testimony of U.S. Attorney General Holder, saying, "If it is true he did not know, then he should have known." The Terry family's attorney, Lincoln Combs, also said in a statement: "The fact of the matter is that the men who killed Brian Terry were armed with brand new military-grade assault weapons and ammunition. The weapons were allowed to be purchased with the full approval of ATF and the U.S. Attorney's office in Arizona, both agencies falling under the control of the attorney general."

© 2016 Cengage Learning®

INTERNAL REVENUE SERVICE The Internal Revenue Service (IRS), the nation's primary revenue-collection agency, is charged with the enforcement of laws regulating federal income tax and its collection. The investigative arm of the IRS is its Criminal Investigation Division (CID). The CID agents investigate tax fraud, unreported income, and hidden assets. As part of its efforts to fight organized crime and drug dealing, the federal government often uses the CID to target major crime figures and drug dealers with the goal of prosecuting them for tax evasion. Many other law enforcement agencies also solicit the help of the CID in their attempts to prosecute major drug dealers and other criminals who possess large amounts of undeclared income.

EXECUTIVE OFFICE FOR ASSET FORFEITURE The Executive Office for Asset Forfeiture (EOAF) administers programs that apply the forfeiture laws to the infrastructure of criminal enterprises, limiting the ability of these organizations to continue their illegal activities. The EOAF primarily directs its efforts against drug cartels, criminal syndicates, and terrorist organizations by removing their assets and minimizing their profits.

EXECUTIVE OFFICE FOR TERRORIST FINANCING AND FINANCIAL CRIME
The Executive Office for Terrorist Financing and Financial Crime (EOTF/FC) develops and implements U.S. government strategies to combat terrorist financing domestically and internationally. It also develops and implements the National Money Laundering Strategy.

OFFICE OF FOREIGN ASSETS CONTROL
The Office of Foreign Assets Control (OFAC) administers and enforces economic and trade sanctions based on U.S. foreign policy and national security goals against targeted foreign countries, terrorists, international narcotics traffickers, and those engaged in activities related to the proliferation of weapons of mass destruction.

FINANCIAL CRIMES ENFORCEMENT NETWORK
The Financial Crimes Enforcement Network (FinCEN) coordinates information sharing among law enforcement agencies to deal with the complex problem of money laundering.

Department of Homeland Security

After much study following the terrorist attacks of September 11, 2001, the cabinet-level Department of Homeland Security (DHS) was established in March 2003.[85] The new agency merged 22 previously disparate domestic agencies into one department to protect the nation against outside threats. At its inception, the new agency consisted of more than 170,000 employees. See Chapter 15 for a complete description of the DHS and other governmental efforts to prevent terrorism and ensure homeland defense.

The creation of the DHS was the most significant transformation of the U.S. government since 1947 when President Harry S. Truman merged the various branches of the U.S. armed forces into the Department of Defense to better coordinate the nation's defense against military threats. The DHS, which represents a similar consolidation in both style and substance, has assumed the former duties of the U.S. Coast Guard, the U.S. Customs Service, the Secret Service, the Immigration and Naturalization Service, the Transportation Security Administration, and numerous other federal communications, science, and technology agencies. The DHS does not include the FBI, CIA, or National Security Agency. The major enforcement agencies within the DHS include Customs and Border Protection (CBP) and Immigrations and Customs Enforcement (ICE).[86] Each of the separate units of the DHS and their functions will be fully discussed in Chapter 15.

The major priority of the DHS is the protection of the nation against further terrorist attacks. The department's units analyze threats and intelligence, guard our borders and airports, protect our critical infrastructure, and coordinate the responses of our nation to future emergencies.

U.S. SECRET SERVICE
The primary mission of U.S. Secret Service is the protection of the president and his or her family, as well as other government leaders and foreign dignitaries. The Secret Service also provides security for designated national events and preserves the integrity of the nation's financial and critical infrastructures. It is the primary agency responsible for protecting U.S. currency from counterfeiters and safeguarding Americans from credit card fraud, financial crimes, and computer fraud. The agency uses prevention-based training and methods to combat cybercriminals and terrorists who attempt to use identity theft, telecommunications fraud, and other technology-based crimes to defraud and undermine American consumers and industry.

In its role of protecting the president, vice president, and other government officials and their families, along with former presidents and presidential and vice presidential candidates, the Secret Service coordinates all security arrangements for official presidential visits, motorcades, and ceremonies with other federal government agencies and state and local law enforcement agencies. The Secret Service has uniformed and nonuniformed divisions. The uniformed division provides protection for the White House complex and other presidential offices, the Main Treasury Building and Annex, and foreign diplomatic missions.

Department of the Interior

The Department of the Interior's myriad law enforcement agencies provide services for the property under its purview utilizing the National Park Service, the U.S. Park Police, the Bureau of Indian Affairs, the Fish and Wildlife Service, the Bureau of

Land Management, and the Bureau of Reclamation. These agencies are responsible for protecting most of the nation's historic icons, such as Mount Rushmore, the Washington Monument, the Hoover and Grand Coulee Dams and 350 other dams, and millions of acres of uninhabited wilderness in national parks, preserves, and other lands controlled by the federal government.

Enforcement agents for the National Park Service are known as commissioned park rangers. They are responsible for law enforcement, traffic control, fire control, and search and rescue operations in the 30 million acres of the National Park Service. Additional rangers serve seasonally as part-time commissioned rangers. The Park Service also uses Park Police officers, mainly in the Washington, D.C., area, but others serve at the Statue of Liberty in New York and the Golden Gate Bridge in San Francisco as well. Enforcement agents for the Department of the Interior's Fish and Wildlife Service are called wildlife law enforcement agents. They investigate people who are illegally trafficking in government-protected animals and birds, such as falcons.

The Fraternal Order of Police has argued for management changes and a bigger budget for the U.S. Park Police. In 2004, the chief of the Park Police, Teresa C. Chambers, was fired after publicly raising concerns about staffing, budgets, and security.[87] In a 2008 report, the Interior Department's inspector general concluded that the U.S. Park Police have failed to adequately protect such national landmarks as the Statue of Liberty, the Lincoln Memorial, and the Washington Monument, and that the agency is plagued by low morale, poor leadership, and bad organization. The inspector general's report further disclosed that the agency is understaffed, insufficiently trained, and woefully equipped, and that important sites on the Washington Mall are weakly guarded and vulnerable to terrorist attack. The report was based on more than 100 interviews of law enforcement personnel and staff as well as surveillance conducted in 2007.[88]

Chambers, who is now chief of the Riverdale Park police force in Prince George's County, Virginia, stated in 2008, "It's exactly the type of thing I was trying to warn my bosses about four or five years ago. I feel for the officers who are trying to do their jobs with the diminishing resources. There is no pleasure in having a report vindicate you when you have officers and visitors at risk. Not only have things not improved, they have gotten worse."[89]

Department of Defense

Each branch of the U.S. military has its own law enforcement agency. The military police agencies are organized in a manner similar to the civil police, using uniformed officers for patrol duties on military bases and investigators to investigate crimes. The Army's investigative arm is the Criminal Investigation Division (CID); the investigative arm of the Navy and Marines is the Naval Criminal Investigative Service (NCIS); and the Air Force's is the Air Force Office of Special Investigations (OSI).

U.S. Postal Service

The Postal Inspections Division of the U.S. Postal Service is one of the oldest of the federal law enforcement agencies, created in 1836. Postal inspectors investigate illegal acts committed against the Postal Service and its property and personnel, such as cases of fraud involving the use of the mails; use of the mails to transport drugs, bombs, and firearms; and assaults upon postal employees while exercising their official duties. Postal inspectors are responsible for criminal investigations covering more than 200 federal statutes related to the postal system. Postal police officers provide security for postal facilities, employees, and assets; escort high-value mail shipments; and perform other protective functions.[90]

Other Federal Enforcement Agencies

Many other federal agencies have law enforcement responsibilities.[91] The Department of Agriculture has enforcement officers in its U.S. Forest Service, and its Office of Investigation investigates fraud in the areas of food stamps and subsidies to farmers and rural home buyers. The Department of Commerce has enforcement divisions in its Bureau of Export Enforcement and the National Marine Fisheries Administration. The Department of Labor has the Office of Labor Racketeering as an enforcement division.[92]

The Food and Drug Administration (FDA) oversees the enforcement of the laws regulating the sale and distribution of pure food and drugs. Criminal law enforcement divisions are also found in the Securities and Exchange Commission (SEC), the Interstate Commerce Commission (ICC), the Federal Trade Commission (FTC), the Department of Health and Human Services (DHHS), the Tennessee Valley

Authority (TVA), the Environmental Protection Agency (EPA), the Veterans Health Administration (VHA), and the Library of Congress. The Department of State has the Bureau of Diplomatic Security to investigate matters involving passport and visa fraud.[93] The U.S. Supreme Court has its own police department. Even the National Gallery of Art has its own law enforcement unit.

The U.S. Capitol Police employs more than 1,200 officers to provide police services for the grounds, buildings, and area immediately surrounding the Capitol complex. The U.S. Mint has a police department that provides police and patrol services for U.S. Mint facilities, including safeguarding the nation's coinage and gold bullion reserves. The Bureau of Engraving and Printing has a police department providing police services for their facilities, including those where currency, stamps, securities, and other official U.S. documents are made. The National Railroad Passenger Corporation, better known as Amtrak, has officers who provide police response, patrol, and investigative services for the railroad.

See Table 2.3 for a summary of federal law enforcement agencies.

TABLE 2.3   Major Federal Law Enforcement Agencies

Department of Justice	Department of Defense
Federal Bureau of Investigation	Army Criminal Investigation Division
Drug Enforcement Administration	Naval Criminal Investigative Service
U.S. Marshals Service	Air Force Office of Special Investigations
Bureau of Alcohol, Tobacco, Firearms, and Explosives	**U.S. Postal Service**
Department of the Treasury	Postal Inspections Service
Internal Revenue Service—Criminal Investigation Division	**Department of Agriculture**
Executive Office for Asset Forfeiture	U.S. Forest Service
Executive Office for Terrorist Financing and Financial Crime	**Department of Commerce**
Office of Foreign Assets Control	Bureau of Export Enforcement
Financial Crimes Enforcement Network	National Marine Fisheries Administration
Department of Homeland Security	**Department of Labor**
Federal Emergency Management Agency, Security Branch	Office of Labor Racketeering
U.S. Customs and Border Protection	**Department of State**
U.S. Immigration and Customs Enforcement	Diplomatic Security Service
U.S. Secret Service	**Other Federal Law Enforcement Agencies**
Department of the Interior	Amtrak Police
National Park Service	Bureau of Engraving and Printing Police
Fish and Wildlife Service	U.S. Capitol Police
U.S. Park Police	U.S. Mint Police
Bureau of Indian Affairs	U.S. Supreme Court Police
Bureau of Land Management	Library of Congress Police
Bureau of Reclamation	National Gallery of Art Police
	Veterans Health Administration

Source: Brian A. Reaves, *Federal Law Enforcement Officers, 2008* (Washington, D.C.: Bureau of Justice Statistics, 2012).

Working Together Toward a Common Goal

Law enforcement agencies around the country have expanded their use of multiagency task forces over the last few decades. The law enforcement leaders have realized there is much to share and that working together produces the best outcomes. Many examples of very successful efforts abound, involving local, state, and federal agencies. This gives the task forces choices in how they address a particular crime, offender, charging decision, or prosecution. It also provides for ample resources, as well as objective and varying opinions during the investigation.

When I was a detective, I participated as part of a regional task force known as the Vice President's Task Force on Drugs that had been assembled to fight the growing drug trade in south Florida. It was my first experience on a task force, and I was very excited for the opportunity to work with agents representing DEA, ATF, and Customs as well as investigators from Dade, Broward, and Palm Beach Counties. Many of the agents we worked with were on a temporary assignment by the federal government to south Florida for a year or so; their home bases were in states all across the country.

I was pulled into the task force due to a home invasion robbery that I was investigating. The victims—a family with a young baby—were confronted upon their return from a dinner out. The masked intruders had broken into their house and were waiting for them. They ordered the husband to open a large gun safe, threatening to cut the baby's fingers off if he did not. Due to his nervousness, it took a while for him to get it open, but the suspects then took a cache of large automatic weapons from the safe. The parents were tied up and the suspects left the house in a vehicle. After some time, the victims freed themselves and called the police.

I received a call the next evening from a neighboring agency: One of the suspects had tried to board a train to New York City. He had consented to having his bag searched, and these guns were discovered and connected to the robbery via their serial numbers. We were able to make a couple of arrests and gather intelligence that became part of the task force investigation.

This was a fun and challenging assignment as it took me to locations I had not patrolled before and enabled me to work with a great group of dedicated detectives. For the next couple of months, we did a lot of surveillance and tracked down leads. With so many agents involved, targets to follow, and leads to explore, there were many task force members involved that I never actually met.

Anytime you're dealing with automatic weapons that are being bought, sold, traded—many to go outside the country—the element of danger is heightened. Tragically, during the existence of this task force, two ATF agents were murdered in cold blood during a gun deal. While this strengthened the resolve of everyone involved, there was also a lot of anger about the loss of these dedicated agents. The whole drug world and its associated tangled web of crime were a source of frustration, and on many days it felt like we were losing the war.

Most of the task force travelled to Puerto Rico to bury the agents, who had come from a rural area in the outskirts of San Juan. It was a dangerous three-hour trip up in the hills. The one- and sometimes two-lane dirt roads we took into the mountains were not meant for a charter bus and there were times I thought the bus was going to topple over the side of the mountain. I later found out that Fuerzas Armadas de Liberacion Nacional (Armed Forces of National Liberation or FALN), a paramilitary organization that advocated complete independence for Puerto Rico, had declared an interest in doing harm to our group of mostly federal agents. I was blissfully ignorant of this as we made our way to the cemetery. This trip allowed us to show our support and gratitude to the families of the slain agents, and it also solidified our resolve in seeing that the people responsible faced justice for the deaths of these two agents as well as the many civilians who happened to get in their way.

The task force was in place for many months after the deaths: Good arrests were made, property recovered, items confiscated, and undoubtedly lives saved through the hard work of everyone involved. For me personally, the experience served as a great learning process and it also enhanced my career as I moved up the ladder. It made me realize the tremendous results a good task force can accomplish and how sharing information and strategies and working together toward the same goal can have a significant impact on crime.

—Linda Forst

Joint Federal and Local Task Force Approach to Law Enforcement

In the 1970s, federal enforcement agencies implemented an innovative approach to law enforcement by using **joint federal and local task forces** involving local, state, and federal law enforcement officers acting as a team. In these task forces, investigators from local police departments and state police agencies are temporarily assigned to a federal law enforcement agency to work with federal agents in combating particular crimes. The local and state officers provide knowledge of the area, local contacts, informants, and street smarts, and federal agents provide investigative experience and resources. The DEA has been using joint drug enforcement task forces in many areas of the country since the early 1970s. The joint task force approach has also been used successfully in ongoing programs to investigate bank robbery, arson, kidnapping, and

joint federal and local task forces Use of federal, state, and local law enforcement agents in a focused task force to address particular crime problems.

terrorism.[94] See Chapter 15 for a complete description of the Joint Terrorism Task Forces.

International Police

Interpol, the International Criminal Police Organization, is a worldwide organization established for the development of cooperation among nations regarding common police problems. Interpol was founded in 1923, and the United States became a member in 1938. The mission of Interpol is to track and provide information that may help other law enforcement agencies apprehend criminal fugitives, thwart criminal schemes, exchange experience and technology, and analyze major trends of international criminal activity. Interpol attempts to achieve its mission by serving as a clearinghouse and depository of intelligence information on wanted criminals.

The main function of Interpol is informational; it is neither an investigative nor an enforcement agency. Police officials of any member country may initiate a request for assistance on a case that extends beyond their country's jurisdiction. Interpol headquarters are in France, and its U.S. representative is the U.S. Treasury Department.[95]

SUMMARY

- For the latest reporting year, local, state, and federal agencies spent approximately $260 billion for criminal justice agencies, including police, corrections, and judicial services.

- Local, state, and federal criminal justice agencies employed about 2.4 million people for the latest reporting period—57.5 percent at the local level, 31 percent at the state level, and 11.5 percent at the federal level.

- Police protection spending amounted to about $95.4 billion from the total national criminal justice budget. Local policing expenditures alone accounted for about 45 percent of the nation's entire criminal justice budget.

- The United States does not have a national police force, unlike most other countries.

- Law enforcement in the United States has developed over the years based on a philosophy of local control, which is the formal and informal use

of local neighborhood forms of control to deter abhorrent behaviors.

- Every few years the Bureau of Justice Statistics (BJS) attempts to paint a picture of law enforcement personnel and practices through its Law Enforcement Management and Administrative Statistics (LEMAS) program.

- For the latest reporting period, state and local governments in the United States operated almost 17,985 full-time law enforcement agencies. These agencies included 12,501 local police departments, almost 3,063 sheriff's offices, and 50 primary state police departments, as well as approximately 1,733 special jurisdiction police departments and about 638 constable/marshal agencies. Federal law enforcement agencies employed more than 105,000 full-time federal law enforcement personnel authorized to make arrests and carry firearms.

- The U.S. law enforcement industry is enormous in both size and scope, tremendously diverse and fragmented, and predominantly local.
- The federal government responded to 9/11 by creating the huge cabinet-level Department of Homeland Security (DHS), which merged and improved the many disparate federal agencies concerned with terrorism, homeland defense, and response to catastrophic emergencies. Local, state, and private agencies also have reengineered themselves to address the need for homeland defense.

KEY TERMS

centralized model of state law enforcement

decentralized model of state law enforcement

joint federal and local task force

LEMAS

local control

National Criminal Justice Reference Service (NCJRS)

National Institute of Justice (NIJ)

straw buyers

sworn law enforcement employee average

walking

REVIEW EXERCISES

1. You have been given the opportunity to create a new town or city based on your specifications. To do this, you must also create the institutions that will govern this town or city. What type of police agency would you create to ensure a safe and orderly environment? You must assume that crime and disorder are possible, even in your new city or town. Consider the qualifications you want the officers in this agency to possess and what power you would give them.

2. Your professor schedules a class debate on the pros and cons of the enforcement of federal immigration laws by the local police. Which side would you take in this debate: the local police must be involved in the enforcement of federal immigration laws, or the local police should not be involved in the enforcement of federal immigration laws? Prepare a list of talking points to argue your side in this debate.

3. Interview a local police officer or sheriff's deputy. Ask the officer or deputy how his or her duties compare and contrast with members of the state police.

WEB EXERCISES

1. Search the Internet and obtain the Bureau of Justice Statistics' latest updates regarding the number of law enforcement agencies in the United States, including local police departments, sheriff's offices, state police agencies, and federal law enforcement agencies.

2. Search the Internet and obtain the Bureau of Justice Statistics' latest updates on the personnel statistics regarding employment in law enforcement agencies in the United States, including local police departments, sheriff's offices, state police agencies, and federal law enforcement agencies.

3. Search the Internet for employment opportunities in federal law enforcement agencies. Prepare a résumé and cover letter applying for a position in one of these agencies.

END NOTES

1. Tracey Kyckelhahn and Tara Martin, *Justice Expenditure and Employment Extracts, 2010 — Preliminary*, (Washington, D.C.: Bureau of Justice Statistics, July 1, 2013),.

2. David H. Bayley, *Forces of Order: Police Behavior in Japan and the United States* (Berkeley: University of California Press, 1976).

3. Brian A. Reaves, *Census of State and Local Law Enforcement Agencies, 2004* (Washington, D.C.: Bureau of Justice Statistics, 2007), p. 2.

4. Brian A. Reaves, *Federal Law Enforcement Officers, 2008* (Washington, D.C.: Bureau of Justice Statistics, 2012), p. 1.

5. U.S. Department of Labor, Bureau of Labor Statistics, *Occupational Outlook Handbook*, "Police and Detectives," retrieved September 7, 2008, from www.bls.gov/oco/ocos160.htm.

6. Brian A. Reaves, *Census of State and Local Law Enforcement Agencies, 2008* (Washington, D.C.: Bureau of Justice Statistics, July 2011), p. 3.

7. Ibid.

8. Sewell Chan, "Counting Heads Along the Thin Blue Line," *New York Times*, March 26, 2006, p. D4.

9. Ibid.

10. Ibid.

11. Ibid.

12. Ibid.

13. Karl Bickel and Ed Connors, "Planning and Managing Security for Major Special Events: Best Practices for Law Enforcement Administrators," *Police Chief* (December 2007): 100–107.

14. Tracey Kyckelhahn, *Justice Expenditures and Employment, 1982–2007–Statistical Tables*, December 16, 2011, p. 2.

15. Reaves, *Census of State and Local Law Enforcement Agencies, 2008*, p. 2.

16. Ibid., p. 4.

17. Brian A. Reaves, *Local Police Departments, 2007* (Washington, D.C.: Bureau of Justice Statistics, 2010), p. 14.

18. Ibid.

19. Reaves, *Census of State and Local Law Enforcement Agencies, 2008*, p. 2.

20. Ibid., p. 17.

21. Ibid., p. 34.

22. Brian A. Reaves, *Local Police Departments, 2007*, p. 9.

23. Reaves, *Census of State and Local Law Enforcement Agencies, 2008*, p. 8.

24. Richard A. Staufenberger, *Progress in Policing: Essays on Change* (Cambridge, Mass: Ballinger Publishing, 1980), pp. 8–9.

25. Reaves, *Census of State and Local Law Enforcement Agencies, 2008*, p. 19.

26. Reaves, *Census of State and Local Law Enforcement Agencies, 2008*, p. 5.

27. Ibid., p. 19.

28. John Hoffman, "Rural Policing," *Law and Order* (June 1992): 20–24.

29. Ibid.

30. "Many Villages in Alaska Lack Police," *Associated Press*, February 7, 2008, retrieved February 7, 2008, from www.officer.com.

31. Ibid.

32. Christopher S. Wren, "The Illegal Home Business: 'Speed' Manufacture," *New York Times*, July 8, 1997, p. A8.

33. Erick Ortiz, "Danger on wheels: Cops grapple with rise in rolling meth labs as more addicts employ 'one-pot' cooking method", *New York Daily News*, April 19, 2013, accessed May 12, 2014 from: http://www.nydailynews.com/news/crime/u-s-grapples-rise-rolling-meth-labs-article-1.1320625.

34. James C. Howell and Arlen Egley, Jr., *Gangs in Small Towns and Rural Counties* (Tallahassee, Fla.: National Youth Gang Center, 2005).

35. Dennis Lindsey and Sean Kelly, "Issues in Small-Town Policing: Understanding Stress," *FBI Law Enforcement Bulletin* (July 2004): 1–7.

36. John M. Violanti, "Study Concludes Police Work Is a Health Hazard," *American Police Beat* (November 2002).

37. Lindsey and Kelly, "Issues in Small-Town Policing," pp. 1–7.

38. Ibid.

39. "Serving the Needs of Rural Law Enforcement," Criminal Justice Institute, National Center for Rural Law Enforcement, University of Arkansas System, retrieved June 9, 2006, from www. ncrle.net; Lee Colwell, "The National Center for Rural Law Enforcement: One Part of the Greater Whole," *Community Policing Exchange* (March/April 1997): 6.

40. Laurence French, "Law Enforcement in Indian Country," *Criminal Justice Studies* 18 (2005): 69–80. This article contains an excellent history of policing in Indian country.

41. National Institute of Justice, *Public Law 280 and Law Enforcement in Indian Country—Research Priorities*, retrieved September 7, 2008, from www.ojp.usdoj.gov/nij/pubs sum/209839.htm.

42. M. Wesley Clark, "Enforcing Criminal Law on Native American Lands," *FBI Law Enforcement Bulletin* (April 2005): 22–31.

43. Steven W. Perry, *Census of Tribal Justice Agencies in Indian Country, 2002* (Washington, D.C.: U.S. Department of Justice, 2005), pp. 1–5; also see Clark, "Enforcing Criminal Law on Native American Lands," pp. 22–31.

44. See Federal Bureau of Investigation, *Indian Country Crime*, retrieved June 9, 2006, from www.fbi.gov.

45. Brian A. Reaves, *Tribal Law Enforcement, 2008*, (Washington, D.C.: Bureau of Justice Statistics, 2011), p. 3.

46. Kay Falk, "Indian Country—Where Wide Open Spaces and Boundaries Blur," *Law Enforcement Technology* (February 2006): 18, 20–27.

47. Michael Riley, "Promises, Justice Broken," *Denver Post*, November 13, 2007, retrieved November 14, 2007, from www.denverpost.com.

48. Ibid.

49. Associated Press, "New Efforts in Fighting Crime on Indian Reservations," *New York Times*, January 12, 2010, retrieved January 12, 2010, from www.nytimes.com; U.S. Department of Justice, *Attorney General Announces Significant Reforms to Improve Public Safety in Indian Country* (Washington, D.C.: U.S. Department of Justice, January 12, 2010).

50. Brian A. Reaves, *Campus Law Enforcement, 2004–2005* (Washington, D.C.: Bureau of Justice Statistics, 2008), pp. 1–5.

51. Ibid.

52. Alfonso Chardy, "Officers in S. Fla. Help Immigration Agents Make Arrests," *Miami Herald*, May 25, 2006.

53. Daniel Gonzalez, "Illegal-Immigration Foes Want Police to Change Rules," *Arizona Republic*, November 4, 2007, retrieved November 5, 2007, from www.azcentral.com.

54. Ibid.; Pamela Constable, "Many Officials Reluctant to Help Arrest Immigrants," *Washington Post*, August 23, 2008, p. B1.

55. Marisa Taylor, "Local Police Split over Immigration Enforcement," *McClatchy Newspapers*, December 6, 2007, retrieved December 7, 2007, from www.mcclatchydc.com. Also see Kristin Collins, "North Carolina Leads in Illegal Immigrant Crackdown," *News & Observer*, October 18, 2007, retrieved October 18, 2007, from www.officer.com; "Missouri Troopers Step Up Immigration Duties," *Kansas City Star*, December 19, 2008, retrieved December 18, 2007, from www.officer.com; James Pinkerton, "Police Chief Defends His Immigration Law Stance," *Houston Chronicle*, January 31, 2008, retrieved February 1, 2008, from www.chron.com; Maria Sacchetti, "U.S. Extends Immigrant Database to Police," *Boston Globe*, December 12, 2007, retrieved December 12, 2007, from www.boston.com; U.S. Immigration and Customs Enforcement, "ICE ACCESS," retrieved January 20, 2008, from www.ice.gov.

56. Daniel C. Vock, "Police Join Feds to Tackle Immigration," retrieved November 28, 2007, from www.stateline.org.

57. Taylor, "Local Police Split over Immigration Enforcement."

58. Harold Hurtt as quoted in James Pinkerton, "Police Chief Defends His Immigration Law Stance."

59. Juan Jorge as quoted in Pinkerton, "Police Chief Defends His Immigration Law Stance."

60. International Association of Chiefs of Police, *Police Chiefs Guide to Immigration Issues* (Alexandria, Va.: International Association of Chiefs of Police, 2007).

61. Anita Khashu, *Role of Local Police: Striking a Balance between Immigration Enforcement and Civil Liberties* (Washington, D.C.: Police Foundation, 2009).

62. Julia Preston, "Report Faults Training of Local Officers in Immigration Enforcement Program," *New York Times*, April 2, 2010, retrieved April 3, 2010, from www.nytimes.com.

63. Randal C. Archibold, "U.S.'s Toughest Immigration Law Signed in Arizona," *New York Times*, April 23, 2010, retrieved April 24, 2010, from www.nytimes.com; Associated Press, "Revision to Arizona Law Sets Conditions for Questions by the Police," *New York Times*, April 30, 2010, retrieved May 1, 2010, from www.nytimes.com; Randal C. Archibold, "Judge Blocks Arizona's Immigration Law," *New York Times*, July 28, 2010, retrieved July 30, 2010, from www.nytimes.com.

64. U.S. DOJ COPS, *The Impact of the Economic Downturn on American Police Agencies*, October 2011.

65. Police Executive Research Forum (PERF), "Is the Economic Downturn Fundamentally Changing How We Police?" *Critical Issues in Policing Series*, vol. 16 (Washington, D.C.: Police Executive Research Forum, 2010).

66. Gloria Hillard, "In Tight Times, L.A. Forced to Rely on Volunteer Police," *NPR*, May 19, 2011.

67. Reaves, *Census of State and Local Law Enforcement Agencies, 2008*, p. 6.

68. Reaves, *Census of State and Local Law Enforcement Agencies, 2008*, p. 7.

69. Reaves, *Federal Law Enforcement Officers, 2008*, June 2012, p. 1.

70. Hughes, *Justice Expenditure and Employment in the United States*, p. 1.

71. Ibid.

72. Federal Bureau of Investigation, *FBI Homepage*, retrieved February 26, 2008, from www.fbi.gov.

73. Scott L. Salley, "Preparing Law Enforcement Leaders: The FBI Academy's Leadership Fellows Program," *FBI Law Enforcement Bulletin* (July 2005): 20–23.

74. See, for example, Althan Theorharis and John Stuart Cox, *The Boss* (Philadelphia: Temple University Press, 1988). There are many books in college libraries and local public libraries regarding the history and operations of the FBI and the history of Director Hoover. An interesting class project or research paper might be to compare and contrast the treatment of the FBI and Hoover in the books published before his death in 1972 and those published after his death. Most authors needed the approval of Hoover and his officials prior to publication, so the books published after Hoover's death generally paint a much different picture of Hoover and the FBI than those published during his time.

75. See, for example, Tony Proveda, *Lawlessness and Reform: The FBI in Transition* (Pacific Grove, Calif.: Brooks/Cole, 1990).

76. Vernon M. Keenan and Marsha O'Neal, "National Crime Information Center Identity Theft File," *Police Chief* (May 2007): 32–34.

77. Federal Bureau of Investigation, *National Incident-Based Reporting System*, retrieved June 9, 2006, from www.fbi.gov.

78. Peter Grier, "Corruption Crackdown: The FBI Has Sharpened Its Focus on Public Graft," *Christian Science Monitor*, May 30, 2006.

79. Leonard G. Johns, Gerard F. Downes, and Camille D. Bibles, "Resurrecting Cold Case Serial Homicide Investigations," *FBI Law Enforcement Bulletin* (August 2005): 1–7.

80. Eugene Rugala, James McNamara, and George Wattendorf, "Expert Testimony and Risk Assessment in Stalking Cases: The FBI's NCAVC as a Resource," *FBI Law Enforcement Bulletin* (November 2004): 8–17.

81. Federal Bureau of Investigation, www.fbi.gov/pressrel/ speeches/speech052902.htm.

82. Suzel Spiller, "The FBI's Field Intelligence Groups and Police," *FBI Law Enforcement Bulletin* (May 2006): 1–6.

83. For a complete description of the DEA and many of its major programs, as well as a complete discussion of controlled substances and drug offenses, see John S. Dempsey, *Introduction to Investigations*, 2nd ed. (Belmont, Calif.: Wadsworth, 2003), Ch. 12.

84. Pete Yost, September 20, 2012, *Justice Dept. Faulted In Operation Fast And Furious*, Associated Press; retrieved 9/27/12, http://www.officer.com/news/10782565/justice-dept -faulted-in-operatin-fast-and-furious?utm_source=Officer .com+Newsday+E-newsletter&utm.

85. See Rand Corporation, *Organizing for Homeland Security* (Santa Monica, Calif.: Rand Corporation, 2002); Randall A. Yim, *National Preparedness: Integration of Federal, State, Local and Private Sector Efforts Is Critical to an Effective National Strategy for Homeland Security* (Washington, D.C.: U.S. General Accounting Office, 2002); David M. Walker, *Homeland Security: Responsibility and Accountability for Achieving National Goals* (Washington, D.C.: U.S. General Accounting Office, 2002); Michael Barletta, *After 9/11: Preventing Mass-Destruction Terrorism and Weapons Proliferation* (Monterey, Calif.: Center for Nonproliferation Studies,

2002); JayEtta Hecker, *Homeland Security: Intergovernmental Coordination and Partnership Will Be Critical to Success* (Washington, D.C.: U.S. General Accounting Office, 2002). All of these documents are available from NCJRS at www.ncjrs.gov.

86. U.S. Department of Homeland Security, *DHS Organization*, retrieved February 26, 2008, from www.dhs.gov/.

87. Allison Klein, "Union Calls Department a 'Mess,' Seeks New Management, Funding," *Washington Post*, February 5, 2008, p. B2.

88. Michael E. Ruane, "Park Police Rebuked for Weak Security," *Washington Post*, February 4, 2008, p. A1.

89. Teresa C. Chambers as quoted in Klein, "Union Calls Department a 'Mess.'"

90. See Douglas Bem, "Postal Inspectors: Not Secret, No Longer Silent," *Police Chief* (December 2007): 38–41.

91. Reaves, *Federal Law Enforcement Officers, 2004*.

92. Ibid.

93. For further information on the U.S. Department of State's Bureau of Diplomatic Security, see Richard J. Griffin, "Operation Triple X: Hitting Hard at Illegal Document Trade," *Police Chief* (October 2007): 30–36.

94. For an interesting article on joint terrorist task force resources, see James Casey, "Managing Joint Terrorism Task Force Resources," *FBI Law Enforcement Bulletin* (November 2004): 1–6; also see Dempsey, *An Introduction to Investigations*, pp. 365–367.

95. Information retrieved February 29, 2008, from www.interpol .int. For further information on Interpol, access their website at www.interpol.int.

Organizing the Police Department

Bruce R. Bennett/The Palm Beach Post/ZUMAPRESS/Newscom

OUTLINE

Organizing the Department:
Managerial Concepts
Division of Labor
Managerial Definitions
Managers, Supervisors… or
   Leaders?
Ethical Leadership
Traditional Organizational Model
   and Structure
Chain of Command
Span of Control
Delegation of Responsibility and
   Authority
Unity of Command
Rules, Regulations, and Discipline
Alternative Organizational Models
and Structures

Organizing by Personnel
The Civil Service System
Sworn and Nonsworn (Civilian)
   Personnel
Rank Structure
Other Personnel
Lateral Transfers
Police Unions
Organizing by Area
Beats
Precincts/Districts/Stations
Organizing by Time
The Three-Tour System
Tour Length: 8 Hours, 10 Hours, or
   12 Hours
Tour Conditions
Steady (Fixed) Tours
Organizing by Function or Purpose
Line and Staff (Support) Functions
Police Department Units

LEARNING OBJECTIVES

- Identify the major managerial concepts that must be considered when organizing a police department.

- Describe some recent examples of shared leadership in policing.

- Explain the benefits and drawbacks of civil service regulations in policing.

- Describe the differences between sworn and nonsworn or civilian police department members, and list some ways in which civilianization can benefit a police department.

- Discuss the special problems that must be dealt with in organizing a police department that operates seven days a week, 24 hours a day.

INTRODUCTION

Some of you reading this text want to become members of a police or other law enforcement department, while some of you are just interested in what the police do and how they do it. In either case, this chapter will give you good insight into how a police department actually works. The term *police department* is used in this chapter as a generic term that includes other law enforcement agencies, such as those at the federal, state, and county level, as well as sheriff's offices.

In any organization, someone must do the work the organization is charged with doing, someone must supervise those doing the work, and someone must command the operation. Certain commonly accepted rules of management must be followed to accomplish the goals of the organization. Therefore, this chapter includes a discussion of leadership and some important organizational concepts. It also offers alternatives to the traditional organizational model of policing and discusses methods for organizing police departments, including by personnel (rank), area, time, and function or purpose. Various organizations use different words to describe these organizational issues, so here the terminology used tends to be generic rather than specific.

This chapter is designed to give you an awareness of the complexities involved in policing seven days a week, 24 hours a day. Not all police organizations are as complex as what is described here. Actually, as we saw in Chapter 2, most police departments in the United States are small. The intent of this chapter, however, is to cover as many complexities of the police organization as possible to give you the broadest possible view of policing in the United States—what the police do and how do they do it.

Organizing the Department: Managerial Concepts

Before discussing the organization of a police department, some managerial concepts common to most organizations should be understood. These concepts include division of labor; managerial definitions; leadership; organizational model or structure; chain of command (hierarchy of authority); span of control; delegation of responsibility and authority; unity of command; and rules, regulations, and discipline.

Division of Labor

All the varied tasks and duties performed by an organization must be divided among its members in accordance with some logical plan. In police departments, the tasks of the organization are divided according to personnel, area, time, and function or purpose. Work assignments must be designed so that similar tasks, functions, and activities are given to a particular group for accomplishment. In a police department, patrol functions are separate from detective functions, which are separate from internal investigative functions. Geographic and time distinctions are also established, with certain officers working certain times and areas. The best way to think of the division of labor in an organization is to ask the question, "Who is going to do what, when, and where?"

The division of labor should be reflected in an organization chart, a pictorial representation of reporting relationships in an organization (see Figure 3.1). A good organizational chart is a snapshot of the organization. Workers can see exactly where they stand in the organization: what functions they perform, whom they report to, and who reports to them.

Managerial Definitions

To understand the contents of this chapter, you should be familiar with several managerial concepts.

ORGANIZATION Nicholas Henry of Georgia Southern University, in his classic text *Public Administration and Public Affairs*, gives us two definitions of **organization**, "a highly rationalized and impersonal integration of a large number of

---

organization A deliberate arrangement of people doing specific jobs, following particular procedures to accomplish a set of goals determined by some authority.

Police Department

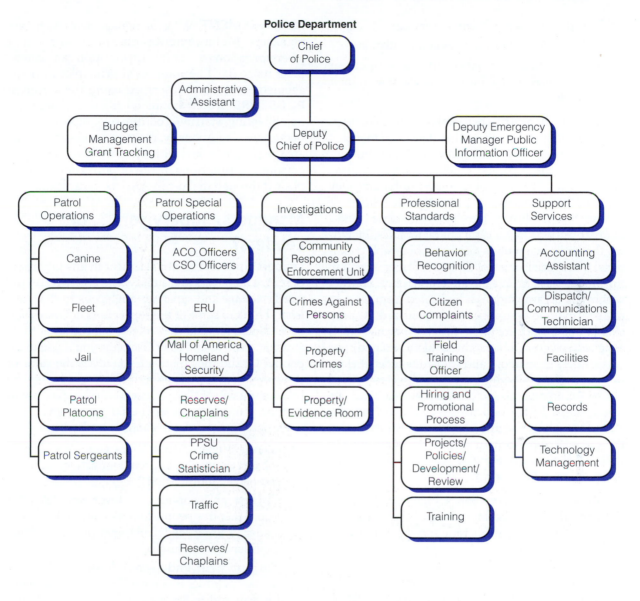

FIGURE 3.1 Organizational Chart: Bloomington, Minnesota, Police Department
Source: Reprinted by permission of the Bloomington, MN Police Department.

specialists cooperating to achieve some announced specific objective," and "a system of consciously coordinated personal activities or forces of two or more persons."[1] In 2005, Patrick O'Hara, in "Why Law Enforcement Organizations Fail: Mapping the Organizational Fault Lines in Policing," gives us a simpler, but no less useful, definition:

> Organizations consist of a deliberate arrangement of people doing specific jobs, following particular procedures in order to accomplish a set of goals determined by some authority.[2]

BUREAUCRACY Max Weber, who many call "the father of sociology," gave us the classic features of the **bureaucracy**:

- Hierarchy
- Promotion based on professional merit and skill

bureaucracy An organizational model marked by hierarchy, promotion on professional merit and skill, the development of a career service, reliance on and use of rules and regulations, and impersonality of relationships among career professionals in the bureaucracy and with their clientele.

- The development of a career service
- Reliance on and use of rules and regulations
- Impersonality of relationships among career professionals in the bureaucracy and with their clientele[3]

Nicolas Henry further explains the principles of bureaucracy as he tells us that the closed model of organizations goes by many names, including bureaucratic, hierarchical, formal, rational, and mechanistic, and reports that *bureaucratic theory* or bureaucracy is one of the most common permutations, schools, or theories that has thrived. He says that the closed model of organizations has several characteristics, including the following: routine tasks occur in stable conditions; task specialization or division of labor is central; the proper ways to do a job are emphasized; conflict within the organization is adjudicated from the top; one's formal job description is emphasized; responsibility and loyalty are to the subunit to which one is assigned; structure is hierarchical (like a pyramid); one takes orders from above and transmits orders below, but not horizontally; interaction is directed toward obedience, command, and clear superior–subordinate relationships; loyalty and obedience to one's superior and the organization are emphasized, sometimes at the expense of performance; and personal status in the organization is determined largely by one's formal office and rank.[4] Henry says,

> Bureaucracy is in our bones. Prehistoric evidence unearthed at archeological digs suggests that the rudiments of a bureaucratic social order were in place 19,000 years ago. Bureaucracy predates, by many millennia, *Homo sapiens*'s earlier experiments with democracy, the emergence of the globe's great religions, and the dawn of civilization itself. Bureaucracy may not be basic to the human condition, but it is basic to human society.[5]

Surely, as you will find in this chapter, modern police organizations can be considered bureaucracies.

management The process of running an organization so that the organization can accomplish its goals.

PODSCORB Acronym for the basic functions of management: planning, organizing, directing, staffing, coordinating, reporting, and budgeting.

leadership An influence relationship among leaders and followers who intend real changes that reflect their mutual purposes.

MANAGEMENT What is management? Who are managers? **Management** is the process of running an organization so that the organization can accomplish its goals. The traditional principles of management have been described using the acronym **PODSCORB**, which stands for planning, organizing, directing, staffing, coordinating, reporting, and budgeting. Traditionally, managers and supervisors are the people tasked with the duty of managing—getting the functions of the organization accomplished through the members of the organization.

Managers, Supervisors... or Leaders?

Leadership is an essential element in any organization. Are managers and supervisors leaders? Are the words *manage* and *supervise* analogous to the word *lead*? Think of some of the supervisors or bosses you have worked for. Did they merely tell you what to do and how to do it, and then discipline you if you did it poorly? Or did they motivate you to see the value of the work you were performing and how you fit into the broader mission of the organization and inspire you to perform your job to the very best of your ability?

Consider these descriptions of leadership.

- Scholar William Arthur Ward wrote, "Leadership is based on inspiration, not domination; on cooperation, not intimidation."
- Chinese philosopher Lao Tzu wrote, "A good leader inspires people to have confidence in the leader; a great leader inspires people to have confidence in themselves."
- Entrepreneur and author John C. Maxwell wrote, "A leader is one who knows the way, goes the way, and shows the way."
- Former Chairman of the U.S. Joint Chiefs of Staff and U.S. Secretary of State Colin Powell described the absences or failure of leadership: "The day soldiers stop bringing you their problems is the day you have stopped leading them. They have either lost confidence that you can help them or concluded that you do not care. Either case is a failure of leadership."
- Even former professional football quarterback Joe Namath, the winner of Super Bowl III, gave us an example of leadership: "To be a leader, you have to make people want to follow you, and nobody wants to follow someone who doesn't know where he is going."

As you can see, people from diverse occupations agree on certain aspects of leadership, including motivation, teaching, team coordination, communication, inspiration, and example. Police departments need leaders, not merely managers and supervisors. By reading this textbook, you are certainly learning about policing. We hope you will take advanced courses that will teach you about leadership. The accomplishments of the police are brought about by leaders and their personnel; the failures of the police are brought about by managers and supervisors who are not leaders, and the performance of their personnel reflects that lack of leadership.

Leadership is essential in police management. Leaders, by teaching and setting examples, develop new leaders. Many law enforcement agencies are providing leadership training for their supervisors and managers, and this training is creating better agencies and better delivery of services to the communities they serve.[6]

Ethical Leadership

What is ethical leadership? Ethical leaders demonstrate integrity on a daily basis in every decision that is made. The ethical leader is the one to whom others are drawn, the one whom others want to emulate. The life and actions of an ethical leader demonstrate integrity, character, credibility, honesty, fairness, loyalty, and respect.

To make ethical decisions, you must have integrity, credibility, responsibility of character, and the courage necessary to make "tough" decisions. You will not be universally praised, but you will, eventually, be respected by those who are affected by your decisions. Ethical decision making requires you to stand your ground, rely on your core ethical principles and values, and make the best decisions for the individuals and the organization. The ethical leader sets the tone for those who follow.

Ethical leadership starts at the top. If you see a law enforcement agency embroiled in constant unrest, constantly portrayed in a negative light in the press, you are looking at an organization that has an ethical leadership problem. The officers in a department want to be ethical, but they will drift to the most comfortable level, which in many cases leads to mediocrity. When you see a department like this, you need to look to the top. The leader has set a tone that has led to problems.

In contrast, when you see a department that has a positive public image and that officers want to work for, you see an organization that has established itself with good leadership at the top. Such leaders are flexible and know their "people." These departments are the ones that other departments look to for their future command staff and chiefs. These are the departments that become models of a good organization within the law enforcement community.

As you read this text, you might want to look at your local law enforcement agency and ask yourself what kind of department you have in your community.

Traditional Organizational Model and Structure

The U.S. police are a civil, as opposed to a military, organization. Despite this, our police departments are **quasi-military organizations** (organizations similar to the military). Like the military, the police are organized along structures of authority and reporting relationships; they wear military-style, highly recognizable uniforms; they use military-style rank designations; they carry weapons; and they are authorized by law to use force. Like the military, police officers are trained to respond to orders immediately.

Despite similarities, however, the police are far different from the military. They are not trained as warriors to fight foreign enemies but instead are trained to maintain order, serve and protect the public, and enforce the criminal law. Most important, the power of the police is limited by state laws and the Bill of Rights.

Recall from Chapter 1 the formation of the London Metropolitan Police. Although Sir Robert Peel wanted his police to be a civil agency as opposed to a military one, he ensured that they would be under strict military-like discipline, as evidenced by the selection of veteran military leader Colonel Charles Rowan as one of the first London Metropolitan Police commissioners. Also, early European police models used military organizational structures that were separate from local politics and supervised by the state.

The trend toward military models of police organizations in the United States was part of police reform in the progressive era of government. Progressives tended to apply the ideas of scientific management and corporate organizational models to running city governments, but they believed that the military model seemed more fitting to what the

---

quasi-military organizations An organization similar to the military along structures of strict authority and reporting relations.

GUEST LECTURE

DR. JEFFREY S. MAGERS

Dr. Jeffrey S. Magers is an assistant professor in the Law and Public Policy Program at California University of Pennsylvania. He retired as a captain with the Jefferson County Police Department in Louisville, Kentucky (now called the Louisville Metro Police Department). Dr. Magers is a Lieutenant Colonel in the U.S. Army Reserve (retired). He attended the Southern Police Institute Administrative Officers' Course and the FBI National Academy.

THE MESSAGE

The criminal justice system relies upon the credibility, integrity, and professional conduct of police officers under the supervision of ethical police leaders. Police leaders often underestimate the influence they have on the ethical climate of an organization and the ethical conduct of individual police officers under their command. This essay will present a true story illustrating how much influence a single, determined, ethical police leader can have when he or she takes the opportunity to demonstrate the conviction of strong moral character and ethical leadership.

Early in my police career, I was a detective in the violent crime unit of a 450-officer county police department. At that time, I worked the evening shift with four other detectives and a sergeant. One evening, early in the shift, I was sitting at my desk writing reports. The other detectives with whom I worked were doing the same. I looked up from my report for a moment and saw our lieutenant walking into the squad room with a determined look on his face. Visits from the lieutenant were not unusual; he worked the day shift and often visited us in the squad room before departing for the day. This evening, with no greeting, he walked directly to the chair in front of my desk. Without prelude, the lieutenant immediately began a speech that I will never forget. He said, "I hate liars, I will not tolerate liars under my command, and anyone under my command whom I catch lying, I will personally do everything I can to see to it that they are terminated."

Needless to say, he had my attention, but I wondered, "Is he talking to me?" I quickly discerned that he had not focused on me alone. His gaze was scanning the room. I realized he was making a blanket statement to all who could hear, and without a doubt he had our undivided attention. He continued to elaborate by saying he would not tolerate lying to him, to the sergeant, to the captain, to other officers, to the media, to prosecutors; I expected him to say "and to our parents, spouses, and children," but he left that out of his speech. He did, however, continue speaking on this theme for several more minutes. He was not happy about something, and it was apparent he felt that someone in his command had lied. He was angry and disappointed.

To this day, I think he suspected that someone had lied about some aspect of a politically sensitive case we had been working on. I suspect he did not know who the culprit was, because no one lost their job that day. The lieutenant finished his tirade, lifted himself from the chair, and left the room abruptly. I remember the general comments in the room after he left focused on what had the lieutenant bent out of shape. That was not what I was thinking. I had just heard the most definitive, firm stance on police ethics ever in my relatively short police career. He left no doubt in my mind as to his expectations of ethical conduct for his detectives and for all police officers in general. Although the speech was impressive, at that moment I did not fully realize how much it would influence my career.

Months later, I was assigned a particularly difficult investigation. It was an unusual case because it was one that to my knowledge no one in our unit had ever tried to investigate and prosecute. Because this was an extraordinary case, I was investigating without much help or guidance. During the course of the investigation I made a serious mistake. The mistake was one I should not have made, but I had not intentionally done so. I came to work one day as the investigation of this case was nearly complete and we were beginning the prosecution phase. I was confronted with my error by the lieutenant. He informed me of my mistake in no uncertain terms and asked me to explain. I could have lied that day and told the lieutenant a story that maybe would have shifted the blame, but I was looking into the eyes of the man who just a few months earlier had given "the speech." My parents had taught me not to lie, and this value was reinforced by an honor code as a commissioned officer in the U.S. Army: but under pressure, the temptation to lie is intense. If we are truthful with ourselves, we know this temptation all too well. Looking at the lieutenant, I realized lying was not an option, and never should have been.

I told the lieutenant the truth about my error, because when presented with the facts, I knew I had to be responsible for my actions involving this investigative mistake. I know you want to know what the mistake was, but that is irrelevant to this story. It was not criminal; it was just a procedural error that could have jeopardized the case and certainly caused everyone working on the case more work. I still obtained a conviction in the case.

After I had confessed my error, the lieutenant gave me a vigorous oral reprimand, as did the captain, the major, and the deputy chief of police. Thank goodness the chief was off that day and I was spared that nightmare, although I must admit I was undeserving of a break. When the ordeal was over, I went about the task of correcting my error. It was only days later that I realized that I had faced a crucial moment in my career. Had I lied that day, I truly believe it would have been the end of my police career. Without the lieutenant's speech, I may have had the strength of character to tell the truth that day, but maybe I would not have. I will never know. I do know the words of the lieutenant echoed in my head, setting the standard for ethical policing. The lieutenant's definitive ethical message was the support I needed at that critical moment. I do not know if the other detectives in the squad room heard the message in the same way I did, but the influence it had on me was profound.

After this incident I thought about three officers in my recruit class who had been terminated for separate ethical lapses. If they had heard this same message, would they have heeded the warning and lived up to the ethical expectations so effectively expressed by my lieutenant, a police leader who took the time to clearly set the standard for ethical conduct of the police officers in his command? We will never know.

Years later, as a sergeant, I was selected for an assignment by that same lieutenant, who by then was a major and the commander of a joint city–county narcotics unit. He chose me to be the asset forfeiture manager for the unit. After I was with the unit for a while, I asked him why he chose me for the job. He said I was the one sergeant he knew he could trust for this highly sensitive position, involving the handling of considerable amounts of cash.

While still working as a police officer, I returned to college to earn a doctorate in leadership education. A considerable amount of my coursework concerned ethics and leadership. I began teaching basic and in-service training ethics classes for police officers and police supervisors in my department, the state, and various venues throughout the country. In every class I have told this story, repeating the lieutenant's message each time. All police leaders, police officers, police recruits, and criminal justice students in college must hear the same message.

Because ethical decision making for police officers is such an important issue, I chose to complete my doctoral dissertation on the topic of how police supervisors influence police officers to lie to cover up unethical behavior. Needless to say, my research indicated what the lieutenant intuitively knew: Police supervisors have a significant effect on the ethical behavior of police officers.

The burden to create an ethical police environment rests not just with police leaders. Individual officers are responsible for their conduct. Leaders can set the tone, but each officer must make a conscious decision to accept or not accept the wise counsel of ethical police leaders. In this era when people often blame others for their crimes or ethical lapses, one should not shift the blame entirely to supervisors for the ethical conduct of their subordinates. Police leaders providing clear ethical messages certainly help those who would choose to make sound, ethical decisions in the course of their daily police lives. Ultimately, however, it is an individual decision. It is your decision to hold yourself accountable and to hold other officers accountable for their actions when police leaders are not physically present.

I retired from policing; I now teach in a masters program at a regional state university in Pennsylvania and provide seminars for police officers and leaders. Every time I tell this story, I hope there are those who hear the same clear, concise, ethical message I heard from the lieutenant to whom I owe so much.

Source: Reprinted by permission of Dr. Jeffrey S. Magers.

TABLE 3.1   Taylor's Four Scientific Management Principles

1. Replace working by "rule of thumb," or simple habit and common sense, and instead use the scientific method to study work and determine the most efficient way to perform specific tasks.
2. Rather than simply assign workers to just any job, match workers to their jobs based on capability and motivation, and train them to work at maximum efficiency.
3. Monitor worker performance, and provide instructions and supervision to ensure that they're using the most efficient ways of working.
4. Allocate the work between managers and workers to that the managers spend their time planning and training, allowing the worker to perform their task efficiently.

Retrieved March 28, 2014, from http://www.mindtools.com/pages/article/newTMM_Taylor.htm

police were supposed to be doing—fighting a war against crime. Police departments were reorganized according to military structure, and ranks, uniforms, weapons, insignia, salutes, and other symbols reflected the military analogy. The progressives felt this was a way to separate the police from partisan politics and political machines. In this era, many departments searched for former military officers to lead their departments. Departments continued to be or were remolded to become more centralized, specialized, and staffed with more administrative and operational support, much like a military unit.[7]

As one example, in 1923 a renowned Marine Corps general, Smedley Butler, a veteran of the Spanish-American War, the Boxer Rebellion, and other campaigns, was given leave from the Marines to become director of public safety in the corruption-laden and politically connected Philadelphia Police Department. "Within forty-eight hours, 75 percent of the thirteen hundred saloons in Philadelphia had been closed." Butler organized a special "bandit squad" armed with armored cars and sawed-off shotguns to raid prostitution houses and suspected crime dens. He was quoted as saying, "The only way to reform a crook is to kill him."[8]

Robert C. Wadman and William Thomas Allison report that the military analogy did prove effective as it helped further the separation between politics and police and made the administrative and operational aspects of police organization more efficient and effective.[9] Todd Wuestewald and Brigitte Steinheider tell us a paramilitary model of policing evolved in response to the widespread corruption and

political interference that threatened the credibility of U.S. policing. In an effort to instill discipline, police leaders utilized authoritarian hierarchy as a tool against both political cooptation and low-level corruption. The scientific management principles of Frederick Taylor were applied to professionalize the police, and his management philosophy persists today (see Table 3.1).[10]

Chain of Command

The managerial concept of **chain of command** (also called hierarchy of authority) involves the superior–subordinate or supervisor–worker relationships throughout the department, wherein each individual is supervised by one immediate supervisor or boss. Thus, the chain of command as pictured in organizational charts shows workers which supervisor they report to; the chain of command also shows supervisors to whom they are accountable and for whom they are responsible (see Figures 3.2 through 3.4).

Example of a Small Police Department

FIGURE 3.2   Organizational Chart: Wickenburg, Arizona, Police Department

Source: Reprinted by permission of the Wickenburg Police Department.

chain of command Managerial concept stating that each individual in an organization is supervised by and reports to only one immediate supervisor.

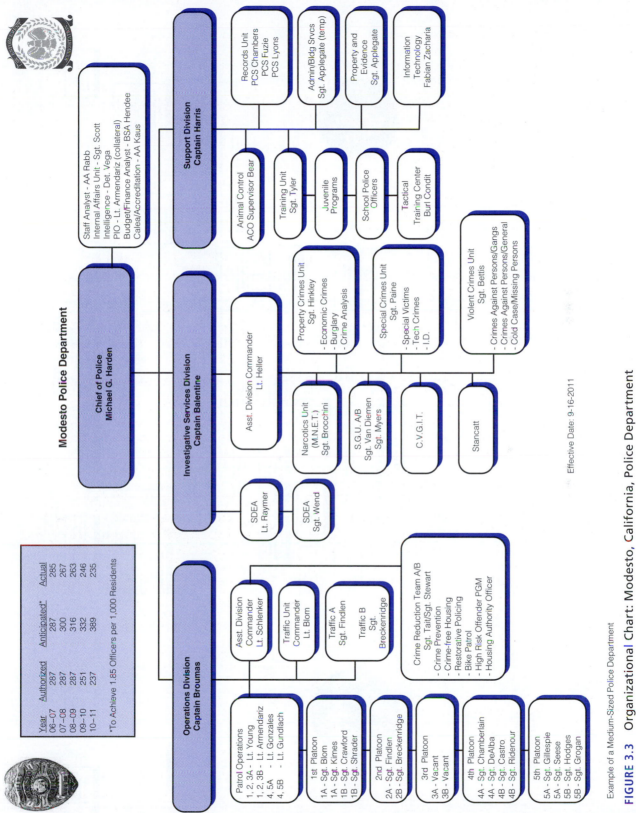

Modesto Police Department

Chief of Police
Michael G. Harden

Staff Analyst - AA Rabb
Internal Affairs Unit - Sgt. Scott
Intelligence - Det. Vega
PIO - Lt. Armendariz (collateral)
Budget/Finance Analyst - BSA Hendee
Calea/Accreditation - AA Kaus

Support Division
Captain Harris

Records Unit
PCS Chambers
PCS Fuzie
PCS Lyons

Admin/Bldg Srvcs
Sgt. Applegate (temp)

Property and
Evidence
Sgt. Applegate

Information
Technology
Fabian Zacharia

Animal Control
ACO Supervisor Bear

Training Unit
Sgt. Tyler

Juvenile
Programs

School Police
Officers

Tactical
Training Center
Burl Condit

Investigative Services Division
Captain Balentine

Asst. Division Commander
Lt. Heller

Property Crimes Unit
Sgt. Hinkley
- Economic Crimes
- Burglary
- Crime Analysis

Special Crimes Unit
Sgt. Paine
- Special Victims
- Tech Crimes
- I.D.

Violent Crimes Unit
Sgt. Bettis
- Crimes Against Persons/Gangs
- Crimes Against Persons/General
- Cold Case/Missing Persons

Narcotics Unit
(M.N.E.T.)
Sgt. Brocchini

S.G.U. A/B
Sgt. Van Diemen
Sgt. Myers

C.V.G.I.T.

Stancatt

SDEA
Lt. Raymer

SDEA
Sgt. Wend

Operations Division
Captain Broumas

Asst. Division
Commander
Lt. Schlenker

Traffic Unit
Commander
Lt. Blom

Traffic A
Sgt. Findlen

Traffic B
Sgt.
Breckenridge

Crime Reduction Team A/B
Sgt. Tait/Sgt. Stewart
- Crime Prevention
- Crime-free Housing
- Restorative Policing
- Bike Patrol
- High Risk Offender PGM
- Housing Authority Officer

Patrol Operations
1, 2, 3A - Lt. Young
1, 2, 3B - Lt. Armendariz
4, 5A - Lt. Gonzales
4, 5B - Lt. Gundlach

1st Platoon
1A - Sgt. Blom
1A - Sgt. Kimes
1B - Sgt. Crawford
1B - Sgt. Shrader

2nd Platoon
2A - Sgt. Findlen
2B - Sgt. Breckenridge

3rd Platoon
3A - Vacant
3B - Vacant

4th Platoon
4A - Sgt. Chamberlain
4A - Sgt. DeAlba
4B - Sgt. Castro
4B - Sgt. Ridenour

5th Platoon
5A - Sgt. Gillespie
5A - Sgt. Seese
5B - Sgt. Hodges
5B - Sgt. Grogan

Year	Authorized	Anticipated*	Actual
06–07	287	287	285
07–08	287	300	267
08–09	287	316	263
09–10	251	332	246
10–11	237	389	235

*To Achieve 1.85 Officers per 1,000 Residents

Effective Date: 9-16-2011

Example of a Medium-Sized Police Department

FIGURE 3.3 Organizational Chart: Modesto, California, Police Department

Source: Reprinted by permission of the Modesto Police Department.

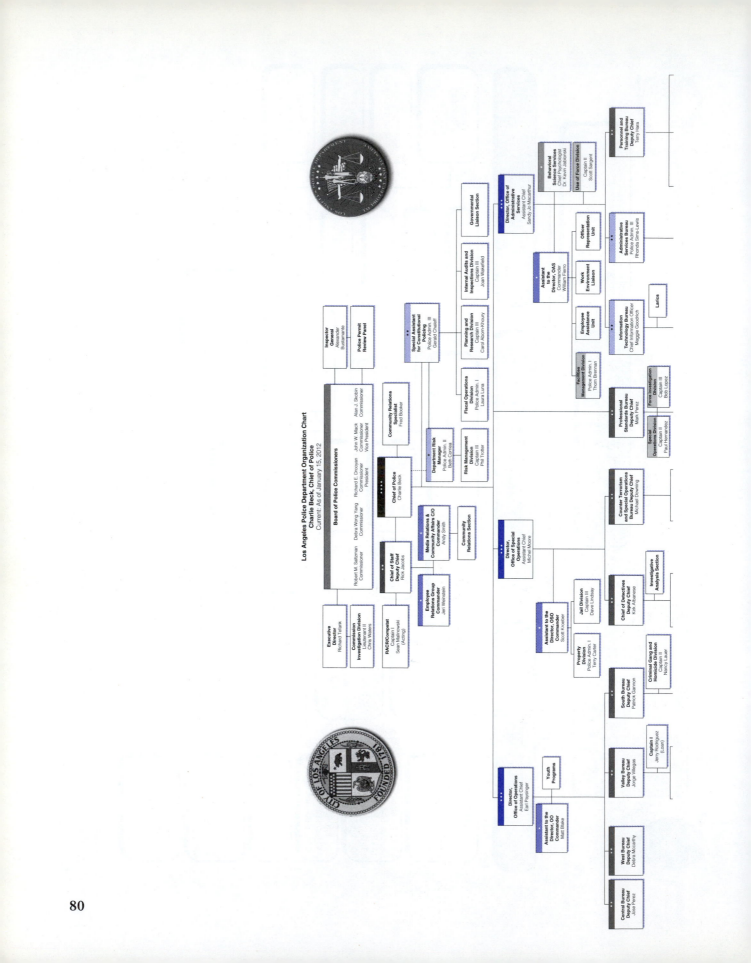

Los Angeles Police Department Organization Chart
Charlie Beck, Chief of Police
Current: As of January 15, 2012

Board of Police Commissioners

| Robert M. Saltzman Commissioner | Debra Wong Yang Commissioner | Richard E. Drooyan Commissioner President | John W. Mack Commissioner Vice President | Alan J. Skobin Commissioner |

Inspector General
Alexander Bustamante

Police Permit Review Panel

Executive Director
Richard Tefank

Commission Investigation Division
Lieutenant II
Chris Waters

Chief of Police
Charlie Beck

Community Relations Specialist
Fred Booker

Special Assistant for Constitutional Policing
Police Admin. III
Gerald Chaleff

Chief of Staff Deputy Chief
Rick Jacobs

RACR/Compstat
Captain I
Sean Malinowski (Acting)

Media Relations & Community Affairs CIO Commander
Andy Smith

Employee Relations Group Commander
Jeri Weinstein

Community Relations Section

Department Risk Manager
Police Admin. II
Beth Correia

Risk Management Division
Captain III
Phil Trotter

Fiscal Operations Division
Police Admin. I
Laura Luna

Planning and Research Division
Captain III
Carol Aborn-Khoury

Internal Audits and Inspections Division
Captain III
Joan Wakefield

Governmental Liaison Section

Director, Office of Administrative Services
Assistant Chief
Sandy Jo Macarthur

Assistant to the Director, OAS
Commander
William Fierro

Employee Assistance Unit

Work Environment Liaison

Officer Representation Unit

Information Technology Bureau
Chief Information Officer
Maggie Goodrich

Larics

Facilities Management Division
Police Admin. I
Thom Brennan

Professional Standards Bureau
Deputy Chief
Mark Perez

Special Operations Division
Captain I
Paul Hernandez

Force Investigation Division
Captain III
Bob Lopez

Behavioral Science Services
Chief Psychologist
Dr. Kevin Jablonski

Use of Force Division
Captain II
Scott Sargent

Administrative Services Bureau
Police Admin. III
Rhonda Sims-Lewis

Personnel and Training Bureau
Deputy Chief
Terry Hara

Director, Office of Special Operations
Assistant Chief
Michel Moore

Assistant to the Director, OSO
Commander
Scott Kroeber

Property Division
Police Admin. I
Terry Carter

Jail Division
Captain III
Dave Lindsay

Chief of Detectives Deputy Chief
Kirk Albanese

Investigative Analysis Section

Counter Terrorism and Special Operations Bureau Deputy Chief
Michael Downing

Director, Office of Operations
Assistant Chief
Earl Paysinger

Assistant to the Director, OO Commander
Matt Blake

Youth Programs

Central Bureau Deputy Chief
Jose Perez

West Bureau Deputy Chief
Debra McCarthy

Valley Bureau Deputy Chief
Jorge Villegas

Captain I
Jerry Rodriguez (Loan)

South Bureau Deputy Chief
Patrick Gannon

Criminal Gang and Homicide Division
Captain II
Nancy Lauer

80

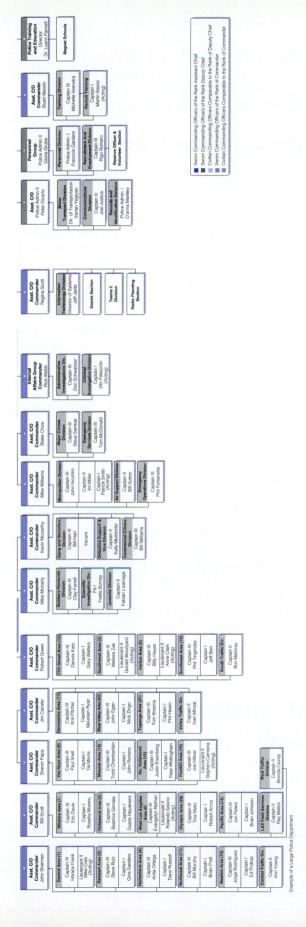

Example of a Large Police Department

FIGURE 3.4 Organizational Chart: Los Angeles Police Department

Source: Reprinted by permission of the Los Angeles Police Department.

81

All members of the organization should follow the chain of command. For example, a patrol officer should report to his or her immediate sergeant, not to the captain. Chain of command may be violated, however, when an emergency exists or speed is necessary.

Regardless of the size of the department, the chain of command always starts with the chief of police. As the size of the agency grows larger in personnel, the chain of command from the chief of police to the patrol officer becomes more distant. The smaller the department, the more intimate the relationships between the chief of police and her or his patrol officers.

Span of Control

The number of officers or subordinates that a superior can supervise effectively is called the **span of control**. Although no one can say exactly how many officers a sergeant can supervise or how many sergeants a lieutenant can supervise, most police management experts say the chain of command should be one supervisor for every 6 to 10 officers of a lower rank. It is best to keep the span of control as limited as possible so that the supervisor can more effectively supervise and control. The number of workers a supervisor can effectively supervise is affected by many factors, including distance, time, knowledge, personality, and the complexity of the work to be performed.

Delegation of Responsibility and Authority

Another important managerial concept in police organizations is delegation of responsibility and authority. Tasks, duties, and responsibilities are assigned to subordinates, along with the power or authority to control, command, make decisions, or otherwise act in order to complete the tasks that have been delegated or assigned to them.

Unity of Command

The concept of **unity of command** means that each individual in an organization is directly accountable to only one supervisor. This concept is important,

---

span of control The number of officers or subordinates a superior can supervise effectively.

unity of command A managerial concept that specifies that each individual in an organization is directly accountable to only one supervisor.

---

because no one person can effectively serve two supervisors at one time. Even in large organizations, this principle holds true. Unity of command may be violated in emergency situations.

Rules, Regulations, and Discipline

Most police organizations have a complex system of rules and regulations designed to control and direct the actions of officers. Most departments have operations manuals or rules and procedures designed to show officers what they must do in most situations they encounter. Rule books are often complex and detailed. In some major police departments, the police rule book is one foot thick.

Police departments have disciplinary standards that are similar to, but less stringent than, the military's. Violation of department standards in dress, appearance, and conduct can lead to sanctions against officers such as reprimands, fines, or even dismissal from the department.

Managing problem employees is a common issue in policing, as it is in every occupation. Thomas Q. Weitzel, an assistant chief who heads the Riverside, Illinois, Police Department's Administrative Division, writes,

> Identifying and managing problem employees can prove difficult. However, it is crucial that departments identify such individuals and handle them efficiently, objectively, and fairly. These workers can have a negative impact both inside and outside the department. Supervisors may find situations involving problem employees intimidating. However, they can follow effective procedures to identify who these individuals are and to work with them to improve their performance or, if this is not possible, to take more drastic measures.[11]

Alternative Organizational Models and Structures

In the face of continued corruption scandals, police administrators have tended to maintain an almost phobic preoccupation with accountability and conformity. But according to Wuestewald and Steinheider, these control-oriented approaches fail to recognize that police work is and always has been highly discretionary. The basic paradox of police hierarchy, they write, is that discretionary authority tends to be greater at the bottom of the police organization, where officers apply laws, policy, and regulations to situations that do not fit neatly into the rule book. Further, these discretionary choices are made in the field, far removed from the direct scrutiny of managers and supervisors. Many have lamented the apparent disjuncture between historically autocratic police management approaches and the requirements of community policing.[12]

A national survey of police departments revealed that although 70 percent of agencies had decentralized some operations in support of community policing, only 22 percent had reduced bureaucratic hierarchy or pushed authority and decision making down in the organization to any significant degree.[13] A five-year study of police in Australia and New Zealand found that officers felt their organizations were not supportive of them and did not exhibit trust, respect, or recognition of their experience in decision-making processing.[14] As we will see later in Chapter 12, "Community Policing: The Debate Continues," community-oriented policing calls for more decision-making processes by frontline patrol officers.

For many years, the corporate world has been moving toward more democratic processes such as shared leadership and participative management models as they try to improve their competitiveness by tapping the knowledge, talents, and creativity of their employees. In this process, organizational hierarchies have tended to flatten as autonomous work teams have replaced managerial levels. Scientific management theories have been replaced by methods of participative management, which have greatly improved organizations in terms of productivity, quality, and worker satisfaction.[15] However, these power-sharing methods have found little acceptance in police organizations. While police have been emphasizing proactive, community-oriented approaches to crime reduction and service providing, employee empowerment and shared leadership may offer significant advantages over traditional top-down police administration.

Shared leadership is known by many names: participative management, employee empowerment, job involvement, participative decision making, dispersed leadership, total quality management (TQM), quality circles (QC), and others. These basic concepts involve any power-sharing arrangement in which workplace influence is shared among

individuals who are otherwise hierarchical unequals. Such arrangements may include various employee involvement schemes resulting in code termination of work conditions, problem solving, and decision making.[16]

Shared leadership attained interest in the 1980s and 1990s in response to the success Japanese industry seemed to be having with empowerment strategies such as TQM and QC. Research in both the public and private sectors has revealed that participative leadership has resulted in many improvements in job satisfaction, increased productivity, organizational citizenship behavior, labor–management relations, and overall organizational performance. In the context of shared leadership, the implementation of the following team leadership principles will help to facilitate the success of the team: "(a) the work team resolves difference to reach agreement, (b) work is distributed properly to take advantage of members' unique skills, (c) information about the company and its strategy is shared, (d) teamwork is promoted with the team itself, and (e) the team works together to identify opportunities to improve productivity and efficiency."[17]

Despite some reluctance, there are several examples of shared leadership being successfully implemented within a police department. In 2006, Todd Wuestewald, chief of the Broken Arrow, Oklahoma, Police Department (BAPD), a 164-person, full-time department that provides a full spectrum of police services to a metropolitan community of 91,000 in northeastern Oklahoma, and Brigitte Steinheider, director of organizational dynamics at the University of Oklahoma, reported on a program designed to incorporate frontline personnel into the important decision-making processes of the BAPD. Since 2003, the BAPD has had participative management in the form of a steering committee called the Leadership Team, composed of 12 members of the BAPD who represent the police union, management, and most of the divisions, units, ranks, and functions in the department. The Leadership Team is an independent body with authority to make binding decisions on a wide range of policy issues, working conditions, and departmental strategies. The chief's office is not represented on the

shared leadership Power-sharing arrangement in which workplace influence is shared among individuals who are otherwise hierarchical unequals.

team, and all decisions are made democratically. The chief retains control of the team's agenda, but once an issue is referred to the team, its decisions are final and binding on all concerned. The team was trained by experts in organizational dynamics in order to facilitate team interactions and communication. An independent evaluation of the effects of the Leadership Team on departmental functioning, using quantitative and qualitative comparisons of the department before and after the establishment of the team, revealed a dramatic improvement in employee relations in such areas as discipline, promotions, hiring, recognition, rewards, and incentives, as well as employee organizational commitment, pride, morale, motivation, productivity, leadership development, and the acceptance of community policing methods. The productivity of the BAPD also improved with increases in arrests of all types, traffic citations, field interview reports, and crime clearance rates.[18]

As another example, Vincent E. Henry, former New York Police Department (NYPD) sergeant and a 2003 Rhodes scholar, describes the shared leadership features of the NYPD's CompStat program, a management process through which the department identifies problems, devises problem-solving strategies, and then measures the results of these problem-solving activities. Henry writes that this program's key strategy is to decentralize an organization's management structure by increasing the authority, responsibilities, and accountabilities of frontline officers and mid-level managers. In reflecting community policing concepts and their problem-oriented focus, officers on the street and their immediate supervisors work with community leaders and residents to identify public safety concerns, analyze crime problems specific to each precinct, and develop proactive strategies for addressing them.[19]

Another example of shared leadership programs in policing is found in a 2006 article by Gregory P. Rothaus, chief of police in San Carlos, California, in which Rothaus discusses team-building workshops (TBW). He asserts that no management fact is more obvious and more critical than the operations of the team. In organizations, members depend on each other for support, ideas, leadership, and encouragement; and in law enforcement, this is especially critical because often lives are at stake.[20]

Officers are looking for leadership characteristics in their managers that will positively influence them in their police career. The leaders these officers look up to primarily operate using task-centered and structured leadership styles. However, some studies show that female officers prefer leaders who are considered "transformational" and "democratic"—who allow subordinates freedom of action and who respond to their concerns.[21]

Organizing by Personnel

A police department faces the same organizational challenges as any organization, and a major challenge is personnel. The civil service system plays a large role in police hiring. This section will describe that role, along with sworn versus nonsworn personnel, rank structure, and other personnel issues.

The Civil Service System

The **civil service system** is a method of hiring and managing government employees that is designed to eliminate political influence, favoritism, nepotism, and bias. Civil service rules govern the hiring, promoting, and terminating of most government employees. The **Pendleton Act** created a civil service system for federal employees in 1883, following the assassination of President James Garfield, who was killed in 1881 by someone who had been rejected for appointment to a federal office. Eventually, many state and local governments adopted their own civil service systems.

Wadman and Allison discuss the history of political influence, patronage, and corruption in police departments before the civil service system, saying, "Police became one of the plums of boss patronage as well as a sure means to economic security for the individual policeman."[22] The corruption of police organizations and officers is a central theme in police history. Before civil service, the competition for police jobs was intense and required

---

civil service system A method of hiring and managing government employees that is designed to eliminate political influence, favoritism, nepotism, and bias.

Pendleton Act A federal law passed in 1883 to establish a civil service system to test, appoint, and promote officers on a merit system.

the approval of the local political machine. As an example, appointment to the New York Police Department required the blessing of the local Tammany Hall (Democratic Party machine) block boss plus a $300 bribe.[23]

Although several cities adopted civil service reforms relatively quickly by the early 20th century, many did not. In 1907 in Louisville, Kentucky, a change of political parties in an election resulted in the demotion of all Democratic captains to patrolmen, replacing them with Republican ones. In 1917, the Democrats resumed power in city hall and eliminated 300 patrol officers from the force of 491. In Salt Lake City, Utah, changeover in police personnel ran as high as 85 percent with each change of political party in power.[24] Civil service regulations regarding hiring, promoting, and firing helped to remove the police from the partisan control of corrupt city political machines. By 1920, only 10 of the 63 cities in the United States with a population of more than 100,000 did not have a civil service system in place.[25]

Today, the vast majority of all government employees at the federal, state, and local levels are covered by the civil service system. Most police departments, particularly larger ones, are governed by civil service regulations, although a few still operate outside them. An example of a non–civil service police department is the Hanson, Massachusetts, Police Department, whose 26 sworn and 6 nonsworn members are hired on the local level without a civil service process.[26]

Civil service has reduced political interference and paved the way for merit employment, a system in which personal ability is stressed above all other considerations. However, some civil service systems seem to guarantee life tenure in the organization and provide an atmosphere of absolute employee protection instead of stressing the merit that the system was initially designed to emphasize. Critics have complained that the civil service system creates many problems for police administrations because a chief or commissioner cannot appoint or promote at will but must do so according to civil service lists. Additionally, it is often difficult to demote or terminate employees under the civil service system.[27] However, it must be remembered that despite the criticism, civil service rules have helped to reduce political influence and to eliminate the autocratic power of a supervisor to hire, fire, or transfer employees on a whim.

Sworn and Nonsworn (Civilian) Personnel

People who work for police departments fall under two major classifications: sworn members of the department, or police officers, and nonsworn members of the department, or civilians.

SWORN MEMBERS **Sworn members** are those people in the police organization we usually think of as police officers, troopers, or deputy sheriffs. They are given traditional police powers by state and local laws, including penal or criminal laws and criminal procedure laws. Upon appointment, sworn members take an oath to abide by the U.S. Constitution and those sections of state and local law applicable to the exercise of police power.

The best example of police power is the power to arrest. Police officers need only probable cause (not definite proof) to make an arrest for any crime or offense, whether committed in their presence or not. *Probable cause* is a series of facts that would indicate to a "reasonable person" that a crime is being committed or was committed and that a certain person is committing or did commit it. A good example of facts leading to probable cause follows:

1. At 3:00 a.m., screams from a female are heard in an alley.
2. An officer sees a man running from the alley.
3. Upon the officer's command, the man refuses to halt and rushes past the officer.

This situation gives the officer probable cause to stop the man, even though there is no "proof" yet of a crime. If it later turns out that no crime was committed, the officer has done nothing wrong, because he or she acted under probable cause.

Citizens, in contrast, cannot use probable cause to arrest fellow citizens. The crime must have actually happened. Additionally, citizens can only arrest for offenses actually committed in their presence, unless the offense is a felony. Nevertheless, citizens who make arrests leave themselves open for false arrest lawsuits.

In addition to the power of arrest, police officers have the power to temporarily stop and question

---

sworn members Police employees given traditional police powers by state and local laws, including penal or criminal laws and criminal procedure laws.

people in public places, to stop vehicles and conduct inspections, and to search for weapons and other contraband. Arrest and stopping issues are covered in more detail in Chapter 5, "The Police Role and Police Discretion," and in Chapter 13, "Police and the Law." Police officers also have significantly more power to use physical force, including deadly physical force, than do citizens.

NONSWORN (CIVILIAN) MEMBERS Nonsworn (civilian) members of police departments are not given traditional police powers and can exercise only the very limited arrest power given to ordinary citizens. Thus, they are assigned to nonenforcement duties in the department. They serve in many different areas of a police organization and in many roles. When we think of nonsworn members, we usually think of typists, 911 operators, and police radio dispatchers. However, nonsworn members serve in many other capacities as well, including clerical, technical, administrative, and managerial jobs. Their rank structure is generally not as vertical as that of sworn officers.

Recognizing the outstanding performance of officers is one of the many aspects of the police chief's job.

Rank Structure

Sworn members generally have a highly organized rank structure (chain of command). At the highest level in most police organizations are chiefs or commissioners. The lowest sworn rank in the police organization is usually the police officer (or in sheriff's offices, the deputy sheriff). To say the police officer has the lowest rank in a police department may sound demeaning, but it only refers to the relative rank in the organizational chart, not to the police officer's power or to the quality and importance of the service performed. Many organizations do have lower-ranked sworn officers, such as cadets or trainees, who generally perform duties similar to nonsworn members or assist sworn members in performing nonenforcement duties. Many cadets or trainees aspire to an eventual sworn position or are in training for one. In most organizations, those in training at the police academy are known as recruits or cadets and generally have the same legal authority as regular officers, except that they usually are not assigned to enforcement duties while still in training.

The following sections describe the various ranks in the police organization using generic terms. (For an example of a specific organizational chart showing some of these ranks, see Figure 3.5.) Most departments use the titles *police officer*, *detective*, *sergeant*, *lieutenant*, and *captain*. However, some organizations, such as state police departments and county sheriff's offices, use different terms to describe their members. In a state police force, the rank of trooper is almost identical to the rank of police officer. In some state police organizations, military ranks such as major or colonel are used. In a sheriff's office, the rank of deputy sheriff is synonymous with the rank of police officer. In federal law enforcement organizations, nonmilitary terms are used to reflect rank structure, such as agent, supervisor, manager, administrator, and director.

Although police officers, troopers, and deputy sheriffs are low in the rank structure in the department, they are the most important people in the police organization. They are the people who are actually working on the streets, attempting to maintain order and enforce the law. A police agency is only as good as the quality of the men and women it employs.

nonsworn (civilian) members Police employees without traditional police powers generally assigned to noncritical or nonenforcement tasks.

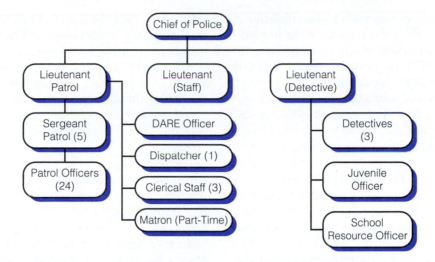

FIGURE 3.5   Organizational Chart: Vestal, New York, Police
Department

Source: Reprinted by permission of the Vestal Police Department, Vestal, NY. http://www
.vestalny.com/DeptPage.aspx?pID=10

POLICE OFFICER Police officers serve as the workers in the police organization. The average police officer is assigned to patrol duties (see Chapter 9, "Patrol Operations," for a complete discussion of the activities of patrol officers). Police officers perform the basic duties for which the organization exists. They are under the control of supervisors, generally known as ranking officers or superior officers. Ranking officers are usually sergeants, lieutenants, and captains.

CORPORAL OR MASTER PATROL OFFICER
Many police departments have established the corporal or master patrol officer rank as an intermediate rank between the police officers and the first-line supervisor, the sergeant. Often this intermediate rank is given to an officer as a reward for exemplary service or for additional services performed, such as training or technical functions.

DETECTIVE/INVESTIGATOR Some police officers in a department are designated as detectives, investigators, or inspectors. (The various names for ranks may be confusing—investigators in the San Francisco Police Department are called inspectors, whereas in the NYPD and many other departments, the rank of inspector is that of a senior manager.) The role of the detective or investigator is to investigate past crimes (see Chapter 10, "Investigations,"

for a complete discussion of this role and the activities involved). Detectives exercise no supervisory role over police officers except at a crime scene, where they are in charge and make most major decisions. In many departments, the assigned, case, or primary detective or investigator is the senior ranking officer at crime scenes and even outranks uniformed supervisors.

The role of the detective is generally considered more prestigious than that of police officer. Detectives commonly receive a higher salary and do not wear uniforms. They are usually designated detectives by appointment, generally for meritorious work rather than through the typical civil service promotional examination. Often detectives do not possess civil service tenure and can be demoted back to the police officer rank without the strict civil service restrictions applicable to the other ranks in a police organization. In agencies where detectives must compete for the position through a civil service exam, the detectives enjoy protections from arbitrary demotions.

SERGEANT The first supervisor in the police chain of command is the *sergeant*. The sergeant is the first-line or frontline supervisor and, many say, the most important figure in the police supervisory and command hierarchy. To most police officers, the sergeant is the boss.

The sergeant has two main responsibilities in police operations. First, the sergeant is the immediate supervisor of a number of officers assigned to his or her supervision. This group of officers is generally known as a **squad**. Usually a squad is made up of 6 to 10 officers, and several squads may work on a particular tour of duty. The sergeant is responsible for the activities and conduct of members of his or her squad. In addition, the sergeant is responsible for decisions made at the scene of a police action until he or she is relieved by a higher-ranking officer.

Because the sergeant is responsible for getting the job done through supervising the actions of other people, he or she must possess personal qualities such as intelligence, integrity, and dedication. The sergeant also must draw on numerous organizational, motivational, and communication skills.

Promotion to sergeant generally results in a pay raise and an increase in prestige, but the transition from police officer to sergeant can be a difficult adjustment, and often the job itself is very difficult. As Scott Oldham, supervisory sergeant with the Bloomington, Indiana, Police Department, says, "As sergeants, it is incumbent upon us to set the standards for our shifts."[28] Sergeants must make decisions regardless of whether they are popular; that is their job. Oldham tells other sergeants, "It is up to the sergeants to teach others the right way to do things and to pass along the knowledge that has been gained from those that have gone before. Yes, doing things this way is hard. Making unpopular decisions is hard, but it is something that must be done for the good of everyone."[29]

LIEUTENANT Just above sergeant in the chain of command is the *lieutenant*. Whereas the sergeant is generally in charge of a squad of officers, the lieutenant is in charge of an entire platoon. The **platoon** consists of all the people working on a particular tour (shift or watch). The lieutenant is in charge of the employees working and all police operations occurring on a particular tour.

Keep in mind that, as in previous discussions, terms used here such as *squad, platoon, tour, shift,* and *watch* are used in this textbook as generic terms. Many departments use different terms to identify these same concepts.

---

squad A group of officers who generally work together all the time under the supervision of a particular sergeant.

platoon All of the people working on a particular tour or shift.

CAPTAIN Next in the chain of command above the lieutenant is the *captain*. The captain is ultimately responsible for all personnel and all activities in a particular area, or for a particular unit, on a 24-hour-a-day basis. The captain must depend on the lieutenant and sergeants under his or her command to communicate his or her orders to the officers and to exercise discipline and control over the officers.

The captain's role, however, is not merely administrative. According to Captain Robert Ray Johnson, a 35-year veteran of the Chicago Police Department and an adjunct professor in the Law Enforcement Management Program at Calumet College of Saint Joseph in Chicago, captains must always be cognizant of what is going on in their commands. He indicates that captains should have an open-door policy in which officers feel comfortable knowing they can stop in and talk to the captain, and that captains need to step out and mingle with their officers. Johnson says that interpersonal interaction with the rank and file is the key to being accurately informed and that a captain who holes up in the office and tends only to administrative duties will soon lose touch.[30]

RANKS ABOVE CAPTAIN Many larger municipal agencies have a hierarchy of ranks above captain. Commanders may perform the same role and functions as inspectors in other agencies. Inspectors generally have administrative control over several precincts or geographic areas, whereas assistant chiefs or chiefs have administrative control of major units, such as personnel, patrol, or detectives.

CHIEF OF POLICE/POLICE COMMISSIONER
The head of the police agency is usually termed the *chief of police* or the *police commissioner*. The mayor, county executive, or governor will generally appoint chiefs of police for a definite term of office. These positions are considered "at-will"; generally, chiefs and commissioners do not have civil service tenure.

Chiefs of police must take an active role in their agencies and properly communicate with employees, including labor representatives. John M. Collins, general counsel for the Massachusetts Chiefs of Police Association, writes that in states with collective bargaining, police chiefs who intend to implement a new rule or make material changes to an existing set of rules and regulations should involve the unions representing various officer bargaining units prior to the effective date of the change in the rules and regulations. Collins also says that even in organizations without bargaining units, chiefs should involve employees in the development and implementation of rules and regulations, since involving employees helps to ensure a sense of teamwork, provides recognition of the value of input and experience, and can produce a sincere commitment to the rules and regulations.[31] The police chief is possibly the key figure in the police organization, as she or he will set the vision and tone for the department.

Other Personnel

Police departments are increasingly using non-sworn employees and civilians to perform tasks in the police department. This effort can both increase efficiency in the use of human resources and cut costs. Community service officers and police auxiliaries also help some departments operate more efficiently.

CIVILIANIZATION The process of removing sworn officers from noncritical or nonenforcement tasks and replacing them with civilians or nonsworn employees is **civilianization**. Civilians with special training and qualifications have been hired to replace officers who formerly did nonenforcement jobs (traffic control, issuing parking tickets, taking past crime reports, and so on). Additionally, civilians with clerical skills have been hired to replace officers who were formerly assigned to desk jobs. Approximately one-quarter of all local police department employees are civilians.

The replacement of sworn officers by civilians in nonenforcement jobs is highly cost-effective for police departments because civilian employees generally earn much less than sworn officers. This strategy also enables a department to have more sworn personnel available for patrol and other enforcement duties.[32]

A study of civilianization programs found that managers and officers were favorably impressed with the use of civilians for nonenforcement duties. Many officers observed that civilians performed some tasks better than the sworn officers they replaced. Additionally, many officers tended to consider some of the noncivilianized jobs as confining, sedentary, a form of punishment, and not proper police work. Others in the study pointed out that

some civilians want careers in police work, and a sizable number of officers recommended that more civilians be hired.[33]

COMMUNITY SERVICE OFFICERS The President's Commission on Law Enforcement and Administration of Justice recommended that three distinct entry-level police personnel categories be established in large and medium-sized police departments: (1) police agents, (2) police officers, and (3) **community service officers (CSOs)**.[34] Police agent would be the most knowledgeable and responsible entry-level position. These officers would be given the most difficult assignments and be allowed to exercise the greatest discretion. The commission suggested a requirement of at least two years of college and preferably a bachelor's degree in the liberal arts or social sciences. Some departments have adopted this recommendation and give these officers the title of corporal or master patrol officer.

Police officers would be the equivalent of the traditional and contemporary police officer. They would perform regular police duties, such as routine preventive patrol and providing emergency services. The commission recommended that a high school degree be required for this position.

Community service officers would be police apprentices, youths 17 to 21 years of age, preferably from minority groups. They would have no general law enforcement powers and no weapons. The commission reasoned that because of their social background and greater understanding of inner-city problems, CSOs would be good police–community relations representatives. The commission suggested that the CSOs work with other youths, investigate minor thefts, help the disabled, and provide community assistance. The commission recommended that the lack of a high school diploma and the existence of a minor arrest record not bar CSOs from employment and also that CSOs be allowed to work their way up to become regular police officers.

civilianization The process of removing sworn officers from noncritical or nonenforcement tasks and replacing them with civilians or nonsworn employees.

community service officers (CSOs) Entry-level police employees without general law enforcement powers, as suggested by the President's Commission on Law Enforcement and Administration of Justice.

We're All Working Together

In many police departments, a disparity arises between the sworn and nonsworn personnel. Our department was no different. Smart police officers realize how important the support personnel are to their mission. Whether you can get the help you need when you need it from these essential areas of the department can make an officer's life much easier or harder.

Think of the difference it can make when you're running late for a court appearance and need to pick up some crucial evidence or paperwork, and the individual who supplies that evidence or paperwork is very busy, with lots of people before you. You didn't plan ahead and allow the time for the request that the department requires. If you're on good working terms with that employee, he or she might go out of the way and make the extra effort to help you out so you don't get in trouble. On the other hand, if you have treated that employee as a second-class citizen, that will be remembered and you will wait your turn; no special effort will be made.

During my career, I encountered a few officers who didn't see the relationship between the jobs we were all doing and treated some of the support personnel in a less-than-equal manner. Whenever I saw this behavior, I would sit the officer down and we'd have a chat about human relations, about how we all work together, and how these coworkers can make officers look good or bad. Officers usually heeded this advice, but some had to learn the hard way.

When I became a patrol captain and went from five years on the midnight shift to working days, with 100 people in my division and all the politics and events involved with day shift, I relied very heavily on my secretary, Lori. She had been working as the uniform division secretary for many years and had a great depth of knowledge and command of the history of the department. Perhaps she spoiled me, but for any question I asked, she was able to pull out a file with all the backup documentation I needed to understand and plan. She was a crucial part of the working of the department, and luckily I had realized her expertise early in my career when I was a sergeant and appreciated all she did. She greatly eased my transition to uniform division captain and contributed to my success in that role.

—Linda Forst

POLICE RESERVES/AUXILIARIES Personnel shortcomings in police departments may be perennial or seasonal, depending on the jurisdiction. Some resort communities face an influx of vacationers and tourists during a particular season that can more than double the normal size of the population. In response to this annual influx, some communities employ "summertime cops"—an example of police reserves.

The term **reserve officer** can be confusing. In many jurisdictions, reserve officers are part-time employees who serve when needed and are compensated. In other jurisdictions, reserves are not compensated. The key element regarding the reserve officer is that he or she is a nonregular but sworn member of the department who has regular police powers. Other volunteer officers, sometimes referred to as auxiliaries, do not have full police powers.

In a 2006 article in the *FBI Law Enforcement Bulletin*, Karey Hedlund and Tod W. Burke define the reserve officer this way:

> A volunteer, nonregular, sworn member of a law enforcement agency who serves with or without compensation and has regular police powers ... and who participates on a regular basis in agency activities, including ... crime prevention or control, and the preservation of the peace and enforcement of the law.[35]

Reserve officers augment the regular force in police departments throughout the nation. Whether paid or not, they have full police powers. Many provide law enforcement services, including

---

reserve officer Either part-time compensated or noncompensated sworn police employees who serve when needed.

patrol, traffic control, assistance at natural and civil disasters, crime prevention, dispatch operations, and numerous other functions.[36] A 2006 estimate counted about 400,000 reserve officers serving in the United States.[37]

Each state varies in its requirements to become a reserve officer. South Carolina, for example, requires a minimum of 60 hours of police instruction and a firearms qualification conducted by a certified firearms instructor. The reserve candidate must then pass a rigid examination conducted by the South Carolina Criminal Justice Academy. The reserve officer in South Carolina cannot be paid. In North Carolina, however, a reserve candidate must receive the same training as a full-time officer. He or she must attend the Basic Law Enforcement Training Course, which consists of 488 hours of instruction at a host of community colleges or at the central North Carolina Justice Academy at Salemburg, North Carolina. Upon completion of the basic training, the student must pass a state board examination. Reserve officers in North Carolina can receive a salary from their employer.

In some cities, auxiliary officers are unpaid volunteers. Although they wear police-type uniforms and carry batons, these auxiliaries are citizens with no police powers and they do not carry firearms. They usually patrol their own communities, acting as a deterrent force and providing the police with extra eyes and ears. Chapter 11, "Police and the Community," provides coverage of police volunteer programs.

Lateral Transfers

Lateral transfers, or lateral movement, in police departments can be defined as the ability and opportunity to transfer from one police department to another. Some states allow lateral transfers from one department to another department and from out-of-state departments, some states allow only in-state lateral transfers, and some states do not allow lateral transfers at all.

Factors that must be considered in lateral transfers include any differences in policing philosophy between the department the officer is transferring from and the new department, how well the officer will fit with the image of the new department, and the degree to which the transferring officer must change in complying with the policies and procedures of the new department. Also, the transferring

officer must be fully trained in the laws, procedures, and technology of the new department.[38]

The major problem with lateral transfers is that many police pension systems are tied into the local government, and money put into those funds cannot be transferred. Thus, lateral transfers in such departments can cause officers to lose some or all of their investments. The President's Commission on Law Enforcement and Administration of Justice has recommended developing a national police retirement system that would permit the transfer of personnel without the loss of benefits. A few experiments with portable police pensions have also been tried.[39]

Police Unions

Unions exist in order to harness the individual power of each worker into one group, the union, which can then speak with one voice for all the members. Unions in the private sector have been on the decline, but public-sector unionism is growing, particularly among police. Police unions have become increasingly political, endorsing and actively campaigning for candidates at the local, state, and federal level.

Police unions are predominantly local organizations that bargain and communicate with the local police department and the mayor's or chief executive's office. Local unions often join into federations on a state or federal level to lobby state and federal legislative bodies, but collective bargaining may still be at a local level. As an example, all 55 sworn members of the town of South Kingstown, Rhode Island, Police Department, with the exception of the chief, are members of the International Brotherhood of Police Officers (IBPO), but their contracts are negotiated with the town.[40]

According to a government report, approximately 38 percent of all police departments have some form of collective bargaining. Police departments serving larger populations tend to have collective bargaining agreements more often than departments serving smaller populations, ranging from 85 percent for departments serving one million or more residents, to 11 percent for those serving populations under 2,500.[41] In 1997, researchers

lateral transfers The ability and opportunity to transfer from one police department to another.

found that the existence of a collective bargaining mechanism in large police agencies was significantly correlated with supplemental pay benefits such as hazardous duty pay, differential shift pay, education incentive pay, and merit pay.[42]

Police unionism has a long and colorful history. Police employee organizations started as fraternal associations to provide fellowship for officers, as well as welfare benefits (death benefits and insurance policies) to protect police families. The Fraternal Order of Police (FOP), the first of the police fraternal organizations, was founded in 1915 by two Pittsburgh, Pennsylvania, patrol officers, and 21 other officers, for the purpose of bringing their grievances to the mayor and council of Pittsburgh. They were recognized for their "strong influence in the legislatures in various states, [and] their considerate and charitable efforts."[43] In other cities, labor unions began to organize the police for the purpose of collective bargaining, and by 1919, 37 locals had been chartered by the American Federation of Labor (AFL). The Boston police strike of 1919, as we saw in Chapter 1, was triggered by the refusal of the city of Boston to recognize the AFL-affiliated union. In response to the strike, Calvin Coolidge, then the governor of Massachusetts, fired all of the striking officers—almost the entire police department. Because of the Boston strike, the police union movement stalled until the 1960s, when it reemerged. During the 1960s, Patrolmen's Benevolent Associations (PBAs) in major cities, using their rank-and-file officers, increased their lobbying and job actions, which ultimately weakened and reversed the political pressure against union recognition, leading to a major victory scored by New York City's PBA in 1964. Since then, the PBAs and the FOP have transformed from pressure groups into labor unions.[44]

The ultimate bargaining tool of the union has traditionally been the strike. Members of many organizations, such as telephone companies, department stores, factories, and so on, strike to win labor concessions from their employers. Should police officers be allowed to strike? Many feel that police officers are special employees and should not have the right to strike. In fact, most states have laws that specifically prohibit strikes by public employees.

Despite such laws, there have been strikes by police employees. In 1970, members of the New York Police Department staged a wildcat strike, for which all officers were fined two days' pay for each day they participated in the strike. Police strikes have also been staged in Baltimore, San Francisco, and New Orleans.

New Orleans police officers went on strike twice in February 1979. The first walkout lasted for 30 hours and was designed to gain recognition of the union, bring the city to the bargaining table, and force agreement on selected economic demands. It was successful. That strike emboldened officers to try another to seek additional concessions, using the approaching Mardi Gras holiday as a bargaining chip. It was intended that this walkout would also include ranking officers in the bargaining unit and would compel the city to enter into a collective bargaining agreement with the union. The second strike, however, which forced the cancellation of the Mardi Gras festivities, lasted 16 days and was unsuccessful.[45]

W. J. Bopp writes that states lacking collective bargaining agreements for public employees are creating a climate in which strikes flourish. Even in cities that voluntarily negotiate with their police employees in the absence of enabling legislation, confusion and misunderstanding are likely to occur. Trouble is also likely to result when hostility, bitterness, distrust, and cynicism become dominant characteristics of the relationships between police labor and management.[46]

To avoid the penalties involved in a formal police strike, police union members occasionally engage in informal job actions to protest working conditions or other officer grievances. Such job actions include contracting the **blue flu** (where officers call and report in sick), refusing to perform certain job functions such as writing traffic summonses, and working "by the rule," which means that officers follow precisely the policies and procedures of a department in order to slow down the work without anyone actually missing work. These actions tend to upset citizens, as response time to routine calls is usually extended.

National umbrella police organizations tend to advocate adversarial tactics and rely on formal, legal redress of grievances.[47] Some of the major local police unions are the International Union of Police Associations (IUPA), the Fraternal Order of Police (FOP), the International Conference of

---

blue flu Informal job actions by officers in which they call in sick and/or refuse to perform certain job functions in an attempt to win labor concessions from their employers.

Police Associations (ICPA), and the International Brotherhood of Police Officers (IBPO). Some officers are also members of national federations of civil service workers, such as the American Federation of State, County and Municipal Employees (AFSCME).

According to a 2006 survey, police chiefs and union officials are not that far apart in their perceptions of the roles that labor and management play in the law enforcement profession. However, they differ in their perceptions of their respective willingness to confer on citizen complaints, scheduling, communication channels, relations with political entities, and the response to racial profiling. Despite the potential for animosity, a majority of executives on both sides described their relationship with labor or management as cooperative and friendly. Neither police chiefs nor union officials believed that labor and management working together would result in alienating unions from their membership.[48]

OTHER POLICE AFFILIATIONS Police officers affiliate on levels other than unions. The two major types of affiliations are fraternal and professional.

Police fraternal organizations generally focus on national origin, ethnic, or gender identification. Some examples in a specific very large urban police department include the Emerald Society (Irish American officers), the Columbian Society (Italian American officers), the Guardian Association (African American officers), the Schomrin Society (Jewish officers), the Policewoman's Endowment Society (female officers), and the Gay Officers Action League (gay, lesbian, and transgender officers).

Major professional organizations for police officers, designed as forums in which to exchange professional information and provide training, are the International Association of Chiefs of Police (IACP); the Police Executive Research Forum (PERF), which is a research-oriented organization; and the National Organization of Black Law Enforcement Executives (NOBLE).

Organizing by Area

Police departments must be organized by personnel functions and by the geographic area they serve. Each officer and group of officers must be responsible for a particular well-defined area. Geographic areas may be beats or posts, precincts, stations, or districts. Various organizations have different words to describe these geographic groupings, so note that the terminology used here is generic rather than specific. Figure 3.6 is a map of a geographic breakdown of a precinct into beats or sectors.

Beats

The **beat** is the smallest geographic area that a single patrol unit—one or two people in a car or on foot—can patrol effectively. A beat may be a foot beat, patrol car beat, mounted beat, motorcycle or scooter beat, or even bicycle beat. Obviously, patrol car beats can be much larger than foot beats.

The beat officer ideally should know everyone living or doing business on his or her beat, as well as conditions of concern and problems on the beat that require police assistance. For this reason, a beat should be as geographically limited as possible, without being so small that it is nonproductive or boring to the officer.

Precincts/Districts/Stations

A **precinct/district/station** is generally the entire collection of beats in a given geographic area. In a small department, generally only one precinct serves as the administrative headquarters for the entire department. In a 2007 survey, Kimberly D. Hassell discovered that a significant proportion of police patrol officers believed that police practices varied by precinct. Hassell attributed the differences in practices to individual officers' personalities and levels of experience; the culture, nature, and expectations of the citizens; the nature of the calls for service, the call loads, and officer safety concerns; and command precinct rules and norms. She concluded that the precinct is an important level of analysis within police organizations.[49]

The building that serves as the administrative headquarters of a precinct is generally called a *precinct house* or *station house*. The station house usually contains detention cells for the temporary

---

beat The smallest geographical area an individual officer can patrol.

precinct/district/station The entire collection of beats in a given geographic area; the organizational headquarters of a police department.

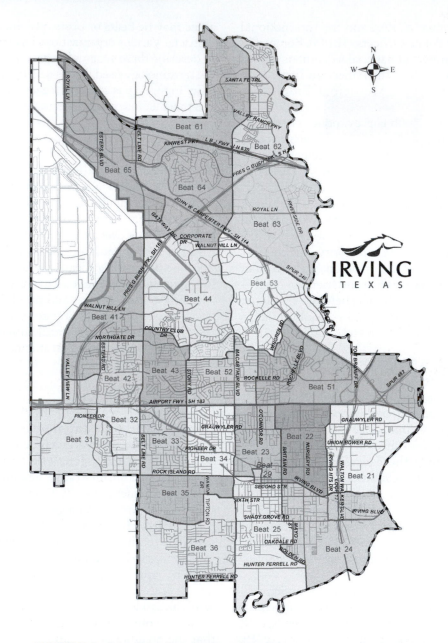

FIGURE 3.6   Map Dividing Precinct into Beats

Source: Reprinted by permission of the City of Irving, Texas. http://cityofirving.org/police/beats/
beatmap.html

detention of prisoners awaiting a court appearance after an arrest, locker rooms in which officers can dress and store their equipment, administrative offices, meeting rooms, and clerical offices.[50]

Often in large urban departments, particularly in the Northeast, the *desk* serves as the centerpiece of the precinct/station/district. The desk is usually an elevated platform near the entrance of the station house, where all major police business is carried on. Prisoners are booked at the desk, and officers are assigned to duty from it. A ranking officer, generally a sergeant or lieutenant, is assigned as the *desk officer* and supervises all activities in the station house.

The desk officer is usually in charge of the *police blotter*, a record in chronological order of all police activities occurring in a precinct each day. The blotter traditionally has been a large bound book in which all entries are handwritten by the desk officer. Although some departments still maintain the classic handwritten form, the term *blotter* is now used more generically as the written record of all activity in a precinct, which can include typed and computerized reports.

Organizing by Time

In addition to being organized by personnel and by area, a police department must organize its use of time. The following section will describe the tour system, including the common three-tour system, tour length, tour conditions, and steady (fixed) tours. Again, remember that various organizations have different words to describe these groupings of schedules, so the terminology used here is generic rather than specific.

The Three-Tour System

Common sense dictates that police officers, like other workers, can work only a certain number of hours and days before fatigue sets in and they lose their effectiveness. Tradition and civil service rules have established the police officer's working day as 8 hours. The traditional police organization separates each day or 24-hour period into three tours (also called shifts or watches): a midnight or night tour, which generally falls between the hours of 12:00 midnight and 8:00 a.m.; a day tour, which generally falls between the hours of 8:00 a.m. and 4:00 p.m.; and an evening tour, which generally falls between the hours of 4:00 p.m. and 12:00 midnight. Shifts, tours, or watches do not necessarily have to fall between these exact hours; they can be between any hours, as long as all 24 hours of the day are covered.

Some departments have shifts that last longer than 8 hours, and they use the overlapping time as training time. Another example of use of longer shifts is the 4-10 schedule, consisting of four 10-hour days on and four 10-hour days off. This is a good tool to build officer morale but, as most supervisors and managers discover, is a scheduling nightmare. It also splits the patrol force into two separate departments, and officers working one half of the schedule rarely see the other half.

Some departments use a variation of the three-tour system, such as three 12-hour tours or the previously mentioned four 10-hour tours a week. An example of a department using 12-hour tours is the Nassau County, New York, Police Department, which uses a 7:00 a.m. to 7:00 p.m. and a 7:00 p.m. to 7:00 a.m. tour system. This department and others that use 12-hour tours have only two platoons, as opposed to the traditional three-platoon system.

When the traditional three-tour system is used, it takes three officers to cover each day: one on the night tour, one on the day tour, and one on the evening tour. When days off, vacation time, and sick time are factored into the three-tour system, approximately five officers are required to cover each beat 24 hours a day, 7 days a week, 365 days a year. Formulas that can be used to allocate personnel are available in police organization and management texts.

Historically, police officers have been allocated evenly during the three tours of duty each day, with equal numbers of officers assigned to each of the tours. However, academic studies of police beginning in the 1960s discovered that crime and other police problems do not fit neatly into the three-tour system. Studies indicated that the majority of crime and police problems in the United States occurred during the late evening and early morning hours. Thus, many police departments began to change their methods of allocating police personnel and most now assign their personnel according to the demand for police services, putting more officers on the street during those hours when crime and calls for police officers are highest.

Tour Length: 8 Hours, 10 Hours, or 12 Hours

The 8-hour tour is the most commonly used tour in police departments, although it is decreasing in popularity. The 8-hour tour is easy for departments to schedule, as most civilian workplaces operate on an 8-hour schedule. It allows officers to be like their civilian counterparts to some degree and spend more time with their families (if they work the day tour).

The 10-hour tour has the benefit of providing a regular workweek of four set days (usually Sunday through Wednesday or Wednesday through Saturday), allowing for three days off with Wednesday being an overlap day to be used for training or other duties. This is the least efficient of the three tours.

The 12-hour tour is gaining in popularity and has the benefit to officers of being predictable like the 10-hour tour. The officers usually work the 12-hour shift rotation in such a way that in a two-week period, officers will work a total of 80 hours, but not necessarily 40 hours in a week. A weakness of this plan is the increase in officer fatigue. At the end of the 12-hour tour, officer effectiveness may be reduced, which may have an adverse effect on officer safety. Officer safety and fatigue are legitimate management concerns with the 12-hour tour.

On the plus side of 10-hour and 12-hour tours, these shifts provide an increase in officer morale. They are also cost-effective. In this time of limited budgets, increasing the use of these longer tours may be worth the additional management headaches they bring. As seen in Table 3.2, although the use of the 8-hour shift decreased from November 2005 to November 2009 by 10.8 percent, use of the 10-hour shift decreased by only 4.9 percent and use of the 12-hour shift actually increased (by 2.3 percent) over the same period. These figures represent a move away from the traditional 8-hour shift and an increased preference for 10-hour and 12-hour shifts.

One intangible factor that cannot be fully accounted for in scheduling is officer overtime. When officers are on a call, they cannot stop in the middle and leave the call just because their shift has ended. The call must be completed. If it involves a major case (for example, a homicide or felony assault), the amount of time the officer has to spend finishing the task may cause him or her to work into the next shift and incur overtime. One of management's functions is to try to control these overtime costs.[51]

Tour Conditions

As any police officer can testify, each of the three shifts in the three-tour system has its own characteristics.

The midnight tour is sometimes called the overnight or the graveyard shift. Most people are sleeping during this time, although in some large cities a good deal of commerce and business occurs. The most common problems for police officers during this tour are disorderly and intoxicated people at home and on the street, domestic violence, disorderly tavern patrons, commercial burglaries, prostitution, and drug sales. In addition to handling these specific problems, the police provide their normal duties, such as routine patrol, response to emergency calls, aiding the sick and injured, and solving disputes.

The day tour occurs during the normal business hours in the United States. Stores and offices are open, highway and construction crews are working, and children are in school and at play. The most common activities for police officers during this tour are facilitating traffic flow and ensuring the safety of those traveling to and from work by enforcing parking and moving violations, ensuring the safety of children walking to and from school and entering and leaving school buses, preventing robberies and other property thefts in commercial areas, and providing other normal police services.

The evening tour is generally the busiest for the police. The workday and school day are over, the sun goes down, and the hours of darkness are

TABLE 3.2 Patrol Shift Length and Patrol Shift—Fixed/Rotating

November 2005 Agencies (287)		November 2009 Agencies (287)	
Fixed	**Rotating**	**Fixed**	**Rotating**
54%	46%	75.3%	24.7%

Agencies (262)*			Agencies (234)**		
8-hour shifts	**10-hour shifts**	**12-hour shifts**	**8-hour shifts**	**10-hour shifts**	**12-hour shifts**
40.1%	27.2%	24%	29.3%	22.3%	26.3%

Note: Totals do not add to 100% for the following reasons: *There were 5 (1.7%) agencies with 9-hour shifts; 3 (1%) agencies with 11-hour shifts; and 17 (5.9%) agencies that employed multiple shifts. Two agencies had fewer than 50 officers. **There were 14 (4.7%) agencies with 9-hour shifts; 16 (5.3%) agencies with 11-hour shifts; 4 (1.3%) agencies with 13-hour shifts; and 32 (10.7%) agencies that employed multiple shifts. Twelve agencies had fewer than 50 officers.

Source: Karen L. Amendola, David Weisburd, Edwin E. Hamilton, Greg Jones, and Meghan Slipka, with Anneke Heitmann, Jon Shane, Christoper Ortiz, and Eliab Tarkghen, *The Impact of Shift Length in Policing on Performance, Health, Quality of Life, Sleep, Fatigue, and Extra-Duty Employment 2012* (Washington, D.C.: National Institute of Justice, Office of Justice Programs, U.S. Department of Justice, December 2011).

here. During the evening hours, normal adherence to acceptable ways of behavior often gives way to alcohol and drug abuse, fights, and disputes. The most common activities of the evening tour are facilitating traffic for the home-ward-bound commuter; dealing with bar fights, violence at home, and violence on the streets; preventing and dealing with street and commercial robberies; and providing normal routine police services. The largest amount of police activity occurs on this tour, and the majority of officers are assigned to it.

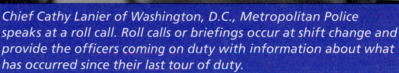

Chief Cathy Lanier of Washington, D.C., Metropolitan Police speaks at a roll call. Roll calls or briefings occur at shift change and provide the officers coming on duty with information about what has occurred since their last tour of duty.

Steady (Fixed) Tours

Traditionally, some police departments have assigned their officers to rotating tours of duty: one or several weeks or months (or other periods) of night tours, one or several weeks or months (or other periods) of day tours, and one or more weeks or months (or other periods) of evening tours. Officers' days off are rotated to accommodate the three-tour system. This practice has caused problems for police officers in both their on-duty and off-duty lives. The strain of working different shifts repeatedly has a negative effect on eating, living, sleeping, and socializing. It creates tremendous levels of stress.

There has been a move in recent years, therefore, to place officers on steady, or fixed, tours of duty, much like most other workers in the United States. Today, officers in many jurisdictions are assigned to steady night tours, day tours, or evening tours based on seniority or the officer's own choice. Table 3.2 shows an increase in fixed shifts from 54 percent in November 2005 to 75.3 percent in November 2009, which is an increase of 21.3 percent. The table also shows a concurrent reduction in rotating shifts of 21.3 percent. These changes demonstrate increased understanding by police leadership of the effect these types of shifts have on the patrol force. Police administrators hope that these steady tours will make officers' on-duty and off-duty lives more normal, thus eliminating the many problems created by shift work.

Organizing by Function or Purpose

The best way to organize a police department by function or purpose is to place similar functions performed by the police into similar units. Thus, all members of the department performing general patrol duties are placed into a patrol division, and all officers performing detective duties are placed into a detective division. Again, different organizations use different words to describe functions or units, so the terminology used here is generic rather than specific.

Line and Staff (Support) Functions

The simplest grouping of units or divisions of a department differentiates between line functions and staff (support) functions. Line functions are those tasks that directly facilitate the accomplishment of organizational goals, whereas staff (support) functions are those tasks that supplement the line units in their task performance.

One of the organizational goals of a police department is order maintenance. The patrol officers who actually patrol the streets to preserve order are grouped under a patrol unit or patrol division. Another organizational goal of a department is to investigate past crimes. The detectives charged with investigating past crimes are grouped together under a detective unit or detective division. Patrol and detective units directly facilitate the accomplishment of the organizational goals of a police department; thus, they perform line functions.

Staff (support) functions are those functions of the police department that are not directly related to the organizational goals of the department but nevertheless are necessary to ensure the smooth running of the department. Investigating candidates for police officers and performing clerical work are examples of staff (support) functions.

Police Department Units

In very large police departments, separate units may be established to perform each task. In smaller departments, the tasks may be grouped together in various ways to be performed by certain units or people.

OPERATIONAL UNITS Operations are activities performed in direct assistance to the public. These are the duties most of us think about when we think of police departments, including crime fighting, crime detection, and providing services to citizens. Operational units include patrol, traffic, criminal investigations, vice, organized crime, juvenile services, community services, crime prevention, and community relations.

The *patrol* unit performs the basic mission of the police department: maintaining order, enforcing the law, responding to calls for assistance, and providing services to citizens. Patrol officers, who are usually on auto or foot patrol, are the backbone of the police service. They are the most important people in police service.

The *traffic* unit performs traffic control at key intersections and in other heavily traveled areas, enforces the traffic laws, and investigates traffic accidents. The *criminal investigations* unit investigates past crimes reported to the police in an effort to identify and apprehend the perpetrators of those crimes. The *vice* unit enforces laws related to illegal gambling, prostitution, controlled substances and other illegal drugs, pornography, and illegal liquor sales. The *organized crime* unit investigates and apprehends members of criminal syndicates who profit from continuing criminal enterprises, such as the vice crimes just mentioned, extortion, loan sharking, and numerous other crimes. The *juvenile services* unit provides a multitude of services to juveniles, including advice and referral

to appropriate social agencies designed to assist youth, particularly youthful offenders. This function also investigates cases of child abuse and neglect.

The *community services* unit provides a multitude of services to the community, including dispute resolution, crime victim assistance, counseling, and other routine and emergency services. It also coordinates relationships between the police and the community, including numerous partnership programs. The police *crime prevention* unit attempts to organize and educate the public on methods people can use on their own and in conjunction with the police to lessen their risk of being victims of crime. Some of these techniques include target hardening, neighborhood watch programs, and operation identification programs. The *community relations* unit attempts to improve relationships between the police and the public so that positive police–community partnerships can develop to decrease crime and improve the quality of life in U.S. neighborhoods.

A rather recent type of police operational unit is the *police paramilitary unit* (PPU), which is similar, in a way, to police SWAT units. The goal of these units is to address extremely serious violent criminal events such as hostage situations, terrorist acts, and sniper shootings. PPUs are equipped with an array of military-like equipment and technology and are focused on the possibility of applying force. Peter B. Kraska and Victor E. Kappeler conducted a survey of 690 U.S. law enforcement agencies and found that fewer than 10 percent of them had PPUs in the early 1970s, but by 1995, more than 89 percent had them.[52] Both PPUs and SWAT teams will be discussed further in Chapter 9.

ADMINISTRATIVE UNITS Administration in a police department is defined as those activities performed, usually from 9:00 a.m. to 5:00 p.m., five days a week, that are not in direct assistance to the public but for the benefit of the organization as a whole. Administrative units include personnel, training, planning and analysis, budget and finance, legal assistance, public information, clerical/secretarial, inspections, internal affairs, and intelligence.

The *personnel* unit performs the duties generally associated with corporate personnel departments, including recruiting and selecting candidates for police positions and assigning, transferring, promoting, and terminating police personnel. The *training* unit provides entry-level training to newly hired recruits and in-service training for veteran officers. The *planning and analysis* unit conducts crime analyses to determine when and where crimes occur so they can be prevented. This unit also conducts operational and administrative analyses to improve police operations and the delivery of police services.

The *budget and finance* unit of the police department is involved in the administration of department finances and budgetary matters, including payroll, purchasing, budgeting, billing, accounting, and auditing. The *legal assistance* unit provides legal advice to members of the department, including patrol officers. The *public information* unit informs the public, through the news media, about police activities, including crime and arrests. This unit also informs the public about actions they can take to reduce their chances of becoming crime victims.

The *clerical/secretarial* unit prepares the necessary reports and documents required to maintain police record keeping. The *inspections* unit conducts internal quality control inspections to ensure that the department's policies, procedures, and rules and regulations are being followed. The *internal affairs* unit investigates corruption and misconduct by officers. Finally, the *intelligence* unit conducts analyses of radical, terrorist, and organized crime groups operating in a police department's jurisdiction.

AUXILIARY SERVICES UNITS Auxiliary services are defined as activities that benefit other units within the police department, but on a more regular and frequent basis than do administrative activities. Auxiliary services functions are usually available to assist the police officer 24 hours a day. Auxiliary services units include records, communications, property, laboratory, detention, identification, alcohol testing, facilities, equipment, supply, and maintenance.

The *records* unit of a police department maintains department records, including records of crimes and arrests, statistics and patterns regarding criminal activity, and records of traffic accidents. The *communications* unit answers incoming calls to the department's 911 telephone lines and assigns police units to respond to emergencies and other requests for police services. The *property* unit inventories and stores all property coming into the custody of the police, including evidence, recovered property, and towed and recovered vehicles.

The *laboratory* unit examines and classifies seized evidence, including drugs, weapons, and evidence found at crime scenes (for example, fingerprints, fibers, and stains). The *detention* unit provides temporary detention for prisoners awaiting their appearance in court. The *identification* unit fingerprints and photographs criminals, classifies prints, and maintains identification files. The *alcohol testing* unit administers driving-while-intoxicated tests for court prosecution.

The *facilities* unit of a police department maintains buildings designed for police use, such as station houses, offices, and detention facilities. The *equipment* unit maintains the numerous types of equipment necessary for the department's effective operation. The supplies necessary for the proper operation of the department are purchased by the *supply* unit. Finally, the *maintenance* unit keeps all facilities and equipment serviceable.

SUMMARY

- Organizations consist of a deliberate arrangement of people doing specific jobs and following particular procedures to accomplish a set of goals determined by some authority.

- The major managerial concepts and definitions common to most organizations include organizational model or structure; division of labor; chain of command (hierarchy of authority); span of control; delegation of responsibility and authority; unity of command; and rules, regulations, and discipline.

- There is a drastic difference between mere managers or supervisors and leaders. In addition to managing and supervising, leaders motivate, teach, coordinate, communicate, inspire, and serve as role models by setting an example.

- Most police organizations use quasi-military or military models of organization, which has led to the professionalization of the police but resulted in a lack of participation by the rank and file. This military-like approach has also caused a paradox of leadership in policing, since most decisions in policing are actually made by police officers acting autonomously on the street.

- Power-sharing methods have found little acceptance in police organizations, although police have been emphasizing proactive, community-oriented approaches to crime reduction and service providing. Employee empowerment may offer significant advantages over traditional top-down police administration.

- The civil service system has eliminated much of the political influence, favoritism, nepotism, and bias formerly found in police employee management.

- Sworn members of police organizations are those given traditional police powers—such as arrest and the ability to stop, question, and search—by state and local laws. Nonsworn members are those without these traditional police powers who perform managerial, administrative, technical, and clerical duties in police organizations.

- Civilianization is the process of removing sworn officers from noncritical or nonenforcement tasks and replacing them with civilians or nonsworn employees.

- Unionization has a long and colorful history in policing. Today, most police unions are local, and many American rank-and-file officers are covered by some form of collective bargaining agreement.

- The size of the geographic area many police agencies cover forces them to subdivide the area into smaller areas of responsibility, such as beats.

- Because of the responsibility of being available 24 hours a day, seven days a week, the police often employ a three-tour system.

- The functions the police are charged with performing are complex and diverse: maintain order, enforce the law, and provide services to citizens. These functions are generally charged to a department's operational units—patrol, criminal investigations, traffic, and community services units. The police also perform administrative duties and auxiliary services.

KEY TERMS

beat

blue flu

bureaucracy

chain of command

civilianization

civil service system

community service officers
    (CSOs)

lateral transfers

leadership

management

nonsworn (civilian) members

organization

Pendleton Act

platoon

PODSCORB

precinct/district/station

quasi-military organization

reserve officer

shared leadership

span of control

squad

sworn members

unity of command

REVIEW EXERCISES

1. You have been appointed the new commissioner of the Anycity Police Department. Anycity is a suburban city 60 miles from a major U.S. city; it has a population of 30,000 people and a police department of 100 officers. The major police problems in Anycity are disorderly teens making unnecessary noise at night, parking and traffic problems in the commercial district during business hours, and daytime residential burglaries.

    The former commissioner's assistant tells you that the department has no organizational chart, no written rules and procedures, and "has always done a great job in the past." Anycity's city manager, however, tells you that the former commissioner was incompetent and that the department is totally disorganized and ineffective.

    You review the department's personnel records and find that of the 100 officers in the department, 30 percent are patrol officers, 30 percent are detectives, and 40 percent are supervisors. In view of what you have learned in this chapter, would you reorganize the department? Why or why not? If you would reorganize, how would you do it?

2. You have been appointed an assistant to your local police chief or sheriff. She tells you that the department has a leadership crisis in its supervisory ranks and asks you to advise her on what qualities she should look for when appointing new supervisors. What advice would you give her?

3. Your criminal justice professor arranges for a class debate. The topic of the debate is the pros and cons of civil service systems in policing. Select a side: Is it better to have a police department based on civil service regulations or not? Prepare a list of talking points to support the side you take.

WEB EXERCISES

1. Find information on civilian or nonsworn employment opportunities in several police departments in your area. Select one department and one advertised employment opportunity and prepare a résumé and cover letter applying for that position.

2. Find information on uniform or sworn employment opportunities in several police departments in your area. Select one department and one advertised employment opportunity and prepare a résumé and cover letter applying for that position.

3. Find personnel information for your local police or sheriff's department. Determine how many sworn and nonsworn personnel are employed in that agency.

END NOTES

1. Nicholas Henry, *Public Administration and Public Affairs,* 9th ed. (Upper Saddle River, N.J.: Pearson Education, Inc., 2004), p. 58 (citing Victor A. Thompson, *Modern Organization* [New York: Knopf, 1961], p. 5); Chester I. Barnard, *The Functions of the Executive* (Cambridge: Harvard University Press, 1938), p. 11.

2. Patrick O'Hara, "Why Law Enforcement Organizations Fail: Mapping the Organizational Fault Lines in Policing," *Crime and Justice International* (March/April 2006): 23–26.

3. Max Weber, "Bureaucracy," in Hans H. Gerth and C. Wright Mills, eds., *Essays in Sociology* (London: Oxford University Press, 1946), renewed 1973 by Hans H. Gerth.

4. Henry, *Public Administration and Public Affairs,* pp. 59–60.

5. Ibid., p. 1. Henry credits the first two lines of this paragraph to Ken Auletta, "The Lost Tycoon," *New Yorker,* April 23 and 30, 2001, p. 154.

6. See, for example, David S. Corderman, "What Is Leadership?" *Police Chief* (February 2006): 13; Daniel W. Ford, "The Impact of Leadership Communication," *Police Chief* (May 2006): 7; Tracey G. Gove, "Praise and Recognition: The Importance of Social Support in Law Enforcement," *FBI Law Enforcement Bulletin* (October 2005): 14–19; Jeff Green, "The Leadership Paradox," *Police Chief* (March 2006): 13; Wayne McFarlin, "Jump-Starting a Leadership Team," *FBI Law Enforcement Bulletin* (April 2006): 1–9; Thomas Q. Weitzel, "Managing the Problem Employee: A Roadmap for Success," *Police Chief* (November 2004): 25–32; Todd Wuestewald and Brigitte Steinheider, "Shared Leadership: Can Empowerment Work in Police Organizations?" *Police Chief* (January 2006): 48–55; Wuestewald and Steinheider, "The Changing Face of Police Leadership," *Police Chief* (April 2006): 26–32; Wuestewald and Steinheider, "How to Implement Shared Leadership," *Police Chief* (April 2006): 34–37.

7. Robert C. Wadman and William Thomas Allison, *To Protect and to Serve: A History of Police in America* (Upper Saddle River, N.J.: Pearson/Prentice Hall, 2004), pp. 76–77.

8. Samuel Walker, *A Critical History of Police Reform: The Emergence of Professionalization* (Lexington, Mass.: Lexington Books, 1977), p. 67.

9. Wadman and Allison, *To Protect and to Serve,* p. 77.

10. Wuestewald and Steinheider, "Shared Leadership," pp. 48–55.

11. Weitzel, "Managing the Problem Employee," pp. 25–32.

12. Wuestewald and Steinheider, "Shared Leadership," pp. 48–55.

13. Lorie Fridell, "The Results of Three National Surveys on Community Policing," in Fridell, *Community Policing: Past, Present, and Future* (Washington, D.C.: Police Executive Research Forum, 2004).

14. K. Beck, "Optimizing the Organizational Commitment of Police Officers," *National Police Research Unit* (2005).

15. Peter Drucker, *Managing in the Next Society* (New York: St. Martin's, 2002).

16. S. Kim, "Participative Management and Job Satisfaction: Lessons for Management Learning," *Public Administration Review* 62 (2, 2002): 231–241. Shared leadership concepts can be traced back to Elton Mayo's Hawthorne studies of the Western Electric Plant during the 1920s and 1930s in which worker job involvement emerged as an important aspect of job production. They can also be connected with humanist traditions of organizational psychology, including the groundbreaking work of Abraham Maslow. See Henry, *Public Administration and Public Affairs,* p. 64, and Abraham H. Maslow, "A Theory of Human Motivation," *Psychological Review* 50 (July 1943): 370–396.

17. Michael D. Kocolowski, "Shared Leadership: Is It Time for a Change?" *Emerging Leadership Journeys* 3 (1, 2010): 25

18. Wuestewald and Steinheider, "Shared Leadership," pp. 48–55; also see Wuestewald and Steinheider, "Changing Face of Police Leadership," pp. 26–32; Wuestewald and Steinheider, "Shared Leadership," pp. 34–37.

19. Vincent E. Henry, *The CompStat Paradigm: Management Accountability in Policing, Business and the Public Sector* (Flushing, N.Y.: Looseleaf Law, 2002).

20. Gregory P. Rothaus, "6 Strategies for Successful Team-Building Workshops," *Police Chief* (May 2006): 48–52.

21. Viviana Andreesci and Gennaro F. Vito, "Exploratory Study on Ideal Leadership Behavior: The Opinions of American Police Managers," *International Journal of Police Science & Management* 12 (4, Winter 2010), retrieved February 26, 2012, from www.ncjrs.gov/App/AbstractDB/AbstractDBDownload.aspx.

22. Wadman and Allison, *To Protect and to Serve,* p. 64.

23. James F. Richardson, *Urban Police in the United States* (Port Washington, N.Y.: Kennikat Press, 1974), p. 51.

24. Wadman and Allison, *To Protect and to Serve*, p. 64.

25. Raymond B. Fosdick, *American Police Systems* (New York: Century, 1920; reprint Montclair, N.J.: Patterson Smith, 1969), pp. 269–285.

26. Information received June 26, 2006, from Professor Pat Faiella of Massasoit Community College, Massachusetts. Pat is also a part-time police officer with the Hanson Police Department.

27. George W. Griesinger, Jeffrey S. Slovak, and Joseph J. Molkup, *Civil Service Systems: Their Impact on Police Administration* (Washington, D.C.: U.S. Government Printing Office, 1979); Dorothy Guyot, "Blending Granite: Attempts to Change the Rank Structure of American Police Departments," *Journal of Police Science and Administration* 7 (1979): 253–284.

28. Scott Oldham, "Sergeant: Apathy Kills," *Law and Order* (January 2006): 30.

29. Scott Oldham, "Sergeant: Decision Making 101," *Law and Order* (March 2006): 16.

30. Robert Roy Johnson, "Captain: Workplace Dissent," *Law and Order* (April 2006): 16; also see Johnson, "Captain: Humor," *Law and Order* (May 2006): 14.

31. John M. Collins, "Labor Relations: Promulgating a New Rule," *Police Chief*, retrieved June 12, 2006, from www.policechiefmagazine.org.

32. See, for example, Larry Sandler, "More Staff for Police Backed: Consultants Say Hiring Civilians Would Free Sworn Officers for Street Duty, Save Money," *Milwaukee Journal Sentinel*, October 25, 2007.

33. National Institute of Law Enforcement and Criminal Justice, *Employing Civilians for Police Work* (Washington, D.C.: U.S. Government Printing Office, 1975), preface.

34. President's Commission on Law Enforcement and Administration of Justice, *Task Force Report: The Police* (Washington, D.C.: U.S. Government Printing Office, 1967), p. 123.

35. Karey Hedlund and Tod W. Burke, "Reserve Officers: A Valuable Resource," *FBI Law Enforcement Bulletin* (December 2006): 12. For more information on reserve officers, see the web page of the National Reserve Law Officers Association at www.nrlo.net.

36. Randall Aragon, "Does Your Agency Need a Reserve Officer Program?" *Police Chief* (November 1994): 27–29.

37. Karey Hedlund and Tod W. Burke, "Reserve Officers: A Valuable Resource." Also see the National Reserve Law Officers Association, www.nrlo.net.

38. Tim Blakeley, "Overcoming Lateral Transfer Training Issues," *Police Chief* (December 2005): 92–96. Also see Carole Moore, "New Day, New Challenges: Looking for Solutions in All the Right Places," *Law Enforcement Technology* 34 (10, 2007): 12–20.

39. Geoffrey N. Calvert, *Portable Police Pensions Improving Inter-Agency Transfers* (Washington, D.C.: U.S. Government Printing Office, 1971); President's Commission on Law Enforcement and Administration of Justice, *The Challenge of Crime in a Free Society* (Washington, D.C.: U.S. Government Printing Office, 1967), p. 112.

40. Information received June 26, 2006, from Denise Owens, project coordinator for the Roger Williams University Justice System Training and Research Institute, and Sergeant Tom Owens, detective sergeant, South Kingstown, Rhode Island, Police Department.

41. Brian A. Reaves, *Local Police Departments, 2007* (Washington, D.C.: Bureau of Justice Statistics, 2010).

42. J. Zhao and N. Lovrich, "Collective Bargaining and the Police: The Consequences for Supplemental Compensation Policies in Large Agencies," *Policing: An International Journal of Police Strategies and Management* 20 (3, 1997): 508–518.

43. Retrieved March 30, 2014 from www.fop.net/about/history/index.shtml

44. See Anthony V. Bouza, "Police Unions: Paper Tigers or Roaring Lions?" pp. 241–280; James B. Jacobs, "Police Unions: How They Look from the Academic Side," pp. 286–290; Robert B. Kliesmet, "The Chief and the Union: May the Force Be with You," pp. 281–285, all from William A. Geller, ed., *Police Leadership in America* (New York: Praeger, 1985). Also see M. J. Levine, "Historical Overview of Police Unionization in the United States," *Police Journal* (October/December 1988): 334–343; Edward A. Thibault, Lawrence M. Lynch, and R. Bruce McBride, *Proactive Police Management*, 6th ed. (Upper Saddle River, N.J.: Prentice Hall, 2004), p. 425; Wadman and Allison, *To Protect and to Serve*, pp. 85–89.

45. W. J. Bopp, "Year They Cancelled Mardi Gras: The New Orleans Police Strike of 1979," in Charles A. Salerno, *Police at the Bargaining Table* (Springfield, Ill.: Charles C. Thomas, 1981), pp. 201–221.

46. Bopp, "Year They Cancelled Mardi Gras," pp. 201–221.

47. W. Hurd, "In Defense of Public Service: Union Strategy in Transition," *Working USA* 7 (January 2005); David Klingner and J. Nalbandian, *Public Personnel Management: Contexts and Strategies* (Upper Saddle River, N.J.: Prentice Hall, 1988).

48. Ronald G. DeLord, Jerry Sanders, Mark Alley, Jerry Hoover, Harold Hurtt, Philip D. Cameron, Michael D. Edwards, Jerry Dowling, and Larry Hoover, *Police Labor-Management Relations (Volume 1): Perspective and Practical Solutions for Implementing Change, Making Reforms, and Handling Crises for Managers and Union Leaders* (Washington, D.C.: U.S. Department of Justice, Office of Community Oriented Policing Services, 2006).

49. Kimberly D. Hassell, "Variation in Police Patrol Practices: The Precinct as a Sub-Organizational Level of Analysis," *Policing: An International Journal of Police Strategies and Management* 30 (2, 2007): 257–276.

50. Patrick Solar, "The Economics of Patrol Scheduling, Part 1," *Law and Order Magazine* 57 (September 2009): 116–118 and 120–122.

51. Robert Sheehan and Gary W. Cordner, *Introduction to Police Administration*, 2nd ed. (Cincinnati: Anderson, 1989), pp. 113–162.

52. Peter B. Kraska and Victor E. Kappeler, "Militarizing American Police: The Rise and Normalization of Paramilitary Units," *Social Problems* 44 (1, 1997): 1–18.

The Personal Side of Policing

Photo by Scott Whittemore/Wellesley Police

CHAPTER 4
Becoming a Police Officer

CHAPTER 5
The Police Role and Police Discretion

CHAPTER 6
Police Culture, Personality, and Stress

CHAPTER 7
Minorities in Policing

CHAPTER 8
Police Ethics and Police Deviance

Becoming a Police Officer

LEARNING OBJECTIVES

- Explain the arguments for and against requiring higher education for police officers.

- Describe the policing recruitment process, particularly the recent changes and current challenges.

- Discuss why the job analysis is such a vital phase in the police hiring practice.

- Explain the typical selection process most police departments use to identify and select qualified police officers.

- Discuss why field training programs and probationary periods are vital phases in the police training practice.

Scott Olson/Staff/Getty Images

OUTLINE

Finding Information on Jobs in Policing

Standards in Police Selection
Physical Requirements
Smoking
Age Requirements
Education Requirements
Prior Drug Use
Criminal Record Restrictions

The Recruitment Process

The Job Analysis

The Selection Process
Characteristics of Good Police Officers

Written Examination
Physical Agility Test
Polygraph Examination
Oral Interview
Background Investigation
Psychological Appraisal
Medical Examination

The Police Training Process
Recruit Training
The Police Academy
Field Training
Probationary Period
Firearms Training
In-Service, Management, and Specialized Training

INTRODUCTION

Becoming a police officer is very different from obtaining most other jobs. The men and women applying for police jobs in the United States must be carefully screened to determine if they have the necessary attributes for this challenging position. Why? Because we trust these individuals with our liberty and safety.

Many of you reading this textbook are interested in becoming police officers. Some want to become officers because it is a secure job with a good salary and good benefits. Some are attracted to police work because they find the work exciting or because of the opportunity to help others. When police officer candidates are asked why they are seeking a career in law enforcement, they often cite these reasons.

Researchers have found, however, that among the new generation of police recruits, these work values have shifted. Newer candidates value their active participation in the workplace. They are less compelled by loyalty to a company or organization and do not want to be limited to taking orders and adhering to strict job duties. They want work that is meaningful, in which they can actively participate, and in which they feel valued. They want to be actively involved in the decision-making processes at the workplace.[1] They realize that the police role can fill these requirements.

There are also some students who want to go into the criminal justice field for the reasons just discussed but are not sure they want to be sworn police officers carrying guns and making arrests. In recent years, many agencies have increased the use of civilians in their departments. Roles traditionally filled by sworn officers have been turned over to civilians as departments have analyzed these jobs and determined that it is not necessary to have an officer with a badge and a gun performing them. When faced with budgetary challenges and unfilled police officer positions, this civilianization process has allowed departments to put more police officers on the street. Though they vary from department to department depending on size and location, these civilian positions may include crime analysts, community service officers, telecommunicators, crime prevention specialists, evidence technicians, accident investigators, victim liaisons, records clerks and managers, and crime scene technicians.

The Largo, Florida, Police Department took this idea one step further. The department is reaching out to "people with abilities," a term that those with disabilities use to remind others that they possess talents and capabilities to fill many positions. Individuals interested in the criminal justice field but physically unable to perform the job of police officer can be "reasonably accommodated" as defined by the **Americans with Disabilities Act** and serve their communities by filling a role behind the scenes, freeing sworn officers to work on the street. For example, a criminal justice student who was paralyzed in a car accident was hired to work in the planning and research division and thus contributes in a valuable way to the department's mission.[2]

Civilianization of positions within police agencies opens opportunities to individuals wanting to serve their community and be involved in an exciting profession but not necessarily in an enforcement capacity. This movement has been encouraged by the federal Office of Community Oriented Policing Services (COPS) grants that fund increased use of technology and civilians to put more sworn police officers on the street. This trend also allows the department to employ people with abilities as well as older workers and make the workplace more representative of the community. However, because of the sensitive nature of the civilian positions, they are subject to most of the same requirements, standards, and hiring procedures as police officer positions.

This chapter is designed to show how the average person begins a police career. We will discuss the recruitment process, the job analysis, standards (the necessary qualifications to become a police officer), the selection process, the police training process, and the probationary period. The chapter also contains some examples of standards, testing procedures, and requirements for selected police departments.

Today's officer is better educated, better trained, and more representative of the entire community. Educational levels have risen; training programs, both preservice and in-service, have improved; and department personnel are more diverse than ever before.

Americans with Disabilities Act Signed into law in 1990, the world's first comprehensive civil rights law for people with disabilities. The act prohibits discrimination against people with disabilities in employment, public services, public accommodations, and telecommunications.

Finding Information on Jobs in Policing

Where do you find information about available jobs in policing or criminal justice in general? All government entities have human resource or personnel departments with job postings for both police officer and civilian positions. You can also usually obtain information regarding the next police examination by visiting or calling the local police station or headquarters. Many police departments, in an effort to recruit college-educated men and women, participate in college job fairs, and many high school career days include representatives from local police departments or other criminal justice agencies.

In recent years, the Internet has become a favorite choice among employers to get the message out about their job openings. Searching the Internet for "law enforcement job opportunities" results in numerous websites with links to job listings. Recently, the International Association of Chiefs of Police (IACP) together with the Bureau of Justice Assistance launched the Discoverpolicing.org site. It is the official job board of IACP and provides comprehensive information on law enforcement jobs. Hiring agencies can post openings and candidates can post their résumés. Potential candidates can read profiles of in-service officers from around the country and search for jobs by state.

In addition, most police departments have their own websites with employment information and a wealth of other information provided to the public. These websites can even allow potential officers to get an idea of the department's organizational culture to help determine whether they feel they would fit in. Most departments also provide information about their requirements and the hiring process. Many address frequently asked questions, give advice on training for the physical agility portion of the test, and provide contact information for further clarification.

Recently, some agencies have sought to personalize their websites, allowing candidates to consult with their recruiter via e-mail, phone, or text message. The Internet provides a time-saving and non-threatening way of obtaining information about a law enforcement career. There are also websites for private enterprises that have assumed the testing role for many smaller law enforcement agencies in various regions of the country. They provide current information regarding their process and requirements.

Word-of-mouth advertising by family members and friends is a common way people receive information about jobs in policing and criminal justice. Many police departments view their current officers as effective recruiters with an accurate perception of the job and what it entails. Through their daily interactions with citizens, officers come into contact with individuals who could be good officer candidates. These recruiters can informally provide valuable information to interested individuals and encourage them to consider a law enforcement career. With the increased competition among departments in the last few years for qualified candidates, some departments are providing financial incentives, such as

YOU ARE THERE

Indiana State Police Qualifications

Basic Eligibility Requirements

1. Must be a U.S. citizen
2. Must be at least 21 and less than 40 years of age when appointed as a police employee
3. Must have vision correctable to 20/50
4. Must possess a valid driver's license
5. Must have earned a high school diploma or GED
6. Must be willing, if appointed, to reside and serve anywhere within the State of Indiana

Selection Process

1. Submission of completed application form
2. Written exam
3. Physical ability tests
4. Oral interview
5. Polygraph
6. Background investigation
7. Medical and psychological examinations
8. Toxicology screening
9. Superintendent's review
10. Recruit Academy examination

Source: Indiana State Police website, 2014, www.in.gov/isp/28772368.htm.

bonuses or paid time off, to officers who recruit successful candidates.

An added bonus for college students is the intern program that is required by many criminal justice programs. Students work for a local government agency for a semester while earning college credit. These programs are valuable for two reasons: (1) Students see firsthand what working in a particular agency is like and thus are better equipped to make well-informed decisions regarding future career plans; and (2) students may obtain inside information regarding job opportunities that may not be available to the general public.

Standards in Police Selection

Each police department sets standards, or necessary qualifications, that it requires in prospective police officers. In recent decades, these standards have changed to allow a greater number of females and minorities to become police officers, but they are still more stringent than standards in most other professions. The police standards cover physical, age, and education requirements, as well as criminal record restrictions.

Physical Requirements

At one time, the main requirement for becoming a police officer was the size of a young man's body and his physical strength and courage. Over the years, we have come to realize that brains are more important than brawn in police work. Also, the former physical requirements discriminated against women and minorities. Today, physical requirements are still stringent, but departments are under pressure to demonstrate that these requirements are job-related and not arbitrary. With the passage of the Americans with Disabilities Act, departments are required to make "reasonable accommodations" for physically challenged employees. The changing role of police officers coupled with rapid technological advances make it incumbent upon police administrators to examine whether their physical requirements for police candidates are valid in today's environment or whether they actually keep excellent potential candidates out of the process.

HEIGHT AND WEIGHT REQUIREMENTS Height and weight requirements for police department applicants have changed dramatically in recent years. Only a few decades ago, most departments required officers to be at least 5 feet 8 inches tall. This is no longer a requirement; consequently, women and minorities can enter the police ranks more easily.

In 1977, in *Dothard v. Rawlinson,* the Supreme Court threw out a 5-foot 2-inch, 120-pound minimum height and weight hiring qualification for a correctional officer, stating that the employer failed to demonstrate this requirement as necessary for performance of the job.[3] Courts typically do not support minimum height and weight requirements but do support the need for maximum weight standards or a weight-to-height proportion ratio.

VISION REQUIREMENTS Many police departments require an applicant to be free from color blindness and to have very good uncorrected vision that must be correctable to 20/20 vision with eyeglasses or contact lenses. These requirements have created a roadblock for some otherwise qualified candidates. Many police officers wear glasses, and police work does not require perfect uncorrected vision. Still, most agencies require vision that is correctable to 20/20, as illustrated by the Madison, Wisconsin, vision requirement as described on its website: "binocular vision correctable to 20/20; normal peripheral vision and no significant eye disease."

It has long been thought that a police officer should have relatively good vision because of the potential for officers to lose their glasses during an altercation with a suspect or have their glasses get fogged up or spotted with rain. The popularity of contact lenses and the increased utilization and success of vision correction surgery make this less of a concern for applicants today than it was even five years ago.

Smoking

Though over the years many police departments have prohibited smoking in public because of concerns for a professional appearance, health and monetary considerations have now become issues for law enforcement agencies as well. In an effort to respond to rising medical costs for personnel and to keep officers healthy and productive for a longer time, many departments have implemented no-smoking policies. Generally, current officers are grandfathered in, but new hires must sign affidavits stating they have not smoked tobacco for a year and will not smoke tobacco once employed by the agency. This prohibition applies on or off duty, and it is a condition of employment. Some departments are afraid of the civil rights implications in these types of rules but prohibit smoking in police facilities and vehicles in an effort to reduce smoking and to minimize exposure to secondhand smoke for other employees. Some departments have had no-smoking policies in place for more than 10 years, and so far, they have withstood court challenges. Courts have traditionally upheld that public safety employers have a legitimate interest in the health and fitness of their employees.[4]

Age Requirements

Until recently, most police departments required that an officer be between the ages of 21 and 29 at the time of appointment. Anyone over the age of 29 was considered too old to begin employment, though exceptions were sometimes made for those with previous military or police experience. The number of years a candidate served in the military or in previous police employment was added to the maximum age limit. The percentage of departments with maximum age limits has dropped significantly in recent years, largely because of age discrimination issues. Many police departments, however, still do not want to accept candidates past a certain age.

On May 31, 1997, a Manhattan Supreme Court justice upheld the NYPD's policy of limiting new officers to applicants under age 35. The judge said that age limits on public safety jobs are acceptable exceptions to laws against age discrimination. Due to this ruling, 80 applicants were denied appointment, even though they had passed the necessary physical, psychological, and educational tests. An older city law setting a maximum age of 34 for new recruits had expired in 1993 and had not been renewed, but the court argued that police work is stressful and physically demanding and therefore better left to people younger than 35.[5] Despite this court ruling,

most departments do not have an official upper age limit. Their concerns in hiring revolve around pensions and health issues and the related medical costs. Some departments will hire officers retiring after 20 years with another department, and it is not unusual to see officers enjoy two lengthy police careers in two different departments. Actually, many law enforcement agencies have come to value the more mature and experienced candidate. They have had positive experiences with older officers they have hired, leading them to be open to this valuable segment of the workforce. Some departments noticed an increase in older applicants after September 11, 2001, perhaps fueled by a feeling of patriotism. Many older applicants are retired from the military and are particularly well suited to the discipline and demands of a law enforcement career.

Education Requirements

Among local law enforcement agencies in 2007, as reported by the Bureau of Justice Statistics (BJS), 82 percent of local departments required a high school diploma, 6 percent had some type of college requirement (non-degree), 9 percent required a two-year college degree, and only 1 percent required a four-year college degree. However, the same report indicated that the percentage of officers employed by a department with some type of college requirement was 29 percent in 2007—three times as many as in 1990. The minimum high school diploma requirement may not reflect actual selection practices because many departments value education for their officers and favor applicants who meet more than the minimum standards. According to the BJS local police report, 32 percent of departments offer educational incentive pay and 37 percent provide **tuition reimbursement** to their officers.[6]

In reviewing requirements nationally, it appears that most departments with college requirements have major universities nearby, perhaps giving them a larger pool of candidates to draw from as well as providing access to higher education for in-service personnel. As we saw earlier in the text, most federal law enforcement agencies require a four-year college degree for employment. The more sought-after departments, with better pay and benefits, are more likely to require college degrees.

The development of college programs for the police was first stimulated by the recommendations of the National Commission on Law Observance

tuition reimbursement Money a police department will pay officers to reimburse them for tuition expenses while they are employed by the police department and are pursuing a college degree.

and Enforcement (*Wickersham Commission Report*) in 1931, which discussed, among other police problems, the poor state of police training in the United States.[7] The idea of proper training can be traced back to Sir Robert Peel, who advocated good training as a way to decrease crime. However, the real impetus behind the relatively high levels of police education in recent decades was the **Law Enforcement Education Program (LEEP)**, a federal scholarship and loan program operated by the U.S. Department of Justice between 1968 and 1976. LEEP spent more than $200 million in grants and loans to students in "law enforcement–related" college programs. LEEP funds supported more than 500,000 "student years" of college education. About 90 percent of the students in the program were in-service sworn officers.[8]

Considerable debate has arisen over the desirability of college education for police officers. Many experts believe that all police officers should have a college degree. As early as 1967, the President's Commission on Law Enforcement and Administration of Justice recommended, "The ultimate aim of all police departments should be that all personnel with general enforcement powers have baccalaureate degrees."[9] Though more than 40 years have passed, this goal is far from becoming a reality. Despite support from the federal courts, the American Bar Association (ABA), and the Commission on Accreditation for Law Enforcement Agencies (CALEA), this ideal of college-educated police officers has remained elusive.

The belief behind the support for college education is that educated officers will be better equipped to serve in today's dynamic and challenging environment, promote the department's professional image and reputation, and minimize costs and negative publicity resulting from disciplinary issues. These officers also will be comfortable in the community policing atmosphere, which encourages critical-thinking, problem-solving, and communication skills.[10] As police officers confront complex social issues and, in this era of community policing, are expected to be problem solvers rather than reactive agents, higher education is valuable. College-educated officers will be better able to understand and analyze cultural issues and societal problems and communicate about these with the community and government leaders.[11]

Educational opportunities have expanded to be more accessible to pre-service or in-service officers. Online and distance courses have made balancing education with a work schedule, family responsibilities, and access to a physical college less critical. The concern among law enforcement administrators with this increased availability of online education is the potential decline in interpersonal communication skills. Most seem to advocate for a mixture of online education and face-to-face classes to help ensure that officers enhance their communication skills, which are a crucial part of the police role.

As part of the debate against requiring higher education in the police force, a recent concern for law enforcement agencies is the ability to have an adequate applicant pool from which to select their candidates. Administrators believe that the higher the education requirement, the smaller their applicant pool will be. There is also a concern for possibly discriminating against minorities when a higher education requirement is imposed. Department administrators are in a quandary as they strive to have both a large, diverse, and high-quality applicant pool and a highly educated police force. Recently, the St. Louis Police Department conducted their own internal study and found that their less educated police officers were more likely to get into career-ending situations. The department consequently entered into an agreement with three local universities with the goal to do all their recruiting through the universities and to require a two-year degree for applicants. They determined that it cost an average of $400,000 to get an officer to the seventh year of service including salary, training, and benefits. The fact that the department lost one-third of every recruitment class by the seven-year mark added up to a $5 million dollar loss of talent.[12]

Studies to date on higher education in policing have been inconclusive and contradictory. Some studies have found a positive correlation between higher education and job performance and a negative correlation with citizen complaints.[13] Others have found no relationship between education levels and job performance, commendations, or complaints.[14] Recently, a study in Florida examined disciplinary cases decided by the state's Criminal Justice Standards and Training Commission (CJSTC) over

Law Enforcement Education Program (LEEP) A federal scholarship and loan program operated by the DOJ between 1968 and 1976. LEEP put money into developing criminal justice programs in colleges and provided tuition and expenses for in-service police officers to go to college.

a five-year period. The data revealed that the higher the education level of the officer, the lower the level of discipline.[15]

The 1978 report of the National Advisory Commission on Higher Education for Police Officers, often called the *Sherman Report,* stated that some evidence shows that officers with more education become dissatisfied with policing as a career more often than do officers with less education. The report also said that the lack of career opportunities for the educated and ambitious officer is a serious problem in law enforcement agencies, and that new officers with college degrees are often resented by veteran officers with no college experience. The report concluded that evidence indicates that some departments punish officers with more education by denying them career opportunities. The Sherman Report criticized current police higher education programs for "servicing the status quo." It suggested that higher education programs for the police should offer them a "broadening" experience, which would enable them to expand their abilities to deal with their professional problems. The Sherman Report also recommended recruiting college-educated young people, rather than sending recruits to college, and argued that police departments should recruit students from liberal arts programs rather than law enforcement programs.[16]

There is some research to dispute this argument. Though liberal arts programs produce desirable candidates, many officers and departments today also target students from criminal justice programs. In the 30 years since the Sherman Report, college criminal justice programs have abandoned the purely vocational orientation of early programs and now stress critical thinking, ethics, and problem solving as well as providing an overall understanding of the criminal justice system. Though there has not been much research regarding the benefits of a criminal justice degree as compared to a liberal arts degree, police officers from criminal justice programs value their degrees and believe they are beneficial for personal and professional advancement. In a survey administered to law enforcement agencies in Alabama, officers overwhelmingly believed the criminal justice degree made significant contributions to their abilities as a law enforcement officer. Law enforcement managers highly supported the value of the criminal justice degree over other degrees. The managers believed the degree contributed positively to the officers' understanding of the

law and the criminal justice system as well as to their administrative, critical-thinking, and communication skills.[17]

Anecdotally, many students have reported that having majored in criminal justice has made their police academy and recruit training less stressful and the learning curve less steep as they have had more of a foundation on which to build. They believe they are better able to assimilate new information and comprehend the finer points of their occupation.

This issue is unlikely to go away. Overall, society, police administrators, and police officers see the value in having an educated police force. At times, the real-world problems and practical matters of recruitment and selection might interfere with the desired goal of more education. However, the demands placed on officers as our society rapidly changes will necessitate educational requirements being constantly reassessed by departments and state Peace Officer Standards and Training (POST) commissions. More and better incentives and requirements may need to be put in place to speed the realization of the goal for a fully college-educated police force.

Prior Drug Use

Departments have continually faced the problem of a candidate's prior drug use. Should a candidate be disqualified because of prior drug use? Is experimentation with marijuana enough to dismiss a candidate? What about cocaine? How many prior uses of drugs are acceptable?

Recently, many departments around the country have liberalized their policies regarding drug use because of a smaller applicant pool as well as societal changes. According to John Firman, the research director for the International Association of Chiefs of Police (IACP), the most common restriction is 10 years free from using hard drugs and 5 years free from marijuana.[18] A recent study found there is no consensus among departments, but 35 percent of the departments surveyed did not reject outright candidates who had used marijuana. Outright rejection of otherwise suitable candidates for smoking marijuana is felt to be counterproductive to recruiting efforts. Departments may have written guidelines, but the word used most often regarding whether marijuana use will disqualify an applicant is *may*—there is a considerable amount of flexibility in putting the policies in practice. Applicants are usually given an opportunity to explain their drug use; and the circumstances, the number of times, and the age at use are examined by the hiring agency. It remains to be seen how the recent legalization of recreational marijuana in Colorado and Washington will impact this issue in the future.

The FBI essentially followed the same procedure when they relaxed their drug standards in 2007 in an effort to expand their candidate pool. Previously, candidates were automatically eliminated due to a scoring system that was somewhat arbitrary. The FBI believes their new policy "encourages honesty and candor" and allows the agency to look at the whole person and the totality of the circumstances. Local agencies have followed their lead and developed similar guidelines.

Drug restrictions vary widely from agency to agency and will require research by interested applicants for whom this is an issue. A policy or action that is too liberal can raise issues of liability for agencies. Most departments also have random drug testing, and officers can be fired and stripped of their state certificate if found to be using drugs.

Criminal Record Restrictions

People wishing to become police officers must respect and adhere to the rules of society. The lack of a significant criminal record is a requirement for becoming a police officer. However, many police departments recognize that people may make mistakes, especially when young, that might result in an arrest. Police departments also distinguish between arrests and convictions.

A Justice Department survey discovered that 100 percent of all police departments conduct criminal record checks for all applicants and 99 percent conduct background investigations.[19] Most departments will reject a candidate with a felony conviction, but a misdemeanor conviction does not necessarily prohibit a person from employment. As with drug use, the severity and violence of the crime, the circumstances surrounding the crime, the time elapsed since the crime, and the age of the individual when the crime was committed will be examined.

Applicants who have concerns about their criminal records should check the websites of the agencies in which they are interested. Most will post exactly what the disqualifying crimes are. Agencies usually make that information available, as they do not want to waste an applicant's or the agency's time. Remember that in the U.S. criminal justice system, a person is not considered guilty until convicted in court.

Along with the issue of criminal records is undetected criminal activity. This will be explored later in this chapter during the discussions of background investigations, polygraph exams, and interviews.

The Recruitment Process

According to Gary W. Cordner, Kathryn E. Scarborough, and Robert Sheehan, some police departments seem to discourage applicants from applying with their lengthy and challenging hiring process. These authors also point to the low esteem in which police are held in some communities and the fictitious television image of the police as other factors that discourage qualified applicants from applying for police jobs.[20] Some potential candidates may perceive the physical attributes as being beyond their reach, whereas others may have negative images of police. Since September 11, 2001, however, the law enforcement profession has been more favorably viewed; watching the media coverage of the terrorist attacks, many people realized the heroes were simply everyday people with a desire to help and contribute to society who, with dedication and hard work, had attained their goals.

In recent years, the **recruitment process** to attract adequate numbers of qualified police candidates has become increasingly challenging. In its 2004 report *Hiring and Keeping Police Officers*, the National Institute of Justice found that since 2000, more than half of small agencies (in areas with population less than 50,000) and two-thirds of large agencies (population greater than 50,000) reported that a lack of qualified candidates has made it difficult to fill vacancies.[21] Some possible explanations cited by that report as well as by others include the following:

- The economy luring candidates into the private sector
- Increased education requirements

recruitment process The effort to attract the best people to apply for the police position.

- High attrition because of retiring baby boomers
- The deployment of qualified candidates in Iraq and Afghanistan
- The booming homeland security industry after 9/11 luring officers and candidates away from law enforcement

The economy's downturn, which began in 2008, may have actually helped recruitment efforts in some ways, although the resulting budget cuts have contributed to jobs remaining unfilled.[22] As the economy improves and the baby boomers retire, new officers will be in high demand.

Successful police recruiters operate in high schools and colleges, among other places. Recruiters also often attend church gatherings, career exhibitions and trade shows, and athletic events to reach others who may not have considered a law enforcement career. Numerous departments throughout the United States use the local media (especially television and radio) to recruit for their examinations.

Rapid changes in U.S. demographics have made recruiting minorities for police careers more essential than ever before. The U.S. Census Bureau predicts that by 2050, minorities will comprise 54 percent of the general population.[23] The age of the U.S. population is also changing, and the percentage between the ages of 16 and 24 (the ages traditionally recruited from for police jobs) is declining. Therefore, the traditional recruiting pool will continue to shrink.

Despite some of the recent recruiting challenges faced by departments, in the long term, law enforcement is a good career choice for many people. It is an opportunity to serve the public and offers a steady income despite the ups and downs of the economy. Individuals who choose to progress up the ranks will have an opportunity to make a good salary and, ultimately, receive an excellent pension. Those who move into positions of leadership will also have an opportunity to shape law enforcement policies into the future.

Recruiters will have to tap into the desires of "Generation Next" or "Millennials"—the labels

given to the current generation of 18- to 25-year-olds. At first glance, it might seem that this generation, who grew up with interactive technology and spend much of their time on the Internet, sending text messages, and using social networking sites, might be vastly different from previous generations entering the workforce. In fact, they value many of the same things their predecessors did, including family, work, and public service. By tapping into their strengths, which include multitasking, problem solving, and group work, law enforcement can benefit from their technical abilities as well as their ability to think outside the box. Recruiters can take advantage of their desire for public service and meaningful work by making agency and career opportunities less traditional and more in keeping with the changing society, and by promoting career paths, meaningful group projects, social outlets, flexibility, and activities consistent with heroism. Agencies that learn to be flexible will better meet the crime-fighting challenge, and if they are adept at recruiting and retaining this Generation Next, they will thrive.[24]

Recently, agencies have expressed an interest in attracting and building relationships with potential candidates years before the candidates may be eligible to be police officers. With increased "tracking" and selection of "majors" in high schools around the country, some public service advocates believe they need to reach students before some of these decisions have been made. The hope is that by presenting the benefits and rewards of public service, students who otherwise might not consider a law enforcement career might be attracted to the field. Some propose taking these efforts even further. Implementing a school-based public safety curriculum would be helpful to creating a pipeline of students interested in a public safety career and would keep them focused on what will make them successful in the selection process. A public safety curriculum beginning as early as elementary school would lead to increased involvement and interest in policing as a career option, eventually giving employers a bigger pool to recruit from. If nothing else, it would increase knowledge among the general public about criminal justice and the governmental process.[25]

Many departments also are expanding or returning to their explorer and cadet programs in an effort to promote loyalty to their department among talented potential applicants. The **police cadet** position is generally a nonsworn, paid,

police cadet A nonsworn law enforcement position for young adults over 18. Generally, these positions are part-time, paid, education-oriented positions in police departments, and the targeted candidates are college students interested in moving into a law enforcement career.

part-time position for young adults 18 years of age and older who are interested in a law enforcement career. It is considered a learning position for potential police candidates while they are pursuing their education; sometimes the agency provides tuition reimbursement.

Police departments always want to attract the best police officer candidates possible to their departments, meaning they have to compete with the private sector for employees. In recent years, however, law enforcement agencies around the country have also found themselves in the unusual position of having to compete with one another to fill vacancies. This situation has led to departments reexamining their employment requirements as well as employing new and smarter recruitment techniques, including signing bonuses to obtain new recruits and increasing salaries to keep officers and reduce turnover. Although the use of these techniques has diminished during the recent economic downturn, we may see them reemerge as the economy improves. Agencies also are conducting more targeted advertising; making recruiting trips across the country, sometimes to areas with layoffs in other industries; targeting lateral transfers; and emphasizing the benefits and quality of life in their jurisdictions.

Within the membership of the IACP and other police organizations, recruiters are being encouraged to think outside the box in their efforts to reach qualified candidates. This may mean improving benefits and incentives such as salary, signing bonuses, uniform allowances, training dollars, educational incentives, overtime opportunities, take-home vehicles, and so forth. Agencies also are striving to make their hiring process more user-friendly and convenient to the applicant by continually accepting applications, explaining the testing process on the agency website, and offering help throughout various stages of the process.[26] Another approach is to examine why recruits are attracted to law enforcement careers and build on that. The New York State Police (NYSP) found that two issues affect this decision: the ability to help others and the ability to serve the community. The NYSP stresses these elements in their vision and mission statements as well as in their recruitment efforts.[27]

The current recruitment challenge is leading departments to "work smarter" in various ways. One method is civilianization, or the use of civilian personnel to fill nonhazardous positions in an effort to put more sworn officers on the street. Civilianization is increasing the availability of jobs for individuals seeking public service positions in law enforcement, but not as police officers. It also assists departments in increasing staffing in agencies with temporary vacancies caused by police officers being called up for military duty or hiring freezes due to budget issues.

The Job Analysis

Before the selection process for new members can actually begin, a police department must know what type of person it is interested in hiring. To determine this, the department must first perform a **job analysis** to identify the important tasks that must be performed by police officers and then identify the knowledge, skills, and abilities necessary to perform those tasks.

In the past, women and members of minority groups were often rejected from police departments because they did not meet certain standards, such as height, weight, and strength requirements. A good job analysis can avoid that situation by measuring what current police officers in a department actually do. From this study, the department then can establish the standards and qualifications necessary for new officers to perform the needed duties.

If a competent job analysis is performed, the knowledge, skills, and abilities necessary for performance in that department are judged to be **job related**. If a certain qualification is deemed to be job related, that requirement can withstand review by the courts, and the specific test measuring for that knowledge or those skills or abilities is nondiscriminatory.

The case of **Guardians Association of New York City Police Department v. Civil Service Commission of New York** (1980) is a landmark appellate court decision regarding the job analysis.[28]

job analysis Identifies the important skills that must be performed by police officers, and then identifies the knowledge, skills, and abilities necessary to perform those tasks.

job relatedness Concept that job requirements must be necessary for the performance of the job a person is applying for.

Guardians Association of New York City Police Department v. Civil Service Commission of New York A landmark appellate court decision on the issue of job analysis.

In this case, the federal courts accepted the job analysis of the New York City Department of Personnel and the New York City Police Department. Two researchers outlined these departments' procedures in preparing the job analysis, which was considered nondiscriminatory.

First, the Department of Personnel identified 71 tasks that police officers generally perform; the department based the choice of tasks on interviews with 49 officers and 49 supervisors. Second, a panel of seven officers and supervisors reviewed the list of tasks to add any tasks that might have been omitted and to eliminate or combine duplicate tasks and tasks not performed by entry-level officers. This process resulted in a final list of 42 tasks commonly performed by entry-level police officers. Third, a questionnaire was sent to 5,600 officers requesting them to rate each of the 42 tasks on the basis of frequency of occurrence, importance, and the amount of time normally spent on performing the task. The 2,600 responses received were analyzed by computer to yield a ranking of the 42 tasks. The ranking was confirmed by observations made by professors from the John Jay College of Criminal Justice in New York City.

Next, the Department of Personnel divided the list of 42 ranked tasks into clusters of related activities. Each of the clusters was analyzed by a separate panel of police officers to identify the **knowledge, skills, and abilities (KSAs)** for the cluster as a whole.[29] KSAs are standards used by police departments and agencies to complete job analyses: Candidates are not expected to know how to do police work, but they must have the KSAs to learn how to perform the duties of the profession. Examples of KSAs include mental abilities such as reading, writing, reasoning, memorization, and communication, and physical abilities such as agility and endurance. The fact that the New York City job analysis and the entrance examination based on it successfully passed the court's examination of job relatedness shows that a police department must carefully construct its entrance examinations based on the duties actually performed by police officers.

knowledge, skills, and abilities (KSAs) Talents or attributes necessary to do a particular job.

selection process The steps or tests an individual must progress through before being hired as a police officer.

The Selection Process

The police **selection process** is lengthy, difficult, and competitive. It involves a series of examinations, interviews, and investigative steps designed to select the best candidate to appoint to a police department from the many who apply. Practitioners relate that in many agencies only 1 out of 100 applicants makes it into the employment ranks. This process can be intimidating to young applicants. The number of steps and all the rules and expectations can make them apprehensive. Reading texts like this will help to educate and prepare candidates about what to expect.

According to a Bureau of Justice Statistics (BJS) report, municipal police agencies used the following screening procedures:

- Written aptitude test (used by 48 percent of agencies)
- Personal interview (99 percent)
- Physical agility test (60 percent)
- Polygraph exam (26 percent)
- Voice stress analyzer (5 percent)
- Psychological evaluation (72 percent)
- Drug test (83 percent)
- Medical exam (89 percent)
- Background investigation (99 percent)[30]

The report also indicated that the percentage of departments using the various screening techniques has increased since the last survey in 2003 and that the percentage of departments using the screening methods increased significantly as the size of the department increased.

In perusing police department websites, it is clear that the protocol indicated by the BJS report is widespread among all types of law enforcement agencies. Typically a candidate has to pass each step before going on to the next step in the process and must pass all steps to become a police officer. The order of the steps in the selection process varies by department depending on its philosophy and financial and personnel resources. However, it is fairly universal that the written and physical agility tests come at the beginning of the screening process and the psychological and medical evaluations are the last screening procedures after a conditional offer of employment has been made to the applicant.

A crucial element of the police selection process is that each step be defensible in court and have validity to the job performance of a police officer. Under the U.S. Equal Employment Opportunity Commission (EEOC) guidelines, **adverse impact** or a different rate of selection occurs when the selection rate for any gender, race, or ethnic group is less than 80 percent of the selection rate for the group with the highest selection rate. If adverse impact is noted and the test or selection criteria cannot be shown to be valid, the EEOC will classify the test as impermissible discrimination, which could result in legal problems for a police agency.

In addition to sworn or uniformed members of law enforcement agencies, nonsworn or civilian members of many departments—for example, 911 operators, community service officers, crime scene technicians, and so on—often receive preemployment screening similar to that of police officers.

According to its website, the Madison, Wisconsin, Police Department has numerous recruiting and hiring goals. The department seeks men and women who reflect the diversity of their community. They want to recruit applicants who can communicate effectively both verbally and in writing. They also seek individuals who are committed to improving the quality of life and who can enforce the law while protecting the constitutional rights of all. They value the diversity of all academic, work, and life experience. By state law positions are open to individuals over 18, but the department has found that the most successful applicants tend to have an average age of 27 or 28 with previous work experience in various professions.

Applicants to the Madison department fill out an extensive application form; after it is reviewed, they are invited to take a written exam testing reading comprehension, vocabulary, and the ability to organize thoughts and communicate them on paper. After the successful completion of the written test, an internal review panel determines which applicants will proceed. These candidates continue to the physical agility exam, after which the internal panel meets again to determine which applicants will proceed to the oral interview in front of a panel. The remaining steps include a thorough background investigation, an interview with the chief of police, a ride-along with a field training officer, a discussion with one of the department's psychiatrists, a personality assessment, and other interviews with departmental personnel. Eventually, a conditional job offer will be made to the selected candidates, followed by a thorough medical exam conducted at city expense. For out-of-town applicants, Madison tries to condense some of these steps to minimize the cost and time to the applicant.[31]

Characteristics of Good Police Officers

What are the "right" characteristics police administrators should look for when selecting future police officers? Efforts have been made to determine the specific criteria that predict future police performance, but the results have been inconclusive in light of the shifting demands placed on police officers in our rapidly changing society and the changing demographics of the officers themselves.

One of the first issues to be examined has to be "What exactly is a good police officer?" Police supervisors and administrators have confronted this question for years as they struggle with performance evaluations. Is the good officer the one who writes lots of tickets, or is it the officer who gives more warnings than citations and builds community relationships? Should officers be encouraged to make arrests whether or not that will solve the problem, or should they be able to solve the problem regardless of whether arrests are made? Exactly what an agency and community wants its officers to do is the first thing that has to be determined.

The second consideration is the type of individual who could best fill this role. A former Harvard Business School professor, Hrand Saxenian, advocated the theory that the selection process should emphasize the person and select the most mature, intelligent, stable applicant without concern for exactly what the job is. The individual could then be taught the particular tasks needed for the job. Saxenian believed that maturity was the most important criterion and attempted to measure it by looking at the ability of a person to express his or her feelings and convictions while considering the thoughts and feelings of other people. He interviewed police recruits at the start of a police academy term and ranked them for maturity level. At the end of the 12-week term,

adverse impact A form of de facto discrimination resulting from a testing element that discriminates against a particular group, essentially keeping members of that group out of the applicant pool.

the recruits were ranked in performance by the academy staff. The rankings were statistically correlated. Follow-up studies also verified that the more mature recruits were the top performers.[32]

Police administrators seem to agree with the importance of maturity in a police recruit. Many agencies have tended toward hiring the more mature applicants in recent years. With the removal of upper age limits and the desire not to discriminate because of age, many departments have been very pleased with the performance of older recruits who, having more life experience, are able to make well-thought-out decisions when faced with difficult issues on the street.

Other characteristics often mentioned by police administrators include a high ethical standard and integrity, the ability to communicate well with all types of people, and the ability to make good decisions and think on one's feet. Recently, police administrators, especially those involved with community policing, have discussed the importance of **emotional intelligence (EI)** for police officers. Emotional intelligence is the ability to interpret, understand, and manage one's own and others' emotions, which encompasses many competencies that are valued in law enforcement, such as self-awareness, self-control, conflict management, and leadership. These competencies coincide with the desired skills for the community policing environment as well as the emerging problem-based-learning recruit training system, which will be discussed later in the chapter.[33]

It is hard to define and measure—and consequently defend in court—personal characteristics such as judgment and decision-making abilities. To assist in this area and to further embrace the community policing philosophy, some agencies are systematically seeking input from the community about what types of police officers citizens are looking for in their community. This is a radical change in the selection process that, if it continues to spread, could significantly affect the process. It also has the potential to enhance the relationship between the community and the police.[34]

The Department of Justice Office of Community Oriented Policing Services (COPS) published a report in 2006 presenting the findings from the Hiring in the Spirit of Service project. This federally funded project involved the community in the recruiting and hiring of service-oriented law enforcement personnel. Five agencies of various sizes and locations and facing various challenges were chosen to participate: Sacramento, California, Police Department; Burlington, Vermont, Police Department; Hillsborough County, Florida, Sheriff's Office; Detroit, Michigan, Police Department; and King County, Washington, Sheriff's Office. These agencies employed advisory committees to participate in activities and provide feedback regarding the recruiting and hiring process. They also used focus groups to engage community support and vision. The objectives of the Hiring in the Spirit of Service strategy included developing an agency image, revising the screening process, and incorporating hiring practices that coincided with the new trends in police service. Conclusions across all sites were that including the community in the recruitment and hiring process was not easy, nor was identifying service-oriented traits that all stakeholders could agree on.[35]

Written Examination

With large numbers of individuals needing to be screened in this first step of the selection process, written tests are generally used to minimize the time and cost to the agency. These tests are often conducted on a regular basis so there is a list of candidates from which to choose when an opening occurs. The tests may be held at schools, community buildings, and military bases for the applicants' convenience. Sometimes these tests are contracted out to private enterprise, with the cost to be borne by the applicant.

Because large numbers of applicants are screened out at the written examination stage, the exams are often subject to litigation. Until recently, cognitive tests were most commonly used and have been found to be correlated with successful job performance.[36] Today, however, departments that are working to improve testing and find the individual best suited to law enforcement are looking beyond cognitive skills.

A written exam can be fair and unbiased when developed from a job analysis that incorporates the expertise of law enforcement practitioners in an effort to determine the KSAs required for the police position. Fairness is the degree to which all ethnic and gender groups are evaluated consistently.[37]

emotional intelligence (EI) The ability to interpret, understand, and manage one's own and others' emotions, which encompasses the competencies valued in law enforcement such as self-awareness, self-control, conflict management, and leadership.

Many departments use tests specifically developed for the police selection process, and often these are administered through the use of computer simulations. Law enforcement agencies may purchase computer systems, contract with private providers, or turn the testing (or certain aspects of it) over to a private enterprise with the cost to be absorbed by the applicant.

Assessment centers have been found to be excellent tools in predicting job performance,[38] and they ensure that candidates will be fairly and objectively evaluated based on their performance of the tasks needed in their potential position.[39] Unfortunately, assessment centers tend to be costly in human and dollar resources, and although many departments use them for promotional exams, most do not use them for hiring selection.

Many departments have found the testing process to be costly, time-consuming, and legally challenging. They also have found that applicants are willing to absorb the cost of testing, especially when it results in less inconvenience. Consequently, private enterprises have arisen to fill this niche and provide legally defensible consolidated testing for many agencies (typically smaller agencies) within a region. One such company, Public Safety Testing in Washington, provides written and physical agility testing for many agencies in the Pacific Northwest. Its website stresses the convenience for applicants, including convenient testing venues with one application, one written test, and one physical agility test, which will be accepted by more than one agency. The company will then send the applicant's scores to all the agencies the applicant wants to pursue.

Physical Agility Test

Police departments are interested in candidates who are physically fit. During the past 20 years, **physical agility testing** has been criticized for discriminating against some candidates, particularly women and physically small members of certain minority groups. Some argue that the tests relate to aspects of the police job that are rarely performed. Others argue that, although these aspects of the police job are not routinely and frequently performed, they are critically important. Not possessing the strength, endurance, or flexibility needed for the job could result in injury or death to the officer or a citizen. It also may increase the likelihood of an officer having to resort to deadly force.

YOU ARE THERE Sample Agility Tests

Arlington, Texas, Police Department

1. Rapid-acceleration agility course (includes hurdles, walls, and actions simulating low hedges, fences, storm drains, bridges, and running through crowds)
2. Trigger squeeze
3. Dummy drag
4. Ladder climb with shotgun
5. Endurance run

Arlington also provides tips and guidelines on its website about preparing for the test.

Fairfax County, Virginia, Police Department

1. Weapon manipulation (trigger pull and slide manipulation)
2. Obstacle course simulating chasing, apprehending, and handcuffing a suspect
3. Obstacle course simulating exiting a vehicle and responding to rescue an occupant of a vehicle
4. Leg endurance test
5. Arm strength test

Sources: Arlington, Texas, Police Department, www .arlingtonpd.org/; Fairfax County, Virginia, Police Department, www.fairfaxcounty.gov/police/jobs/police -officer.htm.

Sometimes candidates do not adequately prepare for the exam and assume they can pass it. Other candidates simply have a problem with a particular area of the physical agility test. Rather than lose an otherwise quality candidate, departments often provide training or guidance before the agility test.

Law enforcement agencies need to first answer the question of how fit officers must be and then prove job relatedness to the standards, or the courts will find against them. One study, conducted over 15 years and collecting data from 34 physical fitness standards validation studies performed on

---

physical agility testing A test of physical fitness to determine if a candidate has the needed strength and endurance to perform the job of police officer.

more than 5,500 officers from federal, state, and local law enforcement, enables law enforcement to document that fitness areas underlie specific task performance. Using several police officer job scenarios, the authors were able to tie in the need for aerobic power (1.5-mile run), anaerobic power (300-meter run), upper-body absolute strength (bench press), upper-body muscular endurance (push-ups), abdominal muscular endurance (sit-ups), explosive leg power (vertical jump), and agility (agility run) to the police job.[40]

A related issue that is often raised by officers, applicants, unions, and scholars is maintaining fitness once someone is employed as a police officer. How can an agency justify having rigorous agility tests for hiring if nothing is done to follow through on this stated job qualification once the officer is hired? Traditionally, police officers have had no standards to adhere to once they were hired. With the inherent physical demands that can be placed on an officer in a moment's notice, this is a recipe for disaster. This situation is slowly changing, but it is a complicated issue involving standards, discipline, incentives, compensation for time, and liability regarding injuries.

Most officers keep themselves in top shape, motivated by personal pride as well as a desire to be healthy, minimize their chance for injury, and better serve the community. This effort is facilitated by departments providing on-site workout facilities or contracts with fitness facilities, on-duty time to work out, and various incentives for maintaining certain levels of fitness. Some employ fitness coordinators to guide employees in their efforts.

In most cases, civilian or nonsworn personnel are not required to take a physical agility test.

Polygraph Examination

The **polygraph**, often called a lie detector, is a mechanical device designed to ascertain whether a person is telling the truth. It was first used by the Berkeley, California, Police Department in 1921. The polygraph records any changes in such body measurements as pulse, blood pressure, breathing rate, and galvanic skin response. The effectiveness of the polygraph is based on the belief that a

person is under stress when telling a lie. Therefore, if a person lies, the machine will record that stress in the body measurements. The polygraph's accuracy depends on the subject, the equipment, and the operator's training and experience. In some cases, the polygraph may fail to detect lies because the subject is on drugs or is a psychopathic personality. In the past, the polygraph was used extensively within private industry for screening job applicants and preventing employee theft.

The use of the polygraph was severely limited by the Employee Polygraph Protection Act (EPPA), signed into law in June 1988. The EPPA prohibits random polygraph testing by private-sector employers and the use of the polygraph for preemployment screening. However, the law exempts the U.S. government and any state or local government from its provisions and restrictions. Although the results of polygraph tests are not admissible in court because of doubts about their reliability, they are still used in the police selection process. Many experts believe there is value in the polygraph because people believe it works and therefore make admissions during testing.[41]

Some departments have switched from the polygraph to the voice stress analyzer because they find it to be easier to administer and less intrusive to the candidate. It operates under a similar theory that stress will be registered in an individual's voice. According to the BJS 2010 report on local police departments, 26 percent of all local police departments use the polygraph in the screening process, and 5 percent use the voice stress analyzer.

Oral Interview

Oral boards can be used to examine a candidate's characteristics that might be otherwise difficult to assess, including poise, presence, and communication skills. The oral interview in the police selection process can be conducted by a board of ranking officers, a psychologist, the police chief, or an investigator. There often are multiple oral boards or interviews conducted by numerous representatives of the department. Stakeholders in the process may include representatives of other city, county, or state departments, such as personnel or community development, that may also actively participate on the board. As mentioned earlier, members of the community also may serve on the oral board when the department is engaged

---

polygraph Also called a lie detector; a mechanical device designed to ascertain whether a person is telling the truth.

The Oral Interview

When students ask me about interviews, I give them advice similar to what Professor Dempsey provides in the "On the Job" box in this chapter entitled "Some Advice to Police Candidates." I will add a couple of examples gathered over my many years of participating in oral boards and conducting background investigations.

The number-one piece of advice is don't lie—that includes exaggerating facts and omitting information. You will be found out. Investigating is law enforcement's strong point. I was constantly amazed by applicants who would lie in interviews or in their background information, sometimes about trivial things that would not have affected their chances and sometimes about big things that were very easy to verify. Once a candidate lies, he or she is out of the game. No second chances.

As Professor Dempsey recommends, dress appropriately. I remember participating on oral boards as a lieutenant with a well-dressed male captain who frequently was heard to exclaim to candidates, "Look how I'm dressed, and I have a job!" The common (and in my experience, accurate) perception among law enforcement executives is that the candidate's demeanor, appearance, and attitude are likely to be the best they will ever be during the hiring process. If they are not top-notch at that time, the future is bleak. How will the applicant dress for future court appearances?

Showing respect for the position of the interviewers is an excellent idea. I have been called both "sir" and "ma'am." In the case of the former, the applicant either had a vision problem, was extremely nervous, or, in the worst-case scenario, was a sexist trying to make a point. Personally, I have never liked to be referred to as "ma'am" because it makes me feel old, and I have heard other female executives make similar comments. I believe if it is at all possible, the preferred method of address is making note of the interviewer's rank or title and using that. It shows respect for the time and effort required to attain the rank and shows a basic understanding of police organizations and the rank structure.

I also recommend you prepare for the interview. Know the organization. Research the jurisdiction and the agency on the Internet. Be aware of the vision of the agency as well as specific goals and initiatives in which the department is involved. This preparation will allow you to ask good questions of the interviewers (most oral boards allow questions at the end of the interview), illustrate your understanding of the agency and its challenges and philosophies, and allow you to show your initiative. The board will view this positively.

Lastly, be yourself. Trying to project an image or persona that you think the board members want to see, but that is not you, will result in a less than positive interview process. It is better to let your true personality come through, and thereby determine whether or not it is a good fit with the agency.

—Linda Forst

in the process of Hiring in the Spirit of Service or the community policing philosophy. The goal is to solicit input from many stakeholders in the organization and to minimize the chance of a personality conflict that might result in an applicant being kept out of the selection pool.

The oral interview may merely discuss the candidate's application and background or may be used to test the candidate's ability to deal with stressful situations. Agencies have always valued this step in the process, as it is extremely important that officers be able to communicate well with people in their community. The oral interview has become even more critical than in the past, since younger applicants are now showing an increased dependence on texting and social media to communicate and seem to have less experience in face-to-face communication than their predecessors.

Through hypotheticals presented during the oral interview, board members can observe the candidate's decision-making process and watch the candidate prioritize and defend his or her choices. The hypotheticals are scenarios an officer could actually face on the street. The candidate's demeanor while under pressure can be assessed.

The oral board is a more structured and court-defensible process than an unstructured one-on-one oral interview. Generally, the oral board will consist of three to six members who develop specific, standardized questions. All candidates are asked the same questions and rated on their responses.

Background Investigation

In an effective **background investigation**, a candidate's past life, past employment, school records, medical records, relationships with neighbors and others, and military record are placed under a microscope. The investigator looks for evidence of incidents that might point to unfavorable traits or habits that could affect the individual's ability to be a good police officer. Such factors include poor work habits, dishonesty, use of alcohol or drugs, or a tendency to violence. Thorough background investigations by a hiring agency are critical to avoid hiring the wrong person for the job.

During the background investigation, the investigator looks for both officially documented incidents and unreported or undetected questionable activity and deception. Though the process may vary between agencies, a good investigation will include the following:

1. *Background interview.* The investigator advises the applicant about the process and meets the candidate for an initial impression.

2. *Background investigation form.* The applicant is given a detailed form to fill out regarding his or her entire life, including residences, schools, jobs, driving, military experience, and criminal activity—detected and undetected.

3. *Release of information form (waiver).* This form is signed by the applicant and notarized, allowing the individual to share information with the investigator.

4. *Photos and fingerprints.* These are used for identification purposes and criminal records checks.

5. *Educational records.* These records are used to verify completion and degree and to determine attendance and disciplinary issues.

6. *Employment records.* These are used to verify or examine jobs, titles, absenteeism, job performance, honesty, initiative, and work relationships.

7. *Credit check.* This check verifies past behavior of fulfilling obligations as well as determining the risk of being susceptible to graft. The credit check is also helpful for investigating the possibility of addictions.

8. *Criminal history.* Every law enforcement agency that has jurisdiction over areas in which the candidate lived, went to school, or worked is contacted.

9. *Driving record.* The applicant's record of accidents and traffic infractions is reviewed.

10. *Military history.* This is used to determine any discipline issues while in the military, as well as the type of discharge.

Although it can be costly, the investigator will usually travel to the applicant's previous areas of residence for the background investigation, since conducting interviews in person results in obtaining more detailed and honest information than that which can be obtained by telephone or in writing.

Psychological Appraisal

The preemployment psychological evaluation is an invaluable tool in the selection process and aids in assessing an individual's current level of functioning as a potential police officer. The psychological appraisal can assist in identifying individuals who may not adjust well to the law enforcement profession. This evaluation is typically done after a conditional offer of employment and examines many factors, including personality disorders that might affect an individual's functioning in a law enforcement agency and/or interacting with the public. This evaluation also considers issues such as substance abuse, self-management skills (anger management, team functioning abilities, impact of prior experiences and traumas), and intellectual abilities.[42]

Over the years, the trend has moved away from using general psychologists and psychiatrists and toward using those in the field who specialize in

---

background investigation The complete and thorough investigation of an applicant's past life, including education, employment, military, driving, and criminal history, as well as relationships and character. It includes verification of all statements made by the applicant on the background form and the evaluation of both detected and undetected behavior to determine whether the candidate is the type of person suited to a career in law enforcement.

law enforcement hiring and fitness-for-duty exams. Because of their expertise and open communication with the agencies hiring them, these specialists understand the unique requirements of law enforcement personnel and the major issues involved in fitness for duty as well as the constraints of conforming to the requirements of the Americans with Disabilities Act (ADA).[43] These psychologists will typically make one of three recommendations to a law enforcement agency regarding an applicant—"recommended," "recommended with reservations," or "not recommended"—or rate the applicant from A to E, with A being the best recommendation. The agency will then choose whether to follow this recommendation. There could be legal problems in the future if an agency hires an individual against the psychologist's recommendation and that officer becomes involved in a questionable situation.

Medical Examination

Police departments generally want candidates who are in excellent health, without medical problems that could affect their ability to perform the police job. There are long-range and short-range reasons for using medical examinations in the police selection process. The short-range purpose is to ensure that candidates can do the police job. The long-range purpose is to ensure that candidates are not prone to injuries that may lead to early retirement and an economic loss to the department. Individuals who are unfit tend to have less energy and might not be able to work the sometimes-demanding hours

and assignments required of the police job. Drug testing is also part of the medical exam because departments want to ensure the candidates are drug-free.

The ADA, signed into law in 1990, extended the basic protection of the Rehabilitation Act of 1973 to government and private industry. This law took effect in 1992 and mandated that discrimination on the basis of disability is prohibited by all governmental entities and all but the smallest private employers. The ADA prohibits discrimination against disabled persons who can perform the essential functions of the job despite their disabilities. If a police agency rejects a disabled person for employment, it must show that the disabled person cannot adequately perform the job. The law provides an affirmative duty for employers to reasonably accommodate qualified disabled persons unless doing so would create an undue hardship. Areas covered by the ADA include physical agility tests, psychological tests, and drug testing.[44]

The Police Training Process

Once an individual has been chosen to be a member of a police department, he or she begins months of intensive training. Recruit training and in-service training programs vary from department to department, and, in reality, police training never ends. Veteran police officers continue their education and training in many areas to keep up with the latest trends in fighting crime as well as changing laws and procedures. Police officers also receive training in preparation for serving in specialized units or managerial positions.

Recruit Training

Recruit training is the initial training a police officer receives. It teaches officers state laws and educates them in the goals, objectives, and procedures of their state and later their individual department. It provides them with the knowledge, skills, and abilities to do the job. Recruit training starts with the police academy, moves on to field training, and ends with the completion of the probationary period.

The Police Academy

The recruit **police academy** provides most of the average police officer's formal career training. It is often the beginning of the socialization process for the new officer, which will be discussed in a later chapter.

Most big cities in the United States have their own police academies. Although only 3 percent of departments operate their own academies, approximately 90 percent of the agencies serving populations greater than 250,000 do so.[45] Localities without their own academies often use a nearby state or regional police academy. Many academies are also based at colleges, community colleges, technical schools, or universities.

Academies may be residential in nature, where the students only go home on weekends, or commuter facilities where the students commute on a daily basis from their homes. The instructors may be full-time academy instructors or police officers on loan from their agencies to the academy for a predetermined amount of time. There is debate about which type of academy, residential or commuter, is the better option for new officers. The residential academy is generally more militaristic in nature and often has more physical and discipline emphasis. Some recruits may view this as more stressful, and it often places more of

a hardship on the recruit's family. The commuter program is more "college-like" and not as stressful on the recruits and their families. The officer generally does not devote any evenings or weekends to the program.

Currently there are approximately 650 police academies nationwide, divided between state, regional, or county-run academies and academies administered in colleges, universities, and technical schools. Forty-five percent are operated by academic institutions, approximately 22 percent by cities or municipalities, 9 percent by sheriffs' offices, 7 percent by state police, and 4 percent by State Peace Officer Standards and Training (POST) commissions. The remainder are hosted by county police, multiagency, or by other arrangements.[46] Academies have come to rely on some external funding to make ends meet; in 2006, 52 percent of academies received at least part of their funding from student tuition, and about a third charged student fees for use of certain facilities or equipment.

In the last decade, another option has grown more popular. Some states (more than 35 offer some variation of this) are allowing aspiring police officers to complete their physical and classroom training in an academy the candidates pay for, and then take those credentials with them to the selection process. There is debate about whether this is a good option. Some agencies view it as a way to keep their costs down (academy costs as well as the salary of an officer for the many months in the academy) and expedite filling a vacancy. The newly hired officer is ready to go on the street much sooner.[47] Considerations that need to be examined, however, are whether the background investigations conducted to get into the academy conform to what the agencies are doing, as well as the cost of the academy and its possible effect on the diversity of the candidates who are able to afford that type of program while not working for several months. Some programs address this latter concern by offering a part-time program.

During the last four decades, there has been a dramatic increase in the quality and quantity of police training, and departments are paying more attention to curriculum, training methods, and the development of training facilities. Perhaps the improvement in police training can be traced to the 1967 recommendation by the President's Commission on Law Enforcement and

police academy The initial formal training that a new police officer receives to learn police procedures, state laws, and objectives of law enforcement. The academy gives police officers the KSAs to accomplish the police job.

Field Training

Field training is on-the-job training for recently graduated recruits from the police academy. The training is provided by specially selected patrol officers and is designed to supplement the theory taught at the police academy with the reality of the street. The length of field training can vary greatly among departments. The average number of hours of field training is 309 hours, with the smallest departments averaging 153 hours. The departments with the largest number of hours are those serving populations of 500,000 to a million, which average 720 hours of field training.[50]

Michael Nagle/Redux

Education and training for police officers do not end after the academy. New officers rely on more experienced officers during the field training process and for mentoring once they are on their own on the streets.

The San Jose, California, Police Department created a field training program as early as 1972. The San Jose program consists of two phases of training: 16 weeks of regular police academy classroom training and 14 weeks of field training. During the field training phase, a recruit is assigned to three different **field training officers (FTOs)**. Recruits receive daily evaluation reports by their FTOs and weekly evaluation reports by the FTO supervisor. Many departments around the country use the San Jose program or a variation of it.

However, in 1996, at a conference on field training held in Boulder, Colorado, the issue of reexamining the San Jose program was raised because trainers felt it had not kept up with changing times. Police chiefs were looking for ways to implement community policing into their agencies and saw the field training program as a logical place to start. After a study funded by the COPS office and conducted by the Police Executive Research Forum (PERF) and the Reno Police Department, the Police Training Officer (PTO) program, also known as the "Reno model," was born.

The objectives of the PTO program are to provide learning opportunities for the officer that meet or exceed the needs of both the police agency and the

Administration of Justice that police departments provide "an absolute minimum of 400 hours of classroom work spread over a four- to six-month period so that it can be combined with carefully selected and supervised field training." The commission also recommended in-service training at least once a year, along with incentives for officers to continue their education.[48] The number of hours devoted to recruit training since then has increased dramatically.

In 2006, new police officers in cities across the nation averaged 761 hours of academy training. In general, the larger police departments and county agencies had the most academy hours. Most states have mandated a minimum number of hours for their academies, but most academies exceed this number in an effort to provide the most comprehensive training possible to their new officers.[49]

The basic law enforcement academy in the state of Washington is representative of what is being offered around the country. Recruits are provided with 720 hours of instruction, including criminal law and procedures, traffic enforcement, cultural awareness, communication skills, emergency vehicle operator's course, firearms, crisis intervention, patrol procedures, criminal investigation, and defensive tactics.

field training   An on-the-job training program that occurs after the police academy under the direction of an FTO.

field training officers (FTOs)   An experienced officer who mentors and trains a new police officer.

GUEST LECTURE

MICHELLE BENNETT

Michelle Bennett has worked for the King County Sheriff's Office since 1990, and she is currently the Chief of Police for the City of Maple Valley Police Department. Michelle has a bachelor's degree in law and justice, a master's degree in psychology/organizational development and behavior, and a doctorate in education. She is a graduate of Northwestern University School of Police Staff and Command and of the FBI National Academy.

In her career as a law enforcement officer, Michelle has been a school resource officer, field-training officer, master police officer, Washington State Criminal Justice Training Academy tactical officer and instructor, field training sergeant, bicycle sergeant, street crimes sergeant, school resource officer sergeant/coordinator, community police sergeant/coordinator, and Youth Explorer sergeant, administrative captain, and operations captain.

Michelle has taught criminal justice classes since 1998 in colleges including Shoreline Community College, Highline Community College, and Central Washington University. She also teaches part time for the School of Police Staff and Command for Northwestern University.

THE LEARNING PROCESS CONTINUES

March 25, 1991, was my first day on patrol, and as a brand-new deputy, I was really excited. I'd spent three months in the basic academy, then a month in a post-academy class learning about our department, and finally a week sitting on my hands riding with a seasoned veteran officer and observing what I could. Now, after months of training, I was ready to get into a patrol car and inflict my newfound knowledge of the law on unsuspecting citizens. Little did I know I would be the one learning most of the lessons that day.

I walked into the precinct roll-call room and was greeted by my first field training officer, another female deputy. "Hi, I'm Diana," she said, and suddenly paused. "How old are you, anyway?"

"Twenty-one," I replied excitedly.

She groaned, "Great," and then said, "C'mon, let's go. It's getting busy out there."

I got into the passenger seat of her patrol car. As a first-month deputy, I was told I was not allowed to drive yet. We were immediately dispatched to help an apparently disoriented senior citizen who was wandering around a residential neighborhood. We arrived, and Diana explained that I was to handle this; she would jump in if I needed any help. I put on my best professional face and proceeded to try out my best problem-solving skills as I began to ask this elderly gentleman a series of questions in order to determine where he lived. He ignored me and continued rambling on, not listening to a word I said. He finally turned to look me in the eye. Raising a craggy, wrinkled finger, he pointed to my face and said, "I think you're a little too young to be troubleshooting, missy!" Diana began laughing behind me as my façade of composure faded. Diana

finished the questioning and was able to locate the man's family.

Okay, so it was my first call. Overall, it could have been worse. I could not help my youth; I would just show them all that it was not the age, but the seasoning that mattered. Our second call was an area check for criminal activity in a local park. We walked through a construction site to get into the park and were greeted by the construction workers, "Hey, Cagney, Lacey, come arrest me!" "No, come arrest me, will you hand-cuff me?" "No, come over here and search me!" I was embarrassed and shocked that any person would address a police officer in such a way. We arrived on the scene to find nothing but were greeted on our way back out by another construction worker. "Would you like to share my cupcakes with me, cup-cake?" he said as he pulled some Hostess cupcakes out of his lunch box. Diana ignored him and continued walking. "No, thank you," I said politely and ran to catch up with my trainer. "You had better get used to this," she said. "It will get worse."

Next, we took a tour of the precinct area. We drove down the main highway, a street laced with seedy motels, strip bars, and taverns. We came upon a group of juveniles jaywalking across the highway. They turned away quickly when they saw us. "Let's go talk to them," Diana said. "You start, and I'll jump in if you need help." No problem, I thought—after two years of college and four months of training, I can handle a group of misguided kids. I began speaking to the youth I felt was the ringleader. He largely ignored what I was saying and began mouthing off to me in an apparent attempt to impress his peers. "Don't you be flippant with me, young man," I said, pointing my finger in his face. Diana interrupted me at that point and finished the questioning, satisfied that we could find nothing on them. When we got back into the car, she turned to me with an incredulous look and said, "'Don't be flippant with me, young man?' Look, I don't even know what 'flippant' means. How in the hell is that kid going to know what it means? You've really got to dumb down, or this isn't going to work! I need a break. Let's get lunch."

As we drove to the nearest cozy diner, I sat immersed in thought about my first day. It was nothing like I thought it was going to be. Respect had to be earned. I had no idea how to talk to people. All of my logical, pragmatic thought processes and problem-solving abilities seemed lost upon the public. To make matters worse, my new bulletproof vest was so tight and uncomfortable that it was hard to breathe. I voiced this last concern to Diana. "Well," she said, "you need to get one with boobs built into it." After some clarification, I realized that I had received a male-fitted vest from our property management unit; the female vests actually had a curved chest, allowing the female wearer to breathe. "I'll take care of this first thing tomorrow," I thought to myself.

We sat down to eat, and I noticed that it seemed as though everyone in the restaurant was staring at us. Then people started coming up to us, asking questions while we were trying to enjoy the meal. "This is why I usually get food to go and sit behind a building somewhere," Diana said. I thought about that for a minute.... Wow, here we were public servants, and yet we needed to hide from the people we were supposed to be serving? It would take me years to understand that concept.

Our next call was a three-car accident blocking the roadway. Upon our arrival, I learned the importance of multitasking at a scene. Who needs aid? Who will block the roadway? Who will call the tow trucks? When do we get the driver's information, and how do we write the report? As all of these things were running through my mind, things got even worse when I realized the driver who caused the accident was intoxicated. I performed field sobriety tests and decided to take the driver into custody. I told her she was under arrest. I soon realized it was a big mistake not to handcuff her first (and was duly chastised later). Suddenly, the fight was on. I could not believe someone would actually fight with a police officer. Weren't we there to protect the public? Were we not there to help and

serve? Did we not command the respect of all those we dealt with? After all, we had guns!

As the woman and I struggled, I utilized my newly learned defensive tactics and techniques to put the woman into custody. Diana yelled for me to call for backup, and I did as I was instructed. A few days later I was given a private speech from a male officer warning me about how it sounds when female officers call for backup. He told me to not do it too often, as the men will think I can't handle myself (another lesson it took me years to unlearn). However, before backup arrived, Diana and I were able to subdue the extremely drunk and agitated woman. The woman hurled every nasty name in the book at me, another huge shock. "Get used to it," Diana said. "Drunk women always want to fight female officers." Over the course of my career, I realized how true her statement was. In my years of police work, approximately 85 percent of my physical confrontations have been with women, and approximately 84 percent of those women were under the influence of an intoxicating substance.

We drove back to the precinct and finished the case report and booking information on our arrested female. It was then I learned another important fact about police work. For every two minutes of excitement on the job, there are at least two hours of paperwork. We spent the rest of our shift completing all of the paperwork from our DUI accident, and I ended up staying late trying to get things done. "I'm going home," Diana said. "See you tomorrow, and we'll start all over again."

I could barely sleep that night, just thinking about the day's events. I wrote everything down in a journal just to get my thoughts out on paper. I was excited about the job, but it was so different from what my perceptions had been. It was so real and exciting, yet at times so tedious, difficult, embarrassing, and dangerous. To me, as a woman, it seemed like there was a whole set of unwritten rules and lessons that I had yet to learn. I have learned and will continue to discover many of those lessons for years to come. I started my first day thinking about all the things I had to teach people and all the knowledge I could impart about the law. In the end, I discovered that little of the job had to do with the law; most of it had to do with people, emotion, respect, and wisdom. The learning process continues....

Source: Reprinted by permission of Michelle Bennett.

GUEST LECTURE

Courtesy of Sue Rahr

BY SUE RAHR, KING COUNTY SHERIFF (RET.)

Sue Rahr joined the King County Sheriff's Office as a deputy in 1979 and for 25 years worked her way up through the ranks until she was elected sheriff in 2005. She served as sheriff for 7 years, responsible for over 1,000 employees, a $150 million budget, and contract police services to 12 cities and transit policing for the Seattle/Puget Sound region.

In April 2012, the day after she retired as sheriff, she was appointed executive director of the Washington State Criminal Justice Training Commission and is now responsible for training all city and county law enforcement and corrections officers in the state. She graduated Cum Laude with a BA in Criminal Justice from Washington State University and is a graduate of the National Sheriff's Institute and the FBI National Executive Institute. She also served as the president of the Washington Association of Sheriffs and Police Chiefs.

FROM WARRIORS TO GUARDIANS

Should we train cops using a military boot camp model like we do soldiers? On the surface it makes sense. Both wear uniforms and carry guns. Both need to be proficient in the use of weapons and physical control tactics. Both have dangerous jobs, and both have to be prepared for attack by human predators.

It's when you look below the surface, at their fundamental missions, that the two are not so similar. Soldiers conquer; police protect. Soldiers deploy in groups and follow the orders of a leader. In policing, deployment is usually done with a single officer and there is rarely a supervisor on scene to give orders. In war, the rules of engagement are known before going into battle. In policing, the rules of engagement evolve as the incident unfolds, and it's up to the judgment of the individual officer to make that call.

Both the police and military have used a boot camp model for basic training. The main purpose of this model is to instill unquestioning obedience to orders and automatic submission to authority. I don't know about you, but during my three decades in law enforcement I can't think of many situations where I had to unquestioningly follow orders from a supervisor about how to handle a call. Usually the first officer on scene at a patrol call decides how to handle it. There are rarely orders to follow. In reality police officers most often operate in the field as independent thinking leaders. Why do we train them using a model designed to create obedient followers?

But don't cops have to follow rules and policies? Of course they do! But they have to figure out how to *apply* the rules and policies to the infinite number of variables at each individual call.

When I was hired to be the executive director of the Washington State Criminal Justice Training Commission last year, I accepted the responsibility to train the next generation of cops. I have taken that responsibility very seriously and feel personally responsible for preparing them to do their jobs effectively and to go home alive at

community. The program, which was designed so that it can be modified to fit individual organizations, uses an adult-learning and problem-based-learning model that teaches transferable skills to the recruit. It is designed to produce graduates capable of providing customer-centered, responsible, community-focused police services. The PTO programs stress community involvement in all training activities. The evaluations are primarily narrative and are worked on by teams during the 15-week program. Outcomes are developed around four modes of policing—emergency response, nonemergency response, patrol activities, and criminal investigations—and officers are instructed and evaluated in these areas.

This "Reno model" is seen as an important innovation in police training and has the support of the National Association of Field Training Officers (NAFTO), which also continues to support the San Jose model. The Reno model is intended to be used as a variation of the San Jose model or in addition to it. The Reno model would not benefit all departments, and the San Jose model is still an important one in the field training process.[51] The PTO program, however, is growing in popularity, as police the end of their shifts. It is with this motivation that I started to question how we train recruits.

I believe if we expect our new recruits to be critical thinkers who can make quick life-and-death decisions, we need to have higher expectations and demand they demonstrate sound judgment. We need to do training that is more in line with military *leadership* than boot camp. We're not making the academy easier; we're actually making it harder.

We're not backing off from the physical standards either. Rather, we're focusing more training time on practicing tactical skills than general physical fitness. We only have 720 hours to teach our recruits to be safe. We can't afford to use limited training hours on general fitness. That's something recruits should do on their own time.

There is also a nonscientific but deeply felt reason that I personally support moving away from the boot camp model—many police recruits are former members of the military. These are the courageous warriors that fought our wars and made great personal sacrifices for our country. Frankly, it just isn't right for our trainers to treat them like beginners. We've had recruits who are graduates of West Point, who have been combat pilots, and who were members of Special Forces. It's embarrassing for civilian trainers to employ pseudo military tactics on these former soldiers who have already paid their dues on the battlefield.

This common sense training approach aligns with our overarching shift in philosophy best described as moving from a culture of warriors to guardians. It's important that I clarify what is meant by the term *guardian*. A guardian is not a customer service rep or a kinder, gentler version of warrior. The role of a guardian is much more complex, requiring a higher level of maturity and greater skill. A guardian has to be just as tough and fight just as fiercely as a warrior when necessary, but has to do it with skill, within the law, and under relentless scrutiny. The "warrior spirit" is one facet of the guardian's role, but it is not the primary identity.

The idea of cops as guardians is not new. We've all known good cops who kept these competing roles in balance. It only makes sense to teach that balance in basic training. We do our recruits no favor if we train them to approach every situation as a war. To do so sets them up to create unnecessary resistance and risk of injury. Teaching them the appropriate balance improves their safety.

We're not making the academy kinder and gentler. We're not trying to placate politicians or the public. We're making the training more germane to the reality of police work. Our recruits should be prepared to go out in the field with greater confidence and stronger critical-thinking skills so they will go home alive at the end of their shift. I know I'm challenging deeply held beliefs and traditions, and I expect some will disagree with me. That's okay. Cultural change doesn't happen overnight, and I don't mind debating the finer points of how we should train the next generation of cops.

chiefs believe its emphasis on problem solving, self-directed learning, and lifelong learning will better prepare officers to adjust to the changing needs and demands of law enforcement in the future.[52]

Probationary Period

A **probationary period** is the period of time following recruit training that a department has to evaluate a new officer's ability to perform his or her job effectively. Generally, a probationary officer can be dismissed at will without proof of specific violations of law or department regulations. Once officers are off probation, civil service rules often make it very difficult to dismiss them. Probationary periods can last anywhere from six months to three years. Today, the average probationary period ranges from 12 to 18 months. It has lengthened in recent years because of the increased time devoted to academy training

probationary period The period in the early part of an officer's career in which the officer can be dismissed if not performing to the department's standards.

AP Images/Steve Perez

Police recruits practice their defensive moves as part of academy training.

officer to interact verbally in the scenario, and the situation can be altered accordingly. The simulations can use local schools, businesses, and streets in the scenarios; allow for more than one officer to participate; and even shoot rubber bullets back at the officers. They provide enlightening and realistic training for officers new to the position as well as for those who have been working the street for some time.

Departments nationwide are reviewing actual shooting incidents and, in an attempt to increase officer safety and minimize litigation, are attempting to make their training as realistic as possible and incorporate stressors that occur in street situations. Administrators have realized that shootings rarely occur with warnings in sterile and controlled situations involving stationary targets, so inclement weather, realistic dress, flashing lights, blaring sirens, multiple individuals or targets, and other distractions involved in the scenarios have been included. Administrators have found that training in this manner, together with stressing the decision to shoot or not shoot, is better equipping officers when they confront situations on the street.

and field training. Agencies want to have enough time to evaluate officers' performance while they are performing on the street on their own.

Firearms Training

In the 1960s, most police firearms training in the United States consisted of firing at bull's-eye targets. Later, training became more sophisticated, using more realistic silhouette targets shaped like armed adversaries. The FBI's Practical Pistol Course began to modernize firearms training; the course required qualification from different distances and different positions, such as standing, kneeling, and prone positions. As firearms training progressed, "shoot/don't shoot" training was introduced using **Hogan's Alley** courses. Targets depicting "good guys" and "bad guys" would pop up, requiring officers to make split-second decisions.

Today, many agencies have replaced Hogan's Alley programs with computer-controlled visual simulations.[53] These simulations allow the officer to shoot at a target, and a laser indicates where the shot went. Some of these computer simulations allow the

In-Service, Management, and Specialized Training

Police training generally does not end at the recruit level. In many departments, **in-service training** is used to regularly update the skills and knowledge base of veteran officers. Because laws and developments in policing are constantly changing, officers need to be kept up to date. Many states have chosen to mandate a required number of in-service training hours for officers to maintain their state certification. Primarily, this has been done as a way to ensure that departments are keeping their officers updated on the latest laws and procedures and ensure some degree of uniformity among jurisdictions. The average annual number of hours required for in-service officers was 35 hours in 2007, with cities with populations between 50,000 and 100,000 requiring 42 hours a year.[54] Some popular topics for in-service

Hogan's Alley A shooting course in which simulated "good guys" and "bad guys" pop up, requiring police officers to make split-second decisions.

in-service training Training that occurs during a police officer's career, usually on a regular basis and usually within the department; often required by department policy or state mandate.

training around the country include ethics, use of force, cultural awareness, stress, domestic violence, workplace harassment, critical incidents, hate crimes, victim assistance, hostage situations, pursuits, interviews and interrogations, fraud, identity theft, and computer crime.

In addition to in-service training, many departments use management training programs to teach supervisory and management skills to newly promoted supervisors and managers. Some of them send supervisors and managers to regional or state sites for this training. There are several well-known law enforcement leadership and administrative officers' courses around the country that departments may use to improve the managerial skills of their mid- and upper-level managers. These include the FBI Academy in Quantico, Virginia; the Southern Police Institute at the University of Louisville, Kentucky; the Center for Public Safety at Northwestern University in Evanston, Illinois; the Senior Management Institute for Police in Boston; the Law Enforcement Leadership Institute at the Federal Law Enforcement Training Center in Glynco, Georgia; and the Institute for Law Enforcement Administration in Plano, Texas. Typically, administrators attend these schools for anywhere from 8 to 13 weeks and are paid a salary while they attend. The managers obtain the latest information concerning law enforcement practices and network with other managers from around the country. This is a valuable source of information and subsequent resources for mid- and upper-level managers who often spend their entire careers in one department.

Many departments also offer specialized training programs for officers assigned to new duties. Training units may be anything from 10-minute training segments to use during or after roll call or several hours for a more in-depth discussion of a topic. These may be conducted on-site or at other locations. Recently, many of these training opportunities have been offered online. While the digital training format can help expand access to information, it needs to be thoughtfully accomplished. There is an increasing variety of formats, including iTunes U and other educational platforms, which enhance availability for the officer and effectiveness for the topic. The attraction for agencies is that the training can be worked in around an officer's schedule, and transportation costs as well as time away from duty are minimized or eliminated when the training is done at the station instead of having to drive to a training facility. This also minimizes the cost of overtime for officers working the night shift if they can fit training in around their work, rather than having to go during the day and get overtime or filling in their work shift at night with an officer on overtime. In addition, this training can increase consistency of training across the particular state or region.

Opportunities for specialized training are often located at and facilitated by the state or regional training academy. In Florida, community colleges are the site of these regional training opportunities. They routinely host in-service training for officers who need to learn new skills to specialize in new assignments. These include drug investigations, traffic homicide investigations, radar, surveillance, investigation, DARE, school resource officer, firearms instructor, crowd control, instructor certification, crime scene investigation, child abuse, sex crimes, robbery investigations, interview and interrogation, and other classes that police chiefs request.

SUMMARY

- Many jobs are available in policing at the federal, state, and local levels, including a growing number of civilian positions.

- The most convenient way to find out about law enforcement jobs, department standards, and the testing process is through law enforcement websites.

- The standards for recruiting and hiring police officers have changed in recent years to facilitate the inclusion of more females, minorities, and older candidates.

- The percentage of departments with maximum age limits has declined, and police departments are finding older, more mature candidates to be excellent police officers.

- In an effort to have the largest possible applicant pool, many departments are not requiring a college degree; however, education is valued, encouraged, and often required for promotion.

- A job analysis is conducted by the law enforcement agency to determine the knowledge, skills, and abilities (KSAs) needed for the job, and these are incorporated into the selection process.

- The selection process is lengthy and usually includes a written exam, physical agility test, polygraph, oral board, background investigation, psychological evaluation, and a medical evaluation.

- In the past, physical agility tests were often found to keep minorities or women out of law enforcement, and consequently departments have worked hard to make the tests more job related and less discriminatory.

- The background investigation that candidates go through is extensive in an effort to screen out candidates with undetected criminal behavior, deception, or unfavorable traits or habits that might affect their ability to be good police officers.

- Recruit training consists of training in a police academy followed by field training.

- Recruits will then complete a probationary period usually lasting from 12 to 18 months.

- Police training will continue throughout an officer's career and may include mandatory in-service training, specialty training, and supervisory and management training.

KEY TERMS

adverse impact

Americans with Disabilities Act

background investigation

emotional intelligence (EI)

field training

field training officer (FTO)

Guardians Association of New York City Police Department v. Civil Service Commission of New York

Hogan's Alley

in-service training

job analysis

job relatedness

knowledge, skills, and abilities (KSAs)

Law Enforcement Education Program (LEEP)

physical agility test

police academy

police cadet

polygraph

probationary period

recruitment process

selection process

tuition reimbursement

REVIEW EXERCISES

1. Prepare a cover letter and résumé for a law enforcement agency. Research the department through its website and look at résumé websites for help with your format if you have never done a résumé before.

2. Your chief has asked you to develop an in-service training plan for the department for the next year. What classes/topics would you include, how many hours would they be, and would they be mandatory or voluntary? Explain your rationale for all of these decisions.

3. Develop a fitness test for police officer candidates. What activities would you include and why? Would all applicants have the same expected standards or would you follow a philosophy that has standards that vary by gender or age, with the goal being that the individual be more fit than most of his or her peers?

WEB EXERCISES

1. Visit the websites of three different law enforcement agencies, preferably from different states. Do the requirements to be a police officer vary? What are the steps in the hiring processes? Is there variation among the three departments regarding what the steps are or where they occur in the process?

2. Visit the website for PublicSafetyTesting.com in Washington. Examine their site and the services they offer. Do you think this concept is a good one for the officer or the agency or both? Why or why not?

3. Examine the website for the Cooper Institute in Dallas, Texas. What kind of fitness programs do they offer? What do you think of their philosophy and their programs?

END NOTES

1. Troy Mineard, "Recruiting and Retaining Gen-X Officers," *Law and Order* 51 (2003): 94–95.

2. Jim Weiss and Mickey Davis, "People with Abilities: The Untapped Resource," *Law and Order* (September 2003): 70–73.

3. John C. Klotter, Jaqueline R. Kanovitz, and Michael I. Kanovitz, *Constitutional Law*, 9th ed. (Cincinnati: Anderson, 2002).

4. Ibid.

5. Mike Pearl, "'Age' Ruling Backs Cops in Battle of Blue & Grey," *New York Post*, May 31, 1997, p. 12; "Age Before Duty? Police Brass Alter Ground Rules, Leaving Some Over-35 NYPD Rookies Standing at the Altar," *Law Enforcement News*, April 1997, p. 5.

6. Brian A. Reeves, *Local Police Departments, 2007* (Washington, D.C.: Bureau of Justice Statistics, 2010), NCJ#231174.

7. National Commission on Law Observance and Enforcement, *Lawlessness in Law Enforcement* (Washington, D.C.: U.S. Government Printing Office, 1931).

8. James B. Jacobs and Samuel B. Magdovitz, "At LEEPs End: A Review of the Law Enforcement Education Program," *Journal of Police Science and Administration* 5 (1977): 1–17.

9. President's Commission on Law Enforcement and Administration of Justice, *The Challenge of Crime in a Free Society* (Washington, D.C.: U.S. Government Printing Office, 1967), p. 110.

10. Louis Mayo, "Support for College Degree Requirements: The Big Picture," *Police Chief* 8 (2006), retrieved February 1, 2008, from www.theiacp.org.

11. M. Napier, "The Need for High Education," *Law and Order* (September 2005): 86–94.

12. Christine Byers, "St. Louis Police Increasing Education Requirements for Recruits," *St. Louis Post-Dispatch*, September 20, 2012.

13. J. D. Dailey, "An Investigation of Police Officers' Background and Performance: An Analytical Study of the Effect of Age, Time in Service, Prior Military Service, and Educational Level in Commendations," Ph.D. dissertation, Sam Houston State University, 2002; V. E. Kappeler, A.D. Sapp, and D. L. Carter, "Police Officer Higher Education, Citizen Complaints and Department Rule Violations," *American Journal of Police* 11 (1992): 37–54; B. J. Palombo, *Academic Professionalism in Law Enforcement* (New York: Garland, 1995); S. M. Smith and M. G. Aamodt, "The Relationship between Education, Experience, and Police Performance," *Journal of Police and Criminal Psychology* 12 (1997): 7–14.

14. C. R. Baratta, "The Relationship between Education and Police Work Performance," master's thesis, East Tennessee State University, 1998; S. E. Buttolph, "Effect of College Education on Police Behavior: Analysis of Complaints and Commendations," master's thesis, East Tennessee State University, 1999; D. S. Peterson, "The Relationship between Educational Attainment and Police Performance," Ph.D. dissertation, Illinois State University, 2001.

15. Scott Cunningham, "The Florida Research," *Police Chief* 9 (2006), retrieved February 1, 2008, from www.theiacp.org.

16. Lawrence W. Sherman and the National Advisory Commission on Higher Education for Police Officers, *The Quality of Police Education* (San Francisco: Jossey-Bass, 1978), pp. 185–188.

17. Philip Carlan, "Do Officers Value Their Degree?" *Law and Order* 12 (2006): 59–62.

18. Kevin Krause, "Police Agencies Mellow on Applicant's Drug Use," *South Florida Sun-Sentinel*, December 11, 2002.

19. Reaves, *Local Police Departments*, 2010.

20. Gary W. Cordner, Kathryn E. Scarborough, and Robert Sheehan, *Police Administration*, 6th ed. (Cincinnati: Anderson, 2007), p. 156.

21. C. S. Koper, *Hiring and Keeping Police Officers* (Washington, D.C.: National Institute of Justice, 2004), NCJ#202289.

22. John Pomfret, "Police Finding It Hard to Fill Jobs," *Washington Post*, March 27, 2006.

23. U.S. Census Bureau Public Information Office, retrieved November 18, 2011, from www.census.gov.

24. Bob Harrison, "Gamers, Milliennials, and Generation Next: Implications for Policing," *Police Chief* 10 (2007), retrieved February 1, 2008, from www.theiacp.org.

25. Paul Cappitelli and Greg Kyritsis, "Establishing a Career Pipeline in Public Schools," *Police Chief* (November 2011), pp. 24–27.

26. B. Taylor, B. Kubu, L. Fridell, C. Rees, T. Jordan, and J. Cheney, *Cop Crunch: Identifying Strategies for Dealing with the Recruiting and Hiring Crisis in Law Enforcement* (Washington, D.C.: U.S. Department of Justice, National Institute of Justice, 2005), NCJ#213800.

27. "Hiring Problem? What Hiring Problem? NYSP Has Answers to Recruiting Slump," *Law Enforcement News*, November 30, 2000, p. 1.

28. *Guardians Association of NYC Police Department v. Civil Service Commission of New York*, 23 FEP 909 (1980).

29. D. Thompson and T. Thompson, "Court Standards for Job Analysis in Test Validation," *Personnel Psychology* 35 (1982): 865–874.

30. Reaves, *Local Police Departments*, 2010.

31. City of Madison, Wisconsin, Police recruiting website, retrieved January 13, 2014, from www.cityofmadison.com/police/jointheteam/applicant/cfm.

32. Cordner, Scarborough, and Sheehan, *Police Administration*, p. 158.

33. Gregory Saville, "Emotional Intelligence in Policing," *Police Chief* 11 (2006), retrieved January 31, 2008, from www.theiacp.org.

34. Cordner, Scarborough, and Sheehan, *Police Administration*, p. 159.

35. E. Scrivner, *Innovations in Police Recruitment and Hiring: Hiring in the Spirit of Service* (Washington, D.C.: Department of Justice, 2006), NCJ#212984.

36. K. Dayan, R. Kastan, and S. Fac, "Entry-Level Police Candidate Assessment Center: An Efficient Tool or a Hammer to Kill a Fly?" *Personnel Psychology* 4 (2002): 827–849.

37. C. Legel, "Evaluating an Entry-Level Exam," *Law and Order* (December 2005): 66–69.

38. M. Bromley, "Evaluating the Use of the Assessment Center Process for Entry-Level Police Officer Selection in a Medium Sized Police Agency," *Journal of Police and Criminal Psychology* 4 (1996): 33–40; Dayan et al., "Entry-Level Police Candidate Assessment Center"; C. Hale, "Candidate Evaluation and Scoring," *Law and Order* (December 2005): 66–69.

39. Hale, "Candidate Evaluation and Scoring."

40. Thomas R. Collingwood, Robert Hoffman, and Jay Smith, "Underlying Physical Fitness Factors for Performing Police Officer Physical Tasks," *Police Chief* (March 2004): 32–37.

41. Dan Eggen and Shankar Vendantam, "Polygraph Results Often in Question," *Washington Post*, May 1, 2006.

42. Arnold Holzman and Mark Kirschner, "Pre-Employment Psychological Evaluations," *Law and Order* (September 2003): 85–87.

43. IACP Police Psychological Services Section, "Guidelines for Police Psychological Service," *Police Chief* 9 (2005).

44. The Americans with Disabilities Act (ADA), available at www.eeoc.gov/ada.

45. Matthew J. Hickman and Brian A. Reaves, *Local Police Departments 2003* (Washington, D.C.: Bureau of Justice Statistics, 2006), NCJ#210118.

46. Brian A. Reaves, *State and Local Law Enforcement Training Academies, 2006* (Washington, D.C.: Department of Justice, February 2009 and updated April 2009), NCJ#222987.

47. Jennifer Nislow, "Who Wins with 'Pay as You Go' Pre-Academy Training Programs?" *Law Enforcement News*, Fall 2004, pp. 1, 10.

48. President's Commission on Law Enforcement and Administration of Justice, *The Challenge of Crime*, pp. 112–113.

49. Reaves, *State and Local Law Enforcement Training Academies*, 2009.

50. Ibid.

51. Jerry Hoover, "The Reno Model Police Training Officer (PTO) Program," *NAFTO News*, December 2004, pp. 10–17.

52. Steve Pitts, Ronald Glensor, and Kenneth Peak, "The Police Training Officer Program: A Contemporary Approach to Postacademy Recruit Training," *Police Chief* 8 (2007), retrieved January 31, 2008, from www.theiacp.org.

53. Reaves, *Local Police Departments*, 2010.

54. Ibid.

The Police Role and Police Discretion

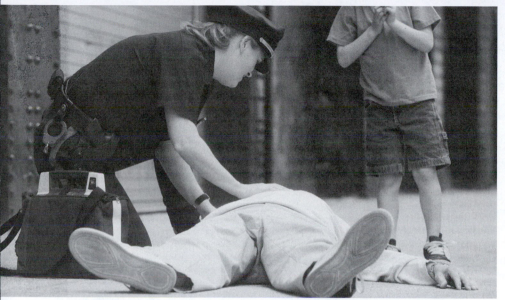

Huntstock/Getty Images

OUTLINE

The Police Role
Crime-Fighting Role
Order-Maintenance Role

Ambiguity of the Police Role
The Police Role in the Aftermath of 9/11

Goals and Objectives of Policing
Primary Goals and Objectives
Secondary Goals and Objectives

Police Operational Styles

Police Discretion
What Is Discretion?
How Is Discretion Exercised?
Why Is Discretion Exercised?

What Factors Influence Discretion?
How Can Discretion Be Controlled?
CALEA Standards

Police Shootings and the Use of Deadly Force
Police Use of Force
Number of Citizens Shot by the Police
Do Police Discriminate with Their Trigger Fingers?
Departure from the "Fleeing Felon" Rule
Firearms Training
Less-than-Lethal Force

LEARNING OBJECTIVES

- Discuss the ambiguity of the police role, including the distinctions between crime fighting and order maintenance.

- List the different definitions of police operational styles and how they address the major goals and objectives of policing.

- Explain police discretion and the importance of knowing factors that affect it.

- Identify the historical changes and current practices in police use of force.

- Discuss how discrimination can be seen to influence police discretion and use of force.

INTRODUCTION

The role of the police and the exercise of police discretion are among the most important issues in policing. Who are the police? What do they do? How do they do what they do? What should they do instead?

This chapter will look at the role of the police in society, including the crime-fighting role, the order-maintenance role, the ambiguity of the police role, and the effects of the September 11, 2001, terrorist attacks on the United States. It will discuss the goals and objectives of the police, as well as various police operational styles discovered by researchers who study the police. The chapter will also examine police discretion—what discretion is, how and why discretion is exercised, what factors influence discretion, and how discretion can be controlled by police administrators. Finally, it will discuss the concept of discretion and police use of force, including police shootings and deadly force.

The Police Role

What is the **police role**? This is a very difficult question to answer. The scholar Herman Goldstein warns, "Anyone attempting to construct a workable definition of the police role will typically come away with old images shattered and a newfound appreciation for the intricacies of police work."[1]

Two major views of the role of the police exist:

- The police are crime fighters concerned with law enforcement (**crime fighting**).
- The police are order maintainers concerned with keeping the peace and providing social services to the community (**order maintenance**).

Though officers do not spend the majority of their time as crime fighters, it is an important role for them. Procedures and safety are important considerations even when officers have backup.

Aristide Economopoulos/Star Ledger/Corbis News/Corbis

Crime-Fighting Role

Movies and television shows about the police emphasize the police crime-fighting role. If we believe these stories, the police engage in daily gunfights, car chases, and acts of violence, and they arrest numerous people every day. Fictional books about police work also emphasize the crime-fighting role. Even the news media emphasize this role; television news shows and newspaper headlines dramatize exciting arrests and action by the police.

The police themselves also emphasize the crime-fighting aspects of their jobs. As a former professor turned police officer, George L. Kirkham, states,

> The police have historically overemphasized their role as crime fighters and played down their more common work as keepers of the peace and providers of social services, simply because our society proffers rewards for the former (crime fighting) but cares little for the latter (peace-keeping and providing services). The public

---

police role The concept of "what do the police do."

crime fighting A major view of the role of the police that emphasizes crime fighting or law enforcement.

order maintenance A major view of the role of the police that emphasizes keeping the peace and providing social services.

accords considerable recognition and esteem to the patrol officer who becomes involved in a shoot-out with an armed robber or who chases and apprehends a rapist, and therefore so do the officer's peers and superiors.[2]

At first glance, there appears to be some truth to the belief that police are primarily crime fighters. Statistics for the latest reporting year reveal that the U.S. police made about 12.4 million arrests for all criminal infractions, excluding traffic violations. An analysis of the arrests, however, shows that about 534,704 of them were for violent crimes (murder, forcible rape, robbery, and aggravated assault) and about 1.64 million of the arrests were for property crimes (burglary, larceny/theft, motor vehicle theft, and arson). The following accounted for the other arrests:

- Driving under the influence (DUI) or driving while intoxicated (DWI)—about 1.21 million arrests
- Drug abuse violations—about 1.53 million arrests
- Misdemeanor assaults—about 1.24 million arrests
- Liquor law violations, drunkenness, disorderly conduct, vagrancy, and loitering—about 1.27 million arrests
- A large variety of lesser offenses, excluding traffic offenses (see Table 5.1)

From the analyses of the arrests made by police, we can see that the vast majority of the arrests are not serious Index crimes but, rather, what we might call crimes of disorder or actions that annoy citizens and

TABLE 5.1 Arrests in the United States, by Crime Committed, 2011

Total[a]	12,408,899		
Murder and nonnegligent manslaughter	10,832	Weapons: carrying, possessing, and so forth	153,519
Forcible rape	19,491	Prostitution and commercialized vice	57,345
Robbery	106,674	Sex offenses (except forcible rape and prostitution)	69,225
Aggravated assault	397,707		
Burglary	296,707	Drug abuse violations	1,531,251
Larceny-theft	1,264,986	Gambling	8,596
Motor vehicle theft	66,414	Offenses against the family and children	116,723
Arson	11,776		
Violent crime[b]	534,704	Driving under the influence	1,215,077
Property crime[b]	1,639,883	Liquor laws	500,648
Other assaults	1,241,722	Drunkenness	534,218
Forgery and counterfeiting	70,211	Disorderly conduct	582,218
Fraud	168,217	Vagrancy	29,203
Embezzlement	16,190	All other offenses	3,532,195
Stolen property: buying, receiving, possessing	93,234	Suspicion	1,424
		Curfew and loitering law violations	76,942
Vandalism	237,638		

[a] Does not include suspicion.

[b] Violent crimes are offenses of murder and nonnegligent manslaughter, forcible rape, robbery, and aggravated assault. Property crimes are offenses of burglary, larceny-theft, motor vehicle theft, and arson.

Source: Federal Bureau of Investigation, *Uniform Crime Reports, 2010*, retrieved March 5, 2012, from www.fbi.gov.

negatively affect their quality of life (for example, offenses involving drugs and alcohol). Even the vast majority of crime fighting the police do is related to order maintenance rather than serious crime.

Furthermore, the 2011 report *Contacts between Police and the Public, 2008*, revealed that approximately 40 million citizens had contacts with the police during the previous reporting year. Among those who had face-to-face contact in 2008, about one in four had more than one contact during the year. The most common contact was as the driver during a traffic stop (44.1 percent). Only about 1.4 percent of all contacts involved the use of or threat of force by the police.[3]

Order-Maintenance Role

If police are not primarily crime fighters, then what are they? In an effort to determine the proper role of the police, researchers have conducted numerous studies to determine what police do and why people call on their services. As far back as 1965, Elaine Cumming and her colleagues reported that the ordinary work routines of police officers included relatively little law enforcement and comprised a large variety of other activities that came to be known as peacekeeping and order maintenance.[4] Since then researchers have consistently reinforced Cumming's findings.

The police must be able to gain the cooperation of the citizens if they are to maintain order within the community. As Wilson and Kelling's broken windows theory suggests, if an area of the community is allowed to deteriorate without some remedy, crime will increase.[5] Looking through almost any city in the United States, you will find areas of the community that have deteriorated and are suffering from neglect. These areas may be filled with graffiti, broken windows, and neglected buildings; even the local government may not pay as much attention to the needs of the community. This leaves the police in the position of responding to "low-level" calls that are generally regarded more as a social function rather than a crime-fighting function. The broken windows theory is discussed more fully in Chapter 12, "Community Policing."

In a classic study of patrol activities in a city of 400,000, John Webster found that providing social

service functions and performing administrative tasks accounted for 55 percent of police officers' time and 57 percent of their calls. Activities involving crime fighting took up only 17 percent of patrol time and amounted to about 16 percent of the calls to the police.[6] Robert Lilly found that of 18,000 calls to a Kentucky police department made during a four-month period, 60 percent were for information, and 13 percent concerned traffic problems. Less than 3 percent were about violent crime, and approximately 2 percent were about theft.[7]

In the Police Services Study (PSS), a survey of 26,000 calls to police in 24 different police departments in 60 neighborhoods, researchers found that only 19 percent of calls involved the report of a criminal activity.[8] Similar studies were conducted by Michael Brown in California, Albert J. Reiss in Chicago, and Norman Weiner in Kansas City with similar results.[9] Additionally, Stephen Meagher analyzed the job duties of 531 police officers in 249 municipal departments and found that regardless of their size, most police agencies and police officers have similar functions and do pretty much the same thing.[10]

In 2004, David Thacher, assistant professor of Public Policy and Urban Planning at the University of Michigan wrote, "A backlash has set in against order maintenance policing strategies, if not among policymakers and the public, then at least among criminologists."[11] While academics may see a backlash, the general public and police may see order maintenance as embodied in the "broken windows" theory as working to keep their communities safe.

Ambiguity of the Police Role

The police role is extremely diverse, **ambiguous**, and dynamic. Egon Bittner has stated that from its earliest origins, police work has been a "tainted" occupation, meaning "that policemen are viewed as the fire it takes to fight fire, that in the natural course of their duties they inflict harm, albeit deserved, and that their very existence attests that the nobler aspirations of mankind do not contain the means necessary to insure survival."[12]

Carl B. Klockars, in *Idea of Police*, broadly defines the basic function of the police as dealing with all those problems that may require the use of

ambiguous The concept that the police role is very diverse and dynamic.

coercive force. He emphasizes that democratic societies give the police the right to use morally dangerous, dirty, and illegal means to achieve good ends because in most cases, noble institutions do not contain the means to ensure their survival.[13]

We must remember that England's Sir Robert Peel, who arranged for the organization of the first paid, full-time, uniformed police department, conceived of the police role as a conspicuous community-oriented patrol designed more for prevention and deterrence than for enforcement. Peel designed the police to be an alternative to the repression of crime and disorder that could have been achieved through military might and severe legal sanctions (see Chapter 1, "Police History").

The early American settlers brought Peel's ideas on the role of the police with them. As Alan Coffey tells us, however, as the United States began to pass more and more statutory laws, the police role expanded from maintaining order to enforcing the law. Coffey states, "It is this combination of role expectations that generates controversy, particularly with those who emphasize the peacekeeping segment of police work as opposed to actual enforcement."[14]

One way of defining the police role may be to say that it is whatever the community expects the police to be. However, we must remember that most communities consist of many diverse groups with different goals and interests. One group in the community may expect police to do something entirely different from what another group expects. For example, older people in a community or store owners may want the police to hassle teenagers hanging out on the street, yet the teenagers, for their part, may feel that if the police do hassle them, the officers are abusing them. Parents in a community may want the police to search and arrest drug dealers and drug users, yet not want the police to search their own children. In these and many other ways, the police are often in a no-win situation.

George Pugh, writing on the expansive and varied role of the police, states that a good police officer must have the qualities of common sense and mature judgment, and must react quickly and effectively to problem situations. A good police officer, Pugh says, must be able to adopt the appropriate role of policing to the situation he or she encounters. Common roles include law enforcer, maintainer of social order, and public servant.

Finally, a good police officer must have the appropriate concepts of policing that guide and prioritize the role the officer should employ in particular situations. The concepts governing police work, Pugh says, are (1) an effort to improve the welfare of the community and (2) a respect for the individual's rights, worth, and dignity.[15]

Robert Sheehan and Gary W. Cordner, using the work of previous scholars, offer the following synopsis of the police role:

1. The core of the police role involves law enforcement and the use of coercive force.

2. The primary skill of policing involves effectively handling problem situations while avoiding the use of force.

3. Skillful police officers avoid the use of force primarily through effective, creative communication.[16]

In summing up the police role, we might agree with Joseph J. Senna and Larry J. Siegel. They say that the police role has become that of a social handywoman or handyman called to handle social problems that citizens wish would simply go away.[17]

The Police Role in the Aftermath of 9/11

The ambiguous role of the police was further complicated by the September 11, 2001, terrorist attacks against the United States. Since 9/11, many have seen the police as the frontline of homeland defense against further terrorist attacks, and many police departments and officers are viewing themselves similarly. Police departments have responded to this by forming specialized, military-like antiterrorist units that appear in public as a strong deterrent force against would-be terrorists. This has concentrated attention on the law enforcement role of the police.

The order maintenance role and social service role of the police have also been reemphasized, as the police are the first responders to all emergencies and unusual occurrences in the nation. They are tasked with the many duties this entails, including crowd control, emergency medical response and treatment, and maintenance of public order in often catastrophic conditions. See Chapter 15, "Homeland Security," which discusses the new duties placed on the police for homeland defense.

GUEST LECTURE

BY BRIAN LEWIS

Detective Brian Lewis joined the Kent Police Department in 2007 after four years in the United States Marine Corps. He began focusing his efforts on domestic sex trafficking and conducted several successful investigations while serving as a patrol officer. In 2010 he was assigned to the special investigations unit and has worked both under-cover and as lead investigator in dozens of complex sex trafficking cases. Detective Lewis is also assigned to the FBI Child Exploitation Task Force and provides training on sex trafficking at the Basic Law Enforcement Academy. Detective Lewis also serves as a team leader on the Valley Swat Team.

TRAFFICKING INVESTIGATIONS CAN INVOLVE EXPANDING POLICE ROLES

The first thing most people think of when they hear about human trafficking is immigrant slaves being smuggled across the ocean in cargo containers. Mention the term *sex trafficking*, and images of Liam Neeson shooting his way through a European city in search of his kidnapped daughter from the Hollywood hit *Taken* play through one's mind. Either way, the threat seems far removed. The trouble is that domestic sex trafficking is a clear and present threat to America's children, and they are being forced into the illegal sex trade in our own backyards.

Unfortunately, pop culture has successfully glamorized the sex trade industry and warped the harsh reality of this life. When I was growing up, Jay-Z rapped "Big Pimpin'," while Nelly spit clever lyrics in his hit "Pimp Juice." These songs played at high school dances with no opposition from school, staff, or parents. Turn on the radio today and you will probably hear Macklemore rapping about having a "ho" snorting coke in the back seat of his Cadillac. This artist has been recognized for his efforts in spreading awareness for human rights, and at the same time, ironically, he is making money off of a song that glorifies the life of a "ho." It's not just hip-hop music, either. I was trick-or-treating with my son last year and a coworker (yes, a cop) was walking around the neighborhood dressed as a

pimp. Hanging on his arm was his wife, dressed as his prostitute.

When I started my career in law enforcement, I was assigned to patrol an area of the city well known for its prostitution activity. Highway 99 ran north to south through my district and on its east border flowed the Green River. Just a few decades prior, Gary Ridgway preyed upon prostitutes, and his first five victims were discovered in this waterway, giving him the name "The Green River Killer."

As I patrolled these streets, I noticed prostitutes walking up and down the "track." "They're just hookers," veteran officers would say. "It's their choice. Prostitution is the oldest profession in history," others proclaimed. After countless contacts and arrests, my conversations with these "hookers" shed light on the truth. One face in particular made it clear to me that this was not a voluntary profession. Her name was Tay, and she was 15 years old.

One evening, I watched Tay walking along the track. With no apparent destination, she wandered until a pickup truck pulled over. She got in and the truck drove away, most likely headed to a hotel or secluded parking lot. I stopped the truck and contacted the driver, a middle-aged blue-collar type. His hands shook nervously, causing his wedding ring to tap the steering wheel. "Just giving my friend a ride," he claimed.

While inside the truck, Tay's eyes were stone cold; it appeared from the outside that street life had erased all evidence of her youth. We got Tay out of the truck and she was of course reluctant to talk to the police. However, by just treating her with dignity and respect—as a human worth more than a $50 car date—she took her mask off and I was able to reach the young girl underneath. We built a rapport, and my partner soon realized she knew this girl from a prior job at a youth correctional facility. Tay began to cry and expressed the need to be rescued from her desperate situation in three words: "I want help."

We could have contacted Tay that day and just arrested her for prostitution. It would have been a quick drive to jail, a two-paragraph report, and something to list on the weekly activity report. The problem is that this method of combating "prostitution" is often counterproductive. Tay's pimp had told her many times that the police were the bad guys and all they wanted to do was put her in jail. Had we done that, he would have been empowered because her trust in him would have grown, while her trust in law enforcement would have diminished.

Instead, we talked to Tay for hours that night. She told us her story and we opened an investigation into a pimp named "Cash" who had been selling teenagers to men for the majority of his adult life. The nearly one-year investigation revealed victims who had been trafficked throughout the past decade. A search warrant at Cash's house revealed sickening, yet phenomenal evidence in his master bedroom. His bed was adorned with Lion King–themed sheets sporadically riddled with his victims' underwear. At the foot of the bed was a chrome stripper pole and above the headboard was an airbrushed mural of a modified $100 bill.

As if this pimp's nickname didn't sum up his mindset, the $100 bill on the wall literally painted the picture of Cash's motivation. Money is one of the primary things that drives a pimp to sell young girls. Pimps also seek prestige, sex, power, and the ability to have complete control over another person.

Cash forced his juvenile victims to prostitute themselves on the streets. When they weren't making him money, they were forced to clean the house, do laundry, and tend to Cash and his friends as they smoked and played video games. The roster on Cash's virtual basketball game was a compilation of his victims' names. These girls were his slaves, and they did everything he told them to do. But why?

Pimps use a variety of control tactics once they have successfully recruited and trained a girl. Some pimps find something in the girl's life she is missing and act as if they can fill that void. Others choose to find something the girl has always wanted and "sell the dream" by promising to provide those wishes. Pimps often use romance as a tactic to gain the trust and loyalty of a girl. Teenage minds are easily manipulated, and girls can easily fall for an older man, especially if he has a car, money, drugs, and a place to stay away from home.

Cash, like many pimps, also used force, fraud, and coercion to get his victims to work as prostitutes and turn their earnings over to them. If a girl is "out of pocket" by disobeying the pimp's rules, they are sometimes beaten, raped, strip searched, threatened, or killed. Pimps also isolate their victims from their comfort zones and families by moving them from city to city on what is known as "the circuit." This way, the girl is unable to establish friends and reach out to family, making her totally reliant on and loyal to her pimp.

Whether you work for one of the large metropolitan cities on "the circuit," or maybe in a rural county between two of these cities, there are certain things you can look for to identify potential victims of sex trafficking. Many victims, like Tay, are runaways, making them desperate and vulnerable to a pimp's manipulation. If you happen to recover a runaway, go beyond the routine: Ask probing questions and look for signs of prostitution and abuse.

Remember, for every face you see looking down at the sidewalk as you drive by in your patrol car, there is a story. These stories often go unheard because the girl has an "attitude," or there isn't enough time, or whatever the excuse may be. That story needs to be heard. Tay's story was heard. My partner and I listened, and her pimp, the slave master who beat, raped, and forced her and over a dozen other teenagers to sell their bodies, is now serving 15 years in federal prison.

Goals and Objectives of Policing

Much study and research has gone into determining the proper goals and objectives of a police department. This topic can be discussed more easily by thinking in terms of primary and secondary goals and objectives.

Primary Goals and Objectives

The two primary goals and objectives of police departments, according to Sheehan and Cordner, are maintaining order and protecting life and property.[18] These are among the most basic roles of government, and the government hires the police to perform these services. As Senna and Siegel say,

> Police are expected to perform many civic duties that in earlier times were the responsibility of every citizen: keeping the peace, performing emergency medical care, and dealing with civil emergencies. Today, we leave those tasks to the police. Although most of us agree that a neighborhood brawl must be broken up, that the homeless family must be found shelter, or the drunk taken safely home, few of us want to jump personally into the fray; we'd rather "call the cops."[19]

Secondary Goals and Objectives

Sheehan and Cordner also list six secondary goals and objectives toward which police resources and activities are used to meet the primary two objectives:

1. Preventing crime
2. Arresting and prosecuting offenders
3. Recovering stolen and missing property
4. Assisting the sick and injured
5. Enforcing noncriminal regulations
6. Delivering services not available elsewhere in the community[20]

omnipresence   The impression of always being there.
police operational styles   Styles adopted by police officers as a way of thinking about the role of the police and law in society.

The police attempt to prevent crime by trying to create a sense of **omnipresence** through routine patrol, responding to calls by citizens to deal with problems that may cause crime, and establishing and participating in police–citizen partnerships designed to prevent crime. Arresting offenders and assisting prosecutors in bringing charges against defendants is one of the main methods used by the police to maintain order and protect life and property.

When people find property on the street, they often bring it to a police officer or to a police station. The police then attempt to find the owner. If that is not possible, they store the property in case the rightful owner comes in to claim it. When people lose valuable property, they generally go to the police station in the hopes that someone has turned it in. Besides all of their other duties, then, the police serve as society's foremost lost-and-found department.

Because they are available 24/7 and are highly mobile, the police generally are the closest government agency for any problem. In many jurisdictions, the police are called to emergency cases of sickness and injury to assess the situation before an ambulance is dispatched, or they are called to assist ambulance, paramedical, or other emergency response personnel.

In the absence of other regulatory personnel or during the times they are not available, the police enforce numerous noncriminal regulations, including parking regulations, liquor law regulations, and many others. The police are generally the only government officials available every day, around the clock. When government offices close, the police become roving representatives of the government who assist people with problems no one else is available to handle. When the lights go off in an apartment building, people call the police. When the water main breaks, people call the police. When your neighbor's dog barks all night and keeps you awake, who do you generally call? The police. Who else can you call at three o'clock in the morning? The police respond and take whatever action they can to ameliorate problems and to deal with emergencies. They direct traffic, evacuate residents, and decide who else to call for assistance.

Police Operational Styles

People who research the police write about **police operational styles**—styles adopted by police officers as a way of thinking about the role of the police and law in society and how the police should perform their jobs. The findings of several leading researchers, including John J. Broderick, James Q. Wilson, William Muir, Ellen Hochstedler, and John Van Maanen, will be discussed here.

The concept of operational styles is useful in analyzing the police role and police behavior (see Table 5.2). However, no officer conforms solely to one of these styles to the exclusion of the others. Many officers show characteristics of several of these styles.

Siegel and Senna tell us that several studies have attempted to define and classify police operational styles into behavioral clusters. These classifications or typologies attempt to categorize officers by groups, each of which has a unique approach to police work. Siegel and Senna report that the purpose of these classifications is to demonstrate that the police are not a cohesive, homogeneous group, but rather individuals with differing approaches to their work.[21] They present four basic styles of policing or typologies. Borrowing from the work of Wilson and Muir, Siegel and Senna define the four basic styles as:

- *Crime fighters* investigate serious crimes and apprehend criminals.
- *Social agents* perform a wide range of activities without regard for their connection to law enforcement.
- *Law enforcers* enforce the law "by the book."
- *Watchmen* maintain public order.[22]

Broderick, in his *Police in a Time of Change*, also presents four distinct police operational styles:

- *Enforcers* maintain order on their beat, keep society safe, and protect society by arresting criminals.
- *Idealists* are similar to enforcers but place a higher value on individual rights and the adherence to due process as required by the U.S. Constitution.
- *Realists* concentrate their efforts on the concept of police loyalty and the mutual support of their fellow officers; they put relatively low emphasis on both social order and individual rights.
- *Optimists* place a relatively high value on individual rights and see their job as people oriented, rather than crime oriented.[23]

TABLE 5.2   The Police Role, Police Operational Styles, Styles of Policing, and Policing Ideals

The Police Role
Crime fighting (law enforcement)
Order maintenance (peacekeeping)

Police Operational Styles
Larry J. Siegel and Joseph J. Senna
Crime fighters
Social agents
Law enforcers
Watchmen
John J. Broderick
Enforcers
Idealists
Realists
Optimists
William K. Muir, Jr.
Professional
Enforcer
Reciprocator
Avoider

Styles of Policing
James Q. Wilson
Watchman style
Legalistic style
Service style

Policing Ideals
Claudia Mendias and E. James Kehoe
Law enforcement
Peace maintenance
Procedural compliance
Protagonist acceptance of responsibility

Sources: Larry J. Siegel and Joseph J. Senna, *Introduction to Criminal Justice*, 10th ed. (Belmont, Calif.: Thomson/Wadsworth, 2005), p. 211. Siegel and Senna cite, in this regard, John J. Broderick, *Police in a Time of Change*, 2nd ed. (Prospect Heights, Ill.: Waveland Press, 1987); Claudia Mendias and E. James Kehoe, "Engagement of Policing Ideals and Their Relationship to the Exercise of Discretionary Powers," *Criminal Justice and Behavior* (February 2006), pp. 70–92; William K. Muir, Jr., *Police: Streetcorner Politicians* (Chicago: University of Chicago Press, 1977); and James Q. Wilson, *Varieties of Police Behavior: The Management of Law and Order in Eight Communities* (Cambridge: Harvard University Press, 1968).

In his seminal work *Varieties of Police Behavior: The Management of Law and Order in Eight Communities*, Wilson described three distinct styles of policing that a police department can deploy in maintaining order and responding to less serious violations of law: the watchman style, the legalistic style, and the service style. (Within each style, the police treat serious felonies similarly.)[24] He found that the political culture of a city, which reflects the socioeconomic characteristics of the city and its organization of government, exerts a major influence on the style of policing exercised by the police.

- *Watchman style.* This style is primarily concerned with order maintenance—maintaining order and controlling illegal and disruptive behavior. Officers in a watchman-style department exercise a great deal of discretion and ignore many minor violations, especially those involving juveniles and traffic. Officers use persuasion and threats, or even "hassle" or "rough up" disruptive people, instead of making formal arrests. This style is generally found in working-class communities with partisan mayor–city council forms of government.

- *Legalistic style.* This style enforces the letter of the law strictly by issuing many citations and making many misdemeanor arrests. Police proceed vigorously against illegal enterprises. This style of enforcement occurs in reform administrations' government styles. Furthermore, this style often occurs in the aftermath of a scandal in a watchman-type department that results in the hiring of a "reform" police chief.

- *Service style.* In this style the emphasis is on serving the needs of the community. The officers see themselves more as helpers than as soldiers in a war against crime. This service style is generally found in more affluent suburban areas.

Muir, in *Police: Streetcorner Philosophers*, observed the behavior of 28 young police officers in an American city during the 1970s to attempt to explain how police adjust to their coercive role in society and how they cope with society's irrationality and violence. Based on his observations, he theorized that a good officer develops two virtues: intellectually grasping the nature of human suffering, and morally resolving the contradiction of achieving just ends with coercive means. He proposed a typology of four general types into which police officers can be grouped: the professional, the enforcer, the reciprocator, and the avoider. These types represented combinations of the officer's view of the nature of mankind and the officer's view of the moral justification of the use or threat of coercion. The typologies were designed to address the need to find police personnel who can perform their duties in a democratic yet efficient manner.[25]

However, Hochstedler, in her doctoral dissertation at the State University of New York at Albany, failed to support Muir's typology, reporting that Muir's dimensions did not predict the types he proposed. She concluded that his typology had not been shown to describe anything beyond mere logical possibilities and could not yet be considered for practical applications. Hochstedler's study included attitudinal and behavioral items of 1,134 police officers. She chose 45 criterion to indicate the officers' job satisfaction, attitudes about the parameters of their task, the role of the officer, and personal conduct.[26]

Claudia Mendias and E. James Kehoe discuss four policing ideals—law enforcement, peace maintenance, procedural compliance, and protagonist acceptance of responsibility. In a 2006 study, they reported that 66 percent of participating police officers from 12 police stations in Sydney, Australia, employed two combinations of policing ideals to justify decisions to arrest: keeping the peace/procedural compliance ideals, and law enforcement/procedural compliance ideals.[27]

Police Discretion

The use of discretion is one of the major challenges facing U.S. police today. The following sections will discuss the meaning of police discretion, how and why it is exercised, what factors influence discretion, and how it can be controlled. The use of discretion by police clearly impacts other crucial areas covered in this textbook, including biased-based policing; police misconduct, brutality, and corruption; and the liability of the police for their conduct. See Chapter 8, "Police Ethics and Police Deviance," for further discussion of these topics.

What Is Discretion?

Discretion means the availability of a choice of options or actions one can take in a situation. We all exercise discretion many times every day in our lives. At a restaurant, we have discretion in selecting a steak dinner or a fish dinner. When we want to watch a movie, we have discretion in picking a mystery or a comedy to view. Discretion involves making a judgment and a decision. It involves selecting one from a group of options.

The criminal justice system involves a tremendous amount of discretion. A judge exercises discretion in sentencing. He or she can sentence a defendant to a prison term or to probation. A judge can release a defendant on bail or order the defendant incarcerated until trial. Prosecutors exercise discretion: They can reduce charges against a defendant or drop the charges entirely. Parole boards exercise discretion: They can parole a person from prison or order him or her to serve the complete sentence. The entire criminal justice system is based on the concept of discretion.

Why is there so much discretion in the U.S. system of criminal justice? In our system, we tend to treat people as individuals. One person who commits a robbery is not the same as another person who commits a robbery. Our system takes into account why the person committed the crime and how he or she committed it. Were there any mitigating or aggravating circumstances? The U.S. system is interested in the spirit of the law as well as the letter of the law.

When a judge, a prosecutor, or a parole board member exercises discretion, they generally have sufficient time and data necessary to make a careful, reasoned decision. The judge can read the presentence report prepared by the probation department or consult with the probation department staff member preparing the report. The judge can also consult with the district attorney or the defense attorney. The prosecutor and parole board member also have sufficient data and time in which to decide what action to take in a case.

However, most crucial decisions made in the criminal justice system are not made through informed and lengthy reasoning. The most important decisions do not take place within an ornately decorated courtroom or a wood-paneled conference room. They take place on the streets, at any time of the day or night, and generally without the opportunity for the decision makers to consult with others or to carefully consider all the facts. These split-second decisions are often based on little information. The police officer is generally the first decision maker in the U.S. criminal justice system and often the most important.

Wilson described the police officer's role in exercising discretion as being "unlike that of any other occupation . . . one in which sub-professionals, working alone, exercise wide discretion in matters of utmost importance (life and death, honor and dishonor) in an environment that is apprehensive and perhaps hostile."[28] Researchers Michael and Don Gottfredson state:

> The police really suffer the worst of all worlds: They must exercise broad discretion behind a facade of performing in ministerial fashion; and they are expected to realize a high level of equality and justice in their discretionary determinations though they have not been provided with the means most commonly relied upon in government to achieve these ends.[29]

Kenneth Culp Davis, an expert on police discretion, says, "The police make policy about what law to enforce, how much to enforce it, against whom, and on what occasions."[30]

Not much happens in the U.S. criminal justice system without the use of discretion by the police. How does a police officer exercise discretion on the street?

Before we look at how discretion is exercised, it is important to understand police-committed and police-uncommitted time. Police are often directed by the 911 dispatcher to crimes, emergencies, and other calls requesting police services. Often supervisors will assign police during particular hours to specific areas to perform duties. These are examples of committed time. However, most of police patrol time is left to the individual officers' discretion; this is uncommitted time.

In his pioneering work, "Police Patrol Work Load Studies: A Review and Critique," Gary W. Cordner stated:

> Patrol officers have the opportunity to determine what their workload will be during the uncommitted portion of their patrol time.

discretion Freedom to act or decide a matter on one's own.

[This proactive] component of patrol work is also largely ambiguous, because the conduct and effect of preventive patrol are not clear, and many of the self-initiated activities undertaken are not strictly crime- or non-crime-related.[31]

In 2005, Christine N. Famega of California State University, San Bernardino, James Frank of the University of Cincinnati, and Lorraine Mazerolle of Griffith University confirmed Cordner's early work. They found that more than three-quarters of a patrol officer's shift is unassigned. Their study concerned three districts of the Baltimore Police Department. During this time, officers primarily self-initiated routine patrol, or backed up officers on calls to which they were not dispatched.[32] In another 2005 report, Famega wrote that a literature review of 11 studies of police workload published between 1970 and 2001, using data from either dispatch records or systematic social observation of patrol officers, indicated that patrol officers "clearly had a lot of downtime."[33]

Most of the research literature concerning police workload has involved large, municipal police agencies. In 2014, however, Jeremy M. Wilson and Alexander Weiss laid out four basic approaches to workforce levels specifically intended for smaller departments: per capita, minimum staffing, authorized level, and workload based. A fifth approach is the coverage-based approach, where agencies determine what coverage is needed during any given time, taking into account calls for service, types of calls, time of day, time of year, and officer safety. It is possible that for a small department only two officers would be needed at any given time.[34]

How Is Discretion Exercised?

The police exercise discretion to perform the following crucial actions:

- Arrest
- Stop, question, or frisk
- Use physical force
- Use deadly force
- Write traffic summonses
- Use certain enforcement tactics (moving loiterers, warning, and so on)
- Take a report on a crime
- Investigate a crime

An example of how discretion is exercised is the current stop-and-frisk policies in cities like New York and Seattle. In Seattle, new policies were finally adopted after addressing key issues from a 2012 settlement agreement between the city and the Department of Justice, which found officers routinely used excessive force most often against people of color and the psychologically or chemically impaired.[35] In this instance police discretion created a rift between the officers and the community; when exercised effectively, however, discretion is a crucial component of policing.

Why Is Discretion Exercised?

Discretion is an extremely necessary part of police work. Sheehan and Cordner tell us that the police exercise discretion for seven reasons:

1. If the police attempted to enforce all the laws all the time, they would constantly be in the station house or court instead of on the street maintaining order and protecting life and property.

2. Because of political realities, legislators pass some laws that they do not intend to have strictly enforced all the time.

3. Lawmakers pass some laws that are vague and ill-defined, making it necessary for the police to interpret these laws and decide when to apply them.

4. Most violations of the law are minor (for example, traffic violations) and do not require full enforcement.

5. The complete enforcement of all the laws all the time would alienate the public from the police and the entire criminal justice system.

6. The full enforcement of all the laws would overwhelm the courts, jails, and prisons.

7. The police have so many duties to perform and such limited resources that good judgment must be exercised in when, where, and how they enforce the law.[36]

Police also have to take into consideration the paradox of enforcing federal laws that are in conflict with state and local laws.

What Factors Influence Discretion?

We know that officers practice discretion, and we know that discretion is necessary. Are there factors that cause the police to exercise discretion in a certain way? Scholars have been studying this issue for quite a while.

Herbert Jacob wrote that four major factors influence police officers in determining the exercise of discretion:

1. *Characteristics of the crime*. A serious crime gives the police less freedom or ability to ignore it or exercise discretion regarding it.

2. *Relationship between the alleged criminal and the victim*. Generally, the police tend to avoid making arrests when a perpetrator and a victim have a close relationship. In recent years, however, many departments have limited discretion in domestic violence or family assault cases and have adopted pro-arrest policies. Domestic violence will be discussed in Chapter 11, "Police and the Community."

3. *Relationship between police and the criminal or victim*. Generally, a respectful, mannerly complainant is taken more seriously and treated better by the police than an antagonistic one. In the same way, a violator who acts respectfully to the police is also less likely to be arrested than an antagonistic one.

4. *Department policies*. The preferences of the police chief and city administration, as expressed in department policy, generally influence the actions of the officer.[37]

In *Varieties of Police Behavior*, Wilson found that an officer's discretion varied depending on the type of situation he or she encountered. Wilson found that police have wide latitude in self-initiated situations, such as the enforcement of traffic or drug violations, because there is usually no complainant or victim demanding police action. However, in citizen-initiated situations, an officer has less discretion, and the preferences of the citizen will often influence the officer's decision about whether or not to arrest.[38]

Research has identified several specific factors that could possibly influence police discretion to arrest, including the subject's offense, attitude, race, socioeconomic status, gender, officer race, and police peer group pressure. Many studies considering these factors are discussed in this chapter.

Studies of police discretion have shown that the most significant factor (66 percent) in forming a suspicion about a suspect is the suspect's behavior. This factor is supplemented by other information, such as

that provided by a dispatcher (18 percent) or a fellow officer. Officers who worked in the same beat continually said they could tell if a person "belonged" in the area due to their familiarity with the people in the neighborhood.[39]

Suspect characteristics most influential in making an arrest after a traffic stop was whether the suspect was under the influence of alcohol or drugs. In those cases, the suspect was more likely to be searched and also arrested. Citizens who were disrespectful when stopped were more than twice as likely to be ticketed or arrested compared to citizens who showed respect to the officer.[40]

In a 2005 article, John D. McCluskey of the University of Texas at San Antonio, William Terrill of Northeastern University, and Eugene A. Paoline III of the University of Central Florida found that collective peer group attitudes toward aggressive patrol do not influence police use-of-force behavior. The researchers examined almost 1,500 police–suspect encounters.[41]

Numerous studies have looked at police discretion as it relates to race. A 2009 study found that the racial makeup of an area does matter to law enforcement and may guide officers' decision making and discretion in enforcement actions, especially if the residents are black. Law enforcement administration should acknowledge these issues and provide organizational constructs that will counteract these concerns.[42]

A 2005 study by Arrick L. Jackson of the University of North Texas in Denton, Texas, and Lorenzo M. Boyd, formerly a deputy sheriff in Suffolk County, Massachusetts, and presently a professor of criminal justice at Fayetteville State University in North Carolina found a significant direct relationship between the numbers of black residents in a community and whether the policing was lenient (ignoring minor crimes). Using a sample of 353 police officers from a midwestern police agency and census tract data, the researchers discovered that patrol divisions with more minority residents are less likely to be lenient than officers in districts that have a majority of white residents. Jackson and Boyd also found that as the percentage of minorities increased in the population, police were less likely to use lenient policing.[43]

In the first half of 2013, New York City Police Department (NYPD) statistics showed that 74 percent of shooting victims were black and 70 percent of those arrested for shooting someone were black.

Those who advocate for the black community are frustrated, as they have seen no measurable change in these statistics since 2009. They attribute these shootings and arrests to the poor economic conditions in the black communities of New York City, a "battle between the haves and have-nots," said Tony Herbert, president of the National Action Network's Brooklyn East Chapter.[44]

In 2011, the Bureau of Justice Statistics (BJS) issued *Contacts between Police and the Public, 2008*, reporting on 40 million contacts between police and citizens. The BJS reported that the likelihood of being stopped by the police while driving did not differ significantly between white (8.4 percent), black (8.8 percent), and Hispanic (9.1 percent) drivers. However, the study disclosed that during the traffic stop, police were three times as likely to carry out some type of search on a black person (12.3 percent) and two times as likely to search a Hispanic person (5.8 percent) than they were to carry out a search on a white person (3.9 percent).[45]

The BJS report also indicated that about 1.4 percent of the 40 million contacts involved police use or threat of force. Blacks (3.4 percent) and Hispanics (1.6 percent) were reported to be more likely than whites (1.2 percent) to experience police threat or use of force.[46]

In a 2008 review of domestic violence cases in state courts, 100 percent of those charged in domestic sexual assault cases and 95.4 percent of nondomestic sexual assault cases were male. Racial characteristics of sexual assault suspects in a domestic situation were 55.6 percent white and 31.1 percent black. Domestic sexual assault cases were more likely to be prosecuted (89 percent) than nondomestic sexual assault (73 percent). In either case, race did not appear to be a deciding factor in prosecution, but behavior of the suspect was.[47]

Some research also has been done on the effect of an officer's race on police discretion. A 2006 article by Robert A. Brown of Indiana University in Indianapolis and James Frank of the University of Cincinnati disclosed a study that found that officer race had a direct influence on arrest outcomes and that there were substantive differences between white and black officers in the decision to arrest. Based on systematic social observations of police–citizen encounters in Cincinnati, Ohio, white officers were more likely to arrest suspects than black officers, but black suspects were more likely to be arrested by a black officer.[48]

Minority groups have alleged that they are the victims of race-based police discretion. The New York Police Department's stop-and-frisk policy is one such example of this deeply held belief. NYPD statistics from 2012 robbery arrests show that 55.8 percent were black and 42.6 percent were white; for aggravated assault, 36.9 percent of those arrested were black and 60.4 percent were white. For all crimes in 2012, blacks were 30.3 percent of those arrested and whites were 67 percent.[49] Based on these comparisons, it would appear the perceived racial bias in policing is not supported by statistical facts. However, this does not minimize the real perceptions or feelings of racial bias by law enforcement toward the black community. These perceptions and feelings need to be addressed.

In 2003, Lundman and Kaufman suggested that women were significantly less likely than men to report being stopped by the police but were more likely than men to report that they were stopped for legitimate reasons and that the police acted properly during the stop.[50] In 2004, Engel and Calnon found that gender played an important role in citations, searches, arrests, and use of force. They said that being male increased the odds by 23 percent of respondents reporting a traffic citation, 300 percent for a search, 180 percent for an arrest, and 230 percent for force.[51] A 2007 study based on a 2005 national survey of contacts between the police and the public revealed that men were more likely to be subject to vehicle stops than were women and were more likely to be subject to the use of force.[52]

In a 2006 study, Michael R. Smith, a former police officer and currently a professor at the University of South Carolina, Geoffrey P. Alpert of the University of South Carolina, and Matthew Makarios, a PhD student at the University of Cincinnati, drawing on more than 66,000 traffic stop records from the Miami-Dade County Police Department, suggested that police may develop unconscious, cognitive schemas that make them more likely to be suspicious of population subgroups they repeatedly encounter in street-level situations involving crime and violence. In this study, police were found to be significantly more suspicious of men than of women in traffic stop encounters, and this suspicion was strongly associated with the decision to arrest.[53]

To add to the confusion, also in 2006, Alpert, Roger G. Dunham, and their colleagues discussed their 2004 study based on observations and debriefings of police officers in Savannah, Georgia, regarding factors causing officers to make stops of individuals and vehicles. They made the following observations:

- Characteristics of the person stopped were not a significant factor in why an officer decided to make the stop. Officers were equally likely to stop individuals who were male or female, black or white, or of low or high socioeconomic status based on appearances.

- In most of the cases where stops were made, the behavior of the suspect was what concerned the officer.

- Appearances of individuals and vehicles only became important in stops when they matched descriptions of suspects for traffic violations or crimes that had been reported.

- Officer observation of a traffic violation, obvious efforts to avoid the officer, and acting nervous in the officer's presence were common behaviors that caused officers to stop individuals.

- Time and place were not significant in officers' decisions to make stops. Officers did not make stops impulsively based upon initial notice of an individual or vehicle. They were not usually made until after continued observations confirmed an initial suspicion that a stop might be required.[54]

As you can see, the factors influencing police discretion and police decision making are complicated, and they continue to be studied and discussed. A literature review points to the tremendous complexity of this issue and the concern we all should have regarding it.[55]

How Can Discretion Be Controlled?

In recent years, much attention has been given to the need to prepare police for the appropriate use of discretion. This preparation begins while the officer is in training in the academy and continues later during field training. Use of discretion is stressed on a regular basis in agencies during daily briefings and after critical incidents with "lessons learned" training. Experts believe that discretion itself is not bad, but that the real problem is uncontrolled or unregulated discretion. The experts feel that discretion cannot and should not be abolished but believe that police departments should attempt to control or regulate it.[56]

Most researchers believe that discretion should be narrowed to the point where all officers in the same agency are dealing with similar issues in similar ways. They feel there should be limits on discretion that reflect the objectives, priorities, and operating philosophy of the department. The limits on discretion should be sufficiently specific to enable an officer to make judgments in a wide variety of unpredictable circumstances in a proper, unbiased manner that will achieve a reasonable degree of uniformity in handling similar incidents in the community.[57]

One approach to managing police behavior involves requiring obedience to a formal set of policies or guidelines that can ensure the just administration of the law. Many police departments established written policies regarding the use of deadly force as far back as the early 1970s, even before the U.S. Supreme Court decision *Tennessee v. Garner*, which will be discussed later in this chapter.[58] These policies dramatically reduced the number of shootings of civilians by the police and the number of officers shot by civilians. Since the 1980s, many departments have established formal procedures for dealing with emotionally disturbed persons, police pursuits, and other critical issues discussed in this text.

One way of controlling discretion, particularly improper application of discretion, is the establishment of employee early warning systems. These automated systems detect significant events in an officer's statistics, such as a high number of use-of-force incidents, vehicle pursuits, sick days, involvement in significant events, or low numbers of arrests or citizen contacts. These systems provide a warning to managers and supervisors, who can then investigate any irregular patterns. The Phoenix, Arizona, Police Department has had such a system in place for several years.[59]

Another method of controlling policing discretion is the use of police internal control mechanisms, such as continual review of officers' actions by police supervisors, managers, internal affairs, and citizen review investigators. There are also external methods of controlling policing discretion, such as local legislatures, independent citizen review boards, and the courts through their process of judicial review. Chapter 8 contains many examples of reviewing and controlling police discretionary actions.

Most importantly, however, controlling discretion involves more than just establishing policies and ensuring that they are obeyed. Managing discretion

You Decide

Think about what you would do as a police officer under the following circumstances. This is a perfect example of a case calling for the exercise of police discretion.

Facts

You receive a call to respond to a boy who is bleeding on the street. You arrive at the location, and you find a 14-year-old Asian boy, naked and with blood on his buttocks; a male in his late 20s or early 30s; and two women. The two women tell you that the man must be trying to kill the boy. The boy is too dazed to respond and remains mute. The man tells you that he and the boy are lovers and were having an argument.

What Would You Do?

If you were the police officer at the scene, which of the following actions would you take?

- Further question all parties at the scene.
- Bring all parties to the station house for further investigation.
- Request that your supervisor or the detectives meet you at the scene.
- Arrest the man for assault and sexual relations with a minor.
- Ignore the situation and let these people solve their own problems.

The Actual Case

The previous facts are from an actual case you probably will recognize. Shortly after midnight on May 27, 1990, two women saw a man chasing a 14-year-old Asian boy, naked and with blood on his buttocks, down an alley behind the Oxford Apartments in a low-income area of Milwaukee, Wisconsin. The women called the police. Two police officers arrived in a patrol car. The man told the police officers that he and the boy were gay lovers having a spat. The officers told all parties to go home and resumed patrol.

The boy was later identified as Konerak Sinthasomphone after his remains were found amid the carnage at Apartment 213 of the Oxford Apartments in 1991. This apartment belonged to Jeffrey Dahmer, who was identified as the man at the scene with Sinthasomphone. When the police searched Dahmer's apartment, they found parts of at least 11 bodies—including three severed heads in the refrigerator, decomposed hands and a genital organ in a lobster pot, and five full skeletons—as well as the remains of six other bodies, three of which were in a chemical-filled, 57-gallon plastic drum in the basement. Dahmer later confessed to the murder of 17 males.

© 2016 Cengage Learning®

---

involves an effort by management to instill a proper value system in officers. According to Wilson, controlling discretion "depends only partly on sanctions and inducements; it also requires instilling in them a shared outlook or ethos that provides for them a common definition of the situations they are likely to encounter and that to the outsider gives to the organization its distinctive character or 'feel.'"[60]

CALEA Standards

Created in 1979 as a credentialing authority, the purpose of CALEA (Commission on Accreditation for Law Enforcement Agencies) is to:

improve the delivery of public safety services, primarily by: maintaining a body of standards, developed by public safety practitioners, covering a wide range of up-to-date public safety initiatives; establishing and administering an accreditation process; and recognizing professional excellence.[61]

CALEA Standard 1.2.7 says that a "written directive governs the use of discretion by sworn officers."[62] The directives that are written by the agency (operation orders, general orders, or policies) should define the limits of discretion and provide guidelines for the exercise of discretion by officers.[63]

Why is this important? The guidelines an agency maintains regarding use of force (discussed in the next section) and other issues of officer discretion are public documents that are often subpoenaed in a court trial. These directives, if followed by the

The issue of the police culture and the police role really hit home with me when I was a road patrol lieutenant working the midnight shift. I had been working the midnight shift for several years. As we know, the types of police work you do can vary somewhat depending on the shift you work, the district you work, and the assignment you have.

On the midnight shift, you spend a lot of time working with "bad guys," because most average citizens are home in bed. Obviously, there are exceptions to this, but, overall, officers on midnights are dealing with people on the street who are up to no good. This observation or feeling starts to ingrain itself in an officer's head, and he or she becomes suspicious of everyone encountered. What are they really doing? Are they lying? Why? The officer develops a protective attitude physically and mentally when approaching and talking to people during the shift. He or she will assume the worst. This is not necessarily a negative trait in terms of officer safety and survival, but it can have an impact on the officer's interactions with people he or she encounters.

I remember one night seeing a car driving in an area of warehouses where we had numerous burglary problems during the midnight shift hours. I watched the vehicle for a few minutes and then pulled it over. I approached the young male driver and asked him what he was doing out here at this time of day—in other words, what was he really up to? He looked at me quizzically and replied that he was just going to work. He was able to produce paperwork that documented this (which of course doesn't necessarily mean he wasn't doing burglaries in the area).

I allowed him to go on his way and thought about the encounter. Though it was still dark, it was just after 6:00 a.m., and good, hardworking people were in fact getting up and going to work, but I was still thinking of "bad guys" being out and about and up to no good.

—Linda Forst

officers, provide protection to the officers and the public. These standards can act as a "conscience" for officers who may be tempted by **noble cause corruption**, which is when officers do the wrong thing for the right reasons, or when police officers act according to their own personal values instead of what the law says.[64]

Police Shootings and the Use of Deadly Force

Police shootings or the use of **deadly force** by the police might be considered the ultimate use of discretion. Sometimes, officers are forced into making a split-second decision about whether to use deadly force. If they hesitate, they run the risk of being killed or seriously injured themselves, or allowing a fellow officer or an innocent citizen to be killed or seriously injured. If their decision is later found to be wrong and it is determined that they misused their discretion, they face public and legal criticism and perhaps even arrest. They are also criticized by the press and the community. Worse still is that they have to live with this mistaken decision for the rest of their life.

Being a police officer and using necessary discretion is not an easy job. Sometimes government officials understand this. Former Mayor John F. Street of Philadelphia, in a 2006 press conference, expressed indignation about those who "second-guess" officers who have fatally shot civilians and said that in some cases their criticism is "unconscionable":

> When we ask people to put on a uniform and to go out and fight crime and to go out into some of the most difficult and the most troubling areas of our community, under circumstances that most of us really wouldn't want to even think about, it is unfair for people to second-guess everything they do, every time they do it.[65]

noble cause corruption Stems from ends-oriented policing and involves police officers bending the rules to achieve the "right" goal of putting a criminal in jail.

deadly force Force that can cause death.

Police Use of Force

In 2011, the BJS, in its *Contacts between Police and the Public, 2008*, reporting on 40 million contacts between police and citizens, noted that only about 1.4 percent of all of the contacts involved the police use or threat of force. About 74.3 percent of people experiencing the threat or use of force felt that the police used excessive force; about 28.4 percent of the people involved in a police force incident reported that they did something to provoke the officer to use force, such as threatening the police or resisting arrest.[66]

According to a 2006 BJS special report, *Citizen Complaints about Police Use of Force*, during 2002 a total of 26,556 citizen complaints about police use of force were received by 5 percent of the agencies nationwide, representing 59 percent of officers. The number of complaints was equal to an overall rate of 6.6 per 100 full-time sworn officers.[67]

Statistics clearly indicate that police officers do not overuse force. In a 2002 report, covering research in six law enforcement agencies, it was disclosed that officers used some physical force in about 17 percent of the adult custody arrests they made, and suspects used some physical force in about 12 percent of their arrests. The researchers found that the officers' use of force was low—weapons were used in only 2.1 percent of all arrests (the weapon most often used was pepper spray).[68]

The Public's Perception

ON THE JOB

It is difficult to know at the outset of a call how people are going to respond to your commands. We constantly need to adjust our perception of the situation and the amount of force that may be necessary to solve the problem. We also need to be aware that as officers, we are always being watched, and that citizens may perceive things differently than we do.

I remember handling a call on a Friday evening during the height of tourist season in Boca. We received a call at a local restaurant advising of an elderly female threatening to slash the bartender with a knife. I was the first officer on the scene and contacted the bartender. He told me that the woman had left. He briefly described her and said that she did in fact show a kitchen knife and threaten to slash his face if he didn't serve her another drink. He felt she was unstable.

As I was talking to him, we got a similar call at a restaurant a few blocks away. This was a large chain-type bistro, and there was an elderly female in the restaurant yelling, acting irrationally, and stating she had a knife. I hopped in my car and drove to the restaurant. The restaurant was packed with families and tourists. I spoke with the manager, who directed me to the woman in the back of the restaurant. By this time, two other officers had arrived. Two of us walked to the back and talked to the woman while the third officer waited by our cars. The woman was agitated but agreed to come out front with us to discuss the situation.

While we were talking, she became increasingly irrational and started screaming that she was going to slash us. I patted her down and was attempting to take her knife from her when she went nuts and started fighting with us and screaming. This woman was only about 5 feet 4 inches tall, 65 to 70 years old, and frail looking. We didn't want her to get hurt, and we didn't want one of us to get hurt, and we felt that by using three officers, we could handcuff her and minimize the chance of injuries by each officer taking an arm and another one doing the cuffing. She struggled and fought us, but we got her cuffed without hurting her.

This happened right in front of the big plate-glass window of the restaurant, and lots of people were watching. We used only as much force as we needed. Even though she was old and frail, she was a danger to herself and others, but we knew it didn't look good—three officers in uniform handcuffing one elderly female. In fact, one person leaving the restaurant made a comment to the effect that we were bullies. But we knew we had done the best we could under the circumstances and, despite outward appearances, were able to keep anyone from getting hurt. Officers are always going to be questioned about the amount of force they use in any given situation.

—Linda Forst

Number of Citizens Shot by the Police

Historically, the shooting of a citizen by the police has been a major problem facing the police. Police shootings have a serious negative impact on police–community relations. Numerous incidents of civil unrest have followed police shootings of civilians. Wilson states, "No aspect of policing elicits more passionate concern or more divided opinions than the use of deadly force."[69]

Police shootings receive tremendous media attention. However, the late James J. Fyfe, a former New York City police lieutenant and deputy commissioner for training and one of the leading experts on the police use of deadly force in the United States, reported that the systematic examination of the use of deadly force was largely neglected until a series of police shootings and other police problems precipitated some of the urban violence of the 1960s.[70]

According to the *Uniform Crime Reports: Crime in the United States 2010*, an average of 390 people per year were killed justifiably by police officers from 2006 to 2010.[71] In the longer term, the general homicide rate (including both justifiable and otherwise) trended up from the 1950s, peaked in the 1980s, and then trended down in 2010 to rates similar to those in the 1960s. The general homicide rate between 1980 and 2008 can be categorized by the following:

- 76.8 percent of *homicide victims* were male, 50.3 percent were white, and 47.7 percent were black. By age, the 18–34 age group was the highest (53.2 percent); and 24 percent of homicide victims were gang related and under age 18.

- 89.5 percent of *homicide offenders* were male, 45.3 percent were white, and 53.5 percent were black. By age, the 18–34 age group was the highest (65.5 percent).[72]

Do Police Discriminate with Their Trigger Fingers?

Numerous studies have been conducted to determine if there is, in fact, racial discrimination in the police use of deadly force. If one considers only total numbers, the overwhelming difference in the percentage of African Americans shot over the percentage of whites shot could lead to the conclusion that discrimination does indeed exist.

In 2012, New York Police Department officers were involved in 16 shootings in which a person was killed and 14 shootings in which a person was accidentally shot. Thirteen officers were injured in the line of duty. No officers were killed. Of those subjects killed by gunfire by NYPD, 69 percent were black, 12.5 percent were Hispanic, and 12.5 percent were white. [73]

There is another side, however, to the analysis of race and police shootings. Two studies indicate that people who engage in violent crime or who engage the police in violent confrontations are much more likely to be the victims of police shootings. In one study, participation in violent crime was used as a relevant variable in police shootings because it generally places a person at risk of being confronted by the police and being shot by the police. The Chicago Law Enforcement Study Group examined shootings by Chicago police over a five-year period. The group first analyzed the rate at which whites, African Americans, and Hispanic Americans were shot and killed relative to their number in the population, and then the rate at which the same groups were shot and killed while participating in violent crimes. The data indicated that African Americans were shot and killed six times as often as whites relative to the total population, but the disparity disappeared when participation in violent crimes was a factor. Whites were shot and killed at a rate of 5.6 per 1,000 arrests for forcible felonies, compared with 4.5 African Americans shot and killed per 1,000 arrests for the same category of crime.[74] David Lester, pointing to the jurisdictional variation of police use of deadly force, reported that police officers killed more people in communities with high violence rates and during years in which the homicide rates were highest.[75]

In a 2004 study, Michael D. White reported that many factors are involved in the quick decision-making process that takes place in a police shooting, including the victim's actions, the officer's actions, the type of assault against the officer, and the type of weapon involved, as well as other options available to the officer besides deadly violence. These are in addition to environmental factors such as community characteristics and organizational factors such as the department's policies and organizational climate.[76]

Tennessee v. Garner

The *Garner* case finally ended the fleeing felon rule. On October 3, 1974, at about 10:45 p.m., two Memphis police officers, Elton Hymon and Leslie Wright, responded to a report of a prowler. Upon reaching the location, they were met by a neighbor, who told them she had heard someone breaking into the house next to hers. Officer Wright radioed for assistance as Officer Hymon went to the rear of the house. As the officer approached the backyard, he heard a door slamming and observed someone running across the backyard. The fleeing person stopped at a 6-foot-high chain link fence at the end of the yard. The officer shone his flashlight and saw what appeared to be a 17- or 18-year-old youth about 5 feet 7 inches tall. The officer yelled, "Police! Halt!" However, the youth began to climb the fence.

If You Were Officer Hymon, What Would You Do?

The officer, thinking that the youth would escape, fired a shot at him, which struck him in the back of the head. The youth later died on the operating table. Ten dollars and a purse taken from the house were found on his body. The dead youth was identified as Edward Garner, a 15-year-old eighth grader. At the trial, the officer admitted that he knew that Garner was unarmed and was trying to escape. The officer testified that he was acting under the provisions of Tennessee law that stated that an officer may use all the necessary means to effect an arrest if, after notice of the intention to arrest, the defendant either flees or forcibly resists.

The U.S. Supreme Court ruled 6 to 3 that the use of deadly force against apparently unarmed and nondangerous fleeing felons is an illegal seizure under the Fourth Amendment. The Court ended the common law fleeing felon rule by stating:

> The use of deadly force to prevent the escape of all felony suspects, whatever the circumstances, is constitutionally unreasonable. It is not better that all felony suspects die than they escape. Where the suspect poses no immediate threat to the officer and no threat to others, the harm resulting from failing to apprehend him does not justify the use of deadly force to do so. It is no doubt unfortunate when a suspect who is in sight escapes, but the fact that the police arrive a little late or are a little slower afoot does not always justify killing the suspect. A police officer may not seize an unarmed, nondangerous suspect by shooting him dead.

If you had been a member of the Court, would you have agreed with this ruling?

Source: Based on *Tennessee v. Garner*, 471 U.S. 1 (1985).

Departure from the "Fleeing Felon" Rule

Before the great amount of attention given to police shootings in the wake of the civil disorders of the 1960s, most U.S. police departments operated under the common law **fleeing felon doctrine**, which held that law enforcement officers could, if necessary, use deadly force to apprehend any fleeing felony suspect. This doctrine evolved from the common law tradition of medieval England, when all felonies were capital offenses (liable for the death penalty). Because there was very little official law enforcement in those days and very few escaping felons were apprehended, the law allowed a person who had committed a felony to be killed while fleeing the scene.

The fleeing felon rule, like most of England's common law, migrated to the United States. Today, however, there is little need for the fleeing felon rule in the United States, because we have sufficient armed police and modern communications systems to aid in the apprehension of fleeing felons. Also, the legality and morality of the fleeing felon rule comes into question because of the U.S. legal concept of presumption of innocence. Most U.S. states, however, maintained the fleeing felon rule well into the 1960s and 1970s. In 1985, the fleeing felon rule

fleeing felon doctrine Doctrine widely followed prior to the 1960s that allowed police officers to use deadly force to apprehend a fleeing felon.

Alternatives to the Fleeing Felon Rule

In the 1970s, the American Law Institute proposed a Model Penal Code, which included new policies on the use of deadly force. Many states replaced their existing penal codes with this model code. During the same period, the Police Foundation proposed its own policies regarding the use of deadly force, which were adopted by many police departments.

Model Penal Code

The Model Penal Code, developed by the American Law Institute, permits the use of deadly force by police officers if an officer believes that (1) the felony for which the arrest is made involved the use, or the threatened use, of deadly force; or (2) there is a substantial risk that the suspect will cause death or serious bodily injury if not immediately apprehended; and (3) the force employed creates no substantial risk of injury to innocent people.

The Police Foundation Standard

After studying the deadly force policies of numerous police departments, including those of Birmingham, Alabama; Detroit, Michigan; Indianapolis, Indiana; Kansas City, Missouri; Oakland, California; Portland, Oregon; and Washington, D.C., the Police Foundation recommended that police departments develop rules governing the use of deadly force after consultation with citizens and police line officers. It recommended that officers be allowed to shoot to defend themselves and others, as well as to apprehend suspects in deadly or potentially deadly felonies. The Police Foundation also recommended several internal police policies that could lead to an improved use of deadly force by the police. These policies included carefully screening recruits to eliminate both unstable and violence-prone officers, dismissing probationary officers who demonstrate instability or propensity to violence, and providing more meaningful training in the rules of deadly force.

The Police Foundation proposed the following deadly force rules that departments might adopt:

- Officers might use deadly force to defend themselves or others from what the officers reasonably perceive as an immediate threat of death or serious injury, when there is no apparent alternative.

- Officers also might use deadly force to apprehend an armed and dangerous subject when alternative means of apprehension would involve a substantial risk of death or serious injury, and when the safety of innocent bystanders would not be additionally jeopardized by the officers' actions.

- Any of the following could make an armed subject dangerous enough to justify the use of deadly force: (1) The subject has recently shot, shot at, killed, or attempted to kill someone, or has done so more than once in the past; (2) the subject has recently committed a serious assault on a law enforcement officer acting in the line of duty; and (3) the subject has declared that he or she will kill, if necessary, to avoid arrest.

Source: Adapted from American Law Institute, Model Penal Code, Section 307(2)(b); and Catherine H. Milton, Jeanne Wahl Halleck, James Lardner, and Gary L. Abrecht, *Police Use of Deadly Force* (Washington, D.C.: Police Foundation, 1977).

---

was declared unconstitutional by the U.S. Supreme Court in the landmark case ***Tennessee v. Garner***.[77]

Although many agreed with the *Garner* decision—that the use of deadly force on an unarmed fleeing felon is unconstitutional unless it is necessary to prevent escape and the officer has probable cause to believe that the suspect poses a significant threat of death or serious physical injury to the officers or others—one critic argued that the standard is much too restrictive, ambiguous, and unrealistic, in that it imposes an impossible burden on an officer to determine in a split second whether a fleeing felon is dangerous to the officer or to others.[78]

Before the *Garner* case and subsequent to the urban riots of the 1960s, many states replaced the fleeing felon rule with new state laws, internal rules of police departments, and court decisions. During the 1970s, many police departments developed an

---

Tennessee v. Garner U.S. Supreme Court case that ended the use of the fleeing felon rule.

alternative to the fleeing felon doctrine based in part on recommendations by the American Law Institute and the Police Foundation. This rule used the **defense of life standard**, which allowed police officers to use deadly force against people who were using deadly force against an officer or another person, as well as in certain violent felony situations. Replacing the common law fleeing felon rule with the defense of life standard changed the incidence of police shootings. Lawrence O'Donnell found that police departments with effective deadly force rules showed sharp decreases in citizen deaths and in officer deaths. In Kansas City, Missouri, for example, after the department adopted a rule that prohibited police from shooting juveniles except in self-defense, the number of youths younger than 18 shot by the police dropped dramatically.[79]

In 1995, after tremendous negative publicity and detailed investigations into the actions of federal agents at the deadly siege of the Branch Davidian compound in Waco, Texas, and at the home of antigovernment separatist Randy Weaver in Ruby Ridge, Idaho, the federal government announced that it was refining the deadly force policy used by federal agents and adopted the **imminent danger standard**, basically the same defense of life standard that law enforcement agencies had been following for years. The imminent danger standard restricts the use of deadly force to only those situations where the lives of agents or others are in imminent danger, although it does permit deadly physical force against a prisoner attempting escape who was being held in or sentenced to a high-security prison. The new policy also forbids the firing of warning shots and shooting at moving vehicles in an attempt to disable such vehicles.[80]

Review of the application of the use-of-force standards should not be taken in isolation, but in the totality of the circumstances. Officers do not operate in a vacuum and in many instances the agency, the courts, the media, and the public tend to review and study these events as a single incident, forgetting the prior circumstances or events preceding the use of force.

---

defense of life standard Doctrine allowing police officers to use deadly force against individuals using deadly force against an officer or others.

imminent danger standard The standard that allows the use of deadly force if the officer feels in immediate danger of great bodily harm or death.

When reviewing use-of-force incidents, several issues must be taken into consideration and fully understood by the agency:

1. The nature of the contact the officer had with the individual.
2. Understanding by the officer of why force was used. The answer may be obvious; however, officers must be sure to have a thorough understanding of their agency's use-of-force policy *prior* to its use.
3. The seriousness of the offense and the officer's consideration of this during the incident. This does not mean a traffic stop cannot turn into the use of deadly force.
4. The characteristics of the suspect and any prior contacts the officer may have had with the suspect.

Having all these points in mind when conducting a use-of-force review will assist agencies in determining whether policy or law was violated and will help in developing new policies and procedures in the future.[81]

Realizing the importance of this issue and the need for guidance for officers, 97 percent of all local police departments and 97 percent of all sheriff's offices have a written policy on use of deadly force.[82] (See Chapter 2, "Organizing Public Security in the United States.")

Firearms Training

During the 1970s and 1980s, police departments came to the realization that officers needed more realistic firearms training and weapons at least equal to those of the criminals on the street. By 1990, 73 percent of all local departments had authorized the use of some type of semiautomatic weapon, and by 2000, that number had increased to almost all local police departments and sheriff's offices.[83]

In 1970, the NYPD began utilizing a "Firearms Discharge Report" to document all gunshots by NYPD officers. By compiling this data, they were hoping to document where, when, and under what conditions officers were firing their guns. Over the years, other departments followed suit in order to analyze shooting incidents and address training needs in an effort to keep officers safe. Data showed that the old style of standing or kneeling at a range and firing at bull's-eye targets 25 or 50 yards downrange was not preparing officers for the real-life conditions they encountered on the street. Most departments are now attempting to incorporate real-life conditions such as low light, noise, sirens, flashing lights, and weather conditions into their training. They are also stressing the "shoot/don't shoot" aspect of shooting as much as accuracy. Although agencies are striving to make firearms training as realistic as possible, it is difficult to simulate randomly moving targets and the emotional, life-threatening dynamics of the real thing; but the effort must continue. [84]

In the most recent study of state and local law enforcement training academies, academy recruits spent an average of 60 hours in firearms training, 51 hours in self-defense training, and 12 hours in nonlethal weapons training. The "soft skills"— mediation and conflict management (8 hours), cultural diversity instruction (11 hours), and basic strategies (8 hours)—were not emphasized as much as the weapons and self-defense skills.[85] Most police departments now train their officers in the use of force using the "use-of-force continuum" in which police officers are taught to escalate their force to the same extent that the subject is using, and to only use deadly force as a final option and only when the subject is using deadly force against the officer or a third party. Special Agent Thomas D. Petrowski of the FBI criticizes this practice, claiming that it results in hesitation in the officer to use force. He writes that such hesitation on the part of the officer is the cause of many officer injuries and deaths. He argues further that policies and training must focus on overcoming instinctive hesitation in using force rather than encouraging it, that the cornerstone of use-of-force training should be threat assessment, and that officers must be trained to respond to the threat of violence and not to the actual violence itself.[86]

Less-than-Lethal Force

In 2005, the U.S. Government Accountability Office, in a report to the U.S. Congress, reported that the growing popularity of **less-than-lethal weapons** (LTLW) by police officers in the United States virtually ensured their increased use in the law enforcement community.[87] In 2007, the Department of Justice reported that 96 percent of all local departments and 89 percent of all sheriff's departments had a policy regarding nonlethal force, and almost all departments authorized the use of one or more nonlethal weapons:

- *Chemical sprays*—authorized by 97 percent of local police departments
- *Batons of some type*—authorized by 93 percent of local police departments
- *Electronic devices (stun guns or Tasers) of some type*—authorized by 60 percent of local departments
- *Choke holds, carotid holds, or neck restraints*—authorized by 15 percent of local police departments
- *Less-lethal kinetic energy rounds,* more commonly called "bean bag" rounds—authorized by 28 percent of police departments[88]

Departments have turned to these less-than-lethal weapons in an effort to give officers options other than deadly force when faced with a combative subject. Various forms of chemical sprays have been in the police arsenal for years. Electronic devices have also given officers an alternative to deadly force, allowing a subject to be temporarily subdued without a gun. There have been several deaths in Taser or stun-gun situations, though none have been blamed on the Taser itself; most of the time, drugs were found to be the primary cause of death. Supporters of these weapons believe that the use of the Taser or stun gun has saved many lives. The International Association of Chiefs of Police (IACP), which has a model policy regarding the use of Tasers and other electronic devices, states that their purpose is to save lives.[89] A spokesperson for Taser International, which makes the Taser, reported that more than 8,000 law enforcement agencies in the United States use it and that in Cincinnati, Ohio, where the Taser was used 1,000 times, police officials noted a 56 percent drop in injuries to officers and a 35 percent drop in injuries to suspects.[90]

Choke holds, carotid holds, and neck restraints became a source of controversy after some deaths were associated with their use. Many departments have removed this option for officers from their

less-than-lethal weapons Innovative alternatives to traditional firearms, such as batons, bodily force techniques, chemical irritant sprays, and Tasers or stun guns.

Brian Nguyen/Reuters

Police at the University of California–Davis use pepper spray in a stand-off against campus protesters.

policies. Some also consider the use of K-9 units to be less-than-lethal force, and there is a concern by some that they are utilized in a biased manner. One report found that 29 percent of local departments use dogs for law enforcement purposes; the bigger the department, the more likely they are to use dogs, with 94 percent of departments serving more than 100,000 people using dogs. Fifty-five percent of sheriff's offices use canines.[91]

Many less-than-lethal weapons, including the baton, oleoresin capsicum (OC, or pepper spray), and the Taser or stun gun, are not control-and-restraint techniques; for example, a person sprayed with OC must still be controlled and then handcuffed. These weapons are useful in temporarily distracting a subject long enough for control and handcuffing to be achieved.[92] Stun guns or Tasers shoot two barbs attached to wires that reach up to 35 feet. The barbs deliver a five-second electrical jolt that seizes the body's major muscle groups and temporarily incapacitates the person, allowing the police to approach a dangerous suspect more closely.

Charles S. Petty, MD, of the University of Texas Southwestern Medical Center, in a 2002 report for the U.S. Department of Justice, reported on the pathological and toxicological information on 63 deaths occurring after the use of OC. Petty's analysis found that drugs, disease, and drugs and disease combined with confrontational situations

were the primary causes of deaths in these situations. His results showed that there is no evidence that OC, as used by law enforcement officers in these confrontational situations, was a total or contributing cause of death. He wrote that the use of OC is relatively innocuous.[93]

However, the use of Tasers or stun guns, also known as conducted energy devices (CEDs), has caused some controversy. Amnesty International reports that more than 150 people have died after being hit by a Taser since 2001 and that it was officially ruled at least a contributing factor in 23 deaths nationwide.[94]

In June 2006, the National Institute of Justice (NIJ) reported that it was reviewing the deaths of as many as 180 people who died after law enforcement officers used stun guns or other electroshock devices to subdue them. Glenn Schmitt of the NIJ said that the review was prompted after law enforcement authorities, including the IACP, expressed concern about the increasing numbers of deaths of subjects when stun guns were used against them by the police. He said that the review would enlist the help of the National Association of Medical Examiners, the American College of Pathologists, the Centers for Disease Control and Prevention, and the IACP.[95] In June 2008, the NIJ released their interim report, *Study of Deaths Following Electro Muscular Disruption*, which concluded that:

> Although exposure to CED is not risk free, there is no conclusive medical evidence within the state of current research that indicates a high risk of serious injury or death from the direct effects of CED exposure. Field experience with CED use indicates that exposure is safe in the vast majority of cases. Therefore, law enforcement need not refrain from deploying CEDs, provided the devices are used in accordance with accepted national guidelines.[96]

See Chapter 14, "Computers, Technology, and Criminalistics in Policing," for further information on less-than-lethal force and less-than-lethal weapons.

SUMMARY

- The two major ways of looking at the police role are the crime-fighting role (law enforcement) and the order-maintenance role (peacekeeping and providing social services).

- The two primary goals and objectives of police departments are maintaining order and protecting life and property. Secondary goals include preventing crime, arresting and prosecuting offenders, recovering stolen and missing property, assisting sick and injured people, enforcing noncriminal regulations, and delivering services not available elsewhere in the community.

- Many researchers suggest that police officers adopt a police operational style in thinking about their role in society and how they should do their jobs.

- An important aspect of a police officer's job is the exercise of discretion, what it means, how and why it is exercised, what factors influence the use of discretion by the police, and how police departments can attempt to control discretion.

- Research has identified many factors that may influence police discretion to arrest, including characteristics of the crime; relationship between the alleged criminal and the victim; relationship between police and the criminal or victim; department policies; the subject's offense, attitude, race, socioeconomic status, and gender; the officer's race; and police peer group pressure.

- In recent years, much attention has been given to the need to prepare police for the appropriate use of discretion.

- Despite common perceptions, police rarely use force. Police shootings or the use of deadly force by the police might be considered the ultimate use of discretion by the police.

- In 1985, the U.S. Supreme Court in *Tennessee v. Garner* declared the fleeing felon rule unconstitutional. Current law generally allows the police to use deadly force only against those using it against them or another person.

- Almost all local police departments and sheriff's offices use less-than-lethal weapons, most commonly chemical sprays, batons, or electronic devices such as stun guns or Tasers.

KEY TERMS

ambiguous	fleeing felon doctrine	order maintenance
crime fighting	imminent danger standard	police operational styles
deadly force	less-than-lethal weapons	police role
defense of life standard	noble cause corruption	*Tennessee v. Garner*
discretion	omnipresence	

REVIEW EXERCISES

1. Interview or ride with some officers from your local police or sheriff's department and determine the following:

   a. To which role—crime fighting or order maintenance—do the officers seem to subscribe?

   b. To which of Siegel and Senna's styles or typologies of policing do the officers seem to subscribe?

   c. Which of Broderick's police operational styles do the officers' styles most resemble?

   d. Which of James Q. Wilson's styles does the officers' department seem to resemble?

   e. What factors influence the decisions the officers make regarding stopping, summonsing, and arresting persons?

   Write a five- to six-page report based on your findings.

2. Your professor states, "Police work is primarily social work, rather than crime fighting." She asks the class to debate her statement. Prepare a list of talking points to defend or counter her comment.

3. Prepare a five- to six-page report on the factors that influence police discretion.

WEB EXERCISES

1. Search the Internet for the website of a police or sheriff's department near your home. Review and analyze the content of the website and attempt to determine which role this department seems to reflect: the crime-fighting role or the order-maintenance role.

2. Search the Internet for the latest arrest statistics for the United States as reported to the FBI. Then search for the arrest statistics for a local police or sheriff's department near your home. Determine how the local statistics compare and contrast to the national statistics.

3. One of your fellow students says to the class that she feels that police tend to discriminate against minorities in their traffic stops. Search the Internet for some studies to determine whether this is true or not.

END NOTES

1. Herman Goldstein, *Policing a Free Society* (Cambridge, Mass.: Ballinger, 1977), p. 21.

2. George L. Kirkham and Laurin A. Wollan, Jr., *Introduction to Law Enforcement* (New York: Harper & Row, 1980), p. 336.

3. Christine Eith and Matthew R. Durose, *Contacts between Police and the Public, 2008* (Washington, D.C.: Bureau of Justice Statistics, U.S. Department of Justice, 2011).

4. Elaine Cumming, I. Cumming, and L. Edell, "Policeman as a Philosopher, Friend and Guide," 1965, in Abraham S. Blumberg and Elaine Niederhoffer, eds., *The Ambivalent Force: Perspectives on the Police*, 3rd ed. (New York: Holt, Rinehart and Winston, 1985), pp. 212–219.

5. James Q. Wilson & George L. Kelling, "Broken Windows: The Police and Neighborhood Safety," *Atlantic Monthly*, March 1982.

6. John Webster, "Police Task and Time Study," *Journal of Criminal Law, Criminology, and Police Science* 61 (1970): 94–100.

7. Robert Lilly, "What Are the Police Now Doing?" *Journal of Police Science and Administration* 6 (1978): 51–53.

8. Eric J. Scott, *Calls for Service: Citizen Demand and Initial Police Response* (Washington, D.C.: National Institute of Justice, 1981), pp. 28–30.

9. Michael Brown, *Working the Street* (New York: Russell Sage Foundation, 1981); Albert J. Reiss, *The Police and the Public* (New Haven: Yale University Press, 1971); Norman Weiner, *The Role of Police in Urban Society: Conflict and Consequences* (Indianapolis: Bobbs-Merrill, 1976).

10. Stephen Meagher, "Police Patrol Styles: How Pervasive Is Community Variation?" *Journal of Police Science and Administration* 13 (1985): 36–55.

11. David Thacher, "Order Maintenance Reconsidered: Moving Beyond Strong Causal Reasoning," The *Journal of Criminal Law & Criminology*, 94 (2), retrieved April 12, 2014

12. Egon Bittner, *The Functions of the Police in Modern Society* (Cambridge, Mass.: Oelgeschlager, Gunn, and Hain, 1979), p. 8.

13. Carl B. Klockars, *Idea of Police* (Thousand Oaks, Calif.: Sage, 1985).

14. Alan Coffey, *Law Enforcement: A Human Relations Approach* (Englewood Cliffs, N.J.: Prentice Hall, 1990), p. 247. The author cites as an excellent example Bruce J. Terris, "The Role of the Police," *Annals of the American Academy of Political and Social Science* (November 1967): 58–69.

15. George Pugh, "The Police Officer: Qualities, Roles and Concepts," *Journal of Police Science and Administration* 14 (1986): 1–6.

16. Robert Sheehan and Gary W. Cordner, *Introduction to Police Administration*, 2nd ed. (Cincinnati: Anderson, 1989), p. 62. In stating this core role, the authors cite the work of Egon Bittner, *The Functions of the Police in Modern Society*; Carl B. Klockars, ed., *Thinking about Police: Contemporary Readings* (New York: McGraw-Hill, 1983), pp. 227–231; and William K. Muir, Jr., *Police: Streetcorner Politicians* (Chicago: University of Chicago Press, 1977).

17. Larry J. Siegel and Joseph J. Senna, *Introduction to Criminal Justice*, 10th ed. (Belmont, Calif.: Thomson/Wadsworth, 2005).

18. Sheehan and Cordner, *Introduction to Police Administration*, p. 16.

19. Siegel and Senna, *Introduction to Criminal Justice*, p. 217.

20. Sheehan and Cordner, *Introduction to Police Administration*, pp. 16–21.

21. Siegel and Senna, *Introduction to Criminal Justice*, p. 211. Siegel and Senna cite, in this regard, Jack Kuykendall and Roy Roberg, "Police Manager's Perception of Employee Types: A Conceptual Model," *Journal of Criminal Justice* 16 (1988): 131–135.

22. Siegel and Senna, *Introduction to Criminal Justice*, p. 211. Siegel and Senna cite, in this regard, William Muir, *Police: Streetcorner Politicians*, and James Q. Wilson, *Varieties of Police Behavior: The Management of Law and Order in Eight Communities* (Cambridge: Harvard University Press, 1968).

23. John J. Broderick, *Police in a Time of Change*, 2nd ed. (Prospect Heights, Ill.: Waveland Press, 1987).

24. The discussion of Wilson's police operational styles is based on Wilson, *Varieties of Police Behavior.*

25. Muir, *Police: Streetcorner Politicians*. Note: Carl B. Klockars, in his final chapter of *Idea of Police*, discusses Muir's theories of good police and good policing and his typology of four police types by using examples from the television program *Hill Street Blues.*

26. Ellen Hochstedler, "Police Types—An Empirical Test of a Typology of Individual Police Officers," PhD dissertation, State University of New York at Albany, 1980; Hochstedler, "Testing Types—A Review and Test of Police Types," *Journal of Criminal Justice* 6 (1981): 451–456.

27. Claudia Mendias and E. James Kehoe, "Engagement of Policing Ideals and Their Relationship to the Exercise of Discretionary Powers," *Criminal Justice and Behavior* (February 2006): 70–92.

28. Wilson, *Varieties of Police Behavior*, p. 187.

29. Michael R. Gottfredson and Don M. Gottfredson, *Decision Making in Criminal Justice: Toward the Rational Exercise of Discretion* (Cambridge, Mass.: Ballinger, 1980), p. 87.

30. Kenneth Culp Davis, *Police Discretion* (St. Paul, Minn.: West, 1975).

31. Gary W. Cordner, "Police Patrol Work Load Studies: A Review and Critique," *Police Studies* 4 (1979): 50–60.

32. Christine N. Famega, James Frank, and Lorraine Mazerolle, "Managing Police Patrol Time: The Role of Supervisor Directives," *Justice Quarterly* 4 (2005): 540–559.

33. Christine N. Famega, "Variation in Officer Downtime: A Review of the Research," *Policing: An International Journal of Police Strategies and Management* 3 (2005): 388–414.

34. Jeremy M. Wilson & Alexander Weiss, "Staffing the "Small" Department: Taking Stock of Existing Benchmarks and Promising Approaches," *The Police Chief Magazine*, April 2014, retrieved April 2014, www.policechiefmagazine.org/magazine/index .cfm?fueaction=print_display&article_id_2906&issue_id=42013

35. Mike Carter & Steve Miletich, "Stop and Frisk Policies Approved in Seattle," *The Seattle Times*, January 21, 2014, retrieved January 22, 2014, http://www.officer.com/ news/11297357/stop-and-frisk-policies-approved-in-seattle

36. Sheehan and Cordner, *Introduction to Police Administration*, pp. 52–53.

37. Herbert Jacob, *Urban Justice* (Boston: Little, Brown, 1973), p. 27.

38. Wilson, *Varieties of Police Behavior*, pp. 83–89.

39. Geoffrey Alpert, Roger Dunham, Meghan Stroshine, Katherine Bennett, and John McDonald, *Police Officers' Decision Making and Making a Stop*, February 2006, NCJRS.

40. Ibid.

41. John D. McCluskey, William Terrill, and Eugene A. Paoline, III, "Peer Group Aggressiveness and the Use of Coercion in Police-Suspect Encounters," *Police Practice & Research: An International Journal* 1 (2005): 19–37.

42. Cynthia Lum, *Does the "Race of Places" Influence Police Officer Decision Making?*, December 2009, NCJRS, September 2010.

43. Arrick L. Jackson and Lorenzo M. Boyd, "Minority-Threat Hypothesis and the Workload Hypothesis: A Community-Level Examination of Lenient Policing in High Crime Communities," *Criminal Justice Studies* 18 (2005): 29–50.

44. Thomas Tracy, "NYPD Stats: 70% of Shooting Suspects in First Half of 2013 Were Black," *New York Daily News*, November 19, 2013, retrieved April 19, 2014, http://www.nydailynews.com/news/ crime/blacks-70-shooting-suspects-2013-nypd-article-1.1522917

45. Eith and Durose, *Contacts between Police and the Public, 2008*, p. 1.

46. Ibid.

47. Erica Smith, Matthew Durose, and Patrick Langan, *State Court Processing of Domestic Violence Cases*, February 2008, revised March 2008, U.S. Department of Justice, Office of Justice Programs, Bureau of Justice Statistics Special Report.

48. Robert A. Brown and James Frank, "Race and Officer Decision Making: Examining Differences in Arrest Outcomes between Black and White Officers," *Justice Quarterly* 1 (2006): 96–126. For another study focused on the race of the officer, see David Eitle, Lisa Stolzenberg, and Stewart J. D'Alessio, "Police Organizational Factors, the Racial Composition of the Police, and the Probability of Arrest," *Justice Quarterly* 1 (2005): 30–57.

49. Crime in the United States 2012, Uniform Crime Reports, FBI, Table 49.

50. R. J. Lundman and R. L. Kaufman, "Driving While Black: Effects of Race Ethnicity and Gender on Citizen Self-Reports of Traffic Stops and Police Actions," *Criminology* 1 (2003): 195–220.

51. Engel and Calnon, "Examining the Influence of Drivers' Characteristics," *Justice Quarterly* 1 (2004): 49–90.

52. Christine Eith, Matthew R. Durose, *Contacts between Police and the Public, 2008* (Washington, D.C.: Bureau of Justice Statistics, U.S. Department of Justice, 2011), pp. 7, 12.

53. Michael R. Smith, Matthew Makarios, and Geoffrey P. Alpert, "Differential Suspicion: Theory Specification and Gender Effects in the Traffic Stop Context," *Justice Quarterly* 2 (2006): 271–295.

54. Geoffrey P. Alpert, Roger G. Dunham, Meghan Stroshine, Katherine Bennett, and John MacDonald, *Police Officers' Decision Making and Discretion: Forming Suspicion and Making a Stop* (Washington, D.C.: National Institute of Justice, 2006).

55. See Sandra Lee Browning, et al., "Race and Getting Hassled by the Police: A Research Note," *Police Studies* 17 (1994): 1–10; Darlene Conley, "Adding Color to a Black and White Picture: Using Qualitative Data to Explain Racial Disproportionality in the Juvenile Justice System," *Journal of Research in Crime and Delinquency* 31 (1994): 135–148; David Klinger, "Demeanor or Crime? Why 'Hostile' Citizens Are More Likely to Be Arrested," *Criminology* 32 (1994): 475–493; Larry Miller and Michael Braswell, "Police Perception of Ethical Decision Making: The Ideal vs. the Real," *American Journal of Police* 11 (1992): 27–45; Eric Riksheim and Steven Cermak, "Causes of Police Behavior Revisited," *Journal of Criminal Justice* 21 (1993): 353–382.

56. Davis, *Police Discretion*; Herman Goldstein, "Police Discretion: The Ideal vs. the Real," *Public Administration Review* 23 (1963): 148–156.

57. Goldstein, *Policing a Free Society*, p. 112.

58. *Tennessee v. Garner*, 471 U.S. 1 (1985).

59. Lori Rhyons and David C. Brewster, "Employee Early Warning Systems: Helping Supervisors Protect Citizens, Officers, and Agencies," *Police Chief* 11 (2002): 32–36.

60. Wilson, *Varieties of Police Behavior*, p. 33.

61. CALEA, www.Calea.org, 2010.

62. CALEA Accreditation Standards, 4th ed., 2001.

63. Ibid.

64. Thomas J. Martinelli, "Noble Cause Corruption and Police Discretion," *The Police Chief* (March 2011): 60–62.

65. Robert Moran, "Street: Police Critics 'Unfair,'" *Philadelphia Inquirer*, May 4, 2006.

66. Eith and Durose, *Contacts between Police and the Public, 2008*, pp. 13–14.

67. Matthew J. Hickman, *Citizen Complaints about Police Use of Force*, Bureau of Justice Statistics, June 2006, p.1, p.2

68. Joel H. Garner and Christopher D. Maxwell, *Understanding the Prevalence and Severity of Force Used by and Against the Police, Executive Summary* (Washington, D.C.: National Institute of Justice, 2002); Garner and Maxwell, *Understanding the Prevalence and Severity of Force Used by and Against the Police, Final Report* (Washington, D.C.: National Institute of Justice, 2002).

69. James Q. Wilson, "Police Use of Deadly Force," *FBI Law Enforcement Bulletin* (August 1980): 16.

70. James J. Fyfe, "Police Use of Deadly Force: Research and Reform," *Justice Quarterly* 5 (1988): 164–205.

71. Federal Bureau of Investigation, *Uniform Crime Reports: Crime in the United States, Justifiable Homicide, by Weapon, Law Enforcement, 2006–2010*, retrieved March 6, 2012, from www.fbi.gov.

72. Alexia Cooper and Erica L. Smith, *Homicide Trends in the United States, 1980–2008* (Washington, D.C.: Bureau of Justice Statistics, 2011).

73. New York City Police Department Annual Firearms Discharge Report, 2012, http://www.nyc.gov/html/nypd/downloads/pdf/analysis_and_planning/nypd_annual_firearms_discharge_report_2012.pdf

74. William A. Geller and Kevin J. Karales, *Split-Second Decisions* (Chicago: Chicago Law Enforcement Study Group, 1981), p. 119.

75. David Lester, "Predicting the Rate of Justifiable Homicide by Police Officers," *Police Studies* 16 (1993): 43.

76. Michael D. White, "Identifying Situational Predictors of Police Shootings Using Multivariate Analysis," *Policing: An International Journal of Police Strategies and Management* 4 (2004): 726–752.

77. *Tennessee v. Garner*, 471 U.S. 1 (1985).

78. Michael D. Greathouse, "Criminal Law—The Right to Run: Deadly Force and the Fleeing Felon, *Tennessee v. Garner*," in Michael J. Palmiotto, ed., *Police Misconduct: A Reader for the 21st Century* (Upper Saddle River, N.J.: Prentice Hall, 2001), pp. 243–255.

79. Lawrence O'Donnell, *Deadly Force* (New York: William Morrow, 1983), p. 14. Also see Abraham Tennenbaum, "The Influence of the *Garner* Decision on Police Use of Deadly Force," *Journal of Law and Criminology* 85 (1994): 241–260.

80. *Law Enforcement News*, November 15, 1995, p. 1.

81. David J. Spotts, "Reviewing Use-of-Force Practices," *The Police Chief Magazine*, August 2012, www.policechiefmagazine.org

82. Brian A. Reaves, *Local Police Departments, 2007* (Washington, D.C.: Bureau of Justice Statistics, 2010), p. 18; Hickman and Reaves, *Sheriff's Offices, 2003* (Washington, D.C.: Bureau of Justice Statistics, 2006), p. 4.

83. Ibid.

84. Thomas Aveni, "Special Report: Firearms Following Standard Procedure—A Long Term Analysis of Gunfights and Their Effects on Policy and Training," *Law and Order* 8 (2003): 78–87.

85. Brian A. Reaves, *State and Local Law Enforcement Training Academies, 2006*, U.S. Department of Justice, Office of Justice Programs, Bureau of Justice Statistic, Special Report, February 2009.

86. Thomas D. Petrowski, "Use of Force Policies and Training: A Reasoned Approach—Part 1," *FBI Law Enforcement Bulletin* 10 (2002): 25–32.

87. U.S. Government Accountability Office, *Taser Weapons: Use of Tasers by Selected Law Enforcement Agencies* (Washington, D.C.: U.S. Government Accountability Office, 2005).

88. Brian A. Reaves, *Local Police Departments, 2007*, (Washington, D.C.: Bureau of Justice Statistics, U.S. Department of Justice, 2010), pp. 18, 38.

89. Karen Krause, "Boca Police Find Taser Guns Help Subdue Suspect, but Some Questions Remain," *South Florida Sun–Sentinel*, April 26, 2002.

90. Christina Jewett, "CHP Weighs Adding Tasers," *Sacramento Bee*, April 7, 2006, p. A3; Mike Saccone, "Local Taser Use Outpaces Most State Agencies," *Daily Sentinel*, June 17, 2006.

91. Hickman and Reaves, *Local Police Departments, 2007*; Hickman and Reaves, *Sheriff's Offices, 2003*.

92. David Standen, "Use of Force Options," *Law and Order* 8 (2005): 88–92.

93. Charles S. Petty, M.D., *Deaths in Police Confrontations When Oleoresin Capsicum Is Used* (Washington, D.C.: National Institute of Justice, 2002).

94. Christina Jewett, "CHP Weighs Adding Tasers," p. A3; Kevin Johnson, "Justice Department Looks into Deaths of People Subdued by Stun Guns," *USA Today*, June 13, 2006. Also see Tal Abbady and Akilah Johnson, "Report Reveals Delray Man Died of Drugs, Not Taser," *Sun–Sentinel*, March 16, 2005; Alex Berenson, "The Safety of Tasers Is Questioned Again," *New York Times*, May 25, 2006; Kevin Johnson, "Federal Bureaus Reject Stun Guns," *USA Today*, March 18, 2005, p. 3A.

95. Kevin Johnson, "Justice Department Looks into Deaths," *USA Today*, June 13, 2006.

96. National Institute of Justice, *Study of Deaths Following Electro Muscular Disruption: Interim Report* (Washington, D.C.: National Institute of Justice, 2008), p. 3.

Police Culture, Personality, and Stress

AP Images/Wilfredo Lee

OUTLINE

The Police Culture or Subculture
The Blue Wall of Silence
The Police Personality
What Is the Police Personality?
Is the Police Personality Innate or
   Learned?
Police Cynicism
The *Dirty Harry* Problem
Police Stress
What Is Stress?
Nature of Stress in Policing

Factors Causing Stress in Policing
Effects of Stress on Police Officers
Stress and Police Families
Police Departments Dealing with
   Stress
Police Suicide
Police Danger
Officers Killed in the Line of Duty
Officers Assaulted in the Line of
   Duty
Police and Contagious Diseases

LEARNING OBJECTIVES

- Explain the police subculture and why it results in the blue wall of silence.

- Characterize the police personality and how it is expressed.

- Explain why levels of stress are higher in policing than other occupations.

- Identify ways police departments can address the high levels of stress exhibited by their officers.

- Describe and discuss the occupational dangers to the health and safety of police officers.

INTRODUCTION

On September 11, 2001, police officers throughout New York City, many responding while off duty, raced through the streets to respond to a 911 call reporting that a plane had crashed into New York City's World Trade Center. Many rushed into the building to help while regular citizens rushed out. Thirty-seven Port Authority of New York/New Jersey police officers, 23 New York City police officers, and 3 New York court officers lost their lives in their valiant effort to protect and serve. In the 1995 bombing of the Federal Building in Oklahoma City, officers rushed courageously into the building to help others get out. In fact, every day in cities and towns all over the United States, law enforcement officers put their own safety and lives at risk in order to protect and serve. Are these brave officers displaying the traits of the police culture?

Many experts and researchers studying the police write about such concepts as a distinct police culture or subculture and a distinct police personality. Are the police different from most other people? Much research indicates that they are.

This chapter will discuss such concepts as the police culture or subculture, the police personality, police cynicism, the *Dirty Harry* problem, police stress, "suicide by cop," and police danger. Police stress is a very serious issue facing officers. Therefore, this chapter will attempt to define it and to show why it occurs, how it exhibits itself, and how police agencies can deal with it.[1]

The Police Culture or Subculture

Numerous academic studies have indicated that the nature of policing and the experiences officers go through on the job cause them to band together into their own group, which many researchers call the police culture or subculture.[2] For example, if someone who was not a police officer walked into a bar at 1:00 a.m. and overheard a group of men and women engaged in animated conversation using such words as *collars, mopes, skells, perps, vics, edps,* and *shoeflies,* he or she would have great difficulty understanding the conversation. However, to the off-duty police officers having a few drinks and talking about their previous tour of duty, each word has a precise meaning.

The word *culture* refers to patterns of human activity or the way of life for a society. It includes informal codes or rules of manners, dress, language, behavior, rituals, and systems of belief.[3] The key components of culture consist of values, norms, and institutions. Values comprise ideas about what in life seems important. They tend to guide the rest of the culture. Norms consist of expectations of how people will behave in various situations, and each culture has methods (sanctions) for enforcing its norms. Institutions are the structures of a society within which values and norms are transmitted.[4]

Large societies often have subcultures, or groups of people with distinct sets of values, attitudes, behaviors, and beliefs that differentiate them from a larger culture of which they are a part. Sometimes subcultures can be defined by religious, occupational, or other factors. The **police culture or police subculture** is a combination of shared norms, values, goals, career patterns, lifestyles, and occupational structures that is somewhat different from the combination held by the rest of society, although in most important respects police share the dominant values of the larger culture. The police subculture, like most subcultures, is characterized by clannishness, secrecy, and isolation from those not in the group. Police officers work with other police officers during their tours of duty. Many socialize together after work and on days off, often to the exclusion of others—even old friends and family. When socializing, off-duty officers tend to talk about their jobs.

Working strange shifts of duty, especially 4-to-12 (4:00 p.m. to 12:00 midnight) and midnights (12:00 midnight to 8:00 a.m.), and working weekends and holidays make it difficult for the police officer to socialize with the average person working a 9-to-5 job Monday through Friday. Many police officers find it difficult to sleep after a tense, busy evening tour. If officers want to socialize or relax after work, instead of going home to a house whose

police culture or police subculture A combination of shared norms, values, goals, career patterns, lifestyles, and occupational structures that is somewhat different from the combination held by the rest of society.

Courtesy Special Olympics Washington

Police officers often primarily socialize with each other due to their challenging work schedules. Although this might increase officers' isolation from society, coupling this socialization with a good cause like the Special Olympics provides an opportunity to reduce stress through exercise and to bond with other officers. Chief Rex Caldwell leads by example as he plunges into frigid water hourly during the Polar Plunge Special Olympics fundraising event.

inhabitants have to get up at 6:00 a.m. to go to regular jobs, many tend to socialize with their comrades from the job. When officers work weekends, their days off fall during the average person's workweek, so, again, many tend to socialize with other officers. Police spouses tend to socialize with other police spouses, and police families tend to associate with other police families. After a while, the police world is the only world for many officers.

Michael K. Brown, in *Working the Street*, tells us that police officers create their own culture to deal with the recurring anxiety and emotional stress that is endemic to policing. Brown believes that the police subculture is based on three major principles: honor, loyalty, and individuality.[5]

Honor is given to officers for engaging in risk-taking behavior. An example of risk-taking behavior is being the first one in the door to challenge an armed adversary, when taking cover and waiting for backup would have been the more prudent course of action.

Loyalty is a major part of the police subculture, and police loyalty is extremely intense. The word

backup occurs often in police officer conversations. Backup involves assisting other officers in emergency situations and coming to their aid when they are challenged, criticized, or even charged with wrongdoing. Brown explains the importance of backup by pointing out that the violence that police must deal with and the strong bonding that occurs among police officers "places the highest value upon the obligation to back up and support a fellow officer."[6]

The ideal officer, according to the police subculture, takes risks (honor), is first on the scene to aid a fellow police officer (loyalty), and is able to handle any situation by doing it her or his own way (individuality). (See Table 6.1.)

The idea of danger permeates the police subculture. George L. Kirkham, a college professor who became a police officer to better understand his police students, discusses the police mistrust of civilians and police reliance upon their own peer-group support to survive on the streets: "As someone who had always regarded policemen as a 'paranoid lot,' I discovered in the daily round of violence which became part of my life that chronic suspiciousness is something that a good cop cultivates in the interest of going home to his family each evening."[7]

Egon Bittner, a police researcher, also has said that an *esprit de corps* develops in police work as a function of the dangerous and unpleasant tasks police officers are required to do. Police solidarity, a "one for all, and all for one" attitude, Bittner says, is one of the most cherished aspects of the police occupation.[8]

John M. Violanti, a former police officer and expert on police suicide, writes that entry into law enforcement involves an abrupt change from citizen to police officer. This process is very strong in basic police training and continues to dominate officers' lives throughout their careers. Police officers can

TABLE 6.1   Traits of the Police Culture/Subculture

• Clannishness
• Secrecy
• Isolation from the public
• Honor
• Loyalty
• Individuality

become addicted to excitement and danger, which can decrease their ability to assess the nature of current challenges and can interfere with rational decision processes. Police officers, through psychological and physiological mechanisms, become ingrained in police work and isolated from other life roles such as family, friendships, or community involvement.[9]

Eugene A. Paoline III, in his *Rethinking Police Culture: Officers' Occupational Attitudes*, discusses the ways in which police officers perceive and cope with aspects of their working environments in contemporary police departments. He says that the occupational attitudes associated with police culture include distrust and suspiciousness of citizens, assessing people in terms of their potential threat, a "we versus they" attitude toward citizens, and loyalty to the peer group.[10]

The police personality is reflected in the many coping strategies officers use to deal with stress, including humor and keeping an emotional distance from themselves and stressful events.[11] Often, officers tend to use "gallows humor" or appear disinterested in the suffering of others. Sometimes, citizens wrongly assume that this attitude of appearing disinterested indicates that the police are uncaring.

Paoline wrote that the conventional wisdom about police culture rests on descriptions of a single occupational phenomenon in which the attitudes, values, and norms of members are homogenous. He believes, however, that as departments continue to diversify and as community policing becomes part of the philosophy of policing, there will be more cultural variations. He urges researchers to focus their efforts on studying this increased cultural variation of the traditional police culture and how it expresses itself.[12] Other researchers also see changes in the traditional concept of the police culture as changing employment patterns have diversified police departments and brought significant changes to and within departments.[13]

A student interested in studying police culture should look on the Internet, where active and retired police officers from all over the nation and abroad have created their own home pages. Often, retired officers will contact former colleagues through the Internet.

blue wall of silence A figurative protective barrier erected by the police in which officers protect one another from outsiders, often even refusing to aid police superiors or other law enforcement officials in investigating wrongdoing of other officers.

The Blue Wall of Silence

Studies of the police culture indicate that police officers protect one another from outsiders, often even refusing to aid police superiors or other law enforcement officials in investigating wrongdoing by other officers. This produces a protective barrier known as the **blue wall of silence**.[14] Writing about the police subculture and the blue wall of silence, Bittner says, "Policing is a dangerous occupation and the availability of unquestioned support and loyalty is not something officers could readily do without."[15]

Robert Sheehan and Gary W. Cordner write about how this aspect of the police subculture can destroy the reputation and integrity of a police department: "The influence of dominant police subcultural role expectations can have a devastating effect on a police department. Actually, the existence of such unofficially established, negative, institutionalized role expectations is the primary reason that so many police departments are held in such low esteem by the public."[16] They give two examples of how the police subculture can create a blue wall of silence and adversely affect a police department in two fictional cities, Cod Bay and Tulane City.[17]

In Cod Bay, Sheehan and Cordner's first fictional city, a police sergeant is dealing with an irate motorist whose car was towed because it was parked illegally. As the sergeant talks to the officer who wrote the summons that caused the car to be towed, the sergeant realizes that the motorist's car was indeed parked legally, and the towing was in error. The sergeant, however, following the dominant police subcultural expectation that he must back the officer whether he was right or wrong, tells the motorist that in order to get his car back, he must pay the towing charge.

In Sheehan and Cordner's other fictional city, Tulane City, politics rule the police department. A police chief appointed by local politicians accepts corruption, incompetence, and brutality by his officers because he realizes that when another mayor takes office, that mayor will select his own police chief, and he himself will return to the department in a lower rank. If he tries to reform the police department while chief, he will be ostracized by officers when he returns to a lower status. Failing to adhere to the existing police subculture would be dangerous to the chief in the future.

A real-life example of the police subcultural blue wall of silence is demonstrated in William

Westley's classic study of the Gary, Indiana, Police Department, in which he found a police culture that had its own customs, law, and morality. Westley says these values produce the **blue curtain**—a situation in which police officers only trust other police officers and do not aid in the investigation of wrongdoing by other officers. Westley calls the blue curtain a barrier that isolates police officers from the rest of society.[18]

The blue wall of silence was brought to the forefront during the interview of a corrupt New York City police officer by the Mollen Commission to Investigate Police Corruption in the 1990s. The officer, when questioned about whether any fellow officers might report his corruption, replied, "Never.... Because it was the Blue Wall of Silence. Cops don't tell on cops."[19] This code of silence was also mentioned in the 1991 Christopher Commission investigation of the Los Angeles Police Department. In the commission's report, a Los Angeles police officer commented, "It is basically a nonwritten rule that you do not roll over, tell on your partner, your companion."[20]

Dr. Neal Trautman, Director of the National Institute of Ethics, presented a research paper to the legal officers' section of the International Association of Chiefs of Police (IACP) at the 2000 IACP conference. His study of 2,698 currently employed officers in 21 states found that 46 percent of those officers had witnessed misconduct but did not report it. This same study also found that 73 percent of the individuals who were "pressuring the individuals to keep quiet" were supervisors. In addition, the study found that 79 percent of police academy recruits in 25 basic law enforcement academies believed that a code of silence exists.[21]

Trautman proposed a solution to the problem of a code of silence with his "Code of Silence Antidote" (COSA). According to Trautman, if the 32 standards included in his code are implemented and followed, "scandals involving multiple officers can be practically eliminated."[22] Prevention of scandals begins during recruitment and is reinforced by the administration. Training officers at police academies reinforce integrity by modeling the behavior and addressing the ethical lessons to be learned from each topic taught. A code of ethics exam can be given to all recruits. By establishing patterns early in the process, the officer knows what is expected, and patterns of integrity are built and reinforced.[23]

The Police Personality

The police culture or subculture leads to what scholars call the **police personality**, or traits common to most police officers. Scholars have reported that this personality is thought to include such traits as authoritarianism, suspicion, hostility, insecurity, conservatism, and cynicism.[24] (See Table 6.2.)

What Is the Police Personality?

Jerome Skolnick coined the term "working personality of police officers."[25] Skolnick stated that the police officer's working personality is shaped by constant exposure to danger and the need to use force and authority to reduce and control threatening situations.[26] He wrote,

> The policeman's role contains two principal variables, danger and authority, which should be interpreted in the light of a "constant" pressure to appear efficient. The element of danger seems to make the policeman especially attentive to signs indicating a potential for violence and law-breaking. As a result the policeman is generally a "suspicious person." Furthermore, the character of the policeman's work makes him less desirable as a friend since norms of friendship implicate others in his work. Accordingly the element of

TABLE 6.2 Traits of the Police Personality

• Authoritarianism
• Suspicion
• Hostility
• Insecurity
• Conservatism
• Cynicism

© 2016 Cengage Learning®

blue curtain A concept developed by William Westley that claims police officers only trust other police officers and do not aid in the investigation of wrongdoing by other officers.

police personality Traits common to most police officers. Scholars have reported that this personality is thought to include such traits as authoritarianism, suspicion, hostility, insecurity, conservatism, and cynicism.

danger isolates the policeman socially from that segment of the citizenry whom he regards as symbolically dangerous and also from the conventional citizenry with whom he identifies.[27]

Elizabeth Burbeck and Adrian Furnham identified three important features of an officer's working personality: danger, authority, and isolation from the public.[28] They reviewed the literature comparing the attitudes of police officers with those of the general population and found that police officers place a higher emphasis on terminal values (such as family security, mature love, and a sense of accomplishment) than on social values (such as equality).

One example of the studies Burbeck and Furnham looked at is the 1971 Rokeach study. Social psychologist Milton Rokeach and his colleagues studied police officers in Lansing, Michigan. They compared the officers' personality traits with a national sample of private citizens and concluded that police officers seemed more oriented toward self-control and obedience than the average citizen. Also, police were more interested in personal goals, such as "an exciting life," and less interested in social goals, such as "a world of peace." Rokeach also compared values of veteran officers with those of recruits and discovered no significant differences. Rokeach concluded that individuals who become police officers have a particular value orientation and personality even before they start their police career.[29]

Regarding the requirements of the police profession and the police personality, Michael Pittaro wrote,

> Police officers are continuously challenged with a number of internal and external stressors, most of which can wreak havoc on the officer's physical and emotional well-being over time. Police work is essentially a dangerous profession in which danger looms in virtually every call for help. The profession requires someone with distinctive personality traits to be both law enforcer and social worker, which is not as simple as one would think.[30]

Is the Police Personality Innate or Learned?

Two opposing viewpoints exist on the development of the police personality. One viewpoint, as demonstrated in the Rokeach study, says that police departments recruit people who by nature possess those traits that we see in the police personality. The second point of view holds that officers develop those traits through their socialization and experiences in the police department.[31]

Edward Thibault, Lawrence M. Lynch, and R. Bruce McBride tell us that most studies have found that the police working personality derives from the socialization process in the police academy, field training, and patrol experience.[32] John Van Maanen also asserts that the police personality is developed through the process of learning and doing police work. In a study of one urban police department, he found that the typical police recruit is a sincere individual who becomes a police officer for the job security, the salary, the belief that the job will be interesting, and the desire to enter an occupation that can benefit society. He found that at the academy, highly idealistic recruits are taught to have a strong sense of camaraderie with fellow rookies. The recruits begin to admire the exploits of the veteran officers who are their teachers. From their instructors, the recruits learn when to do police work by the book and when to ignore department rules and rely on personal discretion.[33]

Van Maanen says that the learning process continues when the recruits are assigned to street duty and trained by field training officers. The recruits listen to the folklore, myths, and legends about veteran officers and start to understand police work in the way that older officers desire them to. By adopting the sentiments and behavior of the older officers, the new recruits avoid ostracism and censure by their supervisors and colleagues.[34]

A recently completed longitudinal study of police attitudes over time, as the officers were exposed to police work, certainly showed a socialization effect. The study tested police recruits during the first week of the academy and then at several follow-up periods up to almost four years after the academy. The testing included the Minnesota Multiphasic Personality Inventory (MMPI), standard demographic questions, questions concerning the respondent's physical exercise program and tobacco use, an alcohol consumption assessment, and Arthur Niederhoffer's cynicism scale (described further in the next section). This study provided clear evidence that the personality characteristics of the officers started to change shortly after their induction into the policing environment. With rare exceptions, officers tended to become more cynical, more paranoid, more depressed, angrier, more dominant, and more hostile the longer they were in the policing environment. White females were the least affected group, and black females were the most affected group. Black males were more affected by their exposure to policing than were white males.[35]

Conversely, several researchers have found little evidence that a "typical" police personality actually exists. Studies by sociologists Larry Tifft, David Bayley and Harold Mendelsohn, and Robert Balch have indicated that even experienced police officers are quite similar to the average citizen.[36] Nevertheless, the weight of existing evidence generally points to the existence of a unique police personality that develops from the police socialization process. Some researchers have found that police officers are actually psychologically healthier, less depressed and anxious, and more social and assertive than the general population.[37]

Police Cynicism

Police cynicism is an attitude that there is no hope for the world and a view of humanity at its worst. This is produced by the police officer's constant contact with offenders and what he or she perceives as miscarriages of justice, such as lenient court decisions and plea bargaining.

Arthur Niederhoffer described police cynicism as follows:

> Cynicism is an emotional plank deeply entrenched in the ethos of the police world and it serves equally well for attack or defense. For many reasons police are particularly vulnerable to cynicism. When they succumb, they lose faith in people, society, and eventually in themselves. In their Hobbesian view, the world becomes a jungle in which crime, corruption, and brutality are normal features of terrain.[38]

Niederhoffer, a former New York City Police Department (NYPD) lieutenant and a professor at John Jay College of Criminal Justice, wrote what is one of the best-known studies of the police personality, *Behind the Shield: The Police in Urban Society*. He examined the thesis that most police officers develop into cynics as a function of their experience as police officers,[39] and he tested Westley's assumption that police officers learn to mistrust the citizens they are paid to protect as a result of being constantly faced with keeping people in line and believing that most people are out to break the law or injure a police officer.[40] Niederhoffer distributed a survey measuring attitudes and values to 220 New York City police officers. Among his most important findings were that police cynicism increased with length of service in the police department, that police officers with a college education became quite cynical if they were denied promotion, and that quasi-military police academy training caused new recruits to become cynical about themselves quickly. For example, Niederhoffer found that nearly 80 percent of first-day recruits believed that the police department was an "efficient, smoothly operating organization." Two months later, fewer than a third held that belief. Also, half the new recruits believed that a police superior was "very interested in the welfare of his subordinates." Two months later, that number declined to 13 percent.[41]

Cynicism may hurt the relationship between the police and the public, but it may help advance an officer in his or her career within the department. In a longitudinal study of police officers in Georgia, Richard Anson, J. Dale Mann, and Dale Sherman found that the officers with the most cynical attitudes were the ones most likely to get high supervisory ratings. The researchers concluded that "cynicism is a valued quality of the personality of the police officer and is positively evaluated by important individuals in police organizations."[42]

The *Dirty Harry* Problem

Police officers are often confronted with situations in which they feel forced to take certain illegal actions to achieve a greater good. Indeed, one of the greatest and oldest ethical questions people have ever faced is this: "Do good ends ever justify bad means?"

Carl B. Klockars has dubbed this moral dilemma of police officers as the **Dirty Harry problem**, from the 1971 film *Dirty Harry*, starring Clint Eastwood as Detective Harry Callahan.[43] In the film, a young girl has been kidnapped by a psychopathic killer named Scorpio, who demands $200,000 in ransom. Scorpio has buried the girl with just enough

---

police cynicism An attitude that there is no hope for the world and a view of humanity at its worst.

Dirty Harry problem A moral dilemma faced by police officers in which they may feel forced to take certain illegal actions to achieve a greater good.

oxygen to survive a few hours. Harry eventually finds Scorpio and tortures him to find out where the girl is. Finally, Scorpio tells Harry her location. Harry finds her, but she has already died from lack of oxygen.

Let's change the plot of the movie and say that Harry's action resulted in his finding the girl and saving her life. This would be a great Hollywood ending, but think about it. Harry had a good end in mind (finding the girl before she died), but what about the means he used (torturing Scorpio and not giving him his constitutional rights before interrogation)?

Harry was wrong, right? He violated police procedure. He violated the precepts of the Fifth Amendment to the U.S. Constitution, which he swore an oath to obey. He committed crimes, the most obvious of which was assault.

Harry was wrong, right? If Harry had used proper police procedure, had not violated the law, had not violated the Constitution of the United States, and had advised Scorpio of his right to an attorney, there is no doubt the attorney would have told Scorpio to remain silent, and the little girl would have died.

Thus, the question is raised: Is it more morally wrong to (1) torture Scorpio, thereby violating the police oath of office and legal obligations but finding the girl and saving her life, or (2) act in accordance with the rules of the system and not make every effort, illegal or not, to force Scorpio to talk and thus permit the girl to die?

Sure, this is only Hollywood. You would never be faced with this dilemma as a police officer, would you? As Klockars writes,

> In real, everyday policing, situations in which innocent victims are buried with just enough oxygen to keep them alive are, thankfully, very rare. But the core scene in *Dirty Harry* should only be understood as an especially dramatic example of a far more common problem: real, everyday, routine situations in which police officers know they can only achieve good ends by employing dirty means. Each time a police officer considers deceiving a suspect into confessing by telling him that his fingerprints were found at the scene or that a conspirator has already confessed, each time a police officer considers adding some untrue details to his account of probable cause to legitimate a crucial stop or search . . . that police officer faces a Dirty Harry Problem.[44]

We can sympathize with Harry Callahan, and surely we can sympathize with the plight of the little girl about to die. However, despite Hollywood portrayals, police officers must operate within the boundaries of the law, because the law is what the people, through their representatives, want to be governed by. The police cannot make their own laws. Harry Callahan, although he attempted to save the life of the child, was wrong. In our system of law, we cannot use unlawful means to achieve worthy goals. Police work is a tough business. Tough choices must be made. As Klockars says,

> Dirty Harry Problems are an inevitable part of policing. They will not go away. The reason they won't is that policing is a moral occupation which constantly places its practitioners in situations in which unquestionable good ends can only be achieved by employing morally, legally, or politically dirty means to their achievements.
>
> The effects of Dirty Harry Problems on real police officers are often devastating. They can lead officers to lose their sense of moral proportion, fail to care, turn cynical, or allow their too passionate caring to lead them to employ dirty means too readily or too crudely. They make policing the most morally corrosive occupation.[45]

Can the *Dirty Harry* (or *Dirty Harriet*) problem lead to a serious ethical problem facing our police? Certainly. Police officers must be always alert to the fact that bad means are never justified by good ends. The police swear allegiance to their oath of office and the U.S. Constitution and their state constitution. Although it may be tempting, police cannot solve all the problems of this world and they certainly cannot solve them by violating their oath of office and their dedication to our Constitution. Ethics will be discussed in much more detail in Chapter 8, "Police Ethics and Police Deviance."

Police Stress

Police officers are often faced with stressful situations during a routine tour of duty. The dispatcher may assign them to respond to a "gun run." (A gun run orders patrol units to respond to a certain location because of a 911 report that a person has a gun in his or her possession. These calls receive immediate police response.) Citizens may stop them to report a crime or dangerous condition. Officers may find an open door to a factory and search for a possible burglar. They may wait in a stakeout for an armed felon to appear. Every tour of duty, police officers must always be ready to react. Their bodies' response to these stressful situations is good in that it prepares them for any emergency, but the stress response takes its toll on officers' physical and mental states.

What Is Stress?

Stress is the body's reaction to internal or external stimuli that upset the body's normal state. A stimulus that causes stress (a stressor) can be physical, mental, or emotional. The term *stress* is used to refer to both the body's reaction and the stimuli that caused it.

The body's reaction to highly stressful situations is known as the **flight-or-fight response**. Under stressful circumstances, quantities of adrenaline, a hormone produced by the adrenal glands, are released into the bloodstream. This stimulates the liver to provide the body with stored carbohydrates for extra energy. It also results in quickened heartbeat and respiration, as well as increased blood pressure and muscle tension. The body is getting prepared for extraordinary physical exertion; this is good. However, if the need for this extraordinary exertion does not materialize, the frustrated readiness may cause headache, upset stomach, irritability, and a host of other symptoms.[46]

Some experts say that stress alone probably does not cause illness, but it contributes to circumstances in which diseases may take hold and flourish. Stress weakens and disturbs the body's defense mechanisms and may play a role in the development of hypertension, ulcers, cardiovascular disease, and cancer.[47]

Nature of Stress in Policing

Although most people have some stress in their lives or careers, studies have found evidence of particularly high rates of stress in certain professions. Some researchers have called policing the most stressful of all professions. The American Institute of Stress ranked police work among the top 10 stress-producing jobs in the United States.[48]

A reporter riding with the police addressed the stress that officers experience:

The world inside the patrol car is a world of its own, two officers who are slaves to the dispatcher on the crackling radio who can send

them speeding into adrenaline overdrive racing to catch a suspect with a gun and then can order "slow it down" after enough cars are already at a crime scene. The result is an emotional up and down in just six blocks.[49]

In an excellent 2008 comprehensive article on police occupational stress and its impact on community relations, Michael Pittaro, former executive director of the Council on Alcohol and Drug Abuse, wrote,

The research strongly suggests and most people would agree that a certain amount of stress is evident in most, if not all, professions; however, law enforcement has the dubious honor of being recognized as one of the most stressful professions in the world. The harmful effects and debilitating impact of stress, particularly chronic stress, can lead to a multitude of physical, emotional, psychological, and behavioral problems that not only affect the individual officer, but also the officer's family, partner, fellow officers, and of particular interest, the community with which the officer has sworn to serve and protect are also at risk.[50]

Some studies indicate that police have higher rates of divorce, suicide, and other manifestations of stress than do other professions.[51] One writer said, "It would be difficult to find an occupation that is subject to more consistent and persistent tension, strain, confrontations, and nerve wracking than that of the uniformed patrolman."[52]

Researchers have identified four general categories of stress with which police officers are confronted: external, organizational, personal, and operational.[53] While differences in scope can certainly be identified between urban and small-town policing, the idea that stress does not affect all officers—as some have asserted—is fallacious. No matter the size of the department, all officers face the same stresses to varying degrees and with similar consequences for the officer and their families.

EXTERNAL STRESS External stress is produced by real threats and dangers, such as responding to gun runs, taking part in auto pursuits, and other

---

flight-or-fight response The body's reaction to highly stressful situations in which it is getting prepared for extraordinary physical exertion.

dangerous assignments. A recent study of police stress in Canada involving full-shift ride-alongs with randomly selected officers from 12 municipal departments in British Columbia found significant levels of physical stress among police officers. Using heart rate coupled with observed physical-activity data, researchers found the highest physical stress to occur during officers' physical enforcement activities and marked psycho-social stress when responding to critical incidents, particularly during an interaction with a suspect, both during the critical incident and then during each subsequent interaction with suspects for the remainder of the shift. The average heart rate of those involved in a critical incident remained elevated for the remainder of the shift for all tasks, including report writing in the last hour of the shift. The evidence also suggests that officers anticipate stress as they conduct their work, experiencing anticipatory stress at the start of each shift.[54]

Consider the external stress faced by members of the New Orleans Police Department in the aftermath of Hurricane Katrina. Many of them were flooded out of their own homes and separated from their families and loved ones, and they had to face constant attacks by armed assailants looking to loot and plunder the little that was left in New Orleans.[55]

Police officers also experience stress from their belief that the criminal justice system does not seem to help them. In 2008, a Nashville, Tennessee, police commander reflected on the recent arrest of a man arrested for pulling a box cutter on an undercover decoy officer. Since 1982, the 60-year-old man has been arrested 416 times for an array of offenses. The commander, Andy Garrett, stated, "The biggest frustrating thing is the amount of resources I have to commit on this one person that has an extensive criminal history where I could be proactive in another area."[56]

ORGANIZATIONAL STRESS Organizational stress is produced by elements inherent in the quasi-military character of the police service, such as constant adjustment to changing tours of duty, odd working hours, working holidays, and the strict discipline imposed on officers. Organizational stress also results from workplace conditions, the lack of influence over work activities, and workplace bias.

In a 2006 study, Merry Morash, Robin Haarr, and Dae-Hoon Kwak found that several workplace conditions cause police stress. They found that the most predictive stressors were lack of influence over

work activities and biases against one's racial, ethnic, or gender group. Their findings also indicated that a lack of influence by officers on how police work is accomplished is a considerable stressor.[57]

In a 2006 article, James D. Sewell, formerly an assistant commissioner of the Florida Department of Law Enforcement, wrote that some management practices, unfortunately, also create stress in the lives of officers. He noted that although contemporary leadership and supervisory courses foster effective management techniques, some managers, often trained in traditional policies or management practices, or perhaps more interested in their own advancement, forget that their actions can create a stressful work environment and impact the success and well-being of a work unit or organization.[58]

PERSONAL STRESS Personal stress is produced by the interpersonal characteristics of belonging to the police organization, such as difficulties in getting along with other officers.

OPERATIONAL STRESS Operational stress is produced by the police officer's daily confrontation with the tragedies of urban life: the need to deal with derelicts, criminals, the mentally disturbed, and the drug addicted; the need to engage in dangerous activity to protect a public that appears to be unappreciative of the police; and the constant awareness of the possibility of being legally liable for actions performed while on duty.

Most studies on police stress have focused primarily on urban and suburban officers, with scant research done on rural and small-town police. Some researchers assert that the public and scholarly view of the concerns of the rural and small-town officer as being merely "small" versions of the urban problems is wrong, and that the tendency to extrapolate findings has led to questions about the ability to generalize them. Also, some researchers argue that an urban bias in our society is perpetuated in academic research.[59]

In 2004, in order to bridge this gap, Yolanda M. Scott of Roger Williams University in Rhode Island produced a study of the stress experiences of 135 rural and small-town officers employed in 11 Pennsylvania municipal police agencies. Her research suggests that the widespread public assumption of rural and small-town officers resembling media portrayals of "Mayberry" law enforcement grossly misrepresents the level and types of stress experienced by these officers. Officers in these agencies were indeed distressed by several factors. She found that organizational stress was among the most problematic for officers and that their perceptions of the organizational setting, specifically administrative changes, were significantly predictive of all forms of officer stress. These officers perceived that changes to the department's top administrative positions would interrupt every part of their lives and work, including their treatment within the department, situations of danger or violence, and the impact of the job on their family. She also found that media criticism was linked to officer stress, and that it was particularly upsetting to officers because it disrupted their credibility with the community of which they are a part. She explains that they are recognizable people in the community and have difficulty finding privacy whether on or off duty. As Scott says, "In contrast to many of their urban counterparts, rural and small-town officers' service area is also the place they call 'home.'" Overall, her findings suggest that rural and small-town police officers would benefit from and likely respond to stress intervention programs such as peer support and mental health counseling.[60]

Scott has also studied coping mechanisms in response to stress among rural and small-town police officers and found that they tend to use a variety of healthy or adaptive coping mechanisms, such as physical exercise, activities or hobbies, and sharing their problems. However, a substantial proportion of the officers utilized maladaptive or unhealthy forms of coping, including absenteeism, avoiding discussion with supervisors, sleeping, drinking alcohol, and tobacco use.[61]

Factors Causing Stress in Policing

According to researchers, many factors lead to stress in police work, including poor training, substandard equipment, poor pay, lack of opportunity, role conflict, exposure to brutality, fears about job competence and safety, and lack of job satisfaction. Researchers also say that the pressure of being on duty 24 hours a day leads to stress and that the police learn to cope with that stress by becoming emotionally detached from their work and the people they are paid to serve.[62]

Fatigue can also affect officers' stress. Working long hours and overtime produces fatigue and consequently stress in officers.[63] In a 2007 study of

shift work and sleep using 111 randomly selected police officers from the Buffalo, New York, Police Department, researchers discovered that shift work and night work were significantly and independently associated with decreased sleep duration. Night shift workers experienced a 44 percent greater likelihood of getting fewer than seven hours of sleep in comparison to day or afternoon shift workers.[64] Bryan Vila, a professor of criminal justice and author of the book *Tired Cops: The Importance of Managing Police Fatigue*, stated, "Many police officers in the United States can't do their jobs safely or live healthy lives because of long and erratic work hours, insufficient sleep, and what appears to be very high levels of sleep disorders among experienced cops."[65]

AP Images/Douglas C. Pizac

The life-and-death decisions an officer makes as well as more routine decisions are a constant source of stress. Even receiving an award for bravery can elicit mixed emotions as the officer relives the stressful event that led to the act being recognized.

One researcher attributed stress problems to a lack of emphasis on physical fitness once an officer leaves the police academy: "Without police fitness standards, a police department has too many 'loose wires' to account for. It is unfair to place the burden of quality effectiveness on each individual without presenting a plan that will achieve these goals."[66]

Do officer race and gender matter in police stress? This is the subject of several recent studies. In 2005, Ni He, Jihong Zhao, and Ling Ren studied more than 1,100 police officers from each of Baltimore's nine police precincts and police headquarters to determine the effects of officer race and gender on police stress. For the purposes of the study, the sample of officers was divided into four subgroups: white males, African American males, white females, and African American females. They were compared on stressors, coping mechanisms, and multiple psychological symptoms of stress. The researchers discovered that white males reported higher levels of physical symptoms of stress, anxiety, and depression than did their African American male counterparts. Levels of psychological stress reported by females were higher than were those reported by males. There was no statistically significant difference between white and African American female officers. Both male and female African American officers were more likely to use constructive coping than were their white counterparts.[67] Another recent study revealed that female officers had higher levels of depression compared with male officers, but that male and female police officers did not differ statistically in clinically developed measures of anxiety.[68]

Some recent research suggests that female officers' baseline rate of work-related stress may compound their trauma reaction to events such as the 9/11 attacks. Female officers may experience added stress from working in a male-dominated environment where they are constantly exposed to the belief that female officers perform less effectively than male officers. Female officers are particularly reluctant to seek counseling in the management of stress, because of the fear that this would reinforce male officers' belief that women are not tough enough to handle police work.[69]

SUICIDE BY COP Compounding the stress problems of police officers is the phenomenon known as **suicide by cop**, in which a person wishing to die deliberately places an officer in a life-threatening situation, causing the officer to use deadly force against that person.[70]

Perhaps the classic case of suicide by cop occurred in 1997 on a Long Island, New York, expressway, when a 19-year-old man, despondent over a gambling debt, drove recklessly, causing the police to pull him over. He then pulled a "very real-looking gun" (actually a $1.79 toy revolver) on them. Police fatally shot him. Inside the youth's car were good-bye cards for his friends and a chilling suicide note addressed "To the Officer Who Shot Me," in which he apologized for getting the police involved.[71]

Another example occurred on January 25, 2012, when Brad Morgan of Portland, Oregon, climbed on the top of an elevator shaft next to a downtown parking garage, called 911, and made statements about "suicide by cop." When asked if he had a gun, he said, "Possibly." After officers arrived on scene, they made the proper calls for assistance from their Project Respond crisis workers and the crisis negotiation team to assist in talking the man down. Unfortunately, before help arrived, the officers were placed in the position of having to shoot Morgan after he pointed a firearm (which later turned out to be a replica firearm) at them. This was the first officer-involved shooting in Portland in more than a year. Later, in grand jury testimony, it was reported that Brad Morgan had said: "What happens if I pull a gun out right now?" In response, one of the officers said: "Brad, you would ruin our lives."[72]

When officers are placed in a situation where deadly force may be used, and especially a "suicide by cop" situation, the police become victims as well, although not all the public agrees that the police are victims in these situations. James Mazzocco, a member of the Advisory Council of the Mental Health Association of Portland, believed the officers named in the Portland grand jury report in the Brad Morgan case should have been held and tried for "assisting suicide."[73]

The effect on police officers involved in these cases is devastating. According to David Klinger, a former police officer, now a professor at the University of Missouri at St. Louis, "Police find out after the fact that they did not need to shoot to protect themselves. It angers them that they hurt or killed someone." Klinger said even though police

....

suicide by cop The phenomenon in which a person wishing to die deliberately places an officer in a life-threatening situation, causing the officer to use deadly force against that person.

officers are trained to use deadly force, actually using it on someone, especially someone who has a death wish, can be life altering for the officers involved: "Police officers generally can develop a bit of a thick skin about dealing with individuals who have killed themselves, but when you are the instrument of that death, it can take quite a toll."[74]

In addition to leaving the police with feelings of guilt and of being tricked into using deadly force, these situations are often compounded by media accounts that depict the deceased as the victim. In a case in St. Charles, Missouri, the daughter of a man who had caused the police to shoot him questioned the officers' use of force because the man had never fired at the police. She said that the police should have wounded him. St. Charles Police Chief Tim Swope determined that the officers' actions were justified, saying, "These officers have families; they want to go home at the end of the day. It's unfortunate that they had to do this, but that's part of the job." St. Charles County Sheriff Tom Neer agreed, saying, "We are trained to eliminate the threat. I know it sounds cold, but we aren't trained to wound people because wounded people kill others."[75]

The suicide by cop phenomenon became widely reported in 1996 by a Canadian police officer, Richard B. Parent, in a landmark report on victim-precipitated homicide. Parent, who interviewed cops after they were involved in such incidents, said many of the officers quit the police department, got divorced, or abused drugs or alcohol after the killings.[76]

A study in the *Annals of Emergency Medicine*, an analysis of 437 deputy-involved shootings that occurred in the Los Angeles County Sheriff's Department, disclosed that suicide by cop incidents accounted for 11 percent of the shootings and 13 percent of all deputy-involved justifiable homicides. The victims in these cases enacted elaborate schemes, including doing something to draw officers to the scene, disobeying commands to put down the weapon, continuing to threaten officers and other individuals, and escalating the encounter to the point where police felt that they had to use deadly force to protect themselves, their partners, and civilians. The study indicated that most of the subjects in these cases were male and had a history of domestic violence, suicide attempts, and alcohol and drug abuse. Police officers involved in these incidents experienced emotions ranging from shock and remorse to shame, anger, and powerlessness. The report concluded that suicide by cop constitutes an actual form of suicide.[77]

A study of the psychological effects of suicide by cop on involved officers revealed that the short-term effects of these incidents seem to entail the same psychological impacts experienced by officers involved in most critical incidents, including mentally replaying the event repeatedly, disruption of sleep, feelings of irritability and detachment, being hypercritical, sensory disturbance, and hypervigilance. The most dominant short-term emotion experienced by the officers was anger toward the subject for controlling the situation and forcing the officer to use deadly force. Long-term effects included feelings of vulnerability, being more protective of family, and being less trusting of the general public. More than half of the officers interviewed seriously considered retiring or quitting the department. Often these thoughts were reinforced by family members, who experienced intensified fears of their loved one being killed in the line of duty. Officers reported that psychological debriefing was particularly important in helping them through the impact of the suicide by cop incident.[78]

In 2005, Anthony J. Pinizzotto, senior scientist and clinical forensic psychologist in the FBI's Behavioral Science Unit (BSU), Edward F. Davis, a retired police officer and instructor at BSU, and Charles E. Miller III, a retired police captain and coordinator and instructor in the FBI's Criminal

YOU ARE THERE

A Cop's Suicide by Cop

When Officer Kline went to work one day in January 2012, he had no idea that he would shoot and kill Alberto Covarrubias, his best friend, his best man, and a fellow officer. Officer Covarrubias had been assigned to a DUI checkpoint and was working with fellow officers and members of the Police Explorers.

Officer Covarrubias was also the subject of an internal investigation for allegedly having sex with a teenage girl. When officers attempted to arrest Covarrubias that day, he pulled his weapon and started shooting at no clear target. Officer Kline, coming to assist the other officers, returned fire and killed Covarrubias.

Rebecca Stincelli, in a statement to ABC News, said: "It is suicide by cop, even if it was a split-second decision to die."

Justice Information Services Division, recommended instituting a national reporting process for suicide by cop incidents, similar to the UCR reporting process.[79]

Effects of Stress on Police Officers

Too much stress affects health. Police officers face the stress created by always being ready for danger day in and day out. In addition, the working hours of police officers and the resultant living conditions have a further negative effect on their health. One writer reports that police officers may be among those with the unhealthiest diets in the United States because of a very high rate of consumption of fast food and junk food.[80] In fact, Dorothy Bracey found that because of a poor diet and lack of exercise, a significant sample of U.S. police possessed a body composition, blood chemistry, and general level of physical fitness greatly inferior to that of a similarly sized sample of prison convicts.[81]

A National Institute of Justice report has listed the following as consequences of job-related stress commonly reported by police officers:

- Cynicism and suspiciousness
- Emotional detachment from various aspects of daily life
- Reduced efficiency
- Absenteeism and early retirement
- Excessive aggressiveness (which may trigger an increase in citizen complaints)
- Alcoholism and other substance abuse problems
- Marital or other family problems (for example, extramarital affairs, divorce, or domestic violence)
- Posttraumatic stress disorder
- Heart attacks, ulcers, weight gain, and other health problems
- Suicide[82]

An early study of 2,300 police officers in 20 U.S. police departments revealed that 37 percent had serious marital problems, 36 percent had health problems, 23 percent had problems with alcohol, 20 percent had problems with their children, and 10 percent had drug problems.[83] Other researchers estimate that between 20 and 30 percent of all police officers have alcohol problems. The typical drinker was described as single, older than 40 years of age, with 15 to 20 years of police experience.[84]

In an extremely important 2004 article, Chad L. Cross, a research scientist, and Larry Ashley, an internationally recognized expert on combat trauma and addictions, both faculty members at the University of Nevada, Las Vegas, wrote that studies have estimated that nearly 25 percent of law enforcement officers are alcohol dependent as a result of on-the-job stress, but these authors indicated that this estimate probably falls well below the true number because of incomplete reporting.[85] A study of 852 police officers in New South Wales, Australia, found that almost 50 percent of male and 40 percent of female officers consumed excessive amounts of alcohol (defined as more than 8 drinks per week at least twice a month or more than 28 drinks a month for males, and more than 6 drinks per week at least twice a month or 14 drinks a month for females), and that nearly 90 percent of all officers consumed alcohol to some degree.[86] Recent reports indicate that drug use also is on the rise in law enforcement agencies.[87]

Cross and Ashley assert that the unique subculture of the law enforcement profession often makes alcohol use appear as an accepted practice to promote camaraderie and social interaction among officers. They wrote that what starts as an occasional socializing activity, however, later can become a dangerous addiction as alcohol use evolves into a coping mechanism to camouflage the stress and trauma experienced by officers on a daily basis. When the effects of the alcohol wear off, the stress or trauma that led to the drinking episode still exits.[88]

Other studies have indicated that police officers are 300 percent more likely to suffer from alcoholism than the average citizen;[89] the average life expectancy of a police officer is 57 years, compared with 71 for the general public; and officers rank at the top among professions in rates of heart disease, hypertension, and diabetes.[90]

Critical incidents and critical incident responses, particularly police shootings, are extremely stressful. Two recent studies revealed the prevalence of acute traumatic dissociative responses in officers who have been involved in these critical incidents.[91] Professors at Michigan State University found that officers who have had to kill someone in the line of duty suffer post-shooting trauma that may lead to severe problems, including the ruin of their careers.

Studies have indicated that 70 percent of these officers leave the police force within seven years after the shooting.[92]

However, in a 2006 report, David Klinger explored the emotional, psychological, and physical reactions of 80 officers and sheriffs' deputies during and after 113 incidents in which they had shot someone. He found evidence that most suffered few long-term negative emotional or physical effects after shooting a suspect.[93]

POST-TRAUMATIC STRESS DISORDER Police officers move from one crisis situation to another and are required to be constantly on the alert and make split-second decisions. Officers witness gruesome situations and are required to provide detailed reports about these incidents; in some cases they personally know or work with the individuals involved. It is not uncommon that officers will bring their work home with them, affecting not only their off-duty time but their family life as well.[94]

Often after a traumatic event or critical incident, officers can suffer from post-traumatic stress disorder (PTSD). The United States Department of Labor, Occupational Safety and Health Administration has listed the signs and symptoms of critical incident stress (see Table 6.3) and recommended steps that can be used to reduce significant stress. These steps should be followed if the signs and symptoms of stress are identified after a critical incident: (1) limit exposure to noise and orders; (2) dictate an immediate 15-minute rest break; (3) provide noncaffeinated fluid to drink; (4) provide low sugar and low fat food; (5) get the person to talk about his or her feelings; and (6) do not rush the person back to work.[95]

Organizations dealing with PTSD are up against built-in resistance in trying to address the symptoms. Officers themselves are the biggest barriers in seeking out treatment, since they do not want to be thought of as "weak" and so will rein in their emotions and try to appear in control. Terry Bykerek, a retired Grand Rapids, Michigan, police officer, notes that individuals may react differently to a single traumatic incident: "What can be a minor experience to one person can be traumatic for another; there may be a higher risk with someone who is an introvert, less social, less physical. They tend to be gatekeepers with their emotions."[96]

Departments that have mandatory counseling after a critical incident are far ahead in addressing these issues. Individuals involved in a traumatic event should attend a critical incident stress debriefing (CISD) as soon as possible. This should include any personnel on scene at the time of the incident, dispatchers, emergency medical personnel, and firefighters. The attendance at a CISD should be mandatory, paid for by the agency (if there are costs), and should be the result of a written agency policy that will help to remove any stigma of attending a CISD.

TABLE 6.3 Signs and Symptoms of Post-Traumatic Stress Disorder

Physical	Cognitive	Emotional	Behavioral
Fatigue	Uncertainty	Grief	Inability to rest
Chills	Confusion	Fear	Withdrawal
Unusual thirst	Nightmares	Guilt	Antisocial behavior
Chest pain	Poor attention	Intense anger	Increased alcohol consumption
Headaches	Poor decision-making ability	Apprehension and depression	Change in communications
Dizziness	Poor concentration/memory	Irritability	
Loss/increase in appetite	Poor problem solving ability	Chronic anxiety	

Source: United States Department of Labor, Occupational Safety & Health Administration, Critical Incident Stress Guide; retrieved from www.osha.gov/SLTC/emergencypreparedness/guides/critical.html.

Stress and Police Families

Police work not only affects officers, but also their families, loved ones, and friends. An early study of stress in the immediate families of police officers revealed that between 10 and 20 percent of all police wives are dissatisfied with their husband's job and would like to see their husband leave the police department.[97] In addition, rotation shift work interferes with planning and celebrating holidays and important family events, such as birthdays and anniversaries. Rotating shifts also make it difficult for a spouse to pursue another career.[98]

Ellen Scrivner, the former director of the Psychological Services Division of the Prince George's County, Maryland, Police Department and president of the Psychologists in Public Service Division of the American Psychological Association, identified a number of job-related issues that contribute to dysfunction in police families:

- *Family disruption due to rotating shifts.* Problems caused by rotating shifts include providing child care, unavailability on holidays and at other family events, and physical problems caused by overtime and shift work, which lead to irritability and increased tension.

- *Unpredictable work environment.* The constantly changing work setting of the police officer leads to crisis and emergency responses, as well as fear of death or injury and of being the target of internal investigations.

- *Job-related personal change and family relationships.* An officer is forced to see much human tragedy and is always personally affected. Changes in the officer's personality and attitudes, in turn, affect the family.

- *Community expectations and demands.* The public seems to hold police officers to a higher standard of behavior in comparison with other workers. Neighbors often expect their police officer neighbors to take care of neighborhood problems and be available for emergencies.

- *Intrusion into family life.* The police officer may have to carry parts of his or her job home. For example, police officers generally carry weapons, which they must secure in a safe place at home. Officers also must be available 24 hours a day.[99]

Additionally, as indicated earlier by Professor Scott, officers in small towns and rural areas are particularly affected by stress, since they live and work in the same area.[100]

Police Departments Dealing with Stress

A 1981 report by the U.S. Commission on Civil Rights emphasized the need to provide stress management programs and services for police. The commission noted that most police departments lack such programs, despite the recent emphasis on stress as "an important underlying factor in police misconduct incidents." The commission recommended the following: "Police officials should institute comprehensive stress management programs that include identification of officers with stress problems, counseling, periodic screening, and training on stress management."[101]

Since then, many police departments around the nation have developed stress programs for their officers. For example, in 1986, the NYPD responded to the problem of police suicides by training 100 officers as peer counselors. The NYPD also established telephone hotlines in four precincts; officers needing help in stressful situations could call for help 24 hours a day, seven days a week.[102] A 1998 summary report on this program revealed a reduction in the number of police suicides, numerous telephone calls on the help line, referrals to mental health clinicians, and families participating in family support seminars.[103]

In 1996, the NYPD and its Patrolman's Benevolent Association, responding to the fact that 26 NYPD officers had committed suicide in the previous two years, created the Police Organization Providing Peer Assistance (POPPA) program to address the problems of police stress and suicide. The program consists of a trained group of volunteer officers who serve as peer support officers (PSOs) to provide support on a 24/7 basis to officers who are experiencing personal or professional problems, such as trauma, stress, depression, alcohol abuse, or family problems. POPPA offers counseling, professional referrals, and a help line for all officers wishing to use its services. The PSOs meet with any caller to the help line, immediately if needed or on the following day. They listen and assist their fellow officers in securing the right professional services, and services are confidential.[104] Since POPPA was implemented in 1996, the suicide rate for NYPD officers has been cut by more than half, from 19 suicides (32/100,000) in 1994–1995 to 11 suicides (15/100,000) in 2008–2009.[105] In 2006, POPPA extended its program to NYPD retirees.[106]

Responding to the needs of its law enforcement officers returning from deployment in military war zones in Iraq and Afghanistan, the South Carolina Law Enforcement Assistance Program (SCLEAP) has created the Post Deployment Peer Support Team. This team of volunteer officers, who are also combat veterans, confidentially counsel their fellow officers in an attempt to help them make the transition from the war zone to their local law enforcement agency. The program offers post-deployment debriefings and seminars, one-on-one peer support, and referrals to mental-health resources in the officers' communities. SCLEAP also offers critical incident stress management assistance, post–critical incident seminars, law enforcement stress management programs, and alcohol rehabilitation services for law enforcement employees in South Carolina.[107]

Stress management has a physical as well as a psychological component. The FBI's Training Division Research and Development Unit mailed a training needs survey packet to 2,497 police agencies across the nation. The survey results indicated that handling personal stress and maintaining an appropriate level of physical fitness ranked first and second in programs most requested by police officers. In another survey, 90 percent of the nearly 2,000 officers questioned reported that they were in favor of a department-sponsored physical fitness program.[108] Speaking of the need for physical fitness, James J. Ness and John Light state,

> The adverse effects of the lack of fitness are overwhelming, while the positive benefits of fitness are often overlooked. Being physically fit diminishes stress, promotes self-esteem, improves firearms accuracy, increases an officer's confidence in confrontations, makes him more effective with impact weapons and defense tactics, and generally improves his quality of life.[109]

Some departments have instituted health and fitness programs to ensure their officers' physical and emotional well-being. For example, the Ohio State Patrol has implemented a mandatory health and fitness program for all its officers. The Ohio program is designed to ensure a "high quality of life

during the troopers' active career period and into retirement."[110]

Following the terrorist attacks of September 11, 2001, the NYPD ordered all 55,000 of its employees to attend mental health counseling to deal with the stress brought about by this event.[111] A similar program of mental health counseling was implemented to help Oklahoma City rescue workers in 1995 following the terrorist attack in that city.[112]

The Worcester, Massachusetts, Police Department has used peer counselors as "stress responders" to assist other officers in dealing with stressful incidents for more than 20 years. A 2002 book outlines the work of police peer counselors and presents their history, describes their strategies and tactics, and identifies the obstacles police officers face in their work.[113] High among the counselors' recommendations is the need for immediate response to critical incident stress events, including immediate critical incident stress debriefings for officers who have been exposed to potentially traumatic circumstances. The counselors report that this can help minimize or eliminate the secondary trauma that often occurs. The counselor can provide an understanding listening ear, and often a strong bond may be forged between the officer and the counselor that can foster follow-up care.[114]

The National Institute of Justice has created the Corrections and Law Enforcement Family Support program to deal with some of the problems of police stress. It has sponsored research and program development in some 30 agencies and related organizations (labor unions and employee professional organizations, for example). These projects include developing innovative treatment and training programs as well as research into the nature and causes of stress.[115]

Today, numerous training programs and support groups for police officers and their families exist. Many of them have a presence on the Internet. In 2006, Samuel Walker, retired professor of criminal justice at the University of Nebraska at Omaha, Stacy Osnick Milligan, a criminal justice consultant, and Anna Berke, a research assistant for the Police Executive Research Forum, produced a comprehensive report regarding strategies for early intervention systems. The report stresses the need for counseling by the immediate supervisor, training, professional counseling on personal or family problems, peer support programs, crisis intervention teams, and reassignment and relief from duty.[116] However, it has been reported that some officers avoid using employee assistance programs (EAPs) because they feel that such programs do not provide enough confidentiality, that staff do not understand law enforcement, and that stigma is attached to using an EAP.[117]

Some researchers believe that the highest amount of stress for the officer is organizational stress—stress from the organizational and management policies and procedures of the agency and its supervisors and managers. Scott writes that this problem is compounded for rural and small-town officers because their departments often lack adequate economic and social service resources to address officers' stress. She adds that efforts must be made to fund programs to address these officers' specific needs, particularly coping with changes in administration and managing stigmatization resulting from media criticism.[118]

Ronnie Garrett has written that an organization that runs well—smoothly, confidently, and consistently—can reduce stress for its employees. He stated that police organizations can cultivate the need to change and provide organizational health to change the stress culture. Ways to do this include:

- Manage in an efficient manner.
- Place people in command who are clear in their goals and in their commands to officers and who are highly supportive of officers.
- Pay close attention to an officer's reactions after an incident and make sure that her or his feelings of stress are not discounted or ignored.[119]

In a 2002 article, Hans Toch stressed that no matter what else may be done to prevent and ameliorate stress, organizational change may hold the key to improving the lives of police officers.[120]

Police administrators must take the lead in helping those in their organization or department deal with the stress that comes with police work. Emphasizing the importance of police administrators' dealing with the problems of police stress through organizational change, Pittaro has written:

> Police occupational stress is widespread and particularly troublesome, yet it can be eliminated, or at the very minimum, controlled as long as police administrators admit that a

problem exists and commit to making changes within the organization. Avoiding stress is unlikely, but learning to cope with the internal and external stressors commonly associated with police occupational stress will minimize the potentially damaging effects of chronic stress. To be truly effective, change must begin within the organization since this appears to be the catalyst to police occupational stress. The dangerousness of the profession is something beyond the organization's control; however, police administrators can begin by creating an organization-wide culture that is committed to reducing stress within the organization. Education and awareness are two key elements that must be factored into any strategic plan in that officers need to understand and recognize the symptoms commonly associated with stress and the coping skills necessary to combat stress.[121]

Police Suicide

Closely associated with the problem of stress in policing is the problem of **police suicide**, which seems to have worsened over the years. Despite all the programs existing to deal with officer problems that may cause suicide, the toll has continued to mount. Studies indicate that the suicide rate among police officers is much higher than that of the general population, and the rate of police suicides has doubled in recent decades.[122]

In 2006, Miller wrote that the suicide rate for police officers is three times that of the general population, and three times as many officers kill themselves as are killed by criminals in the line of duty. According to Miller, "This makes officer suicide the most lethal threat in police history."[123] Other studies show that police officers are six times more likely to kill themselves than average members of the public—60 for every 100,000 police officers each year, compared with 10 for every 100,000 members of the general public. This figure more than triples after retirement. Officers who are disabled are 45 times more likely to commit suicide than the average person.[124]

In 2006, based on data from the Centers for Disease Control and Prevention, Robert Douglas of the National P.O.L.I.C.E. Suicide Foundation estimated that police officers commit suicide at a rate

---

police suicide The intentional taking of one's own life by a police officer.

of 300 to 400 a year.[125] In a 2007 article, Michelle Perin wrote that the National P.O.L.I.C.E. Suicide Foundation projected that an officer kills himself or herself every 17 hours and that 97 percent of officers use their own service weapon in committing suicide. The foundation also reported that many elements of law enforcement contribute to stress reactions with the potential to lead to suicide, including shift work, pending retirement, unsupportive management, and physical ailments.[126] According to forensic psychologist Cindy Goss of New York, the typical profile of a police officer who commits suicide is "male, white, 35, working patrol, abusing alcohol, separated or seeking a divorce, experiencing a recent loss or disappointment."[127]

John M. Violanti, a professor in the Criminal Justice Department of the Rochester Institute of Technology in Rochester, New York, and a member of the Department of Social and Preventive Medicine, University of New York at Buffalo, works on the problem of police suicide. Violanti, who also served 23 years with the New York State Police, has noted that the police culture and the reluctance of police officers to ask for help complicate the problem of police suicide. His research revealed that police are at higher risk for committing suicide for

Losing a Good Friend   ON THE JOB

Suicide is something that happens to other people. You think that it is never going to happen to someone you know and that you will never experience suicidal thoughts. Over my police career and through my interactions with the families of suicide victims as well as people who experienced thoughts of suicide or attempted suicide, I sadly found that this is not true.

One of the saddest times of my career was when a friend and coworker committed suicide. Bernie was in his mid-40s when I joined the department. He was a detective and highly respected within the agency and throughout our local criminal justice system. He was known as a great investigator and interviewer and worked relentlessly to get to the truth and then pursue the case to its conclusion. He had the highest ethical standards and never took shortcuts.

I was very fortunate when Bernie took me under his wing and became my mentor when I joined the department. He said he saw a lot of potential in me and wanted to help me in any way he could. He worked "crimes against persons" and had become our resident expert in sex crimes. He called me out whenever he was called in for a sex crime. We worked together regularly, and I learned a tremendous amount from Bernie. The strongest impact he made on me was demonstrating how to interact with people. He had an unassuming and compassionate style that made people feel comfortable and encouraged them to talk. This resulted in many confessions to sex crimes that other officers were surprised he had obtained.

I can only guess that though Bernie was able to encourage others to talk, he was not as able to open up to others. We spent some off-duty time together, and I knew that he was divorced and his children were up north. But he was dating someone and seemed well adjusted to his lifestyle.

After I had been in the department five years, Bernie took some leave time for minor surgery, and a friend took care of taking him to and from the hospital. I talked to the friend; Bernie didn't want any visitors while he was home recuperating and would see us when he got back to work. A week later, that friend (a detective bureau supervisor) came to my door in the evening. I could tell by the look on his face that something was wrong, but I assumed it was an official visit. We sat down, and he told me that Bernie was dead. Sometime that day Bernie had shot himself with his service weapon.

I had the feelings of guilt that survivors often experience. I should have seen something, I should have visited him even though he didn't want visitors, I should have spent more time with him, I should have encouraged him to talk more… all the things survivors wish they'd done.

Bernie has had a lasting impact not only on all the victims and families he worked with, but also on the many officers he trained and the officers they went on to train. I have taught many investigators Bernie's techniques and philosophies, so he lives on in the efforts of many.

—Linda Forst

a variety of reasons, including access to firearms, continuous exposure to human misery, shift work, social strain and marital difficulties, drinking problems, physical illness, impending retirement, and lack of control over their jobs and personal lives. Violanti's work indicates that police commit suicide at a rate up to 53 percent higher than other city workers.[128]

According to Violanti, police officers become ingrained in police work and isolated from other life roles such as family, friendships, and community involvement; tend to view reality as a black-and-white situation; and are inflexible in their thinking. Violanti has stated that good adjustment involves being able to view frustrating life situations from many angles rather than as simply black and white. Police officers tend to have problems with personal relationships, and these problems may increase their potential for suicide.[129]

Traditionally, no matter what their problems, police officers refrain from asking for help. There are various reasons for this reluctance. The primary reason, however, is that officers do not wish to appear weak or vulnerable in front of their peers. Police suicide is rarely, if ever, talked about publicly. Individuals who perceive themselves as problem solvers often have great difficulty admitting that they have problems of their own. As a result, some officers who feel they can no longer tolerate psychological pain choose to solve the problem themselves through suicide rather than by asking others for help.[130]

In 2003, Daniel W. Clark and Elizabeth K. White wrote that the factors that may interfere with an officer seeking help include the stigma of suicide, confidentiality concerns, job impact worries, personality traits, the stigma of emotional problems, alcohol, mistrust of the psychological field, and the negative perception of taking medication as treatment.[131] Miller, noting that the risk of suicide is greatest in officers with prior histories of depression and those who have recently faced debilitating stressors linked to feelings of hopelessness and helplessness, has said that much can be done by law enforcement agencies to counter and prevent officer depression and suicide. His recommendations include the following:

1. Acknowledge and openly address the severity of the problem, and provide instruction to both command and line officers in occupational stress, signs of impairment, and how to cope with stress in positive ways.

2. Provide officers with training in crisis intervention skills that they can use with fellow officers.

3. Train supervisors to be alert to signs of depression and other problems that may signal the possibility of suicidal thoughts.

4. Provide a convenient and nonstigmatizing system for referring distressed officers for psychological help.

5. When the acute crisis has passed, provide a referral to a mental health clinician to determine the officer's fitness for duty and to help the officer build mental and emotional resources to prevent subsequent crises.[132]

In a 2006 article, Patricia Kelly and Rich Martin suggested that if law enforcement agencies spend time and money equipping and training officers to protect themselves while on duty, they should be equally, if not more, committed to doing what is required to prevent officer suicides. Kelly and Martin argued that agency personnel who observe warning signs in fellow officers and family members of officers at risk should be encouraged to contact the officer's supervisor. They wrote that a clear indication of the intent to commit suicide warrants immediately taking the officer to a hospital emergency room for a full psychological evaluation.[133]

By 2008, the Milwaukee Police Department had suffered six suicides in less than three years. Among the six were four active-duty officers, one retired sergeant, and one 911 dispatcher; two were women.[134] The California Highway Patrol suffered eight trooper suicides in eight months in 2006, and a total of thirteen between September 2003 and 2006.[135]

Robert Douglas, the executive director of the National P.O.L.I.C.E. Suicide Foundation, stated in 2007 that no more than 2 percent of the nation's law enforcement agencies had suicide prevention programs.[136]

Teresa T. Tate, in her article "Police Suicide, What Can Be Done?" said, "As the widow of a police officer who committed suicide in 1989, I know of the stress that is placed upon law enforcement officers in this violent society. Many officers believe that seeking help from a mental health professional is a sign of weakness."[137] Removing the stigma of seeking professional help should be the goal of every department. Recognizing the human need of employees is not only morally and ethically the responsible thing to do for the police supervisor, it also makes good business sense to take care of a valuable resource for the department and the community.

Police Danger

How often are police officers killed or injured in the line of duty? What are the specific threats to the police regarding personal safety? No one would disagree with the statement that police work is dangerous. Unfortunately, its dangers are increasing. Each year many officers are injured or killed in the line of duty. The chances of contracting life-threatening diseases, such as AIDS, are increasing as more of the general population is affected. This section puts these dangers into perspective.

Police officers perform necessary and often dangerous tasks. They deal constantly with what may be the most dangerous species on this planet—humans—often in the most stressful and dangerous situations. They regularly respond to people shooting at each other, stabbing each other, and beating each other. In a typical tour of duty, officers can deal with the full range of human emotions. They respond to calls where they may meet armed adversaries during robberies in progress or hostage situations. Most frequently, officers respond to "unknown problems" or "unknown disturbances" types of calls, where someone is calling for help but the officers are unable to gather further information and really do not know what they are walking into.

The dangerous conditions facing U.S. police officers are compounded by the irrationality produced by alcohol and drugs. The urban drug business since the 1980s has been characterized by an emphasis on tremendous inflows of cash and instant gratification. The proliferation of young, urban, uneducated, and unemployable males armed with a plethora of weapons (including military-like automatic assault weapons) has made officers more and more fearful for their safety. As Barbara Raffel Price of the John Jay College of Criminal Justice wrote, "It would be foolish not to recognize that the violence associated with the drug business puts the police and citizens in greater jeopardy and that it makes the job of policing almost impossible."[138]

Also, the risk of exposure to dangerous chemicals in police work is always present. Deputies and police officers are always subject to the possibility of contamination from a variety of toxic chemicals, such as lye, iodine, and lithium, when they must enter methamphetamine (meth) labs to place offenders under arrest or while processing those under arrest who are contaminated themselves.[139]

Advancing trends and technology also pose threats to police officers' safety. In 2006, it was reported that felons in Minneapolis were increasingly donning body armor in the form of bullet-resistant vests when they hit the streets. Body armor, although expensive, has been becoming cheaper and more easily available on the Internet, and criminals have been getting more violent. According to Minneapolis Captain Rich Stanek, "Wearing it is almost a fashion statement to some of these guys."[140] In 2007, Lieutenant Mike Wallace of the Palm Beach County Sheriff's Office, discussing the shootings of four Broward County Sheriff's deputies, three of whom died within 12 months, stated, "You used to just see a guy turn around and flee before they'd ever take a shot at a cop. Now there's no hesitation. They don't think twice before shooting at the police."[141]

Officers Killed in the Line of Duty

The FBI (which maintains records of law enforcement officers murdered, accidentally killed, and injured in the line of duty each year) reported that 48 law enforcement officers were feloniously slain in the line of duty during 2012. In 2012, of the law enforcement officers murdered in the line of duty, 6 were ambushed; 12 were involved in arrest situations; 8 were investigating suspicious persons or circumstances; 8 were performing traffic stops/pursuits; 4 were answering disturbance calls; 5 were in tactical situations; 1 was conducting activity such as surveillance, searches, or interviews; 1 was handling a person with a mental illness; and 3 were handling or transporting prisoners. Of the 48 officers murdered in 2012, 44 were killed with firearms; 23 were wearing body armor at the time. One officer was killed

Cliff Despeaux/*The Seattle Times*

Funeral for four officers shown on the banner, who were murdered in a Lakewood, Washington, coffee shop in November 2009.

with his or her own weapon. More officers were killed from felonious assaults (8) in August than any other month in 2012, and more officers were involved in fatal accidents (10) on Tuesday than any other day of the week. [142]

The **National Law Enforcement Officers Memorial (NLEOM)** is located in Washington, D.C., and has the names of about 17,500 slain officers inscribed on its walls. Its website is visited by more than 200,000 people each year and enhances public knowledge of and appreciation for law enforcement officers and the dangers they face. The NLEOM Fund collects and catalogs information on law enforcement fatalities in an effort to educate the public about officer safety and with the goal that no officer slain in the line of duty will ever be forgotten.[143]

National Law Enforcement Officers Memorial (NLEOM)
A memorial in Washington, D.C., established to recognize the ultimate sacrifice of police officers killed in the line of duty.

The organization Concerns of Police Survivors Inc. (COPS) was started in 1984 to provide resources to relatives, fellow officers, and other survivors of law enforcement officers killed in the line of duty. Its website provides information to survivors and police agencies. COPS also provides training and assistance to departments in how to respond to a law enforcement death in their department in the hopes of reducing the trauma suffered by coworkers. COPS states on its website, "There is no membership fee to join COPS, for the price paid is already too high."[144]

When one looks at the number of police officer–citizen contacts each year—about 40 million, according to the Bureau of Justice Statistics (BJS)—and the dangerous situations in which officers often find themselves, the police have relatively low murder rates.[145] What accounts for this, given the constant possibility of violence with which they are faced? There are several explanations.

People who would not think twice about shooting a fellow citizen might hesitate in shooting a police officer, knowing that society places a special value on the lives of those they depend on for maintaining law and order on the streets. People also know that the criminal justice system reacts in a harsher way to a "cop killer" than to an ordinary killer. Professional criminals, including organized crime members and drug dealers, know that killing a police officer is "very bad for business." Such a killing will result in tremendous disruption of their business while the police hunt for, and prosecute, the killer.

Another reason is police officers' awareness of the dangers they face every day and the resultant physical and mental precautions they take to deal with such dangers. The discussion of the police personality earlier in this chapter characterized it as suspicious, loyal, and cynical. Most experts believe that the police personality is caused by the dangers of police work. It is possible that the negative aspects of the police personality keep officers relatively safe. Advances in medical science, and improved training and equipment, have also helped to save the lives of police officers. Officers are now trained not to blindly rush into situations but to obtain as much information as possible (aided by improved records systems) while en route and upon arrival. Obtaining cover and waiting for backup are also stressed.

Another possible explanation for the decrease in officer murders is the increased use of body armor. In 2008, statistics indicated that most departments require their field officers to wear protective body armor—75 percent of local police departments, compared with 30 percent in 1990.[146] Recall, however, that 23 officers murdered by people with firearms in 2012 were wearing body armor at the time of their death. Three of the slain officers wearing body armor died from torso wounds caused by bullets entering their bodies despite the armor.[147] This reinforces the fact that body armor is not "bulletproof."

Claire Mayhew, an Australian criminologist, discussed the risk of death, homicide, assault, communicable disease, stress and fatigue, and injuries to officers. Mayhew noted the relatively constant rate of police homicides in a time of increased availability of firearms and illicit drugs, and suggested that body armor, medical technology, and training strategies have kept pace with the threats. She also noted that the risk of assaults far exceeds fatalities and is probably increasing. Assaults on officers in Australia are relatively common; approximately 10 percent of officers are assaulted each year.[148]

Officers Assaulted in the Line of Duty

As we have seen, police officers have relatively low murder rates, but how often are officers injured by criminal assaults in the line of duty? In 2012, 52,901 assaults were committed against state and local police officers. The assaults most commonly involved personal weapons such as hands, feet, and fists (29.7 percent). Firearms were used against officers in 9.8 percent of assaults, and knives or cutting instruments in 13.2 percent of the assaults. Other types of dangerous weapons were used in 23.9 percent of the assaults.[149] About 32.5 percent of the assaults occurred while officers were responding

to disturbance calls, 15.2 percent while attempting arrests, and 13.6 percent while handling, transporting, or otherwise having custody of prisoners.[150]

It might seem that despite the numbers of assaults of police officers, the actuality of these events is relatively low considering that the police generally have face-to-face contact with more than 45 million persons a year, sometimes in extremely tense and stressful encounters.[151] But perhaps the statistics do not tell the complete story. According to Rich Roberts, a former police officer and spokesperson for the International Union of Police Associations, "Police are a stoic breed. Often they take their lumps and don't make a big deal about it. They limp around for a couple of days. But no one's charged, and they don't miss any work."[152]

Police and Contagious Diseases

Since the 1980s, human immunodeficiency virus (HIV), acquired immune deficiency syndrome (AIDS), and hepatitis B and C have become sources of great concern to U.S. police officers, as well as to everyone else. **AIDS**, a deadly disease, is transmitted mainly through sexual contact and the exchange of body fluids. Although AIDS was formerly associated mainly with male homosexuals, intravenous drug users, and prostitutes, it is now known that anyone can be subject to infection by this disease.

The impact of HIV/AIDS is readily apparent. According to the Centers for Disease Control and Prevention (CDC), the estimated cumulative number of AIDS diagnoses in the United States for the latest reporting year was 984,155, with 9,101 of those being children younger than 13. The estimated cumulative number of deaths from AIDS in the United States was 550,394, including 4,865 children younger than 13. In 2005, in the United States alone, 433,760 people were living with AIDS and the estimated deaths from AIDS totaled 17,011.[153]

These figures do not include individuals infected with HIV who may carry the disease for years before any symptoms of AIDS appear. These individuals are still contagious. Though there is no cure for AIDS, advances have been made in the treatment of the disease, allowing infected individuals to live longer lives.[154]

AIDS Acquired immune deficiency syndrome.

GUEST LECTURE

Photo courtesy of Karla D. Swim

DAVID H. SWIM

David H. Swim is a retired captain from the Stockton, California, Police Department, having spent 22 years with that agency. While there, he worked the street as a police officer, sergeant, and lieutenant. He was also assigned to SWAT, serving six years as the SWAT unit's commander. He received his doctorate in public administration from the University of Southern California and is currently an associate professor of criminal justice administration and leadership at California State University, Sacramento. He teaches upper-division courses in police administration, critical issues, and leadership, and two graduate courses in the history of criminal justice in America and collective bargaining.

IN THE LINE OF DUTY

In front of the Stockton Police Department stands a 10-foot-high gray granite monument. It stands as a sentinel, to acknowledge those officers of our community who gave their all for law enforcement in the line of duty. The 14 names etched into the granite will endure as long as the granite. They are enduring in the sense that the absence of these officers and their untimely deaths echo eternally; enduring in the sense that spouses, children, parents, and siblings will constantly feel their absence; enduring in the fact that each day, as officers arrive at work, they pass by this solemn sentinel, reminding them that they, too, could fall in the line of duty.

The chiseled reality of loss is softened by a plaque occupying the top portion of the obelisk. The police officer holding a small child in his arms contrasts the kindness of the calling of police officer with the harshness of reality. Death in the line of duty is not attended by some euphoric national pride or sense of mission. In fact, more than 100 officers are killed annually, silently, simply doing their job. While we are not paid to die, it is a harsh reality of police work.

During my 22 years at the Stockton PD, seven names were added to that monument. Five were killed by gunfire, one was beaten to death, and one died during a foot pursuit. All were friends, some more so than others. Each had a family, most that I personally knew. Each death weathered my soul, extracted tears not cried, and demanded resolution of my shortcomings. Each death reminded me of my own mortality, but, most of all, my inadequacy to properly return to my maker.

One was killed during the exchange of gunfire at the end of a vehicle pursuit. Two were SWAT members whom I had trained to be the "best of the best"; the assailant's bullet pays no respect to training, skill, and finesse. One was ambushed from inside a residence with a rifle that no body armor could stop. One was shot in the face during an exchange of gunfire that also killed his assailant. At the hospital three of us stood around a gurney, silently weeping, knowing that, in the line of duty, real cops cry.

Two were narcotics officers killed on search warrants, by bullets that went over

---

Police officers frequently come into contact with all types of people—including those with infectious diseases—and officers often have contact with blood and other body fluids. Therefore, officers are at special risk for catching communicable diseases. They must take precautionary measures during searches and other contacts with possible carriers of infectious diseases, as well as at crime scenes, where blood and other body fluids may be present.[155]

The model policy of the International Association of Chiefs of Police on HIV/AIDS prevention defines an exposure as "any contact with body fluids including, but not limited to, direct contact with skin, eyes, nose and mouth, and through needle sticks." The policy stresses prevention of HIV/AIDS exposure and recommends behaviors and procedures to minimize the chance of becoming exposed. It also addresses the supplies that departments should have on hand and procedures to be used for cleanup in the event of a body fluid spill or deposit in a patrol vehicle or booking area. In addition, the policy discusses the importance of documenting and following through on an exposure for educational purposes and to ensure the officers are covered if the disease the top of or through the nonexistent side panel of body armor of the 1970s. One of these narcotics officers was the son of our chief of police, who responded to the hospital to find his pride and joy expired on the gurney. As we wept together, how does one console a father, let alone the chief of police? The other narcotics officer's father was working as a reserve that day and expired of a heart attack when he heard of his son's death.

During a several-block foot pursuit of a fleeing suspect, a rare and undiagnosed heart malady stopped the heart of the pursuing officer, making him the sixth of those added to the list during my years with the department. Death was instantaneous, yet absolutely confusing to his attending officers until the postmortem. A nighttime traffic stop of a parolee, bulked up by prison yard weight lifting, resulted in a beating with the seventh officer's own flashlight, so severe that the officer expired days later, never recovering from his comatose state.

Of the seven deaths, six were instant, and finality came over us as immediately as the summer sun is eclipsed by clouds. The expiration of the beaten officer took days as the family and officers anticipated the eventuality of death. Each day was torture as we were literally or figuratively part of the death watch. Ironically, finality brought peace, commensurate with the immense pain.

Each of these deaths left widows and orphans. Each of these deaths tore the heart out of parents, for no parent should have a child precede him or her in death. Each left a community shocked, at least for the moment. Each created an atmosphere where spouses felt the visceral impact and fear for their loved one, in the line of duty. Each reminded us that we were mortal.

Seven viewings with the attendant honor guard in Class A uniforms at each end of the casket. Seven funerals with their respective masses or services. Seven funeral processions with hundreds of marching officers, with labor and management, for the moment, united in step and purpose. Miles of police vehicles with emergency lights beaconing heaven that another chosen servant was on his way. Seven postfuneral receptions where officers attempted to absorb some of the pain and loss of the family of the deceased and yet were confused as they sorted out their own personal loss. I was asked by family to speak at two of those funerals. How does one comfort the family, his fellow officers, and express any justification at all for an officer's life being cut short in the line of duty? Notwithstanding the nobility of the calling, the price is too high.

Policing is a noble calling. It is true that "on the eighth day God created cops." The heroism of the many and the sacrifice of these few are tarnished by any who accept this calling and do not live up to the ethic required of this noble profession. We live in an era when our profession is under the greatest scrutiny and oftentimes disdain from an ambivalent public, due to the actions of those who disrespect their oath of office. Nonetheless, as with the centurions of old, the world is a better place because the noble are willing to be in the line of duty.

Source: Reprinted by permission of David H. Swim.

---

has been contracted. It stresses education and the use of "universal precautions," or generic precautionary rules, which include treating all body fluids as potentially hazardous, routinely using gloves and plastic mouthpieces for CPR, and adopting policies and behaviors that minimize the chance of being exposed to HIV/AIDS. Universal precautions mitigate the fact that, because of confidentiality issues in most states, officers will likely not know who is infected with a communicable disease.[156]

The FBI has published numerous recommendations on how to collect and handle evidence that might be infected with the viruses, bacteria, and germs of infectious diseases.[157] The National Institute of Justice has also published recommendations on dealing with possibly infected evidence.[158] Despite serious medical risks, police officers are not permitted to refuse to handle incidents involving persons infected with the AIDS virus or with other infectious diseases. Failing to perform certain duties—such as rendering first aid, assisting, or even arresting a person—would be a dereliction of duty, as well as discrimination against a class of people.[159]

SUMMARY

- The police culture or police subculture is a combination of shared norms, values, goals, career patterns, lifestyles, and occupational structures that is somewhat different from the combination held by the rest of society, and it is characterized by clannishness, secrecy, and isolation from those not in the group.

- Police officers protect one another from outsiders, often even refusing to aid police superiors or other law enforcement officials in investigating wrongdoing of other officers, producing a protective barrier known as the blue wall of silence or blue curtain.

- The police subculture leads to the police personality, or traits common to most police officers, such as authoritarianism, suspicion, hostility, insecurity, conservatism, and cynicism.

- Police cynicism is an attitude that there is no hope for the world and a view of humanity at its worst.

- The *Dirty Harry* problem refers to the reality that police officers are often confronted with situations in which they feel forced to take certain illegal actions to achieve a greater good.

- Stress is the body's reaction to internal or external stimuli that upset the body's normal state. The body's reaction to highly stressful situations is known as the flight-or-fight response.

- Police officers are confronted with four general categories of stress: external stress, organizational stress, personal stress, and operational stress.

- Many factors lead to stress in police work, including poor training, substandard equipment, poor pay, lack of opportunity, role conflict, exposure to brutality, fears about job competence and safety, lack of job satisfaction, the pressure of being on duty 24 hours a day, and fatigue. Police officers learn to cope with that stress by becoming emotionally detached from their work and the people they are paid to serve.

- The phenomenon of "suicide by cop" is a very serious problem for police officers. Many officer-involved shootings are the result of suicide by cop incidents.

- The suicide rate for police officers is three to six times that of the general population, and three times as many officers kill themselves compared with the number of officers killed by criminals in the line of duty.

- In 2012, 48 state and local law enforcement officers were feloniously slain in the line of duty. Forty-four of them were slain with firearms.

- In 2012, 52,901 assaults were committed against state and local police officers.

- Increasingly, police officers must take special precautions to avoid infection when handling people with HIV/AIDS or hepatitis B or C.

KEY TERMS

AIDS
blue curtain
blue wall of silence
Dirty Harry problem
flight-or-fight response

National Law Enforcement Officers Memorial (NLEOM)
police culture or police subculture

police cynicism
police personality
police suicide
suicide by cop

REVIEW EXERCISES

1. Interview a police officer and tell her or him what you have read about the police culture or subculture in this chapter. Discuss with the officer how your reading compares or contrasts with her or his actual police experience.

2. Discuss what you have read about police stress in this chapter with someone who is not a police officer. Ask this person how stress is similar or different in his or her occupation.

3. Research the issues of police suicide and suicide by cop. Discuss the differences between these two concepts.

WEB EXERCISES

1. Access some police officers' personal pages at a police officer website (www.officer.com is a good source) and try to get a sense of the content and flavor of a few of the personal pages. Do their stories and comments remind you of anything you have read about in this chapter? Do the officers show the features of the police culture and the police personality?

2. Access several websites relating to organizations dealing with police stress. Prepare a brief report naming these sites and discussing the services they offer to police officers.

3. Find the latest statistics on the number of police officers killed or injured in the line of duty.

END NOTES

1. Richard Lezin Jones, "New York Police Officers Face Counseling on September 11 Events," *New York Times*, November 30, 2001, p. A1.

2. See, for example, Egon Bittner, *The Functions of Police in Modern Society* (Cambridge, Mass.: Oelgeschlager, 1980); Michael K. Brown, *Working the Street* (New York: Russell Sage Foundation, 1981); Malcolm Sparrow, Mark Moore, and David Kennedy, *Beyond 911: A New Era for Policing* (New York: Basic Books, 1990); William Westley, *Violence and the Police: A Sociological Study of Law, Custom, and Morality* (Cambridge: MIT Press, 1970).

3. David Jary and Julia Jary, *The HarperCollins Dictionary of Sociology* (New York: Harper Perennial, 1991), p. 101.

4. Thomas Ford Hoult, *Dictionary of Modern Sociology* (Totowa: N.J.: Littlefield, Adams, 1969), p. 93.

5. Brown, *Working the Street*, p. 82.

6. Ibid.

7. George L. Kirkham, "A Professor's Street Lessons," in R. Culbertson and M. Tezak, eds., *Order Under Law* (Prospect Heights, Ill.: Waveland Press, 1981), p. 81.

8. Bittner, *Functions of Police*, p. 63.

9. John M. Violanti, "Suicide and the Police Culture," in Dell P. Hackett and John M. Violanti, eds., *Police Suicide: Tactics for Prevention* (Springfield, Ill.: Charles C. Thomas, 2003), pp. 66–75.

10. Eugene A. Paoline III, *Rethinking Police Culture: Officers' Occupational Attitudes* (New York: LFB Scholarly, 2001).

11. Robin N. Haarr and Merry Morash, "Gender, Race, and Strategies of Coping with Occupational Stress in Policing," *Justice Quarterly* 2 (1999): 303–336.

12. Eugene A. Paoline III, "Taking Stock: Toward a Richer Understanding of Police Culture," *Journal of Criminal Justice* 3 (2003): 199–214.

13. See, for example, Robin N. Haarr, "Patterns of Interaction in a Police Patrol Bureau: Race and Gender Barriers to Integration," *Justice Quarterly* 1 (1997): 53; and Steve Herbert, "Police Subculture Reconsidered," *Criminology* 2 (1998): 343–368.

14. See Richard Harris, *The Police Academy: An Inside View* (New York: Wiley, 1973); Jonathan Rubenstein, *City Police* (New York: Farrar, Straus and Giroux, 1973); and John Van Maanen, "Observations on the Making of a Policeman," in Culbertson and Tezak, eds. *Order Under Law*, p. 81.

15. Bittner, *Functions of Police*, p. 63.

16. Robert Sheehan and Gary W. Cordner, *Introduction to Police Administration*, 2nd ed. (Cincinnati: Anderson, 1989), p. 286.

17. Ibid., pp. 286–289.

18. Westley, *Violence and the Police*.

19. Mollen Commission to Investigate Allegations of Police Corruption, *Commission Report* (New York: The Mollen Commission, 1994), p. 53.

20. Christopher Commission, *Report of the Independent Commission to Investigate the Los Angeles Police Department* (Los Angeles: City of Los Angeles, 1991), pp. 168–171.

21. Neal Trautman, *Police Code of Silence Facts Revealed*, Legal Officers' Section, Annual Conference, International Association of Chiefs of Police, 2000, retrieved March 12, 2012, from www.aele.org.

22. Neal Trautman, *The Code of Silence Antidote: If Successful, Systematic Corruption Will Seldom Occur*, National Institute of Ethics, retrieved March 12, 2012, from www.ethicsinstitute.com.

23. Ibid.

24. Richard Lundman, *Police and Policing* (New York: Holt, Rinehart & Winston, 1980); also see Jerome Skolnick, *Justice without Trial: Law Enforcement in a Democratic Society* (New York: Wiley, 1966).

25. Skolnick, *Justice without Trial*.

26. Ibid.

27. Ibid.

28. Elizabeth Burbeck and Adrian Furnham, "Police Officer Selection: A Critical Review of the Literature," *Journal of Police Science and Administration* 13 (1985): 58–69.

29. Milton Rokeach, Martin Miller, and John Snyder, "The Value Gap between Police and Policed," *Journal of Social Issues* 27 (1971): 155–171.

30. Michael Pittaro, "Police Occupational Stress and Its Impact on Community Relations," *Police Forum: Academy of Criminal Justice Sciences* 1 (2008): 4.

31. Richard Bennett and Theodore Greenstein, "The Police Personality: A Test of the Predispositional Model," *Journal of Police Science and Administration* 3 (1975): 439–445.

32. Edward A. Thibault, Lawrence W. Lynch, and R. Bruce McBride, *Proactive Police Management* (Englewood Cliffs, N.J.: Prentice Hall, 1985).

33. Ibid.

34. Ibid. Also see Lundman, *Police and Policing*, pp. 73, 82, for similar observations.

35. Larry A. Gould, "Longitudinal Approach to the Study of the Police Personality: Race/Gender Differences," *Journal of Police and Criminal Psychology* 2 (2000): 41–51.

36. Robert Balch, "The Police Personality: Fact or Fiction?" *Journal of Criminal Law, Criminology, and Police Science* 63 (1972): 172; David Bayley and Harold Mendelsohn, *Minorities and the Police* (New York: Free Press, 1969); Larry Tifft, "The 'Cop Personality' Reconsidered," *Journal of Police Science and Administration* 2 (1974): 266–278.

37. Bruce Carpenter and Susan Raza, "Personality Characteristics of Police Applicants: Comparisons across Subgroups and with Other Populations," *Journal of Police Science and Administration* 15 (1987): 10–17; Richard Lawrence, "Police Stress and Personality Factors: A Conceptual Model," *Journal of Criminal Justice* 12 (1984): 247–263; James Teevan and Bernard Dolnick, "The Values of the Police: A Reconsideration and Interpretation," *Journal of Police Science and Administration* 1 (1973): 366–369.

38. Arthur Niederhoffer, *Behind the Shield: The Police in Urban Society* (Garden City, N.Y.: Doubleday, 1967), pp. 41–42.

39. Ibid.

40. Westley, *Violence and the Police*.

41. Niederhoffer, *Behind the Shield*, pp. 216–220.

42. Richard Anson, J. Dale Mann, and Dale Sherman, "Niederhoffer Cynicism Scale: Reliability and Beyond," *Journal of Criminal Justice* 14 (1986): 295–307.

43. Carl B. Klockars, "The Dirty Harry Problem," *Annals of the American Association of Political and Social Science* (November 1980): 33–47.

44. Ibid.

45. Ibid.

46. Edwin S. Geffner, ed., *The Internist's Compendium of Patient Information* (New York: McGraw-Hill, 1987), Sec. 30.

47. Ibid.

48. "Stress on the Job," *Newsweek*, April 25, 1988, p. 43.

49. Alison Mitchell, "A Night on Patrol: What's Behind Police Tensions and Discontent," *New York Times*, October 19, 1992, pp. B1, B2.

50. Michael Pittaro, "Police Occupational Stress and Its Impact on Community Relations," *Police Forum: Academy of Criminal Justice Sciences* 1 (2008): 1.

51. W. Clinton Terry, "Police Stress: The Empirical Evidence," *Journal of Police Science and Administration* 9 (1981): 67–70. This article has a substantial bibliography and discussion of the issue of police stress.

52. Clement Milanovich, "The Blue Pressure Cooker," *Police Chief* 47 (1980): 20.

53. Robert J. McGuire, "The Human Dimension in Urban Policing: Dealing with Stress in the 1980s," *Police Chief* (November 1979): 27; Joseph Victor, "Police Stress: Is Anybody Out There Listening?" *New York Law Enforcement Journal* (June 1986): 19–20.

54. Gregory S. Anderson, Robin Litzenberger, and Darryl Plecas, "Physical Evidence of Police Officer Stress," *Policing: An International Journal of Police Strategies and Management* 2 (2000): 399–420.

55. See David Griffith, "Hell in High Water," *Police* 11 (2005): 32–36; Melanie Hamilton, "Taking a Toll," *Police* 11 (2005): 38–42.

56. Andy Garrett, as quoted in "Police Arrest Same Man 416 Times," *WKRN, Nashville Tennessee*, February 25, 2008, retrieved February 25, 2008, from www.wkrn.com.

57. Merry Morash, Robin Haarr, and Dae-Hoon Kwak, "Multilevel Influences on Police Stress," *Journal of Contemporary Criminal Justice* 1 (2006): 26–43.

58. James D. Sewell, "Dealing with Employee Stress: How Managers Can Help or Hinder Their Personnel," *FBI Law Enforcement Bulletin* (July 2006): 1–6.

59. Yolanda M. Scott, "Stress among Rural and Small-Town Patrol Officers: A Survey of Pennsylvania Municipalities," *Police Quarterly* 2 (2004): 237–261.

60. Ibid.

61. Yolanda M. Scott, "Non-Urban Police Officers' Subjective Assessments of Coping with Stress," paper presented at the 43rd annual meeting of the Academy of Criminal Justice Sciences, Baltimore, 2006.

62. Nancy Norvell, Dales Belles, and Holly Hills, "Perceived Stress Levels and Physical Symptoms in Supervisory Law Enforcement Personnel," *Journal of Police Science and Administration* 6 (1978): 402–416.

63. Dennis Lindsey, "Police Fatigue: An Accident Waiting to Happen," *FBI Law Enforcement Bulletin* (August 2007): 1–8; Bryan Vila, "Tired Cops: Probable Connections between Fatigue and the Performance, Health, and Safety of Patrol Officers," *American Journal of Police* 2 (1996): 51–92.

64. Luenda E. Charles, Cecil M. Burchfiel, Desta Fekedulegn, Bryan Vila, Tara A. Hartley, James Slaven, Anna Mnatsakanova, and John M. Violanti, "Shift Work and Sleep: The Buffalo Police Health Study," *Policing: An International Journal of Police Strategies & Management* 2 (2007): 215–227.

65. Bryan Vila, as quoted in "Exhaustion May Have Played a Role in Fatal California Crash," *San Jose Mercury News*, March 18, 2008, retrieved March 19, 2008, from www.officer.com. Also see Bryan Vila, *Tired Cops: The Importance of Managing Police Fatigue* (Washington, D.C.: Police Executive Research Forum, 2000).

66. B. Healy, "The Aerobic Cop," *Police Chief* (February 1981): 67–70.

67. Ni He, Jihong Zhao, and Ling Ren, "Do Race and Gender Matter in Police Stress? A Preliminary Assessment of the Interactive Effects," *Journal of Criminal Justice* 6 (2005): 535–547.

68. Ni He, Jihong Zhao, and Carol A. Archbold, "Gender and Police Stress: The Convergent and Divergent Impact of Work Environment, Work-Family Conflict, and Stress Coping Mechanisms of Female and Male Police Officers," *Policing: An International Journal of Police Strategies and Management* 4 (2002): 687–708.

69. Ibid.

70. See John M. Violanti and Stephanie Samuels, *Under the Blue Shadow: Clinical and Behavioral Perspectives on Police Suicide* (Springfield, Ill.: Charles C. Thomas, 2007), pp. 134–148. Also see John M. Violanti and James J. Drylie, *Copicide: Concepts, Cases, and Controversies of Suicide by Cop* (Springfield, Ill.: Charles C. Thomas, 2008).

71. Denise Buffa and Linda Massarella, "Suicide Teen Tricked Cops into Shooting Him: Dear Officer… Please Kill Me," *New York Post*, November 17, 1997, p. 3.

72. Maxine Bernstein, "Portland Police Fatally Shoot Brad Lee Morgan After He Points What Looks Like a Handgun at Officers," *The Oregonian*, January 25, 2012; "Grand Jury Testimony: Reports Detail Portland Police Shooting That Killed Brad Lee Morgan," *The Oregonian*, February 29, 2012, retrieved March 14, 2012, from www.blog.oregonlive.com.

73. James Mazzocco, "'Suicide by Cop' Means Manslaughter," March 10, 2012, retrieved March 11, 2012, from www.blueoregon.com.

74. Susan Weich, "Suicide by Cop Takes Toll on Police," *St. Louis Post-Dispatch*, February 7, 2006.

75. Ibid.

76. John O'Mahony, "'Suicide by Cop' Not So Odd: Docs," *New York Post*, November 17, 1997, p. 3; Richard B. Parent, "Aspects of Police Use of Deadly Force in British Columbia: The Phenomenon of Victim-Precipitated Homicide," master's thesis, Simon Fraser University, 1996.

77. H. Range Huston, M.D., Diedre Anglin, M.D., et al., American College of Emergency Physicians, "Suicide by Cop," *Annals of Emergency Medicine* 6 (1998). Also see Ronnie L. Paynter, "Suicide by Cop," *Law Enforcement Technology* 6 (2000): 40–44; Anthony J. Pinizzotto, Edward F. Davis, and Charles E. Miller III, "Suicide by Cop: Defining a Devastating Dilemma," *FBI Law Enforcement Bulletin* (February 2005): 8–20; and Weich, "Suicide by Cop Takes Toll on Police."

78. J. Nick Marzella, "Psychological Effects of Suicide by Cop on Involved Officers," in Donald C. Sheehan and Janet I. Warren, eds., *Suicide and Law Enforcement* (Washington, D.C.: Federal Bureau of Investigation, 2001). Also see Vivian B. Lord, *Suicide by Cop: Inducing Officers to Shoot* (Flushing, N.Y.: Looseleaf Law, 2004). In this book, experts in the fields of law, psychology, and police tactics discuss how to recognize, resolve, and deal with the aftermath of suicide by cop cases.

79. Pinizzotto, Davis, and Miller, "Suicide by Cop," pp. 8–20.

80. Sue Titus Reid, *Criminal Justice*, 3rd ed. (New York: Macmillan, 1993), p. 230.

81. Dorothy Bracey, "The Decline of the Vaccination Model: Criminal Justice Education for a Changing World," *CJ, The Americas* (April 1988): 1.

82. "On-the-Job Stress in Policing—Reducing It, Preventing It," *National Institute of Justice Journal* (January 2000): 18–24. Also see Peter Finn and Julie Esselman Tomz, *Developing a Law Enforcement Stress Program for Officers and Their Families* (Washington, D.C.: National Institute of Justice, 1997).

83. John Blackmore, "Are Police Allowed to Have Problems of Their Own?" *Police* 1 (1978): 47–55.

84. Charles Unkovic and William Brown, "The Drunken Cop," *Police Chief* (April 1978): 18.

85. Chad L. Cross and Larry Ashley, "Police Trauma and Addiction: Coping with the Dangers of the Job," *FBI Law Enforcement Bulletin* (October 2004): 24–32. Also see John M. Violanti, *Dying from the Job: The Mortality Risk for Police Officers*, Law Enforcement Wellness Association, Inc., retrieved August 5, 2003, from www.cophealth.com/articles/articles_dying_a.html.

86. Cross and Ashley, "Police Trauma and Addiction"; R. L. Richmond, A. K. Wodak, and L. Heather, "Research Report: How Healthy Are the Police? A Survey of Lifestyle Factors," *Addiction* 93 (1998): 1729–1737.

87. Cross and Ashley, "Police Trauma and Addiction"; Roger G. Dunham, L. Lewis, and G. P. Alpert, "Testing the Police for Drugs," *Criminal Law Bulletin* 24 (1998): 155–166.

88. Cross and Ashley, "Police Trauma and Addiction." In their article, they cite B. A. Arrigo and K. Garsky, "Police Suicide: A Glimpse Behind the Badge," in Roger G. Dunham and Gordon P. Alpert, eds., *Critical Issues in Policing: Contemporary Readings*, 3rd ed. (Prospect Heights, Ill.: Waveland Press, 1997), pp. 609–626; Richmond, Wodak, and Heather, "How Healthy Are the Police?" pp. 1729–1737; and H. W. Stege, "Drug Abuse by Police Officers," *Police Chief* 53 (1986): 53–83.

89. James Hibberd, "Police Psychology," *On Patrol* (Fall 1996): 26.

90. "Dispatches," *On Patrol* (Summer 1996): 25.

91. See J. Michael Rivard, Park Dietz, Daniel Martell, and Mel Widawski, "Acute Dissociative Responses in Law Enforcement Officers Involved in Critical Shooting Incidents: The Clinical and Forensic Implications," *Journal of Forensic Sciences* 5

(2002): 1093–1120; and Susan Taylor, "Post Shooting Emotional Meltdown?" *Police* 9 (2001): 40–43.

92. *Justice Assistance News*, 4 (1983): 5.

93. David Klinger, "Police Responses to Officer-Involved Shootings," *National Institute of Justice Journal* 253 (2006): 21–24.

94. William May, "PTSD—The Killer Among Us," *Law Enforcement Today*, April 22, 2013, retrieved March 9, 2014; www.lawenforcementtoday .com/.2013/04/22/;ptsd-the-killer-among-us/.

95. United States Department of Labor, Occupational Safety & Health Administration, *Critical Incident Stress Guide*; retrieved from www.osha.gov/SLTC/emergencypreparedness/guides/ critical.html

96. Mark W. Clark, "Police and PTSD, Once Thought to Only Affect War Veterans, PTSD Is Now Known to Be a Common Affliction among First Responders," *Police*, February 22, 2013, retrieved March 9, 2014, www.policemag.com/channel/careers-training/articles/2013/02/police-and-ptsd.aspx.

97. David Rafky, "My Husband the Cop," *Police Chief* (August 1984): 65.

98. Peter Maynard and Nancy Maynard, "Stress in Police Families: Some Policy Implications," *Journal of Police Science and Administration* 10 (1980): 309.

99. Ellen Scrivner, "Helping Families Cope with Stress," *Law Enforcement News*, June 15, 1991, p. 6.

100. Scott, "Stress among Rural and Small-Town Patrol Officers."

101. U.S. Commission on Civil Rights, *Who Is Guarding the Guardians? A Report on Police Practices* (Washington, D.C.: U.S. Government Printing Office, 1981).

102. *USA Today*, September 15, 1986, p. 3.

103. National Criminal Justice Reference Service, *Program for the Reduction of Stress for New York City Police Officers and Their Families, Final Report* (Washington, D.C.: National Criminal Justice Reference Service, 1998).

104. Police Organization Providing Peer Assistance (POPPA) website, retrieved February 8, 2008, from www.poppainc.com.

105. Bill Genet and Frank Dowling, "POPPA: Using Volunteer Peer Officers for Building Resiliency and Preventing Suicides of Warriors," January 14, 2010, retrieved March 17, 2012, from www.dcoe.health.mil.

106. Personal communication with the NYPD Retirees Organization (www.poppainc.com), February 8, 2008.

107. South Carolina Law Enforcement Assistance Program (SCLEAP) website, retrieved February 10, 2008, from www.scleap.org.

108. James J. Ness and John Light, "Mandatory Physical Fitness Standards: Issues and Concerns," *Police Chief* (August 1992): 74–78.

109. Ibid., p. 75

110. Ibid., p. 77

111. Richard Lezin Jones, "New York Police Officers Face Counseling on September 11 Events," *New York Times*, November 30, 2001, p. A1.

112. "Can We Talk? Officials Take Steps to Head Off 9/11 Post-Traumatic Stress," *Law Enforcement News*, November 30, 2001, p. 1.

113. John M. Madonna, Jr., and Richard E. Kelly, *Treating Police Stress: The Work and the Words of Peer Counselors* (Springfield, Ill.: Charles C. Thomas, 2002).

114. Richard Kelly, "Critical Incident Debriefing," in Madonna and Kelly, *Treating Police Stress*, pp. 139–149. Also see "Tactical Officers Get Help from Those Who've Been There," *Law Enforcement News*, April 15, 2002.

115. "On-the-Job Stress in Policing—Reducing It, Preventing It." Also see Finn and Tomz, *Developing a Law Enforcement Stress Program*.

116. Samuel Walker, Stacy Osnick Milligan, and Anna Berke, *Strategies for Intervening with Officers through Early Intervention Systems: A Guide for Front-Line Supervisors* (Washington, D.C.: Office of Community Oriented Policing Services, 2006). Also see Violanti and Paton, *Who Gets PTSD?*; Samuel Walker, *Early Intervention Systems: A Guide for Law Enforcement Chief Executives* (Washington, D.C.: Office of Community Oriented Policing Services, 2003); and Samuel Walker, Stacy Osnick Milligan, and Anna Berke, *Supervision and Intervention within Early Intervention Systems: A Guide for Law Enforcement Chief Executives* (Washington, D.C.: Office of Community Oriented Policing Services, U.S. Department of Justice, 2005).

117. "On-the-Job Stress in Policing—Reducing It, Preventing It."

118. Scott, "Stress among Rural and Small-Town Patrol Officers."

119. Ronnie Garrett, "Don't Cowboy Up," *Law Enforcement Technology* 2 (2006): 40, 42–48, 50–51.

120. Hans Toch, *Stress in Policing* (Washington, D.C.: National Institute of Justice, 2002). For recent studies on police stress, see Hasan Buker and Filip Wiecko, "Are Causes of Police Stress Global? Testing the Effects of Common Police Stressors on the Turkish National Police," *Policing: An International Journal of Police Strategies & Management* 2 (2007): 291–309; M. Martinussen, A. M. Richardsen, and R. J. Burke, "Job Demands, Job Resources, and Burnout among Police Officers," *Journal of Criminal Justice* 3 (2007): 239–249; Adriana Ortega, Sten-Olof Brenner, and Phil Leather, "Occupational Stress, Coping and Personality in the Police: An SEM Study," *International Journal of Police Science & Management* 1 (2007): 36–50; and Judith A. Waters and William Ussery, "Police Stress: History, Contributing Factors, Symptoms, and Interventions," *Policing: An International Journal of Police Strategies & Management* 2 (2007): 169–188.

121. Michael Pittaro, "Police Occupational Stress and Its Impact on Community Relations," *Police Forum: Academy of Criminal Justice Sciences* 1 (2008): 12.

122. Recently, significant attention is being addressed to police suicide and the stresses that can be attributed to it. See,

for example, Thomas E. Baker and Jane P. Baker, "Preventing Police Suicide," *FBI Law Enforcement Bulletin* (October 1996): 24–27. Also see Kevin Barrett, "More EAPs Needed in Police Departments to Quash Officers' Super-Human Self-Image," *EA Professional Report* (January 1994), p. 3; Barrett, "Police Suicide: Is Anyone Listening?" *Journal of Safe Management of Disruptive and Assaultive Behavior* (Spring 1997): 6–9; Julia Dahl, "The Police Suicide Problem," *Boston Globe*, January 24, 2010, retrieved January 25, 2010 from www.boston.com; Hackett and Violanti, *Police Suicide*; Steven R. Standfest, "The Police Supervisor and Stress," *FBI Law Enforcement Bulletin* (May 1996): 10–16; "The Greatest Threat to Cops' Lives—Themselves," *Law Enforcement News*, December 31, 1997, p. 22; John M. Violanti, *Police Suicide: Epidemic in Blue*, 2nd ed. (Springfield, Ill.: Charles C. Thomas, 2007); Violanti and Samuels, *Under the Blue Shadow*; Violanti, "Police Suicide: Current Perspectives and Future Considerations"; Violanti, "The Mystery Within: Understanding Police Suicide," *FBI Law Enforcement Bulletin* (February 1995): 19–23; and "What's Killing America's Cops? Mostly Themselves, According to New Study," *Law Enforcement News*, November 15, 1996, p. 1.

123. Laurence Miller, "Practical Strategies for Preventing Officer Suicide," *Law and Order* 3 (2006): 90–92.

124. Meg Kissinger, "Milwaukee Department Hit Hard by Officer Suicides," *Milwaukee Journal Sentinel*, January 22, 2008, retrieved January 23, 2008, from www.officer.com.

125. Patricia Kelly and Rich Martin, "Police Suicide Is Real," *Law and Order* 3 (2006): 93–95.

126. Michelle Perin, "Police Suicide," *Law Enforcement Technology* 9 (2007): 8, 10, 12, 14–16. The website for the National P.O.L.I.C.E. Suicide Foundation is www.psf.org.

127. Monroe Dugdale, *Every Police Department's Nightmare: Officer Suicide*, August 1, 1999, retrieved from www.tearsofacop.com/police/articles/dugdale.html

128. John M. Violanti, as quoted in "What's Killing America's Cops?" Also see Violanti, *Police Suicide: Epidemic in Blue*, 2nd ed.; and Violanti and Samuels, *Under the Blue Shadow*.

129. Violanti, "Suicide and the Police Culture."

130. Violanti, "The Mystery Within: Understanding Police Suicide," p. 22.

131. Daniel W. Clark and Elizabeth K. White, "Clinicians, Cops, and Suicide," in Hackett and Violanti, eds., *Police Suicide: Tactics for Prevention*, pp. 16–36.

132. Miller, "Practical Strategies for Preventing Officer Suicide." Also see Kelly and Martin, "Police Suicide Is Real."

133. Kelly and Martin, "Police Suicide Is Real." Also see Violanti, *Police Suicide: Epidemic in Blue*, 2nd ed.; and Violanti and Samuels, *Under the Blue Shadow*, pp. 173–177.

134. Kissinger, "Milwaukee Department Hit Hard by Officer Suicides."

135. John Ritter, "Suicide Rates Jolt Police Culture," *USA Today*, February 8, 2007, retrieved February 21, 2007, from www.usatoday.com.

136. Robert Douglas, as cited in Ritter, "Suicide Rates Jolt Police Culture."

137. Teresa T. Tate, *Police Suicide, What Can Be Done?*, retrieved March 9, 2014, from www.tearsofacop.com/police/articles/tate.html.

138. Barbara Raffel Price, as quoted in Karen Polk, "New York Police: Caught in the Middle and Losing Faith," *Boston Globe*, December 28, 1988, p. 3.

139. Michael S. McCampbell, "Meth and Meth Labs: The Impact on Sheriffs," *Sheriff* 1 (2006): 16–20, 77.

140. Rich Stanek, as quoted in Mara H. Gottfried, "More Armor, Tougher Crooks," *Pioneer Press*, July 2, 2006.

141. Tim Collie, "South Florida Police Facing More Criminals Not Afraid to Shoot at Them," *South Florida Sun Sentinel*, November 11, 2007, retrieved November 13, 2007, from www.sun-sentinel.com.

142. Federal Bureau of Investigation, *Law Enforcement Officers Feloniously Killed and Assaulted, 2012* (Washington, D.C.: Federal Bureau of Investigation, 2013), retrieved March 12, 2014, from www.fbi.gov.

143. National Law Enforcement Officers Memorial Fund, *Law Enforcement Facts*, retrieved February 10, 2008, from www.nleomf.com/TheFund/fund.htm.

144. Concerns of Police Survivors, Inc., retrieved February 10, 2008, from www.nationalcops.org.

145. Christine Eith, and Matthew R. Durose, *Contacts between Police and the Public, 2008* (Washington, D.C.: Bureau of Justice Statistics, 2011). The statistics of these approximately 40 million contacts yearly include only persons age 16 years or older.

146. Brian A. Reaves, *Local Police Departments, 2007* (Washington, D.C.: Bureau of Justice Statistics, 2010), p. 19.

147. Federal Bureau of Investigation, *Law Enforcement Officers Feloniously Killed and Assaulted, 2012.*

148. Claire Mayhew, *Occupational Health and Safety Risks Faced by Police Officers* (Canberra ACT: Australian Institute of Criminology, 2001).

149. Federal Bureau of Investigation, *Law Enforcement Officers Killed and Assaulted, 2012.*

150. Ibid.

151. Matthew R. Durose, Erica L. Schmitt, and Patrick A. Langan, *Contacts between Police and the Public: Findings from the 2002 National Survey* (Washington, D.C.: Bureau of Justice Statistics, U.S. Department of Justice, 2005).

152. Rich Roberts as quoted in William Kates, "Violence Against Police Is Again on the Rise," *Associated Press*, April 15, 2006.

153. Centers for Disease Control and Prevention, U.S. Department of Health and Human Services, *HIV/AIDS Surveillance Report: HIV Infection and AIDS in the United States*, retrieved March 19, 2008, from www.cdc.gov/hiv/topics/surveillance/basic.htm.

154. International Association of Chiefs of Police, *HIV/AIDS Prevention: Concepts and Issues Paper* (Alexandria, Va.: International Association of Chiefs of Police, 2000).

155. Theodore M. Hammett and Walter Bond, *Risks of Infection with the AIDS Virus through Exposures to Blood* (Washington, D.C.: National Institute of Justice, 1987).

156. International Association of Chiefs of Police, *HIV/AIDS Prevention.* Also see R. A. Thompson and J. W. Marquart, "Law Enforcement Responses to the HIV/AIDS Epidemic: Selected Findings and Suggestions for Future Research," *Policing: An International Journal of Police Strategies and Management* 4 (1998): 648–665. Thompson and Marquart conducted the first study analyzing police officers' beliefs, perceptions, and attitudes about HIV/AIDS.

157. Federal Bureau of Investigation, "Collecting and Handling Evidence Infected with Human Disease-Causing Organisms," *FBI Law Enforcement Bulletin* (July 1987): 1–5.

158. Theodore M. Hammett, *Precautionary Measures and Protective Equipment: Developing a Reasonable Response* (Washington, D.C.: National Institute of Justice, 1988).

159. Theodore M. Hammett, *AIDS and the Law Enforcement Officer: Concerns and Policy Responses* (Washington, D.C.: National Institute of Justice, 1987). Also see John Cooney, "HIV/AIDS in Law Enforcement: What-If Scenarios," *FBI Law Enforcement Bulletin* 2 (2000): 1–6. The author emphasizes management's role in providing their officers with proper knowledge and training regarding HIV/AIDS to reduce their fears that may result from the dissemination of false information.

Minorities in Policing

Hill Street Studios/Blend Images/Alamy

OUTLINE

Discrimination in Policing
Discrimination Against Women
Discrimination Against African
Americans

**How Did Women and Minorities
Strive for Equality?**
The Civil Rights Act of 1964
The Omnibus Crime Control and
Safe Streets Act of 1968
The Equal Employment Opportunity
Act of 1972
The Civil Rights Act of 1991
Federal Courts and Job Discrimination
Affirmative Action Programs

White Male Backlash

**Minorities Proving Themselves
on the Job**
Academic Studies

Minorities in Policing Today
Female Representation
African American Representation
Hispanic Representation
Asian Representation
Muslim Representation
Gay and Lesbian Representation

**Challenges Persist for Minorities in
Policing**
Challenges for Women
Challenges for African Americans
Challenges for Other Minorities

LEARNING OBJECTIVES

- Identify the various minority groups and the issues involved in the recruitment of these groups.

- Describe the role legislation and the federal government played in removing equal employment opportunity barriers to minorities in policing.

- Explain how affirmative action policies have affected white males in hiring and promotional policies.

- Discuss the impact of the police recruitment and testing processes on certain minority groups.

- Summarize the representation of minorities in policing today.

- Identify ways in which minorities still face challenges in policing.

INTRODUCTION

Female police officers on uniformed patrol duty are common today, as are officers who are African American or members of other minority groups. In fact, all races and ethnic groups are represented in U.S. police departments. However, this was not always the case. Until quite recently, white males dominated the ranks, and both women and African Americans were traditionally excluded from U.S. police departments.[1] This underrepresentation of minorities in police departments was not limited to southern cities; northern jurisdictions also have a history of discriminating against African Americans and limiting their job responsibilities in law enforcement.[2]

Although the United States has had organized, paid police departments since the 1840s, the first female police officer was not appointed until 1910 when Alice Stebbins Wells was hired by the Los Angeles Police Department (LAPD).[3] As more women were hired by police departments, they were given only clerical duties or duties dealing with juveniles or female prisoners. Women were not permitted to perform the same patrol duties as men until the late 1960s.[4]

This chapter will focus on the roles of minority groups in U.S. police departments. We will review their experience and the methods they used to secure the same job opportunities as white men. The chapter will also show the extent to which minorities have influenced today's police departments and will explore the capabilities of women in performing what has traditionally been viewed as a male occupation. Finally, we will examine the status of minorities in U.S. law enforcement today.

Discrimination in Policing

The United States has a long history of job **discrimination** against women and minorities. Discrimination is the unequal treatment of persons in personnel decisions (hiring, promotion, and firing) based on their race, religion, national origin, gender, or sexual orientation. Only in the past several decades have women and minorities been able to share the American dream of equal employment. Their treatment in police departments was not much different from their treatment in other jobs and in society in general. The federal government admitted this fact in 1974 in an affirmative action guidebook for employers: "American law guarantees all persons equal opportunity in employment. However, employment discrimination has existed in police departments for a long time. The main areas of discrimination are race/ethnic background and gender."[5]

Discrimination Against Women

In 1910, Los Angeles appointed the nation's first "officially designated" policewoman, Alice Stebbins Wells, a social worker in the city. According to the

LAPD website, Wells was assigned to work with the department's first juvenile officer, Officer Leo W. Marden. Subsequent to her appointment the following order was issued: "No young girl can be questioned by a male officer. Such work is delegated solely to policewomen, who, by their womanly sympathy and intuition, are able to gain the confidence of their younger sisters." Wells and other women who followed her embodied the concept of policewoman-as-social-worker and tended to be educated and upper-middle-class, as opposed to male officers who were largely working-class immigrants. Policewomen were often called "city mothers" and were employed to bring order and assistance to the lives of women and children who needed help and correction. These women separated themselves from male police officers and did not view the males as their equals in class, education, or professionalism. They avoided the trappings of the male officers and did not wear a uniform or carry a gun. The police establishment did not seek to hire them, but, rather, their entrée was usually the result of outside forces, which added to their isolation from their male peers.[6]

After World War II, there was the emergence of middle-class female policing careerists, sometimes called "Depression babies," many of whom were not college-educated and did not want to be social workers. Their police duties expanded, but they were frustrated with their limited roles and opportunities.

discrimination Unequal treatment of persons in personnel decisions on the basis of their race, religion, national origin, gender, or sexual orientation.

Though generally still of a higher class and more educated than male officers, these women were more like their male peers than their predecessors were. They were a bridge generation from the early pioneers to today's female police officer.[7]

In 1968, the Indianapolis Police Department assigned Betty Blankenship and Elizabeth Coffal to patrol. They were the first females to wear a uniform and a gun belt and to drive a marked patrol car, responding to calls for service on an equal basis with men. Blankenship and Coffal broke the "mothering" link for police officers, and though they eventually went back to more traditional "women's roles" in policing, the stage had been set for the modern women-on-patrol era. Today, female officers are much like their male colleagues, entering law enforcement with similar concerns and goals, including salary, benefits, and opportunities as crime fighters to enforce the law, keep the peace, and provide public safety functions.[8]

Women have faced an enormous uphill struggle for the right to wear the uniform and perform the same basic police duties that men performed for years. Why were women excluded from performing regular police work? Until the 1970s, it was presumed that women, because of their gender and typical size, were not capable of performing the same type of patrol duty as men. Social forces also contributed to the discrimination against women. If women could be police officers, that challenged the macho image of the job. Men did not want to have their behavior inhibited in any way by the presence of women on the job. They did not want to be overshadowed by or take orders from women, and they did not want to be supported by women in the performance of potentially dangerous work. The issue of jealousy from police officers' wives was also brought up at times. The most commonly heard comment by male police officers during the 1970s as women entered the patrol arena had to do with the fear of female officers being beaten up and their guns taken. This would endanger the female officers, citizens, and the male officers who would be backing up the women. The men feared that law enforcement would be forever changed and the world as they knew it would come to an end.[9]

From World War II until the 1970s, women constituted only a very small percentage of U.S. police officers. The early female officers were restricted to issuing parking tickets or performing routine clerical tasks. As mentioned earlier, in the early days of female policing, women were normally used in only three actual police-related jobs: vice, juvenile work, and guarding female prisoners.[10] Even O. W. Wilson, writing in his *Police Administration* text, considered by many to be the bible of law enforcement managers, proposed that women were an asset in certain police positions, but not all. Through all four editions of his text, from 1950 to 1977, he conceded that women had value as juvenile officers and in other limited areas but contended that they did not have what it took to be leaders. Men had more experience and were "less likely to become irritable and overcritical under emotional stress" than women.[11]

In the late 1960s and early 1970s, the role of women in U.S. police departments began to change. To some degree, this change was facilitated by the 1964 Civil Rights Act, which barred discrimination on the basis of sex. The change also can be attributed to the women's rights movement and efforts by

Alice Stebbins Wells, who became one of the first policewomen in the United States when she joined the Los Angeles, California, Police Department in 1910.

female officers themselves to perform patrol duty and to achieve equality with male officers.[12] Even as late as the mid-1970s, however, female officers in some jurisdictions experienced different sets of rules than their male counterparts as their administrators and coworkers fluctuated between endorsing their full equality and wanting to "protect" them.

Discrimination Against African Americans

In 1867, after receiving numerous complaints from the *New Orleans Tribune*, Governor Wells appointed Charles Courcelle, a "newly enfranchised" citizen, to the board of police commissioners in New Orleans. Three days later the paper reported that Dusseau Picot and Emile Farrar, both African Americans, had been appointed to the police department. These two pioneers seem to be the first documented African American police officers in the nation. Within 10 years, numerous other cities began appointing blacks to police departments, and just after the turn of the 20th century, significant appointments began taking place in St. Louis, Dayton, Berkeley, and Atlanta.[13]

In 1910, the U.S. Census Bureau reported 576 blacks serving as police officers in the United States, most in northern cities. African Americans had all but disappeared from southern police forces. Though Houston, Austin, Galveston, San Antonio, and Knoxville continued to employ African American police officers, these officers often had no uniforms, could not arrest whites, and worked exclusively in black neighborhoods. Until the 1940s, not a single black police officer worked in the Deep South—including South Carolina, Georgia, Louisiana, Mississippi, and Alabama—and yet, in the 1930s and 1940s, these states had most of the black population in the United States.[14] Most blacks were eliminated from the hiring process because they posed a threat to white supremacy.

Even in the North, African Americans faced discrimination in assignments and promotions. Black police officers felt their issues were not addressed by their administrations and took matters into their own hands. Though not identified as such at the time, an early form of double marginality (discussed shortly) led the black officers to socialize with each other and teach each other how to successfully deal with the discrimination and dual system of law enforcement. This situation led to increased camaraderie and organization within their groups. Black officers formed the Texas Negro Peace Officers Association in 1935. This first formal police association organized by black officers in the United States was followed by others in the 1940s and 1950s. In 1943, the Guardians Association was organized by black New York City officers to "recognize the views and ideals of black policemen in New York City."[15]

In his classic study of African American police officers in the New York City Police Department (NYPD) in 1969, *Black in Blue: A Study of the Negro Policeman*, Nicholas Alex discovered that African Americans were excluded from the department's detective division. Alex also found that African American officers were usually accepted by white officers as fellow police officers but were socially excluded from the white officers' off-duty activities.[16] Alex's major finding was that African American police officers suffered **double marginality**—the simultaneous expectation by white officers that African American officers would give members of their own race better treatment and hostility from members of the African American community who considered black officers to be traitors to their race. African American officers also were subjected to racist behavior from white cops. Alex found that, to deal with this pressure, African American officers adapted behaviors ranging from denying that African American suspects should be treated differently from whites to treating African American offenders more harshly to prove their lack of bias. Thus, Alex found, African American cops suffered from the racism of their fellow officers and were seen to be rougher on African Americans to appease whites. In a repeat of his study in 1976, *New York Cops Talk Back*, Alex stated that he found more aggressive, self-assured African American police officers, and that the officers he studied were less willing to accept any discriminatory practices by the police department.[17]

Stephen Leinen, in his book *Black Police, White Society*, found significant institutionalized

---

double marginality The simultaneous expectation by white officers that African American officers will give members of their own race better treatment and hostility from members of the African American community who consider black officers to be traitors to their race.

discrimination in the NYPD until the 1960s. African American police officers were assigned only to African American neighborhoods and were not assigned to specialized, high-profile units. Leinen also noted that disciplinary actions against African American officers were inequitable when compared with those against white officers. He found, however, that institutional discrimination largely disappeared in subsequent years. He attributed this to the legal, social, and political events of the civil rights era, along with the efforts of African American police officer organizations, such as the NYPD's Guardians.[18]

NATIONAL COMMISSIONS TO STUDY DISCRIMINATION   In the 1960s and early 1970s, the U.S. government recognized the problems caused by the lack of minorities in policing. Various national commissions were established to study and make recommendations toward improving the criminal justice system.

The National Advisory Commission on Civil Disorders stated that discriminatory police employment practices contributed to the riots of the middle and late 1960s. It found that in every city affected by riots, the percentage of minority group officers was substantially lower than the percentage of minorities in the community. The commission noted that in Cleveland, minorities represented 34 percent of the population but only 7 percent of the sworn officers, and, in Detroit, minorities represented 39 percent of the population but only 5 percent of the sworn officers. Although African Americans made up at least 12 percent of the U.S. population, they represented less than 5 percent of police officers nationwide. The commission also reported that minorities were seriously underrepresented in supervisory ranks in police departments. Another commission formed at this time, the President's Commission on Law Enforcement and Administration of Justice, also commented on the low percentage of minorities in police departments: "If police departments, through their hiring or promotion policies, indicate they have little interest in hiring minority group officers, the minority community is not likely to be sympathetic to the police."[19]

Another group, the **National Advisory Commission on Criminal Justice Standards and Goals**, recognized the need to recruit more minorities into U.S. police departments. This presidential commission, which was formed to study the criminal

justice system, issued standards to which police agencies should adhere to reduce job discrimination based on race and gender. On the employment of women, the commission stated that every police agency should immediately ensure that no agency policy discouraged qualified women from seeking employment as sworn or civilian personnel or prevented them from realizing their full employment.[20] Minority recruiting also was discussed:

> Every police agency immediately should [e]nsure that it presents no artificial or arbitrary barriers (cultural or institutional) to discourage qualified individuals from seeking employment or from being employed as police officers.

All departments should engage in positive efforts to employ ethnic minority group members. When a substantial ethnic minority population resides within the jurisdiction, the police agency should take affirmative action to achieve a ratio of minority group employees in approximate proportion to the makeup of the population.[21]

The National Advisory Commission on Civil Disorders, also known as the Kerner Commission, recommended, among other things, that police departments "intensify their efforts to recruit more Negroes," examine their promotional policies, and increase the use and visibility of integrated patrol in minority neighborhoods.[22] This report together with increased pressure from the public led to more aggressive recruiting efforts in police agencies during the 1970s and 1980s.

How Did Women and Minorities Strive for Equality?

Despite pronouncements by national commissions, minorities were forced to take their cases to the U.S. courts in an attempt to achieve equality with white men in U.S. police departments. The primary instrument governing employment equality, as well

National Advisory Commission on Criminal Justice Standards and Goals Presidential commission formed to study the criminal justice system and recommend standards for police agencies to adhere to in order to reduce discrimination.

as all equality, in U.S. society is the **Fourteenth Amendment** to the U.S. Constitution. This amendment, passed in 1868, guarantees "equal protection of the law" to all citizens of the United States:

> Section 1. All persons born or naturalized in the United States, and subject to the jurisdiction thereof, are citizens of the United States and of the State wherein they reside. No State shall make or enforce any law which shall abridge the privileges or immunities of citizens of the United States; nor shall any State deprive any person of life, liberty, or property, without due process of law; nor deny to any person within its jurisdiction the equal protection of the law.

More than the Fourteenth Amendment was needed, however, to end job discrimination in policing (and other governmental agencies). In addition to the Fourteenth Amendment, the path to equality had as milestones the Civil Rights Act of 1964, the Omnibus Crime Control and Safe Streets Act of 1968, the Equal Employment Opportunity Act of 1972 (EEOA), the Civil Rights Act of 1991, federal court cases on discrimination, and government-mandated affirmative action programs.

The Civil Rights Act of 1964

Despite the existence of the Fourteenth Amendment, discrimination by U.S. government agencies continued. In an effort to ensure equality, the **Civil Rights Act of 1964** was passed by Congress and signed into law by President Lyndon B. Johnson.[23] Title VII of this law was designed to prohibit all job discrimination based on race, color, religion, sex, or national origin. It covered hiring, promotion, compensation, dismissal, and all other terms or conditions of employment.

....

Fourteenth Amendment Amendment to the U.S. Constitution passed in 1868 that guarantees "equal protection of the law" to all citizens of the United States; frequently used to govern employment equality in the United States.

Civil Rights Act of 1964 Prohibits job discrimination based on race, color, religion, sex, or national origin.

Omnibus Crime Control and Safe Streets Act of 1968 Enacted to aid communities in reducing the crime problem, it created the Law Enforcement Assistance Administration (LEAA), which provided grants for recruitment, training, and education.

YOU ARE THERE

The Path to Equality: Court Cases

1971	*Griggs v. Duke Power Company*
1973	*Vulcan Society v. Civil Service Commission*
1976	*Mieth v. Dothard*
1979	*Vanguard Justice Society v. Hughes*
1979	*United States v. State of New York*
1980	*Guardians Association of New York City Police Department v. Civil Service Commission of New York*

© 2016 Cengage Learning®

The Omnibus Crime Control and Safe Streets Act of 1968

The **Omnibus Crime Control and Safe Streets Act of 1968** was enacted with the goal of assisting local governments in reducing the incidence of crime by increasing the effectiveness, fairness, and coordination of law enforcement and the criminal justice system. Legislators felt that to prevent crime and ensure greater safety for people, law enforcement efforts would be better coordinated and intensified at the local level, as crime is a local problem. Legislators wanted the federal government to give assistance through grants but not interfere in the efforts. The Law Enforcement Assistance Administration (LEAA) was created to assist with this process. Grants would be awarded in many areas, including the recruitment of law enforcement personnel and the training of these personnel. Money was also allocated to the area of public education relating to crime prevention and encouraging respect for law and order, including school programs to improve the understanding of and cooperation with law enforcement agencies.[24] A major goal of this act (after the trials of the 1960s) was improved community relations and the involvement of the community in crime prevention and public safety. This act encouraged the recruitment of minority personnel to better represent and improve relations with minority communities.

The Equal Employment Opportunity Act of 1972

The **Equal Employment Opportunity Act of 1972 (EEOA)** extended the 1964 Civil Rights Act and made its provisions, including Title VII, applicable to state and local governments.[25] The EEOA expanded the jurisdiction and strengthened the powers of the federal Equal Employment Opportunity Commission (EEOC). The EEOA allowed employees of state and local governments to file employment discrimination suits with the EEOC, strengthened the commission's investigatory powers by allowing it to better document allegations of discrimination, and permitted the U.S. Department of Justice to sue state and local governments for violations of Title VII. The EEOA stated that all procedures regarding entry and promotion in agencies—including application forms, written tests, probation ratings, and physical ability tests—are subject to EEOC review, in order to determine whether there has been any unlawful act of discrimination.

The Civil Rights Act of 1991

The Civil Rights Act of 1991, also administered by the EEOC, allows for the awarding of punitive damages regarding civil rights violations under certain conditions based on the number of employees in a company. Although this act does not apply to governmental agencies, it is a significant development in the civil rights movement and influences behavior throughout the community.

Federal Courts and Job Discrimination

Job discrimination may take several forms. The most obvious, of course, is where there is a clear and explicit policy of discrimination—for example, separate job titles, recruitment efforts, standards, pay, and procedures for female or minority employees. The second, and probably most prevalent, form of job discrimination is **de facto discrimination**, which is discrimination as the indirect result of policies or practices that are not intended to discriminate, but which do, in fact, discriminate.

Under EEOC guidelines, discrimination in testing occurs when there is a substantially different rate of selection in hiring, promotion, or another employment decision that works to the disadvantage of members of a particular race, gender, or ethnic group. Let's say that a substantially different rate of passing a particular examination occurs for different racial or ethnic minority groups or members of a certain gender and that this works to the disadvantage of a particular group. For example, if a certain examination results in almost all women failing that test and almost all men passing it, the particular examination is said to have an adverse impact on women. Adverse impact can be seen as a form of de facto discrimination. In the 1970s and 1980s, women and minorities began to use Title VII and the courts (particularly the federal courts) to attempt to achieve equality.

JOB RELATEDNESS The first important job discrimination case was *Griggs v. Duke Power Company* in 1971, which declared that the practices of the Duke Power Company were unconstitutional because the company required that all of its employees have a high school diploma and pass a standard intelligence test before being hired.[26] The court ruled that these requirements were discriminatory unless they could be shown to measure the attributes needed to perform a specific job. The decision in *Griggs v. Duke Power Company* established the concept that job requirements must be job related—they must be necessary for the performance of the job for which a person is applying.

De facto discrimination or adverse impact was found to be most prevalent in employment standards and entrance examinations. These standards and tests discriminated against certain candidates, particularly women and minorities. To eliminate the discriminatory effect of recruitment and testing practices, the EEOC required that all tests and examinations be job related. To prove that a test or standard is job related, an agency must provide evidence that the test or standard measures qualifications and abilities that are actually necessary to perform the specific job for which an applicant is applying or being tested. In the words of the EEOC, to be job related, a test must be "predictive or significantly correlated

----

Equal Employment Opportunity Act of 1972 (EEOA) Extended the 1964 Civil Rights Act and made it applicable to state and local governments.

de facto discrimination The indirect result of policies or practices that are not intended to discriminate, but which do, in fact, discriminate.

with important elements of work behavior which comprise or are relevant to the job or jobs for which candidates are being evaluated."[27]

How did all these regulations apply to police departments? Candidates who formerly were denied acceptance into police departments because they could not meet certain standards (height and weight) or could not pass certain tests (strength) began to argue that these standards were not job related— that is, the standards did not measure skills and qualifications needed to perform police work.

The requirement that officers not be less than a certain height (height requirement) was probably the strongest example of discrimination against women candidates. With very few exceptions, police departments lost court cases involving the height requirement. In *Mieth v. Dothard* (1976), a lawsuit against the Alabama Department of Public Safety, the court ruled:

> Evidence failed to establish.... that tall officers hold an advantage over smaller colleagues in effectuating arrests and administering emergency aid; furthermore, the contention that tall officers have a psychological advantage was not, as a measure of job performance, sufficient constitutional justification for blanket exclusion of all individuals under the specified height.[28]

In another court case regarding height, the court in *Vanguard Justice Society v. Hughes* (1979) noted that the Baltimore Police Department's height requirement of 5 feet 7 inches was a prima facie case of sex discrimination because it excluded 95 percent of the female population, in addition to 32 percent of the male population.[29] (*Prima facie*, which is Latin for "at first sight," refers to a fact or evidence sufficient to establish a defense or a claim unless otherwise contradicted.)

Previous forms of physical ability testing were also challenged and found discriminatory by the courts. Newer tests, known as physical agility tests, were developed to reduce adverse impact. These tests required much less physical strength than the former tests and relied more on physical fitness. Some researchers who studied these physical agility tests found that some of them still had an adverse impact

on women. One study discovered that women were four times more likely than men to fail physical agility testing for deputy sheriff positions.[30] Another study concluded that these physical agility tests did not represent realistic job samples because they related to aspects of the job that were rarely performed.[31] In cases in which the courts decided that these tests still discriminated against females, the police departments were ordered to create new ones. This issue is still being examined throughout the country.

Although most people recognize that it is crucial for police officers to be fit, law enforcement administrators have struggled with exactly how to define *fit*. A recent study conducted over the past 15 years that examined validation studies from more than 5,500 police officers from federal, state, and local law enforcement allowed job-related fitness areas to be documented. This study and the results are discussed in Chapter 4, "Becoming a Police Officer."

THE JOB ANALYSIS Today, as indicated in Chapter 4, to ensure that entry and promotion examinations are job related, police departments perform a job analysis for each position. An acceptable job analysis, declared constitutional by the courts, includes identification of tasks officers generally perform. This identification is based on interviews of officers and supervisors; reviews by another panel of officers and supervisors; computer analyses of questionnaires to determine the frequency of tasks performed; and analyses of the knowledge, skills, and abilities needed to perform the task.

The courts have issued numerous rulings regarding testing and the job analysis. In *Vulcan Society v. Civil Service Commission* (1973), the court rejected personnel tests because of the lack of a job analysis.[32] However, in the case of *Guardians Association of New York City Police Department v. Civil Service Commission of New York* (1983), which is considered a landmark ruling, the court actually accepted the job analysis of the New York City Department of Personnel and the New York City Police Department as being nondiscriminatory.[33] This ruling showed that police departments had begun to follow the mandates of the federal courts without being ordered to do so.

Affirmative Action Programs

The most controversial method of ending job discrimination is the concept of **affirmative action**. In 1965, in Executive Order 11246, President Lyndon

---

affirmative action An active effort to improve employment or educational opportunities for minorities that includes ensuring equal opportunity as well as redressing past discrimination.

B. Johnson required all federal contractors and sub-contractors to develop affirmative action programs. Subsequent orders have amended and expanded the original executive order. In essence, the concept of affirmative action means that employers must take active steps to ensure equal employment opportunity and to redress past discrimination. Affirmative action is an "active effort" to improve the employment or educational opportunities of members of minority groups. This concept differs from that of equal opportunity, which ensures that no discrimination takes place and that everyone has the same opportunity to obtain a job or promotion.

Affirmative action must be result-oriented—it must focus on the result of employment practices. It is not enough for an agency merely to stop discriminating; the agency must take steps to correct past discrimination and give jobs to those against whom it has discriminated in the past.[34] Basically, affirmative action is designed to make up for, or to undo, past discrimination.

Affirmative action programs involve several major steps. First, the agency must study its personnel makeup and determine a proper level of minority and female representation. If it does not meet that level, the agency must establish goals, quotas, and timetables to correct the lack of female and minority representation. It must make every effort to advertise job openings and actively seek out and encourage female and minority applicants. All tests and screening procedures must be validated as being job related, and any potentially discriminatory procedures must be eliminated.

The major concept behind affirmative action, and possibly the most disturbing concept to many people, is the establishment of **quotas**. To implement affirmative action plans, departments incorporate goals and objectives involving numbers and timetables to correct past underrepresentation. These plans do not necessarily involve rigid quotas, just hiring and promotion goals for which to strive. Some people believe that affirmative action plans and quotas lead to **reverse discrimination**. Under a quota arrangement, a certain percentage of openings are reserved for particular groups, and some agencies may have separate promotional lists for different minorities and hire or promote alternately off each list. Individuals hired or promoted off one list might have scored lower than someone who does not rank high enough on another list to be hired or promoted. The argument is that this involves reverse

discrimination against whites or males in violation of the 1964 Civil Rights Act and the equal protection clause of the Fourteenth Amendment.

In cases stemming from lawsuits over the admission process at the University of Michigan's Law School, the Supreme Court ruled that the use of affirmative action is acceptable as long as it treats race as one factor among many in order to achieve a "diverse" class, but it is unconstitutional if it automatically increases an applicant's chances over others due to race. This ruling means that the concept of affirmative action does not violate the Constitution as long as it is narrowly used to assist in achieving diversity.[35]

In a 2005 publication by the Department of Justice, researchers advocated that police departments direct their efforts into attracting larger numbers of qualified minorities into the applicant pool rather than implementing quotas or changing hiring requirements to reach goal numbers desired.[36] A survey of 281 police agencies also found that affirmative action plans had only a minor impact on the number of African American officers employed and that the most important determinant was the size of the African American population within the community.[37] In the late 1990s and early 2000s, the concept of affirmative action was under attack on numerous fronts, ranging from U.S. Supreme Court cases to state and local laws.

White Male Backlash

As more police jobs and promotions began to go to minorities, fewer white males received those jobs and promotions. White males were passed over on entrance and promotion examinations by minorities, some of whom had received lower test scores. This situation resulted in turmoil, with angry white males voicing anger and resentment, and counter-lawsuits followed.

Though the EEOC prohibits all discrimination and consequently does not use the theory of "reverse discrimination," some individuals label the preferential treatment received by minority groups as

---

quotas Numbers put into place as part of goals and objectives in affirmative action plans.

reverse discrimination The label used by those who believe quotas discriminate against whites and males to describe the preferential treatment received by minority groups and women under affirmative action.

The Walls Come Tumbling Down

Throughout the years, numerous lawsuits involving affirmative action have been filed by and on behalf of women and minorities. The judicial findings and consent decrees (agreements between parties before, and instead of, a final decision by a judge) have done much to ease the way for women and minorities into U.S. police departments. A sampling of these cases follows.

A lawsuit filed against the San Francisco Police Department resulted in a federal court order establishing an experimental quota of 60 women as patrol officers. The department also revised the height and weight requirements that had barred women from patrol jobs. In response to a lawsuit filed by the Department of Justice, Maryland agreed to recruit more female state police officers. Similarly, the New Jersey State Police agreed to establish, within a year of a court ruling, hiring goals for women in both sworn and nonsworn positions.

A rejected female applicant filed suit against the California Highway Patrol, charging that its male-only standards unlawfully discriminated against women under Title VII of the Civil Rights Act. Following the results of a two-year feasibility study, a decision was made in the plaintiff's favor. As a result, the California Highway Patrol officially began accepting qualified women for state trooper positions, ending a 46-year tradition of using only men as traffic officers.

With the threat of a lawsuit in the offing, the New York City Police Department ended its height requirements, unfroze its list of female applicants, and increased its female officers on patrol to 400 in a brief period of time.

The Los Angeles Police Department signed a consent decree with the Justice Department awarding $2 million in back pay to officers who were discriminated against, agreeing that 45 percent of all new recruits would be African American or Hispanic American and that 20 percent of all new recruits would be women. A consent decree also required that one-third of all promotions in the Miami Police Department be given to women and minorities.

Sources: Adapted from Anthony V. Bouza, "Women in Policing," *FBI Law Enforcement Bulletin* (September 1975): 4–7; Glen Craig, "California Highway Patrol Officers," *Police Chief* (January 1977): 60; *Criminal Justice Newsletter* (December 1980): 6; *New York Times*, September 14, 1976, p. 8; *New York Times*, October 8, 1975, p. 45; Dianne Townsey, "Black Women in American Policing: An Advancement Display," *Journal of Criminal Justice* 10 (1982): 455–468.

reverse discrimination.[38] They argue that selecting police officers based on their race or gender actually violates the 1964 Civil Rights Act and is discriminatory. Critics also argue that selecting officers who have scored lower on civil service tests lowers the personnel standards of a police department and will result in poorer performance by the department. Some of these individuals view affirmative action as a threat to their job security.

Even in law enforcement, with the loyalty that generally exists and where officers depend on each other when responding to calls, tensions can arise between various groups in the workplace. In Chicago, white officers intervened on the side of the city when an African American police officer organization filed suit to change promotion criteria.[39] The Detroit Police Officers Association filed suit to prevent the police department from setting up a quota plan for hiring African American police sergeants.[40]

In 1995, a sergeant with the Los Angeles County Sheriff's Department formed the Association of White Male Peace Officers to protect the rights of white male officers through zero discrimination in hiring, promotion, or assignment. The sheriff's department said it could not prevent officers from joining the group but reported that it did not sanction the group or understand the reason for its formation.

The continued need for affirmative action programs is under renewed challenge from critics who contend that the original goals of ending discrimination against minorities and providing parity with white males have been achieved. In April 1995, the Maryland State Police agreed to provide approximately $250,000 in back pay to 99 white male troopers who claimed they were unfairly passed over for promotions in 1989 and 1990.[41] In 1999, the courts ruled that the Dallas quota system of allowing minorities to be promoted even if they scored lower on promotional exams was unconstitutional, causing the elimination of the "skip promote" policy the city council had implemented in 1988.[42]

In March 2005, a jury ruled against former Milwaukee Police Chief Arthur Jones, charging he was discriminating against 17 white male lieutenants when he used his own subjective criteria to promote allegedly less qualified blacks and females to the rank of captain. Jones was the first African American to head the Milwaukee Police Department and took over the agency just before the end of a consent decree imposed by the courts in 1984 that imposed a hiring quota: 40 percent of new officers had to be minorities and 20 percent had to be female. Before that, only 8 percent had been black, and there were no black officers in supervisory positions. When Jones took command, 22 of 25 captains were white males, but in 2003, just 9 of 24 were white. This led to allegations of reverse discrimination. The chief's supporters stated he did nothing differently from previous chiefs, and that the suit was going to have high costs for the city of Milwaukee, both monetarily (more than $5 million to promote 13 of the plaintiffs and pay damages) and socially (because of morale issues).[43]

In 2009, the U.S. Supreme Court issued a ruling with an impact on reverse discrimination cases. In *Ricci v. DeStefano,* the Supreme Court heard a case brought by 17 white and 2 Hispanic firefighters, who had passed the lieutenant's test, against the city of New Haven, Connecticut. The city invalidated the results of the exam because no black firefighters passed with a high enough score to be considered for promotion. The city stated that they invalidated the results because they feared a lawsuit over the test's disparate impact on a protected minority. The 19 firefighters claimed they were denied their promotions because of their race—a form of racial discrimination. The Court held that the city's decision to invalidate the test violated Title VII of the Civil Rights Act of 1964.[44]

Minorities Proving Themselves on the Job

Much of the discrimination against women in police departments was based on a fear that they could not do police work effectively because of their gender and size. Discrimination against minorities was often based on a fear that they would not be accepted by nonminority citizens. The academic studies and anecdotal evidence presented in this section, however, show that women and minorities do indeed make effective police officers.

Academic Studies

In the 1970s, many police officials argued that female officers could not handle the tasks of patrol duty effectively. According to this traditional perspective, policing required physical strength and a tough, masculine attitude. Two important academic studies, however—one by the Police Foundation and the other by the Law Enforcement Assistance Administration (LEAA, the precursor to the National Institute of Justice)—found that women were just as effective on patrol as comparable men.[45]

The study performed by the Police Foundation, *Policewomen on Patrol: Final Report,* evaluated and compared the performance of female recruits during their first year on patrol in Washington, D.C., with that of a matched group of new male officers in the same department. This was the first time a police department had integrated a substantial number of women into the backbone of the department. This research project was designed to determine (1) the ability of women to perform patrol work successfully, (2) their impact on the operations of a police department, and (3) their reception by the community. The study found that women exhibited extremely satisfactory work performance. The women were found to respond to similar types of calls as men, and their arrests were as likely as the men's arrests to result in convictions. The report also found that women were more likely than their male colleagues to receive support from the community, and they were less likely to be charged with improper conduct.[46]

The LEAA study was titled *Women on Patrol: A Pilot Study of Police Performance in New York City.* It involved the observation of 3,625 hours of female police officer patrol in New York and included 2,400 police–citizen encounters. The report concluded that female officers were perceived by citizens as being more competent, pleasant, and respectful than male officers. This study found that women performed better when serving with other female officers and that women, when serving with male partners, seemed to be intimidated by their partners and were less likely to be assertive and self-sufficient.[47]

Thus, the first two large-scale studies of female patrol officers dispelled the myth that they were not able to do the job. Follow-up anecdotal evidence and empirical studies further bolstered the assertion that women make effective patrol officers.

In addition to the studies cited earlier, numerous other academic studies of job performance by women police officers have been conducted, with similar results. James David studied the behavior of 2,293 police officers in Texas and Oklahoma and found that the arrest rates of men and women were almost identical, despite the stereotype that women make fewer arrests than men. David also found that women were more inclined to intervene than were their male counterparts when violations of the law occurred in their presence.[48] A study of police perceptions of spousal abuse by Robert Homant and Daniel Kennedy concluded that women were more

A New York City police officer prepares to have a vehicle towed.

Peter Titmuss/Alamy

understanding of, and sympathetic to, the victims of spousal abuse than were men, and women were more likely than men to refer those victims to shelters.[49]

Loretta Stalans and Mary Finn supported this finding when their study revealed that although there was no difference between men and women in arrest rates on domestic violence calls, experienced female officers were more likely to recommend battered women's shelters and less likely to recommend marriage counseling than were their male counterparts. This difference did not occur among rookie officers. Was this variation the result of their experience over the years with domestic violence calls or because they were willing to act contrary to the men's norms?[50]

In an analysis of the existing research on female police officers, Merry Morash and Jack Greene found that the traditional male belief that female officers could not be effective on patrol was not supported by existing research. Morash and Greene concluded that evidence existed showing that women make highly successful police officers.[51]

Former New York City police detective Sean Grennan's study of patrol teams in New York City found no basic difference between the way men and women, working as a patrol team, reacted to violent confrontations. Grennan also found that female police officers, in most cases, were far more emotionally stable than their male counterparts. The women lacked the need to project the macho image, which, Grennan believed, seemed to be inherent in the personality of most of the men he studied. He found that the female officer, with her less aggressive personality, was more likely to calm a potentially violent situation and less likely to cause physical injury. She was also less likely to use a firearm and no more likely to suffer on-the-job injuries.[52]

An investigation involving male and female officers from six departments indicated that female officers tended to use less force than the situation could dictate and that this did not necessarily lead to an increased likelihood of the officer being injured.[53] However, when compared to male officers, female officers were at increased risk for being assaulted in family conflicts, especially when the subject involved was impaired.[54]

The Christopher Commission found similar results in 1991 while conducting a review of the practices of the Los Angeles Police Department (LAPD) after the Rodney King incident. The commission reported that, of the 120 officers with the most allegations concerning the use of force, all were men.[55] A councilman for the city of Los Angeles introduced five motions following the Christopher Commission report that would encourage the hiring of more women and substantially decrease police violence in the LAPD, including making the police department and the police commission more gender balanced and making gender balance an important issue in the selection of the new chief of police. He believed that this would result in true change in the philosophy of the department.[56]

This was supported by a study conducted in a large police department in the Southeast in which 527 internal affairs complaints of misconduct over a three-year period were examined. These incidents translated into 682 allegations of wrongdoing (more than one officer was involved in some incidents). The analysis revealed that men were overrepresented in these complaints. Women accounted for 12.4 percent of those employed by the agency, but they accounted for only 5.7 percent of the allegations.[57]

A study was conducted in Syracuse, New York, in which 40 patrol officers (20 men and 20 women) were observed during a 10-week period while working the 3-to-11 shift. Their attitudes were assessed using surveys and scenarios. Results indicated there were no differences in how the officers viewed or performed their jobs.[58]

Despite these indications that women are performing no differently than men—or perhaps better, in some situations—resistance or lack of acceptance still exists, though to a lesser degree than in the past, among fellow police officers and the public. Kristen Leger found that there has been a growing acceptance by the public for women in the law enforcement role. Especially noteworthy is that the unfounded skepticism concerning women's ability to handle violent encounters, which often has been raised, no longer exists among most citizens. The public attitude toward women in law enforcement is changing, and police officers and administrators should take note of that.[59]

Although citizens are more accepting, they do have certain preconceived notions about men's and women's strong and weak areas within law enforcement. These stereotypes affect citizen expectations and, consequently, their reactions to police officers. The International Association of Chiefs of Police (IACP) conducted a study of 800 police departments in 1998. The researchers found that law enforcement administrators felt overwhelmingly that women possess exceptional skills in the area of verbal and written communications as well as outstanding interpersonal skills in relating to all types of people—whether victims, witnesses, or suspects—and being sensitive to their needs.[60] A recent study examined officer gender in order to determine if it influenced arrest decisions and determined there was little difference between male and female officers regarding arrest rates. The only interesting difference the study noted was that female officers were significantly more likely to arrest when observed by supervisors.[61]

The National Center for Women and Policing has agreed that women offer unique advantages to the contemporary field of law enforcement, with its emphasis on community policing, the high volume of calls involving diversity issues and violence against women, and the strengths that will prevail in these situations.[62] An examination of use of excessive force as related to officer gender found that women were significantly underrepresented compared with men in both citizen complaints and sustained allegations of excessive force. Women also cost their departments significantly less than men in civil liability payouts involving excessive force. In the LAPD between 1990 and 1999, when the men outnumbered the women on patrol by a ratio of 4 to 1, the payouts for excessive force for males exceeded those for females by a ratio of 23 to 1.[63]

Although women have been assigned to patrol duties for only three decades, evidence exists that they are very effective as patrol officers. The former belief that they lacked the size, strength, and temperament to do the job has given way to a realization that being a patrol officer requires more than size, strength, and a tough attitude.

Unlike the situation for women, there have been no studies regarding the ability of African Americans to do police work. This lack of study seems somewhat unusual given the controversial history of African Americans in police work. What research has been done is old and tends to have involved small numbers of patrol officers in New York City.[64] Anecdotal evidence, however, suggests that African American officers perform as well as any other group.

There have been some inquiries regarding the attitudinal beliefs of African American officers as well as examinations of the early career experiences of current black police administrators. Studies seem to indicate that African American officers and white police officers have very different attitudes. African American officers tend to believe that police use excessive force against racial and ethnic minorities

GUEST LECTURE

Courtesy of Ruth Roy

BY INSPECTOR RUTH ROY, RCMP

Ruth Roy started her career with the RCMP in 1981. In 2001, she was commissioned to the rank of inspector in Ottawa. Currently, Inspector Roy is a travel officer responsible for the security of the Prime Minister of Canada and his family while in Canada and abroad. In 2005, Inspector Roy was recognized by her fellow policewomen and awarded the Officer of the Year Award. Again in 2013, she was recognized by the National Association of Women in Law Enforcement Executives (NAWLEE) as the Woman Law Enforcement Executive of the Year. Ruth received her bachelor's degree in business administration from Mount Saint Vincent University in 2010.

NO PRINCE CHARMING

My first posting with the Royal Canadian Mounted Police 32 years ago was to the west coast of Canada, far from my family, my home, my east coast. It was quite daunting being on my own, being 19 years old, being in a profession with high expectations. I remember being lonely at first and being worried that I would not be able to do the work. I quickly learned that police work is more about being able to deal with people than it is about being physically tough. However, it was in the first six months on the job that I learned the most valuable lesson of my career. That lesson was that how I treated others would often be reflected back in how they reacted to me as a person and as a police officer.

My trainer was "old school" and did not believe that women should be police officers. I considered him to be a bully, a man who liked to strong arm people—basically a beat-them-down and ask-questions-later kind of guy. My initial on-the-job training was prior to the *Canadian Charter of Rights and Freedoms*, and my trainer was not challenged for his treatment of people. It was not unusual for him to choke someone out (a term used for the carotid control technique) and then look at me and say, "Why didn't you do that?" I was intimidated by my trainer and most times, while thinking that that level of force was uncalled for, I would remain silent. After three months of training I was permitted to work on my own and to drive around without my trainer yelling at me. One morning, early in my first summer, I met a man who would change my life. Not my Prince Charming, but someone who did have a huge impact on who I became as a police officer and as a person.

Just as the shift was starting and my watch was preparing for the day ahead, a call came in of a disturbance at the local gospel mission. The mission provided meals to homeless and street people and was a known hangout for some unsavory characters. Their key rule was that visitors had to be sober, so the police would often get calls to remove someone from the property who was intoxicated. That particular morning I responded to the call. When I arrived at the mission, I could hear raised voices coming from the eating area in the rear of the mission. I headed that way and could see the back of a large Aboriginal man who was having words with the minister who managed the place. The part of the conversation I heard was the minister telling the fellow that the police were coming and his reply was, "F*** the police." I'm 5 feet 9 inches tall and my boots add another inch or two, so most of the time I can look men eye to eye. Not this fellow: he was at least 6 feet 5 inches, and big. He wore a leather vest and had his hair cut in a mohawk style. He was intimidating, and I was scared. I knew

and poor people, and consequently are supportive of citizen oversight. They often speak out regarding brutality; the National Black Police Officers Association published a pamphlet urging its members to report misconduct by other officers. Black officers are also more supportive of innovation and change within the policing occupation and are generally more supportive than are white officers of community policing.[65]

Recently, a study examined the attitudes of 638 police officers in Indianapolis and St. Petersburg. These officers were involved in the Project on Policing Neighborhoods (POPN) study that analyzed how police function in a community policing environment. It was found that black officers responded more favorably to quality-of-life policing issues and in essence placed more value on fear of crime, neighborhood conditions, and family and neighborhood that my backup was at least 5 to 10 minutes away and being the only one there in uniform, I was expected to do something.

To this day, I am not sure what prompted me to approach the fellow the way I did. I reached way up and put my hand on his shoulder to get his attention. I looked him square in the eye and said, "You're not going to f*** any police officer today." He probably could have taken me out with one swipe of his big arms but instead looked at me and started to laugh. To my relief he had a sense of humor. I asked him his name and he replied, "Alex." I explained to him that he could not stay, as the owner had asked him to leave. I also told him that he could come into cells and sleep it off and that I would let him out when he had sobered up. This giant—who had obviously been a frequent guest of the police—agreed, and with head hung low he followed me to the police car and squeezed himself into the back seat. I treated him kindly and with respect, and he in return did not give me any problems throughout the booking-in process.

As the summer progressed, Alex became quite well known to most of the police officers. He was not from the community so had no family there and was just hanging around. He was often arrested for fighting or causing a disturbance, or just for being drunk in a public place. Alex was known to give the male officers a good fight every time he was arrested. I would often see Alex in our cells, and each time I would ask him what he had done. His usual response was to hang his head, look at me rather sheepishly, and say, "I'm sorry, I was bad." He always seemed to be genuinely remorseful. I felt sorry for Alex and tried my best to connect him with the agencies in town that could help him. My efforts and treatment toward Alex were to be rewarded, but not in the way I had imagined.

That same fall, the city was clearing out a block of homes to create space for a new development. There was one home left on the lot, and it was propped up on blocks ready to be moved.

Given that the evenings were starting to get cold, some of the local transients decided to use this old house to bunk in for the night. Although they were trespassing, in my opinion, they were out of the way, off the streets, and no one had complained about it, so I did not bother them. One night shift I heard my trainer call in on the police radio that he was going to check this house and roust out the transients. I naturally started heading in that direction in case there were any problems. It didn't take long before my trainer called for backup (a rare event for him). Being the closest car, I responded that I was on my way.

I could almost hear my trainer's sigh of disappointment, hearing that I was responding rather than one of the guys. After arriving at the house, I worked my way through the piles of garbage to a back bedroom where I could hear a commotion. When I entered the room I could see shadows of people in sleeping bags cowering against the walls. My trainer and Alex were in the middle of the room squaring off ready to do battle. Alex towered over my trainer. I calmly asked Alex what was going on; he instantly hung his head and apologized to me. Looking from my trainer to me, he turned away from my trainer and followed me out to the police car. My trainer was left standing there jaw hung open and probably composing himself. He never did thank me for helping him out of what could have been a very bad situation.

After that night I did not see Alex again. I presume he either went home or moved on to another community. The life-changing lesson he taught me, however, stayed with me throughout my career. That summer I learned that I could never approach my work like one of the guys. I had to do police work my own way—a female way—an approach that proved for me to be much more effective than the strong-arm tactics. I also learned that when I treated people with respect they would in turn treat me with respect, and if I was honest with people about what was going to happen to them, they trusted me.

disputes. Addressing these issues within a community could go a long way toward strengthening the police–community relationship and developing a more positive perception of the police.[66]

In his study of African American police executives, R. Alan Thompson reported some common experiences these executives went through in their earlier careers. Many of these experiences correlate with some common assumptions held because of

anecdotal evidence, while others do not. Thompson found that most black police executives perceived a lack of social acceptance by white officers and felt that white officers viewed them as "tokens" and not equals during the first five years of their career. However, he also found that the police culture, professionalism, and loyalty issues overcame those perceived differences when the chips were down. Most officers believed that their coworkers would come to their aid and would respond when needed regardless of race.

In Thompson's study, almost half of the black executives felt resentment by the white community, but just over half felt that they were fully accepted by the white citizens. There was more confusion regarding the relations with the black community. Most black executive officers felt there was ambiguity within the black community regarding support of the police and acknowledgment of the black police officer's authority. More than 80 percent of the executives felt that black police officers experienced a unique form of tension between their roles as members of the black community and as enforcers of the law, exemplifying the "double marginality" issue.

Despite some of the troubling findings in Thompson's study, most of the executives felt that interracial working relations within law enforcement had improved during the past decade, though gradually. Many cited the fact that old-time police officers with more prejudiced views had retired over the years and that newer, younger officers did not share those negative attitudes toward black officers, making the workplace more comfortable.[67]

Minorities in Policing Today

As this chapter has shown, during the past three decades, U.S. police departments have attempted to better reflect the communities they serve. Police administrators have intensified the recruitment of minorities to have more balanced police departments. They also have directed their efforts toward the retention of these officers. Many departments have links on their websites that provide additional information and outreach as well as mentoring services for the targeted population.

Discoverpolicing.org, the career exploration arm of the International Association of Chiefs of Police, addresses the diversity issue on their website. They inform viewers that today's law enforcement agencies are looking to fill their ranks with a diverse group of officers who will reflect the communities they serve. Agencies are also expanding their definition of diversity to include religion, sexual orientation, age, family background, and even neighborhoods. Law enforcement is an occupation that respects individuality and diversity matters in the service to the community. The website stresses that the traits sought after in police officers include empathy, communication skills, intelligence, and compassion. These are traits that anyone can bring to the service regardless of their background.[68]

Departments have altered their entry requirements and training curriculums—sometimes willingly and sometimes under court mandate—to facilitate the hiring and training of minority officers. Today minorities serve in all aspects of police work and in all neighborhoods of towns and cities across the United States.

Female Representation

A 2010 Bureau of Justice Statistics (BJS) publication reports that 11.9 percent of all full-time sworn officers in local law enforcement in 2007 were women, up from 10.6 percent in 2000 and 7.6 percent in 1987. Numbers ranged from 17.9 percent in departments serving populations of one million or more to approximately 6 percent in departments serving fewer than 2,500.[69] To put these percentages into perspective, although the presence and status of women in law enforcement have risen, the percentage of women officers is still below 46.7 percent, the percentage of the labor force that women currently occupy.[70] Women in policing appear to be lagging behind women in other traditionally male professions.

More women are now attaining the length of service and breadth of experience typically associated with command positions. Consequently, recent years have seen a significant increase in the numbers of women in administrative positions and serving as chiefs and sheriffs. The numbers of female police chiefs and sheriffs doubled from 1994 to 2004 compared to the previous 10 years.[71] These women have come to their leadership positions in various ways. Some have stayed with the department where they began their careers and moved up through the ranks. Others have changed departments, particularly in states with liberal lateral transfers. Others have left law enforcement for brief stints in school or in law and returned to law enforcement in upper administration.

Women have been or are currently executives in all sizes of municipal agencies, sheriff's departments, state police, campus police, transit police, and federal agencies. Elizabeth Watson became the first woman to lead a police department in a city of greater than a million population when she headed the Houston, Texas, Police Department from

1990 to 1992; upon leaving Houston, she became the first woman to head the Austin, Texas, Police Department. Paula Meara headed the Springfield, Massachusetts, Police Department starting in 1996 after working her way up the ranks of that department. Annette Sandberg was appointed to head the Washington State Patrol in 1995 after leaving the agency for a time to practice law. She retired in 2002, leaving Anne Beers, the head of the Minnesota State Patrol, as the only female head of a state agency at the time.[72] African American women also have headed major agencies, even in the South. These include Beverly Harvard, who headed the Atlanta Police Department from 1994 to 2002; Annetta Nunn, who was sworn in as chief of the Birmingham, Alabama, Police Department in 2003; and Ella Bully-Cummings, who was named as chief of the Detroit Police Department less than a year later.[73]

Anne Kirkpatrick, current undersheriff in King County Sheriffs Office in Washington, has moved between departments. She began her career at the Memphis, Tennessee, Police Department and moved to the Redmond, Washington, Police Department. After obtaining her law degree and spending time as a professor in a community college, she became the head of the Ellensburg, Washington, Police Department and later the director of public safety in Federal Way, Washington, before serving as the chief of police in Spokane. Colleen Wilson was named the chief of police in Monroe, Washington, in 1993 after rising through the ranks. In 2004, she was named chief of the Sumner, Washington, Police Department and later moved to the Port of Seattle Police Department.[74]

In 2002, Connie Patrick became the director of the Federal Law Enforcement Training Center in Glynco, Georgia, after a long and distinguished law enforcement career. In 2003, Nannette H. Hegerty became the first female chief in the history of the Milwaukee Police Department. In 2004, Heather Fong was named chief of police in San Francisco; soon after, Kathleen O'Toole was appointed chief of the Boston Police Department. In 2006, O'Toole left the Boston Police Department to accept a chief inspector position in the Irish National Police.[75] In 2014, she was named chief of police in Seattle, Washington.

Another groundbreaking event that occurred in 2006 was the swearing in of Chief Mary Ann Viverette of the Gaithersburg, Maryland, Police Department as the president of the International Association of Chiefs of Police. Cathy L. Lanier was officially named chief of police of the Washington,

D.C., Metropolitan Police Department in 2007 after rising from the ranks and obtaining advanced degrees during her career. In 2011, Mayor Cory Booker of Newark, New Jersey, appointed Sheilah Coley as the city's first female police chief after she rose through the ranks during a successful 22-year career.[76]

Val Demings, the first female chief of police in Orlando, Florida, was appointed in November 2007 and retired in 2011. She is believed to be the first police chief to follow in the footsteps of a spouse, former Police Chief Jerry Demings, who retired in 2002 to become Orange County's public safety director. Reports are also being received of mothers and daughters serving in the same police departments, which may lead to the tradition of women following in other family members' footsteps in a police career as men have traditionally done. A recent noteworthy accomplishment was the 2013 appointment by President Obama of Julia Pierson as the first female director of the Secret Service in its 148-year history.

A recent study found that consent decrees during the last couple of decades have been very effective in increasing the numbers of women in law enforcement. A **consent decree** is an agreement that binds the agency to a particular course of action in regard to hiring and promoting women and minorities in law enforcement. The study reported that the representation of female officers in agencies with a consent decree was substantially higher than in agencies without consent decrees and higher than the national average for that type of department. Municipal agencies with consent decrees were found to employ 17.8 percent sworn females (25 percent higher than the national average for municipal agencies), county agencies 12 percent (9 percent higher than the national average for counties), and state police agencies 7.2 percent (23 percent higher than the national average for state police agencies). Unfortunately, the report also stated that once the consent decree ends, the progress for women tends to slow in the agency. The authors of the study believe the consent decree may be a worthwhile tool to stick with until agencies progress on their own in this area.[77]

Others believe this is unnecessary. Though the percentages of women in law enforcement today are nowhere near the 50 percent that women represent

consent decree An agreement binding an agency to a particular course of action for hiring and promoting women and minorities.

in society, many argue that this is, to some degree, a result of self-selection and that law enforcement is simply not a career for everyone. The current numbers of women in law enforcement are a big improvement, considering the fact that women have been actively engaged in the profession for only a few decades. There is some concern, however, that the growth appears to have slowed in the last decade. Some attribute this stagnation in advances to bias in the hiring and selection process (in particular the physical fitness testing), as well as inadequate recruitment policies and the image of police officers and agencies as macho and militaristic.

It is encouraging, however, that law enforcement executives are currently addressing all of these issues in a desire to recruit and retain more women. Some innovative strategies being used are discussed later in this chapter. The slow, steady increase in numbers already seen, coupled with new efforts to eliminate bias in the hiring process and with proactive police administrators, will help increase the numbers of women in law enforcement. This will be greatly aided by women attaining rank in agencies, as shown earlier, and becoming more visible as well as having increased input regarding policies and procedures.

African American Representation

In the 1970s and 1980s, African Americans were appointed as police commissioners or chiefs in some of the nation's biggest city police departments. Among them were William Hart, Detroit; Lee P. Brown, Atlanta, Houston, and New York City; and Benjamin Ward, New York City. In the 1990s, this trend continued with Willie Williams in Los Angeles in 1992. In 1997, Melvin H. Wearing was named police chief of New Haven, Connecticut, the first African American to hold that post. Also in 1997, Mel Carraway became the first African American to be appointed to head the Indiana State Police.

By 2004, many police departments had African Americans in their command staff or serving as chiefs of police. These departments included Arlington, Texas, with Dr. Theron Bowman as chief of police; Madison, Wisconsin, with Chief Noble Wray; and Atlanta, Georgia, with Chief Richard Pennington. In 2005, John Batiste was appointed as the head of the Washington State Patrol after having retired from that agency to be an assistant chief in another agency. Several African American women also have headed major agencies, as noted in the previous section.

According to a BJS Report, in 2007, 25 percent of full-time local law enforcement officers were members of a racial or ethnic minority, an increase from 14.6 percent in 1987. African American officers represented 11.9 percent of all law enforcement officers, an increase when compared with 9.3 percent in 1987. Their representation was highest in agencies serving more than 250,000 people, where they composed more than a third of all officers.[78]

At the end of 2010, 53 percent of the rank-and-file police officers in the NYPD came from minority communities, which brought the department's makeup closer to the ethnic makeup of the city. Although whites overwhelmingly made up the higher ranks within the department, the percentage of minorities in upper ranks had increased 4.5 percent since 2002. As these rank-and-file officers mature with time, their representations should increase accordingly.[79]

Diversity is evident in police departments across the country. Here an officer works at a Cinco de Mayo festival.

© Steve Skjold/Alamy

Progress in the representation of African Americans in U.S. police departments is occurring, but the process has been slow and gradual from the 1960s into the 21st century and has sometimes been accompanied by failures. Strides are being made, however, and police departments are becoming more representative of the people they serve.

Hispanic Representation

The number of Hispanic American officers has increased significantly in the last two decades, as has their percentage in the general U.S. population. According to the Department of Justice, Hispanic or Latino officers accounted for 10.3 percent of police officers nationwide in 2007. The highest percentage of Hispanic officers was in departments serving populations of greater than one million, in which they represented 22.9 percent of the officers. This was an increase over the year 2000 in which 8.3 percent of officers were Hispanic and 1987 in which only 4.5 percent of police officers were Hispanic.[80]

Although there is little empirical research regarding Hispanic officers, these officers are extremely valuable to law enforcement agencies. The diversity of the department is a plus, and the officers' ability to relate to the Hispanic community is an asset, as they can help bridge the language and cultural barriers. These officers serve as ambassadors to the large Latino population and greatly facilitate the communication process in emergency situations and when members of the community request assistance.

A major issue regarding Hispanic officers, both in counting their numbers and in determining their role and fit in the community, is simply determining what is meant by Hispanic. The Hispanic culture encompasses many cultural groups, including Mexicans, Cubans, South Americans, Central Americans, and Puerto Ricans. These groups are not homogeneous; there are many cultural differences and, in some cases, tensions between the groups. Considering all of these groups as one does a disservice to both the ethnic communities and the officers. Different groups predominate in different parts of the country. South Florida is dominated by Cubans, but with increasing numbers of Mexicans and South and Central Americans. Mexicans are the largest group of Hispanics in the states that border Mexico, including Arizona, California, and Texas.

Many Hispanic officers are not bilingual, and many do not necessarily share the cultural experiences of most of the residents in an ethnic community. To assume all Hispanic officers are the same is inaccurate. So, what makes someone Hispanic when we are looking at classifications and numbers? There appears to be no clear consensus, and it is up to the individual officer to declare. According to some officers, whether or not they are considered Hispanic can make a difference in the way they perceive their jobs and their communities and in the way their communities perceive them.

Consider the border states of Arizona, California, and Texas, where Mexican Americans predominate. There is a definite difference among officers and their ability to relate to the community as well as the community's trust in them based on the three types of Hispanic officers. First are the officers who are of Hispanic descent but were born and raised in the United States, are not fluent in Spanish, and do not share the cultural knowledge and experience of having lived in Mexico in their formative years. Second are Hispanic officers who are bilingual and were born in Mexico but raised in the United States.[81] These officers have the ability to communicate with other Hispanics but may not have the cultural awareness that the third group of Hispanic officers has. This third group was born and raised in Mexico, recently came to the United States, and became citizens. They share with newly arrived residents the cultural knowledge and experience of having lived in Mexico. These officers are often best able to build a relationship of trust with residents.

Hispanic officers, like African American officers, can experience a type of double marginality. Sometimes they feel pressure to behave in a different manner because they are Hispanic or of a specific ethnicity such as Mexican. For example, newly arrived Mexicans may expect to be given a break or treated more leniently when interacting with a Mexican American officer. The officers can experience role conflict and emotional challenges when interacting with newly arrived hardworking immigrants who are looking for a better life and trying to get ahead. As one officer stated, "I see my parents in their early, struggling days when I stop an old beat-up pickup truck with red tape over the brake light, and I really don't want to write them a ticket and add to their financial troubles."[82]

The assimilation of Hispanic officers has not been without controversy. These officers have been involved in discrimination issues and affirmative action plans. Several organizations have arisen to serve as support groups for Hispanic officers and to facilitate communication between them around the country. The Hispanic American Police Command Officers Association (HAPCOA) is a national organization established in 1973 with goals of meeting the challenge of selecting, promoting, and retaining Hispanic American men and women in criminal justice agencies. The organization supports applicants and offers agencies guidance and support to address the concerns of Hispanic officers and improve community relations within the Latino community. The National Latino Peace Officers Association was established in 1972; one of its major goals is recruiting Latinos into law enforcement and promoting equality and professionalism in law enforcement. These organizations are not common among smaller departments, and many officers can be hesitant to start or join organizations such as these because they often prefer to blend in with fellow officers.

Usually there does not appear to be overt discrimination against Hispanic officers, but many of these officers feel that commonly held stereotypes impede their progress in doing their job or assimilating within the department. Some Hispanic officers appear Caucasian and can be privy to these stereotypes when comments are made by other officers or citizens who are not aware of the officer's ethnicity.[83] Issues can sometimes arise that are similar to those that appear in discussions with African American officers. Hispanic officers sometimes feel discriminated against when asked to patrol certain areas of their city simply because they are Hispanic, or when they are frequently called away from their duties, simply because they are bilingual, so they can translate for other officers. This second issue has led many jurisdictions to provide additional enhancement pay to officers who are bilingual, which makes it easier for the organization to consider it part of the officers' job to translate and which should minimize any resentment that may exist among officers who are constantly called to translate. Enhancement pay is also a way for the department to let prospective candidates know that their skills are solicited and valued and that they will be fairly compensated for these skills, and it ensures a ready supply of officers able to communicate with the Spanish-speaking community.

Hispanics are the fastest-growing ethnic group in the United States, increasing at a rate of more than 55 percent every 10 years. The Census Bureau predicts that Hispanics will constitute 24.4 percent of the U.S. population by 2050.[84] As Assistant U.S. Attorney General Deborah J. Daniels stated in her speech to the HAPCOA training conference, rather than being viewed as a minority, Hispanics should be seen as an "emerging majority group."[85] With this prediction in mind, police organizations must develop recruitment programs within the Hispanic community.

Recruiting Hispanic officers can present challenges. As with other minorities, some Hispanics have had negative interactions with police in their native lands. In Mexico and some other Central and South American countries, the police are corrupt and abusive. There is often no mechanism in place to make a complaint or even to get help from local law enforcement. Consequently, newly arrived immigrants often do not trust police in the United States, will not contact the police when they need help, and will not assist police officers when asked for help. In the border states that deal with numerous Mexican immigrants, officers see the barriers start to come down when the officer speaks Spanish, and a desire to assist becomes apparent when Mexican American citizens find out the officer is also from Mexico. Typically, these residents will call specific officers whom they know are Mexican rather than call the police department. A major challenge is and will continue to be to reach out to these communities to educate them about what the police in the United States are like and what they do, and to encourage immigrants to pursue law enforcement as an occupation to help make their communities safer and to serve their fellow Mexican Americans.[86]

Asian Representation

Though their numbers have increased slightly during the last few years, Asian Americans are poorly represented in police departments across the country. According to the latest statistics, ethnic minorities aside from African American and Hispanic—including Asians, Pacific Islanders, and Native Americans—constituted only 2.7 percent of local police officers in 2007, compared with 2.8 percent in 2003 and 0.8 percent in 1987.[87]

The biggest challenge concerning Asian Americans in law enforcement appears to be recruitment. Despite dramatic increases in the Asian population across the nation, most police departments have few, if any, Asian officers. According to police administrators, Asian Americans are just not applying for the jobs. It seems to be a cultural issue. Parents are not encouraging their children to seek this type of employment. In some homelands, police officers are looked upon as corrupt, brutal, or uneducated.

Police departments are making efforts to overcome these cultural barriers. Their goal is to have their departments mirror their communities and to facilitate trust in the police and encourage the exchange of information. In 2000, the U.S. Census reported that Asians composed 4.2 percent of the U.S. population but only 1.6 percent of officers and deputies across the United States. In New Jersey, where Asians make up 7.1 percent of the population, they are only 1.1 percent of the state troopers. The NYPD has managed to double its Asian representation to 3.5 percent of the department.

Of the Asians who do pursue law enforcement careers, most experience no blatant bias from colleagues. One Asian FBI agent commented that he does not note any discrimination from coworkers or the public but often does encounter surprise, especially in smaller towns, by people who have never before encountered an Asian FBI agent.[88]

California agencies tend to lead the way with the employment of Asian Americans in law enforcement. The agencies are reaching into their ethnic communities to improve communication and build credibility. Because a law enforcement career is not generally part of many Asians' culture, recruiting seems to occur most often when the potential candidate is a student or through police–community interactions.

This type of effort was instrumental in leading San Francisco's former chief, Heather Fong, to choose a law enforcement career. As mentioned earlier, she was named chief of the San Francisco Police Department in 2004. She was recruited to the department by San Francisco's first Asian American chief, Fred Lau, who lived near her and mentored her career. While an undergraduate at the University of San Francisco, she took the police exam and worked as a cadet. Her parents supported her career choice partly because Chief Lau stressed the importance to the city of women and minorities joining the police department.[89]

The effort toward recruitment should prove more successful as Asian Americans become more visible in departments and are able to reach into the community for qualified recruits.

Muslim Representation

A small but increasingly visible group that has experienced discrimination is Muslim officers. Since September 11, 2001, this group has received increased attention from the media, the public, and their coworkers. Recently, cases have arisen in which Muslim officers have claimed they have been discriminated against. These claims usually involve grooming issues, including the wearing of untrimmed beards by male public safety personnel and the wearing of head coverings by Muslim females. These conventions are an important part of Muslim religious and cultural tradition. However, departments usually back their policies, claiming it is a safety and discipline issue. It is believed to be most important for the community and the citizens who encounter their police officers that the officers have a uniform appearance. Police officers have worn uniforms for most of their history because it is critical that the public readily identify them. Although it is beneficial for the public to see officers as part of other communities, their role as public servants to protect and serve citizens takes priority. There should be no hesitation or doubt about who is or is not a police officer.

Gay and Lesbian Representation

Another group with a challenging history in law enforcement is gay and lesbian officers. Police departments have had a history of discriminating against job applicants because of their sexual orientation. Until the beginning of the focus on equal employment opportunity, many police departments discriminated against homosexuals in employment decisions, and the International Association of Chiefs of Police (IACP) maintained a policy of opposing the employment of gay officers until 1969, when it rescinded this policy. By 1990, an estimated 20 percent of the sworn officers in the San Francisco County Sheriff's Department and perhaps 10 percent of officers in the Los Angeles Police Department were gay men or lesbians.[90]

The percentage of gay and lesbian officers is a difficult number to determine. Many departments do not ask about sexual orientation, and because of a fear of making their sexual orientation known to their coworkers, many police officers hide the fact that they are gay or lesbian. Police work has traditionally been thought of as a "macho" occupation, and the perception was that gay male officers did not fit the mold.

In 2011, when questioned about the lack of openly gay male officers above the rank of sergeant while openly lesbian women have been regularly promoted, Chief Greg Suhr of the San Francisco

Police Department attributed this disparity to the fact that the AIDS epidemic in the 1980s caused a generation of officers who would now be lieutenants and captains to be lost. He also stated that the department has many competent openly gay male officers and anticipates promotions to be made in the next testing processes.[91]

In the past, many departments succeeded in keeping gays out of police departments while keeping the moral issue out of the discussion. They focused instead on behavior. Most states had sodomy laws and criminalized homosexual sex, thereby eliminating these applicants from the candidate pool due to their criminal behavior. This proved effective especially after the *Bowers v. Hardwick* case in 1986 in which the U.S. Supreme Court upheld a Georgia law by not finding a constitutional protection for sexual privacy.[92]

The tide changed in 2003 with the landmark case *Lawrence v. Texas*. In this case, the U.S. Supreme Court reexamined the issue and struck down the Texas sodomy law that had criminalized homosexual sex. The Court held that intimate consensual sex is part of the liberty protected by due process under the Fourteenth Amendment.[93] As a result of this decision, departments could no longer use participation in criminal activity as a reason not to hire gays or to discriminate against them.

Even before this decision, many police administrators had decided not to make an issue of sexual orientation in the background investigation. It is believed that this decision may have reflected an overall change in society's social and sexual mores, as well as a concern by police administrators that if they did not voluntarily take the lead, the federal courts might be called upon to intercede on behalf of the gay community, as the courts had already done in the case of other minorities. These factors, coupled with the federal government's "don't ask, don't tell" policy with the military, the rise of gay and lesbian police officer groups, and the rescinding of the IACP policy opposing the hiring of gays, contributed to police departments' laissez-faire attitudes.[94]

Though departments are examining their history regarding discrimination as well as their efforts at integrating minorities, little has been studied about the gay and lesbian experience. Studies indicate that officers weigh the costs and benefits before deciding whether or not to "come out." Most found acceptance among officers that are already familiar with other homosexuals, though 67 percent experienced homophobic comments and 48 percent felt socially isolated. These officers also found that they felt most discriminated against in the areas of promotions, assignments, and evaluations. Overall, gay and lesbian officers report similar obstacles as the racial minorities and women when integrating into law enforcement agencies, which can result in lowered job satisfaction.[95]

Some cities are recruiting openly gay officers in an attempt to bridge a perceived gap with their gay community. The Key West Police Department has a large number of openly gay officers relative to the city's population. Sergeant Alan Newby, an openly gay officer with Key West and former president of the Florida chapter of Law Enforcement for Gays and Lesbians, states that though officers may receive training in diversity and sexual orientation, "the important thing is that the agency support gay and lesbian police officers and let that officer know he is going to be judged on work product, not sexual orientation." Though Newby sees no need for publicizing officers' sexual orientation, he believes that gay officers are needed in any city with a significant gay population. A gay officer may be more sensitive to issues that arise in the gay community. In advising other departments that are interested in actively recruiting openly gay officers, Newby relates that more attitude adjustments may need to be made for gay men than for lesbians joining the department: "Police work traditionally is viewed as a macho job, and departments are usually more accepting of lesbian officers than gay officers."[96]

Changes are coming slowly. In 2008, Donald J. Lee, Jr., was appointed chief of police of the Key West Police Department after rising up through the ranks. Chief Lee states he is gay and is open about his sexual orientation, although he prefers to refer to himself not as a gay police chief, but rather as a police chief who happens to be gay. He has been told that he may be the only police chief who is gay and open about it, although he does not know whether that is the case.[97]

Gay officers in law enforcement say that the sexual orientation issue is one of the last civil rights battles being fought. Most states provide no special job protection for gay workers, but some departments are providing benefits to same-sex partners. In the 1970s, gay officers in California started the Golden State Peace Officers Association (GSPOA). Another of the nation's first gay officers' associations was the NYPD's Gay Officers Action League (GOAL), which was established in 1981 and, as explained on their website, holds yearly conferences and provides links with 10 U.S. and 8 international gay and lesbian police organizations. Law Enforcement Gays and Lesbians International (LEGAL) and similar support groups around the country also offer support to gay, lesbian, bisexual, and transgender workers in the criminal justice system. They hope to improve the environment within law enforcement agencies for gays and ultimately improve the relationship between the police and the gay community. Organizations such as GOAL and LEGAL serve as support groups and advocates for gay and lesbian officers.[98]

Some departments believe that providing a welcoming climate for gay officers is important but that recruitment is not necessary. Miami Beach Police Department Detective Bobby Hernandez states that they have hired their openly gay officers by doing what they always do: "We hire the most qualified applicants. It's not an issue, and quite frankly, it's none of our business." Perhaps an openly gay citizen in Wilton Manors, Florida, a town looking to actively recruit openly gay officers, summed it up best: "It does not matter to me whether a police officer is openly gay, closeted, or straight, as long as the police department keeps my neighborhood safe."[99]

Challenges Persist for Minorities in Policing

Minorities have made great strides in the law enforcement field. Some are represented within the rank and file of law enforcement agencies in numbers increasingly representative of their presence in their communities. This increase in numbers, together with the passage of time, has allowed minorities to acquire the needed time in rank, which has resulted in a larger pool of competent minority candidates for higher-ranking positions. Consequently, more women and minorities now occupy high-ranking positions within law enforcement agencies up to and including the rank of police chief or sheriff. This gives these individuals increased opportunities to have an impact on the policies and procedures of their departments and have input in the decision-making process within their departments and their communities. It also provides them opportunities to serve as mentors and role models to others. This support and mentoring will lead to a workplace climate that will be more comfortable for minorities.

In examining the workplace experiences of various minorities and the resulting stress, studies have found that the group with the greatest representation within the department has the most favorable workplace climate. Though subgroups of officers share many of the same concerns and problems, including lack of support and influence, these concerns and challenges are experienced more frequently by some groups than by others. In particular, being female and an ethnic or racial minority results in substantially different experiences from those of male and white officers. These different experiences lead to corresponding differences in stress levels. Researchers note that police managers can change the workplace climate through management, supervision, training, and mentoring along with clear policy and proper supervision and sanctions when necessary.[100] Implementing changes will assist in improving the organizational culture for minorities, and thereby enhance the recruitment and retention of minorities.

Minorities and women have made progress in law enforcement, but in addition to the organizational climate issues mentioned earlier, specific minorities face specific challenges. Some of these problems are the same as ones they have traditionally faced, while others are new challenges that have arisen as a result of their new roles.

Challenges for Women

Women in law enforcement have progressed tremendously during the last three decades, but challenges remain. These include recruiting and hiring, acceptance of women, workplace harassment, dating, pregnancy, and family issues. The IACP believes the recruitment of women is an important issue for law enforcement today. This group is involved in investigating the climate in law enforcement regarding women and has actively educated departments on recruiting and retaining female officers. To further this effort, the IACP launched the Women's Leadership Institute in 2013 and offers courses around the country to assist in developing the talent of female supervisors and mid-managers. The programs are interactive and designed to enhance the effectiveness and skills of female leaders. A crucial aspect of this institute is the development and promotion of a mentoring relationship with a successful female law enforcement executive.[101] Departments are also addressing these challenges internally.

The first challenge encountered by female police officers is the recruitment and hiring issue. Agencies need to reach out to women and provide an opportunity for them to see themselves in the role of police officer. Proactive and targeted marketing may help to attract women who have not considered a police career. Ads placed in women's magazines as well as computer and TV ads stressing the community service aspect of law enforcement might encourage women to see themselves in that role. As former Detroit Police Department Chief Ella Bully-Cummings says, visibility of female police officers is important: "If you can't see it, you can't dream it."[102] As these women are seen on the street and in the media, the recruitment effort will be furthered, since women will have the opportunity to discount some of the myths they have held related to women in the public domain.

Many departments provide this visibility through their websites, where they profile female officers and address women's issues. The Los Angeles Police Department website has biographies of female officers, including pioneer Alice Stebbins Wells, and the department has implemented programs to support women, such as the Candidate Assistance Program, Academy Trainee Program, and the Women's Coordinator.[103] The Madison, Wisconsin, Police Department website has many women visible on the website. That department reached a new milestone in May 2011 when 8 of 15 new recruits being sworn in were female. Although the percentage of females in law enforcement nationally hovers at 11 to 12 percent, the Madison Police Department boasts that more than 30 percent of its officers are women.[104]

Once they decide to apply, female applicants may be challenged by the physical agility part of the testing process. Agencies are addressing this issue by examining their requirements and providing information and training to assist women in developing the necessary competencies.

The police culture and socialization process are important to new recruits. For female officers, they require a constant balancing act between their more feminine characteristics that have been encouraged by their socialization process, such as compassion, warmth, and accommodation, and their more masculine traits, such as assertiveness, competitiveness, and no-nonsense approaches. Sometimes the police environment seems to present a no-win situation for women, as they can be and are criticized by male coworkers regardless of which traits they emphasize. Women are perceived either as too soft and weak for the job if they display "feminine" characteristics or as overbearing, bossy, and pushy if they behave in a more "masculine" fashion. Female officers may have to walk a fine line as they discover what works best for them. Many successful female officers recommend developing good communication skills, a strong work ethic, flexibility, the ability to be a team player, a good sense of humor, and a "thick skin."[105]

The state of Vermont has implemented a recruitment strategy in its program entitled Step Up to Law Enforcement. The program is a joint effort between law enforcement, corrections, the U.S. Department of Labor, the Vermont Department of Labor, and Vermont Works for Women (VWW), an organization whose mission is to help females explore and succeed in nontraditional careers. This nine-week training program introduces women to law enforcement and has three primary components: physical conditioning, career planning, and technical training related to the law enforcement profession. Recruits have regular interaction with female officers, as well as post-program support and mentoring. The program has resulted in a significant increase in the number of female applicants and a placement rate of more than 50 percent. It appears to have reached qualified women who had previously not considered a law enforcement career.[106]

Sometimes a female employee can be a target for workplace harassment. This can occur as a personal issue where a particular employee is the target, but other times it can be an organizational, pervasive sense of an "unwelcoming" atmosphere toward female employees. The harassment can come in obvious forms such as inappropriate cartoons, jokes, and posters. However, there also can be subtle harassment in areas such as job, shift, or zone assignment; vehicle or equipment assignment; and even grooming or uniform policies. To work on this issue, departments are clarifying their working conditions and writing policies concerning workplace harassment, which includes harassment because of gender, racial or ethnic background, or sexual orientation. These policies are disseminated, and training is conducted for all personnel so that employees, supervisors, and administrators are well versed in what is acceptable behavior and what is not.

Two other issues challenging departments concern workplace romances and pregnancy. Many departments have not addressed these issues at all, which has resulted in some lawsuits, while other departments have feverishly drafted policies in an attempt to insulate themselves from such litigation.[107]

Policies on pregnancy and job assignment need to be developed by police agencies for legal reasons as well as for the message these policies send to female officers. Departments have to offer the same benefits to pregnant officers as to officers with other conditions, such as a temporary back injury or recovery from surgery. If officers in those situations are allowed to work limited or light-duty assignments, then pregnant officers must be allowed the same choice. Policies and benefits must be equitable. The Pregnancy Discrimination Act (PDA), which amended Title VII of the Civil Rights Act of 1964, states that discrimination on the basis of pregnancy constitutes a type of sex discrimination.

Many departments are allowing the pregnant officer to choose whether to take light or limited duty or to stay in her job assignment. Vicky Stormo, chief of the Oregon Health and Science University and former president of the National Association of Women Law Enforcement Executives (NAWLEE), agrees that the officer should make the decision and the department should not dictate when or if an officer will go on limited duty.[108] Some officers elect to remain in their job assignments throughout the pregnancy, whereas some assume limited duty after the first trimester and others wait until the last trimester. It depends on what their job assignment is and how they feel physically. Some departments even provide maternity uniforms for officers who will be in the public eye.

In the past, some agencies forced pregnant officers to take sick leave or to go to a limited-duty assignment despite their desires. Besides the potential liability this can create if the situation is different from what is offered to an officer who is injured in some way, this action also sends a message to the officer and her female coworkers. Administrators interested in recruiting and retaining females have noticed that many female officers left after giving birth, not necessarily because they wanted to stay home with their babies but, rather, because of the atmosphere and workplace culture. They felt unwelcome and as if they were a burden to the agency.

A New York case illustrates the challenges involved in the pregnancy issue. The Suffolk Police Department's policy of not giving limited duties to officers who cannot patrol because of non–work-related injuries was found to be unfair to pregnant officers, a jury decided in federal court. Officers filed suit after a policy was enacted in 2000 causing pregnant officers to either work their regular assignment while pregnant or use their sick time. Though this was the policy for men with non–duty-related injuries, the jury felt it placed an unfair burden on pregnant women, forcing them to make a difficult decision between potential danger to their unborn child and economic security.[109]

There is a concern among chiefs and sheriffs for the safety of the unborn child. This issue is a bit murky, according to Sam Marcosson, professor at the Brandeis School of Law at the University of Louisville, who served as a litigator in the Appellate Division of the Equal Employment Opportunity Commission. He believes that in a circumstance where a department has to allow a pregnant officer to continue at her job until such time that she or her doctor requests limited duty, the courts will probably not hold the department liable for job-related injuries. However, many departments are taking a conservative approach regarding exposure to lead, which results from firearms qualification exercises, by allowing pregnant officers to forego firearms training until they come back from maternity leave.[110] Having a fair and equitable policy in place will aid the department in creating a supportive and welcoming atmosphere for women and is likely to lead to more applicants and a higher rate of retention for female officers.

The implementation of family-friendly policies, including a favorable pregnancy policy, is crucial in attaining the goals of increased recruitment and retention of women. In recognition of this need, the International Association of Chiefs of Police (IACP) has sought to develop a policy that supports parenthood but does not compromise operations, does not unfairly impose on nonpregnant employees, and is in compliance with all antidiscrimination laws. The organization recently released a model pregnancy policy to guide law enforcement agencies in addressing the pregnancy issue and thereby supporting gender diversity.[111]

Workplace dating is another murky area that some agencies are trying to address. Some sexual harassment cases have arisen from relationships that have soured, leading some departments to want to prohibit fraternization. Though this situation is not unique to the law enforcement workplace, it can be a bit more problematic in the police environment because of the lack of supervision and the variety of locations and situations in which law enforcement can place officers. The issue is complicated by the police culture and the need to socialize with coworkers, regardless of gender. Departments are struggling with this tough issue in an effort to forestall bad situations.

Family issues and conflicts between personal and professional demands also pose a challenge for women and the advancement of their careers. Time taken off for maternity leave and choice of job assignment to better accommodate family life may detract from an officer's active career and put the officer on the "mommy track," which may impede her rise through the ranks. Dual policing careers—having a husband in a police department—also can create unique challenges, especially if both spouses are in the same department. Police leaders are recognizing that all of these issues should be discussed and addressed in order to facilitate recruiting and retaining women.

Another challenge for administrators is the issue of advancement of women in their law enforcement careers. As women obtain seniority by accruing more years in law enforcement, it is important for them to advance themselves in the agencies for which they work; however, women do not pursue the promotional process as often as they could or should. In an effort to avoid tokenism, many women shun high-profile positions and strive to just blend in with the rank and file. They seek to be judged by their work and, in fact, may avoid promotions for fear that others may perceive them as having obtained advancement due to their gender rather than their abilities. Women have avoided the promotional process even when they have been strongly encouraged by a male supervisor to pursue it. Some women feel promotions draw unwanted, negative attention from male police officers, resulting in a stigma for other women who test for promotions.[112] This perception is self-defeating because the more that women move into the supervisory and administrative ranks, the better the environment will become for female officers.

Researchers have examined the strategies and techniques successful female officers have used that facilitated their retention in the department and their upward mobility in the organization. These women reported that they always felt compelled to respond to officers' challenges and tests to their abilities by working hard and proving themselves over and over. Moving up allowed them to develop their own view of success and of their abilities. It was found that the power that comes with rank allowed women to take unique approaches in addressing workplace discrimination and harassment, and their abilities

to utilize these strategies enhanced their chances of promotion. These strategies included avoiding and disengaging from negativity (75 percent); defining themselves in their own views, usually outside of the law enforcement community (87.5 percent); and, if necessary, taking formal action, from speaking up all the way to filing grievances (62.5 percent). This may show that organizational conditions that require women to "cope" are also part of the problem.[113] Real change will occur as more women move into the policy-making positions in law enforcement and have the ability to substantively affect the working conditions women face.

Realistic books (even fiction), movies, and news and magazine articles are another way to respond to the curiosity that women may have about the profession. Books such as Marion Gold's *Top Cops: Profiles of Women in Command* and Patricia Lunneborg's *Women Police: Portraits of Success* portray women who have risen to the top in the law enforcement culture and provide their perspective on law enforcement as a career. Former police officer and now college professor Donna Stuccio turned her talent for playwriting into a way to spread the word about women in law enforcement. Her play *Blue Moon* takes place predominantly in the women's locker room of a police department and brings out some of the issues and challenges women face.[114] In 2010, a couple of "reality" cop shows emerged documenting female officers on the job; time will tell what kind of impact shows such as these will have.

In the last few decades, state, regional, national, and international organizations have been started to lend support to female officers and to address and present a unified voice on issues that affect women in law enforcement. The International Association of Women Police (IAWP) is committed to its mission of strengthening, uniting, and raising the profile of women in criminal justice internationally. The group does this by serving as a support system and source of information and referral, providing networking and training opportunities, and recognizing outstanding female officers with awards. Many states and regions around the country also have women police officer organizations. Since 1995, the National Center for Women and Policing has been working to educate criminal justice policy makers, the media, and the public about the impact of increasing the representation of women in policing.

Despite the challenges women still experience in police departments, they have shown that they can do the job and will do all that is necessary to attain it. Many have given the ultimate sacrifice, their lives. There are currently 245 women's names included among those of the more than 19,000 law enforcement officers who have been killed, listed on the National Law Enforcement Memorial in Washington, D.C. These names include 11 female officers killed in 2011.

Tragically, 2012 began with Mt. Rainier Park Ranger Margaret Anderson being murdered on New Year's Day by a heavily armed man who had been involved in a shooting incident in Seattle on New Year's Eve. It is believed she saved the lives of those at the visitor center when she blocked his car and he abandoned his arsenal to flee into the woods.

We've Come a Long Way!   ON THE JOB

While in college at Florida Atlantic University (FAU), I participated in a "field experience" at the Boca Raton Police Department. I was impressed with the individuals I met there and the progressive chief, Charles McCutcheon, who also taught at FAU. I knew that going into law enforcement as a woman in the mid-1970s would be a challenge and I would not be uniformly welcomed. But I felt that Boca, with its high percentage of college-educated officers and a progressive, educated chief, would be less of a hurdle than many other departments. It was the only department I applied to.

After graduating from the police academy, I was assigned a platoon and field training officer. It was common knowledge that I would be going to C Platoon, as there were already three female officers in the department, one on every platoon except C. The consensus was that the department wanted to evenly distribute the female officers. I was happy with the way this worked out, as I knew a lot of the guys on C Platoon, and we'd become friends. My field training officer was chosen because he was the only married officer on the platoon, and the administration didn't want two young, single officers riding around together for eight hours a day ... who knew what might happen? The chosen officer had no training in being a training officer, didn't particularly want to be one, and, in fact, seemed to not be very much in favor of female officers on the road.

During my first couple of years, I was touched inappropriately and propositioned by a couple of superiors, had a snake put in my patrol car and a rat in my briefcase, and was locked in the men's restroom and the back of a patrol car. These were things I put up with to be "one of the guys."

I watched as the department grew and more women came to the job. I met personally with each one to offer support and a shoulder if they needed it. I offered to serve as a mentor in any way that I could and always encouraged them to apply for new assignments and take promotional exams. When I became the uniform division captain in 1991, there were many women working the road among the 100 or so personnel in the division. One of my proudest moments came one day when I was looking at the deployment of personnel and realized some squads were 50 percent female and some even higher, while others had lower percentages—an officer's race or gender had ceased to be an issue. Everyone was simply an officer choosing a schedule by seniority, and gender, race, or ethnicity was never brought up by anyone in the process.

By that time, we also had a workplace harassment policy in place that was strictly adhered to. Employees were disciplined and even fired for inappropriate comments or behavior, depending on the severity of the offense. There were department representatives designated for employees who had harassment issues, and each incident was investigated. We strived to make all employees feel safe, and we educated all employees on what constituted harassment in the workplace. Employees didn't have to quietly go through what I did in my early career.

Later in my career, when I was involved in the hiring process and did a report regarding female and minority representation, I realized we had greatly diversified our employees with our major efforts aimed simply at hiring the best employees possible. We had female FTOs, supervisors, and specialists in all areas. I was proud of the fact that someone could drive down the streets of Boca, go into a DARE classroom, walk into a community policing outreach center, or get pulled over by an officer on a motorcycle, and be likely to see a female officer or an officer of color. We've come a long way!

—Linda Forst

As women continue to serve and contribute to law enforcement in this country, the face of law enforcement will evolve. The future of women in policing will be dynamic and interesting.

Challenges for African Americans

As with female officers, recruitment of qualified African American candidates is the first challenge to be faced, and it is as formidable as ever. In recent years, there has been less of an issue with African Americans seeing themselves as police officers and even police executives, as significant role models exist. The problem lies with the extensive competition for these talented African Americans, not only within law enforcement but from the private sector, which offers less media scrutiny, safer working conditions, and more money.[115]

Another issue that arises with African American police officers more than other officers is the issue of friendly fire or fraternal fire shooting incidents. These officers are often in the undercover or off-duty capacity and intervening in a situation with their weapons. As they are taking action or detaining a suspect with the aid of their weapons, they are often mistaken for an offender by responding on-duty uniformed personnel. This typically occurs in large organizations or when the off-duty officer is outside his jurisdiction and unknown by responding officers. Several officers have been killed in this manner, which is devastating for all concerned. The FBI reported that 43 police officers were killed by friendly fire from 1987 to 2005; some of those cases fit this description. Though the number is small, it is unnecessary and preventable.

Because of these tragedies, police departments are examining their policies that require officers to always be armed and ready to respond and examining the issuing of more visible badge holders. They also are stepping up their training both for uniformed responding officers and for officers who may be working in an undercover capacity and find themselves in the situation of being mistaken for a suspect due to the role they are playing. But, despite this training, most police administrators will admit that this is a serious risk for minority officers and that some underlying assumptions of white officers need to be examined and addressed. One woman filed a civil rights lawsuit in Rhode Island after her son was killed. She alleged that the rookie officer who shot her son had not received adequate training to recognize plainclothes or off-duty colleagues. The IACP also recommends that off-duty officers who witness a crime call for assistance rather than pull a weapon.[116]

Another challenge that persists for African American officers is the perception of tokenism by themselves, their coworkers, and the public. In their efforts to promote diversity and enhance recruiting, departments often use African Americans in recruiting literature or at recruiting events where it is hoped their visibility will help other African Americans see themselves in the job and wearing the uniform. Unfortunately, this can lead to the perception that black officers are getting particular assignments because they are African American, which may feel like tokenism. Their various assignments may lead to excessive publicity or attention in a desire by the administration or media to promote role models.

This apparent quest for publicity can cause the feeling among white officers that the department's goal is improved public relations with the minority community rather than the department's interests. In the past, this has led some white officers to believe that black officers did not deserve to be on the job but that they were tokens to appease the community.[117] The normal competition for limited promotional opportunities can cause conflicts between groups even in the best of situations. In the study of African American police executives mentioned earlier, those executives interviewed by Thompson noted that overall working relationships with white officers have improved, but they still believed that some white coworkers continue to hold negative views about them and their abilities.[118]

The National Organization of Black Law Enforcement Executives (NOBLE) is trying to address some of these issues and further the status of African Americans in law enforcement. According to its website, the organization's mission is "to serve as the conscience of law enforcement by being committed to justice by action." The NOBLE group aggressively pursues its goals by conducting research, speaking out, and performing outreach activities, and it plays a major role in shaping policy in areas of importance to minorities and the law enforcement community, including recruiting, retaining, and promoting minority officers. It is hoped that efforts of organizations such as NOBLE, as well as those of individual police organizations and the increased visibility of minority officers in uniform, will help to improve the situation for African Americans in law enforcement.

Challenges for Other Minorities

Other minority groups seem to face issues similar to those of African Americans and women, but since their rise in law enforcement is relatively more recent, the challenge of getting more representation in the command structure of police departments is even greater. That comes with time in the department and time in rank. As numbers increase, such opportunities should continue to grow, especially within the Hispanic officer population, which already has big numbers in the rank and file.

The issue of recruitment is related to this issue of representation, particularly command representation in departments. Minority officers need to get out in the community and establish relationships of trust with community members, helping them realize that law enforcement is a viable career for them and their children and that police in the United States are different from what police may have been like where they came from. Minority officers need to show residents that programs, policies, and protections are in place to assist community members who may feel wronged and that police officers follow rules, guidelines, and laws when doing their jobs. The community policing philosophy is a valuable tool in this undertaking. One Mexican American police officer in a border city felt that one of his most important roles was to "build bridges" with the Mexican American community, educate them about the police in the United States, and mentor youth to become police officers.[119]

Minority groups continue to be faced with stereotypes that people, both other officers and community members, hold but do not vocalize. Generally these stereotypes are not expressed overtly, and minority officers may not even be aware that particular people hold them, making them difficult to challenge. Minority groups may still be hesitant to make waves and challenge issues they do not agree with, particularly when they are small in number or new to their careers. Although it is rare for any type of retribution to take place, most do not want to be labeled as troublemakers or to stand out. In keeping with the police culture, they want to be known as team players and to attain their advancement through their hard work, job performance, attitude, and accomplishments.[120] Most minorities do not want anyone to believe or comment that they are where they are because they are a minority; they want to make it clear it is on merit.

Minorities also may be more closely scrutinized than other officers. Minority officers know that they are under the microscope and that often any error they make may be generalized to their minority group. They usually have to work longer and harder to get ahead, but generally they are devoted to their chosen profession and serve as great role models for the community.

SUMMARY

- Law enforcement agencies in the United States have a long history of discrimination against minorities.
- This discrimination has occurred in the hiring process, after minorities have been employed in their job assignments, and in regard to promotions.
- Though employed in law enforcement since the early 1900s, women were not given full patrol duties until the 1970s.
- Even though the first African American police officer was hired in 1867, African American officers were often restricted in the types of functions they could perform.
- The fight for equality was facilitated by the 1964 Civil Rights Act, which barred discrimination on the basis of gender, race, color, religion, or national origin.
- Although it may not be intentional, discrimination can occur as a result of de facto discrimination and adverse impact.
- Despite recommendations by national commissions, minorities have been forced to take their cases to the U.S. courts.
- Affirmative action programs are one of the most controversial methods of ending job discrimination and have given rise to white male backlash.
- Academic studies have proven that women can perform the duties involved in the patrol function.
- The representation of minority officers across the country has increased significantly in the last 20 years.

- Minorities are now making their way into administrative positions in law enforcement agencies.
- Challenges remain to achieve appropriate representation of underrepresented groups in law enforcement.

- Great progress has been made by minorities in law enforcement, and we hope that discrimination in U.S. police departments will soon be completely eliminated.

KEY TERMS

affirmative action
Civil Rights Act of 1964
consent decree
de facto discrimination
discrimination
double marginality

Equal Employment
    Opportunity Act of 1972
    (EEOA)
Fourteenth Amendment
National Advisory
    Commission on Criminal
    Justice Standards and Goals

Omnibus Crime Control
    and Safe Streets Act of 1968
quotas
reverse discrimination

REVIEW EXERCISES

1. You have been assigned to the recruiting division of your police department. Your chief is concerned because not many women are applying to be police officers with your department. You currently have 10 women in your department of 250 sworn officers, but that is below the number the chief would like to see. Your chief asks you to determine how many women you should strive to hire to put the agency in line with the national average. The chief also requests that you research why women are not applying, what might be keeping them from seeking the job, and what efforts you can put forth to increase the numbers. Come up with a recruitment plan addressing all these issues.

2. Many officers today do not realize the past struggles of the minority pioneers and some of the hurdles that have been overcome. Prepare a presentation for new recruits outlining the obstacles that used to keep certain groups out of law enforcement, the progress minorities have made over the years, and the interventions and court rulings that have facilitated these gains.

3. Your city has an Asian American population of approximately 8 percent of the total population, yet there are only 2 Asian American officers in your department of 250 sworn officers. Your chief would like the department to more closely reflect the population of the city and would like you to determine how to increase the number of Asian American applicants and (ultimately) police officers. Research why members of this group are not applying for law enforcement jobs and what the barriers might be, and then determine how you will work with the community to encourage applicants and facilitate their employment with your department.

WEB EXERCISES

1. Go to the National Organization of Black Law Enforcement Executives (NOBLE) website and review the organization's guiding principles. Do any of these principles tie into the community policing philosophy?

2. Visit the International Association of Women Police (IAWP) website and the National Association of Women Law Enforcement Executives (NAWLEE). What are some of the similarities and differences between these organizations?

3. Go to the IACP's job board website, discover-policing.org. Research their policies and information regarding diversity. Do they address the issue of gays in law enforcement? What impact do you think this will have?

END NOTES

1. W. Marvin Dulaney, *Black Police in America* (Bloomington: Indiana University Press), p. 30.

2. Ibid.

3. Dorothy Moses Schulz, *From Social Worker to Crimefighter: Women in United States Municipal Policing* (Westport, Conn.: Praeger), p. 21.

4. Ibid., p 115.

5. U.S. Department of Justice, *Civil Service System: Affirmative Action and Equal Employment: A Guidebook for Employers* (Washington, D.C.: U.S. Government Printing Office, 1974).

6. Schulz, *From Social Worker to Crimefighter.*

7. Ibid.

8. Ibid.

9. Doug Ward, "Much to Male Cops' Surprise, the World Didn't Come to an End," *Law Enforcement News*, May 2005, p. 12.

10. Chloe Owings, *Women Police* (Montclair, N.J.: Patterson Smith, 1969, originally published in 1925).

11. Schulz, *From Social Worker to Crimefighter*, p. 120.

12. Samuel Walker and Charles M. Katz, *Police in America: An Introduction*, 5th ed. (New York: McGraw-Hill, 2005), p. 47.

13. Dulaney, *Black Police in America.*

14. Ibid., p. 30.

15. Ibid., p. 69.

16. Nicholas Alex, *Black in Blue: A Study of the Negro Policeman* (New York: Appleton-Century-Crofts, 1969), pp. 87, 111.

17. Nicholas Alex, *New York Cops Talk Back* (New York: Wiley, 1976).

18. Steven Leinen, *Black Police, White Society* (New York: New York University Press, 1984).

19. National Advisory Commission on Civil Disorders, *Report* (Washington, D.C.: U.S. Government Printing Office, 1968).

20. National Advisory Commission on Criminal Justice Standards and Goals, *Police* (Washington, D.C.: U.S. Government Printing Office, 1973), p. 343.

21. Ibid., p. 329.

22. R. Alan Thompson, *Career Experiences of African American Police Executives: Black in Blue Revisited* (New York: LFB Scholarly, 2003).

23. *Civil Rights Act of 1964*, Public Law 88–352, 88th Cong., *U.S. Statutes at Large* 78 (July 2, 1964), p. 241.

24. U.S. Department of Justice, Civil Rights Division, www.usdoj.gov/crt/ and www.ojp.usdoj.gov/about/offices/ocr.htm (both sites accessed September 21, 2008).

25. *Equal Employment Opportunity Act of 1972*, Public Law No. 92–261.

26. *Griggs v. Duke Power Company*, 401 U.S. 424 (1971).

27. U.S. Equal Employment Opportunity Commission, *Affirmative Action and Equal Employment*, vol. 2 (Washington, D.C.: U.S. Government Printing Office, 1974), p. D-2.

28. *Mieth v. Dothard*, 418 F. Supp. 1169 (1976).

29. Larry K. Gaines, John L. Worrall, Mittie D. Southerland, and John E. Angell, *Police Administration*, 2nd ed. (New York: McGraw-Hill, 2003), p. 367.

30. Ibid.

31. P. Maher, "Police Physical Ability Tests: Can They Ever Be Valid?" *Public Personnel Management Journal* 13 (1984): 173–183.

32. *Vulcan Society v. Civil Service Commission*, 490 F.2d 387, 391 (2d Cir. 1973).

33. *Guardians Association of New York City Police Department v. Civil Service Commission of New York City*, 463 U.S. 582 (1983).

34. U.S. Equal Employment Opportunity Commission, *Affirmative Action and Equal Employment*, vol. 2, pp. D15–D23.

35. Grutter v. Bollinger 539 US 306, 2003; Gratz V. Bollinger 539 U.S. 244, 2003.

36. B. Taylor, B. Kubu, L. Fridell, C. Rees, T. Jordan, and J. Cheney, *Cop Crunch: Identifying Strategies for Dealing with the Recruiting and Hiring Crisis in Law Enforcement* (Washington, D.C.: U.S. Department of Justice, National Institute of Justice, 2005).

37. Zhao Jihong and Nicholas Lovrich, "Determinants of Minority Employment in American Municipal Police Agencies: The Representation of African American Officers," *Journal of Criminal Justice* 4 (1998): 267–278.

38. Charles R. Swanson, Leonard Territo, and Robert W. Taylor, *Police Administration*, 5th ed. (Upper Saddle River, N.J.: Prentice Hall, 2001).

39. *Afro-American Patrolmen's League v. Duck*, 538 F.2d 328 (1976).

40. *Detroit Police Officer Association v. Young*, 46 U.S. Law Week 2463 (E.D. Mich. 1978).

41. "Affirmative Action Programs Looking a Little Black and Blue," *Law Enforcement News*, April 30, 1995, pp. 1, 7.

42. Retrieved February 21, 2008, from www.adversity.net/policefire_6.htm.

43. "Jury Rules Against Ex-Chief in Bias Case," *Law Enforcement News*, May 2005, p. 5.

44. *Ricci v. DeStefano*, 530 F.3d 87 (2009).

45. Peter B. Bloch and Deborah Anderson, *Policewomen on Patrol: Final Report* (Washington, D.C.: Police Foundation, 1974); Joyce L. Sichel, Lucy N. Friedman, Janet C. Quint, and Michael E. Smith, *Women on Patrol: A Pilot Study of Police Performance in New York City* (Washington, D.C.: Department of Justice, 1978).

46. Sichel et al., *Women on Patrol*, Foreword.

47. Ibid.

48. James David, "Perspectives of Policewomen in Texas and Oklahoma," *Journal of Police Science and Administration* 12 (1984): 395–403.

49. Robert Homant and Daniel Kennedy, "Police Perceptions of Spouse Abuse: A Comparison of Male and Female Officers," *Journal of Criminal Justice* 13 (1985): 49–64.

50. Loretta J. Stalans and Mary A. Finn, "Gender Differences in Officers' Perceptions and Decisions about Domestic Violence Cases," *Women and Criminal Justice* 3 (2000): 1–24.

51. Merry Morash and Jack Greene, "Evaluating Women on Patrol: A Critique of Contemporary Wisdom," *Evaluation Review* 10 (1986): 230–255.

52. Sean Grennan, "Findings of the Role of Officer Gender in Violent Encounters with Citizens," *Journal of Police Science and Administration* 15 (1988): 75–78.

53. Amie M. Schuck and Cara Rabe-Hemp, "Women Police: The Use of Force by and against Female Officers," *Women and Criminal Justice* 4 (2005): 91–117.

54. Cara E. Rabe-Hemp and Amie M. Schuck, "Violence Against Police Officers: Are Female Officers at Greater Risk?" *Police Quarterly* 4 (2007): 411–428.

55. *Report of the Independent Commission on the Los Angeles Police Department* (Los Angeles: Independent Commission on the Los Angeles Police Department, 1991).

56. Zev Yarolslavsky, "Gender Balance in Los Angeles Police Department," *WomenPolice* 3 (1992): 14–15.

57. Kim Michelle Lersch, "Exploring Gender Differences in Citizen Allegations of Misconduct: An Analysis of a Municipal Police Department," *Women and Criminal Justice* 4 (1998): 69–79.

58. Richard M. Seklecki, "A Quantitative Analysis of Attitude and Behavior Differences between Male and Female Police Officers toward Citizens in a Highly Conflictive and Densely Populated Urban Area," paper presented at the Academy of Criminal Justice Sciences Annual Meeting, Washington, D.C., April 2001.

59. Kristen Leger, "Public Perceptions of Female Police Officers on Patrol," *American Journal of Criminal Justice* 2 (1997): 231–249.

60. International Association of Chiefs of Police, "The Future of Women in Policing: Mandates for Action," November 1998, retrieved April 24, 2004, from www.theiacp.org/pubinfo/researchcenterdox.htm.

61. Kenneth J. Novak, Robert A. Brown, and James Frank, "Women on Patrol: An Analysis of Differences in Officer Arrest Behavior," *Policing: An International Journal of Police Strategies and Management* 34 (4, 2011): 565–587.

62. Kimberly Lonsway, "The Role of Women in Community Policing: Dismantling the Warrior Image," September 2001, retrieved April 12, 2004, from www.lib.msu.edu/harris23/crimjust/commpol.htm.

63. National Center for Women and Policing, "Men, Women, and Police Excessive Force: A Tale of Two Genders, A Content Analysis of Civil Liability Cases, Sustained Allegations and Citizen Complaints," 2002, retrieved April 12, 2004, from www.womenandpolicing.org.

64. Thompson, *Career Experiences of African American Police Executives.*

65. Walker and Katz, *Police in America*, p. 161.

66. Lorenzo M. Boyd, "Light Blue v. Dark Blue: Attitudinal Differences in Quality of Life Policing," *Journal of Ethnicity in Criminal Justice* 8 (1, 2010): 37–48.

67. Thompson, *Career Experiences of African American Police Executives*, pp. 81–154.

68. discoverpolicing.org, 2014.

69. Brian Reaves, *Local Police Departments, 2007* (Washington, D.C.: Bureau of Justice Statistics, 2010).

70. Bureau of Labor Statistics, *Current Population Survey,* "Table 3 Employment Status of the Civilian Non-Institutional Population by Age, Sex, and Race," Annual Averages 2010 (Washington, D.C.: U.S. Government Printing Office, 2011).

71. Dorothy Moses Schulz, *Breaking the Brass Ceiling: Women Police Chiefs and Their Paths to the Top* (Westport, Conn.: Praeger, 2004), p. 29.

72. Ibid., p. 28.

73. Ibid., p. 84.

74. Ibid., p. 72.

75. Donovan Slack, "'I Don't Envy My Successor': O'Toole's Departure Leaves Menino with Critical Decision on Police Leadership," *Boston Globe,* May 10, 2006.

76. James Queally, "Newark's First Female Police Chief Brings No-Nonsense Approach to City Police Force," *The Star-Ledger,* NJ.com, September 2, 2011.

77. National Center for Women and Policing, "The Effect of Consent Decrees on the Representation of Women in Sworn Law Enforcement," Spring 2003, retrieved April 15, 2010, from www.womenandpolicing.org.

78. Reaves, *Local Police Departments, 2007.*

79. Tamer El-Ghobashy, "Minorities Gain in NYPD Ranks," *Wall Street Journal,* January 7, 2011.

80. Reaves, *Local Police Departments, 2007.*

81. Obtained from an interview with Sergeant Cesar Fazz of the Yuma, Arizona, Police Department on July 26, 2006.

82. Ibid.

83. Ibid.

84. U.S. Census Bureau, *Population Projections,* January 6, 2012.

85. Remarks of the Honorable Deborah J. Daniels, Assistant Attorney General, at the Hispanic American Police Command Officers Association 29th Annual Training Conference, August 22, 2002, Albuquerque, New Mexico.

86. Interview with Sergeant Fazz.

87. Reaves, *Local Police Departments, 2007.*

88. Joseph Berger, "Influx of Asians in NJ Is Not Reflected in Police Ranks," *New York Times,* May 1, 2006.

89. Schulz, *Breaking the Brass Ceiling,* pp. 177–179.

90. *Law Enforcement News,* October 1990, p. 1.

91. Seth Hemmelgarn, "New SF Police Chief Discusses Pink Saturday, Gay Officers," *Bay Area Reporter*, June 9, 2011, retrieved January 6, 2012, from www.ebar.com/news/article .php?sec=news&article=5758.

92. *Bowers v. Hardwick*, 478 U.S. 186 (1986).

93. *Lawrence v. Texas*, 539 U.S. 558 (2003).

94. M. L. Dantzker, *Understanding Today's Police Officer*, 3rd ed. (Upper Saddle River, N.J.: Prentice Hall, 2003).

95. Roddrick Colvin, "Shared Perceptions Among Lesbian and Gay Police Officers: Barriers and Opportunities in the Law Enforcement Work Environment," *Police Quarterly* 12 (1, 2009): 86–101.

96. Karla D. Shores, "Manors Should Hire an Openly Gay Officer, Mayor Says," *South Florida Sun-Sentinel*, January 22, 2002.

97. Personal correspondence with Chief Donald J. Lee Jr., January 7, 2012.

98. Wanda J. DeMarzo and Steve Rothaus, "Despite Some Progress, Many Gay Officers Still in the Closet," *Miami Herald*, January 28, 2006.

99. Shores, "Manors Should Hire."

100. Kimberly D. Hassell and Steven G. Brandl, "An Examination of the Workplace Experiences of Police Patrol Officers: The Role of Race, Sex, and Sexual Orientation," *Police Quarterly* 12 (4, 2009): 408–430.

101. theiacp.org/-WOMENS-LEADERSHIP-INSTITUTE-WLI-

102. Donna Leinwand, "Lawsuits of '70s Shape Police Leadership Now," *USA Today*, April 26, 2004, p. 13A.

103. lapdonline.org.

104. Teresa Mackin, "A First for Madison Police Department Recruiting Class," WKOW.com, May 31, 2011.

105. Sandra K. Wells and Betty L. Alt, *Policewomen: Life with the Badge* (Westport, Conn.: Praeger, 2005), pp. 39–42.

106. Lianne Tuomey and Rachel Jolly, "Step Up to Law Enforcement: A Successful Strategy for Recruiting Women into the Law Enforcement Profession," *Police Chief*, June 2009, pp. 68–73.

107. Lance D. Jones, "Matrons to Chiefs in One Short Century: The Transition of Women in U.S. Law Enforcement," *WomenPolice* (Summer 2003): 6–9.

108. Carole Moore, "Pregnant Officer Policies," *Law and Order* 9 (2003): 73–78.

109. Jennifer Sinco Kelleher, "Suffolk Female Cops Win Case," *Newsday.com*, June 15, 2006.

110. Moore, "Pregnant Officer Policies," p. 76.

111. Deborah Campbell and Karen Kruger, "IACP Policy Assists Agencies to Define Pregnancy Policies," *Police Chief*, July 2010, pp. 12–14.

112. Carol Archibald and Dorothy Moses Schulz, "Making Rank: The Lingering Effects of Tokenism on Female Police Officers' Promotion Aspirations," *Police Quarterly* 1 (2008): 50–73.

113. Haarr and Morash, "The Effect of Rank on Police Women Coping with Discrimination and Harassment," *Police Quarterly* 16 (4, 2013): 395–419.

114. Marion Gold, *Top Cops: Profiles of Women in Command* (Chicago: Brittany, 1999); Patricia Lunneborg, *Women Police: Portraits of Success* (New York: iUniverse, 2004); Donna Stuccio, "Blue Moon," *Women and Criminal Justice* 1 (2002).

115. Dantzker, *Understanding Today's Police Officer*.

116. "Always Armed, Always on Duty Questioned in Rhode Island Case," *Providence Journal*, November 28, 2005.

117. Thompson, *Career Experiences of African American Police Executives*, p. 32.

118. Ibid., p. 154.

119. Interview with Officer Eric Cazares of the Yuma, Arizona, Police Department on July 27, 2006.

120. Interview with Sergeant Fazz.

8

Police Ethics and Police Deviance

LEARNING OBJECTIVES

- Identify some of the forms and extent of police deviance.

- Explain various reasons for police corruption, including why corruption may be more likely in policing than in other professions.

- Discuss various responses to police brutality and corruption, both within departments and agencies and in the community.

- Explain how officers can be held legally liable for their conduct, including the reasons for and results of legal action brought against officers.

- Describe the effects of allegations of corruption on the officer, the agency, law enforcement in general, and the community.

amc/Alamy

OUTLINE

Ethics and the Police
The Dilemma of Law Versus Order
Review of the Police
Police Corruption
  Corruption Makes Good Books and Films
  Examples of Police Corruption
  Reasons for Police Corruption
  Types and Forms of Corruption
  Noble Cause Corruption
  Effects of Police Corruption
Other Police Misconduct
  Drug-Related Misconduct
  Sleeping on Duty
  Police Deception

  Sex-Related Misconduct
  Domestic Violence in Police Families
Biased-Based Policing
Police Brutality
Responses to Police Corruption
  Investigations
  Discipline and Termination
  Preventive Administrative Actions
  Citizen Oversight
Police Civil and Criminal Liability
  State Liability
  Federal Liability
  Reasons for Suing Police Officers
  Effects of Lawsuits on Police Departments and Officers
  The Emotional Toll of Police Lawsuits

INTRODUCTION

Police officers in the United States are given tremendous authority and wide latitude in using that authority. In addition, to the average citizen, the police are the most visible symbol of not only the U.S. criminal justice system but also the U.S. government.

Many police officers complain that the press overdoes coverage of corrupt or brutal police officers. The home videotape of the 1991 beating of African American motorist Rodney King by four white Los Angeles police officers was broadcast over every television network in the United States for weeks. The 1997 Abner Louima case (in which a New York City police officer allegedly inserted a stick into the rectum of a prisoner and then put the feces- and blood-covered stick into the prisoner's mouth) was worldwide news. Sometimes it can seem like the media is only covering the bad things and ignoring all the good work that police officers do on a daily basis.

We must remember that the media operate under the following philosophy: If a dog bites a person, that is not news. Dogs bite people every day of the week. But if a person bites a dog, that is news. Newsworthy items are the events that are different and not normal. Police officers across the United States do thousands of good acts every day. They arrest lawbreakers, find lost children and people suffering from Alzheimer's, walk the elderly across the street, bring the sick and injured to the hospital, deliver babies, stop fights and arguments, and counsel the confused. That is their job, and they do it well, but that is not news. But when the very people we trust to uphold our law—to serve as the model of what our law is and what it stands for—violate that law, that is news. That is the person biting the dog. It is healthy that police misconduct is news. Imagine if this misconduct were so common that it did not qualify as news.

It must be remembered, before reading this chapter, that the vast majority of the more than 800,000 men and women in our nation's law enforcement agencies are extremely ethical. Unfortunately, a few are not, and therefore, this chapter must exist. However, it is indeed about the person biting the dog, not the dog biting the person. This chapter will discuss ethics and police deviance, including police **corruption** and other misconduct such as police sexual violence, domestic violence in police families, police deception, and police brutality.

Ethics and the Police

What is ethics? **Ethics** is defined as the study of what constitutes good or bad conduct. The term is often used interchangeably with *morals*, which is understandable because they came from similar root meanings pertaining to behavioral practices or character. Applied ethics is concerned with the study of what constitutes right and wrong behavior in certain situations.[1] Basic ethics are the rather broad moral principles that govern all conduct, whereas applied ethics focuses these broad principles on specific applications. For example, a basic ethical tenet assumes that lying is wrong, and applied ethics would examine under what conditions such a wrong would occur.

Aristotle defined virtue as what he called the Golden Mean or *Nicomachean ethics*. This philosophy suggests that life circumstances trigger a natural range of response that includes a mean between excessive and defective responses. A person's character traits" are the individual's habitual ways of responding, and individuals who are the most admirable are those who find the norm between the two extremes regularly. The virtues cited by Aristotle more than 2,000 years ago include courage, self-control, generosity, high-mindedness, gentleness, truthfulness, and modesty.[2] These traits are still looked upon as evidence of good character.

Over the past few decades, there has been a growing interest in ethics in the academic and law enforcement literature, including textbooks, studies, journal articles, and media articles. Many departments and law enforcement organizations are

---

corruption   Acts involving misuse of authority by a police officer in a manner designed to produce personal gain for the officer or others.

ethics   The study of what constitutes good or bad conduct.

promoting in-service training in the area of ethics. The International Association of Chiefs of Police (IACP) offers courses in ethics, including "Ethical Standards in Police Service, Force Management, and Integrity Issues" and "Value-Centered Leadership: A Workshop on Ethics and Quality Leadership." The IACP and the Office of Community Oriented Policing Services (COPS) have made an "Ethics Toolkit" resource available on the IACP website for increasing awareness of law enforcement ethics. Additionally, the FBI Virtual Academy has partnered with COPS to provide a free online course for law enforcement personnel on ethics for the individual officer. Many departments have incorporated ethics into their mission statements, core values, and hiring process. They also have stressed ethics training as part of their commitment to community policing. These departments recognize that trust is a vital element of community policing and that ethical people inspire trust but unethical people do not. They realize that ethics training will help departments recognize their full potential.

It is important for police officers to study ethics for many reasons. Police officers use a lot of discretion, and one of their duties is the enforcement of the law. It is their duty to protect the constitutional safeguards, such as due process, and the equal protection that are the basis of our system. They are public servants, and their behavior involves the public trust. Education and training that address the issue of ethical decision making will aid officers in the decision-making process. As mentioned, the IACP and police departments across the nation have recognized the importance of this topic, and ethics training takes place both in academies and as part of in-service training.

How do we measure police ethical standards? What standards have been established to determine how police officers should act? Joycelyn Pollock, in her excellent book *Ethical Dilemmas and Decisions in Criminal Justice*, identified some of these standards:

- Organizational value systems or codes of ethics designed to educate and guide the behavior of those who work within the organization

- An oath of office, which can be considered a shorthand version of the value system or code of ethics

- The Law Enforcement Code of Ethics, as promulgated by the International Association of Chiefs of Police (IACP)[3]

Other standards governing police ethics are the U.S. Constitution and the Bill of Rights, case law as determined by appellate courts and the U.S. Supreme Court, and federal and state criminal laws and codes of criminal procedure.

Although these standards appear to set a perfect example for police officers and mandate exemplary performance by them, how widely accepted and followed are they by individual officers and departments? As Pollack explains, the police subculture often works against these official ethical precepts.[4] The informal code of conduct that is taught through socialization includes doing the right amount of work, keeping a cool head, backing up fellow officers, not giving up another cop, not volunteering information, not making waves, covering their butts, and not trusting administration to look out for their best interests. This subculture and these values, however, may be breaking down in police departments today due to increased diversity among officers, police unions' formalization of grievance processes, and the threat of civil litigation when covering up for other officers.

Evidence exists that the U.S. public believes to a great extent that our police are good, are ethical, and do the right thing. Although the public has less confidence in all institutions than they did in past years, the police ranked third in a recent poll on public trust, with 57 percent of respondents rating the police either very high or high in honesty and ethical standards. The two institutions ranking higher were the military with 76 percent and small business with 65 percent. Only 10 percent had confidence in Congress (ranking it lowest) and only 22 percent in big business.[5]

In a report prepared by the Administration of Justice Program at George Mason University for the IACP in October 2001, the authors found that not only do the police consistently rank among the institutions and occupations in which the public expresses the highest confidence and trust, but also most citizens are satisfied with police service in their own neighborhoods. Interestingly, most citizens have not had face-to-face contact with police, and therefore their opinions are based primarily on secondhand information and media accounts.[6]

In a sad turn of events, this respect, support, and caring for police officers was painfully obvious in late 2009 when the state of Washington had six police officers murdered within weeks. During the funerals, massive numbers of citizens attended the services, lined the procession route, and donated money to show their support for the officers putting their lives on the line every day for the community. Most of these community members did not know the officers but felt it was important to show support for law enforcement, stand up for what was right, and share the message with their children. The emotion evident in these citizens' faces and voices was touching, and police officers were humbled by the love and support their community showed them.

The Dilemma of Law Versus Order

Police corruption and police brutality have always been part of policing. The names, places, and times change, but corruption and brutality remain. The role of the police in maintaining law and order in U.S. society has always contained an inherent conflict.[7] It would be very easy to maintain law and order by ensuring that our cops were bigger, meaner, and tougher than our criminals, and by letting the cops just beat up all the criminals to ensure a safe society. Of course, we cannot do that. We must have our police comply with the same laws they are paid to enforce.

Police officers face ethical dilemmas every day. They make difficult decisions on a daily basis using discretion. Every situation is different, and circumstances surrounding an incident may determine whether an arrest is made. Officers have to weigh

many variables and sometimes contemplate accomplishing the most good for the greatest number of people. Whenever they do this, they are open to questions and criticism. If they consider the wrong factors (race, ability to gain influence, payoffs) in making these decisions, they may be on the slippery slope to corruption. The slippery slope concept suggests that when people begin to deviate, they do it in small ways, but once they have deviated, they begin to slide down a slope that leads to greater and more pronounced types of deviance. Therefore, there is no such thing as "minor" unethical behavior.[8]

Review of the Police

Possibly because of the dilemma of law versus order, the police are constantly under review by government agencies, including federal, state, and local agencies; the courts; academics; the media; and the general public. Numerous national commissions have looked into the operations of the police. Among the most noteworthy were the National Commission on Law Observance and Enforcement, more popularly known as the Wickersham Commission (1931); the President's Commission on Law Enforcement and Administration of Justice (1967); the National Advisory Commission on Civil Disorders, commonly referred to as the Kerner Commission (1968); the National Advisory Commission on Criminal Justice Standards and Goals (1973); and the Commission on Accreditation for Law Enforcement Agencies (1982).[9]

In addition to the national commissions, state and local commissions, panels, and hearings have looked into the behavior and operations of the police. The most notable was the Knapp Commission to Investigate Allegations of Police Corruption in New York City, commonly known as the **Knapp Commission**.[10] The Knapp Commission was created in 1970 by New York City Mayor John V. Lindsay in response to a series of articles in the *New York Times* detailing organized, widespread police corruption in New York City. The Knapp Commission held public hearings, and its findings caused widespread changes in the policies and operations of the New York City Police Department (NYPD).

YOU ARE THERE

National Commissions Overseeing the Police

1931   National Commission on Law Observance and Enforcement (Wickersham Commission)

1967   President's Commission on Law Enforcement and Administration of Justice

1968   National Advisory Commission on Civil Disorders (Kerner Commission)

1973   National Advisory Commission on Criminal Justice Standards and Goals

1982   Commission on Accreditation for Law Enforcement Agencies

© 2016 Cengage Learning®

Knapp Commission Commission created in 1970 to investigate allegations of widespread, organized corruption in the New York City Police Department.

YOU ARE THERE

The Knapp Commission Discovers Corruption

The Knapp Commission was created in 1970 by New York City Mayor John V. Lindsay in response to allegations brought by New York City police officers Frank Serpico and David Durk of widespread corruption in the New York City Police Department (NYPD). These allegations were detailed in several articles in the *New York Times* and received national attention. The hearings conducted by the commission also received national attention in the media. The committee's final report was issued in 1972, and its findings were responsible for widespread changes in the policies and operations of the NYPD.

The types of corruption in the NYPD discovered by the Knapp Commission through its hearings, investigations, and informants were so many and so varied that they could fill volumes. The Knapp Commission discovered corruption in the following areas:

- *Gambling.* Officers assigned to plainclothes (antigambling) units received regular monthly payments from the operators of illegal bookmaking, policy, and other gambling operations. The regular monthly payments were called "the pad." Other payments that involved one-time-only payments were called "scores."

- *Narcotics.* Officers assigned to narcotics units extorted money and other bribes, including drugs, from drug addicts and dealers. The officers also conducted illegal wiretaps and used other unlawful investigatory techniques. In addition, officers engaged in flaking people (claiming someone was in possession of narcotics when he or she was not—the drugs used for evidence were from the officer's own supply) and padding arrests (similar to flaking, but involving adding enough extra narcotics, or felony weight, to the defendant's total to raise the charge to a felony).

- *Prostitution.* Officers involved in plainclothes units maintained pads and received scores from houses of prostitution, prostitute bars, and prostitutes.

- *Construction.* Uniformed officers received payoffs from contractors who violated city regulations or who did not possess proper licenses and permits.

- *Bars.* Officers received payoffs from licensed and unlicensed bars to overlook crimes and violations.

- *Sabbath law.* Officers received payoffs from food store owners to allow the owners to violate the Sabbath law, a former New York City law that required certain food stores—such as delicatessens, groceries, and bodegas—to close down on Sundays.

- *Parking and traffic.* Officers received payoffs from motorists who wanted to avoid traffic summonses, as well as from business establishments to discourage officers from issuing summonses for illegal parking in front of their businesses.

- *Retrieving seized automobiles from the police.* Officers at city automobile storage yards received payments from owners to retrieve their automobiles.

- *Intradepartmental payments.* Certain officers received payments for doing paperwork for other officers and for temporary assignments, permanent assignments, and medical discharges.

- *Sale of information.* Officers received payments for the sale of confidential police information to criminals and private investigation firms.

- *Gratuities.* Officers received free meals, drinks, hotel rooms, merchandise, Christmas payments, and other gifts and tips for services rendered.

- *Miscellaneous.* Officers received payments from fortune-tellers, loan sharks, automobile theft rings, hijackers, and peddlers. Officers stole money and property from dead bodies (DOAs) and their apartments. They burglarized stores and other premises.

The Knapp Commission's report distinguished between two types of corrupt officers: *grass-eaters* and *meat-eaters*. Grass-eating, the most common form of police deviance, was described as illegitimate activity that occurs from time to time in the normal course of police work, such as taking small bribes or relatively minor services offered by citizens seeking to avoid arrest or to get special police services. Meat-eating, in contrast, was a much more serious form of corruption involving the active seeking of illicit moneymaking opportunities. Meat-eaters solicited bribes through threat or intimidation, whereas grass-eaters made the simpler mistake of not refusing those that were offered.

Source: Adapted from Knapp Commission, Report on Police Corruption (New York: Braziller, 1973), pp. 1–5.

The police are also under constant review by the U.S. judicial system through judicial review. **Judicial review** is the process by which the actions of the police in such areas as arrests, search and seizure, and custodial interrogation are reviewed by the U.S. court system at various levels to ensure the constitutionality of those actions. Judicial review has resulted in such landmark Supreme Court cases as *Mapp v. Ohio* (1961) and *Miranda v. Arizona* (1966). In addition, the police are reviewed daily by the media: newspapers, magazines, radio, and television. Finally, they are under constant review by citizens, many of whom do not hesitate to report what they consider to be deviant conduct to the media, to the police themselves, or to other legal authorities. Officers' high visibility often puts them under the microscope.

The police today act in many types of situations, and it is difficult for courts or police administrators to predict every possible situation that could arise. This, coupled with the fact that the legal authority of the police and the interpretation of the constitutional limitations of the police by the courts are constantly changing, leads to a dynamic and challenging situation.[11]

Police Corruption

Police corruption has many definitions. Herman Goldstein defines it as "acts involving the misuse of authority by a police officer in a manner designed to produce personal gain for himself or others."[12] Carl B. Klockars defines it as the abuse of police authority for personal or organizational gain.[13] Michael J. Palmiotto explains that police officers involved in corruption gain economically by providing services they should already be performing or by failing to perform services that are required by their position.[14] Richard J. Lundman defines police corruption as "when officers accept money, goods, or services for actions they are sworn to do anyway. It also exists when police officers accept money, goods, or services for ignoring actions they are sworn to invoke legal procedures against."[15]

Although these definitions differ, we can find enough commonalities to define corruption for our purposes as follows: A police officer is corrupt when he or she is acting under his or her official capacity and receives a benefit or something of value (other than his or her paycheck) for doing something or for refraining from doing something.

Is giving an officer a free cup of coffee or a sandwich an act of corruption? It can be difficult to distinguish between genuine gifts (such as Christmas gifts), gratuities, bribes, and corruption. At times, accepting any kind of gift is the beginning of the slippery slope syndrome where it becomes easier to accept other, larger gratuities in the future and, eventually, bribes.

Corruption Makes Good Books and Films

Police corruption is a popular topic in literature and film. Does life imitate art, or does art imitate life? This eternal question is easily answered when we discuss police corruption: Art imitates life.

As an example, the novel *Serpico,* by Peter Maas, and the movie starring Al Pacino were great successes.[16] *Serpico* tells the true tale of an honest NYPD plainclothes officer, Frank Serpico, who roams the police department and city government in an attempt to report corruption in his division in the Bronx. Serpico tells his supervisors, his commanders, the chief of personnel, an assistant to the mayor, and the city's department of investigation his tale, and nothing is done; corruption remains rampant. Finally, frustrated in his efforts, Serpico and a friend, Sergeant David Durk, report their allegations to a reporter for the *New York Times.* This leads to the formation of the Knapp Commission and widespread changes in the NYPD's policies and procedures initiated by Commissioner Patrick V. Murphy, who was appointed soon after the allegations were made.

The 1997 movie *L.A. Confidential* portrays life in 1940s Hollywood. Police corruption and other types of corruption are portrayed throughout the story. Some of the factors that contribute to or facilitate police corruption can be seen throughout the movie, including power, financial gain, and job advancement.

In 2001, *Training Day,* written by David Ayer, was released. Denzel Washington stars as a cop in Los Angeles who becomes involved in corruption on the street level of the organization. Ayer wrote another film, released in 2003, *Dark Blue,* which stars Kurt Russell. This film examines morality and corruption and is set during the time of the Rodney

....

judicial review Process by which the actions of the police in areas such as arrests, search and seizure, and custodial interrogation are reviewed by the court system to ensure their constitutionality.

Mike Blake/Reuters

Police officers must be aware that their behavior is always being observed and subject to public scrutiny. It is commonplace for people on the street to use their smartphones to record police activity and interaction.

King riots. The movie focuses a bit more on the internal corruption of the agency.

The many current TV shows and cable shows concerning crime and police also frequently involve "crooked" cops to add an interesting twist to the story. Police corruption makes for good TV as well as film.

Examples of Police Corruption

Despite all the attention police corruption has received and the efforts by police administrators to detect and eradicate it, numerous examples of serious police corruption can be found. During the 1980s and 1990s, many large-scale corruption cases occurred around the country, in some cases fueled by thirst for drugs. Officers in cities such as Miami, New York, and New Orleans were involved in and later charged with drug dealing, robberies, batteries, and even murder.

In February 2000, more than 70 Los Angeles Police Department (LAPD) officers were investigated in what came to be known as the "Rampart" scandal. These officers committed crimes, covered up unjustified beatings and shootings, planted evidence, and committed perjury. The situation started as an aggressive policing effort to clean up the gangs, lower the crime rate, and make the streets safe. The corrupt behavior took hold after officers were commended by the department and the community for their efforts

and results in cleaning up the streets. The officers who were working hard to put bad guys in jail and turn the streets over to law-abiding citizens began to circumvent the law to accomplish their noble purpose.[17]

In 2003, a federal jury convicted three Miami officers of conspiracy for covering up questionable shootings that occurred from 1995 to 1997. Eleven officers had been indicted; two had previously pleaded guilty and testified at the trial, three were found not guilty, and mistrials were declared for the remaining three officers. The convicted officers received sentences ranging from 13 months to 37 months in prison coupled with three years of supervised release.[18]

After Hurricane Katrina in 2005, there were allegations that New Orleans police officers participated in the large-scale looting spree that overtook the city. News reports indicated officers were at the scene of some of the heaviest looting in the city, and some witnesses stated that officers were taking items from the shelves of a Walmart. Though this allegation reportedly involved fewer than 20 officers, more than 200 officers abandoned the city during the hurricane and were fired or suspended.[19] Additionally, in 2011, a federal jury convicted five New Orleans police officers of various roles in gunning down civilians during the aftermath of Hurricane Katrina and then covering it up. Five others pleaded guilty in what came to be called the Danziger Bridge case.[20]

Corruption is not limited to rank-and-file police officers. In 2001, a city manager in Miami was charged with taking almost $70,000 from a youth anticrime group while serving as police chief during the 1990s. He was on the charity's board of directors for nine years. He served a year in prison, was ordered to repay the money, and lost his police pension.[21]

Bernard Kerik, the former New York City police commissioner and brief nominee to the cabinet post of head of the Department of Homeland Security in 2004, was indicted in 2009 for making false statements to White House officials regarding some abnormalities that occurred while he was on the city payroll. Kerik was a familiar face to Americans immediately following 9/11 as he flanked then-Mayor Rudolph Giuliani at press conferences as the NYPD police commissioner. Shortly after being nominated by President Bush to head Homeland Security, he was forced to withdraw because of tax problems with the family's nanny. Later investigation revealed that Kerik failed to report that he accepted $200,000 in renovations to his Bronx apartment from a New Jersey company long accused by the city of having ties to organized crime. He also intervened and attempted to help that company get a New York City license, and his brother was given an $85,000-a-year job with the company.[22] Kerik was released in 2013 after serving three of his four years in a federal facility.

Federal law enforcement agents also have succumbed to the temptation of corruption and misconduct. A customs agent was charged for allowing drug smugglers to cross the border from Mexico to the United States with large loads of marijuana. Investigators believe he took more than $1 million in bribes while waving through more than 50 tons of drugs. When the customs inspector came under suspicion in 2003, investigators found he lived way beyond his means. Though they declared bankruptcy in 2000 and essentially had no assets, the inspector and his wife were spending more than $400,000 a year in cash with only his $55,664 yearly salary reported as income in 2003. Their purchases included expensive jewelry, a car dealership, 10 classic muscle cars, and payments toward a very luxurious home in Texas.[23] In 2007, he was sentenced to 14 years in prison.

Police deviance and corruption is an issue of concern both for law enforcement and society in general and is being studied and examined by academics and practitioners.

Reasons for Police Corruption

When we consider the enormous authority given to our police officers, the tremendous discretion they are allowed to exercise, and the existence of the police personality and police cynicism, it is easy to see that police work is fertile ground for the growth of corruption. To this environment we can add the constant contact police have with criminals and unsavory people, the moral dilemma they face when given the responsibility of enforcing unenforceable laws regarding services people actually want (illegal drugs, gambling, alcohol, and prostitution), and the enormous amount of money that can be made by corrupt officers. Based on all these factors, it is little wonder that corruption emerges in police departments.

Samuel Walker and Charles Katz cite several possible explanations for corruption:

- *Individual officer explanations.* The blame for corruption is placed on the "rotten apple" in the department. This is the most convenient explanation for the agency but not widely accepted because hiring has improved and because some departments seem to experience more corruption than others do.

- *Social structural explanations.* Certain social structures in the United States tend to encourage and sustain corruption, including the criminal law (regulations prohibiting activities many consider legitimate and ordinances that serve conflicting purposes), cultural conflict (some outlawed behavior is considered appropriate in certain cultures), and local politics (if the local government and community are corrupt, the police department will also tend to be corrupt).

- *Neighborhood explanations.* Neighborhoods with social disorganization have higher levels of poverty, lower levels of social control, and higher levels of corruption.

- *The nature of police work.* Police work takes place with officers working alone or in pairs and with little or no supervision, and the conditions of work often cause the officer to become cynical. Constant exposure to wrongdoing can lead the officer to believe that everyone is doing it.

- *The police organization.* Corruption flourishes in departments in which the organizational culture tolerates it and the departmental integrity and expectations of being disciplined for certain acts are low.

- *The police subculture.* The police subculture's emphasis on loyalty and group solidarity can lead to lying and cover-ups.[24]

Any or all of these explanations can be at work in influencing the existence and extent of corruption in police agencies, but some view the police subculture and the values associated with that subculture as particularly problematic in regard to the corruption issue. The informal code of policing seems to contradict the formal codes as presented by the IACP.[25]

The code of silence, often referred to as the "blue curtain" or "blue veil," is the tendency of law enforcement personnel to not share information with others. This code can make it difficult to get at the truth. The belief that others outside the police profession could not possibly understand the challenges that officers face is absorbed early in the training and socialization process and reinforced with time on the job. At the risk of being harshly judged, officers are reluctant to share their experiences and feelings with outsiders. Officers need to protect and rely on each other in dangerous or tenuous situations. They feel solidarity with other officers and sense the need to stick together and back each other up. They may see group administrators or supervisors as outsiders who do not "need to know," since the perception is often that administrators do not share the same goals as the rank and file. Consequently, these feelings of loyalty and solidarity can become even stronger in the face of administrative efforts to control and monitor behavior, which can result in stronger resistance to administrative oversight.[26] This blue curtain is a factor that needs to be acknowledged and addressed in the formulation of any policies involving the corruption issue.

Types and Forms of Corruption

Corruption is not limited to the present day. Lawrence W. Sherman reports, "For as long as there have been police, there has been police corruption."[27] Goldstein says, "Corruption is endemic to policing. The very nature of the police function is bound to subject officers to tempting offers."[28]

As discussed earlier, when the Knapp Commission reported on the police corruption in New York City in the early 1970s, it distinguished two primary types of corrupt police officers. **Grass-eaters** are more passive and will accept what is offered to them. **Meat-eaters** are more aggressive and search out opportunities to exploit for financial gain. Most officers who accept bribes are grass-eaters.[29]

There are four general types of police corruption: taking gratuities, taking bribes, theft or burglary, and internal corruption.[30] **Gratuities** are small tips or discounts on goods purchased. In many communities, taking gratuities is not considered corruption but merely the showing of goodwill to the police (with, of course, the hope that the police might perform their

duties a little better for the person who shows them goodwill). Pollack defines gratuities as items of value received by someone because of his or her role or job rather than because of a personal relationship.[31]

Whether to define the acceptance of gratuities as corruption has been and continues to be hotly debated by both police professionals and the community. The concern by those who feel it is corruption is that it may be the beginning of a slippery slope and make it easier for officers to justify participating in more serious acts of wrongdoing. It may lead officers to feel they are entitled to special privileges. It may also lead the public or the person providing the gratuity to expect differential treatment. The opposing argument that many businesses provide, especially 24-hour businesses or businesses in more crime-prone areas, is that if providing officers with a free cup of coffee causes them to hang around the business a little longer or a little more frequently, it is a form of preventive patrol. Some view it as an enhancement of the community policing philosophy, with officers spending time in the business and finding out about the issues and problems of the area. Though many departments have policies against the acceptance of gratuities, many do not. Often the policies that do exist are not clear and are frequently ignored by the rank and file, many times with knowledge of the administration.

Police corruption also may involve taking **bribes**—the payment of money or other consideration to police officers with the intent to subvert the aims of the criminal justice system. This is a far more serious form of corruption and often involves payment for non-enforcement of laws or ordinances. According to Walker and Katz, bribes may take two forms: (1) the pad (formal, regular, periodic payments to the police to overlook continuing criminal enterprises) and (2) the score (a one-time payment to avoid arrest for illegal conduct). The pad is the type of bribe that would be used by meat-eaters after identifying good targets. Grass-eaters would most commonly be involved in the acceptance of one-time payments that come their way.[32]

Theft or burglary—the taking of money or property by the police while performing their duties—is another form of police corruption. The police have access to numerous premises, including warehouses and stores, while investigating burglaries, open doors, and alarms. They also have access to homes while on official business. Theft may be especially tempting at narcotics investigations. Often there are huge amounts of cash or drugs lying

---

grass-eaters Police officers who participate in the more passive type of police corruption by accepting opportunities of corruption that present themselves.

meat-eaters Officers who participate in a more aggressive type of corruption by seeking out and taking advantage of opportunities of corruption.

gratuities Items of value received by someone because of his or her role or job rather than because of a personal relationship.

bribe Payment of money or other contribution to a police officer with the intent to subvert the aim of the criminal justice system.

around, and no one, not even the suspects, knows exactly how much is there. Until an official cash count or drug inventory is done (which can be hours after discovery), the exact amounts of contraband are unknown. A corrupt police officer has plenty of opportunity to take property from others.

The final type of police corruption is internal corruption. Officers pay members of their departments for special assignments or promotions.

Sherman discusses three general levels of police corruption based on the pervasiveness of the corruption, the source of the bribes, and the organization of the corruption.[33] The first is the "**rotten apples** and rotten pockets" theory of police corruption, which holds that only one officer or a very small group of officers in a department or precinct is corrupt. At first thought, this may not seem very serious: A department needs only to arrest the officer or group and use the arrest as an example to other officers of what might happen to them if they were to become corrupt. The dangerous part of this theory is that if police commanders believe that only a few officers are bad, they will not take the tough, proactive measures necessary to uncover and eradicate corruption in the entire precinct or department.

The second level of corruption that Sherman found is pervasive, unorganized corruption, where most of the officers are corrupt but are not actively working with one another on an organized or planned basis. Sherman's third level of corruption is pervasive, organized corruption, where almost all members of a department or precinct are working together in systematic and organized corruption.

Several stages of the moral decline of police officers have been identified. Sherman tells us about certain stages in an officer's moral career. The first stage involves the acceptance of minor gratuities, such as free meals. Peer pressure from other officers is extremely important at this stage. The second and third stages involve accepting gratuities to overlook regulatory offenses, such as accepting money to allow bars to remain open past regular closing hours or accepting money from a motorist instead of giving him or her a summons. Peer pressure from other officers is also very important at this stage. The final stage involves changing from passively accepting gratuities to actively seeking bribes. As the corruption continues, it becomes more systematic. It involves larger amounts of money and includes numerous types of crimes, ranging from gambling violations and prostitution to dealing in narcotics.[34]

Noble Cause Corruption

Noble cause corruption, often called the *Dirty Harry syndrome*, refers to situations where a police officer bends the rules to attain the "right" result. In the extreme situation, an officer might justify violating a suspect's rights to save someone's life. More commonly, the rights violation would be justified in the officer's mind by the ultimate good of putting the bad guy in jail where he or she belongs. These behaviors involve police officers misusing their legal authority, but they are not doing it for personal gain. They rationalize the behavior to get the bad guys behind bars and consider their actions to be a noble cause type of corruption.[35]

According to Michael A. Caldero and John P. Crank in their book *Police Ethics: The Corruption of Noble Cause*, noble cause corruption is a more significant problem than economic corruption, and it is increasing in U.S. police departments today. Because of past reforms targeting corruption, we have some safeguards in place to minimize the chances of rotten apples obtaining law enforcement careers. Today's officers are morally committed to their work and to making their community a better place. They believe in enforcing the law and putting criminals in jail. However, the professionalism movement with this commitment to the police mission may have unintentionally contributed to the growth of noble cause corruption: the corruption of belief from caring about police work too much.[36]

In this ends-oriented view of policing, officers will do what it takes to get bad guys off the street. One means of doing this is the use of "creative report writing," in which officers write up an incident in such a way as to criminalize a subject or make the incident more serious. The officers believe this type of action does more harm to the bad guy and is less risky to themselves than hitting him or her and leaving marks.

Traditionally, we have looked at the rotten apples—the officers rotten to the core—as being responsible for incidents of police corruption. With this perspective, corruption is an easy issue to solve—we just throw them out. Today, however, our

---

"rotten apple" theory Theory of corruption in which it is believed that individual officers within the agency are bad, rather than the organization as a whole.

noble cause corruption Stems from ends-oriented policing and involves police officers bending the rules to achieve the "right" goal of putting a criminal in jail.

screening process keeps most of these individuals out of law enforcement. In keeping with their theory of the prevalence of noble cause corruption, Crank and Caldero speak of "golden apples," the intelligent, hardworking officers who are committed to the noble cause and who value efficiency and effectiveness. These officers become too focused on the good ends and break the law or violate policy to "do something about the crime problem." These apples are more difficult for agencies or chiefs to deal with because this issue is more complicated and may involve departmental policies.[37]

Crank and Caldero have revisited the slippery slope model in the venue of noble cause corruption. The model acts out what the officers have been psychologically prepared for in the academy and through their early socialization process. It is primarily a test of loyalty to the group. Crank and Caldero call the initial step the "Mama Rosa's" test. A new rookie officer is out to dinner with his training officer and other officers. At the end of the meal, he takes out his money and asks the others how much he should leave. The other officers tell him to put away his money and be quiet. The cops have been eating at Mama Rosa's for free for years, and it has never been robbed, unlike the other establishments in the area. Mama Rosa is very appreciative. Now the recruit is being tested—if he goes along, he is tainted, but if he does not, he will not be trusted as a team player. If he goes along, he will be tested again in the field. This is a test for loyalty to the team and the "good" they are accomplishing by keeping Mama Rosa's safe. The second test will involve backing up another officer's version of events, another test of loyalty. The stakes will now be higher. Loyalty to each other and commitment to the noble cause are viewed as intertwined. Crank and Caldero's view of the slippery slope model can be summarized as follows:

1. Free meals (a test of loyalty)
2. Loyalty backup (loyalty with higher stakes such as false testimony, finding evidence in plain sight that was originally found in an unlawful search, or making a false call of a crime)
3. Physical violence against citizens (much more serious)
4. Flaking drugs (planting drugs or adding drugs to make the crime a more serious one—very serious and generally very limited)

Noble cause corruption, then, becomes a gateway for material reward or financial corruption.[38]

If noble cause corruption is the most prevalent type of corruption in law enforcement today, then this is where our efforts to eliminate corruption should be directed. We must strive to educate officers and to intervene early in the socialization process.

Effects of Police Corruption

For the past few decades, police misconduct has made headlines far too often. This media attention has given a black eye to officers who have never, and would never, consider any type of misconduct, as well as to agencies with similar standards. Police misconduct affects the reputations of police officers and police agencies in general. Misconduct committed by an officer affects not only that officer, but also the department for which the officer works, the community in which the officer serves, and every police department and police officer throughout our country.

Police misconduct also affects the police–community relationship in general, undermining the public's trust in the police. Law enforcement has come to the realization that it can be far more effective in its mission with the help of the community. Citizens will not help the police if they do not trust the police. Citizens must feel that they will be treated fairly and with respect.

Morale within the department will suffer from misconduct, as officers may feel they are "painted with the same wide brush." This effect occurs not only with local incidents, but with incidents that happen in other jurisdictions and even other states. Many officers will tell you they were questioned by citizens for months after the Rodney King incident, regardless of what state or what type of agency they worked for.

An incident that occurs within an officer's organization is often complicated by rumors and lack of official information. During an investigation, the fact that an investigation is occurring quickly becomes common knowledge, and rumors fly. Departments typically do not release any information or discuss the investigation before it has been concluded. Officers are left with rumors as their source of information, and everyone is nervous about what is going on, what will happen next, who else is involved, and whether or not they will be questioned. Officers do not know whom to trust, and morale plummets. The air of suspicion can last for months while the investigation is conducted. This type of atmosphere is emotionally draining for officers and will greatly contribute to the stress they experience.

Officers may find their work or personal lives made more difficult or complicated in an inappropriate manner due to an incident involving someone else. For example, an incident of corruption can result in an organization writing a policy or implementing training that might have prevented this particular incident from occurring, but which is not a realistic policy or training session that is needed for most of the personnel.

Just one or two incidents of corruption can ruin a department's reputation and destroy the trust the community has in the department. It can take years to overcome the bad publicity, and the department will be affected in many ways. There will be a lack of trust, resulting in a lack of cooperation and information, from the community. The department also will be less attractive to highly qualified police officer candidates as well as to police administrators, and it

Deviance and the Job

ON THE JOB

Police departments strive to hire the most ethical individuals they can. In my opinion, they do an outstanding job. The fact that officers have vast opportunities to do the wrong thing and yet very few choose to follow that path says something about the quality of the individuals working the street. Officers are confronted on a daily basis with ethical issues.

I remember as a police officer working the street being constantly challenged by citizens and business owners who wanted to show their appreciation for the job we were doing. The crime rate was very high, and citizens were grateful when we gave them the service they deserved, even in matters they may have perceived as minor. Half-price meals and free coffee were fairly common offerings. The arguments that ensued over payment were embarrassing and usually resulted in my leaving the full price of the meal on the table or counter; they could use it as a tip if nothing else. Unfortunately, these encounters sometimes resulted in my avoiding that restaurant and going elsewhere, which of course was the exact opposite of what the business owner wanted.

In this book, we mention that studies have found that often the biggest complaint citizens had about officers' behavior toward them was abusive or derogatory language rather than excessive force. Though I feel that everyone should be treated with respect, I was also concerned with the safety of the community and my own safety as well as that of other officers. There were times when people I encountered on the street did not respond to my requests. There were times when I resorted to crazy language, bad language, or harsh orders to avoid the need for a physical confrontation. One time I spotted an unarmed robbery suspect while I was patrolling the edge of town. I confronted him, and the chase was on. Because I was out in the woods on the edge

of town, I knew there would be no backup anywhere close. I yelled all sorts of things at this guy, because I wanted him to think I was crazy and might not play by the rules. It worked. He stopped and put his hands up, and I was able to cuff him and take him in.

I feel that public education can help in complaint situations and aid in smoothing misunderstandings between the police and the community. I remember as a road patrol captain, I used to get calls from angry citizens complaining about the harsh treatment they received from an officer. I explained the officer's point of view and police procedure, including the officer's need to control the situation. I also explained that the officer encounters all types of people during the day and that many officers get killed or injured during car stops. I found that after being made aware of these factors, the citizen usually no longer wanted to make a complaint.

Lastly, I think it is critical that departments make it as difficult as possible for officers to be tempted to deviate from their good ethical conduct. They need to have good, solid policies and procedures in place to protect the officers from temptation and from any possible allegations of wrongdoing. I went to many scenes as a road supervisor where the narcotics unit had made some arrests. There were often bags of money and drugs all around, with no one sure exactly how much was there. Once there was a half million dollars in duffle bags. How tempting it might be for an officer having trouble paying the mortgage to take some cash from bad guys that no one would even miss—or how easy for someone to make that accusation. Policies must be in place to provide checks and balances and protect the officers on the scene. Police departments owe it to their organization and their officers.

—Linda Forst

can stagnate for years under this perception unless drastic and highly visible changes are made.

Other Police Misconduct

Police corruption and police brutality are the most serious forms of police deviance. Police brutality will be discussed later in the chapter. Other types of police deviance also exist. Chief among them are drug-related misconduct, sleeping on duty, police deception, sex-related misconduct, and domestic violence.

Drug-Related Misconduct

Drug-related misconduct is similar to other types of corruption, but it is an added concern to modern law enforcement agencies because of the frequency with which these incidents can occur. Drug users and dealers make good targets for corrupt officers because they are less likely to report being victimized. There is also an opportunity to make a lot of money simply by looking the other way.

In a report to the U.S. House of Representatives, the General Accountability Office (GAO) found that although there was no central data source from which to gather information, some valuable insight on the topic of drug-related police corruption could be provided through research and interviews. The GAO report found that most police officers are honest, but noted the potential for drug-related misconduct in cities where drug dealing is a concern. Typically, this type of corruption involves small groups of officers who assist and protect each other in criminal activities, including protecting criminals or ignoring their activities, stealing drugs or money from drug dealers, selling drugs, and lying about illegal searches. Profit was the most frequent motive.[39]

The report cited four management-related factors associated with drug-related corruption, including a culture characterized by a code of silence and cynicism, officers with less education and maturity, ineffective supervision, and a lack of emphasis on integrity and internal oversight within the department. Without proper procedures, close supervision,

and oversight in place, it is easier for officers to fall victim to the lure of the quick buck surrounding the drug trade and to use their power and opportunities to steal from those they feel will never report it.

Sleeping on Duty

Fatigue is an issue for all involved in police work, and, consequently, sleeping on duty intentionally or unintentionally is an issue. With officers working the night shift and the rest of the world functioning on a day-shift schedule, conflicts arise. Officers attend court and meetings during the day when they should be sleeping. Their sleep is interrupted by phones, delivery personnel, repair people, and family responsibilities. Because of the nature of police work and the lack of activity and supervision during the early morning hours, it can be easy for an officer to find a "hiding place" and attempt to sleep for a while. This is clearly inattention to duty and is hazardous for the officer and his or her coworkers.

Most departments have policies in place to minimize the fatigue issue, including restrictions on the number of hours of extra-duty jobs that an officer can work and attempts to streamline court procedures, particularly traffic court. This misconduct can arise if officers decide to work as many extra-duty jobs as possible or maximize their overtime hours for economic reasons with the expectation that they will catch a little sleep while working the street. If an officer is involved in activity that is in any way questioned, such as a shooting, pursuit, or violent confrontation, the issue of impaired judgment because of fatigue may be raised. The fatigue issue and the resulting liability is part of the police culture, and professional departments are making every effort to address it.

Police Deception

Another form of police misconduct is **police deception**, which includes perjury while testifying in court, attempts to circumvent rules regarding searches and seizures of evidence, and falsifying police reports.

Skolnick states that police deception, if it occurs, usually occurs at three stages of the police detection process: investigation, interrogation, and testimony in court. "Particularly objectionable," says Skolnick, "is the idea that a police officer would not be truthful when testifying under oath in court. However,

police deception Form of misconduct that includes perjury and falsifying police reports.

much evidence suggests that there are 'tolerable' levels of perjury among police officers when testifying in court."[40]

Columbia University law students analyzed the effect of the landmark U.S. Supreme Court case *Mapp v. Ohio* (1961) on police practices in the seizure of narcotics. This case severely restricted the power of the police to make certain searches of persons or premises. The students found that before *Mapp v. Ohio*, police officers typically testified that they found narcotics hidden on the defendants' persons. After the *Mapp* case, police officers testified that the narcotics they found were dropped on the ground by the defendants. This became known as *dropsy* (from "drop-see testimony"). Before the *Mapp* case, narcotics evidence obtained from suspects by police, even when illegally seized, was admissible in court. After *Mapp*, this was no longer so. Hence, the researchers said, police officers began to commit perjury to circumvent the illegal seizure of evidence rule and to ensure that their testimony and the evidence would be admissible against defendants charged with narcotics possession.[41]

Deception is a serious issue. Police administrators will tell you that honesty is the most crucial trait in a police applicant and police officer. Deception in the hiring process will disqualify applicants, no questions asked, and deception by police officers will result in termination. With officers routinely swearing to the truth in everything they do and write, deception cannot be tolerated. Yet, as administrators will tell you, deception can be difficult to prove, as it often comes down to one person's word against another. When deception is discovered in any aspect of the job, it can taint any case in which that officer has ever been involved.

A U.S. Supreme Court decision, *Brady v. Maryland*, requires prosecutors to notify defense attorneys whenever a cop involved in their case has a record of knowingly lying in an official capacity.[42] These cops have become known as "Brady cops" and can be liabilities to their agencies.

In the last two decades or so, increased attention has fallen on departments that have altered some of their crime statistics. There have been scandals in large and small cities around the country. In some cases, officers or supervisors have lost their jobs. Generally, this misconduct has been part of the organizational culture, where there has been a desire to make the city appear safer or possibly more dangerous than it is. Transferring crime statistics into

Uniform Crime Reports (UCR) data is not always a precise science. Officers and administrators within a department may elect to err on a particular side when making decisions about the numbers. Often these errors or discrepancies have been good faith errors, but sometimes they have been an effort to make the city appear safer for tourism or business reasons. On occasion, cities have wanted to make it appear that their crime problem was more severe so they could qualify for federal grants to implement a crime-fighting program or initiative.

In June 2006, it became known that the Washington, D.C., Police Department had 119 cases in 2005 that were not properly classified as robberies or other crimes but, rather, were classified as incidents that were not crimes. This exposure occurred after a *New York Times* reporter was robbed and murdered, and prior robbery victims indicated the suspects could have been arrested had the previous reports been properly investigated as crimes. To put things in perspective, however, the 119 cases were less than 1 percent of the district's felonies.[43]

In a major scandal in Broward County, Florida, several deputies were clearing cases that should not have been cleared. This was done to make the clearance rate of the sheriff's office look extremely high in comparison with other jurisdictions with which the sheriff was negotiating contracts for service. These actions made the sheriff's office as well as the individual detectives look good. Some officers in these cases faced criminal charges because reports were falsified, confessions made up, and people charged with the crimes who could not have been involved.[44]

Sex-Related Misconduct

Police sexual violence incorporates many behaviors and involves "those situations in which a citizen experiences a sexually degrading, humiliating, violating, damaging or threatening act committed by a police officer, through the use of force or police authority."[45] This type of misconduct is a very serious offense against the public trust. Most police officers detest this behavior by the few who perpetrate it. The community is shocked to think an officer would use his position of trust to violate some of the most vulnerable citizens. The average officer has a hard time believing this type of abuse occurs, but a perusal of newspapers across the country indicates that it does occur.

GUEST LECTURE

CHARLES L. JOHNSON

Charles L. Johnson is a retired California Highway Patrol officer, having worked in East Los Angeles and Oakland, California. He received his bachelor's and master's degrees from California State University, Sacramento, and his doctorate in criminal justice from Washington State University. Dr. Johnson is currently an assistant professor of criminal justice at Western New England University in Springfield, Massachusetts. He is also chair of the police section of the Academy of Criminal Justice Sciences. His publication, research, and teaching interests include intelligence-led policing, police deviance, and police administration.

SEXUAL DEVIANCE BY POLICE

I had just turned 23 when I entered the California Highway Patrol academy in 1977, so I must say that I was a bit shocked when I first heard an academy instructor's admonitions about sexual deviance while on patrol. The instructor, an old salt who had many years on the road before "retiring" to academy training, began by telling the cadet class that women, alcohol, and bribes were the downfall of many good officers. I remember wondering what he meant, not only by the words he spoke, but in the tone used in his delivery. There were fewer than 10 women in our cadet class, so it was obvious that his words were specifically targeted at men. He went on to explain that he had worked with several officers who had lost their jobs due to "sins of the flesh." The training officer's words, however, rang true once I landed in the field.

It is fairly easy for an officer to recognize signs that other officers are taking gratuities, or that they are drinking or on drugs while on duty, but sexual deviance may not be so clearly identifiable. Having been trained well at the academy, I was prepared to recognize such occurrences on the road. The first memory I have of sexual indiscretion while on duty involved a beat partner who received a complaint from a motorist whom he had cited. The complainant reported that my partner had called his girlfriend and taken her on a date. The girl had been a passenger in the car driven by the complainant, and she had given the officer her phone number on a matchbook during the stop. The duty sergeant handled the complaint, which ended in the exoneration of the officer because the girlfriend corroborated the officer's story that the date and subsequent sex had been both consensual and while the officer was off-duty.

That incident started me thinking about the ethical lines regarding relationships between police officers and the public. Did the fact that the officer met and received the girl's phone number in the line of duty matter, regardless of the circumstances of the actual date? The sergeant admonished my beat partner that similar incidents would not be tolerated. I realized that the officer was a serial offender when, about a year

The IACP recently reviewed a study that identified an unprecedented number of cases of sex-related misconduct. The data was gathered via the Google News search engine from published news stories reporting arrests of police officers involving sexual misconduct. The study indicated that the sexual misconduct most frequently involved victims who were minors and victims who were strangers to the officers. This data strengthens the IACP's recommendations that law enforcement agencies and departments develop policies specifically addressing sexual misconduct and effective oversight, including the use of early intervention systems for monitoring and preventing this behavior.[46]

Police administrators need to be aware of this type of violation and be vigilant in looking for warning signs. Often, behavior can signal a potential problem; if that behavior is handled quickly and effectively, administrators can avert a bigger problem or give the organization documentation of behavior for a discipline case. Examples of warning signs might include a male officer who disproportionally pulls over female drivers, spends a lot of time outside bars at closing time, spends an inordinate amount of time at any place women tend to congregate, or conducts inappropriate follow-ups that he would not conduct for the average citizen. Most of these activities can be explained away in the context later, I stopped a young lady who asked for the officer by name, stating that she wanted me to tell him that she was pregnant with his child. By that time the officer had transferred out of our duty station.

Securing dates from people officers met while on duty was not as uncommon as I had expected. There seemed to be a general acceptance level of activity that included getting phone numbers from people encountered while on duty. As it was explained to me by older officers, many police officers have ended up dating and subsequently marrying waitresses, nurses, and other people (including civilians) whom they met while on duty simply because of their availability.

My observations, however, soon expanded beyond consensual dates to more explicitly deviant sexual escapades. Some officers specialized in voyeurism, which involved routinely patrolling lover's lane and other "necking" spots. Others knew which windows on specific homes would yield a view from the street at a given time of night. Such incidents were not the most disconcerting, however. One afternoon while working swing shift, I received a call from a beat partner to rendezvous for an "exchange of information." On arrival, I saw an attractive young woman standing by his patrol car. Without notice, the officer told the woman to "show him your assets," and she pulled up her top. Later when I recounted the incident over coffee with the officer, he responded, "You aren't a real highway man until you have had sex in a patrol car." That was the moment I realized that the line in the sand regarding acceptable behavior was drawn differently by each officer. Consensual sexually related activity between people is one thing, professional ethics aside, but coerced sexual activity is a problem for police agencies as well.

Now that I am retired, I have had the time to dedicate to my research in the area of police deviance. A significant concern for police administrators involves nonconsensual (coerced) sexual deviance perpetrated by police officers while on duty. Incidents of rape and other forms of sexual assault by on-duty officers occur frequently, based on reports I have examined over the past six years. What distinguishes these cases from those witnessed by me in the 1970s and 1980s is that some officers are now brazen about committing sexually criminal activity with impunity. The result is ruined lives—both of the victims and of the criminal officers and their families. Many of these cases end in multimillion-dollar liability settlements by the hiring department, as well as lengthy prison sentences for the officers following the finding in court of civil rights violations.

Deviance by police officers cannot be tolerated. Best practices in hiring officers include careful psychological screening and exhaustive background checks that may give the hiring agency a heads-up that a prospective officer might be susceptible to committing deviant acts, but some misfits will still manage to secure positions of power as police officers. Increased vigilance by officers, coupled with the increase in numbers of women on patrol, may help to alleviate the problem.

Source: Reprinted by permission of Charles L. Johnson.

of performing good police service, but together they can be a pattern of behavior worth watching. Administrators need to be cognizant that these women are generally not going to come forward of their own volition as they are fearful of retribution by the officer and his friends.

Law enforcement agencies also need to communicate to all personnel a zero tolerance for this type of violation. The efforts of an early warning system together with a well-written policy outlining the process for reporting, documenting, and investigating these incidents as recommended by the IACP will further strengthen the agency's position and minimize the chances of these incidents occurring.

Domestic Violence in Police Families

Some studies indicate that domestic violence may be more prevalent in police families than in the general population.[47] It has traditionally been a hidden problem because victims are hesitant to report it. Domestic violence is only beginning to be addressed, and it is an uphill battle. If the victim is a spouse of a police officer, then the offender has friends and supporters in the department who may not believe the allegations, the offender has a gun, and the offender knows the system and where the shelters are.

A victim who is a police officer must deal with all sorts of psychological issues as to why he or she cannot handle this problem alone. The victims fear for their safety and for the economic future of their family because an act of domestic violence could cost the officer his or her job.

Many departments that get a report of domestic violence involving one of their officers choose to handle it informally in an effort to protect the officer. This has resulted in tragedy. How departments handle domestic violence has been found to be inconsistent between departments and even within departments. A survey of 123 police departments documented that 45 percent had no specific policy for handling officers involved in domestic violence, and the most common form of discipline for sustained allegations was counseling.[48]

The IACP has developed a model policy regarding police-involved domestic violence, and some departments are building on that policy and becoming proactive. The IACP policy stresses that zero tolerance toward domestic violence should be established in agencies through education and training of all personnel as well as development of clear and comprehensive policies and procedures. However, a survey indicated that after the issuance of the IACP model policy, only 21 percent of 282 agencies contacted had heard of the IACP model policy and only 11 percent had implemented a policy for police-involved domestic violence. Out of a random sample of 100 large agencies a couple of years later, fewer than 29 percent had a police domestic violence policy.[49] It appears that the situation has improved somewhat, as the latest data indicates that 25 percent of the 56 largest departments in the nation have a policy for domestic violence involving police officers.[50]

A 1996 federal law (18 U.S.C. 925), widely referred to as the Lautenberg Act, prohibits anyone convicted of a misdemeanor domestic violence offense from owning or using a firearm. This further complicates the police domestic violence law enforcement issue. Some argue that an abusive police officer should not lose his or her job (which being prohibited from carrying a gun would effectively accomplish), but others feel the law as written is ineffective and are challenging the constitutionality of it. They feel it is too harsh a punishment for an incident that may be nothing more than a misdemeanor battery (such as touching or grabbing) on an incorrigible teen.[51]

In 1997, a task force studying the LAPD found that 91 of 227 cases of alleged domestic violence investigated between 1990 and 1997 were sustained. In more than 75 percent of the 91 cases, the sustained allegations were not mentioned in the officer's yearly evaluations, and in fact, 26 of these officers were promoted.[52] As recently as 2011 it was discovered that the Milwaukee Police Department was ignoring crucial elements of the IACP model policy as well as Wisconsin's model policy, and, consequently, though 16 officers were disciplined for domestic violence, only 3 were charged with a crime and none of those were domestic violence charges. One of the goals of model policies is to eliminate police bias by removing discretion governing the response, notification, and documentation of the incident. Milwaukee did not implement this policy, and therefore police bias influenced the handling of these calls and they were not appropriately handled.[53] Research in Florida found that between 2008 and 2012 more than a quarter of Florida law enforcement officers accused of domestic violence were still working at the same department one year after the complaint, compared to 1 percent of those who failed a drug test and 7 percent accused of theft.[54]

A case that exemplifies this type of response ended tragically in Tacoma, Washington. On April 26, 2003, David Brame, the Tacoma chief of police, fatally shot his wife and then himself in front of his children in a parking lot in a neighboring community. This came several days after allegations of abuse and impending divorce became public and despite his wife's efforts to minimize his anger and embarrassment by filing the divorce papers in a neighboring county. Brame's wife, Crystal, had filed for divorce and moved out of the home with the children in February, alleging that her husband was abusive and possessive. Brame was assistant chief and a 20-year veteran of the department when he was named chief in December 2001. There are allegations that the city manager knew of rumors of abuse and an acquaintance rape issue in Brame's past but did not investigate them thoroughly before appointing him chief. The state of Washington concluded an investigation of the incident in November 2003 and found no grounds for criminal charges but significant evidence of mismanagement within the city of Tacoma. Relatives of Crystal Brame filed a $75 million wrongful-death civil suit, with the belief that the city's inaction or inappropriate actions ultimately led to Crystal's death.[55] The family settled the suit, with the city of Tacoma paying the family $12 million in addition to the establishment of a city–county domestic violence center named after Crystal and the implementation of new policies and procedures regarding police officer–involved domestic violence.

Another relevant case is that of Drew Peterson, a former sergeant and 29-year police veteran with the Bolingbrook, Illinois, Police Department. In late 2007, when his 24-year-old fourth wife, Stacy, went missing and left her two young children, Peterson quickly became a suspect and subsequently resigned from his police position. Oddly enough, he made the talk show rounds proclaiming his innocence. He maintained his wife had run away with a boyfriend, but her family disputed that. It also came to light that Stacy had voiced a concern for her safety regarding her husband. Pursuant to her disappearance, the death of Peterson's third wife, Kathleen Savio, in 2004 was reopened. It had been recorded as a drowning, but her body was exhumed and an autopsy determined that she died as a result of a struggle, drowning when her unconscious body was placed in the bathtub. She had filed an order of protection against Peterson, and her family had long suspected it was not an accident. Peterson's second wife also raised issues of increasingly controlling behavior, threats, and abuse. The police did in fact respond to some calls, but the officers were his friends and no report was ever written. Peterson was convicted of killing Savio in 2013 and is currently serving a 38-year sentence.[56] Stacy is presumed dead, and though he has not been charged, Peterson is a suspect.

Biased-Based Policing

Biased-based policing has emerged as an important issue in communities in the last two decades. But, in reality, the government has faced this problem since *Plessy v. Ferguson* (1896) and *Brown v. Board of Education of Topeka* (1954). Providing equal protection and equal opportunity is a critical issue to the American people, but sometimes police behavior seems to contradict those values. When this behavior increased in frequency and severity in the 1980s and 1990s in an attempt to fight the rising crime rate and escalating drug problem, the community began to notice and speak out. The issue of whether this was proper police procedure or ethical police behavior was raised.

Racial profiling, the term commonly used for bias-based policing, is generally defined as any police-initiated activity that relies on a person's race

or ethnic background rather than on behavior as a basis for identifying that individual as being involved in criminal activity. Police may not use race or ethnicity to decide whom to stop or search, but they may use it to determine whether an individual matches a specific description of a suspect.[57] The difficulty arises in the validity of stops when police are investigating a crime committed by a group of individuals who may share ethnic or racial characteristics. Some criminal enterprises are composed of persons with similar ethnic, racial, or national origins, but under this definition, using this characteristic as a determining factor could be interpreted as racial profiling.[58]

During the 1990s, racial profiling became a hot topic in the media. New terms were coined, such as "driving while black (DWB)." The media attention brought the topic up for discussion in communities. A survey indicated that 53 percent of Americans believed that police engaged in racial profiling, and 69 percent disagreed with the practice.[59] The perception of the prevalence of the problem varied slightly by race, with 56 percent of whites and 77 percent of African Americans responding that racial profiling was widely used by police. Six percent of whites and 42 percent of African Americans felt they had been stopped by the police because of their race, and a staggering 72 percent of African American males between 18 and 34 believed they had been stopped because of their race.

The perception of racial profiling correlates with animosity toward police in a community. According to a Gallup poll, African American respondents had a lower opinion of police (58 percent had a favorable opinion of local police, and 64 percent favorably viewed state police) than white respondents (85 percent and 87 percent, respectively). Fifty-three percent of African American males between 18 and 34 said they had been treated unfairly by police.[60] Recently, the Department of Justice found that among all traffic stops nationwide, though all races were stopped at similar rates by police, African American (12.3 percent) and Hispanics (5.8 percent) were more likely to be searched during their stops than whites (3.9 percent). Of those drivers who were physically searched, over 36 percent felt the search was not legitimate and almost 21 percent of those whose vehicle

biased-based policing Any police-initiated activity that relies on a person's race or ethnic background rather than on behavior as a basis for identifying that individual as being involved in criminal activity.

was searched felt police had no reason to conduct the search.[61] As mentioned, these perceptions add to the animosity already felt by community members at large who perceive this biased policing to exist and disagree with the practice. This hampers police–community interactions and makes it less likely for community members to come forward and share information with the police or help in investigations when police need it. If they don't feel they can trust officers in uniform, the relationship will deteriorate.

Most recently, the issue of biased-based policing has often involved individuals of Muslim descent. In the aftermath of 9/11, the community as well as the police began to report an increased awareness of the activities of people who appear to be of Middle Eastern descent. In the summer of 2007, this became an issue in the state of Washington when two men with dark hair and olive skin were reported to have been asking unusual questions and acting suspiciously on several ferries. The FBI released their pictures to the media in an attempt to identify them in order to clear the matter up. Members of the Muslim community were outraged and believed it amounted to profiling, since the men could be perceived as Middle Eastern. They were also concerned that it raised the fear factor in the community and could result in a backlash.[62] This continues to be an issue, as can be seen by the more recent controversy in New York City in which the police department was criticized for conducting undercover surveillance in Muslim cafés and other gathering spots as part of their counterterrorism investigations.

The president of the United States has even weighed in on the issue of profiling. In July 2009, Henry Louis Gates Jr., a Harvard University scholar, accused a Cambridge, Massachusetts, sergeant of racism after he was arrested at his own home. The incident reignited the discussion of profiling. Gates had just returned home from a trip to China and was locked out of his house, and he and his limo driver were trying to jimmy the door to the house when the police responded to a call from a neighbor about a burglary in progress in the early morning hours. Gates ended up being arrested for disorderly conduct after the situation deteriorated and he accused the sergeant of racism and racial profiling. The department maintained that race had nothing to do with the incident and that if Gates had cooperated and answered the officers' questions, the situation could have been settled. Though the charges were eventually dropped, the department stands by its handling of the situation. President Obama, who said it is "just a fact" that African Americans and Hispanics are disproportionately stopped by police, accused the Cambridge officers of acting "stupidly," though he admitted he did not have all the facts. This angered police officers and police unions across the country. Ultimately, the president sat down with both Gates and the sergeant at the White House to clear the air and mend bridges.[63]

Most people believe that police do engage in racial profiling, but most police chiefs do not believe their personnel engage in this behavior.[64] Regardless of whether it occurs, the mere perception of its existence can result in problems with the community. Realizing this, many states have instituted legislation requiring the gathering of data and the implementation of racial profiling policies. According to the Department of Justice's Survey of Local Police Departments in 2007, 67 percent of all departments and 100 percent of departments serving populations over one million had written policies about racial profiling by officers.[65]

Police officers have a lot of discretion in their jobs, and this is particularly evident in traffic stops. First, officers decide whether or not to stop a car, and then they decide how to handle the stop—that is, remove occupants from the vehicle, call for a drug dog, ask for a consent search, and so on. Citizens have questioned how officers make these discretionary decisions, and some allege that the decisions are based on race or ethnicity. Many members of minority groups feel they are being stopped for petty traffic violations, such as failure to use a turn signal or an equipment violation, so that officers can use the opportunity to question occupants or search vehicles.

Research on bias-based policing or racial profiling has been used in lawsuits. John Lamberth of Temple University analyzed police searches by Maryland State Police along I-95. He found that 74 percent of speeders were white and 17.5 percent were African American, yet African Americans made up 79 percent of the drivers searched. He was also asked to analyze New Jersey data when there were complaints that African American drivers were being stopped disproportionately by state troopers. He analyzed data from 1988 through 1991 and found that African Americans constituted 13.5 percent of New Jersey Turnpike traffic and 15 percent of the drivers speeding, yet they represented 35 percent of those stopped and 73.2 percent of those arrested. Lamberth concluded that African Americans were much more likely to be stopped and arrested than were whites. The Superior Court of New Jersey used these data when it suppressed evidence seized by troopers and agreed that troopers were relying on race in stopping and searching vehicles. In April 1999, the attorney general of New Jersey issued a report indicating that New Jersey troopers had participated in racial profiling on the New Jersey Turnpike; people of color were 40.6 percent of those stopped on the turnpike and 77.2 percent of the people searched. The report also found that 80 percent of consent searches involved minority motorists.[66]

Jim Ruiz and Matthew Woessner conducted a study in Louisiana in an effort to examine the profiling issue. They reviewed arrest statistics of the Louisiana State Police–Criminal Patrol Unit and some St. Martin Parish sheriff's deputies and observed significant discrepancies consistent with demographic and racial profiling when compared with the baseline group, the Louisiana State Police–Traffic Patrol. The researchers believed that those officers were conducting focused traffic stops on targeted populations in a drug interdiction effort along I-10.[67]

The Rand Corporation was hired to analyze the NYPD's pedestrian stops for 2006, which amounted to half a million stops. They found slight racial differences in certain areas of the city but overall found the majority were not race-related stops. They flagged a few officers for stopping more minority pedestrians and also recommended some training and record-keeping changes to improve the police–pedestrian interactions.[68]

These limited studies together with anecdotal evidence have helped criminal justice practitioners as well as community activists understand what is happening. More data are needed to better determine if there is a specific problem in various cities and states across the country. In response to the community outcry, most states have implemented some type of data collection system. Collecting these data will either help the community see there is no problem with the activities of their police or help the police

and community understand the scope of the problems. This data collection will also send a message to all concerned that racial profiling is unacceptable.

Analyzing the data and initiating an early warning system can also help identify particular officers or squads who may be prone to inappropriate stops. There is a likelihood of initial resistance from officers asked to compile these data, but many have come to accept this collection process, especially when the data are used to examine trends rather than target individual officers. The data should be looked at as part of a big picture, however. Characteristics of a particular jurisdiction can skew the data—major highways, large shopping centers, and large employers can affect the amount of nonresidential population traveling to or through a jurisdiction. Some agencies may not be pleased with the analysis of their data, but others will be reassured.

If analysis of these data reveals a problem, it can be addressed. New procedures, training, or counseling can be employed to make changes. Some departments are reassured when they find there is not a bias-based policing problem, and the data can help them counter allegations of unfair treatment. Having the data available is a starting point toward improvement, if there is a need for it, and documentation to defend the department's practices, if no problem is detected.

Racial profiling and police brutality continue to be of concern to both the public and the police. Departments have procedures, reporting systems, and discipline in place to help prevent, respond to, and address these issues.

Marmaduke St. John/Alamy

Community support and relationships can be enhanced when the community has faith in the unbiased behavior of their police officers. A community that trusts its department is more likely to work with the police in making the community safe, a good thing for all concerned.

Police Brutality

Use of force is a necessary part of police work. Officers are allowed to use the level of force necessary to counter a suspect's resistance and get the suspect to comply with a lawful order. Use of force can range from a loud, commanding voice to deadly force. The use of force must be reasonable and it must be appropriate. When officers exceed this necessary level of force to achieve compliance, they are using excessive force. Excessive force occurs when an officer uses more force than is necessary to counter a subject's resistance. Police brutality is more severe and represents a significant disparity between the level of compliance by the citizen and the level of police force used.

When an officer uses physical violence against citizens, it is a significant occurrence. When it is excessive, not warranted, or qualifies as brutality, it is farther along on the slippery slope of corruption. Police brutality involves significant risk, including injury or death to the suspect, officer, or other officers, as well as the risk of citizen retaliation.

Police brutality has existed as long as there have been organized police departments. In 1931, the Wickersham Commission noted the problem of police lawlessness and abuses to obtain confessions. Subsequent commissions in the 1940s and 1960s also raised the issue of police brutality.[69] Claims of police brutality were common during the civil disorders of the 1960s and 1970s, and continued to be significant in the 1980s and 1990s. Shootings of African American men in Miami between 1980 and 1989 resulted in three race riots. As recently as the 1990s, people in the United States were stunned by the use of excessive force by police officers in the Abner Louima and Rodney King cases. In fact, the 1992 Los Angeles riots came on the heels of not-guilty verdicts in the trials of the four LAPD officers accused of beating Rodney King.

Police brutality still exists. According to the Department of Justice, 26,556 complaints of excessive force were reported in 2002 with state and local law enforcement agencies that have at least 100 full-time officers. A year after the complaints were lodged, 94 percent had a final disposition:

- Twenty-five percent were unfounded (excessive force did not occur).
- Twenty-three percent of the complaints exonerated the officers (officers performed lawfully).
- Thirty-four percent turned up insufficient evidence to prove the allegation.
- Eight percent were sustained (there was sufficient evidence to justify disciplining the accused officers).
- The remainder had some other type of disposition, such as withdrawal of the complaint.

This is an average of one incident per 200 full-time officers. Interestingly, the rate was higher for agencies with a civilian complaint review board (11.9 versus 6.6 per 100 officers). Advocates of civilian review boards have long maintained that citizens are more willing to bring abuse complaints forward to civilians than to officers.[70]

The issue of excessive force received a lot of media attention with the "Occupy" movement occurring recently around the country. Though there were some violent confrontations between police and the occupy protesters leading to allegations of excessive force—most notably in Oakland, California; Seattle, Washington; New York City; and at the University of California at Davis—most evictions were relatively peaceful. Many people credit this to improved training and communication both with the protesters and with other law enforcement agencies as to what approach works best, as compared to the way protests were handled during the civil rights movement in the 1960s.

Overall, some of the excessive force incidents can be attributed to noble cause corruption and ends-oriented thinking. Officers involved in chases with subjects who run from them or try to fight them often believe that these individuals need to be taught a lesson to make the streets safer for everyone else. The officer believes he or she is doing a good thing for society. But what happens when this officer's actions are caught on tape and aired on the evening news? Now the officer is seen as the bad guy, the bad guy is seen as the victim, more harm has been done to the larger society, and the bad guy gets the benefit. Noble cause corruption, with the ends justifying the means, has backfired.

Responses to Police Corruption

Investigations

The most important step in eliminating or reducing police corruption is to admit that corruption exists. The need for candor, Goldstein argues, is paramount. Police officials have traditionally attempted to ignore the problem and deny that it exists.[71] Many police departments have established **internal affairs divisions** as their major department resource to combat corruption. Internal affairs divisions or units are the police who police the police department. Although it can vary by department, depending on the organizational climate in the agency, sometimes internal affairs investigators are not very popular with other members of the department because many officers see them as spies who only want to get other officers in trouble.

Police corruption and internal affairs investigations can be particularly problematic for small and rural agencies for several reasons. The more frequent, intimate contact with residents can present more opportunities for unethical behavior, and because of this close relationship, residents may be less likely to bring a complaint against an officer. If an investigation is initiated, it is difficult to keep it quiet and confidential, and relationships are such that employees are probably too close to the investigation, if not involved themselves. There may be no intentional bias, but the investigators may find it difficult to believe the allegations, and consequently may not be capable of conducting an objective internal affairs investigation. For this reason, most small and rural departments work out arrangements for another agency and possibly the state to conduct internal investigations for their departments.

Understanding both the negative connotations of the "internal affairs" title and the need for systematic preventive initiatives regarding corruption, many departments have implemented "professional standards" units, "compliance" units, or "integrity" units. These divisions within the police department investigate allegations of wrongdoing but are also actively involved in developing and implementing policies and procedures to minimize the chances of corruption occurring. Such units conduct audits and inspections to ensure that safeguards are in place and that procedures are being adhered to. Good record keeping is essential in preventing corruption and is helpful in the investigative process if corruption does occur.

Internal affairs divisions can attack corruption in two ways: reactively and proactively. In a reactive investigation, the investigator waits for a complaint of corruption from the public and then investigates that specific complaint using traditional investigative techniques. In a proactive investigation into police corruption, investigators provide opportunities for officers to commit illegal acts, such as leaving valuable property at a scene to see if officers follow normal procedures regarding found property. Proactive investigations are often called **integrity tests**.

Police corruption also can be investigated by local district attorneys, state and federal prosecutors, and special investigative bodies, such as the Knapp Commission (New York City police corruption, 1970s), the Mollen Commission (New York City police corruption, 1990s), and the Christopher Commission (Los Angeles police brutality, 1991).

The NYPD has had a series of corruption scandals that have occurred in approximately 20-year cycles. In the 1970s, the Knapp Commission found institutionalized corruption within the NYPD, primarily involving officers taking bribes in order to allow some criminals to avoid arrest. Reforms followed this investigation, including the reorganization of the internal affairs division and the establishment of a special prosecutor to prosecute officers involved in corruption. This position was eliminated in 1990, but in 1992, there were new allegations of corruption.

Concern about the new allegations of corruption as well as the apparent ability of corruption to exist undetected within the NYPD led to the formation of the **Mollen Commission**, which found some serious corruption among patrol officers in high-crime areas of the city, including protection of narcotics traffickers, unlawful search and seizure, deception, and even direct involvement in drug dealing

internal affairs divisions The unit of a police agency that is charged with investigating police corruption or misconduct.

integrity tests Proactive investigation of corruption in which investigators provide opportunities for officers to commit illegal acts.

Mollen Commission A commission created in the 1990s to investigate corruption allegations in the New York City Police Department.

and robberies. The commission also found that the administration of the department had failed to monitor, supervise, and investigate these officers. In the "us-versus-them" high-crime environment where the officers depended on each other for support and even for their safety, officers who did report problems or concerns encountered hostility and lack of cooperation.

Consequently, the Mollen Commission again recommended reorganizing the internal affairs division into a centralized bureau and instituting procedures for monitoring officers. The commission also suggested changes in recruitment and training. Though the department would retain primary responsibility for investigating corruption, an independent permanent oversight agency would be created to continually assess the NYPD's anticorruption measures and, if necessary, conduct investigations. The Commission to Combat Police Corruption (CCPC) was created in 1995 and is made up of six commissioners appointed by the mayor. According to the New York City government website, the commission continues to publish yearly reports on corruption.[72]

In addition to other bodies that investigate police corruption, the FBI has jurisdiction to investigate corruption in police departments. Investigations by the FBI have had a major effect on several police departments, including the Philadelphia and New Orleans departments.

Discipline and Termination

When corruption has been discovered in an agency, discipline is in order. This discipline will start with any individuals directly involved and move up the chain to "clean house." Typically, anyone who knew or should have known there was a problem (and either chose to look the other way and ignore it, or was simply an ineffective leader) will be terminated. Usually this will include the chief. At times, this process can be problematic. Officers, like everyone, are entitled to due process. With civil service protections and union representation, what can appear to administrators as a clear violation worthy of discipline or termination (especially in the case of noncriminal misconduct) can be ultimately overturned by arbitrators, civil service boards, or courts. A department can be in a state of limbo as these cases move through various stages and appeals. Often the department is unable to fill the apparent vacancy because if the individual is granted his or her job back on appeal, the individual hired to fill the position would have to be demoted or laid off.

Departments often choose to put officers accused of corruption on administrative leave, give them administrative assignments, or allow them to continue in their assignments while awaiting the final outcome of their discipline. Agencies may also allow the officer to resign rather than be fired to save the costs of going through expensive litigation. Both of these options, however, allow the officer to continue to benefit from tax dollars in salary or pension benefits, which can greatly anger taxpayers.

Decertification is another option for law enforcement agencies. This is an administrative action coordinated through the state police standards organization that will determine if cause exists to strip an officer of his or her state certification to be a police officer. This action prevents problem officers from moving from agency to agency. In the past, some smaller agencies did not conduct thorough background investigations and thus were unaware of, or unconcerned about, an officer's past wrongdoing. States want to ensure some uniformity in who continues to wear a badge in the state. These state agencies regulating police standards also oversee revocation of officers' licenses for serious misbehavior in 44 states. They attempt to minimize the chance of a smaller, more cash-strapped town from hiring a rogue officer from another department.

Preventive Administrative Actions

The ideal way for police agencies to handle the deviance and corruption issue is through prevention. The hiring and screening process is the first step in preventing police corruption and misconduct. By screening applicants out of the process who might be prone to violence, have a quick temper, hold inappropriate attitudes, show a tendency to be "badge-heavy," or already have committed criminal acts, many problems can be avoided. This screening is accomplished through the use of the polygraph, psychological evaluation, background investigation, and, if necessary, the field training process and probationary period. Hiring the wrong person can have disastrous results for an agency both monetarily and in terms of morale. Because of the difficulty in terminating employees, problem employees can work and receive payouts for years before the agency has enough documentation to terminate them.

Another administrative tool to prevent corruption or misconduct is a good policy and procedure manual that lets officers, supervisors, administrators, and the public know what behavior is allowed and what is not acceptable. Some agencies have gone one step further and, in addition to having the policies printed in a book (which, of course, every officer should read), have chosen certain "high-liability" policies to discuss verbally one-on-one with officers early in their careers. These discussions are usually built systematically into the orientation and training process, and officers have an opportunity to clarify any questions regarding the policies. Often officers must sign a statement that they have read and understood the policies. Such policies should be written as clearly as possible so that everyone knows what is expected. Officers may view such policies as a way to "hang" an officer if they are too vague or too much is left to the discretion of the supervisor. Developing policies that are relevant to every possible contingency is an ongoing challenge for agencies.

Training is a follow-up to the development of good policies. Ongoing training is necessary as laws and policies change. Officers need to be aware of the latest policies and changes in the law and need to review these policies, role-play particular scenarios, and problem-solve different situations. This training will assist officers in making decisions as situations arise on the street.

In addition to being made aware of the department's policies and procedures, citizens should be informed of the procedure for making a complaint against a departmental employee. They should be allowed to make complaints via phone, by mail, or in person. The department should have a procedure in place to govern these complaints to make sure that all of them are investigated and that a determination is made regarding the validity of each complaint. There also should be a system for tracking cases. Problems and bad press are caused when citizens refer to former complaints that were made and claim that nothing was done about them. If a complaint has not been properly documented or recorded, the department and the officers cannot properly defend themselves, even though the officers might have been cleared of wrongdoing or the behavior might have been justified. Proper documentation and tracking show the community that the department is not afraid to examine allegations and then take disciplinary action when an officer has done something wrong, which promotes a feeling of trust between the police and the community.

Some departments take this a step further and hold mediation meetings between the complainant and the involved officer, though only if both agree to it. This is only used in minor complaints. It has been found that sitting down and talking about the incident in a nonemotional way and in a nonthreatening environment can greatly defuse the situation. By each side explaining their point of view, it can open up the eyes of the other person and lead to increased understanding and sometimes put a quick end to the complaint. On rare occasions some departments—again only with officer approval—may publicize disciplinary hearings. In following through in the community policing philosophy, this can enable the community to feel like a part of the discipline process and help them to see the officer is a real human being who made a mistake rather than just a "uniform." This can also lead to improved relationships, reduced complaints, and increased empathy. It takes a strong, positive organizational culture for officers to accept this option.

Computerized early warning systems, now generally referred to as early intervention systems, have been developed in recent years. These systems make it easier to identify officers who might have a problem. Typically these computer programs flag officers who may be prone to problems when interacting with the public. In most agencies, only a small percentage of officers cause most of the problems and generate most of the complaints from citizens. Early intervention systems look at any number of criteria, including use of force and citizen complaints, that a department deems appropriate to determine which officers can benefit from early intervention before they become problem officers. The department can intervene through counseling or training and can monitor the officer's performance in the future. These systems are particularly valuable in larger agencies, where supervisors may not be as familiar with individual officers and their personalities, work habits, and reliability; but they must be coupled with the common sense of supervisors and management. For example, officers with more aggressive assignments and generally working the nighttime shifts or areas of town with high crime rates will generate the most complaints because their assignment is to be proactive and prevent crime.

Adequate supervision can help prevent misconduct that may occur during slow times of the shift, in certain areas of town, or on particularly problematic types of calls. The knowledge that a supervisor will or could show up may keep officers from making the wrong decision, and the knowledge that they will have to explain their actions also helps officers "do the right thing" on their calls. If officers feel their behavior is not being monitored or that certain actions do not receive discipline, they may determine that misdeeds will not be caught or that they are condoned. This supervision is of particular importance with new officers and with officers assigned to particularly sensitive and discretionary assignments such as narcotics. These days, a reminder that a video or still camera could be overhead, on an apartment balcony, or on an individual's cellphone may help officers make the right decision.

Some departments have begun to use what is often referred to as "uniform cams." These small cameras can be worn on officers' sunglasses, caps, or lapels, and record all police–citizen interactions. These are believed to be a valuable tool for police officers despite their initial reluctance to use them. These cameras for the most part serve to protect officers from malicious accusations and to clear the air and the record when conflicting recollections result from interactions. The biggest asset is that incidents can be seen through the eyes of the officer. Proponents of these cameras feel that in the long run the savings in potential litigation and loss of goodwill will far outweigh the high cost of these cameras and data storage. There are still some ethical and constitutional issues to iron out in order to ensure no one's rights are violated. These cameras potentially will also serve as "remote" supervision by keeping officers on the straight and narrow and encouraging them to model the best behavior when involved in citizen encounters.

The organizational culture can help prevent corruption and misconduct. If a department takes a proactive stance toward promoting integrity throughout the entire agency, the environment will not be conducive toward the development of corruption or deviance. If officers know where the chief stands and the chief models ethical behavior, officers will know which behaviors will not be tolerated. The late Carl Klockars and his associates found that an agency's culture of integrity may be more important in shaping the ethics of police officers than hiring

the right officers. This culture is defined by clearly understood and implemented policies and rules. If unwritten rules conflict with the written rules, the confusion that results undermines the department's integrity-enhancing efforts. The officers will gauge the integrity of the department by the department's diligence in detecting and disciplining those who engage in misconduct.[73]

First-line supervisors are also critically important in modeling ethical behavior because they are the personnel who interact most frequently with road officers on a daily basis. Even officers acknowledge the importance of this type of modeling. Ethical behavior from supervisors, together with rewarding good officer behavior such as the reporting of wrongdoing by other officers, will help establish an ethical climate in the agency. Administrators must work to ensure that officers who report or confirm misconduct do not suffer retribution or alienation by their coworkers.

By incorporating all these preventive methods, working to promote integrity, and working with the community to solve problems and reduce crime, a department can create an improved environment for all. In her introduction to the U.S. Department of Justice report on integrity, former Attorney General Janet Reno called attention to the inscription on the side of the Justice Department building in Washington, D.C., which reads, "The common law is derived from the will of mankind, issuing from the people, framed through mutual confidence, sanctioned by the light of reason." She concluded with the comment, "Policing at its best can do more than anything to frame that confidence and bring together all of the people, in the knowledge that the law speaks fairly to them."[74]

Citizen Oversight

Citizen oversight (also referred to as civilian review, citizen complaint boards, or external review) is a method designed to allow for independent citizen review of complaints filed against the police through a board or committee that independently reviews allegations, monitors the complaint process, examines procedures, and makes recommendations regarding procedures and the quality of the investigations in the department. Citizen oversight generally has been implemented in communities that were unhappy with their police department and believed that citizens had not had adequate input into how

citizen oversight Also referred to as civilian review or external review. A method that allows for the independent citizen review of complaints filed against the police through a board or committee that independently reviews allegations of misconduct.

the department was operated. When communities have felt that internal affairs was not doing its job, citizens' rights groups have demanded some type of citizen oversight to ensure that complaints against the police are adequately investigated.

Citizen review boards rose in popularity after the civil disturbances of the 1960s and 1970s. Today, most major cities have some type of citizen oversight in place. It is often recommended that agencies use an open complaint process for enhancing integrity in a department, provide a process by which it is convenient for citizens to file complaints against members of the organization, and ensure that citizens can have confidence that the complaints will be fairly investigated.

There are four basic models of oversight systems:

- Citizens investigate allegations of misconduct and make recommendations to the head of the agency.

- Officers or a nonsworn police employee conduct the investigations and develop findings that the citizens then review, recommending to the head of the agency to approve or reject the findings.

- Officers investigate misconduct and render recommendations, but citizens can appeal the findings to citizens who are designated to make recommendations to the head of the agency.

- An auditor investigates the process the department uses to investigate misconduct and reports on the fairness and thoroughness of the process to the community.

- Citizen review boards can play several general roles:

- The board can provide an independent review of complaints. The belief is that an independent review board with no ties to the police will provide a fair and unbiased investigation, and the mere perception of this will provide greater public confidence in the complaint process.

- The board can monitor both the complaint process and general police department policies and practices.

- The board can provide policy review for the department when looking into the underlying problems that resulted in the citizen's complaint.

In general, citizens are in favor of the citizen review process. Police can be somewhat resistant regarding the use of civilian review boards, but often come to see the value when they realize the effect the process can have on the community's perception of their department. However, most departments like to have the final say in what discipline, policies, and training the department will implement. The concept of individuals who know nothing about police work making such important decisions and recommendations for departments makes administrators and officers alike nervous. Depending on the model used, the board can duplicate the work of internal affairs and cause unnecessary expense and time to the community, and citizens may question a review board's power if the board is only advisory and has no real clout. Generally, however, citizens feel that community input into the running of their police organization will help make the department more representative of the community.

Despite the valid arguments on both sides of the issue of citizen oversight, processes involving citizens are widely used. Therefore, the issue of whether citizen reviews are valuable may already have been settled from the public's point of view. The only decision to be made is what type of review system to incorporate. As viewed from the police perspective, these types of boards are most often implemented after a highly publicized and emotionally charged incident has occurred. Consequently, they are sometimes hastily put together and may not be the system best designed to serve the particular police department. In order to have more time and input in choosing the system that best complements the police organization, many departments are taking a proactive approach and putting a system in place before a crisis erupts. Ultimately, this may contribute to the success of the system for all concerned.

Police Civil and Criminal Liability

Misconduct by police officers can lead to civil and criminal liability. Police officers may be held legally liable—arrested, sued, and prosecuted—for their conduct. This concept of police legal liability comes in many different forms. Police **civil liability** means

---

civil liability Potential liability for payment of damages as a result of a ruling in a lawsuit.

that a police officer may be sued in civil court for improper behavior, using such civil law concepts as negligence and torts. Civil liability is a relatively new approach to correcting improper actions by the police through lawsuits and the resultant monetary judgments. Officers also may be sued under the provisions of a state civil rights law for violation of a person's civil rights.

Rolando V. del Carmen has identified several major sources of police legal liability: Under state law, police are subject to (1) civil liabilities, including state tort laws and state civil rights laws; (2) criminal liabilities, including state penal code provisions applicable only to public officials and general state penal law provisions; and (3) administrative liabilities. Under federal law, police are subject to (1) civil liabilities, including three sections of Title 42 of the U.S. Code; (2) criminal liabilities, including three sections of Title 18 of the U.S. Code; and (3) administrative liabilities.[75]

State Liability

Police may be sued in state civil courts for torts. A tort is a private wrong, as opposed to a crime that is considered a public wrong. Torts can be classified as intentional or negligence. As for **criminal liability**, many states have provisions in their penal codes that make certain actions by police officers or other public servants a crime. Police officers, like everyone else, are subject to being charged with violations of the state penal law, such as murder, assault, or larceny.

Police officers are also subject to administrative liability. They are liable for the rules and regulations established by their department to govern the conduct of its officers. Officers charged with violations of a department's internal rules and regulations may be subject to discipline in the form of fines, demotions, and even dismissal from the department.

Federal Liability

In recent years, an increasing number of lawsuits against police officers have been brought to federal courts on civil rights grounds. These federal suits are known as 1983 suits, because they are based on Section 1983 of Title 42 of the U.S. Code (Civil Action for Deprivation of Civil Rights):

> Every person who, under color of any statute, ordinance, regulation, custom, or usage, of any State or Territory, subjects or causes to be subjected, any citizen of the United States or other persons within the jurisdiction thereof to the deprivation of any rights, privileges or immunities secured by the Constitution and laws, shall be liable to the party injured in an action at law, suit in equity, or other proper proceeding for redress.

This law was passed in 1871 by Congress to ensure the civil rights of individuals. It requires due process of law before any person can be deprived of life, liberty, or property and provides redress for the denial of these constitutional rights by officials acting under color of state law (under the authority of their power as public officials).[76]

Section 1983 of Title 42 of the U.S. Code was originally known as Section 1 of the Ku Klux Klan Act of April 20, 1871, enacted by Congress as a means of enforcing the Fourteenth Amendment guarantee of rights to the newly freed slaves. This law originally was given a narrow interpretation by the courts and was seldom used. Between 1871 and 1920, only 21 cases were decided under Section 1983.[77] Police officers who violate a person's civil rights by unlawfully searching or detaining a person can be sued under this law. It can also be used in abuse-of-force cases.

Two other sections of Title 42 of the U.S. Code also apply to police officers. Section 1985 (Conspiracy to Interfere with Civil Rights) can be used against two or more officers who conspire to deprive a person of the equal protection of the law. Section 1981 (Equal Rights under the Law) can also be used against officers. In addition to being sued by a plaintiff civilly for violation of a person's civil rights, a police officer can face criminal charges by the government, using Title 18 of the U.S. Code, Section 242 (Deprivation of Rights under Color of Law), and in conspiracy cases, Title 18 of the U.S. Code, Section 241 (Conspiracy Against Rights). Title 18 of the U.S. Code, Section 245 (Federally Protected Activities), may be used against officers who interfere with certain activities such as voting, serving as a juror in a federal court, and other federally regulated activities.

In 2011, the Department of Justice investigated civil rights issues in 17 police and sheriffs'

---

criminal liability Subject to punishment for a crime.

departments, the largest number in its 54-year history. These departments included the Seattle Police, Portland (Oregon) Police, Maricopa County (Arizona) Police, Puerto Rico Police, Alamance County (North Carolina) Police, New Orleans Police, and Newark (New Jersey) Police. Experts are not sure whether this number reflects a true increase in civil rights violations and the use of excessive force or whether violations are now more likely to be exposed. It is also possible that issues such as the state of the economy and weaknesses in the mental health system could be causing more dangerous encounters for police.[78]

Just as state officers are subject to the rules and regulations of their departments, federal law enforcement officers also are subject to administrative liability for violating the rules and regulations of their agencies. The violation of these regulations may lead to such disciplinary action as fines, demotions, or dismissal.

Reasons for Suing Police Officers

The major sources of police civil liability include: failure to render proper emergency medical assistance, failure to aid private citizens, false arrest, excessive force or inappropriate use of deadly force, malicious prosecution, patterns of unfair and inequitable treatment, negligence in the care of suspects in police custody, failure to prevent a foreseeable crime, lack of due regard for the safety of others, false imprisonment, violations of constitutional rights, and racial profiling.[79] Typically, the issue of excessive force is the most widely publicized and well-known basis for civil liability because of the media attention it receives.

In *Civil Liabilities in American Policing: A Text for Law Enforcement Personnel*, del Carmen includes chapters on the following types of liabilities affecting law enforcement personnel: liability for nondeadly and deadly use of force; liability for false arrest and false imprisonment; liability for searches and seizures; liability for negligence, and specific instances of negligence in police work; liability for jail management; liabilities of police supervisors for what their subordinates do; and liabilities of police supervisors for what they do to their subordinates.[80]

In his text *Critical Issues in Police Civil Liability*, Victor Kappeler addresses the issue of negligence and discusses areas of concern to law enforcement

officers. These areas of potential liability include negligent operation of emergency vehicles; negligent failure to protect; negligent failure to arrest; negligent failure to render assistance; negligent selection, hiring, and retention; negligent police supervision and direction; negligent entrustment and assignment; and negligent failure to discipline and investigate. Some of these issues are of more concern to law enforcement administrators, but many should be of concern to the street officer as well. Kappeler further discusses areas of concern to officers in regard to the liability associated with excessive force, high-risk drug enforcement, abandoning citizens in dangerous places, failure to arrest intoxicated drivers, and negligence at accident scenes.[81]

Civil lawsuits are filed against the police for several reasons, as the following examples show. In 2006, the city of Oakland, California, agreed to pay $2 million to antiwar protesters injured three years earlier by police use of less-than-lethal force. The police fired less-than-lethal rounds (rubber and wooden bullets) at the demonstrators, some of whom had thrown rocks at the police, which resulted in 58 people being injured.[82]

In 2012, a jury awarded $5.7 million to a convicted felon left paralyzed in a police shooting. Robert Contreras, a known gang member pleaded no-contest to attempted murder in a drive-by shooting. Officers responding to the drive-by shooting chased Contreras into a dark driveway as he was fleeing the scene. When he turned toward them with an object in his hand (which turned out to be a cell phone), the officers opened fire.[83]

A month later, a federal jury handed down a $3.2 million verdict against the LAPD after officers shot a mentally ill woman and used a Taser on her. In the 2009 confrontation, a 37-year-old woman suffering from bipolar disorder went into a manic episode and wandered city streets for hours, half naked and talking incoherently. When officers pulled up, she rushed their patrol car, banging on the windows, and then struck one officer with a wooden stake. The other officer shot her three times. She survived her wounds; the jury felt the officers were "malicious" and excessive in how they treated the mentally ill woman.[84]

As mentioned earlier, the city of Tacoma, Washington, agreed to pay the family of Crystal Brame $12 million after she was murdered by her husband, David Brame, the chief of police in Tacoma, following a pattern of abusive behavior.

Effects of Lawsuits on Police Departments and Officers

The use of civil lawsuits against the police has been increasing at a rapid rate and is having a dramatic effect on the treasuries of some counties and cities. Advocates of police civil damage lawsuits see these lawsuits as a vehicle for stimulating police reform. They assume that the dollar cost of police misconduct will force other city officials to intervene and force improvements in the police department through discipline, policy change, or training.

Increased media attention, coupled with some high judgments and out-of-court settlements, has encouraged individuals and lawyers to go after the most visible arm of the criminal justice system—the police. Seminars held around the country instruct attorneys on how to sue police departments, in addition to seminars for government entities and police managers on how to avoid or protect themselves against lawsuits. There is the perception that the government has "deep pockets" and the ability to pay these judgments and settlements. The cost to taxpayers for civil suits is extremely high when factoring in the cost of liability insurance, litigation, out-of-court settlements, and punitive damage awards. It is unfortunate, but because of the high costs, many governments pay minimal out-of-court settlements to get rid of the case and avoid the costs of litigation. This angers police officers who feel that they did nothing wrong and that the government should always defend them and stand up for what is right, rather than just looking at the least expensive way to resolve the situation. Police also fear that settlements encourage frivolous lawsuits.

This issue of settling lawsuits is often viewed by the rank and file and even police administrators as an additional ethical issue. Cities or counties frequently settle lawsuits simply because it makes sense financially due to the high cost of employing specialist lawyers and beginning a defense strategy. Officers and supervisors believe that when everything was done correctly, and yet the city agrees to settle with an accuser, it sends the wrong message—that the officers were wrong and the accuser is right, which is usually far from the truth. Officers have noted that they are held to high ethical standards and encouraged to do the right thing; this standard should also hold for the governing entity, which should not settle cases just to save money. The government should back their officers when they have behaved appropriately in the performance of their job.

The city of Chicago recently implemented a program that considered this issue. Their new strategy was to go to trial with all defensible lawsuits against their officers rather than settling the cases to save money. After a year, the results of this policy were "astonishing," with lawsuits filed against officers and settlements falling dramatically as word of this policy change spread.[85] So many suits have been filed against the police that the U.S. Supreme Court, in *Canton v. Harris* (1989), made it more difficult for victims to sue for damages. The Court ruled that to be liable, police departments must be deliberately indifferent to the needs of the people with whom police come in contact.[86]

Officers and administrators need to be aware of the issue of civil liability and the police. Sometimes the threat of civil suits and large penalties proves to be an effective deterrent to excessive force, but unrealistic fears of civil liability have a number of negative effects, including morale problems, alienation from the public, and sometimes misunderstandings. Some officers may develop a reluctance to take action that should be taken as part of their job because of the fear of being sued. Such fears and reluctance could result in an ineffective police agency, with many officers just doing enough to get by and stay out of trouble.

The increase in litigation does have a positive side in that it allows for proper redress of police wrongdoing and promotes better police training and more responsible police practices; it also sets the standard for police behavior.[87] Officers should be as educated in this area as possible to have a realistic view and accurate understanding of the issue. Kappeler's text, *Critical Issues in Police Civil Liability*, is a good place to begin that education.

The Emotional Toll of Police Lawsuits

The emotional toll that internal affairs investigations can cause is a subject often ignored by academics. Although it is important to receive, document, and track complaints against the police for many reasons, people have all sorts of reasons for complaining about police officers. Many mistakenly hope to get out of whatever charges they face, from traffic tickets to arrests. Often the person charged is not even the one to make the complaint. He or she tells someone about it, and that third party may decide to make an issue of it.

Complaints against the police can generate a lot of media attention. The media love to report on "bad cops," sometimes even before all the facts have been ascertained. When the public reads about an alleged misconduct incident in the paper or hears about it in the news, a statement such as "Officer Smith would not comment" is often included, which the public may view negatively. Generally the press does not mention that usually departmental policy, and sometimes state law, prevents an officer from discussing an ongoing investigation. Thus, the citizen complainant gets to tell his or her story, often repeatedly, without the account being disputed by the police until the investigation has been concluded. Unfortunately, this procedure can take weeks or months, depending on how involved the investigation is, by which time the public or the press no longer cares about the case.

This kind of publicity has a drastic impact on the psychological well-being of the officers involved, as well as their families, as they see their names trashed in the papers and on the news. Sometimes fellow officers unintentionally distance themselves from an accused officer, wanting to avoid any negative publicity by association. Command staff and supervisors also may avoid contact with the officer in hopes of not contaminating the investigation, and frequently the involved officer is placed on administrative leave. Hence, the officer may feel abandoned and alone, with no one to talk to about the incident. Often departments do not consider this aspect of the situation because their most pressing concern becomes distancing the department and its policies from the officer's behavior if necessary.

Both administrators and officers need to remind themselves that police officers go into law enforcement to serve the public and do the right thing, and if by being wrongly accused or by making a mistake they are now vilified, the effects can be devastating. The worst-case scenario is the officer who commits suicide as his or her world crumbles; lesser problems can include increased use of alcohol, marital problems, or extreme cynicism for the remainder of his or her career. Police administrators need to be cognizant of the emotional toll of internal investigations and have some procedures in place to help minimize those effects.

SUMMARY

- Ethics is defined as the study of what is good or bad conduct and is critical in understanding and confronting police misconduct.

- Police behavior is governed by the U.S. Constitution, the Bill of Rights, the Supreme Court, case law, state laws, department policies and procedures, the Law Enforcement Code of Ethics, and an oath of office.

- The media highlights incidents of police corruption or misconduct.

- Police corruption has been around for many years, and several high-profile incidents have led to the formation of commissions to study the problem.

- Noble cause corruption refers to situations where officers bend the rules to attain the "right" result.

- There are many different responses to police corruption, including investigations, discipline, and preventive actions.

- Preventive actions used to minimize the occurrences of corruption and misconduct include hiring processes, policies and procedures, training, supervision, promoting integrity within the department, and early intervention systems.

- Other forms of police deviance include drug-related misconduct, sleeping on duty, police deception, sex-related misconduct, domestic violence in police families, and biased-based policing.

- Although use of force is a necessary part of the job, it must be reasonable and appropriate. When officers cross the line, force becomes excessive, and brutality is even more severe, with a significant disparity between the level of compliance and the amount of force used.

- Citizen oversight is often demanded by the community when citizens believe the police department is not being responsive to their concerns and investigations are not being fairly conducted.

- Police may be held liable for their actions through the state courts or the federal courts.

- Only a very small percentage of officers are involved in misconduct, and police deviance will probably never be entirely eliminated. Nevertheless, police departments must do all that they can to prevent police deviance.

KEY TERMS

biased-based policing

bribe

citizen oversight

civil liability

corruption

criminal liability

ethics

grass-eaters

gratuities

integrity test

internal affairs division

judicial review

Knapp Commission

meat-eaters

Mollen Commission

noble cause corruption

police deception

"rotten apple" theory

REVIEW EXERCISES

1. It has come to your new chief's attention that officers are receiving free meals and coffee at a couple of restaurants in town. Many officers have been doing this for years and do not see a problem with it. The chief is concerned about this practice and the perception it may cause among businesses, the officers, and the public at large. She assigns you the task of writing a policy that will address gratuities and training the officers in this policy. She also requests that you write a letter she can send to business owners informing them of this new policy. Draft a policy the officers can understand and adhere to, as well as an hour-long training session explaining the rationale for the policy to the officers. Lastly, draft a letter to the business owners for the chief's signature.

2. Your city has decided to address the issue of biased-based policing proactively. With your current assignment in the planning division, your chief has asked you to develop an instrument for collecting data on car stops that could be analyzed on a regular basis to determine if there may be a problem and to help reassure your citizens that you are working to fairly represent the community and provide equitable services. Consider that the form should be concise and exact to facilitate its use by officers, and yet it needs to collect the data that will answer the questions. Explore instruments used by other agencies and states to help you clarify what type of questions to ask, and prepare the instrument for collecting the data.

3. Develop a policy that outlines what police officers should do if they arrive on a domestic violence call involving a police officer. Outline the investigative and administrative follow-up that will occur.

WEB EXERCISES

1. Go to the websites of three police departments and summarize their instructions for citizens desiring to make a complaint against an officer. Can the citizen report it online, over the phone, in the mail, in person, or any of these? Who will review and investigate the complaint? Do you get a feeling that a complaint will be fairly investigated or does the site discourage people who want to make a complaint?

2. Go to the website of the Washington State Office of the Attorney General and look at the information on domestic violence involving law enforcement officers. Examine their model policy and compare it to the one in your state.

3. Go to the website for your state patrol agency. Analyze their traffic stop data regarding biased-based policing. What do the data show? Is the state patrol in your state stopping and searching people in a manner consistent with the population of the state? If there appears to be a problem, what are they doing to rectify it? What are some of the challenges they mention for tracking and analyzing this information, such as a high percentage of transient workers, proximity to a state or national border, and so on?

END NOTES

1. Joycelyn M. Pollock, *Ethical Dilemmas and Decisions in Criminal Justice*, 6th ed. (Belmont, Calif.: Thomson/Wadsworth, 2010), p. 7.

2. Douglas W. Perez and J. Alan Moore, *Police Ethics: A Matter of Character*, 2nd ed. (Clifton Park, NY.: Delmar/Cengage, 2013), p. 86.

3. Pollock, p. 189.

4. Ibid., p. 195.

5. Gallup, Inc., The Gallup Poll online, June 2013, available at www.gallup.com/poll/1597/confidence-institutions.apx.

6. Catherine Gallagher, Edward Maguire, Stephen D. Mastrofski, and Michael D. Reisig, "The Public Image of Police," 2001, retrieved April 21, 2010, from www.theiacp.org.

7. Frank Schmalleger, *Criminal Justice Today*, 9th ed. (Upper Saddle River, N.J.: Prentice Hall, 2007), p. 18.

8. Perez and Moore, *Police Ethics*, p. 193.

9. National Advisory Commission on Criminal Justice Standards and Goals, *Police* (Washington, D.C.: U.S. Government Printing Office, 1973); National Commission on Law Observance and Enforcement, *Report on Police* (Washington, D.C.: U.S. Government Printing Office, 1931); President's Commission on Law Enforcement and Administration of Justice, *The Challenge of Crime in a Free Society* (Washington, D.C.: U.S. Government Printing Office, 1968); *Standards for Law Enforcement Agencies*, 2nd ed. (Fairfax, Va.: Commission on Accreditation for Law Enforcement Agencies, 1987).

10. Knapp Commission, *Report on Police Corruption* (New York: Braziller, 1973).

11. Vincent J. Palmiotto, "Legal Authority of Police," in Michael J. Palmiotto, *Police Misconduct* (Upper Saddle River, N.J.: Prentice Hall, 2001), pp. 3–14.

12. Herman Goldstein, *Police Corruption: A Perspective on Its Nature and Control* (Washington, D.C.: Police Foundation, 1975), p. 3.

13. Carl B. Klockars, Sanja Kutnjak Ivkovic, William E. Harver, and Maria R. Haberfeld, "The Measurement of Police Integrity," *National Institute of Justice Research in Brief* (Washington, D.C.: National Institute of Justice, 2000), p. 1.

14. Michael J. Palmiotto, "Police Misconduct: What Is It?" in Palmiotto, *Police Misconduct*, p. 37.

15. Richard J. Lundman, "Police Misconduct," in Abraham S. Blumberg and Elaine Niederhoffer, eds., *The Ambivalent Force: Perspectives on the Police*, 3rd ed. (New York: Holt, Rinehart and Winston, 1985), p. 158.

16. Peter Maas, *Serpico* (New York: Bantam Books, 1974).

17. John P. Crank and Michael A. Caldero, *Police Ethics: The Corruption of Noble Cause*, 3rd ed. (Cincinnati: LexisNexis, 2010), p. 141.

18. "Sentencing in City of Miami Cops Case," press release from U.S. Department of Justice, U.S. Attorney for Southern District of Florida, October 29, 2003.

19. Christopher Drew, "Police Struggles in New Orleans Raise Old Fears," *New York Times*, June 9, 2006.

20. John Burnett, "Verdict in Katrina Shooting Buoys Police Reform," NPR online, www.npr.org/2011/08/18/139668648/verdict-in-katrina-shooting.

21. Associated Press, "Former Miami City Manager Warshaw Loses Pension—Again," *South Florida Sun-Sentinel*, August 6, 2003.

22. William K. Rashbaum, "Kerik Described as Close to Deal on a Guilty Plea," *New York Times*, June 29, 2006.

23. James Pinkerton, "Customs Agent Let Drugs Slip Through," *Houston Chronicle*, March 26, 2006.

24. Samuel Walker and Charles M. Katz, *Police in America: An Introduction*, 6th ed. (New York: McGraw-Hill, 2008), pp. 455–460.

25. Pollack, *Ethical Dilemmas and Decisions in Criminal Justice*, p. 195.

26. Crank and Caldero, *Police Ethics*, pp. 77–79.

27. Lawrence W. Sherman, ed., *Police Corruption: A Sociological Perspective* (Garden City, N.Y.: Doubleday, 1974), p. 1.

28. Herman Goldstein, *Policing a Free Society* (Cambridge: Ballinger, 1977), p. 218.

29. Knapp Commission, *Report on Police Corruption*, p. 4.

30. Walker and Katz, *Police in America*, pp. 452–454.

31. Pollack, *Ethical Dilemmas and Decisions in Criminal Justice*, p. 226.

32. Walker and Katz, *Police in America*, p. 452.

33. Sherman, *Police Corruption*, p. 7.

34. Ibid., pp. 191–208.

35. Perez and Moore, *Police Ethics*, p. 194.

36. Crank and Caldero, *Police Ethics*, pp. 105–110.

37. Ibid., p. 137.

38. Ibid., p. 138.

39. U.S. General Accounting Office, *Information on Drug-Related Police Corruption* (Washington, D.C.: U.S. General Accounting Office, 1998), GAO/GGD-98-111.

40. Jerome H. Skolnick, "Deception by Police," in Frederick A. Elliston and Michael Fieldberg, eds., *Moral Issues in Police Work* (Totowa, N.J.: Rowman and Allanheld, 1985), pp. 76–77.

41. Ibid.

42. *Brady v. Maryland*, 373 U.S. 83 (1963).

43. Petula Dvorak, "Police Reclassify 119 Injury Reports as Crimes," *Washington Post*, June 2, 2006.

44. Paula McMahon, "Broward Deputy's Trial Under Way for Allegedly Blaming Crimes on Wrong People," *South Florida Sun-Sentinel*, May 17, 2006.

45. P. B. Kraska and V. E. Kappeler, "To Serve and Pursue: Exploring Police Sexual Violence Against Women," *Justice Quarterly* 1 (1995): 85–111.

46. Philip M. Stinson and John Liederbach, "Sex-Related Misconduct," *Police Chief* (August 2013): 14–15.

47. National Center for Women and Policing, *Police Family Violence Fact Sheet*, retrieved February 22, 2008, from www.womenandpolicing.org.

48. Ibid.

49. Kimberly A. Lonsway, "Policies on Police Officer Domestic Violence: Prevalence and Specific Provisions of Large Police Agencies," *Police Quarterly* 4 (2006): 397–422.

50. Sarah Cohen, Rebecca Ruiz, and Sarah Childress, "Departments Are Slow to Police Their Own Abusers," *The New York Times*, November 23, 2013.

51. Kenneth Peak, *Policing America: Methods, Issues, Challenges*, 5th ed. (Upper Saddle River, N.J.: Prentice Hall, 2006).

52. National Center for Women and Policing.

53. Gina Barton, "Police Department Ignores National Standards for Officers Accused of Domestic Violence," *Journal Sentinel*, October 30, 2011, www.jsonline.com.

54. Cohen et al.

55. Michael Ko, "Brame Inquiry: Poor Judgment but No Charges," *Seattle Times*, November 18, 2003.

56. "Drew Peterson Sentenced: Ex-Cop Gets 38 Years in Kathleen Savio's 2004 Drowning Death," *The Huffington Post*, February 22, 2013, http://www.huffingtonpost.com/2013/02/21/drew-peterson-sentenced-e_n_2735356.html.

57. U.S. Department of Justice, *A Resource Guide on Racial Profiling Data Collection Systems: Promising Practices and Lessons Learned* (Washington, D.C.: Department of Justice, 2000), NCJ#184768.

58. Ibid.

59. *Sourcebook of Criminal Justice Statistics*, retrieved November 19, 2006, from www.albany.edu/sourcebook.

60. U.S. Department of Justice, *A Resource Guide on Racial Profiling Data Collection Systems*.

61. Christine Eith and Mathew R. Durose, *Contacts between Police and the Public, 2008* (Washington, D.C.: Department of Justice, 2011), NCJ#234599.

62. William Yardley, "Debate Swirls Around Two Men on a Ferry," *New York Times*, August 26, 2007.

63. Jonathan Saltzman, "Sergeant Gets Backup: Cambridge Chief Defends Arrest but Promises a Review," *boston.com*, July 24, 2009, retrieved August 21, 2009, from www.boston.com/news/local/massachusetts/articles/2009/07/24/cambridge_police.

64. Joyce McMahon, Joel Gomer, Ronald Davis, and Amanda Kraus, *How to Correctly Collect and Analyze Racial Profiling Data: Your Reputation Depends on It* (Washington, D.C.: Department of Justice, 2003), retrieved October 12, 2008, from www.ncjrs.gov.

65. Brian Reaves, *Local Police Departments, 2007* (Washington, D.C.: Bureau of Justice Statistics, 2010), NCJ#231174.

66. U.S. *Department of Justice, A Resource Guide on Racial Profiling Data Collection Systems*.

67. Jim Ruiz and Matthew Woessner, "Profiling, Cajun Style: Racial and Demographic Profiling in Louisiana's War on Drugs," *International Journal of Police Science and Management* 3 (2006): 176–197.

68. Alison Gendar, "Review Says Half-Million NYPD Stop-and-Frisk Cases Not Racial Profiling," *New York Daily News*, November 21, 2007.

69. Crank and Caldero, *Police Ethics*, p. 86.

70. Michael J. Sniffen, "Study Tracks Police Brutality Claims," *Washington Post*, June 25, 2006.

71. Goldstein, *Police Corruption*, pp. 6–8.

72. New York City government website, www.nyc.gov.

73. Carl B. Klockars, Sanja Kutnjak Ivkovic, and Maria R. Haberfeld, *Enhancing Police Integrity* (Washington, D.C.: Department of Justice, December 2005), NCJ#209269, retrieved October 12, 2008, from www.ncjrs.gov/pdffiles1/nij/209269.pdf.

74. Klockars, Ivkovic, and Haberfeld, *Enhancing Police Integrity*, NCJ#209269.

75. Rolando V. del Carmen, *Civil Liabilities in American Policing: A Text for Law Enforcement Personnel* (Englewood Cliffs, N.J.: Prentice Hall, 1991), pp. 7–14.

76. Schmalleger, *Criminal Justice Today*, p. 317.

77. Del Carmen, *Civil Liabilities in American Policing*.

78. Jerry Markon, "Justice Department Boosts Activity to Police the Police," *Washington Post*, September 17, 2011.

79. Schmalleger, *Criminal Justice Today*, p. 315.

80. Del Carmen, *Civil Liabilities in American Policing*, pp. 2–3.

81. Victor Kappeler, *Critical Issues in Police Civil Liability*, 3rd ed. (Prospect Heights, Ill.: Waveland Press, 2001), p. 26.

82. "Oakland to Pay $2 Million to Protesters Injured by Cops," *New York Times*, March 20, 2006.

83. Rong-Gong Lin II and Joel Rubin, "LAPD Chief Urges Appeal of $5.7 Million Jury Award to Paralyzed Felon," *Los Angeles Times*, September 22, 2012.

84. Joel Rubin, "Jury Awards $3.2 Million to Woman Shot by LAPD," *Los Angeles Times*, October 2, 2012.

85. Frank Main, "'Astonishing' Drop in Lawsuits Against City Cops," *Chicago Sun-Times*, November 10, 2010, www.suntimes.com.

86. *Canton v. Harris*, 489 U.S. 378 (1989).

87. Kappeler, *Critical Issues in Police Civil Liability*.

Police Operations

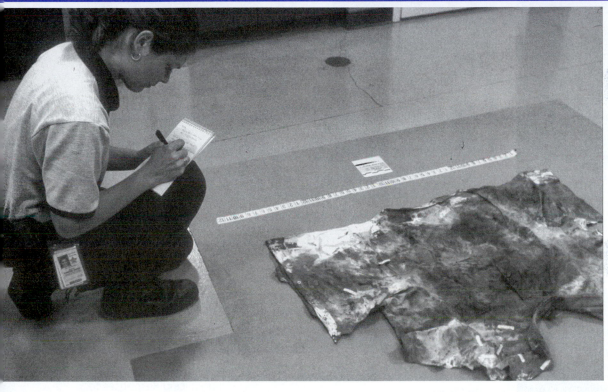

© Joel Gordon

CHAPTER 9
Patrol Operations

CHAPTER 10
Investigations

CHAPTER 11
Police and Their Clients

CHAPTER 12
Community Policing

CHAPTER 13
Police and the Law

Patrol Operations

LEARNING OBJECTIVES

- Describe the three traditional patrol methods and what the results of the Kansas City study revealed about their effectiveness.

- Discuss the value of various patrol innovations, including evidence-based policing, predictive policing, and smart policing.

- Discuss the issues and perspectives behind decisions on how to deploy personnel on patrol.

- Explain alternative strategies in use to better combat certain types of crime.

- Describe police traffic operations, including efforts against distracted, drunk, and aggressive drivers, and the debate surrounding police pursuits.

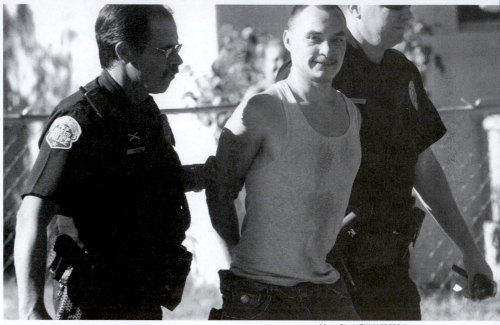

Marty Bicek/ZUMAPRESS/Newscom

OUTLINE

Traditional Methods of Police Work
Police Patrol Operations
  Activities of the Patrol Officer
  The Legacy of O. W. Wilson
Evaluating the Effectiveness of Police Work
Random Routine Patrol: The Kansas City Study
Rapid Response to Citizens' 911 Calls
  Academic Studies of the Police Patrol Function
  From the Foot Beat to the Patrol Car
  One-Officer Versus Two-Officer Patrol Cars
  Return to Foot Patrol
Patrol Innovations: Working Smarter
  Evidence-Based Policing
  Predictive Policing
  Smart Policing
Personnel Deployment
  Directing Patrol Efforts
  Differential Response to Calls for Service and the 911 System

  Reverse 911
  Smart911
Allocation of Resources
  Personnel
  Vehicles
Alternative Strategies
  Tactical Operations
  Specialized Policing Responses to Individuals with Mental Illness
  Decoy Vehicles
  Alternative Vehicle Deployment
Police Traffic Operations
  Video Camera Traffic Enforcement
  The Challenge of Distracted Drivers
  Efforts Against Drunk Drivers and Impaired Drivers
  Fighting Aggressive Driving
  Police Automobile Pursuits
Other Police Operational Units
  SWAT Teams and Police Paramilitary Units
  K-9 Units

INTRODUCTION

This chapter is about police operations: what the police do and how they do it. It covers police patrol operations, responding to 911 calls, allocation of resources, alternative crime-fighting strategies, traffic operations, and other police operational units.

The chapter will discuss the academic studies of the 1960s and 1970s, particularly the Kansas City study, which has changed our understanding of the effectiveness of the traditional methods of doing police work. The Kansas City study, as well as other studies, has forced academics and progressive police administrators to look closely at their operations to see if there are better, more effective ways to do police work. We will examine some of the changes that have taken place as a result of these studies and some of the new, more effective ways of policing.

Most of this chapter will be related to police patrol operations, the core of policing. Patrol operations involve the activities and role of the patrol officer and the various methods of doing patrol work, including motorized and foot patrols. Additionally, the chapter will discuss traffic operations and special operations, including SWAT teams and K-9 units.

Traditional Methods of Police Work

The three cornerstones of traditional police work are (1) random routine patrol, (2) rapid response to citizens' calls to 911, and (3) retroactive investigation of past crimes by detectives.[1]

The average U.S. police officer arrives at work at the beginning of his or her shift and receives the keys and the patrol car from the officer who used it on the previous tour. The officer then drives around a designated geographic area (**random routine patrol**). When the officer receives a call from the police dispatcher, he or she responds to the call and performs whatever police work is required—an arrest, first aid, breaking up a fight, taking a crime report, and so on (**rapid response to citizens' calls to 911**). If the call involves a crime, the officer conducts a preliminary investigation and often refers the case to a detective, who conducts a follow-up investigation of the crime (**retroactive investigation of past crimes by detectives**). As soon as the officer is finished handling the call, he or she resumes patrol and is ready to respond to another call.

These are the methods of traditional police work. However, are random routine patrol, rapid response to citizens' calls to 911, and retroactive investigation of past crimes by detectives the best ways for the police to safeguard our communities? Are these methods effective? Is this combination of methods the only way to do police work? This chapter will address these issues with the exception of retroactive investigation of past crimes, which will be examined in depth in Chapter 10.

Police Patrol Operations

When we think of the police, often our first image is that of the man or woman in uniform driving a police car at rapid speeds with lights and siren to the scene of a crime or an accident. We also may think of the uniformed officer on foot patrol ("walking a beat") in a downtown business area, moving a drunk and disorderly citizen away from a group of ordinary shoppers. (**Foot patrol** is a method of deploying police officers that gives them responsibility for all policing activity by requiring them to walk around a defined geographic area.) We may think of a police officer on horseback or one on a motorcycle. All these officers have one thing in common: they are patrol officers.

Since the time of Sir Robert Peel (the promoter of the first organized, paid, uniformed police force in London in 1829), patrol has been the most important and visible part of police work to the public.

---

random routine patrol Officers driving around a designated geographic area.

rapid response to citizens' calls to 911 Officers being dispatched to calls immediately, regardless of the type of call.

retroactive investigation of past crimes by detectives The follow-up investigation of crimes by detectives that occurs after a crime has been reported.

foot patrol Police officers walk a beat or assigned area rather than patrolling in a motor vehicle.

Peel's major innovation and contribution to society was the idea of a continuous police presence throughout a community that is organized and delivered by means of regular patrol over a fixed beat by uniformed officers. Patrol is the essence of policing.

Activities of the Patrol Officer

Patrol is known as the foundation of the police department. Patrol officers are the uniformed officers who respond to calls for service, emergencies, and all sorts of disturbances that occur. They are the most visible arm of the criminal justice system as well as the gatekeepers to the system. Almost without exception, all police officers begin their careers in patrol, and this is where they garner the bulk of their police experience. Patrol is where most sworn personnel are assigned and carry out the mission of the police agency. Generally, 60 to 70 percent of law enforcement officers spend their time patrolling, so how this time is used is of critical importance.

The patrol function has changed little since 1829 and has three main goals:

- The deterrence of crime
- The maintenance of a feeling of public security
- Twenty-four-hour availability for service to the public

Traditionally, the primary services provided by the patrol function include enforcing laws, deterring crime, maintaining order, keeping the peace, enforcing traffic laws and keeping traffic flowing, investigating accidents, conducting preliminary investigations, responding to calls for assistance, and assisting those who cannot help themselves.

The patrol officer is the police department's generalist and foremost representative to the public. He or she performs numerous and varied duties in and for the community. Patrol officers face numerous complex problems on a daily basis and see things that most people never see. Patrol officers respond to calls about overflowing sewers and lights being out, reports of attempted suicides, domestic disputes, neighborhood disputes, dogs running loose, reports of Martians trying to gain entry to people's homes, reports of people banging their heads against brick walls, requests to check on the welfare of elderly people who have not been seen for a few days,

requests to check out strange smells, requests to "do something about" the aggressive person on the street corner, and requests for information and help with almost anything you can think of. When citizens do not know whom to call or other businesses or services are not available, they call the police.

The Legacy of O. W. Wilson

Until the 1970s, most of what we knew about patrol was written by O. W. Wilson, former dean of the School of Criminology at the University of California at Berkeley and a former police chief in Wichita and Chicago, and his associate, Roy Clinton McLaren, in the classic book *Police Administration*. Wilson called patrol "the backbone of policing" and stated that patrol is designed to create "an impression of omnipresence," which will eliminate "the actual opportunity (or the belief that the opportunity exists) for successful misconduct."[2] The word **omnipresence** can be defined as "the quality of always being there." Thus, if the police are always there or seem to be always there, criminals cannot operate. Wilson's patrol ideas were designed to make the police appear to be as omnipresent as possible.

Wilson defined the distribution of patrol officers as the "assignment of a given number of personnel according to area, workload, time, or function."[3] Under Wilson's theory, some police officers work the day shift, some work the evening shift, and others work the night shift. Officers are assigned to certain areas based on the workload (number of crimes, arrests, and calls for service) in a particular area. Patrol officers are also assigned according to the type of work they perform—foot, radio car, traffic, canine, or some other type of patrol function. Professional police management has consistently followed Wilson's ideas on emphasizing the rational distribution of patrol officers according to a workload formula.

Evaluating the Effectiveness of Police Work

Evaluating the effectiveness of police work is very difficult. If a city has a high crime rate, does it follow that its police department is not effective? If a city has a low crime rate, does it follow that its police

---

omnipresence The impression of always being there.

department is an effective one? When we talk about crime, we are talking about many different and complex variables. The police cannot control all the variables that might produce crime, such as social disorganization; anger; poverty; hostility; revenge; psychological, social, or biological problems; and the desire to commit crime as an alternative to the world of work.

Despite the difficulties and problems associated with conducting academic and scientific research in policing, the research has been influential in the development of policing strategies during the last three decades. Although systematic research on policing is relatively new, it has influenced how police departments operate as well as public perceptions of policing. Changes in policy and practice around the country suggest that research has had particularly important conceptual and operational effects in patrol operations. Most of all, the research that has been conducted, though somewhat limited, has caused law enforcement personnel to reexamine their beliefs about crime and preventing crime and to consider more creative ways to address the crime issue.

Can we have controlled experiments to see if a police department is effective? Can we eliminate police patrols from one neighborhood and compare the crime rate in that neighborhood with the crime rate in the neighborhood where there are police patrols? A myriad of problems accompany controlled experiments with crime. Is such experimentation ethical? Is it legal? This chapter will look at several controlled experiments with crime to see how they have affected our traditional concepts of doing police work.

Random Routine Patrol: The Kansas City Study

Random routine patrol, otherwise known as preventive patrol, involves a police officer driving around within a community when he or she is not on an assignment from the radio dispatcher or a supervisor. Tradition has held that random routine patrol creates a sense of omnipresence and deters crime because a criminal will not chance committing a crime if a police officer might be just around the corner. Random routine patrol was believed to enable police officers to catch criminals in the act of

committing their crimes. Just how effective is random routine patrol? The **Kansas City patrol study** was the first attempt to actually test the effectiveness of random routine patrol.

During 1972 and 1973, the Kansas City, Missouri, Police Department, under the leadership of Chief Clarence Kelly (who later became the director of the FBI) and with the support of the Police Foundation, conducted an experiment to test the effects of routine preventive patrol. This yearlong experiment was both influential and controversial.

Fifteen patrol beats in Kansas City's South Patrol Division were used for the study. Five of these beats were assigned to a control group with no changes in normal patrol staffing or tactics. Five other beats were chosen as reactive beats, and all preventive patrolling was eliminated. Outside patrol units handled calls in the reactive beats, and units left the beats once they had handled the calls. The final five beats in the experiment were proactive beats, in which two to three times the usual level of preventive patrolling was provided. Thus, the reactive beats (with all routine patrol eliminated) and the proactive beats (with routine patrol increased) were the experimental groups. If random routine patrol is an effective way of policing our communities, we would expect to see changes in the reactive and proactive beats.[4]

When the Kansas City study was finished, the researchers concluded, "Decreasing or increasing routine preventive patrol within the range tested in [the] experiment had no effect on crime, citizen fear of crime, community attitudes toward the police on the delivery of police service, police response time, or traffic accidents."[5] In effect, the study failed to demonstrate that adding or taking away police patrols from an area made any difference within the community.

The conclusions of the Kansas City study shocked many people and differed from the assumptions made regarding police patrol. It had been commonly believed that putting more officers on patrol would cause a decrease in crime, and taking away police would cause it to increase.

In summary, the Kansas City study indicated that our traditional three cornerstones of policing might not be the most effective way to do police

Kansas City patrol study The first study conducted to test the effectiveness of random routine patrol.

work. The study definitely led the way for the academic study of policing, which in turn has caused tremendous changes in our thinking about policing.

Rapid Response to Citizens' 911 Calls

Rapid response to citizens' calls to 911 has traditionally been thought of as a way in which the police could catch criminals while they were in the act of committing their crimes or as they were escaping from their crimes. The ideal scenario is this: A citizen observes a person committing a crime and immediately calls 911. The police respond in seconds and arrest the perpetrator. This sounds great, but it rarely works that way.

Another scenario follows: A citizen is mugged and, just after the mugging, immediately calls 911 and reports the crime. The police respond in seconds and catch the perpetrator as he or she is at the crime scene or in immediate flight from it. This also sounds great, but again, it rarely works that way. The traditional approach of rapid response to 911 calls was based on unexamined assumptions about police patrol. Research during the past 20 years has pointed out that we cannot depend on this television portrayal of police work.

In 1967, the President's Commission on Law Enforcement and Administration of Justice, in its *Task Force Report: Science and Technology*, found that quick response to a citizen's report of a crime to 911 made an arrest more likely. However, the commission emphasized that only extremely quick response times were likely to result in arrest. The commission discovered that when police response time was one or two minutes, an arrest was likely, and improvements in the response time of even 15 to 30 seconds greatly improved the likelihood of an arrest. In contrast, when response time exceeded three or four minutes, the probability of an arrest dropped sharply.[6]

In 1973, the National Advisory Commission on Criminal Justice Standards and Goals recommended, "Urban area response time... under normal conditions should not exceed 3 minutes for emergency calls and 20 minutes for nonemergency calls." The commission stated, "When the time is cut to 2 minutes, it can have a dramatic effect on crime."[7]

In time, further studies of rapid response to citizens' calls to 911 were carried out. These studies took into account the complexity of response time, which the earlier research by the two commissions had failed to do. Total response time (from the moment of the crime to the arrival of the first police officer) consists of three basic components:

1. The time between when the crime occurs and the moment the victim or a witness calls the police

2. The time required for the police to process the call

3. Travel time from the time the patrol car receives the dispatcher's call until it arrives at the scene

Two studies looked even more carefully at response time and at the different types of situations that spur calls to 911 for police assistance. These studies found that victims often delay calling the police after a crime or other incident occurs. Sometimes no phone is available; sometimes the victims are physically prevented from calling by the perpetrator. Often, victims of crime are temporarily disoriented, frightened, ashamed, or even apathetic. Some people in one study reported that they first called parents, insurance companies, or their doctors. Later studies reported that the average citizen delay in calling the police for serious crimes was between 5 and 10 minutes. The discovery that citizens often wait several minutes before calling the police, as well as the fact that some victims discover the crimes after the fact, puts response time in a different light and suggests that rapid response may not be as significant as was once thought.[8]

We will always need some type of rapid police response to citizens' calls to 911, even though we have to realize that a one- or two-minute response is highly unrealistic. We will always need rapid response to calls where someone is in danger or the perpetrator is still on the scene or is in immediate flight from it. Also, quick response improves the chances for finding and interviewing possible witnesses and securing and retrieving physical evidence for analysis. However, as the academic studies have indicated, alternative strategies to rapid response to citizens' calls to 911 are needed to make better use of police officers.

Academic Studies of the Police Patrol Function

Before the 1960s, there was little study of the police patrol function—what patrol officers do and how they do it. For years, O. W. Wilson's writings were the bible of policing. It took many years of study to realize that much of what Wilson taught us about police patrol was based on faulty assumptions. Despite the fact that many of Wilson's ideas have been replaced by new ideas and concepts based on the subsequent research revolution in policing, we still owe a tremendous thanks to him as the first researcher to really study and write on police operations.

George L. Kelling and Mary A. Wycoff, in their 2001 *Evolving Strategy of Policing: Case Studies of Strategic Change*, wrote that during the era dominated by O. W. Wilson and his colleagues, roughly the 1920s through the 1970s, police strategy and management emphasized bureaucratic autonomy, efficiency, and internal accountability through command and control systems that focused on countering serious crime by criminal investigation, random preventive patrol by automobile, and rapid response to calls for service.[9] During the 1970s, however, research into police practices challenged the core competencies of police preventive patrol and rapid response to calls for service.

What do the police hope to accomplish through the use of patrol? William G. Gay, Theodore H. Schell, and Stephen Schack define the goals of patrol as follows: "crime prevention and deterrence, the apprehension of criminals, the provision of non–crime-related service, the provision of a sense of community security and satisfaction with the police, and the recovery of stolen property." They then divide routine patrol activity into four basic functional categories:

- *Calls for service.* Responding to citizens' calls to 911 relative to emergencies or other problems accounts for 25 percent of patrol time.
- *Preventive patrol.* Driving through a community in an attempt to provide omnipresence accounts for 40 percent of patrol time.
- *Officer-initiated activities.* Stopping motorists or pedestrians and questioning them about their activities account for 15 percent of patrol time.
- *Administrative tasks.* Paperwork accounts for 20 percent of patrol time.[10]

James Q. Wilson's pioneering work, *Varieties of Police Behavior: The Management of Law and Order in Eight Communities*, resulted from an attempt to study what police officers do. Wilson concluded that the major role of the police was "handling the situation" and believed that the police encounter many troubling incidents that need some sort of "fixing up." He said that enforcing the law might be one tool a patrol officer uses; threats, coercion, sympathy, understanding, and apathy might be others. Most important to the police officer, Wilson said, "is keeping things under control so that there are no complaints that he is doing nothing or that he is doing too much."[11]

For many years, the major role of police patrol was considered to be law enforcement. However, research conducted in the 1960s and 1970s by academics showed that very little of a patrol officer's time was spent on crime-fighting duties.

PATROL ACTIVITY STUDIES To determine what police actually do, researchers have conducted patrol activity studies. This research has involved studying four major sets of data: data on incoming calls to police departments (calls to 911), calls radioed to patrol officers, actual activity by patrol officers, and police–citizen encounters.

The nature of incoming calls to police departments reveals the kinds of problems or conditions for which citizens call 911. Data from these calls can usually be retrieved from telephone logs or from recordings of conversations between callers and 911 operators. The calls radioed to patrol officers, or assignments given to police patrol units by 911 dispatchers, reveal the types of problems for which people call the police and the types of problems the police feel deserve a response by patrol units.

The data regarding the actual activity of patrol officers during each hour of their tours can usually be retrieved from officers' activity reports and observations by researchers riding with police patrol officers.[12] Data on what occurs when an officer encounters a citizen—either when the officer is on assignment from the dispatcher or is on self-initiated activities—can best be retrieved from researcher observations.

The patrol activity studies that were conducted in the 1960s, 1970s, and 1980s reported generally that patrol officers spend less than 20 to 30 percent of their time on crime-related calls. Gary

Cordner, commenting on these studies, writes that most patrol work involves not doing anything very specific, but rather taking breaks, meeting with other officers, and engaging in preventive patrolling. He states that administrative duties are the most common in police patrol, and the remaining time is divided among police-initiated activities (33 percent) and calls from the police dispatcher (67 percent). Cordner says the police-initiated activities are mostly related to law enforcement (particularly traffic enforcement). The calls from the dispatcher involve a blend of crimes, disputes, traffic problems, and service requests, with crimes and disputes being the most common.[13]

Jack R. Greene and Carl B. Klockars described a survey of a full year's worth of computer-aided dispatch (CAD) data for the Wilmington, Delaware, Police Department. Their survey found, as did many of the previous studies regarding police activity, that much of police work deals with problems that are not related to crime.[14] The study revealed that the police spent 26 percent of their time on criminal matters, 9 percent on order maintenance assignments, 4 percent on service-related functions, 11 percent on traffic matters, 2 percent on medical assistance, and 12 percent on administrative matters. Five percent of their time, they were unavailable for service, and almost 30 percent of the time was clear or unassigned, when the officers performed random routine patrol.

Two significant findings emerged from this study. First, when the percentages of time involved in unavailable, administrative, and clear time are excluded from the data, the data indicate that the police spent almost 50 percent of their time on criminal matters, 16 percent on order maintenance, 8 percent on service, 21 percent on traffic, and 4 percent on medical assistance. Second, 47 percent of the officers' time was spent on activities other than actual assignments.

We have seen that the police spend their time performing numerous types of duties. They spend significant time on criminal matters, but the measurement of this time varies, depending on the study. In looking at all of the police activity studies, it is obvious why most experts today agree that the bulk of police patrol work is devoted to what has been described as random routine patrol, administrative matters, order maintenance, and service-related functions. However, Cordner and Scarborough have stated that although the studies

have performed a valuable function by challenging the crime-fighting image of police work, by the late 1970s, many police chiefs and scholars had carried them too far in downplaying and deemphasizing the crime-related and law enforcement aspects of police work. These authors believe a middle-of-the-road position is advisable.[15]

A former police chief gives a vivid description of police patrol work that may point more to the truth of the matter than can academic studies:

Cops on the street hurry from call to call, bound to their crackling radios, which offer no relief—especially on summer weekend nights. That is the time when the ghetto throbs with noise, booze, violence, drugs, illness, blaring TVs, and human misery. The cops jump from crisis to crisis, rarely having time to do more than tamp one down sufficiently and leave for the next. Gaps of boredom and inactivity fill the interims, although there aren't many of these in the hot months. Periods of boredom get increasingly longer as the night wears on and the weather gets colder.[16]

From the Foot Beat to the Patrol Car

Patrol allocation models give the police answers as to where and when to assign officers. Over the years, however, different methods of deploying police officers have been used. The two major deployments are motorized patrol and foot patrol.

Police patrol, as we saw in Chapter 1, is a historical outgrowth of the early watch system. The first formal police patrols were on foot, and the cop on the beat became the symbol and very essence of policing in the United States. Furthermore, the cop on the beat became the embodiment of American government to most citizens. However, as early as the 1930s, foot patrols were beginning to vanish in favor of the more efficient and faster patrol car.[17] By the late 1930s and 1940s, police management experts stressed the importance of motorized patrol as a means of increasing efficiency, and the number of cities using motorized patrol grew.

By the 1960s, the efficiency of the remaining foot patrols was being challenged. Foot patrols were considered geographically restrictive and wasteful of personnel. Foot officers, who at the time had no portable radios (not available until

Rushing to the Scene   ON THE JOB

When I entered policing, responding to calls with lights and siren was not that uncommon. We did it a lot more frequently than officers do today. I can remember responding to bar fights with lights and siren, as was the procedure at the time. After responding to many of these calls in this manner, I began to question the rationale of running red lights and driving over the speed limit, with cars pulling over in every direction to get out of my way. I began to wonder why I was risking my life and the lives of other motorists, as very rarely was there still a fight going on when I got there. Most of the time, friends had separated the individuals involved, and it was usually a situation of mutual (drunk) combatants. It didn't seem to be a call worth risking lives over. Over the years, police departments looked at this situation and came to similar conclusions. Our department started to strictly limit which calls we could respond to in an emergency mode because of the potential for injuries and death and the liability involved.

But early in my career we were very cognizant of police response times, and a bar fight was a call with potential injuries; we wanted to have a good response time. We were not considering the fact that often the fight had been going on for a while or might even have been over before someone—usually management—decided to call the police, which was often the threat made by management when the subjects wouldn't leave the lounge. If the subjects didn't leave, management picked up the phone and called the police, the subjects saw the management was serious and left, and, consequently, they were often gone or leaving when we got there.

When police departments started examining the philosophy of immediate response and response time, it became apparent that factors outside our control, such as the common delay before making a call to the police, determined whether our response was, in fact, immediate; and thus our "immediate" response lost a lot of its value. When departments weighed the issues of danger to the public and officers, they began to severely restrict the types of calls that require an emergency response.

It took a long time to make adjustments in procedure; officers still like to respond as an emergency vehicle and would like to do it more often. They sometimes argue that it's better to get to most situations earlier rather than later, but with streets increasingly more crowded at all hours of the day and night, speeding to every call in emergency response mode just isn't safe.

—Linda Forst

the 1970s), were inefficient in terms of covering large areas or being available to be signaled and sent on assignments. Thus, to management experts, foot patrols were not as efficient as the readily available radio cars.

At about this time, many cities had shifted almost totally away from foot patrols, replacing them with more deployable two-person car patrols. However, as a report of the Kansas City, Missouri, Police Department pointed out, in 1966, the number of foot patrol beats per shift in Boston, Baltimore, Pittsburgh, and other major urban centers remained in the hundreds.[18]

The International Association of Chiefs of Police (IACP) went one step further than the cities that were moving toward patrol cars, strongly advocating a conspicuous patrol that conveyed a sense of police omnipresence, which this association believed could be best achieved by using a highly mobile force of one-person cars:

> The more men and more cars that are visible on the streets, the greater is the potential for preventing a crime. A heavy blanket of conspicuous patrol at all times and in all parts of the city tends to suppress violations of the law. The most economical manner of providing this heavy blanket of patrol is by using one-man cars when and where they are feasible.[19]

The next section explores the debate about one-person versus two-person patrol cars in more detail.

The change from foot to motor patrol revolutionized U.S. policing. It fulfilled the expectations of the management experts by enabling police departments to provide more efficient patrol coverage—that is, covering more areas more frequently and responding more quickly to calls for service. However, one major unforeseen consequence of the shift to motorized patrol continues to haunt us. Motorized patrol was very efficient in coverage, but achieving that efficiency involved a trade-off in the relationship between the police and the community.

With the advent of motor patrol, police officers, who drove quickly through the streets to respond to the calls for service, became isolated from the community and had few contacts with ordinary citizens in normal situations. Most calls to which the police responded involved problems, either crime or order maintenance problems. The personal contact between citizens and the officer on the foot beat was lost, and a growing rift began to develop between the police and the public. Few people noticed this change in policing until the riots of the 1960s dramatized the problem of police–community relations.[20]

Around 1968, experts began to realize the problems created by the emphasis on the efficiency of the patrol car and by the absence of the foot officer's closeness to the community. The *Task Force Report* of the President's Commission on Law Enforcement and Administration of Justice noted, "The most significant weakness in American motor patrol operations today is the general lack of contact with citizens except when an officer has responded to a call. Forced to stay near the car's radio, awaiting an assignment, most patrol officers have few opportunities to develop closer relationships with persons living in the district."[21] Despite the drawbacks, by 1978, the *Police Practices Survey* found that more than 90 percent of all beats were handled by motor patrol. Foot patrol accounted for less than 10 percent.[22]

One-Officer Versus Two-Officer Patrol Cars

Along with the IACP recommendation mentioned above, O. W. Wilson's concept of random routine patrol by marked police vehicles included his insistence that the cars should contain one officer, rather than the two officers that were commonly used earlier. This was quite controversial at the time and remains so. Wilson believed that one-officer patrols could observe more than two-officer patrols, that one-officer patrols would respond more quickly to calls for service, and that officers patrolling by themselves were actually safer than were officers patrolling in pairs.

There has been an ongoing debate about whether having one officer or two officers in a patrol car is better. Typically, the larger urban departments such as New York, Chicago, Washington, D.C., and Los Angeles have deployed two-officer cars. Most suburban and rural departments have preferred one-officer cars, since that allows them to better deploy their limited number of officers. Since many calls for service do not necessitate two officers, they believe they get more coverage this way. The theory is that if an officer goes to a dangerous call or encounters a dangerous situation, he or she will automatically have a backup dispatched or can call for backup from a neighboring beat or zone. Having one officer in a car allows departments to maximize their resources and have the ability to respond to more calls for less money. This advantage is especially relevant today with declining budgets and the difficulty in recruiting officers and filling vacancies. Some agencies have compromised by using primarily one-officer cars supplemented by two-officer cars in high-crime areas or during peak hours.

In a study of police officer attitudes toward one-officer versus two-officer patrol, officers generally agreed that they would perform the same regardless of whether they were in a one- or two-officer patrol car; however, they believed that two-officer units should be used during the evening or midnight shift as well as in areas of the city where people mistrust the police, and that two-officer patrols are generally more effective.[23] Many officers state that police departments are compromising officer safety in an effort to save money. They believe that officers are safer when working in pairs and that they are less likely to be assaulted or killed if there are two officers present. Though there is some anecdotal evidence to support this claim, the empirical research has been unclear. Some officers have related that if not for their partner being present, they would be dead or seriously injured. Others who have been injured have indicated that perhaps they would not have been assaulted or injured had they not been alone in a car with no backup immediately available. It can be difficult to ascertain the deterrent effect that seeing two officers together might have on someone who might consider assaulting an officer or trying to escape.

On the other hand, it is thought that when officers work in pairs, they may become distracted by their conversation and not be quite as observant as they might be on their own. They also may become overly confident and have a false sense of security about their abilities as a team. In addition, beats may have to go unattended when an agency doubles up officers in cars and does not have enough officers available for staffing, and this, too, can result in a dangerous situation.

This discussion of one- versus two-officer patrol cars has become an issue again with felonious attacks on officers on the upswing. Police unions and state and local officials in some parts of the country are advocating reexamining the issue of two-officer cars. Criminals seem to have become even more brazen and well-armed, and less hesitant to hurt or kill an officer. After several murders and attempted murders of officers in South Florida, the use of traditional one-officer cars has been questioned, though it appears unlikely there will be changes due to budget and staffing issues.[24] St. Louis and Kansas City also are discussing this issue, as they have had officers recently murdered and almost murdered, and it is believed the incidents might not have occurred had the officers been in two-officer cars. Agencies are trying to analyze this issue, but it is complex and challenging, and it may be difficult to come to a definitive solution.[25]

Return to Foot Patrol

Police officers on motorized patrols are more efficient than foot officers. Cars get to locations much more quickly, they can cover much larger areas, and they provide the officers more comfort in inclement weather. Cars also allow the transport of all the equipment that officers of today have in their arsenals. However, as we have seen, some police managers and other experts feel that automobile patrolling has led to a distancing of police officers from the community that they serve.

In the mid-1980s, in an attempt to get the police closer to the public and to avoid the problems caused by the alienation of radio car officers from the community, an emphasis on foot patrol began to return. By 1985, foot patrol had been reinstituted in many cities, and approximately two-thirds of medium-sized and large police departments used foot patrol in some form. Researchers arrived at the following conclusions about the reinstitution of foot patrol in Newark, New Jersey, and Flint, Michigan:

- When foot patrol is added in neighborhoods, levels of fear decrease significantly.

- When foot patrol is withdrawn from neighborhoods, levels of fear increase significantly.
- Citizen satisfaction with police increases when foot patrol is added in neighborhoods.
- Police who patrol on foot have a greater appreciation for the values of the neighborhood residents than do police who patrol the same area in automobiles.
- Police who patrol on foot have greater job satisfaction, less fear, and higher morale than do officers who patrol in automobiles.[26]

A thorough study conducted in Newark regarding foot patrols was unable to demonstrate that either adding or removing foot patrols affected crime in any way. However, Newark citizens involved in this study were less fearful of crime and more satisfied with services provided by officers on foot patrol than services by officers on motorized patrol. Also, Newark citizens in this study were aware of additions and deletions of foot patrol from their neighborhoods, in contrast with the Kansas City study, where citizens did not perceive changes in the level of motorized patrol. Thus, the **Newark foot patrol study** does not prove that foot patrols reduce crime but, rather, that foot patrols actually make citizens feel safer. Experience indicates that citizens want to see a return to the old "cop on the beat."[27]

When a similar foot patrol study was conducted in Flint, residents believed the police on foot patrol were more responsive to their needs than had been the case before the experimental program. Interviews over a four-year period disclosed that the Neighborhood Patrol program improved relationships between the police and the community.[28]

Citizens want and like foot patrol officers. Why does this more expensive form of policing seem to be more effective than the traditional radio car patrol? It is not necessarily the implementation of foot patrol itself but, rather, the relationship that develops between the officer and the community because of the officer's increased accessibility. Through relationships with the community members, the officer feels like a part of the community and will work to address the true underlying issues affecting the community, and the citizens experience an

Newark foot patrol study A study conducted to determine the effectiveness of foot patrol officers in preventing crime.

improved sense of safety when they feel they can trust their police officers.

Recently, Philadelphia added some support to the effectiveness of implementing foot patrol. The department stressed foot patrol, setting up small, 6- to 10-block beats, in its efforts to target high-crime neighborhoods in the city. After several months, the agency noted a decrease in shootings and the overall crime rate. The success of this endeavor won the officers over to the idea, and since then they have worked even harder to strengthen their relationships with the community.[29]

Patrol Innovations: Working Smarter

The various patrol studies and the resulting challenges to long-term beliefs regarding policing in general and patrol in particular have caused law enforcement to examine traditional ways of doing things. If random patrol produces no real benefit, how can that time be better spent? Is there another type of patrol activity that might prove to be more productive? If responding immediately and in emergency mode is not necessarily beneficial, how can we organize our response so that it will be appropriate to the call for service and reduce the potential danger to the officer and the public? Can we combine these issues and come up with blocks of time that can be better spent in other ways in an effort to address crime problems? The answers to these questions are especially critical given the current economic challenges and the fact that law enforcement has to do more with much less.

In the overall realization that the crime problem is not entirely under the control of law enforcement, the importance of involving the community in the crime-fighting effort has become clear. Much of the police role involves order maintenance and service activities. Developing a partnership and a working relationship with the community can help address these issues and make the law enforcement mission

successful. This is the driving force behind community policing, which will be more thoroughly discussed in Chapter 12.

Evidence-Based Policing

The revelation that some experimentation could be conducted and could possibly challenge long-held beliefs led some researchers to stress that using scientific research could provide great information for improving police response to and tactics in various situations. To the extent that relevant scientific research can be conducted without endangering the community or raising ethical issues, it could provide an excellent scientific basis for future activities and programs.

Noted criminologist Lawrence W. Sherman, who proposed this concept in 1998, called this approach **evidence-based policing** (*evidence* refers to scientific evidence, not criminal evidence). Sherman defines this type of policing as "the use of the best available research on the outcomes of police work to implement guidelines and evaluate agencies, units, and officers." To successfully make use of evidence-based policing, departments will have to let go of the traditional wisdom that has become part of department history and be willing to deviate from "the way we've always done it." Sherman recommends that departments access the "best practices" from the literature and adapt them to their specific laws, policies, and communities. He then advocates monitoring and evaluating the projects to determine if they are working and if they can be improved. The sharing of the information with other agencies will continue to add to the knowledge available.[30]

Predictive Policing

Predictive policing is the application of analytical techniques to identify targets for police attention and interaction and to prevent crime or solve past crimes. This process is sometimes referred to as forecasting. Smaller departments can accomplish this on a small scale using crime analysis, and bigger departments can address it via data analysis and statistical predictions. The more simple and conventional approach to crime analysis and investigation has led the way to the more complex "predictive analytics" that expand on the conventional method with the use of mathematical formulas to analyze larger data sets. Small departments are best served by approaching

---

evidence-based policing Using available scientific research on policing to implement crime-fighting strategies and department policies.

predictive policing The application of crime analysis, data analysis, and statistical predictions to identify targets for police attention, also called forecasting.

predictive policing in a low-cost simple manner that can aggregate and analyze small amounts of data. Large departments with a larger geographical area, more officers, and more crime would be advised to use more sophisticated analytical methods.

Predictive policing is a somewhat recent phenomenon and though it has been done on a limited basis, the practice is growing across the country. Predictive methods can be divided into four broad categories: methods for predicting crimes, methods for predicting offenders, methods for identifying offenders, and methods for predicting victims of crimes.[31]

Predictive policing strives to link various clues that data reveal to potential suspects or victims by identifying at-risk groups, individuals associated with various types of crime, and proximity to at-risk locations. After a prediction is made, the agency must implement some interventions that lead to reduced crime or solved crimes. These interventions start with simple generic intervention, then increasing in complexity to crime-specific intervention and problem-specific intervention. Many of the analysis processes that inform predictive policing have been done for many years under other names; looking at those efforts can assist in anticipating possible pitfalls and addressing them before they occur.

Before departments implement the analysis of data and proceed on a course of action, they should be aware of the strengths and weaknesses of the data and the data collection as well as understand the importance of assessing the actions taken and evaluating the results. Once an intervention or approach is implemented, departments should still be prepared and open to modifying the approach and deploying the appropriate resources. They should also be cognizant of individuals' civil rights and privacy rights, in particular as they pertain to emerging technology. It is hoped that by using predictive policing as recommended and being aware of the limitations and the potential pitfalls, agencies can work toward ensuring that predicted crime risks do not become real crimes.

Smart Policing

Smart policing is an emerging paradigm that advocates expanding on the use of an evidence base for policing with the goal of reducing crime. It was launched in 2009 with a new funding initiative from the Department of Justice, Bureau of Justice Administration (BJA).[32] Faced with significant budget reductions as a result of the recession in 2008, many law enforcement agencies stopped hiring, eliminated positions, and put equipment upgrades on hold. Some found that to cope with their demands for service with fewer personnel, they had to either stop responding to minor calls or come up with alternative ways of servicing the public. In 2009, BJA solicited for Smart Policing Initiatives (SPI), hoping that local agencies would identify effective and efficient solutions to chronic crime problems, and awarded SPIs with funding to 10 local law enforcement agencies to work with academics to develop sound methods of assessing and evaluating these initiatives.[33] The hope was that all of law enforcement would benefit from the increased understanding and innovative ideas that arose from the police–academic partnership that developed through SPI funding to address these pressing crime problems.

Smart policing builds on previous improvements in the delivery of police services and looks for innovative ideas to policing. The premise of the program is that the agencies themselves are in the best position to know their specific crime problems; thus, they are best equipped to work with researchers to examine the problems and come up with effective solutions that can be measured and evaluated.

There are currently more than 30 funded SPI projects in progress around the country. They address crimes from quality-of-life issues to gang and drug-related crime to homicide and other violent crime. The strategies researched are varied and include place-based policing, such as **hot spot** policing, and offender-based policing, which targets known offenders through deterrence programs and social support networks. Most follow the problem-solving approach and adhere to community-oriented policing ideology. Technology is often the focus of the SPI, such as uniform cameras and surveillance technology.[34]

Findings from the original 10 SPI sites awarded in 2009 seem to indicate that offender-based programs can significantly reduce violent crime (Philadelphia), as can the creative use of crime analysis together with targeted problem-solving approaches (Los Angeles).

----

smart policing A funding initiative from the Bureau of Justice Administration that partners local law enforcement agencies with academics to develop and evaluate solutions to chronic crime problems.

hot spot An area receiving a high volume of calls for service.

Data also suggests that problem-solving teams can prevent violence in chronic high crime areas (Boston) and reduce calls for service in problematic convenience stores (Glendale). Current projects are looking at body-worn cameras (Phoenix), video camera surveillance in order-maintenance areas (Pullman, Washington), links between traffic violations and vehicle crashes and other criminal activity (Shawnee, Kansas, and York, Maine), and predictive policing (Cambridge, Massachusetts, and Indio, California).[35]

The Los Angeles Smart Policing Initiative, known as Los Angeles' Strategic Extraction and Restoration (LASER) program, is particularly interesting as it incorporated both a chronic offender component and a chronic location component in some of the most violent neighborhoods in the city. Results indicated that a reduction in gun crime was significant only in neighborhoods in which both components were utilized to address the problem. The city reported a 19 percent decrease in violent crimes and attained an all-time low of 16 homicides in 2012 (compared to 36 in 2011).[36]

The assessments of these various strategies and continued research on other innovative tactics should help clarify the issue of addressing crime in the most effective and cost-efficient ways that will exist long after the fiscal challenges have subsided.

Personnel Deployment

Police have responded to the challenges of smarter deployment of personnel in several ways, including the direction given to patrol officers as well as the differential response to calls for service by the agency as a whole. These innovative approaches to policing are designed to make better use of officers' patrol time and department resources.

Directing Patrol Efforts

An alternative to random routine patrol is **directed patrol**, in which officers are given specific directions to follow when they are not responding to calls.

directed patrol Officers patrol strategically to address a specific crime problem.

split-force patrol A method in which the patrol force is split; half responds to calls for service and the other half performs directed patrol activities.

The directed patrol assignments are given to officers before they begin their tour and are meant to replace uncommitted random patrol time with specific duties that police commanders believe will be effective. Directed patrol assignments can be based on crime analysis, specific problems, or complaints received from the community. In departments using the community policing philosophy, patrol officers are often given the freedom of determining where and when their patrol efforts (often with input from the community) should be directed based on crime analysis and their experiences.

A successful example of a directed patrol program that achieved positive results was the Kansas City gun experiment. Working with the University of Maryland, the Kansas City, Missouri, Police Department focused extra directed patrol attention to gun crimes in a hot spot area that was determined by computer analysis. The goal was to determine whether vigorously enforcing gun laws could reduce gun crimes. A special unit was assigned to the area: They did not respond to radio calls, but instead removed guns from citizens following searches incident to arrest for other crimes and other valid stop-and-frisk situations. During the 29-week experiment, the gun patrol officers made thousands of car and pedestrian checks, traffic stops, and more than 600 arrests. The gun patrol efforts did affect crime rates. There was a decrease of 49 percent in gun crimes in the target area compared with a slight increase in a nontargeted area. Drive-by shootings and homicides decreased significantly. Interestingly, none of the seven contiguous beats showed a significant increase in gun crime, indicating that there was little crime displacement effect (crime being moved to another area).[37]

Community surveys conducted before and after the program was initiated indicated that citizens in the target area were less fearful of crime and more satisfied with their neighborhood than were residents in companion areas. After the extra directed patrols were ended, crime rates went back to their normal levels.

While directed patrol is designed so officers can pay particular attention to specific crimes and disorder while they are not on assignment from the police dispatcher, calls for service often interrupt the performance of directed patrol assignments. **Split-force patrol** offers a solution to this problem. One portion of the patrol force is designated to handle all calls dispatched to patrol units. The rest of the officers working that tour are given directed patrol assignments with the assurance that, except for serious emergencies, they will not be interrupted. This approach has the potential to cause resentment among the officers handling the calls for service, and it would not be a popular strategy in today's economic climate.

Hot-spot policing takes this directed response to crime problems even further. This strategy targets a particular geographic area that receives a high volume of calls for service and proactively addresses the problem. Often agencies couple these deployment techniques with various alternative patrol strategies discussed later in this chapter to most effectively reduce crime.

In 2011, the Sacramento Police Department identified 42 hot spots on street corners where the highest percentage of violent crimes was occurring. Officers were assigned to visit these locations for 15-minute periods each day and to combat crime in a highly visible, proactive manner. Results indicated a reduction in both violent and property crimes in these hot spots, and displacement was not a factor. These results were achieved without any additional funding, and thus this form of directed patrol presents itself as a cost-effective way to combat crime in the future according to the police department.[38]

Differential Response to Calls for Service and the 911 System

Differential response to calls for service abandons the traditional practice of responding to all calls for service. In differential response, responses to citizens' calls to 911 for service are matched to the importance or severity of the calls. Reports of injuries, crimes, or emergencies in progress, as well as reports of serious past crimes, continue to receive an immediate response by sworn police. However, less serious calls are handled by alternative methods. Conditions for which delayed or alternative responses are appropriate include burglaries, thefts, and vandalisms reported after the perpetrator is gone, as well as lost property and insurance reports.

Differential response alternatives can replace sending a patrol unit to investigate a past crime. A patrol unit can be sent later, when there are fewer calls for service, or the caller can be asked to come into the precinct headquarters to report the crime. In some cases, the call can be transferred to a nonsworn member, who then takes the report over the phone; in some departments, the report can be made online. Finally, the dispatcher can make an appointment for a nonsworn department member to respond to the caller's home to take a report. Differential response to calls for service is designed to reduce and better manage the workload of patrol officers. It gives patrol officers more time to devote to directed patrol, investigations, and crime prevention programs.

The idea of differential response to calls arose from the studies that looked at the value of rapid response for police officers. The program also makes sense when looking at the overall use of resources, including both personnel and equipment (such as police vehicles and fuel). Perhaps rapid response is good for police public relations— "See how fast we respond when you call!"—but the allocation of scarce patrol resources should depend on police effectiveness rather than on public relations. Research has shown that most citizens will accept explanations of alternative police responses if the explanations are politely and logically presented. Departments have different ways of presenting this information and educating the public about their policies, and the Internet has increased the available options. Some departments post their policy regarding response to 911 calls, and how and why the department prioritizes calls, on their website.

Departments suffering from financial difficulties that prevent them from hiring additional officers may benefit most from differential response. They can spread out the workload while ensuring that all emergency calls are responded to and all reports related to past crimes and incidents are recorded and investigated. They also make use of less-expensive civilian personnel, and perhaps even volunteers, in some of this report taking. By stacking nonpriority calls until the beat car is available, rather than sending an adjacent beat car immediately, a department can save gas and possibly identify a need to realign the beats if a disparity in workload becomes apparent. This will facilitate

differential response to calls for service The police response to calls for service varies according to the type and severity of the call.

using resources more effectively in the future. In addition to the benefits to the departments, citizens are not unhappy with delayed response from police departments when they are aware that there will be a delay and the rationale is explained. Many citizens find the new options, including online reporting, phone reporting, and referrals, more convenient for their busy schedules.

An example of this process is the trend for most cities to minimize the time and resources spent responding to false alarm calls. Not that long ago, law enforcement responded to every alarm that went off, whether it was one of 20 going off during a thunderstorm or at a residence with a faulty alarm system set off on a daily basis by the family pet. By legislating ordinances and working with alarm companies, most departments have been able to decrease or at least keep the number of alarm calls constant even though the use of alarm systems has risen greatly. These efforts include ordinance development, registration of alarms, graduated fine structure, new equipment standards, suspension of response to chronic abusers, and the use of enhanced call verification where the alarm company makes numerous phone calls before calling the police agency with what appears to be a needed response. In an effort to manage police resources as well as enhance officer safety (officers can develop a "false alarm" mentality that leads to injury or death on the real call), cities saw the necessity to change their response methods.[39]

The 911 system has evolved over the years to make police departments more effective and to assist their efforts to manage their resources. Traditionally, the 911 call has determined the police department priorities. When the 911 number was introduced by AT&T in 1968, the concept was very exciting. By 2000, 93 percent of all larger local law enforcement agencies participated in an enhanced 911 system where the caller's location could be identified automatically, an increase from only 57 percent in 1990.[40] Calls to 911 have skyrocketed over the years because of the promotion and advertising regarding this number. Police departments strive to educate their citizens to use 911 only in true emergencies, and that is often the first question the call takers ask the caller. Unfortunately, when someone needs help but does not know who to call, 911 is often the number the person remembers.

In the mid- to late 1990s, jurisdictions began to introduce the 311 system to relieve overburdened 911 systems. A 311 system takes some of the demand off the 911 lines and keeps them available for true emergencies by allowing nonemergency calls to be redirected to other referral or government agencies, either by citizens directly calling 311 or by 911 operators quickly rerouting the appropriate calls to 311. Baltimore and Dallas were studied to determine how the addition of a 311 system affected the 911 system as well as officer workload. The study found that when accompanied by an effective public awareness campaign, a 311 system can greatly reduce the 911 call burden by removing nonemergency calls for service or information from the queue and sending them to more appropriate agencies. In these two cities, even though the system appeared to free time for police officers, most officers did not notice an increase in discretionary time. The researchers believe the system can affect officers' free time but recommend to departments that, to have that occur, they should not have officers respond to 311 calls but simply transfer them to an alternate referral agency.[41]

Reverse 911

With the advancement in communications technology as well as the progression of mapping abilities, the use of reverse 911 systems has expanded. This type of system allows police departments to call citizens in the entire jurisdiction or limit calls to a particular neighborhood where something is occurring. The department can disseminate emergency information to residents within minutes. Reverse 911 is a valuable tool when there are in-progress events or a pursuit or manhunt in a certain neighborhood.

The system can call the phone numbers of residents; the program also has been expanded to include cell phone numbers. The expansion of the system to cell phones was hastened by the Virginia Tech shootings, when it became apparent that such a notification system would have helped students know what was going on and respond appropriately. The program has become widespread among colleges and cities where residents sign up to receive text messages or calls about crime incidents occurring. This reverse 911 arrangement allows the community to work together with the police to solve crimes as well as to minimize injury and death to innocent bystanders. This increased public awareness allows the police to work more effectively and ultimately to better serve the public and improve the safety of their communities.

Smart911

Many jurisdictions across the country are now offering Smart911. This new system allows individuals to voluntarily register their phone numbers and enter associated personal, medical, and disability information into a secure website. When an individual calls 911 from that registered number, the additional data will display at the Public Safety Answering Point (PSAP). This will allow addresses to be linked to wireless phones that previously had no address information attached. This technology will become increasingly important as more people do away with their landlines.

This can help first responders provide service more quickly and more effectively based on the information individuals have chosen to provide. For example, medical conditions will help responders when the person needing help can't communicate. Citizens create their own "safety profile" on the Smart911 website and can choose to enter their vehicle description, the number of people in the house, work and school addresses, or whatever information they feel would help when they need emergency assistance. Photos can be attached, which could help in a situation of a missing child or a person with Alzheimer's. Knowing how many people reside in a house—and, in particular, the number of children—would be helpful in a fire department response. It can also expedite response: Responders can know what type of car to look for when they get GPS information and know a location to head to when GPS information is hard to get. Smart911 can also let public safety personnel know if another language is spoken, so they can expedite arrangements to bring the appropriate translators to the call.

This service is backed by public safety personnel, community organizations, and municipalities, and the cost is born by local municipalities. There is no cost to the individual subscriber. Though not all 911 centers are currently able to utilize this profile, as their equipment gets updated they will be. Public safety is encouraging the registration of this information even if local 911 centers aren't yet using it, as it will be helpful when traveling. The Smart911 website provides all the information about the services as well as a place to enter your zip code to see if and where it is used in your area. The site will prompt registered individuals to verify their information every six months or the information will be deleted.[42]

Allocation of Resources

Considerations in the allocation of resources revolve around personnel, including the scheduling of officers, and the use of vehicles.

Personnel

Personnel are the most expensive part of a police department's budget. In this day of shrinking budgets, agencies must allocate their personnel in the most efficient way possible and consider nontraditional ways of doing things. Most departments have reexamined their roles and tasks and are questioning whether certain jobs need to be done, how they might be better done—for example, over the phone or online—and who should do them. Many departments have increased their use of civilians for nonhazardous jobs such as evidence technician, accident investigator, property technician, call taker, and front desk attendant. This allows the sworn officers to be used for the more hazardous duties and puts more officers on the street in an effort to combat crime and keep the residents safe.

Scheduling officers is also a big issue. Departments do not want to have too many officers on duty at one time so they are climbing all over each other to respond to calls, nor do they want to be understaffed should a significant emergency occur. Unfortunately, law enforcement is a very unpredictable field. It can be extremely quiet and boring one minute, but in the second it takes for an alert tone to come over the radio, the day or night can become crazy. Scheduling is especially important if the department wants to conduct directed patrol activities to address certain crime problems.

Traditionally, departments used equal staffing for every shift. In other words, there were 10 officers on days, 10 officers on evenings, and 10 officers on midnights. Officers and administrators alike knew the workload was not the same, but it was difficult to quantify before computers. Now there is plenty of data available as long as departments know how to collect it and analyze it. Departments can determine workload by types of calls and areas of the city, which can help them design beats or zones so that the workload is more evenly divided between officers. Departments also can determine what kinds of calls are happening at what hours of the day, how much time particular calls take, and whether they can be handled by one officer, two officers, or perhaps even more.

A zone or beat with a big mall in it might be extremely busy during the day with shoplifter calls, stolen vehicles, vehicle burglaries, robberies, and so on. This might require one, two, or even three officers during certain hours of the day. During the midnight shift, the mall area could be made part of another zone or handled by an officer who is also handling the adjacent zone. Likewise, in certain areas of town, the calls for service will increase significantly at night because of local drinking establishments, people hanging out on the street, or gang activity. These beats or zones may require more than one car or possibly two-officer cars.

Departments also have instituted staggered shift changes and briefings. Besides the obvious issue of the criminal element quickly figuring out when shift changes occur by seeing all the patrol cars heading in at the end of a shift, there is also the issue of responding to emergency calls that come in around shift changes. How this situation is handled will affect the overtime budget and personnel costs. If the patrol cars are all close to or in the station when a call comes in, for example, 20 minutes before a shift change, the response time will be delayed even if a car responds immediately. In addition, the determination has to be made of who should handle the call. Should an officer who is getting off be held over to handle it on overtime, should an oncoming unit be sent out early, or should the call be held for the oncoming beat car after briefing? If several calls come in, conceivably most of the units from a new shift could be tied up as soon as they hit the street. By staggering shifts and briefings for half the force by an hour, these problems can be solved. Cars will be scattered around the city to respond to emergencies, overtime costs can be minimized, and oncoming units will not be immediately tied up with calls. In the past, conducting more than one briefing per shift was more of a concern, but with the use of computers and mobile digital terminals, this concern is now lessened because officers can brief themselves if necessary.

In general, officers working the day and evening shifts are going to have more time devoted to calls for service and little "free time" in which to conduct activity aimed at discovering suspicious activity or individuals. During the midnight shift when most residents are asleep, there will be far fewer calls for service received through dispatch and much more officer-initiated activity as officers drive their beats looking for suspicious activity, checking on businesses, and so forth. These officer-initiated activities, however, also frequently involve arrests that can keep an officer tied up for several hours on paperwork and possibly transporting prisoners. Cities that want officers to conduct proactive efforts need to make sure enough people are working so that there is enough discretionary time for officers to make such efforts.

A city that correctly analyzes all the data will have a better working knowledge of how many officers are needed per shift and by the day of the week. The issue is very complicated, however, because this information and these needs must be tempered by proper or humane work schedules and contract or collective bargaining restrictions. If officers like particular shifts—say the 12-hour shift—they will often try to get it in the union contract so that it cannot be changed arbitrarily.

Another issue to contend with is how officers choose their schedules. Is it by seniority, where perhaps the most senior officers all end up working days with weekends off and all rookies work midnights on the weekends? Should officers work fixed schedules for a certain amount of time (for example, midnight shift with Sunday, Monday, and Tuesday off for six months) or should squads rotate together (work a month of days followed by a month of midnights) in an effort to make the schedules more fair?

Scheduling of personnel is very challenging, with many competing factors to be considered. Studies are being conducted to look at the health ramifications of shift work in general and whether it is better to rotate forward or backward, or to have two days or three days off. But in a 24/7 service such as law enforcement, there is no getting around the fact that all shifts must be appropriately covered. Fortunately, computer programs and models can now accommodate 8-, 10-, and 12-hour shifts to help administrators with this task.

Vehicles

Most departments use fleet vehicles—that is, patrol vehicles that are used by different officers around the clock. This allows the jurisdiction to get the most use of its vehicles and have the fewest number of vehicles needed to patrol the streets. This system is viewed as an efficient use of resources when all officers report to the same location for the start and end of their shifts. However, agencies that cover a bigger geographical area, such as sheriffs' departments and state patrols, often find this system impractical. They issue officers their own vehicles, which the officers then take home with them at the end of every shift. This allows officers to go into service from their homes and start responding to calls immediately. Officers also have all of their equipment already loaded and stowed in the vehicle. The vehicle loading and inspection time is greatly reduced for these officers, and their in-service time is maximized.

Some cities with a central shift change area have also looked at and implemented take-home vehicle plans. Although initially significantly more expensive than fleet programs, these patrol vehicles last longer because they receive less wear and tear that comes from 24-hour usage. It is also believed that officers take better care of these vehicles when they are "theirs"; they maintain them well and drive them more carefully. Added incentives for cities to undertake such programs are the ability to attract quality candidates with the lure of the extra benefit of a take-home vehicle and the increased police visibility while these vehicles are driven around town, to and from work, and parked in neighborhoods. Some also believe there might be a benefit in improved community relations as citizens see their officers (with vehicles) at the park running the fitness trail or coaching a Little League team and realize officers are just like everyone else and are actually part of the community.

The allocation of police vehicles is a significant part of the police budget and, consequently, how to best accomplish this task is a big decision. Motor vehicles are a major part of most police departments' operations, so many policies and procedures govern usage and maintenance of the vehicles, regardless of which plan the department may elect to follow.

Alternative Strategies

Police departments use varying strategies to combat the crime problem. These include tactical operations, Specialized Policing Responses, decoy vehicles, and the deployment of various types of vehicles for patrol.

Tactical Operations

Tactical operations involve the use of traditional patrol operations in a more aggressive manner. The two basic kinds of tactical operations are aggressive patrol tactics and saturation patrol. Tactical units are made up of officers who are relieved of routine patrol responsibilities, such as random routine patrol and handling calls for service, so they can concentrate on proactive crime control. They often saturate an area that is experiencing a serious crime problem. The tactical units are proactive and make numerous pedestrian and vehicle stops to increase the likelihood of encountering offenders. These officers are often in full uniform but may be in a tactical uniform or in plain clothes, depending on the situation.

These specially assigned officers make numerous field interrogations. A field interrogation or interview is a contact with a citizen initiated by a patrol officer who stops, questions, and sometimes searches a citizen because the officer has reasonable suspicion that the subject may have committed, may be committing, or may be about to commit a crime. These contacts are valuable because they let law enforcement know who was present in a given area at a given time and who may be a suspect if a crime is discovered. They also let the people contacted know the police are aware of their presence, which may deter them from committing illegal acts.

A study in San Diego tested the effects of field interrogations. In this study, field interrogation activity was suspended for nine months in one experimental area but maintained at normal levels in two control areas. Crime in the area where field interrogations were suspended increased by a substantial amount, but it remained about the same in the control areas where field interrogations continued to be used. With the resumption of field interview activity in the experimental area, crime decreased to about the same level it had been before the experiment.[43]

Some bigger cities have large tactical units able to heavily patrol many areas of the city, but most departments have smaller tactical units that may be full time or may be assembled on a temporary basis in response to a particular crime problem. Typically, these units work flexible schedules and employ varying techniques, depending on the particular problem they are addressing.

AGGRESSIVE PATROL Aggressive patrol tactics are sometimes used in high-crime areas to stop people and vehicles in an attempt to find evidence that they may have committed a crime or may be committing a crime. Aggressive patrol tactics using field interrogations can be very effective in reducing crime. However, they often cause problems with the community because of their potential for abusing citizens' rights.

Many claim that the drastic drop in crime rates in the mid-1990s, particularly in cities like New York, was the result of aggressive, zero-tolerance anticrime policies. During this period, New York City's crime rates dropped to 30-year lows under the administration of Police Commissioner William J. Bratton. As part of his crime-fighting strategy, he ordered his officers to crack down on such minor offenses as public urination, loitering, loud radios, and unlicensed street vending to improve the city's quality of life. He told his uniformed street officers to resume making low-level drug arrests and not leave them to specialized units, which the NYPD had done for many years for fear of corruption scandals. Under his policies, all minor offenders were frisked for guns and checked for outstanding warrants. Computer-plotted maps were made daily to track crime in every block in the city. Bratton said, "I want to challenge the old idea that policing can't make a substantial impact on social change. American policing has been swatting at mosquitoes for 20 years. In New York we've learned how to drain the swamp."[44]

In growing numbers, police executives are convinced that effective policing can decrease crime, and even a growing cohort of criminologists is conceding that police work was responsible for the notable decline in crime throughout the 1990s and early 2000s. Nationwide, there are clear signs of departments reorganizing and implementing anticrime strategies and targeting and attacking problems.

The evidence seems to suggest that proactive, aggressive police strategies are effective in reducing crime, at least in target areas. However, many claim that these patrol tactics breed resentment in minority areas; citizens there often believe they are the target of police suspicion and reaction. This leads to a serious conflict for police administrators. Do they reduce crime rates by using effective yet aggressive police techniques and thereby risk poor relationships with lawful members of the community? In addition, despite the credit paid to the police in reducing crime, many criminologists and other students of crime and criminal justice point to other possible reasons for crime reduction, including the aging of the criminal-prone population, increased prison and jail populations, and increased commitment of community groups in addressing crime conditions.

SATURATION PATROL Another kind of tactical operation is **saturation patrol**. When this type of patrol is used, a larger number of uniformed officers than normal is assigned to a particular area to deal with a particular crime problem. A program in Jersey City, New Jersey, examined by Weisburg and Green in 1995 found that drug trafficking was reduced, rather than merely displaced, with a neighborhood crackdown coupled with police surveillance in high-crime and drug-trafficking locations.[45]

In 2007, faced with an increasing violent crime rate in Washington, D.C., Chief Cathy Lanier employed an aggressive saturation patrol operation called All Hands on Deck. The goal of the operation was to increase police presence during concentrated time periods to deter crime and improve community relations. Administrative and desk officers were added to the patrol force for a total of 3,500 officers on the street on selected weekends. Results were positive, particularly one weekend when the city had no shootings, which was a significant accomplishment. That was the fifth weekend of saturation patrol activity that year, and violent crime dropped sharply over the weekend. Police made more than 400 arrests and seized $94,000 in cash and $52,000 worth of drugs. This number of arrests was in fact fewer than they had made on other All Hands on Deck weekends, but it was noteworthy due to the lack of shootings and homicides.[46]

The saturation patrol weekends in Washington, D.C., have continued despite an arbitrator's ruling in 2009 that this practice violates the union contract. To supplement the officer numbers, the department now draws from recruits in the police academy. After seven years in operation, this program has produced mixed results. In addition to resistance from the police union, opinions from the community have varied in regard to whether the program is effective. Most citizens like seeing the extra police officers out during an operation but are concerned it is just a temporary fix. They would prefer to see more officers on the street all of the time.[47]

saturation patrol Assigning a larger number of uniformed officers than normal to an area to deal with a particular crime problem.

A more specific type of saturation patrol is a **crackdown**, which generally targets a specific violation of the law. Although these crackdowns can focus on crimes such as drugs or prostitution, they may, depending on the organization and the needs of the community, be used for traffic violations such as speeding, seat belt violations, construction zone violations, and impaired driving.

Nationwide, police agencies continue to consider saturation patrols as an option in addressing problems such as narcotics, robberies, burglaries, and auto thefts in an effort to make arrests and deter criminal activity.

Specialized Policing Responses to Individuals with Mental Illness

The issue of mental illness in the population, how society in general is providing for these individuals, and, more specifically, how law enforcement is responding to calls involving the mentally ill has become a major issue. For the last few decades our nation has failed the mentally ill after shutting down many mental institutions and reducing the availability of community mental health programs. This has led to an increase in untreated mentally ill people living on the streets or in the community with loved ones. Police officers now come into contact with mentally ill people on a more frequent basis, often when they are in crisis and out of control. This has resulted in some tragic incidents. These tragedies have led to outrage by both the community and law enforcement; these groups have begun to come together to address the issue of the mentally ill population and attempt to come up with a solution to keep more tragedies from happening. Some communities have come up with some very innovative responses.

Specialized Policing Responses (SPRs) to the mentally ill population involve training responders in crisis de-escalation and prioritizing treatment over incarceration in order to improve the outcomes in these encounters.[48] These responses tailor specifics to the local community depending on its unique needs, resources, and limitations. The responses vary depending on whether the community is rural or urban, if the community has a high percentage of homeless people, and the resources and facilities the community has available. The process starts with comprehensive planning, involving a wide variety of stakeholders.

Two predominant models of these SPRs include the Crisis Intervention Team (CIT) and the co-responder model. The first law enforcement-based CIT program was started in Memphis, Tennessee, in 1988 after an officer killed a person with mental illness. This strategy was designed to improve safety during these encounters by arming officers with de-escalation techniques and providing community alternatives to incarceration. Los Angeles and San Diego use the co-responder model, in which officers and treatment professionals respond together to calls for service in an effort to connect the mentally ill individuals more effectively with community-based treatment. Many jurisdictions around the country use these two models or versions of them with adjustments made to better match their community needs.

Some agencies have developed programs using aspects of both approaches. The Houston Police Department instituted a program in 2007 that overhauled how they dealt with mentally ill people after some police encounters ended tragically. Their program is often held up as a model as it combines a CIT program with a co-responder program, called the Crisis Intervention Response Team (CIRT), which partners a police officer and a licensed mental health professional. The vast majority of calls related to individuals with mental illnesses are handled by CIRT officers.[49]

The King County Sheriff's Office in Washington has taken response to another level: They focus on the individual as well as the response through their RADAR program. The office identifies individuals at risk for future contacts and encourages voluntary sharing of information during a noncrisis time that will follow the individual regardless of where he or she is in the area and facilitate the most appropriate response by law enforcement. The more information officers have, the more options they have in responding to future incidents and the less likely they will have to respond to a situation with force.

All jurisdictions working on this problem and implementing the various solutions hope to contribute to solving this raging problem of untreated individuals roaming the streets without the help they

crackdown An enforcement effort targeting a specific violation of the law.

Specialized Policing Responses (SPRs) A tailored law enforcement response to individuals with mental illness that involves trained first responders and prioritizes crisis de-escalation and treatment over arrest and incarceration.

RADAR at the King County Sheriff's Office

"Come quick! Someone's fighting, there's blood everywhere…the male has a knife…a female is outside with cuts to her hand…barricaded subject with a hostage"

- King County Sheriff's Office (KCSO) dispatch relaying information to responding deputies

"There may be a loaded rifle in the house"… "Drop the gun, Drop the gun!"

- KCSO Deputy Erik Soderstrom and other responding deputies speaking to each other and then screaming at an armed young man prior to taking his life

"Every call is a risk assessment… you're doing it in your head as you go there… we need more information and more options."

- KCSO Deputy Erik Soderstrom testifying at his shooting inquest

As I watched Deputy Soderstrom testify in the shooting inquest, I was reminded of how little information we have when responding to dangerous and unpredictable scenes. At the inquest we learned for the first time that in the weeks prior to his death, this now deceased young man had spoken openly to both his girlfriend and his family (what we refer to as his "circle of support"), about his paranoia of the police killing him and his preoccupation with suicide. Those who loved him had witnessed his mental health decompensate. All too often this dynamic of violence is repeated in counties and cities across our country, frequently ending in the same tragic result. Afterwards, we ask ourselves the same questions: How could this have been prevented? Why was this person not on our radar? How can we in law enforcement be better prepared to de-escalate this specific person and lessen the likelihood of use of force? If force is required, how can we best minimize the force used?

Every day, law enforcement professionals are called to America's "front porches" in times of crisis. We accept that challenge—it's what we do. But as alluded to by Deputy Soderstrom in his inquest testimony, we must do everything in our power to increase the odds of safe, properly conducted, and effective response to those in crisis. As Deputy

Soderstrom stated, when responding to an individual in crisis, "We need more information, we need more options." Our communities expect officers to perform with a high level of professionalism. Command staff has an obligation to provide our officers with the tools they need to meet these expectations. Would access to "subject-specific" de-escalation information have changed the outcome of the particular scenario that Deputy Soderstrom found himself facing? It's impossible to say for certain. However, when responding to our citizens in times of crisis, more information is always preferable to less.

We at the King County Sheriff's Office are exploring a three-pronged response to this challenge with an effort we call "RADAR" (Risk Awareness, De-escalation, and Referral). RADAR voluntarily establishes channels of communication between challenged individuals (and/or their COS) and local law enforcement who are tasked with safely and effectively responding to crisis events.

Risk awareness is achieved by identifying those members of our communities that have demonstrated an increased likelihood of being involved in a use-of-force encounter with police. The identification process may include documentation of previous use of force, assaultive behavior, threats, or complaints involving citizens with such challenges as severe or untreated mental illness, cognitive disabilities, or behavior management challenges as the result of chronic substance abuse. These individuals are brought to our attention through prior documented behavior, not their particular diagnosis.

"Subject-specific" de-escalation planning is achieved through a collaborative effort normally initiated by law enforcement to engage the subject and/or his COS in a candid conversation to identify violent behavior triggers and inhibitors. Every individual that law enforcement encounters behaves in his or her own distinctive manner. Our de-escalation approach is based on research that indicates that "people's pre-existing views (of police) shape their perceptions of future encounters." It is our responsibility as community caretakers to put forth the time and effort required to build trusting and empathetic relationships with these behaviorally challenged individuals and reshape negative preexisting views into positive ones.

A *referral* is the real-time sharing of risk aware-ness and de-escalation planning information with other law enforcement and aid personnel. This is achieved via a web-based IT system that allows selected first responders and dispatchers immedi-ate access to preplanned, cooperatively designed, subject-specific de-escalation strategies. Unlike typ-ical sterile information sharing systems, RADAR is a dynamic platform designed to allow first respond-ers the ability to share timely and subject-specific de-escalation information among themselves. RADAR becomes a force multiplier in terms of build-ing and sharing positive interpersonal relationships between the challenged individual, the COS, and law enforcement. These relationships are built on a foundation of trust and empathy—one officer, one contact at a time.

Through outreach by both conventional and social media, RADAR is encouraging families and loved ones of our challenged populations to step forward and work with local law enforcement to break through natural tensions and demystify each other's role in addressing a crisis event.

Deputy Soderstrom voiced the need for more information and more options. We believe RADAR is the right tool to meet those needs.

Captain Scott D. Strathy
King County Sheriff's Office
Shoreline, Washington

need. Hopefully, the attention these efforts are raising around the country will result in preventing future tragedies like the movie theater shooter in Colorado, the Sandy Hook Elementary School shooter, the Café Racer killer in Seattle, the Naval Yard shooter in Washington, D.C., or the woman shot by police after trying to ram the barricades by the White House.

Decoy Vehicles

Although individuals have been used as decoys for years, typically by investigations units but some-times by and with the assistance of patrol, another type of decoy operation has also been used with success and involves no danger to officers. Its pri-mary goal is preventing crime violations, rather than catching criminals. This decoy operation, which involves using unoccupied marked police vehicles in strategic locations to give the perception of omni-presence, has been used successfully to address less serious but demanding crime problems and traffic violations in the least resource-intensive way.

Police agencies may park a marked vehicle on a roadside where there is a problem with speeding. Drivers see the unit in the distance and slow down. Even if they see that the vehicle is unoccupied, it serves as a reminder that it could have been occupied and they could have gotten a ticket. This technique helps drivers become more aware of their driving habits, slows them down, increases awareness, and educates drivers, much like the portable radar devices that post the speed limit and show drivers their speed. It allows police agencies to address traffic problems without tying up an officer for extended periods.

This idea can be and has been expanded upon. When faced with numerous and persistent "smash and grabs" at exclusive women's clothing stores, the Boca Raton, Florida, Police Department had a problem. There was no discernible pattern to these burglaries, which were occurring throughout Dade, Broward, and Palm Beach counties, yet store own-ers were outraged by repeated victimization that occurred over many months. With a limited num-ber of midnight shift officers, many square miles of territory, and a high number of women's clothing stores, the police department had to come up with a method to address this problem and reassure the community that they considered it a priority. They started parking unoccupied marked vehicles in front of some of the more vulnerable targets. The hope was that the offender driving on the main roadways looking for a target would bypass these stores, think-ing that there was an officer in the car, in the store, or in the area. Unfortunately, as is common with law enforcement efforts at crime prevention, it was dif-ficult to measure success. However, businesses with police vehicles in the area were not broken into and store owners appreciated police efforts.

Although this decoy strategy alone would not solve all crimes, in this instance if a surveil-lance effort were put into effect at the remaining stores, the criminals might be displaced to those

GUEST LECTURE

Photo courtesy of Chief John Lekan, Yuma Police Department

CLAUDIA LEYVA

Claudia Leyva is a lieutenant with the Yuma, Arizona, Police Department. She has been with the department for 20 years, spending 8 years working gang investigations. She is currently working as a patrol bureau watch commander. She graduated as a dean's scholar from the 115th Administrative Officer's Course at Southern Police Institute.

GANG INVESTIGATION

Gang investigations were handed over to me soon after I became a detective. It was an assignment no one really wanted, including me. I quickly learned these types of cases could be time-consuming and challenging. I didn't have enough seniority to be a homicide detective but soon found that gang investigations were going to bring a wide variety of cases my way, including high-profile cases. I worked graffiti cases, assault cases, and narcotics cases, as well as shootings and stabbings. The assignment that nobody wanted and the one that I was unsure of soon became one I was grateful to have.

A simple case can be magnified in complexity once you determine that more than one gang member participated in the event. In a nongang case, you usually have a victim and a suspect. The victim reports the circumstances of how he or she was victimized, and when the suspect is located, we try to get his or her version of the events, with the goal of developing probable cause for an arrest.

In a gang-related investigation, there are often two or more opposing groups involved in an offense in an attempt to promote their gangs. Generally, we call the group on the losing end of the incident the "victims," but there may not be any true victims in gang-related cases. These "victims" won't readily report all the circumstances surrounding their "victimization," even if they are lying in pools of their own blood. They may give us bits and pieces of the facts but rarely tell us everything up front. Often they aren't forthcoming because they have committed a crime themselves, during the event or in the past, to contribute to the gang rivalry.

The next step is usually trying to find a witness. We try to find one who is not afraid of retaliation, one who will tell us what the

establishments, and arrests could result. At the very least, it was a preventive technique for the businesses and led to displacement of the crime to another area or town. Unfortunately, as with "target-hardening" prevention techniques, sometimes this is all we can hope to accomplish.

Alternative Vehicle Deployment

Although most police patrol today is performed by uniformed officers in radio-equipped patrol cars or on foot, police also patrol on motorcycles, scooters, boats, planes, helicopters, horses, and bicycles. Some patrol in golf carts or all-terrain vehicles, and in 1997, the city of Philadelphia actually started a patrol unit using officers on in-line roller skates.[50] In 2003, many police departments began experimenting with patrols using the battery-operated self-balancing vehicle, the Segway.[51] Departments have been willing to explore new ways of providing their

services, especially methods that will assist them in being among the people, responding more quickly, and, in this time of escalating fuel costs, saving money on the cost of fuel.

A 2003 article explains the versatility of certain specialized vehicles for patrol:

- The police motorcycle's maneuverability and acceleration make it ideal for traffic enforcement, escort details, and crowd control.

- Bicycles are quiet and efficient and provide a bridge between motorized vehicles and foot patrol. They provide efficient transportation to areas that are normally available only by walking, such as parks, public housing developments with limited street access, tourist areas, college campuses, business plazas, and sports arenas.

- Electric bikes provide all of the advantages of the pedal bicycle but require less physical effort by the rider.

"victim" wouldn't. We hope to learn enough about the incident to lead us to the suspects. During the course of identifying and interviewing everyone, we often learn new information that will necessitate reinterviewing everyone. This sometimes happens more than once, which helps to explain why these cases are so time-consuming and complicated.

In a simple nongang-related case, we may need to obtain and serve a search warrant on a home or vehicle. In a gang case, however, the number of search warrants to be served is multiplied by the number of suspects and "victims." Because the "victims" in these cases are often suspects as well, properly articulated search warrants could grant us access to all participants' homes in search of gang indicia and any other evidence of the crime. This part of the case contributes to its complexity but also can be invaluable, especially when evidence of other crimes, such as narcotics or stolen property, is found.

During the course of one case, I wrote an affidavit for search warrants on 21 homes. It took two days and the assistance of more than 70 officers from many different law enforcement agencies in the area to carry out these warrants. This action, however, made my case, and I was also happy with the message sent to the citizens, making it clear that we were addressing the widespread gang issue.

In another case, my coworkers and I were at a home serving a warrant and were amazed to find graffiti carved into furniture and painted or marked on items throughout the house. It was difficult for me to understand why gang members would do that to their own home. I saw two toddlers playing with a toy covered in graffiti and noticed a three-dot tattoo on the mother's hand and a teardrop tattoo on her face. I then realized just how challenging the fight would be. How could we make a gang member believe the gang lifestyle was wrong when family members lived it and accepted it? And when would we be dealing with those toddlers as gang members?

Gang investigations are complicated and challenging. Being a female investigator dealing mostly with young Hispanic males was part of the challenge. I was able to use the situation to my advantage by getting them to identify with me as their sister, aunt, or even mother. I had some successes in getting the bad guys off the streets and some successes in luring young people away from the gang lifestyle. On the bad days, it was those successes that motivated me to continue my efforts and to be grateful for the assignment.

Source: Reprinted by permission of Claudia Leyva.

- Scooters are more maneuverable than cars, yet offer many of the features of a car in a compact space. They also may provide shelter from the weather and enable officers to carry more equipment than bicycles do. They are especially suited for parking enforcement and specialized patrol on college campuses and business premises.

- Multiterrain vehicles are useful when officers are required to travel into remote areas such as mountains and beaches. Their low-pressure, high-flotation tires, motorcycle-type engines, and handlebar steering provide maneuverability in traversing rough terrain. They can often be used for search and rescue missions.

- Mobile substations or precincts can be driven to a specific area to provide a base of operations for beat officers and to facilitate community interaction. They can function as self-contained

community policing headquarters and be used in daily community policing programs. They can also be used as a command center at the scene of a crime or disaster.[52]

A common method of transportation used by police officers in many different jurisdictions around the country is the **bike patrol**. It is hard to imagine that as recently as two decades ago, police officers were rarely seen on bicycles. Now there are bicycle "police packages" recommended for officers using bikes to patrol, and training programs are conducted around the country to teach new bike officers techniques for policing and ways to stay safe.

The bicycle patrol movement is believed to have started in 1987, when former Seattle police officer

bike patrol Officers patrol an assigned area on bicycle rather than in a patrol car.

Paul Grady, sitting in traffic and unable to respond to a call, observed bike messengers weaving their way through the traffic jam to get to their destinations. He thought that mode of transportation might work for patrolling downtown and approached his commander, who approved his idea. Grady and his partner, Mike Miller, began to patrol downtown Seattle on their personal mountain bikes, and a movement was born. The idea spread quickly, and bicycle patrols are now used across the country.[53] Currently, 32 percent of municipal law enforcement agencies regularly use bicycle patrol.[54]

Bike patrols are used for congested downtown areas, major sporting events and community gatherings, beach and park properties, and even residential areas. Bicycles are very adaptable and can be moved around town on bike racks on the back of patrol vehicles. They consume no fuel, emit no pollution, are quiet, give the officers time to interact with the public, and can even enhance officers' fitness and health. They seem to be an ideal solution for many situations.

Bicycles also are employed by many departments in their tactical policing efforts. They are used in covert surveillance by plainclothes officers, who will have a better ability to blend in with their surroundings on bicycles. They can also prove valuable for officers in uniform, allowing them to maneuver in crowded conditions, such as parades, street fairs, and downtown streets when workers are arriving or leaving work, and to quietly and quickly approach individuals they suspect are involved in suspicious activity. Officers on the midnight shift can use bicycles to check businesses in areas where there are burglary problems. In the quiet of the early morning hours, approaching police vehicles are easily identified, but an officer on a bike can get around quickly and quietly and surprise the criminals.

As mentioned earlier in the chapter, foot patrol is a popular option for citizens and consequently police departments. It appears to make citizens feel safer and enhances the police–community relationship. Many departments believe strongly in this benefit, and in fact, in 2007, 55 percent of all municipal departments routinely used foot patrol.[55] The police–community relationship is an important part of the philosophy behind the community policing movement, which is discussed in Chapter 12.

Police Traffic Operations

Although some people may underestimate the importance of the traffic function in policing, it always ranks high as an area of concern among the public. Being able to get where you need to go in a fluid manner as well as having the confidence that drivers are driving through your neighborhood responsibly is important. Feeling safe in your vehicle as you go about your daily life is part of what defines the concept of "quality of life." Controlling the movement of vehicular traffic and enforcing the traffic laws are important activities in which the police engage.

Traffic stops are a large part of what patrol officers do. They also are a dangerous part of the job, as many officers are hurt or killed while making traffic stops. Officers do not always know what drivers have done or how they may react to a show of authority. Though most stops are for minor traffic offenses, with no indication of their being "felony" car stops, precautions still must be taken to keep everyone safe and prevent traffic stops from escalating into serious incidents.

Officers should always radio in the car stop information to the dispatcher, including the location, license plate number, vehicle description, and any other pertinent information; pick a safe location in which to pull the vehicle over; and make sure they are visible and positioned in a way as to be safe from traffic. In order to stay safe, officers must constantly be focused on the vehicle and its occupants, yet cognizant of traffic and other activity in the area. When officers pull over a vehicle believed to be involved in a felony, they intensify their protective actions by letting dispatch and other officers know the circumstances, limiting radio traffic, and waiting for a backup officer if possible.

Traffic stops are part of the mission of police departments to keep the public safe by investigating suspicious activity, enforcing traffic laws, and educating the public regarding traffic safety. Police officers are trained early in their careers on how to conduct traffic stops in a courteous and safe manner, maximizing safety and minimizing the likelihood of citizen complaints due to misunderstandings. When crash investigations are also part of a patrol or traffic officer's role, a professional, objective investigation protects the public, enforces the laws, and enhances public safety.

Although traffic stops are one of the primary tasks of patrol officers, most law enforcement agencies also have traffic units that spend time on traffic education and enforcement. The traffic unit is typically assigned to the same bureau or division as patrol, so the officers in that unit work closely with the uniformed patrol officers. Usually there are not enough traffic officers to handle all traffic incidents, but they can lend expertise and handle the more complicated and serious incidents.

Traffic incidents can place a significant demand on officers' time; consequently, departments are always exploring better ways of handling them as well as ways to prevent incidents from occurring. Working with city departments to improve traffic engineering and signage can help prevent accidents, and working with the public information office, if there is one, or community groups directly to educate the public can also help to reduce accidents. Using new techniques and equipment to address traffic issues can make things work more smoothly and efficiently.

The International Association of Chiefs of Police (IACP) realizes the importance of the traffic function as well as the importance of sharing information among police agencies. The IACP has a Highway Safety Committee that works closely with the National Highway Traffic Safety Administration (NHTSA) and offers numerous publications. An article by the chair of the IACP Highway Safety Committee addressing the top 10 trends in traffic enforcement provided the following list of concerns for law enforcement in 2005:

- *Speed enforcement.* Speed is involved in one of every three fatalities in the United States.
- *Dangerous work zones.* Every year, highway workers are needlessly killed or injured because of inattentive drivers.
- *Fatigued or distracted drivers.* Many drivers are sleep deprived, and many others are multitasking—using driving time to talk on cell phones, read the paper, put on lipstick, or eat chili dogs. Part of the effort to reduce this problem includes keeping rest areas safe with high-visibility patrol, so drivers view them as an alternative when tired.
- *Sleep-deprived officers.* Because of court appearances, overtime, and extra jobs, police officers are often sleep deprived. Combating this

problem would include policies and procedures restricting the amount of overtime officers can work.

- *Safer traffic stops.* Many officers are injured or killed while writing citations, speaking with drivers, or working accidents. Departments must educate officers in the newest techniques to minimize their chances of being hurt.
- *New laws and tactics.* Keeping up to date on court decisions and the newest techniques and procedures for safe and legal enforcement is challenging and time-consuming.
- *New types of vehicles.* Hybrids and electric vehicles pose new safety concerns.
- *Drugged drivers.* A significant number of drivers that police encounter are under the influence of drugs or alcohol. Departments should have an adequate number of officers certified as drug recognition experts (DREs).
- *Traffic officers and homeland security.* Officers must know how to recognize suspicious activities or information while on traffic stops.
- *Incident clearance.* Interdisciplinary traffic teams should be formed with all agencies involved in traffic incidents in order to develop protocols for responding quickly and effectively and minimizing the disruption to the public.[56]

The proliferation of cars, motorcycles, and trucks in the United States has been accompanied by a tremendous number of traffic fatalities, injuries, and property damage. In 2012, there were 33,561 traffic fatalities, an increase of 3.3 percent from 2011. The fatality rate for 2012 was 1.13 fatalities per 100 million vehicle miles traveled (VMT), up from a historic low 1.10 fatalities per 100 million VMT in 2011. The NHTSA attributes the decrease in traffic fatalities to the safety features in cars and to the use of seat belts. Currently, the NHTSA estimates seat belt compliance to be over 85 percent nationwide.[57]

States have enacted numerous laws dealing with vehicle use, and it falls upon the police to enforce those laws. Police investigate accidents and identify their causes, identify traffic hazards and attempt to neutralize them, and strive to educate the public. States and police agencies use the statistics that the NHTSA gathers to determine where their efforts would best be directed. The effort in many states is on seat belt enforcement, as the data indicate that increased seat belt usage can decrease the number of fatalities. The state of Washington highly publicizes its "Click It or Ticket" campaign to increase public awareness of the penalty for violating the law and to let the public know that seal belt use is a priority.

In recent years, states have changed their laws regarding new drivers after being frustrated by the high numbers of unnecessary deaths among teen drivers. Most states have various forms of graduated licensing, which restricts the hours that teen drivers can operate a motor vehicle as well as placing restrictions on who and how many people may be in the vehicle with a new driver. Efforts in this area appear to be paying off.

Recently, in an effort to do more with less and to enhance traffic safety in a time of staffing challenges, some jurisdictions have allowed volunteers to use radar guns. There are regulations governing this usage, such as operating in groups of at least two or three and being associated with a homeowners' group. These volunteers set up a highly visible presence and monitor traffic speed. They are not allowed to issue citations, but letters can be mailed to the owners of the vehicles. The goal is public education and increasing voluntary compliance, which increases traffic safety.

Video Camera Traffic Enforcement

Taking traffic surveillance a step further, some agencies are employing the use of **red light cameras** and, on occasion, cameras coupled with electronic speed monitoring. Violators can receive citations, though generally the offenses do not go on their driving record. This is a controversial program. Although public opinion surveys repeatedly find that 75 to 80 percent of the public support red light cameras, opponents are very vocal and have concerns about the constitutionality of these cameras, as they put the violator in the position of fighting accusations from a technological device. They also view this as nothing more than a cash cow for cities needing revenue rather than a true traffic safety strategy.

red light cameras Automated cameras mounted on poles at intersections. The cameras are triggered when a vehicle enters the intersection after the light has turned red. The camera records the violation and the license plate number. A citation and the photos are sent to the owner of the vehicle along with instructions on how to pay the fine or contest the ticket.

Studies, however, seem to indicate that driver behavior changes when red light cameras are used. A study conducted in Virginia Beach examined signal violations at four intersections before cameras were installed, while they were being used, and after they were removed. Researchers found that violations more than tripled after the cameras were removed. Similar results were found in Philadelphia when a significant drop in red light violations occurred after cameras were installed.

Nevertheless, legal challenges to this form of traffic enforcement are pending around the country.[58] In fact, many cities have outlawed these cameras after their voters have rejected their use.

The Challenge of Distracted Drivers

Many states as well as the federal government have recently targeted the issue of distracted driving. This movement has been propelled by accidents and fatalities caused by drivers who are texting or talking on their cell phones, behavior that has even been referred to as the new DUI. Some studies indicate that drivers who text have even slower reaction times than drunken drivers.

The fear is that with the increasing popularity of texting and smartphone apps, crashes could reach an epidemic level. Society has become obsessed with electronic devices and can't seem to put them down. In 2011, 3,331 people died nationwide in crashes involving a distracted driver, up from 3267 in 2010. Studies indicate that though texting while driving is illegal in 39 states and the District of Columbia, almost half of adult drivers admit to texting while driving, as do 43 percent of teenagers. The hope is that additional enforcement including undercover enforcement, together with an increased interest in robust driver education programs, will be able to help curb this problem that enforcement doesn't seem to be able to control by itself.[59]

The U.S. secretary of transportation is escalating efforts to stop drivers from texting or talking on cell phones by pushing for tougher federal rules, possibly as part of a highway-funding bill. The Department of Transportation is currently funding pilot programs to ticket distracted drivers in New York and Connecticut that will be modeled after the "Click It or Ticket" campaign used to prod motorists to use safety belts. The slogan is "Phone in one

Drivers distracted by their cell phones are a serious safety issue that has led most states to legislate against cell phone use while driving.

AP Images/Jim Cole, File

hand. Ticket in the other." The programs highlight ticketing blitzes and use ads to highlight the risks of distracted driving.[60]

Efforts Against Drunk Drivers and Impaired Drivers

During the 1990s, much attention was paid to the tremendous damage done on our highways by impaired drivers, including drunk drivers. Efforts by groups such as Mothers Against Drunk Driving (MADD) and Students Against Drunk Driving (SADD) caused the police to pay particular attention to the problem. According to the NHTSA, there has been a decline in alcohol-related fatalities since 1982, the earliest year for which NHTSA has the data. This decline can be attributed to increased and high-visibility enforcement, increased sanctions, and decreased public acceptance.

Despite these efforts, the alcohol and driving issue remains a concern. In 2012, more than 10,000 people died in alcohol-impaired driving crashes, more than one every 51 minutes.[61] It can be difficult for patrol officers to deal effectively with the problem of drunk drivers, because so much of their time is occupied by other duties. To enforce the laws against DWI or DUI, the police have resorted to sobriety checkpoints.

The following describes the typical DWI checkpoint or roadblock: Officers conducting the roadblock may stop all traffic or every car after a set number, such as every fifth vehicle. After a vehicle is directed to the side of the road, an officer may request to see an operator's license, registration, and insurance card. The officer may ask several questions to observe the driver's demeanor, and if the officer detects signs of inebriation, the motorist may be directed to move the vehicle to a secondary area and submit to a roadside sobriety test or Breathalyzer test. The failure to pass either test constitutes sufficient probable cause for arrest. Police are also using saturation patrol or crackdowns to combat the drunk driving problem. Officers will saturate a predesignated area with roving police officers to monitor traffic for signs of impaired driving. They are also emphasizing speeding and seat belt violations.

Studies indicate that laws establishing administrative license revocation (ALR) have reduced alcohol-related crashes by almost 40 percent.[62] Police can continue to work with legislative bodies to implement these types of driver's license sanctions.

Recently, alcohol-monitoring ankle bracelets have been issued to DUI offenders in order to keep track of drunk driving defendants. These bracelets, which test alcohol secreted from a person's skin, are regarded as a cost-effective way to monitor individuals convicted of drunk driving or those awaiting trial.

The NHTSA supports all of these efforts to target impaired drivers. In an effort to assist departments in running saturation patrols and sobriety checkpoints, the NHTSA provides guidelines on its website and delineates the issues that need to be addressed to successfully run checkpoints.[63]

In 2006, MADD expanded its previous efforts in the DUI battle. With the approach of the holidays in December, MADD announced a new campaign in its fight against drunk driving. An integral strategy in this campaign was the push for states to enact laws requiring breath-test interlock devices in the vehicles of all those convicted of drunk driving, including first-time offenders. This device prevents the car from starting if alcohol is detected on the driver's breath. Studies have indicated that these devices can decrease repeat DUI offenses by 64 percent. Most states allow this device for repeat offenders, but New Mexico led the way in 2005 by making the interlock device mandatory for all convicted drunk drivers. Today 20 states require or highly incentivize the use of the interlock for every convicted drunk driver. As of July 2013, there were 305,000 interlocks in use compared to 100,000 in 2006 when MADD launched their campaign.[64]

The Department of Justice (DOJ) has published a guide for law enforcement to address drunk driving using the problem-oriented approach. The guide, available on the DOJ website, advocates that law enforcement personnel analyze their community's DUI problem: where and when people are drinking, who is doing the drinking, and what approach is the best to address these specifics. The most effective approach could be through legislation, enforcement, training, education, sanctions, environmental design, or a combination of some or all of these techniques. Law enforcement personnel should monitor and evaluate the effectiveness of these strategies and follow up appropriately. This approach is an example of Sherman's evidence-based policing. The challenge will be in isolating the effectiveness of the various strategies independently, if that kind of information is desired.[65]

In following this advice, many states are trying some new tactics. A few states have begun to gather "last drink" data as a means of coming up with names of lounges or bars that consistently serve that last drink to people who are apparently impaired. The information goes into a database, and the state may pursue sanctions involving investigations or licensing with the biggest offenders. The state also may explore providing training to employees. The goal is to get the word out and prevent violations, thereby keeping the streets safe.

The recent legalization of recreational marijuana in Washington and Colorado as well as the previously passed legalization of medical marijuana in many states presents challenges to law enforcement trying to keep our streets safe from impaired drivers. According to Jonathan Adkins, the executive director of the Governors Highway Safety Association, this is the next big issue in highway safety.[66]

There seems to be a perception that using marijuana is no big deal, but it does in fact cause impairment. A study examining marijuana's effect on driving ability showed that the effects of marijuana affect the complex processes necessary for driving. People under the influence of marijuana tend to have trouble staying in lanes, doing multiple tasks at once, and concentrating on long drives. There isn't much definitive data yet on how this translates to crashes, and there is no agreement or data on how various amounts of marijuana in the driver's system affects driving. With drinking behavior, drinkers know how much alcohol they are ingesting; scientific evidence helped to determine the .08 standard for traffic safety in the nation. Marijuana potency varies from source to source and its impact on an individual is also variable.

At this time, officers are relying on driving behavior as the primary basis of a charge of driving under the influence. If the driver is ambulatory, officers will have the support of the roadside test. Building a strong case can be problematic and the process is ever evolving, as marijuana and its effects as well as more efficient methods of detecting the amount of tetrahydrocannabinol (THC) in the system are explored. This issue is being watched closely by law enforcement.

Fighting Aggressive Driving

Road rage has become a serious problem. People have been assaulted and even murdered in road rage incidents. Sometimes road rage takes the form of aggressive driving, and innocent people have died because of the recklessness of aggressive drivers.

Aggressive driving is not necessarily defined as a specific offense but, rather, is a combination of several violations, including speeding, tailgating, driving on the shoulder, and not signaling when changing lanes. The NHTSA defines aggressive driving as "the commission of two or more moving violations that is likely to endanger other persons or property, or any single intentional violation that requires a defensive reaction of another driver." According to the Washington State Patrol website, the state of Washington defines road rage as "an assault with a motor vehicle or other dangerous weapon by the operator or passenger(s) of one motor vehicle on the operator or passenger(s) of another motor vehicle caused by an incident that occurred on a roadway."[67]

The frustration caused by heavy traffic, traffic jams, and drivers who make errors because of inattention results in some individuals resorting to driving behavior to "get back" at the other driver. Such behavior may include passing a vehicle and then stopping suddenly or tailgating a vehicle the driver perceives as moving too slowly. If the other driver begins to adapt this behavior as well, a verbal or physical confrontation at a traffic light can result.[68]

Sometimes drivers are just frustrated with traffic and will do whatever they feel will help them move faster, such as passing cars, quickly changing lanes, or tailgating to intimidate other drivers into changing lanes. Inappropriately passing vehicles has resulted in fatal head-on crashes. Many states are targeting such aggressive driving in an effort to reduce crashes and make the roads safer.

A somewhat recent phenomenon that might be classified as a type of aggressive driving is motorcycle swarms. These have been described by some as one of the newest urban public safety threats. It involves large groups of people who take to major highways and busy streets on motorcycles for the thrill of it or to do stunts. This issue was brought to the attention of the public when the media focused on a horrific example in the fall of 2013 as one of these swarms was caught on video. A driver in an SUV was attacked and beaten with his family in the car after allegedly causing a biker to crash.

Motorcycle swarms are difficult to police as their smaller, nimbler vehicles can easily elude police. Furthermore, officers cannot use the same tactics to stop these motorcycles that they might use on other vehicles driving aggressively and threateningly to stop their progress and place them under arrest. The public finds these swarms intimidating and frightening; they impede the public's movement and in fact pose a danger or threat in many instances. Large groups of motorcyclists can materialize quickly and massively with the help of social media. States are struggling with how to curb and prevent these dangerous gatherings.

Police Automobile Pursuits

The police practice of using high-powered vehicles to chase speeding motorists, or **police pursuits**, has resulted in numerous accidents, injuries, and deaths to innocent civilians, police officers, and the pursued drivers. Geoffrey Alpert and Patrick R. Anderson characterize the police high-speed automobile pursuit as the most deadly force available to the police.

Alpert and Anderson define a high-speed pursuit as "an active attempt by a law enforcement officer operating an emergency vehicle to apprehend alleged criminals in a moving motor vehicle, when the driver of the vehicle, in an attempt to avoid apprehension, significantly increases his or her speed or takes other evasive action." They point out several possible outcomes of such a chase:

- The pursued driver stops the car and surrenders.
- The chased vehicle crashes into a structure, and the driver and occupants are apprehended, escape, are injured, or are killed.
- The chased vehicle crashes into another vehicle (with or without injuries to the driver and other occupants in the chased vehicle or another vehicle).
- The vehicle being chased strikes a pedestrian (with or without injuries or death).
- The police use some level of force to stop the pursued vehicle, including firearms, roadblocks, ramming, bumping, boxing, and so on.
- The police car crashes (with or without injuries to officers or civilians).[69]

Not all of these possible outcomes are acceptable for the police or innocent civilians.

A current debate questions whether the police should pursue fleeing vehicles, especially when such a pursuit could risk injuries to the police or innocent civilians. Certainly, no one wants officers or civilians injured. However, people on the other side of the debate say that if the police do not pursue fleeing drivers, they are sending a message to violators that they can get away with traffic violations by fleeing.

STUDIES INVOLVING POLICE PURSUITS

Studies have been conducted to determine what happens in a rapid pursuit. This information may help police administrators establish policies on rapid pursuits.

A review by the California Highway Patrol of nearly 700 pursuits on its highways during a six-month period revealed the following about the typical pursuit:

- It starts as a traffic violation.
- It occurs at night.
- It covers only a mile or so.

police pursuits The attempt by law enforcement to apprehend alleged criminals in a moving motor vehicle when the driver is trying to elude capture and increases speed or takes evasive action.

- It takes approximately two minutes to resolve.
- It involves at least two police cars.
- It ends when the pursued driver stops his or her vehicle.
- It results in the apprehension of more than three-fourths of the pursued drivers.
- It ends without an accident 70 percent of the time.

The study also revealed that drivers failed to stop for the following reasons, based on the judgment of the pursuing officer:

- To avoid an arrest for driving while intoxicated (DWI) or a drug arrest (19 percent)
- To avoid a summons for a traffic infraction (14 percent)
- Because the driver was driving a stolen vehicle (12 percent)
- To avoid an arrest for a law violation (11 percent)
- Because of unknown or miscellaneous reasons, such as the driver being afraid of the police, disliking the police, or enjoying the excitement of the chase (44 percent)[70]

The California Highway Patrol study concluded that although there are risks in high-speed pursuits, the pursuits are worth the risks:

> Attempted apprehension of motorists in violation of what appear to be minor traffic infractions is necessary for the preservation of order on the highways of California.... One can imagine what would happen if the police suddenly banned pursuits. Undoubtedly, innocent people may be injured or killed because an officer chooses to pursue a suspect, but this risk is necessary to avoid the even greater loss that would occur if law enforcement agencies were not allowed to aggressively pursue violators.[71]

Alpert and Roger G. Dunham studied 952 pursuits in Dade County, Florida, by the area's two major police departments, the Metro-Dade Police Department and the City of Miami Police Department. The researchers found that 38 percent of the pursuits resulted in an accident, 17 percent in injury, and 0.7 percent in death. Of the 160 pursuits with injury, 30 involved injury to the police officer, 17 involved injury to an innocent bystander, and 113 involved injury to the fleeing driver or the passengers or both. Alpert and Dunham also concluded that 54 percent of the pursuits were initiated for traffic offenses, 2 percent for reckless driving or impaired driving, 33 percent for serious criminal activity, and 11 percent for "be on the lookout" (BOLO) alarms.[72]

A study conducted in Minnesota indicated that 44 percent of pursuits resulted in accidents, and 24 percent resulted in injuries. The causes of the pursuits included traffic (76 percent), suspicion of driving under the influence (6 percent), and suspicion of a felony (16 percent).[73]

In 2004, the University of Washington released a study conducted by two researchers at the Harborview Medical Center's Injury Prevention and Research Center. The researchers examined all traffic fatalities in the nation from 1994 through 2002 and found 2,654 fatal crashes with 3,146 deaths resulting from police pursuits. Of those deaths, 1,048, or one-third, were not people in the fleeing vehicles. They were drivers or occupants of other vehicles, pedestrians, or bicyclists; 40 were police

A patrol car is abandoned in the middle of an intersection in Grand Rapids, Michigan, after it was involved in a pursuit subsequent to a shooting incident.

Ryan M.L. Young/Grand Rapids Press /Landov

officers. The report did not determine how many police chases do not end in deaths or analyze the reasons for the pursuits, but the researchers did state that police chase fatalities make up 1 percent of all motor vehicle–related deaths in the United States.[74] Clearly, this is a serious safety issue for police and citizens that requires further intensive study.

THE EVOLUTION OF PURSUITS Departments are examining their long-standing policy of actively pursuing anyone who fails to stop for a police officer. These pursuits cause a lot of injury, death, damage, emotional pain, and economic costs. With today's technology, offenders can often be apprehended in safer ways.

The number of accidents and injuries resulting from police high-speed pursuits has led many U.S. police departments to establish formal **police pursuit policies** (policies regulating the circumstances and conditions under which the police should pursue or chase motorists driving at high speeds in a dangerous manner). Most departments have examined this issue closely in the last few years, and many have come to the conclusion that the dangers to officers, citizens, and even the individual being pursued often indicate that pursuits are not an effective tactic and the dangers far outweigh the benefits. Police pursuit policies provide clear guidelines to officers and supervisors about what their roles are. Some departments are even telling their officers to discontinue a pursuit under certain circumstances. In 2003, nearly all departments had pursuit policies: 61 percent of local police agencies had a restrictive pursuit policy (restrictions based on speed, type of offense, and so on); 25 percent of departments had a judgmental pursuit policy, leaving it to the officer's discretion; and 6 percent discouraged all vehicle pursuits.[75]

Pursuit policies can cause conflicts between departments in neighboring towns or counties when their policies differ; one jurisdiction may initiate a pursuit that crosses a boundary into another jurisdiction where officers will not pursue. Agencies need to communicate their policies and plan how to handle any conflicts that arise.

Considering the widely televised beatings of individuals after pursuits, a proposal by Alpert, a professor of criminology at the University of South Carolina, seems to make a great deal of sense. In a 1996 study of police pursuit policies, Alpert recommended that suspects be apprehended by backup officers other than those who led the chase. Alpert found that officers chasing suspects experience an adrenaline high that can lead to the use of excessive force once they have caught up with the fleeing suspects.[76]

In 2007, the U.S. Supreme Court ruled on the issue of reasonableness in using force to terminate a pursuit. The case, *Scott v. Harris*, involved a deputy pursuing Harris and ultimately ramming the back of his vehicle to get him to stop. (This case is discussed in Chapter 13.) This action caused Harris to lose control of his vehicle. His vehicle left the roadway, rolled, and crashed, causing injuries that resulted in Harris becoming paraplegic. Harris sued Deputy Scott, alleging that excessive force was used against him in violation of his Fourth Amendment rights. The case made its way to the U.S. Supreme Court, and the Court issued an opinion that held that police officers may use potentially deadly force to end a high-speed chase of a suspect whose actions risk the safety of other drivers and pedestrians.[77] Though this ruling would seem to strengthen law enforcement's position in pursuits, departments still prefer to avoid these kinds of situations if at all possible. Consequently, as mentioned earlier, the vast majority of departments have some restrictions in their pursuit policies.

One of the best alternatives that departments are exploring is the use of technology. Law enforcement air units commonly assist in pursuits and track the offender to a stopping place, often with the added element of video. Many departments have good working relationships with the TV media and can request this kind of monitored assistance. Many departments also use tire deflation spikes in appropriate situations, and some are exploring emerging GPS tracking systems.

Other Police Operational Units

Other operational units that are part of today's police department include SWAT teams, police paramilitary units, and K-9 units.

police pursuit policies Policies regulating the circumstances and conditions under which the police should pursue or chase motorists driving at high speeds in a dangerous manner.

SWAT Teams and Police Paramilitary Units

SWAT teams were created in many cities during the 1960s, generally in response to riots and similar disturbances. The first SWAT team was the Philadelphia Police Department's 100-officer SWAT squad, which was organized in 1964 in response to the growing number of bank robberies throughout the city.[78] SWAT teams are commonly used around the country but sometimes have other names. Some people believe that the name SWAT sounds a little too aggressive and militaristic, and some cities have chosen variations of the title for the same type of team, such as special response unit (SRU) or special response team (SRT).

Police paramilitary unit (PPU) is a term made popular by Peter Kraska and Victor Kappeler in the 1990s to refer to units within police departments that are organized in a more militaristic manner, with their primary function to threaten or use force collectively and not necessarily as a last resort. The term includes units, also referred to as SWAT teams or special response units, that are "distinguished by power and number of weapons." These units are highly trained as use-of-force specialists.

The number of PPUs has grown tremendously since the 1970s, when fewer than 10 percent of police departments had them; in 1995, 89 percent of departments had such a unit.[79] The use of these units over the years also has changed from handling the occasional dangerous situation callouts to being involved on a more routine basis in such things as serving high-risk search warrants and arrest warrants. Kraska and Kappeler found that 20 percent of the departments they surveyed used PPUs for patrolling urban areas on a somewhat regular basis.

Members of these teams are carefully chosen and trained in the use of weapons and strategic invasion tactics. They are used in situations involving hostages, serious crimes, airplane hijackings, and prison riots, as well as in other situations requiring specialized skills and training. When serving warrants, it is safer to use these highly trained officers to make the entry than using the narcotics investigators who may be working the case and getting the warrants, since members of these units can be better trained and have more experience.

Most departments are too small to have a full-time SWAT team; such departments often have a SWAT team composed of officers with varying assignments throughout the department. Officers have their regular assignments, but when a SWAT callout occurs, they respond from wherever they are. Unless a city is very large and busy, there are not enough SWAT calls to justify having a full-time unit. Some departments have difficulty justifying having a SWAT team even when it is composed of officers on other job assignments. In these situations, the departments in an area may collaborate to form a regional SWAT team, with officers coming from several departments. The most important issue in this situation is determining who has control of the unit and who is in charge. There can be no confusion regarding command on a SWAT call.

No matter how the SWAT team or PPU is formed, training is of utmost importance. Deploying a PPU is expensive, primarily because of the training requirements. The members of these units must be constantly training and working together so that any action they take will be appropriate and court defensible.

Most of these units were created in the 1980s and 1990s, and their use has become more prevalent due to the increasing violence in our communities and the use of more lethal weapons by criminals. Their effect on the organizational culture of departments is unknown, but Kraska and Kappeler believe this interaction should be closely scrutinized. The effect of these paramilitary units can be particularly relevant when they are seen patrolling the streets with all their militaristic equipment or are present at public gatherings or demonstrations, as in the recent "Occupy" movement around the country.

Some critics believe that use of paramilitary units and military-like equipment is becoming more prevalent and is resulting in cases of unnecessary force and the intimidation of residents. However, law enforcement would rather overreact in terms of resources than have someone get hurt. In fact, in some cases, police departments have been criticized when they served what should have been perceived as a high-risk warrant without using one of these highly trained teams and it resulted in someone getting hurt or killed.

SWATTING   Unfortunately, a prank activity becoming more prevalent in recent years is now leading to

---

police paramilitary unit (PPU)   A term popularized in the late 1990s to refer to police units organized in a more militaristic manner (such as SWAT teams), with their primary function to threaten or use force collectively.

unsafe SWAT deployment. **Swatting** is making a hoax 911 call to elicit a law enforcement response, usually by a SWAT team. Typically, these calls are made using technology to make it appear that the emergency call is coming from the "victim's" residence. These calls are commonly made as a prank or for revenge. Politicians and private company executives have been targeted when the caller wants retribution for some offense. Often the perpetrators want to see or hear about the dramatic response.

Swatting calls can have very dangerous consequences. The FBI has arrested several individuals for this crime, although local agencies tend to investigate and process most incidents themselves with support from the FBI when necessary.

One of the earliest swatting conspiracies began in 2004, when 14-year-old Matthew Weigman convinced a 911 operator that he was holding a girl and her father at gunpoint in their home in Colorado, prompting a SWAT call. Weigman had met the girl through an online chat room, and her refusal to participate in phone sex with him prompted his swatting call. Weigman later began operating as a phone hacker in Washington state; he pulled off dozens of swatting calls by scamming telecommunications employees and manipulating phone systems until he was arrested in 2009. Weigman, then 19, was sentenced to more than 11 years in federal prison.

Not only do these calls divert significant resources from other needed responses and duties, it is only a matter of time before one ends in tragedy. There have already been several close calls: Whenever numerous officers and units respond to a potentially dangerous emergency call, the risk of accidents and injuries en route is high. The officers respond to swatting calls with the expectation that there is a violent suspect on the scene or that victims are in life-threatening danger. Once they arrive, unsuspecting residents might try to defend themselves, raising the possibility for serious injuries and deaths. Some residents have suffered heart attacks as a result of the fear and scare resulting from the SWAT unit's arrival. The worst-case scenario would be a misunderstanding with the responding officers using deadly force against those they suspect are offenders.

Although there are no nationwide statistics on swatting incidents, an estimated 100 calls are made per year. There have been swatting incidents targeting major sporting events, hotels, and public gathering spaces. A recent trend is celebrity swattings, with Ashton Kutcher, Justin Bieber, Clint Eastwood, and Ryan Seacrest among those already targeted. These individuals often have armed security details that raise the risk of danger to an even higher level.

People that perpetrate these calls are often serial offenders involved in other cybercrimes. It is critical that law enforcement and the general public be aware of these types of calls to recognize when they are occurring.[80]

K-9 Units

Most departments today employ K-9 (canine) units. Talented dogs have been used by the police for many years, but during the last few years, their role has expanded and the need for them has grown.

Traditionally, K-9 units have supplemented the patrol function by responding to burglary calls or open doors where a premises search is needed. The dogs can search more safely and accurately than human officers, particularly when the area to be searched is large or difficult to reach, such as a crawl space. This aids in the effort to keep officers safe. The dogs also have been used for tracking when a crime has just occurred. They can help officers know the direction of travel of a suspect or if the suspect got in a vehicle. In the best-case scenario, the dog will lead officers to the suspect's home, vehicle, or hiding place. K-9s also can assist in convincing a suspect to surrender. People know they cannot reason with a dog, so when a dog is set loose to apprehend them, they may be more likely to give up peacefully. This can save an officer from getting injured trying to take a noncompliant suspect into custody.

Dogs have been a big asset in the war on drugs, sniffing vehicles and packages and signaling if drugs are present. Since September 11, 2001, there has been an increase in the demand for dogs that sniff bombs and explosives. These dogs are used routinely at airports, train stations, ferry terminals, ports, subways, highways, bridges, and tunnels.

The dogs are also a public relations asset and a great tool for bridging the gap between the community and the officers at special events. Departments that cannot justify having their own dog often have arrangements with other local agencies or the county or state to have a dog respond when needed.

---

swatting A growing and dangerous trend of making a hoax call to incite SWAT deployment or other law enforcement response.

SUMMARY

- The three cornerstones of traditional police work are random routine patrol, rapid response to citizens' calls to 911, and retroactive investigation of past crimes by detectives.

- Before the academic studies of the 1960s and 1970s, particularly the Kansas City study, most of what we knew about police work and the way it was done in the United States relied on untested assumptions.

- The Kansas City study forced academics and progressive police administrators to look closely at police operations to see if there were better, more effective ways to do police work. This self-examination occurred after the Kansas City study indicated that the amount of random patrol had no effect on crime or citizens' fear of crime.

- Rapid police response to calls was found to be not as critical as once thought because of delays outside police control. The determination that there is often a delay between the occurrence of a crime and when a citizen reports it negated the advantage of a quick police response in these situations.

- After moving from foot patrol to vehicle patrol, law enforcement has realized the value of foot patrol and is once again using it. Reactions by both police officers and the community indicate that foot patrol enhances the relationship between the police and the community and leads to improved exchange of information.

- Departments should use evidence-based policing to determine which methods to employ in solving the problems they encounter.

- Officers and departments can better use discretionary time to fight crime through directed patrol activities.

- Police can better manage their resources by responding to calls based on the severity and importance of the calls and employing differential response alternatives.

- Police departments are exploring new approaches to calls involving the mentally ill in order to better serve their needs and to minimize the chances for injury to all parties.

- Police officers can use a variety of methods to fight crime and serve their community, including vehicle patrol, foot patrol, bicycle patrol, mounted patrol, and other innovative methods, such as scooters, multiterrain vehicles, and mobile substations.

- Law enforcement is using more innovative techniques in an effort to attack the distracted driving, DUI, and aggressive driving problems.

- Police departments are restricting the use of pursuits and using alternative methods to catch individuals who attempt to elude police officers.

- SWAT teams and K-9 units supplement the patrol mission in fighting crime.

KEY TERMS

bike patrol

crackdown

differential response to calls for service

directed patrol

evidence-based policing

foot patrol

hot spot

Kansas City patrol study

Newark foot patrol study

omnipresence

police paramilitary unit (PPU)

police pursuit policies

police pursuits

predictive policing

random routine patrol

rapid response to citizens' calls to 911

red light cameras

retroactive investigation of past crimes by detectives

saturation patrol

smart policing

Specialized Policing Responses (SPRs)

split-force patrol

swatting

REVIEW EXERCISES

1. Recently, your city had five officers involved in a pursuit that resulted in an accident when a citizen was struck by the fleeing suspect's vehicle. The incident caused a lot of bad publicity, and the officers have mixed feelings on whether the police should have been pursuing the vehicle in the first place. You are the training lieutenant for your department, and your chief has asked you to put together a committee to develop a policy regarding pursuits. Who would you appoint to this committee and why? When and under what conditions would you allow officers to pursue vehicles? Factors to consider include the number of vehicles involved in a pursuit, the rank of officers and their responsibilities, what to do when the vehicle leaves your jurisdiction, whether officers are in uniform or plainclothes and whether they are in a marked or unmarked vehicle, speeds involved in the pursuit, and alternative methods or procedures to employ and when.

2. Your community has recently experienced tragic accidents involving teen drivers. On two separate occasions, a car with several teens in it was traveling at a high rate of speed in the late evening hours and the driver lost control of the vehicle. Teens in both accidents were thrown from the vehicles and killed. They were not wearing seat belts. The community is concerned about the well-being of its teenagers, and representatives have come to the police chief wanting something to be done to protect or educate the young people in your community. The chief has turned to you, since you are a long-time traffic officer. What types of programs would you implement to address this problem? Prepare a report for the chief including the background and supporting information she needs to address the community's concerns.

3. Your city council has come to the chief requesting an answer to the burglary problem. Many homes are being broken into while the residents are at work during the day. The method of entry most commonly used is coming in through an unlocked door. Items targeted include cash, jewelry, iPods, and laptops. What methods should the chief employ in order to combat this problem?

WEB EXERCISES

1. Go to the Manatee County, Florida, Sheriff's Office website and look at their Teen Driver Challenge. What do you think of this program? Do you think this is a valuable program that other departments should emulate? Examine their enforcement bureau. What types of units do they employ? Do you think this is good information to post on their site? Why or why not?

2. Visit the Kirkland, Washington, Police Department website. Look at the department's mission as well as the chief's message. Do they complement each other? Examine their crime-mapping feature and the prevalence of certain kinds of crimes.

3. Go to the Seattle Police Department website. Look in their policy and procedure manual and read their pursuit policy. What kind of policy do they have and under what conditions can an officer pursue a vehicle? What are the officers' responsibilities when involved in a pursuit?

END NOTES

1. Gary W. Cordner and Kathryn E. Scarborough, *Police Administration*, 6th ed. (Cincinnati: Anderson, 2007), p. 383.

2. O. W. Wilson and Roy Clinton McLaren, *Police Administration*, 4th ed. (New York: McGraw-Hill, 1977). A fifth edition was published in 1997, authored by three major researchers, in addition to Wilson and McLaren: James J. Fyfe, Jack R. Greene, William F. Walsh, O. W. Wilson, and Roy Clinton McLaren, *Police Administration*, 5th ed. (New York: McGraw-Hill, 1997).

3. Wilson and McLaren, *Police Administration*, p. 320.

4. George L. Kelling, Tony Pate, Duane Dieckman, and Charles E. Brown, *The Kansas City Preventive Patrol Experiment: A Summary Report* (Washington, D.C.: Police Foundation, 1974).

5. Ibid., p. 16.

6. H. H. Isaacs, "A Study of Communications, Crimes, and Arrests in a Metropolitan Police Department," in President's Commission on Law Enforcement and Administration of Justice, *Task Force Report: Science and Technology* (Washington, D.C.: U.S. Government Printing Office, 1967).

7. National Advisory Commission on Criminal Justice Standards and Goals, *Police* (Washington, D.C.: U.S. Government Printing Office, 1973), p. 194.

8. Kansas City Police Department, *Response Time Analysis: Executive Summary* (Washington, D.C.: U.S. Government Printing Office, 1978); William Spelman and D. K. Brown, *Calling the Police: Citizen Reporting of Serious Crime* (Washington, D.C.: Police Executive Research Forum, 1981).

9. George L. Kelling and Mary A. Wycoff, *Evolving Strategy of Policing: Case Studies of Strategic Change* (Cambridge, Mass.: Harvard University Press, 2001).

10. William G. Gay, Theodore H. Schell, and Steven Schack, *Routine Patrol: Improve Patrol Productivity*, vol. 1 (Washington, D.C.: National Institute of Justice, 1977), p. 2.

11. James Q. Wilson, *Varieties of Police Behavior: The Management of Law and Order in Eight Communities* (Cambridge, Mass.: Harvard University Press, 1968).

12. Gary W. Cordner, "The Police on Patrol," in Dennis Jay Kenney, ed., *Police and Policing: Contemporary Issues* (New York: Praeger, 1989), pp. 60–71.

13. Cordner, "Police on Patrol," p. 65.

14. Jack R. Greene and Carl B. Klockars, "What Police Do," in Carl B. Klockars and Stephen D. Mastrofski, eds., *Thinking about Police: Contemporary Readings*, 2nd ed. (New York: McGraw-Hill, 1991), pp. 273–284.

15. Cordner and Scarborough, *Police Administration*, p. 31.

16. Anthony V. Bouza, *Police Mystique: An Insider's Look at Cops, Crime, and the Criminal Justice System* (New York: Plenum, 1990), p. 84.

17. Bruce Smith, *Police Systems in the United States*, 2nd ed. (New York: Harper & Row, 1960), p. 14.

18. Police Department of Kansas City, *1966 Survey of Municipal Police Departments* (Kansas City, Mo.: Police Department of Kansas City, 1966), p. 53.

19. International Association of Chiefs of Police, *A Survey of the Police Department of Youngstown, Ohio* (Washington, D.C.: International Association of Chiefs of Police, 1964), p. 89.

20. Walker and Katz, *Police in America*, p. 315.

21. President's Commission on Law Enforcement and Administration of Justice, *Task Force Report: The Police*, p. 54.

22. John Heaphy, ed., *Police Practices: The General Administrative Survey* (Washington, D.C.: Police Foundation, 1978), p. 11.

23. Alejandro del Carmen and Lori Guevara, "Police Officers on Two-Officer Units: A Study of Attitudinal Responses Towards a Patrol Experiment," *Policing: An International Journal of Police Strategies and Management* 1 (2003): 144–161.

24. Todd Wright, "Officials Push for a Return to Police Partners," *Miami Herald*, September 10, 2007.

25. Christine Vendel, "KC Officer Reacted Quickly in Tight Spot," *Kansas City Star*, June 12, 2007.

26. George L. Kelling, *Foot Patrol* (Washington, D.C.: National Institute of Justice, 1988).

27. Police Foundation, *The Newark Foot Patrol Experiment* (Washington, D.C.: Police Foundation, 1981).

28. Robert C. Trojanowicz and Dennis W. Banas, *The Impact of Foot Patrol on Black and White Perceptions of Policing* (East Lansing: National Neighborhood Foot Patrol Center, School of Criminal Justice, Michigan State University, 1988).

29. Allison Steele, "Walking the Walk to Cut City's Crime," retrieved March 7, 2010, from Philly.com.

30. Lawrence W. Sherman, "Evidence-Based Policing," in *Ideas in American Policing* (Washington, D.C.: Police Foundation, 1998); Carl J. Jensen III, "Consuming and Applying Research: Evidence-Based Policing," *Police Chief* 2 (2006): 98–101.

31. Walter L. Perry, Brian McInnis, Carter C. Price, Susan C. Smith, John S. Hollywood, *Predictive Policing: The Role of Crime Forecasting in Law Enforcement Operations*, National Institute of Justice and the Safety and Justice Program within Rand: DOJ # 2010-IJ-CX-K007, 2013.

32. James R. Caldren, Jr., Alissa Huntoon, and Michael Medaris, "Introducing Smart Policing: Foundations, Principles, and Practice," *Police Quarterly* 16 (3): 275–286, 2013.

33. Ibid.

34. Ibid.

35. Ibid.

36. Craig D. Uchida and Mar L. Swatt, "Operation LASER and the Effectiveness of Hotspot Patrol: A Panel Analysis," *Police Quarterly* 16 (3, 2013): 287–304.

37. Lawrence Sherman, James Shaw, and Dennis Rogan, *The Kansas City Gun Experiment* (Washington, D.C.: National Institute of Justice, 1994).

38. "'Hot Spot' Policing Reduces Crime," City of Sacramento Police Department website, Media Relations office, News Release #20111004-166, October 4, 2011.

39. Glen M. Mowrey and Derek Rice, "Alarm Industry Steps Up to Reduce False Alarm Calls through Enhanced Call Verification," *Police Chief* 9 (2004): 14, 15.

40. *Law Enforcement Management and Administrative Statistics, 2000* (Washington, D.C.: Bureau of Justice Statistics, 2004), NCJ#203350.

41. Lorraine Mazerolle, Dennis Rogan, James Frank, Christine Famega, and John E. Eck, *Managing Calls to the Police with 911/311 Systems* (Washington, D.C.: U.S. Department of Justice, National Institute of Justice, 2005), NCJ#206256.

42. www.smart911.com.

43. J. E. Boydstun, *San Diego Field Interrogation: Final Report* (Washington, D.C.: Police Foundation, 1975).

44. *Law Enforcement News*, October 31, 1995, p. 1.

45. Larry K. Gaines and Victor Kappeler, *Policing in America*, 4th ed. (Cincinnati: Anderson, 2003), p. 531.

46. Allison Klein, "D.C. Has Weekend Free of Shootings," *Washington Post*, December 11, 2007, p. B1.

47. Theola Labbe'-DeBose, "All Hands on Deck Police Effort Gets Mixed Reviews," *Washington Post*, October 31, 2011.

48. Melissa Reuland, Laura Draper, and Blake Norton, "Improving Responses to People with Mental Illnesses: Tailoring Law Enforcement Initiatives to Individual Jurisdictions," Council of State Governments Justice Center: New York, 2010.

49. www.nami.org.

50. American Society for Industrial Security, "Innovations in Patrol," *Educator* (Spring/Summer 1997): 3.

51. Charles E. Higinbotham, "Spotlight On: Specialized Patrol Vehicles," *Police Chief* 70 (2003): 53–54, 56, 59–60, 62–63.

52. Ibid.

53. Seattle Police Department, *Annual Report* (Seattle, Wash.: Seattle Police Department, 2005), p. 8.

54. Brian A. Reaves, *Local Police Departments*, 2007 (Washington, D.C.: U.S. Department of Justice, 2010), NCJ#231174.

55. Ibid.

56. Earl M. Sweeney, "Top Ten Trends: Traffic Enforcement," *Police Chief* 9 (2005). From *The Police Chief*, vol. 72, no. 9, September 2005. Copyright held by the International Association of Chiefs of Police, 515 North Washington Street, Alexandria, VA 22314 USA. Further reproduction without express written permission from IACP is strictly prohibited.

57. National Highway Traffic Safety Administration (NHTSA) website, retrieved May 7, 2014, from www.nhtsa.gov.

58. Larry Copeland, "Red Light Cameras Work," *USA Today*, February 15, 2007.

59. Larry Copeland, "New York Has Increased Undercover Patrols to Catch Drivers Texting While Driving," *USA Today*, August 13, 2013.

60. Joseph B. White, "More Enforcement Planned Against Distracted Driving," *Wall Street Journal*, retrieved April 8, 2010, from wsj.com. in looking now—that also appears to be the date published—I often get word of relevant articles and go to them that day.

61. www.nhtsa.gov/impaired

62. "Alcohol and Highway Safety 2001: A Review of the State of Knowledge," National Highway Traffic Safety Administration, 2001, retrieved November 28, 2006, from www.nhtsa.dot.gov/people/injury/research/alcoholhighway.

63. National Highway Traffic Safety Administration website, www.nhtsa.gov.

64. "Ignition Interlocks," retrieved March 24, 2014, from Mothers Against Drunk Driving, www.madd.org.

65. "Drunk Driving: Problem-Oriented Guides for Police," *Problem Specific Guides Series* #36 (Washington, D.C.: U.S. Department of Justice, 2006), available at www.popcenter.org and www.cops.usdoj.gov.

66. "No Easy Answers for DUI Concerns as Marijuana Gains Support," NPR, February 23, 2014, www.npr.org/2014/0223/280310526.

67. Washington State Patrol website, www.wsp.wa.gov.

68. Ibid.

69. Geoffrey Alpert and Patrick R. Anderson, "The Most Deadly Force: Police Pursuits," *Justice Quarterly* 3 (1986): 1–14.

70. California Highway Patrol, *Pursuit Study* (Sacramento: California Highway Patrol, 1993).

71. Ibid., p. 21.

72. Geoffrey P. Alpert and Roger G. Dunham, "Research on Police Pursuits: Applications for Law Enforcement," *American Journal of Police* 7 (1988): 123–131.

73. Geoffrey P. Alpert and Lorie A. Fridell, *Police Vehicles and Firearms: Instruments of Deadly Force* (Prospect Heights, Ill.: Waveland Press, 1992).

74. Michael Ko, "Harborview Researchers Tally Police Chase Toll," *Seattle Times*, April 8, 2004.

75. Matthew J. Hickman and Brian A. Reaves, *Local Police Departments*, 2003 (Washington D.C.: U.S. Department of Justice, 2006).

76. "Life, Liberty and Pursuits," *Law Enforcement News*, December 31, 1996, p. 26.

77. International Association of Chiefs of Police website, www.theiacp.org.

78. *Philadelphia Bulletin*, March 26, 1976, sec. 3, p. 1.

79. Larry Gaines and Victor Kappeler, *Policing in America*, 5th ed. (LexisNexis, 2005), pp. 243–247.

80. FBI Stories, www.fbi.gov, September 2013.

10 Investigations

AP Images/Joseph Kaczmarek

LEARNING OBJECTIVES

- Discuss the innovations to police detective operations motivated by the Rand study and other research.

- Identify alternatives to retroactive investigation of past crimes by detectives.

- Explain how crime analysis and information management benefits law enforcement, including examples of recent technology in this area.

- Describe some of the proactive tactics employed by investigators.

- Define entrapment and give examples, including how the entrapment defense is treated in court.

OUTLINE

Retroactive Investigation of Past Crimes by Detectives
Detective Operations
The Investigative Process
What Detectives Do
The Detective Mystique
Alternatives to Retroactive Investigation of Past Crimes by Detectives
Improved Investigation of Past Crimes
Managing Criminal Investigations (MCI)
Mentoring and Training
Crime Analysis and Information Management
Crime Analysis
Information Management

Multiagency Investigative Task Forces
Repeat Offender Programs (ROPs)
Internet Registries
Global Positioning System (GPS) Technology, Smartphones, and Social Media
Surveillance Cameras
Cold-Case Squads
Proactive Tactics
Decoy Operations
Stakeout Operations
Sting Operations
Cybercrime Investigations
Undercover Operations
Police Undercover Investigations
Federal Undercover Investigations
Drug Undercover Investigations
Entrapment

INTRODUCTION

After an unprecedented crime decrease in the 1990s, crime rates across the country remained relatively flat from 2000 to 2004. Since 2005, the rates have fluctuated, depending on the type of crime as well as size of city. The *Uniform Crime Reports* (UCR) keep track of these figures nationally as well as regionally. To average citizens, what matters most is what is happening in their community and whether they or their friends have been victimized.

Smaller cities often feel immune to big-city problems and perhaps never put programs into place to combat the crime problem as the bigger cities have. The difficult challenges that police departments face include determining why exactly their crime rates go up and developing ways to combat crime and keep their citizens safe. Crime-rate increases in middle America attract the attention of the community. If citizens do not feel safe in their hometowns, they let their elected officials know and demand tactics and solutions. This issue has received and will continue to receive media attention. On the positive side, taxpayers may be more likely to fund initiatives that cities develop to address the crime problem.

Police departments throughout the nation have learned that they must be more specific and focused in addressing crime and disorder problems. Departments have created new policies, procedures, and units to address these concerns. The previous chapter discussed new ways of addressing the crime problem in general, and this chapter will examine some of the new approaches in investigating crimes that have occurred or are occurring. Traditional detective operations have been modified in response to academic studies that indicate new methods for investigating past crimes and apprehending career criminals. Investigations of past crimes have improved as a result of changes made in detective operations in response to research conducted by the Rand Corporation and other think tanks, as well as the use of cold-case squads. Increased attention to career criminals has led to a proliferation of repeat offender programs (ROPs) throughout the United States. Furthermore, the use of multiagency investigative task forces has facilitated information management and information sharing.

New tactics and operations have been developed during the past two decades in an attempt to provide more effective crime investigation and to keep up with the changing face of crime and criminals. This chapter discusses both these innovations and the more tried-and-true methods, including decoy operations, stakeout operations, and sting operations. The major types of undercover operations also are covered. The chapter concludes with a discussion of the legal aspects of entrapment and how it relates to undercover work and other law enforcement tactics.

Retroactive Investigation of Past Crimes by Detectives

Before the Rand study *The Criminal Investigation Process*, it was common for police departments to have policies and procedures in place that emphasized the retroactive investigation of past crimes by detectives. The investigation of almost all felonies and of some misdemeanors was the sole responsibility of the detective division of a police department.[1] The patrol officer merely obtained information for a complaint or incident report and referred the case to the detectives for follow-up investigation. Theoretically, detectives would interview complainants and witnesses again, respond to the scene of the crime, and search for clues and leads that could solve the crime.

In 1975, the Rand Corporation think tank found that much of a detective's time was spent in nonproductive work—93 percent was spent on activities that did not lead directly to solving previously reported crimes—and that investigative expertise did little to solve cases. The Rand report said that half of all detectives could be replaced without negatively influencing crime clearance rates:

The single most important determinant of whether or not a case will be solved is the information the victim supplies to the immediately responding patrol officer. If information that uniquely identifies the perpetrator is not present at the time the crime is reported, the perpetrator, by and large, will not be subsequently identified. Of those cases that are ultimately cleared but in which the perpetrator is not identifiable at the time of the initial police incident report, almost all are cleared as a result of routine police procedures....

Our data consistently reveal that an investigator's time is largely consumed in reviewing reports, documenting files, and attempting to locate and interview victims on cases that experience shows will not be solved. For cases that are solved (i.e., a suspect is identified), an investigator spends more time in post-clearance processing than he does in identifying the perpetrator.[2]

The effectiveness of detectives was also questioned by a Police Executive Research Forum (PERF) study in 1981. Data from the study disclosed that if a crime is reported while it is in progress, police have about a 33 percent chance of making an arrest. However, the probability of arrest declines to about 10 percent if the crime is reported one minute later and to 5 percent if more than 15 minutes elapse before the crime is reported. In addition, as time elapses between the crime and the arrest, the chances of a conviction are reduced, probably because the ability to recover evidence is lost. Once a crime has been completed and the investigation is put into the hands of detectives, the chances of identifying and arresting the perpetrator diminish rapidly.[3]

Mark Willman and John Snortum duplicated the Rand and PERF findings in a study of detective work in 1984. The researchers analyzed 5,336 cases reported to a suburban police department and found that most cases were solved when the perpetrator was identified at the scene of the crime; scientific detective work was rarely necessary.[4]

Though the Rand finding regarding detectives' value in the investigative process was controversial, and the investigative process itself has not changed much in the years since the study, most researchers feel the detectives' role is an important one. The key variable among departments is whether they utilize the more traditional model with patrol officers doing little investigative work or subscribe to the model advocated by the Rand study where patrol officers take a great deal of the workload off of the detectives. Several studies indicate that, as reported in the *National Survey of Police Practices Regarding the Criminal Investigations Process: Twenty-Five Years After Rand*, detectives

"play critical roles in routine case resolutions and in post-arrest activities, and many of their duties require highly specialized skills."[5] It is generally believed that the patrol officer–detective relationship and their roles in an investigation are complementary and symbiotic and make for successful investigative outcomes. This chapter will explore some of the newer, more efficient techniques that departments have developed to investigate past crimes.

Detective Operations

Most of the activities of a police department involve police patrol operations. As we saw in earlier chapters, however, the police engage in numerous other activities. Detective operations and investigations are an important part of police work.

The Investigative Process

The investigative process begins with the patrol officer. The officer who responds to the scene performs a crucial function that initiates the investigation. The officer will conduct a preliminary investigation, which the detective will use as the basis for follow-up investigation.

The preliminary investigation includes many tasks that will be performed by the responding officer or by others at the responding officer's direction. These tasks will be accomplished as more resources arrive on the scene and as staffing allows and the incident requires. A smaller agency may want to request assistance from neighboring jurisdictions. The tasks in the preliminary investigation include:

- Responding safely and looking for possible fleeing suspects
- Assessing the situation and summoning assistance as needed and as available such as emergency medical assistance, K-9 units, crime scene personnel, supervisors, SWAT team, hostage negotiator, press information officer, and officers from neighboring jurisdictions if needed
- Locating key parties such as the victim, witnesses, and any suspects, and making sure they are controlled and separated
- Identifying and securing the crime scene
- Documenting everything the officers observe and do

The documentation mentioned at the end of the list consists of the officer's **field notes**, which will serve as the basis for the incident report that the officer writes. The **incident report** is a crucial part of the investigation and is the document the detective will use when starting the follow-up investigation. It will also be the department's official memory, and anyone who needs access to the information can retrieve the file even when the reporting officer or the detective is no longer available.

The incident report must answer the questions of who, what, where, when, how, and why regarding the crime and must be written accurately and in a clear manner that will enable readers to know exactly what happened and what has been done. It can ensure that others do not repeat tasks that have already been taken care of, thus minimizing duplication of effort by investigators. When examining the facts of the case and what information is available, either the responding officer or a detective will follow up on the case. In a small department, an investigator or investigative team from another agency may conduct the follow-up investigation.

What Detectives Do

The detective division of a police department is charged with solving, or clearing, reported crimes. In traditional detective operations, detectives conduct a follow-up investigation of a past crime after a member of the patrol force takes the initial report of the crime and conducts some sort of preliminary investigation.

According to police tradition, a detective or investigator reinterviews the victim of the crime and any witnesses, collects evidence, and processes or oversees the processing of the crime scene (searches the scene of a crime for physical evidence, collects the evidence, and forwards it to the police laboratory for analysis). The detective or investigator also conducts canvasses (searches areas for witnesses), interrogates possible suspects, arrests the alleged perpetrator, and prepares the case, with the assistance of the district attorney's or prosecutor's office, for presentation in court.

As mentioned earlier, the detective generally begins an investigation upon receipt of an incident report prepared by the officer who conducted the initial interview with the victim. The incident report contains identifying information regarding the victim, details of the crime, identifying information regarding the perpetrators or suspects (or a description of them), and identifying information regarding any property taken.

As the detective begins the investigation, he or she maintains a file on the case, using follow-up reports for each stage of the investigation. The incident report and the follow-up reports are generally placed in a case folder and serve as the official history of the crime and its investigation. This information or a report compiled from it is then used by the prosecutor to prosecute the case in court. The incident report and the follow-up reports also may be subpoenaed by a defendant's defense attorney under the legal process known as discovery, which allows a defendant, before a trial, to have access to the information the police and prosecutor will use at the trial.

Detective units may be organized on a decentralized or centralized basis. In a decentralized system, each precinct in a city has its own local detective squad, which investigates all crimes occurring in the precinct. Detectives or investigators in a decentralized squad are considered generalists.

In a centralized system, in contrast, all detectives operate out of one central office or headquarters and each is responsible for particular types of crime in the entire city. These detectives are considered specialists. Some departments separate centralized or specialty squads into crimes against persons squads and crimes against property squads. Some departments operate specialized squads or units for most serious crimes; for example, they may have separate squads for homicide, sex crimes, robbery, burglary, forgery, auto theft, bias crimes (that is, crimes that are motivated by bigotry or hatred of a person's race, ethnic origin, gender, or sexual orientation), and, most recently, computer crimes.

Some cities use both decentralized and centralized investigatory units. The decentralized squads operate out of local precincts and refer some of their cases to the specialized centralized squads, such as sex crimes, homicide, or arson squads. The decentralized squads then investigate less serious cases themselves. In smaller departments, detectives tend

---

field notes The brief written record made by an officer from the time of arrival on a scene until completion of the assignment.

incident report The first written investigative report of a crime, usually compiled by the officer conducting the preliminary investigation.

to be generalists. There may be one detective with expertise and special training in sex crimes, juvenile crimes, cybercrimes, and homicide crimes. Or one or two detectives may receive all of this training and conduct all major investigations in their jurisdiction. In some cities, the police department may call for assistance from county or state law enforcement when confronted with a homicide or rash of sex crimes. It really does not matter which approach the jurisdiction uses as long as the individuals who investigate the major crimes have the latest training available and have current information about the legal issues.

For instance, there are very specific guidelines regarding juvenile investigations. When juveniles are victims of a crime—whether it is neglect, abuse, an Internet crime, or a sex crime—it is beneficial to have an investigator specially trained in interviewing children to be able to elicit the needed information. In addition, special rules exist regarding the detention and questioning of juveniles arrested for a crime; investigators need to be aware of these special rules or they can jeopardize the investigation and subsequent prosecution. Although the procedures may vary from state to state, some of the issues in juvenile law of which investigators must be aware include photographing and fingerprinting, storage and confidentiality of a juvenile's records, right to counsel or parents being present during questioning, and separation of juveniles and adults while the juvenile is in custody.

The investigator and prosecutor have the same ultimate goal in mind—a conviction brought about by a good, solid case. Strong trusting relationships between the detectives and the prosecutors enhance case preparation. Having someone to call when an unusual legal question arises can provide detectives guidance on their actions early in the case. Therefore, it is helpful when detectives work closely with the prosecutor's office as early in the investigation as possible. This reciprocal arrangement can also assure prosecutors that there is an investigator who will help them out quickly should a fact-finding issue arise during trial preparation.

The Detective Mystique

Detectives work out of uniform, perform no patrol duties, and are sometimes paid at a higher rate than regular uniformed officers. In the past, the assignment to detective duties was a promotion that an officer attained through a promotional examination process, but that has changed during the last couple of decades. In larger, big-city departments, it is still a promotion with higher pay. In most small and mid-sized departments, a detective is a plainclothes police officer with the same rank as a police officer, but having attained an assignment in the detective bureau or division through a competitive process. These detectives may be paid more in the form of assignment pay or clothing allowance required by their union or collective bargaining contract.

The important distinction between the detective as a plainclothes police officer versus the detective as a person with promotional rank is that when the position is not a rank, it is a temporary assignment. If it does not work out or the department needs to downsize the detective division, the officer can be transferred back to the road without being demoted or violating the contract. Often, officers are chosen for transfer to the detective bureau based on their performance as patrol officers; but there is no guarantee that the individuals chosen will be the same high performers as detectives, and most departments prefer the flexibility of being able to assign those who do not perform as well in the detective position back to the road.

Conversely, the officer may not be satisfied with the position. Though the jobs of patrol officer and detective are very similar, some different skill sets are needed, and the work conditions vary enough that the fit may not be right for some people. An officer may love the job of patrol officer and enjoy conducting the occasional investigation and the preliminary investigations that come his or her way, but not like doing it every day. Sometimes patrol officers do not realize exactly what the detective job involves before they actually do it. They may miss the day-to-day contact with citizens and being able to help them in small ways. They may miss the excitement of responding at the time of the crime. Most noticeably, new detectives may tire of the constant stress of conducting investigations and never feeling as if they have finished their job. As a road officer, most officers start their shift with a clean slate; whereas at the start of each tour, detectives find themselves facing the cases and work that they left the day before. They tend to take their cases home with them and think about them at night and sometimes even dream about them. This does not create a problem for many detectives who learn to cope in their own ways, but it makes some prefer to go back to the patrol division.

When the patrol and detective positions are the same rank, moving someone back to patrol can be done with minimal embarrassment and impact on the person's career and financial status. Why would there be embarrassment? Even in police departments, not to mention in the general community, detectives generally enjoy much greater status and prestige than patrol officers do. Detectives have historically been seen as the heroes of police work in novels, on television, and in the movies—consider Sherlock Holmes, Cagney and Lacey, Andy Sipowicz, Crockett and Tubbs, Dirty Harry Callahan, Olivia Benson, Steve McGarrett, Kono, and other fictional detectives. Are real-life detectives as heroic, smart, individualistic, tough, hardworking, and mysterious as their fictional counterparts? Or is there a mystique attached to the detective position?

The **detective mystique** is the idea that detective work is as glamorous, exciting, and dangerous as it is depicted in the movies and on television. In reality, however, detectives spend most of their time filling out reports and reinterviewing victims on the telephone. Commenting on the detective mystique, Herman Goldstein wrote:

> Part of the mystique of detective operations is the impression that a detective has difficult-to-come-by qualifications and skills, that investigating crime is a real science, that a detective does much more important work than other police officers, that all detective work is exciting and that a good detective can solve any crime.... [In] the context of the totality of police operations, the cases detectives solve account for a much smaller part of police business than is commonly realized. This is so because in case after case, there is literally nothing to go on: no physical evidence, no description of the offender, no witness and often no cooperation, even from the victim.[6]

Before the Rand study *The Criminal Investigation Process*, the detective mystique was considered an accurate representation of reality. It was believed that each crime was completely investigated, that all leads and tips were followed to their logical conclusion, and that each case was successfully solved. This is not true, as we will see when we discuss the Rand study. The reality of detective work usually has little in common with its media representations. Much of what detectives do consists of routine and simple chores and is somewhat boring; according to

Herman Goldstein, it is arguable as to whether any special skills are required to be a detective.[7]

Because of the Rand study and other studies, police administrators can now make some generalizations about detective operations. First, the single most important determinant of whether or not a crime is solved is not the quality of the work performed by the detectives but the information the responding officers obtain from the victim and witnesses at the scene.[8] Next, traditional detective work has not proved very effective in solving crimes. Nationally, police are only able to clear (solve) 46.8 percent of all violent crimes (murder, forcible rape, robbery, aggravated assault) and 19 percent of property crimes (burglary, theft, and motor vehicle theft) reported to them. These figures are relatively consistent from year to year. The difference between the clearance rates for violent versus property crimes is because of the vigorous investigation put forth in the more serious cases and because the violent crimes often have a victim or witness available to assist police with information.[9] Furthermore, because not all cases are reported to the police, the clearance rate is actually even lower; police cannot clear crimes not reported to them. Finally, patrol officers, not detectives, are responsible for the vast majority of all arrests, which they generally make at the scene of the crime.

Alternatives to Retroactive Investigation of Past Crimes by Detectives

Current popular alternatives to retroactive investigation of past crimes by detectives are improved investigation of past crimes and repeat offender programs. These innovative techniques are designed to concentrate investigative resources on crimes that have a high chance of being solved. Managing investigations effectively and maximizing the use of technology and science is especially important in these days of budget cuts and personnel reductions.

detective mystique The idea that detective work is glamorous, exciting, and dangerous, as it is depicted in the movies and on television.

Improved Investigation of Past Crimes

The National Advisory Commission on Criminal Justice Standards and Goals has recommended the increased use of patrol officers in the criminal investigation process. The commission recommended that every police agency direct patrol officers to conduct thorough preliminary investigations and that agencies establish written priorities to ensure that investigative efforts are spent in a manner that best achieves organizational goals. The commission further recommended that investigative specialists (detectives) only be assigned to very serious or complex preliminary investigations.[10]

Managing Criminal Investigations (MCI)

As a consequence of the Rand study and other studies, the Law Enforcement Assistance Administration (LEAA) funded research that led to the publication and wide dissemination of a new proposal regarding methods that should be used to investigate past crimes.[11] This proposal, **Managing Criminal Investigations (MCI)**, offers a series of guidelines that recommend (1) expanding the role of patrol officers to include investigative responsibilities and (2) designing a new method to manage criminal investigations by including **solvability factors**, case screening, case enhancement, and police and prosecutor coordination.[12] Under an MCI program, the responding patrol officer is responsible for a great deal of the follow-up activity that used to be assigned to detectives. These duties include locating and interviewing the victim and witnesses, detecting physical evidence, and preparing an initial investigative report that will serve as a guide for investigators. This report must contain proper documentation to indicate whether the case should be assigned for continued investigation or immediately suspended for lack of evidence.[13]

The other major innovation under MCI involves the use of a managerial system that grades cases according to their solvability; detectives then work only on cases that have a chance of being solved. Though it can vary by department, the road supervisor often makes the decision about whether the case will be followed up by the road officer or a detective or whether the case will be "inactivated" based on these solvability factors. Some solvability factors include the following:

1. Is there a witness?
2. Is a suspect named or known?
3. Can a suspect be identified?
4. Will the complainant cooperate in the investigation?

Each solvability factor is given a numerical weight. In the next process, case screening, the total weight of all solvability factors—the total score—determines whether or not the case will be investigated.[14]

The MCI method of managing investigations is designed to put most of an investigator's time and effort into only very important cases and into cases that actually can be solved. Research conducted by numerous police departments has demonstrated that scoring systems using checklists and point scores successfully screen out cases with a low probability of being solved and identify promising cases.[15]

Over the years, departments using the MCI approach have redesigned their crime reports to highlight these solvability factors. An education component aids the success of the program. Detectives and patrol officers must be educated about the philosophy and the goals of the program as well as the techniques to employ. It can be a difficult hurdle to overcome generations of the expectation of detectives "solving" all crimes. Citizens also must be informed by the responding officer about what to expect to happen to their case. Because most cases (especially property crimes) have little or no significant evidence, the percentage screened out for no follow-up is considerable.[16]

Sometimes the solvability factors may be disregarded and—because of officers' concern, for political reasons, or due to concern about public safety—a case will be investigated that does not meet the numerical criteria. Some cases are so important or serious that they demand a follow-up regardless of their potential solvability based on the solvability factors. Nevertheless, the MCI approach has given

---

Managing Criminal Investigations (MCI) Proposal recommended by the Rand study (research funded by the LEAA) regarding a more effective way of investigating crimes, including allowing patrol officers to follow up cases and using solvability factors in determining which cases to follow up.

solvability factors Factors considered in determining whether or not a case should be assigned for follow-up investigation.

investigators more manageable caseloads and an opportunity to be more organized and methodical in their efforts. Investigators are more efficient when they are working 15 to 20 cases a month with strategic investigative activities than when they are carrying 40 to 50 cases a month, many of which are not solvable and for which detectives can do little more than keep reviewing them and hoping evidence will appear.

Even with all the changes recommended by the Rand and other studies, and even though police departments have implemented many changes in the investigatory process, the police are still not very successful in clearing crimes reported to them. The improved methods of investigation, however, have resulted in less waste and more efficiency in police detective operations and have allowed departments to use personnel in more proactive policing.

Mentoring and Training

Training for investigators or detectives has long been viewed as a way to improve their productivity. Specialized investigations require specialized training, and these include investigations in the areas of homicide, sex crimes, juvenile crime and juvenile offenders, cybercrime, white-collar crime, and even auto theft. Detectives or investigators are usually sent to specialized schools as soon as practical after, or perhaps even before, they are appointed as investigators.

Informal **mentoring** programs have been used for years, as experienced detectives have taught new detectives what they know. Often detectives see potential in a patrol officer, and then mentor or work with that officer, even while he or she is still a patrol officer. These patrol officers may come in when they are not on shift to work a case with detectives, or manage to talk their road supervisors into freeing them to work with detectives on an investigation, thereby gaining experience.

Some departments also have implemented formal mentoring programs. Typically, a mentor is a role model, teacher, motivator, coach, or advisor who invests time in facilitating another person's professional job growth. A mentor program allows a noninvestigator to be paired with an experienced investigator to become familiar with the investigative process. It strengthens noninvestigators' preliminary investigation skills, eases the transition

should they become detectives, and allows them to "try out" the role of investigator to see if they would like it. Overall, mentoring improves the quality of investigations throughout the department and improves the skills of all personnel involved.[17] It also helps to keep the knowledge pool current to prepare for the inevitable job turnover. When police detectives retire, they take a wealth of information with them. A good mentoring program allows that information to be shared with others.[18]

Crime Analysis and Information Management

Crime Analysis

Crime analysis is the process of analyzing the data collected in a police organization to determine exactly what the crime problem is and where, when, and possibly even why it is happening. Crime analysis has grown tremendously in the last two decades and goes hand in hand with community-oriented policing and problem-oriented policing. Analysis allows the smarter use of information and, consequently, the smarter use of personnel and resources to address the true crime problem. Law enforcement leaders have coined the phrase **intelligence-led policing** to describe this strategy of using data analysis and other intelligence to focus police efforts on incidents and offenders causing the most harm to the community. The importance of gathering, analyzing, and sharing this information will become evident throughout the rest of this section.

Many departments employ full-time civilian crime analysts, but others have their investigators do the crime analysis as part of their investigative responsibility. The goal of crime analysis is to determine crime patterns and problems.[19] It begins with

---

mentoring Filling a role as teacher, model, motivator, coach, or advisor in someone else's professional growth.

crime analysis The use of analytical methods to obtain pertinent information on crime patterns and trends that can then be disseminated to officers on the street.

intelligence-led policing Using data analysis and other intelligence to focus police efforts on incidents and offenders causing the most harm to the community.

collating the information that comes into the police department. This includes information from dispatch, police reports, and intelligence information, as well as information gathered from parking citations, traffic citations, and field interviews. Crime analysis allows police to make links between incidents that have occurred and people and vehicles passing through town. This is especially critical for bigger departments where various shifts and beats may not know what the others are doing.

Historically, before computers and formal crime analysis, officers often did this function on their own. They knew who on their beats did burglaries, what their *modus operandi* (MO, or mode of operation) was, and whether they were in or out of jail. As crime increased and cities and towns grew, it became more difficult for officers to do this on their own. With the advent of computers, it became possible to formally perform this function to allow better deployment of police resources. With incident reports and citations formatted to collect the relevant data, data can be retrieved to look for trends or patterns. For instance, when burglaries increase, analysts can look at the reports and query via the computer to see where in town they are occurring, what time they are occurring, what is being taken, and how the burglars are gaining entry. Analysts also may be able to come up with possible suspects based on past burglaries or vehicle descriptions, and they can generate reports detailing this information and telling patrol officers what to look for.

This crime analysis information helps the agency, and the beat officer in particular, know how to direct their efforts in directed patrol activities on particular shifts. It also helps shift supervisors know how to allocate their personnel and helps the appropriate division determine the best strategy to address a particular crime pattern, such as decoys, stings, or public notification and education. This means "working smarter" with the resources at hand. Ultimately, the information can be used for budgetary purposes to request more personnel or equipment as the particular crime patterns and trends may dictate and, in these days of budget cutting, can enhance the agency's ability to do more with less.

Information Management

The key to police work, and investigations in particular, is information. Obtaining good information is critical. Whether information comes from complainants, victims, witnesses, the suspect, or all the various files of data that are kept, it can all enhance and strengthen the investigation.

In this computer age, we have a lot of information at our fingertips. Sometimes, it may seem that there is too much information, and we may experience information overload. Although this increased information generally helps with solving crimes, it also can require many hours of work to go through and discern which data are valuable and pertinent to a case. The computer age has allowed law enforcement agencies to share information with each other, which has enhanced investigations and assisted with detecting patterns and similar MOs.

Detectives can obtain information from a number of sources and share it in several ways. The Internet provides an opportunity for police personnel to research topics and to share knowledge with other officers through internal e-mail lists, expert directories, professional organizations, and outside e-mail lists that pertain to certain areas of interest. Journals, trade magazines, and newspaper articles that are available online can provide a wealth of information regarding what strategies are being used in other departments and also alert investigators to crime trends in neighboring communities, something that traditionally has been done and continues to be done in person as well.[20] Investigators hold monthly meetings with investigators from other agencies who work similar types of crime (such as sex crimes, auto thefts, and so forth) and compare and share information. Information acquired on the Internet and through e-mail, however, is often more current than that obtained through a meeting. As an example, in an effort to get important information to the public in a timely manner, Facebook has teamed with police agencies to create AMBER Alert pages; users can opt to receive notifications when an AMBER Alert has been posted in their area.[21]

Do these methods of sharing information over the computer help law enforcement be more efficient? In a recent study, the officers using an automated information system in the San Diego area strongly believed that this information sharing made them more productive. They participated in a Web-based network of criminal justice agencies called the Automated Regional Justice Information System (ARJIS) that allowed them to gather information for tactical analysis and investigations. The system could be requested to notify them when information they needed about a person, vehicle, or location became available from another agency or officer. Though officers felt the information system made them more productive, when compared with the control group in an area of the country without an automated regional system, the data did not indicate this. The investigators with the automated regional system had lower clearance rates and arrest rates than the control group without the system; however, the control group was using CompStat as part of its management system, which might have accounted for the higher clearance and arrest rate.[22]

The ARJIS has a presence online where San Diego law enforcement agencies can connect for information, and citizens are encouraged to interact with law enforcement via crime mapping and crime alerts. The goal of the program is to partner with the community, using technology to anticipate public safety issues and working together to solve these problems.[23]

Whereas crime analysis addresses routine crime, intelligence analysis tends to emphasize organized crimes (usually involving narcotics, human smuggling, gambling, and terrorism). Like the information used for crime analysis, the intelligence can be obtained from many sources, evaluated for reliability and validity, and used in a proactive manner.[24] Police in Kansas City, Missouri, created a task force to see if there were any common threads among the increased number of murders that occurred in 2005. They analyzed all the data available on the 127 murders and found that 85 percent of the victims had some type of criminal record and that the use of guns in homicides was up (105 of the homicides were shootings). In response to this information, the agency doubled the number of detectives assigned to investigate assaults, with the goal of stopping the assaults before they became homicides; in 2006, the murder rate was down 28 percent for the first half of the year.[25]

In Dallas, the police department used a $1.5 million Homeland Security grant to purchase software and equipment to link 28 databases within the police department and city to facilitate "intelligence-led policing," which is being implemented in cities around the country. In the past, units such as narcotics, homicide, and sex crimes had their own databases and only individuals with a "need to know" had access to those files. In following successes from around the country, the Dallas police recognized that criminals do not confine themselves to one type of crime. By making all the information available to all types of investigators, a better overall understanding of crime patterns and connections can be achieved, giving investigators better ammunition in combating the crime problem. The Dallas databases at the Metro Operations Support and Analytical Intelligence Center (MOSAIC), which began operations in January 2007, collect tips and trends from all over and make them available to investigators and officers in the field. The center also works closely with federal, state, and other local departments as well as private and corporate security. The information in the databases, coupled with that from mundane databases such as water records and traffic tickets, allows a full view of available information. This facilitates law enforcement's ability to effectively direct their efforts to the most serious crime problems.[26] This fusion center (see Chapter 12) seeks to provide timely intelligence to officers in the field and to share information internally and through networking.[27]

New technologies have improved information management. It is hoped that by being better able to record, analyze, share, and disseminate information to the parties who need it, more crimes can be solved, more offenders jailed, and more incidents prevented.

Multiagency Investigative Task Forces

In recent years, the use of multiagency **investigative task forces** has increased. With the realization that criminals know no boundaries, and often intentionally cross jurisdictional lines to commit crimes, the importance of sharing information and working together has been increasingly recognized. Palm Beach County, Florida, instituted the 13-member Palm Beach County Violent Crime Task Force, which consists of 7 full-time and 6 part-time detectives from various agencies in the county as well as the sheriff's office and the school district police (public schools are organized in a countywide school district that has its own police department). A full-time prosecutor is assigned to the task force, and investigators from the FBI, the U.S. Marshals Service, the federal Bureau of Alcohol, Tobacco, Firearms and Explosives, and the Florida Department of Law

investigative task forces A group of investigators working together to investigate one or more crimes. These investigators are often from different law enforcement agencies.

Enforcement are available to assist. Local agencies call on the unit when they have difficulty solving a homicide, drive-by shooting, violent home invasion, or armed robbery that appears to involve gangs or career criminals. The unit consists primarily of veteran violent-crime and gang detectives who are actively involved in each other's cases. With the free flow of information about these individuals and gangs, detectives are often able to make connections they were unable to make before this unit was instituted. Detectives gather information from their informants and use it to solve these cases, regardless of jurisdiction. It has also proved beneficial to have a prosecutor involved from the beginning, helping investigators build stronger cases to get and keep these offenders off the street.[28]

Multiagency investigative task forces have led the way in the investigation of human trafficking. In 2000, the U.S. Trafficking Victims Protection Act made human trafficking a crime and created protections and services for victims of trafficking. A hotline at the National Human Trafficking Resource Center (NHTRC) received more than 9,000 cases of human trafficking between 2007 and 2012.[29] These trafficking victims include citizens and noncitizens, adults and juveniles, and men and women who are exploited in domestic servitude, construction work, restaurant work, agriculture, small businesses, and commercial sex. Though trafficking is a relatively hidden crime, these victims and offenders are in all areas of the country—in cities, suburbs, and rural areas.

In 2010, an effort by the U.S. Department of Homeland Security to combat human trafficking was developed to bring together law enforcement agencies at all levels to conduct effective investigations, train local law enforcement, and bring these crimes out in the open. This effort was named the Blue Campaign, and it strives to protect the basic right of freedom for all and bring offenders to justice. The Federal Law Enforcement Training Centers (FLETC) are an integral part of this multiagency effort to train officers in awareness and investigation of this crime.[30]

The U.S. Attorney's Office for the Western District of Washington convened the Washington Advisory Committee on Trafficking (WashACT) in 2004. Together with the Seattle Police Department and the Washington Anti-Trafficking Response Network (WARN), they work with a myriad of local, state, and federal agencies as well as nongovernmental organizations to combat human trafficking. This collaboration has served over 200 victims with the prosecution of more than 40 cases at the federal level as well as additional cases at the local level, an accomplishment that would never have been possible to individual agencies acting alone. WashACT serves as a model nationwide in conducting training in the area of human trafficking, collaborating on investigations, and providing services to the victims and survivors of human trafficking.[31] One of the largest multiagency task forces involved the Washington, D.C., area sniper investigation in 2002. As mentioned in Chapter 1, this manhunt and investigation, which led to the capture of two individuals, involved more than 20 local, 2 state, and at least 10 federal law enforcement agencies. This investigation spanned 23 days in October 2002 while the Virginia, Maryland, and D.C. areas were terrorized by snipers with high-powered rifles shooting

Multiagency task forces facilitate sharing information and coordinating efforts to solve crimes quickly and ensure the safety of the community.

AP Images/Alex Brandon

at people indiscriminately. John Allen Muhammad and Lee Boyd Malvo were arrested at a rest area in Myersville, Maryland, but not before shooting 14 people, 10 of whom died. In 2004, Muhammad was sentenced to death (and executed in November 2009) and Malvo (a teenager) was sentenced to life in prison.[32]

The Police Executive Research Forum (PERF) issued a report entitled *Managing a Multijurisdictional Case: Identifying Lessons Learned from the Sniper Investigation*, which identified the challenges faced by law enforcement personnel in this particular incident, including conducting criminal investigations simultaneously on each incident, trying to prevent more from occurring, and responding to the scenes as new ones occurred.[33] The report identified information management and teamwork or relationships as being the most critical issues in a major investigation such as this. The difference between a quick apprehension and a prolonged frustrating effort, said the report, lay in the development of an effective information management system.[34] This included communication between leaders of the agencies, communicating with the rank and file, and communicating with the public. These efforts were probably enhanced in this particular area of the country because the federal agencies work with state and local law enforcement more than they might in other regions.

The PERF report also recommended that agencies have a plan for investigating incidents such as the sniper case. Although the same plan may not exactly apply to each situation, it can be tweaked and put into place. One of the crucial aspects is defining roles and responsibilities. The agencies involved in the sniper case did an exemplary job considering the unprecedented nature of the incident, though there is always room for improvement.

Crucial to an investigation like the sniper case is providing a daily briefing to staff to curtail rumors and sharing regular and honest communication among the leaders of the agency. This was accomplished in the sniper case via a daily or more frequent conference call with the leaders of the organizations and daily briefings within their organizations. An automated and efficient way of receiving tips (they received almost 10,000 tips a day) is critical to minimize duplication of effort and to make sure a crucial lead is not lost. There also have to be regular conversations regarding what information will be released to the public to allow citizens to protect themselves and possibly contribute to the investigation, yet not spark panic and mass hysteria. Overall, during the sniper investigation, it seemed that organizational barriers and power and control issues that ordinarily might have arisen were overridden by the seriousness of the crimes and everyone's desire to do whatever it took to solve the crime, arrest the offenders, and make the public safe.[35]

This sniper incident and response, as well as the PERF report, can serve as important guides to agencies in developing a plan for any similar situation that might arise. In today's extremely mobile society, with copycat crimes common as well as individuals wanting their 15 minutes of fame, a well-thought-out plan for law enforcement can greatly enhance the likelihood of a quick resolution to a serious incident.

Repeat Offender Programs (ROPs)

American criminologist Marvin Wolfgang discovered that only a few criminals are responsible for most of the predatory street crime in the United States. Most Americans do not commit street robberies; only a relatively small group of people does, but they commit a tremendous amount of crime each year. Borrowing from Wolfgang's research, police started to address their investigative resources to the career criminal using **repeat offender programs (ROPs)**. These programs can be conducted in two major ways.

First, police can identify certain people as the target of investigation. Once a career criminal is identified, the police can use surveillance techniques, follow the criminal, and wait to either catch the person in the act of committing a crime or catch him or her immediately after a crime occurs. These target offender programs are labor intensive.

The second way police can operate the ROP is through case enhancement. Specialized career criminal detectives can be notified of the arrest of a robbery suspect by other officers and then determine from the suspect's conviction or arrest rate whether or not the arrest merits enhancement. If the case is enhanced, an experienced detective assists the arresting officer in preparing the case for presentation in court and debriefs the suspect to obtain further information. A major tactic behind case

repeat offender programs (ROPs) Enforcement efforts directed at known repeat offenders through surveillance or case enhancement.

GUEST LECTURE

MICHAEL K. KEHOE

Michael K. Kehoe is the chief of the Newtown, Connecticut, Police Department, which has 45 sworn officers and 15 civilian staff. Chief Kehoe has over 36 years of law enforcement service with the Newtown Police Department and has received his MBA from Renselear Polytechnic Institute and BA from Western Connecticut State University. He is currently an adjunct professor at Post University in Waterbury, Connecticut.

THE SANDY HOOK ELEMENTARY SCHOOL SHOOTING INVESTIGATION AND RESPONSE

Newtown, Connecticut, is a town of 60 square miles located just 90 miles from the city of New York. Newtown is a typical small suburban New England town with a population of 28,000 located between urban Connecticut centers. On December 14, 2012, at approximately 9:34 a.m., I was involved in an event I never thought I would encounter. I was walking to my office when I was notified that emergency communications personnel were sending my officers to an elementary school shooting. We've trained for mass shooting incidents for years now, but I never really thought we'd have one. We had all heard of Columbine, Virginia Tech, and many others, but our belief was not in our town and certainly not at an elementary school.

As we would later learn, a lone male gunman, aged 20 and equipped with four different weapons, forcibly shot his way into a neighborhood elementary school and murdered 20 first-grade children and 6 adults. Prior to murdering 26 people at the school, the young adult murdered his mother at their home in the Sandy Hook district of Newtown. This incident was the second deadliest mass shooting by a single person in American history, surpassed only by the 2007 Virginia Tech massacre. In this case, as with many mass casualty violence events, the perpetrator committed suicide just before we got there or as we were arriving.

Initially, we weren't sure what was going on because so many calls were coming in at once. We had units heading toward the school and officers from all over were volunteering to render mutual aid, but we weren't even sure what we were dealing with. This incident, like so many calls for service whether routine or not, unfolded with much conflicting information being relayed to responding officers and not enough accurate and timely information being relayed. We needed accurate information in order to handle the situation in the safest way possible for all concerned. Initial calls indicated that possibly two shooters were present, but later it was determined to be a lone shooter.

Our protocol for any active shooter mandates a rapid coordinated response of all available law enforcement officers. The next protocol mandates an immediate confrontation of the threat. The approach and tactics that responding officers use is based upon information already received as well as the observations the officers make as they are arriving. History has taught us that the "typical" active shooter only stops when confronted; as a result, the quicker the confrontation by police, the better, but tactics play a unique role in any meaningful and rapid confrontation.

In this case, my officers began arriving at the scene in less than three minutes and made entry into the school as soon as practicable. Officers were on scene less than one minute before the shooter committed suicide. Unfortunately, this was not enough time to assess the situation, confront the exterior threats, tactically enter the locked building, and engage the shooter. The first arriving officers did what they could with the little information they did receive.

Policing today mandates all law enforcement be trained in similar fashions to mitigate the loss of life and to enhance the coordinated response. Luckily, we had trained similarly with our neighboring agencies and were all on the same page as to how to handle these types of calls. Tactics training after the Columbine massacre had been given to all law enforcement in the state, making our initial response organized. Training with all types of first responders is important and a must, as recent history indicates a trend of more frequent active shooter events with mass casualties. In these types of events, law enforcement takes the lead response, which is critical to all responders. Other mass casualties, such as terrorism, plane crashes, and environmental catastrophes, frequently dictate fire service taking the lead with assistance from law enforcement.

The shooting at Sandy Hook Elementary School touched off an initial massive response with all available law enforcement in the region descending upon the tiny community of Newtown. Through social media, parents learned of a potential threat and shooting at the school and began arriving at the school, creating additional chaos and alarm. The media also descended quickly and in great numbers. All media groups and personnel were initially directed to a nearby park for briefings. The media was advised early to muster at the park for briefings, and this freed up valuable real estate and personnel for additional responding units and agencies.

Arriving officers successfully identified and created a hot zone and a warm zone and also established a reunification area. Due to our previous training for these situations, officers knew to form contact teams, rescue teams, clearing teams, and evacuation teams. Over 450 students and over 50 adults were evacuated in an orderly fashion and successfully reunited with families. We had established a heavily guarded perimeter to ensure this could be safely accomplished before we moved any children and adults to the reunification zone, since at that time we were concerned there could be a secondary shooter.

It was important to have a unified command as many federal, state, and local government entities needed to successfully and cooperatively handle the incident and its aftermath. We had to set up a command structure as soon as possible that would be appropriate for the varied demands placed upon first responders and ensure that we all knew who was in charge and how to negotiate follow-through.

The investigation of the homicides at Sandy Hook Elementary School and the shooter's residence were handled by the Connecticut State Police Department with the help of the Newtown Police Department. A small agency like the Newtown Police Department is under-equipped to investigate a homicide and often contacts the state police for a variety of forensic and specialized services. The partnerships and relationships built before the tragic shooting at Sandy Hook made the combined initial investigation of the murders run smoothly. The homicide investigations were supported by various state and federal entities. Thankfully, we had worked on developing and strengthening our working relationships with our neighboring agencies for years. Smaller agencies tend to rely on these relationships more than bigger urban departments, but in our state, most agencies would have needed to rely on mutual aid for an event of this magnitude. Our teamwork in this situation was crucial to the success of this investigation.

Our work continued long after the immediate danger and critical response had passed. Other investigations of various types were spun out of the initial massacre. Threats to harm hospitals, churches, schools, and families began to filter in. Financial frauds and use of the incident to bogusly acquire money quickly emerged. Many of these investigations were handled by federal law enforcement. Under the direction of the U.S. Attorney, the FBI, the U.S. Marshall's Service, the ATF, and other federal partners worked closely with all state and local law enforcement to ensure the unity and thoroughness of the investigations and.

There were many challenges in the days following the incident. Visits by the president of the United States and other elected or appointed officials became a frequent occurrence requiring an extraordinary law enforcement presence. In addition to the personnel required to conduct a massive homicide scene along with the security needed to prevent unwanted persons entering on or near the school, extra law enforcement personnel were needed to guard victims' family homes, churches, vigils, schools (private and public), and municipal buildings. Law enforcement was needed to maintain traffic safety and control throughout the town.

A nice gesture but yet a huge challenge we had not anticipated was the outpouring of gifts and donations to the victims, survivors, and community. How would we handle that? How would we make sure the donations were distributed fairly and to the right people, and who would handle that? Where would we store all these items until we could deal with it? The community was quickly overwhelmed by the generosity of gifts, mail, and well-wishers from all over the country. In addition, mental health care givers and advisors descended upon Newtown to deliver and provide necessary services to the community, officials, and responders. All of these created added responsibilities for law enforcement and community leaders, necessitating an unprecedented statewide mutual aid response.

All sorts of roadside memorials were set up all over town. What should we do with them? This was a question asked very early on. We needed to get traffic moving freely throughout town again and restore commercial and retail store activity, for they were hurt by the extraordinary amount of traffic. At the same time, we had to be sensitive to the needs of the families and the community. Shielding and protecting the victims' families became a full-time law enforcement effort. All funerals,

(continued)

wakes, and interments required a unique and active police presence to protect, shield, and deliver families to their respective venues. Traffic control and traffic management became a priority for law enforcement for several weeks after the initial event. The average daily staffing levels for all law enforcement services provided in Newtown during the days following December 14, 2012, rose from approximately 6–9 officers per day shift to 60–100 officers. How would we accommodate all

of these helpers? How would we protect the victims' families from the media and outside pressures?

There were many lessons learned from this event that could impact law enforcement's ability to render capable services to any community. There is no doubt that law enforcement has trained to respond effectively to an active shooter. However, more training is needed to include other responder disciplines so that effective and important services are rendered as quickly

---

enhancement is liaison with the district attorney's office to alert the prosecuting attorney to the importance of the case and to the suspect's past record. Such information helps ensure zealous efforts by the prosecutor.

Marcia Chaiken and Jan Chaiken, in their report *Priority Prosecutors of High-Rate Dangerous Offenders*, distinguished between persistent offenders (those who commit crimes over a long period of time), high-rate offenders (those who commit numerous crimes per year), and dangerous offenders (those who commit crimes of violence).[36] These authors suggest that the most accurate way to identify high-rate dangerous offenders is using a two-stage screening process. The first stage should look for evidence of a serious previous felony conviction, failure to complete a previous sentence, arrests while in pretrial release, or a known drug problem. The authors state that defendants who fall into three out of four of these categories have a 90 percent chance of being high-rate dangerous offenders and should be further screened. The second screening involves looking for evidence of the following: use of a weapon in the current crime, one or more juvenile convictions for robbery, or status of wanted for failure to complete a previous sentence.[37] The presence of any of these aggravating factors would cause the defendant to be considered a high-rate dangerous offender. The authors suggest that any defendant considered a high-rate dangerous offender should receive special attention by investigators and prosecutors.

An initiative with pilot programs involving the federal government and local agencies called the Violent Crime Impact Teams (VCIT) found that during the first six months of operation, 13 of

the 15 pilot programs reported decreases in homicides committed with firearms. The programs were designed to identify, target, disrupt, arrest, and prosecute the worst criminal offenders in high-crime areas throughout the country. The strategy relied heavily on a team effort between the federal, state, and local law enforcement agencies in the area, which is believed to be the most crucial factor in the long-term success of the initiative. Overall, the VCIT areas reported that firearm-related homicides decreased by 17 percent, 500 targeted individuals were arrested, 3,000 firearms were confiscated, more than $2 million was seized, and 2,500 other criminals were arrested. The initiative appears to be a success, and other cities are being added.[38]

Internet Registries

Some jurisdictions are enacting laws requiring the registration of various types of criminals. For years, sex offenders have been tracked in most states. This tracking primarily serves as a public notification system so parents know if there are any sex offenders living in their neighborhood, allowing them to take the proper precautions to keep their children safe. These registries also notify local law enforcement of individuals residing in their community with a past in this particular type of crime. If a crime occurs, the officers have individuals they can contact, possibly increasing the chances of a successful investigation.

Some states have added to the information they provide on the registry. The state of Florida recently added vehicle and boat information as well as more detailed crime information to its sex offender website to assist citizens in more accurately assessing their and professionally as possible. Mass casualty training must also include the chaotic aftermath and management using the widely accepted NIMS (National Incident Management System) and ICS (Incident Command System) tools.

The greatest challenge for law enforcement and our communities will be how to prevent these mass casualties. American law enforcement has been equal to such tasks in the past, and I suspect they will be able to make significant inroads

on this unpleasant but increasingly common societal phenomenon. Law enforcement's response that day and in the weeks that followed was extraordinary considering the many challenges involved. But as with any major incident, we critically reviewed our response and determined what could have been done better and what was done really well; then we shared our knowledge with other law enforcement agencies to help them if it ever is necessary.

risk.[39] Though much more information is available through the Internet to the public and police than before, it is unknown whether the registries have actually discouraged offenders from committing new crimes. There is also concern that these registries may create a false sense of security, as the public often assumes that having these registries means the offenders are closely monitored.

Exactly how sex offender cases are handled varies from state to state. There is now a National Sex Offender public website coordinated by the Department of Justice and located on the FBI website that allows citizens to search the latest information from all 50 states, the District of Columbia, the U.S. territories, and numerous Indian tribes for the identity and location of known sex offenders.[40]

Recently, some states have created a similar registry for meth offenders. The governor of Minnesota signed an executive order creating an online registry for people convicted of making or selling methamphetamine. It is modeled after a similar registry in Tennessee. The Minnesota governor stated, "When you have public awareness of the presence of these individuals, there will be further accountability by neighbors, by people who are interested in making sure that their areas of work or residence are safe." Many states now have similar registries in place, and the U.S. Drug Enforcement Administration maintains a National Clandestine Laboratory Registry on their website that allows the public to access the information on labs in their state. In Illinois, the purpose of the law is to expedite law enforcement's research regarding conviction records rather than to inform the public, but the public is not barred from accessing the information.[41] The hope is that neighbors

and citizens will be extra vigilant and perhaps help in investigations, allowing law enforcement to get these offenders off the streets for longer periods.[42]

Global Positioning System (GPS) Technology, Smartphones, and Social Media

Surveillance of offenders is extremely labor intensive and costly. Today, technology has improved to a degree to allow law enforcement to track offenders without having them physically followed 24 hours a day. Global positioning system (GPS) technology has allowed many states to implement programs monitoring offenders. It saves the state the money of incarcerating the offenders, and most states require offenders to pay for the monitoring unless they are indigent. Though some states are using GPS technology to monitor paroled gang members, most are using it to monitor sex offenders. Some states have named their laws after Jennifer Lunsford, a nine-year-old Florida girl who was kidnapped, raped, and killed in February 2005, by a convicted sex offender who had not reported that he lived across the street from her family. He fled after her murder, and it took a month to find him.

Many states have passed laws on GPS monitoring, and others have bills pending, because it appears to have tremendous support among elected officials. At least 23 states have implemented programs to monitor sex offenders by satellite, and most are reporting success with their programs. In California, in just under a year, 45 monitored offenders (out of 430) were arrested for violating parole, and no new crimes were committed by those offenders. Massachusetts arrested 8 of its 192 high-risk offenders in the same period. A study by Florida State University released in February 2006 found that offenders tracked by GPS were 90 percent less likely to abscond or reoffend than were those not monitored. Most states plan to continue and possibly expand their programs.[43]

OnStar, the General Motors emergency rescue and recovery service, has been used to assist accident victims, locate stolen vehicles, and disable stolen vehicles. This program has helped to protect the community, minimize injury to others, and recover property. A similar system, LoJack, has worked with local law enforcement for years and has also been used to locate stolen vehicles that have been outfitted with their GPS device.

Smartphones also have proven to be a valuable crime-fighting tool. They have been used to take photos or videos of suspects, vehicles, and crimes and other violations in progress, where it would be likely that the actions would have been concluded or the suspects would have fled by the time police arrived. Victims or witnesses might be reluctant to confront a violator, but taking a photo can allow them to assist their community and remain relatively anonymous, depending on the situation. Victims or witnesses can text messages when they are unable to speak or afraid of being heard. The phone can be tracked to find the location of the owner of the phone, or the phone itself if it has been removed from the owner. People who were victims of crime have been rescued from harm and people who have been involved in accidents and were unable to communicate have been found. Additionally, smartphones can provide information regarding the ongoing location of the phone, phone and e-mail contacts, locations indicating where photos were taken, and information from other applications that may have been downloaded.

Social media are being used increasingly by law enforcement agencies to reach out to the public in order to solicit their input regarding crime information and suspect identification. The use of videos has proven to be an asset to investigations that would most likely not have had successful conclusions if not for the public coming forward in response to images captured on tape. The use of social media to disseminate information was particularly evident in the Boston Marathon bombing in April 2013. Together with the use of surveillance cameras and cell phone footage by marathon spectators, the information disseminated by average citizens sometimes appeared more timely than the information shared by the authorities. As events unfolded, the conventional media could be seen checking their cell phones and obtaining updated information from tweets shared by various investigative agencies both to garner leads from the public and to share developments in the case. This case seemed to be a game changer in the way major events are covered by the media and the partnership between traditional media outlets, investigative agencies, and citizens. Some chiefs have recounted that their agency must release information via social networks quickly, or others will release it and it might not be accurate. Many officers have arrived on scenes to find photos or videos already being shared by witnesses or passersby, sometimes to the detriment of the investigation. Law enforcement must rise to the challenge of using social media in a positive and productive manner as technology and communication methods evolve if they want to remain in control of the investigation but also make the best use of a very beneficial partnership with the community such as that seen during the Boston Marathon bombing investigation.

Surveillance Cameras

Surveillance cameras are everywhere today; despite some challenges, most courts have upheld their use, stating that they are not a violation of individuals' rights because there is no expectation of privacy in most of the locations. Although these cameras have been touted as a crime prevention tool, they have been critical in solving some major cases. Many cities across the country, large and small, are allocating budget dollars to install surveillance cameras and to purchase license plate scanners both mobile (on police vehicles) and on fixed locations in the jurisdiction. These cameras and scanners have assisted in all types of criminal investigations by tracking particular vehicles. This topic is discussed in more detail in Chapter 14.

Some critics dispute the value of surveillance cameras in crime fighting and crime prevention, and even their constitutionality.[44] However, it is hard to dispute the contribution they have made in some high-profile cases that may not have been solved had it not been for surveillance cameras installed by property owners. When 11-year-old Carlie Brucia was reported missing in Sarasota, Florida, on February 1,

2004, there were few leads other than where she had been and that she was believed to be heading home. Detectives obtained a surveillance video from a car wash located along Carlie's route home. The video showed Carlie walking along the rear of the car wash, where a man was seen approaching her and forcibly walking her out of view of the camera. This video was released to the media and an AMBER Alert system was activated. Numerous phone calls were received identifying the suspect, Joseph Smith, and he was subsequently arrested[45] and convicted[46] of raping and murdering Carlie.

In 2010, a robbery and assault by four teens on a 15-year-old girl in a Seattle bus tunnel was caught on surveillance video and aired nationally, primarily due to the lack of response by uniformed security personnel within a few feet of the attack. The teens were identified and charged due to the surveillance tape. Other videotapes have captured robbers, burglars, and vandals on tape and, when aired on TV, have resulted in some arrests.

Law enforcement has also started to take the surveillance tapes they acquire in their investigation of crimes to the Internet-savvy public by posting them on YouTube. Typically, they will do this when they have footage of the suspect but cannot identify him or her. They then may notify selected groups or individuals that they have posted the clip or attach a request for help to the clip and hope someone will recognize the offender. Sometimes, frustrated business owners or homeowners who have been victimized in less serious ways post their surveillance tapes on YouTube themselves. They post the clip of the suspect breaking into their business or car or vandalizing their property with the hope that someone may watch their video and recognize the offender. With social media and the sharing of information via smartphones and Facebook, surveillance cameras also greatly facilitated solving the crime of the Boston Marathon bombing.

The use of YouTube in solving crimes has taken another turn. Individuals desiring their 15 minutes of fame have posted videos of fights and assaults on

AP Images/Chip Litherland, Pool

Mike Evanoff, owner of Evie's Car Wash, testifies about this security video footage from his business, which was used in the trial of Joseph Smith. Smith was charged in the death of 11-year-old Carlie Brucia after he was identified in the security video footage approaching Brucia and taking her forcibly by the arm.

the site. Those videos have then been used as evidence by law enforcement to prosecute the individuals committing the assaults. A case that attracted a lot of attention was the Florida case involving six teenage girls accused of beating a 16-year-old cheerleader and filming the attack for the Internet. Shortly after the case hit the press, 6 of the 20 most-viewed videos on YouTube were related to the attack.[47]

Cold-Case Squads

Advances in DNA technology have led to the increased use of cold-case squads to solve crimes. **Cold-case squads** reexamine old cases that have remained unsolved. They use the passage of time coupled with a fresh set of eyes to help solve cases that have been stagnant for years and often decades.

Over time, relationships change. People may no longer be married, may no longer be friends, or may no longer be intimidated by or afraid of the same

---

cold-case squads Investigative units that reexamine old cases that have remained unsolved. They use the passage of time coupled with a fresh set of eyes to help solve cases that have been stagnant for years and often decades.

people. Someone who was reluctant to talk because of either fear or loyalty may decide to tell the truth years later. Individuals may have found religion or changed their lifestyle, and years later realize that what they did, witnessed, or knew about was bad and they want to set the record straight. Cold-case detectives reinterview all individuals involved and hope someone has had a change of heart over the years or forgotten what was said initially, allowing police to uncover new information.

Cold-case detectives also benefit from the passage of time in another way. In the last couple of decades, there have been tremendous advances in forensic science, especially DNA testing, which have greatly enhanced the investigative process. Much smaller samples are necessary now to get a more definitive match through DNA than even a few years ago. Cold-case detectives are able to solve many cases solely by reexamining the evidence.

In 1977, a six-year-old girl was reported missing in Reno, Nevada; 23 years later, the detectives had her clothes retested, found previously undetected DNA evidence, and tied the crime to a convicted felon.[48] In 2003, Jesus Mezquia, a 48-year-old resident of Florida, was arrested for the 1993 rape and murder of Mia Zapata in Seattle. King County cold-case detectives submitted the DNA profile found on Zapata's body to the National DNA Index System and found that it matched a DNA sample obtained from Mezquia as a result of a previous, unrelated arrest in Florida. The Seattle crime had been a random sexual assault and murder; Mezquia and Zapata had no connection save location, so this crime would have likely remained unsolved without DNA analysis.

Investigators who make up the cold-case squad must not be afraid to use whatever means may help their case, including the media. Some departments use shows such as *America's Most Wanted* to help bring a suspect or a crime back into the mind of the public. In 2011, when the show was canceled by the Fox network, President Obama commented on its "remarkable record" in apprehending more than 1,000 suspects in its two-decade run.[49] A strategy that has had some success recently is the use of "cold-case" playing cards and drink coasters to highlight unsolved murders and missing persons cases to inmates and others with the goal of generating leads and solving the cases.

Recently, an FBI task force launched a media blitz in their hunt for James "Whitey" Bulger, an infamous Boston crime boss who had been the subject of a 16-year international manhunt. They posted television spots on shows like *Ellen*, *The View*, and *Live with Regis and Kelly*, targeting individuals who might have had encounters with Bulger's girlfriend. They received more than 200 tips, and Bulger was in custody within days.[50]

Detectives use innovative ideas to obtain the evidence they may need for comparison purposes. A man from New Jersey was recently arrested for a decades-old murder of a teenage girl in Seattle, when he too was a teen. He had been a prime suspect, but investigators had no evidence linking him to the crime. In 2003, they sent him a form to fill out to participate in a suit regarding parking fines in Seattle. He filled out the form, put it in the envelope, licked the envelope, and mailed it back to Seattle. Detectives were able to match the DNA from his saliva to that found on evidence, and he was arrested. That case has withstood several challenges by the defendant's attorneys, and he is in prison.

The National Institute of Justice (NIJ) has awarded more than $73 million since 2005 to more than 100 law enforcement agencies across the country through its "Solving Cold Cases with DNA" competitive grant program. This funding has allowed more than 119,000 cases to be reexamined and over 4,000 DNA profiles to be added into the FBI's combined DNA index system, resulting in more than 1,400 hits. In 2013, the Boston Police Department was finally able to link Albert DeSalvo, the Boston Strangler, to the rape and murder of Mary Sullivan in 1964. She was one of 11 young women that DeSalvo confessed to killing. The help of this grant and the DNA link provided the ability to reopen the cold case and close this mystery.[51]

Cold-case squads are providing great hope and comfort to families of victims of old, unsolved crimes. The community also experiences a sense of justice when detectives are able to solve these long-dormant cases and hold the defendants accountable for their actions.

Proactive Tactics

Decoy Operations

One of the primary purposes of police patrol is to prevent crime by creating a sense of omnipresence; potential criminals are deterred from crime by the presence or potential presence of the police.

Omnipresence does not always work well, however. We have crime both on our streets and in areas where ordinary police patrols cannot see crime developing, such as the inside of a store or the hallway of a housing project. We also have seen that retroactive investigations of crimes, with the intent to identify and arrest perpetrators, are not very effective.

One proactive approach to apprehending criminals in the course of committing a crime is **decoy operations**. Decoy operations take several forms, among them blending and decoy. In **blending**, officers dressed in civilian clothes try to blend into an area and patrol it on foot or in unmarked police cars in an attempt to catch a criminal in the act of committing a crime. Officers may target areas where a significant amount of crime occurs, or they may follow particular people who appear to be potential victims or potential offenders. To blend, officers assume the roles and dress of ordinary citizens—construction workers, shoppers, joggers, bicyclists, physically disabled persons, and so on—so that they can be close enough to observe and intervene should a crime occur without first being recognized as officers.

In decoy, officers dress as, and play the role of, potential victims—drunks, nurses, businesspeople, tourists, prostitutes, blind people, isolated subway riders, or defenseless elderly people. The officers wait to be the subject of a crime while a team of backup officers is ready to apprehend the violator in the act of committing the crime. Decoy operations are most effective in combating the crimes of robbery, purse snatching, and other larcenies from the person; burglaries; and thefts of and from automobiles.

Police officers around the country have responded creatively to crime problems by playing many roles. Some have filled in as coffee shop employees or as baristas at espresso stands. They have worked at convenience stores, nail salons, and video stores in an effort to catch robbers in the act. Many successful arrests have been made in such situations, and the surrounding publicity creates uncertainty for criminals about whether their intended victim might be a police officer. A man who had posted a fraudulent ad for "models" and "actresses" in a South Florida newspaper and then proceeded to fondle and molest female applicants was shocked after one of his "applicants" came back to the office wearing a badge and reading him his rights.

Anticrime and decoy strategies focus on reducing serious and violent street crimes, apprehending criminals in the act, making quality arrests, and maintaining a high conviction record. In achieving successful prosecutions in their cases, decoy operations overcome the problem police encounter when witnesses and victims are reluctant to cooperate with police and prosecutors because of fear or apathy. There is a concern for potential injury to the officer as well as the perception of entrapment by individuals not knowledgeable of the legal boundaries.

As mentioned in Chapter 9, decoy vehicles can be used in solving crimes and enhancing investigations. When an agency has a lot of vehicles being broken into in a particular place, such as a mall or hospital parking lot, they can set up a decoy vehicle with similarities to the vehicles that appear to be the target. Investigators can watch the vehicle, and when the perpetrator breaks in, they can quickly make an arrest.

Stakeout Operations

Many crimes occur indoors, where passing patrol officers cannot see their occurrence. To catch some of these criminals, stakeouts are used. A **stakeout** is the hidden surveillance of a location or person. For example, a stakeout might consist of a group of heavily armed officers who hide in an area of a store building waiting for an impending holdup. If an armed robber enters the store and attempts a robbery, the officers yell "Police!" from their hidden areas. If the perpetrator fails to drop the weapon, the officers open fire.

Stakeouts are effective in cases in which the police receive a tip that a crime is going to occur in a commercial establishment or in which the police discover or come upon a pattern. A typical pattern would be a group of liquor stores in a certain downtown commercial area that have been robbed at gunpoint in a way that is consistent enough to indicate it might happen again.

Stakeouts are extremely expensive in terms of police personnel. They are also controversial because they can be dangerous for all involved. The situations are always dynamic, and officers have to

---

decoy operations Operations in which officers dress as and play the role of potential victims in the hope of attracting and catching a criminal.

blending Plainclothes officers' efforts to blend into an area and attempt to catch a criminal.

stakeout The hidden surveillance of a location or person.

Jogging on the Job

Decoy work varies tremendously in challenge and desirability. In large departments, it can be an officer's regular assignment, but in most mid-sized and smaller departments, it will be used as necessary, depending on crime issues that arise. In these cases, it will usually be a break from an officer's regular assignment. During my police career, I had many occasions to work decoy assignments in which females were targeted victims. I found these assignments to be a challenge and a welcome break to my routine, whether I was assigned to patrol or the detective bureau at the time.

One June we had a couple of incidents of indecent exposure at a popular but somewhat isolated jogging trail. We then had an incident where a female was grabbed at 8:00 a.m. and pulled into the bushes along this jogging trail. She fought her attacker off and managed to get away, but it was clearly an attempted rape. We decided that for two weeks, we would put a female officer out jogging this same trail in the early morning hours. Since I was known to be a runner, I was chosen for the

assignment. It sounds pretty cool, getting paid to run and work out on duty, but the conditions were less than ideal.

June in South Florida is *very* hot and humid, and this trail was in a scrub area with lots of bushes but not many trees; consequently, there was little shade. I put on a wire so that I had voice communication when I was out of sight of the two backup officers along the three-mile course. I had to be covered up enough to hide the wire, which meant I would be even warmer. I ran and walked for about two hours a day around this course. As I sweated profusely, jumped over and avoided snakes, and was bitten by the biggest horseflies I had ever seen, I started singing Helen Reddy's song "Ain't No Way to Treat a Lady" for the entertainment of my backup officers (and perhaps to make a point). We saw nothing of interest during the two weeks, and there were never any more attacks there, so the offender must have moved on or been arrested for something else. Or maybe he heard me singing and got scared off?

—Linda Forst

decide how far to let these incidents progress. There are so many variables that police can never know when violence may erupt, even in a previously nonviolent pattern of crimes. Law enforcement personnel do not want to risk standing by and having innocent people get hurt.

Sting Operations

Sting operations are undercover police operations in which police officers pose as criminals in order to arrest law violators. They can be used, for example, to apprehend thieves and recover stolen property. In this case, the police might rent a storefront and put the word out on the street that they will buy any stolen property—no questions asked. The police would set up hidden video and audio recorders that could be used to identify "customers," who then would be located and placed under arrest several months later.

These audio and video recorders make excellent evidence in court.

Sting operations are often used to purchase stolen vehicles or car parts. Electronic devices are also targeted in sting operations in an effort to catch the individuals committing crimes to get these items. Depending on the size and scope of the targeted criminal organizations, sting operations may be multijurisdictional in nature or in fact organized by the FBI.

Another type of sting operation is directed against people wanted on warrants. These wanted persons are mailed a letter telling them that they have won an award (such as tickets to an important ball game) and that they should report to a certain location (usually a hotel) at a certain time to pick up the prize. When the person appears, he or she is arrested.

Traditionally, sting operations involved setting up false storefronts to deal in stolen property, but over the years the definition of sting operations has expanded. Now they often are used in situations of corruption, prostitution, car theft, drug dealing, child pornography, child sexual abuse, and tobacco

---

sting operations Undercover police operations in which police pose as criminals to arrest law violators.

and alcohol sales to minors. Generally, a sting operation includes four elements:

- An opportunity or enticement to commit a crime
- A targeted likely offender or offender group
- An undercover or hidden police officer or surrogate, or some form of deception
- A "gotcha" climax when the operation ends with arrests [52]

Studies of sting operations have found that they account for a large number of arrests and the recovery of a significant amount of stolen property. However, the studies have failed to demonstrate that the tactic leads to reductions in crime. [53] A major drawback to sting operations is that they can serve as inducements to burglary and theft because they create a market for stolen goods.

Frustrated with increasing gun violence and the perception that the federal government was not taking any action, New York City decided to take on gun dealers in other states. The city sent teams of private investigators posing as gun buyers to stores in five states and caught 15 dealers making illegal sales. These businesses had been the source of 500 guns that were used in the commission of crimes in New York City. The operatives went into the stores with hidden cameras. One investigator looked at the guns, talked with the sales staff, and made the decision. This investigator then called the second investigator over (usually a female), who had not been involved in any way, to fill out the background paperwork, and then the first investigator paid for the gun. This practice is referred to as using a "straw buyer," someone with no criminal record, to fill out the background paperwork to purchase a gun from a dealer.

Other cities around the country have followed New York's lead, including Minneapolis, which discovered that some of its gun dealers were selling many guns to the same "straw buyers" repeatedly. Local gangs were using female "straw buyers" for the purchases. [54] These types of suits may be a way to increase accountability among gun dealers and sellers and help bring down the violent crime rate.

Sting operations targeting lewd behavior have often been used around the country, particularly in parks and areas frequented by children in an effort to protect them from inadvertently seeing something they should not see. Many agencies have discovered that some public locations become known as meeting places for inappropriate sexual activity, and the use of sting operations has helped to curtail these activities and shield children and unsuspecting members of the public.

Another kind of sting operation that has been a point of discussion is the child predator sting aired on NBC. Law enforcement has been working with the media in operating some of these child pornography stings. From 2004 to 2007, *Dateline* on the NBC network aired "To Catch a Predator," where a sting is set up in a rented home. When the operation began, *Dateline* staff members worked with an organization from Portland, Oregon, called Perverted Justice, whose volunteer members posed as young boys and girls in Internet chat rooms and waited to be contacted by adult men seeking sex with minors. The volunteers lured the men to the rented house, where they were confronted by a *Dateline* reporter on camera. In many situations, NBC did not notify local law enforcement. After seeing the popularity of the show, NBC formalized its relationship with Perverted Justice and started working more closely with law enforcement, which resulted in police making more arrests after the confrontations. Other networks have aired similar shows since 2007 when NBC stopped producing "To Catch a Predator."

These relationships and operations are not without controversy, as roles and relationships have become blurred. [55] The public seems hungry for this type of story and eager to put pedophiles behind bars. Legal outcomes and court challenges will help to determine whether these types of arrangements and stings will continue. Despite the attention these operations have received, detectives are continually surprised by the abundance of child predators on the Internet. Investigators frequently go into chat rooms or onto social media sites and pose as young teens. It does not take long for them to be approached by suspected predators and have these predators progress to proposing an in-person meeting.

Sting operations may appear to be an attractive option for some crime investigations, but law enforcement should carefully weigh all of the options before deciding on this approach. They may not in fact reduce or prevent recurring crime problems and in this era of reduced budgets, the cost in both dollars and resources may be prohibitive. There are also ethical and entrapment issues that need to be considered. There may be other more effective problem-solving techniques.

Cybercrime Investigations

The world today is changing quickly as a result of ever-evolving technology. This includes criminals and how they choose to commit their crimes or obtain the goods or financial gain they seek. With the advent of technology, the criminals are able to commit the same types of crimes but with the added assistance of anonymity and a vast resource of potential victims. **Cybercrime** is any type of criminal activity involving computers and networks, ranging from fraud to viruses to infiltrating networks or sites to obtain personal information for identity theft or to shut systems down. Cybercrime trends change regularly and quickly, which can make them difficult for law enforcement to keep up with. Many databases are interrelated and in a digital format in order to be able to share information and avoid duplication. These databases no longer catalog just financial information, but include a lot of personal data and even medical and health information. This information in the wrong hands can be extremely harmful with significant consequences. The Internet and social media can also cause psychological damage through the posting of threats toward an individual or group or the practice of cyberbullying.

All types of criminals use the Internet and social media sites to facilitate their crimes, whether to fence stolen goods or to meet underage boys and girls for sexual gratification. With smartphone technology, they also are leaving digital evidence of their crimes: Incriminating information can now be found in personal smartphones and sometimes on the more public social media sites. Just knowing where to find this evidence and how to access it involves a certain amount of expertise.

Law enforcement agencies must add the capability of conducting effective and productive cybercrime investigations to their crime-solving toolbox. Historically, police agencies have been slow to keep up with new demands, especially in the area of technology. Considering the exponential growth of technology and its rapidly changing face, law enforcement has significant demands placed upon

---

cybercrime Criminal activity involving computers and networks, ranging from fraud to viruses to infiltrating networks or sites to obtain personal information for identity theft or to shut systems down.

undercover investigation A covert investigation involving plainclothes officers.

YOU ARE THERE The Legality of Police Undercover Drug Investigations: *Gordon v. Warren Consolidated Board of Education, 1983*

High school officials had placed an undercover officer in regular classes to investigate student drug use. After the investigation, several students were arrested and convicted of participating in the drug trade. They appealed their convictions, claiming that the actions of the school officials violated their rights under the First Amendment of the U.S. Constitution. Their appeal was dismissed by an appellate court ruling that the presence of the police officer working undercover did not constitute any more than a "chilling" effect on the students' First Amendment rights, because it did not disrupt classroom activities or education and it did not have any tangible effect on inhibiting expression of particular views in the classroom.

Source: Based on *Gordon v. Warren Consolidated Board of Education*, 706 F.2d 778 (6th Cir. 1983).

---

the investigations unit, especially when you factor in recent budget cuts and reductions in personnel. It is a constant struggle to train and retain officers educated in this area. Departments need to find ways to train as many officers as possible in the basics of cybercrime investigations and to have at least one expert available within the department to advise and guide these investigations as they arise. This is critically important, especially as the cybercrime numbers continue to grow and the impact on the community becomes more widespread.[56]

Undercover Operations

An **undercover investigation** may be defined as one in which an investigator assumes a different identity to obtain information or achieve another investigatory purpose. The undercover investigator generally plays the role of another person. In an undercover investigation, the investigator can be doing many things, including merely observing or performing certain actions that are designed to get other people to do something or to react to or interact with the investigator in a certain way.

One dangerous consequence of the undercover job and the officer's ability to blend into the criminal subculture is the fact that the undercover officer may be mistaken for a suspect by uniformed officers who are responding to a scene. This is especially true in big agencies and when undercover officers end up out of their jurisdiction. These officers receive additional training in how to respond to uniformed officers who may respond with guns drawn and treat them as suspects. The goal is for all to come out of the situation unhurt. The primary function of the investigator in these cases is to play a role without anyone realizing that he or she is playing a role, and officers must learn to safely handle the unintended consequences of this function. In policing, the primary purpose of the undercover operation most often is the collection of evidence of crimes.

Police Undercover Investigations

Undercover investigations generally include drug undercover investigations; stings, including warrant stings and fencing stings that involve the buying and selling of stolen goods and other contraband; decoy operations targeted against the crimes of robbery, burglary, and assault; antiprostitution operations; and operations involving the infiltration and arrest of people involved in organized crime, white-collar crime, and corruption. Police undercover officers have a dangerous yet often rewarding job. It can be rewarding as well as a relief when the undercover officer gets to arrest the offender at the end of the investigation. Offenders are often very surprised when they realize the role an undercover officer played in their arrest.

Undercover investigations can present some significant challenges to police officers and police organizations. Officers who infiltrate the criminal lifestyle are living a lie. They spend their working hours in a role quite contrary to who they are. The difficulty involved in this will vary with the assignment and the length of the assignment. Hanging around with criminals and attempting to become their friends and fit in with their lifestyle can lead to a socialization process very different from what officers experienced growing up and preparing for the police job. This situation is further complicated because undercover officers receive little supervision and often little training in preparation for their roles. Eventually their bonds to other officers and even to family and friends may be cut or weakened, depending on the assignment. This has contributed to some

officers becoming deviant, adhering to the subculture, breaking the law, and ending their careers, which is a real tragedy for all concerned.

Realizing the difficult challenges and conditions that undercover officers face, departments are implementing policies to minimize the chance of officers going astray and to protect them and the department. The Commission on Accreditation for Law Enforcement Agencies (CALEA) requires departments to have policies and procedures in place concerning undercover and decoy operations as well as vice, drug surveillance, and investigations.[57]

Federal Undercover Investigations

Federal undercover investigations generally include efforts at detecting and arresting people involved in political corruption, insurance fraud, labor racketeering, and other types of organized conspiracy-type crimes. Federal agencies, including the Drug Enforcement Administration (DEA), Customs, and the Bureau of Alcohol, Tobacco, Firearms and Explosives (ATF), often form joint task force investigations with local, county, and state law enforcement agencies. Some of the agents work undercover and others work surveillance. This allows them to pool resources and expertise. This approach has been particularly successful in South Florida. Many major drug or arms smuggling operations have been broken up, arrests made, and property worth millions of dollars confiscated.

Drug Undercover Investigations

Drug enforcement is a priority in law enforcement and a vital part of the law enforcement mission. Drugs contribute to a myriad of social problems and quality-of-life issues in communities. There is a strong correlation between drugs and criminal activity and acts of violence. Almost everyone knows someone who has had their life impacted in some way by drugs.

The drug problem consumes a lot of police resources and puts both police officers and community members at risk. It also poses a significant financial burden for society. Though we all strive for the same goals—safe communities and highways, drug-free workplaces and schools, babies born free of addiction, and a peaceful quality of life—individual values often dictate different ways of achieving these goals. Add in political agendas, availability of resources, conflicting laws, the changing trends in drug usage, and the influence of organized crime, and law enforcement is charged with an extremely difficult job.[58]

Law enforcement must constantly assess the drug issue—including changing laws, changing usage, alternate manufacturing techniques, and evolving distribution patterns—and determine the safest and most effective way of attacking the problem and keeping citizens safe. Many of the chosen tactics are under constant scrutiny to ensure that constitutional safeguards are being upheld. Recently, medical marijuana laws have been passed in many states and recreational marijuana laws have been passed in Colorado and Washington, which has further complicated the issue, as these laws are in direct conflict with the federal drug laws. In addition, "synthetic" drugs that mimic the effects of various drugs are frequently being developed but are not legally prohibited until lawmakers catch up with these substances and enact new laws. Law enforcement must follow these trends and disseminate information to the street officers and investigators, as they are charged with investigating the drug law violations and keeping the public safe.

Prescription drug fraud, or the illegal acquisition of prescription drugs for personal use or profit, is a popular way to get around some of the enforcement efforts targeting other controlled substances and yet build on the profits of the drug trade. This can take the form of covert or overt crimes, including Medicaid fraud; theft (of prescription pads or the drugs themselves) from pharmacies, doctors' offices, and patients; or even robberies of these same parties; doctor shopping or consulting multiple doctors to obtain prescriptions; using prescriptions legally prescribed to family members or friends; or altering prescriptions to increase the quantity of medication. Some parts of the country are known to have less restrictive laws regarding pain clinics or prescriptions and have become a target destination for addicts desiring these drugs or individuals eager to take advantage of addicts' needs. South Florida has acquired the reputation as the epicenter of the problem due in part to the prevalence of pain-management clinics, many of which dispense medications inappropriately. After a city has examined their problem, they can analyze whether it can be addressed via enforcement actions or if it is a bigger problem requiring a task force approach with medical personnel and treatment facilities.[59]

Drug investigations can be approached in the same manner as any other investigation, but they involve some additional risks due to the nature of drug trafficking and the violence associated with it. Most drug investigations involve an undercover component, which can be very dangerous. Drug dealers are usually armed, the encounter may be a rip-off and not an actual deal, and the dealers may be in a paranoid state or under the influence of narcotics at the time of the deal. Caution also needs to be taken to make sure that the deal is not being done between two law enforcement agencies, which has happened in the past. Most agencies now have procedures in place to check whether that may be the case before the deal goes down.

At least three general methods can be used in conducting drug undercover investigations. The first involves infiltrating criminal organizations that sell large amounts of drugs. The method is to buy larger and larger amounts of drugs so the buyer can reach as high as possible into the particular organizational hierarchy. Lower members of the criminal hierarchy have access only to a fixed quantity of drugs. To obtain larger amounts, they have to introduce the investigator to their source or connection, who is generally someone in the upper echelon of the organization or a member of a more sophisticated organization. These operations usually require sophisticated electronic surveillance measures and large sums of money. Such investigations can be very lengthy and dangerous to the undercover investigators.

The next method that can be used to attack drug syndicates or drug locations is the process of staking out a particular location and making detailed observations of the conditions that indicate drug sales, such as the arrival and brief visit of numerous cars and people. These observations are best if recorded on video to establish probable cause for obtaining a search warrant. If a judge agrees with the probable cause, he or she can issue a search warrant, which can then be executed against a particular person, automobile, or premises. These investigations can be very lengthy and involve extensive sophisticated electronic surveillance.

The third method is the undercover "buy-bust," an operation in which an undercover police officer purchases a quantity of drugs from a subject and then leaves the scene, contacts the backup team, and identifies the seller. The backup team, in or out of uniform, responds to the location of the sale and arrests the seller, based on the description given by the undercover officer. The legal basis of the arrest is probable cause to believe that a crime was committed and that the subject was the perpetrator of the crime. Based on the legal arrest, the backup team can search the subject and seize any illegal drugs. If the arrest occurs inside the premises, the backup team can seize any illegal substances that are in plain view. The undercover officer then goes to the police facility to which the subject has been transferred and makes a positive identification of the subject from a hidden location, generally through a one-way mirror or window. By viewing the suspect through the one-way mirror or window, the undercover officer cannot be seen and thus can be used again in the same role.

The buy-bust is generally used in low-level drug operations that receive numerous complaints from the community. The purpose is to take the person into custody as quickly as possible to relieve the quality-of-life problem in the neighborhood. A sufficient number of officers is extremely important in undercover buy-bust operations. Buy-bust operations usually include the following officers:

- *The undercover officer (U/C).* This officer poses as a drug user and purchases the drugs from the dealer.
- *The ghost officer.* This officer closely shadows or follows the U/C as she or he travels within an area and approaches the dealer.
- *The backup team.* This team should consist of at least five officers, if possible, who can watch from a discreet location to ensure the safety of the U/C and the ghost and who can move in when it is time to arrest the dealer.
- *The supervisor.* This critical member of the team plans and directs the operation and makes all key decisions.

Often, the undercover officer makes numerous purchases over time and then obtains an arrest warrant for the dealer, and a team goes in to make the arrest. This is a good strategy because the dealer is less likely to make a connection to the buyer/officer, and it allows the officer to build probable cause and a stronger case.

Sometimes law enforcement then conducts a reverse-sting operation. After the buy-bust, an officer poses as the drug dealer and arrests the buyers who come to purchase drugs. This operation is usually done in areas that readily attract buyers. As soon as an exchange is made, the backup team makes the bust. Reverse-sting operations often lead to accusations of entrapment, so officers must be thoroughly versed in their state laws and court rulings regarding entrapment.

Entrapment

Often people believe that undercover operations by the police are entrapment. **Entrapment** is defined as inducing an individual to violate a criminal statute he or she did not contemplate violating, for the sole purpose of arrest and criminal prosecution.[60] Entrapment is a defense to criminal responsibility that arises from improper acts committed against an accused by another, usually an undercover agent. *Inducement* is the key word; when police encouragement plays upon the weaknesses of innocent persons and beguiles them into committing crimes they normally would not attempt, the police action can be deemed improper as entrapment and the evidence barred under the exclusionary rule.

Entrapment is an affirmative defense and can be easily raised at trial. It is based on the principle that people should not be convicted of a crime that was instigated by the government, and it arises when "government officials 'plant the seeds' of criminal intent."[61] However, when police simply give a person the opportunity to commit a crime, they are not guilty of entrapment. For example, an undercover officer sitting on the sidewalk, apparently drunk, with a $10 bill sticking out of his or her pocket, is not forcing a person to take the money but giving a person the opportunity to take the money. A person who takes advantage of the apparent drunk and takes the money is committing a larceny. The entrapment defense is not applicable to this situation, but it may apply when the police action is outrageous and forces an otherwise innocent person to commit a crime.

In *Jacobson v. United States* (503 U.S. 540, 1992), the U.S. Supreme Court ruled that the government's action of repeatedly, for two and a half years, sending a man advertisements of material of a sexual nature, causing the man to order an illegal sexually oriented magazine, constituted entrapment. It ruled that law enforcement officers "may not originate a criminal design, implant in an innocent person's mind

---

entrapment A legal defense that holds that police originated the criminal idea or initiated the criminal action.

the disposition to commit a criminal act, and then induce commission of the crime so that the government may prosecute." The issue of entrapment is a contentious one, with the defendant's predisposition being evaluated against the government activities. The defendant's predisposition is very subjective, but the government activities are more objective and easier to evaluate.

The American Law Institute's Model Penal Code looks at the entrapment defense in this way: "If the government employed methods of persuasion or inducement which create a substantial risk that such an offense will be committed by persons other than those who are ready to commit it," then the defense is available despite the offender's predisposition.[62] The Supreme Court, however, has predominantly focused on the predisposition of the defendant and ruled that the entrapment defense did not apply.[63] Although in *Hampton v. United States* the Court held that the defendant's predisposition, rather than government conduct, matters regarding the entrapment defense, justices did state in a concurring opinion that if government behavior "shocks the conscience," it could violate due process.[64] Certainly, such behavior as instigating robberies or beatings to gather evidence would cross the line. The Supreme Court has failed to identify specific actions that cross the line, but some lower courts have. If officers "use violence, supply contraband that is wholly unobtainable or engage in a criminal enterprise," defendants often succeed with an entrapment defense.[65]

YOU ARE THERE

Jacobson v. United States, 1992

In February 1984, a 56-year-old Nebraska farmer (hereinafter, the defendant), with no record or reputation for violating any law, lawfully ordered and received from an adult bookstore two magazines that contained photographs of nude teenage boys. Subsequent to this, Congress passed the Child Protection Act of 1984, which made it illegal to receive such material through the mail. Later that year, the U.S. Postal Service obtained the defendant's name from a mailing list seized at the adult bookstore, and, in January 1985, began an undercover operation targeting him.

During the next two and a half years, government investigators, through five fictitious organizations and a bogus pen pal, repeatedly contacted the defendant by mail, exploring his attitudes toward child pornography. The communications also contained disparaging remarks about the legitimacy and constitutionality of efforts to restrict the availability of sexually explicit material and, finally, offered the defendant the opportunity to order illegal child pornography. Twenty-six months after the mailings to the defendant commenced, government investigators sent him a brochure advertising photographs of young boys engaging in sex. At this time, the defendant placed an order that was never filled.

Meanwhile, the investigators attempted to further pique the defendant's interest through a fictitious letter decrying censorship and suggesting a method of getting material to him without the "prying eyes of U.S. Customs." A catalog was then sent to him, and he ordered a magazine containing child pornography. After a controlled delivery of a photocopy of the magazine, the defendant was arrested. A search of his home revealed only the material he received from the government and the two sexually oriented magazines he lawfully acquired in 1984. The defendant was charged with receiving child pornography through the mail in violation of 18 U.S.C. 2252(a)(2)(A). He defended himself by claiming that the government's conduct was outrageous, that the government needed reasonable suspicion before it could legally begin an investigation of him, and that he had been entrapped by the government's investigative techniques.

The lower federal courts rejected these defenses, but in a 5–4 decision, the Supreme Court reversed the defendant's conviction based solely on the entrapment claim. In *Jacobson*, the Supreme Court held that law enforcement officers "may not originate a criminal design, implant in an innocent person's mind the disposition to commit a criminal act, and then induce commission of the crime so that the government may prosecute."

Sources: Based on *Jacobson v. United States*, 503 U.S. 540 (1992); and Thomas V. Kukura, J.D., "Undercover Investigations and the Entrapment Defense: Recent Court Cases," *FBI Law Enforcement Bulletin* (April 1993): 27–32.

SUMMARY

- Traditionally, investigations have been conducted by detectives.

- The Rand study *The Criminal Investigation Process* revealed that a lot of detectives' time was being spent unproductively and consequently investigations were not being efficiently conducted.

- Alternatives to traditional retroactive investigation of past crimes by detectives include improved case management, mentoring and training of detectives, and improved crime analysis and information management.

- Multiagency task forces, repeat offender programs, cold-case squads, and the use of closed-circuit TV or surveillance cameras have led to improved case clearance.

- Repeat offender programs may identify certain individuals to be targets of an intensified investigation through surveillance and other strategies or may seek case enhancement by working closely with the prosecutor in the hopes of obtaining stronger sentences.

- Global positioning system technology, smartphones, and social media allow investigators to obtain information for their investigations without having to be physically present.

- With the tremendous advances in technology during the last couple of decades, cold-case squads have had significant success in investigating old, dormant cases.

- Proactive tactics in police investigations include decoy operations, stakeout operations, and sting operations.

- Other traditional proactive techniques include undercover operations.

- The legal concept of entrapment and how it affects undercover operations and proactive tactics is an important concept for officers to understand.

KEY TERMS

blending

cold-case squads

crime analysis

cybercrime

decoy operations

detective mystique

entrapment

field notes

incident report

intelligence-led policing

investigative task forces

Managing Criminal
   Investigations (MCI)

mentoring

repeat offender programs
   (ROPs)

solvability factors

stakeout

sting operations

undercover investigations

REVIEW EXERCISES

1. You are the lieutenant in the detective bureau and your chief has requested that you consider using a sting operation to help combat the growing crime problem in your city. Research the topic, including what other agencies have done, which crimes they have targeted in this way, and whether or not the operations were successful. You may want to start with government websites (such as the Department of Justice and the NCJRS) to research any publications they have on stings, as well as state sites or even law enforcement agencies that have used sting operations successfully.

2. Consult law enforcement in your area and determine what crime problems they are facing. Determine which types of crimes might benefit from multijurisdictional task forces and draw up a plan for a task force. Determine which departments would be represented and by whom within each department, how often the members would meet, and what type of activities (if any) they would put together.

3. Pick an individual department in your area and examine its crime statistics (most departments have these available online). Determine which crimes appear to be the biggest problems. How would you propose to address them? What strategies would you employ to attempt to lower these numbers?

WEB EXERCISES

1. Go to the Department of Justice website and review the PERF report entitled *Managing a Multijurisdictional Case: Identifying Lessons Learned from the Sniper Investigation*. What were some of the challenges faced in this case, and how were some of these challenges successfully handled? Are there things that agencies might want to do differently in the future?

2. Go to the website for the Unified Government of Wyandotte County and Kansas City, and look at the information they have posted for residents regarding identifying a "drug house." What is their goal in making this information available for their residents? What do they indicate are warning signs of a possible drug house and what do they recommend residents do? Do you think this approach will help combat the drug problem or solve crimes?

3. Go to the Department of Justice website—the Office of Community Oriented Policing Services—and review their Problem-Oriented Guides for Police, Response Guides Series, No. 24, on Prescription Drug Fraud and Misuse, 2nd Edition. What kinds of crimes does this guide discuss?

END NOTES

1. Peter W. Greenwood and Joan Petersilia, *The Criminal Investigation Process, Vol. I: Summary and Policy Implications* (Santa Monica, Calif.: Rand Corporation, 1975).

2. Ibid., p. vii.

3. William Spelman and D. K. Brown, *Calling the Police: Citizen Reporting of Serious Crime* (Washington, D.C.: Police Executive Research Forum, 1981).

4. Mark Willman and John Snortum, "Detective Work: The Criminal Investigation Process in a Medium-Size Police Department," *Criminal Justice Review* 9 (1984): 33–39.

5. *A National Survey of Police Policies and Practices Regarding the Criminal Investigations Process: Twenty-Five Years After Rand*, as cited in Charissa L. Womack, *Criminal Investigations: The Impact of Patrol Officers on Solving Crime*, master's thesis, University of North Texas, 2007, retrieved April 23, 2008, from http://digital.library.unt.edu/permalink/meta-dc-3594:1.

6. Herman Goldstein, *Policing a Free Society* (Cambridge, Mass.: Ballinger, 1977), pp. 55–56.

7. Ibid.

8. Greenwood and Petersilia, *Criminal Investigation Process*, p. vii.

9. FBI, *Uniform Crime Reports: Crime in the United States*, retrieved April 3, 2014, from www.fbi.gov.

10. National Advisory Commission on Criminal Justice Standards and Goals, *Police* (Washington, D.C.: U.S. Government Printing Office, 1973).

11. Donald F. Cawley, H. J. Miron, W. J. Aranjo, R. Wassserman, T. A. Mannello, and Y. Huffman, *Managing Criminal Investigations: Manual* (Washington, D.C.: National Institute of Justice, 1977).

12. Ibid.

13. Ibid.

14. Ilene Greenberg and Robert Wasserman, *Managing Criminal Investigations* (Washington, D.C.: National Institute of Justice, 1975).

15. John E. Eck, *Managing Case Assignments: The Burglary Investigation Decision Model Replication* (Washington, D.C.: Police Executive Research Forum, 1979).

16. Gary W. Cordner and Kathryn E. Scarborough, *Police Administration*, 6th ed. (Cincinnati: LexisNexis, 2007), p. 396.

17. Frank A. Colaprete, "The Case for Investigator Mentoring," *Police Chief* (October 2004): 47–52.

18. Frank A. Colaprete, "Knowledge Management in the Criminal Investigation Process," *Law and Order* (October 2004): 82–89.

19. G. H. Reiner, T. J. Sweeney, R. V. Waymire, F. A. Newton III, R. G. Grassie, S. M. White, and W. D. Wallace, *Integrated Criminal Apprehension Program: Crime Analysis Operations Manual* (Washington, D.C.: Law Enforcement Assistance Administration, 1977).

20. Colaprete, "Knowledge Management in the Criminal Investigation Process."

21. Andrew Seaman, "Facebook Teams with Agencies for Amber Alert Pages," *USA Today*, January 12, 2011.

22. "Automated Information Sharing: Does It Help Law Enforcement Officers Work Better?" *National Institute of Justice Journal* 253 (January 2006).

23. ARJIS public website, April 3, 2014.

24. Cordner and Scarborough, *Police Administration*, p. 334.

25. Paulson and Llana, "After Long Decline."

26. "Dallas Police Developing Intelligence Hub," *Dallas Morning News*, January 16, 2007; MOSAIC, *Public Safety Update*, retrieved October 30, 2008, from www.dallascityhall.com/committee_briefings/briefings0108/PS_010708_MOSAIC.pdf.

27. Memo on Dallas PD Fusion Center, June 12, 2009, retrieved February 11, 2012, from www.scribd.com/doc/25038660/Dallas-2009-Fusion-Center.

28. Leon Fooksman, "Detectives from Different Agencies in Palm Beach County Team Up to Tackle Violence," *South Florida Sun-Sentinel*, June 2, 2006, retrieved April 9, 2010, from the Palm Beach County Sheriff's Office website, www.pbso.org/index.cfm?fa5violentcrimetf.

29. "Report: Rampant Human Trafficking in America," *The Crime Report*, December 4, 2013.

30. Scott Santoro, "DHS' Unified Effort to Combat Human Trafficking," *The Police Chief Magazine* (November 2013): 53–55.

31. WashACT informational brochures, funded by DOJ – Bureau of Justice Assistance/grant # 90ZV0091 from Department of Health and Human Services and #2004-VT-BX-K007 from the Office of Victims of Crime, U.S. Department of Justice.

32. Jennifer Nislow, "Working Together: A Case Study," *Law Enforcement News*, January 2005, pp. 1, 11. Report by the Police Executive Research Forum is available on the Department of Justice website, www.ojp.usdoj.gov/BJA/pubs/SniperRpt.pdf.

33. Nislow, "Working Together."

34. Ibid.

35. Ibid.

36. Marcia Chaiken and Jan Chaiken, *Priority Prosecutors of High-Rate Dangerous Offenders* (Washington, D.C.: National Institute of Justice, 1991), as cited in Stephen Goldsmith, "Targeting High-Rate Offenders: Asking Some Tough Questions," *Law Enforcement News*, July/August 1991, p. 11.

37. Goldsmith, "Targeting High-Rate Offenders."

38. David Chipman and Cynthia E. Pappas, *Violent Crime Impact Teams (VCIT) Initiative: Focus on Partnerships* (Washington, D.C.: Department of Justice, February 2006), NCJ#214168, retrieved April 9, 2010, from the Bureau of Alcohol, Tobacco, Firearms and Explosives website, Public Affairs Division, "Fact Sheet" dated March 2010, www.atf.gov/publications/factsheets/factsheet-violent-crime-impact-teams.htms.

39. Associated Press, "FDLE Sex Offender Site Adds Crime Detail, Vehicle Info," *South Florida Sun-Sentinel*, July 25, 2006.

40. FBI website, retrieved February 11, 2012, from www.fbi.gov/scams-safety/registry.

41. Elizabeth Wilkerson, "States Fight Meth Plague with Registries," retrieved June 9, 2006, from www.stateline.org.

42. Laura McCallum, "Pawlenty's Meth Registry: Good Policy or a Gimmick?" Minnesota Public Radio, July 27, 2006, retrieved August 3, 2006, from http://minnesota.publicradio.org.

43. Wendy Koch, "More Sex Offenders Tracked by Satellite," *USA Today*, June 6, 2006.

44. Robert Moran, "City Voters Approve Anticrime Cameras," *Philadelphia Inquirer*, May 17, 2006.

45. Information obtained from probable cause affidavit filed in Sarasota County by Detective Chris Hallisey.

46. Associated Press, "Man Guilty of Killing Girl," *Everett Herald*, November 18, 2005, retrieved July 25, 2006, from www.heraldnet.com.

47. Damien Cave, "Eight Teenagers Charged in Internet Beating Have Their Day on the Web," *New York Times*, April 12, 2008.

48. Christina Lewis, "Solving the Cold Case: Time, Ingenuity and DNA Can Help," retrieved December 17, 2002, from wwwcnn.com.

49. Slate.com, May 27, 2011.

50. Jonathan Saltzman, "Ad Blitz Brought an End to FBI Quest," *Boston Globe*, June 24, 2011.

51. Philip Bulman, "Solving Cold Cases with DNA: The Boston Strangler Case," *NIJ Journal* (February 2014): No. 273, http://nij.gov/journals/273/pages/boston-strangler.aspx.

52. "Problem-Oriented Guides for Police, Response Guides Series, No. 6: Sting Operations" (#2005CKWXK001, October 2007), available from the Department of Justice, Office of Community Oriented Policing Services, www.usdoj.gov.

53. Carl B. Klockars, "The Modern Sting," in *Thinking about Police: Contemporary Readings*.

54. Paul McEnroe, "Illegal Guns Flooding into Minneapolis," *Minneapolis Star Tribune*, April 29, 2006.

55. Paul Farhi, "'Dateline's Pedophile Sting: One More Point," *Washington Post*, April 9, 2006.

56. Terry Sult, "Facing the New World of Digital Evidence and Cybersecurity," *Police Chief* (February 2014): 50–51.

57. Commission on Accreditation for Law Enforcement Agencies, *Standards for Law Enforcement Agencies* (Fairfax, Va.: CALEA, 1987).

58. Michael D. Lyman, *Drugs in Society: Causes, Concepts and Control*, 6th ed. (Burlington, Mass.: Anderson Publishing, 2011).

59. Julie Wartell and Nancy G. LaVigne, "Prescription Drug Fraud and Misuse," 2nd edition #24, Center for Problem Oriented Policing, Community Oriented Policing Services, U.S. Department of Justice, 2013, www.cops.usdoj.gov.

60. David N. Falcone, *Dictionary of Criminal Justice, Criminology and Criminal Law* (Upper Saddle River, N.J.: Pearson/Prentice Hall, 2005).

61. Craig Hemmens, John L. Worrall, and Alan Thompson, *Significant Cases in Criminal Procedure* (Los Angeles: Roxbury, 2004), p. 147.

62. Ibid.

63. *United States* v. Russell, 411 U.S. 423 (1973).

64. *Hampton v. United States*, 425 U.S. 484 (1976).

65. Hemmens, Worrall, and Thompson, *Significant Cases in Criminal Procedure*, p. 148.

Police and Their Clients

LEARNING OBJECTIVES

- Describe the meaning of police–community relations and their importance to the safety and quality of life in a community.

- Explain the issues experienced by various minority populations with regard to their interactions with the police, including the efforts of law enforcement to mitigate these issues.

- Identify special populations and police efforts being made to better serve these populations.

- Discuss community crime prevention programs and how they address reducing crime and improving the quality of life in communities.

- Explain the legal and ethical questions surrounding police–business partnerships.

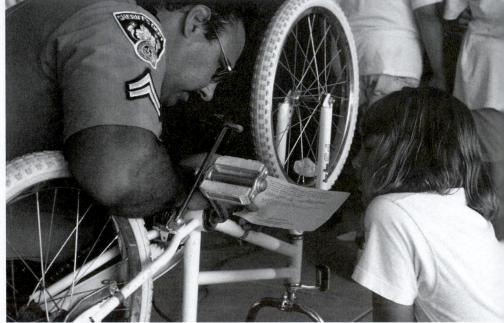

FOTOSEARCH RM/Age Fotostock

OUTLINE

The Need for Proper Police–Community Relationships

Human Relations, Public Relations, Community Relations

Public Opinion and the Police

Police and Minority Communities
Multiculturalism
African Americans
Hispanic Americans
Asian Americans
Native Americans
Arab Americans and Muslims
Jews
Women
Gays and Lesbians
New Immigrants

Police and Special Populations
The Physically Challenged
The Aging Population
Young People
Crime Victims

Victims of Domestic Violence
The Mentally Ill
The Homeless

Community Crime Prevention Programs
Neighborhood Watch Programs
National Night Out
Citizen Patrols
Citizen Volunteer Programs
Home Security Surveys and Operation Identification
Police Storefront Stations or Ministations
Crime Stoppers
Mass Media Campaigns
Chaplain Programs
Citizen Police Academies
Other Police-Sponsored Crime Prevention Programs

Police and Business Cooperation

INTRODUCTION

This chapter deals with relationships between the police and the citizens they are paid to protect: the community. The community makes up the client base of the police department. This chapter, along with Chapter 12, forms the focus of the police and community section of this text. Chapter 12 will deal with the philosophies of community policing and problem-solving policing, and this chapter will discuss the relationships between the police and their clients. We will describe numerous programs being implemented by police agencies to better serve various populations within the community.

The chapter, which emphasizes the need for proper relationships between the police and their clients, presents definitions of police human relations, police public relations, and police–community relations. We will explore public opinion of the police, the challenges presented by an increasingly diverse population, and the relationships between the police and minority communities (including African Americans, Hispanic Americans, Asian Americans, Native Americans, Arab Americans and Muslims, Jews, women, gays and lesbians, and new immigrants). We also will look at relationships between the police and some special populations, including the aging population, young people, the homeless, crime victims, domestic violence victims, and physically and mentally challenged individuals.

In addition, the chapter discusses community crime prevention programs, including Neighborhood Watch programs, National Night Out, citizen patrols, citizen volunteer programs, home security surveys and Operation Identification, police storefront stations or ministations, Crime Stoppers, mass media campaigns, chaplain programs, citizen police academies, and other police-sponsored crime prevention programs, as well as police and business and citizen initiatives.

The Need for Proper Police–Community Relationships

The police are needed to handle emergencies, maintain order, regulate traffic, and promote a sense of security within the community. To accomplish this, the police must be part of the community. They cannot be viewed as mercenaries or as an army of occupation. When the police see themselves as an occupying army or are seen as one by the community, urban unrest results. The police can best serve the community when they are regarded as part of the community by both the residents and themselves.

The police and community need each other to help communities be as vibrant and safe as possible. Police–community relationships must be two-way partnerships. In a democratic society, the legitimacy of the police depends on broad and active public acceptance and support. Police chiefs or police commissioners have the responsibility and obligation to educate the public about the many

Peter Casolino/Alamy

To strengthen their relationships with people they serve, police departments are striving to make themselves more diverse and representative of their communities.

causes of crime and the inability of the police acting alone to control crime. The more educated a community is concerning the role of the police and the challenges the police face in meeting multiple demands, the more supportive and helpful the citizens can be.

Although it is very important for a chief to seek the support and cooperation of the public to improve efforts to police the community, the most important person in the police department, in terms of improving police–community relations, is the individual police officer. Patrol officers, traffic officers, and detectives are the individuals within the department who come into contact with the public on a regular basis. Most people receive their impression of a particular police department through the actions of the police officers they encounter. A person who has a bad experience with a particular officer may believe that the entire department mirrors that officer. Because of the high visibility of uniformed officers, many citizens will form opinions based on behavior they may observe in restaurants and stores, on car stops, at crime scenes, or even by police driving their marked police vehicles. Most likely the officer will not even be aware that he or she is being scrutinized in these situations. Officers are constantly serving as ambassadors for their departments.

Human Relations, Public Relations, Community Relations

A tremendous emphasis on police–community relations has arisen since the civil disorders of the 1960s. Numerous textbooks and courses exist on police–community relations and police human relations.

---

human relations Everything done with each other as human beings in all kinds of relationships.

police public relations Activities performed by police agencies designed to create a favorable image of themselves.

police–community relations The relationships involved in both human relations and public relations between the police and the community.

police–community relations (PCR) movement Beginning in the 1950s and 1960s, a few officers in a department were assigned as community affairs or community relations specialists to interact with the public and reduce tension between the public and the department.

What do these terms mean? Are they interchangeable? Are community relations and human relations the same as police public relations?

Steven M. Cox and Jack D. Fitzgerald perhaps best define these terms. They define police **human relations** as follows: "In the most general sense, the concept of human relations refers to everything we do with, for, and to each other as citizens and as human beings."[1] Human relations thus connotes treating others with respect and dignity and following the Golden Rule—acting toward others as you would want others to act toward you. Cox and Fitzgerald define **police public relations** as "a variety of activities with the express intent of creating a favorable image of themselves . . . sponsored and paid for by the organization." Then, using these two definitions, they define **police–community relations** as follows:

> Community relations are comprised of the combined effects of human and public relations. Police community relations then encompass the sum total of human and public relations, whether initiated by the police or other members of the community. . . . Police community relations may be either positive or negative, depending upon the quality of police interactions with other citizens (human relations) and the collective images each holds of the other (which are derived from public as well as human relations).[2]

In 1967, the President's Commission on Law Enforcement and Administration of Justice reported that "police relations with minority groups had sunk to explosively low levels." The commission defined police–community relations in its summary report, *The Challenge of Crime in a Free Society:*

> A community relations program is not a public relations program "to sell the police image" to the people. . . . It is a long-range, full-scale effort to acquaint the police and the community with each other's problems and to stimulate action aimed at solving these problems.[3]

Louis A. Radelet, a pioneer in studying the role of the police in the community, traced the development of the **police–community relations (PCR) movement** to an annual conference begun in 1955.[4] However, some believe that the PCR movement grew out of the riots and civil disorders of the 1960s. The PCR movement should not be confused

Law Enforcement and Special Olympics

Officer, deputy, trooper, agent, or marshal—whatever title they carry, the men and women of law enforcement, whether commissioned or civilian, paid or volunteer, believe deeply in service to their community. Knowing that their commitment to the common good means giving back to those who rely on them, the law enforcement family frequently supports others on and off duty. It is the individual desire to serve their community that leads many to the career in the first place and fuels the collective desire to improve lives and better situations for others.

Such is the motivation for members of the profession involved with the Special Olympics Law Enforcement Torch Run® (LETR). An organization of police agency representatives that support Special Olympics athletes around the world, LETR began in 1981 with the Wichita, Kansas, Police Department supporting a local event. LETR has grown to nearly 100,000 volunteers in 46 countries raising nearly a half billion dollars by the end of 2013. It has been described as one of the largest and most successful grassroots fundraising efforts in the world. Supported by the International Association of Chiefs of Police (IACP) and many state level organizations such as the Washington Association of Sheriffs and Police Chiefs, LETR is the charity of choice for a large number of agencies.

The inaugural event involved a few officers running with Special Olympics athletes to raise awareness of the local games. Officers now run with the official Flame of Hope® torch in all 50 states. In Washington State, three separate torches converge from the furthest corners of the state in June each year to light the flame for the Summer Games. Passed from jurisdiction to jurisdiction across miles and, often, international borders, these torches carry the vision of Special Olympics: "to help bring all persons with intellectual disabilities into the larger society under conditions whereby they are accepted, respected, and given the chance to become useful and productive citizens." It's quite a sight—a long caravan of flashing lights protecting a slow-moving group of officers and athletes jogging along with the torch across towns and rural roads, all to draw attention to the wonderful work Special Olympics does.

LETR conducts thousands of events year-round reaching millions of people. Events range from a few officers and support staff from a single agency conducting a garage sale to regional events like Polar Plunge bringing hundreds of police and civilian community members together in a common cause of service. Popular events include Tip-a-Cop, where officers supplement wait staff in restaurants to collect tips; Cops on Donut Shops, where officers sit atop bakeries; and, beginning in Washington State in 2013, an event titled Run from the Cops where participants run a 5K within a 30-minute time limit to "outrun" the officers or pay "bail" in the form of a promise to support Special Olympics.

Many of the larger events have medical screenings for

The official "Flame of Hope" torch is carried by law enforcement officers across the country in the Law Enforcement Torch Run to raise awareness and funds for the Special Olympics.

Courtesy Special Olympics Washington

(continued)

YOU ARE THERE

Law Enforcement and Special Olympics (continued)

athletes that can lead to the discovery of underlying health issues. Team member families coming together has led to lifelong friendships and support groups beyond the games as well.

Each year a select group of LETR representatives from around the world gather to complete the Final Leg of the event to opening ceremonies for international Summer or Winter Games. Carrying the Flame of Hope®, athletes and police officers crisscross the host country to raise awareness. Runners must undergo a rigorous selection process to be chosen for the Final Leg team.

My personal philosophy is "leave things better than you found them." This is one of the many reasons I have for both supporting LETR as an agency head and for being personally involved as an active participant in many of the events that occur each year. Another reason is the close relationship I have with friends who have Special Olympics athletes in their families. Witnessing the positive impact these sporting events have for athletes and families up close is overwhelming. Working with local coaches and athletes is just one of the benefits provided by law enforcement to their community.

As a career criminal justice professional with more than three decades of experience to date, I've been fortunate to be involved with LETR and other charitable causes since the early 1980s. Having waited tables, plunged into frigid lake waters 22 times in a day as a Super Plunger, organized and competed in Run from the Cops 5K events, bowled with athletes, and exchanged hugs and high-fives with hundreds of athletes at games around the state, I feel lucky to be a small part of helping them enjoy their games and supporting their families.

A particular memory stands out from my time working in Germany for the World's Fair EXPO 2000 as part of an international task force of officers dedicated to the safety of the event. A group of about 30 of us ran the torch more than eight miles around Hannover, Niedersachsen, and onto the EXPO grounds to build excitement for Special Olympics and raise money. It was the first such event held in Germany and since I had done many similar events in the United States, they asked me to assist with organizing the run. It was a great honor to help out, but I will admit it was the longest run I had ever done to that date. No one dared drop out and our pace was not exactly world-class, but it was a wonderful morning and the shocked stares we got running across the EXPO grounds singing and clapping was worth the pain.

As a police chief, I talk with potential criminal justice candidates and students nearly every day. Most applicants for police officer jobs tell me at oral boards that they want to help people. If you choose a career in criminal justice, this is a great opportunity to do exactly that!

Chief Rex Caldwell
Mukilteo, Washington, Police Department

with today's community policing endeavors. The PCR movement involved assigning a few officers in a department as community affairs or community relations specialists. These officers attended community meetings and tried to reduce tensions between members of the department and the public. Some of the programs were shams or merely public relations attempts. The PCR movement had no real effect on the philosophy or culture of most police departments. Egon Bittner has said that for PCR programs to be effective, they need to reach to "the grassroots of discontent," where citizen dissatisfaction with the police exists.[5] In short, police human relations skills are needed.

Since the urban disorders of the 1960s, training in human relations has become part of the police academy and in-service training in many departments. Sensitivity training—sometimes referred to as T-groups or encounter groups—is designed to give participants an opportunity to learn more about themselves and their impact on others, as well as to learn to function more effectively in face-to-face situations. In a typical encounter group, officers may engage in a role play face-to-face with a group of minority citizens, teenagers, or others who have had problem relationships with the police. The police officers play the role of the other group, and the members of the other group play the role of the police. The goal of this training is to facilitate the ability of police officers to understand the perceptions and behaviors of the citizen group.

The **International Association of Chiefs of Police (IACP)** understands the importance of public relations and the interactions between the police and the community. The IACP has issued training keys on managing anger, police–citizen contacts, dealing with the mentally ill, elderly victimization, and hate crimes. There is also an understanding that crucial to police–community relations is the community's faith in the police department to police itself. It must be understood by all that allegations of police misconduct will be thoroughly and fairly investigated. The IACP has also issued several training keys on this topic.

Public Opinion and the Police

Although it is well known the police have a difficult job, the role of the police has always been somewhat ambiguous. The perception of the police mission by police leaders as well as community leaders has varied during the last few decades. With the adoption of the community policing philosophy (discussed in the next chapter), many law enforcement agencies have seen their roles expand to include activities that previously were not viewed as police functions. Despite this reassessment, the police role continues to be viewed as existing in three primary areas: crime fighters, order maintainers, and service providers. Though views differ, it is a common refrain from police and citizens alike that there are not enough police officers on the streets.

Given the difficult job the police have, it is easier for them to perform their duties if they have the support of the public. The media often portray a police force that is not liked by the public. However, this is a false perception. In a nationwide poll asking people how much confidence they have in the police, 56 percent answered "a great deal," 28 percent answered "some," 15 percent answered "very little," and 1 percent answered "none."[6] The public's opinion of the police has remained relatively constant over time, with most of the public giving favorable ratings to the police. Whites and older citizens generally give the police better ratings than do African Americans and younger people.

Generally, however, the police feel that the public does not like them or support them. James Q. Wilson, acknowledging this fact, concluded that the police "probably exaggerate the extent of citizen hostility."[7] Perhaps one reason many officers believe the public does not like them is that officers, particularly in high-crime areas, spend a significant proportion of their time dealing with criminals and unsavory people. Further confusing their perceptions is the way in which any conflict or negative issue that arises will be played out repeatedly in the media and the community.

Often the public's opinion of the police is formed by their perceptions and the biases they attach to what they see and has nothing to do with the behavior of the officers. For instance, as mentioned in Chapter 9, there has been an increase in the use of police paramilitary units, which means more officers are outfitted in military-looking regalia. After 9/11, it has become more common to see officers heavily armed and wearing uniforms, boots, and equipment that may appear more militaristic than the traditional uniform. This may be especially true when officers are working large special events, a forum in which they are seen by more citizens. This military-like appearance may offend people, who may feel that these officers look more like an occupying army than peace officers. In these situations, officers may be perceived as more aggressive and perhaps even threatening in nature. Both officers and administrators need to be aware of this effect.

In these days of escalating gasoline prices and the return of strong environmental concerns, how an officer uses energy resources and treats the environment will be noticed. As has always been true, police officers in uniform are very visible symbols of the government, and everything they do is seen and scrutinized. How "green" or environmentally responsible police officers are can have an impact on the public's opinion of the police. Police officers have often taken it upon themselves to investigate complicated environmental crimes, and they routinely enforce nuisance-type laws that are also environmentally related, such as littering. The use of hybrid vehicles when possible, enacting recycling programs, using rechargeable battery-operated flares, and using "paperless" report systems will all reduce an agency's impact on the environment. All of these efforts will be viewed favorably by the community.

Police and Minority Communities

One of the most significant problems facing the police during the past three decades has been the tension, and often outright hostility, between the police and minority group citizens. Most of this tension has focused on relationships between African Americans and the police. However, tension has existed between police and Hispanic Americans, Native Americans, Asian Americans, and other minority groups, including women and the gay community.

One of the best ways to improve relationships between the police and minority groups is to ensure that minority groups are adequately represented in a jurisdiction's police department. Over the last few decades, minority representation has increased significantly in U.S. police departments. However, as Chapter 7 discussed, African Americans, Hispanic Americans, and other minorities (including women) are still seriously underrepresented in U.S. police departments.

Although increasing diversity within the law enforcement workforce will facilitate cultural awareness and understanding with various minority populations, law enforcement can make other efforts. Having and conveying respect for these cultures is critical. Opening the lines of communication with the informal leaders of these communities to discuss their issues and their needs also will result in greater cooperation.

Officers should be trained in the background and cultures of the various communities to aid in understanding. If language is a barrier, the identification of reliable, honest translators within the community will be helpful. The Department of Justice's Office of Community Oriented Policing Services (COPS) has joined with the Vera Institute of Justice and published a booklet entitled "Overcoming Language Barriers: Solutions for Law Enforcement," which is available on the COPS website and has many cost-effective strategies to help police departments with this challenge.[8] In turn, education of the community in police goals and operations will increase residents' understanding and reduce their fears.

Multiculturalism

The 2010 U.S. Census reported that 12.5 percent of the total U.S. population is foreign born, accounting for 38.5 million people. Of these, 54 percent were born in Latin America, 27 percent in Asia, and 12 percent in Europe, with the remainder coming from other areas of the world, including Africa. Approximately 20 percent of American households now report that they speak a language other than English at home.[9] These factors have implications for police officers responding to calls involving these residents. Not only is there likely to be a communication problem, but there also may be a lack of trust and understanding of police, possibly resulting in fear.

Racial and ethnic minorities accounted for 90 percent of the population growth in the United States from 2000 to 2010, and the United States is very rapidly becoming even more diverse. The growth in the minority populations is no longer limited to the border and southern states. The immigration issue has affected every state in the union. Minority groups make up an increasing share of the population in every state except West Virginia, possibly because of its struggling economy and lack of history in attracting immigrants. "This is just an extraordinary explosion of diversity all across the United States," said William Frey, a demographer at the Brookings Institution, a Washington think tank. "It's diversity and immigration going hand in hand."[10] Non-Hispanic whites are now a minority in four states (Hawaii, New Mexico, California, and Texas, as well as the District of Columbia) and are below 60 percent in Maryland, Georgia, and Nevada. Nationally, the percentage of non-Hispanic whites declined from 70 percent in 2000 to 67 percent in 2005. Immigrants have shown they will go where the jobs are, and for the first time have moved to many states not typically challenged with immigration issues. South Carolina's immigrant population has increased 47 percent since 2000, and Arkansas's Hispanic population has increased 48 percent.[11]

This rapid increase in the minority population has led to some backlash and challenges for law enforcement in communities that have not previously faced this issue. Multicultural understanding is critical, as currently members of racial and ethnic minorities account for more than one in three Americans, and projections indicate that members of minorities will constitute a majority of the nation's population by 2050.[12] Numerous training programs have been developed to address the issues of cultural diversity. Law enforcement is aggressively looking for, developing, and implementing relevant training programs for officers as well as outreach programs for the minority communities to increase multicultural understanding. It is believed that increasing understanding of the cultures of the various minority groups will facilitate improved relations with them.

African Americans

The face of the U.S. population is changing as it has continued to become more diverse year after year. Whereas in 1950 Caucasians represented approximately 87 percent of the U.S. population, by 2030 they will make up only 59 percent of the American population. African Americans currently are 13 percent of the population, compared with 10 percent in 1950, but their percentage of the population is expected to remain relatively constant.

African Americans have historically faced discrimination in U.S. society. Not until 1954, with the landmark Supreme Court case of *Brown* v. *Board of Education of Topeka*, was legal segregation of the races officially declared unconstitutional.[13] This case overturned the old "separate but equal" doctrine regarding race and public schools. A decade later, Congress passed the Civil Rights Act of 1964, which strengthened the rights of all citizens regardless of race, religion, or national origin.

Access to equal rights did not come easily, and, as discussed in Chapter 1, there were clashes between the police and the African American community in the 1950s and 1960s, and even as late as the early 1990s as a result of the Rodney King incident. Despite the elimination of legal racism and the increased acceptance of minorities into mainstream society, the problems of African Americans did not disappear. Racism and hatred still exist in our society. Many African Americans in the inner cities remain unemployed or underemployed. Many live below the poverty level and remain in a state of chronic anger or rage.

There continues to be a concern among individuals in the African American community about unfair treatment by law enforcement and the criminal justice system. The terms *racial profiling* and *driving while black* have become commonplace. Racial profiling or biased-based policing is a form of discrimination that singles out people of racial or ethnic groups due to the belief that these groups are more likely than others to commit certain types of crimes. This kind of policing is illegal. This issue was discussed in Chapter 8.

The relationship between police and African Americans remains an area that needs to be addressed. Police officers must make efforts to understand the attitudes of all community members and work with them for fair law enforcement and to protect all community members, regardless of race or ethnicity, from the criminals who victimize law-abiding citizens.

Hispanic Americans

The Hispanic community is composed of many different cultures. The Census Bureau uses the term *Hispanic* for people with ethnic backgrounds in Spanish-speaking countries. Hispanics can be of any race, and most in the United States are white. (To differentiate between white Hispanics and Caucasians, the term *non-Hispanic whites* is often used.) Officers must understand and acknowledge this diversity.

In 1950, Hispanics made up approximately 3 percent of the U.S. population, but in 2005 they surpassed African Americans as the largest minority group when they reached 14.5 percent of the population. In 2012, Hispanics represented 16.9 percent of the population.[14] Officers cannot assume that all Hispanic groups share the same culture and beliefs. Though there are similarities, each is unique. If police officers group all Hispanics together because of a lack of understanding or knowledge, this can lead to resentment within the community.

Hispanic Americans have suffered discrimination, and many are also handicapped by language and cultural barriers. Their relationships with the police have often been as tense as the relationships between the police and the African American community. Though knowing Spanish may ease the communication process, it does not necessarily do anything to facilitate a deeper relationship with the community, except perhaps show community members that the officers and department are willing to put forth an effort to learn their language. Many departments do provide basic "police-language" training to police officers to minimize the problems that might occur because of a lack of understanding of rudimentary commands.

Spanish or Latino citizen police academies and victim liaison programs have exploded across the country as the Hispanic population has increased. Fueled by the belief in the value of these popular academies, many cities have chosen to build on their success. Some citizen police academies, especially those targeting newer immigrants, have included information on the U.S. government and history and governmental procedures and rules. These efforts have led to improved relationships as both groups share information.[15]

Asian Americans

In 2011, 29 percent of the foreign-born population in the United States was born in Asia. The Asian population grew significantly from 2000 to 2010 and now makes up 5 percent of the U.S. population.[16] These Asian Americans include many distinct and separate cultures—China, Japan, Korea, Vietnam, Laos, Cambodia, Thailand, and other countries of the Far East. Chinese Americans are among the most visible of the Asian American community, and many large U.S. cities have an area known as Chinatown. Pockets of Koreans, Vietnamese, and Cambodians have also grown in certain areas of the country and have become strong economic and cultural forces in certain cities and towns.

Many departments are strengthening their relationships with the Asian population by reaching out to the community and educating Asian Americans about the role of police in the United States. Misperceptions and misunderstandings about what the police do and why they do it often exist, especially given what people from various cultures have experienced in their homelands. Police departments also have made concerted efforts to recruit more Asian Americans, as discussed in Chapter 7.

Opening the lines of communication with the various groups and understanding their histories, beliefs, and cultures go a long way toward facilitating an open relationship. Particularly important for officers to understand is the political culture of the native countries, including the police role, both formal and informal. This will help officers understand reactions they are encountering on the street and minimize the opportunity for misunderstandings. Establishing a liaison program between the police department and community leaders with the goal of educating both the residents and police officers will have a positive effect on the relationship.

Native Americans

In the 2012 Census, Native Americans accounted for 1.2 percent of the U.S. population.[17] Native American nations, reservations, colonies, and communities with criminal jurisdiction have traditionally been policed in two ways: by federal officers from the Bureau of Indian Affairs (BIA) or by their own police departments, like any other governmental entity. American Indian tribes operate 171 law enforcement agencies and employ about 2,300 full-time, sworn officers.[18]

Throughout the United States, there are more than 500 different tribal groups, all with distinct histories, cultures, and often a separate language.[19] The various cultural beliefs filter the residents' perceptions of information they receive from governmental personnel or law enforcement. These beliefs also influence how Native Americans interact with others, including law enforcement, and may result in misunderstandings if officers are not aware of these cultural differences.

Law enforcement in tribal areas is typically very complex. There are overlaps as well as gaps in law enforcement, depending on whether the officer is Native American or not and whether the individual involved is a tribal member or not. In addition, two Bureau of Justice Statistics (BJS) studies indicated high victimization and offender rates for Native Americans in the 1990s when the crime rate in the rest of the U.S. population was declining. Problems that were being addressed outside Indian country were not being adequately addressed inside.

The complexity of law enforcement in tribal areas, coupled with the alarming statistics regarding an increased crime rate involving American Indians, spurred the IACP to address this issue with tribal communities through the summit "Improving Safety in Indian Country."[20] The summit was held to develop some ideas about how to reverse this trend. Recommendations included cross-jurisdictional cooperation, elimination of jurisdictional authority issues that impede law enforcement, improved crime prevention programs and funding, training for law enforcement working in or near tribal country regarding Native American culture, improved data collection and information sharing, and improved victims' services to minimize revictimization. Considering the fact that Native Americans are victims of violent crimes at greater than twice the national average, issues can arise frequently, and consequently, police officers will have regular contact with Native Americans.[21]

Despite the recent efforts, however, the violent crime rate has continued at unacceptable levels, and in fact the rate of Native American female murder victims is 10 times the national average. The attorney general has launched an initiative in the Department of Justice on public safety in tribal communities in an effort to address the high violent crime rate in Indian country. Limited tribal law enforcement resources coupled with isolation has led to the federal government initiating and facilitating the development of a program involving strategic personnel, including FBI agents, U.S. Attorneys, and victims' specialists, to help the state, local, and tribal agencies in addressing the crime problem.[22]

Many reservations employ both Native Americans and non–Native Americans as police officers. Some prefer Native American officers because of cultural issues, but many agencies have found that with training and communication on both sides, ethnic background should not be a factor. Many are also involved in community relations programs in an outreach effort to residents of the tribal lands. Law enforcement is continuing to examine pressing issues involving Native Americans and what efforts can be undertaken to address those issues.

Arab Americans and Muslims

Since September 11, 2001, there has been an increased awareness of the needs and issues of the Middle Eastern community. After it was revealed that the 9/11 terrorists had lived, worked, and gone to school in many South Florida communities without arousing any suspicion, many residents became alarmed at any individual of Middle Eastern descent living in their neighborhoods. The Muslim community has raised concerns for their civil rights and the suspicion that seems to have been generated within their communities.

Many Muslims have asked law enforcement for extra protection because they fear hate crimes being perpetrated because of their ethnicity. The Community Relations Service of the Department of Justice has written a guide to help

law enforcement respond to this issue.[23] The guide recommends conducting a community assessment to determine the vulnerable targets. Increasing high-visibility patrol in those areas is one strategy, as is opening the lines of communication with the Muslim community to determine their fears, concerns, and tensions. A proactive approach by the police department, speaking out against hate crimes and promising vigorous investigation and prosecution, will set the tone for the community. The guide also recommends initiating dialogues via task forces or committees among representatives of the various ethnic and religious groups within the community. This will help to break down barriers and stereotypes among residents. Training for police officers and education for community residents in Muslim beliefs and traditions is also advocated for spreading the truth and minimizing misunderstandings. Having access to community leaders and good translators will help the communication process.

From 2003 to 2005, the Vera Institute of Justice conducted a study funded by the Justice Department that involved interviewing both law enforcement personnel and members of the Arab American community. Both groups felt the primary problem was a lack of trust between law enforcement and the Muslim community. The events of 9/11 considerably derailed the relationships that had been built during the previous decades to encourage new immigrants to trust the police. Both groups expressed dismay at the reporting of false information in the

Los Angeles police officers pray with Muslims at an Islamic Center.

Ann Johansson/The New York Times/Redux

form of anonymous tips that were actually the result of petty disputes, business competition, and dating rivalries. The police often feel as victimized as the community when placed in the middle of these "tips." The primary recommendation coming out of the study was that the best way to maintain or enhance relationships is the continued use of the community policing philosophy and the use of partnerships between the Muslim community and law enforcement to address the homeland security mission.[24]

In addition, for the long term, increasing recruiting efforts within these ethnic minorities will facilitate understanding. All these efforts should help community members of Middle Eastern descent feel less threatened and less ostracized.

Jews

Since September 11, 2001, there has been fear among the Jewish population, particularly in cities with large Jewish populations, of being a "soft" terrorism target. This fear and concerns for the safety of Jewish residents, synagogues, temples, schools, and group homes has caused a surge in demand for police protection in some communities.

Programs are being put in place in areas with large Jewish populations to make the community feel safer and to make police officers and non-Jewish residents of the community more sensitive to the needs of the Jewish population. The Metropolitan Police Department in Washington, D.C., has implemented a police training program for police recruits. Through a partnership with the Anti-Defamation League (ADL) and the U.S. Holocaust Memorial Museum (USHMM), former Chief Charles Ramsey mandated that all police recruits attend a tour of the museum as part of the "hate crimes" component of their training. This program was a 2001 IACP award winner in the education and training section. Many departments around the country have followed their lead and are working with the Anti-Defamation League to provide training for their officers and commanders on terrorism, and many of these utilize the Law Enforcement Agency Resource Network on the Anti-Defamation League website.

Members of the Jewish community are teaming up with their police departments for guidance and instruction regarding responding to a gun threat, dealing with suspicious packages and threatening phone calls, and responding to catastrophic events. This partnership with the police department is important to the Jewish community and helps them to feel empowered in providing for their security and safety.

Women

Women make up approximately 50 percent of the population, so police officers have frequent interactions with women. Unfortunately, law enforcement often becomes involved with women when they are victims of crimes. In the last decade, however, officers' contact with women offenders has increased as statistics indicate there are more women being arrested for crimes.

Although women are often victims of the same types of crimes as men, they also are more vulnerable to certain crimes that men usually do not have to be overly concerned about. It can be difficult for men to understand what it is like to feel vulnerable and to sometimes fear 50 percent of the population. That does not happen to men under ordinary living conditions. Although men can be victims of sex offenses, it is far more common for women to be sexually assaulted or raped. Women also are involved in domestic violence cases most frequently as the victim of an assault, rather than as the offender. Police officers who encounter them as victims need to be aware of the psychological aspects of this victimization.

Many women have been critical of police methods for handling domestic violence cases and have complained of insensitivity by the police in rape and other sexual assault cases. Law enforcement has heeded their complaints regarding the handling of domestic violence cases by increasingly adopting pro-arrest policies in these cases. Also, since the 1970s, the police have become much more sensitive to women in rape and sexual assault cases. Numerous police departments have formed special investigating units to handle sex crimes (often using female investigators), and many departments conduct training sessions to help officers understand the concerns of women.

With the increased numbers of women in law enforcement and the slowly increasing number in the upper administration of police organizations, the policies and procedures in place are now more reflective of the female perspective than ever before. As female officers become more visible in communities, the perception of the police as being supportive of women should increase. Another way many departments around the country have shown their support is through victim/witness services. In these departments, individuals or units receive specialized training in crime victimization, including domestic and sexual violence. Police departments are using these units within their own agencies to better serve the victims and witnesses of crime, many of whom are women. This effort also represents a desire to be more receptive to women's needs within the criminal justice system.

Gays and Lesbians

In cities with visibly large gay populations, there have been numerous verbal and physical attacks on members of the gay community (sometimes called "gay bashing"). Police departments across the United States have created bias units to investigate crimes that are the result of racial, religious, ethnic, or sexual orientation hatred. In Chapter 7, we discussed the efforts to recruit gay police officers. These efforts have certainly improved relationships between the police and the gay community. Publicized efforts of police departments to recruit homosexuals have reduced fears of reporting crimes among many members of the gay community. The gay and lesbian unit of the Washington, D.C., Metropolitan Police Department was the only law enforcement program to be named a finalist for the "Innovations in American Government" award in 2005, an award presented each year by Harvard University's Kennedy School of Government. The unit investigates crimes committed by and against homosexuals, bisexuals, and transgendered individuals and advises the police chief on issues affecting D.C.'s gay residents.[25]

The murder of Matthew Shepard made it clear that hate-motivated violence is still a problem for the gay community. The Lambda Legal Defense and Education Fund—a legal organization dedicated to the civil rights of lesbians, gay men, people with HIV and AIDS, and the transgendered community—proposes increased prevention efforts to target antigay attitudes and violent tendencies that start at a young age.[26] Hate crime legislation seeks to appropriately punish individuals perpetrating such crimes, but it is felt that if attitudes and socialization issues can be changed, we could reduce the number of these types of crimes and allow these minority populations to live free of fear.

It is believed that violent crime against individuals identifying themselves as lesbian, gay, bisexual, or transgender (LGBT) has increased recently, although much of it has not been reported. Many victims have stated they did not file reports due to a perceived indifference or even abusive attitudes by police.[27]

New Immigrants

A great proportion of new immigrants, particularly in larger cities and border states, are Mexican, Chinese, Haitian, and Cuban. The numbers of people arriving on Florida shores seeking political asylum and improved economic conditions have proven challenging for the local governments and schools. These immigrants often bring with them strong religious and cultural beliefs with which law enforcement is unfamiliar. These beliefs and rituals can affect police services and have presented challenges to police, resulting in the desire of police to learn as much as possible about these cultures to minimize misunderstandings and danger to both officers and immigrants.

In seeking to make a new life for themselves, new immigrants also must shed their ingrained beliefs concerning police officers. The police in their native lands often operate much differently than do the police in the United States; to gain their trust, law enforcement personnel need to educate these new immigrants in the U.S. system.

Large cities and border states are not the only places confronting the immigrant issue any more. Census data show the most dramatic increase in new immigrants to be in the South and Midwest. This is affecting smaller towns in a dramatic way. The immigrant population in these new immigrant growth states is disproportionately composed of new arrivals, which correlates with them having a limited ability to speak English.[28]

Law enforcement procedures have evolved over the years as immigrants have arrived in larger numbers. Police are striving to serve the new arrivals better and to minimize the impact on police services. Law enforcement agencies are addressing the challenge of newly arrived immigrants from all over the world who do not speak English or understand the culture of the United States. Police are trying to educate immigrants about what the police do in the United States compared with their countries of origin and to build a relationship between the community and the police.

Risking All for the American Dream

ON THE JOB

I was a police officer in Boca Raton, Florida, when Haitians started to arrive on our shores. I was a sergeant on the road when the issue first presented itself in the mid-1980s. It was something we had never dealt with before, and we had no idea how to address this new challenge. The first time it happened was around 4:00 or 5:00 a.m.; we got a call from a citizen that there was a group of people, soaking wet, walking up to State Road A1A from the beach.

Previously, we had been confronted with drug dealers using boats to smuggle marijuana and cocaine to the beaches. At times, their boats broke up and people and drugs scattered; other times, the drugs were dumped offshore as the occupants of the vessel were scared by the possibility of law enforcement being in the area, either on the water or in the air. When word got out of drugs washing up, there was often a response by locals trying to gather up some of the drugs.

Because this had been my previous experience, I made a similar assumption regarding the call as I responded to back up the zone officer. When we arrived, we found about eight black men and women walking in two different directions on A1A. We stopped them and attempted to communicate with them. None of us knew Creole, and the Haitians did not speak English well. One Haitian knew a little English, and we were able to ascertain that they had come from Haiti on a small boat that had broken up a few hundred yards offshore, and that they had swum and then walked to shore. These people were wet, cold, tired, hungry, and scared. We tried to talk to them as best we could, but, in addition to the language barrier, they would not look us in the eye, which made us suspicious that they were perhaps lying to us.

We ended up using several police vehicles to transport them to the police station. Once at the station, we searched all of them (there were those drug smuggling fears again) and ultimately ended up transporting them to Miami where U.S. Immigration and Naturalization Services (INS) took custody of them.

This began to happen with increased regularity, and the numbers of people got larger and larger. Tragedy resulted on several occasions with

people drowning on their way to shore. We also saw pregnant women and children arriving with these groups. We learned some things about these new arrivals with each group that came, and we sat down as a police organization and with other groups such as the INS to decide how these situations should be handled.

We found that economic conditions in Haiti were deplorable, and people were fleeing to the United States for an opportunity to work. Others were persecuted by the dictatorship in Haiti and in fear for their lives. The police were different in Haiti and often shot citizens for no reason. Knowing this, I was surprised these people were so docile and cooperative when we stopped them. I can only attribute it to fear. In fact, their reluctance to look us in the eye was a cultural sign of respect.

For the most part, reports of Haitians sailing the ocean in the rickety boats they were getting off were false. Most were transported part of the way by smugglers and then placed on the old boats to go the rest of the way, or they were simply forced to jump off the smugglers' boats, often resulting in death.

When I searched the women early on in this process, I found that they were wearing several layers of clothing in an effort to bring as many clothes with them as possible. They carried nothing. They literally came to this country with just the clothes on their backs.

Our procedures changed as encountering immigrants became a more regular occurrence and involved larger groups. We stopped bringing them to the station and searching them and began calling INS to respond directly to the beach. We often had groups of more than 100 Haitians, and we would have officers stay with them in a designated area on or near the beach and await buses that INS sent. Most of these arrivals spent months in the Krome Detention Center in Miami waiting for their cases to be heard and decided by immigration.

South Florida has a large population of Haitians, and, as a police officer, I frequently interacted with them. They quickly went to work at any job they could find. Overall, I found them

(continued)

to be a very hardworking, peaceful group of people. They were happy to be able to work and send money home to Haiti to their families, and they often spent their nonworking time studying English. They also brought some unique cultural beliefs, in particular concerning voodoo, that were new to me as well as to other officers. It was something we learned about and had to be aware of when we were investigating crimes.

The department provided us with training in the Haitian culture as well as some basic Creole to facilitate communication.

It was an eye-opening experience for me to witness these people risking everything, including their lives, for an opportunity to work at (usually) very menial positions. The situation reminded me how lucky we are here in the United States.

—Linda Forst

As the rate of new immigrants, including many illegal immigrants, has increased tremendously in the last two decades and presented many new challenges to law enforcement, there also has been some backlash in towns and cities around the country. Many states and communities have enacted immigration-related laws. The laws are aimed at curbing illegal immigration, targeting businesses that employ illegal immigrants and landlords who rent to illegal immigrants. Community leaders state they are passing these local laws because of inaction by the federal government in enforcing immigration laws. They believe these actions are legal because "states and localities bear a significant amount of the burden for dealing with illegal immigrants, but the federal government bears the brunt of enforcing the law, and when they don't, states and local governments pay the price."[29]

Law enforcement, however, has been thrown into the middle of this controversy. In the towns and cities that want something done and see the federal government as unresponsive, it falls to law enforcement personnel to enforce the local ordinances and state laws and also intervene in disturbances that arise over their implementation. Also, according to the Southern Poverty Law Center's report "The Year in Hate," there is a link between anti-immigration activism and the significant rise in hate crimes against Latinos in recent years.[30]

The immigration issue has created a lot of debate and turmoil in the law enforcement community and in local and state governments. Some jurisdictions instruct their officers to investigate immigration status on all calls, others only allow them to determine status after someone has been arrested, and still others believe that local government should not get involved at all. This issue and how it is handled will continue to evolve.

Police and Special Populations

As we have seen, the community the police serve is extremely diverse. Special populations offer unique challenges for police departments. Some of the groups with special needs are the physically challenged, the aging population, young people, crime victims, victims of domestic violence, the mentally ill, and the homeless.

The Physically Challenged

Depending on the definition of *physically challenged*, there are between 40 million and 70 million physically challenged people in the United States. According to the 2010 Census, there are 36 million people with disabilities, or about 12 percent of the population, and the likelihood of a disability increases with age.[31] Those with disabilities include the deaf and hard of hearing; those who use wheelchairs, walkers, canes, and other mobility aids; the blind and visually impaired; those with communication problems; and the mentally ill.

The National Crime Victimization Survey, which examines crimes against people with disabilities, indicates that, when adjusted for age variations, people with disabilities experience violence at about twice the rate of people without a disability. It is imperative that law enforcement ensure that this segment of the community will feel comfortable interacting with the police and reporting their victimization.[32]

The deaf community can present a difficult challenge to law enforcement, particularly in a crisis situation. Communication is always a vital part of police response, so being unable to communicate with a member of the deaf community can be a significant hurdle. There have been scattered incidents where individuals have been injured or killed by police officers who misinterpreted the individual's lack of response to commands. Many departments across the country have implemented training for police officers to increase their understanding of the hurdles of the deaf community and have conducted informational sessions for the deaf community.

Diabetics also have significant problems of which the police should be aware. Because of the prevalence of drug abuse in our society, officers frequently confront people who are in possession of hypodermic syringes and needles or are actually using a hypodermic needle. Some, however, may be people suffering from diabetes, treating themselves by injecting insulin. Diabetics often wear easily recognizable identification alerting first responders and police that they have insulin-treated diabetes. Officers might also encounter diabetics who are in need of insulin but appear to be suffering from drug- or alcohol-related impairment, are confused, combative, unconscious, or are suffering from seizures. With education and awareness, officers will be able to summon the necessary medical assistance as early as possible for these individuals.

The Office for Victims of Crime offers several training guides and informational articles through their website that will enhance the police response to individuals with disabilities. It is designed to help law enforcement professionals gain a deeper understanding of the lives and abilities of individuals with disabilities and thereby enhance their relationship with this segment of the community.

The Aging Population

America is getting older. In 2010, the 40.4 million people aged 65 and older represented 13.1 percent of the population, an increase of 15.3 percent since 2000.[33] By the year 2020, it is expected that the number will be 55 million.

Senior citizens experience particular problems that necessitate special attention from the police.

Many police officers find it rewarding to work with the Special Olympics during their off-duty hours.

© Steve Skjold/Alamy

Although seniors have the lowest criminal victimization rates of all age groups, they experience a tremendous fear of crime, often refusing to leave their homes because of the fear of becoming a victim. Many senior citizens are infirm and require emergency services. Police often provide special programs and services for senior citizens.

Also of concern to older Americans is the desire to retain their independence. An AARP (originally, the American Association of Retired Persons) study found that 85 percent of people over the age of 60 want to remain living independently as they age. Only one in eight lives with other relatives.[34]

Although there are many innovative programs to assist the aging population, law enforcement leaders have realized that education and training of their officers must occur for officers to foster a good relationship with this segment of the population. As mentioned earlier, the patrol officer is the ambassador for the department. The way officers treat older people will affect what seniors think of the department.

It is important for officers to understand the physical, emotional, and social challenges that people face as they age. Officers can then adapt some of their procedures to minimize the effect of some physical challenges (for example, changes in vision, hearing, and mobility) on their interactions with older people. An officer who understands the psychological and social issues will be able to understand an unexpectedly emotional reaction to what he or she perceives as a routine event. An example would be an overreaction by an older person to being involved in an automobile crash. To the person involved, this accident could be seen as a threat to his or her independence. A citation could affect a senior's ability to keep his or her license and consequently to remain independent. The social issues confronting older Americans include adjusting to retirement, losing family and friends to death, coping with illness and impairments, and perhaps facing a terminal illness. To have these things happen in close proximity to each other enhances the effects.

Line officers also need to be aware of special issues facing the older person, including deterioration of driving skills, fraud, self-neglect, and elder abuse. If officers are alert for signs of such problems, this awareness will help the officers take action or make the proper referrals as well as help the department develop appropriate programs to address these issues.

Today, police departments have created numerous special programs to assist with the challenges faced by the aging population. One such program is **Triad**, a partnership between the police and senior citizens to address specific problems seniors encounter with safety and quality-of-life issues. Triad was started by the International Association of Chiefs of Police (IACP) in cooperation with AARP and the National Sheriffs' Association (NSA). Triads are involved in training police officers to interact with seniors and advising departments on various programs.

AARP has cooperated with law enforcement by publishing several brochures on crime prevention for the elderly. The brochures contain practical advice about how to reduce criminal opportunity. Crime prevention information as well as driving information for older people is available through the AARP website.

Alzheimer's is a disease that does and will continue to affect police officers' jobs as they encounter Alzheimer's victims wandering or receive reports from concerned citizens regarding missing family members. Symptoms of Alzheimer's include memory loss, disorientation, loss of language skills, impairment of judgment, and personality changes. Patients have been known to wander aimlessly. Because of these factors, law enforcement personnel frequently encounter Alzheimer's sufferers. There are more than 5 million Alzheimer's victims in the United States. Most victims are older than 65, but this disease can strike people in their 40s and 50s. As the population ages, it has been estimated that the number of people affected will reach 14 million by the middle of this century unless a cure or treatment is found. In recent years, locating and ensuring the safety of Alzheimer's victims has been significantly assisted by GPS technology and tracking devices.

Young People

Young children are a special target of police–community relations programs because they are impressionable: It is believed that if children learn something early enough in life, it will stay with them forever. The problem of crime and young people has been a concern for decades.

During the 1980s and early 1990s, crime involving juveniles soared. The nation responded by implementing many different types of programs to try to address this issue. Programs were implemented addressing family issues and living conditions, educational and school programs were started, and law enforcement implemented programs. Factors studied included educational attainment, substance abuse, mentors and role models, and supervision. Police felt that if the American public cared about the crime problem, then programs targeting children and youth needed to be undertaken. In general, the arrest rate for crimes by juvenile offenders has steadily declined, possibly influenced by the youth programs.[35]

Many departments have realized that by getting involved in young people's lives, they can have a positive impact and minimize the chances of the youth making bad choices. Such involvement is also viewed as a way of grooming "good citizens" and possibly of molding future police candidates. For this reason, many agencies have explored offering many of the programs that they have for adults to younger age groups. These young people may have more time than their working parents to participate in such programs, improve the quality of their own lives and the community they live in, and assist the police department at the same time. Such programs include crime watch for youth, crime prevention, Internet safety, citizen police academies, and Community Emergency Response Team (CERT) programs. In addition, there are the more traditional youth programs targeting defined youth problems as well as at-risk youth.

Triad A joint partnership between the police and senior citizens to address specific problems seniors encounter with safety and quality-of-life issues.

GUEST LECTURE

JOHN LOVICK

John Lovick was recently pro-moted to county executive in Snohomish County while serv-ing his second term as sheriff of Snohomish County, Washington. He served 13 years in the U.S. Coast Guard and 31 years with the Washington State Patrol. He also served nine years in the Washington state legislature. He is originally from Robeline, Louisiana, and has an AA degree in criminal justice from Shoreline Community College in Shoreline, Washington.

DON'T GIVE UP

I grew up in a small town in Louisiana during the turbulent 1960s. My grandmother raised me, along with her nine chil-dren, after my grandfa-ther died. Our house sat in the middle of a large cotton field. There was no running water in the house and no electricity until after I reached the fifth grade. I spent my days going to school and working in the cotton fields.

Segregation was not only a way of life in Louisiana, but it was the law of the land. My school was completely segregated. I experi-enced many devastating setbacks during my school years, some that would cause even the most optimistic person to give up. Then, during my fourth grade year, a police officer visited our school to talk about things that were occur-ring in town. He told us how important our education was, how important it was to stay in school, and how important it was to stay out of trouble. He encouraged us to work hard at whatever we set our minds on and to believe in ourselves. I was sitting on the floor about 20 feet away from him as he spoke.

I would later learn that this police officer was Sheriff Earl K. Morris of Natchitoches Parish, Louisiana. As Sheriff Morris spoke, I was thinking like any fourth grader would think dur-ing those times. I was dreading how hot it was going to be in the fields when I got home. I was also hoping we would

be able to afford to stay in our house for the rest of the year. Near the end of his talk, the sheriff paused, looked around at all the students, and said something that would stay with me for the next 50 years. He said, "Don't give up." He said he knew things were difficult and life was hard. He said don't give up on school, don't give up on our families, and never ever quit.

Now at that point in my life, I had witnessed several of my uncles drop out of school, some before the ninth grade. There was little expectation I would ever graduate from high school. However, the message delivered by Sheriff Morris that day impacted my life and that of several other students. With those three simple words, "don't give up," he changed my life and became a hero of mine. It was also the way in which he told us not to give up. Sheriff Morris demonstrated how he cared for each of us.

Sheriff Morris treated everyone with kindness, dignity, and respect. His values and ethics inspired me to finish school. I would later enlist in the U.S. Coast Guard, become a state trooper with the Washington State Patrol, be elected to the Washington state legislature, and, eventually, get elected sheriff of Snohomish County, Washington.

I share my story because as a law enforcement officer, we are held to some very high standards. We are also held in high esteem by the general public. Our words and actions, as dem-onstrated by Sheriff Morris, can have a huge impact on many people, but especially on our youth. Our children and young adults look to us for guidance and leadership.

There have been many, many times in my life where I wanted to simply give up when it appeared the odds were stacked against me. But I didn't quit, thanks in large part to that visit from Sheriff Morris to my tiny school house on that hot day in Louisiana. I will never forget those three encouraging words, and I will share those words with as many young people as possible in the hope that others will never give up.

Source: Reprinted by permission of John Lovick.

ANTIDRUG PROGRAMS FOR YOUNG PEOPLE

Currently, the most popular antidrug program aimed at children is **Drug Abuse Resistance Education (DARE)**. In DARE programs, police officers teach students in their own classrooms about the dangers of drug abuse. The program is designed to help children and teens (1) build self-esteem, (2) build self-confidence, (3) manage youthful stress, (4) redirect behavior to viable alternatives, and (5) see police officers as positive role models.

The DARE program has received mixed reviews, and some departments have cut their programs, especially in these tight budget years. In a continuing effort to improve its program and address concerns regarding benefits, DARE has developed some new curricula and joined forces with the University of Akron to conduct further research.[36] They have added online safety, bullying, choosing good role models, and other current topics to their programs. The new DARE program for substance abuse and violence prevention is high-tech, interactive, and decision-model based. DARE officers serve as "coaches" to support kids, using research-based refusal strategies to give them the skills and information they need to make good life choices. Students are actively involved and use brain imagery, mock courtroom role-play, and discussion groups to enhance comprehension of the consequences of drug use and violence.[37]

Some antidrug programs are appealing to the vanity of teenagers. A computer program called Face2Face shows teens what they would look like six months, one year, and even three years into a meth habit, including the scabs, droopy skin, thinning hair, and rotting teeth. When these programs are presented in high schools, they seem to have a dramatic effect on the teens.

Despite the mixed reviews, many parents and teachers believe such programs are crucial if children are to learn to resist peer pressure and stay away from drugs. Researchers seem to believe that the programs cannot be one size fits all and cannot condemn outright either legitimate medications or alcohol in moderation, which may confuse the students and conflict with what they learn at home.[38] It will take continued study of DARE and other similar programs to determine what components of the program are most effective and in what way.

OTHER PROGRAMS FOR YOUNG PEOPLE

Police programs for young people exist to address concerns other than drugs. In this section, we discuss some of the most popular programs.

The **Gang Resistance Education and Training (GREAT)** program is modeled after DARE but specifically addresses the issues of gangs. According to their website, GREAT is a school-based, police officer–instructed classroom curriculum with prevention of delinquency, youth violence, and gang membership as its primary objective. There are programs for elementary and middle school students as well as summer programs and family training.[39]

Youth Crime Watch of America is a youth-led movement to create a crime-free, drug-free, and violence-free environment in the schools and neighborhoods.[40] Recently they have renamed their organization "Ignitus Worldwide" to emphasize their goal of mobilizing and empowering youth and giving them a voice in their own communities. They continue to stress safety programs as well as leadership development, substance abuse prevention, peer mentoring, and civic engagement.

Antibullying programs are becoming more prevalent. In the wake of recent school violence, many schools and communities are addressing the area of bullying in their schools with various education and prevention programs. State legislatures are also addressing this issue due to an increased frequency of these types of incidents and the tragic results, including some recent suicides. With increased use of technology and social networking sites, bullying has become even more of a problem. It is now facilitated during nonschool hours and in a less private manner through social network sites and cell phone texting. Therefore, the consequences of cyberbullying can be far more devastating.

CERT training has been made available to high school students in many schools throughout the country (more on CERT is included later in this chapter under crime prevention programs). After 9/11, there was increased awareness of the importance of

---

Drug Abuse Resistance Education (DARE) The most popular antidrug program in which police officers teach students in schools about the dangers of drug use.

Gang Resistance Education and Training (GREAT) An educational program designed after DARE that addresses the issue of gangs.

civilians being trained in basic emergency response, first aid, and search and rescue. It was also realized that students would be a great asset to improving safety in their schools in the event of a disaster. Students view this as an opportunity to learn valuable skills that could enhance their chances of obtaining employment in police and fire departments.

Officer Friendly and other programs designed to help children see and talk to police officers are popular with schools and police administrators alike. The intent of the Officer Friendly programs is to encourage young children to view police officers as friends by getting to know some. Some officers dress up as clowns or old-time police officers and perform clown-type tricks with balloons. This has proven to be popular with young children. Police officers also have been involved in literacy programs at schools where they read with or to young students. In addition, K-9 demonstrations in classrooms have proven to be beneficial in building relationships with children. Some departments use music to reach out to young people and have officers who perform together in rock bands, jazz groups, or singing groups.

The **Police Explorer** program is part of the Boy Scouts and is a popular program available around the nation. Police Explorer programs are a win-win endeavor for all concerned. They give young people an opportunity to explore the law enforcement field. The Explorers receive training in various areas of law enforcement either through their sponsoring agency or sometimes through regional or state training opportunities. They are also sometimes involved in competitions with other posts. The Explorers help to supplement the workforce of the department and can assist with community festivals, parades, and emergencies in areas such as directing traffic and assisting the public. They also have been found to be valuable in emergency preparedness. Being an Explorer is a great way to determine if a law enforcement career is right for a young person, and the department gets an opportunity to look at a potential candidate. These Explorers will provide for a future workforce that is well trained and educated in the law enforcement field. Most Police Explorer units have Web pages attached to their police department's site with information regarding their post.

Police Explorers A program for young adults between the ages of 14 and 20 in which they work closely with law enforcement and explore the police career.

Police trading cards are another popular youth program. Trading cards in the format of baseball cards feature the photographs and personal information of officers in the department. Young people often go to the police station to find officers from whom they want a card or autograph. Some officers use them as their business cards. Officers may provide their favorite quote or inspirational saying on the backs of the cards as well as their professional background. Some agencies have cards for particular units, such as the bicycle unit, motor unit, or K-9s, in addition to individual cards. Some police departments feature a "card of the week" or "card of the month," which is printed in the local paper and available at the front desk for pickup. The cards provide a good icebreaker for officers as well as the youth to initiate conversations.

The school resource officer, a position designed to combat the increase of juvenile crime and improve relationships between school children and the police, has proven to be effective. Nationally, 38 percent of local police departments used full-time school resource officers in 2007, although this percentage was much higher for larger departments serving populations of between 25,000 and 500,000 (more than 80 percent).[41] The school resource officer program assigns uniformed police officers to schools, generally junior and senior high schools, to provide a wide variety of services. These officers build bridges and become friendly with the students. By being available to and familiar with students, they can discuss students' problems and give advice that might help students make good choices. The school resource officer also functions as a good resource person for the teachers and administrators and in an emergency can serve as a first responder with a good working knowledge of the school, its personnel, and its layout.

Anti–child abduction programs are also popular. Many law enforcement agencies provide parents with free photo ID documents and crucial information about safety for their children. Some departments have begun to facilitate the collection of DNA from children via a swabbing kit; the parents then retain the specimen. In 2003, President Bush signed the Protect Act. Although many states have had AMBER Alert systems in place since this program originated in Texas in 1996, the Protect Act formally established the federal government's role in the AMBER Alert system. The goal is to get entire communities involved in the search for missing

Police Exploring

Students can find out firsthand what police work is all about in several ways. If your school has an intern program with the local government, try to get into it and request to work with the police department. If your police department has an auxiliary program that allows you to contribute your time to the department, try that out. If your police department has a ride-along program, take advantage of it. Being a Police Explorer will make you more aware of the needs and problems of your community. The program can strengthen or clarify your decision to become a police officer.

The Law Enforcement Exploring program involves young men and women, ages 14 to 20, in a hands-on look at law enforcement as a potential career. Youths interested in Law Enforcement Exploring join posts sponsored by a law enforcement agency. The law enforcement agency provides a sworn officer as the post leader. Liability insurance is provided by the Boy Scouts of America (BSA), which offers Law Enforcement Exploring as a program for older youths. The BSA also operates regional and national events for Explorers.

In a typical post, Explorers are required to work approximately 20 hours a month to maintain their eligibility, but they may work more hours if they wish.

Some of the ways in which Explorers work with the police include assisting in crowd, traffic, and parking control at parades and festivals; staging crime prevention programs for neighborhood associations and assisting with Operation Identification by marking citizens' valuables; assisting the police in performing clerical functions; and serving as role models for younger children and assistants for officers teaching DARE. Explorers can attend regional events in which they compete in pistol shooting, crime scene searches, hostage negotiations, report writing, traffic accident investigations, and other events based on aspects of law enforcement. Every other year, a national conference with an interpost competition is held.

According to the BSA, approximately 40 percent of Explorers become either law enforcement officers or lawyers.

—John S. Dempsey

---

children by joining the efforts of law enforcement and the media. Using the media to quickly alert the public to the descriptions of individuals endangering children has already had a number of successes.[42] In conjunction with these efforts, many departments offer Internet safety brochures and programs to guide parents in keeping their children safe on the computer. This is an emerging safety issue because online predators seem to be multiplying and naïve preteens are posting too much personal information on social media sites, making themselves easy targets.

Police athletic programs or **Police Athletic Leagues (PALs)** have long been some of the most popular programs involving the police and youth. These programs include boxing, baseball, football, and basketball leagues (including midnight basketball) as well as summer camps. Some prominent former members of PALs around the nation include boxers Mohammed Ali and Evander Holyfield and entertainer Bill Cosby. PAL is the largest organization of law enforcement agencies, using athletics, recreation, and education to instill positive life principles and character-building tools to deter crime and violence. By 2008, there were more than 400 chapters serving over 700 cities and more than 2 million youths nationwide.[43]

Crime Victims

"Victim issues and concerns are becoming an integral part of policing in the 21st century. We have to prioritize this in our law enforcement mission," said Chief Frank Winters, chair of the IACP Victim Services Committee.[44] As many as 31 million people are victims of violent or property crime in the United States annually.[45] Many efforts have been undertaken to assist victims of crime, including victims' rights laws, victim assistance programs, and crime compensation funds.

Police Athletic League (PAL) A large sports program involving police officers and youth.

Law enforcement realizes that by working more closely with victims, they can not only better serve the victims and enhance community support, but they can also help advance the law enforcement mission and goal of reducing and solving crime and reducing fear of crime. Traditionally, victims have been considered to be law enforcement clients because they receive law enforcement services, but the criminal justice system has now recognized that victims also are powerful and resourceful stakeholders in the system. By working more closely with them and incorporating their assistance, police can have a greater impact on crime and the perception of community safety.

Many departments around the country have established victims' services units within their agencies and have found this to be a very positive undertaking. Victims' services staff can have a more rapid response and consequently obtain more and better information regarding the crime and the victim's needs than they would by reading the report the next day or even later. Crisis counseling can be initiated earlier, and police time can be devoted to investigation. This supportive atmosphere may also encourage citizens to report more crime and cooperate more fully, and consequently may increase conviction rates.

Police also have instituted special investigative units and are using special tools to make the investigative process less threatening to victims of crime, such as trying to minimize the number of times a victim or witness has to talk to someone, making any meetings as convenient as possible for the victims and witnesses, and striving to keep victims informed of the status of their cases. Keeping victims informed has proven to be especially critical among homicide victims' families, where often the detective who is working very hard on the homicide case does not have the time (and in the past did not consider it a priority) to keep the family informed. The family frequently perceived this as the investigator either not caring or not working on their loved one's case. Many departments have now initiated programs through which they regularly exchange information with the families or loved ones of homicide victims, and these programs have proven to be very successful and greatly improved relationships within communities.

Washington, D.C., implemented "open house" gatherings following the suggestion of an activist who suffered through the murder of two sons. These events allowed the families to see how difficult the investigations are and the challenges involved in obtaining witnesses and leads. On the other hand, they were also a reminder to detectives and investigators about what is important to the community and the victims' families, and that even though a homicide case may be 1 of 20 cases an investigator is working, it is a major, significant, life-altering trauma to the family.[46] At times, some family members left as angry as they came, but in most instances they were pleased to discover their case had not been forgotten and was in fact being followed up.

Victims can have a powerful voice in their community. Elizabeth Smart has emerged as a strong voice for victims and has made an impact on many as she has stepped forward and been open and forthcoming about her eight-month ordeal of abduction and sexual assault at the hands of Brian David Mitchell, who abducted her from her bedroom when she was 14. (Her rescue is discussed later in the section on Crime Stoppers.) She has confidently testified as the case has progressed through the system. She refuses to be a victim and wants to encourage other victims to speak out and stand up to their offenders. She is currently partnering with ABC to help empower other victims and to be a voice in child advocacy issues.

Victims of Domestic Violence

There has been increased demand on law enforcement to be responsive to the needs of domestic violence victims. Family violence is one of the most frequent types of violence that police encounter, and though it is not necessarily considered the most dangerous police call (because of improved training and procedures), it is one filled with danger and emotional trauma for all concerned.

Although police once dismissed domestic disputes as a "civil matter," the latest statistics indicate the seriousness of this violence. According to the National Crime Victimization Survey, domestic violence accounted for 21 percent of all violent crime over a 10-year period from 2003 to 2012; 76 percent of those victims were women.[47] According to the National Coalition Against Domestic Violence (NCADV) website, one in every four women will experience domestic violence in her lifetime, and an estimated 1.3 million women are victims of physical assaults by an intimate partner each year. Even more alarming is the fact that in 70 to 80 percent of intimate partner homicides, no matter which partner was killed, the man physically abused the woman before the murder. There is also a significant economic impact, as it is estimated that the cost of intimate partner violence exceeds $5.8 billion each year, including the medical and mental health services. Additionally, the societal cost is huge, as the culture of violence is passed on to the next generation of children who may witness this violence.[48]

This violence between intimate couples of opposite gender may start very early. In a survey of 635 suburban, middle-class high school students, about 36 percent of girls and 37 percent of boys said they had experienced physical abuse from a date. Half of the girls—and just 4 percent of the boys—said their worst abusive experience "hurt a lot." Among the other key findings were that 44 percent of the girls stayed with boys after moderate violence, including slapping, and 36 percent stayed after severe abuse, including choking and punching.[49] With the advancement of technology, abusers have acquired a new way to control their victims digitally with text messages and using photos to obtain proof of what their victims are doing, who they are with, and where they are. Twenty-six percent of teens in romantic relationships report being intimidated and controlled with the assistance of smartphones and social media sites.[50] It is clear that this type of violence is a very real problem demanding innovative police response.

Traditionally, the criminal justice system took a hands-off policy toward domestic violence, treating it as a private affair that should be handled within the family, and police did not make arrests even when it qualified as a felony. Two assumptions prevailed: (1) that the arrest would make life worse for the victim, because the abuser might retaliate, and (2) that the victim would refuse to press charges. Most police departments had no formal policies regarding domestic violence, and officers used many different techniques to deal with the problem.

Two important lawsuits—brought forward by women's groups in New York City (*Bruno v. Codd*, 396 N.Y.S.2d 974, 1977) and Oakland, California (*Scott v. Hart*, No. C-76-2395, N.D. Cal., 1976)—followed by the **Minneapolis Domestic Violence Experiment**, conducted by the Police Foundation in 1981 to 1982, began to change the police response in domestic violence cases. The findings indicated that arrest prevented further domestic violence more effectively than did separation or mediation.

Though the study authors Lawrence Sherman and Richard Berk recommended further research and data before implementing any changes, mandatory arrest laws were adopted around the country, fueled by women's rights groups and battered women's advocates. Mandatory arrest is still the preferred method of handling domestic violence, and it aids the individuals involved in getting into the system and getting help as well as educating the public that domestic violence is a crime.

Despite the lack of a clear consensus regarding the effectiveness of arrest in domestic violence cases, most departments have a domestic violence policy.

In response to the demands placed on law enforcement because of domestic violence calls and the desire to be more sensitive to the needs of the victim, many police departments throughout the country employ domestic violence specialists or coordinators to oversee the domestic violence cases the department handles. The specialist ensures that all victims are aware of the services available and assists them in obtaining these services. The specialist also attempts to make sure that no cases slip through the cracks because of inaccurate reporting and assists the officers in handling these situations when requested. Women's perceptions of how they were treated by police affect whether or not they will call the police again.

As domestic violence is chronically underreported, it is imperative that the public be educated about the warning signs and dangers involved. It would be nice to be able to predict which cases are going to escalate, but at this time that is impossible. The Orlando Police Department has initiated a program with the intent to break the spiral of domestic violence. They have partnered with domestic violence centers in forming the InVEST Services (Intimate Violence Enhanced Services Team) to provide intensive service management and assistance to individuals identified to be in potentially lethal situations.[51] When officers respond to domestic violence calls, they complete a threat assessment checklist in an effort to determine which cases are similar to previous cases that have resulted in death. Those cases receive additional intervention and attention.[52]

Minneapolis Domestic Violence Experiment An experiment conducted in Minneapolis, Minnesota, to determine the deterrent effect of various methods of handling domestic violence, including mandatory arrest.

Other departments around the country are following similar paths and using various lethality assessments of domestic violence incidents in an attempt to protect the most vulnerable victims.

The trend is to deal with domestic violence as part of the bigger picture involving family violence and provide a coordinated effort to all members of a family plagued by violence. The impact of violence on our society, especially when witnessed or experienced at a young age, is becoming apparent, and service providers and criminal justice practitioners see the importance of intervening as early as possible.

The Mentally Ill

Police officers frequently encounter people with mental illness, which poses a significant challenge for law enforcement. Approximately 10 to 15 percent of jail inmates have severe mental illness. In jurisdictions with populations greater than 100,000, approximately 7 percent of police contacts involve the mentally ill.[53]

The calls involving people with mental illness can be some of the most dangerous that officers face. Often the calls come from family members who have tried to handle the situation themselves but find they are unable to do so. This is often an ongoing problem; they have been able to handle it many times in the past and do not wish to involve the police if they do not have to. If, however, they start to fear for their safety or the safety of the mentally ill person, they will call the police. The other way that officers encounter mentally ill persons is when they are causing some type of disruption in public and a citizen or businessperson observes this odd or threatening behavior and calls police. Sometimes officers encounter individuals acting strangely out in public and believe they need to take some type of action. Often, the mentally ill person is in the process of committing a crime.

Officers dealing with a mentally ill individual have several difficult decisions to make. First, they must decide if the person needs to be restricted in some way. If they feel they have calmed an individual down so that the individual is not a danger to himself or herself or to others, officers may leave the individual where that person is or with family. If the individual cannot safely be left, the officer can take the person to jail or a mental health facility. This decision will depend on what mental health facilities are available. If the community does not have competent mental health facilities or if they are full and refusing any new patients, an officer may find a way to make an arrest to keep the person safe and get some mental health care in jail.[54]

Since police officers are limited in what they can do with people who are acting strangely, they frequently use creative problem solving when nothing else seems available. (In these situations, officers were using a form of problem-oriented policing even before the term was popularized.) However, in the most serious and dangerous cases, officers believe they need to take action. Unless they can adequately document that the individual is a danger to self or others, they cannot involuntarily commit the individual. Sometimes, it can be difficult to define exactly when that occurs, but officers encounter these decisions frequently and often respond repeatedly to the same individuals and locations. Many officers become frustrated as they attempt to bring someone to the mental health crisis facility only to have the crisis center staff say they are full or that the person does not meet the facility's criteria, or they may take the individual in and conduct an evaluation only to release the person within a few hours.

Though mental health issues are not a police job per se, they have become one because these individuals are in the community and get involved in suicide attempts, disturbances, assaults, or other criminal actions. Confrontations with people who may be delusional often end with the individual, the officer, or a bystander being injured or killed. Police departments across the country are implementing creative approaches and teaming up with other service providers in an attempt to minimize these negative outcomes. Some of these approaches were discussed in Chapter 9.

Police departments have worked hard to develop these policies and procedures, as well as weapons and technology, to minimize tragic outcomes. Three problems that are closely related to the challenge of people with mental illness are homelessness, drug abuse, and alcohol abuse.[55] An additional concern that needs to be examined and addressed is the mental health challenge of combat veterans returning from Afghanistan and Iraq and the lingering effects of post-traumatic stress disorder (PTSD). Law enforcement organizations report that war veterans may be in need of mental health help. Society needs to have all sectors of the community that deal with these problems work together to develop proactive solutions.

The Homeless

Police departments are generally the only agencies available 24 hours a day, seven days a week. Therefore, the police are frequently called to deal with alcoholics, the mentally ill, and the homeless. Large numbers of people live on the streets today. Many of these people are often in drug or alcoholic stupors or frenzies, or they exhibit wild and chaotic behavior. The roots of the homeless problem are many and include the following: the policy in the 1960s and 1970s of releasing the institutionalized mentally ill, today's jail overcrowding, the decriminalization of public intoxication, the breakdown of the traditional family, and the lack of affordable housing.

Anchorage police officers attempt to gather information from inebriated subjects living in a tent in the woods.

Community residents often call the police and insist they remove homeless people from the streets. Residents do not realize, do not understand, and perhaps do not care that the police have very few options for dealing with these needy members of the community. The public is fearful, or at least uncomfortable, in the presence of strangers loitering and asking for money, and this generates calls to the police. The police are also concerned about the high degree of victimization of the homeless and their inability to quickly report incidents to the police. Additionally, over the years, the homeless population has grown to include more women and children.

Nationally, 49 percent of homeless people are homeless for the first time, 28 percent of the homeless have been homeless for three months or less, and 30 percent have been homeless for more than two years.[56] The homeless are no longer living just in subways, along railroad tracks, or in urban downtown areas. They are in suburban and rural towns, living along rivers, in wooded areas, and in business districts. They live almost anywhere in cars, trucks, tents, and under tarps. It can be difficult to locate these individuals to even offer various available services.

Many of the homeless who come to the attention of the police do so as a result of committing a crime or being the victim of a crime. Typically, these incidents include drinking in public, disturbing the peace, fighting, thefts, panhandling, and more serious offenses, including sex crimes, robberies, and murders.

Businesses frequently call the police to remove these members of the population when the business owners believe the homeless are keeping customers away because of begging, harassment, odors, urine or excrement in the area, noise, litter, and narcotics usage. Business owners believe that this population poses a health and public safety concern to themselves and the community.

The homeless issue today is a multifaceted one and requires many organizations working together to attempt to solve the underlying problems. Many police departments have realized this and have taken a proactive approach. Police leaders differ in their beliefs about how to best address the situation. They may want to restrict the ability of the homeless to gather and arrest them for any possible violation, or they may work with local government leaders to enact laws that will outlaw camping, sleeping, and such activities in a way that will drive the homeless out of the area. Generally, the courts do not look favorably on these types of laws and allow them only if they are narrow in scope, such as during certain hours or for a particular area of town and for good reasons. The outright banning of the homeless is unconstitutional. Other departments try to address the issue by looking at what the underlying causes are and seeing if they can work with social service agencies to put programs together to address these causes.

The vulnerability of this population has become more evident after several high-profile attacks on the homeless. Cities are working on strategies to protect this most vulnerable population, open the lines of communication in order to discover their true problems and needs, encourage reporting of victimization, and facilitate their movement out of homelessness.

The media attention that this issue has received in recent years has increased awareness and sensitivity among most community members, including police officers. A photo taken by an impressed tourist of a New York City Police Department (NYPD) officer giving boots and thermal socks to a homeless man in November 2012 ended up posted to the NYPD Facebook page. It became an instant hit and the story was featured on many major news networks as an example of the sensitivity of some police officers. Though these types of encounters occur often, they are rarely documented and seldom highlighted by the media.

Community Crime Prevention Programs

Police expert George L. Kelling has written that citizens have "armed themselves, restricted their activities, rejected cities, built fortress houses and housing complexes both inside and outside the cities, and panicked about particular groups and classes of citizens" in response to criminal activity.[57] Surely, citizens are worried about crimes and have taken measures to protect themselves against it, and the police have an obligation to help them do so. It is obvious that the police cannot solve the crime and disorder problems of the United States by themselves. However, the police also cannot let citizens take the law into their own hands.

To address the crime and disorder problems, the police must turn to the public for its support and active participation in programs to make the streets safer and improve the quality of life for all. Community crime prevention programs include Neighborhood Watch, National Night Out, citizen patrols, citizen volunteer programs, home security surveys and Operation Identification, police storefronts, Crime Stoppers, mass media campaigns, chaplain programs, citizen police academies, and other police-sponsored programs.

Neighborhood Watch Programs

Citizen involvement in crime prevention programs has increased greatly during the past three decades. The idea behind these various programs goes back to the early days of law enforcement in the United States when citizens were the eyes and ears of the community and worked with their neighbors to keep it safe. Community-based crime prevention programs require strong, committed leadership. The partnership between the police and the community will empower citizens with an active role in crime prevention activities.

The IACP Crime Prevention Committee encourages police agencies to base this crime prevention strategy on the organizational philosophy and policy of the department.[58] Most departments have customized programs to their community and post information on their websites inviting citizens to become involved in their various neighborhood watch programs.

Crime prevention programs in which community members participate have different names in various parts of the country. Examples are Crime Watch, Block Watch, Community Alert, and, most commonly, **Neighborhood Watch**. Neighborhood Watch was launched in 1972 and is sponsored by the National Sheriffs' Association (NSA). In this organization, citizens organize themselves and work with law enforcement personnel to keep trained eyes and ears on their communities. Within 10 years of its beginnings, Neighborhood Watch programs involved more than 12 percent of the population nationally.[59] These groups engage in a wide range of specific crime prevention activities, as well as community-oriented activities. Citizens watch over activities on their block and alert the police to any suspicious or disorderly behavior. Neighborhood Watch blocks have clear signs alerting people that the block is protected by a Neighborhood Watch group. Some groups are taking advantage of technology and using Twitter or texts to disseminate

---

Neighborhood Watch A specific crime prevention program, and also a generic term for crime prevention programs in which community members participate and engage in a wide range of specific crime prevention activities, as well as community-oriented activities.

information to each other and to communicate while watching suspicious behavior.

In some jurisdictions, regular service providers have gotten involved in various crime watch programs. Providers such as postal employees, power company employees, and delivery personnel who are routinely out in residential areas are trained in identification of suspicious activity. They radio or call in this activity to their dispatchers, who in turn notify the police. These efforts have produced positive outcomes.

In keeping with changing technology, many departments around the country are allowing residents to sign up to receive text message alerts on crime trends as well as particular incidents either citywide or in particular neighborhoods. Residents can also send anonymous tips to the police. Voluntary community organizations are often more successful in middle-class or high-income neighborhoods and neighborhoods with a strong sense of community and a certain degree of stability. One of the keys is the community's degree of transience. The more rooted the residents feel, the more they have invested in the community. Their tendency would be to get involved to maintain the highest level of quality of life. If the residents envision living there for only a few months, they do not care about the long-term future of the area. Therefore, the more stable the residents, the more successful a program will be.

National Night Out

Every year citizens are encouraged to turn on all outside lighting and step outside their homes between 8:00 p.m. and 9:00 p.m. on a well-publicized, designated night, called National Night Out. Though the exact date may vary by community, National Night Out is generally held during the first week in August. In addition, a growing number of residents are expanding their participation by staging parades and concerts and securing corporate sponsors for the annual event. One of the program's primary objectives is to enable neighbors to get to know one another so suspicious people and activities can be detected and reported as soon as possible. Other objectives include generating community support for, and participation in, local anticrime efforts, strengthening community spirit, and placing criminals on notice that neighborhood residents are watching them.

Citizen Patrols

Citizen patrols are very popular around the nation. They involve citizens patrolling on foot or in cars and alerting the police to possible crimes or criminals in the area, thus being the eyes and ears of the police. One of the best-known citizen patrols is the Guardian Angels. The group, begun by Curtis Sliwa in 1977 to patrol New York City subway cars and stations, now has chapters in many other parts of the United States. The Angels are young people in distinctive red berets and T-shirts who patrol on buses, subways, and streets. They have expanded their group into some of the bigger cities across the country. Their main function is to act as an intimidating force against possible criminals or potentially disruptive people. The Guardian Angels have also expanded their efforts into other community concerns, including youth violence, bullying, Internet safety, and educational programs.

Many police departments are now using citizens as observers in more formal ways. Volunteers with training (often graduates of the citizen police academy) are uniformed and drive in department vehicles. These vehicles are marked but carefully painted differently than police cars. These citizens patrol in teams and are another set of eyes and ears for the police, guided by strict policies on noninvolvement and instructions on how to report suspicious activity.

Citizen Volunteer Programs

Citizen volunteer programs—in which citizens volunteer to do police jobs, thus freeing police officers to return to patrol duties—have become numerous and popular. Citizens perform such jobs as crime analysis, clerical work, victim assistance, crime prevention, patrolling shopping centers, vacant house checks, and fingerprinting children. The program and services provided should be tailored to the department and community.

The use of volunteers in police departments has increased tremendously in the last couple of decades. Departments have realized the value of using the talents of their residents from many perspectives. A police department that does not actively seek to

citizen patrols A program that involves citizens patrolling on foot or in private cars and alerting the police to possible crimes or criminals in the area.

recruit volunteers is not practicing good management. Volunteer programs can help a department accomplish its duties more effectively, maximize existing resources, enhance public safety and services, and improve community relations. Volunteers allow police officers to focus on patrol work and investigations while providing services that citizens may want.

The volunteers feel a vested interest in their police department and can often be counted on for support when departments are trying to expand, start new programs, or hire additional personnel. Police officers can have increased involvement with citizens at times other than crisis situations. Administrators can redirect sworn employees to more hazardous duties when volunteers assume nonhazardous jobs. The department may be able to try new programs they would not ordinarily be able to attempt because of a lack of personnel. The city or county government benefits from reduced or flat expenditures and the ability to maintain the current tax rate in these budget-strapped times. The community benefits with a more educated citizenry and an increased feeling of safety. It is a win-win situation for all involved.

Although there is no salary for citizen volunteers, there are costs associated with the use of them, including salary and benefits for the program coordinator, screening, training, workspace requirements, supplies, equipment, uniforms, and recognition. Most departments that have launched successful programs have found that the value of volunteer hours contributed has far exceeded the costs associated with the program.[60]

One of the most visible uses of volunteers is as Reserve Police Officers. They may be called auxiliary, special, or part-time police officers, but generally they have another source of income and another job besides their hours spent in law enforcement. States regulate their training and authority. Many receive exactly the same training as a police officer and do the same job and consequently are subjected to the same dangers. They are used to supplement staffing during busy summer times in some resort areas or to supplement emergency personnel all year on an as-needed basis. They have become even more valuable to police departments as budget challenges have arisen. Most of these reserve officers will tell you they do the job as a way to give back to their community in a meaningful way.

A Los Angeles Sheriff's deputy who is paid one dollar a year was hailed as a hero when he pulled over and arrested an arson suspect responsible for one of the worst arson sprees in Los Angeles history. Shervin Lalezary, an Iranian-born lawyer who moonlights as a deputy, pulled over a van with a driver who fit the description of a suspect they were looking for in the arson spree and, with the assistance of backup units, placed him under arrest. Nervous LA residents were able to breathe a sigh of relief after being on edge for more than a week. Lalezary credited the extensive training reserve officers receive and humbly deflected attention from himself to the full-time deputies who put their lives on the line on a daily basis in order to protect and serve the public.[61]

Use of volunteers is limited only by the imagination of police managers and volunteers. Nationwide, departments use volunteers for parking enforcement, help at special events, as crime prevention specialists, for telephone follow-ups and pawnshop investigations, as receptionists and in clerical positions, and as tour guides for the facility. Citizens may volunteer with PAL, at communitywide safety fairs conducting fingerprinting, and even for role-play situations in police training. Some retirees have special talents that prove extremely valuable to police departments such as computer expertise, printing know-how, writing abilities for brochures or notices, photographic or video expertise, or even cooking or catering skills to supply refreshments for special occasions. Riding on the wave of the popular *CSI* television programs, some departments are using volunteers in some of the less sensitive areas of those units.[62]

The Volunteers in Police Service (VIPS) program provides support and resources for agencies interested in initiating or expanding a volunteer program as well as for citizens interested in volunteering their time to their local law enforcement agency. The program arose from the Citizen Corps—a vital component of the USA Freedom Corps, a White House office established in 2002 by President Bush to expand volunteer service in America. The Citizen Corps was developed to coordinate volunteer activities to make communities safer. The IACP manages the VIPS program in partnership with the USA Freedom Corps and the Department of Justice. The goals of the VIPS program are to increase the use of volunteers in current programs, expand the number of programs, and assist agencies and individuals interested in these programs. Resources, documents, training, and online discussions can be found on the VIPS website.[63]

Home Security Surveys and Operation Identification

Target-hardening programs have become very popular in the last few decades. Target hardening involves installing burglar alarms, protective gates, and other devices and techniques to make it more difficult for criminals to enter premises to commit crime. To facilitate target hardening, numerous police departments offer home and business security surveys free of charge.

Operation Identification programs involve engraving identifying numbers onto such property as bicycles, televisions, and other personal electronic items with the goal of returning the property to owners if it is stolen and then recovered by the police. The program also involves displaying decals on windows announcing that a house is equipped with an alarm or has participated in an Operation Identification program. Advancements in technology have facilitated the collection, storage, and accessing of this identification information by community members with the hope is that it will reduce the theft problem.

Police Storefront Stations or Ministations

In an effort to get closer to the public, many police departments operate **police storefront stations** or **ministations**. In these programs, a small group of police officers is assigned to patrol in the immediate area of a ministation or storefront station and to engage in crime prevention programs with members of the community. Although they would not be considered ministations, many businesses, such as 7-Eleven, McDonald's, and the pharmacy chain CVS, are opening their stores for the local police to use as temporary community police stations by reserving workstations for them at a table near the front of the store.

Many jurisdictions have consolidated services in their police storefronts or ministations. Their goal is to use their tax dollars more efficiently and make city services as accessible as possible for their taxpayers. They may be able to conduct minor water department or zoning business or obtain various city forms at the station. Paramedics often host "wellness fairs" at these facilities, where health information is distributed along with blood pressure tests and the like.

Crime Stoppers

Crime Stoppers originated in 1975 in Albuquerque, New Mexico, and quickly spread across the country. In the typical Crime Stoppers program, the police ask television and radio stations to publicize an "unsolved crime of the week." Cash rewards are given for information that results in the conviction of the offender. Currently, there are more than 1,200 Crime Stoppers programs around the world. Since the inception of the organization, the program has been responsible for recovering property and seizing drugs totaling more than $7 billion.[64]

Similar to Crime Stoppers programs are programs that provide citizens the opportunity to leave anonymous tips regarding crimes and criminals for the police. Along the same lines, some television shows focus on locating wanted persons. Though recently canceled, one show that enjoyed great success was *America's Most Wanted*, hosted by John Walsh. The show precipitated one of its highest-profile captures on March 12, 2003. Information aired by the show led to citizens calling the police when they spotted Elizabeth Smart and her kidnappers. That call, together with good police work by the officers who responded, led to a happy conclusion. Elizabeth was a 14-year-old girl kidnapped from her bedroom as she slept in Salt Lake City, Utah. She had been missing for many months, and her captors had many contacts with people who did not recognize them. The show put the information back in people's minds, and the country rejoiced when she was safely reunited with her family. This capture was the 747th influenced by the show. This is an example of the public and private sector working together for the good of the community.

Mass Media Campaigns

Mass media campaigns, such as the "Take a Bite Out of Crime" advertisements in newspapers, magazines, and on television, provide crime prevention suggestions for citizens. The "Take a Bite Out of Crime" national media campaign features the crime

---

Operation Identification Engraving identification numbers onto property that is most likely to be stolen.

police storefront station or ministation A small satellite police station designed to serve a local part of the community and facilitate the community's access to its police officers.

Crime Stoppers A program in which a cash reward is offered for information that results in the conviction of an offender.

dog McGruff, a trench-coated cartoon figure, as the "spokes-dog" for the National Crime Prevention Council (NCPC). McGruff advises readers or viewers of actions they should take when they witness criminal activity. Since the inception of the McGruff campaign in 1980, he has become an icon in the crime prevention movement. He still enjoys wide recognition and a positive image among all age groups. The NCPC has extended its goals to keep up with changing technology and is now taking on cyberbullying, identity theft, and cybercrime. The McGruff website is user-friendly and interactive, with downloadable posters and other instructor materials. The organization's emphasis continues to be how individual prevention efforts can make a difference.

The media have taken on a greater role in fighting crime during the last two decades. They are able to respond quickly to calls they hear over police frequencies and are quick to set up their cameras. A good working relationship with the press and the media is essential to get their cooperation, especially when there is particular information they may obtain that should not be released to the public, such as in a hostage or tactical situation. On many occasions, media helicopters have followed suspects and assisted law enforcement in catching them. The media also have taken on active roles in helping to solve crimes,

especially in the case of child abductions. Since the implementation of the AMBER Alert system, media broadcasts of information regarding suspects and vehicle descriptions have facilitated the safe return of many children and the arrest of their abductors.

In addition, the media can be asked to assist with a particular crime problem a community is experiencing by letting the public know the crime is occurring and what steps citizens can take to minimize their chances of becoming a victim. Even the FBI is using digital billboards in visible locations, including Times Square, to highlight their fugitives. The media also air surveillance videos in an attempt to assist law enforcement with the identification of suspects seen on the videos.

Overall, the media can be a great asset to law enforcement, but this depends on relationships that are developed. The more law enforcement can learn about journalists and the more journalists can learn about law enforcement, the more successful the partnership will be. The Poynter Institute (a training institute for journalists) recommends that journalists spend time riding with officers and learning their culture and jargon. Conversely, law enforcement should spend time learning what the goals of the news industry are and ways in which they can work together for mutually successful outcomes. The relationship between law enforcement and the media can be a very fruitful one that will aid in making the community safer.

Recently, social media have played a valuable role in the crime fight as well as in building relationships between police departments and their clients. Departments have begun to embrace Facebook, YouTube, and Twitter as a means to get messages out and to give the community a forum for exchanging information in a timely manner regarding particular crime problems. These formats can be the modern-day version of the wanted poster or crime bulletin, with information shared in a more timely manner and with more people.

In the Los Angeles arson cases mentioned previously, residents were posting photos, videos, and information regarding fires as they were occurring. Law enforcement

McGruff the Crime Dog has become an icon in the crime prevention movement and participates in community events across the country.

Dave Buresh/The Denver Post/Getty Images

and fire agencies joined the conversation on the various social media sites to both disseminate information and track new information coming in from the community. The rapid sharing of information led to a quick resolution of the arson spree, and members of the public as well as law enforcement believe this case may have been a turning point for law enforcement in embracing social media.[65]

In 2013, the use of social media and the traditional media in crime investigation was clearly obvious as the Boston Marathon bombings and subsequent investigation unfolded. Through online forums, scanners, smartphones, and Twitter, residents and community members began assuming the role of armchair detective and police officer and posting information they received from others or from scanners and video feeds. This had positive and negative results as there was misinformation being shared about the suspects in the crime, resulting in wasted time and the promotion of bad information. As events unfolded, media anchors could be seen viewing their phones for the information they were then sharing with the public. In some cases this information had not been verified and later had to be corrected. The Boston Police Department soon realized they had to be an active participant to rein in this information and to make sure that the information released was good and might actually serve the public. The department began to share information in order to calm nerves, keep the public informed about the investigation, and correct misinformation. The massive sharing of information in this investigation was groundbreaking and made all law enforcement take note of how these major incidents might unfold in the future.

As we know from community policing efforts, the police cannot be everywhere, nor do they know the daily habits of neighborhoods as well as community residents do. Thousands of additional eyes armed with good information could have the potential to greatly assist. There is still discussion about the role of social media as it relates to traditional media and what is broadcast to the public. Law enforcement agencies around the country are using the Boston Marathon bombing investigation as a starting point to examine their social media protocols and anticipate potential challenges in the future. Most agencies endorse social media as an expansion on their community policing philosophy and efforts to strengthen their relationships with their community.

On a smaller but significant scale, social media are routinely being used around the country to

further relationships between the police and their community, by informing residents about crime in their neighborhood and posting information about suspicious activity. This provides "real-time" investigation by police in conjunction with the residents who know the neighborhood best. It works to empower the community and to enhance the police–community relationship. It has also strengthened relationships among neighbors and led to a feeling of community cohesiveness.

Chaplain Programs

Departments around the country have discovered the benefits of having an active, involved chaplain program. These volunteers serve as liaisons with various religious institutions in the community. They are indispensable in the event of a tragedy. They can provide counseling and referral services to victims, families, and police officers as needed. When they show up to assist at a suicide or homicide scene, they can help free officers from the emotional demands of the scene to concentrate on their investigation.

A well-rounded chaplain program will attempt to have representatives from all local religious groups. In the event of disharmony in the community, these volunteers can provide calming voices to their constituents and help solve problems. The faith–community concept is believed to be an essential ingredient in making law enforcement more sensitive to the needs of the community.

Citizen Police Academies

Many police departments have established **citizen police academies**. Through these academies, police agencies seek to educate community members about the roles and responsibilities of police officers and to familiarize the public with the departments and how they work within the community. The goal of most citizen police academies is not to provide civilians with law enforcement training but, rather, to create a nucleus of citizens who are well informed about a department's practices and services.

Many departments use their citizen police academy as a form of training and preparation for their

citizen police academies Academies provided by the police department for the citizens of the community to enhance their understanding of the workings of their police department.

volunteer pools. The academy gives the volunteer an excellent overview of the police department. At times, departments may tailor their citizen academies to meet the needs of a specific group, such as older residents or high school students. The academy also may be held off-site to facilitate attendance by groups with transportation problems. Websites often describe the course and provide application materials online.

This concept has spread throughout the country. Typically, a citizen police academy is held one night a week for 8 to 12 weeks, during which each major function of the department will be addressed. The key is that the department uses specialists to teach about their areas of expertise, sharing their passion and enthusiasm with the students. Most officers involved in this endeavor love it. The participants get to meet many officers in the department and learn how the various divisions function. They can be taught why police can and cannot do certain things, resulting in realistic expectations within the community. Departments have begun to conduct these classes for minority populations, particularly new immigrants, to enhance relations and educate them about police in the United States.

Other Police-Sponsored Crime Prevention Programs

To allow citizens to get an inside look at how the police perform their jobs and help them understand the police better, many police departments offer such programs as ride alongs and tours of precincts and other police facilities. In the ride-along programs, citizens actually ride in patrol cars with police officers and respond to calls for police services with the officers. Citizens get a firsthand look at the activities the police perform and the special problems they encounter. Police departments providing ride-along programs require participants to sign a waiver freeing the jurisdiction from civil liability if a participant is injured.

Many departments provide tours of police stations, police headquarters buildings, shooting ranges, and other facilities to allow citizens to see how their tax dollars are spent. Some also allow citizens to participate in their shoot/don't shoot programs using the computer simulator programs

to enhance understanding of the complex situations officers face on the street. As mentioned earlier, many agencies also are using social media sites to interact with their citizens and answer questions about crime or incidents. This helps the citizens feel more vested in their community.

In the last decade, police agencies have facilitated the forming of **Community Emergency Response Teams (CERTs)**. The team members undergo training to help them act in the event of an emergency or a disaster. The training enables them to respond before emergency services arrive on the scene and to assist the emergency service personnel when they do arrive. Many larger departments address this role on their websites and have links to the organization conducting the training. This training provides communities with a pool of trained civilians able to respond in disaster situations. It also encourages a feeling of teamwork in the community.

Police and Business Cooperation

Businesses throughout the United States have become increasingly involved in assisting their local police departments in the last couple of decades. This involvement has become more pronounced in times of tight budgets for governments that do not allow police to offer programs they may wish to provide, attend training they may find beneficial, or buy equipment that could improve the effectiveness of the police department. Businesses may provide vehicles for DARE or crime prevention, donate computers, donate printing for trading cards or brochures, donate food for police-community meetings, provide and outfit bikes for a bicycle unit, provide prizes for children for safety contests such as helmet safety or bike rodeos, fund police dogs or equipment for them, or provide bulletproof vests for officers.

As with other volunteer opportunities, the ideas for business involvement are endless. The problem is that, as with gratuities, the police–business relationship can be a slippery slope. Departments and businesses have to be aware of how a donation might look to the public as well as how it is perceived within the department and the business community. Many cities and towns address this ethical issue for businesses (as well as individuals) that want to donate money or equipment to the police department through the

Community Emergency Response Team (CERT) A program in which civilians are trained in basic emergency response, first aid, and search and rescue.

formation of a private foundation. Concerned citizens and businesses can join to form a charitable foundation that raises money to assist the police department in various ways. It is up to the foundation board how the money is spent. Often these foundations hold fundraisers for people to donate and raise funds for K-9s and their equipment, bikes, training, expenses for officers hurt or killed in the line of duty, and so on. They can be very successful and very helpful to law enforcement agencies as well as individual officers, without particular individuals or businesses being the source of the funding, thereby allowing citizens and businesses to have a positive impact on their communities.

On the positive side of the police–business partnership, business often has the personnel, resources, and know-how to get things done, sometimes more quickly and with less red tape than governments can. Coupled with the view that crime is a community issue, businesses and corporations want to get involved and do their part to contribute to the community good. There is a trend in directing corporate donations at solving societal problems. The retailer Target is an active partner to law enforcement,

applying some of their state-of-the-art technology to various problems and offering training opportunities to FBI and police leaders. A program called "Target and Blue" helps define its approach to partnership with law enforcement. They award public safety grants, share their forensics labs, and promote their annual Heroes and Helpers, which pairs public safety personnel with community youth for holiday shopping sprees at their stores.[66] Certainly, Target has had an impact on crime issues and the safety of the community in a way that might not have been possible without the company's support and financial backing. Critics might question what Target gets out of it. Does the company expect some kind of preferential treatment? Will police respond more quickly to calls for assistance at Target stores?

These are issues that law enforcement and the corporate community must grapple with and clarify before getting involved in police–business partnerships. Overall, there is great potential in these relationships. However, it is incumbent on government to scrutinize the partnership in terms of ethics, fairness, and public perception.

SUMMARY

- It is important for public opinion and police effectiveness that the relationships between the police and minority communities and special groups are positive.

- Partnerships and outreach have occurred between police departments and African Americans, Hispanic Americans, Asian Americans, Native Americans, Arab Americans and Muslims, Jews, women, and gays and lesbians.

- With the increase in immigrant populations and their movement around the country, police agencies are implementing programs to facilitate communication.

- The many groups that make up our communities have specific and varying needs that the police need to be aware of and make efforts to address to build and strengthen their relationships.

- With the aging of the baby boomers, programs directed at and involving the older population are extremely important.

- Police programs involving young people appear to have the greatest potential for success in creating positive relationships with the police and causing youths to develop positive ways of behaving that will lead to future success.

- Police agencies are training their officers so they are better able to serve communities with special needs, such as the physically challenged, crime victims, the homeless, and the mentally ill.

- Community crime prevention programs—including Neighborhood Watch, National Night Out, citizen patrols, citizen volunteer programs, home security surveys, police storefront stations, Crime Stoppers, mass media campaigns, chaplain programs, citizen police academies, and other programs—are designed to assist in the fight against crime and improve the quality of life in U.S. communities.

- The expanded use of volunteers, which in many situations may pull from the aging baby boomer population, is a wise and effective goal for police agencies.

- The business community is a valuable asset and partner in the crime fight, though those partnerships are not without controversy.

KEY TERMS

citizen patrols

citizen police academies

Community Emergency
    Response Team (CERT)

Crime Stoppers

Drug Abuse Resistance
    Education (DARE)

Gang Resistance Education and
    Training (GREAT)

human relations

Minneapolis Domestic Violence
    Experiment

Neighborhood Watch

Operation Identification

Police Athletic League
    (PAL)

police–community relations

police–community relations
    (PCR) movement

Police Explorers

police public relations

police storefront station or
    ministation

Triad

REVIEW EXERCISES

1. Check with the schools and police departments
   in your area. What youth programs do they
   have in place? What are the goals of these programs and who are they targeting? Do they feel
   these programs are successful? How have these
   programs been received by the public?

2. Contact a police department in your area. Do
   they have any programs in place to assist the
   senior population with the challenges they are
   facing? Why or why not? What do they see as
   the benefits of these programs?

3. Contact a law enforcement agency in your
   area. What type of volunteer opportunities
   do they have in place for their residents? What
   do they view as the benefits of these programs?
   If they do not use volunteers in their department, why not? Do they have a citizen police
   academy, and if so, is it a requirement for their
   volunteers to attend it before they volunteer in
   the department?

WEB EXERCISES

1. Go to the website of the Department of Justice
   Office on Violence Against Women. What is
   their mission? When was this office created, and
   what type of grants and initiatives do they have?
   What type of information and links does the site
   provide for individuals seeking more information?

2. Go to the website for the National Association
   of Triads. What is their mission or purpose?

What type of recent news stories do they post?
Using their site, research whether police agencies in your area have Triad programs.

3. Go to the National DARE program website.
   Look at the DARE mission and vision. Read
   about the "Keepin' It Real" program. Does this
   seem like a good program? Who is the target
   audience?

END NOTES

1. Steven M. Cox and Jack D. Fitzgerald, *Police in Community Relations*, 3rd ed. (Madison, Wisc.: Brown and Benchmark, 1996).

2. Ibid.

3. President's Commission on Law Enforcement and Administration of Justice, *The Challenge of Crime in a Free Society* (Washington, D.C.: U.S. Government Printing Office, 1967), p. 100.

4. Louis A. Radelet, *The Police and the Community* (Encino, Calif.: Glencoe, 1980).

5. Egon Bittner, "Community Relations," in Alvin W. Cohn and Emilio C. Viano, eds., *Police Community Relations: Images, Roles, Realities* (Philadelphia: Lippincott, 1976), pp. 77–82.

6. *Sourcebook of Criminal Justice Statistics*, "Reported Confidence in the Police, 2012," www.albany.edu/sourcebook/pdf/t2122012.pdf.

7. James Q. Wilson, *Varieties of Police Behavior* (Cambridge, Mass.: Harvard University Press, 1968), p. 28.

8. "Overcoming Language Barriers: Solutions for Law Enforcement," DOJ website, retrieved April 20, 2014, from www.cops.usdoj.gov/giles/ric/Publications/vera_translating_justice_final.pdf.

9. U.S. Census Bureau, retrieved from www.census.gov.

10. William Frey, as quoted in Stephen Ohlemacher, "Minority Population Increasing in States," *Newsday*, August 15, 2006.

11. Ibid.

12. Sam Roberts, "Rise in Minorities Is Led by Children, Census Finds," *New York Times*, May 1, 2008.

13. *Brown v. Board of Education of Topeka*, 347 U.S. 483 (1954).

14. U.S. Census Bureau, retrieved from www.census.gov.

15. Thomas Kathman and Tim Chesser, "Latino Academy," *Police Chief* (June 2005): 62–63.

16. U.S. Census Bureau.

17. Ibid.

18. *American Indians and Crime: A BJS Statistical Profile, 1992–2002* (Washington, D.C.: U.S. Department of Justice, 2004), NCJ#203097.

19. Ibid.

20. International Association of Chiefs of Police (IACP), *Improving Safety in Indian Country: Recommendations from the IACP 2001 Summit* (Alexandria, Va.: IACP, 2001).

21. *American Indians and Crime.*

22. David W. Ogden, Deputy Attorney General, "Indian Country Law Enforcement Initiative," memorandum for U.S. Attorneys with districts containing Indian country, January 11, 2010, retrieved January 19, 2010, from the U.S. Department of Justice website, www.justice.gov/dag/dag-memo-indian-country.html.

23. U.S. Department of Justice, Community Relations Service, *Twenty Plus Things Law Enforcement Agencies Can Do to Prevent or Respond to Hate Incidents against Arab-Americans, Muslims, and Sikhs* (Washington, D.C.: U.S. Department of Justice), retrieved August 18, 2006, from www.usdoj.gov/crs/twentyplus.htm.

24. Andrea Elliott, "After 9/11, Arab-Americans Fear Police Acts, Study Finds," *New York Times*, June 12, 2006.

25. "D.C.'s Gay-Crime Unit Gets Recognition as It Builds Track Record of Achievement," *Law Enforcement News*, September 2005, p. 6.

26. Ruth Harlow, "Let's Work to Prevent, Not Just Punish, Hate Crimes," *Lambda Legal* (Spring/Summer 1999), retrieved April 19, 2003, from www.lambdalegal.org.

27. Natalie DiBlasio, "Crimes against LGBT Community Are Up, Despite Social Gains," *USA Today*, August 1, 2011.

28. Bharathi Venkatraman, "Lost in Translation: Limited English Proficient Populations and Police," *Police Chief* (April 2006).

29. Oren Dorell, "Towns Take Aim at Illegal Immigration," *USA Today*, August 14, 2006.

30. David Crary, "Hate Crimes Linked to Immigration Debate," *USA Today*, March 10, 2008.

31. U.S. Census Bureau.

32. Erika Harrell and Michael R. Rand, "Crime against People with Disabilities, 2008," Bureau of Justice Statistics: Special Report (Washington, D.C.: U.S. Department of Justice, December 2010), NCJ#231328.

33. Department of Health—Administration on Aging website, retrieved February 20, 2010, from www.aoa.gov.

34. Linda Forst, *The Aging of America: A Handbook for Police Officers* (Springfield, Ill.: Charles C. Thomas, 2000), p. 7.

35. Office of Juvenile Justice and Delinquency Prevention (OJJDP), retrieved May 5, 2010, from http://ojjdp.ncjrs.org.

36. Marnell Jameson, "Anti-Drug Overdose?" *Los Angeles Times*, May 15, 2006.

37. DARE America website, retrieved February 26, 2012, from www.dare.com.

38. Jameson, "Anti-Drug Overdose?"

39. Retrieved February 25, 2012, from www.great-online.org/.

40. Youth Crime Watch of America, retrieved April 17, 2014, from www.ignitusworldwide.org.

41. Brian A. Reaves, *Local Police Departments, 2007* (Washington, D.C.: Bureau of Justice Statistics, 2010), NCJ#231174.

42. "President Signs Protect Act," Department of Justice fact sheet, April 30, 2003, www.usdoj.gov/opa/pr/2003/April/03_ag_266.htm.

43. National Association of Police Athletic Leagues (PAL), retrieved May 1, 2008, from www.nationalpal.org.

44. International Association of Chiefs of Police (IACP), "What Do Victims Want? Effective Strategies to Achieve Justice for Victims of Crime," May 2000, retrieved April 28, 2004, from www.theiacp.org/documents/index.cfm?fuseaction5document&document_id5150.

45. Ibid.

46. Del Quentin Wilber, "An Open House on Open Cases," *Washington Post*, May 18, 2006, retrieved May 6, 2010, from http://mpdc.dc.gov/.

47. Jennifer Truman and Rachel Morgan, "Nonfatal Domestic Violence, 2000–2012," Department of Justice, Bureau of Justice Statistics (April 2014): #NCJ244697.

48. Retrieved February 26, 2012, from www.ncadv.org.

49. Denise Kindschi-Gosselin, *Heavy Hands: An Introduction to the Crimes of Family Violence*, 2nd ed. (Upper Saddle River, N.J.: Prentice Hall, 2003).

50. Kate Santich, "Teen Dating Study Shows Growing Threat of Cyber Abuse," *Orlando Sentinel*, February 20, 2013.

51. www.cityoforlando.net/police/domesticviolence, retrieved April 20, 2014.

52. Mark Schlueb, "Questionnaire Helps Orlando Police Break Spiral of Domestic Abuse," February 11, 2009, retrieved same date from OrlandoSentinel.com.

53. Gary W. Cordner, "People with Mental Illness," *Department of Justice: Problem-Oriented Guides for Police, Guide #40* (Washington, D.C.: U.S. Department of Justice, May 2006).

54. Richard Lamb, Linda Weinberger, and Walter DeCuir, "The Police and Mental Health," *Psychiatric Services* 10 (2002): 1266–1271.

55. Cordner, "People with Mental Illness."

56. Alison Hibbert, "Police Come to the Aid of the Homeless," *Police Chief* (May 2000).

57. George L. Kelling, "On the Accomplishments of the Police," in Maurice Punch, ed., *Control of the Police Organization* (Cambridge, Mass.: MIT Press, 1983), p. 164.

58. IACP Crime Prevention Committee, "Sustaining Crime Prevention and Community Outreach Programs," *Police Chief* (September 2005).

59. National Crime Watch, retrieved April 20, 2014, from National Crime Prevention Council, www.ncpc.org.

60. Nancy Kolb, "Law Enforcement Volunteerism," *Police Chief* (June 2005): 22–30.

61. Lateef Mungin, "Deputy Who Caught Hollywood Arson Suspect Hailed as Hero," CNN.com, January 3, 2012.

62. Rebecca Kanable, "Volunteers Enter the Crime Scene," *Law Enforcement Technology* 3 (2006): 14–23.

63. Volunteers in Police Service, retrieved February 25, 2012, from www.policevolunteers.org.

64. Crime Stoppers USA, retrieved February 25, 2012, from Crime Stoppers International, www.crimestoppersusa.com.

65. Matt Stevens and Richard Winton, "Social Media Sites Are Crucial in Arson Probe," *Los Angeles Times*, January 2, 2012, retrieved from www.latimes.com.

66. Target, retrieved, from http://corporate.target.com. This is still there so you can use May 28, 2014, as the retrieval date.

Community Policing

AP Images/*Northwest Florida Daily News*, Nick Tomecek

OUTLINE

Corporate Strategies for Policing

The Philosophy of Community Policing and Problem-Solving Policing

Community Policing

Problem-Solving Policing

Successful Examples of Community-Oriented Policing

Community Policing Today
Resident Officer Programs: The Ultimate in Community Policing?

The Federal Government and Community Policing
The Crime Bill
Office of Community Oriented Policing Services (COPS)

Some Accomplishments of Community Policing

The Debate Continues on Community Policing

Homeland Security and the Future of Community Policing

LEARNING OBJECTIVES

- Define community policing and problem-solving policing, identifying the philosophy behind these practices and giving examples of each.

- Discuss how the community-policing philosophy is best exemplified in a police department.

- Identify some of the programs administered and supported by the Office of Community Oriented Policing Services (COPS) of the U.S. Department of Justice.

- Explain the opposing viewpoints in the debate on the success and effectiveness of community policing.

- Describe some of the ways community policing is being used or can be used in the fight against terror.

INTRODUCTION

This chapter continues the discussion of relationships between the police and the community that began in Chapter 11 but deals with more philosophical and strategic issues about reducing crime and improving our quality of life. It addresses the concepts of community policing and problem-solving policing. Many consider these to be new strategies, while others argue that they are a return to the policing of the past. In 1988, the scholar George L. Kelling stated,

> A quiet revolution is reshaping American policing. Police in dozens of communities are returning to foot patrol. In many communities, police are surveying citizens to learn what they believe to be their most serious neighborhood problems. Many police departments are finding alternatives to rapidly responding to the majority of calls for service. Many departments are targeting resources on citizen fear of crime by concentrating on disorder. Organizing citizens' groups has become a priority in many departments. Increasingly, police departments are looking for means to evaluate themselves on their contribution to the quality of neighborhood life, not just crime statistics. Are such activities the business of policing? In a crescendo, police are answering yes.[1]

By 1998, 10 years later, many said the face of policing had changed dramatically. Community policing and problem-solving policing had proven to be tremendously popular with some citizens, academics, politicians, and police chiefs. Many continue to believe that community policing and problem-solving policing could be the best strategies to use in policing our nation. These two ideas emphasize community involvement and the building of partnerships between the police and the community. In many areas where community policing and problem-solving policing have been implemented, crime rates have gone down, quality of life has improved, and people have felt safer. Others, however, are not enthusiastic about this new philosophy and argue about its definition and implementation. The discussion and study of community policing continue.

This chapter is intended to present the facts, explore the issues, and continue the debate. We will discuss three corporate strategies for modern policing: strategic policing, community policing, and problem-solving policing. We will also discuss the genesis and underlying philosophy of community policing and problem-solving policing and then provide some examples of how these concepts can be translated into action.

The chapter will also cover the federal government and its influence over community policing, including the 1994 Crime Bill and the Office of Community Oriented Policing Services. We will present some empirical and anecdotal evidence of the accomplishments of community policing but will also show how some scholars and practitioners do not agree with these policing strategies. It is hoped that by presenting the issues and exploring them, we may continue the process begun by Sir Robert Peel in 1829 of making the police an essential part of life in the community.

Corporate Strategies for Policing

For several decades, police chiefs and academics throughout the United States have discussed changes in the traditional methods of policing and have explored new ways of accomplishing the police mission. Many of these strategies have been discussed in this text. Since the mid-1980s, Harvard University's prestigious John F. Kennedy School of Government has held periodic meetings to discuss the current state of policing in the United States. These Executive Sessions on Policing are developed and administered by the Kennedy School's Program in Criminal Justice Policy and Management. At these sessions, leading police administrators and academics gather at Harvard to debate the use and costs of such practices as strategic policing, community policing, and problem-solving policing.

Beginning in 1988, Harvard and the National Institute of Justice (NIJ) produced a series of monographs that shaped the current state of police thinking. These monographs discuss community policing, problem-oriented policing, police values, corporate strategies of policing, crime and policing, policing and the fear of crime, the history of policing, police accountability, and drugs and the police.[2] Harvard's Executive Sessions on Policing have identified three corporate strategies that are presently guiding U.S. policing: (1) strategic policing, (2) community policing, and (3) problem-solving policing.[3]

Strategic policing involves a continued reliance on traditional police operations, but with an increased emphasis on crimes that are not generally well controlled by traditional policing (for example, serial offenders, gangs, organized crime, drug distribution networks, and white-collar crime, and cybercrime). Strategic policing represents an advanced stage of traditional policing using innovative enforcement techniques, including intelligence operations, electronic surveillance, and sophisticated forensic techniques. Much of this textbook, particularly the chapters on police operations and technology, deals with strategic policing issues.

Community policing is an attempt to involve the community as an active partner with the police in addressing crime problems. It involves a true trusting partnership with the community and a willingness to accept and use input from the community.

Problem-solving policing emphasizes that many crimes are caused by underlying social problems and attempts to deal with those underlying problems rather than just responding to each criminal incident. Problem-solving or problem-oriented policing seeks to solve problems and have an outcome.

Community policing and problem-solving policing are very similar approaches to the crime and disorder problems in our communities. These two philosophies or strategies tend to go hand-in-hand: Most departments adopting a community policing program also follow many of the tenets of problem-solving policing.

Getting out in the community and interacting with residents in positive ways is a form of community policing and serves to strengthen the relationship between law enforcement and the community.

The Philosophy of Community Policing and Problem-Solving Policing

In the 1960s, increases in crime, technological advances, and changes in police management thinking led to the abandonment of police foot patrols and their resultant ties to the community. Foot patrols were replaced by highly mobile police officers who could drive from one incident to another in minutes.

At the same time, many urban communities were experiencing drastic demographic changes. Longtime community residents were moving from

strategic policing Involves a continued reliance on traditional policing operations.

community policing Philosophy of empowering citizens and developing a partnership between the police and the community to work together to solve problems.

problem-solving policing Analyzing crime issues to determine the underlying problems and addressing those problems.

the inner city to newly opened suburbs and being replaced by newly arrived people from rural areas and Caribbean and Latin American countries. These people were not used to urban life in the United States and the culture, norms, and mores of their adopted neighborhoods. Often, there was a language barrier between the immigrants and older members of the community. These changes brought severe social problems to our cities and, of course, problems to our police. In addition, the heroin epidemic hit the United States in the 1960s, causing crime, social disorganization, fear, and mistrust. Recall the urban riots of the late 1960s described in Chapter 1.

Many problems developed between the police and the newly arrived residents as rapidly moving police mobile units, with flashing lights and roaring sirens, arrived in a community to answer someone's request for assistance or report of a crime. A lack of communication and mistrust often ensued because of the police officers' need to take quick action and then return to more serious emergencies. The police were no longer seen as members of the community, as the old beat cops had been; they were increasingly seen as an invading or occupying army. As a result, many police departments began to establish community relations units to address problems between themselves and the community. The units were part of what was called the police-community relations (PCR) movement.

Although the community relations units were well intentioned, they did not work in reality. The PCR units were supposed to address this communication gap, but could not do this effectively because they usually only appeared after an ugly incident. The real responsibility for proper police–community relations, as any experienced police officer knows, rests with every police officer, not with a select, small group of community relations officers. Today's community policing is completely different from the earlier PCR movement and should not be confused with it.

Modern community policing, as compared with the PCR movement, entails a substantial change in police thinking. It expands the responsibility for fighting crime to the community as a whole and, through a partnership with the community, addresses the community's concerns and underlying problems that lead to crime. The police and community work toward the ultimate goal of reducing the fear of crime as well as the crime rate.[4]

Many believe that the modern stage of community policing began with the seminal 1982 article in the *Atlantic Monthly* by James Q. Wilson and George L. Kelling, "'Broken Windows': The Police and Neighborhood Safety." Their theory has come to be known as the **broken windows model** of policing.[5] Wilson and Kelling made several very critical points. First, disorder in neighborhoods creates fear. Urban streets that are often occupied by homeless people, prostitutes, drug addicts, youth gangs, and the mentally disturbed, as well as regular citizens, are more likely to have high crime rates than are other areas. Second, certain neighborhoods send out "signals" that encourage crime. A community in which housing has deteriorated, broken windows are left unrepaired, and disorderly behavior is ignored may actually promote crime. Honest and good citizens live in fear in these areas, and predatory criminals are attracted. Third, community policing is essential. If police are to reduce fear and combat crime in these areas, they must rely on the cooperation of citizens for support and assistance.

Wilson and Kelling argued that community preservation, public safety, and order maintenance—not crime fighting—should become the primary focus of police patrol. From this concept, many believe, the modern concept of community policing began. Expanding on the work of Wilson and Kelling, Wesley G. Skogan surveyed numerous neighborhoods and identified two major categories of disorder that affect the quality of life in the community: human disorder and physical disorder. The human behaviors found to be extremely disruptive to the community were public drinking, corner gangs, street harassment, drugs, noisy neighbors, and commercial sex. The physical disorders that Skogan found to be extremely destructive to the community were vandalism, dilapidation and abandonment, and rubbish.[6]

Using the Wilson and Kelling and Skogan ideas as a philosophical and practical framework, many scholars and progressive police chiefs jumped onto the community policing bandwagon.

broken windows model Theory that unrepaired broken windows indicate to others that members of the community do not care about the quality of life in the neighborhood and are unlikely to get involved; consequently, disorder and crime will thrive.

Community Policing

Community policing is an approach toward crime that addresses the underlying causes of crime and endeavors to apply long-term problem solving to the issue through improved police–community partnerships and communication. Robert C. Trojanowicz founded the National Center for Community Policing in East Lansing, Michigan, in 1983 and was the director until his death in 1994. Trojanowicz believed that community policing can play a vital role in reducing three important kinds of violence in the community: (1) individual violence, ranging from street crime to domestic abuse to drug-related violence; (2) civil unrest, which can often include gang violence and open confrontations among various segments of society, specifically the police; and (3) police brutality.[7]

Community policing is not a new concept. As we saw in Chapter 1, policing has always been community oriented from its early English roots. The concept of community policing goes as far back as Sir Robert Peel, who began building his public London police in 1829. In his original principles, he said, "The police are the public and the public are the police; the police being only members of the public who are paid to give full-time attention to duties which are incumbent on every citizen in the interests of community welfare and existence."[8]

The practices and terminology of modern-day community policing did not suddenly materialize, either. David L. Carter of Michigan State University explains that community policing evolved from research conducted by a wide range of scholars and police research organizations. Beginning primarily in the early 1970s, a great deal of research was conducted on police patrol.[9]

Community policing seeks to replace our traditional methods of police patrol with a more holistic approach. Traditional law enforcement held the belief that the "experts" would save us, but over the years this idea has moved to a holistic concept in which we are all partners in the health of our communities. Some scholars liken this to the similar movement toward a holistic medical model. Although there is a need for experts to save us in the emergency room or operating room (just as police save us in making arrests), there is also a need to maintain our health and prevent certain illnesses from happening or intervene before reaching the emergency or critical stage. In this holistic approach to police patrol, a community policing officer working a particular neighborhood fills a role similar to that of a family physician, and the street officer responding to the emergency call is fulfilling the role of society's emergency room physician.

The community policing officer acts as a problem solver and an ombudsman to other social service agencies that can assist in addressing the problem.[10] This model supports Trojanowicz's belief that "community policing is a philosophy of full service personalized policing, where the same officer patrols and works in the same area on a permanent basis, from a decentralized place, working in a proactive partnership with citizens to identify and solve problems."[11]

Some examples of very early attempts at community policing involved experiences in Houston, Detroit, and New York City. A study in Houston that involved patrol officers visiting households to solicit viewpoints and information on community problems reported that both crime and fear decreased in the study area.[12] In Detroit, one approach implemented by community policing advocates was the development of decentralized neighborhood-based precincts that served as "storefront" police stations. The Detroit Mini-Station Program established more than 36 such stations around the city. At first, the community did not accept the program because the officers assigned to the mini-stations seemed to lack commitment. Later, however, officers were chosen for ministation duty on the basis of their community relations skills and crime prevention abilities, and since then the program has met with much greater community acceptance. The program is still going strong, with a mobile ministation added in 2009 and seven new ministations added in 2013.[13] According to the city's website, these ministations increase police presence in the community, improve communication and cooperation between officers and residents, and expand the department's commitment to community policing.[14]

The New York City Police Department began a Community Patrol Officer Program (CPOP) in 1984. Instead of responding to calls from 911, the CPOP officers were directed to identify neighborhood problems and develop short- and long-term strategies for solving them. Each officer kept a beat book in which he or she was expected to identify major problems on his or her beat and list strategies to deal with them. Officers thus were encouraged to think about problems and their solutions.[15]

Regarding community policing, Joseph E. Braun of the U.S. Department of Justice wrote in 1997:

> The traditional role of law enforcement is changing.... Community policing allows law enforcement practitioners to bring government resources closer to the community. Hence, participation and cooperation are key.... [W]e cannot expect law enforcement to solve crime and social disorder problems alone. Community involvement is imperative.... With the implementation of community policing practices, officers and deputies still retain their enforcement duties and powers. Community policing does not mean that authority is relinquished; rather, its proactive nature is intended to reduce the need for enforcement in the long term as problems are addressed up front and much earlier. This can only occur with the cooperation and participation of the community.[16]

Community policing mandates that the police work with the community, rather than against it, to be effective. The foot patrol experiments described earlier in the text are examples of the community policing model suggested by Wilson and Kelling in their broken windows approach to policing.

In *"Broken Windows" and Police Discretion*, Kelling notes that the community policing model expands and encourages the use of discretion among officers at all levels of the organization. The traditional method of telling officers what they can and cannot do, as is commonly found in police manuals, will not greatly improve the quality of policing. He advocates teaching officers how to think about what they should do, do it, and then review their actions with coworkers. With time, this should lead to improved practices and the sharing of values, knowledge, and skills that will prove valuable in the performance of their job.[17] Kelling supports "guideline development" in police agencies to facilitate the discretionary behavior of police officers and enable them to better work with the public in enhancing the quality of life.

Herman Goldstein has offered the following list of the most important benefits of community policing:

1. A more realistic acknowledgment of police functions
2. A recognition of the interrelationships among police functions
3. An acknowledgment of the limited capacity of the police to accomplish their jobs on their own and of the importance of an alliance between the police and the public
4. Less dependence on the criminal justice system and more emphasis on new problem-solving methods
5. Greatly increased use of the knowledge gained by the police of their assigned areas
6. More effective use of personnel
7. An increased awareness of community problems as a basis for designing more effective police response[18]

Under the philosophy of community policing, departments are expanding their efforts to work with their communities, including incorporating new technology and developing new policies and procedures. In some cases, departments are examining the characteristics that make for a good community policing officer and incorporating those characteristics into their hiring and evaluation practices.

The public seems to like this community policing trend. In 1999, the Department of Justice conducted a study of residents in 12 cities across the country. The percentage of residents who were "very satisfied" or "satisfied" with the police ranged from 97 percent in Madison, Wisconsin, to 78 percent in Washington, D.C. More than 50 percent of these residents knew what community policing was, and 54 percent said their departments practiced community policing in their neighborhood. According to then-U.S. Deputy Attorney General Eric Holder:

> The high degree of citizen support for America's neighborhood police officers is a testament to the dedicated men and women who work day in and day out to establish relationships with the residents in their communities. These relationships help citizens and police work together to promote community safety.[19]

At the time of the study, 64 percent of departments had full-time community policing officers. By 2003, that percentage had decreased to 58 percent, and in 2007 it was 47 percent. These statistics may cause some to question law enforcement's support of the community policing concept, but they should actually be interpreted in a positive manner. As mentioned earlier, community policing differs from the police–community relations concept in that it is

Community Policing in the Bronx

When I first started as a police officer in the 41st Precinct in the Bronx in 1966, I was a foot patrol cop, as were most of us. During my first two years there, there were only four radio motor patrol (RMP) sector cars in the entire precinct, plus the sergeant's car. Our foot patrol beats generally covered five or six blocks.

Early in my career there, the precinct earned the nickname Fort Apache because of the wild conditions and crime that permeated the precinct. It was considered the busiest and most dangerous precinct in the city of New York, and probably the world, in the 1960s and 1970s. Later, a movie was made, starring Paul Newman, called *Fort Apache, the Bronx*, detailing life as a police officer in the days I was there. Believe me, the movie made the place seem too tame. It was much crazier than that.

My foot patrol post, Post 28, covered all of Westchester Avenue from Southern Boulevard to Kelly Street, both sides of the streets and all of the side streets, including Simpson Street, Fox Street, Tiffany Street, and Kelly Street. Westchester Avenue, under the el, was the commercial hub of the area, and all of the side blocks were covered by wall-to-wall five-story tenements. It was the height of the heroin crisis in New York City, and crime and disorder were rampant. I patrolled this post alone without the portable radio you see officers carry today. I loved it. I made hundreds of collars (arrests), mostly gun collars and junk (drug) arrests. I also broke up fights, delivered babies, brought kids home to their parents, directed traffic, gave comfort and advice, and helped as many people as I could.

Whatever the time, day or night, whenever I was working, people knew they could talk to me. Whenever they had a problem, they could come to me. The good people on my post loved me—they called me their amigo. The people who wanted to annoy the good people on my post learned to avoid me—they went someplace else. The criminals . . . well, they didn't like me too much. I put them in jail. In summary, I was the *cop*. Everyone knew me.

I was part of the life of that community, part of the life of that little spot of the world—Patrol Post 28 of the 41st Precinct. We didn't have a concept known as community policing then. We were all just cops, doing our job.

As the years went by, the number of patrol car sectors assigned to the precinct increased and increased, until by 1970 we had over 14 sectors, almost four times the number we had when I started. I guess this was due to new management thinking in the department: a radio motor patrol unit can cover so much more territory than a foot cop; thus, officers in a car are more economical, cost-effective, and efficient. Also, 911 had taken over the NYPD by then. We would race from one 911 call to another—handle one incident after another—do what we had to do and then do it all over again, time after time. No longer did we deal with problems. We just dealt with incidents.

Although this change from foot patrol to the more cost-effective motorized patrol may have been necessary because of 911, I think it was a big mistake. Most of us were assigned to regular seats in the radio cars and never walked our foot beats again. What we gained in efficiency, we lost in closeness to the community. Many of the people on my beat felt they had lost their amigo—I was always busy running around the entire precinct handling 911 jobs.

Today's community police officer, I believe and hope, is a return to the past, a return to the cop on the beat who knows, and is known by, everyone. The major difference between today's community officer and the beat cop of my day is structure. Today, the officers receive training and support from the department and other city agencies. They have offices and answering machines and fill out paperwork. I hope they also become what I was on Post 28 in the 41st Precinct—part of life in that little part of the world, the good people's amigo.

—John S. Dempsey

a philosophy that runs throughout the department. It must be believed, supported, and practiced by all levels of the department, especially the line officers. They are the ones in contact with the public on a regular basis. Having a special unit devoted to community policing can enhance the departments' efforts, but it cannot be the basis of the department's efforts. For smaller departments where dollars and personnel are more limited, it would be difficult and highly unlikely that they would be able to allocate full-time personnel to community policing.

Because community policing promotes the use of organizational strategies to address the causes of crime and social disorder through problem solving and police–community partnerships, there are trends other than having a full-time officer or unit that are worth examining. One of these is the indication of departments' interest in providing training in the area of community policing and incorporating problem solving into how they do business. In 2007, 44 percent of local departments provided community policing training to all new recruits. Most departments serving populations greater than 10,000 assigned officers by geographic area, which is a major tenet of the community policing philosophy. Twenty-one percent of all local departments encouraged officers to engage in problem-solving projects in their beats, and most departments serving populations greater than 50,000 had such a policy.

Many departments have both implemented special units to support the agency's community policing efforts and encouraged all officers in their community policing efforts. The Office of Community Oriented Policing Services (COPS), described later in this chapter, reports that this hybrid approach to community policing seems to work well for police agencies.[20]

The partnership with the community is further demonstrated by departments that reach out and encourage input from the community. In 2007, more than 80 percent of departments serving 50,000 or more residents had problem-solving partnerships with community groups and offered citizen police academies, and 38 percent of all departments had partnered with citizen groups to solicit input and develop community policing strategies. Some departments were also institutionalizing community policing into personnel issues; 29 percent of agencies assessed new recruits' analytical and problem-solving abilities, and 20 percent of the departments assessed the recruits' understanding of diverse populations.[21]

Community policing is more easily facilitated with the technology available today, and 25 percent of all departments have taken advantage of this to maximize their outreach to the community. A high-quality interactive website can be a successful way of sharing the department's philosophy, beliefs, and practices with the community, as well as sharing information about the law enforcement personnel, which increases familiarity with employees, facilitates a relationship, and encourages a partnership. Sharing procedures, resources, and crime statistics in an open way can show the community the department's commitment to a partnership and to providing citizens with as much information as possible in an effort to meet their needs. Communication is further enhanced with links, e-mail, a presence on social media sites, and the availability for citizens to make reports online. Departments realize that the use of technology is a crucial element in their outreach to the community and are devoting dollars and personnel to this effort.

Problem-Solving Policing

The idea of problem-solving policing can be attributed to Herman Goldstein, a law professor at the University of Wisconsin, who spent a great deal of time in the trenches with different police departments. The problem-solving approach to policing was first mentioned by Goldstein in a 1979 article calling for a new kind of policing, which he termed problem-oriented policing.[22]

In traditional policing, most of what the police do is incident driven—they respond to incident after incident, dealing with each one and then responding to the next. Problem-solving policing, or problem-oriented policing, forces the police to focus on the problems that cause the incidents. Goldstein's central theory is that the broad types of police roles (crime, order maintenance, and service) can be further broken down into specific crime areas—for example, murder, drunk driving, auto theft. Each of these areas can be addressed and specific strategies or responses can be developed, depending on the underlying social or criminal issues for each one. Instead of the strategy of responding to each incident and resolving it individually, the problem-oriented approach involves officers examining the underlying problems and developing responses to address these problems. The power within the department must be decentralized and the line officer empowered to take action.[23]

With incident-driven policing, officers tend to respond to similar incidents at the same location numerous times—for example, burglaries in a certain housing project, or car thefts in a certain parking lot. Because the police have traditionally focused on incidents, they have rarely sought to determine the underlying causes of these incidents. Problem-oriented policing tries to find out what is causing citizen calls for help and what the underlying issues are.

Historically, beat officers naturally saw crime on their beats in terms of patterns. They were responsible for all incidents on their turf, and a rash of burglaries or overdoses signaled a burglar or a dealer who needed to be dealt with. With the advent of mobile response, officers, tied to their radios, saw crime as an endless string of isolated incidents. Several burglaries in the same general vicinity might draw several different officers.

Problem-oriented policing, like the historical beat approach, involves officers thinking, not just responding to yet another call for duty. It involves officers dealing with the underlying causes of incidents to prevent those incidents from happening again, and it encourages officers to use a wide range of resources (not just police resources) to engage in developing solutions.

The problem-oriented policing strategy consists of four distinct parts: scanning, analysis, response, and assessment—known by the acronym **SARA**. The parts of this process can be summarized as follows:

Scanning: Identifying the neighborhood crime and disorder problems

Analysis: Understanding the conditions that cause the problems to occur

Response: Developing and implementing solutions

Assessment: Determining the impact of the solutions

In the scanning process, groups of officers discuss incidents as "problems" instead of as specific incidents and criminal law concepts, such as "robberies" or "larcenies." Problems are defined as two or more incidents, similar in nature (through location, suspects, targets, or *modus operandi* [Mo]), capable of causing harm, and about which the public expects the police to do something.[24] For example, a robbery, which used to be thought of as a single incident, in the scanning process is thought of as being part of a pattern of robberies, which in turn might be related to another problem, such as prostitution-related robberies in a particular area of the city.

After defining the problem, officers begin analysis. They collect information from a variety of sources, such as members of the business community, other city agencies, or local citizens. The officers then use the information to discover the underlying nature of the problem, its causes, and options for solutions.

After scanning and analysis, the police begin response. They work with citizens, business owners, and public and private agencies to prepare a program of action suitable to the specifics of the particular problem. Solutions may include arrest but also may involve action by other community agencies and organizations. Responses are developed through brainstorming sessions to come up with a plan, followed by determining what needs to be done before the plan can be implemented and who is responsible for these preliminary actions, and then outlining and implementing the plan. Examining what other communities have done to respond to a similar problem is a valuable part of the process. There are several viable expectations for the plan, including eliminating the problem, reducing the problem, reducing the harm, and moving the problem.[25]

In the assessment process—after the police make their response to the problem—they evaluate the effectiveness of the response. They examine the following: Was the plan implemented? What was the goal? Was the goal attained, and how do we know? What will happen if the plan is removed or remains in place? What new strategies can be implemented to increase effectiveness, and how can the response be monitored in the future? Police may use the results to revise the response, collect more data, or even to redefine the problem.[26]

The problem-oriented policing process necessitates improving various skill sets, including communication (agreement to share thoughts and ideas with various groups), coordination (networking), cooperation (two or more parties agreeing to assist each other), and collaboration (a formal sustained commitment to work together to accomplish a common mission). Goldstein defined problem analysis as "an approach/method/process conducted within the police agency in which formal criminal justice theory, research methods, and comprehensive data collection and analysis procedures are used in a systematic way to conduct in-depth examination of, develop informed responses to, and evaluate crime

....

SARA Acronym for the four parts of the problem-oriented policing strategy: scanning, analysis, response, and assessment.

and disorder problems."[27] Many new tools are available to law enforcement today to assist with problem analysis.

The most effective problem analysis occurs within the department, using the latest research to develop appropriate procedures to successfully address problems in the community. Developing partnerships with local universities may prove to be a win-win solution for police organizations. By understanding the underlying factors leading to the problems, the most realistic solutions can be developed.[28] New technology also enhances law enforcement's ability to analyze crime and geography and consider factors such as repeat victimization, repeat offending, and MOs, thereby obtaining the data that will facilitate their ability to successfully address the crime problem. Even with recent budgetary constraints, departments can use improved technology, together with criminological theories and up-to-date research, to find innovative ways to reduce crime.

Successful Examples of Community-Oriented Policing

The concepts of community policing and problem-solving policing have merged in the past decades and are sometimes looked at as one philosophy. This philosophy has been given several names in addition to community policing and problem-solving policing, including community-oriented policing. Whatever the name given to this philosophy, the concept is the same—the involvement of the community as a partner in the policing process and an emphasis on proactive, problem-oriented policing rather than incident-driven policing.

The community-oriented policing concept emphasizes a partnership with the community, problem solving, and organizational transformation.[29] Although community policing and problem-oriented policing are close and go hand-in-hand, there are differences. Community policing is concerned with the relationship between the police and the community, and problem-oriented policing is more concerned with solving a particular problem and having an outcome. It involves making efforts to solve problems and have positive results. Clearly this process will be more successful when there is a good

relationship with the community and a partnership exists that promotes dialogue and teamwork. This section will address several of the methods, techniques, and ways of implementing community-oriented policing to solve problems.

In 1999, the California Highway Patrol (CHP) implemented a program to keep the thousands of farm laborers who are hired to work in the fields safe while being transported to worksites. There had been a large number of collisions with fatalities and injuries, and in the Central Division during peak months, the traffic fatalities were 42 percent higher than in nonpeak months. In examining why there were such high numbers of injuries and fatalities, CHP observed that there were statutory and regulatory shortcomings regarding vehicle safety in California. For instance, farm labor vehicles were exempt from the mandatory seat belt law, and because of language barriers, the outreach and educational efforts were less than optimal. CHP worked with the California State Legislature to get two bills passed to enhance the safety of farm workers and vehicles. The mandatory use of seat belts, stronger safety and inspection programs for the farm vehicles, increased staff within CHP to handle inspections, enforcement of these issues, and an increased public education effort had a significant impact on the issue. In 2000, after one year of implementing this program, there were no fatalities resulting from farm labor vehicle collisions for the first time in eight years, and the number of collisions involving farm labor vehicles dropped 73 percent.[30]

The San Marcos, Texas, Police Department used problem-oriented policing to address noise complaints, which, while not as serious as traffic fatalities, were bothersome to the residents and were generating an increased number of calls for service. As residences near the Texas State University–San Marcos transitioned from resident homeowners to student renters, differences in lifestyles caused tension, particularly regarding late-night party noise. In 2007, the police department responded to 2,833 noise complaints, their most frequent call for service. Department staff analyzed where the complaints were occurring and how the police responded. Representatives of the city, the university, and the community came together to address this neighborhood disorder. They developed the Achieving Community Together (ACT) campaign, which focused on reducing the reliance on law enforcement to address the problem by shifting the emphasis from enforcement to education and community influence. This effort resulted in a 16.3 percent decrease in calls for service regarding loud noise and parties and a 43.6 percent decrease in arrests and citations for noise violations.[31]

The Colorado Springs, Colorado, Police Department implemented a community policing strategy to combat a rising problem with homeless camps on public land adjacent to recreational trails and creek beds. The population of these camps had risen to 500; the camps were generating a tremendous amount of litter and a resulting public health concern, which in turn was generating complaints from citizens. The department partnered with advocacy groups and service providers to form the Homeless Outreach Team (HOT). They solicited extensive public input, developed an enforceable "no camping" ordinance, and established procedures to assist individuals to get out of homelessness. As a result of this initiative, the camps were cleaned up, no arrests were made for violating the ordinance, 229 individuals were sheltered, and 117 people were reunited with family members out of state. The program also documented 100 people becoming employed and self-sufficient.[32]

The Charlotte-Mecklenburg Police Department in North Carolina used problem-oriented policing to address an increase in robbery victimization among the Hispanic population. When officers analyzed the situation, they found the majority of robberies were at a particular apartment complex. After meeting with the residents, the police found that most robberies occurred in the parking lot and near the laundry facilities, that the residents were doing their socializing in the parking lots, and that they frequently had large sums of money because they did not trust banks. The police also discovered that the victimization rate was higher than previously thought because the residents rarely called police, and the offenders were from outside the area. Officers worked with the complex management to improve safety, access, and lighting. They shared information gathered with the robbery unit, arrested several suspects, and worked

Michael Dwyer/Alamy

Bicycle patrol is a strategy that enhances community policing while at the same time effectively fighting crime. It allows officers to get out in the community without the barrier of a car and to patrol in situations that might be difficult for motor vehicles.

to build relationships with the Hispanic residents. Officers partnered with the local banking industry to educate the residents and facilitate banking activities. These efforts produced a 72 percent decline in robbery rates in the apartment complex, and overall calls for service also declined. Police replicated the strategy in five other areas and produced an average decrease of 8 percent in robberies. In addition, residents reported increased trust in police and greater use of bank accounts.[33]

Community Policing Today

Many of the programs and outreach efforts discussed in Chapter 11 are examples of community policing strategies. When departments use storefront substations, ministations, or kiosks, they are encouraging citizens to interact with them on a more frequent basis. The hope is that by decentralizing police operations and making officers and information more available, the residents will become more involved with their police department and local government.

Using various modes of transportation such as bicycles, scooters, all-terrain vehicles (ATVs), and horses also brings the officer into the community, especially at special events, with the goal of enhancing relationships. Citizen police academies, new resident information sessions, police officer trading cards, informational brochures in other languages, and police department tours are all examples of community policing efforts.

Implementing Neighborhood Watch programs, Community Emergency Response Team (CERT) training programs, and volunteer programs is another way to give residents more opportunity to participate in their department and their community in a positive manner. The message is that the quality of life in the community, and consequently the crime rate and fear of crime, is partially the citizens' responsibility; therefore, when citizens work together with the police and supplement law enforcement's efforts, real impacts can be made.

All programs aimed at working with various populations to serve them better also are examples of community policing. Youth programs—including the Police Athletic League (PAL), the recreation and tutoring programs, Drug Abuse Resistance Education (DARE), Gang Resistance Education and Training (GREAT), and the wilderness programs for at-risk youth—all seek to actively involve the youth and their families in improving quality of life in the community and to address and minimize various risk factors. Police work with the senior population in an effort to empower seniors and minimize their fear of crime as well as enhance their ability to contribute to their community and police department in a positive manner.

The outreach that law enforcement provides to the various segments of the diverse community makes those groups feel part of the community and gives them a voice, and the work that is done with crime victims helps empower them and makes the police department more responsive to the needs of crime victims. Most departments today use a multitude of programs to express and demonstrate their community policing philosophy. Citizens can visit their department's website and see the various community policing efforts. Just having a website that allows information to be reported, questions to be asked, and the correct people in the organization to be contacted is a community policing strategy.

Elgin, Illinois, a community of more than 77,000 people located 35 miles northwest of Chicago, has focused its department on numerous products that have supported a comprehensive, innovative community policing philosophy. This philosophy emphasizes that policing is done by everyone in the community and that police officers are the paid professionals who facilitate it. The strategy includes many of the programs discussed in Chapter 11 and the philosophies discussed in this chapter. Among the Elgin programs are:

- The Resident Officer Program of Elgin (ROPE), in which officers live and work in distressed neighborhoods of the city

- The Neighborhood Officer Program of Elgin (NOPE), through which officers are assigned to particular neighborhoods within the city

- A Crime-Free Housing Unit, in which officers work closely with all constituents (renters, managers, owners, neighbors) in rental communities in an effort to decrease crime and improve the quality of life, including a mandatory landlord training program for all rental license holders in Elgin

- An informative website with newsletters, monthly and yearly crime statistics, internal affairs investigations statistics, and crime reporting information

- A liaison officer who works with senior services and the local crisis center to enhance services through better criminal investigation, information, and education, and Cellular Assistance for Seniors (CASE), in which seniors can obtain free cell phones that are programmed for 911 calls

- A youth services bureau that includes an explorer post, a kids united program, and a peer jury program

- A social services coordinator who offers immediate assistance to victims of crime and domestic violence

- Community Emergency Response Training (CERT)

- Online tools for leaving an anonymous tip or reporting a crime in 70 different languages

- Crime prevention and community relations programs, including Neighborhood Watch, Citizens Academy, ride-along program, citizen patrol, and other volunteer activities

- Police officer involvement on numerous community boards and committees that are working to prevent crime, drug use, and gang activity

- A Premise Alert program, which identifies residences where occupants might need special accommodations in an emergency

- A Family Finder Program for identifying and locating people within the community with a propensity to become disoriented or lost

The Elgin Police Department website explains its philosophy by making the mission statements of the department, the ROPE unit, and the Crime-Free Housing Unit available. All speak to the issue of the necessity of the police and the community working together to solve the community's problems. The department also warns that none of these programs is a quick fix. In neighborhoods that have deteriorated and in which crime has risen over the years, reversing the situation will take a long-term investment in time and personnel.[34]

The Chicago Alternative Policing Strategy (CAPS), one of the nation's most ambitious community policing initiatives, also embodies the philosophies discussed earlier in this chapter. In an average month, some 6,000 Chicagoans connect with their beat officers through the 230 community meetings held throughout the city. The purpose of the beat officer is to identify and resolve problems of crime and disorder in Chicago's neighborhoods. Both the police and community members have been trained in problem solving and partnership building, resulting in the formation of meaningful partnerships. Other city agencies have been brought into the process to address quality-of-life issues. Beat officers work the same neighborhood and watch for one year to ensure they become a familiar presence in the community.[35]

According to a report on the Chicago Police website, CAPS has made strides in involving the public in securing neighborhood safety. The majority of the city's population (79 percent) knows about the program, largely because of the TV campaign, and participation has been maintained in the communities that need it most. Though participation in community meetings appears to be low, those who do attend feel positive about the process. One criticism has been that it appears to be the police who propose solutions to the problems rather than the community. Community policing training in the police department is ongoing and progress has been made, but the department is looking to address the concerns and weaknesses in its program.[36]

Although most of the academic and professional writing about policing centers on big cities, many crime and disorder problems occur in small towns

and mid-sized suburbs. Community-oriented policing strategies are also widely and successfully used in the departments serving these cities and towns. The true community policing philosophy is one that permeates the department and is put into action by all officers and personnel who have contact with the public. As the following examples will show, successful community policing initiatives can be undertaken in a community of any size.

In 2009, the Wilson, North Carolina, Police Department received a Community Policing award from the International Association of Chiefs of Police (IACP). The department targeted a four-block area plagued by violence and substandard living conditions. By surveying the community, the police department determined that gangs and drug activities were the residents' primary concerns and that the residents did not trust the police. With help from local churches (the strongest organized link to the community), the police department worked on improving communication and enhancing relationships with the community. They worked with property owners to clean up the area and, together with the clergy, concentrated efforts on youth truancy and drug violations. They also educated the community on the signs of gang recruitment. A follow-up survey indicated a 90 percent approval rating for the police coupled with a 38 percent reduction in calls for service. The department believes that police transparency is the greatest tool for collaboration and building trust within the community.[37]

The city of Suwanee, Georgia, experienced a 262 percent increase in its population from 1990 to 2000. Due to this rapid increase, the officers lost their ability to interact with the residents and became increasingly isolated from the community. In an effort to build relationships with the community, the chief initiated the Police and Citizens Together Initiative (PACT). In the tradition of community policing, officers are assigned to various neighborhoods to integrate themselves into the community and learn about the needs of the individual residents as well as about the neighborhood as a whole. In 2008, they held 94 residential meetings and expanded to 200 businesses. This program is highlighted on the department's website, which lists the liaisons and officers for each neighborhood. The crime rate has gone down, and residents report feeling safer and appreciate their ability to contact "their officer" quickly to work together to resolve problems.[38]

Like many cities, the city of Herndon, Virginia, was significantly affected by the mortgage lender crash. The small community soon had more than 300 foreclosed homes. These abandoned homes were not maintained, causing a look of disorder, and they were often vandalized and became locations for criminal activity. This situation resulted in a significant number of calls for service. Besides working with zoning, public works, realtors, bankers, and homeowners associations (HOAs) to design a program that reduced the number of illegal activities, the police department also addressed the care of these neglected properties by working with banks to secure the properties and with HOAs to maintain them. Calls for service in these vacant homes were successfully reduced by 65 percent in one year, and citizens' quality of life was improved. A town ordinance also was enacted that required banks to pay restitution for any services the town had to provide, thereby allowing the department to recover some of its expenditures.[39]

The Louisville, Kentucky, Division of Police was recognized by the IACP for a community policing initiative developed to improve success on calls involving mental illness. In consulting with mental health professionals in the community, the Louisville police developed a 24-hour proactive citywide crisis intervention team composed of specially trained crisis intervention team (CIT) officers; the program was based on one in place in Memphis, Tennessee. The primary objective of the program included increased training for all officers in the area of mental health issues, a reduction in the use of force, and an increase in options involving less-than-lethal force in the handling of these calls. The program seems to be successful; in a three-month period, CIT officers responded to 503 calls. Of those, 401 of the involved individuals were hospitalized for evaluation or treatment, and 11 were charged with offenses. Force was used in only three cases, and that was "empty-hand control" only. The program continues to be closely monitored and evaluated by the CIT committee initially formed to implement the plan.[40]

The small town of Purcellville, Virginia (population 7,800), implemented a community policing effort in working to illustrate the theory "it takes a village to raise a child." They created community

policing sectors and assigned officers responsible for these sectors, and they implemented programs to partner with the community stakeholders. The police were tasked with providing guidance and positive messages to the community, especially the youth. Some strategies included basketball games with the youth, public safety days, an end-of-school picnic, homework assistance, a scholarship pageant, and Christmas caroling for the elderly. The Homework Assistance Program was held in various apartment complexes throughout the town, with officers serving as tutors for the students. The programs have proven to be very popular; there has been a 30 percent decrease in domestic reports involving youth, a 60 percent decrease in runaway reports, a 70 percent decrease in incidents of graffiti, and a 95 percent decrease in skateboarding complaints since implementing the initiative. Anecdotally, officers report an increase in respect and trust from all residents.[41]

University police agencies and university communities also can be involved in community policing efforts. The University of Vermont Department of Public Safety was given recognition for its community policing initiative, designed to address poor relations with students resulting in tension, lack of crime reporting, and lack of trust. The primary goal was to improve communications and work with the students to solve the problems of the campus community. The department appointed liaison officers for various groups and solicited input from the students, faculty, and staff via surveys regarding issues on the campus. Police services also became more involved in university-wide staff development and training regarding safety issues.[42]

Resident Officer Programs: The Ultimate in Community Policing?

Numerous initiatives generally known as **resident officer programs** have sprung up around the nation since the early 1990s. Supporters of these programs believe resident officer programs capture the essence of community policing: improved relationships between police and their neighbors, who team together to fight crime and address quality-of-life conditions that contribute to crime.

Elgin's ROPE, which started in 1991 with three officers, had grown to eight officers by 1997. The ROPE officers, living in donated or subsidized

---

resident officer programs Programs through which officers live in particular communities to strengthen relations between the police and the community.

Community Policing in Florida

My experience with community policing began when we got a new chief of police from outside the agency in the early 1980s. He used the term *team policing*, but the philosophy was similar to community policing.

I was a road sergeant at the time and was given supervisory responsibility for everything that happened in a particular sector of the city. The chief had divided the city into three sectors, and the supervisory staff was responsible for everything occurring in all the zones within that sector; the lieutenants and captain were accountable for everything that occurred in that sector whether they were on duty or not.

Personnel were assigned to sectors, and this assignment never changed. Staffing was the responsibility of the sector supervisors, and they did not get help from the other sectors. The lieutenants were most affected by this change in philosophy, and some did not like it, but they seemed to accept it well. The new chief also implemented changes in the detective bureau that appeared to diminish some of their authority and autonomy. Patrol officers were following up minor crimes, and some detectives were reporting to sector supervisors. That chief did not last too long because of other issues, but some of his philosophies and changes remained.

When a new chief was appointed who had risen through the ranks, he continued with many of these ideas but also expanded further and implemented various strategies to address problems within our community. He put together task forces to address certain problems and instructed them to work with the community to attempt to come up with solutions. He recognized the need for training when implementing these changes, and the Police Executive Research Foundation (PERF) came to the department to provide training in problem-oriented policing. The training started with the supervisors and then progressed to the officers. We used real problems in our community to practice the steps in problem solving. Later we would actually implement some of these ideas. Most importantly, this training got us thinking outside the box in addressing some of our persistent problems.

My experience as well as that of a lot of other officers and supervisors was that many of the strategies that community policing stressed were in fact things we were already doing and enjoyed doing. Getting out of my police vehicle and talking with business owners, residents, and tourists was something I loved to do. I had found it was also a great way to develop relationships and obtain information. I preferred to work the same zone so that I could get to know the comings and goings of the people living and working there. Most supervisors also believed in this and assigned people to the same zone for extended periods whenever possible. The response of some officers and supervisors to this training was, "What else is new? We already know this and already do this . . . they're just giving it a new name." Most went along with the change and encouraged their coworkers to try new things.

We had a particular section of town called Pearl City, a lower socioeconomic area that was experiencing crime and drug problems. The neighborhood was centrally located along main highways and railroad tracks and had been splintered by road expansion as the city grew. A minority police officer was assigned to foot patrol in this predominantly minority-populated section of town. He spent all his time in the neighborhood and established relationships with the community. He became a friend to older and younger residents, someone they knew and could come to with problems. He worked with them in addressing the problems the community was facing. In 1987, he established the Children and Teens Service (CATS) program in the community. He worked with other resources in the community to provide positive role models, mentors, after-school and summer activities, and educational opportunities. He also worked with other city agencies to clean up the neighborhood. He was a charismatic officer and was good at marketing his program and getting community leaders to donate effort, time, and money. This program grew and became successful in many ways; ultimately, it was used as a model in other neighborhoods in the city.

Eventually, these programs became known as the Neighborhood Improvement Programs, and a variety of programs were encompassed under that

(continued)

Community Policing in Florida (continued)   ON THE JOB

heading. Educational funding for college was guaranteed for students maintaining certain standards in school, computer labs were built and staffed by high school and college students, and tutoring and recreational programs were made available in an effort to provide wholesome activities and to level the school playing field for children from less-affluent homes. These programs were successful and gained national recognition through TV documentaries, magazine articles, and national awards.

This was, of course, great news for the organization, right? Yes, but the fame and attention that this one officer received caused some resentment in other officers. Some officers felt that their efforts at aggressive law enforcement, conducted in addition to these "softer" methods to clean up the area, were ignored. They felt they had risked injury and worked hard to clean up the area, and only one officer was getting the credit. They believed these were good programs but also felt the one officer could not have accomplished what he did without other officers backing him up and covering the calls for service that he would have been handling had he not had this special assignment. Luckily, this resentment was small-scale and did not grow, because most officers realized that the ultimate goal was to improve the quality of life for community residents as well as everyone else in the city and to minimize our repeat responses to problems. Those goals were being accomplished, and most knowledgeable people would realize that it took a coordinated effort throughout the department.

One of the most significant changes within the department occurred when supervisors allowed officers to take risks in addressing problems in unconventional ways. When supervisors truly allowed officers to "fail" without marking them down on their evaluations, this encouraged officers to try new things. One of the most difficult issues to deal with in our department, as it probably is in any department, was that some officers and supervisors just do not want to do the thinking or work involved in problem solving. They would rather just continue to do law enforcement the traditional way and then throw their hands up and blame other conditions or factors when they cannot solve a problem.

The philosophy I have carried with me since leaving law enforcement, and that I look for in other law enforcement agencies and personnel, is the realization that the police department belongs to the community and is an extension of the community. Police organizations need to be responsive to the residents and realize that the residents are actually their "bosses." The effort to improve the quality of life for all residents, not just lower socioeconomic populations, should be ongoing. Making it easier for residents to file reports, obtain reports, understand the department, obtain information, and speak with employees should always be a concern. Whether through the various strategies we have mentioned—such as online reporting, telephone reporting, Web pages, ministations throughout the community, citizen academies, and public forums—or just the philosophy of always giving the citizens the best service possible, we must be willing to go the extra mile to build the partnership between the police and the community.

—Linda Forst

homes or apartments, normally work an 8-hour day, but for all practical purposes, they are on call 24 hours a day for residents needing assistance. They also serve as the liaison with government resources. Everyone understands that community policing is not a "quick fix," and the whole community engages in long-term problem solving to achieve mutually agreed-upon goals. The mission statement for ROPE is: "By working and living in a distressed neighborhood, we will provide police service and be the stimulus that empowers the residents to problem-solve, improve their quality of life and independently take ownership of the neighborhood."[43]

The effectiveness of the program in Elgin can be seen by the change in answers to a survey distributed to one area's residents. When ROPE first started in the neighborhood, a questionnaire asked what problems concerned the residents. Drugs and gangs were the major problems then, but two years later the same residents answered that loud stereos and speeding cars were now their biggest concerns. One of the original ROPE locations closed after only three years because of the sustained decrease in crime in the neighborhood.

The DeKalb, Illinois, Police Department has a resident officer program at an apartment complex in their city. Their website states that the goal of the program is to eliminate problems caused by unauthorized boarders and visitors and to give the residents someone approachable to turn to when in need of law enforcement services or support. The officer is viewed as facilitating proactive problem solving in the community; the program also emphasizes the goal of providing a positive role model to the children in the complex to influence their development in a positive direction.[44]

The city of Pasadena, Texas, has a resident officer program in two sections of the city that has evolved into a comprehensive problem-solving police tool by developing relationships between the residents and city officials to enhance the quality of life in the communities. The officers monitor the code enforcement issues and living conditions in their communities as well as carrying out traditional law enforcement responsibilities. In an interesting twist, the officers allow residents of their communities who have outstanding warrants to perform community service projects in lieu of being confined in jail, and they allow teens who have committed minor traffic or city ordinance violations to perform community service projects in their community; this both enhances the quality-of-life issues in the neighborhoods and allows these violators to give back to their community in a positive and visible manner. The department also reports a decrease in criminal activity and an increase in real estate prices in the ROPE areas of the city, demonstrating the positive impact of the program.[45]

In 1997, President Clinton joined the resident officer bandwagon when he announced a plan to give 50 percent discounts to 2,000 police officers to buy federally foreclosed homes in 500 low-income neighborhoods nationwide. Participating officers had to agree to live in the homes for at least three years. This program, called **Officer Next Door (OND)**, was part of a wide-ranging Urban Homestead Initiative designed to reduce crime and make low-income neighborhoods more attractive to homeowners. OND is now under the Good Neighbor Next Door program. Teachers, firefighters, and emergency medical technicians have been added

to the program over the years. The Department of Housing and Urban Development (HUD) states that having public safety personnel living in these communities contributes to community revitalization, makes communities stronger, and helps to build a safer nation. OND has helped to make these goals a reality by encouraging public servants to become homeowners in revitalization areas.[46]

The Federal Government and Community Policing

In the 1992 presidential race, Bill Clinton championed the concept of community-oriented policing and promised to add 100,000 more police officers to the nation's streets. After the election, the federal government made tremendous contributions to the state of community policing strategies throughout the nation. This section will discuss the 1994 Crime Bill, the Department of Justice's Office of Community Oriented Policing Services (COPS), and the Regional Community Policing Institutes (RCPIs).

The Crime Bill

After much political debate, the Violent Crime Control and Law Enforcement Act (the **Crime Bill**) was signed into law by President Clinton in 1994. The provisions of this bill authorized the expenditure of nearly $8 billion over six years for grants to law enforcement agencies to reduce crime.

Office of Community Oriented Policing Services (COPS)

As the research and evaluation arm of the Department of Justice, the NIJ has mounted a broad agenda to study changes in policing. In the wake of the passage

Officer Next Door (OND) A plan initiated in 1997 allowing police officers to receive 50 percent discounts and low-cost loans to purchase homes in "distressed" areas nationwide. It is now under the umbrella Good Neighbor Next Door program, which also includes teachers, firefighters, and emergency medical technicians.

Crime Bill The Violent Crime Control and Law Enforcement Act, signed by President Clinton in 1994.

of the Crime Bill, Attorney General Janet Reno established the **Office of Community Oriented Policing Services (COPS)**.[47] The COPS office was established to administer the grant money provided by the Crime Bill and to promote community-oriented policing: "The Office of Community Oriented Policing Services is the component of the U.S. Department of Justice responsible for advancing the practice of community policing by the nation's state, local, territory, and tribal law enforcement agencies through information and grant resources."[48]

In an effort to eliminate the atmosphere of fear created by crime as well as to prevent crime, COPS stresses earning the trust of the community and making members of the community stakeholders in their own safety, which allows law enforcement to best address the needs of the community. Over the years, COPS has allocated their funds in three ways: (1) providing three-year grants to hire police officers to work in community policing initiatives; (2) awarding grants for improved productivity through acquiring technology or hiring civilians to free sworn-officer time, which can then be devoted to community policing activities; and (3) awarding grants to agencies for special programs attacking specific crime issues.

To maximize participation by the agencies that need the resources and to facilitate the most equitable distribution of funds throughout the nation, the act establishing COPS required simplified application procedures and equal distribution of funds between jurisdictions with more and less than 150,000 population.

The COPS program appears to have been a success. Though falling short of its original goal to put "100,000 new cops on the beat," it has greatly increased the number of police officers out in the field. The data show that there are many more officers on the street than there would have been without the federal funding, which has greatly aided the fight against rising crime rates. This increase in the number of officers includes both numbers of police officer hires and the full-time equivalents gained through increased productivity because of technology use or the implementation of new programs. Though difficult to document, it is believed that the effort has facilitated the growth of community policing in the country.[49]

The COPS office has continued to fund services over the years. Between 1994 and 2005, COPS awarded more than $11.3 billion in total to local, state, and tribal agencies to hire and redeploy more than 118,000 law enforcement officers. COPS has supported other law enforcement community policing initiatives, including granting $10.9 million in antigang initiatives, $21.7 million in training since 1999 for "COPS in Schools," and $69.6 million for community policing initiatives to combat domestic violence.[50]

In 2012, there was an allocation of $111 million for new grants for hiring police officers in an effort to create and preserve law enforcement jobs and increase community policing activities. A requirement for the most recent round of hiring grants is that agencies must commit to hiring a post-9/11 military veteran in keeping with their VETS to COPS initiative. The COPS website provides resources and publications for interested veterans and police agencies. In 2013, the COPS office awarded $125 million in grants to create 937 law enforcement positions nationwide, with $45 million of that allocated to fund 356 new school resource officer positions.

Unfortunately, funding for the COPS program has decreased in recent years, both because much of the money formerly allocated to COPS is going to homeland security and because of complications due to the economic issues our country has faced. In 2005, the budget for COPS was reduced, and in 2008 the allocation for the program was only $587 million as compared to a high of $1.4 billion in 2000.[51]

Since its inception, COPS has provided many resources for law enforcement. Through its Hiring in the Spirit of Service program started in 2000, the organization has examined the character of police officers, including exploring changes in how law enforcement officers are recruited and hired. COPS also has devoted resources and training to the issues of police integrity and ethics for the individual officer. In 1999, the office provided funding to the Reno, Nevada, Police Department and the Police Executive Research Forum (PERF) to develop an alternative national model for field training that would incorporate community policing and problem-solving philosophies. The resulting program, described in Chapter 4 as the Reno model, was the first new field training program for law enforcement in more than 30 years. Feedback about the program

Office of Community Oriented Policing Services (COPS) Established to administer the grant money provided by the 1994 Crime Bill and to promote community policing.

has been positive as departments have continued on their road to community policing, and the officers who have gone through the program are open to working with the community and also show positive leadership skills. Currently, this program is spreading to more and more agencies around the country. COPS provides training manuals and standards to agencies looking to try this program.

In responding to issues deemed community problems, COPS has allocated financial backing to law enforcement agencies developing innovative community policing responses to problems created by methamphetamine. COPS members believe that a strong relationship between law enforcement and the community can help to combat the methamphetamine problem as well as other issues confronting the community. COPS has developed publications, implemented training programs, and provided grant funding in other areas considered to be community problems as well, including stopping child sexual predators, school safety, bullying in schools, and most recently the "snitching" problem. Since it is believed that communication between law enforcement and the community is critical to successful community policing and consequently healthy communities, they have developed *The Stop Snitching Phenomenon: Breaking the Code of Silence* publication. As we will discuss, the COPS program also is committed to homeland security and has many initiatives in that area, including funding the development of interoperable communication networks, in an effort to keep our homeland safe.

In addition, COPS supports the **Regional Community Policing Institutes (RCPIs)**, which consist of partnerships across a variety of police agencies, community groups, and organizations to create a delivery system for training police officers in community-oriented policing. Each of the more than 30 RCPIs develops innovative, region-specific curricula for community policing training as well as providing technical assistance opportunities for policing agencies and community members. The RCPI network is facilitating the growth of community policing throughout the United States. The COPS program is active in publishing articles, researching strategies, and conducting training (either through the RCPIs or nationally) for law enforcement. Many of its publications can be downloaded from the website.

COPS funding continues to help encourage police–community partnerships. One successful program was developed in Phoenix, Arizona, to facilitate the collaborative partnership between the police and the citizens. The Phoenix Neighborhood Patrol (PNP) empowers neighborhood residents to be the eyes and ears of the Phoenix Police Department. The PNP participants receive eight hours of training in patrol procedures, observation skills, the 911 system, reporting techniques, confrontation avoidance, and safety practices. They also have the opportunity to ride along with a patrol officer. After this training, they are issued an identification card and an official shirt so they are easily identifiable in their communities. Participants patrol their own community with which they are very familiar and report any suspicious activity to the police. To date over 1,500 citizens have been trained, and there are training opportunities and forms on their website. This program, in addition to others the Phoenix PD has employed, has allowed officers and residents to keep the lines of communication strong.[52]

Using a COPS methamphetamine grant, Salt Lake City, Utah, established a task force involving more than 30 government agencies working together to prevent the use and production of methamphetamine. One result of the initiative, the Drug Endangered Children Program (DEC), succeeded in changing the child endangerment statutes to better protect drug-exposed children.[53]

The COPS office continues to respond to the changing needs of law enforcement and the American community. After 9/11, COPS reassessed some of law enforcement's processes and decided to address the information-sharing aspect of law enforcement. COPS funded a project by the IACP to determine ways to improve information sharing among federal, state, local, and tribal law enforcement agencies. The result was a report entitled "Criminal Intelligence Sharing: A National Plan for Intelligence-Led Policing at the Local, State and Federal Levels." Among other things, the report recommended the creation of a Criminal Intelligence Coordinating Council (CICC) to help the Department of Homeland Security share criminal intelligence.[54] COPS members view community policing as a strong weapon in the fight against terror, so they will continue to address the issue.

Regional Community Policing Institutes (RCPIs) Part of the COPS program, the more than 30 RCPIs provide regional training and technical assistance to law enforcement around the country regarding community policing.

In viewing the success of the COPS program, the weak area appears to be the problem-solving and relationship-building initiatives. Relationship building is somewhat dependent on the community and citizens' willingness to participate in the process. In some communities, the residents have been reluctant or unable to participate. Problem solving as a methodology spans a wide continuum. Some departments are truly practicing problem solving as Goldstein defined it. In other agencies, problem solving may occur in name only as things are done in the same traditional law enforcement manner with some additional steps added.

With the tightening of budget dollars because of the Iraq war and the fight against terror, some COPS programs have been scaled back in recent years and more of the money is targeted toward programs in homeland security. The programs do continue, however, and successes can be seen around the country. In fact, one of the biggest studies conducted so far was conducted by Jihong "Solomon" Zhao and Quint Thurman, who found that the COPS program was very effective. They examined almost 6,000 cities during a seven-year period. Zhao and Thurman found that COPS hiring and innovative grant programs have been related to significant reductions in local crime rates for both violent and nonviolent offenses in cities with populations of greater than 10,000.[55] A report released in 2010 also indicated that problem-oriented policing has been associated with reductions in crime and disorder.[56]

Some Accomplishments of Community Policing

As reports of overall crime rate decreases hit the presses in the mid- and late-1990s, some police officials associated this decrease with closer relationships with their communities through community policing, as well as the addition of new community policing officers.

The biggest success often cited is that of New York City. In the mid-1980s, New York's crime rate was escalating and the quality of life was dismal in many areas of the city. Panhandlers intimidated tourists and residents, graffiti was all over the city, vagrants were sleeping on the street, subways overwhelmingly smelled of urine, and peep shows and sex shops took over the streets as more legitimate businesses left town. After some particularly horrendous homicides, New Yorkers had had enough. Mayor Rudolph Giuliani launched an effort to restore public confidence and take back the city. The city condemned properties, enforced new ordinances, removed graffiti, and pursued con artists and loiterers as well as violent criminals. Business associations got involved to provide assistance to the police effort. Judges and courts cooperated, and new counseling, rehabilitation, and community service programs were implemented. Violent and property crime rates are down in New York, and business investors as well as residents and tourists are flocking to Times Square and Grand Central Station as the city flourishes with new investments and businesses and a perception of safety.[57]

Other cities are trying to follow New York City's steps to success. Faced with crime increases in the 2000s, many are eager to hire administrators who came up under William Bratton, former head of the NYPD. Though academics debate how much of the decline in crime in the 1990s can be attributed to the community policing philosophy and its emphasis on CompStat and broken windows policing, many city administrators believe policing made a difference. These administrators, faced with a community worried about crime, are choosing to hire chiefs who believe departments can have an impact on crime with the strategies they have employed in the past. Such cities include Los Angeles, Miami, Philadelphia, Sarasota (Florida), Raleigh (North Carolina), Hartford and Stamford (Connecticut), Ann Arbor (Michigan), Aurora (Colorado), Providence (Rhode Island), and Baltimore. The leaders are producing some significant declines in crime in these cities, though not without some controversies, such as morale problems and a confrontation at an immigration rally in Los Angeles.[58]

The International Association of Chiefs of Police continues to present awards for community policing annually to cities in various size categories to highlight innovative and successful programs and illustrate success in jurisdictions of all sizes in all parts of the community.

In 2011, an IACP Community Policing Award went to the New Rochelle, New York, Police Department for their "Fixing Broken Windows: A Collaborative Approach to Housing Remediation" initiative. With evolving demographic trends, an increase in day laborers and undocumented aliens, transient college students, and early 1900s housing, the atmosphere was ripe for housing abuses. There was an increased number of housing complaints, fire code violations, and overcrowding. The police department partnered with the fire department, building departments, public works, and inspectors to form a multiagency "Quality of Life Task Force" to meet with citizen groups, college administrators, and landlords. By working together to ensure that violations were handled quickly and fairly as well as implementing prevention programs targeting contributing factors, they were able to significantly reduce calls for service and improve the quality of life for all residents. They realized a 16 percent decrease in calls for service in the targeted area from 2007 to 2011 and a reduction in Part I crimes for the whole city by 25 percent.[59]

In 2012, the Duluth, Minnesota, Police Department was one of the winners for their Safety and Accountability Audit of the Response to Native Women Who Report Sexual Assault. The department initiated this program after being approached by two local service organizations concerned about the lack of prosecutions in cases of sexual assault against Native American women. In response to this concern, the Duluth PD began a systematic examination of the criminal justice system's response to reported assaults by this segment of the population. They began this collaborative process in a victim-centered audit and at the end of the process had identified seven problem areas, which they termed "gaps." These gaps continue to be addressed by the multidisciplinary team assembled to represent the stakeholders, and Duluth PD has made substantial improvements in their delivery of services to this segment of the population, including changes to policy, training, and relationship building with all of the stakeholders.

Also in 2012, the Clearwater Police Department in Florida was recognized for their award-winning program entitled Operation Graduate in which they partnered with the United Way, the local school district, and a local college to build a program to prevent youths from becoming part of the criminal justice system. They provide at-risk youth with life and financial skills to build a foundation to become successful and contributing members of society. The program encourages on-time graduation with exposure to colleges, financial education, and a healthy lifestyle through nutrition and exercise programs as well as mentors to help them overcome negative learned behaviors. All participants, both the

youth and the supportive mentors and partners, felt positively about the program; the results have been promising as there was a big decrease in recidivism and 100 percent of the students enrolled in college classes received passing grades. The police department learned that ongoing communication and cooperation among all partners greatly improved successful outcomes and allowed the project to be adapted and changed as necessary as it developed, enhancing success.[60]

Surveys indicate that the public supports community policing and strategies that are indicative of community policing. One survey found that when citizens were queried about strategies that are part of community policing, they overwhelmingly supported the increased use of community meetings with the police as well as the increased use of police programs in schools.[61] Another study found that in cities where the training of police officers in community policing is relatively extensive, victims demonstrate a preference for reporting incidents to the police. The belief is that the community has bought into the philosophy that police and citizens must work together to reduce crime, and there is a sense of mutual trust between the police and the community.[62] Some studies have confirmed this belief by showing that community policing initiatives have led not only to decreases in crime but also to an increase in residents' confidence in policing and feelings of safety, as well as a belief that the police are successfully addressing community problems.[63]

Although many attribute crime reduction to community policing strategies, others do not. Some believe that these new philosophies are merely rhetoric. Others attribute the drastic decrease in crime rates in the mid- and late-1990s to more aggressive, strategic, and legalistic law enforcement, similar to that practiced in New York City and other metropolitan areas, as discussed in Chapter 1.

The Debate Continues on Community Policing

Research on the effectiveness of community-oriented policing has yielded mixed results. Many experts are not overly enthusiastic about the idea of community policing. One of the problems faced in community policing is to define what is meant by *community*. In many community policing projects, the concept of community is defined in terms of "administrative areas" traditionally used by police departments to allocate patrols, instead of in terms of "ecological areas" defined by common norms, shared values, and interpersonal bonds. If the police are using administrative areas instead of ecological areas, they lose the ability to activate a community's norms and cultural values.

Some administrators are also uncomfortable with dividing a community up into "parcels" and possibly having those areas competing against each other for funding, attention, and service. Though it is important for various sections of a city or town to have their say, it is also important for cities and towns to work on problems that affect the entire population communitywide, rather than just a neighborhood. Community members should be able to come together, discuss issues and challenges, and prioritize action plans to address them.[64]

In addition to this issue of community, Merry Morash and J. Kevin Ford, in their book *The Move to Community Policing: Making Change Happen*, cite other challenges that law enforcement agencies face when implementing community policing. The move to community-oriented policing involves major changes in how traditional police organizations operate. They need to take the customer-based approach and constantly learn about and improve their policing efforts. The process of moving into this form of policing is transformational, complex, and long-term. These authors define the stages of the process as follows:

1. Exploration and commitment
2. Planning and implementation
3. Monitoring and institutionalization
4. Developing data-driven approaches
5. Changing the police culture
6. Creating partnerships for community policing
7. Dealing with ongoing challenges in the shift to community policing

As the department progresses through these stages, there are many challenges, including some from stakeholders such as administrators, supervisors, unions, line officers, and even the community. How the department reacts to the challenges and the intended and unintended consequences of the process will affect the likelihood of the community policing philosophy becoming institutionalized.

This, in turn, will affect whether the community policing effort is viewed as a success.[65]

Many feel that community policing can actually have a negative effect on certain people. An analysis of a victim callback program established by the Houston Police Department found that the program, which was originally designed to help victims, had a generally negative effect on some minority groups (Asian Americans and Hispanic Americans), whose members may have been suspicious of the department's intentions.[66]

Another concern that has been raised by some law enforcement leaders is questioning whether the activities that officers are engaging in under the umbrella of community policing (recreational roles, tutoring roles, social work roles) are the type of activities that law enforcement officers should be doing. Departments need to address that issue on a continuing basis.

Yet another concern in the debate about community policing revolves around reverting to the older foot patrol model of close interactions with the community. As discussed earlier in the text, there is always a concern about corruption and unfair influence when officers get too involved or too close to community groups. Are the community policing strategies placing officers in an ambiguous position and perhaps enhancing relationships with (and, consequently, the influence of) one group over another? This issue also leads to the discussion earlier about zero-tolerance policies and aggressive patrolling to clean up the streets, make community groups happy, and improve the quality of life. Can this desire to please and be successful lead to overly aggressive techniques that could possibly cross the line to abuse? These concerns need to be continually considered and examined.

A reassuring report has come from New York City, one of the success stories in the implementation of the broken windows model. When the city saw the crime rate plunge—including murders, which decreased from 2,262 in 1990 to 629 in 1998—complaints against police and police shootings concurrently declined. In fact, police shootings reached their lowest level since the 1970s when the data were first recorded.[67]

On the other hand, an audit of the Houston Police Department by a consulting firm criticized the department's neighborhood-oriented policing (NOP) approach. The audit concluded that although "well-conceived," NOP faced a number of difficulties and had not produced any comprehensive improvements in police services. The report acknowledged that NOP has the potential to enhance the quality of police services without adding costs but claimed that the Houston program did not have tangible effects on citizens' security and quality of life. The report said that the program, which had been implemented at the expense of more proactive law enforcement functions, such as arresting criminals, had resulted in mediocre performance in response time to emergency calls for service.[68]

Some believe the empirical evidence for community policing's effectiveness in solving the crime problem is both limited and contradictory.[69] Other researchers hold that although a number of community policing programs have had documented success, there is also an indication that community policing may merely displace crime. Indeed, several studies have indicated that there has been an increase in crime in the areas surrounding the community policing impact area.[70]

The debate regarding community policing continues to rage, sometimes even among officials of the same agency. Different departments may define community policing in different ways. They may label certain programs as community policing when they are just traditional methods with a new name. A thorough commitment to community policing involves new structures and new responsibilities for the officers in engaging the community in problem solving rather than just using the rhetoric or titles.[71] To effectively use the community policing philosophy, departments need to tailor their responses to their community—it is not "one size fits all." To evaluate community policing initiatives correctly, the initiatives must be examined closely to separate true community policing from "pretenders."[72]

In many agencies, police administrators have used specialization to create special units and call them community policing squads, units, or officers. These officers typically are relieved of regular patrol duties to devote their time to "community policing" efforts. This is despite the general agreement of law enforcement leaders that community policing should be the responsibility of all personnel.[73] Although these units can be part of a community policing effort in a department, street officers will have different opportunities to engage in community policing and different options for those initiatives

depending on what part of town they work in and what hours they work.

To effectively evaluate community policing efforts, everyone needs to understand and agree on what community policing is, what defines "success," and how that success should be measured. A concern for agencies implementing and using community policing is that it may necessitate developing new hiring guidelines, evaluation guidelines, and promotional standards. Departments need to define what type of qualities they are looking for in officers so they can maximize their success in the community policing environment. This may seem like an overwhelming duty for agencies entrenched in traditional evaluation methods and possibly constrained by union or collective bargaining agreements.

Researchers who traveled to St. Petersburg, Florida, to observe changes occurring in police roles and police–community relations after the implementation of community policing found that the citizens seemed satisfied with community policing. The researchers also found high levels of cooperation in everyday police–citizen contact and found that 85 percent of those interviewed were "very" or "somewhat" satisfied with neighborhood policing services. The department seems to be attaining the goal of high visibility because approximately one-third of those surveyed said they had seen the police in the previous 24 hours. Of more interest, the perception of police officers toward community policing had improved, although the researchers noted distinctions between community policing officers and road officers. Generally, community policing officers were more supportive of the importance of assisting citizens and enforcing minor laws than were the officers handling calls for service. An interesting finding was that, among all the police officers, a still rather high 25 percent said they have reason to distrust most citizens.[74]

Recently, the success of the broken windows model was challenged by Bernard Harcourt, a professor in the University of Chicago Law School. Harcourt and Jens Ludwig, an associate professor at Georgetown University, reanalyzed Northwestern University professor Wesley Skogan's *Disorder and Decline: Crime and the Spiral of Decay in American Neighborhoods*, originally presented in 1990. As Bratton and Kelling had noted, Skogan's findings supported the link between disorder and serious crime, fortifying support for the broken

GUEST LECTURE

ADOLFO GONZALES

As chief of police for National City in California, Adolfo Gonzales oversees 92 sworn officers, 34 professional staff, and 26 volunteers. Chief Gonzales earned his doctorate degree in leadership science from the University of San Diego in 1996. He is an adjunct faculty member of University of Phoenix, Argosy University, and Brandman University in San Diego.

POLICING IN THE SPHERE OF ILLEGAL IMMIGRATION

Immigrants, whether legal or illegal, are a defining part of our nation's past, present, and future. U.S. policy makers and the public often question how the new immigrant population will impact social service systems like the educational and health care systems.

Policies shape how we police the streets in National City, California. We are located in San Diego County, about seven miles north of the U.S.–Mexico international border. Though the city is only about nine square miles, illegal immigration is something residents and officers must deal with on a daily basis. As we police our streets, we often see two things in terms of illegal immigration: (1) undocumented persons who are victims of crimes, and (2) undocumented people responsible for committing various crimes.

Some proportion of our city's criminals and victims are in the United States illegally, but it is difficult to gauge the percentage of victims or criminals who are undocumented.

Undocumented people are less likely to report crimes, so crime data on undocumented victimization rates likely underreport the true level of crimes against undocumented people. Similarly, the true number of undocumented criminals may be undervalued. To uphold our respect for individuals and to prevent the propensity to engage in racial profiling, NCPD's policy is to *not* collect data on the immigration status of victims or suspects. Most of our data is based on the individual voluntarily telling us his or her immigration status.

We, like all law enforcement agencies, are responsible for the enforcement

windows theory.[75] Harcourt and Ludwig, however, argued that the "popular crime fighting strategy is, well, wrong" and that it does not work in practice.[76] Harcourt stated that the targeted areas chosen for the initiative were also the areas most affected by the crack cocaine epidemic and that when the epidemic ebbed, so did the crime rate, which would have happened with or without the broken windows policing. He and Ludwig concluded, "In our opinion, focusing on minor misdemeanors is a diversion of valuable police funding and time from what really seems to help—targeted police patrols against violence, gang activity and gun crimes in the highest-crime 'hot spots.' … [I]t's not about being pro-cop or anti-cop. It's about using police officer time and limited resources intelligently."[77]

William J. Bratton and George L. Kelling have criticized Harcourt's analysis, charging that he eliminated two areas from the study that showed strong relationships between disorder and crime.

Bratton was the New York City police commissioner at the time and now heads the Los Angeles Police Department, where he has employed similar strategies: in three years, crime went down 26 percent and homicides decreased 25 percent.[78] Bratton stands firmly behind the broken windows strategy, as do many law enforcement leaders who are employing it.

An initial concern in the early stages of the COPS grants (see information earlier in chapter) was whether departments would permanently retain the police officers hired through the grants and absorb the costs locally. In September 1997, it was reported that the first cycle of U.S. Justice Department grants, begun in 1994, was ending. This would require agencies throughout the nation to fund all of the new officers added since the 1994 Crime Bill without the help of the federal government, which had been funding 75 percent of the cost. Some feared that local officials might be tempted to scrap community of all laws and for the safety and protection of all persons. In National City, our officers will not detain undocumented persons for U.S. Customs and Border Protection if the persons are victims or witnesses of crime, unless they are needed as material witnesses. Additionally, our officers will not detain undocumented persons during family disturbance calls, while on minor traffic enforcement, and if the persons are seeking medical treatment.

Our officers have a duty to contact any person(s) when there is a "reasonable suspicion" to believe they are involved in criminal activity. Officers will arrest a person if the probable cause to arrest exists, regardless of what immigration status the person is perceived to hold. If the arrested individual is found to be in the country illegally, a "hold" will be placed on the person for U.S. Customs and Border Protection. This means that before the individual is released from jail, the U.S. Border Patrol is called and the person is turned over to them for deportation.

As officers in the field, we also see that federal policies often have very real impacts on the local level. Following Operation Gatekeeper, an effort by the U.S. Border Patrol in the 1990s to reduce the number of undocumented persons crossing into the United States, we saw an influx of people attempting to cross into the United States through the mountains and deserts. Attempting to cross through more dangerous terrain, many of these people never survived their journey. Operation Gatekeepers' efforts managed to curtail the flow of people over land, but we saw an increase of underground tunnels. These tunnels are believed to be used by major narcotic traffickers to smuggle drugs into the United States. Moreover, human traffickers also utilize these same tunnels.

In a post-9/11 era, controlling our borders and stopping the flow of undocumented persons is often touted as a critical strategy for homeland security and combating the war on terror. Since the September 11th terrorist attacks, the United States has tripled spending on border enforcement. Despite increased funding, illegal immigration has doubled, and an estimated 21 million undocumented immigrants are now in the United States.... This just goes to show that even with new laws, programs, and funding, we can't always be sure that the outcome will be what we hoped for or expected. Sometimes solving one problem may incite another. As officers, we must always be prepared to adapt to shifts in crime and security trends.

Source: Reprinted by permission of Adolfo Gonzales.

policing programs or shift officers around to avoid retaining COPS hires.[79]

This fear, however, seems to have been unfounded. In mid-1999, 98 percent of respondents indicated they had kept the COPS-funded officers or quickly filled any vacancies that arose. In addition, 95 percent reported that the officers were or would be part of the department's budget by the time grant funding ended.[80] This was a stipulation that the federal government required before granting the money to departments. The grant required the department to gradually take over funding for the officers in the three-year grant period and totally assume the cost at the end. Department leaders and government leaders had to sign off on that stipulation.[81]

The biggest recent threat to community policing—and, consequently, the biggest criticism of the initiatives that have taken place—has concerned the current inability to keep police departments fully staffed and to keep the money flowing to these initiatives. Bratton, speaking at a conference, declared that community policing caused a downward trend in crime nationally in the 1990s, but that crime is beginning to rebound because less money and attention have been devoted to community policing since September 11, 2001. Many of the resources previously devoted to community policing have been siphoned to prevent terrorism. Bratton believes that local jurisdictions as well as states and the federal government need to reexamine this issue.[82] This issue of funding is not just affecting the big cities; for example, Stamford, Connecticut, is cutting back on its community policing efforts because of a lack of funding and a lack of personnel. With lower numbers of officers, increased residents, and the loss of federal and state funding since 9/11, the chief can no longer afford to devote the resources to the more labor-intensive community efforts.[83]

On many fronts, the debate over community policing continues.

Homeland Security and the Future of Community Policing

Since September 11, 2001, some departments have made increased efforts to get back to essential police services. Budget dollars are at a premium and "extra" programs may be viewed as nonessential. Some believe that going back to more traditional law enforcement with more militaristic tactics is the only way to fight the war on terror.

In examining the events leading up to 9/11 and in an effort to prevent these types of informational gaps from happening in the future, community policing could fill a vital role. In an article posted on the COPS website, "Community Policing: Now More than Ever," Rob Chapman and Matthew Scheider illustrate the strengths of community policing and how they would prove beneficial in the war on terror.

One of the primary goals would be the prevention of terrorist acts. Through partnerships with other agencies and the community, "hard" and "soft" targets can be identified, vulnerability assessed, and responses planned. Additionally, with established, positive, trusting relationships, members of the community will be more likely to come forward with good intelligence information, allowing law enforcement to "connect the dots" before it is too late.[84]

Many states and larger cities have created state and local fusion centers to share information and intelligence within their jurisdictions as well as with the federal government. Fusion centers serve as focal points within the local environment for the receipt, analysis, gathering, and sharing of threat-related information between the federal government and state, local, and private sector partners. The Office of Intelligence and Analysis of the Department of Homeland Security (DHS) provides assistance to these fusion centers. These centers can be tailored to the unique needs of the locality, and the goal is to facilitate the flow of classified and unclassified information, provide local awareness and access, and provide expertise. As of May 2014, there were 78 designated fusion centers around the country.[85] More information on fusion centers can be found in Chapter 15, "Homeland Security."

The Salt Lake City Police Department has a Fusion Division devoted to enhancing their interaction with and response to the community and facilitating the exchange and flow of information between the community, the police department, and other entities accountable for action. Their posting indicates they have placed in this division the "best and brightest" individuals who will retain the information and have the necessary skills to facilitate sharing of information as they move into future leadership roles in the department.[86]

If a catastrophic incident were to occur again, knowing the community and neighborhood would prove beneficial. Community leaders—possibly already CERT trained (as discussed in Chapter 11)—could be called to assist with response. Previous relationships and knowledge of the neighborhood would facilitate response. Police officers accustomed to making decisions and not having to rely on superiors would be an advantage in a crisis situation where events are rapidly unfolding, communication is challenged, and innovative responses are needed.[87]

Police agencies are joining with federal law enforcement and state and county agencies to integrate responses to significant events and train personnel from all areas of life to recognize and share appropriate information on a timely basis. The assistant director of the FBI stated, "The FBI fully understands that our success in the fight against terrorism is directly related to the strength of our relationship with our state and local partners."[88] To facilitate this relationship, the Department of Justice Office of Community Oriented Policing Services (COPS) and the Police Executive Research Forum (PERF) have produced a guide for law enforcement entitled "Protecting Your Community from Terrorism: Strategies for Local Law Enforcement," which addresses partnerships to promote homeland security.[89]

As a way of recognizing efforts in this area, the IACP began giving community policing awards in the homeland security category in 2004. In 2005, Tempe, Arizona, was recognized for its efforts in partnering with community members representing business, education, faith, police, elected officials, utility companies, Neighborhood Watch, emergency services, health care, and the local university to form the Citizen Corps Council. The council, which is the bridge connecting all the groups, created the Assistance in Disaster (AID) program to organize and mobilize a community response in the event of a natural disaster or terrorist attack. They have screened and trained volunteers in evacuations, searches, traffic control, evidence preservation, and missing persons.[90]

Departments take this need seriously and are devoting personnel, time, and money to this endeavor. The Massachusetts Law Enforcement Technology and Training Support Center is researching the integration of the homeland security mission into community policing. This is funded through a COPS grant and has brought together first responders to develop a homeland security plan. They have developed training programs, addressed the approachability issue, and explored outreach efforts and communication issues. They came up with many community information sources who can be trained in recognizing and reporting suspicious actions to the appropriate agency. These sources include Neighborhood Watch participants, hotel personnel, real estate agents, storage facility employees, transportation center and tourist attraction employees, custodians, public works and sanitation workers, meter readers, and vehicle rental employees, among others.[91] Homeland security efforts can be greatly enhanced by training these community members to know what constitutes possibly threatening behavior and what to do with this information.

Another community group that can greatly contribute to the mission of keeping the homeland safe is the private security industry. This is a somewhat untapped resource that could prove to be an extremely valuable partner to law enforcement. The number of personnel in this sector has increased since 9/11. Estimates indicate they outnumber their public-sector counterparts by more than two to one and provide oversight to approximately 85 percent of the nation's critical infrastructure. Because of their unique responsibilities, street-level knowledge, and state-of-the-art technology, they are an important community partner in this mission.[92]

Community policing is an excellent vehicle for addressing homeland security. The partnership and the trusting relationship with the community will prove to be invaluable as the entire community—in the largest sense—contributes to keeping our homeland safe.

Though the debate about the value of community policing goes on, research continues adding to the literature and police administrators keep looking to the community policing philosophy to address new issues that arise. Time may be needed to examine these initiatives more closely and over longer periods, but some preliminary research has indicated success. The state of California has conducted statewide research in an effort to answer the big question, "Does community policing work at reducing the crime rate?" The results indicate that broken windows law enforcement strategies can be effective in reducing more serious crime, and agencies that are exploring the issue can be reassured that these strategies are likely to work.[93]

SUMMARY

- Community policing and problem-solving policing have been practiced for almost three decades, and some say they have been tremendously popular and successful.

- Others have disagreed, so the debate continues, which is good for policing.

- The three corporate strategies for modern policing are strategic policing, community policing, and problem-solving policing.

- Problem-oriented or problem-solving policing involves the process of scanning, analysis, response, and assessment (SARA).

- The problem-oriented policing method can be used for almost any type of problem an agency faces to determine what the underlying causes of problems are and how best to address them.

- There are many ways to implement community policing; it is flexible and can be implemented to address the particular problems that an agency faces.

- The resident officer program is one particular form of community policing that many cities are using.

- The federal government has played a role in community policing through, for example, the passage of the 1994 Crime Bill and the creation of the Office of Community Oriented Policing Services (COPS).

- Although both empirical and anecdotal evidence have shown benefits to COPS programs, some scholars and practitioners do not agree with community policing strategies.

- The nature of community policing continues to evolve as it is used to address new issues.

- The future of community policing includes, among other issues, the area of terrorism and the role that community policing can play in homeland security.

KEY TERMS

broken windows model
community policing
Crime Bill
Office of Community Oriented Policing Services (COPS)

Officer Next Door (OND)
problem-solving policing
Regional Community Policing Institutes (RCPIs)

resident officer programs
SARA
strategic policing

REVIEW EXERCISES

1. Your chief requests that you implement a school resource officer (SRO) program at your local high school and middle school in an effort to build better relationships with the young people in your community. The COPS office provides a guide, which was published in 2005 by NIJ, on their website for agencies seeking to start and maintain an SRO program. Read this guide and put together an action plan for your chief on how to go about starting an SRO program tailored to your schools.

2. Your city is experiencing a challenging problem with street-level drug dealing just off a main thoroughfare. Word has spread that this is the place to make a quick score, and it is almost like a drive-through drug store. It is evident to law-abiding citizens that this is going on, and

it even causes traffic backups. Citizens are outraged. The community in which it is happening has not been very helpful, as they are afraid to be seen cooperating with the police. You have tried short-term aggressive policing with limited success. Whom would you meet with and why in studying this problem, and what other strategies might you employ? You may want to peruse websites of police departments as well as the DOJ publications for ideas.

3. How does community policing fit with the Homeland Security initiatives developed since 2001? Is it a good fit or a bad fit? In what ways would you try to use the community policing philosophy to enhance Homeland Security efforts in a police agency?

WEB EXERCISES

1. Go to the Department of Justice's Office of Community Oriented Policing Services website. What is the mission of this office and what do they do? Look at the resources they offer, including the publications. Would this site be of value to a law enforcement agency?

2. Go to the University of California at Irvine website. Read what they have on their site regarding community policing. Does this information help you understand the community policing philosophy? Do you think this information would be valuable to their clients?

3. Go to the Salt Lake City Police Department website. Look at their community intelligence unit. What is the mission of this unit? Look at their "coffee with a cop" program, HOST program, bicycle resources, Operation Safe Passage, volunteer corps, and Citizens Academy. What do these programs and the Salt Lake City PD site tell you about their philosophy regarding community policing?

END NOTES

1. George L. Kelling, *Police and Communities: The Quiet Revolution, Perspectives on Policing*, no. 1 (Washington, D.C.: National Institute of Justice, 1988).

2. The 12 monographs in the *Perspectives on Policing* series were published in 1988 and 1989 by the National Institute of Justice, Washington, D.C.

3. Mark H. Moore and Robert C. Trojanowicz, *Corporate Strategies for Policing, Perspectives on Policing*, no. 6 (Washington, D.C.: National Institute of Justice, 1988).

4. Dennis J. Stevens, *Applied Community Policing in the 21st Century* (Boston: Allyn & Bacon, 2003), p. 13.

5. *James Q. Wilson and George L. Kelling, "'Broken Windows': The Police and Neighborhood Safety," Atlantic Monthly* (March 1982): 29–38.

6. Wesley G. Skogan, *Disorder and Decline: Crime and the Spiral of Decay in American Neighborhoods* (New York: Free Press, 1990), pp. 21–50.

7. Robert C. Trojanowicz, "Building Support for Community Policing: An Effective Strategy," *FBI Law Enforcement Bulletin* (May 1992): 7–12.

8. Charles H. Weigand, "Combining Tactical and Community Policing Considerations," *Law and Order* (May 1997): 70–71.

9. David L. Carter, *Community Policing and DARE: A Practitioner's Perspective* (Washington, D.C.: National Institute of Justice, 1995), p. 2.

10. Bonnie Bucqueroux, *What Community Policing Teaches Us about Community Criminal Justice*, retrieved August 29, 2006, from www.policing.com.

11. Retrieved August 29, 2006, from www.safestreet.org.

12. Mary Ann Wycoff, Wesley G. Skogan, Anthony M. Pate, and Lawrence Sherman, *Citizen Contact Patrol: Executive Summary* (Washington, D.C.: Police Foundation, 1985).

13. "Detroit Mayor Dave Bing: 13 New Police Mini-Stations to Open," from www.freep.com/20121205

14. City of Detroit—News Releases, retrieved March 6, 2014, from www.detroitmi.gov/departmentsandagencies/communicationsandcreativeservices.

15. Michael J. Farrell, "The Development of the Community Patrol Officer Program: Community Oriented Policing in the City of New York," in Jack R. Greene and Stephen D. Mastrofski, eds., *Community Policing: Rhetoric or Reality?* (New York: Praeger, 1988), pp. 73–88.

16. Joseph E. Braun, "Progress through Partnerships," *Community Links* (January 1997).

17. George L. Kelling, *"Broken Windows" and Police Discretion* (Washington, D.C.: U.S. Department of Justice, 1999).

18. Herman Goldstein, "Toward Community-Oriented Policing: Potential, Basic Requirements and Threshold Questions," *Crime and Delinquency* 33 (1997): 6–36, copyright © 1997 by Sage Publications. Reprinted by permission of Sage Publications.

19. U.S. Department of Justice, *Surveys in 12 Cities Show Widespread Community Support for Police* (Washington, D.C.: National Institute of Justice, 1999).

20. "Community Policing: Specialists vs. Generalists," *Community Policing Dispatch* vol. 1, #4: April 2008, cops.usdj.gov.

21. Brian A. Reaves, *Local Police Departments*, 2007 (Washington D.C.: Bureau of Justice Statistics, 2010), NCJ#231174.

22. Samuel Walker and Charles Katz, *Police in America: An Introduction*, 6th ed. (New York: McGraw-Hill, 2008), p. 335.

23. Jack Green, "Community Policing in America: Changing the Nature, Structure, and Function of the Police," in Julie Horney, ed., *Policies, Processes, and Decisions of the Criminal Justice System* (Washington, D.C.: National Institute of Justice, 2000).

24. Police Executive Research Forum (PERF), "The Mechanics of Problem Solving Slides," retrieved September 2, 2006, from www.policeforum.org.

25. Ibid.

26. Ibid.

27. Herman Goldstein, *Problem-Oriented Policing* (New York: McGraw-Hill,1990).

28. Rachel Boba, "What Is Problem Analysis?" *Problem Analysis in Policing: An Executive Summary* 1 (2003): 2.

29. PERF, "The Mechanics of Problem Solving Skills."

30. Police Executive Research Forum (PERF), "2002 Herman Goldstein Award Winners," retrieved September 2, 2006, from www.policeforum.org.

31. Center for Problem-Oriented Policing website, Goldstein Awards, 2011, retrieved March 6, 2014, from www.popcenter.org/library/awards/goldstein.cfm?browse=abstracts.

32. Ibid.

33. Ibid.

34. Elgin Police Department website, retrieved May 1, 2014, from www.cityofelgin.org.

35. Chicago Police Department website, retrieved May 1, 2014, from www.cityofchicago.org.

36. Ibid.

37. IACP, 2009 Community Policing Awards, retrieved April 13, 2010, from www.theiacp.org.

38. Ibid.

39. Ibid.

40. Louisville, Kentucky, website, retrieved May 1, 2014 from www.louisvilleky.gov/metropolice.

41. IACP Community Policing Award, sponsored by Cisco, 2011 awards and finalists, retrieved March 6, 2014, from www.iacpcommunitypolicing.org.

42. Ibid.

43. Elgin Police Department website, retrieved May 1, 2014, from www.cityofelgin.org.

44. City of DeKalb Police Department website, retrieved May 1, 2014, from www.cityofdekalb.com/police/progra-Residentofficer.htm.

45. City of Pasadena Police Department website, retrieved May 1, 2014, from www.ci.pasadena.tx.us/default.aspx?name=pol.resident_officer.

46. Housing and Urban Development website, retrieved May 1, 2014, from www.hud.gov/buying/.

47. Jeffrey A. Roth and Joseph F. Ryan, "The Cops Program after 4 Years: National Evaluation," *Research in Brief* (August 2000): 1.

48. COPS website, retrieved April 13, 2010, from www.cops.usdoj.gov.

49. Department of Justice, *On the Beat* 19 (2002), retrieved April 2, 2004, from www.cops.usdoj.gov.

50. COPS website.

51. Dana Wilkie, "Budgetary Tug of War over Funds for Police," *San Diego Union-Tribune*, February 17, 2008.

52. Phoenix Police Department website, retrieved May 1, 2014, from http://phoenix.gov/police/bwonpa1.html.

53. Salt Lake City Police Department website, retrieved April 13, 2010, from www.slcpd.com/insideslcpd/administativebureau/fusiondivision.html.

54. Department of Justice, retrieved May 1, 2014, from https://it.ojp.gov/cicc.

55. Jihong "Solomon" Zhao and Quint Thurman, *Funding Community Policing to Reduce Crime: Have COPS Grants Made a Difference from 1994 to 2000?* (U.S. Department of Justice, Office of Community Oriented Policing Services, July 2004).

56. David Weisburd, Cody W. Telep, Joshua C. Hinkle, and John E. Eck, "Is Problem-Oriented Policing Effective in Reducing Crime and Disorder? Findings from a Campbell Systematic Review," *Criminology and Public Policy* 9 (1, February 2010).

57. *Historical New York City Crime Data*, retrieved May 5, 2014, from www.nyc.gov/html/nypd.

58. Robert Gurwitt, "Bratton's Brigade," Governing.com, August 2007.

59. IACP Community Policing Award, sponsored by Cisco, 2011 awards and finalists, retrieved March 6, 2014, from www.iacpcommunitypolicing.org.

60. IACP Community Policing Award, sponsored by Cisco, 2012 awards and finalists, retrieved March 6, 2014, from www.iacpcommunitypolicing.org.

61. Ronald Weitzer and Steven A. Tuch, "Public Opinion on Reforms in Policing," *Police Chief* (December 2004): 26–30.

62. Stephen M. Schnebly, "The Influence of Community-Oriented Policing on Crime-Reporting Behavior," *Justice Quarterly* 2 (2008): 223–251.

63. Rachel Tuffin, Julia Morris, and Alexis Poole, "Evaluation of the Impact of the National Reassurance Policing Programme,"

Great Britain Home Office Research Development and Statistics Directorate, January 2006.

64. Natasha Lee, "Chief Rethinks Community Policing Policy," *Stamford Advocate*, April 10, 2006.

65. Merry Morash and J. Kevin Ford, eds., *The Move to Community Policing: Making Change Happen* (Thousand Oaks, Calif.: Sage Publications, 2002), pp. 1–10.

66. Wesley Skogan and Mary Ann Wycoff, "Some Unexpected Effects of a Police Service for Victims," *Crime and Delinquency* 33 (1987): 490–501.

67. William J. Bratton and George L. Kelling, "There Are No Cracks in the Broken Windows," *National Review Online*, February 28, 2006.

68. "Audit Rips Houston's Policing Style as a Good Idea That Falls Short of the Mark," *Law Enforcement News*, September 30, 1991, p. 1.

69. *Gary B. Schobel, Thomas A. Evans, and John L. Daly, "Community Policing: Does It Reduce Crime, or Just Displace It?" Police Chief* (August 1997): 64–71.

70. Lisa M. Reichers and Roy Roberg, "Community Policing: A Critical Review of Underlying Assumptions," *Journal of Police Science and Administration* (June 1990): 110.

71. David Griffith, "Does Community Policing Work?" *Police* 12 (2005): 40, 42, 45.

72. Timothy Oettmeier and Mary Ann Wycoff, "Personnel Performance Evaluations in the Community Policing Context," U.S. Department of Justice and Community Policing Consortium, 2006, retrieved June 9, 2006, from www.policeforum.org, p. 352.

73. Ibid., p. 354.

74. National Institute of Justice, "Policing Neighborhoods: A Report from St. Petersburg," *Research Preview* (July 1999).

75. Bratton and Kelling, "There Are No Cracks in the Broken Windows."

76. Rob McManamy, "Study Authors Find Cracks in 'Broken Windows,'" *University of Chicago Chronicle*, March 30, 2006.

77. Ibid.

78. Bratton and Kelling, "There Are No Cracks in the Broken Windows."

79. Jacob R. Clark, "Time to Pay the Piper: COPS Funded Officers, Departments Near Day of Fiscal Reckoning," *Law Enforcement News*, September 30, 1997, pp. 1, 14.

80. National Institute of Justice, "Policing Neighborhoods."

81. Clark, "Time to Pay the Piper."

82. "Bratton: Terror Fight Diverts Money from Crime Prevention," *Providence Journal*, March 2, 2006.

83. Lee, "Chief Rethinks Community Policing Policy."

84. U.S. Department of Justice website, retrieved May 25, 2004, from www.cops.usdoj.gov/default.asp?item=109.

85. Department of Homeland Security website, retrieved May 1, 2014, from www.dhs.gov/files/programs.

86. Salt Lake City Police Department website, retrieved April 13, 2010, www.slcpd.com/insideslcpd/administrativebureau/fusiondivision.html.

87. Rob Chapman and Matthew C. Scheider, "Community Policing: Now More than Ever," retrieved May 2, 2003, from www.cops.usdoj.gov/default.asp?item=716.

88. Quote from FBI Assistant Director of the Office of Law Enforcement coordinator Louis F. Quijas, retrieved December 13, 2006, from www.cops.usdoj.gov.

89. U.S. Department of Justice website, retrieved May 2014, from www.cops.usdoj.gov.

90. International Association of Chiefs of Police website, retrieved May 3, 2006, from www.theiacp.org.

91. Stephen Doherty and Bradley G. Hibbard, "Special Focus: Community Policing and Homeland Security," *Police Chief* (February 2006).

92. Robert Chapman, "Community Partnerships: A Key Ingredient in an Effective Homeland Security Approach," *Community Policing Dispatch* (February 2008).

93. John L. Worrall, "Does 'Broken Windows' Law Enforcement Reduce Serious Crime?" *California Institute for County Government Research Brief* (2002), p. 9.

Police and the Law

Kevork Djansezian/Getty Images

OUTLINE

Crime in the United States
The Judicial Process
How Do We Measure Crime?
How Much Crime Occurs in the United States?
Arrests in the United States
Crime and Punishment

The Police and the U.S. Constitution
The Bill of Rights and the Fourteenth Amendment
The Role of the Supreme Court in Regulating the Police
The Exclusionary Rule

The Police and Arrest
Probable Cause
Reasonable and Deadly Force in Making Arrests
Police Traffic Stops

The Police and Search and Seizure
Canine Sniffs

The Warrant Requirement and the Search Warrant
Exceptions to the Warrant Requirement

The Police and Custodial Interrogation
The Path to *Miranda*
The *Miranda* Ruling
The Erosion of *Miranda*
The *Dickerson* Ruling and Beyond
Police and Surreptitious Recording of Suspects' Conversations

Police Eyewitness Identification Procedures
Lineups, Showups, and Photo Arrays
Other Identification Procedures

INTRODUCTION

When people think about the police, they generally think about the power to arrest someone, the power to issue a citation for driving violations, or some other enforcement activity. People think of the police in terms of the law. As this text has shown, the police do much more than enforce the law. Although the police role is not limited to law enforcement, that is definitely a major part of the police role.

This chapter will explain the U.S. judicial process and discuss the amount and types of crime in the United States, along with the amount and types of arrests made by the police. It will also discuss the U.S. Constitution and the Bill of Rights, focusing on the relationship between the police and the Bill of Rights as interpreted by the U.S. Supreme Court over the years. We will explore significant areas of police power, including the power to arrest people, to stop people and inquire about their conduct, to search people and places and seize property, and to question people about their participation in a crime. Landmark Supreme Court cases will be used to show how the police have altered their procedures to comply with the provisions of the U.S. Constitution.

The chapter provides the fact pattern behind some of the cases. A *fact pattern* is the events in a criminal case that led to the arrest, as well as the facts of the investigation and arrest. The fact pattern is considered by the courts in adjudicating a case. Reading these fact patterns will help you see that law is not abstract principles but, rather, the result of personal and dynamic events.

This chapter is perhaps the most important one in this text. The role of the police is a very special one in our society. The police enforce the law. When doing so, they sometimes have to arrest people. By arresting people, the police take away what Americans value most highly: their freedom and their liberty. The police must know the law and apply it correctly.

Crime in the United States

Crime is part of life in the United States. We read about crime in newspapers, and often details of crimes are the lead stories on television news broadcasts. The following sections will discuss the judicial process in the United States; examine how we measure crime, how much crime occurs, and how many arrests are made; and review the factors that determine what constitutes crime and the punishment that should be given.

The Judicial Process

The courts of the United States were created under Article III, Section 1, of the U.S. Constitution. Section 1 reads, "The judicial power of the United States, shall be vested in one Supreme Court, and such inferior courts as the Congress may from time to time ordain and establish."[1] The Congress has created the appellate courts and district courts within the federal system.

The states have also created their own court systems in order to handle legal matters at the state level. The state courts in many ways mirror the federal courts. Court cases that start at the state level will move through the state system and may try to appeal to the federal system, starting at the District Court level.

THE FEDERAL SYSTEM Congress has used the power of Article III, Section 1, to create 12 federal Courts of Appeals and 94 U.S. District Courts, the U.S. Court of Claims, the U.S. Court of International Trade, and the U.S. Bankruptcy Court. The process of "moving" a court case from one federal court to the next begins at the lowest level, the U.S. District Court. A party dissatisfied with a ruling made by the District Court may appeal that decision to the next level, the Court of Appeals, for that person's state or territory jurisdiction (see Figure 13.1). If parties are unhappy with the Court of Appeals decision, they may appeal to the U.S. Supreme Court.

The Supreme Court is the lone arbiter of what cases it decides to accept and is under no obligation

crime Any act that the government has declared to be contrary to the public good, that is declared by statute to be a crime, and that is prosecuted in a criminal proceeding. In some jurisdictions, crimes only include felonies and/or misdemeanors.

Geographic Boundaries
of U.S. Courts of Appeals and U.S. District Courts

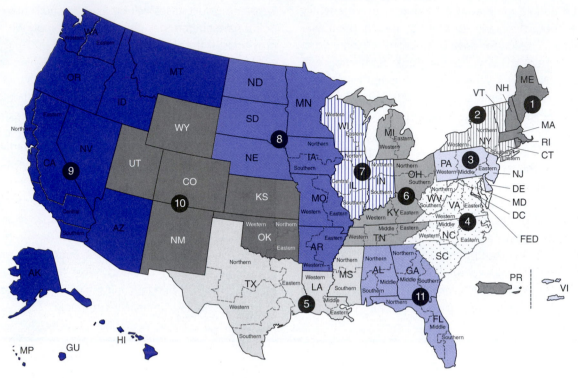

FIGURE 13.1   Federal Appeals Court Jurisdictions
Source: US Courts.gov, retrieved March 23, 2012, from www.uscourts.gov.

to accept any case. The Supreme Court usually will accept cases that have an important constitutional issue that needs to be decided or clarified. A good example of this is the number of cases that have been accepted by the Court with regard to *Miranda* (discussed later in this chapter).[2]

THE STATE SYSTEM   State courts are established by the constitution and laws of each state. Every state in the United States has a trial court level, an appellate court level, and a supreme court level. The state supreme courts mirror the U.S. Supreme Court in responsibility, only on the state level. The state supreme courts accept cases affecting state constitutional issues.

All cases that eventually end up at the U.S. Supreme Court begin in state trial courts. The next level of state courts, after the trial courts, is the appellate level. At this level, state court cases are argued before a panel of judges who will make the final decision. If either party in a case is dissatisfied with the decision, he or she may appeal to the state supreme court. The state supreme court can decide whether or not to hear the case; if it is not heard, the decision of the appellate court is final.[3] If the case is heard, and one of the parties is unhappy with the state supreme court's decision, one or both parties may pursue the appeals process through the federal levels.

Police officers who are on the streets fighting crime are an integral part of the judicial system. An officer who makes an arrest one day may have his or her report read at every court level and eventually may have his or her name published in a U.S. Supreme Court decision for all to read and reference.

How Do We Measure Crime?

Crime is part of life in the United States—but how much crime is there? This section looks at how we measure the amount of crime in the United States. Two major methods are used: (1) the *Uniform Crime Reports* and (2) the National Crime Victimization Survey.

UNIFORM CRIME REPORTS The *Uniform Crime Reports* (UCR) are collected and published by the FBI based on reports of crimes made to the police across the United States. The FBI publishes a yearly report entitled *Crime in the United States* based on all reports made to the police for the year and forwarded to the FBI. The UCR has four major sections: the Crime Index, Crime Index Offenses Cleared, Persons Arrested, and Law Enforcement Personnel.

The FBI's Crime Index consists of data regarding the major Index crimes (murder and nonnegligent manslaughter, forcible rape, robbery, aggravated assault, burglary, larceny/theft, motor vehicle theft, and arson). The Crime Index section of the yearly UCR generally comprises several hundred pages of tables and graphs regarding the Index crimes. Included on these pages are multiyear analyses of each of the crimes using numerous variables, such as the relationship between perpetrator and victim; weapons used; age, race, and gender; crime trends; and crime rates for all offenses reported to the police for the previous year for each of the reporting cities, towns, universities/colleges, and suburban and rural counties.

The Crime Index Offenses Cleared section lists the clearance rates (rates of crimes solved by arrest) for the Index crimes according to certain variables, such as population group and geographic region of the country.

The section on Persons Arrested lists all arrests in the United States for the Index crimes and other crimes according to certain variables. These include geographic area, age, race, and gender.

The Law Enforcement Personnel section lists the number of all uniformed and civilian law enforcement employees for each reporting town, city, and county.

Before 1972, the UCR was the only nationwide measure of crime in the United States. Scholars, however, became skeptical of the crime report data in the UCR because it was based solely on reports made to the police and did not recognize the fact that many crimes are not reported to the police. To get a more accurate account of crime, the National Crime Victimization Survey was started.

NATIONAL CRIME VICTIMIZATION SURVEY The **National Crime Victimization Survey (NCVS)** is prepared by the National Institute of Justice (NIJ), the research arm of the U.S. Department of Justice. The NCVS, as the name implies, is a survey of a random sample of U.S. households, asking them if a crime was committed against anyone in the household during the prior six months. It also asks them certain questions about the incident. Data from the NCVS is published by the NIJ yearly as *Criminal Victimization in the United States*. The NIJ also issues periodic reports regarding trends in particular crimes.

How Much Crime Occurs in the United States?

Crime information for the latest year available for each of the Index crimes is shown in Table 13.1. The data in the UCR are easy to read. For example, when we look at the figures for murder, we see that there were 14,748 murders, which amounts to 4.8 murders for every 100,000 Americans.

TABLE 13.1 *Uniform Crime Reports* Data: 2012

Index Crime	Amount	Crime Rate per 100,000 Residents
Violent Crime	1,214,462	386.9
Murder and nonnegligent manslaughter	14,827	4.7
Forcible rape	84,376	26.9
Robbery	354,520	112.9
Aggravated assault	760,739	242.3
Property Crime	8,975,438	2,859.2
Burglary	2,103,787	670.2
Larceny/theft	6,150,598	1595.3
Motor vehicle theft	721,053	229.7

Note: Regarding arson: Because of the limited reporting of arson offenses by law enforcement agencies, the UCR does not estimate for arson; therefore, arson offenses are not included in this table.

Source: Federal Bureau of Investigation, *Uniform Crime Reports*, 2012, retrieved May 8, 2014, from www.fbi.gov.

Uniform Crime Reports (UCR) Yearly collection of aggregate crime statistics prepared by the FBI based upon citizens' reports of crimes to the police.

National Crime Victimization Survey (NCVS) National Institute of Justice survey of a random sample of U.S. households, asking them if a crime was committed against anyone in the household during the prior six months.

TABLE 13.2   Criminal Victimization, Numbers and Rates, 2012

Type of Crime	Number	Rate per 1,000 People Ages 12 and Older
*Violent Crimes**	6,842,590	26.1
Rape/sexual assault	346,830	1.3
Robbery	741,760	2.8
Aggravated assault	996,110	3.8
Simple assault	4,757,900	18.2
Property Crimes	19,622,980	155.8
Household burglary	3,764,540	29.9
Motor vehicle theft	633,740	5.0
Theft	15,224,700	120.9

Note: Detail may not add to total shown because of rounding.

*Excludes murder because the NCVS is based on interviews with victims and therefore cannot measure murder.

Source: National Institute of Justice, *Criminal Victimization 2012*, Table 1 (Washington, D.C.: Bureau of Justice Statistics, October 2013), p. 2.

The other crime measure, the NCVS, reports the crime data shown in Table 13.2. Notice that the number of incidents for each crime is quite different in the two reports. The UCR data include only incidents actually reported to the police, whereas the NCVS data are based on results of interviews with people, many of whom did not report their criminal victimization to the police. Note that the figures for motor vehicle theft (auto larceny) are closest in both reports. This is because most people in the United States are covered by automobile insurance and thus report an automobile theft to the police in order to make a claim with their insurance company.

malum in se   An act that is "wrong in itself"—that is, illegal in its very nature based on English common law and because it violates the natural, moral, or public principles of a civilized society.

malum prohibitum   A "wrong due to being prohibited"—an act that is made a crime by statute.

Arrests in the United States

For reporting year 2010, police made about 13.1 million arrests for all criminal infractions except traffic violations. About 2.3 million of these arrests were for the FBI's Index or Part I crimes. Of these crimes, about 552,000 were for violent crimes (murder, forcible rape, robbery, and aggravated assault) and about 1.6 million were for property crimes (burglary, larceny/theft, motor vehicle theft, and arson).

The remaining 12.5 million arrests were for various other offenses. The major categories of these arrests and their approximate totals were: simple assaults, 1.3 million; drug abuse violations, 1.63 million; driving under the influence, 1.41 million; weapon law violations, 159,020; liquor laws and drunkenness, disorderly conduct, and vagrancy, 1.72 million; and many other offenses.[4]

Crime and Punishment

In order for a crime to be proved by the government, the elements of the crime must be proven. Without a law, there is no crime; without an act, there is no crime; and without intent, there is no crime. There must be an act and intent for a crime to be committed.[5] In order for a crime to be committed, it must be either a crime that is wrong in itself (**malum in se**) or a crime that is prohibited by statute (**malum prohibitum**).[6]

Whenever there is a crime and a person is arrested and convicted, there will be some form of punishment. The punishment can be anywhere from an admonition by the judge up to life in prison or the death penalty.

How do we determine the punishment for any crime? In the federal criminal justice system, the courts follow the U.S. Sentencing Guidelines (USSG). These guidelines are determined by the U.S. Sentencing Commission. There are minimum and maximum punishments established, and crimes committed at the federal level are assigned "points." Some of the factors to be considered in sentencing are prior criminal record, age, the amount of loss to the victims, whether a weapon was used, and the age of the victims. A higher number of points will result in more severe sentencing; for example, a defendant with a prior criminal history will receive more points than one without a criminal history. The guidelines do not allow for any leniency on the part of the judge other than the minimum sentence allowable.

TABLE 13.3   Crime Classifications and Punishment in Texas

	Classification	Punishment	Alternatives Available
Felonies	Capital	Death by lethal injection or life imprisonment	
	First degree	5–99 years or life in prison, fine up to $10,000	
	Second degree	2–20 years in prison, fine up to $10,000	
	Third degree	2–10 years in prison, fine up to $10,000	
	State jail; fourth degree	180 days to 2 years in jail, fine up to $10,000	Court may impose Class A misdemeanor punishment
Misdemeanors	Class A	1 year in county jail and/or fine up to $4,000	
	Class B	Up to 180 days in county jail and/or fine up to $2,000	
	Class C	Fine not to exceed $500	

Source: Data from Law Offices of Roderick C. White, retrieved March 25, 2012, from www.rcwhitelaw.com.

Prior to any trial, sentencing, or plea bargain, defendants are allowed to present a defense of the charges against them. Some of the most common defenses are: the defendant did not commit the crime; there is reasonable doubt; there is an alibi; or, if the defendant admits to committing the crime, it was self-defense or the defendant is insane. An insanity defense is especially hard to prove, as the burden of proof shifts to the defense. Another defense strategy used is that the defendant was under the influence (did not have the capacity to commit a crime) or that the defendant was entrapped by the police (explained in Chapter 10).[7]

In the federal and state systems, there is the opportunity for a plea bargain. When this takes place, the prosecutor and the defense attorney agree to allow the defendant to plead guilty to a lesser charge in order to obtain a reduced sentence. The results of a plea bargain can range anywhere from a dismissal of all charges, reduced jail time, or, in a death penalty case, life in prison without the possibility of parole. In the federal system, the sentencing guidelines limit the types of plea bargains that can be accepted.[8] Each state, however, sets rules for itself. Table 13.3 shows an example of crime classifications and punishments in the state of Texas.

The Police and the U.S. Constitution

The United States is a nation governed by law. The primary law regulating life in the United States is the U.S. Constitution, including its many amendments. The following sections will discuss the first 10 amendments to the Constitution (the Bill of Rights), the Fourteenth Amendment, the role of the U.S. Supreme Court in regulating the police, and the exclusionary rule and its impact on the police. See Table 13.4 for a list of the amendments to the U.S. Constitution that specifically affect the U.S. criminal justice system.

It must be remembered that the U.S. Constitution is a continuing, dynamic document constantly being reviewed by the U.S. Supreme Court. This chapter discusses hundreds of Supreme Court decisions, "landmark cases," that have affected the police and the entire criminal justice system, as well as our society. Since this judicial review process of the Court is ongoing, with constant reinterpretations of the Constitution and changes in the rules that govern police behavior, all officers must constantly review their own organization's rules and directives in light of the fact that the law is always changing.

Courtesy of Chief Riseling

BY CHIEF SUSAN RISELING

Associate Vice Chancellor Chief Riseling currently leads the police department at the University of Wisconsin–Madison. Chief Riseling is a former IACP vice president. Currently she chairs the Civil Rights committee and is a member of the IACP Executive Committee and the Constitutional Review Committee. Chief Riseling is a past president of the Dane County Chiefs of Police and the Wisconsin Chiefs of Police Association; she the first woman and first university police chief to hold that particular position. She is a past president of the National Association of Women Law Enforcement Executives. In August 2003, Chief Riseling was awarded the Motorola NAWLEE (National Association of Women Law Enforcement Executives) Law Enforcement Executive of the year.

A VIEW FROM THE INTERIOR: POLICING THE PROTESTS AT THE WISCONSIN STATE CAPITOL

On February 11, 2011, a gathering of local police chiefs took place in Madison, Wisconsin, to prepare for what was initially anticipated to be a work stoppage in response to the governor's announcement of a "budget repair bill." The Capitol Square in Madison, Wisconsin, was going to become ground zero of the national Occupy movement protests that would follow across the country in 2011.

Most of the police attendees at these early planning meetings had long-standing professional relationships with one another, going back two decades. Many had trained together; most had come up through the ranks of their organizations together and had watched one another mature into leadership positions. This shared history would serve to help the group ramp up quickly; each knew the others' strengths and capabilities, and communication was smoothed by years of collaboration. And yet, as in any long relationship, there were times when familiarity was a burden. Old tensions did not melt away in a moment of need. If anything, conflicts were intensified with the stress of the protests, especially because the governor's bill would strip bargaining rights for some of the state's police forces, but not all. In addition, each agency brought its own unique style of policing appropriate to its jurisdiction and blending these styles into a coherent whole would prove challenging.

We would try to use the Incident Command System. Following the horrific attack on our country in 2001, the federal government developed the National Incident Management System (NIMS), and as a part of that system the Incident Command System (ICS) became the response structure for all first responders to use.

As originally conceived, the ICS functions well in physical emergencies such as fires and floods. The goals are clear in those situations: preserve life and protect property. The tactics are generally agreed upon: extinguish the fire or restore the levy, dam, or flood gate. Each role in the Incident Command System is defined and has specific responsibilities. Individuals trained in the functions can be changed in or out at the end of an operational period. While ICS is responsive to political leadership, the tactics are left to the first responders. Fires don't burn and floods don't rise because of who the governor might be or what the mayor said in a statement to the city. One doesn't negotiate with a fire or with a flood.

Political and protest demonstrations are different. While law enforcement may use the structure of ICS to organize the first responders and achieve the lofty goals of preserving life and property, there are other significant goals to consider. A key goal is the preservation of constitutionally protected rights of the people to disagree with their elected leadership. Attempting to dialog or negotiate with a burning wildfire would never be considered, but negotiating and talking with demonstrators is vital in a democratic society. Who should have that dialog? What happens when the two sides in a political standoff refuse to talk and the side that controls the police wants aggressive enforcement action against their opponents, not to preserve life but to make their political point? How much autonomy should law enforcement leaders have from their elected civilian leadership?

These were all questions we dealt with during the first week of protests. With crowds from 2,000 to 65,000 as our first week at the Capitol came to a close, our efforts gradually transitioned from the urgent scramble of first response to the deliberate bustle of sustained support. The determination of the protestors to keep the gathering peaceful certainly aided our work, but the size and duration of the protests created complications. Our work was shifting from simply responding to planning and anticipating what might be coming next. Unfortunately, due to politics and rancor between the Democrats and Republicans, much of what was to come caught us by surprise.

The chiefs may have been building on 20 years of shared history, but the officers they oversaw began their day with barely

20 minutes together. During the height of the protests the interior branch drew staff from 198 different agencies. The branch took responsibility for daily briefings for up to 500 visiting officers who would be providing security for the next 12-hour shift. The makeup of any particular group of officers varied from day to day. Some folks were able to serve multiple shifts while others were with us for just one day. Within a half hour each team learned their purpose, their protocols, and where the bathrooms were located! Using three-by-five-inch instruction cards, we communicated to each officer her or his role, supervisor, and radio protocol. While these teams worked their "beat" inside the Capitol, the interior branch, the command post, and the policy group were working toward a shared understanding of the overall goal of this mission.

Twelve days in, an effort to facilitate participation in democracy and allow people to exercise their constitutional rights was competing with a more practical desire to get the building back under control and return some sense of normal government operations. The hands-off approach we were consistently taking made returning to normal difficult to achieve.

There are 5.5 million residents of Wisconsin; all deserve a functioning government. Over the first 12 days of the protests just over a million had come to Madison to make their voices heard. They had met with their representatives and senators, testified, marched, observed, sang, wept, slept, laughed, talked, chanted, posted signs, prayed, and sang the national anthem, and in doing so affirmed their constitutional rights. In that time, remarkably only 12 had been arrested, of which 3 had little or nothing to do with the protests.

We had been planning to close the Capitol at 4:00 p.m. on Day 14—a key step in returning the building to "normal operations." Our hope was to clear the building, clean it, and re-open it to the public the next day. The intent was not to prevent public access to the Capitol, but rather to facilitate that access according to long-established building hours.

In its normal operations, our government reflects a philosophical compromise: that we should be ruled by the will of the majority while protecting the rights of the minority. The inherent tension in that arrangement poses challenges but also provides for the checks and balances so essential to democracy. In the days to come, we would spend much of our time navigating that tricky middle ground. Could we continue to provide daytime access to the public at large, if a few refused to leave at night? How far would voluntary compliance take us? And what options did we have if and when that approach failed? Out of thousands of protesters, 300 decided to stay. Surprisingly the orders from the administration were to not forcibly remove the protesters. Instead we were told to keep the whole building closed as long as any protesters remained inside. This therefore shut out the public, and the much larger crowd outside the venue grew impatient.

At this point, no one from the Republican Party trusted the Democratic Party or vice versa. Many in the crowd did not trust the administration. Everything that was occurring was viewed with cynicism and from a political angle. The thought that the police were acting on the public's behalf had started to erode with significant doubt that our actions were independent of the administration.

It would take the judicial branch of government to decide between the protestors and the administration. The drama unfolded in a Dane County courtroom. All testimony was available in real time for public viewing around the world through "Wisconsin Eye."

The court order seemed to remove the politics from the issue of access to the Capitol. The court ordered the protesters out of the building and to comply with the building hours from this point forward. The remaining protestors left the Capitol without being arrested or carried out and preserved the overall positive feeling between the demonstrators and the police.

The protection of civil rights is easy when everyone agrees. It is in moments of disagreement that our beliefs and principles are tested. It is these moments when law enforcement must be the thin blue line with the Bill of Rights as the guide, with a respect of the rule of law, not political gain or personal bias influencing our actions. Police must act as facilitators safeguarding the exercise of constitutional rights. It is in moments of turmoil that law enforcement leaders must take a stand and resist using force unless absolutely necessary. At times they must speak truth to power, knowing it may require some level of personal sacrifice. After all, courts can rule and politicians can legislate, but it is the police who take those results to the street and enforce the rule of law. It is a complex role, a role few outside law enforcement leadership ever understand. Without a strong sense of principle, without understanding the importance of free expression, without exercising constitutional rights and the police protecting those rights using only reasonable force, we as people will not succeed.

Democracy is intentionally messy. If it were efficient, it wouldn't be a democracy. The ability to redress one's grievances with the government can take many forms. This form of democracy is expensive and cost Wisconsin approximately eight million dollars in wages and expenses. The thing is, to live in a nation where protests take this form without violence, without destruction—well, that's priceless.

The Bill of Rights and the Fourteenth Amendment

The U.S. criminal justice system is based on the Bill of Rights, the first 10 amendments to the U.S. Constitution. Five of the first 10 amendments specifically address freedoms or rights that people possess when involved with the criminal justice system.

To understand the U.S. system of criminal justice, we must go back to the birth of the United States. The early colonists came to escape persecution and to seek freedom. The colonists, however, continued to be persecuted and denied freedom by the British government. They rebelled, wrote the Declaration of Independence, fought for independence from England, and were able to defeat the British troops. As newly freed people, the former colonists wrote the U.S. Constitution to govern themselves. They then wrote the first 10 amendments to the Constitution, which form the basis of our criminal justice system—the rights and freedoms we possess that can be used against government tyranny.

The Fourteenth Amendment also affects the U.S. criminal justice system. The Supreme Court, over the years, has extended the Bill of Rights to the states through the due process clause of the Fourteenth Amendment. The due process clause protects all citizens of the United States against any state depriving them of life, liberty, or property except through the proper legal processes

TABLE 13.4   U.S. Constitution: Amendments Governing the U.S. Criminal Justice System

First Amendment	Sixth Amendment
Congress shall make no law respecting an establishment of religion, or prohibiting the free exercise thereof; or abridging the freedom of speech, or of the press; or the right of the people peaceably to assemble, and to petition the government for a redress of grievances.	In all criminal prosecutions, the accused shall enjoy the right to a speedy and public trial, by an impartial jury of the State and district wherein the crime shall have been committed, which district shall have been previously ascertained by law, and to be informed of the nature and cause of the accusation; to be confronted with the witnesses against him; to have compulsory process for obtaining witnesses in his favor, and to have the assistance of counsel for his defense.
Fourth Amendment	
The right of the people to be secure in their persons, houses, papers, and effects against unreasonable searches and seizures, shall not be violated, and no warrants shall issue, but upon probable cause, supported by oath or affirmation, and particularly describing the place to be searched, and the persons or things to be seized.	**Eighth Amendment**
	Excessive bail shall not be required, nor excessive fines imposed, nor cruel and unusual punishments inflicted.
Fifth Amendment	**Fourteenth Amendment (Section 1)**
No person shall be held to answer for a capital, or otherwise infamous crime, unless on a presentment or indictment of a grand jury, except in cases arising in the land or naval forces, or in the militia, when in actual service in time of war or public danger; nor shall any person be subject for the same offense to be twice put in jeopardy of life or limb; nor shall be compelled in any criminal case to be a witness, against himself, nor be deprived of life, liberty, or property, without due process of law; nor shall private property be taken for public use, without just compensation.	All persons born or naturalized in the United States and subject to the jurisdiction thereof, are citizens of the United States and of the State wherein they reside. No State shall make or enforce any law which shall abridge the privileges or immunities of citizens of the United States; nor shall any State deprive any person of life, liberty, or property, without due process of law; nor deny to any person within its jurisdiction the equal protection of the laws.

Source: www.house.gov/house/Constitution/Amend.html, retrieved April 17, 2012.

guaranteed by the U.S. Constitution. The section has been the vehicle through which much of the Bill of Rights has been interpreted to apply to state courts as well as federal courts.

The Role of the Supreme Court in Regulating the Police

The U.S. Supreme Court, through its policy of **judicial review**, has made a significant impact on the way the police do their job. As early as 1914, in *Weeks v. United States*, the Court influenced the police by regulating how they should conduct their searches and seizures.[9] In 1936, in *Brown v. Mississippi*, the Court ruled certain methods of police interrogation unconstitutional.[10]

Most Supreme Court cases regarding criminal justice try to strike a balance between the rights of the individual and the rights of society. But what do we mean by those rights? A simple example, which could have occurred today in your classroom, might explain it. You and your fellow students want a safe classroom. You do not want a student walking into class with an illegal gun that could be used to shoot you (rights of society). However, which of you would like the police to be at the classroom door each morning, searching you for illegal guns without just cause (rights of the individual)?

The Supreme Court has the difficult task of bringing balance between these two often conflicting goals. There is an inherent inconsistency between protecting the rights of the individual and the rights of society. Having unlimited individual rights presents the risk that the rights of society to be safe from crime will be limited, but having unlimited rights of society to be safe from crime presents the risk of having individual rights taken away. It falls upon the Supreme Court to balance these two precious rights.

In police matters, the Supreme Court hears cases on appeal from people who have been the subject of police actions, including arrest, search and seizure, and custodial interrogation. The justices then decide whether the police action violated the person's constitutional rights. In most cases, they do this by interpreting one of the amendments to the Constitution. Supreme Court decisions can bring about changes in police procedures. Certain significant cases, such as *Mapp v. Ohio*

and *Miranda v. Arizona,* are known as landmark cases.[11] The major method used by the Supreme Court to ensure that the police do not violate people's constitutional rights is the use of the exclusionary rule.

The Exclusionary Rule

The **exclusionary rule** is not a part of the U.S. Constitution. It is an interpretation of the Fourteenth Amendment by the Supreme Court that holds that evidence seized in violation of the U.S. Constitution cannot be used in court against a defendant. Such evidence is suppressed (not allowed to be used in court).

The exclusionary rule evolved in U.S. law through a series of Supreme Court cases. Since at least 1914, the Supreme Court has been concerned with the use of illegal means by the police to seize evidence in violation of the Constitution, and then using that evidence to convict a defendant in court. Because the Bill of Rights, when written, applied only to agents of the federal government, and not to those of local governments, the Court first applied the exclusionary rule only to federal courts and federal law enforcement officers. The Court, however, continually warned state courts and law enforcement agencies that they must amend their procedures in order to comply with the U.S. Constitution or risk the exclusionary rule being imposed on them as well. By 1961, the Supreme Court, noting that states had not amended their procedures to conform to the Constitution, applied the exclusionary rule to state courts and law enforcement agencies, as well as federal ones. The following four landmark cases show how the exclusionary rule developed in this country.

WEEKS v. UNITED STATES *Weeks v. United States* (1914) was the first case in which the exclusionary rule was used.[12] It involved federal law enforcement personnel entering an arrested person's

judicial review Process by which actions of the police in areas such as arrests, search and seizure, and custodial interrogations are reviewed by the court system to ensure their constitutionality.

exclusionary rule An interpretation of the U.S. Constitution by the U.S. Supreme Court that holds that evidence seized in violation of the Constitution cannot be used in court against a defendant.

Weeks v. United States (1914)

Freemont Weeks was arrested at his place of business on December 21, 1911, and charged with using the U.S. mail to conduct an illegal lottery. The police then searched Weeks's house and turned over articles and papers to a U.S. marshal. The marshal, together with the police, then searched Weeks's room and confiscated other documents and letters. All the searches were conducted without a warrant.

Weeks was convicted based on the evidence seized from his home. On appeal to the U.S. Supreme Court, his conviction was overturned, and the exclusionary rule was established.

Source: Based on *Weeks v. United States*, 232 U.S. 383 (1914).

Rochin v. California (1952)

On July 1, 1949, based on information received that Rochin was selling narcotics, three Los Angeles County deputy sheriffs entered Rochin's house without a warrant and forced open the door to his apartment within the house. When the police entered Rochin's bedroom, they saw two capsules on his bedside table and asked him what they were. Rochin picked up the capsules and swallowed them. A struggle ensued between Rochin and the police, and the police attempted to open Rochin's mouth to get to the capsules. Failing to do this, they handcuffed him and forcibly took him to a hospital. At the hospital, under the direction of one of the police officers, a doctor forced an emetic solution through a tube into Rochin's stomach against his will. The stomach pumping caused Rochin to vomit. In the vomited matter were found two capsules, which proved to be morphine.

Source: Based on *Rochin v. California*, 342 U.S. 165 (1952).

---

silver platter doctrine Legal tactic that allowed federal prosecutors to use evidence obtained by state police officers through unreasonable searches and seizures.

home and seizing evidence without a warrant. The evidence was used against him in court, and he was convicted based on it.

On appeal, the Supreme Court overturned the man's conviction and established the exclusionary rule. Expressing the opinion of the Court, Justice William R. Day wrote the following:

> If letters and private documents can thus be seized and held and used in evidence against a citizen accused of an offense, the protection of the Fourth Amendment, declaring his right to be secure against such searches and seizures, is of no value, and so far as those thus placed are concerned, might as well be stricken from the Constitution. The efforts of the courts and their officials to bring the guilty to punishment, praiseworthy as they are, are not to be aided by the sacrifice of these great principles established by years of endeavor and suffering which have resulted in their embodiment in the fundamental law of the land.

The exclusionary rule provided that any evidence seized in violation of the Fourth Amendment could not be used against a defendant in a criminal case. As enunciated in the *Weeks* case, the exclusionary rule applied only to evidence seized in an unconstitutional search and seizure by a federal agent and used in a federal court. It did not apply to state courts.

The exclusionary rule gave rise to another form of police misconduct that has been called the **silver platter doctrine**. Under the silver platter doctrine, federal prosecutors were allowed to use "tainted" evidence obtained by state police officers seized through unreasonable searches and seizures, provided that the evidence was obtained without federal participation and was turned over to federal officers. In *Silverthorne Lumber Co. v. United States* (1920), however, the Court ruled that such tainted evidence is illegal to use in court.[13] In its colorful language, the Court compared the illegal search to a "poisoned tree" and termed any evidence resulting from the illegal search as the "fruit of the poisoned tree."

WOLF v. COLORADO Another case that involved the exclusionary rule was *Wolf v. Colorado* in 1949.[14] Wolf was suspected of being an illegal abortionist. A deputy sheriff seized his appointment book without a warrant and interrogated people whose names appeared in the book. Based on the evidence from

Mapp v. Ohio (1961)

On May 23, 1957, three Cleveland police officers went to the home of Dollree ("Dolly") Mapp to search for a man named Virgil Ogletree, who was wanted in connection with a bombing at the home of Donald King. (Donald King was a well-known boxing promoter who promoted former heavy-weight champion Mike Tyson, among other fighters.) The police knocked at the door and demanded entry. Mapp telephoned her lawyer and, on his advice, refused to allow the police to enter without a warrant.

Three hours later, the police again arrived with additional officers. The police then forced their way into the house. At this point, Mapp's lawyer arrived but was not allowed to see his client or to enter the house. As the police were rushing up the stairs to Mapp's second-floor apartment, Mapp was halfway down the stairs, rushing the police and demanding to see the warrant. In response to Mapp's demand, one of the officers held up a piece of paper purported to be a warrant. Mapp grabbed the piece of paper and stuffed it down the front of her clothing. A struggle ensued, during which the officers retrieved the piece of paper and then handcuffed Mapp because she was acting "belligerent."

The officers then forcibly took her to her bedroom, where they searched a dresser, a chest of drawers, a closet, and some suitcases. They looked through a photo album and some of Mapp's personal papers. The police also searched the living room, dining area, kitchen, and Mapp's daughter's bedroom. They then went to the basement and searched it and a trunk located there. During the search, the police found an unspecified amount of pornographic literature.

Mapp was charged with possession of "lewd and lascivious books, pictures and photographs" and subsequently convicted in court for possessing obscene materials. The warrant was never produced in court.

On appeal, the Supreme Court reversed Mapp's conviction based on the police's violation of the Fourth Amendment. It then extended the exclusionary rule to all state courts and law enforcement personnel.

In 1970, Dollree Mapp was arrested by New York City police for the possession of drugs. Suspecting that Mapp was dealing in stolen property, the police obtained a search warrant. While executing it, they found 50,000 envelopes of heroin and stolen property valued at over $100,000. Mapp was convicted and sentenced to a term of 20 years to life. On New Year's Eve in 1980, the New York governor commuted her sentence.

Source: Based on *Mapp v. Ohio*, 367 U.S. 643 (1961).

these patients, Wolf was arrested, charged with committing illegal abortions, and convicted in court.

On appeal, the Supreme Court issued what could be seen as a rather strange decision. It ruled that although the Fourth Amendment did bar the admissibility of illegally seized evidence, it would not impose federal standards (the exclusionary rule) on state courts. The Court directed that the states create stronger state rules that would prevent illegally obtained evidence from being admitted into state courts. (At the time of the *Wolf* decision, 31 states had rejected the exclusionary rule, and the Court had accepted this, respecting states' rights. By 1961, however, when *Mapp v. Ohio* reached the Supreme Court, many states had accepted the exclusionary rule.) In *Wolf*, Justice Felix Frankfurter, speaking for the Court, wrote, "We hold, therefore, that in a prosecution in a State Court for a State crime the Fourteenth Amendment does not forbid the admission of evidence obtained by an unreasonable search and seizure."

ROCHIN v. CALIFORNIA   In *Rochin v. California* (1952), another landmark case in the development of the exclusionary rule, the police entered Rochin's home without a warrant and, upon seeing him place what they believed to be narcotics into his mouth, forcefully attempted to extract the narcotics from him.[15] Failing this, they brought Rochin to a hospital, where his stomach was pumped. The stomach pumping produced two capsules as evidence of illegal drugs. Rochin was convicted in court and sentenced to 60 days' imprisonment. The chief evidence against him was the two capsules.

The Supreme Court overturned Rochin's conviction, considering the forcible seizure of evidence as a violation of the Fourteenth Amendment's due process clause. Speaking for the Court, Justice Felix Frankfurter wrote,

> This is conduct that shocks the conscience. Illegally breaking into the privacy of Rochin, the struggle to open his mouth and remove what was there, the forcible extraction of his stomach's contents—this course of proceedings by agents of government to obtain evidence is bound to offend even hardened sensibilities. They are methods too close to the rack and screw to permit of constitutional differentiation.

In the *Rochin* case, the Court did not make the exclusionary rule applicable in all state cases, but only in those cases of extremely serious police misconduct—the kind of misconduct that, in Justice Frankfurter's words, shocks the conscience. The Court again urged the states to enact laws prohibiting the use of illegally seized evidence in state courts and threatened that if the states did not enact those laws, the Court might impose the exclusionary rule upon the states.

MAPP v. OHIO *Mapp v. Ohio* (1961) was the vehicle the Supreme Court used for applying the exclusionary rule to state courts.[16] The case involved the warrantless entry of police into a woman's home to search for a man in connection with a bombing. While in her home, the police searched it and found "obscene materials," for which she was arrested and ultimately convicted in court. Speaking for the Supreme Court, Justice Tom C. Clark wrote the following:

> The ignoble shortcut to conviction left open to the State tends to destroy the entire system of constitutional restraints on which the liberties of the people rest. Having once recognized that the right to privacy embodied in the Fourth Amendment is enforceable against the States, and that the right to be secure against rude invasions of privacy by state officers is, therefore, constitutional in origin, we can no longer permit that right to remain an empty promise. Because it is enforceable in the same manner and to like effect as other basic rights secured by the Due Process Clause, we can no longer permit it to be revocable at the whim of the police officer who, in the name of law enforcement itself, chooses to suspend its enjoyment. Our decision, founded on reason and truth, gives to the individual no more than that which the Constitution guarantees him, to the police officer no less than that to which honest law enforcement is entitled, and to the courts, the judicial integrity so necessary in the true administration of justice.

See Table 13.5 for a list of landmark cases regarding the exclusionary rule in search and seizure cases.

IMPACT OF THE EXCLUSIONARY RULE ON THE POLICE Many police officers and citizens believe that the exclusionary rule is unfair—that it is procriminal and antipolice. They believe that the rule allows hardened criminals the chance to escape justice and be released "on a technicality." Since the *Mapp* and *Miranda* decisions, many people have claimed that the Supreme Court has "handcuffed" the police and that the police no longer have the tools to fight crime. (The *Miranda* case is discussed later in this chapter.)

Academic studies of the effect of the exclusionary rule have not confirmed these fears. One study revealed that the exclusionary rule is overwhelmingly used with drug offenses, rather than violent crimes, and that the rule was responsible for evidence being suppressed in less than 1 percent of

TABLE 13.5 Landmark U.S. Supreme Court Decisions: Exclusionary Rule in Police Search and Seizure Cases

Case	Decision
Weeks v. United States (1914)	Exclusionary rule applies to federal law enforcement agents
Wolf v. Colorado (1949)	Exclusionary rule would not be applied in state courts
Rochin v. California (1952)	Exclusionary rule applies in shocking cases
Mapp v. Ohio (1961)	Exclusionary rule applies to all law enforcement agents

---

Many landmark U.S. Supreme Court cases are described in this chapter. You should know the facts of these cases.

The law is not mere theory or the application of reason to problems. To paraphrase Justice Oliver Wendell Holmes, "There is more law in a page of history than in a volume of logic." This means that the law is dynamic. It changes over time because it is responsive to the thoughts, feelings, and needs of society.

The law—specifically, case law—is based on real experiences of real people. *Case law* is the body of law that results from court decisions or court interpretations of *statutory law*, which is law written by the legislative or executive branch of the government.

In discussions of case law, it is common to hear the names Dollree Mapp, Danny Escobedo, Ernesto Miranda, and even Donald or Don King,

Mike Tyson's former boxing promoter. Sure, these people were often on the "other side of the law," but as Justice Felix Frankfurter once observed, "The safeguards of liberty have frequently been forged in controversies involving not very nice people."[17] Thus, even though Dollree Mapp was a small-time gambler and hid a man wanted by the police, Danny Escobedo was a murderer, and Ernesto Miranda was a rapist, they all influenced legal history by exercising their rights under the U.S. Constitution—those very rights that also apply to all of us.

As you further your studies in criminal law, perhaps even in law school, a text or a professor may refer to a "Terry stop" or say "as the Court ruled in *Chimel*," and you will be expected to know what that means. You should know both the facts of the cases and the concepts that have arisen from them.

—John S. Dempsey

---

all criminal cases in the study.[18] Another study—a review of 7,500 felony cases in nine counties in three states—found that only 0.6 percent were dismissed because of the exclusionary rule.[19]

The remainder of this chapter will deal with constitutional limitations on the police in the areas of arrest, search and seizure, custodial interrogation, and identification procedures.

The Police and Arrest

The police authority to **arrest** is restricted by the Fifth Amendment, which forbids depriving citizens of life, liberty, or property without due processes of law. An arrest is also controlled by the Fourth Amendment's restrictions on searches and seizures because an arrest is the ultimate seizure—the seizure of one's body. A state's criminal procedure law defines an arrest and directs who can make an arrest, for what offenses, and when. Most states define an arrest as "the taking of a person into custody, in the manner authorized by law for the purpose of presenting that person before a magistrate to answer for the commission of a crime."

In 2001, in *Atwater v. City of Lago Vista*, the Supreme Court ruled that custodial arrests are reasonable seizures under the Fourth Amendment regardless of the possible punishment for the crime that resulted in the arrest.[20] In this case, police in Lago Vista, Texas, arrested Gail Atwater for driving her vehicle with her two children, ages three and five, in the front seat. Neither Atwater nor the two children had on seat belts, which is a misdemeanor in Texas punishable by a maximum fine of $50. Texas law permits police to make warrantless arrests for misdemeanors. Atwater was handcuffed, transported to the police station for booking, and placed in a cell for an hour before being seen by a magistrate. Atwater, after pleading no contest to the seat belt violation and paying a $50 fine, sued the police and the city of Lago Vista for being subjected to an unreasonable Fourth Amendment seizure. She argued that her offense carried no jail time and there was no need for her immediate detention.

....

arrest The initial taking into custody of a person by law enforcement authorities to answer for a criminal offense or violation of a code or ordinance.

In this case, the Supreme Court ruled that Atwater's arrest satisfied constitutional requirements because it was based on probable cause to believe that Atwater had committed a crime in the arresting officer's presence. Many commentators have criticized this decision by the Court, saying that it gave new unprecedented power to the police. They argue that Atwater could merely have been given a traffic citation or ticket for her offense (no seat belts). However, the decision actually only confirmed the Court's long-standing opinion that the police can make an arrest for any offense committed in their presence, and traffic tickets or citations are only options in lieu of physical arrest. Atwater's actions were a misdemeanor under Texas law and an actual arrest, rather than a traffic citation, was justified in this case.

Arrests can be made with or without a *warrant* (a writ, or formal written order, issued by a judicial officer that directs a law enforcement officer to perform a specified act and affords the officer protection from damage if he or she acts according to the order). In general, police officers can arrest a person (1) for any crime committed in the officers' presence, (2) for a felony not committed in the officers' presence if they have probable cause to believe that a felony has occurred and that the person they have arrested committed the felony, or (3) under the authority of an arrest warrant.

As an example of the first circumstance, officers can arrest a man they observe committing a robbery with a gun. An arrest can also be made in the following scenario, as an example of the second circumstance: An officer is called to a scene where there is a dead body and is told by witnesses that a woman in a black leather jacket was engaged in an altercation with the deceased and took out a gun and shot him. The officer searches the area around the crime scene and finds a woman in a black jacket hiding under a staircase. Upon searching the woman, the officer finds a gun. An example of the third circumstance would be the scenario where the officer does not find the woman after the crime, but witnesses positively identify her. The officer can go to court and obtain an arrest warrant for the woman and a search warrant to find the gun.

However, if a routine arrest is to be made in a suspect's home, an arrest warrant is necessary unless

---

TABLE 13.6 A Police Officer's Power to Arrest

The Tennessee Code, Section 40.803, reads as follows:

Grounds for arrest by officer without warrant—An officer may, without a warrant, arrest a person:

1: For a public offense committed or a breach of the peace threatened in his presence.

2: When the person has committed a felony, though not in his presence.

3: When a felony has in fact been committed, and he has reasonable cause for believing the person arrested to have committed it.

4: On a charge made, upon reasonable cause, of the commission of a felony by the person arrested.

Source: Tennessee Code, Section 40.803.

---

the suspect gives consent or an emergency exists. *Payton v. New York* (1980) ruled on the case of New York City police attempting to arrest Theodore Payton based on probable cause for a murder. They attempted to gain entrance to Payton's apartment, but there was no response to their knocks. Officers then went into the apartment by breaking down the door. Upon entering the apartment, they observed in plain view a .30-caliber shell casing that was used as evidence of the murder. The Supreme Court ruled that this was a routine arrest and the police had ample time to gain a warrant before entry.[21]

See Table 13.6 for a sample state code defining a police officer's power to arrest.

Probable Cause

Most of the arrests made by the average police officer do not involve a warrant, because most crimes an officer becomes aware of on the street necessitate immediate action and do not allow the officer the time necessary to go to court to obtain a warrant. Most of the arrests made by the police are based on the probable cause standard.

Probable cause can be defined as evidence that may lead a reasonable person to believe that a crime has been committed and that a certain person committed it. Probable cause is less than *beyond a reasonable doubt*, which is the standard used by a court to convict a person of a crime. Probable cause

---

probable cause Evidence that may lead a reasonable person to believe that a crime has been committed and that a certain person committed it.

is more than **reasonable suspicion**, which is a standard of proof that would lead a reasonable person (a police officer) to believe a certain condition or fact (that a crime is, will be, or has occurred) exists. This is the standard necessary for police officers to conduct stop and frisks.

The evidence needed for probable cause must be established prior to arrest. For example, if an officer sees a man who is walking down a block adjust his jacket to the extent that a gun can be seen protruding from his waistband, the officer has reasonable suspicion to stop and question the man. If the possession of the gun is illegal, the officer has probable cause to make an arrest. Because the arrest is legal, the search that produced the gun is legal; therefore, the gun can be entered into evidence. In contrast, if an officer stops all people walking down the street and searches them without sufficient justification, any arrest for possession of a gun would be illegal, and the gun would be suppressed in court.

The U.S. Supreme Court has made numerous important decisions on the legality and requirements for arrests. In *Brinegar v. United States* (1949), the Supreme Court ruled that relaxations of the fundamental requirements of probable cause, as it relates to the power of arrest, would leave law-abiding citizens at the mercy of police officers' whims.[22] In 1959, *Henry v. United States* set the precedent that an arrest must be made on firmer grounds than mere suspicion and that the Fourth Amendment applies to searches and arrests.[23] Also in 1959, *Draper v. United States* held that the identification of a suspect by a reliable informant may constitute probable cause for an arrest, where the information given is sufficiently accurate to lead the officers directly to the suspect.[24]

In 1991, in *County of Riverside v. McLaughlin*, the Court ruled that a person arrested without a warrant must generally be provided with a judicial determination of probable cause within 48 hours after arrest, including intervening weekends and holidays, meaning that weekends and holidays could not be excluded from the 48-hour rule.[25]

In *Maryland v. Pringle* (2003), the Supreme Court addressed the constitutionality of arresting a group of companions when the officer has reason to believe that at least one or more of them is involved in criminal activity but does not have information to identify with certainty who is the actual person or persons in the group responsible for the criminal activity.[26] In this case, an officer stopped a car occupied by three men, including Joseph Pringle,

for speeding. The officer requested and was given consent to search the vehicle. During the search, he found five plastic bags of cocaine and more than $700 in rolled-up cash. The three occupants of the vehicle denied any knowledge of the money and drugs, and the officer arrested all three, including Pringle. Pringle later confessed that the cocaine belonged to him and that the others were not aware that drugs were in the car.

At trial, Pringle challenged the use of his confession, arguing that his arrest was not supported by probable cause. The trial court agreed and held that without specific factors establishing Pringle's dominion and control over the drugs, the officer's mere finding that it was in a car occupied by Pringle was insufficient to justify probable cause to arrest.

Upon appeal, the U.S. Supreme Court reversed the trial court and ruled that the officer had sufficient probable cause to arrest Pringle based on the information known to the officer at the time of arrest and the reasonable inferences the officer could draw therefrom. It held that the officer could reasonably infer that one or all of the three occupants of the car had knowledge of, and exercised dominion and control over, the cocaine because all three were riding together in a small vehicle and appeared to be engaged in a common enterprise. The Court noted that a standard higher than probable cause is to be applied later in the criminal justice process and does not apply to the decision to arrest someone.

See Table 13.7 for a list of landmark cases regarding police arrests.

TABLE 13.7 Landmark U.S. Supreme Court Decisions: Arrests by Police

Issue	Cases
Probable cause	*Brinegar v. United States* (1949), *Draper v. United States* (1959), *Henry v. United States* (1959), *Payton v. New York* (1980), *Atwater v. City of Lago Vista* (2001), *Maryland v. Pringle* (2003)
48-hour rule	*County of Riverside v. McLaughlin* (1991)

© 2016 Cengage Learning®

reasonable suspicion The standard of proof that is necessary for police officers to conduct stops and frisks.

Reasonable and Deadly Force in Making Arrests

The amount of force an officer can use when making an arrest is called **reasonable force**. Reasonable force is that amount of force necessary to overcome resistance by the person being arrested by the police. For example, if a person is punching the officer in an effort to avoid the arrest, the officer may use similar force in an attempt to subdue the person and control him or her. As an attacker's force escalates, an officer may escalate his or her use of force.[27]

The best way to define reasonable force may be to define unreasonable force. Punching, kicking, or otherwise using force against a person who is not resisting and who is willingly submitting to an arrest would be the unreasonable use of force. Continuing to strike at a person after he or she is subdued, handcuffed, and under the officer's physical control would be an unreasonable use of force. The Rodney King incident (1991) would appear to be an excellent example of unreasonable force, even though the jury apparently saw it differently in the first trial. In the video, King does not appear to be resisting, yet the officers continue to hit him with their batons.

The use of deadly force (force sufficient to cause a person's death) has long been a controversial topic in policing. The use of deadly force by the police is generally permitted (1) when an officer's life or another's life is at peril from the person against whom the deadly physical force is directed, (2) where the officer has probable cause to believe the suspect has committed a crime involving serious physical harm to another, or (3) in other serious felony cases. The landmark U.S. Supreme Court case relative to use of deadly force by the police is *Tennessee v. Garner* (1985).[28]

In 2007, in *Scott v. Harris*, the U.S. Supreme Court addressed the reasonableness of the use of

© Bill Bachmann/The Image Works

A motorist performs a roadside sobriety test after being stopped for suspicion of drunk driving. The motorist's performance on this test, together with the driving witnessed by the officers, will determine whether he is taken into custody for drunk driving.

force to terminate a motor vehicle pursuit.[29] In this case, a Georgia county deputy attempted to stop a car driven by Victor Harris traveling 73 miles per hour in a 55-miles-per-hour zone. Harris refused to pull over and led police on a chase at speeds exceeding 85 miles per hour. During the pursuit, Deputy Scott applied his push bumper to the rear of Harris's vehicle, causing Harris to lose control of his car, which left the roadway, rolled over, and crashed, causing injuries that made him quadriplegic. Harris sued Deputy Scott, claiming excessive force was used against him in violation of the Fourth Amendment. The court of appeals held that a reasonable jury could find that Scott violated Harris's Fourth Amendment right to be free from an unreasonable seizure.

Scott appealed the decision to the U.S. Supreme Court. The Court noted that the "decision to terminate the car chase by ramming his bumper into [Harris's] vehicle" constituted a Fourth Amendment seizure and decided to determine the case using the reasonableness standard. In determining the reasonableness of the seizure, the Court employed the balancing-of-interest test, which "balances the nature and quality of the intrusion on the individual's Fourth Amendment interests against the importance of the governmental interests alleged to

---

reasonable force The amount of force an officer can use when making an arrest.

justify the intrusion." In deciding on Scott's behalf, the Court stated:

> It was [Harris], after all, who intentionally placed himself and the public in danger by unlawfully engaging in the reckless, high-speed flight that ultimately produces the choice between two evils that Scott confronted. Multiple police cars, with blue lights flashing and sirens blaring, had been chasing [Harris] for nearly 10 miles, but he ignored their warning to stop. By contrast, those who might have been harmed had Scott not taken the action he did were entirely innocent. We have little difficulty in concluding it was reasonable for Scott to take the action he did.[30]

The Court, thus, refused to accept the argument made by Harris that the public would be better protected by having the police terminate the pursuit. The Court commented that ceasing the pursuit was no guarantee that Harris would not continue to pose a danger to the public. In addition, the Court was reluctant to establish a rule requiring the police to allow fleeing suspects to get away whenever they drive *so recklessly* that they put other people's lives in danger. The Court, instead, established the following rule:

> A police officer's attempt to terminate a dangerous high-speed car chase that threatens the lives of innocent bystanders does not violate the Fourth Amendment, even when it places the fleeing motorist at risk of serious injury or death.[31]

Police Traffic Stops

There is no such thing as a "routine traffic stop" for officers, especially for the officer whose primary duty is to make contact with the traffic violator. The Texas Education Agency Law Enforcement Course recommends that officers use a seven-step method when making contact with violators to reduce possible conflict: (1) greet and show identification, (2) state the violation that was committed, (3) ask the driver for identification, (4) state an action before taking it, (5) take the stated action, (6) explain what the violator must do, and (7) leave.[32]

In the past, many officers stated, "It was a routine traffic stop," when testifying in court regarding summonses and arrests for drivers of automobiles. The routine traffic stop came to an end, however, in 1979, with the case of *Delaware v. Prouse*.[33] In this case, the Supreme Court ruled that the police cannot make capricious car stops and that "random spot checks" of motorists are a violation of a citizen's Fourth Amendment rights. The Court, however, stated that police may still stop automobiles based on reasonable suspicion that (1) a crime was being committed or (2) a traffic violation occurred. The Court also said that the police can establish roadblocks as long as (1) all citizens are subject to the stop or (2) a pattern is set such as every third car is stopped.

Can a police officer legally order a driver or a passenger out of the vehicle after he or she has stopped it? Yes, ruled the Supreme Court in two cases. In *Pennsylvania v. Mimms* (1977), the Court ruled that the Fourth Amendment allows a law enforcement officer who has made a lawful routine stop of a vehicle for a traffic offense to order the driver to exit the vehicle without requiring any additional factual justification.[34] In this case, the defendant was stopped for driving with an expired license plate. The officer then ordered the defendant to exit

 YOU ARE THERE

Delaware v. Prouse (1979)

On November 30, 1976, at about 7:30 p.m., a New Castle County, Delaware, police officer stopped an automobile owned by William Prouse. Another man was driving Prouse's car, and Prouse was an occupant. As the officer approached the vehicle, he smelled the odor of marijuana. He then observed marijuana on the floor of the automobile. Prouse was arrested and later went on trial.

At the trial, the officer testified that his stop of Prouse's car was "routine." He stated that he saw the car, and because he was not answering any other calls, he decided to stop the car. He further testified that he saw no traffic violations or vehicle equipment violations.

The trial court ruled that the stop and detention had been capricious and was a violation of Prouse's Fourth Amendment rights. The state of Delaware appealed the case to the Supreme Court, which affirmed the opinion of the trial court. The Supreme Court ruled that random spot checks of automobiles are a violation of citizens' Fourth Amendment rights.

Source: Based on *Delaware v. Prouse*, 440 U.S. 648 (1979).

the vehicle. The officer later testified that he routinely ordered all drivers to exit vehicles following routine traffic stops out of a concern for his safety. When Mimms stepped out of the vehicle, the officer noticed a bulge in his jacket, prompting the officer to conduct a limited search for weapons and leading to the discovery of a handgun.

In *Maryland v. Wilson* (1997), a Maryland state trooper pulled over a vehicle for speeding.[35] The trooper, out of concern for his safety, directed the defendant, Wilson, a passenger in the vehicle, to step out of the vehicle. As the man exited the car, the trooper observed a bag of cocaine fall to the ground.

In both cases, the Court recognized the inherently dangerous nature of the traffic stop. In fact, in *Maryland v. Wilson*, the Court cited statistics showing that in the year in which the *Mimms* stop occurred, almost 6,000 officers were assaulted and 11 were killed during traffic pursuits and stops.[36]

In 1990, the Supreme Court, in *Michigan Department of State Police v. Sitz*, ruled that brief, suspicionless stops at highway checkpoints for the purpose of combating drunk driving are legal.[37] However, in 2000, in *City of Indianapolis v. Edmond*, the Court ruled that when the purpose of the checkpoint is to locate illegal drugs, the seizure involved is unconstitutional.[38] Thus, highway checkpoints for DWI enforcement are constitutional, but for drug enforcement, they are not legal. In the *Edmond* case, the Court reasoned that the drunk driving checkpoint is clearly aimed at reducing the immediate hazard posed by drunk drivers on the highways, while general crime control (such as drug enforcement) stops need some quantum of individualized suspicion.

In 2004, in *Illinois v. Lidster*, the Supreme Court clarified its *Edmond* decision, ruling that *Edmond* does not condemn all highway checkpoints.[39] In *Lidster*, the police had established a highway checkpoint to locate witnesses to a previous hit-and-run death of a bicyclist. Police stopped all vehicles approaching the checkpoint and asked the occupants whether they knew anything about the accident. As Lidster approached the checkpoint, his vehicle nearly struck an officer. The officer approached the vehicle and smelled alcohol on Lidster's breath. Lidster subsequently failed a field sobriety test and was arrested and then convicted for driving under the influence of alcohol. Lidster appealed his conviction, claiming that the information leading to his

arrest was derived from an unlawful seizure because the checkpoint violated the Fourth Amendment based on the *Edmond* ruling. The appellate court agreed with Lidster and suppressed the evidence against him. The U.S. Supreme Court, however, reversed the appellate court and concluded that the use of the checkpoint in *Lidster* differed greatly from the one in *Edmond* because its purpose was to solicit information about a fatal accident as opposed to general crime control.

In *Whren v. United States* (1996), the Supreme Court ruled that pretextual traffic stops, also known as *pretext stops* (the temporary detention of a motorist upon probable cause to believe that he or she has violated the traffic laws even if another reasonable officer may not have stopped the motorist absent some additional law enforcement objective), do not violate the Fourth Amendment. In this case, plainclothes vice officers were patrolling a high drug activity area in an unmarked car when they noticed a vehicle with temporary license plates and youthful occupants waiting at a stop sign. The truck remained stopped at the intersection for what appeared to be an unusually long time while the driver stared into the lap of the passenger. When the officers made a U-turn and headed toward the vehicle, the truck made a sudden right turn without signaling and sped off at an "unreasonable" speed. The officers overtook the vehicle when it stopped at a red light. When one of the officers approached the vehicle, he observed two large plastic bags of what appeared to be crack cocaine in Whren's hands. Whren was arrested. At trial, he sought to suppress the evidence, saying that the plainclothes officer would not normally stop traffic violators and that there was no probable cause to make a stop on drug charges; therefore, the stop on the traffic violation was merely a pretext to determine whether Whren had drugs.[40] Despite his argument, the Court ruled that Whren's stop was not unconstitutional.

In 2007, in *Brendlin v. California*, the Supreme Court ruled that a passenger in a vehicle has the same right as a driver to challenge the constitutionality of a traffic stop.[41] In this case, deputy sheriffs in Yuba City, California, arrested Bruce Edward Brendlin, who was a passenger in a vehicle, on a parole violation and drug charges. Brendlin was eventually convicted and sentenced to four years in prison. The deputies had observed a vehicle in which Brendlin was a passenger, on the morning of November 27, 2001. The vehicle had expired registration tags.

Crime and the Community

The law and enforcement of the law are not always cut and dried. Politics and community values influence what police officers do in their jurisdiction. These are just two of the factors that influence officer discretion.

When I was a detective, we had a robbery go down in our business district. It was a time of very high crime rates; the public was fed up with "bad guys," and they wanted them arrested and punished. They wanted to feel safe in their community and be able to walk the streets without fear of being robbed or of going home and finding their house broken into.

This robbery, in fact, was similar to many we'd been having throughout the city. There was no weapon involved—just physical force. Two young men walked into a jewelry store in a crowded strip mall. It was around 1:00 p.m. on a beautiful day in the middle of December, the height of both the tourist season and the busy holiday shopping season. These two young men asked to look at some gold chains and were shown several by the employees. Leery because they had been victimized on several prior occasions by "snatchers," the employees showed only a couple at a time and didn't stray far from the counter.

After a few minutes of looking at chains and discussing pros and cons, the two "customers" grabbed several and ran out the door. The owner pulled a gun and told them to stop. They did not. They ran out the door, and the owner followed. He let off some rounds and hit one of the subjects in the butt as he exited the store. The owner continued running after the other subject and fired off two more rounds but missed him. Shoppers were diving for cover, and the two rounds lodged in the wall of an adjacent store (the strip mall was L-shaped, with several stores perpendicular to the jewelry store).

When I got to the scene, the injured offender was still there. Though he wasn't seriously injured, he was transported to the hospital, where the bullet was removed, and he was released. The second subject was apprehended not far from the scene. It turned out these two subjects were juveniles—big juveniles (about six feet tall) but only 16 years old. They were charged with their crime and sent to the detention center. I wanted to charge the store owner with firing his weapon, as it was not a case of self-defense and there was a significant potential for harming innocent bystanders. I consulted with the state attorney's office, and the ultimate decision was that we would present the case to a grand jury. The state attorney recognized the political nature of this case (as did I) in this time of soaring crime rates and citizens' anger and impatience with "bad guys." He thought it would be a better move politically to avoid charging the owner outright and, rather, let a grand jury of 21 citizens make the decision.

We took the case to the grand jury; after listening to the testimony, they decided not to charge the owner. With many of the jurors having been crime victims or knowing crime victims, they could relate to the frustration of the business owner. They felt he was justified in doing what he did because he had been victimized so many times and was just trying to protect his business and livelihood. I'm just glad no one got hurt in this reckless action.

—Linda Forst

The deputies radioed dispatch and were informed that an application for renewal of the registration was being processed for the vehicle. Later that day, the deputies observed the same vehicle and noticed a temporary operating permit, indicating that it was legal to drive the vehicle. Despite the display of the temporary permit, the officers pulled the vehicle over. They then noticed the passenger, Brendlin, whom they recognized as a possible parole violator. They ran his name and determined that he had an outstanding warrant for his arrest. They placed him under arrest and conducted a search of his person, which produced a syringe cap. A pat-down of the driver revealed syringes and a plastic bag containing marijuana. A search of the car disclosed items used to manufacture methamphetamine. Brendlin moved to suppress the evidence found during his arrest and the search of the car on the grounds that it was the fruit of an unlawful seizure. He argued that since the deputies did not have a valid reason for stopping the vehicle, his seizure was not supported by sufficient cause as required under the Fourth Amendment. The U.S. Supreme Court agreed with Brendlin's motions and dismissed the evidence.

In an interesting 2008 case, Virginia police officers arrested David Lee Moore for driving with a suspended license—a misdemeanor. Upon searching the vehicle, the officers seized crack cocaine and Moore was arrested for two charges, driving with a suspended license charge and possession of drugs. He was convicted. Upon appeal to the Virginia Supreme Court, the court reversed the conviction, declaring that the search violated the Fourth Amendment because the arresting officers should have issued a citation under state law, and the Fourth Amendment does not permit a search incident to the issuance of a citation. The U.S. Supreme Court unanimously overruled the Virginia Supreme Court, stating that the police have the power to conduct searches and seize evidence, even when done during an arrest that turns out to have violated state law.[42]

The Police and Search and Seizure

Search and seizure is the search for and taking of persons and property as evidence of crime by law enforcement officers. Searches and seizures are the means used by the police to obtain evidence that can be used by the courts to prove a defendant's guilt. Police searches are governed by the Fourth Amendment, which prohibits all unreasonable searches and seizures and requires that all warrants be based on probable cause and that they particularly describe the place to be searched and the persons or things to be seized.

The sanctity of one's home is very important in U.S. legal tradition, and it is commonly assumed that *a person's home is his or her castle*—a concept referred to as the **castle doctrine**. The

search and seizure Legal concept relating to the search for and confiscation of evidence by the police.

castle doctrine Reflects the English common law practice that a person's home is his or her castle; codified in the Fourth Amendment to the U.S. Constitution.

YOU ARE THERE

The Castle Doctrine in "Stand-Your-Ground" Laws

The castle doctrine gives citizens in their homes—and in some states, in their cars and workplaces—the right to protect themselves, others, and their property by force up to and including deadly force.[43] The table below lists how this doctrine is implemented by "stand-your-ground" laws in four states.

On the night of February 26, 2012, Trayvon Martin was shot and killed by George Zimmerman in Sanford, Florida. The ensuing firestorm from all quarters, including the president of the United States, brought into focus "stand-your-ground" laws not only in Florida, but also throughout the United States. States and the federal government started to review their "stand-your-ground" laws and how they can be applied in a more balanced way. In April 2014, Florida passed new "warning shot" legislation aimed at protecting those who point a firearm or fire a warning shot at an intruder. Opponents have said this legislation will open up a Pandora's box of legal problems.[44]

STAND-YOUR-GROUND LAWS		
FLORIDA	Florida Statute 776.032	A person who uses force is immune from criminal civil prosecution.
CALIFORNIA	Penal Code 198.5	If someone enters your home, you can presume your life is in danger and can use deadly force. You do not have a duty to retreat.
NEW YORK	Penal Law 35.15	Allows the use of physical force upon another person when they believe it is necessary to defend themselves or another. You cannot use deadly force if you can retreat.
TEXAS	Penal Code Chapter 9	Specifically states there is "no duty to retreat" before using deadly force if the force is justified.

U.S. Supreme Court has consistently ruled that the police must use due process to enter one's home. In *Payton v. New York* (1980), discussed earlier in this chapter, the Court ruled that the police need a warrant to enter a person's home to make a routine arrest absent consent or emergency situations.[45] In *Minnesota v. Olson* (1990), the Supreme Court held that an overnight guest has a sufficient expectation of privacy in a host's dwelling and is entitled to the Fourth Amendment protection against unreasonable searches and seizures.[46] In *Minnesota v. Carter* (1998), however, the Court refused to extend Fourth Amendment protections to a person who is merely present with the consent of the householder.[47]

In 2002, in *Kirk v. Louisiana*, the Court reaffirmed its previous ruling in *Payton* that the police may not enter a person's home without a warrant, unless emergency or exigent circumstances are present. In this case, police had entered Kennedy Kirk's apartment after observing what they believed to be drug purchases therein and then stopping one of the apparent buyers on the street to verify the drug sales. Officers testified that "because the stop took place within a block of the apartment [they] feared that evidence would be destroyed and ordered the apartment be entered." They immediately knocked on the door of the apartment, arrested Kirk, searched him, found a drug vial in his underwear, and then observed contraband in plain view in the apartment. The Court ruled that police officers need either a warrant or probable cause plus exigent circumstances in order to make a lawful entry into a home.[48]

The 2000 U.S. Supreme Court landmark case *Bond v. United States* provides a good example of the meaning of a legal Fourth Amendment search.[49] In this case, Dewayne Bond was a passenger with carry-on luggage on a bus. When the bus stopped at a Border Patrol checkpoint, a Border Patrol agent boarded the bus to check the passengers' immigration status. In an effort to locate illegal drugs, the agent began to squeeze the soft luggage, which some passengers had placed in the overhead storage space above their seats. The agent squeezed the canvas bag above Bond's seat and noticed that it contained a "bricklike" object. Bond admitted that the bag was his and consented to its search. When the agent looked inside the bag, he discovered a brick of methamphetamine. Bond was arrested and then indicted and convicted for federal drug charges. Upon appeal, the Supreme Court reversed the

conviction and ruled that the agent's manipulation of the bag was an unreasonable search that violated the Fourth Amendment. The Court ruled that the agent did in fact conduct a search and that the search was unreasonable because he conducted it without a warrant and the search did not fall under any of the recognized exceptions to the warrant requirement. Although Bond consented to a search of his bag,

YOU ARE THERE *Katz v. United States* (1967)

Justice Potter Stewart delivered the opinion of the Court:

The petitioner was convicted in the District Court of the Southern District of California under an eight-count indictment charging him with transmitting wagering information by telephone from Los Angeles to Miami and Boston, in violation of a federal statute. At trial the Government was permitted, over the petitioner's objection, to introduce evidence of the petitioner's end of telephone conversations, overheard by FBI agents who had attached an electronic listening and recording device to the outside of the public telephone booth from which he had placed his calls. In affirming his conviction, the Court of Appeals rejected the contention that the recordings had been obtained in violation of the Fourth Amendment, because "there was no physical entrance into the area occupied by the petitioner." We granted certiorari in order to consider the constitutional questions....

Wherever a man may be, he is entitled to know that he will remain free from unreasonable searches and seizures. The government agents here ignored "the procedure of antecedent justification" ... that is central to the Fourth Amendment, a procedure that we hold to be a constitutional precondition of the kind of electronic surveillance involved in this case. Because the surveillance here failed to meet that condition, and because it led to the petitioner's conviction, the judgment must be reversed.

It is so ordered.

Source: Based on *Katz v. United States*, 389 U.S. 347 (1967).

his consent was not an issue. The agent's squeezing of Bond's bag was the issue; Bond argued and the Court agreed that the agent's squeezing of his bag was an illegal search that occurred before any consent given by Bond.[50]

In explaining the legality of a search and seizure, the Court's reasoning in *Bond* was that the search was in violation of the Fourth Amendment in that, according to *Katz v. United States* (1967), a search is a government infringement of a person's reasonable expectation of privacy and that a search must be reasonable to comply with the Fourth Amendment. The Court has ruled that any government search conducted without a warrant is per se unreasonable, unless the search falls under a few recognized exceptions to the warrant requirement (for example, consent searches, emergency searches, motor vehicle searches, inventory searches, searches incident to arrest, and the like).[51]

In a more recent case, *Kyllo v. United States* (2001), the Supreme Court again refined its definition of a search. *Kyllo* was a federal drug prosecution that began in 1992, when two federal agents trained a new thermal imaging device, called an Agema Thermovision 210, on a home in Florence, Oregon, where, on the basis of tips and utility bills, they believed marijuana was being grown under high-intensity lamps. Although the thermal imager cannot see through walls, it can detect hot spots and in this case disclosed that part of the roof and a side wall were warmer than the rest of the building and the neighboring houses. The agents used that information to get a warrant to enter and search the home, where they found more than a hundred marijuana plants growing under halide lights. The resident of the home, Danny Kyllo, was arrested. He contested the validity of the search to the U.S. Supreme Court. The government strongly defended use of thermal imagers on the grounds that in detecting heat loss, the devices neither reveal private information nor violate the "reasonable expectation of privacy" that is the Court's test under the Fourth Amendment.

The issue in *Kyllo* was whether the thermal-imaging device aimed at a private home from a public street constituted a search under the Fourth Amendment. The Court ruled that the use of the surveillance device was a search and that a warrant should have been obtained before its use. It further ruled that a warrant would also be necessary before the police could use other new sophisticated devices already available or being developed that let the police gain knowledge that in the past would have been impossible without a physical entry into the home. The Court applied this rule only to homes and did not address warrantless imaging of other locations.[52]

Canine Sniffs

The U.S. Supreme Court has consistently ruled that canine sniffs by a trained drug dog are not actual searches and seizures controlled by the Fourth Amendment. In 1983, in *United States v. Place*, the U.S. Supreme Court ruled that exposure of luggage in a public place to a trained drug canine did not constitute a search within the meaning of the Fourth Amendment.[53] The Court explained that the dog's alert to the presence of drugs created probable cause for the issuance of a search warrant for drugs. It explained that the dog's sniff is nonintrusive and reveals only the presence of contraband. Many cases have ruled that a dog's positive alert alone generally constitutes probable cause to search a vehicle under the motor vehicle exception to the search warrant requirement.[54]

Special Agent Michael J. Bulzomi, a legal instructor at the FBI Academy, writes that drug detection dogs remain extremely important in drug interdiction. They represent a highly efficient and cost-effective way to establish quickly whether probable cause exists to execute a search for contraband. The use of drug detection dogs has met with few real legal challenges in the courts. The only notable area that has been challenged is a dog's reliability. Drug detection dog handlers should be prepared to establish a dog's reliability by providing prosecutors with a complete record of the dog's training, success rate, and certification in drug detection.[55] Jayme S. Walker, in a 2001 article in the *FBI Law Enforcement Bulletin*, provided many examples of court decisions declaring dog sniffs not searches under the Fourth Amendment in cases involving luggage, packages, warehouses or garages, buses, trains, motel rooms, apartments, and homes.[56]

In an extension of *United States v. Place*, the U.S. Supreme Court in *Illinois v. Caballes* (2005) held that a dog sniff of the exterior of an automobile conducted during the course of a lawful vehicle stop is not a search and may be performed without any suspicion that the vehicle's occupants are engaged in criminal activity.[57] In *Illinois v. Caballes*, an Illinois state trooper stopped Caballes for speeding and radioed his stop in to dispatch. A second trooper overheard the radio transmission and drove to the scene with his narcotics-detection dog. While the first trooper was writing Caballes a warning ticket, the second trooper walked the dog around the vehicle. When the dog alerted to the trunk, both officers searched it and found marijuana. Caballes was then arrested and later convicted on drug charges. The U.S. Supreme Court affirmed the conviction, ruling that the use of the narcotics-detection dog to sniff around the exterior of the vehicle did not constitute any additional infringement on Fourth Amendment rights. The Court ruled that in this case, the traffic stop was not extended beyond the time necessary to issue a warning ticket. It ruled that the use of a well-trained dog "does not expose noncontraband items that otherwise would remain hidden from public view."[58]

This ruling was again upheld in 2013 by *Florida v. Harris*, which involved a traffic stop upon a vehicle driven by Harris. During the stop, Harris was very nervous, arousing the suspicions of Officer Wheetley. Subsequently, Wheetley sought consent to search Harris's vehicle. When Harris refused, Wheetley conducted a sniff test with his trained narcotics dog, Aldo. Aldo alerted at the driver's side door handle. Wheetley concluded he had probable cause to search the vehicle and subsequently found pseudoephedrine and other ingredients for manufacturing methamphetamine. While Harris was out on bail, Wheetley made another stop on Harris and conducted a search, finding nothing. During the suppression hearing, the prosecution presented evidence of Aldo's extensive training in drug detection. Harris's attorney did not contest the training, but did focus on Aldo's certification and performance in the field. The trial court denied the motion to suppress; however, the Florida Supreme Court reversed. The U.S. Supreme Court overturned, saying, "Because training and testing records supported Aldo's reliability in detecting drugs and Harris failed to undermine that

Canine sniffs by trained dogs are frequently conducted by law enforcement during car stops, at airports, and at ferry terminals. Here a Washington State Patrol canine unit checks cars waiting to board a Washington State ferry.

Robert Sumner/Getty Images

evidence, Wheetley had probable cause to search Harris's truck."[59]

See Table 13.8 for a list of landmark cases relative to police traffic stops and canine sniffs.

The Warrant Requirement and the Search Warrant

In the United States, the general rule regarding search and seizure is that law enforcement officers obtain a search warrant before any search and seizure. A **search warrant** is an order from a court, issued by a judge, authorizing and directing the police to search a particular place for certain property described in the warrant and directing the police to bring that property to court.

Generally, to get a search warrant, a police officer prepares a typed affidavit applying for the warrant and then personally appears before a judge. The judge reads the application; questions the officer,

search warrant A written order, based on probable cause and signed by a judge, authorizing police to search a specific person, place, or property to obtain evidence.

TABLE 13.8 Landmark U.S. Supreme Court Decisions: Police Traffic Stops and Canine Sniffs

Issue	Cases
Police Traffic Stops	
Routine traffic stops	*Delaware v. Prouse* (1979), *Brendlin v. California* (2007)
Ordering driver out of vehicle	*Pennsylvania v. Mimms* (1977)
Ordering passenger out of vehicle	*Maryland v. Wilson* (1997)
DWI checkpoints	*Michigan Department of State Police v. Sitz* (1990)
Drug checkpoints	*City of Indianapolis v. Edmond* (2000)
Pretext stops	*Whren v. United States* (1996)
Non-DWI or drug checkpoints	*Illinois v. Lidster* (2004)
Use of force to stop vehicle	*Scott v. Harris* (2007)
What is a search?	*Katz v. United States* (1967), *Bond v. United States* (2000), *Kyllo v. United States* (2001)
Canine Sniffs	
Not a search under Fourth Amendment	*United States v. Place* (1983), *Illinois v. Caballes* (2005), *Florida v. Harris* (2013)

© 2016 Cengage Learning®

if necessary; and signs the warrant if in agreement with the officer that there is probable cause that certain property that may be evidence of a crime, proceeds from a crime, or *contraband* (material that is illegal to possess, such as illegal drugs or illegal weapons) is present at a certain place. Usually, a warrant can be executed only during daylight hours and within a certain time period; however, there are many exceptions. Officers executing a warrant generally must announce their presence before entering. At times, judges may add a "no-knock" provision to the warrant, which allows the officers to enter without announcing their presence.[60]

Most searches by police officers are not made with warrants, because they are performed on the street with no time for an officer to proceed to court to obtain a warrant. Most searches are made in accordance with one of the exceptions to the search warrant requirement—situations involving **exigent circumstances** (emergency situations). Exceptions to the warrant requirement will be discussed at length in the next section.

Often, the cases in which search warrants are used are lengthy investigations in which immediate action is not required. Warrants are also often used in organized crime and other conspiracy-type investigations.

One of the major uses of warrants is after an informant provides information to the police that certain people are engaged in continuous illegal acts, such as drug dealing. For example, a man tells the police that a person is a drug dealer and sells the drugs from her house. The police get as much information as they can from the informant and then dispatch a team of plainclothes officers to make undercover observations of the house. The officers do not see actual drug dealing, because it is going on inside the house, but they see certain actions that go along with the drug trade, such as cars stopping at the house and people entering the house for a short time and then leaving and driving away. Based on these observations, the police can then go to court and request that a judge issue a search warrant. If a search warrant is issued, the police can enter and search the house.

....
exigent circumstances One of the major exceptions to the warrant requirement of the Fourth Amendment. Exigency may be defined as "emergency."

The Supreme Court has had several standards by which to determine what evidence would constitute probable cause for a judge to issue a warrant. The first standard was a *two-pronged* test that mandated that the police show (1) why they believed the informant and (2) the circumstances that showed that the informant had personal knowledge of the crime. This standard was articulated in two major Supreme Court cases, *Aguilar v. Texas* (1964) and *Spinelli v. United States* (1969).[61] There were problems with this standard. To show why the police believed the informant and how the informant obtained the information, the police would have to identify the informant or show how the informant was trustworthy in the past, or both. Identifying the informant and describing past tips could put the informant in danger.

In *Illinois v. Gates (1983)*, the Supreme Court reversed the *Aguilar-Spinelli* two-pronged test[62] and replaced it with the *totality of circumstances test*, which holds that an informant can be considered reliable if he or she gives the police sufficient facts to indicate that a crime is being committed and if the police verify these facts.[63]

Illinois v. Gates (1983)

The Bloomingdale (Illinois) Police Department received by mail the following anonymous handwritten letter:

> This letter is to inform you that you have a couple in your town who strictly make their living on selling drugs. They are Sue and Lance Gates, they live on Greenway, off Bloomingdale Rd. in the condominiums. Most of their buys are done in Florida. Sue his wife drives their car to Florida, where she leaves it to be loaded up with drugs, then Lance flys [sic] down and drives it back. Sue flys [sic] back after she drops the car off in Florida. May 3 she is driving down there again and Lance will be flying down in a few days to drive it back. At the time Lance drives the car back he has the trunk loaded with over $100,000.00 in drugs. Presently they have over $100,000.00 worth of drugs in their basement.
>
> They brag about the fact they never have to work, and make their living on pushers. I guarantee if you watch them carefully you will make a big catch. They are friends with some big drugs dealers who visit their house often.

"Lance & Susan Gates"
"Greenway"
"in Condominiums"

Obviously, the *Aguilar-Spinelli* two-pronged test could not apply to this case. The writer was anonymous; the police could not produce the writer and prove his or her reliability.

Based on this letter, however, the police performed the following investigatory actions:

1. They verified the Gateses' address.
2. They obtained information from a confidential informant about Lance Gates.
3. They obtained information from an O'Hare Airport police officer that "L. Gates" had made a reservation on Eastern Airlines to West Palm Beach, Florida, departing Chicago on May 5 at 4:15 p.m.
4. They arranged for the Drug Enforcement Administration to conduct a surveillance of the May 5 Eastern Airlines flight.

The surveillance resulted in the information that Lance Gates arrived in West Palm Beach and went to a Holiday Inn room registered to one Susan Gates, as well as other information verifying the information in the letter. A judge issued a search warrant for the Gateses' apartment and automobile. Using the warrant, the police seized approximately 350 pounds of marijuana, weapons, and other contraband.

The Gateses were arrested and indicted for violation of state drug laws. The evidence, however, was suppressed in a pretrial motion, as the judge ruled that the affidavit submitted in support of the application for the warrant was inadequate under the *Aguilar-Spinelli* standard. Upon appeal, the U.S. Supreme Court replaced the *Aguilar-Spinelli* standard with the totality of circumstances standard.

Source: Based on *Illinois v. Gates*, 462 U.S. 213 (1983).

In *Michigan v. Summers* (1981), the Supreme Court ruled that officers serving a search warrant for drugs can detain the occupants of the premises during their search to prevent their flight in the event that incriminating evidence is found, to minimize the risk of harm to the officers, and to facilitate the search because the occupants' "self-interest may induce them to open locked doors or locked containers." The court ruled that a warrant to search for contraband carries with it the limited authority to detain occupants of the premises while a search is conducted.[64]

In *Muehler v. Mena* (2005), the Court expanded on *Summers*, concluding that an officer's authority to detain occupants incident to the execution of a search warrant for contraband or evidence was absolute and unqualified and did not require any justification beyond the warrant itself. In this case, police in California obtained a warrant in connection with a drive-by shooting to search a suspected gang member's house for weapons, ammunition, and gang paraphernalia. Because of the high-risk nature of the case, a police special weapons and tactics (SWAT) team made the initial entry. Four occupants, including Iris Mena, were handcuffed at gunpoint and taken to a garage on the premises, where they were detained for the two to three hours it took to finish the search. Mena brought a civil action against officers, alleging a violation of her Fourth Amendment rights. The Supreme Court rejected the civil action.[65]

In 2007, in *Los Angeles County, California v. Rettele*, the Supreme Court held that law enforcement officers acted reasonably while executing a search warrant for a residence when they ordered the naked residents out of their bed and held them at gunpoint for one to two minutes while they verified that no weapons were present and that other persons were not close by.[66] The Court wrote:

> The orders by the police to the occupants, in the context of this lawful search, were permissible, perhaps necessary, to protect the safety of deputies.... The deputies needed a moment to secure the room and ensure that other persons close by did not present a danger. Deputies were not required to turn their backs to allow [the plaintiffs] to retrieve clothing or to cover themselves with sheets. Rather, the "risk of harm to both the police and occupants is minimized if the officers routinely exercise unquestioned command of the situation."[67]

In *United States v. Banks* (2003), the U.S. Supreme Court provided guidance to law enforcement officers in assessing how much time they are required to wait prior to making a forcible entry after knocking and announcing their presence and demanding entry in a warrant case.[68] In this case, officers obtained a search warrant based on information that cocaine was being sold from an apartment. Officers at the front door of the apartment knocked and announced loudly enough to be heard by officers located in the back. After waiting 15 to 20 seconds with no response, officers forcibly entered the apartment using a battering ram. They encountered the defendant walking out of the shower after he heard them enter. Evidence of drug dealing was found during the search, which the defendant sought to suppress, arguing that the officers failed to wait a reasonable time before the forcible entry. The federal Ninth Circuit Court of Appeals agreed with the defendant and suppressed the evidence. The U.S. Supreme Court, however, on appeal, rejected the appellate court's decision and reallowed the evidence, ruling that the delay of 15 to 20 seconds in *Banks* was sufficient given that a reasonably objective law enforcement officer could conclude that the danger of disposal of the drugs had ripened.

In 2006, in what some saw as a controversial decision, the Court, in *Hudson v. Michigan*, ruled that violation of the common law principle that law enforcement officers must announce their presence and provide residents an opportunity to open a door (knock-and-announce rule) does not require the suppression of evidence found in a search (exclusionary rule). In this case, Detroit police were executing a search warrant for narcotics and weapons and entered Booker T. Hudson's home. When the police arrived to execute the warrant, they announced their presence, but waited only a short time—perhaps "three to five seconds"—before turning the knob of the unlocked front door and entering Hudson's home. They discovered large quantities of drugs, including cocaine rocks in Hudson's pocket, and a loaded gun lodged between the cushion and armrest of the chair in which he was sitting.[69] In the Court's decision, Justice Antonin Scalia wrote,

> The social costs of applying the exclusion rule to knock-and-announce violations are considerable; the incentive to such violations is minimal to begin with, and the extant deterrences against them are substantial—comparably

greater than the factors deterring warrantless entries when *Mapp* was decided. Resort to the massive remedy of suppressing evidence of guilt is unjustified.[70]

In 2006, in *United States v. Grubbs*, the U.S. Supreme Court ruled that "anticipatory" search warrants, which are issued in advance of a "triggering condition" that makes them executable, are constitutional.[71] In this case, Jeffrey Grubbs became the subject of an undercover federal investigation and prosecution when he ordered a videotape containing child pornography from a website operated by an undercover U.S. postal inspector. The U.S. Postal Inspection Service then arranged a controlled delivery of the tape to Grubbs and obtained an *anticipatory search warrant* (so called because it is based upon the probable cause that at some time in the future certain evidence of a crime will be located at a specified place—a "triggering condition"). Two days later, the undercover delivery occurred and Grubb's house was searched after the tape was taken inside. The videotape and other items were seized and Grubbs was arrested. Grubbs moved to suppress the evidence seized during the search, arguing that the warrant was invalid because it failed to list the triggering condition. The U.S. Court of Appeals for the Ninth Circuit agreed with Grubbs's motion and declared that the search was illegal. The Supreme Court reversed the Court of Appeals and declared that the warrant and the ensuing search and seizure were valid and constitutional, since they were based upon an affidavit showing probable cause that at some future time certain evidence of a crime would be located at a specific place.

See Table 13.9 for a list of landmark cases regarding search warrants.

Exceptions to the Warrant Requirement

Many exigent circumstances arise in which the police cannot be expected to travel to court to obtain a search warrant. The evidence might be destroyed by a suspect, the suspect might get away, or an officer might be injured. The following are the major exceptions to the search warrant requirement and the rules established by the Supreme Court that govern these exceptions.

INCIDENT TO LAWFUL ARREST In *Chimel v. California* (1969), the U.S. Supreme Court established guidelines regarding searches at the time of arrest.[72] In this case, the Court ruled that incident to (at the time of) an arrest, the police may search the defendant and only that area immediately surrounding the defendant for the purpose of preventing injury to the officer and the destruction of evidence. This has become known as the "arm's reach doctrine."

TABLE 13.9 Landmark U.S. Supreme Court Decisions: Search Warrants

Issue	Cases
Two-pronged test	*Aguilar v. Texas* (1964), *Spinelli v. United States* (1969)
Totality of circumstances test	*Illinois v. Gates* (1983)
Time to wait before forcible entry	*United States v. Banks* (2003)
Authority to detain, handcuff, question	*Muehler v. Mena* (2005), *Los Angeles County, California v. Rettele* (2007)
Can detain occupants during search	*Michigan v. Summers* (1981), *Illinois v. McArthur* (2001)
Need warrant to enter home to arrest	*Payton v. New York* (1980), *Minnesota v. Olson* (1990), *Kirk v. Illinois* (2002)
Violation of knock-and-announce rule does not require suppression of evidence	*Hudson v. Michigan* (2006)
Anticipatory search warrants	*United States v. Grubbs* (2006)

On September 13, 1965, three police officers from the Santa Ana, California, Police Department arrived at Ted Chimel's house with a warrant to arrest him for the burglary of a coin shop. The police showed Chimel the arrest warrant and asked him if they could "look around." Chimel objected, but the officers told him they could search the house on the basis of the lawful arrest. The officers then searched the entire three-bedroom house for 45 minutes. They seized numerous items, including some coins. The coins were admitted into evidence, and Chimel was convicted at trial of burglary.

Upon appeal, the U.S. Supreme Court ruled that the warrantless search of Chimel's home was a violation of his constitutional rights. The Court thus established the "arm's reach doctrine."

In 1973, in *United States v. Robinson*, the Court ruled that because a probable cause arrest is a reasonable Fourth Amendment intrusion, a search incident to that arrest requires no additional justification.[73]

In *Knowles v. Iowa* (1998), the Supreme Court considered the application of the right of the warrantless search incident to arrest to the search of a motor vehicle stopped by the police incident to a traffic citation. Patrick Knowles was stopped for speeding by a police officer in Newton, Iowa. The officer issued Knowles a citation and then conducted a thorough search of Knowles's car without his consent, found a bag of marijuana and a "pot pipe," and arrested and charged Knowles with violation of the controlled substances statutes. The Court ruled that when the police officer stopped Knowles, he had probable cause to believe Knowles had violated traffic laws. He could have arrested Knowles for that violation, but chose instead to issue a citation. The Court ruled that the search incident to an arrest exception does not apply to a traffic citation.[74]

In an interesting 2007 article, FBI Special Agent Michael J. Bulzomi discussed the seizure of personal electronics articles, such as pagers and cellular telephones, under the context of the "incident to arrest" exception to the Fourth Amendment.[75] He cited two cases determined by lower courts that found that the seizure of these electronic articles incident to arrest and the activation of them were constitutional.[76]

FIELD INTERROGATIONS (STOP AND FRISK)

In 1968, the Supreme Court established the standard for allowing police officers to perform a **stop and frisk** (pat down) of a suspect in *Terry v. Ohio*.[77] A stop and frisk is the detaining of a person by a law enforcement officer for the purpose of investigation (**field interrogation**), accompanied by a superficial examination by the officer of the person's body surface or clothing to discover weapons, contraband, or other objects relating to criminal activity. In *Terry v. Ohio*, the Court ruled that a police officer can stop a person in a public place to make reasonable inquiries about the person's conduct. It ruled that when the following five conditions exist, a police officer is justified in patting down, or frisking, a suspect:

1. Where a police officer observes unusual conduct which leads him reasonably to conclude in light of his experience that criminal activity may be afoot ...

2. ... and that the person with whom he is dealing may be armed and dangerous ...

3. ... where in the course of investigating this behavior he identifies himself as a policeman ...

4. ... and makes reasonable inquiry ...

5. ... and where nothing in the initial stages of the encounter serves to dispel his reasonable fear for his own or other's safety ... he is entitled to conduct a carefully limited search of the outer clothing of such persons in an attempt to discover weapons which might be used to assault him. Such search is a reasonable search under the Fourth Amendment and any weapons seized may properly be introduced in evidence against the person from whom they were taken.[78]

The New York City Police Department (NYPD) implemented the practice of increased stop-and-frisk encounters in high-crime areas of the city with the goal of reducing crime. In the second quarter of 2012, police recovered 1,769 weapons. During this same time period, the police department made 34 percent fewer stop-and-frisk encounters compared to the first quarter of 2012. Police Commissioner Raymond Kelly attributed this decline to additional training and oversight, and also to the assignment of fewer rookie officers in those zones most affected by the practice.

stop and frisk The detaining of a person by law enforcement officers for the purpose of investigation, accompanied by a superficial examination of the person's body surface or clothing to discover weapons, contraband, or other objects relating to criminal activity.

field interrogation Unplanned questioning of an individual who has aroused the suspicions of an officer.

Donna Lieberman, the executive director of the New York Civil Liberties Union, said the numbers were "encouraging" but they failed to show the number of innocent people stopped.[79] This practice has come under fire; in a 2008 lawsuit filed in federal court, Vincent Warren, director of the Center for Constitutional Rights, said, "We're putting the NYPD on trial, and the stakes are the constitutional rights of hundreds of thousands of New Yorkers."[80]

In *Hiibel v. Sixth Judicial District Court of Nevada, Humboldt County* (2004), the Supreme Court approved a state statute requiring individuals to identify themselves as part of an investigative detention or field interrogation, ruling that it was not a violation of the Fourth or Fifth Amendment.[81] In this case, a deputy sheriff responding to a call reporting an assault lawfully detained a man, who later turned out to be Hiibel, based on reasonable suspicion of his involvement in the crime. After numerous attempts to determine the man's identity, the deputy arrested him for failing to identify himself during an investigative detention pursuant to Nevada's stop and identify statute. Hiibel was convicted and appealed, challenging the constitutionality of the statute. The Supreme Court rejected Hiibel's appeal and ruled that if a stop is justified at its inception (based on reasonable suspicion) and the request for identity is reasonably related to the purpose of the stop, it is justified.

In 1993, in *Minnesota v. Dickerson*, the Court placed new limits on an officer's ability to seize evidence discovered during a pat-down search conducted for protective reasons when the search itself is based merely upon suspicion and fails to immediately reveal the presence of a weapon.[82] In this case, Timothy Dickerson was stopped by Minneapolis police after they noticed him acting suspiciously while leaving a building known for cocaine trafficking. The officers decided to investigate and ordered Dickerson to submit to a pat-down search. One of the officers testified that he felt no weapon but did feel a small lump in Dickerson's jacket pocket, which he believed to be a lump of cocaine upon examining it with his fingers. Dickerson was arrested and convicted of drug possession. Upon appeal, the U.S. Supreme Court ruled that the search was illegal, saying, "While *Terry* entitled [the officer] to place his hands on the respondent's jacket and to feel the lump in his pocket, his continued exploration of the pocket after he concluded that it contained no weapons was unrelated to the sole justification for the search under *Terry*."

YOU ARE THERE

Terry v. Ohio (1968)

Detective Martin McFadden, a veteran of the Cleveland Police Department's robbery squad, was on routine stakeout duty in a Cleveland downtown shopping district when he observed two men acting suspiciously on the street in the vicinity of Huron Road and Euclid Avenue. One of the suspects looked furtively into a store, walked on, returned to look at the same store, and then joined a companion. The companion, another male, then went to the store, looked in it, and then rejoined his companion. The two men continually repeated these actions and looked into the store numerous times. The two men then met with a third man.

McFadden suspected that the males were casing the store for a stickup and believed that they were armed. He approached the three men, identified himself as a police officer, and asked the men their names. The men mumbled something, whereupon McFadden frisked them, or ran his hands over their outer clothing. His frisk and subsequent search revealed that one of the men, Terry, was in possession of a gun. Another frisk and subsequent search revealed that one of his companions, Richard Chilton, also had a gun.

Terry and Chilton were arrested for possession of a gun and were convicted. Upon appeal, the Supreme Court ruled that McFadden's actions were constitutional.

Source: Based on *Terry v. Ohio*, 392 U.S. 1 (1968).

In *Illinois v. Wardlow* (2000), the Court held that a police officer's initial stop of a suspect was supported by reasonable suspicion if the suspect both was present in an area of expected criminal activity and fled upon seeing the police.[83] In this case, two police officers were investigating drug transactions while driving in an area known for heavy drug trafficking. They noticed Wardlow holding a bag. When Wardlow saw the officers, he fled. The officers pursued and stopped him. One of the officers conducted a protective pat-down search for weapons because, in his experience, it was common for weapons to be in the vicinity of drug transactions. During the pat down, the officers squeezed Wardlow's bag and felt a heavy, hard object in the shape of a gun. When the officer opened the bag, he did in fact discover a handgun with ammunition. Wardlow was arrested.

Upon appeal that the arrest was illegal because the officers did not perform a lawful stop and frisk, the Court held that the initial stop was reasonable and supported by reasonable suspicion, and cited *Terry v. Ohio:* "Under *Terry*, an officer may, consistent with the Fourth Amendment, conduct a brief, investigatory stop when the officer has a reasonable, articulable suspicion that criminal activity is afoot."[84] Thus, in *Wardlow*, the Court ruled that several factors can be used to determine whether an officer has reasonable suspicion to make a **Terry stop**, including (1) whether the stop occurred in a high-crime area; (2) a suspect's nervous, evasive behavior; and (3) a suspect's unprovoked flight upon noticing the police.[85]

Regarding field interrogations and anonymous tips to the police, the Supreme Court has ruled that if an officer is relying on an anonymous tip to make a *Terry* stop, then the tip must be sufficiently reliable to provide the officer with reasonable suspicion to make the stop. Generally, an anonymous tip alone is not sufficiently reliable. The Court explained that an anonymous tip that is suitably corroborated may be sufficiently reliable to provide the officer with reasonable suspicion to make a *Terry* stop, considering two factors: (1) what the officers knew—either by their own observations, their experience, or prior knowledge of the suspect or area—before they conducted their stop; and (2) whether the anonymous tip showed that the informant had predicted accurately the suspect's movements or had knowledge of concealed criminal activity. A tip that merely identifies a specific person is not reliable enough to show knowledge of concealed criminal activity.

In *Florida v. J. L.* (2000), the Court held that an anonymous tip that a person is carrying a gun, without more information, does not justify a police officer's stop and frisk of that person. In this case, an anonymous caller reported to the police that a young black man standing at a particular bus stop and wearing a plaid shirt was carrying a gun. There was no audio recording of the tip and nothing was known about the informant. Officers went to the bus stop and saw three black men. One of the men, J. L., was wearing a plaid shirt. Aside from the tip, the officers had no reason to suspect the three of illegal conduct. The officers did not see a firearm or observe any unusual movements. One of the officers frisked J. L. and seized a gun from his pocket.[86]

EXIGENT CIRCUMSTANCES Although the general rule on searches within a home without a warrant is that they are presumptively unreasonable, the Supreme Court has established a few narrowly crafted exceptions to the warrant requirement.[87] These exceptions allow the police to act when "the public interest requires some flexibility in the application of the general rule that a valid warrant is a prerequisite for a search."[88] The Court has recognized the following "exigent" or emergency circumstances as those in which there is insufficient time to obtain a search warrant:

1. To prevent escape
2. To prevent harm to the officers or others
3. To prevent the destruction of evidence
4. While in hot pursuit of a criminal suspect
5. To render immediate aid to a person in need of assistance[89]

As some examples, in *Warden v. Hayden* (1967), the Court approved the warrantless search of a residence after receiving reports that an armed robber had fled into a building;[90] in *Mincey v. Arizona* (1978), the Court held that the Fourth Amendment does not require police officers to delay an investigation if to do so would gravely endanger their lives or others;[91] in 1990, in *Maryland v. Buie*, the Court extended the warrantless authority of police to search locations in a house (protective sweep) where a potentially dangerous person could hide while an arrest warrant is being served;[92] and in *Wilson v. Arkansas* (1995), the Court ruled that officers need not announce themselves while executing a warrant if evidence may be destroyed, officers are pursuing a recently escaped arrestee, or officers' lives may be endangered.[93] Also, in 2001, in *Illinois v. McArthur*, the Court ruled that officers with probable cause to believe that a home contains contraband or evidence of criminal activity may reasonably prevent a suspect found outside the home from reentering it while they apply for a search warrant.[94]

Terry stop Based on the U.S. Supreme Court decision in *Terry v. Ohio*, the standard for allowing police officers to perform a stop and frisk (pat down) of a suspect.

A call to 911, even an anonymous one, is an example of a possible exigent circumstance. In these situations, however, to make a lawful warrantless, nonconsensual entry and search to render aid, (1) the police must reasonably believe that an emergency situation exists requiring immediate police intervention, (2) the search must not be motivated primarily by intent to arrest and seize evidence, and (3) there must be some reasonable basis, approximating probable cause, to associate the emergency with the area or place to be searched. Michael L. Ciminelli, in a 2003 *FBI Law Enforcement Bulletin*, while acknowledging that officers should not hesitate to act reasonably to preserve life and protect others in a potentially dangerous situation, says officers can use the following guidelines to help support the legal justification to enter a home when answering an anonymous 911 call:

- Take reasonable steps to identify the caller before making the entry if circumstances permit; however, in certain cases—for example, screams for help, sounds of a struggle, or shots fired—this may not always be possible.

- Where safe and feasible, take reasonable steps to investigate and corroborate the anonymous call before acting by speaking to neighbors and other persons in the vicinity.

- Where safe and feasible, attempt to obtain a valid consent to enter.

- Accurately document the information given by the anonymous caller.

- Accurately document conditions found at the scene that may corroborate the anonymous call.[95]

In 2006, in *Brigham City v. Stuart*, the Supreme Court issued another significant decision regarding exigent circumstances.[96] In this case, police officers responded to a call reporting a loud party occurring at a residence. Upon arriving at the scene, the officers heard shouting and what sounded like an altercation from inside the house. The officers looked in the front window of the house and saw nothing. They then walked around to the back and saw two juveniles drinking in the backyard. They also were able to see, through a back screen door, four adults struggling with and punching a juvenile. An officer opened the door and brought the situation under control. The occupants of the house were eventually arrested for intoxication, disorderly conduct,

and contributing to the delinquency of a minor. The defendants filed a motion to suppress the evidence the officers found while inside the residence, arguing that the officers' initial entry into the residence violated the Fourth Amendment prohibition against unreasonable searches and seizures. The motion was granted and the evidence was suppressed. Upon appeal to the Supreme Court, the Court rejected the defendants' motion and ruled that the ongoing violence the officers observed was serious enough to justify the warrantless entry. The Court wrote:

> Nothing in the Fourth Amendment required them to wait until another blow rendered someone "unconscious" or "semi-conscious" or worse before entering. The role of a peace officer includes preventing violence and restoring order, not simply rendering first aid to casualties; an officer is not like a boxing (or hockey) referee, poised to stop a bout only if it becomes too one-sided.[97]

CONSENT SEARCHES   A police officer can also search without a warrant if consent is given by a person having authority to give such consent. Consent searches have some limitations. The request cannot be phrased as a command or a threat; it must be a genuine request for permission. The police must receive an oral reply; a nod of the head is not consent. Also, the search must be limited to the area for which consent is given.[98] The following cases represent some of the most important consent search decisions made by the Supreme Court.

In *Schneckloth v. Bustamonte* (1973), the Supreme Court ruled that a search conducted pursuant to lawfully given consent is an exception to the warrant and probable cause requirements of the Fourth Amendment; however, because a consensual search is still a search, the Fourth Amendment reasonableness requirement still applies. The Court ruled that to determine whether an individual voluntarily consented to a search, the reviewing court should consider the totality of the circumstances surrounding the consent.[99]

In *United States v. Matlock* (1974), the Court ruled that for a consent search to be constitutionally valid, the consent must be voluntarily given by a person with proper authority. In this case, the Court ruled that a person sharing a room with another person had the authority to allow the police to search the room.[100]

An example of a search that was considered unconstitutional occurred in *Bumper v. North Carolina* (1968), in which the police searched a defendant's house by getting the permission of the defendant's grandmother, who also occupied the house.[101] To acquire the grandmother's permission, the police told her that they had a lawful search warrant, which they actually did not have. During the search, the officers found a gun in the house, which was used as evidence in a rape case against the defendant, Bumper. The Court ruled that the government has the burden of proving that an individual voluntarily consented to the search and, in this case, the government did not. The Court ruled that the officers' assertion that they had a search warrant was "coercive—albeit colorably lawful coercion," and the gun was suppressed as evidence.

In 1990, in *Illinois v. Rodriguez*, the Court declared constitutional the actions of the police in entering the defendant's Chicago apartment with his former girlfriend's consent and key after she claimed he had seriously assaulted her.[102] Upon entry, the police found the defendant, Rodriguez, and a quantity of cocaine and drug paraphernalia. Rodriguez's claim that his former girlfriend had no control over the apartment since she had moved out at least a month earlier did not sway the Court.

In 1991, in *Florida v. Bostick*, the Supreme Court reinterpreted consent searches by ruling that police requests to a person to look into his or her luggage do not require that the officer have reasonable suspicion that the person is violating the law.[103]

The Supreme Court also has established a "consent once removed" exception to the search warrant requirement. Under that exception, officers are permitted to make a warrantless entry to arrest a suspect based on the consent to enter given earlier to an undercover officer or informant.[104] An example is the 2000 case of *United States v. Pollard*, in which an informant and an undercover officer entered a residence to purchase four kilograms of cocaine. Upon seeing the cocaine in the apartment, the informant gave the arrest signal. In response to the arrest signal, approximately six officers, without knocking or announcing, immediately broke down the front door and arrested the defendants. The U.S. Court of Appeals for the Sixth Circuit ruled that the entry by the backup officers to arrest the defendants was lawful under the consent once removed doctrine. The court found that once the defendants gave the undercover officer and the informant permission to enter, the entry by the arrest team did not create any further invasion of privacy.[105]

In 2006, the Court ruled in *Georgia v. Randolph* that consent to search a residence was not constitutional when one co-occupant, who was present at the time, refused to consent.[106] This case was substantially different from *United States v. Matlock* (1974) and *Illinois v. Rodriguez* (1990) because in those two cases the co-occupants were not present.[107]

In February 2014, the U.S. Supreme Court's decision in *Fernandez v. California* brought clarity to *Georgia v. Randolph*.[108] *Fernandez v. California* involved police responding to a violent robbery, where a suspect was seen by police running into an apartment building. Police heard screams come from one of the apartments. Officers knocked on the apartment door, which was answered by Roxanne Rojas, who appeared to be the victim of domestic violence. When the officers asked Rojas to step out of the apartment to conduct a protective sweep, Walter Fernandez came to the door and objected to the entry. Suspecting that Fernandez was responsible for the domestic violence, the officers removed him from the apartment. He was later identified as the suspect in the robbery. An officer returned later to Rojas's apartment, obtained written and verbal consent to search the apartment, and found several items linking Fernandez to the robbery. Fernandez's motion to suppress was denied because Fernandez was not present when Rojas gave consent to search the apartment. *Georgia v. Randolph* did not apply. The 6–3 decision delivered by Chief Justice Roberts held that *Randolph* does not extend to this situation, where Rojas's consent was provided well after Fernandez had been removed from their apartment. Justice Ginsburg in her dissent said, "This case calls for a straightforward application of *Randolph*."[109]

See Table 13.10 for a list of landmark cases regarding exceptions to the warrant requirement.

PLAIN VIEW Plain view evidence is unconcealed evidence inadvertently seen by an officer engaged in a lawful activity. If an officer is at a location legally

---

plain view evidence Evidence seized by police without a warrant who have the right to be in a position to observe it.

TABLE 13.10   Landmark U.S. Supreme Court Decisions: Exceptions to the Warrant Requirement in Police Search and Seizure Cases

Issue	Cases
Abandoned property	*Abel v. United States* (1960), *California v. Greenwood* (1988), *California v. Hodari, D.* (1991)
Automobile exception	*Carroll v. United States* (1925), *New York v. Belton* (1981), *Arizona v. Gant* (2009)
Border searches	*United States v. Martinez-Fuerte* (1976)
Buses	*Florida v. Bostick* (1991)
Computer error	*Arizona v. Evans* (1995)
Consent	*Bumper v. North Carolina* (1968), *Schneckloth v. Bustamonte* (1973), *United States v. Matlock* (1974), *Illinois v. Rodriguez* (1990), *United States v. Pollard* (2000), *Georgia v. Randolph* (2006), *Fernandez v. California* (2014)
Exigent circumstances	*Warden v. Hayden* (1967), *Mincey v. Arizona* (1978), *Wilson v. Arkansas* (1995), *Bond v. United States* (2000), *Illinois v. McArthur* (2001), *Kirk v. Louisiana* (2002), *Brigham City v. Stuart* (2006)
Good faith	*Massachusetts v. Sheppard* (1984), *United States v. Leon* (1984), *Illinois v. Krull* (1987), *Maryland v. Garrison* (1987), *Groh v. Ramirez* (2004)
Incident to arrest	*Chimel v. California* (1969), *United States v. Robinson* (1973), *Knowles v. Iowa* (1998)
Inventory	*Colorado v. Bertine* (1987)
Motor homes	*California v. Carney* (1985)
Open fields	*Hester v. United States* (1924), *Oliver v. United States* (1984), *California v. Ciraola* (1986), *Florida v. Riley* (1989)
Plain view	*Coolidge v. New Hampshire* (1971), *Harris v. New York* (1971), *Arizona v. Hicks* (1987)
Protective sweep	*Maryland v. Buie* (1990)
Stop and frisk, field interrogations	*Terry v. Ohio* (1968), *Minnesota v. Dickerson* (1993), *Illinois v. Wardlow* (2000), *Florida v. J. L.* (2000), *Hiibel v. Sixth Judicial District Court of Nevada, Humboldt County* (2004)
Suspicionless search of parolee	*Samson v. California* (2006)
Watercraft	*United States v. Villamonte-Marquez* (1983)

© 2016 Cengage Learning®

doing police work and observes contraband or other plain view evidence, its seizure without a warrant is legal, according to the U.S. Supreme Court in *Harris v. United States* (1968).[110] In *Arizona v. Hicks* (1987), the Court ruled that the evidence must indeed be in plain view without the police moving or dislodging objects to view the evidence.[111]

Many people think that there is a **crime scene** exception to the search warrant. This is not so. In *Mincey v. Arizona* (1978), the Court refused to recognize a crime scene search as one of the

crime scene The location where a crime occurred.

well-delineated exceptions to the search warrant requirement. As a result, crime scenes are given no special consideration under the Fourth Amendment. If a crime occurs in an area where there is a reasonable expectation of privacy, law enforcement officers are compelled to obtain a search warrant before the crime scene search.[112] To obtain a valid search warrant, officers must meet two critical requirements of the Fourth Amendment. First, they must establish probable cause to believe that the location contains evidence of a crime, and second, they must particularly describe that evidence. It is very simple to justify the granting of a search warrant for a crime scene because by its very nature a crime scene establishes the probable cause for obtaining the warrant. Descriptions of the evidence believed to be present at the scene are generally relatively generic, such as blood, a weapon, and the like.[113]

Yet, despite the general requirement to obtain a search warrant, it is very common that most crime scenes do not permit the police sufficient time to obtain a search warrant before making initial entries onto the scene. Consequently, officers are forced to rely on exceptions to the warrant requirement to justify these searches. The most common justifications in these cases are consent, emergencies (exigent circumstances), public place, and plain view.

The consent exception can apply to many crime scenes because often the person who has summoned the police to the scene is someone who can consent to the search. However, for the crime scene search to be constitutional, consent must be given voluntarily by a person reasonably believed by law enforcement officers to have lawful access and control over the premises.[114]

The emergency exception also applies to many crime scenes. Traditionally, courts have recognized three different types of emergencies: threats to life or safety, destruction or removal of evidence, and escape. It is indeed difficult to imagine a crime scene that would not automatically present officers with the necessary belief that at least one of these exigent circumstances exists. However, once officers are inside the premises and have done whatever is necessary to resolve the emergency, the emergency is over. The officers must have a warrant or one of the other exceptions to the warrant requirement must exist for officers to either remain on the premises or continue their search.

Although officers cannot conduct a full-scale search of a crime scene under the emergency exception, there are certain investigative steps that may lead to the discovery of evidence that fall well within its scope. For instance, officers arriving on the scene of a violent crime unquestionably can sweep the premises in an effort to locate other victims or the suspect if they reasonably suspect that either is present. If a body is found at the scene, taking the medical examiner to view and collect the body is deemed a reasonable step. If officers have probable cause to believe a crime scene contains evidence that will be destroyed if not quickly recovered, that evidence may be retrieved as part of the emergency. Officers also may secure doors and control people on the premises to guarantee that the scene is not contaminated. Finally, if the crime scene is in a public place or evidence is in plain view, a warrant is not required.[115]

ABANDONED PROPERTY   In *Abel v. United States* (1960), the U.S. Supreme Court established a standard regarding police searches of abandoned property.[116] A hotel manager gave an FBI agent permission to search a hotel room that had been previously occupied by Rudolf Abel. The agent found incriminating evidence in a wastepaper basket. Abel was arrested and convicted based on this evidence. On appeal to the U.S. Supreme Court, the Court ruled that once Abel vacated the room, the hotel had the right to give law enforcement agents permission to search it.

In *California v. Greenwood* (1988), the Supreme Court extended the abandoned property rule to include garbage left at the curb.[117] In this case, the police in Laguna Beach, California, received information from an informant that Billy Greenwood was engaged in drug dealing from his house. They made observations of the house and found numerous cars stopping there at night. The drivers would exit their cars, enter the house for a short time, and then leave. The police arranged with the local garbage collector to pick up Greenwood's trash, which he left in brown plastic bags in front of his house, and to take it to the station house. The police searched the garbage and found evidence indicating a drug business, including razor blades, straws with cocaine residue, and discarded telephone bills with numerous calls to people who had police records for drug possession. Using this evidence, the police obtained a search warrant.

When they executed the warrant, they found hashish and cocaine, and arrested Greenwood.

The U.S. Supreme Court ruled that searches of a person's discarded garbage are not violations of the Fourth Amendment. Speaking for the Court, Justice Byron White stated, "It is common knowledge that garbage bags left on or at the side of a public street are readily accessible to animals, children, scavengers, snoops and other members of the public. Requiring police to seek warrants before searching such refuse would therefore be inappropriate."

In 1991, in *California v. Hodari, D.*, the Court ruled the police acted properly in arresting a defendant who fled from the police and threw away (abandoned) evidence as he retreated.[118] In this case, a group of youths in Oakland, California, fled when they saw the approach of two police officers. The officers retrieved a rock of crack cocaine thrown away by one of the youths.

INVENTORY In *Colorado v. Bertine*, the Supreme Court ruled in 1987 that the police may enter a defendant's automobile that they have impounded for safekeeping and are planning to return to the defendant after initial police and court processing, and may inventory its contents without a warrant, to ensure that all contents have been accounted for.[119] In this case, Bertine had been arrested for driving while intoxicated. Upon making an inventory of his van's contents, the police found canisters of drugs. Bertine was additionally charged with violation of the drug laws. The Supreme Court ruled that the police action did not violate Bertine's constitutional rights.

OPEN FIELDS In *Hester v. United States* (1924), the Supreme Court established an "open fields exception" to the warrant requirement.[120] The Court said that fields not immediately surrounding a home do not have the protection of the Fourth Amendment and that no warrant is required to enter them and search. Justice Oliver Wendell Holmes, Jr., speaking for the Court, wrote:

The special protection accorded by the Fourth Amendment to the people in their "persons, houses, papers, and effects," is not extended to the open fields. The distinction between the latter and the house is as old as the common law.

In *Oliver v. United States* (1984), the Supreme Court was asked to reexamine its open fields exception under the following circumstances:

Acting on reports that marijuana was being raised on the farm of petitioner Oliver, two narcotics agents of the Kentucky State Police went to the farm to investigate. Arriving at the farm they drove past petitioner's house to a locked gate with a "No Trespassing" sign.... The officers found a field of marijuana over a mile from petitioner's house.[121]

Speaking for the Court, and reaffirming the open fields exception, Justice Lewis F. Powell, Jr., wrote the following: "We conclude that the open fields doctrine, as enunciated in *Hester*, is consistent with the plain language of the Fourth Amendment and its historical purpose."

Two additional cases in the 1980s expanded the power of the police to watch over citizens without a warrant. In 1986, in *California v. Ciraola*, the Court ruled on the actions of the police who had received a tip that marijuana was growing in the defendant Ciraola's backyard.[122] The backyard was surrounded by fences, one of which was 10 feet high. Police flew over the yard in a private plane at an altitude of 1,000 feet in an effort to verify the tip. On the basis of their observations, the police were able to secure and execute a search warrant, which resulted in the seizure of marijuana. Ciraola was convicted on the drug charges, and on appeal, the Court ruled that the police actions were constitutional.

In 1989, in *Florida v. Riley*, the police flew a helicopter 400 feet over a greenhouse in which Riley and his associates were growing marijuana plants.[123] Based on their observations, the police arrested Riley on drug charges. On appeal, the Court ruled that the police did not need a search warrant to conduct such a low-altitude helicopter search of private property because the flight was within airspace legally available to helicopters under federal regulations.

THE AUTOMOBILE EXCEPTION Many students complain about the actions of police officers who search their automobiles. "Don't we have Fourth Amendment rights when we are in our cars?" they ask. "Yes," the professor answers, "but fewer than in your house."

The automobile exception to the search warrant requirement goes all the way back to *Carroll v. United States* in 1925.[124] In this case, the Supreme Court ruled that distinctions should be made between searches of automobiles, persons, and homes, and that a warrantless search of a vehicle, which can be readily moved, is valid if the police have probable cause to believe that the car contains evidence they are seeking. This decision has become known as the **Carroll doctrine**.[125]

In 1981, in *New York v. Belton*, the Supreme Court ruled that a search incident to a lawful arrest of the occupant of an automobile can extend to the entire passenger compartment of the automobile, including luggage boxes or clothing found in it and the glove compartment.[126] This extended the *Chimel* "arm's reach doctrine" in the case of automobiles. In 1983, in *United States v. Villamonte-Marquez*, the Court extended the *Carroll* doctrine to include watercraft; and in 1985, in *California v. Carney*, it extended the doctrine to include motor homes.[127]

In 2009, however, 28 years after the *Belton* decision, the U.S. Supreme Court, in *Arizona v. Gant*, reversed its previous decision in *Belton*. In this case, Rodney J. Gant was arrested on an outstanding warrant for driving with a suspended license. Upon arrest, he was handcuffed in the back of a patrol car and his car was searched. During the search of the vehicle, the police found cocaine and a gun. Gant was subsequently convicted and sentenced to three years in prison. On appeal, the Arizona Supreme Court ruled that the search had violated the Fourth Amendment's ban on unreasonable searches and suppressed the evidence. The U.S. Supreme Court, in a 5-4 decision, affirmed that decision, ruling that the Fourth Amendment does not permit broad authority to search a motor vehicle incident to arrest simply because the arrestee is at the site of the arrest. In the decision, the Court ruled that the need to search the interior of a vehicle incident to arrest is limited to situations involving officer safety and the prevention of the destruction of evidence. Under the facts of the case, Gant was not within reaching distance of the vehicle at the time of the search (he was

Carroll doctrine Based on the landmark 1925 U.S. Supreme Court case *Carroll v. United States*, the legal doctrine that automobiles have less Fourth Amendment protection than other places.

YOU ARE THERE   *Carroll v. United States* (1925)

On September 29, 1921, during Prohibition, two federal agents were in an apartment in Grand Rapids, Michigan, when George Carroll and John Kiro entered. The agents arranged to buy a case of whiskey from them. The two men were to deliver the whiskey the next day, but they never returned. A few days later, on October 6, 1921, the agents observed Carroll and Kiro driving an automobile on a highway. They pursued them but lost them. Two months later, on December 15, 1921, the agents again observed them on the same highway and were able to overtake them and stop them. The agents searched the car and found 68 bottles of whiskey within the upholstery of the seats. Carroll and Kiro were arrested for violation of the Prohibition laws. Upon appeal, the Supreme Court established the automobile exception to the Fourth Amendment.

Source: Based on *Carroll v. United States*, 267 U.S. 132 (1925).

handcuffed and locked inside the police car), and there was no reason to believe the car contained evidence of the crime for which he was arrested (driving with a suspended license).[128]

BORDER SEARCHES   A border search can be made without probable cause, without a warrant, and, indeed, without any articulable suspicion at all.[129] In *United States v. Martinez-Fuerte* (1976), the Supreme Court ruled that border patrol officers do not have to have probable cause or a warrant to stop cars for brief questioning at fixed checkpoints.[130]

GOOD FAITH   The Supreme Court established a "good faith" exception to the exclusionary rule in *United States v. Leon* (1984). It waived the exclusionary rule in cases in which the police act in reasonable reliance and good faith on a search warrant that is later ruled faulty or found to be unsupported by probable cause.[131] Speaking for the Court, Justice Byron R. White stated,

> In the absence of an allegation that the magistrate abandoned his detached and neutral role, suppression is appropriate only if the officers

United States v. Leon (1984)

In August 1981, Officer Cyril Rombach, an experienced and well-trained narcotics investigator, prepared an application for a search warrant to search the homes and automobiles of several suspects in a drug investigation. In September 1981, a search warrant was issued by a state superior judge. The officer executed the search warrant and found large quantities of drugs at three residences and in two automobiles listed on the warrant. Rombach arrested several people, including Alberto Leon, for drug violations.

The defendants were indicted by a grand jury and charged with conspiracy to possess and distribute cocaine. The defendants filed motions to suppress the evidence, and the district court granted the motions to suppress in part. It concluded that the affidavit was insufficient to establish probable cause. The court recognized that Rombach had acted in good faith, but it rejected the government's suggestion that the Fourth Amendment exclusionary rule should not apply where evidence is seized in reasonable good faith reliance on a search warrant.

Upon appeal, the Supreme Court overruled the district court and established the "good faith doctrine." It ruled that evidence obtained in good faith, where the officers reasonably believed they had sufficient probable cause to get a warrant, is admissible in court. The Court said that the exclusionary rule should be applied only in cases in which the police purposely, recklessly, or negligently violate the law.

Source: Based on *United States v. Leon*, 468 U.S. 897 (1984).

were dishonest or reckless in preparing their affidavit or could not have harbored an objectively reasonable belief in the existence of probable cause.

During the 1980s, the Court continued its emphasis on "good faith" exceptions to the Fourth Amendment in *Massachusetts v. Sheppard* (1984), *Illinois v. Krull* (1987), and *Maryland v. Garrison* (1987).[132]

In 1995, in *Arizona v. Evans*, the Court extended the "good faith" exception by creating a "computer errors" exception. In this case, the police arrested Evans for a traffic violation. A routine computer check reported an outstanding arrest warrant for Evans. He was arrested, and a search of his vehicle revealed possession of a controlled substance. Later, it was determined that the arrest warrant should have been removed from the computer a few weeks earlier. However, the Court reasoned that officers could not be held responsible for a clerical error made by a court worker and did, in fact, act in good faith.[133]

In 2004, in *Groh v. Ramirez*, however, the Supreme Court rejected a "good faith" exception in a case involving a warrant to search a residence.[134] The warrant application and affidavit (paperwork presented to the court to obtain the warrant) contained a particular description of the items to be seized; however, the warrant itself did not contain such a description as required by the Fourth Amendment. Although the warrant was reviewed, signed by a judge, and executed, the Supreme Court concluded that it was unconstitutional because any reasonable officer would have concluded from just a cursory look at the warrant that it was invalid.

SUSPICIONLESS SEARCH OF A PAROLEE   In 2006, in *Samson v. California*, the Supreme Court ruled that suspicionless searches of parolees by law enforcement officers are reasonable under the Fourth Amendment.[135] In this case, the defendant was on parole when confronted by a local police officer. The police officer stopped him, believing there was a warrant out for his arrest and also knowing that the defendant was out on parole. After resolving the fact that there was no outstanding warrant, the officer searched the defendant pursuant to a California law that holds that every prisoner eligible for release on state parole agrees in writing to be subject to search and seizure by a parole officer or other peace officer at any time of the day or night, with or without a search warrant and with or without cause. The search revealed that the defendant was in possession of methamphetamine and the officer arrested him. The defendant challenged the search, asserting that the suspicionless search violated the reasonableness principle of the Fourth Amendment. The Supreme Court ruled against the defendant, concluding that the governmental interests at stake in monitoring individuals released on parole outweigh the already reduced privacy interests of the parolee, and that the search was consistent with the Fourth Amendment.

SEARCHES BY PRIVATE PERSONS In *Burdeau v. McDowell* (1921), the Supreme Court ruled that the Bill of Rights applies only to the actions of government agents; it does not apply to private security employees or private citizens not acting on behalf of, or with, official law enforcement agencies.[136] The fact that private security personnel are not bound by the tenets of the Constitution and cannot obtain warrants, however, does not mean that they can indiscriminately violate the rights of offenders. If they do, they can be sued under civil law and suffer severe financial damages.

The Police and Custodial Interrogation

FBI legal instructor Kimberly A. Crawford states that the U.S. Supreme Court has recognized two constitutional sources of the right to counsel during interrogation. One source is the Court's interpretation in *Miranda v. Arizona* of the Fifth Amendment right against self-incrimination; the other is contained within the language of the Sixth Amendment.[137] The impetus for the creation of the *Miranda* rights was the Supreme Court's concern that **custodial interrogations** are intrinsically coercive. The right to counsel contained within *Miranda* applies only when the subject of an interrogation is in custody.[138]

In English common law, the lack of a confession was often viewed as a serious deficiency in the government's case, enough to cause a judge or jury to acquit an accused person. Although confessions are not required to prove guilt, the emphasis on securing a confession from a suspect remains today.[139]

Louis DiPietro, a special agent and legal instructor at the FBI Academy, states that a confession is probably the most substantiating and damaging evidence that can be admitted against a defendant. To be admissible, due process mandates that a confession be made voluntarily and that, in addition, the investigator has scrupulously complied with the U.S. Supreme Court's requirements emanating from the landmark *Miranda* case as well as other constitutional rights of an accused. DiPietro warns that if the government obtains a nonvoluntary confession, the resulting confession will be excludable on the grounds of denial of due process of law.[140]

This section will pay particular attention to cases leading to the *Miranda* ruling, the *Miranda* case and its ruling, cases that seem to have led to the erosion of the *Miranda* rule, the *Dickerson* ruling and cases subsequent to *Dickerson*, and surreptitious recording of suspects' conversations.

The Path to *Miranda*

The police have many crimes to investigate and often not enough resources to accomplish their mission. In many cases, there is not enough physical evidence or there are no eyewitnesses to assist the police in their investigation. Thus, police must seek to gain a confession from a defendant, particularly in murder cases, in order to convict.

The history of methods used by the police to obtain confessions from suspects has been sordid, including beatings and torture that came to be known as the *third degree*. From 1936 until 1966, the Supreme Court issued a number of rulings to preclude this misconduct and ensure compliance with due process as guaranteed by the Bill of Rights. The following landmark cases show the development of rules regarding custodial interrogation during those three decades. See Table 13.11 for a list of landmark cases and rules leading to the *Miranda* decision.

END OF THE THIRD DEGREE In *Brown v. Mississippi* (1936), the Supreme Court put an end to the almost official practice of brutality and violence (the **third degree**) used by the police to obtain confessions from suspects. The case involved the coerced confessions, through beatings, of three men. The Supreme Court suppressed the confessions and

TABLE 13.11 The Path to *Miranda*

Brown v. Mississippi (1936)
McNabb-Mallory rule (1957)
Escobedo v. Illinois (1964)
Miranda v. Arizona (1966)

© 2016 Cengage Learning®

---

custodial interrogation The questioning of a person in police custody regarding his or her participation in a crime.

third degree The pattern of brutality and violence used by the police to obtain confessions by suspects.

Brown v. Mississippi (1936)

On March 30, 1934, Raymond Steward, a white planter, was murdered. On that night Deputy Sheriff Dial went to the home of Ellington, a black tenant farmer and one of the defendants, and requested him to accompany him to the house of the deceased, where a number of white men were gathered and began to accuse the defendant of the crime. Upon his denial, they seized him and hanged him by a rope to the limb of a tree, twice. When they took him down the second time, they tied him to a tree and whipped him. The trial record showed that the signs of the rope on his neck were plainly visible during the trial.

Ellington was again picked up a day or two later, and again severely beaten until he confessed. The other two defendants, Ed Brown and Henry Shields, also black tenant farmers, were also arrested and taken to jail. In order to obtain confessions, the defendants were "made to strip and they were laid over chairs and their backs were cut to pieces with a leather strap with buckles on it and they were likewise made by the said deputy definitely to understand that the whipping would be continued unless and until they confessed, and not only confessed, but confessed to every matter of detail as demanded by those present."

The defendants made their confessions on April 1, 1934. They were indicted on April 4, went on trial on April 5, and were convicted and sentenced to death on April 6, 1934. The deputy sheriff who supervised the beatings, Deputy Sheriff Dial, testifying in court, responded to an inquiry about how severely a defendant was whipped by stating, "Not too much for a negro; not as much as I would have done if it were left to me."

On appeal, the Supreme Court ruled that the actions against the three men were violations of their due process rights.

Source: Based on *Brown v. Mississippi*, 297 U.S. 278 (1936).

McNabb v. United States (1943) and Mallory v. United States (1957)

The McNabb family consisted of five Tennessee mountain people who operated an illegal moonshine business near Chattanooga. During a raid on their business by federal agents, a police officer was killed. The five were arrested and subjected to continuous interrogation for two days. Two of the McNabbs were convicted based on their confessions, and each was sentenced to 45 years in prison for murder. In *McNabb v. United States*, the Supreme Court ruled that these confessions were in violation of the Constitution because they violated the Federal Rules of Criminal Procedure, which required that defendants must be taken before a magistrate without unnecessary delay.

In *Mallory v. United States*, the defendant was a 19-year-old male of limited intelligence who was arrested for rape in Washington, D.C. He was arrested the day after the crime, taken to the police station, and questioned over a 10-hour period. He confessed under interrogation by the police officer administering the polygraph examination. The Supreme Court again ruled that the delay in bringing the defendant before a magistrate was a violation of the Federal Rules of Criminal Procedure.

In both of these cases, the Court did not even consider the question of voluntariness. The new standard that the Court adopted, now called the *McNabb-Mallory* rule, considered only the time element between the arrest and the first appearance before a judge. This rule applied only to actions of federal law enforcement officers.

Source: Based on *McNabb v. United States*, 318 U.S. 332 (1943), and *Mallory v. United States*, 354 U.S. 449 (1957).

unconstitutional.[141] Speaking for the Court, Chief Justice Charles E. Hughes wrote the following:

> Because a State may dispense with a jury trial, it does not follow that it may substitute trial by ordeal. The rack and torture chamber may not be substituted for the witness stand. The State may not permit an accused to be hurried to conviction under mob domination—where the whole proceeding is but a mask—without

emphasized that the use of confessions obtained through barbaric tactics deprived the defendants of their right to due process under the Fourteenth Amendment. The Court, in effect, said that coerced confessions are untrustworthy, unreliable, and supplying corrective process.... The due process clause requires "that state action, whether through one agency or another, shall be consistent with the fundamental principles of liberty and justice which lie at the base of all our civil and political institutions." . . . It would be difficult to conceive of methods more revolting to the sense of justice than those taken to procure the confessions of these petitioners, and the use of confessions thus obtained as the basis for conviction and sentence was a clear denial of due process.

THE PROMPT ARRAIGNMENT RULE *McNabb v. United States* (1943) and *Mallory v. United States* (1957) involved confessions obtained as a result of delays in the "prompt arraignment" of the

Escobedo v. Illinois (1964)

On the evening of January 19, 1960, Danny Escobedo's brother-in-law, Manuel, was shot to death. The next morning the Chicago police arrested Escobedo and attempted to interrogate him. However, his attorney obtained a writ of habeas corpus, requiring the police to free him.

On January 30, Benedict DiGerlando, who was then in police custody, told the police that Escobedo had fired the fatal shots at his brother-in-law. The police rearrested Escobedo and brought him to police headquarters. Escobedo told the police he wanted to consult his lawyer. Shortly after the arrest, Escobedo's attorney arrived at headquarters and attempted to see him, but he was denied access. During their stay at headquarters, the police caused an encounter between Escobedo and DiGerlando during which Escobedo made admissions to the crime. Later a statement was taken from Escobedo. He was never advised of his rights. He was convicted of the murder of Manuel based on his statements.

The Supreme Court reversed Escobedo's conviction based on the fact that the police violated Escobedo's Sixth Amendment rights, rights made obligatory on the states through the Fourteenth Amendment.

Source: Based on *Escobedo v. Illinois*, 378 U.S. 478 (1964).

defendants before a federal judge.[142] The Court did not address whether or not the confessions were voluntary, which was the previous standard for admitting them into evidence. Instead, it considered how long it took for law enforcement agents to bring the suspects before a judge and whether the confessions should be admissible because of this delay.

ENTRY OF LAWYERS INTO THE STATION HOUSE In 1964, the Supreme Court ruled in *Escobedo v. Illinois* that the refusal by the police to honor a suspect's request to consult with his lawyer during the course of an interrogation constituted a denial of his Sixth Amendment right to counsel and his Fifth Amendment right to be free from self-incrimination—rights made obligatory upon the states by the Fourteenth Amendment.[143] The decision rendered any incriminating statement elicited by the police during such an interrogation inadmissible in court. The Court ruled that once a suspect becomes the focus of a police interrogation, is taken into custody, and requests the advice of a lawyer, the police must permit access to the lawyer.

The *Miranda* Ruling

The well-known case of *Miranda v. Arizona* (1966) was the culmination of many Supreme Court decisions focusing on the rights of individuals during police interrogations.[144] The *Miranda* decision was actually a combination of cases involving four persons: Ernesto Miranda, arrested in Phoenix for kidnapping and rape; Michael Vignera, arrested in New York City for robbery; Carl Westover, arrested in Kansas City for robbery; and Roy Stewart, arrested in Los Angeles for robbery. What we now call the *Miranda* rule could have been called the *Vignera*, *Westover*, or *Stewart* rule, but the Court decided to issue their ruling under Ernesto Miranda's case.[145]

In *Miranda*, the Supreme Court ruled that confessions are by their very nature inherently coercive and that custodial interrogation makes any statements obtained from defendants compelled and thus not voluntary. The Court felt that interrogations violate the Fifth Amendment, which guarantees that no one shall be compelled to be a witness against himself or herself in a criminal case, and that this guarantee is violated any time a person is taken into custody and interrogated.

The Court then established the well-known *Miranda* **rule (or** *Miranda* **warnings)**, which states that prior to any interrogation of a person in custody, the police must do the following:

- Advise the suspect that he or she has the right to remain silent
- Advise the suspect that anything he or she says can and will be used against him or her in court
- Advise the suspect that he or she has the right to consult a lawyer and to have the lawyer present during questioning
- Advise the suspect that if he or she cannot afford an attorney, an attorney will be provided, free of charge

The Court further ruled that if before or during the interrogation, the suspect, in any way, indicates a wish to remain silent or to have an attorney, the interrogation may no longer proceed.

The *Miranda* rule applies to all custodial interrogations; however, this does not mean that every police interview requires the warnings. The Supreme Court has made it clear that *Miranda* applies only when the suspect is *both* in custody and subject to interrogation.[146] Even interrogations taking place at the police station may not fall within the meaning of custodial interrogation. For example, in *Oregon v. Mathiason* (1977), the Court held that a suspect who was invited to come to the police station, voluntarily arrived unaccompanied by the police, and was told before the interrogation that he was not under arrest was not in custody for the purpose of *Miranda*.[147] The Court has also found that routine traffic stops and questioning at a suspect's home are noncustodial situations.[148]

When giving the *Miranda* warnings, officers must ensure that a suspect makes a knowing, intelligent, and voluntary waiver of his or her rights as a prerequisite to questioning. Also, if a suspect clearly indicates unwillingness to answer questions and invokes the right to silence, police must scrupulously honor that request. Where a suspect makes a clear request to consult with an attorney, police must immediately cease any further questioning and may not contact the suspect about any crime unless a lawyer is present or unless the suspect initiates the contact with the police.[149] The Court has also ruled that persons who cannot understand the *Miranda* warnings because of their age, mental handicaps, or language problems cannot be legally questioned without an attorney being present.[150] In *Arizona v.*

Roberson (1988), the Court held that the police may not avoid a suspect's request for a lawyer by beginning a new line of questioning, even if it is about an unrelated offense.[151]

The Erosion of *Miranda*

In the aftermath of the *Miranda* decision, there was tremendous confusion in the legal community over its exact meaning. Consequently, a large number of cases were brought to the Court challenging and questioning it. Eventually, the Supreme Court of the 1970s and 1980s under Chief Justice Warren E. Burger began to impose a series of exceptions to the *Miranda* decision. These decisions led noted civil liberties lawyer and Harvard law professor Alan M. Dershowitz to write an article in 1984 entitled, "A Requiem for the Exclusionary Rule," in which he said, "The Burger Court has chipped away at the exclusionary rule—carving out so many exceptions that it is falling of its own weight."[152] Dershowitz added,

> Our twenty-five year experiment with the exclusionary rule may well be coming to an end. We have learned precious little from it, because the exclusionary rule was never really given a chance. The public, spurred by politicians' rhetoric, closed its eyes and ears to facts like the following: that only a tiny fraction of defendants (less than half of one percent, according to a federal study) are freed because of the exclusionary rule; and that there has been a marked improvement both in police efficiency and in compliance with the Constitution since the exclusionary rule was established.[153]

Despite Dershowitz's thoughts, the *Miranda* rule still stands and defendants in custody must still be advised of their constitutional rights before any interrogation. However, the Court does recognize certain exceptions to *Miranda*. A sample of post-*Miranda* cases that have led to the weakening of the *Miranda* rule follows.

HARRIS v. NEW YORK In *Harris v. New York* (1971), the Court ruled that statements that are trustworthy, even though they were obtained without

---

Miranda **rule (or** *Miranda* **warnings)** Rule established by the U.S. Supreme Court in the landmark case *Miranda v. United States* (1966) that requires the police to advise suspects confronting custodial interrogation of their constitutional rights.

Miranda v. Arizona (1966)

On March 2, 1963, in Phoenix, Arizona, an 18-year-old woman walking to a bus stop after work was accosted by a man who shoved her into his car and tied her hands and ankles. He then took her to the edge of the city where he raped her. The rapist drove the victim to a street near her home and let her out of the car. On March 13, the Phoenix police arrested a 23-year-old eighth-grade dropout named Ernesto Miranda and charged him with the crime. Miranda had a police record dating back to when he was 14 years old, had been given an undesirable discharge by the army for being a peeping Tom, and had served time in federal prison for driving a stolen car across a state line.

Miranda was placed in a lineup at the station house and positively identified by the victim. He was then taken to an interrogation room where he was questioned by the police without being informed that he had a right to have an attorney present. Two hours later, police emerged from the interrogation room with a written confession signed by Miranda. At the top of the statement was a typed paragraph stating that the confession was made voluntarily, without threats or promises of immunity, and "with full knowledge of my legal rights, understanding any statement I make may be used against me."

Source: Based on *Miranda v. Arizona*, 384 U.S. 436 (1966).

giving a defendant *Miranda* warnings, may be used to attack the credibility of a defendant who takes the witness stand.[154] The prosecutor accused Harris of lying on the stand and used statements obtained by the police, without *Miranda* warnings, before the trial to prove it.

Justice Burger, speaking for the Court relative to the *Miranda* rule, wrote, "The shield provided by *Miranda* cannot be perverted into a license to use perjury by way of a defense, free from the risk of confrontation with prior inconsistent utterances. We hold, therefore, that petitioner's credibility was appropriately impeached by use of his earlier conflicting statements."

MICHIGAN v. MOSLEY   In *Michigan v. Mosley* (1975), the Court ruled that a second interrogation, held after the suspect had initially refused to make a statement, was not a violation of the *Miranda* decision. In the second interrogation, which was for a different crime, the suspect had been read the *Miranda* warnings.[155]

BREWER v. WILLIAMS   In *Brewer v. Williams*, decided in 1977, the Supreme Court seemed to extend the meaning of the word *interrogation* by interpreting comments made by a police detective as "subtle coercion."[156] This case affirmed *Miranda* but is presented here because of a second decision in the case of *Nix v. Williams* (1984).[157] In this case, the state of Iowa continued to appeal the decision reached in *Brewer v. Williams*. In 1984, the Supreme Court, in *Nix v. Williams*, promulgated the "inevitability of discovery" rule, holding that victim Pamela Powers's body would have been discovered inevitably, so it should be allowed to be used as evidence in the trial despite the subtle coercion of the police.

RHODE ISLAND v. INNIS   In *Rhode Island v. Innis* (1980), the Supreme Court clarified its definition of interrogation by ruling that the "definition of interrogation can extend only to words or actions on the part of police officers that *they should have known* [Court's emphasis] were reasonably likely to elicit an incriminating response."[158] In this case, a man told the police where he had left a shotgun he used in a shooting after the police had made remarks about the possibility of a disabled child finding it. (There was a home for disabled children nearby.)

NEW YORK v. QUARLES   In *New York v. Quarles* (1984), the Supreme Court created a "public safety" exception to the *Miranda* rule.[159] In this case, a police officer, after arresting and handcuffing a man wanted in connection with a crime, and after feeling an empty shoulder holster on the man's body, asked him where the gun was without giving the man the *Miranda* warnings. The gun was suppressed as evidence because the officer's question was not preceded by the warnings. The Supreme Court, however, overruled the state court and said the officer's failure to read the *Miranda* warnings was justified in the interest of public safety. The Court wrote:

We conclude that the need for answers to questions in a situation posing a threat to the public safety outweighs the need for the prophylactic rule protecting the Fifth Amendment's privilege against self-incrimination. We decline to place officers such as Officer Kraft in the untenable position of having to consider, often in a matter of seconds, whether it best serves society for them to ask the necessary questions without the *Miranda* warnings and render whatever probative evidence they uncover inadmissible, or for them to give the warnings in order to preserve the admissibility of evidence they might uncover but possibly damage or destroy their ability to obtain that evidence and neutralize the volatile situation confronting them.

OREGON v. ELSTAD In *Oregon v. Elstad* (1985), the Supreme Court ruled that the simple failure of the police to warn a suspect of his *Miranda* rights (with no indication of misbehavior or coercion on the part of the police) until after obtaining an incriminating statement or confession was not a violation of *Miranda*.[160] In *Elstad*, law enforcement officers went to the home of a burglary suspect, Elstad, to take him into custody. The suspect's mother answered the door and led the officers to the suspect, who was in his bedroom. Before the arrest, one of the officers waited

---

YOU ARE THERE

Brewer v. Williams (1977) and Nix v. Williams (1984)

On Christmas Eve 1968, 10-year-old Pamela Powers was at a Des Moines, Iowa, YMCA with her parents to watch her brother participate in a wrestling match. Pamela told her parents that she was going to use the bathroom. She was never seen alive again. At about the time of Pamela's disappearance, a young boy saw a man, later identified as Robert Williams, walking out of the YMCA carrying a bundle wrapped in a blanket to his car. The boy told police that he thought he saw two legs under the blanket. Robert Williams was a resident of the YMCA, a religious fanatic, and an escaped mental patient. On Christmas Day, Williams's car was found abandoned near the city of Davenport, Iowa, 160 miles from Des Moines. On the day after Christmas, Williams walked into the Davenport police station house and surrendered to the police. The Davenport police notified the Des Moines police, who arranged to pick up Williams.

When Detective Leaming arrived at the Davenport police station to pick up Williams, he was advised by Williams's lawyer, Henry McKnight, that he did not want Williams to be the subject of any interrogation during the trip from Davenport to Des Moines. Leaming agreed to the lawyer's request.

In the car on the way back to Des Moines, Detective Leaming, knowing that Williams was a religious fanatic, addressed him as "Reverend" and made what has become known as the "Christian Burial Speech":

> I want to give you something to think about while we're traveling down the road.... Number one, I want you to observe the weather conditions. It's raining, it's sleeting, it's freezing, driving is very treacherous, visibility is poor, it's going to be dark early this evening. They are predicting several inches of snow for tonight, and I feel that you yourself are the only person that knows where this little girl's body is, that you yourself have only been there once, and if you get a snow on top of it you yourself may be unable to find it. And, since we will be going right past the area on the way into Des Moines, I feel that we could stop and locate the body, that the parents of this little girl should be entitled to a Christian burial for the little girl who was snatched away from them on Christmas Eve and murdered. And I feel we should stop and locate it on the way in rather than waiting until morning and trying to come back out after a snowstorm and possibly not being able to find it at all.

After this speech, Williams directed the police to the young girl's dead body. Williams was convicted of her murder.

On appeal to the Supreme Court, the Court voted 5–4 that Leaming's "Christian Burial Speech" constituted custodial interrogation and that the evidence, the body, was illegally obtained and therefore not admissible in court. But the state of Iowa continued to appeal the *Brewer* decision, and in 1984 the Supreme Court, in *Nix v. Williams*, promulgated the "inevitability of discovery rule," saying in effect that Pamela Powers's body would have been discovered inevitably, and thus it should be allowed to be used as evidence in a trial.

Source: Based on *Brewer v. Williams*, 430 U.S. 222 (1977), and *Nix v. Williams*, 467 U.S. 431 (1984).

for the suspect to get dressed and accompanied him to the living room while the other officer asked the suspect's mother to step into the kitchen where he advised her that they had a warrant for her son's arrest on a burglary charge. The officer who remained with Elstad asked him if he was aware of why they were at his home to arrest him. Elstad replied that he did not know. The officer then asked him if he knew a person by the name of Gross (the subject of the burglary), and Elstad replied that he did and added that

he heard that there was a robbery at the Gross house. The officer then told Elstad that he believed that he (Elstad) was involved in the burglary. Elstad then stated to the officer, "Yes, I was there."

The police then brought Elstad to the police station, where he was advised of his *Miranda* rights and subjected to custodial interrogation. Elstad waived his rights and gave a full confession, admitting to his role in the burglary. In court, Elstad's attorney made a motion to suppress his confession, arguing that the

Rhode Island v. Innis (1980)

On the night of January 12, 1975, John Mulvaney, a Providence, Rhode Island, cabdriver, disappeared after being dispatched to pick up a fare. His body was discovered four days later buried in a shallow grave in Coventry, Rhode Island. He had died from a shotgun blast to the back of his head.

Five days later, shortly after midnight, the Providence police received a phone call from a cabdriver who reported that he had just been robbed by a man with a sawed-off shotgun. While at the police station, the robbery victim noticed a picture of his assailant on a bulletin board and informed a detective. The detective prepared a photo array, and the complainant identified the suspect again.

The police began a search of the area where the cabdriver had brought the suspect. At about 4:30 a.m., an officer spotted the suspect standing in the street. Upon apprehending the suspect, the officer, Patrolman Lovel, advised him of his *Miranda* rights. A sergeant responded and again advised the suspect of his *Miranda* rights. A captain responded and for a third time advised the suspect of his constitutional rights. The suspect stated that he understood his rights and wanted to speak with an attorney. The captain directed three other officers to bring the suspect to the police station in a caged wagon, a four-door police car with a wire screen mesh between the front and rear seats.

While en route to the police station, two of the officers engaged in conversation. One, Patrolman Gleckman, testified at the trial:

At this point, I was talking back and forth with Patrolman McKenna stating that I frequent this area while on patrol and (that because a school for handicapped children is located nearby)

there's a lot of handicapped children running around in this area, and God forbid one of them might find a weapon with shells and they might hurt themselves.

Patrolman McKenna testified:

I more or less concurred with him that it was a safety factor and that we should, you know, continue to search for the weapon and try to find it.

The third officer, Patrolman Williams, did not participate in the conversation but testified about the conversation between the two officers:

He (Gleckman) said it would be too bad if the little—I believe he said a girl—would pick up the gun, maybe kill herself.

According to police testimony, the suspect then interrupted the conversation, stating that the officers should turn the car around so he could show them where the gun was located.

When they reached the crime scene, the suspect was again advised of his *Miranda* rights. The suspect said he understood his rights but that he "wanted to get the gun out of the way because of the kids in the area in the school." The suspect then led the police to the area where the shotgun was located. The defendant Innis was convicted, but upon appeal, the gun was suppressed. In 1980, however, the U.S. Supreme Court heard the case and reversed the Rhode Island appeals court, ruling that the officers' statements were not interrogation, and the gun was allowed to remain in evidence.

Source: Based on *Rhode Island v. Innis*, 446 U.S. 291 (1980).

confession was "tainted" by the unwarned statement made in Elstad's living room. The trial court agreed and held that once the initial *Miranda* violation occurred, all that followed was tainted, including the station house confession, and therefore the confession was inadmissible.

Upon appeal to the U.S. Supreme Court, the Court rejected the lower court's ruling and held that a simple failure to administer the *Miranda* warnings to a suspect, with no indication of behavior on the part of the law enforcement officer that could be interpreted as coercion, compulsion, or an effort to undermine the suspect's ability to exercise free will, should not keep out a statement that the suspect makes that otherwise is voluntary.

MORAN v. BURBINE   In *Moran v. Burbine* (1986), a murder case, the Supreme Court ruled that the police failure to inform a suspect undergoing custodial interrogation of his attorney's attempts to reach him does not constitute a violation of the *Miranda* rule.[161] The Court reasoned that events that are not known by a defendant have no bearing on his or her capacity to knowingly waive his or her rights. Speaking for the Court, Justice Sandra Day O'Connor, commenting on the actions of the police in lying to the lawyer, Munson, wrote:

> Focusing primarily on the impropriety of conveying false information to an attorney, he [Burbine] invites us to declare that such behavior should be condemned as violative of canons fundamental to the "traditions and conscience of our people." ... We do not question that on facts more egregious than those presented here police deception might rise to a level of a due process violation. ... We hold only that, on these facts, the challenged conduct falls short of the kind of misbehavior that so shocks the sensibilities of civilized society as to warrant a federal intrusion into the criminal processes of the States.

ILLINOIS v. PERKINS   In *Illinois v. Perkins* (1990), the Supreme Court further clarified its *Miranda* decision.[162] In the *Perkins* case, police placed an informant and an undercover officer in a cellblock with Lloyd Perkins, a suspected murderer incarcerated on an unrelated charge of aggravated assault. While planning a prison break, the undercover officer asked Perkins whether he had ever "done" anyone. In response, Perkins described at length the details of a murder-for-hire he had committed.

When Perkins was subsequently charged with the murder, he argued successfully to have the statements he made in prison suppressed because no *Miranda* warnings had been given before his conversation with the informant and undercover officer.

YOU ARE THERE

New York v. Quarles (1984)

At 12:30 a.m., police officers Frank Kraft and Sal Scarring were on routine patrol in Queens, New York, when a young woman approached them and told them that she had been raped by a black male, approximately six feet tall, who was wearing a black jacket with the name "Big Ben" printed in yellow letters on the back. She then told the officers that the man had just entered an A&P supermarket located nearby and that the man had a gun. The officers put the woman into the police car and drove to the A&P, where Officer Kraft entered the store while his partner radioed for backup. Kraft observed the suspect, Quarles, approaching a checkout counter. On seeing the officer, Quarles turned and ran toward the rear of the store. Kraft took out his revolver and chased Quarles. When Quarles turned the corner at the end of an aisle, Kraft lost sight of him for several seconds. On regaining sight of Quarles, Kraft apprehended him and ordered him to stop and put his hands over his head.

Kraft then frisked Quarles and discovered that he was wearing an empty shoulder holster. After handcuffing him, Kraft asked him where the gun was. Quarles nodded in the direction of some empty cartons and said, "The gun is over there." Kraft retrieved a loaded .38-caliber revolver from one of the cartons and then formally arrested Quarles and read him the *Miranda* warnings. At trial, the judge suppressed Quarles's statement, "The gun is over there," and suppressed the gun because Kraft had not given Quarles the *Miranda* warnings before asking, "Where's the gun?"

On appeal from the prosecutor to the U.S. Supreme Court, the Court reversed the New York ruling and created a "public safety" exception to the requirement that police give a suspect the *Miranda* warnings before interrogation.

Source: Based on *New York v. Quarles*, 467 U.S. 649, 658 (1984).

Moran v. Burbine (1986)

On March 3, 1977, Mary Jo Hickey was found unconscious in a factory parking lot in Providence, Rhode Island. Suffering from injuries to her skull apparently inflicted by a metal pipe found at the scene, she was rushed to a nearby hospital. Three weeks later she died from her wounds.

Several months after her death, the Cranston, Rhode Island, police arrested Brian Burbine and two others for burglary. Shortly before the arrest, Detective Ferranti of the Cranston police had learned from a confidential informant that the man responsible for Hickey's death lived at a certain address and was known by the nickname "Butch." On learning from the arresting officer that Burbine went by the nickname Butch and that he gave his address as the same one given by the informant, Ferranti advised Burbine of his constitutional rights. Burbine refused to speak to the detective. Ferranti spoke to Burbine's two associates and obtained more incriminating information. Ferranti then called the Providence police, who sent three detectives to Cranston to interrogate Burbine.

That evening Burbine's sister called the Providence Public Defender's Office to obtain legal assistance for her brother. A lawyer from the office, Allegra Munson, called the Cranston detective division. The conversation went as follows:

A male voice responded with the word "Detectives." Ms. Munson identified herself and asked if Brian Burbine was being held; the person

responded affirmatively. Ms. Munson explained to the person that Burbine was represented by attorney and she would act as Burbine's legal counsel in the event that the police intended to place him in a lineup or question him. The unidentified person told Ms. Munson that the police would not be questioning Burbine or putting him in a lineup and that they were through with him for the night. Ms. Munson was not informed that the Providence police were at the Cranston police station or that Burbine was a suspect in Mary's murder.

Less than an hour after Munson's call, Burbine was brought to an interrogation room and questioned about Mary Jo Hickey's murder. He was informed of his *Miranda* rights on three separate occasions, and he signed three written forms acknowledging that he understood his right to the presence of an attorney and indicating that he did not want an attorney called or appointed for him. Burbine signed three written statements fully admitting to the murder. Based on his written statements, Burbine was convicted of murder.

Upon appeal, the Rhode Island appeals court reversed the conviction. The U.S. Supreme Court, however, reversed the court of appeals ruling and ruled that Burbine's constitutional rights were not violated.

Source: Based on *Moran v. Burbine*, 475 U.S. 412 (1986).

On review, however, the Supreme Court reversed the order of suppression. Rejecting Perkins's argument, the Supreme Court recognized that there are limitations to the rules announced in *Miranda*. The Court expressly declined to accept the notion that the *Miranda* warnings are required whenever a suspect is in custody in a technical sense and converses with someone who happens to be a government agent. Rather, the Court concluded that not every custodial interrogation creates the psychologically compelling atmosphere that *Miranda* was designed to protect against. When the compulsion is lacking, the Court found, so is the need for *Miranda* warnings.

The Court in *Perkins* found the facts at issue to be a clear example of a custodial interrogation that created no compulsion. Pointing out that compulsion is determined from the perspective of the suspect, the Court noted that Perkins had no reason to believe that either the informant or the undercover officer had any official power over him, and therefore, he had no reason to feel any compulsion to make self-incriminating statements. On the contrary, Perkins bragged about his role in the murder in an effort to impress those he believed to be his fellow inmates. *Miranda* was not designed to protect individuals from themselves.

PENNSYLVANIA v. MUNIZ In *Pennsylvania v. Muniz* (1990), the Court ruled that the police use of the defendant's slurred and drunken responses to booking questions (he was arrested for driving under the influence of alcohol) as evidence in his trial was not a violation of *Miranda* rights, even though he was never given his *Miranda* warnings.[163]

ARIZONA v. FULMINANTE In 1991, in *Arizona v. Fulminante*, the Supreme Court further weakened *Miranda* by ruling that a coerced confession might be a harmless trial error.[164] In this case, the Court overruled years of precedent to hold that if other evidence introduced at trial is strong enough, the use of a coerced confession could be considered harmless and a conviction upheld. In other words, a coerced confession, by itself, is not sufficient to have a conviction overruled if there is other compelling evidence of guilt.

MINNICK v. MISSISSIPPI In *Minnick v. Mississippi* (1991), the Court clarified the mechanics of *Miranda* by ruling that once a suspect in custody requests counsel in response to *Miranda* warnings, law enforcement officers may no longer attempt to reinterrogate that suspect unless the suspect's attorney is present or the suspect initiates the contact with the law enforcement agents.[165]

MCNEIL v. WISCONSIN In *McNeil v. Wisconsin* (1991), the Court ruled that an in-custody suspect who requests counsel at a judicial proceeding, such as an arraignment or initial appearance, is only invoking the Sixth Amendment right to counsel as to the charged offense and is not invoking the Fifth Amendment right to have an attorney present during the custodial interrogation.[166]

WITHROW v. WILLIAMS In *Withrow v. Williams* (1993), the Supreme Court distinguished *Miranda* violations from Fourth Amendment violations with respect to habeas corpus proceedings.[167] The Court held that criminal defendants can continue to raise *Miranda* violations in **habeas corpus** proceedings, even though it had previously restricted habeas corpus petitions that raised Fourth Amendment issues.

DAVIS v. UNITED STATES In *Davis v. United States* (1994), the Court ruled that after law enforcement officers have obtained a valid *Miranda* waiver from an in-custody suspect, they may continue

questioning the suspect when he or she makes an ambiguous or equivocal request for counsel during the questioning.[168] The Court stated that although it may be a good law enforcement practice to attempt to clarify an equivocal request for counsel, that practice is not constitutionally required.

In *Davis*, Naval Investigative Service (NIS) agents investigating a murder obtained both oral and written *Miranda* waivers from the defendant. After being interviewed for approximately 90 minutes, the defendant said, "Maybe I should talk to a lawyer." After asking some clarifying questions, the NIS agents continued to interrogate him. The Court ruled that the defendant's statement was not sufficiently unequivocal to constitute an assertion of his *Miranda* right to counsel.

STANSBURY v. CALIFORNIA In *Stansbury v. California* (1994), the Court reaffirmed the principle that an officer's uncommunicated suspicions about a suspect's guilt are irrelevant to the question of whether that suspect is in custody for purposes of *Miranda*.[169] Thus, custody for *Miranda* purposes is a completely objective determination based on facts and circumstances known to the suspect.

In *Stansbury*, the Court reiterated its earlier holding in *Oregon v. Mathiason* (1977) that *Miranda* warnings are required only when a person is in custody, which can be defined as either a formal arrest or a restraint on freedom of movement to the degree associated with a formal arrest. The Court then stated that this determination of custody depends on objective factors, and not on the subjective views of the officers or the suspect.

The *Dickerson* Ruling and Beyond

In a much-anticipated case, *Dickerson v. United States* (2000), the Supreme Court ruled that *Miranda* was a constitutional decision that cannot be overruled by an act of Congress.[170] In this case, Charles Thomas Dickerson was charged with conspiracy to commit bank robbery and other offenses. Before trial, he moved to suppress a statement he had made to the FBI on the grounds that he had not received *Miranda* warnings before being interrogated. The district court suppressed the statement.

habeas corpus A writ requiring that an arrested person be brought before a court to determine whether he or she has been legally detained.

The prosecution appealed, arguing that two years after the Supreme Court's *Miranda* decision, Congress passed a new federal criminal procedure and evidence law, 18 U.S.C. Section 3501, providing that a confession shall be admissible in federal court if it is voluntarily given. The law did not require the giving of *Miranda* warnings to suspects in custody. The prosecution felt that Congress intended to overrule *Miranda* because the new law required merely voluntariness—not the four warnings as per *Miranda*—as the determining factor as to whether a statement or confession will be admissible.

After several appellate decisions, the U.S. Supreme Court finally ruled in *Dickerson* that *Miranda* was a constitutional decision—that is, a decision that interprets and polices the Constitution—that cannot be overruled by an act of Congress, such as 18 U.S.C. Section 3501. Though conceding that Congress may modify or set aside the Court's rules of evidence and procedure that are not required by the Constitution, the Court emphasized that Congress may not overrule the Court's decisions, such as *Miranda*, that interpret and apply the Constitution.

The Court cited various other reasons for reaching its conclusion that *Miranda* is a constitutionally based rule. Among them, the Court noted that *Miranda* had become part of our national culture because the warnings were embedded in routine police practice. By holding *Miranda* to be a constitutional decision, the Court reaffirmed that *Miranda* governs the admissibility of statements made during custodial interrogation in both state and federal courts. Given the *Dickerson* decision, a violation of *Miranda* is now clearly a violation of the Constitution, which can result in suppression of statements in both federal and state courts.[171]

Before *Dickerson*, some constitutional scholars had expected that the Court might find a way to use the many cases mentioned in "The Erosion of *Miranda*" section of this chapter to overrule *Miranda*; but the Court expressly declined to do so in *Dickerson*. The Court's decision in this case did not attempt to find and defend an underlying rationale that would reconcile *Miranda* with those previous relevant cases that threatened to undermine or erode *Miranda*.[172]

After *Dickerson*, the Supreme Court continued to make significant rulings regarding custodial interrogation and the *Miranda* rule. In *Texas v. Cobb* (2001), the Court ruled that the Sixth Amendment right to counsel applies only to the case for which that right

was invoked by the suspect, and not to other cases affecting the suspect.[173] After his arrest for burglary and murder, Cobb admitted to the burglary but not the murder. He was indicted and invoked his Sixth Amendment right to counsel. Cobb later waived his *Miranda* rights again and led the police to the grave, confessing to the murder. After being convicted and sentenced to death, Cobb appealed his conviction on the grounds that the interrogation following his arrest on the murder charges violated his Sixth Amendment right to counsel that had attached and been invoked with respect to the burglary charge. An appellate court agreed and Cobb's murder conviction was reversed. The Supreme Court, however, reversed the appellate court and ruled that the interrogation did not violate Cobb's Sixth Amendment right to counsel and that the confession was admissible. The

YOU ARE THERE

Texas v. Cobb (2001)

When Owings returned from work, he found his house burglarized and his wife and daughter missing. After being advised of and waiving his *Miranda* rights, Raymond Cobb, 17, admitted to the burglary but denied any knowledge of the whereabouts of the woman and child. After being freed on bond, Cobb confessed to his father that he had killed the woman and the child. The father reported his son's confession to the police, and a warrant was obtained for the boy's arrest on charges of murder.

After the arrest, Cobb was advised of his *Miranda* rights and again waived them. He admitted to the police that he stabbed the wife to death with a knife he had brought with him and then took her body into a wooded area behind the house to bury her. He then returned to the house and found the 16-month-old child sleeping on her bed. He took the baby into the woods and laid her near the mother, and then obtained a shovel and dug a grave. Before Cobb had put the mother's body in the grave, the child awoke and began stumbling around, looking for her mother. When the baby fell into the grave, Cobb put the mother's body on top of her and buried them both.

After an appeal and multiple reversals of his sentence, Cobb was convicted of capital murder and sentenced to death.

Court argued that the Sixth Amendment right to counsel is "offense specific," and applied to the burglary charge only and not the murder charge.

In 2003, the U.S. Supreme Court decided two more important cases involving confessions. In *Chavez v. Martinez*, the Court held that questioning alone, unrelated to a criminal case, does not violate the Fifth Amendment self-incrimination clause. The Court ruled that the phrase "criminal case," in the Fifth Amendment's self-incrimination clause, at the very least requires initiation of legal proceedings and does not encompass the entire criminal investigatory process, including police interrogations.[174] In this case, Sergeant Chavez was interviewing Martinez while Martinez was being treated in a hospital emergency room suffering from gunshot wounds inflicted by the police. Martinez was not charged with a crime before the questioning, but during the questioning admitted that he had just used heroin and had stolen a police officer's gun. The Court ruled that Sergeant Chavez's questioning was not a *Miranda* violation.

In another 2003 case, *Kaupp v. Texas*, the Court made a different decision and vacated the conviction of a 17-year-old boy who was awakened late at night by the police, taken to the police station in handcuffs in his underwear, and interrogated.[175] The boy had been wakened at 3:00 a.m., and the officer told him, "We need to go and talk," to which the boy responded, "Okay." The boy was taken to the scene of the crime where the victim's body had just been recovered and then was taken to the police station. All parties agreed that the police, at this point, did not have probable cause to arrest the young man. At the police station, the youth was given the *Miranda* warnings, and after a brief interrogation, he confessed to some involvement in the murder. He was subsequently convicted and given a 55-year sentence.

On appeal, Texas courts affirmed the conviction and held that the boy's response of "okay" indicated consent, that his failure to protest was a waiver of rights, and that his transport to the police station was simply routine. The U.S. Supreme Court, in vacating the conviction, concluded that a 17-year-old boy being awakened late at night, taken to the police station in handcuffs in his underwear, and interrogated is indistinguishable from a traditional arrest. And because he was arrested without probable cause, his subsequent confession had to be suppressed absent evidence of intervening events sufficient to purge the taint of the unlawful seizure.

In 2012, a divided U.S. Supreme Court decided that age was a factor that must be considered when *Miranda* is given to a defendant. In *J.D.B. v. North Carolina* (2011), Justice Sotomayor, writing for the majority, said that the age of a subject is relevant when a child is subject to police questioning. J.D.B. was 13 years old when he was questioned by the police for about one-half hour. Prior to questioning, J.D.B. was not advised of his *Miranda* rights and was not told he could contact his mother or that he was free to leave the room. He was questioned about some burglaries that had occurred and about property that was seen in his possession that matched the property that had been stolen. J.D.B. confessed. During his juvenile hearings, his lawyer objected and submitted a motion to suppress his statements, stating that *Miranda* had been violated, that J.D.B. was in custody, and that the officers should have considered his age during questioning. On remand from the U.S. Supreme Court, the North Carolina court was ordered to consider the defendant's age, custody, and other relevant circumstances during interrogation.[176]

In 2004, the U.S. Supreme Court decided two other very important custodial interrogation cases. In *United States v. Patane*, the Court ruled that the failure to provide *Miranda* warnings before engaging in custodial interrogation does not require suppression of physical evidence discovered as a result of the person's unwarned but voluntary statements. The Court held, however, that the unwarned statement itself is inadmissible.[177] In this case, police arrested Patane, sought to question him about his alleged possession of a handgun, and began reading him his *Miranda* rights. Patane interrupted right after he was advised he had the right to remain silent and told the officers that they did not need to read him his rights because he already understood them. In response to the questioning, Patane told the officers where the gun was located and gave them permission to retrieve it. The Supreme Court allowed the gun to remain in evidence.

In another 2004 case involving unwarned statements, *Missouri v. Seibert*, the U.S. Supreme Court clarified its 1985 *Oregon v. Elstad* decision relative to the admission of unwarned statements given before *Miranda* warnings.[178] Recall that in *Elstad*, the Court had held that a simple failure to administer the *Miranda* warnings, with no indication of behavior on the part of the law enforcement officer that could be interpreted as coercion, compulsion, or an effort to undermine the suspect's ability to exercise free will, should not keep out a statement that otherwise is voluntary. In *Seibert*, however, there was a different pattern of behavior by the police, and the Supreme Court made a different decision from the one it made in *Elstad*.

The defendant Seibert gave two statements to the arresting officer during her interrogation, one before the officer had advised her of her *Miranda* rights. The officer testified at the trial that he had purposefully refrained from advising Seibert of her rights even though he knew that he was conducting a custodial interrogation and stated that he had learned this interrogation technique ("two-tier interrogation") during a police training session. The trial court suppressed Seibert's first statement but allowed her second statement to be used under the precedent of *Oregon v. Elstad*. It held that the admissions during the second interrogation were admissible because she was advised of her rights and she provided a signed waiver. The U.S. Supreme Court, however, found that the situation in this case was different from *Elstad* and involved an approach that implicitly encouraged *Miranda* violations. It ruled that the practice of two-tier interrogations, sometimes referred to as "beachheading," violates the purpose of *Miranda* and is unconstitutional. It held that the officer's intentional omission of the *Miranda* warnings was intended to deprive Seibert of the opportunity to knowingly and intelligently waive her *Miranda* rights.

In 2009, the U.S. Supreme Court, in *Montejo v. Louisiana*, ruled that the Sixth Amendment does not preclude law enforcement from initiating contact with a defendant in an effort to obtain a confession following the defendant's request for counsel or the court's appointment of counsel at the initial court appearance. In this case, Jesse Montejo was arrested for a murder, and at a preliminary hearing a judge ordered that a public defender be appointed for him. After the defendant's court appearance, police approached him and advised him of his *Miranda* rights, which he waived. He agreed to accompany police on a drive to locate the murder weapon. During this trip, he confessed to the murder and wrote a letter of apology to the victim's family.[179]

Berghuis v. Thompkins (2010) brought to the forefront the "right to remain silent" that was recognized in *Miranda*. Police questioned Van Chester Thompkins for more than three hours, and he remained almost entirely silent during the questioning. However, in reply to the police asking, "Do you pray to God to forgive you for shooting that boy down?" Thompkins answered in the affirmative, and that statement was used against him in his murder trial.[180] The Sixth U.S. Circuit Court of Appeals overturned the conviction, stating that his *Miranda* rights had been violated. In the 5–4 U.S. Supreme Court decision, Justice Kennedy, writing for the majority of the Court, said that defendants, by remaining silent when asked if they want a lawyer, do not expressly waive their right to remain silent or to have a lawyer present while being questioned; they must make an affirmative statement or action to do so.

Miranda continues to be interpreted and refined on a regular basis by the U.S. Supreme Court. Although controversy has always surrounded the repeated questioning of suspects without their lawyer being present, a refusal to talk to police without a lawyer being present has always indicated to police that any questioning must stop or not take place. However, in a recent U.S. Supreme Court ruling, *Maryland v. Shatzer* (2010), the Court placed a time limit on a request for a lawyer at 14 days from the initial *Miranda* warning given by police. In this case, Michael Shatzer, while he was in prison in 2006, confessed to abusing his son. When first questioned in 2003, he refused to talk about the incident, but new evidence came to light in 2006 when Shazter's son provided the police with more details. An officer obtained a confession to the 2003 crime after advising Shatzer of his *Miranda* rights. The Maryland Supreme Court threw out the confession, stating that the passage of time did not invalidate Shazter's prior assertion of his *Miranda* rights. The U.S. Supreme Court, however, said that enough time had passed between the first and second interrogations to allow the second interrogation.[181]

Though it was decided in 4th Circuit Court, so it did not become a Supreme Court case, *Seremeth v. Frederick County et al.* (2012) was the first case to deal with the Americans with Disability Act (ADA) and police interrogation. Police responded to a possible domestic dispute at the home of Robert Seremeth, who is deaf. Seremeth was handcuffed, preventing him from communicating, and the police did not have a qualified sign language interpreter on staff at the time. Seremeth then filed suit against the officers and Frederick County for violation of his rights under the Rehabilitation Act and Title II of the ADA. The court ruled that the actions of the police were "unreasonable under the circumstances."[182]

Police and Surreptitious Recording of Suspects' Conversations

Crawford reports that the surreptitious recording of suspects' conversations is an effective investigative technique that, if done properly, can withstand both constitutional and statutory challenges.[183] She cites several cases in which the courts have ruled that the surreptitious recording of suspects' conversations did not violate the custodial interrogation rules decided in *Miranda*.

In *Stanley v. Wainwright* (1979), two robbery suspects were arrested and placed in the back seat of a police car. They were unaware that one of the arresting officers had turned on a tape recorder on the front seat of the car before leaving the suspects unattended for a short period of time. During that time, the suspects engaged in a conversation that later proved to be incriminating. On appeal, the defense argued that the recording violated the ruling in *Miranda* because the suspects were in custody at the time the recording was made and the placing of the suspects alone in the vehicle with the activated recorder was interrogation for purposes of *Miranda*. The appeals court summarily dismissed this argument and found that the statements were spontaneously made and not the product of interrogation.[184]

In *Kuhlmann v. Wilson* (1986), the Supreme Court held that placing an informant in a cell with a formally charged suspect in an effort to gain incriminating statements did not amount to a violation of the defendant's constitutional rights, stating,

> Since the Sixth Amendment is not violated whenever—by luck or happenstance—the State obtains incriminating statements from the accused after the right to counsel was attached, a defendant does not make out a violation of that right simply by showing that an informant, either through prior arrangement or voluntarily, reported his incriminating statements to the police. Rather, the defendant must demonstrate that the police and their informant took some action, beyond merely listening, that was designed deliberately to elicit incriminating remarks.[185]

In a 1989 case, *Ahmad A. v. Superior Court*, the California Court of Appeals confronted a Fourth Amendment challenge to the admissibility of a surreptitiously recorded conversation between the defendant and his mother. The defendant, a juvenile arrested for murder, asked to speak with his mother when advised of his constitutional rights. The two were thereafter permitted to converse in an interrogation room with the door closed. During the surreptitiously recorded conversation that ensued, the defendant admitted his part in the murder. Reviewing the defendant's subsequent Fourth Amendment challenge, the California court noted that at the time the mother and her son were permitted to meet in the interrogation room, no representations or inquiries were made as to privacy or confidentiality. Finding the age-old truism "walls have ears" to be applicable, the court held that any subjective expectation that the defendant had regarding the privacy of his conversation was not objectively reasonable.[186] In 2001, in *Belmar v. Commonwealth*, the Virginia Appellate Court, ruling on a case similar to *Ahmad A. v. Superior Court*, wrote that police interrogation rooms are "designed for disclosure, not the hiding, of information."[187]

These cases and others show that the mere placing of a recorder in a prison cell, interrogation room, or police vehicle does not constitute a violation of a suspect's rights. Instead, in order to raise a successful Sixth Amendment challenge, the defense has to show that someone acting on behalf of the government went beyond the role of a mere passive listener (often referred to by the courts as a "listening post") and actively pursued incriminating statements from the suspect.

Crawford suggests that law enforcement officers contemplating the use of this technique comply with the following guidelines:

- To avoid a Sixth Amendment problem, this technique should not be used after formal charges have been filed or the initial appearance in court, unless the conversation does not involve a government actor, the conversation involves a government actor who has assumed the role of a "listening post," or the conversation pertains to a crime other than the one with that the suspect has been charged.
- To avoid conflicts with both Fourth Amendment and Title III of the Omnibus Crime Control and Safe Streets Act, suspects should not be given any specific assurances that their conversations are private.[188]

See Table 13.12 for a list of landmark cases regarding custodial interrogation.

TABLE 13.12   Landmark U.S. Supreme Court Decisions: Custodial Interrogations

Issue	Cases
Physical torture	*Brown v. Mississippi* (1936)
Prompt arraignment	*McNabb v. United States* (1943), *Mallory v. United States* (1957)
Refusal to allow counsel	*Escobedo v. Illinois* (1964)
Must advise of constitutional rights	*Miranda v. Arizona* (1966)
Inevitability of discovery	*Brewer v. Williams* (1977), *Nix v. Williams* (1984)
Public safety	*New York v. Quarles* (1984)
Use of unwarned statement	*Oregon v. Elstad* (1985), *Kaupp v. Texas* (2003), *J.D.B. v. North Carolina* (2011)
Lying to lawyers	*Moran v. Burbine* (1986)
Placing informer in prison cell	*Illinois v. Perkins* (1990)
Harmless trial error	*Arizona v. Fulminante* (1991)
Equivocal request for counsel	*Davis v. United States* (1994)
Miranda as constitutional decision	*Dickerson v. United States* (2000)
6th Amendment as offense-specific	*Texas v. Cobb* (2001)
Unrelated questioning not 5th Amendment violation	*Chavez v. Martinez* (2003)
Suppression of physical evidence in case of unwarned but voluntary statement	*United States v. Patane* (2004)
Use of statements obtained in follow-up interrogation despite an earlier violation of *Miranda* (beachheading)	*Missouri v. Seibert* (2004)
Right to remain silent	*Berghuis v. Thompkins* (2010)

© 2016 Cengage Learning®

Police Eyewitness Identification Procedures

Often, law enforcement officers apprehend suspects based on descriptions given by victims of violent crimes. To ensure that the apprehended person is actually the perpetrator, the police must obtain assistance from the victim or employ other identification procedures. The following sections discuss procedures to identify suspects properly as the actual perpetrators of crimes.

Lineups, Showups, and Photo Arrays

Lineups, showups, and photo arrays are important parts of the police investigation process, as are procedures requiring suspects to give samples of their voice, blood, and handwriting to be used in identification comparison procedures.

A **lineup** is the placing of a suspect with a group of other people of similar physical characteristics

lineup Police identification procedure involving the placing of a suspect with a group of other people of similar physical characteristics so that a witness or victim of a crime can have the opportunity to identify the perpetrator of the crime.

(such as race, age, hair color, hair type, height, and weight) so that a witness or victim of a crime has the opportunity to identify the perpetrator of the crime. Lineups are usually used after an arrest.

A **showup** involves bringing a suspect back to the scene of the crime or another place (for example, a hospital where an injured victim is) where the suspect can be seen and possibly identified by a victim or witness. The showup must be conducted as soon as possible after the crime, and with no suggestion that the person is a suspect. A showup is usually used after an arrest.

A **photo array** is similar to a lineup, except that photos of the suspect (who is not in custody) and others are shown to a witness. Photo arrays are used prior to arrest.

Could these procedures be construed as violating a defendant's freedom against self-incrimination as provided by the Fifth Amendment to the U.S. Constitution? The following cases detail the key landmark decisions of the Supreme Court in lineup, showup, and photo array cases.

UNITED STATES v. WADE In *United States v. Wade*, the Supreme Court in 1967 made two very important decisions about lineups.[189] It ruled that a person can be made to stand in a lineup and perform certain actions that were performed by the suspect during the crime, such as saying certain words or walking in a certain fashion. The Court also ruled that once a person is indicted, that person has a right to have an attorney present at the lineup.

KIRBY v. ILLINOIS In 1972, in *Kirby v. Illinois*, the Supreme Court ruled that the right to counsel at lineups applies only after the initiation of formal judicial criminal proceedings, such as an indictment, information, or arraignment—that is, when a person formally enters the court system.[190] An *information* is a formal charging document drafted by a prosecutor and presented to a judge. An *indictment* is a formal charging document returned by a grand jury based on evidence presented to it by a prosecutor. The indictment is then presented to a judge. Indictments generally cover felonies. An *arraignment* is a hearing before a court having jurisdiction in a criminal case, in which the identity of the defendant is established, the defendant is informed of the charge or charges and his or her rights, and the defendant is required to enter a plea. In *Kirby*, the Court reasoned that because a lineup may free an innocent person, and

YOU ARE THERE

Missouri v. Seibert (2004)

The defendant Seibert's young son, Jonathan, who was afflicted with cerebral palsy, died in his sleep, and the defendant feared that she would be charged with the neglect of her son when the death was reported to the police. In concert with two of her other sons and two of their friends, she concocted a scheme to conceal the true cause of Jonathan's death by setting the mobile home in which they lived on fire with Jonathan's body inside. Concerned with how she would explain leaving her ill son alone and unattended, the group decided to also leave Donald Rector, a mentally ill teenager who lived with the Seibert family, in the mobile home when it was set on fire. Jonathan Seibert and Donald Rector were both found dead in the burned motor home. Upon investigation, Seibert was arrested for murder and arson and transported to the police station for questioning.

Once at the police station, the arresting officer began to question Seibert without advising her of her *Miranda* rights. He questioned her for about 30 to 40 minutes before advising her of her rights under *Miranda*. During this unwarned time, Seibert admitted that before committing the arson, she knew that Donald Rector would die in the fire. Seibert was then given a 20-minute break. The officer then advised Seibert of her rights and obtained a signed waiver of rights from her. During the subsequent custodial interrogation, Seibert admitted to facts of the crime. Based on her statements, she was convicted of second-degree murder. This conviction was reversed by the Supreme Court, citing unconstitutional grounds.

the required presence of an attorney might delay the lineup, it is preferable to have the lineup as soon as possible, even without an attorney.

Thus in a postarrest, preindictment lineup, there is no right to have an attorney present. Many police

showup Police identification process involving bringing a suspect back to the scene of the crime or another place (for example, a hospital where an injured victim is) where the suspect can be seen and possibly identified by a victim or witness of a crime.

photo array Police identification procedure similar to a lineup, except that photos of the suspect (who is not in custody) and others are shown to a witness or victim of a crime.

departments, however, will permit an attorney to be present at a lineup and make reasonable suggestions, as long as there is no significant delay of the lineup.

STOVAL v. DENNO In *Stoval v. Denno* (1967), the Supreme Court ruled that showups are constitutional and do not require the presence of an attorney.[191] The Court addressed the issue as follows:

> The practice of showing suspects singly to persons for purpose of identification, and not a part of a lineup, has been unduly condemned. . . However, a claimed violation of due process of law in the conduct of a confrontation depends on the totality of the circumstances surrounding it, and the record in the present case reveals that the showing of Stoval to Mrs. Behrendt in an immediate hospital confrontation was imperative.

Subsequent to *Stoval v. Denno*, a federal appellate court established a set of guidelines phrased in the form of questions that could decide the constitutionality of a showup. A careful review of the questions reveals that the court clearly prefers lineups to showups but will permit showups if certain conditions are met:

- Was the defendant the only individual who could possibly be identified as the guilty party by the complaining witness, or were there others near him or her at the time of the showup so as to negate the assertion that he or she was shown alone to the witness?
- Where did the showup take place?
- Were there any compelling reasons for a prompt showup that would deprive the police of the opportunity of securing other similar individuals for the purpose of holding a lineup?
- Was the witness aware of any observation by another or any other evidence indicating the guilt of the suspect at the time of the showup?
- Were any tangible objects related to the offense placed before the witness that would encourage identification?
- Was the witness identification based on only part of the suspect's total personality?
- Was the identification a product of mutual reinforcement of opinion among witnesses simultaneously viewing the defendant?
- Was the emotional state of the witness such as to preclude identification?[192]

UNITED STATES v. ASH In *United States v. Ash* (1973), the Supreme Court ruled that the police could show victims or witnesses photographic displays containing a suspect's photograph (photo arrays) without the requirement that the suspect's lawyer be present.[193]

Other Identification Procedures

The Fifth Amendment governs any type of testimony. However, in most cases coming before it, the Supreme Court has declared that procedures that are not testimonial are not under the purview of the Fifth Amendment. *Testimonial* refers to oral or written communication by a suspect, rather than the taking of blood or exemplars, as indicated in this section. Samples of such cases follow.

SCHMERBER v. CALIFORNIA In 1966, in *Schmerber v. California*, the Supreme Court ruled that the forced extraction of blood by a doctor from a man who was arrested for driving while intoxicated was not a violation of that man's constitutional rights.[194] Note the difference between *Schmerber* and *Rochin v. California* (1952), mentioned earlier in this chapter. In *Rochin*, the Court held that the police had engaged in behavior that "shocks the conscience" and thus held their actions to be unconstitutional. In *Schmerber*, the Court found no similar shocking behavior and thus held the doctor's actions to be constitutional.

Recently, in *Missouri v. McNeely* (2013), the Supreme Court ruled that "a compelled physical intrusion beneath McNeely's skin and into his veins to obtain a sample of his blood for use as evidence in a criminal investigation" was "an invasion of bodily integrity" and "implicates an individual's most personal and deep-rooted expectations of privacy." Based on this decision, police must now obtain a warrant before drawing blood from a suspect in a DUI investigation, effectively reversing the *Schmerber* ruling. The Court did, however, leave open the possibility for exigent circumstances.[195]

WINSTON v. LEE In *Winston v. Lee* (1985), the Supreme Court clarified its position on medical provisions regarding prisoners.[196] When the Court decided the *Schmerber* case, it warned, "That we today hold that the Constitution does not forbid the States' minor intrusions into an individual's body under stringently limited conditions in no way indicates that it permits more substantial intrusions, or intrusions under other conditions."[197] The *Lee* case provided the test of how far the police can go in attempting to retrieve evidence from a suspect's body. Rudolph Lee, a suspect in a robbery, was shot by the victim. The police endeavored to have a bullet removed from Lee's body in order to use it for a ballistics examination. Justice William J. Brennan, speaking for the Court, wrote the following:

> We conclude that the procedure sought here is an example of the "more substantial intrusion" cautioned against in *Schmerber*, and hold that to permit the procedure would violate respondent's right to be secure in his person guaranteed by the Fourth Amendment.[198]

UNITED STATES v. DIONISIO   In *United States v. Dionisio*, the Supreme Court ruled in 1973 that a suspect must provide voice exemplars (samples of his or her voice) that can be compared with the voice spoken at the time of the crime.[199]

UNITED STATES v. MARA   In 1973, in *United States v. Mara*, the Supreme Court ruled that it was not a violation of constitutional rights for the police to require a suspect to provide a handwriting exemplar (a sample of his or her handwriting) for comparison with handwriting involved in the crime.[200]

EYEWITNESS IDENTIFICATION   In 2001, the National Institute of Justice produced a guide for law enforcement for the collection and preservation of eyewitness evidence that represented a combination of the best current, workable police practices and psychological research. It describes practices and procedures that, if consistently applied, will tend to increase the overall accuracy and reliability

United States v. Wade (1967)

On September 21, 1964, a man with a piece of tape on each side of his face forced a cashier and a bank official to put money into a pillowcase. The robber then left the bank and drove away with an accomplice, who was waiting outside in a car.

In March 1965, six months after the robbery, an indictment was returned against Wade and an accomplice for the robbery. Wade was arrested on April 2, 1965. Two weeks later, an FBI agent put Wade into a lineup to be observed by two bank employees. Wade had a lawyer, but the lawyer was not notified of the lineup. Each person in the lineup had strips of tape on his face, similar to those worn by the robber, and each was told to say words that had been spoken at the robbery. Both bank employees identified Wade as the robber. Wade was convicted based on the identification by the witnesses.

On appeal, the Supreme Court ruled that placing someone in a lineup and forcing that person to speak or perform other acts at the lineup does not violate the Fifth Amendment privilege against self-incrimination. The Court held, however, that because Wade had been indicted and was represented by counsel, the lawyer should have been allowed to be there.

Source: Based on *United States v. Wade*, 388 U.S. 218 (1967).

Winston v. Lee (1985)

On July 18, 1982, Ralph E. Warkinson was shot during a robbery attempt at his place of business. Warkinson fired at the shooter and believed he hit him in the side. The police brought Warkinson to a local hospital emergency room. Twenty minutes later, the police responded to a reported shooting and found Rudolph Lee suffering from a gunshot wound to the left chest area. Lee said he had been shot during a robbery attempt by two men. When Lee was taken to the hospital (the same one to which Warkinson had been taken), Warkinson identified Lee as the man who had shot him. After a police interrogation, Lee was arrested for the shooting.

In an effort to obtain ballistics evidence, the police attempted to have Lee undergo a surgical procedure under a general anesthetic for the removal of the bullet lodged in his chest. Lee appealed to the courts, which ruled in his favor and against the operation. The Commonwealth of Virginia appealed the case to the U.S. Supreme Court. The Court ruled that such a surgical procedure, without Lee's permission, would be a violation of his Fourth Amendment rights.

Source: Based on *Winston v. Lee*, 470 U.S. 753 (1985).

of eyewitness evidence. Although not intended to state legal criteria for the admissibility of evidence, it sets out rigorous criteria for handling eyewitness evidence that are as demanding as those governing the handling of physical trace evidence. It outlines basic procedures that officers can use to obtain the most reliable and accurate information from eyewitnesses.[201]

See Table 13.13 for a list of landmark cases regarding police identification.

TABLE 13.13   Landmark U.S. Supreme Court Decisions: Police Identification Procedures

Issue	Cases
Lineups	*United States v. Wade* (1967), *Kirby v. Illinois* (1972)
Showups	*Stoval v. Denno* (1967)
Photo arrays	*United States v. Ash* (1973)
Medical procedures	*Schmerber v. California* (1966), *Winston v. Lee* (1985), *Missouri v. McNeely* (2013)

© 2016 Cengage Learning®

SUMMARY

- Two major methods are used to measure crime in the United States: (1) the *Uniform Crime Reports* (UCR), and (2) the National Crime Victimization Survey (NCVS).

- In 2010, the U.S. police made about 13.1 million arrests for all criminal infractions except traffic violations.

- The United States is a nation governed by law. The primary law regulating life in the United States is the U.S. Constitution, including its many amendments.

- The U.S. Constitution is a continuing, dynamic document constantly being reviewed by the U.S. Supreme Court.

- The U.S. criminal justice system is based on the Bill of Rights, the first 10 amendments to the U.S. Constitution. Five of the first 10 amendments specifically address freedoms or rights that people possess when involved with the criminal justice system.

- The U.S. Supreme Court, through its policy of judicial review, has made a significant impact on the way the police do their job. As early as 1914, in *Weeks v. United States*, the Court influenced the police by regulating how they should conduct their searches and seizures. In 1936, in *Brown v. Mississippi*, the Court began to affect the police by ruling certain methods of police interrogation unconstitutional.

- Most Supreme Court cases regarding criminal justice try to strike a balance between the rights of the individual and the rights of society. The Supreme Court has the difficult task of bringing balance between these two often-conflicting goals.

- In police matters, the Supreme Court hears cases, on appeal, from people who have been the subject of police actions, including arrest, search and seizure, and custodial interrogation. The justices then decide whether or not the police action violated the person's constitutional rights, usually by interpreting one of the amendments to the Constitution. Certain significant cases, such as *Mapp v. Ohio* and *Miranda v. Arizona*, are known as landmark cases and can bring about changes in police procedures.

- The major method used by the Supreme Court to ensure that the police do not violate people's constitutional rights is the use of the exclusionary rule, which is an interpretation of the Fourteenth Amendment by the Supreme Court that holds that evidence seized in violation of the U.S. Constitution cannot be used in court against a defendant. The exclusionary rule evolved in U.S. law through a series of Supreme Court cases. By 1961, the Supreme Court, noting that states had not amended their procedures to conform to the Constitution, applied the exclusionary rule to state courts and law enforcement agencies, as well as federal ones.

- Most of the arrests made by the average police officer do not involve a warrant, because most crimes an officer becomes aware of on the street necessitate immediate action and do not allow the officer the time necessary to go to court to obtain a warrant.

- Most of the arrests made by the police are based on the probable cause standard, which can be defined as evidence that may lead a reasonable person to believe that a crime has been committed and that a certain person committed it.

- Reasonable suspicion is a standard of proof that would lead a reasonable person (a police officer) to believe a certain condition or fact exists (that a crime is, will be, or has occurred). This is the standard necessary for police officers to conduct stop and frisks.

- The U.S. Supreme Court has consistently ruled that canine sniffs by a trained drug dog are not actual searches and seizures controlled by the Fourth Amendment.

- Police searches are governed by the Fourth Amendment, which prohibits all unreasonable searches and seizures and requires that all warrants be based on probable cause and that they particularly describe the place to be searched and the persons or things to be seized.

- The major exceptions to the warrant requirement of the Fourth Amendment are: abandoned property, automobile exception, border searches, computer error, consent, exigent circumstances, field interrogations, good faith, incident to arrest, inventory, open fields, and plain view.

- The U.S. Supreme Court has recognized two constitutional sources of the right to counsel during interrogation: the Court's interpretation in *Miranda v. Arizona* of the Fifth Amendment right against self-incrimination and the Sixth Amendment.

- The *Miranda* rule (or *Miranda* warnings) states that prior to any interrogation of a person in custody, the police must do the following:
  - Advise the suspect that he or she has the right to remain silent
  - Advise the suspect that anything he or she says will be used against him or her in court
  - Advise the suspect that he or she has the right to consult a lawyer and to have the lawyer present during questioning
  - Advise the suspect that if he or she cannot afford an attorney, an attorney will be provided, free of charge

- In *Dickerson* v. United States (2000), the Supreme Court ruled that *Miranda* is a constitutional decision that cannot be overruled by an act of Congress.

- The surreptitious recording of suspects' conversations is an effective investigative technique that, if done properly, can withstand both constitutional and statutory challenges.

- Lineups, showups, and photo arrays are important parts of the police investigation process, as are procedures requiring suspects to give samples of their voice, blood, and handwriting to be used in identification comparison procedures.

KEY TERMS

arrest
Carroll doctrine
castle doctrine
crime
crime scene
custodial interrogation
exclusionary rule
exigent circumstances
field interrogation
habeas corpus
judicial review

lineup
malum in se
malum prohibitum
Miranda rule (or *Miranda* warnings)
National Crime Victimization Survey (NCVS)
photo array
plain view evidence
probable cause
reasonable force

reasonable suspicion
search and seizure
search warrant
showup
silver platter doctrine
stop and frisk
Terry stop
third degree
Uniform Crime Reports (UCR)

REVIEW EXERCISES

1. Your criminal justice professor has scheduled a class debate regarding the Supreme Court and the Fourth Amendment. The subject to be debated is "The Supreme Court has swung too far to the left by overemphasizing the rights of society and underemphasizing individual rights." The professor gives you a choice as to which side you take and tells you to be prepared to cite as many cases as possible in the area of search and seizure in order to defend your stand. Prepare yourself for the debate.

2. Your criminal justice professor has scheduled a class debate regarding the Supreme Court and the Fifth and Sixth Amendments. The subject to be debated is "The Supreme Court has swung too far to the left by overemphasizing the rights of society and underemphasizing individual

rights." The professor gives you a choice as to which side you take and tells you to be prepared to cite as many cases as possible in the area of custodial interrogation in order to defend your stand. Prepare yourself for the debate.

3. Your criminal justice professor states, "You have plenty of Fourth Amendment rights against unreasonable search and seizure in your home, fewer on the public streets, and many fewer in your vehicle." Is she right? Cite five cases in each area (home, street, vehicle) to explain your answer.

4. Your criminal justice professor has established a static traffic stop exercise for you to complete. You are to use the seven-step method to contact a violator at the traffic scene. This is not a "felony" traffic stop. What are the seven steps you should use in making contact with a violator?

WEB EXERCISES

1. Search the Web and obtain the latest statistics on the number and types of Index crimes reported to the police in the United States.

2. Search the Web and obtain the latest statistics on the number and types of arrests made by the police in the United States.

3. Search the Web and obtain the latest statistics on the number and types of crimes reported to the National Institute of Justice in the National Crime Victimization Survey.

END NOTES

1. U.S. Constitution, retrieved March 21, 2012, from www.law.cornell.edu.

2. "Comparing Federal and State Courts," retrieved March 20, 2012, from www.uscourts.gov.

3. Ibid.

4. Howard N. Snyder, *Arrest in the United States, 1990-2010*, U.S. Department of Justice, Office of Justice Programs, Bureau of Justice Statistics (October 2012).

5. "Legal Element of a Crime," retrieved March 25, 2012, from www.cliffnotes.com.

6. Dictionary.law.com, retrieved March 25, 2012, from www.law.com.

7. "Defenses to Criminal Charges," retrieved March 26, 2012, from www.nolo.com.

8. "Punishment of Crime," retrieved March 25, 2012, from www.lawyers.com.

9. *Weeks v. United States*, 232 U.S. 383 (1914).

10. *Brown v. Mississippi*, 297 U.S. 278 (1936).

11. *Mapp v. Ohio*, 367 U.S. 643 (1961); *Miranda v. Arizona*, 384 U.S. 436 (1966).

12. *Weeks v.* United States.

13. *Silverthorne Lumber Co. v. United States*, 251 U.S. 385 (1920).

14. *Wolf v. Colorado*, 338 U.S. 25 (1949).

15. *Rochin v. California*, 342 U.S. 165 (1952).

16. *Mapp v. Ohio*.

17. Fred W. Friendly and Martha J. H. Elliot, *The Constitution: That Delicate Balance*, New York: McGraw-Hill, 1984, p. vii.

18. U.S. Department of Justice, National Institute of Justice, *The Effects of the Exclusionary Rule: A Study of California* (Washington, D.C.: National Institute of Justice, 1982), p. 12.

19. Peter Nardulli, "The Societal Cost of the Exclusionary Rule: An Empirical Assessment," *ABF Research Journal* (1983): 585–609.

20. *Atwater v. City of Lago Vista*, 532 U.S. 318 (2001).

21. *Payton v. New York*, 445 U.S. 573 (1980).

22. *Brinegar v. United States*, 338 U.S. 160 (1949).

23. *Henry v. United States*, 361 U.S. 98 (1959).

24. *Draper v. United States*, 358 U.S. 307 (1959).

25. *County of Riverside v. McLaughlin*, 500 U.S. 44 (1991).

26. *Maryland v. Pringle*, 124 S. Ct. 795 (2003).

27. For a comprehensive article on police use of force, see Thomas D. Petrowski, "When Is Force Excessive: Insightful Guidance from the U.S. Supreme Court," *FBI Law Enforcement Bulletin* (September 2005): 27–32.

28. *Tennessee v. Garner*, 471 U.S. 1 (1985).

29. *Scott v. Harris*, 127 S. Ct. 1769 (2007). Also see Carl A. Benoit, "Vehicle Pursuits and the Fourth Amendment: A Roadmap for Police," *FBI Law Enforcement Bulletin* (October 2007): 23–32.

30. Ibid.

31. Ibid.

32. Basic Traffic Stops, Law Enforcement I, Unit XII, Texas Education Agency, 2011.

33. *Delaware v. Prouse*, 440 U.S. 648 (1979).

34. *Mimms v. Pennsylvania*, 434 U.S. 106 (1977).

35. *Maryland v. Wilson*, 117 S. Ct. 882 (1997). For a thorough discussion of *Mimms* and *Wilson*, see Lisa A. Regini, "Extending the *Mimms* Rule to Include Passengers," *FBI Law Enforcement Bulletin* (June 1997): 27–32.

36. *Maryland v. Wilson*, citing Federal Bureau of Investigation, *Uniform Crime Reports: Law Enforcement Officers Killed and Assaulted* (Washington, D.C.: Federal Bureau of Investigation, 1994).

37. *Michigan Department of State Police v. Sitz*, 496 U.S. 444 (1990).

38. *City of Indianapolis v. Edmond*, 121 S. Ct. 447 (2000).

39. *Illinois v. Lidster*, 124 S. Ct. 885 (2004). For a thorough discussion of *Lidster, Edmond*, and *Sitz*, see Martin J. King, "The 'Special Needs' Exception to the Warrant Requirement," *FBI Law Enforcement Bulletin* (June 2006): 21–30.

40. *Whren v. United States*, 116 S. Ct. 1769 (1996).

41. *Brendlin v. California*, 127 S. Ct. 2400 (2007). Also see Richard J. Ashton, "Bridging the Legal Gap between the Traffic Stop and Criminal Investigation," *Police Chief* (July 2007): 42–44, 46, 49–51; William Branigin, "Supreme Court Rules in Favor of Car Passengers," *Washington Post*, June 18, 2007; and John M. Collins, "Recent Decision in *Brendlin v. California* Provides Good 'Law Review' on Seizures of Persons," *Police Chief* (September 2007): 10–11.

42. *Virginia v. Moore*, 553 U.S. 164 (2008).

43. Brendan Purves, *Castle Doctrine from State to State*, New and Noteworthy, retrieved April 5, 2014, from http://source#southuniversity.edu/castle-doctrine-from-state-tostate-46514.aspx.

44. "Got Gun? Florida's 'Stand Your Ground' Law Just Got Teeth," April 4, 2014, accessed May 8, 2014, http://rt.com/usa/florida-guns-bill-nra-333/.

45. *Payton v. New York*.

46. *Minnesota v. Olson*, 495 U.S. 91 (1990).

47. *Minnesota v. Carter*, 119 S. Ct. 469 (1998).

48. *Kirk v. Louisiana*, 536 U.S. 635 (2002).

49. *Bond v. United States*, 529 U.S. 334 (2000).

50. Sophia Y. Kil, "Supreme Court Cases: 1999–2000 Term," *FBI Law Enforcement Bulletin* (November 2000): 28–29.

51. *Katz v. United States*, 389 U.S. 347 (1967).

52. *Kyllo v. United States*, 533 U.S. 27 (2001); Linda Greenhouse, "Justices Say Warrant Is Required in High-Tech Searches of Homes," *New York Times*, June 12, 2001, pp. A1, A29.

53. *United States v. Place*, 462 U.S. 696 (1983).

54. See Michael J. Bulzomi, "Drug Detection Dogs: Legal Considerations," *FBI Law Enforcement Bulletin* (January 2000): 27–31.

55. Ibid.

56. Jayme S. Walker, "Using Drug Detection Dogs: An Update," *FBI Law Enforcement Bulletin* (April 2001): 25–32.

57. *Illinois v. Caballes*, 543 U.S. 405 (2005). Also see Jennifer Ashley, Simon Billinge, and Craig Hemmens, "Who Let the Dogs Out? Drug Dogs in Court," *Criminal Justice Studies* 3 (2007): 177–196.

58. *Illinois v. Caballes*.

59. *Florida v. Harris* 568 US (2013).

60. *Wilson v. Arkansas*, 115 S. Ct. 1914 (1995). For a complete discussion of Fourth Amendment standards on search warrants, see Michael J. Bulzomi, "Knock and Announce: A Fourth Amendment Standard," *FBI Law Enforcement Bulletin* (May 1997): 27–32.

61. *Aguilar v. Texas*, 378 U.S. 108 (1964); *Spinelli v. United States*, 393 U.S. 410 (1969).

62. *Illinois v. Gates*, 462 U.S. 213 (1983).

63. For an excellent article on *Illinois v. Gates* and other cases involving probable cause and search warrants, see Edward Hendrie, "Inferring Probable Cause: Obtaining a Search Warrant for a Suspect's Home Without Direct Information That Evidence Is Inside," *FBI Law Enforcement* Bulletin (February 2002): 23–32.

64. *Michigan v. Summers*, 452 U.S. 692 (1981). For further discussion of *Summers*, see Carl A. Benoit, "Detaining Individuals at the Scene of a Search," *FBI Law Enforcement Bulletin* (December 2006): 16–25.

65. *Muehler v. Mena*, 125 S. Ct. 1465 (2005). For further discussion of *Mena*, see Benoit, "Detaining Individuals at the Scene of a Search."

66. *Los Angeles County, California v. Rettele*, 127 S. Ct. 1989 (2007).

67. Ibid.

68. *United States v. Banks*, 124 S. Ct. 521 (2003).

69. *Hudson v. Michigan*, 126 S. Ct. 2159 (2006); Richard G. Schott, "Knock and Announce Violations: No 'Cause' to Suppress," *FBI Law Enforcement Bullet in* (September 2006): 26–32.

70. *Hudson v. Michigan.*

71. *United States v. Grubbs*, 547 U.S. 90 (2006).

72. *Chimel v. California*, 395 U.S. 752 (1969).

73. *United States v. Robinson*, 414 U.S. 218 (1973).

74. *Knowles v. Iowa*, 119 S. Ct. 484 (1998). For an excellent article on the history of searches incident to arrest, see Thomas D. Colbridge, "Search Incident to Arrest: Another Look," *FBI Law Enforcement Bulletin* (May 1999): 27–32.

75. Michael J. Bulzomi, "Search Incident to Arrest in the Age of Personal Electronics," *FBI Law Enforcement Bulletin* (September 2007): 26–32. Also see M. Wesley Clark, "Searching Cell Phones Seized Incident to Arrest," *FBI Law Enforcement Bulletin* (February 2009): 25–32.

76. *United States v. Chan*, 830 F. Supp. 531 (N.D. Cal. 1993); *United States v. Finley*, 477 F.3d 250 (5th Cir. 2007).

77. *Terry v. Ohio*, 392 U.S. 1 (1968). For further information on *Terry*, see Bulzomi, "Police Intervention Short of Arrest."

78. *Terry v. Ohio.*

79. Joe Kemp, *Stop-and-Frisks Drop 34% in Latest Quarter, report New York Police Dept.*, August 3, 2012, *New York Daily News*, retrieved August 8, 2012, from www.nydailynews.com/new-york/stop-and-frisks-drop-34-latest-quarter-reports-new-yark-police-dept-article-1.1128427?print.

80. Colleen Long, March 18, 2013, *NYPD's 'Stop and Frisk' Heads to Federal Court*, Associated Press, retrieved August 8, 2013 from www.Officer.com (November 2006): 26–32.

81. *Hiibel v. Sixth Judicial District Court of Nevada, Humboldt County*, 124 S. Ct. 2451 (2004). For further information on *Hiibel*, see Michael J. Bulzomi, "Police Intervention Short of Arrest," *FBI Law Enforcement Bulletin* (November 2006): 26–32.

82. *Minnesota v. Dickerson*, 113 S. Ct. 2130 (1993).

83. *Illinois v. Wardlow*, 120 S. Ct. 673 (2000).

84. *Illinois v. Wardlow*, citing *Terry*, 392 U.S. at 30.

85. Kil, "Supreme Court Cases: 1999–2000 Term," pp. 28–32. For an excellent discussion of the *Wardlow* decision and flight as justification for seizure, see Michel E. Brooks, "Flight as Justification for Seizure: Supreme Court Rulings," *FBI Law Enforcement Bulletin* (June 2000): 28–32.

86. *Florida v. J. L.*, 120 S. Ct. 1375 (2000). For an interesting, informative article on *Terry* stops in response to anonymous tips, see Michael J. Bulzomi, "Anonymous Tips and Frisks: Determining Reasonable Suspicion," *FBI Law Enforcement Bulletin* (August 2000): 28–30.

87. *Payton v. New York.*

88. *Arkansas v. Sanders*, 442 U.S. 753 (1979).

89. Michael L. Ciminelli, "Police Response to Anonymous Emergency Calls," *FBI Law Enforcement Bulletin* (May 2003): 23–32.

90. *Warden v. Hayden*, 387 U.S. 294 (1967).

91. *Mincey v. Arizona*, 437 U.S. 385 (1978).

92. *Maryland v. Buie.*

93. *Wilson v. Arkansas.*

94. *Illinois v. McArthur.*

95. Ciminelli, "Police Response to Anonymous Emergency Calls," pp. 23–31.

96. *Brigham City v. Stuart*, 126 S. Ct. 1943 (2006).

97. Ibid.

98. Jayme Walker Holcomb, "Consent Searches: Factors Courts Consider in Determining Voluntariness," *FBI Law Enforcement Bulletin* (May 2002): 25–31; also see Holcomb, "Obtaining Written Consent to Search," *FBI Law Enforcement Bulletin* (March 2003): 26–32; and Carl A. Benoit, "Questioning 'Authority': Fourth Amendment Consent Searches," *FBI Law Enforcement* Bulletin (July 2008): 23–32.

99. *Schneckloth v. Bustamonte*, 412 U.S. 218 (1973).

100. *United States v. Matlock*, 415 U.S. 164 (1974).

101. *Bumper v. North Carolina*, 391 U.S. 543 (1968).

102. *Illinois v. Rodriguez*, 110 S. Ct. 2793 (1990).

103. *Florida v. Bostick*, 111 S. Ct. 2382 (1991).

104. Edward M. Hendrie, "Consent Once Removed," *FBI Law Enforcement Bulletin* (February 2003): 24–32.

105. *United States v. Pollard*, 215 F.3d 643 (6th Cir. 2000).

106. *Georgia v. Randolph*, 126 S. Ct. 1515 (2006).

107. *United States v. Matlock* and *Illinois v. Rodriguez.*

108. *Fernandez v. California*, 571 US#(2014)

109. *Fernandez v. California*, 571 US#(2014), Dissent, p2

110. *Harris v. United States*, 390 U.S. 234 (1968). See also *Horton v. California*, 110 S. Ct. 2301 (1990). For a comprehensive article on plain view evidence, see Devallis Rutledge, "Seizing Evidence in Plain View," *Police* (March 2006): 82–84.

111. *Arizona v. Hicks*, 107 S. Ct. 1149 (1987).

112. *Mincey v. Arizona*, 437 U.S. 385 (1978); also see *Thompson v. Louisiana*, 496 U.S. 17 (1984); John S. Dempsey, *Introduction to Investigations*, 2nd ed. (Belmont, Calif.: Wadsworth, 2003), pp. 48–49; and Kimberly A. Crawford, "Crime Scene Searches: The Need for Fourth Amendment Compliance," *FBI Law Enforcement Bulletin* (January 1999): 26–31.

113. Crawford, "Crime Scene Searches." For a complete discussion of crime scenes and crime scene procedures, see Dempsey, *An Introduction to Investigations*, Ch. 3.

114. *Illinois v. Rodriguez.*

115. Crawford, "Crime Scene Searches."

116. *Abel v. United States*, 362 U.S. 217 (1960). For further information on abandonment of evidence, see Jayme W. Holcomb, "Abandonment of Items Associated with the Person," *FBI Law Enforcement Bulletin* (August 2007): 23–32; Holcomb, "Abandoning Places," *FBI Law Enforcement Bulletin* (October 2008): 22–32.

117. *California v. Greenwood*, 486 U.S. 35 (1988). For further information on abandonment of evidence, see Holcomb, "Abandonment of Items Associated with the Person."

118. *California v. Hodari, D.*, 499 U.S. 621 (1991). For further information on *Hodari, D.*, see Holcomb, "Abandonment of Items Associated with the Person."

119. *Colorado v. Bertine*, 479 U.S. 367 (1987).

120. *Hester v. United States*, 265 U.S. 57 (1924).

121. *Oliver v. United States*, 466 U.S. 170 (1984).

122. *California v.* Ciraola, 476 U.S. 207 (1986).

123. *Florida v. Riley*, 488 U.S. 445 (1989).

124. *Carroll v. United States*, 267 U.S. 132 (1925).

125. *Carroll v. United States.* For a comprehensive recent article on the motor vehicle exception, see Edward Hendrie, "The Motor Vehicle Exception," *FBI Law Enforcement Bulletin* (August 2005): 22–32.

126. *New York v. Belton*, 453 U.S. 454 (1981).

127. *United States v. Villamonte-Marquez*, 462 U.S. 579 (1983); *California v. Carney*, 471 U.S. 386 (1985).

128. *Arizona v. Gant*, 129 S. Ct. 1710 (2009); Richard G. Schott, "The Supreme Court Reexamines Search Incident to Lawful Arrest," *FBI Law Enforcement Bulletin* (July 2009): 22–31; and Adam Liptak, "Supreme Court Cuts Back Officers' Searches of Vehicles," *New York Times*, April 22, 2009, retrieved April 22, 2009, from www.nytimes.com.

129. M. Weseley Clark, "U.S. Land Border Search Authority," *FBI Law Enforcement Bulletin* (August 2004): 22–32.

130. *United States v. Martinez-Fuerte*, 428 U.S. 543 (1976). For a comprehensive article on border searches, see Clark, "U.S. Land Border Search Authority." For further information on *Martinez-Fuerte*, see Martin J. King, "The 'Special Needs' Exception to the Warrant Requirement," *FBI Law Enforcement* Bulletin (June 2006): 21–30.

131. *United States v. Leon*, 468 U.S. 897 (1984).

132. *Massachusetts v. Sheppard*, 468 U.S. 981 (1984); *Illinois v. Krull*, 480 U.S. 340 (1987); *Maryland v. Garrison*, 480 U.S. 79 (1987).

133. *Arizona v. Evans*, 514 U.S. 1 (1995).

134. *Groh v. Ramirez*, 124 S. Ct. 1284 (2004).

135. *Samson v. California*, 126 S. Ct. 2193 (2006).

136. *Burdeau v. McDowell*, 256 U.S. 465 (1921). For further information on *Burdeau*, see John S. Dempsey, *Introduction to Private Security* (Belmont, Calif.: Thomson/Wadsworth, 2008): 94–95; and Dempsey, *Introduction to Private Security*, 2nd ed. (Belmont, Calif.: Wadsworth/Cengage Learning, 2011): 96–97.

137. *Miranda v. Arizona.*

138. Kimberly A. Crawford, "Constitutional Rights to Counsel During Interrogation: Comparing Rights Under the Fifth and Sixth Amendments," *FBI Law Enforcement Bulletin* (September 2002): 28–32.

139. James W. Osterburg and Richard H. Ward, *Criminal Investigation: A Method for Reconstructing the Past* (Cincinnati: Anderson, 1992), p. 377.

140. Louis DiPietro, "Lies, Promises, or Threats: The Voluntariness of Confessions," *FBI Law Enforcement Bulletin* (July 1993): 27–32.

141. *Brown v. Mississippi.*

142. *McNabb v. United States*, 318 U.S. 332 (1943); *Mallory v. United States*, 354 U.S. 449 (1957).

143. *Escobedo v. Illinois*, 378 U.S. 478 (1964).

144. *Miranda v. Arizona.*

145. Based on *Miranda v. Arizona.*

146. Lisa A. Judge, "*Miranda* Revisited," *Police Chief* (August 2003): 13–15.

147. *Oregon v. Mathiason*, 429 U.S. 492 (1977).

148. *Berkemer v. McCarty*, 468 U.S. 420 (1984); *Beckwith v. United States*, 425 U.S. 341 (1976).

149. *Moran v. Burbine*, 475 U.S. 412 (1986); *Michigan v. Mosley*, 423 U.S. 96 (1975); *Edwards v.* Arizona, 451 U.S. 477 (1981); *Arizona v. Roberson*, 486 U.S. 675 (1988); *Minnick v. Mississippi*, 495 U.S. 903 (1991).

150. *Colorado v. Connelly*, 107 S. Ct. 515 (1986).

151. *Arizona v. Roberson.*

152. Alan M. Dershowitz, *Taking Liberties: A Decade of Hard Cases, Bad Laws and Bum Raps* (Chicago: Contemporary Books, 1988), p. 10.

153. Ibid., p. 12.

154. *Harris v. New York*, 401 U.S. 222 (1971).

155. *Michigan v. Mosley.*

156. *Brewer v. Williams*, 430 U.S. 387 (1977).

157. *Nix v. Williams*, 467 U.S. 431 (1984).

158. *Rhode Island v. Innis*, 446 U.S. 291 (1980).

159. *New York v. Quarles*, 104 S. Ct. 2626 (1984).

160. *Oregon v. Elstad*, 470 U.S. 298 (1985).

161. *Moran v. Burbine.*

162. *Illinois v. Perkins*, 110 S. Ct. 2394 (1990).

163. *Pennsylvania v. Muniz*, 496 U.S. 582 (1990).

164. *Arizona v. Fulminante*, 111 S. Ct. 1246 (1991).

165. *Minnick v. Mississippi*, 111 S. Ct. 486 (1991).

166. *McNeil v. Wisconsin*, 111 S. Ct. 2204 (1991).

167. *Withrow v. Williams*, 112 S. Ct. 1745 (1993).

168. *Davis v. United States*, 114 S. Ct. 2350 (1994).

169. *Stansbury v. California*, 114 S. Ct. 1526 (1994).

170. *Dickerson v. United States*, 530 U.S. 428 (2000). See Thomas D. Petrowski, "Miranda Revisited: Dickerson v. United States," *FBI Law Enforcement Bulletin* (August 2001): 25–32.

171. *Dickerson v. United States*; Kil, "Supreme Court Cases: 1999–2000 Term," pp. 28–32.

172. Samuel C. Rickless, *"Miranda, Dickerson,* and the Problem of Actual Innocence," *Criminal Justice Ethics* 2 (2000): 2–55.

173. *Texas v. Cobb,* 121 S. Ct. 1335 (2001); also see Kimberly A. Crawford, "The Sixth Amendment Right to Counsel: Application and Limitations," *FBI Law Enforcement Bulletin* (July 2001): 27–32.

174. *Chavez v. Martinez,* 123 S. Ct. 1994 (2003).

175. *Kaupp v. Texas,* 123 S. Ct. 1843 (2003). For further information on *Kaupp,* see Michael J. Bulzomi, "Police Intervention Short of Arrest," *FBI Law Enforcement Bulletin* (November 2006): 26–32.

176. *J.D.B. v. North Carolina,* 564 U.S._____ (2011).

177. *United States v. Patane,* 124 S. Ct. 2620 (2004).

178. *Missouri v. Seibert,* 124 S. Ct. 2601 (2004). For a comprehensive article on the *Seibert* case, see Lucy Ann Hoover, "The Supreme Court Brings an End to the 'End Run' Around Miranda," *FBI Law Enforcement* Bulletin (June 2005): 26–32.

179. *Montejo v. Louisiana,* 129 S. Ct. 2079 (2009); and David Stout, "Justices Ease Rules on Questioning," *New York Times,* May 27, 2009, retrieved May 27, 2009, from www.nytimes.com.

180. *Berghuis v. Thompkins,* 560 U.S. 370 (2010).

181. *Maryland v. Shatzer,* 559 U.S. (2010).

182. *Seremeth v. Frederick County, et al.,* 573 F.3d 333 (2012).

183. Kimberly A. Crawford, "Surreptitious Recording of Suspects' Conversations," *FBI Law Enforcement Bulletin* (September 1993): 26–32; also see Richard G. Schott, "Warrantless Interception of Communications: When, Where, and Why It Can Be Done," *FBI Law Enforcement Bulletin* (January 2003): 25–31.

184. *Stanley v. Wainwright,* 604 F.2d 379 (5th Cir. 1979).

185. *Kuhlmann v. Wilson,* 106 S. Ct. 2616 (1986).

186. *Ahmad A. v. Superior Court,* 263 Cal. Rptr. 747 (Cal. App. 2d 1989), *cert.* denied, 498 U.S. 834 (1990).

187. *Belmar v. Commonwealth,* 553 S.E.2d 123 (Va. App. Ct. 2001).

188. Crawford, "Surreptitious Recording of Suspects' Conversations," pp. 29–31.

189. *United States v. Wade,* 388 U.S. 218 (1967).

190. *Kirby v. Illinois,* 406 U.S. 682 (1972).

191. *Stoval v. Denno,* 388 U.S. 293 (1967).

192. *United States v. O'Connor,* 282 F. Supp. 963 (D.D.C. 1968).

193. *United States v. Ash,* 413 U.S. 300 (1973).

194. *Schmerber v. California,* 384 U.S. 757 (1966).

195. *Missouri v. McNeely,* 2013 U.S. LEXIS 3160 (2013).

196. *Winston v. Lee,* 470 U.S. 753 (1985).

197. *Schmerber v. California.*

198. *Winston v. Lee.*

199. *United States v. Dionisio,* 410 U.S. 1 (1973).

200. *United States v. Mara,* 410 U.S. 19 (1973).

201. "Eyewitness Evidence," *FBI Law Enforcement Bulletin* (July 2001): 15. Also see Beth Schuster, "Police Lineup: Making Eyewitness Identification More Reliable," *NIJ Journal* 258 (2007): 2–9.

Critical Issues in Policing

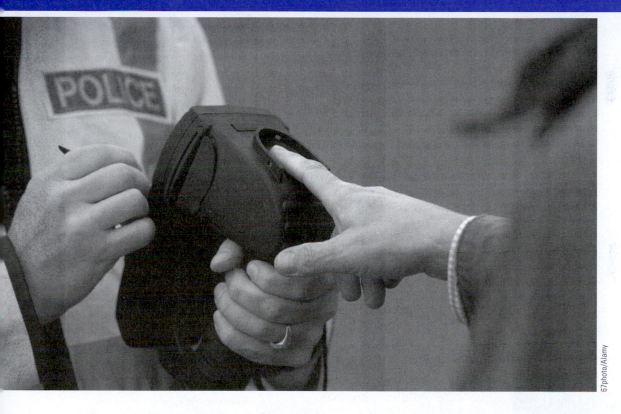

67photo/Alamy

CHAPTER 14
Computers, Technology, and Criminalistics in Policing

CHAPTER 15
Homeland Security

Computers, Technology, and Criminalistics in Policing

© Joel Gordon

LEARNING OBJECTIVES

- List the major uses of computers in police departments today and discuss some of the controversy surrounding their implementation.

- Explain why the use of less-than-lethal weapons can be seen as both necessary and dangerous.

- Identify examples of how modern technology has changed police surveillance practices.

- Explain the functions of crime labs and the need for rigorous accreditation policies.

- Summarize the historical and current use of DNA profiling in policing.

- Discuss the debate regarding technology use in policing and public civil liberties.

OUTLINE

Computer Technology in Policing
Computer-Aided Dispatch (CAD)
Automated Databases
Automated Crime Analysis (Crime Mapping)
Computer-Aided Investigation (Computer-Aided Case Management)
Computer-Assisted Instruction
Administrative Uses of Computers
Computer Networks and the Internet
Mobile Technology

Fingerprint Technology
Basic Categories of Fingerprints
Automated Fingerprint Identification Systems
Automated Palm Print Technology

Less-than-Lethal Weapons
Chemical Irritant Sprays
The Taser and Other Stun Devices
Safety and Effectiveness of Less-than-Lethal Weapons

Surveillance Technology
Surveillance Vans
Vehicle Tracking Systems
Night Vision Devices
Global Positioning Systems
Surveillance Aircraft
Electronic Video Surveillance
Cell Phone Monitoring

Advanced Photographic Techniques
Digital Photography
Aerial Photography
Mug Shot Imaging
Age-Progression Photographs
Composite Sketches

Modern Forensics or Criminalistics
The *CSI* Effect
The Modern Crime Lab
Crime Lab Accreditation
Computer/Digital Forensics

DNA Profiling
The Science of DNA
History of DNA in U.S. Courts
Current Technology
DNA Databases
Other Current DNA Issues

Biometric Identification

Videotaping

Robotics

Concerns About Technology and Civil Liberties

INTRODUCTION

Computers, technology, and modern forensic or criminalistics techniques have revolutionized policing and made the police more effective in crime fighting and other duties. Lee Boyd Malvo, the teenage sniper responsible for the 2002 Beltway Sniper shootings that shocked the Washington, D.C., metropolitan and suburban areas, was identified as a result of a fingerprinting innovation described in this chapter. Dennis Rader, known as the BTK (bind, torture, and kill) killer, who murdered at least 10 people in and around Wichita, Kansas, between 1974 and 1991, was identified and arrested in 2005 based on another innovation mentioned in this chapter.

Video cameras, VCRs, DVDs, microcomputers, laptops, ATMs, smartphones, satellites, and the Internet are all very familiar to the students reading this text. However, many might not be aware that little was known of this technology on the day they were born. The past few decades have seen advances in technology that most of us would never have foreseen.

The computer chip has revolutionized society. The criminal justice system and the police in particular have benefited greatly from this technological revolution. The terrorist attacks of September 11, 2001, and other cases have heightened public awareness of the police and of forensic and scientific evidence to an extent that has never existed before. As you will see in this chapter, policing is adapting to this new technology. As former U.S. Attorney General John Ashcroft stated in 2001:

> The wave of technological advancement that has changed the lives of almost every individual, business, and institution in the nation has also changed the world of criminal justice—from how we fight crime to how we manage law enforcement resources to the types of crimes we face. New technologies can help law enforcement agencies prevent crime, apprehend criminals, manage offender populations, and protect the public from the threat of terrorism.[1]

This chapter will discuss technology in policing, including computers and their application in record keeping, crime analysis, communications, personnel allocation, investigations, administration, and training. It will also discuss fingerprint technology, including basic categories of fingerprints and automated fingerprint and palm print identification systems. Additionally, it will discuss less-than-lethal weapons, such as chemical irritant sprays, the Taser, and other stun devices, as well as the safety and effectiveness of these innovative alternatives to the use of deadly force.

The chapter will cover emerging state-of-the-art surveillance technology, including surveillance vans, vehicle tracking systems, night vision devices, global positioning systems, surveillance aircraft, and electronic video surveillance, and will discuss advanced photographic techniques such as digital photography, aerial photography, mug shot imaging, age-progression photographs, and composite sketches. We will also examine forensics and criminalistics such as the *CSI* effect, modern crime labs, crime lab accreditation, computer/digital forensics, and DNA profiling, including the science of DNA, history of DNA in U.S. courts, current DNA technology, DNA databases, and other current DNA issues. Other topics discussed include biometric identification, videotaping, robotics, and concerns about how the increased police use of modern technology may affect civil liberties.

Computer Technology in Policing

In 1964, St. Louis was the only city in the United States with a computer system for its police department. By 1968, 10 states and 50 cities had computer-based criminal justice information systems, but small and mid-sized agencies were still left behind. Today, almost every law enforcement agency uses computers in many phases of its operations. The most recently available statistics indicate that 90 percent of local police departments serving 25,000 or more residents used in-field computers. Those agencies under 25,000 population used computers on average about 60 percent of the time.[2]

It is not uncommon to see in-car cameras, radios that can scan over several different frequencies and transmission bands, license plate readers, and live scan technology. All of this technology is tied into the in-car computer, making the job of the officer more efficient. The patrol car has truly become a mobile office.[3]

Some people may think that computerization has to be an expensive undertaking available only to large police departments, but this is far from the truth. A small department can become computerized with a basic computer system, including easily available database software management programs. Computers today have become more geared toward law enforcement, giving agencies more choices and a better ability to tailor the technology to their specific needs. Officers are using laptops, embedded or modular systems, and hand-held personal digital assistants (PDAs) for transporting information back and forth between their police vehicle or field assignment and the police station.[4]

The following sections discuss the most commonly used applications of computers in police work.

Computer-Aided Dispatch (CAD)

Before the computer revolution, the police communications system was slow and cumbersome. A citizen would call the police with a seven-digit telephone number. A police telephone operator would take the information, write the phone number on an index card, and put the card on a conveyor belt, where it would travel to the dispatcher's desk. The dispatcher would then manually search maps and records for the police car that covered the area from which the call originated and then call the car, giving the officer all the information from the index card. All records were kept manually.

The 911 emergency telephone number system was introduced by American Telephone and Telegraph (AT&T) in 1968.[5] The most recent available data indicate that 92 percent of local police departments and 94 percent of sheriff's offices

----

computer-aided dispatch (CAD) System that allows almost immediate communication between the police dispatcher and police units in the field.

participate in an emergency 911 system. In addition, 73 percent of local police departments and 71 percent of sheriffs' offices had enhanced 911 systems, capable of automatically displaying information such as a caller's phone number, address, and special needs.[6]

According to Scott Freitag, president of the National Academies of Emergency Dispatch, about a half million 911 calls are placed each day. He said fewer than 1 percent of the calls are prank calls and about 10 to 15 percent are bad calls (hang-ups, misdials, or accidental activation of 911 buttons on cellular phones). About 35 percent of all 911 calls are life-threatening emergencies. Freitag said the three most important rules in handling 911 calls are: (1) treat each call as legitimate until proven otherwise; (2) follow a script, rather than adlibbing a response; and (3) use a professional and encouraging demeanor.[7]

Today **computer-aided dispatch (CAD)** allows almost immediate communication between the police dispatcher and police units in the field. Numerous CAD system software packages are available for purchase by police departments. With typical CAD systems, after a 911 operator takes a call from a citizen, the operator codes the information into the computer, and the information immediately flashes on the dispatcher's screen. The CAD system prioritizes the calls on the dispatcher's screen, putting more serious calls (such as crimes in progress and heart attacks) above less serious calls (such as past crimes and nonemergency requests for assistance). The system verifies the caller's address and telephone number and determines the most direct route to the location. The system also searches a database for dangers near the location to which the officers are responding, calls to the same location within the last 24 hours, and any previous history of calls to that location.

In addition, the CAD system constantly maintains the status of each patrol unit. In this way, the dispatcher knows which units are available and where all units are located. The system also enable dispatchers to quickly determine which patrol units are nearest to a reported emergency incident so the closest units can be dispatched to the scene.[8] Some CAD systems have automatic transponders within patrol units. These enable dispatch personnel to visually monitor all patrol vehicles via computer and to assign them in coordination with this computer-generated information.

ENHANCED CAD (ENHANCED 911, OR E911)

The technology director for the National Emergency Number Association reports that 96 percent of the nation is covered by dispatch centers that have enhanced 911 capabilities. He added that the movement toward 100 percent implementation has been slow because some counties, typically those with a low population, do not have the money to convert to the system. As an example, 24 rural counties in Kentucky have only basic 911 service. Without enhanced 911, dispatchers have to take the time to get precise directions from callers before they can notify police or other emergency responders.[9]

With an E911 system, when a person calls 911 for assistance, vital information is immediately flashed on a screen in front of the operator. The screen gives the exact address of the telephone being used; the name of the telephone subscriber; whether the location is a residence, business, or pay telephone; the police patrol beat it is on; the nearest ambulance; and the closest fire department. This system gives the police the ability to assist people at risk even when people cannot communicate because of illness, injury, or an inability to speak English. For example, if a sick or injured person initiates a call to 911 for assistance and then passes out or can no longer continue the conversation for some other reason, the police, having the information in the computer, are still able to respond with assistance.

Some enhanced CAD systems use **mobile digital terminals (MDTs)** in each patrol unit. In systems using MDTs, voice communications are replaced by electronic transmissions that appear on an officer's MDT, a device put into a police vehicle that allows the electronic transmission of messages between the police dispatcher and the officer in the field. Officers receive messages via a computer screen and transmit messages via a keyboard. The MDT systems offer the following advantages over voice systems:

- A direct interface between the patrol unit and local, county, state, and federal criminal justice information system computers, enabling an officer to query names, license plates, and driver's licenses with almost immediate response, and without interfering with radio communications or requesting the services of a dispatcher

- The elimination of many clerical duties

- The availability of more detailed information, including addresses displayed with the nearest cross streets and map coordinates (and in some cases, even floor plans)

- Better coordination of all emergency agencies, because their movements can be monitored visually by both officers at the scene and dispatchers

- Automatic processing of incident information via a preformatted incident form, eliminating the need for the officer to drop off an incident report at the station house and the need for someone to type up a report

- A dramatic increase in response time as the entire dispatch process, from call to arrival, is fully automated

- The capability for the accumulation of large amounts of data regarding police incidents and personnel, which can be used in crime analysis and staff allocation planning to assign personnel when and where crime is highest or calls for assistance are heaviest[10]

A report on the use of mobile data access to law enforcement databases has revealed that officers with in-car data access technology make more than eight times as many inquiries on driving records, vehicle registrations, and wanted persons or property per 8-hour shift than do officers without in-car computers.

The combination of geographic information systems (GIS), global positioning systems (GPS), and automatic vehicle location (AVL) systems with CAD and MDT software has increased the ability of departments to control and monitor their patrol functions. A department can quickly trace an officer's vehicle location when an officer is incapacitated and cannot verbally communicate his or her location.

---

mobile digital terminal (MDT) A device put into a police vehicle that allows the electronic transmission of messages between the police dispatcher and the officer in the field.

When CAD Systems Do Not Work as Advertised

The Bureau of Emergency Communication (BOEC) in Portland, Oregon, installed a new $14.5 million CAD system in place of its antiquated 17-year-old 911 system. The new system, rolled out in April 2011, immediately met with resistance from user agencies. After two months of operations, more than 400 bugs had been identified in the new system. Officers in the field were complaining about safety issues and poor service for the citizens. At a meeting in May 2011, the governing board announced there would be 67 fixes to the computer system within a week.

The director of the BOEC, Lisa Turley, said the project management team was processing the complaints and admitted that some resulted from lack of training and operator errors. Director Turley's take on the transition from the old system to the new was that it had been a "very smooth transition so far." With any new system, problems are to be expected, and one of the problems was a change of management during the computer transition, which in itself caused problems. Turley said it is management's responsibility to make sure all the parties involved in the transition to the new system are kept informed of what is going on.

Critics say the new CAD system in Portland is just another "botched computer system." They claim the problems and expense could have been avoided by upgrading the old system for around $500,000.

Sources: Maxine Bernstein, "Multnomah County's New 9-1-1 Computer Dispatch System Puts Officers and Public at Risk, Police Say," *The Oregonian*, May 18, 2011, retrieved March 30, 2012, from www.oregonlive.com; Jim Redden, "Critics Jump on City's New 9-1-1 System," *Portland Tribune*, May 8, 2011, retrieved March 30, 2012, from www.portlandtribune.com; Maxine Bernstein, "Portland Board Examining Problems with New 9-1-1 Dispatch System Bars Media from Meeting," *OregonLive.com*, May 19, 2011, retrieved March 30, 2012, from www.oregonlive.com.

CELL PHONE TECHNOLOGY The number of 911 calls placed from cell phones has increased, and most sophisticated 911 systems have the ability to trace the cell phone or get a location from which the call is coming. This aids the police greatly. In July 2006,

an 18-year-old woman was taken from the deserted streets of lower Manhattan in the early morning hours to a seedy hotel in Weehawken, New Jersey, where she was raped and murdered. The suspect stuffed the victim's body into a suitcase and dumped it in a trash bin behind an apartment building two blocks away. He then drove back to New York City and registered at another hotel. Police were able to find the suspect because he had taken the victim's cell phone and used it to make some calls to his mother and girlfriend. Police started their investigation by tracking her cell phone, which led them to the people the killer had called. The cell phone number appeared on caller IDs on the phones the killer had called. The police were able to take him into custody shortly thereafter.[11]

In 2007, it was reported that although more 911 calls were coming from cell phones than from land lines, 40 percent of the nation's counties, mostly rural, still could not pinpoint the location of cell phone callers even though the technology to do so had been available for at least five years.[12] For example, in 2004, a man in Provo died in a botched 911 response when paramedics were sent to a wrong address and had no way to pinpoint the accurate location of the call. The man's body was found four days later. According to Utah's E911 program manager, many rural counties do not have the tax base to sustain their 911 services.[13]

In a 2006 *FBI Law Enforcement Bulletin* article, M. Wesley Clark stated that the legal requirements are still uncertain for acquisition of cell site information by the police for the purpose of identifying the location of a cellular telephone and its user, and that traditional law does not provide law enforcement with clear-cut guidance in the area of cell phone technology. He wrote that traditional law enforcement methods of tracking, whether through the use of a tracking device on a vehicle or other conveyance or the placing of a device inside a container, fit with the analysis provided by the U.S. Supreme Court in *United States v. Knotts* (1983) and *United States v. Karo* (1984). Those cases held that as long as the conveyance or thing to be monitored is out and about on public thoroughfares, open fields, or even on private property—all instances where the information revealed by the target could be observed by visual surveillance engaged in by third parties—no showing of evidence, let alone probable cause, is required.[14] Clark stated that although this analysis holds true today as long as the tracking equipment belongs to the government, it does not resolve the issue when third-party assistance from the service provider is required. Cell phone companies with mounting concerns about liability typically will not furnish cell phone location information to law enforcement without a court order.[15]

IP TELEPHONY Telephone technology is constantly growing. **Internet Protocol (IP) telephony** is a collection of communication technologies, products, and services that can facilitate communication across diverse systems. **Voiceover IP (VoIP)**, a subset of IP telephony, is a set of software, hardware, and standards designed to enable voice transmissions over packet-switched networks, which can be either an internal local area network or the Internet. VoIP is not associated with a physical telephone line but, rather, with an IP address that is linked to a phone number.[16] Many police departments are now using IP telephony.

REVERSE 911 (R911) R911 is a way for the police to contact the community by telephone in the event of an emergency or serious situation, by a simple digital click—much more quickly and over a larger area than if the officers had to go door-to-door to notify residents. This technology was first used in DuPage County, Illinois, in 1996 and has been utilized by many municipalities since the terrorist attacks of September 11, 2001. It was used very successfully in Arlington, Virginia, following the terrorist attack on the Pentagon to enable rapid mobilization of off-duty officers.[17] During the California wildfires of October 2007, San Diego city officials implemented a reverse 911 system with automated warning calls going to residents, urging them to evacuate.[18]

Automated Databases

As we have come into the 21st century, computer technology is doing things previously unimaginable in policing. The availability of automated databases has revolutionized police work. An automated database is an enormous electronic filing cabinet that is capable of storing information and retrieving it in any desired format.

A simple example of how far we have come is a system in Mesa, Arizona. The Mesa Police Department's Cellular Digital Packet Data (CDPD) technology, an automated database, gives officers immediate access, via mobile computers, to critical information contained in the city's mainframe computer. The department's divisions using this system include homicide, pawn detail, auto theft, public information, gang control, and hostage negotiation.[19] In 2006, a pocket PC system, the Advanced Ground Information System (AGIS), was developed that allows the rapid exchange of voice, text, photos, video, and other information from emergency personnel from multiple agencies who are responding to the same event on a cell phone.[20]

The FBI created a major automated database, the **National Crime Information Center (NCIC)**, in 1967. The NCIC collects and retrieves data about people wanted for crimes anywhere in the United States; stolen and lost property, including stolen automobiles, license plates, identifiable property, boats, and securities; and other criminal justice information. The NCIC also contains criminal history files and the status (prison, jail, probation, or parole) of criminals. With its millions of active records completely automated by computer, the NCIC provides virtually uninterrupted operation day or night, seven days a week. Although the NCIC is operated by the FBI, approximately 70 percent of its use is by local, state, and other federal agencies.

In 2000, the NCIC was renamed NCIC 2000 when a major upgrade to the services extended the services down to the patrol car and the mobile officer. With this system, a police officer can identify fugitives and missing persons quickly using automated fingerprint identification system (AFIS) technology, which will be discussed later in this chapter. The officer places a subject's finger on a fingerprint reader in a patrol car, and the reader transmits the image to the NCIC computer. Within minutes, the computer forwards a reply to the officer. A printer installed in patrol cars allows officers to get copies of a suspect's photograph, fingerprint image, signature, and tattoos, along with composite drawings

----

Internet Protocol (IP) telephony A collection of communication technologies, products, and services that can facilitate communication across diverse systems.

Voiceover IP (VoIP) A subset of IP telephony that is a set of software, hardware, and standards designed to enable voice transmissions over packet-switched networks, which can be either an internal local area network or the Internet. VoIP is not associated with a physical telephone line, but rather with an IP address that is linked to a phone number.

National Crime Information Center (NCIC) Computerized database of criminal information maintained by the FBI.

of unknown subjects. The printer can also receive images of stolen goods, including cars. The new system provides for enhanced name searches (based on phonetically similar names); prisoner, probation, and parole records; convicted sex offender registries; and other services.[21]

The FBI also maintains other databases. The National Instant Criminal Background Check System (NICS) provides access to millions of criminal history records from all 50 states and the District of Columbia to match subject information for background checks on individuals attempting to purchase a firearm.[22] The Violent Criminal Apprehension Program (ViCAP) database, which contains information on unsolved murders, has helped local and state law enforcement agencies solve violent crimes for almost 20 years.[23]

In addition to these national databases, local law enforcement agencies maintain their own databases. Police departments and investigators store many different types of archived files onto CD-ROM, such as closed cases, mug shots, fingerprint cards, motor vehicle records, firearm registration information, wanted notices, court decisions, missing person photos and information, and known career criminal files, including photographs and fingerprints.[24]

The Memphis, Tennessee, police department utilizes predictive software called Blue CRUSH (criminal reduction utilizing statistical history). Although not a *Minority Report* software (referring to the movie plot where crime is predicted prior to it happening and arrests are made based on the predictions), it does use prior statistical crime and arrest data, weather forecasts, economic indicators, and other information to "predict" possible crime in certain locales. If the watch commander believes CRUSH is correct, he or she will send officers to those areas. Since Memphis began using the software in 2005, the crime rate has dropped 30 percent.[25]

Two other major automated forensic databases are discussed later in this chapter: the Integrated Automated Fingerprint Identification System (IAFIS) and the Combined DNA Index System (CODIS). Numerous other automated forensic databases are also available to help law enforcement investigators and crime scene personnel in their

---

automated crime analysis The automated collection and analysis of data regarding crime (when, where, who, what, how, and why) to discern criminal patterns and assist in the effective assignment of personnel to combat crime.

YOU ARE THERE

Sample ViCAP Alert—April 2006

On October 24, 2003, deer hunters found the body of a woman lying face down in a wooded area off Devil Dog Road about one mile south of Interstate 40 and six miles west of Williams, Arizona. This area is a popular entrance into the Grand Canyon National Park. The victim died from a single blow to her head and likely was killed someplace other than where her body was discovered. All attempts to identify this woman have been unsuccessful.

The victim is described as a white female, 60 years of age or older, 5 feet 4 inches tall, 150 pounds, with blondish-gray hair in a bob style. The victim had brown eyes and no ear piercings or tattoos. Moles are present on the left side of the forehead, on the tip of the right shoulder, over the left clavicle, on the front of the right lower leg, and on the right ankle. Old scars are noted on the back of the left hand, below the right knee, and on the back of the right forearm. There was evidence of heart disease and also a skin condition (senile ecchymosis), likely requiring dermatological intervention.

An examination of the dental records revealed extensive dental work worth $20,000. These restorations included porcelain fused to metal crowns, four root canals, a full-gold crown, and two three-unit fixed partial dentures (bridges).

Law enforcement agencies should bring this information to the attention of all homicide, missing persons, special victims, and crime analysis units.

Source: "ViCAP Alert, Unidentified Homicide Victim," *FBI Law Enforcement Bulletin*, April 2006, p. 24.

---

criminalistic or forensic work, including databases of bullet and cartridge casings, auto paint, glass, shoe prints, tire and tire tread patterns, text writings, inks, drugs, prescription drugs, ignitable liquids, and chemicals.[26]

Automated Crime Analysis (Crime Mapping)

Numerous software application programs aid the police in **automated crime analysis** or crime mapping. Crime analysis entails the collection and analysis of data regarding crime (when, where, who, what, how, and why) to discern criminal patterns and assist in the effective assignment of personnel to combat crime. The most basic use of crime analysis is to determine where and when crimes occur so that personnel can be assigned to catch perpetrators in the act of committing the crime or to prevent them from committing it.[27]

The forerunner in the use of modern sophisticated automated crime analysis was the New York City Police Department's (NYPD) CompStat program, which was discussed in Chapter 1. CompStat provides instant statistical updating of all reported crimes, arrests, and other police activities, such as traffic and other citations. This program and its movie screen–type visual displays provide the framework for the weekly crime analysis meetings at the NYPD headquarters, during which precinct commanders must account for all increases in crime and provide strategies to combat these crimes.

The keynote of the NYPD reengineering program of the mid-1990s and the envy of police departments throughout the world, the CompStat process began to evolve in early 1994 when, after changes in the leadership of many of the NYPD's bureaus, disturbing information emerged. It appeared that the NYPD did not know most of its own current crime statistics, and there was a time lag of three to six months in its statistical reporting methods. Upon learning this, the department made a concerted effort to generate crime activity data on a weekly basis. CompStat has been credited with causing crime in New York City to drop to levels not seen since the 1960s.[28] Numerous cities are now using CompStat programs and other forms of automated crime analysis and crime mapping.

REGIONAL CRIME ANALYSIS GEOGRAPHIC INFORMATION SYSTEMS (RCAGIS) SPATIAL ANALYSIS Another computer program several police departments have added to their arsenal of anticrime programs is **Regional Crime Analysis Geographic Information Systems (RCAGIS) spatial analysis**. Although still an imprecise science, these computer programs have been able to help police locate crime hot spots, spatially relate a list of potential suspects to actual crimes, profile crime geographically to identify where a serial criminal most likely lives, and even forecast where the next crime in a series might occur. Geographic profiling was developed in the late 1980s. The Baltimore County police department uses a RCAGIS program called CrimeStat.[29]

A 2006 article disclosed that numerous law enforcement agencies throughout the nation are using a wide variety of GIS or spatial analysis software programs. The police use of special forecasting has been spurred by the development of electronic police records, advances in street maps for crime model specification, and improvement in police management that places an emphasis on performance measures and accountability. Currently, the National Law Enforcement Corrections and Technology Center (NLECTC) and several other research bodies are attempting to determine which program is the best.[30] Other countries also are using this type of software. The United Kingdom, for example, uses GIS-based information-sharing systems in its Crime and Disorder Reduction Partnerships (CDRP).[31]

Although the GIS systems show great promise, they cannot be considered a replacement for the experienced crime analyst and investigator. According to Ronald Wilson, program manager of the Mapping and Analysis for Public Safety (MAPS) program at the National Institute of Justice (NIJ), "There is a lot of human behavior that cannot be accounted for by mathematical models."[32]

Computer-Aided Investigation (Computer-Aided Case Management)

The criminal investigation process is being revolutionized by **computer-aided investigation** and **computer-aided case management**. As early as the 1980s, the NYPD's Detective Division created an automated mug shot file called Computer-Assisted Terminal Criminal Hunt (CATCH). Using CATCH, detectives feed the description and *modus operandi* (MO) information of an unknown robbery perpetrator into the computer and receive a computer printout that lists, in rank order, any

Regional Crime Analysis Geographic Information Systems (RCAGIS) spatial analysis Computer programs to help police locate crime hot spots, spatially relate a list of potential suspects to actual crimes, profile crime geographically to identify where a serial criminal most likely lives, and forecast where the next crime in a series might occur.

computer-aided investigation/computer-aided case management The use of computers to perform case management and other functions in investigations.

potential suspects. The detectives can then obtain photographs of possible suspects and show them in photo arrays to victims for possible identification. The Los Angeles Police Department has operated a system similar to that of New York since 1985.[33]

Since the 1990s, British police have operated a computer-aided investigation system called the Home Office Large Major Enquiry System (HOLMES, which is a reference to the legendary fictional detective Sherlock Holmes). It is a sophisticated computer program developed to aid British investigators in managing complex investigations. (In Great Britain, an investigation is called an enquiry.) HOLMES is a complete case management system that can retrieve, process, organize, recognize, and interrelate all aspects of information on a case. It also keeps track of ongoing progress, or the lack of it, in investigations. The system was created in response to the infamous Yorkshire Ripper case, in which 13 women were killed between 1974 and 1981. When the perpetrator was finally apprehended in 1981, it was discovered that he had been detained and questioned by at least six different police departments in connection with the attacks. Because sharing of information on related cases was so cumbersome for the neighboring forces at that time, the connection was never made.[34]

Investigators in Washington State battle violent crime with the Homicide Investigation and Tracking System/Supervision Management and Recidivist Tracking (HITS/SMART). This electronic investigation system stores, collates, and analyzes characteristics of all murders and sexual offenses in Washington. Investigators statewide can then retrieve information from the system on these violent crimes to help them solve related cases. The HITS/SMART system relies on the voluntary submission of information by law enforcement agencies throughout the state. Agencies submit data about murders, attempted murders, missing persons (when foul play is suspected), unidentified dead persons believed to be murder victims, and predatory sex offenders.[35]

Based on the information provided by the detectives, HITS/SMART analysts can query the database for any combination of the victim's gender, race, lifestyle, method and cause of death, geographic location of the crime, the absence or presence of clothing on the body, concealment of the body, and the dates of death and body discovery. In this way, analysts can identify other murder cases with common

elements. Once the database is accessed, analysts can then supply detectives with the names of similarly murdered victims (if known), investigating agencies, case numbers, and the primary investigator's name and telephone number. Designing the query usually takes only a few minutes, as does the data search.

A database connected to HITS/SMART stores information contained in records from the Washington State Department of Corrections. This file gives HITS/SMART immediate access to the identification of present and former inmates with murder and sexual assault convictions. Their physical descriptions can be checked against the physical descriptions of unidentified suspects in recent sexual assault investigations.

As one example of the success of HITS/SMART, after a brutal rape, a detective made a request to the system for information about offenders having certain physical descriptions and MOs. The system staff provided the investigator with a list of known sexual offenders released from prison during the past five years and the areas to which they had been released. Along with this information, the HITS/SMART staff provided a collection of photographs to the detective, and the victim immediately identified one of the former offenders as her assailant.

One of the latest versions of computer-aided investigative technology is the NYPD's Real Time Crime Center (RTCC), which aids patrol officers and investigators in responding to and investigating crimes. This system allows for the accessing of crucial information in a real-time environment. It turns immense amounts of raw data from disparate sources into a cohesive and understandable "big picture" that can be immediately used by officers and detectives in the field.[36] The RTCC's advanced data-mining capabilities provide investigators with rapid access to billions of records, including more than 5 million New York State criminal records and parole/probation files; more than 20 million New York City criminal complaints, emergency calls, and summonses spanning five years; more than 31 million national crime records; and more than 33 billion public records.

The RTCC system also uses satellite imaging and sophisticated city mapping to guide officers to addresses and detect geographic patterns in crimes. It can track suspects to all of their known addresses and the locations where they are most likely to flee. The RTCC is located at NYPD headquarters and is linked to laptop computers in each of the city's precincts and a fleet of 11 computer-equipped vans that can arrive at crime scenes minutes after a crime.

In 2007, a very serious crime was solved in a few days as a result of the RTCC. On April 14, 2007, a 23-year-old university graduate student was tortured for 19 hours by an intruder in her apartment. The woman was raped, burned with bleach, force-fed an overdose of pain relievers, and her eyelids were slit with scissors. Before leaving, the assailant stole the victim's ATM card and also set fire to her apartment. The victim awoke to the smell of smoke and was able to escape.

An immediate response to the case by detectives resulted in a description of the assailant by the victim and another building resident. The resident was taken to an RTCC mobile van where her description and the one given by the victim were used to construct a composite sketch of the assailant that was sent to all members of the NYPD. Detectives tracked down the use of the ATM card to a local bodega where a security camera captured an image of a man who resembled the police composite sketch. After the image was made public, two callers notified the police that it resembled a man who went by the nickname of "Pooh." The RTCC's nickname database linked "Pooh" to a man who had been convicted of attempted murder in 1996 and served eight years in prison. The man's prison photograph was shown to officers at precinct roll calls across the city, and he was arrested later that day after he was spotted by officers walking out of a building where a burglary had been reported.[37]

In 2010, Boston opened their Real Time Crime Center as the latest in the Boston Police Department's efforts to combine shoe-leather police work with technological savvy to monitor and catch criminals. The program uses existing technology such as cameras focused on major city streets, the department's gunshot detection system, and the 911 dispatch center to relay information about a crime almost instantaneously to investigators. Boston is one of a handful of cities nationwide that have developed a center like New York's. Previously police departments in Houston and Memphis opened their own Real Time Crime Centers.[38]

Unfortunately, not all computer-aided investigative technology has been successful. In 2005, the FBI, facing tremendous criticism over its poorly functioning and outdated computer-aided case management system after September 11, 2001, was forced to abandon its planned Virtual Case File that was to be part of a billion-dollar effort to overhaul its systems since the software became outdated before it was even implemented.[39]

Despite the proven effectiveness of the computer in the investigative process, it will never replace the investigator. The successful investigation of crimes and other police incidents will always depend primarily on the intelligence and hard work of investigators and police officers. As a prime example, recall the 2002 Beltway Sniper case, the series of random shootings that terrorized Washington, D.C., and its suburbs. The Beltway snipers killed 10 people and wounded another 3. Although geographic profiling and other computer models were used in this case, which was one of the most intense manhunts in U.S. criminal history, the suspects were identified based on leads provided by one of the snipers about a seemingly unrelated case in Alabama. Moreover, despite the formation of a massive law enforcement dragnet, the suspects were caught after an alert motorist saw them sleeping in their car 50 miles from the closest crime scene.[40]

Computer-Assisted Instruction

Computers are valuable teaching tools in police departments. Computer-assisted instruction (CAI) is a learning process in which students interact one-on-one with a computer, which instructs them and quizzes them. One of the most popular CAI systems is the Firearms Training System (FATS), a computer-driven laser disk mechanism used to train police officers to make decisions in life-threatening situations. The FATS system assists both veteran officers and new recruits in making shoot/don't shoot decisions.

A new type of FATS training system now in use by law enforcement and the military is the "virtual" simulator. One such system, VirTra Systems 300 LE, uses a 300-degree screen with a five-camera setup to provide officers with realistic firearms training through decision-making simulations. The simulations are so realistic that officers believe they are actually in the situations.[41]

Administrative Uses of Computers

Police departments use computers to perform many administrative functions. Management information systems and automated clerical processing systems free personnel to concentrate on serving the public.

Software packages can assist police departments in jail and prisoner management. Automated patrol allocation is also possible.

MANAGEMENT INFORMATION SYSTEMS
Just as businesses use management information systems, so do police departments. Robert Sheehan and Gary W. Cordner define management information systems as "those systems that provide information needed for supervisory, allocation, strategic, tactical, policy and administrative decisions."[42] Sheehan and Cordner list the following management information systems found in police departments: (1) personnel information systems, (2) warranty control information systems, (3) equipment inventory systems, (4) evidence and property control systems, (5) booking information systems, (6) detention information systems, (7) case-tracking systems, (8) financial information systems, and (9) fleet maintenance information systems.[43]

Computers are perfect vehicles for management information systems, especially in larger police departments. Computer use eliminates the need to keep handwritten records and conduct manual searches. Many of the management information systems just listed are now computerized in most large, modern police departments. For example, in 1997, the Prince George's County, Maryland, Police Department joined a growing roster of law enforcement agencies nationwide that have instituted computer-aided early-warning systems to identify officers who are experiencing stress or other problems so that positive interventions can be made before the situation becomes career threatening.[44]

AUTOMATED CLERICAL PROCESSING SYSTEMS
Policing involves a tremendous amount of paperwork, including arrest reports, incident and follow-up reports, and accident and injury reports. The computer simplifies the report-writing process. Many police departments today used automated clerical processing systems, and many officers use these systems in their patrol cars with portable or laptop computers.

JAIL AND PRISONER MANAGEMENT
Many software packages can assist in jail and prisoner management. This application of computers is useful for police departments and sheriff's offices that are responsible for the lodging of prisoners awaiting appearance in court. These packages perform booking, updating, record inquiry, daily logs and audit trails, medical accounting, classification and pretrial release, inmate cash accounting, and billing.[45]

PATROL ALLOCATION DESIGN
Patrol allocation is a very important responsibility for police administrators. Sheehan and Cordner summarize the major issues in patrol allocation as follows:

1. Determining the number of patrol units needed in each precinct, at each time of the day, and for each day of the week
2. Designing patrol beats
3. Developing policies to dispatch and redeploy patrol units
4. Scheduling patrol personnel to match variations in the number of units on duty[46]

Several computerized models are available for automated patrol allocation. These software packages determine the number of patrol units needed by precinct, day of the week, and shift, based on predetermined objectives.

An officer in Alexandria, Virginia, uses license plate recognition technology to scan license plates while on patrol.

AP Images/Pablo Martinez Monsivais

Computer Networks and the Internet

A computer network allows users from many different areas to communicate with one another and access the network's database. The International Association of Chiefs of Police (IACP) has formed a nationwide computer network for the exchange of semiofficial and informal communications among police departments. Today, a great many police departments, large and small, have created their own websites and home pages on the Internet.

Much of the information in this chapter can be accessed through the Internet without taking the time to travel to a library, call a corporation, or look for a book. The Internet has revolutionized policing by enhancing the ability of officers and investigators to access tremendous amounts of data at a moment's notice without leaving their workplace. The ability to surf the Internet through search engines; to access business, media, educational, and government websites; and to explore links attached to many websites is becoming essential in policing. As an example of how the Internet can help the police interact with the public, many cities, counties, and states in all regions of the nation are putting their crime maps on the Web, which enables citizens to view them.

In 2006, it was reported that the San Francisco Police Department (SFPD), which started taking citizen crime reports on the Web two years before, had 10 to 12 percent of their citizen crime reports submitted online. An SFPD spokesperson said, "If we don't have to send an officer out to take a report, the officer is available to respond to more emergency calls." In San Mateo, California, it used to take an officer about 40 minutes to complete a crime report. Taking reports online has saved the equivalent of more than eight officer-workweeks per year. In San Mateo, more than 500 reports were filed by citizens in the first six months after online reporting began.[47]

Mobile Technology

The concept of mobile computing was introduced several decades ago with the development and use of computer-aided dispatch (CAD) systems and mobile data terminals (MDTs), which supplied officers with computer-aided dispatch data. Since then, mobile computerization and technology have expanded exponentially.

Current mobile technology systems give patrol officers the tools they need to function as if they were in an office while remaining out in the community performing police work. These systems provide patrol officers with records management systems (RMSs), CAD systems, MDTs, mobile wireless report entry (MRE), AVL/GPS mapping, and many other capabilities once available only in traditional offices. Mobile technologies enable patrol officers to access real-time data and file reports via laptops in patrol vehicles or through personal communication devices, such as a personal digital assistant (PDA) or BlackBerry. Mobile technology minimizes routine paperwork that must be done at the station house or police headquarters, thus reducing the amount of time that officers must be "out of service."[48]

Mobile technology is expanding into new applications that will further facilitate in-field law enforcement operations. These systems include rugged laptops with digital pens, GPS mapping for airborne operations, and handheld devices that instantly access information about a violator.[49]

By 2008, law enforcement agencies were using the popular PDA BlackBerry. The handheld BlackBerry allows e-mail, voice telephone, wireless Web access, and almost anything else that can be done with a wireless laptop computer. The BlackBerry can be loaded with specialized law enforcement programs, allowing the user to query the NCIC database as well as other state and motor vehicle department databases.[50]

One of the latest mobile technological innovations is **license plate recognition (LPR) technology**, which can be used to search for stolen vehicles, vehicles listed in AMBER Alerts, or vehicles driven by wanted persons. This technology employs cameras and computer software to discern the letters and numbers of vehicle license plates and then compares them with records contained in state and federal databases, including the department of motor vehicles and NCIC records. Imaging cameras can be placed on the front or roof of a patrol vehicle or in its light bar.[51]

license plate recognition (LPR) technology Employs cameras and computer software to discern the letters and numbers of vehicle license plates and then compares them with records contained in state and federal databases, including department of motor vehicles and NCIC records.

GUEST LECTURE

BY TIMOTHY M. LUCKIE

Detective Tim Luckie has been employed by the Seattle Police Department for the past 33 years. He currently is assigned to the Seattle Internet Crimes Against Children (ICAC) Task Force as an investigator and computer forensic examiner. He assisted in the development of the Seattle ICAC Task Force in 1999 and assisted in the implementation of satellite task forces in Washington and Alaska. He has taught ICAC-related subjects to members of law enforcement, prosecutors, probation/parole officers, teachers, parents, and students.

THE EVOLUTION OF TECHNOLOGY AND CHILD PORNOGRAPHY INVESTIGATIONS

The Seattle Internet Crimes Against Children (ICAC) Task Force is one of 61 ICAC lead agencies (with over 2700 partner affiliate agencies) throughout the United States. Each task force is federally funded through grants from the Department of Justice, Office of Juvenile Justice and Delinquency Prevention (OJJDP). Their primary task is to increase the investigative capabilities of state and local law enforcement officers in the detection, investigation, and apprehension of offenses or offenders of Internet crimes against children, including technology-facilitated child exploitation offenses. ICAC investigators develop and deliver public awareness and prevention programs for Internet crimes against children. Today, ICAC has a complicated and evolving mission that wasn't even heard of until the explosive use of today's technology.

It is not often a person can say they have a dream job, but I can and it has been an honor to be a part of this effort since the very beginning. Through it all, I have simply viewed my role as protecting children: protecting them from familial abuse, strangers, predators, Internet content, and, most recently, themselves.

The sexual abuse of children has occurred since there have been children. As societies matured, the practice of having sex with children was met with boundaries and laws were enacted to protect our children. Most civilized cultures have laws criminalizing the sexual abuse of children, including the production, distribution, and possession of any depictions of those acts. These laws are clear. Child pornography is contraband, much like illegal drugs, and punishable by prison. Unfortunately, it is the prime issue that has law enforcement policing the Internet.

For over a hundred years, need-driven deviant offenders seeking child pornography had to overcome their own survival instincts, high costs, and high risks. Those costs and risks include potentially losing family, friends, jobs, and freedom. Prior to the Internet, most commercial child pornography was available only in backrooms and through the mail. A lot of things changed with the advent of affordable personal computers. I know it's hard to believe, but much of the early use of personal computers was for viewing pornography saved on floppy disks. This also included child pornography.

In 1991, I investigated one of the first child rape cases using a computer. A five-year-girl disclosed that her dad had performed an abusive act. She said her dad showed her pictures on a computer with women doing the same thing he was doing to her, and he told her it was normal. During the investigation, we seized a computer and several floppy disks. Since our department didn't have a personal computer to view the floppy disks, we had to use the suspect's computer. We verified that the pictures existed and again used the suspect's computer during the trial. Offenders have long groomed their child victims, but this was our first experience where a computer was used. Obviously, we had no clue about computer forensics and best practices. Nonetheless, he was found guilty and went to prison.

During the 1980s, the public was getting familiar with their new computers and finding evermore useful programs for practical use. But the Internet still remained largely unavailable and untapped for everyday use by the public.

By 1992, the Internet was made available for commercial use by everyone. The use of the Internet quickly expanded with numerous new electronic service providers such as AOL, Yahoo!, and MSN expanding their services and properties to millions of users.

As expected, the pornography business exploded. It was easy to get access, it was cheap, and it was all but anonymous. It was a win-win for pornography business, the user, and Internet growth. Most would agree pornography is big business; most would also agree child pornography is wrong and has no place on the Internet. But even so, there was money to be made. Organized crime worldwide found that child pornography was cheaper to produce and safer to distribute than drugs. Now anyone could download child pornography to their computer.

Why was law enforcement not all over this? First and foremost, law enforcement is generally reactive to criminal trends and as there were few reported offenses, it was not investigated. Second, once awakened to the growing problem, law enforcement was ill prepared to respond. Finally, as early awareness to the problem grew, jurisdictional battles between local, state, and federal agencies slowed the overall response.

Law enforcement saw the need and started to develop investigative protocols using stand-alone computers with dial-up connections. Initially, this was entirely reactive and for a while we reactively investigated on a case-by-case basis, progressing to other methods as the technology developed.

Our first proactive investigations started with the Internet Relay Chats (IRCs) using the DalNets and UnderNets, among others. Our response to computer- and Internet-related investigations was just developing as explosive advances in technology became available to everyone. Computers were getting more affordable, faster, smaller, and easier to use. Data storage capacities were growing exponentially at ever lower costs. The Internet experience was improving as access and connection speeds increased.

In 1998, Congress passed the Child Protection and Sexual Predator Punishment Act. The act was described as the comprehensive response to the horrifying menace of sex crimes against children, particularly assaults facilitated by computers. An important part of the act was the mandatory requirement that electronic service providers report instances of "apparent child pornography" to the Cyber Tipline, with substantial financial penalties for failing to do so.

In 1984, the National Center for Missing and Exploited Children (NCMEC) was opened and dedicated to the recovery of missing and exploited children; in 1998, it assumed the additional task of managing the CyberTipline. The tip line receives reports of suspected child sexual exploitation, processes the information, and refers the Cybertip to the proper jurisdiction. Since its inception in 1998, the CyberTipline has processed over 2.5 million reports concerning crimes against children, including online enticement for sexual acts, sexual molestation, child pornography, and unsolicited obscene material.

In response, Congress also approved the funding and creation of the first group of ICAC Task Forces in 1998. Partnerships were quickly forged with U.S. Customs, the FBI, the U.S. Postal Inspectors, the U.S. Attorney's Office, and numerous local agencies. We learned from our federal partners about the many issues and similarities with early child pornography investigations and applied them to online and undercover

operations. We sought assistance from Microsoft, Yahoo!, AOL, IT specialists, and a long list of computer user groups. This training has constantly improved and is updated as new technologies emerge.

In 2000, just as the ICACs were developing policies, best practices, forensic capabilities, training, and equipment, two events occurred that significantly impacted these efforts. The federal government tightened restrictions and increased oversight on electronic service providers. The three major providers—AOL, Yahoo!, and Microsoft—dumped tens of thousands of stored abuse reports to NCMEC's CyberTipline. This resulted in thousands of Cybertips flooding into the ICACs to investigate. At the same time, a major investigation was unfolding: Operation Avalanche. This investigation by the U.S. Postal Inspectors and the Dallas Police Department took down the largest known online child pornography ring at that time. The website was known as Landslide, Inc., and had over 250,000 subscribers paying $29.95 a month for access to child pornography. Law enforcement seized the website and the customer credit card records. Customer information was referred to the appropriate jurisdictions for follow-up investigation; thousands of subjects were contacted and hundreds arrested. The subjects of the investigation were from all walks of life. The husband and wife behind the operation were arrested and the husband was sentenced to 180 years in prison.

It was during this first major operation we realized anyone could be our target. The customer was no longer solely the pervert child predator whom the public suspected. I investigated police officers, politicians, doctors, lawyers, counselors, teachers, and even a Little League coach I knew. Operation Avalanche was the first of many operations conducted by ICAC, federal, and international partners.

As we developed proactive techniques for undercover online enticement cases and child pornography distribution cases, we were responding to the ever increasing Cybertips involving chat rooms, photo storage, and the exponential growth of teen involvement on the Internet.

Dial-up modems were eventually replaced by DSL high-speed access using phone lines, which were then replaced by satellite and cable connections. Home networks started appearing with wireless access to laptops. With high-speed access to the Internet and low-cost storage, the demand for photo and video content, both legal and illegal, exploded. All electronic service providers had abuse reporting built into their

(continued)

operations; AOL was screening all email attachments for child pornography images. This led to increased reporting to the CyberTipline, taxing all ICAC resources.

As computers, the Internet, and digital cameras were sprinting through the millennium, another technology was developing that posed an even greater risk to our youth: the cell phone. Many parents were buying phones using family plans, and it seemed every teen had a phone so parents could keep in touch. Teens were developing a unique texting shorthand that challenged law enforcement efforts to disrupt predators from communicating with this victim-rich environment. Cell phones are now the main electronic device used by teens.

In 2003, MySpace was introduced to the Internet, becoming the first of many social networking sites. Facebook is currently the number-one social network in the world with 1.28 billion users. Facebook is also the number-one Cybertip reporter. Law enforcement investigation efforts of the all social networks have increased exponentially as teens deal with daily unsolicited sexual content, sexual enticement, cyber stalking, cyberbullying, self-exploitation, and hands-on offenses.

June 29, 2007. Remember this date: The iPhone was released to the public. With that, the smartphone era began, and now everyone has an all-in-one computer, camera, and Web browser tucked in their pocket that can also make a phone call with live video feed. Self-exploitation from teens photographing themselves and sending the images and videos to their BFFs via their smartphone have made teens the leading producers of child pornography. Law enforcement and the judicial system have a problem. When caught, teens are guilty of production, then distribution and possession, of child pornography. Do the laws need to be changed?

ICAC task forces are still reactive to Cybertips, but they now include an aggressive proactive investigative response to the distribution of child pornography. Ninety-three percent of all reported Cybertips are still relative to child pornography. ICAC task forces are actively investigating file sharing networks like Shareaza, Ares, Kazaa, Limewire, Bearshare, BitTorrent, and

Initially LPR technology was designed for use in parking lots (to record the time a vehicle entered), for access control (allowing authorized vehicles into a secure area), and for paying tolls. Now this technology is also being used for border control and traffic fine enforcement.

One of the concerns raised by these useful LPR tools is the issue of privacy. The executive director of the New York Civil Liberties Union, Donna Lieberman, has expressed concern about having a balance between "effective and efficient law enforcement" and the "values of privacy and freedom."[52]

Fingerprint Technology

Fingerprints have historically offered an infallible means of personal identification. Criminal identification by means of fingerprints is one of the most potent factors in apprehending fugitives who might otherwise escape arrest and continue their criminal activities indefinitely. This type of identification makes possible an accurate determination of a person's previous arrests and convictions, which results in the imposition of more equitable sentences by the judiciary. In addition, this system of identification enables the prosecutor to present his or her case in the light of the offender's previous record. It provides probation officers and parole board members with definite information upon which to base their judgment in dealing with criminals in their jurisdiction.[53]

Occasionally, criminals try in vain to alter their fingerprints. In 2007, a plastic surgeon from Pennsylvania pleaded guilty to federal charges of harboring and concealing a fugitive. The surgeon had replaced the fingerprints of an alleged drug dealer, Marc George, with skin from the bottom of his feet to help him avoid apprehension. George had spent several weeks in a hotel in Mexico recuperating from surgery but was still limping badly when arrested crossing into the United States.[54]

Fingerprints may be recorded on standard fingerprint cards or can be recorded digitally and transmitted electronically for comparison. By comparing fingerprints at the scene of a crime with the fingerprint record of suspects, officials can establish absolute proof of the presence or identity of a person.[55]

many others for openly sharing child pornography. ICAC has also developed operations focusing on the highly anonymized Freenet and Darknet sharing networks.

With the advent of cloud storage like Microsoft OneDrive, DropBox, GoogleDrive, and iCloud, law enforcement has had to adapt to the rampant abuse of storing child pornography on the cloud. In 2011, Microsoft announced the development of PhotoDNA. All files stored on their cloud storage Onedrive are scanned for known images of child pornography. This is done through the use of hash values, commonly referred to as "digital fingerprints." Each file has a unique digital fingerprint; when a file is identified as suspicious content, the information is reported to the CyberTipline. Facebook currently scans files using PhotoDNA and other cloud storage businesses are getting on board as well.

With the disclosure of the government spy program PRISM, Internet and cell phone users responded by utilizing available and free data encryption programs. This added an additional challenge to our investigations and digital forensics.

ICAC is facing many challenges. Staying on top of apps (such as SnapChat, Poof, KIK, Face Time, Skype, Omegle, and countless others) that assist teens and offenders as they try to hide activities from parents and law enforcement is a never-ending task. The new tech devices announced weekly are stretching the budgets of law enforcement in an attempt to keep up with investigative techniques. It certainly doesn't help our cause that many investigations are victim-initiated. A large part of the ICAC mission is still community outreach programs, trying to educate parents and children of Internet dangers.

I am still excited about my role with ICAC. To protect children and use new and challenging technologies to do so is rewarding. I try to share that excitement with anyone interested in the criminal justice system, especially students. We have come a long way in recognizing, investigating, and prosecuting these crimes; however, we have further to go and could use the help of interested and talented investigative professionals.

Basic Categories of Fingerprints

There are two basic categories of fingerprints: inked prints or ten-prints and latent prints.

- **Inked prints** or **ten-prints** are the result of the process of rolling each finger onto a ten-print card (each finger is rolled onto a separate box on the card) using fingerprinting ink. Inked prints are kept on file at local police departments, state criminal justice information agencies, and the FBI. When a person is arrested, he or she is fingerprinted and those inked prints are compared with fingerprints on file of known criminals. Inked prints or ten-prints are also taken for numerous other types of investigations such as employment background checks and license applications.

- **Latent prints** are impressions left on evidence. These prints may be "lifted" and then compared with inked prints on file in order to establish the identity of the perpetrator. Latent prints are impressions produced by the ridged skin on human fingers, palms, and soles of the feet. Latent print examiners analyze and compare

latent prints to known prints of individuals in an effort to make identifications or exclusions. The uniqueness, permanence, and arrangement of the friction ridges allow examiners to positively match two prints and to determine whether an area of a friction ridge impression originated from one source to the exclusion of others.

A variety of techniques, including use of chemicals, powders, lasers, alternate light sources, and other physical means, are employed in the detection and development of latent prints. In instances where a latent print has limited quality and quantity of detail, examiners may perform microscopic examinations to make conclusive comparisons.

Sometimes, a latent fingerprint found in dust may be the only lead in an investigation. Even though this kind of print was actually caused by some of the dust being removed—because it adhered to the ridges of the skin that touched there—methods of

inked prints (ten-prints) Result of the process of rolling each finger onto a ten-print card.

latent prints Fingerprint impressions left at a crime scene.

lifting these prints are now available.[56] Lasers can be used to lift prints from surfaces that often defy traditional powder or chemical techniques, including glass, paper, cardboard, rubber, wood, plastic, leather, and even human skin.[57] The use of lasers in fingerprint lifting allowed the FBI to detect a 40-year-old fingerprint of a Nazi war criminal on a postcard.[58] In an article, the special agent in charge of the Forensic Services Division of the U.S. Secret Service cited numerous cases of the successful use of sophisticated fingerprint technology. He mentioned such high-profile cases as the original bombing of the World Trade Center and the killing of two CIA employees in Langley, Virginia.[59]

Innovations in fingerprint analysis continue, including methods for the development of fingerprints on thermal paper, detection of latent fingerprints on fruits and vegetables, obtaining fingerprint impressions using a vacuum box, and improvements in the FBI's latent print processes.[60]

The latest in fingerprinting technology is the development of mobile fingerprint-reading devices. In 2009, in Alexandria, Virginia, the police scanned a dead man's fingers using a mobile fingerprint scanner and identified him within three minutes. Detectives made an arrest days later. Without the device, police would have waited at least 36 hours for an autopsy. This innovative fingerprinting system, based on technology developed for the military, has helped police solve countless cases as officers use the devices on the street and during traffic stops. When a fingerprint is scanned, it is electronically matched against a police database. If there's a hit, it comes back within minutes, often with a picture of the suspect.[61]

 Some Fingerprint Facts

Three Classifications

Three fingerprint classifications form the basis for all ten-print classification systems presently in use:

- *Loops.* Fingerprints characterized by ridge lines that enter from one side of the pattern and curve around to exit from the same side of the pattern. Some 60 percent of fingerprints are loops.

- *Whorls.* Fingerprints characterized by ridge patterns that are generally rounded or circular in shape and have two deltas (triangular shapes). Some 30 percent of fingerprints are whorls.

- *Arches.* Fingerprints characterized by ridge lines that enter the print from one side and flow out of the other side. Some 5 percent of fingerprints are arches.

Three Types

Most people refer to any fingerprint discovered at a crime scene as a latent fingerprint. But there are really three basic types of prints:

- *Visible prints.* Made by fingers touching a surface after the ridges have been in contact with a colored material such as blood, paint, grease, or ink.

- *Plastic prints.* Ridge impressions left on a soft material such as putty, wax, soap, or dust.

- *Latent (invisible) prints.* Impressions caused when body perspiration or oils present on fingerprint ridges adhere to the surface of an object.

Source: Adapted from Richard Saferstein, *Criminalistics: An Introduction to Forensic Science*, 7th ed. (Upper Saddle River, N.J.: Prentice Hall, 2001), p. 401.

 Can a Person Change Fingerprints?

It is impossible to change one's fingerprints, although many criminals have tried to obscure them. Perhaps the most celebrated attempt to obliterate one's fingerprints was the efforts by the notorious 1930s gangster John Dillinger, who tried to destroy his fingerprints by applying a corrosive acid to them. However, prints taken at the morgue after he was shot to death, compared with fingerprints taken at the time of a previous arrest, proved that his efforts had been a failure.

Richard Saferstein, a noted criminalistics expert, has indicated that efforts at intentionally scarring the skin on one's fingerprints can only be self-defeating, for it would be totally impossible to obliterate all the ridge characteristics on the hand, and the presence of permanent scars merely provides new characteristics for identification.

Source: Adapted from Richard Saferstein, *Criminalistics: An Introduction to Forensic Science*, 7th ed. (Upper Saddle River, N.J.: Prentice Hall, 2001), p. 400.

YOU ARE THERE

How to Find and Develop Latent Fingerprints

- *Carbon dusting powders*. When finely ground carbon powder is applied lightly to a surface with a camel's hair or fiberglass brush, it will adhere to perspiration residues left on the surface and can render an invisible impression visible. Generally, the print technician will apply powder of a contrasting color to the color of the surface being dusted. The raised print is photographed, lifted off the surface using transparent tape, and then transferred to a card that has a color in contrast to the color of the powder used on the tape.

- *Iodine fuming*. Crystals of iodine are placed in a glass container called a fumer along with the article suspected of containing latent prints. When the crystals are heated, iodine vapors will fill the chamber and make the latent prints visible. Iodine prints are not permanent and begin to fade once the fuming process is stopped. The resultant fingerprints must be immediately photographed. This method is particularly useful for obtaining prints from paper or cardboard.

- *Silver nitrate*. A solution of silver nitrate in distilled water is sprayed or saturated on paper believed to have latent prints. When the paper is exposed to light, the prints become visible.

- *Ninhydrin*. The chemical ninhydrin is sprayed over large cardboard or paper containers, and if a latent print is present, it will become visible.

- *Super glue fuming*. Super glue (cyanoacrylate) treated with sodium hydroxide is placed within a chamber with an object believed to contain latent prints. The resultant fumes from the glue adhere to the latent prints, making them visible.

- *Ultraviolet light*. An ultraviolet (UV) lamp (black light) can be effective in a darkened environment to expose latent prints.

- *Laser*. The laser, when directed at a surface, can cause the perspiration forming a latent fingerprint to fluoresce, thus making the print visible.

- *Alternative light sources*. An alternative light source (ALS) operates under the same principle as a laser and can make latent fingerprints fluoresce and become visible. It is much more portable than the laser.

Sources: Adapted from Larry Ragle, *Crime Scene* (New York: Avon, 1995), pp. 101–108; Richard Saferstein, *Criminalistics: An Introduction to Forensic Science*, 7th ed. (Upper Saddle River, N.J.: Prentice Hall, 2001), pp. 405–413.

Automated Fingerprint Identification Systems

By the 1980s, **automated fingerprint identification system (AFIS)** began to be developed. The AFIS system enables a print technician to enter unidentified latent prints into the computer. The computer automatically searches its files and presents a list of likely matches, which can be visually examined by a fingerprint technician in order to find the perfect match. Using AFIS technology, a person's prints can be taken and stored into memory without the use of traditional inking and rolling techniques.[62]

The first locally funded, regional automated fingerprint identification system in the United States was NOVARIS (Northern Virginia Regional Identification System).[63] Since then, numerous police departments have developed AFIS systems,

and there are many successful examples of automated fingerprint identification systems in Alaska, California, Idaho, Maryland, Nevada, Oregon, Rhode Island, Utah, Washington, Wisconsin, Wyoming, and Canada.[64]

Initially, AFIS technology was extraordinarily expensive and therefore procured only by the largest agencies. The technology provided excellent high-speed fingerprint matching once fingerprint databases became large enough. Still, a drawback was that each system was stand-alone—that is, systems could not exchange information rapidly. But there are now

automated fingerprint identification system (AFIS) Fingerprinting innovation begun in the 1980s in which a print technician can enter unidentified latent fingerprints into a computer. The computer automatically searches its files and presents a list of likely matches.

software-based systems using open-system architecture, which means that any brand of computer based on the Unix operating system will work with them.[65] These systems are designed to exchange fingerprint and other data over the Internet with other criminal justice information systems, using the widely accepted Henry System of fingerprint classification.

The new AFIS systems designed for use in a booking facility can use ink and paper fingerprints, or can employ **Live Scan**, an optical fingerprint scanning system, to read a suspect's prints. The scanner uses electronic capture of the suspect's fingerprint pattern, using 500 DPI resolution, electronic quality analysis, and automatic image centering. The booking officer begins with a single-finger or dual-digit search, placing the suspect's finger on the scanner

....

Live Scan The electronic taking and transmission of fingerprints as opposed to traditional ink methods.

for reading. If the computer finds a possible match, he or she gets news of a "hit" within minutes. The computer selects the most likely matches, which then must be verified by a human operator. If there is no hit, the computer adds the fingerprint to its database automatically.

These systems also have electronic quality checking, image enhancement, and ten-print system capability. They can scan fingerprint cards, reducing them to electronic records, and store them for future reference. They also can print fingerprint cards from electronically scanned Live Scan fingerprints. A latent fingerprint examiner can link separate crime scenes using single latent prints, which can point to a common perpetrator or a pattern.

The use of Live Scan stations allows fingerprints and demographic information to be electronically captured, stored, and transmitted in minutes. Greater use of applicant fingerprints in the hiring

---

What a Difference Technology Makes

ON THE JOB

During my police career, I saw some great improvements in technology. Many tasks that took hours to complete and document began to be done by computers. When I first started in the department, we handwrote reports that had five copies and were turned in to the supervisor who read them, signed off on them, and sent them to records (after perhaps having us rewrite some a few times). A clerk then entered the data so that very basic information could be retrieved for future reference. When it was time to go to court, the officer went back to records and requested a copy of the report to take to court.

By the time I left the department, officers had been using laptops for several years with state-of-the-art programs; they wrote their reports, and the supervisors retrieved and reviewed them electronically and uploaded them to the main computer system. Much more extensive data was thus available for retrieval without the use of a data entry clerk. Reports were generated on a daily basis to gather needed information for units such as crime analysis, the press information office, and the detective bureau.

In my opinion, the most significant improvement I saw during my career was the advent of the automated fingerprint identification system (AFIS).

When I started with the police department, we had a sworn officer, a sergeant in fact, doing fingerprint comparisons. If we arrested a suspect and thought he or she might have committed some specific crimes, we could request that the suspect's prints be compared with the latents lifted at the scenes. If we worked a scene and had some possible suspects, we could request that the latents be compared with the suspects' prints—if we had them. If we had no suspect, the sergeant could compare the prints with those of some local offenders known to have committed similar crimes, but other than that, we were out of luck. This man spent eight hours a day comparing prints with very few productive results.

Now, when an officer works a scene, he or she turns in any latents, which can be compared with all the latents in the database within minutes, if not seconds. Clearance rates have been greatly enhanced by this technology. Now we don't have to use a sergeant for eight hours a day to look at prints; we are able to put that officer out on the street where he or she is needed. Dusting for fingerprints is no longer seen as an exercise in futility. This is just one way technology has made law enforcement much more productive and effective.

—Linda Forst

process is among the many reasons why the use of ten-print Live Scan stations is increasing nation-wide. Built-in quality-control software helps to reduce human errors. Because there is no ink, there is no smearing. If a mistake is made, a print can be retaken until one high-quality record is obtained. There is no need to print a person again for local, state, and federal agencies because Live Scan can make copies. Higher-quality fingerprints mean a higher likelihood of the AFIS finding a match in its database without human verification.[66]

INTEGRATED AUTOMATED FINGERPRINT IDENTIFICATION SYSTEM (IAFIS)

In 1999, the FBI began its **Integrated Automated Fingerprint Identification System (IAFIS)**. This system provides the capability to search latent fingerprints against the largest criminal fingerprint repository in the world, which contains the fingerprints of almost 55 million individuals. This allows the FBI to make identifications without the benefit of a named suspect to help solve a variety of crimes.[67]

IAFIS is primarily a ten-print system for searching an individual's fingerprints to determine whether a prior arrest record exists and for maintaining a criminal arrest record history for each individual. The system also offers significant latent print capabilities. Using IAFIS, a latent print specialist can digitally capture latent print and ten-print images and perform several functions with each, including enhancing the prints to improve image quality, comparing latent fingerprints against suspect ten-print records retrieved from the criminal fingerprint repository, searching latent fingerprints against the ten-print fingerprint repository when no suspects have been developed, doing automatic searches of new arrest ten-print records against an unsolved latent fingerprint repository, and creating special files of ten-print records to support major criminal investigations.[68]

In 2000, the fingerprint databases of the FBI and the Immigration and Naturalization Service (INS, now part of the Department of Homeland Security) were merged. Formerly federal, state, and local law enforcement officials did not have access to all fingerprint information captured by Border Patrol agents, and INS did not have access

Integrated Automated Fingerprint Identification System (IAFIS) A system for searching an individual's fingerprints against a computerized database of fingerprints.

YOU ARE THERE

DNA Couldn't Find the Suspect, but IAFIS Did

The Georgia Bureau of Identification (GBI) and the Pleasant Prairie, Wisconsin, Police Department (PPPD) were both looking for the same rape suspect in crimes committed in their jurisdictions. The PPPD contacted the GBI because they noted common characteristics in the rapes: The victims all worked as clerks at retail strip malls near interstates. The PPPD sent fingerprint and DNA samples for examination. Through DNA testing, the GBI tied those two rapes to a rape in Florence, Kentucky, but could not identify the suspect.

After exhaustive investigation efforts with the PPPD, including a requested subject analysis by the FBI's Violent Crime Apprehension Program, had yielded no viable leads, the GBI submitted the Wisconsin print for examination by the FBI's Integrated Automated Fingerprint Identification System (IAFIS) database. Within minutes, the search produced the name of a suspect.

The man was located in jail at Lawrenceville, Georgia, where he was being held on an unrelated crime. The GBI was granted a search warrant to obtain a blood sample. Although he denied any involvement in the crimes, his blood was matched to DNA samples from the serial rapes. A few days after the sample was taken, he used a bed sheet to hang himself in his jail cell. He implicated himself in other rapes before his death.

The lesson from this investigation is the value of the IAFIS latent search technique. Despite exhaustive investigative efforts, none of the other organizations' efforts were able to identify a suspect for these serial crimes, but IAFIS did.

Source: Adapted from "Unsolved Case Fingerprint Matching," *FBI Law Enforcement Bulletin* (December 2000): 12–13.

to the FBI's records when its agents apprehended suspects at the border. The merging of the two systems was prompted by the inadvertent release by the INS in 1999 of Angel Maturino-Resendez, a suspected serial killer—known as the "railroad killer"—who was alleged to have stowed away on trains and murdered eight people near rail lines during a three-state killing spree. Border Patrol agents had picked up Maturino-Resendez for illegal entry into the United States and sent him back to Mexico. The agents were unaware that he was wanted by the Houston police and the FBI for questioning in the murders. Within days of his release, Maturino-Resendez killed four more victims. Eventually he surrendered to Texas Rangers in July 1999.[69]

IAFIS serves as an international standard for providing fingerprints electronically. After a criminal ten-print search is submitted electronically, the FBI guarantees a response within two hours and the prints are compared to those of anyone who has been arrested in the United States since the 1920s.[70] IAFIS was instrumental in the capture of Lee Boyd Malvo, one of the two suspects in the 2002 Washington, D.C., area sniper case. A latent print entered into IAFIS matched Malvo—his prints were in the system because he had been previously arrested by the INS.[71]

IBIS A portable handheld device, the Identification Based Information System (IBIS), delivers on-the-spot positive identification when a suspect has no driver's license or seems to be presenting a false identification. The IBIS captures thumbprints and mug shots and receives text and mug shots from databases with criminal histories, warrants, and images. It even has a silent assist button in the event the investigator requires help from fellow officers. The IBIS offers a high-resolution camera to make images of latent fingerprints at a crime scene, a digital voice recorder, and a GIS. Local agencies can connect with state and federal communications and information systems.[72]

Numerous other countries have also made innovations in fingerprinting technology.[73] The International Association for Identification (IAI) is a professional organization for those interested in fingerprint identification, latent prints, and AFIS.[74]

Automated Palm Print Technology

Recent advances in biometrics have made it possible for automated palm print systems to complement standard AFIS technology. The technology works in the same manner as its AFIS counterpart, but instead of fingerprints, it captures the four core areas of the palm and converts them into data for storage in a palm print repository. On arrest, suspects have their palms scanned along with their fingerprints. After a palm print is lifted from a crime scene, it too is scanned and entered into the database for matching. The palm print matching processor then returns a rank-ordered notification of match candidates to the workstation. Before palm print technology, if police did not have a suspect to compare prints to, the only way they could make a palm print match was to manually compare latent palm prints with hundreds of thousands of individual prints sitting in repositories.[75]

Less-than-Lethal Weapons

Police departments are using technological devices to stop and disable armed, dangerous, and violent subjects without resorting to the use of firearms. The term **less-than-lethal weapons**, or nonlethal weapons, is used to identify innovative alternatives to traditional nonfirearm weapons (such as batons and flashlights) and tactics (such as martial arts techniques and other bodily force techniques, including tackles and choke holds). Nonlethal weapons can be seen as shooting-avoidance tools because these weapons can control unarmed but resisting suspects early in a confrontation, before they have the opportunity to become armed and attack an officer. These weapons also can be used against a subject who is armed with less than a firearm—for example, a knife, club, or other instrument that can cause injury to officers.

Although less-than-lethal technology continues to evolve in modern policing, there is still no perfect weapon available that will immediately stop unlawful resistance and cause absolutely no harm to the receiver.[76] Among the most popular nonlethal weapons being used by the police are chemical irritant sprays and conducted energy devices, including the Taser and other stun devices.

---

less-than-lethal weapons Innovative alternatives to traditional firearms, such as batons, bodily force techniques, chemical irritant sprays, and Tasers or stun guns.

Chemical Irritant Sprays

Chemical irritant sprays are handheld liquid products that contain the active ingredients of cayenne pepper, or CS or CN tear gas. They can be sprayed into the face of a resisting suspect from as far away as 15 feet to cause discomfort and temporary disorientation. Thus, officers gain the necessary time to subdue the subject safely.

For many years, the aerosol CN tear gas, originally introduced by Smith and Wesson under the name Chemical Mace, was regarded by law enforcement as the closest thing to a perfect nonlethal weapon. Today, however, police are experimenting with other types of aerosol sprays. Aerosol subject restraints (ASRs), for example, are different from CS or CN sprays in that they do not rely on pain. They cause a subject's eyes to close and double the subject over with uncontrollable coughing. They also cause a temporary loss of strength and coordination. ASRs cause no physical damage and require no area decontamination. Among popular ASRs are oleoresin capsicum (OC, the hot ingredient in chili peppers), Aerko (Punch), Def-Tee (Pepper Mace), Guardian Personal Security Products (Bodyguard), and Zarc (Cap-Stun).[77]

A National Institute of Justice (NIJ) study of officer and arrestee injuries in three North Carolina police jurisdictions before and after pepper spray was introduced found a correlation between pepper spray use and a decline in injuries. The NIJ report also covered another study of 63 cases in which deaths of in-custody suspects followed pepper spray use. The study disclosed that in only two of these cases was pepper spray found to have been part of the reason for death—and in both cases, it was only a factor in the deaths, not the cause of them.[78]

The Taser and Other Stun Devices

The Taser, an acronym for Thomas A. Swift's Electric Rifle, is a handheld electronic stun gun that discharges a high-voltage, low-amperage, pulsating current via tiny wires and darts, which can be fired from as far as 15 feet away. When the darts strike the subject, the electric current causes a temporary incapacitation of the muscles. This gives the officers the necessary time to subdue the subject safely. The electricity can penetrate as much as two inches of clothing. The Taser discharges only a few watts

of power and is not harmful to cardiac patients with implanted pacemakers, nor can it be modified to produce a lethal charge.[79]

In 2009, a decision by the Ninth U.S. Circuit Court of Appeals set judicial standards for police and for people who claim they were victims of excessive force after police hit them with a Taser dart. The court ruled that police need reasons to believe a suspect is dangerous before firing a Taser and cannot use the Taser simply because the person is disobeying orders or acting erratically.[80]

Another increasingly popular less-than-lethal weapon is the "beanbag" gun. The one-inch-square canvas bag, filled with bird shot, has been used by SWAT teams for several years and more recently by regular patrol officers. The beanbag gun produces a velocity of 320 feet per second within a range of a few inches to 30 feet away with nonlethal force.[81] However, in the 2001 *Deorle v. Rutherford* court decision by the U.S. Court of Appeals for the Ninth Circuit, the court decided that firing beanbag rounds at an unarmed suspect without first issuing a verbal warning represented excessive force and ruled that the beanbag round represented force with a significant risk of serious injury.[82]

Safety and Effectiveness of Less-than-Lethal Weapons

J. P. Morgan, chief of the Goldsboro, North Carolina, Police Department, points to a possible drawback of the less-than-lethal weapon: "Sometimes . . . it can give a false sense of security, as evidenced by an officer's response to the offer of a backup. 'I don't need one, I got my OC.'"[83]

Just how safe are less-than-lethal weapons? A study of 502 use-of-force incidents not involving the use of firearms attempted to discover the injury rate to officers and subjects from eight specific types of force used by the officers. The force was used to cause a suspect to fall to the ground so that the officers could safely subdue him or her. The types of force studied were (1) striking with a baton; (2) a karate kick; (3) a punch; (4) striking with a flashlight; (5) swarming techniques, or organized tackles by a group of officers; (6) miscellaneous bodily force, including pushing, shoving, and tackling; (7) chemical irritant sprays (CS and CN); and (8) the Taser.[84]

YOU ARE THERE   Safer Tasers

In 2009 the city of Charlotte-Mecklenburg paid $625,000 to the family of Darryl Wayne Turner, who died in 2008 after a CMPD officer shocked him with a Taser. The officer had shocked Turner with the Taser for 37 seconds, in violation of department policy.

The CMPD Chief of Police, Rodney Monroe, who believed the Taser was an important tool for his officers, recommended to the city council the purchase of a new Taser (X-26) that included safeguards. One feature of the X-26 was limiting the electric shock to five seconds. Another safety feature was that the officer could trigger a "prewarning" visible and audible signal with the Taser. That prewarning signal would stop many people from continuing their activity.

Tasers are not without controversy, as they emit a 50,000-volt charge that temporarily incapacitates subjects, and they have been linked to deaths nationwide. The CMPD policy states that the Taser should be used "to restrain violent individuals where alternative restraint tactics fail or are reasonably likely to fail."

Source: Based on Steve Harrison, "City to Spend $1.83 Million on 1,600 Safer Tasers," 2011, retrieved September 27, 2011, from www.charlotteobserver.com/2011/09/27/2643200/council-oks-safer-tasers.html#storylink=misearch.

The most used types of force in the study were the baton, miscellaneous bodily force, and the Taser; the least used were chemical irritant sprays, flashlights, and punches. (See Table 14.1 for the various types of less-than-lethal weapons.) The Taser was used in 102 cases, and chemical irritant sprays were used in 21 cases. The Taser was about as effective as the other forms of nonlethal force in subduing a subject, and it resulted in fewer injuries to officers and subjects. The researcher concluded, "Expanded use of nonlethal weapons, along with the concurrent development of the next generation of such devices, will lead to fewer and less severe injuries to suspects and officers, reduced civil liability claims and payments, reduced personnel complaints, reduced disability time out of the field, reduced disability pension payments, and an improved public image for law enforcement."[85]

The use of the Taser has been upheld in court. In *Michenfelder v. Sumner* (1988), a federal court found the following: "Authorities believe the Taser is the preferred method for controlling prisoners because it is the 'least confrontational' when compared to the use of physical restraint, billy clubs, mace or beanbag guns.... When contrasted to alternative methods for physically controlling inmates, some of which can have serious after-effects, the Taser compared favorably."[86] As of 2007, U.S. courts had issued 53 written opinions concerning the reasonableness of Taser usage in arrest situations. Most approved of the police using the Taser to control resistant persons.[87]

Recent studies have discovered that less-than-lethal weapons result in fewer officer and suspect injuries.[88] A 2007 study of medical issues regarding less-than-lethal weapons disclosed that although rare cases of sudden in-custody deaths have resulted from the use of these devices, it is unclear what causal connection may exist between these less-than-lethal technologies and reported fatalities. In many instances, individuals were in conditions that placed them at high risk for sudden death regardless of what force was utilized.[89]

A 2009 review of the policies of the Department of Justice (DOJ) regarding the use of less-than-lethal weapons by the Office of the Inspector General resulted in the following four recommendations:

1. The DOJ should coordinate and ensure that its components (BOP, DEA, ATF, FBI, and so on) develop appropriate and consistent policies to specifically address the use of less-than-lethal weapons.

2. The law enforcement components should establish procedures to ensure that state and local task force members are informed and adhere to the component's less-than-lethal weapons policies.

3. The law enforcement components should periodically analyze their use of less-than-lethal weapons.

4. The NIJ and the Civil Rights Division of the DOJ should share the results of any research or investigations concerning the use of less-than-lethal weapons with the DOJ's law enforcement components.[90]

See Chapter 5, "The Police Role and Police Discretion," for further discussion of the use of less-than-lethal force.

TABLE 14.1   Types of Less-than-Lethal Weapons

Type of Less-than-Lethal Weapons	Description
Impact Weapons	
Baton	Round stick of various lengths, made of hardwood, aluminum, or plastic composite materials; "straight" stick, expandable baton, T-type baton
Beanbag Shotgun Rounds	Heavy nylon cloth squares about the size of a tea bag filled with birdshot; also a "sock" configuration that is deployed through a munitions delivery system; deployed using a standard shotgun adapted to fire beanbag rounds
Baton Launcher	Usually a standard shotgun or grenade launcher adapted to fire baton rounds; can fire one long baton or several shorter batons
Rubber Projectiles, Pellets	Rubber projectiles encased in a shotgun shell; usually fired from a 12-gauge shotgun
Chemical Agents	
CS Gas ("Tear Gas")	Causes tears and painful breathing; deployed using a standard shotgun or grenade launcher; either single shot or a multiple-round launcher may be used
Pepper Spray	OC (oleoresin capsicum) gas, or capsicum spray; causes tears, pain, and temporary blindness
Pepper Ball System	Projectile launcher launches up to four projectiles that release hot pepper powder (capsaicin II)
Sting Ball Grenade	Small, soft rubber container includes a bursting charge that distributes more than 100 soft rubber balls; may also disperse oleoresin capsicum
Conducted Energy Devices	
Electronic Custody Control Belt, Stun Belt, or "Band-It" Electronic Restraint	System of bands put on a subject to deliver an incapacitating electric shock if the subject attempts to flee or attack; can be set off automatically on movement or by an operator up to 150 feet away
Taser	Deployment of electrical energy sufficient to cause uncontrolled muscle contractions and override an individual's voluntary motor responses; may be employed while up to 30 feet from the suspect
Ultron II Contact Stun Device	Similar to Taser; deploys electrical energy sufficient to temporarily incapacitate an individual; officer must make physical contact with the individual
Sound Weapons	
Aerial Dispersion Shotgun Round	CO_2 or compressed air round (blank round) fired into the air by a standard shotgun, causing a loud "bang" similar to a warning shot

(continued)

TABLE 14.1   *Continued*

Type of Less-than-Lethal Weapons	Description
Emerging Less-than-Lethal Technologies	
Long Range Acoustic Device (LRAD)	Emits a concentrated, 150-decibel (dB) high-energy acoustic wave that retains a level of 100 dB over distances of 500 meters; wave is focused within a 15-to 30-degree "beam" allowing aim at a specific target; used by NYPD
Electrolaser	Electroshock weapon that forms an electrically conductive laser-induced plasma channel through which powerful electric current is sent to incapacitate subjects; functions as a long-distance version of the Taser; developed for the U.S. military
Dazzler	Employs intense visible light usually generated by a laser to cause temporary blindness or disorientation; used by the U.S. military in Iraq
Active Denial System	Emits electromagnetic radiation at a frequency of 95 GHz toward the subject; waves deter individuals by causing an intense painful burning sensation without actually burning the skin; developed by the Department of Defense's Joint Non-Lethal Weapons Directorate
Sticky Foam Gun	Fires multiple shots of sticky foam, material that entangles and impairs individuals; provided to the U.S. Marine Corps for Operation United Shield
LED Incapacitator	Resembles a large flashlight; uses light emitting diode (LED) lights flashed at several frequencies with multiple colors and random pulses that the brain cannot process, making the suspect physically ill; developed for the U.S. Department of Homeland Security

Source: U.S. Department of Justice, Office of the Inspector General, Evaluation and Inspections Division, "Review of the Department of Justice's Use of Less-Lethal Weapons," May 2009, retrieved April 1, 2012, from www.justice.gov/oig.

Surveillance Technology

Police agencies use surveillance for a variety of reasons. Surveillance might be used to provide cover for an undercover officer and an arrest team in a buy-and-bust narcotics operation, to gather intelligence, or to establish probable cause for arrest. Today's advances in technology provide us with more surveillance devices than ever before.[91]

Formerly, surveillance equipment consisted of a nearly broken-down undercover van used to store the typical surveillance equipment: a camera and a pair of binoculars. Times have changed: Today's police have, among other innovations, high-tech, state-of-the-art listening, recording, and viewing devices; high-tech surveillance vans; night vision devices; vehicle tracking systems; global positioning systems; and surveillance aircraft. Scientific breakthroughs in the areas of surveillance, mobile communications, and illicit drug detection are arming law enforcement agencies with increasingly sophisticated tools in their fight against illegal drug traffickers and other criminals.[92] This section will discuss the latest in surveillance devices.

Surveillance Vans

A vehicle specialist describes today's state-of-the-art surveillance van: "When talking about surveillance vehicles today . . . we tend to think of a van whose interior looks slightly less complex than the bridge of *Star Trek*'s USS Enterprise." The ideal surveillance van has the following equipment: power periscopes operated by a joystick; six cameras to cover 360 degrees of the van's exterior, plus a periscope-mounted observer's camera; CDs to record everything happening on the street; quick-change periscope camera mounts; portable toilets; video printers; motion detection cameras; night vision cameras; cell phones; CB radios, police radios, and police scanners; and other personalized equipment.[93]

Vehicle Tracking Systems

Vehicle tracking systems, sometimes referred to as transponders, bumper beepers, or homing devices, enable officers and investigators to track a vehicle during surveillance. These systems are actually transmitters that can be placed on a subject's vehicle. The tracking system consists of the transmitter on the subject's vehicle and a receiver, which picks up the signal from the transmitter. There are three basic vehicle tracking systems on the market:

- *Radio frequency (RF) tracking systems* are usually short-range systems that operate on a transmitted signal from a transmitter placed on the target vehicle. The receiver receives the signal using three or four antennas and determines the direction of the target vehicle.

- *Cellular tracking systems* work similarly to RF tracking systems but use transmitters that link to cell towers to track the target vehicle. Often, a cell phone serves as the transmitter signal that the tracking system employs. Tracking range is limited to the range of towers in the area.

- *Global positioning system (GPS) tracking systems* use GPS satellites to pinpoint the location of a target vehicle. GPS technology can locate a target vehicle anywhere in the world. Mapping software allows the target vehicle's location to be displayed on detailed street maps.

The ready availability and increasing affordability of GPS devices allow law enforcement agencies to efficiently, accurately, and safely track the movement of vehicles. The results of GPS tracking create a permanent and credible record of precisely where the tracked vehicle was and the time it was there. To use this technology, officers must have lawful access to the target vehicle to install certain equipment such as a GPS receiver, antenna, power supply, and logging device that records where the vehicle has moved. Depending on the equipment installed, officers can remotely obtain data electronically or physically retrieve data from the logging device in the vehicle.

Fourth Amendment considerations apply to the installation and monitoring of GPS devices. If officers need to intrude into an area where people have a reasonable expectation of privacy, they will need a search warrant.[94] Early in 2012, the U.S. Supreme Court decided the fate of law enforcement use of GPS devices without a warrant. In *United States v. Jones*, the unanimous decision delivered by Justice Scalia held that the "government's attachment of the GPS device to the vehicle, and its use of that device to monitor the vehicle's movements, constitutes a search under the Fourth Amendment."[95]

Global positioning systems will be discussed in more detail later in this chapter.

Night Vision Devices

Among the most sophisticated surveillance devices in use today are enhanced **night vision devices**, including monocular devices small enough to hold in one hand, which can be adapted to a camera, video camera, or countersniper rifle. An expert describes the potential of such devices:

> Perhaps an automobile slowly approaches you in the dark with its lights out. With a normal night vision scope you can see it clearly—but you can't see through the windshield to see who's driving the car. Switch on the infrared (IR) laser, and it illuminates a spot through the windshield so you can identify the operator. In another case, at night a man lurks on the porch of a mountain cabin. In normal mode only the cabin and porch are clearly visible. The IR laser illuminates a spot to show the person waiting in the shadows.[96]

As far back as 1800, Sir William Herschel discovered the fact that every object emits thermal energy in the infrared (IR) wavelengths. His son, Sir John Herschel, took the first IR photographs of the sun approximately 40 years later. Infrared surveillance systems appeared toward the end of World War II as a covert way to observe the enemy at night. The Germans were the first to use IR systems as impressive nighttime tank killers. The Soviets developed IR systems in the 1960s and 1970s. Since then,

vehicle tracking systems Transmitters that enable investigators to track a vehicle during a surveillance; also called transponders, bumper beepers, or homing devices.

night vision devices Photographic and viewing devices that allow visibility in darkness.

these systems have been used by the United States during the Korean, Vietnam, Gulf, and Iraq wars.[97]

A more sophisticated form of infrared technology is thermal imaging (TI), which does not require any light at all. Traditional night vision equipment requires minimal light, such as from the moon. Thermal imaging can also see through fog, mist, or smoke and is especially useful in penetrating many types of camouflaging. TI takes advantage of the IR emission but does it passively, so only the user knows when it is in operation, not the subject.[98] IR and TI systems can be mounted on police vehicles and pan possible subjects in all directions. Display screens can be mounted in patrol cars or investigators' cars, and joysticks can be used to direct the panning of the cameras.[99]

Law enforcement agents from the U.S. Department of Homeland Security (DHS) make extensive use of thermal imagers. These heat-sensing cameras detect the presence and location of a human, and then an image intensifier makes the image clearer so that identification is possible. These tools are also used for myriad law enforcement and investigatory purposes, such as search-and-rescue missions, fugitive searches, perimeter surveillance, vehicle pursuits, flight safety, marine and ground surveillance, structure profiles, disturbed surfaces, hidden compartments, environmental hazards, and officer safety. Other emerging uses of TI are obtaining more accurate skid-mark measures at a crash scene and obtaining evidence at a crime scene that cannot be observed with the human eye.[100] DHS officers use many different night vision technologies in their duties, including IR cameras, night vision goggles, handheld searchlights with a band that reaches more than a mile, seismic and infrared sensors, and fiberscopes.[101]

Global Positioning Systems

Global positioning systems (GPS) are the most recent technology available to help law enforcement and investigators. The GPS is a network of 24 satellites used by the U.S. Department of Defense to pinpoint targets and guide bombs. The satellites are equipped with atomic clocks and equally accurate position-measuring telemetry gear. GPS has been used for everything from helping hikers find their way through the woods to guiding law enforcement officers to stolen vehicles.[102]

When GPS is combined with geographic information systems (GIS) and automatic vehicle locations (AVL), officers can tell where they are on a map and the dispatch center can continuously monitor the officers' location. Police departments can determine the location of each patrol vehicle without any communication from the officer who is driving. In a car wreck, such a system could automatically notify the dispatcher of a possibly injured officer at a specific location. Also, if an officer engages in a high-speed chase, such a system would provide the vehicle's location automatically, or if an officer is injured in an encounter with a suspect, it can suggest that help be sent immediately.

GPS is also used by fleet operators in the private sector to track fleets for routing purposes and for rolling emergencies. It can be used to track the route over time and to monitor the vehicle's speed. In addition, GPS is used for crime mapping, tracking, and monitoring the location of probationers and parolees around the clock.[103]

Surveillance Aircraft

Airplanes are being added to law enforcement's arsenal of surveillance devices. Fixed-wing aircraft and rotorcraft complement ground-based vehicles in hundreds of police agencies worldwide and aid search-and-rescue operations, surveillance, and investigative missions. These aircraft do not require extensive landing fields and have proved to be very successful in surveillance operations. Advanced electronic and computer systems for aircraft now include real-time video downlinks and low-light surveillance.[104]

DRONES The domestic use of drones, and even their consideration of use, has become the subject of national debate, including a filibuster in the U.S. Senate in 2013.[105] **Drones** are also known as **unmanned aerial vehicles (UAV)** and are used in combat by the U.S. military. Drones are aircraft remotely controlled by "pilots" situated at a remote location. Control is via radio or other transmission, usually assisted by a video feed. Drone use falls into two different categories: surveillance and reconnaissance. Drones can be armed with missiles and bombs.[106]

Drone technology is transitioning from the battlefield to use in law enforcement and commercial

global positioning system (GPS) A satellite system used to locate any position on the map.

drone/unmanned aerial vehicle (UAV) Unmanned aircraft piloted remotely, used for surveillance and reconnaissance.

endeavors. The Federal Aviation Administration (FAA) is working on new regulations to allow the use of drones to operate in civilian air space.[107] This attempt to authorize civilian use has several states lobbying to become drone test sites, and commercial interests pressing forward to conduct drone research for civilian uses. The FAA is scheduled to pick six sites for testing by the end of 2014.[108]

The FAA Modernization and Reform Act, with a seven-page section known as the Drone Act, was passed in 2012 and requires the FAA to fully integrate unmanned aircraft for civilian use into the airways of the United States by 2015. This has raised both safety and privacy concerns. The number of drones in use could reach 30,000 by the year 2020.[109] In 2011, the FAA levied a $10,000 fine against Raphael Pirker for flying a drone over the University of Virginia to film a commercial for the school. The fine was appealed and the National Transportation Safety Board dismissed it, saying the FAA lacked the legal authority to fine Pirker.[110]

In contrast to the FAA ruling, a court in North Dakota has upheld what is believed be the first use of unmanned drones to assist in the arrest of a U.S. citizen on American soil. Police deployed an unmanned Predator drone on loan from the DHS after obtaining an arrest warrant for Rodney Brossart following a 16-hour standoff at his property.[111] Some have expressed concern about the use of drones by law enforcement, especially with regard to violation of privacy. The ACLU in California has filed a lawsuit against the FAA and the U.S. Department of Transportation due to what the union calls failure to answer Freedom of Information Act requests to determine how drones are being used.[112]

Electronic Video Surveillance

The use of electronic video surveillance (surveillance and security cameras and closed-circuit television [CCTV] systems) has increased rapidly in both the private security industry and public policing. Electronic video surveillance systems can passively record and play back video at certain intervals, be actively monitored by security personnel, or used in a combination of these methods. Some evidence suggests that video surveillance is successful in reducing and preventing crimes and is helpful in prosecuting criminals.

Electronic video surveillance has several objectives, including a reduction in crime and disorder,

making people feel safer, and providing evidence for police investigations.[113] By 2007, as technology continued to advance, many electronic video surveillance systems were converted from analog closed circuit television (CCTV) systems to wireless, digital, IP-based video systems. The advantages of wireless IP-based surveillance include real-time visual data, image clarity, and the ability to incorporate smart video technology.[114]

British police began using surveillance cameras and CCTV technology in the late 1950s to assist in the one-person operation of traffic lights. In the 1960s, the police began discussing the use of CCTV to prevent crime, and by 1969, 14 different police forces were using CCTV with 67 cameras in use nationwide. Only four of the departments were using video recorders at that time.[115] Since then, the use of surveillance cameras has increased exponentially in Great Britain.

Research results in Britain have been somewhat incomplete, confusing, and inconsistent. Instead of discussing each conflicting study in this chapter, we suggest the reader seriously interested in studying this research access the reports cited in the references to this chapter.[116] The most recent information from the British Home Office in 2005 is that academic studies of the effectiveness of electronic video surveillance are still inconclusive.[117] However, a 2005 survey of British police officers revealed that most viewed CCTV as a cost-effective tool that can facilitate the speed of investigations and encourage offenders captured on CCTV to plead guilty, thus saving police and court time. A 2005 survey of the British public revealed that 80 percent of respondents believed CCTV would reduce crimes in their areas.[118]

Testimony before the U.S. Congress in 2002 revealed that there were more than a million video surveillance cameras in use in the United States. This testimony revealed that the reasons for using video surveillance included preventing and detecting crime, reducing citizens' fear of crime, aiding criminal investigations through post-event analysis of surveillance tapes, and countering terrorism.[119] The market research firm IMS estimates that there were over 30 million surveillance cameras sold in the United States from 2001 to 2011.[120]

Some experts believe there is little evidence to date that electronic video surveillance has had a great impact on crime; however, its symbolic impact as a deterrent is believed by police forces to be significant. Further, police favor it as it expands the visual surveillance of the police without having to increase the number of officers.[121]

Eighty percent of 200 U.S. law enforcement agencies that responded to a survey by the International Association of Chiefs of Police (IACP) reported that they have used CCTV technology, and the other 20 percent anticipated using it in the future. Sixty-three percent of those using it found it was useful for investigative assistance, 54 percent found it useful for gathering evidence, and 20 percent found it useful in crime reduction. Ninety-six percent of the agencies did not have a way to measure their crime reduction ability, but of the eight agencies that did, three said it had a great effect in reducing crime.[122]

Electronic video surveillance systems make some law-abiding citizens feel safer while making others very nervous. In 2005, the police commissioner of the Redlands, California, Police Department, which was using 20 cameras at three sites, reported that the department was planning to install more surveillance cameras throughout the city and anticipated having hundreds of them within a decade. Many citizens reported pleasure at the announcement; however, the mayor said he did not think more cameras were necessary—"This is absolutely crazy. In my opinion, it's Big Brother coming in"—and the associate director of the American Civil Liberties Union (ACLU) of Southern California said she had "grave concerns about the proliferation of cameras and the whole Big Brother aspect of every person's movement being captured throughout the day in many locations."[123]

The installation in Washington, D.C., of a network of more than 14 high-tech video cameras caused privacy concerns over the possible misuse of the videotapes by the government, and critics maintained that the cost of installing them could be equal to half of the annual salary of a new police recruit, raising the question of whether it would be more important to hire more police. However, surveillance cameras have been reported to give tourists a feeling of confidence.[124]

In 2005, it was reported that the NYPD monitored 80 surveillance cameras in public places, as well as 3,000 cameras in the city Housing Authority's 15 public housing developments. The cameras in the housing developments were credited by the NYPD as cutting crime by 36 percent, mostly quality-of-life crimes like graffiti and public urination. Other

large cities that were aggressively stepping up surveillance systems at that time included Chicago and Baltimore, financed partly with federal funds. Chicago announced in 2005 that it was linking 2,000 surveillance cameras.[125]

Grant Fredericks, forensic video analyst with the nonprofit Law Enforcement and Emergency Services Video Association, says fingerprints used to play the most important role in crime scene evidence, but that role is now being filled by electronic video surveillance systems. "There's more visual evidence at crime scenes today than any other evidence," he says. Surveillance cameras have been useful in solving many types of cases, including terrorism, robberies, kidnappings, murders, thefts, fraud, and burglaries. One video security firm says there are more than 26 million surveillance cameras in the country, including those at banks, stores, train stations, schools, highways, and rooftops.[126]

The increasing use of video monitoring by law enforcement agencies, public agencies, private businesses, and citizens is providing law enforcement agencies with an unprecedented amount of visual information to aid in investigations. When police are investigating crimes, it is a common practice to view any videotapes that have been captured by businesses or public buildings near the crime scene to retrieve any visual evidence of a suspect committing the crime or fleeing the area. In many cases, videos reveal important leads, such as escape vehicles or accomplices acting as lookouts. Police use evidence and chain-of-custody procedures in these cases and consult with prosecutors.[127]

The proliferation of private surveillance cameras around the nation is transforming police work, and surveillance cameras have become key tools in investigations. "One of the things we do at the scene of any crime is look for cameras, private-sector cameras," said New York City Police Commissioner Raymond W. Kelly. "It was not standard procedure 10 or 15 years ago."[128]

The security tapes can prove more reliable than human witnesses' fuzzy recollections. The improved quality of cameras, recording systems, and digital enhancement means that evidence such as a license plate number or face can be easily singled out and enhanced. The objective nature of cameras has been critical in forcing confessions and gaining convictions. In the 2005 perjury trial of rap performer Lil' Kim, a video shows her standing within a few feet of rap producer Damien Butler, also known as D-Roc, before a shootout, even though she claimed in her grand jury testimony that she did not recall his presence. She was convicted on perjury charges based on her testimony.[129]

Experts say criminals are more likely to make confessions when they realize they have been caught on video. A surveillance video expert from the University of Indianapolis, Thomas C. Christenberry, says, "In the absence of any human witness, the video might be your only witness."[130]

The use of electronic video surveillance has been consistently held by the courts to be constitutional and not a violation of citizens' privacy rights. Although privacy advocates are uneasy about the use of electronic video surveillance to monitor public meetings and demonstrations, courts have generally ruled that people do not have a reasonable expectation of privacy when in public, because their actions are readily observable by others.[131] Also, the use of video surveillance on private property is not a violation of the U.S. Constitution.

Video evidence has been used not just to convict criminals but also to exonerate wrongly accused suspects. As an example, a homeless man arrested in New York City in 2000 for a brutal brick attack on a young woman was released after a week in jail, although he had been picked out of a lineup by three witnesses and made a confession of guilt. A review of security tapes at a Virgin Megastore about 20 blocks from the scene revealed that he was in that store at the time of the assault and thus could not have been the attacker. Police reviewed 15 hours of tapes from 31 surveillance cameras inside the store to obtain this exculpatory evidence.[132]

Norman Siegel, a former executive director of the New York Civil Liberties Union who wants public hearings on the pros and cons of surveillance cameras, says, "You are talking about fundamental freedoms: the right to freely travel, the right of anonymity." An NYPD spokesperson claims, however, "There is no privacy issue here at all. They (the cameras) would only be placed in areas where there is absolutely no expectation of privacy."[133]

Cell Phone Monitoring

With the advent of modern cell phone technology, the ability of government agencies to monitor and retrieve cell phone data has been brought to public attention through revelations about National Security Agency (NSA) practices. These revelations have affected government at all levels, especially law enforcement.

How does law enforcement track and trace phone calls? Matt Blaze lists several ways law enforcement can and does track cell phones:

1. Call Detail Records (CDR) are the official billing records released each month to customers by cell service providers. These records list the time of the call, the length of the call, and the phone number called. These records can be requested by law enforcement with a simple subpoena.

2. Pen Register and Tap and Trace are requests that relate to past activity and are similar to the CDR. These records can determine the number of calls and incoming numbers to a cell phone. A subpoena is the minimum needed to obtain the information.

3. Content wiretaps require a search warrant for law enforcement to be able to tap into the cell phone to record conversations; probable cause must be established to do so. When a content wiretap is requested, a CDR and Pen Register/Tap and Trace are usually included to give context to the wiretap.

4. E911 pings are signals sent by a cell phone when it is powered on. These signals register the cell phone on a cell tower and move from tower to tower as the cell phone moves. This technology can be used to locate missing persons and also to test the veracity of a suspect's alibi. In some cases, the cell phone carrier can trigger the E911 location feature in an attempt to locate the cell phone. Law enforcement usually can request this information without a warrant, especially if it is needed to locate a subject who has been kidnapped or is missing and time is of the essence.

5. Tower dumps are requests by law enforcement for all the cell phone activity from a particular cell phone tower or towers in a certain geographical area. This type of request will provide information on everyone in the area, whether they are the target of an investigation or not.

6. Stingrays/IMSI Catchers will capture all cell phone activity in a particular area, essentially creating a portable cell phone tower that identifies every phone number that can later be used to request CDR information. The law is unclear as to the legality of this method.[134]

As noted above, the law is muddied regarding the requirements for a search warrant to obtain information. In some cases the law is clear (wiretaps) and in others it is still up in the air (stingrays). States in the 4th U.S. Circuit, 5th U.S. Circuit, and 7th U.S. Circuit, as well as Georgia, Alabama, and California, all have said a warrant is *not* required when conducting a cell phone search.[135] Other states have determined that a warrant is required; this has caused the U.S. Supreme Court to take up two conflicting cases, *United States v. Wurie* and *Riley v. California*.[136]

Advanced Photographic Techniques

Photography has always played a major role in policing. Innovations and advanced techniques have increased this role. This section discusses digital photography, aerial photography, mug shot imaging systems, age-progression photography, and composite sketching.

Digital Photography

Digital photography is being increasingly recognized and used in law enforcement as an efficient tool that enables instant viewing and distribution of images that aid in criminal investigations. The major concern about digital photography is its admissibility as evidence in court because it can be manipulated with computer software. Traditional film-based photography can also be manipulated, however, either while taking the original photograph or in developing the film.

Under current rules of evidence, parties seeking to introduce a film-based photograph must demonstrate its relevancy and authenticity. Courts generally require the original (the negative or any print therefrom). A 2005 article recommended that to alleviate fears that digital photographs might elude confirmation of authenticity, police agencies should attempt to establish standard operating procedures that include the preservation of and accountability for the original image on a camera chip prior to

processing via computer software and a printer, as well as evidence of how the image was processed before being admitted into evidence.[137]

Aerial Photography

Aerial photography is extremely useful in documenting certain scenes and their evidence, such as large outdoor crime scenes and vehicle crash scenes. It can provide a superior perspective while providing facts in a more accurate and more easily understood manner than the usual verbal testimony, and it adds a dimension of visual reference.[138] In *Florida v. Riley* (1989), the U.S. Supreme Court overturned a suppression motion upheld by the Florida Supreme Court, stating in the decision delivered by Justice White:

> The Fourth Amendment does not require the police traveling in the public airways at an altitude of 400 feet to obtain a warrant in order to observe what is visible to the naked eye. *California v. Ciraolo*, 476 U.S. 207—which held that a naked-eye police inspection of the backyard of a house from a fixed-wing aircraft at 1,000 feet was not a "search"—is controlling.[139]

Mug Shot Imaging

Mug shot imaging is a system of digitizing a photo of a suspect or arrest and storing the image on a computer. The picture is taken with a video camera and then transferred to a color video monitor, where it appears as an electronic image. When the image is filed, the operator enters the identifying data such as race, gender, date of birth, and the subject's case number. Using this system, victims of crimes can quickly view possible mug shots on a computer screen.[140]

A good example of mug shot imaging is the ALERT (Advanced Law Enforcement Response Technology) system. This system allows a photo of a subject to be transmitted from one police vehicle to others with the necessary equipment, giving officers an immediate view of a wanted suspect or a missing person.[141]

Automated systems that capture and digitize mug shots can incorporate biometric facial recognition. The Los Angeles County Sheriff's Department installed a system that can take the composite drawing of a suspect or a video image of someone committing a crime and search it against its database of digitized mug shots.[142]

---

mug shot imaging A system of digitizing a mug shot picture and storing its image on a computer so that it can be retrieved later.

Age-Progression Photographs

One important development in police photography is **age-progression photos**. The ability to recognize a face may be thwarted by the changes that naturally occur to the face with age. To counter this, two medical illustrators, Scott Barrows and Lewis Sadler, developed techniques in the early 1980s for producing age-progression drawings. Today, thanks to a computer algorithm, the same process that used to take hours using calipers, ruler, and pen can be completed in seconds. Developed by a colleague of Barrows and Sadler, the age-progression program systematizes the knowledge of the anatomy of 14 major bones and more than 100 muscles and how they grow. It also shows the change in relationship, over time, of 48 facial landmarks, such as the corners of the eyes and the nose. Computers have enabled the National Center for Missing and Exploited Children to have thousands of age-progressed pictures printed onto milk cartons and flyers.[143]

The FBI uses its own age-progression program for adult faces. The system allows artists to do such things as thin hair, add jowls, or increase wrinkles while maintaining the basic facial proportions. The FBI's software for aging children's faces allows pictures of parents and older siblings to be fused into photos of missing children to obtain a more accurate image.[144]

Composite Sketches

Police have for many years sought the assistance of forensic artists in preparing **composite sketches**. The FBI began to use composite sketching in 1920; other agencies had been using it even earlier. These portrait-style drawings generally require hours of interview, drawing, and revision. Today the FBI has converted its book of photographs, used for interviewing witnesses for composites, into hand-drawn images using forensic imaging. The hand-drawn images are entered into a computer, where they form the basis of a database that automatically generates images similar to those that are hand drawn. Once the witness selects features from the catalog, the composite image appears on the computer screen in just a few minutes.[145]

The FBI will be activating a new facial recognition service in select states that will allow local police to identify unknown subjects. This has been a multiyear effort to overhaul the existing fingerprint database so as to allow law enforcement to quickly and accurately identify suspects. In many cases officers will have a photo, but not much else, and this new database should help fill that void.[146] Currently the database, known as Next Generation Identification (NGI), has 16 million images and could have up to 52 million by 2015. The FBI has said this database would help track down terrorists and criminals.[147]

Computer software can also allow officers to produce a digitized composite photo of a suspect based on the recollections of victims and witnesses. The resulting photo can then be compared with thousands of digital mug shots stored in the growing number of databases in jurisdictions all over the nation, including those states that now issue digitized photos on driver's licenses. Included in this software is a databank of thousands of facial features from which witnesses select the ones that best fit their description of suspects. Software users, who need no formal artistic training, can adjust the composite by using a scanner to adjust the facial features chosen by the witness.[148] The system can be loaded into a laptop computer to further speed up the process by taking it directly to a crime scene. It can also be accessed via a modem hookup or put online, with an artist or investigator in another city available to prepare the composite while a witness views and suggests changes.

A CD-ROM program called "Faces, the Ultimate Composite Picture" provides nearly 4,000 facial features that can be selected to create billions of faces. The designers used photos taken of approximately 15,000 volunteers, ages 17 to 60, to acquire images of hair, eyes, chins, and more. Instead of a police artist trying to coax the memory of an offender's face from a frightened victim, artists and even victims themselves can create photo-quality composites in about 30 minutes.[149]

There remains a controversy, however, over the value of forensic artistry versus the use of digital imaging composite software. Hand-drawn sketches are seen as having the ability to include subtleties that composite software programs cannot, and can increase the number of unique facial features

---

age-progression photos Photo systems that show changes that will naturally occur to the face with age; also called age-enhanced photos.

composite sketches Sketches prepared by forensic artists or by automated means of people wanted by the police for a crime.

Finding Missing Children through Age-Enhanced Photos

An investigator from Oakland, California, reached out across the United States and Canada with age-enhanced images of two missing brothers. After exhausting every lead, the investigator turned to the television program *Unsolved Mysteries*.

On the evening of the broadcast, hundreds of calls poured in from the Albuquerque, New Mexico, area. Authorities located the children in a trailer on the outskirts of town, where they lived with their mother and her new husband—a known drug dealer. The boys were returned to their father, who had not seen them in several years. Although the aged images of the boys were very accurate, the relentless determination of the investigator and the assistance of the public ultimately solved the case.

Source: Adapted from Gene O'Donnell, "Forensic Imaging Comes of Age," *FBI Law Enforcement Bulletin* (January 1994): 9.

possible. Digital composites, on the other hand, can be made in the field immediately following an incident, printed out, and dispersed to field units almost immediately. Hand-drawn sketches can then be scanned into a digital imaging program.[150] According to a 2006 article, the construction of a composite image based on selections provided by computer graphics software can be useful, but it may be either too limited in its selections of features or provide so many selections that victims or witnesses become confused and frustrated, whereas artist-drawn composites can be flexible and responsive to the distinctive memories of victims and witnesses. Also the author indicates that the cost of computer-generated imaging and all of the required software and equipment makes the training of a composite artist cost-efficient. These artists can also perform other useful functions, such as the creation of demonstrative evidence for courtroom presentations, age progressions, postmortem imaging, and facial reconstruction.[151]

forensic science That part of science applied to answering legal questions.

criminalistics A branch of forensic science that deals with the study of physical evidence related to crime.

In a 2007 article, Donna Rogers reminds us that it is critical to remember that a facial composite gives investigators "a direction but it is not the nail in the coffin; there is additional evidence like DNA or fingerprints." She states that numerous factors affect the accuracy of eyewitness composites, such as a delay following the event, exposure time to the subject, emotion, and stress. She emphasizes that a bad composite can lead an investigation astray and produce wrongful convictions.[152]

Modern Forensics or Criminalistics

The use of scientific technology to solve crime is generally referred to as **forensic science** or **criminalistics**. *Forensic science,* the more general of the two terms, is that part of science applied to answering legal questions. According to Richard Saferstein, former chief forensic scientist of the New Jersey State Police laboratory and the author of eight editions of the leading textbook regarding forensic science and criminalistics, *Criminalistics: An Introduction to Forensic Science,* "Forensic science is the application of science to those criminal and civil laws that are enforced by police agencies in a criminal justice system."[153] Regarding the interchangeability of the terms *forensic science* and *criminalistics,* Saferstein says that for all intents and purposes, the two terms are seen as similar and he uses them interchangeably in his text.

Criminalistics is actually just one of several branches of forensic science. Other branches include forensic medicine, pathology, toxicology, physical anthropology, odontology, psychiatry, questioned documents, ballistics, tool work comparison, and serology.[154] (See Table 14.2.) To simplify the

TABLE 14.2 Forensic Specialties

Forensic pathology	Dead bodies
Forensic physical anthropology	Skeletal remains
Forensic odontology	Teeth formation
Forensic toxicology	Poisons
Forensic entomology	Insects at death scenes

© 2016 Cengage Learning®

information in this chapter for the nonscience student, however, the word *criminalistics* will be used interchangeably with *forensic science*.[155]

Criminalistics has been defined as "the examination, evaluation, and explanation of physical evidence related to crime."[156] The California Association of Criminalists defines criminalistics as "that profession and scientific discipline directed to the recognition, identification, individualization, and evaluation of physical evidence by the application of the natural sciences to law-science matters."[157] Criminalistic evidence includes such clues as fingerprints, blood and blood stains, semen stains, drugs and alcohol, hairs and fibers, and firearms and tool marks. Forensic technicians, forensic scientists, forensic chemists, and criminalists (the more generic term) generally specialize in one or more of the following areas: analysis of trace evidence, serology, drug chemistry, firearms and tool marks, and questioned documents.

The purpose of criminalistics is to take physical evidence from a crime or a crime scene and use it to (1) identify the person who committed the crime and (2) exonerate others who may be under suspicion. For example, was the revolver found on a suspect the one that fired the bullet found in the body of a murder victim? If so, did the suspect fire it? Criminalistic evidence also can be used to establish an element of the crime and to reconstruct how the crime was committed.

In court, criminalistic evidence is presented via laboratory analysis by an expert prepared to interpret and testify to the scientific results, thus distinguishing forensic evidence from other forms of physical or tangible evidence such as stolen goods, articles of clothing, and other personal property. In a study of criminalistic evidence and the criminal justice system, the NIJ discovered that the police are, on average, about three times more likely to clear cases when scientific evidence is gathered and analyzed, prosecutors are less likely to agree to enter into plea negotiations if criminalistic evidence strongly associates the defendant with the crime, and judges issue more severe sentences when criminalistic evidence is presented at trials.[158]

As indicated in Chapter 1, there has been serious criticism of crime labs and scientific evidence; one example is the O. J. Simpson case, but there are many others. In 1997, the Justice Department's inspector general reported that the FBI's renowned crime laboratory was riddled with flawed scientific practices that had potentially tainted dozens of criminal cases, including the bombing of the Federal Building in Oklahoma City and the original bombing of the World Trade Center in New York. The inspector general's findings resulted from an 18-month investigation that uncovered extremely serious and significant problems at the laboratory that had been a symbol of the FBI's cutting-edge scientific sleuthing.[159] The dramatic series of problems associated with the FBI and its alleged bungling of scientific evidence and criminal investigations led *Time* magazine to produce a cover article entitled, "What's Wrong at the FBI?: The Fiasco at the Crime Lab."[160]

In 2001, an Oklahoma City Police Department forensic scientist was accused of a series of forensic errors involving at least five cases in which she made significant errors or overstepped the acceptable limits of forensic science. In response, Oklahoma's governor launched a review of every one of the thousands of cases the scientist had handled between 1980 and 1993. In 12 of these cases, the defendants were awaiting the death penalty, and in another 11, the defendants had already been put to death.[161]

In 2003, DNA evidence in 64 criminal cases from Marion County, Indiana, was challenged because of concerns that a laboratory technician may have cut corners.[162] In 2006, a special investigator assigned to study the Houston Police Department's crime lab indicated that 43 DNA cases and 50 serology cases dating back to 1980 had "major issues." The investigator said the cases contained problems that raised significant doubt as to the reliability of the work performed, the validity of the analytical results, or the correctness of the analysts' conclusions. The DNA division of the Houston crime laboratory had been closed in 2002 after an independent audit had exposed widespread problems with protocols and personnel, but in the following years, errors also were exposed in the lab's firearms, serology, and drug units.[163]

In 2008, the Detroit Police Department closed down its crime laboratory after an audit uncovered serious errors in numerous cases. The audit revealed that sloppy work had probably resulted in wrongful convictions. The inspection found that the laboratory's firearms unit was in compliance with just 42 percent of essential standards. In 2010, it was reported that the closing of the Detroit Police lab was adding to heavy backlogs of forensic evidence at labs across the state and grinding the justice system in Michigan to a halt. The Michigan State Police, which took over from the Detroit crime lab, was sending evidence in violent cases to other state, federal, and private labs, putting local cases on hold. Officials reported a backlog of 12,000 rape kits and 2,700 other pieces of forensic evidence.[164]

Additionally, in March 2010, the San Francisco Police Department said that it would close the drug analysis unit indefinitely after an outside audit concluded that the lab had been sacrificing quality for quantity to deal with an untenable workload. The lab had been closed earlier in response to suspicions that a longtime technician had used cocaine that she was supposed to test. Hundreds of drug cases have been dismissed.[165] The crime lab technician at the center of the scandal was convicted in July 2013 of misdemeanor cocaine possession and sentenced to five years of probation and one year of home confinement.[166]

In 2009, the National Academy of Sciences issued a 328-page report, *Strengthening Forensic Science in the United States: A Path Forward.* The report found serious problems with much of the work performed by crime laboratories in the United States. It concluded that crime labs were overworked, there were few certification programs for investigators and technicians, and the entire field suffered from a lack of oversight. The most serious conclusions found in the report were that many forensic disciplines—including analysis of fingerprints, bite marks, and the striations and indentations left by a pry bar or a gun's firing mechanism—were not grounded in the kind of rigorous, peer-reviewed research that is the hallmark of classic science. DNA analysis was an exception, the report noted, in that it had been studied extensively. Other investigative tests, the report said, had never been exposed to stringent scientific scrutiny. It said that these tests have never been rigorously shown to have the capacity to consistently, and with a high degree of certainty, demonstrate a connection between evidence and a specific individual or source.[167]

Also in 2009, the NIJ issued a report, *The 2007 Survey of Law Enforcement Forensic Evidence Processing.* The survey was conducted to estimate the number of unsolved homicide, rape, and property crime cases in the United States involving forensic evidence that was not submitted to a crime laboratory for analysis, as well as to determine the policies and procedures used in law enforcement agencies for processing, submitting, and retaining forensic evidence. The survey findings showed that 14 percent of all unsolved homicides and 18 percent of unsolved rapes yielded forensic evidence that was not submitted to a crime laboratory for analysis. DNA was the most common form of forensic evidence in these cases. Survey results also indicated that 23 percent of all unsolved property crimes involved unanalyzed forensic evidence. The findings showed that law enforcement agencies were continuing to face substantial forensic evidence caseloads.[168]

The American Academy of Forensic Sciences (AAFS) is a professional society dedicated to the application of science to the law. Its membership includes physicians, criminalists, toxicologists, attorneys, dentists, physical anthropologists, document examiners, engineers, psychiatrists, educators, and others who practice and perform research in the many diverse fields relating to forensic science.

The *CSI* Effect

The popularity of the television series *CSI: Crime Scene Investigation*, and its spin-offs *CSI: Miami* and *CSI: New York,* as well as other television shows and movies that romanticize criminalistics work has produced what many call the **CSI effect**. The *CSI* effect has created challenges for investigators, forensic experts, and juries. According to a Lowell, Massachusetts, police captain, "People are demanding today to see what they see on TV. DNA takes 15 minutes to analyze on TV, but in reality, it takes months." Commenting on the possibility of physical evidence being as prolific as indicated on the *CSI* shows, Lawrence Kobilinsky, a forensic scientist and consultant at John Jay College, said, "Not every case is a case where you've got physical evidence." As an example, in Alabama, cases with hair, fiber, glass, paint, and other trace evidence make up less than 1 percent of the total number of cases submitted to forensic analysis.[169]

Julian Fantino, commissioner of the Ontario Provincial Police, also commented on the *CSI* effect, saying, "Unrealistic portrayals of the science have translated to equally unrealistic expectations from not only the public but also other professions that

---

CSI effect The phenomenon in which the popularity of the television series *CSI: Crime Scene Investigation,* as well as its spin-offs *CSI: Miami* and *CSI: New York,* and other television shows and movies makes the public and jurors believe that the police can do what their television counterparts can.

Criminalistics and Good Old Detective Work Find Suspect in Hit and Run

In January 2001, Marjorie Cordero, the wife of famed jockey Angel Cordero, was struck and killed by an auto driven by a hit-and-run driver as she crossed a road near her home in Greenvale, New York. Among the evidence left at the scene were a headlight and a two-by-three-inch plate of fiberglass from a header panel of the car. Eventually this evidence enabled police to make an arrest in May 2001.

Criminalists from the Nassau County Police Department's Scientific Investigation Bureau analyzed the headlight and the fiberglass and determined that these pieces of evidence came from a 1987 or 1988 black Mercury Cougar. They ran that description through the state Department of Motor Vehicles database and found there were hundreds of cars of that model in the Nassau County and eastern Queens area. During the weeks that followed, investigators looked at more than 300 Mercury Cougars—staking out driveways, glancing at header panels—before zeroing in on the suspect's car. They obtained a warrant to search it, and the piece of black fiberglass recovered at the scene fit into the header panel of the suspect's car like a missing piece of a jigsaw puzzle.

Source: Adapted from Oscar Corral, "Hit-Run Arrest: Cops Find Suspect in Incident That Killed Marjorie Cordero," *Newsday*, May 2, 2001, p. A3.

operate within the justice system who now apparently believe in magic."[170] In 2006, one writer argued that due to the *CSI* effect, the public now expects a 40-minute investigation turnaround, compared with what typically can take months. She said that jurors also are expecting law enforcement to be using the biggest and best equipment like that shown on the TV programs. This phenomenon affects more than just the court system: Those committing the crimes are becoming better educated about what not to leave behind at a crime scene. On a positive note, however, the *CSI* effect is leading many high school and college students to take forensic science or criminalistics courses and prepare for careers in the field.[171]

A very good example of the *CSI* effect was a 2006 case involving the alleged assault and rape of a 27-year-old exotic dancer in Durham, North Carolina, by a group of Duke University lacrosse players at a team party. The case received national attention because it stirred passions regarding class and race differences. The dancer was black and all but one of the 47 lacrosse players were white. The 46 white lacrosse players were the subject of DNA tests, which found no matching DNA. The lawyers representing the players claimed that the absence of DNA indicated that their clients were innocent, and others agreed with this assertion. However, the prosecutor dismissed the DNA findings and three of the players were indicted on rape charges.[172]

The true facts about DNA are as follows: DNA evidence from an attacker is successfully recovered in less than a quarter of sexual assault cases; two-thirds of sexual assault cases are solved without DNA evidence; and tests that pinpoint DNA are often overplayed as a forensic tool.[173]

The Modern Crime Lab

There are hundreds of public and private crime laboratories in the United States today. There are nearly 400 publicly funded labs, including state, regional, county, municipal, and federal labs. The latest available statistics indicate that these public labs employed more than 11,900 full-time personnel, had total budgets exceeding $821 million, and received nearly 2.7 million new cases each year.

Most very large police departments operate their own police laboratories. Smaller departments may contract with large county crime labs or state police crime labs. Some departments use the services of the FBI lab.[174] (See Table 14.3.) The FBI lab reports that it conducts more than one million examinations each year. The FBI opened its $130 million, 500,000-square-foot laboratory on its campus in Quantico, Virginia, in 2003.[175]

One of the latest developments in crime scene technology is the use of mobile crime labs that enable crime scene technicians to conduct extensive evidence collection and processing at crime scene sites, such as homicide scenes, meth lab sites, arson sites, and investigations that involve mass casualties. Most mobile crime labs contain equipment for analyzing chemicals, special hoods for fume disposal, isolated boxes for hazardous material analysis, and supplies

TABLE 14.3 Services Provided by the FBI Laboratory

- Chemistry
- Combined DNA Index System (CODIS)
- Computer analysis and response
- DNA analysis
- Evidence response
- Explosives
- Firearms and tool marks
- Forensic audio, video, and image analysis
- Forensic science research
- Forensic science training
- Hazardous materials response
- Investigative and prosecutive graphics
- Latent prints
- Materials analysis
- Questioned documents
- Racketeering records
- Special photographic analysis
- Structural design
- Trace evidence

Source: Adapted from *FBI Laboratory Services*, retrieved August 1, 2006, from http://www.fbi.gov/about-us/lab.

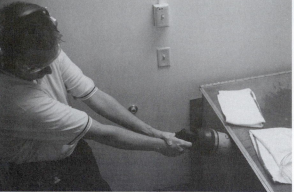

Guns can be tested by firing them into a tank of water. The bullets are collected from the bottom of the tank and then analyzed using microscopes and computers.

Most crime labs have the following sections that concentrate on different criminalistics evidence: ballistics, serology, criminalistics, chemistry, and document analysis. (See Table 14.4.)

BALLISTICS The **ballistics** section of the crime lab conducts scientific analysis of guns and bullets. (Ballistics is the science of the study of objects in motion and at rest.) Examination of firearms evidence involves the identification, testing, and classification of firearms submitted to the lab. Technicians microscopically examine a bullet, cartridge case, or shotgun shell in order to determine

for crime scene investigation. The Pinellas County Sheriff's Office in Florida has purchased such a lab. The rationale for the purchase was to have a mobile crime lab that could be deployed at a crime scene for several days with the capabilities of processing evidence at the scene.[176]

Private (that is, nongovernment) labs are taking on greater importance in the U.S. legal system. Their analyses are increasingly being introduced into criminal and civil trials, often not only as evidence but also to contradict evidence presented by a prosecutor that was analyzed in a police lab.

TABLE 14.4 Police Forensic Laboratories

Major Section	Function
Ballistics	Examination of guns and bullets
Serology	Examination of blood, semen, and other body fluids
Criminalistics	Examination of hairs, fibers, paints, clothing, glass, and other trace evidence
Chemistry	Examination of drugs and alcohol
Document analysis	Comparison of handwriting

ballistics Scientific analysis of guns and bullets.

© 2016 Cengage Learning®

whether it was fired from a specific firearm to the exclusion of any other firearm.

The ballistics examination provides the investigator with such information related to shooting cases as comparison of a spent (fired) bullet to a suspect weapon, the type and model of weapon that may have been used in a shooting, the description and operating condition of a suspect weapon, the trajectory of a bullet wound (the line of fire and firing position of the shooter), the possibility of an accidental discharge of a weapon rather than a purposeful discharge, the trigger pull (amount of force required to fire a particular weapon), the shooting distance in possible suicide cases, and restored serial numbers from a weapon in which the original serial numbers were altered or obliterated.

To determine whether a suspect firearm was used in a particular shooting, ballistics experts test-fire a bullet from it into a tank of water known as a ballistics recovery tank. The spent bullet is then compared to the bullet taken from a victim or the crime scene using a ballistic comparison microscope. The rationale behind this testing is that bullets fired from a gun receive a mark on them from the lands and grooves of the barrel of the gun. These small individualistic markings are called *striae*. Bullets fired from the same gun should have similar markings.

The NYPD's ballistics lab of its Forensics Investigations Division maintains a collection of 720 guns used in previous shootings, including the gun used to kill John Lennon and the one used by the Son of Sam killer, David Berkowitz, that they use for comparison purposes.

The Federal Bureau of Alcohol, Tobacco, Firearms, and Explosives (ATF) maintains the Integrated Ballistics Information System (IBIS). IBIS is a computer identification system that correlates and matches both projectile (bullet) and shell casing ballistic evidence. This unique ballistic comparison system allows firearms technicians to digitize and store bullets and shell casings at a greatly accelerated rate. It stores bullet "signatures" in a database to allow ballistics examiners to quickly determine whether a spent bullet may be linked to a crime. The software-driven system includes a customized microscope, video camera, specimen manipulator, image digitizer, and a series of computers. The video camera and microscope record the unique, telltale markings and grooves made as a soft lead bullet is fired through a gun

barrel, then digitally translate the information for computer storage and future analysis. The system alerts the operator if a possible match has already been entered into the database by providing the examiner with a numerically ranked list. The examiner can then retrieve the stored image for a side-by-side visual comparison, eliminating the need to track down the original specimen. It allows examiners to magnify any portion of the stored images.[177] The ATF also maintains the National Tracing Center (NTC), which provides assistance to law enforcement agencies 24 hours a day, 7 days a week. The NTC traces firearms recovered in crimes worldwide and has more than 100 million firearm records.[178]

By 2000, the various national law enforcement ammunition-tracing databases created since 1993 held more than 800,000 images of bullets and shell casings. More than 8,000 matches have been made in over 16,000 cases. Law enforcement officials say that computer ballistic imaging technology is the most important forensic advancement since the development of the comparison microscope more than 70 years ago.[179]

In September 2005, the FBI lab announced it had stopped making comparative bullet lead analyses (data-chaining), a four-decades-old technique that attempts to link a fired bullet with a particular box of bullets. This action was the result of a study by the National Academy of Sciences that found significant flaws in the techniques used in this test.[180]

In 2006, the FBI lab also announced that it would discontinue analyzing gunshot residue (GSR). GSR is made up of the microscopic particles that explode from a gun when it is fired. The particles can be collected from suspects' hands, analyzed, and used as evidence in court. A spokesperson for the lab said that in recent years the lab had been receiving fewer than 10 requests per year and decided its resources were better used in "areas that directly relate to fighting terrorism." However, there are also problems with GSR that make it somewhat unreliable. The major problem is that the particles float like ash and never disintegrate, making it possible for it to be transmitted from a police officer's hands to lab work tables and contaminate fresh samples. Contamination studies have revealed hundreds of particles consistent with gunshot residue in several areas of the lab that could cast doubts on the origin of the residue in a sample. It also has been claimed that all trace evidence, including GSR, can be presented to jurors with a false degree of certainty.[181]

A professional organization for persons interested in firearms and ballistics examinations is the Association of Firearms and Tool Mark Examiners (AFTE).

SEROLOGY The crime lab's **serology** section analyzes blood, semen, and other body fluids found at a crime scene—important evidence in homicide and sexual assault cases. If blood on a suspect's shirt can be matched to the victim's blood, it can place the suspect at the crime scene. If semen found in a rape victim or on her clothing can be matched to a suspect's, it can link the perpetrator to the crime. Certain tests are useful in this process. The hemin crystal test will determine if a particular stain is actually blood. The precipitin test will determine if the blood is human, animal, or a mixture of both. Other tests can determine the specific blood type of the stain. Tests can also detect the existence of semen in stains, if sperm is present, if the person was a secretor, and match the semen to a particular blood type.

The use of the chemical luminol can produce evidence that blood was at a scene even if the area was meticulously cleaned. When luminol is sprayed on an area, a luminescence or glow is produced if blood has been present. The development of DNA profiling or genetic fingerprinting (which will be discussed later in this chapter) has revolutionized the serology capacity of the crime lab.

CRIMINALISTICS The criminalistics section of the crime lab studies myriad pieces of physical evidence that may connect a suspect to a crime or a crime scene. Often this evidence is crucial to the understanding of the crime scene and the identification of perpetrators. A perpetrator may unknowingly take something from a crime scene (for example, fibers from the victim's carpet may be found on the suspect's clothing) or may leave something at the crime scene (a shoe print in the mud outside the victim's window or marks from a tool used to pry open the victim's window).

The matching of samples of evidence found at the crime scene to a particular subject can be instrumental in the identification and successful prosecution of a suspect. The following are some examples of crime scene evidence that can be of value in an investigation.

- **Glass** Fragments of glass found at a crime scene can give an investigator a great deal of useful information. Traces of blood, clothing, hair, or fingerprints can be found on glass fragments. When a suspect is arrested, these same fragments can conclusively establish the individual's presence at the scene if they are also found on his or her clothing.

  In addition, glass can tell an investigator how a crime was committed. Investigators can study conchoidal fractures, radial fractures, and concentric breaks to determine how the glass was broken, the angle at which a bullet was fired, and even which bullet was fired first through a window with multiple bullet holes.

  Glass offers a wealth of information because of differences in the way it is made. It varies widely in physical and chemical composition, and has numerous impurities. Through the use of refractive index analysis, dispersion analysis, densities analysis, and spectrographic analysis, a crime lab can link glass from a suspect's clothing to that collected at a crime scene, or specify the type of vehicle from fragments collected at a hit-and-run accident.

- **Hairs and Fibers** Hairs and fibers can be vital pieces of evidence. They can be found on a victim's clothing and in objects at the crime scene, such as bed linen, carpets, and furniture. Hair can tell the perpetrator's race and gender. Investigators can tell which part of the body the hair came from, whether it was pulled out forcibly or fell out naturally, and whether it was smashed with a blunt object or sheared with a sharp instrument.

  Fibers are also very specific in the information they reveal. Because they vary dramatically in color, source, shape, and composition, they actually have more identifying characteristics than hair.

- **Fingernail Scrapings** Two types of evidence can be taken from fingernail scrapings and fingernails at a crime scene. First, when fingernails are trimmed and collected from a victim, scrapings of hairs, fibers, skin, or blood from under the nail can reveal a variety of information about the crime and the perpetrator, especially

----

serology Scientific analysis of blood, semen, and other body fluids.

in cases in which the victim struggled with the perpetrator. Second, when a broken fingernail is left at the scene and later compared to the nails of a suspect, it can include or exclude that person from the list of suspects. Much like fingerprints, nails are unique to each individual and rarely change through a person's life. Fingernails can be examined in much the same way as tool marks, bullets, and casings. Because the striae on nails are on the same scale as that found on fired bullets, the same type of comparison microscope is used.

- **Impressions and Casts** Impressions and casts taken of footprints at a crime scene can be very important to the investigator because no two people will wear shoes in precisely the same pattern or show damage in the same places. Footprints can include or exclude a suspect, as well as tell investigators whether he or she was walking or running, was carrying a heavy object, or seemed unfamiliar with the area or unsure of the terrain.

- **Chemistry** The chemistry section studies alcohol and possible drugs or controlled substances gathered in investigations and arrests. This section analyzes most of the cases handled by the crime lab.

  The most commonly used standard for the degree of intoxication in criminal cases such as driving while intoxicated (DWI) or driving while under the influence (DUI) is the measure of alcohol concentration in the suspect's blood. The alcohol concentration level determined by the lab is instrumental in the eventual prosecution of these alcohol-related crimes.

  The chemistry section also tests substances believed to be in violation of drug laws. Using chemical and other tests, chemists can identify the type of drug in a substance, as well as the percentage of a drug in a particular mixture.

  The latest annual report of the National Forensic Laboratory Information System (NFLIS) reported that 1,189,089 million drug items were analyzed by state and local laboratories in the United States in 2012. Cannabis or marijuana was the most frequently identified drug, followed by cocaine, methamphetamine, and heroin.[182]

- **Document Analysis** The document analysis section studies handwriting, printing, typewriting, and the paper and ink used in the preparation of a document to provide investigators with leads to the identity of the writer. The document technician can compare requested handwriting exemplars (samples of the suspect's handwriting requested by the police) with the questioned document. This is a very important type of analysis in investigating ransom notes, anonymous letters, and possible forgeries. Document analysis can also determine if there were any additions, changes, or deletions made. The paper on which a document is written can provide a number of clues to the investigator, such as the manufacturer, date of production, the pH and fiber composition, trace elements, and chemical elements, including fibers, waxes, dyes, fluorescent brighteners, and fillers.

- The Scientific Working Group for Forensic Document Examination (SWGDOC) has adopted guidelines for forensic document examinations outlining the technologies and procedures to be used for professional document examinations.[183] Scientists and technicians are continually making new improvements in document analysis.[184] The American Society of Questioned Document Examiners (ASQDE) is a professional organization for forensic document examiners.[185]

- **Carbon-14 Dating** Normally associated with archeology and "ancient finds" throughout the world, carbon-14 is now being applied to law enforcement in an attempt to identify the age of skeletons or other unidentified human remains. Carbon-14 dating is based on the natural process of radioactive carbon formation that results from cosmic ray bombardment of nitrogen in the earth's upper atmosphere. This radioactivity enters into the human body via the food chain. It is the measurement of the amount of the carbon-14 dating that can determine the year of death.[186]

Crime Lab Accreditation

Crime lab accreditation is designed to ameliorate some of the problems raised earlier in this chapter regarding mistakes made by crime labs.

The American Society of Crime Laboratory Directors (ASCLD) is a nonprofit professional society of crime laboratory directors, devoted to the improvement of crime laboratory operations through sound management practices. Its purpose is to foster the common professional interests of its members and to promote and foster the development of laboratory management principles and techniques. Its Crime Laboratory Accreditation Program is a voluntary program in which any crime laboratory may participate to demonstrate that its management, operations, personnel, procedures, equipment, physical plant, security, and personnel safety procedures meet established standards. The accreditation process is part of a laboratory's quality assurance program that should also include proficiency testing, continuing education, and other programs to help the laboratory give better overall service to the criminal justice system. The ASCLD maintains that the process of self-evaluation is in itself a valuable management tool for the crime laboratory director.[187]

The American Board of Criminalists (ABC) certifies lab employees. Because it ensures that lab personnel are all held to the same standard, certification helps analysts fend off courtroom salvos about their experience, background, and training.

Accreditation and certification are certainly needed in the nation's labs. According to Ron Urbanovsky, director of the Texas Department of Public Safety's statewide system of crime labs, "Part of the [O. J.] Simpson case fallout was that we've seen much longer and stiffer cross-examinations in court. Testimony that used to take two to three hours now takes eight to 12 hours, and it's grueling. We are asked to be perfect in a non-perfect world."[188]

The NIJ has created the Technical Working Group on Crime Scene Investigation (TWGCSI) as a multidisciplinary group of experts from across the United States from both urban and rural jurisdictions. The TWGCSI produced *Crime Scene Investigation: A Guide for Law Enforcement*, which documents and explains the major steps and processes in working a crime scene.[189]

Because of a recent U.S. Supreme Court case, law enforcement is now required to have the forensic laboratory technician in court to testify to the document created at the time of testing, which allows the defendant to directly confront his accuser. The Court, in its 2011 decision in *Bullcoming v. New Mexico*, held that "[t]he Six Amendment's Confrontation Clause gives the accused . . . in all criminal prosecutions . . .

computer/digital forensics The science of identifying, collecting, preserving, documenting, examining, analyzing, and presenting evidence from computers, computer networks, and other electronic devices.

Credibility of Crime Lab in Question

Although many crime labs are participating in accreditation, some labs have suffered massive public relations and credibility disasters due to malfeasance by employees not following procedures or participating in outright criminal behavior. The crime lab in San Francisco, for example, was shut down in 2010 after allegations that a then-retired 29-year veteran of the lab had stolen and used cocaine evidence at the lab. San Francisco District Attorney (later California Attorney General) Kamala Harris said that up to 1,000 cases might be dropped as a result.

The San Francisco Police Department also conducted an internal investigation. A lieutenant in the department, Lyn Tomioka, said that the lab probe had moved beyond the initial allegations and everyone assigned to the lab was under investigation. Police hoped that some of the cases could be salvaged and not dismissed just because of the problems at the lab.

Source: Based on Jaxon Van Derbeken, "Drug Lab Scandal Jeopardized Hundreds of Cases," SFGate.com, retrieved March 29, 2010, from www.sfgate.com/cgi-bin/article .cgi?f=/c/a/2010/03/27/MND91CMCJN.DTL.

the right . . . to be confronted with the witnesses against him. . . . Bullcoming's jury trial on charges of driving while intoxicated (DWI) occurred after *Crawford*, but before *Melendez-Diaz*." The evidence against Bullcoming was a forensic laboratory report certifying that his blood-alcohol level was well above the threshold for aggravated DWI. The Court held that the analyst had to be present in court to testify to the laboratory report.[190]

Computer/Digital Forensics

Computer or digital forensics is the science of identifying, collecting, preserving, documenting, examining, analyzing, and presenting evidence from computers, computer networks, and other electronic devices.[191] With the advent of personal computers, cell phones, the Internet, and an unending variety of electronic devices, computer/digital forensics has become an increasingly important job for law enforcement. Much of an individual's personal information, as well as other evidence, is saved in a potentially fragile digital format. All digital evidence must be collected, preserved, and examined in a forensically sound and pristine manner in order to ensure that the evidence is admissible in court.[192]

Digital media that could contain valuable forensic evidence includes computers, laptops, flash drives, external storage devices, digital cameras, game units, and cell phones. Digital evidence can provide material directly related to an offense, such as digital images of the crime itself or the possession of digital images that are illegal, such as child pornography. Digital evidence may also show intent to commit a crime or premeditation in committing a criminal act. This can be determined from the suspect's Internet searches for information on materials or procedures that were involved in the charged crime. Another possible use of digital evidence is in supporting or refuting witness, victim, or suspect statements.[193]

Computer crime units in law enforcement agencies have grown immensely over the past decade. Even crimes not specifically linked to the computer, such as interpersonal crimes of violence, can be solved by combing through cell phone records, cell phone photographs, and personal computers for evidence about the victim's life and acquaintances.[194] In a 2007 article, Charles I. Cohen wrote, "Computer forensics can provide evidence of motivation, a chronology of events, insight into an offender's interests and activities. . . . Nearly every type of investigation has the potential to benefit from computer forensics."[195] C. M. Whitcomb, the director of the National Center for Forensic Science at the University of Central Florida, wrote in another 2007 article, "Every second, harmless and harmful packets of information pass each other as they fly through the Internet and the airwaves. While trainers are using the Internet to teach cybercrime investigations classes, child predators are sending out their invitations to unsuspecting innocents. Clearly, digital evidence will be a major form of evidence with which society must contend for the foreseeable future."[196]

In 2000, the Scientific Working Group on Digital Evidence (SWGDE) issued standards for the recovery, preservation, and examination of digital evidence to ensure that this evidence is accurate and reliable.[197] In a 2004 article in the *FBI Law Enforcement Bulletin*, Loren D. Mercer discussed the proper storage and preservation of computer-related forensic evidence. Mercer wrote that because digital evidence is especially vulnerable to alteration, examiners must use copies of the original data for their investigations, thus preserving the authenticity of the original digital evidence.[198]

Also in 2004, the NIJ prepared and published *Forensic Examination of Digital Evidence: A Guide for Law Enforcement*, an extensive set of instructions for members of the law enforcement community who are responsible for the examination of digital evidence. In addition, the NIJ has published *Electronic Crime Scene Investigation: A Guide for First Responders*, which deals with common situations encountered during the processing and handling of digital evidence. These guides offer agencies and investigators rules that can be used to develop their own policies and procedures.[199]

In 2005, the National White Collar Crime Center produced a DVD providing instructions for law enforcement officers in dealing with searching, seizing, and preserving digital evidence. It offers instructions for first responders, investigators, and forensics experts who will examine digital information for evidence. Among the topics applying to first responders are the nature of digital evidence and where it may be found; the securing of the crime scene so that digital evidence is not erased or compromised; and procedures for identifying, handling, and transporting digital evidence. The DVD discusses the various methods that criminals use to hide, disguise, or eliminate computer evidence of their crimes, and investigative techniques that can link computer evidence to a suspect, including techniques for conducting interviews with suspects. Among the topics applying to forensic examiners are documentation, copying, and examining the suspect's computer drives, and techniques for obtaining evidence from corrupted drives.[200]

In 2007, the DHS published a pocket guide for first responders regarding best practices for seizing electronic evidence.[201] Generally, after a suspect's computer and various hard drives have been seized, the computer forensic specialist makes a "true copy" or "mirror copy" of the hard drive. The true copy of the data can then be examined using computer forensics software programs.[202]

The keys to solving computer crimes are the traditional investigative skills and techniques, including establishing evidence of a crime, determining how the crime occurred, identifying likely suspects, and developing the case for prosecution. Investigators also need to be knowledgeable about information security and how to preserve evidence.[203] There is a difference between handling traditional, tangible evidence and computer evidence, and that difference is the fragility of computer evidence. It can be altered, damaged, or destroyed simply by turning a computer on or off at the wrong time. This means that the field of computer forensics requires special training and skills.[204]

Several professional organizations provide networking for computer investigators. One is the International High Technology Crime Investigation Association (HTCIA).[205] Another is the Computer Crime Research Center (CCRC).[206]

IDENTITY THEFT Identity theft, while not a new phenomenon in this age of easy access to computers and the Internet, has become a major problem for law enforcement and for the public. Data breaches are an almost common occurrence for retailers and banks with resulting calls for stricter security measures to protect customer accounts. It is considered the nation's top crime against consumers.

The majority of identity theft cases (85 percent) involve the fraudulent uses of credit card or bank information. Victims who have personal information stolen are more likely to have a new account opened in their name than those who just have their credit card or bank data stolen. Direct and indirect losses from identity theft totaled $24.7 billion dollars in 2012.[207]

While these statistics seem staggering, there are actions that can be taken to help reduced the probability of identity theft. Law enforcement recommends individuals watch for these signs that they may be the victim of identity theft:

1. Unexplained withdrawals from your bank account
2. Not receiving your bills or other mail
3. Your checks are refused by merchants
4. Debt collectors are calling you about debts that are not yours

5. You find unfamiliar accounts on your credit report or charges on your credit cards
6. The IRS notifies you that you have not filed one or more tax returns
7. You are arrested for a crime you did not commit by someone using your name

Victims of identity theft should take the following actions to protect themselves and their assets:

1. Place a fraud alert on their credit with the credit reporting agencies
2. Monitor their credit on a regular basis and check their accounts for unusual activity
3. Obtain a free copy of their credit report (everyone is entitled to a free report once per year)
4. Report to the police that they have been a victim of identity theft[208]

Methods of stealing personal information are as many as the imagination of the criminal can produce. Dumpster diving or digging through trash bins is one of the most common ways personal identification is stolen. It is not uncommon for offices in downtown areas, including government institutions, to throw away old files and documents without shredding them prior to disposal. In this way, criminals can obtain name, address, bank account, medical, and other personal information. With this information criminals are able to open up new accounts and create checks and identification allowing them to become someone else.

The United States Supreme Court ruled in *California v. Greenwood* (1988) that the Fourth Amendment does not prohibit the warrantless search and seizure of garbage left outside the curtilage of the home for collection.[209] By extension, this also applied to individuals who dumpster dive as long as the person is not violating trespass laws. In an effort to reduce identity theft, in 2005 Layton, Utah, passed a local ordinance prohibiting dumpster diving.[210]

Criminals will also break into mailboxes in front of residences and mailbox clusters in neighborhoods. They will follow mail delivery trucks and wait until they have left and steal the mail. They will also break into vehicles to obtain driver's licenses, credit cards, computers, and vehicle registration information.

Cybercrime activities such as "**phishing**" attacks, **Trojan horse** viruses, and **spyware** are

---

phishing Fraudulently acquiring private or sensitive information using computer program expertise and techniques.

Trojan horse A computer virus acting or disguising itself as a legitimate program that when opened infects the target computer(s) and then searches for sensitive data.

spyware Computer software that collects personal information, changes computer settings, or generates advertising.

common. The official-looking email from a government agency or a long-lost uncle or other relative asking for your personal information so you can "inherit" millions of dollars is not uncommon in today's Internet age.

CELL PHONES According to the Federal Communications Commission, in 2008 there were over 270,334,000 million cell phone users in the United States.[211] These cell phones, along with records of their use, contain evidence of the nature and timing of the behaviors of their users not only to communicate with others, but also to take pictures, store data, and use the Internet. Evidence related to suspects' cell phone use can be useful in linking them to crime-related events and people. Kanable recommends that first responders be trained in how to handle cell phones as evidence. They should seize the cell phone and its power supply together (if possible), turn off the cell phone, and remove the battery for evidence preservation. She further advises that law enforcement agencies should be familiar with the *Guidelines on Cell Phone Forensics* recommendations of the National Institute of Standards and Technology.[212]

In another 2007 article, Jeannine Heinecke writes that with the evolution of cell phone capabilities to contain vast amounts of useful information and potentially powerful evidence, cell phone seizure devices should be a crucial component of the forensic examiner's toolkit.[213]

In 2009, in *United States v. Murphy*, the court ruled that evidence obtained from a cell phone was admissible, and the motion to suppress was denied. This case gave officers the ability to search a cell phone without a warrant and incident to arrest.[214]

DNA Profiling

DNA profiling, also called **genetic fingerprinting** or **DNA typing**, has shown exponential progress in the last decade in helping investigators solve crimes and ensuring that those guilty of crimes are convicted in court. According to the U.S. Department of Justice, "DNA evidence arguably has become the most well-known type of forensic evidence, probably because it can be uniquely identifying and because it is the genetic blueprint of the human body. For these reasons, DNA evidence has become a highly influential piece of the crime puzzle."[215] This section will cover the science of DNA, the history of DNA in U.S. courts, current DNA technology, DNA databases, and current DNA issues. (See Table 14.5.)

TABLE 14.5 Milestones in the Development of DNA Use in Police Work

Date	Development
1900	A, B, O blood groups discovered
1923	*Frye v. United States*
1983	PCR first conceived by Kerry Mullis
1984	First DNA profiling test developed by Alec Jeffreys
1986	First use of DNA to solve a crime and exonerate an innocent subject (Colin Pitchfork case)
1986	First acceptance of DNA testing in a U.S. civil court
1987	First use of DNA profiling in a U.S. criminal court
1987	*Castro* case
1992	Publication of *DNA Technology in Forensic Science*
1992	*Jakobetz* case
1993	*Daubert v. Merrell Dow Pharmaceuticals, Inc.*
1997	*General Electric Co. v. Joiner*
1998	FBI implements NDIS/CODIS
1998	Creation of the National Commission on the Future of DNA Evidence
2000	Publication of *The Future of Forensic DNA Testing*
2004	Innocence Project nonprofit organization established

Sources: Adapted from National Institute of Justice, *The Future of Forensic DNA Testing: Predictions of the Research and Development Working Group* (Washington, D.C.: National Institute of Justice, 2000); Norah Rudin, "Forensic Science Timeline," retrieved May 12, 2001, from www.forensicdna.com.

DNA profiling/genetic fingerprinting/DNA typing The examination of DNA samples from a body fluid to determine whether they came from a particular subject.

The Science of DNA

Deoxyribonucleic acid (DNA) is the basic building code for all of the human body's chromosomes and is the same for each cell of an individual's body, including skin, bone, teeth, hair, organs, fingernails and toenails, and all body fluids, including blood, semen, saliva, mucus, perspiration, urine, and feces. Every cell of the body contains DNA. Because the characteristics of certain segments of DNA vary from person to person, it is possible to analyze certain bodily substances and compare them with a sample from a suspect.

Forensic science consultant Richard Saferstein tells us that portions of the DNA structure are as unique to each individual as fingerprints. He writes that inside each of the 60 trillion cells in the human body are strands of genetic material called chromosomes. Arranged along the chromosomes, like beads on a thread, are nearly 100,000 genes. Genes are the fundamental unit of heredity. They instruct the body cells to make proteins that determine everything from hair color to susceptibility to diseases. Each gene is actually composed of DNA specifically designed to carry out a single body function. Scientists have determined that DNA is the substance by which genetic instructions are passed from one generation to the next.[216]

DNA profiling has helped investigators solve crimes and ensure that those guilty of crimes are convicted in court. Profiling is the examination of DNA samples from a body substance or fluid to determine whether they came from a particular subject. For example, semen on a rape victim's clothing can be positively or negatively compared with a suspect's semen.

DNA is powerful evidence. Elizabeth Devine, former supervising criminalist in the Scientific Services Bureau of the Los Angeles County Sheriff's Department, says, "The power of what we can look for and analyze now is incredible. It's like magic. Every day we discover evidence where we never thought it would be. You almost can't do anything without leaving some DNA around. DNA takes longer than fingerprints to analyze but you get a really big bang for your buck."[217]

DNA profiling has been used in criminal investigations since 1987, and the FBI has made great progress in improving the technology since opening its first DNA typing laboratory in October 1988.[218] DNA technology in law enforcement has changed rapidly. The current procedure—**polymerase chain reaction-short tandem repeat (PCR-STR)**—has several distinct advantages for law enforcement over **restricted fragment length polymorphism (RFLP)**, an earlier DNA procedure. PCR-STR requires only pinhead-size samples, rather than the dime-size samples needed for RFLP. With the PCR-STR process, samples degraded or broken down by exposure to heat, light, or humidity can be analyzed.[219]

The DNA Analysis Unit of the FBI laboratory analyzes body fluids and body fluid stains recovered as evidence in violent crimes. Examinations include the identification and characterization of blood, semen, saliva, and other body fluids using traditional serological techniques and related biochemical analysis. Once the stain is identified, it is characterized by DNA analysis using RFLP or PCR-STR techniques. The results of the analyses are compared with results obtained from known blood or saliva samples submitted from the victims or suspects.[220] Technological advances have made DNA more reliable and more efficient as the time needed to determine a sample's DNA profile has dropped from between six and eight weeks to between one and two days.[221]

The unit also uses **mitochondrial DNA (MtDNA) analysis**, which is applied to evidence containing very small or degraded quantities of DNA from hair, bones, teeth, and body fluids. The results of MtDNA analysis are then also compared with blood or saliva submitted from victims and suspects. Mitochondrial DNA is not as useful for identification as nuclear DNA, but it does not break down as quickly—and that makes it vitally important to cold cases. Alice Eisenberg, head of the FBI's mitochondrial DNA analysis lab, says cold cases are the meat and potatoes of her unit's operation. Her technicians are dealing with bone and hair samples that have been sitting on evidence room shelves for years.[222] "No one was able to perform DNA analysis on them until we came along with our mitochondrial DNA technology."[223]

---

deoxyribonucleic acid (DNA) The basic building code for all of the human body's chromosomes.

polymerase chain reaction-short tandem repeat (PCR-STR) One of the latest DNA technology systems; requires only pinhead-size samples rather than the dime-size samples needed for RFLP.

restricted fragment length polymorphism (RFLP) Traditional method of DNA technology analysis.

mitochondrial DNA (MtDNA) analysis DNA analysis applied to evidence containing very small or degraded quantities from hair, bones, teeth, and body fluids.

Another current DNA innovation is **Combined DNA Index System (CODIS)** or DNA databases. CODIS contains DNA profiles obtained from subjects convicted of homicide, sexual assault, and other serious felonies. Investigators are able to search evidence from their individual cases against the system's extensive national file of DNA genetic markers.[224] By March 2014, more than 194 public law enforcement laboratories across the United States participated in CODIS and the National DNA Index System (NDIS), which permits data sharing between laboratories.[225] Internationally, more than 40 law enforcement laboratories in over 25 countries use the CODIS software for their own database initiatives.[226]

CODIS provides software and support services so that state and local laboratories can establish databases of convicted offenders, unsolved crime scenes, and missing persons. It allows these forensic laboratories to exchange and compare DNA profiles electronically, thereby linking serial violent crimes, especially sexual assaults, to each other, and to identify suspects by matching DNA from crime scenes to convicted offenders. All 50 states have enacted

DNA database laws requiring the collection of a DNA sample from specified categories of convicted offenders. Most states take samples from convicted felons, but they vary on which types of felons. Some states are trying to pass legislation to take samples from all persons charged with a felony; some are even considering collecting them from people convicted of misdemeanors.

Most federal, state, and local DNA analysts have received CODIS training. The FBI laboratory has also provided CODIS software and training to criminal justice agencies in other countries. The **National DNA Index System (NDIS)** is the final level of CODIS and supports the sharing of DNA profiles from convicted offenders and crime scene

---

Combined DNA Index System (CODIS) Database that contains DNA profiles obtained from subjects convicted of homicide, sexual assault, and other serious felonies.

National DNA Index System (NDIS) The final level of CODIS that supports the sharing of DNA profiles from convicted offenders and crime scene evidence submitted by state and local forensic laboratories across the United States.

 YOU ARE THERE

The Blooding: The First Use of DNA Typing in a Criminal Case

DNA profiling was the subject of *The Blooding* by Joseph Wambaugh. This book describes the case surrounding the brutal beating and murder of two young girls in the English county of Leicestershire. Although the police had no clues to the identity of the killer, eventually a young man whom Wambaugh called only the "Kitchen Porter" confessed to the murder of the first girl and was also charged by the police with the second murder. Hoping to get physical evidence to corroborate this confession, the police asked Alec Jeffreys, a young geneticist at nearby Leicestershire University and the man who discovered genetic fingerprinting, to compare DNA samples from the victims with the DNA of the defendant.

After performing his testing, Jeffreys told the police that their suspect definitely did not commit the murders. He also told them that the same man—not their suspect, however—was responsible for the murders of both girls. The police decided to embark on a campaign of "blooding" to find the killer. They "requested" that all men within a certain

age group who lived, worked, or had business in the area appear at the police station and submit to a venipuncture (the drawing of a vial of blood). The blood was then analyzed using Jeffreys's technique. But even after more than 4,500 men gave samples of their blood, the police had no suspects.

Eventually it was discovered, over a few beers in a local pub, that a young man named Colin Pitchfork had paid another young man, Ian Kelly, to appear and be "blooded" for him. When the police approached Pitchfork, he willingly confessed to both murders. His blood samples were then tested, and the DNA tests revealed that he was, indeed, the murderer of both girls.

The DNA analysis did not solve the case, although it did eliminate a suspect and it did confirm guilt. Even if DNA profiling is fully accepted by the scientific community, it will never replace regular detective work.

Source: Based on Joseph Wambaugh, *The Blooding* (New York: William Morrow, 1989).

evidence submitted by state and local forensic laboratories across the United States.[227]

The current version of CODIS contains two indexes: a convicted offender index and a forensic index. The former index contains DNA profiles from those convicted of violent crimes, and the latter contains DNA profiles acquired from crime scene evidence. The CODIS system is also separated into different segments, from the local to the national level. The system stores the information necessary for determining a match (a specimen identifier, the sponsoring laboratory's identifier, the names of laboratory personnel who produced the profile, and the DNA profile). To ensure privacy, it does not include such things as Social Security numbers, criminal history, or case-related information.[228]

The FBI maintains the national database, whereas each state has one designated database location, and each participating locality maintains its own local database. Thus, it is possible for each locality to cross-reference a DNA profile against other DNA profiles across the country. Furthermore, it is likely that an international DNA database may be implemented, allowing law enforcement officials to identify suspects both nationally and internationally. As of February 2010, NDIS contained more than 7.9 million offender profiles and about 306,000 forensic profiles from the scenes of unsolved crimes, and CODIS had produced about 107,600 hits assisting in more than 109,900 investigations.[229] It has been estimated that the DNA bank is growing by more than 80,000 individual profiles every month.[230]

New technologies regarding DNA evidence emerge constantly. One is Low Copy Number (LCN) DNA, which attempts to provide unprecedented levels of detection by obtaining DNA profiles from objects that were simply touched by a suspect. LCN DNA can be obtained from as little as a fingerprint or residue from the lip of a drinking glass. However, there are still some complications and limitations of this technology. The DNA could be transferred from one person to another (for example, through a handshake) and then to an object. This challenges the reliability of placing a person at a crime scene through this type of analysis. More research is being conducted of this promising technology to reduce the dangers of contamination.[231]

The FBI's nuclear DNA lab at Quantico, Virginia, now does much of its work with robots. The robots allow the FBI to process DNA samples at an exponentially higher rate than humans ever could, since the robots can do 500 samples a day. Jennifer Luttman, who runs the convicted offender program at the FBI lab, says that they still use people to find DNA at a crime scene, but the steps that come after that are easily automated: "We still use humans to look for the stains, to test for blood, to test for semen, to cut out the stains. Only a human can do that because they need to see how much is there and that's all based on experience."[232] As of June 2012, the FBI had over 1,139,065 arrestee profiles (DNA profiles of arrested persons) and 153,215 offender hits (DNA "matches" from the offender profiles).[233]

Researchers from Germany, the United Kingdom, Australia, and the United States are currently engaged in ongoing research that would allow DNA evidence to provide information about suspect height, weight, hair color, eye color, skin pigmentation, and other characteristics. Researchers explain that once scientists learn how to interpret each piece of DNA evidence, a whole new world of identification will open up for law enforcement, security, and medical purposes.[234]

The History of DNA in U.S. Courts

The use of DNA in the U.S. courts has an interesting history. The process has gained popularity at an exponential rate since its introduction in the United States in 1987. It was initially hailed as "foolproof" and 99 percent positive. Most of the positive claims about DNA profiling were based on the testimony of interested parties, such as prosecutors and scientists from companies involved in DNA testing. Defense attorneys were often unable to combat DNA evidence in court or to find experts to testify against it. Generally, defendants, when confronted with a DNA match, pleaded guilty in a plea bargain—until the *Castro* case.

On February 5, 1987, 23-year-old Vilma Ponce and her 2-year-old daughter were stabbed to death in their apartment in the Bronx, New York. There were few leads until police arrested the building's superintendent, Joseph Castro, and found some dried blood in the grooves of his watch. When questioned, he said the blood was his own. Prosecutors sent the blood from the watch, samples of the victims' blood, and a sample of Castro's blood to a firm called Lifecodes for testing.

Lifecodes declared a match between the DNA from the blood on the watch and the DNA from Vilma Ponce's blood. Defense attorneys

Barry Scheck and Peter Neufeld located experts who agreed to testify against the admission of the DNA typing evidence. For 12 weeks the evidence was argued before New York Supreme Court Acting Justice Gerald Sheindlin, who listened to experts from both sides. The experts for the defense were able to uncover such serious blunders committed by Lifecodes in its performance of the tests that the prosecution's expert witnesses recanted their position. In an unprecedented move, two expert witnesses for the defense and two for the prosecution issued a joint statement:

> The DNA data in this case are not scientifically reliable enough to support the assertion that the samples . . . do or do not match. If these data were submitted to a peer-reviewed journal in support of a conclusion, they would not be accepted. Further experimentation would be required.[235]

Ultimately, Justice Sheindlin ruled the evidence of the match inadmissible, and the case against Castro was dismissed.

The main problem with DNA profiling at the *Castro* stage was that it could not pass the **Frye test**. The *Frye* test is based on the Supreme Court case *Frye v. United States* (1923), in which the Court ruled that novel scientific evidence will not be accepted into evidence until it has gained general acceptance in the particular scientific discipline in which it belongs.[236] Although DNA was accepted by some courts and rejected by others, its reliability had to be held in question until it gained general acceptance by the scientific community.[237]

A 1992 unanimous decision by the U.S. Court of Appeals for the Second Circuit began to change court rulings nationwide on DNA evidence. The court approved the use of DNA evidence and affirmed the conviction of Randolph Jakobetz for kidnapping and rape. The evidence on which he was convicted involved an FBI analysis of the DNA from semen recovered from the woman and matched to Jakobetz from a blood test.

Legal experts have said that this decision was the first clear-cut guidance from the federal appellate bench on the use of DNA fingerprinting. Previously, many courts would not allow DNA evidence to be used at a trial unless it was presented first at a pre-trial hearing. Under the new ruling, courts could allow DNA evidence without such hearings and let the jury determine the worth of the evidence. In this case, the court seems to have overruled the *Frye* test

by ruling that "scientific evidence was like any other and that it could be admitted if its 'probativeness, materiality and reliability' outweighed any tendency to mislead, prejudice and confuse the jury."[238]

The *Jakobetz* case was followed by two other important U.S. Supreme Court cases, *Daubert v. Merrell Dow Pharmaceuticals, Inc.* (1993) and *General Electric Co. v. Joiner* (1997), which further undermined the restrictive *Frye* test by ruling that federal courts should generally allow admission of all relevant evidence. This ruling applied to all evidence in civil and criminal cases, including DNA evidence and other forensic science issues.[239]

In 1992, after a two-year study, a 12-member panel consisting of forensic, legal, and molecular biology experts endorsed DNA profiling in the identification of suspects in criminal cases. Conducted under the auspices of the National Academy of Sciences, the study concluded that DNA fingerprinting is a reliable method of identification for use as evidence in criminal trials, but found problems with current methods of sampling, labeling, and general quality assurance. The panel of experts recommended that accreditation be required of forensic laboratories performing this work.[240]

The panel also advised the courts to consider the reliability of new DNA typing techniques on a case-by-case basis when determining the admissibility of DNA evidence. The panel's report called for the creation of a national DNA profile databank that would contain DNA samples and document information on the genetic makeup of felons convicted of violent crimes. This report led to the creation of CODIS, described earlier.

The National Commission on the Future of DNA Evidence was created in 1998 at the request of the U.S. attorney general. The commission's mission is to examine the future of DNA evidence and how the Justice Department can encourage its most effective use. One of the duties of the commission is to submit recommendations to the attorney general that will ensure more effective use of DNA as a crime-fighting tool and foster its use through the entire criminal justice system. Other focal areas for the commission's consideration include crime scene investigation and evidence collection, laboratory funding, legal issues, and research and development.[241]

Frye test Standard to admitting new scientific evidence into U.S. courts; based on the U.S. Supreme Court case *Frye v. United States* (1923).

Current Technology

In 2000, the National Commission on the Future of DNA Evidence reported:

> The great variability of DNA polymorphisms has made it possible to offer strong support for concluding that DNA from a suspect and from the crime scene are from the same person. Prior to this . . . it was possible to exclude a suspect, but evidence for inclusion was weaker than it is now because the probability of a coincidental match was larger. DNA polymorphisms brought an enormous change. Evidence that two DNA samples are from the same person is still probabilistic rather than certain. But with today's battery of genetic markers, the likelihood that two matching profiles came from the same person approaches certainty.[242]

Although the evidence that two samples came from the same person is statistical, the conclusion that they came from different persons is certain (assuming no human or technical errors). As a result of DNA testing, more than 70 persons previously convicted of capital crimes and frequently having served long prison terms have been exonerated. The commission made the following conclusions and projections for the near future:

- Current state-of-the-art DNA typing is such that the technology and statistical methods are accurate and reproducible.

- Methods of automation, increasing the speed and output and reliability of STR methods, will continue. Portable, miniature chips are expected to make possible the analysis of DNA directly at the crime scene. This can be telemetered to databases, offering the possibility of immediate identification.[243]

DNA Databases

Initially, DNA fingerprinting or profiling was used to confirm the identity of an individual already suspected of committing a specific crime; now the use of offender DNA databases has altered the way a criminal investigation can proceed. Very small amounts of DNA recovered from a crime scene can be used to link an otherwise unknown suspect to the crime. The existing offender DNA databases have been upheld over Fourth Amendment challenges

due to the minimal privacy expectations offenders have because of their status as offenders.

By 2010, every state had a DNA database statute that allows collection of DNA from specified offenders. Under a 2005 federal law, the national database (the National DNA Index System) will not only continue to include convicted felons but will also add genetic profiles of people who have been arrested but not convicted and of immigrant detainees.[244] By June 2012, there were over 9.7 million offender profiles in the CODIS database.[245]

Some believe that the growing practice of using voluntary DNA samples to link the donor to other unsolved crimes should be curbed. However, police and prosecutors defend the strategy, claiming that it allows them to take full advantage of the technology to solve crimes. Darrell Sanders, chief of police in Frankfort, Illinois, says, "If we get someone's DNA legally, how can we justify giving him a free pass on something else he once did?" Defense attorneys, such as Barry Scheck, foresee the potential for abuse: "As it is, there's nothing to stop police from setting up a DNA base of 'the usual suspects.'"[246]

Another issue is the implementation of a universal DNA database containing DNA fingerprints from every member of society. Some people believe this would not withstand constitutional scrutiny because free persons have no diminished expectations of privacy, as prisoners do; they hold that allowing a universal DNA database would allow the government to intrude without suspicion on an individual's privacy.[247]

A 2003 report by the Executive Office of the President of the United States praised DNA technology for becoming increasingly vital to identifying criminals, clearing suspects, and identifying missing persons. The report acknowledged, however, that current federal and state DNA collection and analysis need improvement because crime labs are overwhelmed and ill-equipped to deal with the influx of DNA samples and evidence. The president proposed federal funding for the improvement of the use of DNA in these labs. Subsequently, Congress passed a five-year, $1 billion bill, the Justice for All Act of 2004.[248] The NIJ has issued numerous training guidelines regarding DNA and human forensic identification.[249]

In 2006, the FBI began to use its national DNA database system to help identify not only criminals, but also missing persons and tens of thousands of unidentified bodies held by local coroners and medical examiners. The FBI compares genetic profiles taken from unidentified bodies or body parts with DNA submitted by family members of missing persons. The International Homicide Investigators Association estimates that there are more than 40,000 unidentified dead nationally.[250]

Collection of DNA from arrestees has become the practice in some states. In 2012, the ACLU challenged the California practice of DNA collection from arrestees as a result of the California Proposition 69, which allowed police to obtain a genetic sample from every person arrested on felony charges.[251] The U.S. Supreme Court weighed in on the issue when the Court decided *Maryland v. King* (2013). In its decision, the Court held that states may obtain and test DNA samples of defendants arrested for violent crimes.[252]

Other Current DNA Issues

Current issues regarding DNA that are examined in the text that follows include the backlog in cases, contamination of samples, cold hits, storage of and warrants for DNA, dragnets and familial searches, exonerations based on DNA, and the use of DNA in property crimes.

BACKLOG   A major problem with DNA today is the growing backlog of DNA cases. In a 2006 article in the *Criminal Justice Policy Review*, Travis C. Pratt, Michael J. Gaffney, and Nicholas P. Lovrich, professors at Washington State University, and doctoral student Charles L. Johnson, also of Washington State University, revealed that as of 2003, there were 169,229 unsolved rape cases and 51,774 homicide cases that might contain biological evidence that had not yet been sent to a forensic laboratory for DNA testing. This means that this evidence is just sitting around in police property rooms. State and local laboratories reported 57,349 backlogged cases of rape and homicide on hand waiting for DNA analysis. Thus, the combined estimate of rape and murder cases that still required DNA review was 278,352 throughout the nation. The study also estimated that as many as 264,371 property crime cases with possible biological evidence had not yet been subjected to DNA analysis, which put the total backlog of cases with the possibility of DNA evidence at 542,723.

The authors of the article suggested that one reason so many unsolved cases had yet to be subjected

to DNA analysis is police investigators' belief that forensic laboratories cannot process such evidence quickly enough to be helpful. Pratt and colleagues also suggested that local and regional forensic laboratories cannot afford the personnel, equipment, and facilities necessary to increase the volume of DNA analysis.[253]

According to the NIJ, 918,563 DNA samples were received or held pending analysis in U.S. forensic laboratories in 2011. Of these, 711,060 samples were completed by the end of 2011.[254]

CONTAMINATION   Another problem with DNA is the possibility of fingerprinting techniques contaminating DNA results. Testing reported in 2005 revealed the possibility that fingerprint brushes can accumulate DNA from surfaces with which they come into contact, and that they can redeposit this DNA-containing material onto a number of subsequently brushed objects. The chance of this occurring increases after powdering biological samples, such as blood, saliva, skin, or fresh prints.[255]

COLD HITS   A **cold hit** is a DNA sample collected from a crime scene that ties an unknown suspect to the DNA profile of someone in the national or a state's database. To date, the FBI's CODIS DNA database has resulted in more than 239,158 cold hits, California's in 29,989 cold hits, and New York's in 17,289 cold hits. Ohio's CODIS database has offender profiles on 444,352 individuals.[256] The National Police Services of Canada's National DNA Data Bank contains the DNA profiles of more than 46,000 convicted offenders, and about 1,000 cold hits have been made since the database opened in June 2000.[257]

A cold hit is not enough to close a case—an investigator from the jurisdiction where the original crime was committed has to reopen the case, and then locate and apprehend the subject. Often, the subject may be in prison, and the investigator has to go there to process him or her. The investigator also has to confirm the DNA sample and retest the subject to ensure accuracy.[258]

Sometimes errors can occur in this process. In a case involving the sexual assault of a 10-year-old girl, the police received a cold hit in January 2004 but took a year to arrest the subject; in the interim

cold hit   A DNA sample collected from a crime scene that ties an unknown suspect to the DNA profile of someone in the national or a state's database.

he sexually assaulted another 10-year-old. In 2006, it was reported that the Oakland police had 73 unresolved rape or homicide cold-hit DNA cases in which the subject had yet to be apprehended.[259]

In another processing mistake, a Baltimore man entered Maryland's state prison in 2004 on conviction of attempted sale of cocaine to a police officer. A bill had been passed in 2002 requiring the collection of DNA from Maryland's 20,000 state prison inmates serving time for felonies. The man's DNA was never collected despite the law. If proper procedures had been followed, police would have been alerted that his DNA matched two unsolved crimes, a 1999 rape and a 2002 murder. The man escaped in 2004, never having been subjected to a DNA test. During the year he was free, he killed three more persons, assaulted four others, and raped one more woman before being arrested again in 2005. When his DNA was finally taken, it linked him to five murders over six years. A 2004 audit revealed that despite the law, 8,300 inmates had not yet had their DNA collected, and 8,200 samples collected the previous year had not been sent for testing. Numerous similar cases have been reported.[260]

DNA STORAGE The storage of DNA evidence is required in only about half of the states, and 16 states do not have any preservation laws. The strict storage guidelines in Texas were implemented by Dallas District Attorney Henry Wade, who wanted to protect against defendant appeals. Much of that evidence is stored in freezers set to 0 degrees Fahrenheit. Those freezers now hold more than 100,000 pieces of evidence. Even though evidence has been stored dating back to the 1970s, about 30 percent of the evidence is unavailable.[261]

DNA WARRANTS In 1999, the Milwaukee, Wisconsin, county prosecutor made an innovative legal move regarding DNA in an effort to prevent the statute of limitations from expiring in a case against an unknown person suspected in a series of kidnappings and rapes. The prosecutor filed a "John Doe" warrant, not uncommon in cases where a suspect's identity is unknown. What made this case

familial DNA analysis A technique whereby a crime scene profile is deliberately run through the offender databank in the hopes of getting a list of profiles that are genetically similar to the DNA evidence and using this information as an investigative lead to interview family members of the near matches.

different was the means used to identify the suspect. The warrant identified the assailant as "John Doe, unknown male with matching deoxyribonucleic acid (DNA) at five locations."[262] Since then, DNA warrants have been used quite often.

In 2003, New York City criminal justice officials announced a sweeping, innovative plan, termed the "John Doe Indictment Project," in which prosecutors, investigators, and scientists would seek to match the DNA profiles of unknown sexual offenders in the most serious unsolved sexual attacks to specific DNA profiles in the state DNA known offender databank, and then file John Doe warrants before they had linked a name to the DNA or arrested a suspect. Four years later, the police closed the first case submitted in the John Doe Indictment Project with the arrest of a man who was eventually convicted and sentenced to 44 to 107 years in prison. As of 2009, in New York City, prosecutors had secured 117 indictments of DNA samples in rape cases, linked 18 of those profiles to specific people, and obtained 13 convictions, either through trials or negotiated pleas.[263]

DNA DRAGNETS DNA dragnets are requests by the police of persons in an area to give a voluntary DNA sample so that the police can compare their DNA with evidence found at the scene of a crime.[264] DNA lineups give police and grand juries limited authority to test the DNA of small groups of people based on a "reasonable suspicion" standard of probability that each member of the group might be involved in a crime.[265]

FAMILIAL DNA SEARCHES Familial DNA analysis from the daughter of Dennis Rader, the BTK killer, was instrumental in his 2005 arrest for at least 10 homicides.[266] Familial DNA searches are common in Great Britain. Some researchers believe that close relatives of criminals are more likely than others to break the law. This technique has proven successful in several cases.[267] In one case, police retrieved DNA from a brick that was thrown from an overpass and smashed through a windshield, killing the driver. A near-match of that DNA with someone in Britain's DNA base led police to investigate that offender's relatives, one of whom confessed to the crime when confronted with the evidence.

Some, however, see familial DNA searches as being controversial. Troy Duster, a sociologist at New York University, says familial searches would exacerbate already serious racial inequities in the U.S. criminal justice system because incarceration rates are eight times higher for blacks than they are for whites, so any technique that focuses on relatives of people in the databases will just expand that trend.[268] Tania Simoncelli of the American Civil Liberties Union states that expanding DNA databanks and techniques such as familial searches "undermine the inherent notion that one should have privacy in their DNA."[269] Harvard professor David Lazer, a DNA expert, disagrees: "If we prohibited investigative processes that led to the investigation of innocent people, we would just stop investigations altogether, because investigations always yield talking to and suspecting people who turn out not to be guilty."[270]

EXONERATIONS There have been reports of numerous cases of persons who were convicted of serious felonies but later exonerated by DNA evidence.[271] In 2003, Janet Reno, former U.S. attorney general, in a speech to the National Conference on Preventing the Conviction of Innocent Persons, stated that during the previous 30 years, more than 100 people had been exonerated because of DNA or other tests.[272]

The **Innocence Project** was founded in 1992 to assist prisoners who could be proven innocent through DNA testing; as a result of their efforts, 289 people who were serving time in prison have been exonerated by DNA testing.[273] One of the biggest issues facing the Innocence Project is finding old evidence, much of which may have been destroyed, degraded in storage over time, or was improperly stored or labeled. Once evidence is produced, the Innocence Project works with prosecutors and the courts to get the evidence tested. In many of the cases, DNA testing may not have been available at the time of the original trial. When courts and prosecutors agree to testing, the DNA sample is compared to the defendant in the case. The exoneration rate is over 40 percent, and in many cases law enforcement identifies the actual suspect.[274]

USE IN PROPERTY CRIMES Expanding DNA analysis to include biological evidence from property crime scenes is costly, but the result may prove to be worth the costs. Property crime offenders have a high recidivism rate, and people who commit burglary often escalate to more serious crimes. The effort to expand DNA analysis to include property crimes, however, has increased the backlog of untested DNA evidence.[275]

Edwin Zedlewski and Mary B. Murphy reported that three NIJ-funded pilot programs designed to decrease the backlog of DNA samples waiting for analysis in high-volume property crimes have been successful in identifying suspects and also in linking one crime to other crimes. As an example, of 201 DNA samples from New York State burglaries, 86 were matched to offenders already entered in CODIS. The authors wrote that the success of the project underscores the importance of collecting and analyzing DNA evidence from high-volume property crimes, especially given the high recidivism rates and tendency of these persons to engage in violent crime.[276]

Biometric Identification

Fingerprints and palm prints are only two forms of **biometric identification**. Biometric systems use a physical characteristic to distinguish one person from another. Other systems involve the face, the eyes, the hands, and the voice. A study of the accuracy, applications, costs, legal issues, and privacy issues associated with potential uses of biometric identification concluded that such systems have enormous potential for public and private organizations alike.[277]

Biometric systems serve two purposes: identification and authentication. They can help identify criminals, prevent welfare fraud, aid security in corrections, support border control, conduct criminal background checks, and establish identities on driver's licenses. Biometric systems already on the market can identify and authenticate people with a high degree of accuracy.

Fingerprints remain the best choice for applications involving large numbers of users. Iris-based systems (which scan the human eye) may equal or exceed fingerprints in accuracy, but the limited number of vendors and lack of precedent for iris recognition make them less attractive. Hand-geometry systems have proven themselves in physical control, particularly

---

Innocence Project A national litigation and public policy organization dedicated to exonerating wrongfully convicted people through DNA testing and reforming the criminal justice system to prevent future injustice.

biometric identification Automated identification systems that use particular physical characteristics to distinguish one person from another; can identify criminals or provide authentication.

in prisons, which require high levels of accuracy and security. Voice recognition has proven to be least accurate but might be the best alternative to verify someone's identity over the phone. Facial recognition systems create opportunities to identify people unobtrusively and without their cooperation, as in video surveillance, and they can be added to digital photo systems used for mug shots or driver's licenses.[278]

In 2007, it was reported that a growing number of sheriff's departments were using iris scans to identify sex offenders, runaways, abducted children, and missing persons. More than 2,100 departments in 27 states were taking digital pictures of eyes and storing the information in databases that could be searched later to identify a missing person or someone who uses a fake name.[279] Sheriff Greg Solano of Santa Fe County, New Mexico, stated, "This is the wave of the future. This will become as common as fingerprinting."[280] As of September 2013, iris scan services were in the pilot phase and the Iris Tech Spec was in draft.[281]

Also in 2007, the FBI embarked on a $1 billion effort to build the world's largest computer database, Next Generation Identification, of people's biometric physical characteristics, including not only fingerprints, but also iris patterns, face-shape data, scars, and even the unique ways people walk and talk. The FBI has reported that this will help them solve crimes and identify criminals and terrorists.[282]

Facial identification technology and its potential impact on crime control were examined in a study that focused on the history of identification systems, the nature and status of the technology, and privacy issues. The study noted that facial recognition technology compares a real-time picture from a video camera to digital pictures in a computerized database to identify a person. It has the potential for both access security and the identification and apprehension of criminals.[283]

A project funded by the NIJ developed a surveillance system using real-time facial recognition technology to increase the usefulness of currently existing CCTV-compatible surveillance software. The system is a state-of-the-art, automated facial recognition surveillance system that could be extremely useful to law enforcement, intelligence personnel, and CCTV control room officers.[284]

British police used facial recognition software to identify suspects in the UK riots in August 2011.[285] In Britain, more than 200,000 video cameras are used for surveillance, many watching streets and shopping areas. A computer will monitor video cameras set to watch for known criminals. When the system recognizes someone, it will alert the police.[286]

Facial recognition technology, often touted as a promising tool in the fight against terrorism, earned a bad reputation after it failed miserably in some well-publicized tests for picking faces out of crowds. Yet, on simpler challenges, its performance is improving. Major casinos now use facial recognition to spot card counters at blackjack tables. Several states are using facial recognition systems to check for persons who have obtained multiple driver's licenses by lying about their identity.

Facial recognition systems use cameras and computers to map someone's facial features and to collect the data for storage in databases or on a microchip on documents like passports. Making the technology work has required nearly perfect lighting and cooperative subjects, conditions that are not present when trying to spot suspected terrorists and criminals in a crowd.[287]

The most damaging publicity for facial recognition came from tests of the facial recognition software and video surveillance cameras used to spot criminal suspects on the streets of Tampa, Florida, and Virginia Beach, Virginia. The programs did not lead to a single arrest and angered privacy advocates. Another facial recognition system that scanned 100,000 football fans entering the 2001 Super Bowl in Tampa picked out 19 people with criminal records, but none were among those being sought by the authorities.[288]

Analysts and many industry officials say that too much is being expected from the technology, which is still one of the newest methods in biometrics. Advocates of facial recognition have long promoted it as one of the least intrusive biometrics and potentially the most powerful because it can make use of a huge amount of existing data, such as the 1.2 billion digitized photographs of people in databases around the world. Performance in facial recognition plummets in poor lighting, when subjects move past control points without staring directly into the cameras, and when eyeglasses or other objects cover part of the face. Success rates also have declined as the databases of potential matches have grown and as the photos used have gotten older.[289]

In 2005, the DHS announced its first biometric standard for facial recognition. It provides technical criteria vendors can use to design equipment such as cameras and software for facial recognition. The standard is designed to be consistent with international biometric standards for travel documents and other applications.[290]

In 2007, in the world's first large-scale, scientific study on how well facial recognition works in a crowd, the German government found that, although promising, facial recognition was not yet effective enough to allow its use by the police. The study, which was conducted over three months at a train station in Mainz, Germany, that draws 23,000 passengers daily, found that the technology was able to match travelers' faces against a database of volunteers more than 60 percent of the time during the day, when lighting was best; however, the rate fell to 10 to 20 percent at night.[291]

Videotaping

The use of handheld compact videotaping equipment is an example of the growing use of technology as a policing tool. For many years, the police have been using videotape in investigations, undercover operations, and recording the confessions of suspects. The latest available statistics indicate that 60 percent of all local police departments and 66 percent of all sheriffs' offices have used video cameras on a regular basis. The most common use of video cameras has been in patrol cars, with 55 percent of local police departments and 58 percent of sheriffs' offices using video cameras in this application. Local police departments have used 48,800 in-car cameras, and sheriffs' offices have used 17,700.[292]

The Franklin County, Ohio, Sheriff's Office and the Columbus, Ohio, Police Department were the recipients of several video cameras donated by insurance companies and Mothers Against Drunk Driving (MADD). The cameras are mounted to the dashboards of police cars. When an officer sees a vehicle that appears to be operated by an alcohol-impaired driver, the officer begins to record the suspect's driving and notes on tape the location and the circumstances raising suspicions of drunk driving. When the vehicle is stopped, the officer approaching the car wears an activated wireless microphone that is able to record conversations up to 500 feet from the camera. The videotape provides corroborating evidence to the officer's testimony.[293]

Another example of a promising application of videotaping involves departments equipping their patrol vehicles with video recorders. These cameras automatically record everything said or done within their range. The system was originally intended to aid in drug interdiction cases, in prosecuting alcohol-impaired drivers, and in accident investigations. However, the police discovered that the video cameras provided reliable, unbiased evidence in citizen complaint cases. In one case, a trooper was accused of being rude and using profanity during a traffic stop. The videotape proved that the charges were unfounded. In another case, a trooper was accused of shooting an unarmed motorist, who in fact was armed with a gun. The videotape revealed that the trooper had issued at least 26 warnings for the person to drop his gun before the officer fired. Videotapes also can confirm wrongdoing by officers. In one case in which a trooper was accused of raping a motorist he had stopped for a traffic violation, the videotape was admitted into evidence against him.[294]

In numerous cases, patrol vehicle video recorders have caught officers being assaulted, and even feloniously killed. In one case in 1997, Deputy Sheriff Henry Huff, a member of the Walton County, Georgia, Sheriff's Office, was shot at point-blank range during a traffic stop by a 16-year-old wielding a 9-mm gun. Huff's squad car was equipped with an automatic surveillance camera, and the entire incident was recorded on videotape. Fortunately, despite being shot twice in the chest, Huff was spared serious injury by his bullet-resistant vest and was able to return to duty.[295]

Robotics

Robotics is the science of using robots to perform operations formerly done by human beings. Robots have been available to law enforcement since the early 1970s, but because of their high cost, they were seldom purchased for law enforcement use. Since the mid-1980s, however, robots have become very popular in police departments for bomb disposal or explosive ordinance disposal (EOD).

Bomb robots can be operated by an electric cable or by radio control. They can take X-rays, photograph packages, search suspect locations, and place explosive devices into a transport vessel, thus keeping bomb personnel safely away from the immediate area. Robots can have closed-circuit video systems, audio systems, and spotlights. Some of the more sophisticated robots can climb stairs, cross ditches, and knock down doors.[296]

....

robotics The science of using robots to perform operations formerly done by human beings.

In a series of studies, law enforcement officials indicated that they had other uses for robots, including the functions of small-item delivery, passive remote communication, and remote surveillance. The features of the robots considered most important were stair-climbing ability, a robust communication link, low cost, and longer battery life. A study by the U.S. Department of Defense's Defense Advanced Research Projects Agency (DARPA) indicated that no single robot could meet all of the demands of law enforcement beyond EOD work. DARPA recommended that any robots developed for police work be modular, with application-specific mission packages or tool sets that can be tailored to the needs of a particular user.[297]

Carnegie Mellon University's Robotics Institute has a 4-foot, 160-pound helicopter that can perform search and rescue, surveillance, aerial cinematographing, and mapping functions. It operates with vision-guided systems that can visually lock on to ground objects and sense its own position in real time. These vision-guided robot helicopters can be used for law enforcement applications, such as patrol. They also can be used in hostage negotiations or SWAT operations.[298]

Robots were used at Ground Zero in New York City in two basic applications. Small, tethered robots (about the size of a shoebox) were used on the rubble pile for the first two weeks to locate voids where survivors might be found. During the next two weeks, the robots focused more on structural inspection. Researchers are currently working on more functions for police robots, such as crawling under closed doors to detect biological chemicals and detecting illegal drugs.[299]

Concerns About Technology and Civil Liberties

Some people fear that technological developments, such as improved computer-based files and long-range electronic surveillance devices, will give the police more power to intrude into the private lives of citizens. A congressional report found reason to believe that DNA fingerprinting may work against a suspect's reasonable expectation of privacy.[300] Even the magazine *Popular Mechanics* has expressed concern about the civil liberties issues of enhanced police technology:

> Along with the advantages, however, has come new potential for abuse. For example, the same computer databases that make AFIS possible could also be used for random searches that might focus suspicion on people because they have stayed in a homeless shelter, or because they fall into certain categories based on age, race or other discriminatory criteria.[301]

The noted civil liberties lawyer Alan M. Dershowitz, of Harvard University Law School, in *Taking Liberties: A Decade of Hard Cases, Bad Laws, and Bum Raps*, commented on the 1986 U.S. Supreme Court case *California v. Ciraolo*.[302] In this case, the Court ruled that evidence obtained by the police flying over and photographing a person's property was not a violation of the person's Fourth Amendment rights. Dershowitz wrote, "You can be sure that our Constitution's Founding Fathers would have been appalled at this breach of privacy. A person's home—whether it be a walled estate, a plantation, or small cottage—was regarded as his castle, free from the intruding eye of government, without a warrant based on probable cause."[303]

Commenting on the call by some for a national registry of every American's DNA profile against which the police could instantly compare crime scene specimens, many civil libertarians have expressed concern. "These databases are starting to look more like a surveillance tool than a tool for criminal investigation. A universal database will bring us more wrongful arrests and possibly more wrongful convictions," says Tania Simoncelli of the ACLU in New York. Carol Roses of the Massachusetts ACLU says, "We don't know all the potential uses of DNA, but once the state has your sample and there are no limits on how it can be used, then the potential civil liberty violations are as vast as the uses themselves."[304]

SUMMARY

- Tremendous improvements have been made in the police use of technology in the fields of computers, communications, criminal investigation, surveillance, and criminalistics. Computers have enabled the police to dispatch officers immediately to any calls for service. They have also aided the police in the investigation process by enabling officers to feed descriptions and MOs into the computer and to receive almost instantaneous printouts on possible suspects. Computers have enabled police to maintain better records more easily.

- The computer also has caused a revolution in the processing of fingerprints through automated fingerprint identification system (AFIS) terminals.

- In recent years, the police have used science to develop less-than-lethal weapons, such as Tasers and chemical irritant sprays, as an alternative to using deadly force.

- Other technology, including improved surveillance devices and improved forensic techniques (such as DNA profiling), is enhancing the ability of the police to solve crime.

- The *CSI* effect makes the public and jurors believe that the police can do what their television counterparts can. The modern crime lab, however, still has limitations, including the rigorous accreditation process to attempt to minimize lab error.

- DNA profiling, also called genetic fingerprinting or DNA typing, has shown exponential progress in the last decade in helping investigators solve crimes and ensuring that those guilty of crimes are convicted in court. However, significant backlogs exist in DNA testing; an estimated 600,000 to 700,000 criminal cases with possible biological evidence remain in the hands of law enforcement or have been backlogged at forensic labs.

- Despite the advances that science brings to police work, the key to police work will always be people—the men and women we hire to serve and protect us.

KEY TERMS

age-progression photos

automated crime analysis

automated fingerprint identification system (AFIS)

ballistics

biometric identification

cold hit

Combined DNA Index System (CODIS)

composite sketches

computer-aided dispatch (CAD)

computer-aided investigation/ computer-aided case management

computer/digital forensics

criminalistics

CSI effect

deoxyribonucleic acid (DNA)

DNA profiling/genetic fingerprinting/DNA typing

drone/unmanned aerial vehicle (UAV)

familial DNA analysis

forensic science

Frye test

global positioning system (GPS)

inked prints (ten-prints)

Innocence Project

Integrated Automated Fingerprint Identification System (IAFIS)

Internet Protocol (IP) telephony

latent prints

less-than-lethal weapons

license plate recognition (LPR) technology

Live Scan

mitochondrial DNA (MtDNA) analysis

mobile digital terminal (MDT)

mug shot imaging

National Crime Information Center (NCIC)

National DNA Index System (NDIS)

night vision devices

phishing

polymerase chain reaction-short tandem repeat (PCR-STR)

Regional Crime Analysis Geographic Information Systems (RCAGIS) spatial analysis

restricted fragment length polymorphism (RFLP)

robotics

serology

spyware

Trojan horse

vehicle tracking systems

Voiceover IP (VoIP)

REVIEW EXERCISES

1. Your professor arranges for a class debate regarding concerns about the increasing use of technology and civil liberties. He asks you to select a position on the following statement: "The increased use of technology by the police poses a significant threat to the civil liberties of the public." Select a position on this debate and prepare a set of talking points to argue on behalf of your position.

2. Conduct research on a recent criminal case in your area and show how forensic or criminalistic evidence resulted in a conviction or acquittal in court.

3. You have been assigned to investigate a homicide in your community. There is substantial public outrage over the victim of the homicide and there are racial overtones to this case. There is significant evidence for you to collect. Describe how you would do the following: (1) establish a perimeter; (2) account for personnel who have entered/exited the crime scene; (3) locate and develop latent prints at the scene; and (4) collect, preserve, and document possible DNA evidence that may be present. What time lines will you have to meet in order to make sure the evidence is not contaminated?

WEB EXERCISES

1. The honors program of your school is sponsoring a symposium entitled "The Challenge to Privacy Faced by Increased Law Enforcement Technology." Your professor has selected you to research this subject and present some background information to your class before the symposium. She asks you to search the Internet for several sites on this topic and to prepare a brief report on some major issues that might arise at the symposium.

2. Search the Internet for three professional associations for persons interested in forensic science and criminalistics. Prepare a list of them and add a brief description of each.

3. You are working as an intern with a local police department that does not have a crime lab. The department sends its evidence to the state lab. The chief, knowing of your interest in forensic science and computers, asks you to help her understand DNA. She says she uses the Internet and would like to look at a few sites that will increase her understanding of it as a layperson. Select at least three sites that may help the chief. Provide her with the names and Internet addresses and a few sample pages of each site's coverage of DNA.

END NOTES

1. John Ashcroft, *A Resource Guide to Law Enforcement, Corrections and Forensic Technologies* (Washington, D.C.: U.S. Department of Justice, 2001), p. iii.

2. David J. Roberts, "Technology Is Playing an Expanding Role in Policing," Technology Talk, *The Police Chief* 78 (January 2011): 72–73, http://www.nxtbook.com/nxtbooks/naylor/CPIM0111/#/72.

3. Ibid.

4. Christa Miller, "Mobile Computing Options for 21st Century Law Enforcement," *Law Enforcement Technology* (July 2002): 34, 36–39, 40.

5. Charles E. Higginbotham, "High-Tech Solutions to Police Problems," *Police Chief* (February 2003): 32, 34–35, 36; Donna Rogers, "CAD Selection 101: The Nuts and Bolts of Finding a CAD System That Works for You," *Law Enforcement Technology* (October 2001): 120–124, 126–127.

6. Bureau of Justice Statistics, *State and Local Law Enforcement Statistics* (Washington, D.C.: Bureau of Justice Statistics, 2006), p. 2; Matthew J. Hickman and Brian A. Reaves, *Local Police Departments, 2003* (Washington, D.C.: Bureau of Justice Statistics, 2006); Matthew J. Hickman and Brian A. Reaves, *Sheriffs' Offices, 2003* (Washington, D.C.: Bureau of Justice Statistics, 2006).

7. Paul Egan, "Expert: 911 Rules Were Broken," *Detroit News*, April 11, 2006.

8. Brad Brewer, "AVL/GPS for Front Line Policing," *Law and Order* (November 2007): 46–54; Greg Wandrei, "Instant Access to Vital Information: The Role of GIS," *Law Enforcement Technology* 11 (2007): 56–61.

9. Roger Alford, "24 Counties Have Only Basic 911 Service," *Associated Press*, March 13, 2006.

10. Charles R. Swanson, Leonard Territo, and Robert W. Taylor, *Police Administration: Structures, Processes and Behavior* (New York: Macmillan, 1988), pp. 381–383.

11. Al Baker, "Night Out in City Ends in Slaying of Woman, 18," *New York Times*, July 28, 2006, pp. A1, B5; John Mazor and John Doyle, "Cellphone Trace Led to 'Killer,'" *New York Post*, July 28, 2006, p. 6; Murray Weiss, Larry Celona, and Lenny Greene, "Doomed Teen's Chilling Call," *New York Post*, July 28, 2006, pp. 6, 7; Michael Miller, "Being Alone Raises Perils in a Night on the Town," *New York Times*, July 28, 2006, p. B5; Anne Barnard, "Growing Presence in the Courtroom: Cellphone Data as Witness," *New York Times*, July 6, 2009, retrieved July 7, 2009, from www.nytimes.com.

12. Shaila Dewan, "An SOS for 911 Systems in Age of High-Tech," *New York Times*, April 6, 2007.

13. Matthew D. LaPlante, "Utah Slow on 911 Tracing," *Salt Lake Tribune*, March 14, 2006.

14. M. Wesley Clark, "Cell Phone Technology and Physical Surveillance," *FBI Law Enforcement Bulletin* 5 (2006): 25–32; *United States v. Knotts*, 460 U.S. 276 (1983); *United States v. Karo*, 468 U.S. 705 (1984).

15. Ibid. Also see Barnard, 2009.

16. Marc Robins, "Special Report: New IP Telephony Solutions for the Government Enterprise," *Homeland Defense Journal* 1 (2006): 22–27.

17. Elizabeth Daigneau, "Calling All Citizens: A Growing Number of Municipalities Are Using 'Reverse 911' to Alert Residents in the Event of an Emergency," *Governance* (July 2002): 44–45.

18. "Special Report/Wildfires," *Time*, November 5, 2007, p. 35.

19. "Cellular Digital Packet Data (CDPD) Technology Assists Plainclothes Officers," *Police Chief* (March 1997): 14–15.

20. Sam Simon, "Pocket PC Goes Tactical," *Law Enforcement Technology* 5 (2006): 112–119.

21. Federal Bureau of Investigation, *NCIC: National Crime Information Center*, retrieved August 17, 2002, from www.fbi.gov/hq/cjisd/ncic.htm. Also see Stephanie L. Hitt, "NCIC 2000," *FBI Law Enforcement Bulletin* (July 2000): 12–15; Christopher Swope, "Sherlock Online," *Governing* (September 2000): 80–84.

22. Federal Bureau of Investigation, *NICS: National Instant Criminal Background Check System*, retrieved July 17, 2001, from www.fbi.gov/hq/cjisd/nics.htm.

23. For the latest on ViCAP, see Eric W. Witzig, "The New ViCAP: More User-Friendly and Used by More Agencies," *FBI Law Enforcement Bulletin* (June 2003): 1–7. For a further description of ViCAP and sample ViCAP alerts, see John S. Dempsey, *Introduction to Investigations*, 2nd ed. (Belmont, Calif.: Wadsworth, 2003), Ch. 10.

24. Bill Clede, "Storing Massive Records," *Law and Order* (January 1994): 45.

25. Lauren Cox, "Software Aims to Prevent Crime," *Technology Review*, retrieved December 15, 2010, from www.technologyreview.com.

26. Robin Bowen and Jessica Schneider, "Forensic Databases: Paint, Shoe Prints, and Beyond," *National Institute of Justice Journal* 258 (2007): 34–38.

27. See Ed Burnett, "Crime Analysis Reporting and Mapping for Small Agencies," *FBI Law Enforcement Bulletin* (October 2007): 15–22.

28. See William J. Bratton, "Great Expectations: How Higher Expectations for Police Departments Can Lead to a Decrease in Crime," paper presented at the National Institute of Justice's Research Institute's "Measuring What Matters" conference, Washington, D.C., November 28, 1995; William Bratton and Peter Knobler, *Turnaround: How America's Top Cop Reversed the Crime Epidemic* (New York: Random House, 1998); Rudolph W. Giuliani, Randy M. Mastro, and Donna Lynne, *Mayor's Management Report: The City of New York* (New York: City of New York, 1997); Vincent E. Henry, *The Compstat Paradigm: Management Accountability in Policing, Business and the Public Sector* (New York: Looseleaf Law, 2002); Howard Safir, *The CompStat Process* (New York: New York City Police Department, n.d.); Jeremy Travis, "Computerized Crime Mapping," *NIJ News* (Washington, D.C.: National Institute of Justice, 1999).

29. "Predicting a Criminal's Journey to Crime," *NIJ Journal* 253 (January 2006): 11–13.

30. Donna Rogers, "Map Quest: While Most Agree the Time Has Come for GIS Tactical Crime Analysis, the Million-Dollar Question Is Which Methodologies Are Most Accurate," *Law Enforcement Technology* 1 (2006): 60–69. Also see Greg Donahue, "Location Intelligence: The Next Trend in Mapping Technology," *Law Enforcement Technology* 9 (2007): 84–91.

31. Spencer Chainey and Chloe Smith, *Review of GIS-Based Information Sharing Systems* (London: Great Britain Home Office Research Development and Statistics, 2006).

32. "Predicting a Criminal's Journey to Crime," pp. 11–13.

33. Preston Gralla, "Hollywood Confidential: PC Crime Fighters," *PC Computing* (January 1989): 188.

34. Sharon Hollis Sutter, "Holmes … Still Aiding Complex Investigations," *Law and Order* (November 1991): 50–52.

35. Robert D. Keppel and Joseph G. Weis, "HITS: Catching Criminals in the Northwest," *FBI Law Enforcement Bulletin* (April 1993): 14–19; Terry Morgan, "HITS/SMART: Washington State's Crime-Fighting Tool," *FBI Law Enforcement Bulletin* (February 2002): 1–10.

36. Christopher Kane, "IBM Fighting Crime in Real Time," *Law and Order* (September 2007): 18–22; Thomas J. Lueck, "From Database to Crime Scene: Network Is Potent Police Weapon," *New York Times*, June 7, 2007; Michael S. Schmidt, "Have a Tattoo or Walk with a Limp? The Police May Know," *New York Times*, February 17, 2010, p. A19.

37. Lueck, "From Database to Crime Scene"; Javier C. Hernandez, "422 Years for a Rapist Who Tortured His Victim," *New York Times*, July 25, 2008.

38. Maria Cramer, "City's Police Sharpen Their Watch on Crime: New Center Links Monitors, Officers," *Boston Globe*, March 3, 2010, retrieved March 3, 2010, from www.boston.com.

39. "FBI Throws in the Towel on Overdue, Problem-Plagued Computer Upgrade," *Law Enforcement News*, January 2005, p. 1; Jonathan Krim, "FBI Rejects Its New Case File Software," *Washington Post*, January 2005, p. A05, accessed June 4, 2014.

40. "Predicting a Criminal's Journey to Crime," pp. 11–13.

41. VirTra Systems, VirTra 300LE Product Overview, retrieved March 30, 2012, from www.virtrasystem.com.

42. Robert Sheehan and Gary W. Cordner, *Introduction to Police Administration*, 2nd ed. (Cincinnati: Anderson, 1989), p. 419.

43. Sheehan and Cordner, *Introduction to Police Administration*, p. 422.

44. "PG County Police Opt for Computer-Aided System to Red-Flag Stressed-Out Officers," *Law Enforcement News*, June 30, 1997, p. 5.

45. Swanson, Territo, and Taylor, *Police Administration*, pp. 380–381.

46. Sheehan and Cordner, *Introduction to Police Administration*, p. 428.

47. Beth Winegarner, "Police Say Online Crime Reporting Saves Officers Time," *Examiner*, April 17, 2006. Also see William Gitmed, "Citizens Reporting Crimes Online: The San Francisco Experience," *Police Chief* (August 2007): 124–131.

48. Brad Brewer, "ABCs of Mobile Reporting," *Law and Order* (November 2007): 36–44; David McDonald, "10 Things Every Police Chief Needs to Know . . . About Mobile Technology," *Law and Order* (November 2007): 56–59; Calie Voorhis, "RIMS Case Studies," *Law and Order* (November 2007): 60–61.

49. Mary Schacklett, "Creating the Mobile Office: Michigan Departments Take Technology on the Road," *Law Enforcement Technology* 10 (2007): 108–117.

50. James Careless, "The BlackBerry: A Surprisingly Powerful Crime-Fighting Tool," *Law and Order* (January 2008): 13–16.

51. Arthur Gordon and Ross Wolf, "License Plate Recognition Technology: Innovation in Law Enforcement Use," *FBI Law Enforcement Bulletin* (March 2007): 8–13. Also see Jacques Billeaud, "License Plate Scanners Help Recover Stolen Cars, Raise Concerns," *North County Times*, December 19, 2007, retrieved December 19, 2007, from www.nctimes.com; Michael Frazier, "Police Conduct Second Drug Raid in Hempstead Neighborhood," *Newsday*, January 14, 2008; "L.A. Experience," *Techbeat* (Spring 2006): 2; Trevor Hughes, "Police Partner with License Plate Readers," *USA Today*, March 4, 2010, retrieved March 4, 2010, from www.usatoday.com; Thomas Manson, "Automatic License Place Recognition Systems," *Law and Order* (December 2006): 72–77; Matt Zapotosky, "Cruiser-Top Cameras Make Police Work a Snap," *Washington Post*, August 2, 2008, p. A1.

52. Al Baker, "Camera Scans of Car Plates Are Reshaping Police Inquiries," *New York Times*, retrieved April 12, 2011, from www.nytimes.com.

53. For a brief but interesting history of the use of fingerprints as identification, see Dempsey, *Introduction to Investigations*, pp. 123–124.

54. Mimi Hall, "Criminals Go to Extremes to Hide Identities," *USA Today*, November 6, 2007; Peter Jackson, "Pennsylvania Doctor Guilty of Helping Alleged Drug Dealer Remove Fingerprints," *Associated Press*, November 3, 2007; Mark Levy, "Doc Gets 18 Months for Removing Prints," *Associated Press*, February 13, 2008.

55. Federal Bureau of Investigation, *Fingerprint Identification: An Overview*, retrieved June 12, 2001, from www.fbi.gov/hq/cjisd/ident.htm.

56. Curtis C. Frame, "Lifting Latent Prints in Dust," *Law and Order* (June 2000): 75; also see Frame, "Picking Up Latent Prints in Dust," *Police Chief* (April 2000): 180.

57. J. Zonderman, "High-Tech Crime Hunters," *Popular Mechanics* (December 1991): 30.

58. T. F. Wilson and P. L. Woodard, *Automated Fingerprint Identification Systems—Technology and Policy Issues* (Washington, D.C.: U.S. Department of Justice, 1987), p. 5.

59. Harold J. Grasman, "New Fingerprint Technology Boosts Odds in Fight Against Terrorism," *Police Chief* (January 1997): 23–28.

60. Rongliang Ma and Qun Wei, "Chemical Fuming: A Practical Method for Fingerprint Development on Thermal Paper," *Journal of Forensic Identification* 3 (2006): 364–373; Stephen H. Ostrowski and Marc E. Dupre, "Fingerprint Impression Development Using a Vacuum Box," *Journal of Forensic Identification* 3 (2006): 356–363; Gagan Deep Singh, G. S. Sodhi, and O. P. Jasuja, "Detection of Latent Fingerprints on Fruits and Vegetables," *Journal of Forensic Identification* 3 (2006): 374–381; Melissa Anne Smrz et al., "Review of FBI Latent Print Processes and Recommendations to Improve Practices and Quality," *Journal of Forensic Identification* 3 (2006): 402–434.

61. Allison Klein, "Solving Crimes with Simply the Snap of a Finger," *Washington Post*, October 25, 2009, retrieved October 26, 2009, from www.washingtonpost.com. Also see Leo M. Norton, "Who Goes There? Mobile Fingerprint Readers in Los Angeles County," *Police Chief* (June 2009): 32–39.

62. Allison Klein, "Solving Crimes with Simply the Snap of a Finger," *Washington Post*, October 25, 2009, retrieved October 26, 2009, from www.washingtonpost.com. Also see Leo M. Norton, "Who Goes There? Mobile Fingerprint Readers in Los Angeles County," *Police Chief* (June 2009): 32–39.

63. William Folsom, "Automated Fingerprint Identification Systems," *Law and Order* (July 1986): 27–28.

64. See John Ryan, "AFIS Pays Big Dividends for a Small City," *Law and Order* (June 2000): 70–72; Judith Blair Schmitt, "Computerized ID Systems," *Police Chief* (February 1992); "Something for Everyone in High-Tech," *Law Enforcement News*, December 15/31, 1998, p. 17; William Stover, "Automated Fingerprint Identification—Regional Application of Technology," *FBI Law Enforcement Bulletin* 53 (1984): 1–4.

65. Tony Lesce, "Verafind AFIS System: Flexible and Software Based," *Law and Order* (December 1994): 53–54.

66. Rebecca Kanable, "Live-Scan Is Making Its Print," *Law Enforcement Technology* (April 1999): 77–81.

67. Federal Bureau of Investigation, *Integrated Automated Fingerprint Identification System (IAFIS)*, retrieved February 23, 2008, from www.fbi.gov/hq/cjisd/iafis.htm.

68. Federal Bureau of Investigation, *Latent Print Unit*, retrieved June 2, 2001, from www.fbi.gov.

69. "INS, FBI Plan a $200M Wedding—Of Their Fingerprint Databases," *Law Enforcement News*, March 31, 2000, p. 7.

70. Federal Bureau of Investigation, *Integrated Automated Fingerprint Identification System (IAFIS)*, retrieved April 16, 2010, from www.fbi.com.

71. Rebecca Kanable, "Fingerprints Making the Case: AFIS and IAFIS Are Helping Find Matching Prints, but There Are More to Be Found," *Law Enforcement Technology* (March 2003): 48, 50–53.

72. Rebecca Kanable, "Grip on Identification Information," *Law Enforcement Technology* (June 2000): 122–126.

73. Dominic Andrae, "New Zealand Fingerprint Technology," *Law and Order* (November 1993): 37–38; "NAFIS Launched in South Wales," *Law and Order* (June 2000): 74.

74. The website for the International Association for Identification is www.theiai.org.

75. Tony Doonan, "Palmprint Technology Comes of Age," *Law and Order* (November 2000): 63–65.

76. See Charlie Mesloh, Ross Wolf, Mark Henych, and Frank L. Thompson, "Less Lethal Weapons for Law Enforcement: Performance-Based Analysis," *Law Enforcement Executive Forum* 1 (2008): 133–149; Ronnie Paynter, "Less-Lethal Weaponry," *Law Enforcement Technology* (October 1999): 78–84; Lois Pilant, *Less-than-Lethal Weapons: New Solutions for Law Enforcement* (Alexandria, Va.: International Association of Chiefs of Police, 2000).

77. Bill Clede, "A Banquet of Aerosol Sprays," *Law and Order* (September 1992): 57–59; Christopher Reilly, "The Science of Pepper Spray," *Law and Order* (July 2003): 124–130.

78. "Pepper Sprays Get Yet Another Shake," *Security Management* (August 2003): 18.

79. For a recent report on the Taser, see George T. Williams and Richard V. Simon, "Tasertron's 95HP: The Law Enforcement Taser," *Law and Order* (November 2001): 80–83.

80. Bob Egelko, "Federal Ruling Establishes Taser Standards," *San Francisco Chronicle*, December 30, 2009, retrieved December 30, 2009, from www.officer.com; Randy Means and Pam McDonald, "TASER and the 9th Circuit Decision," *Law and Order* (April 2010): 52–56.

81. John Graham, "Officers Armed with Beanbags," *Law and Order* (June 1997): 67–68.

82. Joan A. Hopper, "Less-Lethal Litigation: Departments and the Courts React to Less-Lethal Standards," *Law and Order* (November 2001): 87–91.

83. J. P. Morgan, "Oleoresin Capsicum Policy," *Police Chief* (August 1992): 26.

84. Greg Meyer, "Nonlethal Weapons vs. Conventional Police Tactics: Assessing Injuries and Liabilities," *Police Chief* (August 1992): 15–16.

85. Ibid., p. 18.

86. *Michenfelder v. Sumner*, 860 F.2d 328 (9th Cir. 1988).

87. Michael R. Smith, Matthew Petrocelli, and Charlie Scheer, "Excessive Force, Civil Liability, and the Taser in the Nation's Courts: Implications for Law Enforcement Policy and Practice," *Policing: An International Journal of Police Strategies and Management* 3 (2007): 398–422.

88. Raymond L. Downs, "Less Lethal Weapons: A Technologist's Perspective," *Policing: An International Journal of Police Strategies and Management* 3 (2007): 358–384; Ronnie Garrett, "CEDs Stop Suspects in Their Tracks," *Law Enforcement Technology* 5 (2007): 60, 62–68; Kenneth Adams and Victoria Jennison, "What We Do Not Know About Police Use of Tasers," *Policing: An International Journal of Police Strategies and Management* 3 (2007): 447–465; Michael R. Smith, Robert J. Kaminski, Jeffrey Rojeck, Geoffrey P. Alpert, and Jason Mathis, "Impact of Conducted Energy Devices and Other Types of Force and Resistance on Officer and Suspect Injuries," *Policing: An International Journal of Police Strategies and Management* 3 (2007): 423–446.

89. Gary M. Vike and Theodore C. Chan, "Less Lethal Technology: Medical Issues," *Policing: An International Journal of Police Strategies and Management* 3 (2007): 341–357.

90. U.S. Department of Justice, Office of the Inspector General, "Review of the Department of Justice's Use of Less-than-lethal Weapons," 2009, retrieved April 1, 2012, from www.justice.gov/oig.

91. For a comprehensive article on advanced surveillance devices, see Lois Pilant, "Spotlight on … Achieving State-of-the-Ar Surveillance," *Police Chief* (June 1993): 25–34.

92. Albert E. Brandenstein, "Advanced Technologies Bolster Law Enforcement's Counterdrug Efforts," *Police Chief* (January 1997): 32–34.

93. Tom Yates, "Surveillance Vans," *Law and Order* (December 1991): 52, 56.

94. Keith Hodges, "Tracking 'Bad Guys': Legal Considerations in Using GPS," *FBI Law Enforcement Bulletin* (July 2007): 25–32.

95. *United States v. Jones*, 565 U.S. _____ (2012).

96. Yates, "Surveillance Vans," p. 53.

97. Bill Siuru, "Seeing in the Dark and Much More: Thermal Imaging," *Law and Order* (November 1993): 18–20.

98. Ibid.

99. Tom Yates, "'Eyes' in the Night," *Law and Order* (November 1993): 19–24.

100. Donna Rogers, "Contraband Cops: U.S. Customs and Border Patrol Agents Stem the Tide of Smuggling with High-Tech Tools," *Law Enforcement Technology* (April 2000): 68–72.

101. Ronnie Paynter, "Images in the Night: Law Enforcement Sheds Light on Applications for Night Vision Technologies," *Law Enforcement Technology* (May 1999): 22–26.

102. Donna Rogers, "GPS: Getting the Proper Positioning," *Law Enforcement Technology* (September 2000): 44–50; also see U.S.

Department of Justice, *GPS Applications in Law Enforcement: The SkyTracker Surveillance System, Final Report* (Washington, D.C.: National Institute of Justice, 1998).

103. Keith Harries, *Mapping Crime: Principle and Practice* (Washington, D.C.: National Institute of Justice, 1999); Ron Mercer, Murray Brooks, and Paula T. Bryant, "Global Positioning Satellite System: Tracking Offenders in Real Time," *Corrections Today* (July 2000): 76–80; Bill Siuru, "Tracking 'Down': Space-Age GPS Technology Is Here," *Corrections Technology and Management* (September–October 1999): 1–14.

104. National Sheriffs' Association, "Law Enforcement Aircraft: A Vital Force Multiplier," *Sheriff* (January–February 2000): 32–60.

105. Ashley Parker, *Republicans, Led by Rand Paul, Finally End Filibuster*, March 6, 2013, *New York Times*, The Caucus, retrieved April 19, 2014, http://thecaucus.blogs.nytimes.com/2013/03/06/rand-paul-does-not-go-quietly-into-the-night/

106. Chris Cole, Jim Wright, *What are drones?*, Drone Wars UK, January 2010, retrieved April 19, 2014, http://dronewars.net/aboutdrone/

107. Byron King, *The Shocking New Use for Drone Technology*, retrieved March 10, 2014, http://dailyreckonong.com/drones-not-just-for-killing-terrorists-anymore/

108. Audrey Cheng, Alyssa Howard and Tom Meyer, *With Billions at Stake, States Lobby for Drone Test Sites*, The Dome Drone Project, April 30, 2013, retrieved March 10, 2014, http://droneproject.nationalsecurityzone.org/with-billions-at-stake-states-lobby-for-drone-test-sites

109. Josh Solomon, *Drones in the U.S.: A Special Student Report*, retrieved March 10, 2014, http://thedroneproject.nationalsecurityzone.org/uncertainties-remain-as-faa-integrates-drones-in-us-skies-number-of-drones-may-hit-30000-by 2020.

110. *US Aviation Agency to Appeal Drone Ruling*, March 7, 2014, UAV News, retrieved March 10, 2014, http://www.spacewar.com/reports/US_aviation_agency_to_appeal_drone-ruling_999.html

111. Jason Koebler, *Court Upholds Domestic Drone Use in Arrest of American Citizen*, August 2, 2012, US. News & World Report, retrieved August 5, 2012, http://www.usnews.com/news/articles/2012/08/02/court-upholds-domestic-drone-use-in-arrest-of-american-citizen

112. Josh Smith, *Domestic Drone Programs Spark Civil-Liberties Lawsuit*, January 11, 2012. National Journal, retrieved March 10, 2014, http://www.nationaljournal.com/tech/domestic-drone-programs-spark-covil-liberties-lawsuit.

113. Deena Kara, Jonathan Kilworth, and Martin Gill, "What Makes CCTV Effective?" *Intersect: The Journal of International Security* 9 (2003): 293–296.

114. Douglas Page, "Video Surveillance Networks: Lights, Camera, Controversy," *Law Enforcement Technology* 6 (2007): 106–114.

115. Chris A. Williams, "Police Surveillance and the Emergence of CCTV in the 1960s," *Crime Prevention and Community Safety: An International Journal* 3 (2003): 27–37.

116. "Anti-Crime Cameras Help in 180 Arrests," *Gloucester Citizen*, February 25, 2005; Ben Brown, *CCTV in Town Centres: Three Case Studies: Crime Detection and Prevention Series*

Paper 68 (London: Home Office, 1995); Michael R. Chatterton and Samantha J. Frenz, "Closed-Circuit Television: Its Role in Reducing Burglaries and the Fear of Crime in Sheltered Accommodation for the Elderly," *Security Journal* 5 (1994): 133–139; Martin Gill and Karryn Loveday, "What Do Offenders Think About CCTV?" *Crime Prevention and Community Safety: An International Journal* 3 (2003): 17–25; Barry Poyner, "Situational Crime Prevention in Two Parking Facilities," *Security Journal* 2 (1991): 96–101; Anya Sostek, "Here's Looking at You: Electronic Surveillance Systems Make Some Law-Abiding Citizens Feel Safer, They Make Others Very Nervous," *Governing* 11 (2002): 44–45; Nicholas Tilly, *Understanding Car Parks, Crime and CCTV: Evaluation Lessons from Safer Cities: Crime Prevention Unit Paper* 42 (London: Home Office, 1993); Brandon C. Welsh and David P. Farrington, "Surveillance for Crime Prevention in Public Space: Results and Policy Choices in Britain and America," *Criminology and Public Policy* 3 (2004): 497–525; Stig Winge and Johannes Knutson, "Evaluation of the CCTV Scheme at Oslo Central Railway Station," *Crime Prevention and Community Safety: An International Journal* 3 (2003): 49–59.

117. Martin Gill and Angela Spriggs, *Assessing the Impact of CCTV* (London: Great Britain Home Office Research Development and Statistics Directorate, 2005).

118. Tom Levesley and Amanda Martin, *Police Attitudes to and Use of CCTV* (London: Great Britain Home Office Research Development and Statistics Directorate, 2005); Angela Spriggs, Javier Argomaniz, Martin Gill, and Jane Bryan, *Public Attitudes Towards CCTV: Results from the Pre-Intervention Public Attitude Survey Carried Out in Areas Implementing CCTV* (London: Great Britain Home Office Research Development and Statistics Directorate, 2005).

119. John D. Woodward, Jr., *Privacy vs. Security: Electronic Surveillance in the Nation's Capital* (Santa Monica, Calif.: Rand Corporation, 2002).

120. Allison Linn, *Post 9/11, Surveillance Cameras Everywhere*, August 23, 2011, NBCNEWS.com, http://www.nbcnews.com/id/44163852/ns/business-us_business/t/post-surveillance-cameras-everywhere/#.U2rvb8ZCVFw, retrieved May 7, 2014.

121. Williams, "Police Surveillance and the Emergence of CCTV in the 1960s," pp. 27–37.

122. Laura J. Nichols, *Use of CCTV/Video Cameras in Law Enforcement, Executive Brief* (Alexandria, Va.: International Association of Chiefs of Police, 2001).

123. Leonor Vivanco, "More Surveillance Cameras Planned Throughout Redlands," *San Bernardino County Sun*, March 24, 2005.

124. Sostek, "Here's Looking at You: Electronic Surveillance Systems," pp. 44–45.

125. Jennifer Lee, "Police Seek to Increase Surveillance; Want 400 Cameras for Public Access," *New York Times*, May 31, 2005, p. B3.

126. Grant Fredericks, as quoted in Michael E. Ruane, "Security Camera New Star Witness," *Washington Post*, October 8, 2005, p. B1.

127. Grant Fredericks, "CCTV: A Law Enforcement Tool," *Police Chief* 8 (2004): 68–74.

128. Jennifer Lee, "Caught on Tape, Then Just Caught: Private Cameras Transform Police Work," *New York Times*, May 22, 2005, pp. 33, 36.

129. Ibid.

130. Ruane, "Security Camera New Star Witness," p. B1.

131. Jolene Hernon, "CCTV: Constant Cameras Track Violators," *National Institute of Justice Journal* 249 (2003): 16–23.

132. Katherine E. Finkelstein, "Officials Admit Wrong Man Was Held in Street Attack: Morgenthau Calls Evidence Overwhelming," *New York Times*, July 27, 2000, p. B3; Joyce Purnick, "The Truth, as Always, Is Stranger," *New York Times*, July 27, 2000, p. B1.

133. Lee, "Police Seek to Increase Surveillance," p. B3.

134. Matt Blaze, *How Law Enforcement Tracks Cellular Phones*, Exhaustive Search, Science, Security, Curiosity, Dec 13, 2013, retrieved April 14, 2014, http://www.crypto.com/blog/celltapping.

135. *U.S. v. Murphy*, 552 F. 3d 405; *Hawkins v. State*, 732 SE 2d 924; *Gracie v. State*, 92 So. 3d 806; *U.S. v. Flores-Lopez*, 670 F 3d 803; *U.S. v. Curtis*, 635 F. 3d 704; *People v. Taylor*, Colo: Court of Appeals, 5th Div 2012; *People v. Diaz*, 51 Cal. 4th 84 (2011).

136. *State v. Smith*,124 Ohio St. 3d 163; *U.S. v. Wurie*, Court of Appeals, 1st Circuit 2013; *Smallwood v. State*, Fla: Supreme Court 2013; Lawrence Hurley, *U.S. Supreme Court to Weight Cell Phone Searches by Police*, January 17, 2014, retrieved April 14, 2014, http://www.reuters.com/assets/print?aid=USBREA0GIH320140117

137. David P. Nagosky, "Admissibility of Digital Photographs in Criminal Cases," *FBI Law Enforcement Bulletin* 12 (2005): 1–8.

138. Matthew Langer and Mark Dunaski, "Aerial Photography: An Elevated Perspective," *Evidence Technology Magazine* (July–August 2007): 28–33. Also see Catherine Sapp, "The Benefits of Aerial Photography," *FBI Law Enforcement Bulletin* (September 2008): 6–7.

139. *Florida v. Riley*, 488 U.S. 445 (1989).

140. John J. Pavlis, "Mug-Shot Imaging Systems," *FBI Law Enforcement Bulletin* (August 1992): 20–22.

141. "Picture This: Digital Photos Beam from Texas to Virginia via High-Tech Patrol Cars," *Law Enforcement News*, June 15, 1997, p. 1; Darrel L. Sanders, "The Critical Role of Technology," *Police Chief* (July 1997): 6.

142. Stephen Coleman, "Biometrics: Solving Cases of Mistaken Identity and More," *FBI Law Enforcement Bulletin* (June 2000): 13.

143. Zonderman, "High-Tech Crime Hunters," p. 31.

144. Ibid. Also see Gene O'Donnell, "Forensic Imaging Comes of Age," *FBI Law Enforcement Bulletin* (January 1994): 5–10.

145. Zonderman, "High-Tech Crime Hunters," p. 31. Also see Charles Jackson, "Drawing without a Net," *Forensic Magazine* (April/May 2007): 32–37; O'Donnell, "Forensic Imaging Comes of Age."

146. Aliya Sternstein, "FBI to Launch Nationwide Facial Recognition Service," 2011, retrieved October 10, 2011, from www.nextgov.com.

147. *Massive FBI Facial Recognition Database Poses Threat to Privacy*, Group Says, April 16, 2014, Fox News, retrieved May 4, 2014, http://www.foxnews.com/tech/2014/04/16/massive-fbi-facial-recognition-database-threat-to-privacy-group-says/

148. "No More Pencils, No More Books?" *Law Enforcement News*, January 31, 1998, p. 5.

149. "The Face Is Familiar—and Computer-Generated," *Law Enforcement News*, October 31, 1999, p. 7.

150. Donna Rogers, "Drawing the Line," *Law Enforcement Technology* (May 2003): 44–50.

151. Charles Jackson, "Hand-Drawn Composites," *Law and Order* 3 (2006): 36–39. Also see Charles T. Jackson, "Guide for the Artist," *Journal of Forensic Identification* 3 (2006): 388–401.

152. Donna Rogers, "Forensic Composite Imaging," *Law Enforcement Technology* 11 (2007): 76–83.

153. Richard Saferstein, *Criminalistics: An Introduction to Forensic Science*, 8th ed. (Upper Saddle River, N.J.: Pearson/Prentice Hall, 2004), p. 2. Saferstein recommends the following two works as excellent references for the definition and application of forensic science: Andre A. Moenssens, Fred E. Inbau, James Starrs, and Carol E. Henderson, *Scientific Evidence in Civil and Criminal Cases*, 4th ed. (Mineola, N.Y.: Foundation Press, 1995), and Werner U. Spitz, ed., *Medicolegal Investigation of Death*, 3rd ed. (Springfield, Ill.: Charles C. Thomas, 1993).

154. Dempsey, *Introduction to Investigations*, p. 133.

155. Saferstein, *Criminalistics*, p. 2.

156. Marc H. Caplan and Joe Holt Anderson, *Forensic: When Science Bears Witness* (Washington, D.C.: National Institute of Justice, 1984), p. 2. For an interesting history of criminalistics, see Dempsey, *Introduction to Investigations*, pp. 122–125. Also see Saferstein, *Criminalistics*, pp. 2–6.

157. Peter R. DeForest, N. Petraco, and L. Koblinsky, "Chemistry and the Challenge of Crime," in S. Gerber, ed., *Chemistry and Crime* (Washington, D.C.: American Chemical Society, 1983), p. 45.

158. Joseph L. Peterson, *Use of Forensic Evidence by the Police and Courts* (Washington, D.C.: National Institute of Justice, 1987).

159. David Johnston, "Report Criticizes Scientific Testing at FBI Lab: Serious Problems Cited," *New York Times*, April 16, 1997, pp. A1, D23; Mireya Navarro, "Doubts About FBI Lab Raise Hopes for Convict: On Death Row, but Seeking a New Trial," *New York Times*, April 22, 1997, p. A8.

160. "What's Wrong at the FBI?: The Fiasco at the Crime Lab," *Time*, April 28, 1997, pp. 28–35.

161. Belinda Luscombe, "When the Evidence Lies: Joyce Gilchrist Helped Send Dozens to Death Row. The Forensic Scientist's Errors Are Putting Capital Punishment under the Microscope," *Time*, May 21, 2001, pp. 37–40.

162. "Indiana: DNA Evidence Under Review," *New York Times*, July 19, 2003, p. A10.

163. Roma Khanna and Steve McVicker, "Police Lab Tailored Tests to Theories, Report Says," *Houston Chronicle*, May 12, 2006; Steve McVicker and Roma Khanna, "More Problems Found in HPD Crime Lab Cases," *Houston Chronicle*, May 11, 2006. See also Richard Willing, "Errors Prompt States to Watch over Crime Labs," *USA Today*, April 3, 2006.

164. Nick Bunkley, "Detroit Police Lab Is Closed After Audit Finds Serious Errors in Many Cases," *New York Times*, September 26,

2008; Mark Hornbeck, "Detroit Crime Lab Closure Ripples through Michigan Justice System," *Detroit News*, February 19, 2010, retrieved February 19, 2010, from www.detnews.com.

165. Jesse McKinley, "Hundreds of Drug Cases Are at Risk in San Francisco," *New York Times*, April 2, 2010, retrieved April 5, 2010, from www.nytimes.com; Jaxon Van Derbeken, "Overworked S.F. Drug Lab Was Sloppy, Audit Says," *San Francisco Chronicle*, March 31, 2010, retrieved March 31, 2010, from www.sfgate.com.

166. Bay City News, *No Prison for Technician At Center Of SFPD Crime Lab Scandal*, July 19, 2013, accessed May 4, 2014, http://sfappeal.com/2013/07/no-prison-for-technician-at-center-of-sfpd-crime-lab-scandal

167. National Academy of Sciences, Committee on Identifying the Needs of the Forensic Science Community, *Strengthening Forensic Science in the United States: A Path Forward* (Washington, D.C.: National Academy of Sciences, 2009); Henry Fountain, "Plugging Holes in the Science of Forensics," *New York Times*, May 12, 2009, retrieved May 12, 2009, from www.nytimes.com.

168. Kevin J. Strom, Jeri Ropero-Miller, Shelton Jones, Nathan Sikes, Mark Pope, and Nicole Horstmann, *The 2007 Survey of Law Enforcement Forensic Evidence Processing* (Washington, D.C.: National Institute of Justice, 2009).

169. "Life Imitates Art with the 'CSI Effect.'" *Law Enforcement News*, June 2005, pp. 1, 11.

170. Julian Fantino, "Forensic Science: A Fundamental Perspective," *Police Chief* (November 2007): 26.

171. Jennifer Mertens, "Smoking Gun: When Real-Life CSI and Hollywood Collide," *Law Enforcement Technology* 3 (2006): 52–61.

172. Michael Biesecker, "DNA Doesn't Offer Magic Key to Case," *News & Observer*, April 12, 2006; Patrik Jonsson, "Duke Lacrosse Case: No DNA, but Old-Fashioned Sleuthing," *Christian Science Monitor*, April 19, 2006.

173. Ibid.

174. Matthew R. Durose, *Census of Publicly Funded Forensic Crime Laboratories, 2005* (Washington, D.C.: National Institute of Justice, 2008).

175. Federal Bureau of Investigation, *FBI Laboratory*, retrieved August 1, 2006, from www.fbi.gov/hq/lab/labhome.htm.

176. Rebecca Kanable, "Forensics on the Move: Mobile Crime Labs Allow Evidence Processing on Scene and More," *Law Enforcement Technology* (July 2009): 18–22.

177. Bureau of Alcohol, Tobacco, Firearms, and Explosives, *Integrated Ballistic Identification System*, retrieved August 4, 2006, from www.atf.gov/firearms/; "Hey Buddy, Got a Match?: New System Does for Bullets What AFIS Did for Prints," *Law Enforcement News*, April 30, 1994, p. 1.

178. Bureau of Alcohol, Tobacco, Firearms, and Explosives, *Integrated Ballistic Identification System*.

179. "ATF Tightens Screws on Illicit Gun Sales with Gun- & Bullet-Tracing Databases," *Law Enforcement News*, February 14, 2000, pp. 1, 6; Tracy Hite, "Developments in Forensic Science: The National Integrated Ballistics Information Network," *Police Chief* 4 (2000): 173–174.

180. Julie Bykowicz, "FBI Lab Scraps Gunfire Residue," *Baltimore Sun*, May 26, 2006; "Going Ballistic: Serious Flaws Seen in FBI Bullet-Matching Test," *Law Enforcement News*, February 2004, pp. 1–10. Also see John Solomon, "FBI's Forensic Test Full of Holes," *Washington Post*, November 18, 2007, p. 1.

181. Bykowicz, "FBI Lab Scraps Gunfire Residue."

182. U.S. Drug Enforcement Administration (DEA), Office of Diversion Control, *National Forensic Laboratory Information System (NFLIS) 2012 Annual Report* (Washington, D.C.: Drug Enforcement Administration, 2012).

183. Scientific Working Group for Forensic Document Examination, "Guidelines for Forensic Document Examination," *Forensic Science Communications* 2 (2000): 1–4.

184. Atul K. Singla and Mukesh K. Thakar, "Establishing the Sequence of Intersecting Ballpoint Pen and Felt-Tipped Marker Strokes," *Journal of Forensic Identification* 3 (2006): 382–387.

185. The website of the American Society of Questioned Document Examiners (ASQDE) is www.asqde.org.

186. Philip Bulman and Danielle McLeod-Henning, "Applying Carbon-14 Dating to Recent Human Remains," U.S. DOJ, OJP, NIJ, The Research, Development, and Evaluation Agency of the U.S. Department of Justice, retrieved March 30, 2012, from www.nij.gov/nij/journals/269.

187. American Society of Crime Laboratory Directors, retrieved August 4, 2006, from www.ascld.org. For further information on accreditation in the forensic sciences, see Frank Fitzpatrick and Terence Ely, "Ensuring the Quality of Forensic Service Providers through Accreditation: The Illinois State Police Crime Scene Services Command Experience," *Police Chief* (November 2007): 50–53.

188. Lois Pilant, "Crime Laboratory Developments," *Police Chief* (June 1997): 31.

189. Technical Working Group on Crime Scene Investigation, *Crime Scene Investigation: A Guide for Law Enforcement* (Washington, D.C.: National Institute of Justice, U.S. Department of Justice, 2000).

190. *Bullcoming v. New Mexico*, 564 U.S. _____ (2011).

191. National Institute of Justice, *Technical Working Group for Education and Training in Digital Forensics* (Washington, D.C.: National Institute of Justice, 2007).

192. C. M. Whitcomb, "Evolution of Digital Evidence in Forensic Science Laboratories," *Police Chief* (November 2007): 36–42.

193. National Law Enforcement and Corrections Technology Center, *Digital Evidence: Its True Value* (Rockville, Md.: National Law Enforcement and Corrections Technology Center, 2009); Christa Miller and Kipp Loving, "Crime Scene Evidence You're Ignoring: Computers and Cell Phones Aren't the Only Digital Devices That Hold Evidence," *Law Enforcement Technology* (October 2009): 36–45.

194. Pamela Mills-Senn, "Hidden Messages: Computers and Other Technology Have Much to Say About a Case, If Investigators Take the Time to Look," *Law Enforcement Technology* 4 (2006): 8–16.

195. Charles I. Cohen, "Growing Challenges of Computer Forensics," *Police Chief* (March 2007): 24–29.

196. C. M. Whitcomb, "Evolution of Digital Evidence in Forensic Science Laboratories," *Police Chief* (November 2007): 41–42.

197. Scientific Working Group on Digital Evidence, *Digital Evidence: Standards and Principles* (Washington, D.C.: Scientific Working Group on Digital Evidence, 2000).

198. Loren D. Mercer, "Computer Forensics: Characteristics and Preservation of Digital Evidence," *FBI Law Enforcement Bulletin* (March 2004): 28–32.

199. National Institute of Justice, *Forensic Examination of Digital Evidence: A Guide for Law Enforcement*, retrieved November 8, 2004, from www.ojp.usdoj.gov/nij/pubs-sum/199408.htm; National Institute of Justice, *Electronic Crime Scene Investigation: A Guide for First Responders*, 2nd ed. (Washington, D.C.: National Institute of Justice, 2008).

200. National White Collar Crime Center, *Cyber Crime Fighting II: Digital Evidence Search, Seizure, and Preservation* (Morgantown, W.V.: National White Collar Crime Center, 2005).

201. U.S. Department of Homeland Security, *Best Practices for Seizing Electronic Evidence: A Pocket Guide for First Responders* (Washington, D.C.: U.S. Department of Homeland Security, 2007).

202. David Griffith, "How to Investigate Cybercrime," *Police* (November 2003): 18–20, 22; Angelique C. Grado, "Internet Investigations: The Crime Scene of Cybercrime," *Evidence Technology Magazine* (July/August 2005): 12–15, 38; Jon Berryhill, "Finding a Qualified Computer Forensic Analyst," *Law Enforcement Technology* (May 2005): 122–127.

203. R. L. Mendell, *Investigating Computer Crime: A Primer for Security Managers* (Springfield, Ill.: Charles C. Thomas, 1998).

204. Lois Pilant, "Electronic Evidence Recovery," *Police Chief* (February 1999): 37–48.

205. International High Technology Crime Investigation Association, retrieved February 15, 2008, from www.htcia.org.

206. Computer Crime Research Center, retrieved February 15, 2008, from www.crime-research.org.

207. Erika Harrell, Lynn Langton, *Victims of Identity Theft*, 2012, U.S. Department of Justice, Office of Justice Programs, Bureau of Justice Statics, December 2013.

208. *Taking Charge, What to Do If Your Identity Is Stolen*, Federal Trade Commission, 2012, www.FTC.gov/ID Theft

209. *California v. Greenwood*, 486 U.S. 35 (1988)

210. Jon Dunn, *Layton Outlaws Dumpster Diving*, KSL.com, November 7, 2005, accessed April 12, 2014, http://www.ksl.com/?nid=148&sid=126132

211. Trends in Telephone Service, September 2010, Chart 11-1, p. 11–4, http://hraunfoss.fcc.gov/edocs_public/attachmatch/DOC-301823A1.pdf, accessed May 7, 2014

212. Rebecca Kanable, "New Frontier in Digital Evidence: With Cell Phones Ringing Everywhere, Agencies Need to Know How to Answer This New Call of Duty," *Law Enforcement Technology* 7 (2007): 16–25. Also see Don L. Lewis, "Examining Cellular Phones and Handheld Devices," *Forensic Magazine*, August/September 2009, pp. 12–16; Christa Miller, "More than a Cell Phone," *Law Enforcement Technology* 4 (2003): 82–86. Note: The *Guidelines on Cell Phone Forensics* report issued by the National Institute of Standards and Technology (NIST) in May 2007 is available on the NIST website at www.nist.gov, retrieved February 16, 2008.

213. Jeannine Heinecke, "Evolution in Cell Forensics," *Law Enforcement Technology* 11 (2007): 62–70.

214. Carl Milazzo, "Searching Cell Phones Incident to Arrest: 2009 Update," *Police Chief* (May 2009): 12; *United States v. Murphy*, 552 F.3d 405, 412 (4th Cir. 2009).

215. National Criminal Justice Reference Center, "In the Spotlight: Forensic Science: Summary," retrieved July 27, 2006, from www.ncjrs.gov/spotlight/forensic/Summary.html. For an excellent recent article on the impact of DNA on police operations, see Raymond J. Prime and Jonathan Newman, "The Impact of DNA on Policing: Past, Present, and Future," *Police Chief* (November 2007): 30–35. The authors are with the Centre of Forensic Sciences, Toronto, Ontario, Canada.

216. Saferstein, *Criminalistics*, pp. 353–394.

217. Elizabeth Devine, as quoted in Judith Martin, "The Power of DNA," *Law and Order* (May 2001): 31–35.

218. Peter J. Neufeld and Neville Colman, "When Science Takes the Witness Stand," *Scientific American* (May 1990):46.

219. C. Thomas Caskey and Holly A. Hammond, *Automated DNA Typing: Method of the Future?* (Washington, D.C.: National Institute of Justice, 1997), p. 1.

220. Federal Bureau of Investigation, *DNA Analysis*, retrieved June 2, 2001, from www.fbi.gov.

221. National Criminal Justice Reference Center, *In the Spotlight: Forensic Science: Summary*; National Institute of Justice, *Improved Analysis of DNA Short Tandem Repeats with Time-of-Flight Mass Spectrometry* (Washington, D.C.: National Institute of Justice, 2001).

222. Dina Temple-Raston, "FBI's New Technology Revolutionizes DNA Analysis," retrieved January 28, 2008, from www.npr.org.

223. Alice Eisenberg, as quoted in Temple-Raston, "FBI's New Technology Revolutionizes DNA Analysis."

224. CODIS was officially created by Congress through the 1994 DNA Identification Act. See Nicolas P. Lovrich, Michael J. Gaffney, Travis C. Pratt, and Charles L. Johnson, *National Forensic DNA Study Report* (Washington, D.C.: National Institute of Justice, 2003); Terry Knowles, "Meeting the Challenges of the 21st Century," *Police Chief* (June 1997): 39–43.

225. Federal Bureau of Investigation, CODIS-NDIS Statistics, retrieved May 7, 2014 from http://www.fbi.gov/about-us/lab/biometric-analysis/codis/ndis-statistics

226. Federal Bureau of Investigation, "CODIS—Crime," retrieved April 16, 2010, from www.fbi.gov/hq/lab/html/codis3.htm.

227. Federal Bureau of Investigation, Combined DNA Index System (*CODIS*), retrieved June 2, 2001, from www.fbi.gov; Federal Bureau of Investigation, "CODIS—Crime"; National Criminal Justice Reference Center, *In the Spotlight: Forensic Science: Facts and Figures.*

228. Federal Bureau of Investigation, "CODIS—Crime"; National Commission on the Future of DNA Testing, *The Future of Forensic DNA Testing: Predictions of the Research and Development Working Group* (Washington, D.C.: National Institute of Justice, 2000): 19–20; National Criminal Justice Reference Center, *In the Spotlight: Forensic Science: Facts and Figures.*

229. Federal Bureau of Investigation, "NDIS Statistics," retrieved April 16, 2010, from www.fbi.gov/hq/lab/codis/clickmap.htm.

230. Rick Weiss, "Vast DNA Bank Pits Policing vs. Privacy," *Washington Post*, June 3, 2006, p. A1.

231. Jeff Wise and Richard Li, "The Future of DNA Evidence," *Crime and Justice International* 70 (2003): 31–32.

232. Jennifer Luttman, as quoted in Temple-Raston, "FBI's New Technology Revolutionizes DNA Analysis."

233. Federal Bureau of Investigation, CODIS Brochure, retrieved May 7, 2014, from http://www.fbi.gov/about-us/lab/codis/codis-and-ndis-fact-sheet

234. Doug Hanson, "DNA Evidence: A Powerful Tool," *Law and Order* (April 2007): 95–99.

235. Janet C. Hoeffel, "The Dark Side of DNA Profiling: Unreliable Scientific Evidence Meets the Criminal Defendant," *Stanford Law Review* 42 (1990): 465–538.

236. *Frye v. United States*, 293 F. 1013 (1923).

237. "DNA Fingerprinting ID Method May Streamline Investigations," *Current Reports: BNA Criminal Practice Manual* 19 (1987): 1.

238. Ronald Sullivan, "Appeals Court Eases Rules on Genetic Evidence," *New York Times*, January 11, 1992, p. 8.

239. "Supreme Court Clarifies Ruling on Admitting Scientific Evidence," *Criminal Justice Newsletter*, December 1, 1997, p. 1; *Daubert v. Merrell Dow Pharmaceuticals*, 509 U.S. 579 (1993); *General Electric Company v. Joiner*, 522 U.S. 136 (1997).

240. "DNA Typing Endorsed by National Academy of Sciences," *CJ Update* (Fall 1992): 1.

241. National Commission on the Future of DNA Evidence, *The Future of Forensic DNA Testing*, p. v.

242. Ibid., p. 1.

243. Ibid., pp. 3–6.

244. Solomon Moore, "In a Lab, an Ever-Growing Database of DNA Profiles," *New York Times*, May 12, 2009, retrieved May 12, 2009, from www.nytimes.com; Solomon Moore, "F.B.I. and States Vastly Expand DNA Databases," *New York Times*, April 19, 2009, retrieved April 19, 2009, from www.nytimes.com; Sarah B. Berson, "Debating DNA Collection," *National Institute of Justice Journal* 264 (November 2009): 9–13.

245. Federal Bureau of Investigation, CODIS Brochure, retrieved May 7, 2014 from http://www.fbi.gov/about-us/lab/biometric-analysis/codis/codis_brochure

246. "The Truth Is in Your Genes," *Law Enforcement News*, December 15/31, 2000, p. 7.

247. Rebecca S. Peterson, "DNA Databases: When Fear Goes Too Far," *American Criminal Law Review* 3 (2000): 1219–1237.

248. Executive Office of the President of the United States, *Advancing Justice through DNA Technology* (Washington, D.C.: National Institute of Justice, 2003); U.S. Department of Justice, *Justice for All Act* (Washington, D.C.: U.S. Department of Justice, 2006); Edwin Zedlewski and Mary B. Murphy, "DNA Analysis for 'Minor' Crimes: A Major Benefit for Law Enforcement," *National Institute of Justice Journal* 253 (2006).

249. National Commission on the Future of DNA Evidence, *What Every Law Enforcement Officer Should Know About DNA Evidence* (Washington, D.C.: National Institute of Justice, 2000); National Institute of Justice, *Understanding DNA Evidence: A Guide for Victim Service Providers* (Washington, D.C.: National Institute of Justice, 2001); National Institute of Justice, *Mass Fatality Incidents: A Guide for Human Forensic Identification* (Washington, D.C.: National Institute of Justice, 2006).

250. Richard Willing, "FBI Adds Uses for Its DNA Database," *USA Today*, May 30, 2006.

251. Paul Elias, *Calif. DNA Collection from Arrestees Challenged*, Associated Press, Sep. 17, 2012, retrieved Sep 17, 2012, http://www.officer.com/news/10780331/calf-dna-collection-from-arrestee-challenged?utm_source=Officer.com+Newsday+E+Newsletter&utm_m...

252. *Maryland v. King*, 133 S.Ct. 1958

253. Lovrich, Pratt, Gaffney, and Johnson, *National Forensic DNA Study Report*; Travis C. Pratt, Michael J. Gaffney, Nicholas P. Lovrich, and Charles L. Johnson, "This Isn't CSI: Estimating the National Backlog of Forensic DNA Cases and the Barriers Associated with Case Processing," *Criminal Justice Policy Review* 1 (2006): 32–47. Also see Tom McGhee, "Felons' DNA Clogs System," *Denver Post*, February 4, 2008; Solomon Moore, "Progress Is Minimal in Clearing DNA Cases," *New York Times*, October 25, 2008; Richard Pinchin, "Eliminating DNA Backlog," *Forensic Magazine* (August/September 2007): 32–36; Ari Shapiro, "Crime Labs Struggle with Flood of DNA Samples," retrieved December 12, 2007, from www.npr.org; Richard Winton and Patrick McGreevy, "LAPD Far Short of Funds for DNA Tests," *Los Angeles Times*, November 30, 2007.

254. Mark Nelson, Ruby Chase, and Lindsay DePalma, Making Sense of DNA Backlog, 2012—Myths vs. Reality, National Institute of Justice Special Report, December 2013, accessed May 7, 2014, from https://www.ncjrs.gov/pdffiles1/nij/243347.pdf

255. Roland A. H. van Oorschot, Sally Treadwell, et al., "Beware of the Possibility of Fingerprinting Techniques Transferring DNA," *Journal of Forensic Sciences* 6 (2005): 1417–1422.

256. Federal Bureau of Investigation, CODIS-NDIS Statistics, accessed May 7, 2014, http://www.fbi.gov/about-us/lab/biometric-analysis/codis/ndis-statistics

257. Katherine Aldred, "RCMP Furthers Innovation in the Forensic Sciences," *Gazette* 3 (2003): 10–13.

258. See Jim Markey, "After the Match: Dealing with the New Era of DNA," *FBI Law Enforcement Bulletin* (October 2007): 1–4.

259. Dearen, "DNA Cases Expose Problems in Oakland."

260. Stephen Kiehl, "Evidence Uncollected, Crimes Undeterred," *Baltimore Sun*, July 16, 2006.

261. Kevin Johnson, "Storage of DNA Evidence Crucial to Exonerations," *USA Today*, March 28, 2011, retrieved March 28, 2011, from www.usatoday.com.

262. Tod W. Burke and Jason M. Rexrode, "DNA Warrants," *Law and Order* (July 2000): 121–124.

263. William K. Rashbaum, "New York Pursues Old Cases of Rape Based Just on DNA," *New York Times*, August 5, 2003, pp. A-1, B-6; Al Baker, "Indicting DNA Profiles Is Vital in Old Rape Cases," *New York Times*, October 19, 2009, retrieved October 19, 2009.

264. Weiss, "Vast DNA Bank Pits Policing vs. Privacy," p. A1.

265. Angus J. Dodson, "DNA 'Line-ups' Based on a Reasonable Suspicion Standard," *University of Colorado Law Review* 1 (2000): 221–254.

266. Ari Shapiro, "Police Use DNA to Track Suspects through Family," retrieved December 12, 2007, from www.npr.org.

267. Rick Weiss, "DNA of Criminals' Kin Cited in Solving Cases," *Washington Post*, May 12, 2006, p. A10.

268. Ibid.

269. Tania Simoncelli, as quoted in Shapiro, "Police Use DNA to Track Suspects through Family."

270. David Lazer, as quoted in Shapiro, "Police Use DNA to Track Suspects through Family."

271. Ibid.

272. Janet Reno, "Preventing the Conviction of the Innocent: A Compelling and Urgent Need," *Judicature* 4 (2004): 163–165.

273. Innocence Project, retrieved March 28, 2012, from www.innocentproject.org.

274. Ibid.

275. Susan Geoghegan, "Forensic DNA," *Law and Order* (June 2009): 49–53.

276. Zedlewski and Murphy, "DNA Analysis for 'Minor' Crimes."

277. Stephen Coleman, "Biometrics: Solving Cases of Mistaken Identity and More," *FBI Law Enforcement Bulletin* (June 2000): 13. Also see Al Varga, "Biometrics Is Scientific Help," *Law and Order* (June 2009): 44–48.

278. Ibid.

279. Wendy Koch, "Iris Scans Let Law Enforcement Keep Eye on Criminals," *USA Today*, December 6, 2007.

280. Greg Solano, as quoted in Koch, "Iris Scans Let Law Enforcement Keep Eye on Criminals."

281. Federal Bureau of Investigation, Biometric Specifications (BioSpecs), accessed May 7, 2014, https://www.fbibiospecs.org

282. Federal Bureau of Investigation, "Press Release: FBI Contract Award for Next Generation Identification System,"

retrieved February 24, 2008, from www.fbi.gov; Ellen Nakashima, "FBI Prepares Vast Database of Biometrics," *Washington Post*, December 22, 2007, p. A1. Also see Ellen Nakashima, "Lockheed Secures Contract to Expand Biometric Database," *Washington Post*, February 13, 2008, p. D1.

283. Jo Ann West, *Facial Identification Technology and Law Enforcement* (Sacramento, Calif.: California Commission on Peace Officer Standards and Training, 1996).

284. Visionics Corporation, *Adaptive Surveillance: A Novel Approach to Facial Surveillance for CCTV Systems, Final Progress Report* (Jersey City, N.J.: Visionics Corporation, 2001). Also see Christopher A. Miles and Jeffrey P. Cohn, "Tracking Prisoners in Jail with Biometrics: An Experiment in a Navy Brig," *National Institute of Justice Journal* 253 (2006): 6–9.

285. Brent Rose, Police Used Facial Recognition Software to ID Suspects in UK Riots, August 15, 2011, http://gizmodo.com/5831119/police-used-facial-recognition-software-to-id-suspects-in-uk-riots

286. Coleman, "Biometrics: Solving Cases of Mistaken Identity and More," p. 13.

287. Barnaby J. Feder, "Technology Strains to Find Menace in the Crowd: Face Recognition Attempts to Heal Its Black Eye," *New York Times*, May 31, 2004, pp. C-1, C-2. Also see Kay Falk, "Putting a Name to a Face: Facial Recognition Systems Help Officers Make Timely Decisions," *Law Enforcement Technology* 7 (2007): 32, 34–40.

288. Feder, "Technology Strains to Find Menace in the Crowd," pp. C-1, C-2.

289. Ibid.

290. "News and Trends," *Security Management* (January 2005): 12.

291. Nakashima, "FBI Prepares Vast Database of Biometrics."

292. Bureau of Justice Statistics, *State and Local Law Enforcement Statistics*, p. 2; Hickman and Reaves, *Local Police Departments*, 2003; Hickman and Reaves, *Sheriffs' Offices*, 2003.

293. Michael Giacoppo, "The Expanding Role of Videotape in Court," *FBI Law Enforcement Bulletin* (November 1991): 3.

294. Giacoppo, "The Expanding Role of Videotape"; Ronnie L. Paynter, "Patrol Car Video," *Law Enforcement Technology* (June 1999): 34–37; Dale Stockton, "Police Video: Up Close and Personal," *Law and Order* (August 1999): 78–82.

295. Joseph G. Estey, "2,000 Survivors' Club Hits: In the Past 10 Years, 2,000 Officers Have 'Dressed for Survival,'" *Police Chief* (May 1997): 19.

296. H. G. Nguyen and J. P. Bott, *Robotics for Law Enforcement: Beyond Explosive Ordinance Disposal* (San Diego, Calif.: SPAWAR Systems Center, 2000); Douglas Page, "Get Smart: A Bomb Robot with Know-How," *Law Enforcement Technology* (July 2002): 136–142; Douglas Page, "Small Fry Robots Becoming Big Law Enforcement Deal," *Law Enforcement Technology* (May 2002): 34–37; Lois Pilant, "Spotlight on. . . Equipping a Bomb Unit," *Police Chief* (October 1992): 58–67.

297. Nguyen and Bott, *Robotics for Law Enforcement*.

298. Page, "Get Smart," pp. 136–142.

299. Ibid.

300. U.S. Congress, Office of Technology Assessment, *Criminal Justice*.

301. Zonderman, "High-Tech Crime Hunters," p. 31.

302. *California v. Ciraolo*, 476 U.S. 207 (1986).

303. Alan M. Dershowitz, *Taking Liberties: A Decade of Hard Cases, Bad Laws, and Bum Raps* (Chicago: Contemporary Books, 1988), p. 209.

304. Tania Simoncelli and Carol Roses in Weiss, "Vast DNA Bank Pits Policing vs. Privacy," p. A1.

Homeland Security

15

AP Images/Kathy Willens

OUTLINE

Homeland Security

Terrorism
International Terrorism
Domestic Terrorism

Methods of Investigating Terrorism
Proactive Methods
Reactive Methods

Post-9/11 Response to Terrorism and Homeland Defense
9/11 Commission's Review of Efforts for Homeland Security

Federal Law Enforcement Efforts for Homeland Security
Department of Homeland Security (DHS)
Federal Bureau of Investigation (FBI)
Secure Communities: DHS and FBI
Office of the Director of National Intelligence (ODNI)
Other Federal Agencies

State and Local Law Enforcement Efforts for Homeland Security

Security Versus Civil Liberties

LEARNING OBJECTIVES

- Define terrorism, including threats posed to the United States both internationally and domestically.

- Describe the response of the U.S. government immediately following the September 11, 2001, terrorist attacks.

- Identify and explain federal law enforcement efforts for homeland security.

- Identify and explain state and local law enforcement efforts for homeland security.

- Summarize both sides of the debate between security and civil liberties.

INTRODUCTION

On September 11, 2001, our world changed. A series of unthinkable and incomprehensible events led to ultimate disasters in New York City, Washington, D.C., and a grassy field in Pennsylvania. Those events shocked the world and changed history.

The swiftness, scale, and sophisticated coordination of the operation, coupled with the extraordinary planning required, launched new awareness of terrorism and mass murder in the United States and, indeed, the world. In the immediate aftermath of the attacks, it was reported that almost 5,000 people were missing and more than 400 confirmed dead. Eventually, it was determined that the missing persons included 23 New York City police officers, 35 New York and New Jersey Port Authority officers, 3 New York State court officers, and more than 300 New York City fire fighters. These attacks shocked us, even though there had been similar events before, although not as massive.

Terrorism is, sadly, not new to the United States. In 1993, there was the first terrorist attack on New York City's World Trade Center, killing 6 and wounding 1,000. In 1995, there was the bombing of the Alfred P. Murrah Federal Building in Oklahoma City, killing 168 persons and injuring 675 others. The 1996 bombing at the Olympic Games in Atlanta, Georgia, killed 1 person and wounded 111 others. During these years, there were also terrorist acts committed against churches and family planning clinics that provide abortions, as well as many other depraved, senseless incidents. All of these events awakened Americans to the fact that terrorism had actually come ashore. However, no other day in America's history had been quite like September 11, 2001. The attacks jolted Americans out of a sense of complacency, and perhaps lethargy. The need for a strong homeland defense has been a primary interest of U.S. law enforcement since then.

This chapter will discuss terrorism directed against Americans and American interests abroad, including foreign and domestic terrorism. We will discuss the immediate aftermath of September 11, and the rapid, unprecedented efforts made by the U.S. government. The chapter will describe federal, state, and local efforts for homeland security and the issue of security versus individual rights—how we can ensure a safe environment without threatening our civil liberties and individual freedoms granted under the U.S. Constitution.

Homeland Security

The term **homeland security** has been used since the September 11 terrorism acts to describe defensive efforts within the borders of the United States. Officials use it to separate the U.S. Department of Homeland Security's (DHS) operations from those of the U.S. Department of Defense.[1] Following 9/11, the U.S. government prepared and published the *National Strategy for Homeland Security* to mobilize and organize the United States to secure its homeland from terrorist attacks. The objectives of the strategy are to prevent terrorist attacks against the United States, to reduce America's vulnerability to terrorism, and to minimize the damage and recover from attacks that do occur. The strategy provides direction to the federal government departments and agencies that have a role in homeland security and suggests steps that state and local governments, private companies and organizations, and individual Americans can take to improve our security.[2]

According to Jonathan R. White, professor of criminal justice and executive director of the Homeland Defense Initiative at Grand Valley State University in Grand Rapids, Michigan,

> America has no common definition of homeland security. Issues surrounding homeland security are confused because the country is dealing with a new concept, a new meaning of conflict, and a change in the procedures used to defend the United States. In the past, military forces protected the homeland, projecting power beyond U.S. borders.[3]

White, however, explains that *homeland security* simply means keeping the country safe. It protects lives, property, and infrastructure and is designed to secure the United States.[4]

homeland security Efforts made since the terrorist acts of September 11, 2001, to protect the United States against terrorist acts.

The events of September 11, 2001, were an unprecedented challenge to the rescue personnel who responded. They tried to restore some order and calm, despite their own physical and emotional responses to viewing the tragedy and its effects up close.

Terrorism

Terrorism has many definitions. The Federal Bureau of Investigation (FBI) defines **terrorism** as "the unlawful use of force or violence against persons or property to intimidate or coerce a government, the civilian population, or a segment thereof, in furtherance of political or social objectives." The U.S. Defense Department defines it as "the unlawful use or threatened use of force or violence against individuals or property to coerce or intimidate governments or societies, often to achieve political, religious, or ideological objectives."[5] Jonathan R. White sums up terrorism simply: "Terrorism uses violence or threatened violence against innocent people to achieve a social or political goal."[6] The National Counterterrorism Center defines terrorism as "premeditated, politically motivated violence perpetrated against noncombatant targets by subnational groups or clandestine agents."[7]

Terrorism has a long tradition in world history. Terrorist tactics have been used frequently by radical and criminal groups to influence public opinion and to attempt to force authorities to do their will. Terrorists have criminal, political, and other nefarious motives. Some may remember the 1972 Olympic Games in Munich, Germany, when terrorists attacked and took hostage the Israeli Olympic team and killed all of them; the 1988 explosion of Flight 103 in the air over Lockerbie, Scotland, killing all 270 persons aboard; and the actions of the Unabomber.

Many Americans and most major U.S. firms have been targeted by terrorists in some way. Political extremists and terrorists use the violence and suspense of terrorist acts such as bombing, kidnapping, and hostage situations to put pressure on those in authority to comply with their demands and cause the authorities and public to recognize their power. Extremists and terrorists use their activities to obtain money for their causes, to alter business or government policies, or to change public opinion. Attacks against executives are common in Latin America, the Middle East, and Europe, and they have spread to the United States. Successful terrorist techniques employed in one country have spread to others. Governments and corporations have had to develop extensive plans to deal with terrorism.

According to Louis J. Freeh, former director of the FBI,

> Terrorists are among the most ruthless of criminals, but their motivation rarely stems from personal need or a desire for material gain. Unlike the majority of violent criminals, terrorists do not know their victims; in fact, one of the hallmarks of terrorism is its indiscriminate victimization. Also, unlike most serious criminal activity, terrorism invites—and even depends upon—media attention to ensure a maximum yield of terror.[8]

The **National Counterterrorism Center (NCTC)** was created in 2004, under the Intelligence Reform and Terrorism Prevention Act (IRTPA), to

terrorism Premeditated, politically motivated violence perpetrated against noncombatant targets.

National Counterterrorism Center (NCTC) The National Counterterrorism Center was created in 2004, under the Intelligence Reform and Terrorism Prevention Act (IRTPA), to serve as the primary organization in the U.S. government for integrating and analyzing all intelligence pertaining to terrorism and counterterrorism and for conducting strategic operational planning by integrating all instruments of national power.

serve as the primary organization in the U.S. government for integrating and analyzing all intelligence pertaining to terrorism and counterterrorism and for conducting strategic operational planning by integrating all instruments of national power. The NCTC has the statutory mission to serve as the U.S. government's knowledge bank on international terrorism and to provide the Department of State with required statistical information. It is under the administrative control of the Office of the Director of National Intelligence (DNI).[9]

The NCTC reported that there were over 10,000 terrorist attacks worldwide in 2011 that resulted in more than 12,500 deaths. These attacks were almost a 12 percent decrease from 2010 and nearly a 29 percent decrease from 2007.[10]

International Terrorism

According to John F. Lewis, Jr., retired assistant director of the FBI's National Security Division, the FBI divides the current international threat to the United States into three categories.[11]

First, there are threats from foreign sponsors of international terrorism. These sponsors view terrorism as a tool of foreign policy. Their activities have changed over time. Past activities included direct terrorist support and operations by official state agents. Now these sponsors generally seek to conceal their support of terrorism by relying on surrogates to conduct operations. State sponsors remain involved in terrorist activities by funding, organizing, networking, and providing other support and instruction to formal terrorist groups and loosely affiliated extremists.

Second, according to Lewis, there are threats from formalized terrorist groups, such as al-Qaeda, the Lebanese Hezbollah, Egyptian al-Gama'a al-Islamiyya, and the Palestinian Hamas. These autonomous organizations have their own infrastructures, personnel, financial arrangements, and training facilities. They can plan and mount terrorist campaigns overseas as well as support terrorist operations inside the United States. Some groups use supporters in the United States to plan and coordinate acts of terrorism. In the past, these formalized terrorist groups engaged in such criminal activities in the United States as illegally acquiring weapons, violating U.S. immigration laws, and providing safe havens to fugitives.[12]

Third, there are threats from loosely affiliated international radical extremists, such as those who attacked the World Trade Center in 1995. These extremists do not represent a particular nation. Loosely affiliated extremists may pose the most urgent threat to the United States at this time because they remain relatively unknown to law enforcement. They can travel freely, obtain a variety of identities, and recruit like-minded sympathizers from various countries.[13]

In 2005, the DHS reported that the threat of countries facilitating or supporting terrorism had diminished. It said that ideologically driven actors, particularly al-Qaeda, are the top terrorist threat against the United States today. The DHS also named several visual symbols such as the White House and the Statue of Liberty as the most likely targets of terrorism, and truck bombs and small explosives-laden boats as the most likely terrorism weapons.[14]

Many cases of international terrorism have involved the United States, primarily by targeting U.S. citizens and interests abroad. Some memorable attacks in addition to those mentioned earlier include the abduction of hostages in Lebanon in the mid-1980s; the 1996 detonation of an explosive device outside the Khobar Towers in Dhahran, Saudi Arabia, in which 10 U.S. military personnel were killed; the 1998 bombings of the U.S. embassies in Nairobi, Kenya, and Dares Salaam, Tanzania,

YOU ARE THERE

Fazul Abdullah Mohammed Killed in Somalia

The mastermind of the 1998 U.S. Embassy bombings in Tanzania and Kenya, Fazul Abdullah Mohammed, was killed in Somalia. Mohammed was considered the longest-serving and most senior al-Qaeda operative in East Africa.

Fazul Abdullah Mohammed had been instrumental in bringing the extremist al-Shabab groups in Somalia into the al-Qaeda fold as well as attracting other militant groups from Africa. Counterterrorism chief advisor Brennan said that Mohammed's death was a "huge setback" for al-Qaeda.

Source: Based on Brian Bennett, "Al-Qaeda Operative Key to 1998 U.S. Embassy Bombings Killed in Somalia", June 12, 2011, retrieved June 13, 2011, www.latimes.com/news/nationworl/world/la-fg-embassy-bombings-20110612,0,10.

which resulted in the deaths of 12 Americans and 200 others; the terrorist attack on the U.S.S. *Cole* in the waters of Aden, which killed 19 U.S. sailors; and the abduction and subsequent murder of *Wall Street Journal* journalist Daniel Pearl in 2002. Before the September 11, 2001, attack, the most recent case of international terrorism occurring on our shores was on February 26, 1993, when foreign terrorists bombed the World Trade Center.

Foreign terrorism has continued since 9/11. Nearly every day, terrorist acts occur in many parts of the world, including Iraq, Afghanistan, and Israel. In 2002, terrorist nightclub bombings in Bali, Indonesia, killed more than 200 people. The Indonesian capital of Jakarta was targeted by suicide bombings during 2003 and 2004.[15] In 2004, Russia lost at least 425 people in terrorist attacks, including a bombing at a Moscow subway station, two bombed passenger jets, and a massacre at an elementary school in which 32 terrorists seized the school, taking more than 1,000 hostages.[16] Also in 2004, terrorist attacks on commuter trains in Madrid, Spain, killed hundreds.

On July 7, 2005, during rush hour, a series of at least six explosions occurred on the London transportation network, including five attacks on the underground system and one on a bus in the city's center, causing 56 deaths and more than 700 injuries. This was London's worst attack since World War II. The incidents took place on the day after it was announced that the 2012 Olympic summer games were awarded to London. The attack also coincided with a meeting of the leaders of the G8 (major officials from eight highly industrialized nations) at Gleneagles, Scotland.[17] Four suspects were arrested within a week; all were British citizens, three British-born and one Jamaican-born, and all were Islamic fanatics. Three lived in Leeds, an industrial city in Northern England.[18] A few weeks later, four bombs went off almost simultaneously on London undergrounds trains and a bus again, but only the detonators blew up.[19]

Subsequent to the London bombings, three bombings in the Egyptian resort town of Sharm el-Sheikh, a vacationing hot spot for Europeans, Israelis, and Arabs, killed at least 88 and wounded more than 200.[20] Also in 2005, three suicide bombers wearing explosive vests blew themselves up in three crowded restaurants in the tourist resort of Bali, Indonesia, killing about 25 people and wounding 101 others.

In April 2006, suicide bombers killed 24 persons and wounded 100 at a Sinai resort.[21] In June 2006, Canadian police charged 12 men and 5 youths with planning a wave of terrorist attacks, ranging from blowing up the Toronto Stock Exchange to storming the national public broadcaster and Parliament buildings in Ottawa and beheading the prime minister.[22] Also in June 2006, 6 men were arrested in Miami and 1 in Atlanta for plotting to destroy Chicago's Sears Tower. The arrest was the result of an FBI sting involving an informant who posed as an al-Qaeda operative.[23] In July 2006, about 190 persons were killed and about 600 were injured when bombs exploded on seven commuter trains during the evening rush hour in Mumbai, India. A few days earlier, a series of grenade explosions struck Srinagar, the summer capital of Indian-administered Kashmir, hitting a tourist bus and killing 8 persons and wounding more than 40.[24] Also in 2006, extreme violence was reported in Somalia by Islamist militias operating under an umbrella group calling itself the Council of Islamic Courts.[25]

In August 2006, British authorities arrested 24 extremists who planned to use liquid explosives to blow up airplanes flying from Britain to the United States. The men were planning to carry the liquids in drink bottles and combine them into explosive cocktails to commit mass murder aboard as many as 10 flights over the Atlantic. The arrests caused massive alerts at airports and new rules regarding what could be brought aboard a plane.[26]

In June 2007, bungled terrorist attacks occurred in London and Glasgow, Scotland. In the London incident, two terrorists parked two vehicles laden with gas canisters and explosives near a popular nightclub. The cars, apparently positioned to strike people leaving the nightclub, failed to ignite. The next day, the two terrorists rammed a Jeep Cherokee loaded with gas canisters into the Glasgow airport. The vehicle erupted in flames; the driver was severely burned and died several weeks later.[27]

In December 2007, twin car bombs exploded in Algiers near United Nations offices and an Algerian government building, killing dozens of people.[28] Also in December 2007, Benazir Bhutto, former Pakistan prime minister and the leader of Pakistan's largest political party, was assassinated in a terrorist attack in Rawalpindi, Pakistan, as she left a political rally. A suicide attacker detonated a bomb, damaging one of the cars in Bhutto's motorcade, killing more than 20 people, and wounding 50. Just two months earlier, in October 2007, Bhutto had survived a suicide bombing that killed 150 people in Karachi, Pakistan.[29]

In March 2008, Pakistani police formally accused militant leader Baitullah Mehsud of planning Bhutto's assassination. Mehsud was the leader of the Tehrik-e-Taliban, an umbrella movement of Pakistani Taliban groups.[30] Terrorist attacks and attempts have continued in Pakistan since the 2007 assassination of Benazir Bhutto; hundreds of people have been killed by terrorists, mostly in suicide bombings.[31]

Terrorist attacks have continued in other countries as well. In February 2008, a suicide bomber blew himself up in a large crowd just outside the city of Kandahar, Afghanistan, killing more than 100 people and wounding more than 90 others in the country's worst single bombing since 2001.[32] On November 26, 2008, in Mumbai, India, at least 170 people were killed and several hundred injured in a series of well-coordinated attacks by a terrorist group at two five-star hotels, the city's largest train station, a Jewish center, a movie theater, and a hospital.[33] Mumbai was targeted again in July 2011 when a rush-hour triple bombing killed 18 people. In a statement released through the media, Prime Minister Manmohan Singh said, "I understand the shock and outrage of the people of Mumbai. I share their pain, anguish and anger."[34]

In September 2009, authorities arrested Najibullah Zazi and others for an al-Qaeda plot to detonate a bomb in the New York City subways. Zazi, an Afghan immigrant, pled guilty in February 2010 to what authorities described as one of the most serious threats to the United States since 9/11.[35]

On Christmas Day in 2009, in another al-Qaeda attempted attack, Umar Farouk Abdulmutallab, a Nigerian, was arrested aboard a Northwest Airlines aircraft on its final approach to Detroit Metropolitan Airport for placing a destructive device on the aircraft. Interviews of the passengers and crew revealed that prior to the incident, Abdulmutallab went to the bathroom for about 20 minutes. Upon returning to his seat, he stated

that his stomach was upset and pulled a blanket over himself. Passengers then heard popping noises similar to firecrackers, smelled an odor, and observed his pants leg and the wall of the airplane on fire. Passengers and crew subdued Abdulmutallab and used blankets and fire extinguishers to put out the flames. It was revealed later that the U.S. intelligence community had early signals of the terrorist plot but, curiously, ignored them.[36] In January 2010, President Barack Obama ordered intelligence agencies to take a series of steps to streamline how terrorism threats are pursued and analyzed, saying the government had to respond aggressively to the failures that allowed Abdulmutallab to ignite his explosive.[37]

In March 2010, huge explosions during the morning rush hour in two subway stations in central Moscow killed more than 33 people and injured hundreds. The investigation revealed that the bombings were attributed to two young women, "black widow" suicide bombers, who were linked with the Islamist underground in the North Caucasus.[38]

In July 2011, a single individual bombed the government center in Oslo, Norway, killing 7 people, and then went to an island summer camp for young members of the Labor Party and killed at least 80 more people. This was the deadliest attack on Norwegian soil since World War II. Acting Police Chief Sveinung Sponheim said the suspect had written Internet postings that suggested he had "some political traits directed toward the right, and anti-Muslin views." The suspect, a 32-year-old Norwegian identified as Anders Behring Breivik, had posted on his Twitter account that "one person with a belief is equal to the force of 100,000 who have only interests."[39]

One significant concern that falls under the umbrella of terrorism is bioterrorism or **biological weapons**. The anthrax attacks of 2001 caused numerous deaths and sicknesses, as well as significant panic in our nation. Mailed letters containing alleged anthrax paralyzed the nation's postal system and forced the government to spend billions to install sophisticated detection equipment at postal centers throughout the country.

Four types of biological agents can be weaponized: natural poisons or toxins that occur without human modification, viruses, bacteria, and plagues. The Centers for Disease Control and Prevention (CDC) classify the most threatening agents as smallpox, anthrax, plague, botulism, tularemia,

---

biological weapons Weapons made from live bacterial, viral, or other microorganisms.

and hemorrhagic fever. Smallpox is a deadly contagious virus. Anthrax is a noncontagious bacterial infection, while plague is transmitted by insects. Botulism is a food-borne illness. Hemorrhagic fevers are caused by viruses. One of the best-known hemorrhagic fevers is the Ebola virus.[40]

The U.S. General Accountability Office (GAO) reported in 2004 that the CDC, learning from the anthrax incidents, had developed databases and expertise on biological agents likely to be used in a terrorist attack.[41] In 2004, the president signed a bill creating Project BioShield to help the United States purchase, develop, and deploy cutting-edge defenses against biological weapons attacks. The bill authorized the expenditure of $5.6 billion over 10 years for the government to purchase and stockpile vaccines and drugs to fight anthrax, smallpox, and other potential agents of bioterror. Project BioShield also purchased 75 million doses of an improved anthrax vaccine for the Strategic National Stockpile.[42]

Fortunately, a major drawback in the use of biological weapons is that they cannot be controlled. This means, for example, that if terrorists were to release a weaponized strain of smallpox, the disease might spread to the terrorist group and its allies.[43]

Involvement in Major Incidents

ON THE JOB

I have always felt it is important for everyone in law enforcement to be aware of what is going on in their jurisdiction as well as nationally—to know about crime trends, unusual incidents, investigations, and court rulings.

I was no longer working for the police department when the attacks of September 11, 2001, occurred. Like everyone, I was glued to the TV, and we discussed it quite a bit in class. When the anthrax threat occurred several weeks later and we didn't know whether there was a relationship or not, again I watched events unfold.

The anthrax incidents held particular interest because the American Media building is located in Boca Raton, where I was teaching. When an employee died, another went to the hospital, and almost 1,000 lined up in the hot sun at the Health Department to obtain testing and precautionary antibiotics, I also looked at the situation as a former police administrator in that city.

The logistics and cost to the agency to serve in this highly unusual and unexpected situation created a challenge that agency personnel had to meet quickly. Securing the building 24 hours a day, documenting who came and went, interviewing employees, conferencing with other emergency response personnel and federal agencies, maintaining order among the anxious employees waiting for testing in the hot and humid conditions, collating information, and disseminating that information to a demanding press and a concerned public would tax their resources to the maximum. The city still required protection, but clearly all sworn personnel suspended their normal activities except those of an emergency nature. The calls for service were also increased with citizens bringing in "suspicious" packages and substances as well as calling in information regarding "suspicious" individuals who might be accomplices to the terrorists, some of whom had been living in the South Florida area.

These demands required the administration to reassign personnel, change schedules, examine vehicle demands, devise procedures for handling the suspicious substances, define roles among the multiple investigatory agencies, establish procedures for handling the American media scene, and clarify and disseminate information regarding the health risks to the public. These demands lasted quite a while, and though they eventually deescalated, the unusual level of activity continued. As the emergency nature of the situation slowly decreased, concern about paying for all these services did not.

It was exciting to watch the coverage and see friends and former coworkers being interviewed, giving press conferences, and walking around at the scene. It would have been an exciting and challenging time to be on the Boca Raton Police Department.

—Linda Forst

YOU ARE THERE

Some Major International Terrorism Cases Affecting the United States

1993 World Trade Center Attack

Six people were killed and more than 1,000 injured in the blast on February 26, 1993, in New York City. In 1994, four men were convicted of bombing the World Trade Center. Abdel Rahman, also known as Omar Ahmad Ali Abdel Rahman, a blind Egyptian religious leader, was charged with being one of the planners of the bombing conspiracy and leading a terrorist organization that sprang up in the United States in 1989. Investigators say he also participated in conversations involving the planned bombing of the United Nations building and the assassination of Egyptian President Hosni Mubarak. Rahman and 11 others were convicted in federal court on charges of trying to assassinate political leaders and bomb major New York City landmarks. In 1995, another man, Ramzi Ahmed Yousef, was arrested as the main plotter behind the World Trade Center bombing.

U.S. Embassy bombings

On August 7, 1998, simultaneous bombings occurred in the U.S. embassies in Dares Salaam, Tanzania, and Nairobi, Kenya. These attacks killed more than 200 people, including 20 Americans. Osama bin Laden—who also used the aliases of Usama bin Muhammad bin Ladin, Shaykh Usama bin Ladin, the Prince, the Emir, Abu Abdallah, Mujahid Shaykh, Hajj, and the Director—was wanted by the FBI in connection with these bombings.

Millennium Bomb Plot

On December 14, 1999, as the world was preparing to celebrate the year 2000 millennium, an Algerian terrorist attempted to enter the United States from Canada with the intention of setting off a bomb at the Los Angeles International Airport during the celebrations. The would-be bomber, Ahmed Ressam, was arrested at the border near Seattle with a trunk full of explosives. The FBI started a sweeping search for other suspects and information about the plot. Investigators developed information that the plot was linked to a worldwide network of terrorists orchestrated by Osama bin Laden. Ressam was convicted and sentenced to prison in May 2000.

In July 2001, an Algerian-born shopkeeper, Mokhtar Haouari, age 32, who ran a gift shop in Montreal and as a sideline dealt in false identification documents and check and credit card scams, was also convicted in the conspiracy. A third suspect, Abdel Ghani Meskini, offered testimony against the other plotters in exchange for a reduced sentence. The suspects said they were trained in guerrilla camps in Afghanistan that were run by bin Laden.

Bombing of the U.S.S. *Cole*

On October 12, 2000, two suicide bombers attacked the U.S. destroyer *Cole* in the waters off Aden, killing 17 American sailors. The FBI linked the bombing once again to Osama bin Laden, the fugitive Saudi, who had declared a worldwide "holy war" against the United States. Six men were arrested soon after the bombing.

© 2016 Cengage Learning®

Domestic Terrorism

According to Lewis, **domestic terrorism** involves groups or individuals who operate without foreign direction entirely within the United States and target elements of the U.S. government or citizens. He states that the 1995 federal building explosion in Oklahoma City and the pipe bomb explosion in Centennial Olympic Park during the 1996 Summer Olympic Games underscore the ever-present threat that exists from U.S. residents determined to use violence to advance their agendas.[44]

Lewis reports that domestic terrorist groups today represent extreme right-wing, extreme left-wing, and special-interest beliefs. The main themes espoused today by extremist right-wing groups are conspiracies having to do with the New World Order, gun control laws, and white supremacy. Many of these extremist groups also advocate

domestic terrorism   Terrorism committed by citizens of the United States in the United States.

The Hunt for Bin Laden

After 9/11, Osama bin Laden was Public Enemy No. 1 for all in law enforcement and the military. Every effort was expended to either capture or kill bin Laden. In May 2011, U.S. Navy Seals infiltrated Pakistan in four helicopters and entered a secure compound 35 miles from the Pakistani capital. A short gunfight took place and five people were killed, among them bin Laden.

Osama bin Laden was found on the third floor of his house and was shot while resisting capture. One of his wives identified the body, and later DNA analysis provided 99.9 percent confirmation. Bin Laden's body was transported back to the carrier U.S.S. *Carl Vinson* and buried at sea in a weighted bag. The 10-year hunt for bin Laden was over.

Source: Based on Mark Mazzetti, Helene Cooper, and Peter Baker, "Behind the Hunt for Bin Laden," May 2, 2011, retrieved May 4, 2011, from www.nytimes.com/2011/05/03/.world/asia/03intel.html.

antigovernment, antitaxation, or antiabortion sentiments and engage in survivalist training, with their goal to ensure the perpetuation of the United States as a white, Christian nation.

The Nationwide Suspicious Activity Reporting (SAR) Initiative (NSI) established a national capacity for gathering, documenting, processing, analyzing, and sharing information on suspicious activities. The Office of Justice Program's (OJP) Bureau of Justice Assistance (BJA) runs the NSI Program Management Office (PMO) to facilitate implementation of NSI at all levels of the government. The PMO assists agencies with adopting consistent processes, policies, and standards, while ensuring that privacy rights and civil liberties are protected.[45]

In November 2009, a self-radicalized U.S. Army psychiatrist, Major Nidal Malik Hasan, facing deployment to one of America's war zones, killed 13 people and wounded 30 others in a shooting rampage with two handguns at the huge Fort Hood Army post in central Texas. Fort Hood is about 100 miles south of Dallas–Fort Worth and is the largest active duty military post in the United Sates. Hasan, who had been in the Army since 1995, sprayed his bullets inside a crowded medical processing center

for soldiers returning from or about to be sent overseas. Sergeant Kimberly Denise Munley, a civilian police officer at Fort Hood, interrupted the attack and shot Hasan four times. She was wounded herself in an exchange of gunfire with him.[46] Hasan, who is currently undergoing court-martial, is said to have shown signs of mental instability prior to the shootings but was also allegedly influenced by the writings of Anwar al-Awlaki, a U.S.-born al-Qaeda leader.[47] After a two-year manhunt, Anwar al-Awlaki was killed in a village in southwestern Yemen. Unmanned, armed drones were able to target al-Awlaki while he was driving in Yemen. The missiles launched from a drone killed al-Awlaki and Samir Khan, the editor of the al-Qaeda English-language online magazine *Inspire*.[48]

Domestic terrorism was also responsible for the bombing in Centennial Olympic Park at the Atlanta Olympics Games on July 27, 1996. The media reported that the FBI originally suspected security guard Richard A. Jewell of complicity in the bombing, but the FBI later indicated there was no evidence that he had any criminal part in it. In June 1997, an FBI task force linked the Olympic bombing to the 1997 bombings at the Sandy Springs Professional Building (housing the Atlanta Northside Family Planning Services clinic, an abortion clinic) and an Atlanta lesbian nightclub.[49]

The FBI determined the primary suspect in the Atlanta bombings to be Eric Rudolph. Rudolph was arrested in 2003, after hiding in the mountains of North Carolina for five years. He had defeated all efforts to find him and was found not by an elite squad but by a rookie police officer in Murphy, North Carolina. The concern of the government is that it is doubtful that Rudolph was able to survive and hide in the wilderness unaided for five years; it is believed that he had help, illustrating, at the very least, that sympathy and support for some domestic terrorist groups does exist.[50]

One particularly troubling element of rightwing extremism is the militia, or patriot, movement. Militia members want to remove federal involvement from various issues. They generally are lawabiding citizens who have become intolerant of what they perceive as violations of their constitutional rights. Membership in a militia organization is not entirely illegal in the United States, but certain states have legislated limits on militias, including on the types of training (for example, paramilitary training) that they can offer. The FBI bases its interest in the militia movement on the risk of violence or the potential for violence and criminal activity.

Experts have traced the growth of the militia movement partly to the effective use of modern communication mediums. Videos, Internet forums, and other online platforms have been used with great effectiveness by militia sympathizers. Pro-militia networks disseminate material from well-known hate group figures and conspiracy theorists. Organizers can promote their ideologies at militia meetings, patriot rallies, and gatherings of various other groups espousing antigovernment sentiments.

FBI Special Agents James E. Duffy and Alan C. Brantley give us this profile of the typical militia member:

> Most militia organization members are white males who range in age from the early 20s to the mid-50s. The majority of militia members appear to be attracted to the movement because of gun control issues. . . . Militia members generally maintain strong Christian beliefs and justify their actions by claiming to be ardent defenders of the Constitution.[51]

In March 2010, nine suspects tied to a Christian militia were charged with conspiring to kill an unidentified local police officer, and then attack a police funeral in the hopes of killing more law enforcement personnel who would come to the funeral. Members of the group Hutaree, based about 70 miles southwest of Detroit, were charged in the case, including their leader, David Brian Stone, also known as Captain Hutaree. Stone and his wife made no secret about the fact that they were part of a militia. They frequently let visitors in military fatigues erect tents in front of their trailer home, and the sound of gunfire was routine. According to investigators, the Hutaree view local, state, and federal law enforcement as an enemy, and they planned to attack them as part of an armed struggle against the U.S. government. An undercover federal agent attended training exercises with the Hutaree militia for at least eight months before the arrest. The charges followed FBI raids on locations in Michigan, Ohio, and Indiana.[52]

Terrorism experts have reported that the number of paramilitary militia groups in the United States dwindled substantially after the Oklahoma City bombing in 1995 because of public backlash and intense pressure from law enforcement. They say, however, that the terrorism threat posed by

YOU ARE THERE — The Ohio Defense Force

The Ohio Defense Force is a private militia claiming more than 300 members who train all year for ambushes, sniper missions, close-quarters battle, and other infantry staples. The unit motto is "Today's Minutemen," and they have conducted practice and training around the abandoned Roseville State Prison near Zanesville, Ohio.

In 2010, the group claimed that one exercise was designed against an "enemy" identified as an Islamic army that had traveled through the United States unchecked on orders from the president, but the exercise looked more like it was designed to combat the Bureau of Alcohol, Tobacco, Firearms and Explosives (ATF). Brian Vandersall, who designed the exercise, said, "I don't know who the redcoats are. It could be U.N. troops. It could be federal troops. It could be Blackwater, which was used in Katrina. It could be Mexican troops who are crossing the border." In any case, Vandersall said, "Whoever they are, we have to be ready."

Source: Based on Barton Gellman, "Locked and Loaded: The Secret World of Extreme Militias," September 30, 2010, retrieved September 30, 2010, from www.time.com/time/printout/0,8816,2022516,00.html.

individual "lone wolf" extremists has remained strong, and that far-left environmental and animal rights groups also pose a serious threat.[53]

Another domestic terrorist movement is the "sovereign citizen" movement. Sovereign citizens are antigovernment extremists who believe that even though they physically reside in the United States, they are separate or "sovereign" from the country. As a result, they believe they do not have to answer to any government authority, including courts, taxing entities, motor vehicle departments, or law enforcement. According to the FBI, the sovereign citizens commit murder and physical assault; threaten judges, law enforcement professionals, and government personnel; impersonate police officers and diplomats; use fake currency, passports, license plates, and driver's licenses; and engineer various white-collar scams, including mortgage fraud.[54]

While not all sovereign citizens commit crimes of violence, in August 2013 the Las Vegas Metro Police Department (LVMPD) arrested two sovereigns, David Allan Brutsche and Devon Campbell Newman, on charges of attempted murder and conspiracy to commit murder. Brutsche and Campbell had met with undercover LVMPD officers over several months, expressing their hatred for law enforcement and describing how they wanted to kidnap cops from traffic stops, arrest them, try them in their court, and then kill them. Brutsche said he had the right to "stop cops by killing them because we as the people are kings and cops are servants."[55]

Left-wing extremist groups represent another domestic terrorism threat. Generally these groups profess a revolutionary socialist doctrine and view themselves as protectors of the American people against capitalism and imperialism. They aim to change the nation through revolutionary means rather than by participating in the regular political and social process. During the 1970s, leftist-oriented extremist groups posed the predominant domestic terrorist threat in the United States. Beginning in the 1980s, however, the FBI dismantled many of these groups by arresting key members for their criminal activities. The transformation of the former Soviet Union also deprived many leftist groups of a coherent ideology or spiritual patron. As a result, membership and support for these groups have declined.

Special-interest terrorist groups are also domestic threats. They differ from both extreme left-wing and right-wing terrorist groups because their members seek to resolve specific interests rather than pursue widespread political change. Members of such groups include animal rights advocates, supporters of environmental issues, and antiabortion advocates. Although some consider the causes that these groups represent understandable or even worthy, the groups remain separated from traditional law-abiding special-interest groups because of their criminal activity.

Groups such as the Animal Liberation Front (ALF) and the Earth Liberation Front (ELF) have used violent actions to attempt to force various segments of society, including the general public, to change their attitudes about issues they consider important. These groups have released caged animals into the wild, targeted buildings where experimentation on animals has been conducted, damaged vehicles they feel are not environmentally friendly, and burned down new residential communities. In 1998, ELF members were linked to the destruction of the Vail Ski Resort in Colorado, a fire that caused $12 million in damage. ELF members were

"Justice Department" Makes Threats Against UCLA Animal Researcher

A group called the "Justice Department," an offshoot of the Animal Liberation Front (ALF), sent a package containing razor blades to David Jentsch, an animal researcher at UCLA. This was a clear attempt to intimidate Jentsch.

Jentsch is a frequent target of animal rights groups due to his research work using primates. A cofounder of the North American Animal Liberation Press Office, Jerry Vlasak, said Jentsch has "made himself an even bigger target" by saying he will continue "torturing" animals in his research. Jentsch had his car fire-bombed in March 2009 while parked in the driveway of his home. He has also been the target of regular harassment and demonstrations outside his home.

The "Justice Department" has also claimed responsibility for mailing needles covered with rat poison to two primate researchers at Wake Forest University in North Carolina, and razor blades covered with rat poison to at least one other primate researcher at UCLA.

Source: Based on "'Justice Department' Claims Responsibility for Threats Against UCLA Animal Researcher," December 3, 2010, retrieved on April 4, 2012, from www.adl.org/learn/extremism_in_america_updates/movements/ecoterrorism/justice_department_ucla.htm.

also charged with firebombing the University of Washington's Center for Urban Horticulture in 2001.[56] In August 2003, several car dealerships in Southern California were targeted by ELF members who burned dozens of SUVs, as well as an auto dealership warehouse, and spray-painted vehicles with sayings such as "Fat, Lazy Americans." ELF has claimed responsibility for many arsons against commercial establishments that ELF members say damage the environment.[57]

In December 2005, federal agents made the most extensive arrest of eco-saboteurs in U.S. history, charging seven people with a series of arsons and vandalism that plagued the Pacific Northwest for nearly three years. Agents took six men and one woman into custody from Oregon to New York, tying them to nearly $5 million in arson and vandalism damage from 1998 to 2001. Several were members of ELF and ALF. Agents used a provision of the USA Patriot Act to close in on them by getting search warrants from a U.S. magistrate in Oregon to search in other states for evidence.[58] In 2008, ELF was linked to fires that gutted five multimillion-dollar model homes in Seattle, Washington, that were marketed as "built green."[59]

Researchers presenting at the annual meeting of the American Association for the Advancement of Science in February 2008 reported that, while most people in the United States focus on foreign-based radical groups when thinking about terrorism, it is actually domestic extremists committing violence in the name of their cause that account for most of the damage from terrorist incidents in the United States. The researchers stated that these homegrown groups are seven times more likely than overseas groups to commit some kind of violence in the nation.[60]

Radical, extremist, and hate groups have long presented a serious problem to society. Throughout a major part of our history, the Ku Klux Klan terrorized and killed thousands of citizens. In the 1960s and 1970s, radical hate groups, such as the Black Panthers and the Black Liberation Army, raged urban warfare against the police, maiming and killing scores of police officers. Also during that period of our history, militant student and antiwar groups caused tremendous problems for the police. Historically, radical groups have been involved in assassinations, bombings, terrorism, and other crimes and acts of violence to protest the policies of the United States and to attempt to impose their views on all members of our society.

One noted extremist group was the Branch Davidians. A 51-day siege of the Branch Davidian compound in Waco, Texas, ended in April 1993 when 80 members of the sect died after a fire and a shootout with police and federal agents. David Koresh, leader of the group, died of a gunshot wound to the head sometime during the blaze. The FBI's actions in Waco prompted much criticism. Another controversial action against an extremist group occurred in 1992 when U.S. Marshals tried to arrest white separatist Randall C. Weaver on firearms charges. During the resulting siege in Ruby Ridge, Idaho, Weaver's unarmed wife, Vicki, and his 14-year-old son, Sammy (as well as U.S. Marshal William Degan), were killed. In 1995, the U.S. government, without admitting guilt in the case, agreed to pay $3.1 million to Weaver and his

three surviving children.[61] One news source stated, "Like Waco, Ruby Ridge long ago entered the political mythology of the ultraright. Like Waco, it attests to the emergence of a reckless mentality that sullies the image of the FBI and plays straight into the hands of those who like to demagogue the federal government."[62]

Anarchists also have been operating in the United States protesting global and trade issues. Some of their members advocate violence and destruction of property and travel to trade meetings with the goal of disrupting the meetings and causing chaos and destruction in the streets.

An example of a "lone wolf" (an individual who operates alone without ties to any group) extremist is Jared Loughner who, in January 2011, gunned down U.S. Representative Gabrielle Giffords and at least 17 others in Arizona. Six of the victims died, including U.S. District Court (Arizona) Chief Judge John M. Roll and a nine-year-old girl.[63] In a search of Loughner's home, the FBI recovered evidence from his safe indicating that Loughner had planned an assassination attempt specifically targeted on Giffords and that it was not the work of an extremist group.[64]

Recently, attention has focused on homegrown terrorists who reflect violent Islamic extremism. In 2007, Willie T. Hulon, the executive assistant director of the National Security Branch of the FBI, after acknowledging that al-Qaeda has been the driving force of terrorism for the past decade, wrote that he has increasingly seen the emergence of individuals and groups that will carry out attacks on their own soil:

> Homegrown terrorists or extremists, acting in concert with other like-minded individuals or as lone wolves, have become one of the gravest domestic threats we face. Largely self-recruited and self-trained, these terrorists may have no direct connection to al-Qaeda or other terrorist groups.[65]

A 2007 article by Carol Dyer, Ryan E. McCoy, and Joel Rodriquez, intelligence analysts in the FBI's Counterterrorism Division, and Donald N. Van Duyn, the deputy assistant director of the FBI's Counterterrorism Division, reflected on the disruption of recent terrorist plots in the United Kingdom, Canada, and the United States. In addition to the 2005 terrorist bombings in London, the authors reported that significant attention is now being

YOU ARE THERE

Some Major Domestic Terrorism Cases in the United States

Oklahoma City Federal Building

At 9:05 A.M. on April 19, 1995, an explosion occurred at the Alfred P. Murrah Federal Building in Oklahoma City. The bombing destroyed the structure, killed 168 people, and injured 675. Later that day, an Oklahoma state trooper arrested Timothy McVeigh on Interstate 35 for driving without license plates. Several days later, McVeigh was charged with the bombing. He was alleged to have links to white supremacist and patriot groups. McVeigh was convicted for his crimes in 1997 and executed in 2001.

Atlanta Olympic Games

On July 27, 1996, a bombing occurred in Centennial Olympic Park at the Atlanta Olympic Games; a woman was killed and 111 other people were injured. In June 1997, the FBI linked the Olympic bombing to the January 16, 1997, bombing at the Sandy Springs Professional Building, which housed the Atlanta Northside Family Planning Services clinic (a clinic that provided abortions) and the February 2, 1997, bombing of an Atlanta lesbian nightclub. The FBI claimed that letters mailed to the press by a militant religious cell known as the Army of God connected the group to the bombings.

After a five-year manhunt, Eric Robert Rudolph was arrested in the small town of Murphy, North Carolina, on May 31, 2003, by rookie police officer Jeff Postell. Rudolph was charged with these crimes, which killed and injured hundreds.

Sources: "FBI Ten Most Wanted Fugitives: Eric Robert Rudolph," retrieved from www.fbi.gov; Kevin Sack, "Officials Link Atlanta Bombings and Ask for Help," *New York Times*, June 10, 1997, p. A1; Jo Thomas, "McVeigh Guilty on All Counts in the Oklahoma City Bombing," *New York Times*, June 3, 1997, p. A1.

given to the concept of homegrown radicalization, particularly violent Islamic extremism. They stated that the exploitation of religion by Islamic extremists to use violence both overseas and at home is one of the gravest dangers facing the United States today.[66]

The authors of the article concluded that the Islamic radicalization of U.S. persons, foreign-born or native, increasingly concerns law enforcement leaders because of its potential to lead to violent action. The key to success in countering violent Islamic extremists, they wrote, lies in identifying patterns and trends of extremist behavior in its early stages. They argued that law enforcement professionals must convey that, as part of a fair and compassionate government, they also share the interests of communities and must respond aggressively to hate crimes and discrimination against any ethnic populations.

Methods of Investigating Terrorism

As with many types of investigations, there are two primary methods of investigating acts of terrorism: proactive and reactive. In addition, there is the federal–local Joint Terrorism Task Forces concept. These three methods together can help prevent and detect acts of terrorism before they occur or, when that is not possible, investigate their occurrences, determine who was involved in their commission, and bring the offenders to justice.[67]

Proactive Methods

Much of this chapter discusses proactive techniques that are constantly in use to prevent acts of terrorism before they occur. These methods include ongoing and coordinated planning, intelligence gathering, and investigating activity by various agencies. Despite all of the proactive efforts, however, terrorist events do occur; thus, reactive techniques must be employed as well.

Reactive Methods

Numerous reactive methods can be used to investigate acts of terrorism after they occur, including response to the incident, crime scene processing and analysis, following up on leads and tips, use of informants, surveillance, and other normal investigative activities.

RESPONSE TO THE INCIDENT The local law enforcement agency is usually the first responder to scenes of terrorist crimes—just as it is on any crime scene. These officers must follow the normal first-responder duties of rendering aid to the injured, arresting suspects, questioning witnesses, and other immediate response and investigatory issues. It is essential that they safeguard the scene and preserve the evidence for processing by laboratory personnel and arson and terrorist specialists. As with the crime of arson, much of the evidence is present in the debris that follows a terrorist explosion.

CRIME SCENE PROCESSING AND ANALYSIS

Crime scene specialists and trained personnel from the various federal, state, and local investigating units use their special skills to seek the means used to commit the crime and any evidence that might connect the crime to the persons responsible for it. As an example of the importance of crime scene processing and analysis, two small pieces of evidence were the keys to determining the cause of the Pan Am explosion over Lockerbie, Scotland. Investigators had painstakingly searched a crime scene of more than 845 square miles of debris to find this evidence.

How extensive are terrorist crime scenes? Consider the 2001 World Trade Center attack. When the jumbo jets crashed into the buildings,

several things occurred. First, the explosive force of the planes entering the buildings destroyed much of the immediate internal structure and the victims within. The planes, just refueled for their flights, contained thousands of pounds of fuel. The ensuing fireball, reaching incredibly high temperatures, incinerated all in its path. The fuel then worked its way down to lower floors, continuing its destruction. Shortly after the initial explosions, the weakened buildings, with some of their steel infrastructure actually melting in the intense heat, collapsed under the weight of the crumbling upper floors. The result: millions of pounds of crime scene material and evidence.

The crime scene investigation was extensive. The first concern of this investigation was to account for and identify as many victims as possible. But before any identifications could be made, the remains had to be recovered. This required the detailed sifting of all the debris and material collected from the crime scene. Sifting was also conducted during the examination of the Oklahoma City bombing incident.

After suspected human remains were recovered from the debris, determinations needed to be made

---

YOU ARE THERE

A Domestic Terrorist: The Unabomber

Thomas J. Mosser, an executive with the Young and Rubicam advertising firm in Manhattan, was killed by a mail bomb on December 10, 1994. The parcel had been mailed to his home. The explosion and Mosser's murder were attributed to the work of a serial bomber known as the Unabomber, who was believed to be responsible for 14 other bombings or attempted bombings beginning in 1978. The FBI reports that 2 people died and 23 others were injured in these explosions, which occurred over some 16 years, as this man terrorized his fellow American citizens.

The sequence of events related to the Unabomber is:

- A bomb exploded at Northwestern University in Illinois, May 25, 1978; a security guard was injured.

- A second person at Northwestern was injured on May 9, 1979, when a bomb exploded in the technical building.

- On American Airlines Flight 444 (Chicago to Boston), 12 persons suffered smoke inhalation injuries on November 15, 1979, when a bomb placed in a mailbag in the cargo bay failed to detonate.

- The president of United Airlines, Percy Wood, was injured by a bomb on June 10, 1980. The bomb was in a package mailed to his home.

- A bomb in a business classroom at the University of Utah exploded on October 8, 1981.

- At Vanderbilt University in Nashville, a secretary was injured on May 5, 1982, when a bomb mailed to the head of the computer science department exploded.

- Two people were injured, one seriously, at the University of California, Berkeley, as a result of bombings: an electrical engineering about their origin and identity. Efforts to identify recovered remains included such forensic disciplines as pathology, odontology, biology, and anthropology. For the most part, DNA was used to establish the identities of the deceased. Personal items found at the crime scene—such as jewelry and clothing—were also used for identification, but were considered presumptive in nature, because many of these items are not unique. Still, personal items provided investigators with some information on the identities of the missing.

FOLLOWING UP ON LEADS AND TIPS There must be canvasses and recanvasses, and interviews and reinterviews. Anyone with any information at all must be interviewed immediately. All leads must be followed through to their logical conclusions. Tip lines must be established and all tips must be followed up.

USE OF INFORMANTS Informants can be very important in the investigation of terrorist incidents. A good example of the value of an informant's information was the February 1995 arrest of Ramzi Ahmed Yousef, ranked at the time as number one on the FBI's Most Wanted List and believed to be the main plotter behind the 1993 World Trade Center bombing. Yousef was the target of an international manhunt spanning several countries and thousands of miles. He was located and arrested based on information provided by an unexpected informer who simply walked into the American Embassy in Islamabad, Pakistan. Authorities believed the informer was seeking to collect the $2 million reward that the U.S. State Department was offering for information resulting in Yousef's arrest. After receiving the informant's information, a team of Pakistani police and U.S. law enforcement officials was assembled and sent to the hotel room where Yousef was believed to be; the team broke down the door and rushed into the room and found Yousef lying on his bed, a suitcase of explosives nearby.[68]

SURVEILLANCE Surveillance is used in terrorist investigations to follow suspects identified as involved in the crime. Other methods of surveillance or information-gathering techniques also can be used for intelligence purposes. Flight recorders in aircraft cockpits provide investigators with

professor on July 2, 1982, and a student on May 15, 1985.

- Alert employees of the Boeing Company in Washington State had a bomb safely dismantled on May 18, 1985, when they realized a mailed package contained an explosive device.

- On November 15, 1985, the research assistant to a psychology professor at the University of Michigan at Ann Arbor was injured when a bomb received at the professor's home exploded.

- On December 11, 1985, Hugh Campbell, the owner of a computer rental store in Sacramento, California, was killed by a bomb left at his store.

- In Salt Lake City, another employee in the computer industry was maimed by a bomb placed in a bag in the company parking lot on February 20, 1987.

- A geneticist at the University of California at San Francisco sustained injuries when he opened a package received in the mail at his home on June 22, 1993.

- A computer scientist at Yale University opened a package mailed to his office and was injured by a bomb on June 24, 1993.

The FBI was certain that these bombings were related and attributable to one suspect, the Unabomber. The bombs were all built from similar materials and had a comparable, sophisticated design.

In 1996, based on a tip provided by his brother, Theodore Kaczynski was arrested and charged with all the Unabomber attacks. At trial, he was found guilty and sentenced to life imprisonment.

Source: John S. Dempsey, *An Introduction to Public and Private Investigations* (Minneapolis/St. Paul, Minn.: West, 1996), pp. 16–17.

a multitude of details about a hijacking. Security cameras in public locations provide details on a terrorist's actions. Timothy McVeigh's truck was recorded on a security camera, and terrorists involved in the September 11 attack were recorded on airport security systems. These types of surveillance systems are invaluable for the investigation of terrorist activities.

In 2011, New York City Mayor Michael Bloomberg said the New York City Police Department's surveillance had not unfairly targeted any group in an effort to root out possible terror connections. Bloomberg said, "I believe we should do what we have to do to keep us safe. And we have to be consistent with the Constitution and with people's rights."[69]

Post-9/11 Response to Terrorism and Homeland Defense

In the immediate aftermath of the 9/11 terrorist attacks, strict security procedures were instituted at airports, government buildings, cultural centers, and many other facilities. The FBI advised state and local law enforcement agencies to move to their highest level of alert and be prepared to respond to any further acts of terrorism. Armed National Guard troops supplemented airport security officers and local and state police in many jurisdictions. Military aircraft flew protective patrol over U.S. cities, and the Coast Guard patrolled coastlines and ports. Some other immediate responses included expanding the intelligence community's ability to intercept and translate messages in Arabic, Farsi, and other languages; fortification of cockpits to prevent access by hijackers; placing federal air marshals on commercial flights; and more intensive screening of luggage.

Approximately 4,000 FBI special agents were assigned to the 9/11 attacks case nationwide, and by early October, the FBI was handling more than a quarter million potential leads and tips. The FBI sent all law enforcement agencies a list of more than 190 witnesses, suspects, and others the agency wanted to interview, and in the two months following the attacks, the Justice Department arrested more than 1,000 people suspected of having links to terrorist groups.[70] The 9/11 terrorist acts were attributed to the multinational terrorist group al-Qaeda (Arabic for "the base") operated by Osama bin Laden, a known terrorist residing in Afghanistan, sheltered by the ruling Taliban government.

On October 7, 2001, the United States launched a full-scale military assault—a war—against Afghanistan, the Taliban and its allies, al-Qaeda, and Osama bin Laden. As a result of this military action, the Taliban government was replaced in Afghanistan, and many members of al-Qaeda were killed or arrested. Osama bin Laden remained at large for 10 more years until May 2011 when he was tracked down in Pakistan and killed by U.S. forces.

Much has been written about the failure of U.S. law enforcement, particularly federal law enforcement, to deal with terrorism. Some have reported that the failure to follow up leads and analyze information has made the efforts of terrorists to commit terrorist attacks against the United States easier. Others have reported that a major flaw of counterterrorism measures has been a lack of interagency cooperation and data sharing.[71]

To address these concerns, on October 8, 2001, President Bush signed Executive Order 13228, which established the Office of Homeland Security.[72] The office's mission was to develop and coordinate the implementation of a comprehensive national strategy to secure the United States from threats and attacks. The office coordinated the executive branch's efforts to detect, prepare for, prevent, and respond to terrorist attacks within this country. The president also established a Homeland Security Council that was responsible for advising and assisting him with all aspects of security. The council consists of the president and vice president, the secretary of the treasury, the secretary of defense, the attorney general, the secretary of health and human services, the secretary of transportation, the director of the Federal Emergency Management Agency (FEMA), the director of the FBI, the director of the Central Intelligence Agency (CIA), and the assistant to the president for homeland security.[73] In 2009, President Obama merged the Homeland Security Council with the National Security Council creating the National Security Staff,[74] and by Executive Order issued on February 10, 2014, the name of the National

Security Staff was changed to the National Security Council staff.[75]

On October 26, 2001, President Bush signed into law the **USA Patriot Act** (Uniting and Strengthening America by Providing Appropriate Tools Required to Intercept and Obstruct Terrorism), which gave law enforcement personnel new abilities to search, seize, detain, or eavesdrop in their pursuit of possible terrorists.[76] The law expanded the FBI's wiretapping and electronic surveillance authority and allowed nationwide jurisdiction for search warrants and electronic surveillance devices, including legal expansion of those devices to e-mail and the Internet. The Patriot Act also included money-laundering provisions and set strong penalties for anyone harboring or financing terrorists. It established new punishments for possession of biological weapons and made it a federal crime to commit an act of terrorism against a mass transit system. The bill allowed law enforcement agents to detain terrorism suspects for up to seven days without filing charges against them.[77] The Patriot Act is covered more thoroughly later in this chapter.

In November 2001, the president signed into law the Aviation and Transportation Security Act, which among other-things established the Transportation Security Administration (TSA) within the Department of Transportation to protect the nation's transportation systems and ensure freedom of movement for people and commerce. This new agency assumed the duties formerly provided by the Federal Aviation Administration (FAA). The TSA recruited thousands of security personnel to perform screening duties at commercial airports and significantly expanded the federal air marshals program. It also created the positions of federal security directors to be directly responsible for security at airports, developed new passenger boarding procedures, trained pilots and flight crews in hijacking scenarios, and required all airport personnel to undergo background checks.[78] Polls conducted immediately following the 9/11 attacks revealed that an overwhelming majority of Americans—approximately 75 percent—thought it necessary to give up some personal freedoms for the sake of security.[79]

Later, in June 2002, the president proposed creating a new cabinet-level agency, the U.S. Department of Homeland Security (DHS), to replace the Office of Homeland Security. With the new cabinet agency, duties formerly belonging to other government agencies were merged, including border and transportation security; emergency preparedness and response; chemical, biological, radiological, and nuclear countermeasures; and information analysis and infrastructure protection.[80] The new DHS went into effect in 2003.

In the six months following September 11, 2001, $10.6 billion was spent on creating new mechanisms for homeland security, responding to and investigating terrorist threats, and providing security for likely terrorist targets.[81] In 2002, in response to public demand, the president and Congress appointed a blue ribbon national commission to investigate the attacks. It was called the National Commission on Terrorist Attacks upon the United States, popularly known as the 9/11 Commission. Its charge was to investigate how the nation was unprepared for these terrorist attacks, how they happened, and how the nation could avoid a repeat tragedy. Its report, the *9/11 Commission Report: The Final Report of the National Commission on Terrorist Attacks upon the United States*, was released in 2004.

9/11 Commission's Review of Efforts for Homeland Security

In 2004, the *9/11 Commission Report: The Final Report of the National Commission on Terrorist Attacks upon the United States* was released by the National Commission on Terrorist Attacks.[82] The members of the commission met for two years, reviewed more than 2.5 million pages of documents, and interviewed more than 1,200 individuals in 10 countries. It held 19 days of hearings and took public testimony from 160 witnesses. It made 41 main proposals to improve homeland security and prevent future acts of terrorism against

USA Patriot Act Public Law No. 107-56, passed in 2001, giving law enforcement new ability to search, seize, detain, or eavesdrop in their pursuit of possible terrorists; full title of the law is USA Patriot Act—Uniting and Strengthening America by Providing Appropriate Tools Required to Intercept and Obstruct Terrorism.

YOU ARE THERE

Career Opportunity Areas with the Department of Homeland Security (DHS)

The DHS reports the following career opportunity areas, among others:

- *U.S. Citizenship and Immigration Services (USCIS).* Employees are responsible for adjudicating and processing the host of applications and forms necessary to ensure the immigration of people and their families to the United States, from initial stages through their transition to permanent residence, and finally to citizenship.

- *U.S. Coast Guard.* Civilian employees work together with military personnel to save lives, enforce the law, operate ports and waterways, and protect the environment.

- *U.S. Customs and Border Protection (CBP).* Employees prevent terrorists and terrorist weapons from entering the United States while facilitating the flow of legitimate trade and travel.

- *Federal Emergency Management Agency (FEMA).* Employees prevent losses from disasters wherever possible, and assist when they do happen. [This is] an intensely focused team dedicated to helping our country prepare for, prevent, respond to, and recover from disasters.

- *U.S. Immigration and Customs Enforcement (ICE).* Employees enforce immigration and customs laws, safeguard U.S. commercial aviation, and protect federal facilities.

- *U.S. Secret Service.* Employees have the dual missions of protecting our nation's leaders, and criminal investigation involving law enforcement, security, information technology, communications, administration, intelligence, forensics, and other specialized fields.

- *U.S. Transportation Security Administration (TSA).* Employees help secure our transportation infrastructure from future terrorist acts in intelligence, regulation enforcement, and inspection positions.

- *Federal Law Enforcement Training Center (FLETC).* Employees develop the skills, knowledge, and professionalism of law enforcers from 801 federal agencies in this unique interagency training organization.

Source: U.S. Department of Homeland Security, retrieved May 14, 2014, from www.dhs.gov/component-careers.

---

our nation. Some of the commission's recommendations were accepted and implemented by the government.

In December 2005, the former commission, which re-created itself as a private nonprofit organization to pressure Congress and the White House to act on its recommendations, issued a report card as its last official act, giving the federal government largely failing and mediocre marks as well as "incompletes" in its implementation of the panel's 41 main proposals. It gave its highest mark, an A2, for the government's vigorous efforts against terrorist financing, and Bs and Cs for other efforts, such as the creation of a director of national intelligence and the ongoing presence in Afghanistan. However, the commission heavily criticized the government for numerous failures

that the commission claimed were largely caused by political wrangling and bureaucracy. It particularly mentioned the failure of Congress to focus homeland security funding on risk assessments and gave the FBI a C because it was restructuring itself too slowly.[83]

The panel chairperson wrote, "We believe that the terrorists will strike again. If they do, and these reforms that might have prevented such an attack have not been implemented, what will our excuses be?"[84] The chairperson also stated before the release of the report, "It's not a priority for the government right now. More than four years after 9/11 . . . people are not paying attention. God help us if we have another attack." Another former commission member said the country was "less safe than we were 18 months ago."[85]

Federal Law Enforcement Efforts for Homeland Security

The major federal law enforcement efforts for homeland security involve the Department of Homeland Security, the FBI, the Office of the Director of National Intelligence (ODNI), and some other federal agencies.

Department of Homeland Security (DHS)

After much debate, study, and planning in the aftermath of 9/11, the cabinet-level U.S. **Department of Homeland Security (DHS)** was established in March 2003.[86]

The creation of DHS was the most significant transformation of the U.S. government since 1947 when President Harry S. Truman merged the various branches of the U.S. Armed Forces into the Department of Defense to better coordinate the nation's defense against military threats. DHS represents a similar consolidation, both in style and substance. The DHS includes former duties of 22 domestic agencies, including the Coast Guard, U.S. Customs Service, the Secret Service, the Immigration and Naturalization Service, and the Transportation Security Administration, along with numerous other federal communications, science, and technology agencies. (See Table 15.1.) The DHS does not include the FBI, CIA, or National Security Agency, but these agencies are required to share their data with the department's intelligence center. In 2014, the DHS reported it had 240,000 employees.[87]

The department's first priority is to protect the nation against further terrorist attacks. The department's agencies analyze threats and intelligence, guard our borders and airports, protect our critical infrastructure, and coordinate the responses of our nation for future emergencies. In 2004, the National Incident Management System (NIMS) was created as a result of Homeland Security Presidential Directive-5 (HSPD-5) to provide a consistent nationwide approach for federal, state, tribal, and local governments to work together to prepare for, prevent, respond to, and recover from domestic incidents, regardless of cause, size, or

TABLE 15.1 U.S. Department of Homeland Security (DHS)

Components and Agencies
Directorate for National Protection and Programs
Directorate for Science and Technology
Directorate for Management
Office of Policy
Office of Health Affairs
Office of Intelligence and Analysis
Office of Operations Coordination
Federal Law Enforcement Training Center
Domestic Nuclear Detection Office
Transportation Security Administration (TSA)
U.S. Customs and Border Protection (CBP)
U.S. Citizenship and Immigration Services
U.S. Immigration and Customs Enforcement (ICE)
U.S. Coast Guard
Federal Emergency Management Administration (FEMA)
U.S. Secret Service

Source: U.S. Department of Homeland Security, retrieved April 20, 2010, from www.dhs.gov.

complexity.[88] To understand the importance of the DHS to our homeland security, consider that 730 million people travel on commercial aircraft each year; more than 700 million pieces of baggage are screened for explosives; 11.2 million trucks and 2.2 million rail cars cross into the United States; and 7,500 foreign flagships make 51,000 calls in U.S. ports annually.[89]

One of the DHS's priorities is combating terrorism overseas. A Government Accounting Office (GAO) Report to Congressional Requesters in September 2013 said that DHS has not established the mechanisms necessary to ensure that decisions

Department of Homeland Security (DHS) Federal cabinet department established in the aftermath of the terrorist attacks of September 11, 2001.

to deploy resources abroad, made at the individual unit level, are in keeping with the strategic priorities of DHS.[90] The DHS also faces challenges of coordinating domestic DHS management with their partners abroad and the U.S. missions in foreign countries having an understanding the role of DHS.[91] This lack of coordination and complete understanding of the mission can lead to serious consequences in the battle against terrorism.

The DHS controls immigration into the United States through its US-VISIT (United States Visitor and Immigrant Status Indicator Technology) program. US-VISIT is part of a continuum of security measures that begins outside U.S. borders and continues through a visitor's arrival in and departure from the United States. The program applies to all visitors entering the United States and is a top priority for DHS because it enhances security for our citizens and visitors while facilitating legitimate travel and trade across our borders. The program helps secure the borders, facilitate the entry and exit process, and ensure the integrity of our immigration system while respecting the privacy of our visitors.[92]

The TSA is on the front lines of the nation's efforts to secure air transportation from terrorism. Since 2002, federal rules have required that the TSA conduct security inspections of all air passengers and air travel. By 2014, TSA had about 50,000 transportation security officers (TSOs). TSA's air marshals are deployed on flights around the world. The number of marshals is classified. They blend in with passengers and rely on their training, including investigative techniques, criminal terrorist behavior recognition, firearms proficiency, aircraft-specific tactics, and close-quarters self-defense measures to protect the flying public. Air marshals work in plainclothes, in teams of two or sometimes more. They board airplanes before passengers, survey the cabin, and watch passengers as they walk toward their seats.[93]

TSA federal air marshals used fatal force for the first time in December 2005 at the Miami International Airport when they shot and killed an airline passenger who claimed to have a bomb and was running out of a plane onto a jetway. The man's wife, who was traveling with him, claimed he was mentally ill.[94]

The **terrorist watchlist** is a list maintained by the federal government of individuals who are not allowed to fly on airlines. They are placed on this list due to suspected terrorism ties or tendencies. On December 25, 2005, Northwest Flight 253 was subject to a terrorist-bombing attempt by extremist Umar Farouk Abdulmtallaba. This attempted bombing exposed weaknesses in how the federal government nominated individuals to be on the watchlist and how agencies used the watchlist to screen individuals to determine if they posed s security threat. As a result of a classified study conducted by the GAO in 2010, the federal government changed procedures, which led to more individuals being added to the terrorist watchlist.[95]

U.S. Customs and Border Protection (CBP) is responsible for securing our borders while facilitating the flow of legitimate trade and travel. It protects 5,000 miles of border with Canada, 1,900 miles of border with Mexico, and 95,000 miles of shoreline. It employs about 61,000 employees, including the following enforcement personnel: 12,058 officers, more than 20,000 border patrol agents, over 2,200 agriculture specialists, and nearly 1,000 air and marine officers and pilots.[96] In 2014, the DHS reported that in 2013 at 329 U.S. ports of entry, CBP officers inspected 351 million pedestrians and passengers, including over 107 million conveyances; processed over 98 million aircraft passengers; seized 206, 246 pounds of cocaine and 3,895,381 pounds of marijuana; and intercepted more than 170,967 agricultural items and pests.[97]

U.S. Immigration and Customs Enforcement (ICE) is responsible for the enforcement of federal immigration laws, customs laws, and air security laws. It targets illegal immigrants; the people, money, and materials that support terrorism; and other criminal activities. As of 2014, ICE had about 20,000 employees in 50 states and 47 foreign countries.[98]

On the front lines of our efforts in maritime security is the U.S. Coast Guard (USCG). The Coast Guard is a military branch of the U.S. armed forces involved in maritime law, mariner assistance, and search and rescue. The USCG patrols in any maritime region in which U.S. interests may be at risk, including international waters and America's coasts, ports, and inland waterways. It became part of the DHS in 2003.[99]

The biggest challenge for law enforcement agencies is the small group or "lone wolf" operators who do not usually have formal contacts or connections

---

terrorist watchlist A list maintained by the federal government of individuals who are not allowed to fly on airlines.

with al-Qaeda or other large terrorist organizations. Michael Chertoff, former head of the Department of Homeland Security and founder of the security firm Chertoff Group, said, "The more people are out there trying, the greater the chances one of them will get through."[100]

Federal Bureau of Investigation (FBI)

The Federal Bureau of Investigation (FBI) has traditionally been the lead federal agency in the response to and investigation of terrorism. In May 2002, in the wake of massive criticism that the FBI had failed to properly handle information that could have led to the prevention of the September 11 attacks, FBI Director Robert S. Mueller completely reorganized the Bureau and created a new strategic focus for the agency. The FBI's new focus placed the following as its three priorities: (1) protecting the United States from terrorist attack, (2) protecting the United States against foreign intelligence operations and espionage, and (3) protecting the United States against cyber-based attacks and high-technology crimes.

The reorganization Mueller implemented involved a complete restructuring of the **counterterrorism** activities of the Bureau and a shift from a reactive to a proactive orientation. The main organizational improvements were the development of special squads to coordinate national and international investigations; a reemphasis on the **Joint Terrorism Task Forces (JTTF) concept**; enhanced analytical capabilities with personnel and technological improvements; a permanent shift of additional resources to counterterrorism; the creation of a more mobile, agile, and flexible national terrorism response; and targeted recruitment to acquire agents, analysts, translators, and others with specialized skills and backgrounds.[101] In 2005, the FBI created its National Security Branch (NSB), which combines the missions, capabilities, and resources of the counterterrorism, counterintelligence, and intelligence elements of the FBI.[102]

Possibly the most important unit in investigating terrorism in the United States is the FBI–local Joint Terrorist Task Forces (JTTF). Before the establishment of these task forces, ad hoc task forces of local and federal authorities would be established to investigate each new terrorist case as it occurred and then disbanded after the investigation. The

new concept ensures that the unit remains in place, becoming a close-knit, cohesive group capable of addressing the complex problems inherent in terrorism investigations. Because federal, state, and local law enforcement resources have been combined in these task forces, there is effective maximization of resources, provision of sophisticated investigative and technological resources, and linkage to all federal government resources in the United States and worldwide.[103]

The objectives of the JTTF are twofold: to respond to and investigate terrorist incidents or terrorist-related criminal activity (reactive measures), and to investigate domestic and foreign terrorist groups and individuals targeting or operating in the area for the purpose of detecting, preventing, and prosecuting their criminal activity (proactive measures). The key to the success of these task forces is the melding of personnel and talent from various law enforcement agencies in a single, focused unit. The local police members bring the insights that come from years of living and working with the people in their area. They have usually advanced through their careers from uniformed precinct patrol to various detective duties before being assigned to the task force. Each of the participating agencies similarly contributes its own resources and areas of expertise to the team. The integration of the many agencies, each bringing its own unique skills and investigative specialties to the task force, makes these units formidable in combating terrorism.

In an article in the *FBI Law Enforcement Bulletin*, Robert A. Martin, former deputy inspector for the New York City Police Department (NYPD) and former member of the FBI–NYPD JTTF, describes the operation of the task force:

The FBI special agents bring vast investigative experience from assignments all over the world. The FBI legal attachés, assigned to U.S. embassies throughout the world, provide initial law enforcement information on international terrorism cases. Since many terrorist events are committed by suspects from other countries,

counterterrorism Enforcement efforts made against terrorist organizations.

Joint Terrorism Task Forces (JTTF) concept Use of single-focused investigative units that meld personnel and talent from various law enforcement agencies.

YOU ARE THERE

Seeking a Job with the U.S. Department of Homeland Security (DHS)

Those interested in applying for Department of Homeland Security positions should visit the USA Jobs electronic portal to government-wide opportunities. From that site, they can search for current DHS employment opportunities by job category, location, salary, and more.

DHS job announcements provide important information about job qualifications, duties, salary, duty location, benefits, and security requirements. Potential applicants can view these announcements to determine if their interests, education, and professional background will make them good candidates for the job.

All DHS jobs require U.S. citizenship, and most require successful completion of a full background investigation. Applicants may also be required to submit to drug tests.

Source: U.S. Department of Homeland Security, "Get a Homeland Security Job," retrieved May 6, 2014, from www.dhs.gov.

it is necessary to gain the cooperation of law enforcement agencies from the countries of origin. Interagency cooperation is essential when investigating crimes committed internationally. The FBI will work in tandem with other agencies to develop investigative leads.[104]

Before September 11, 2001, the United States had 35 formal JTTFs. After the attacks, JTTFs were added to each of the FBI's 56 field offices, as well as 10 stand-alone formalized JTTFs in the FBI's largest resident agencies (resident agencies are maintained in smaller cities and towns across the county).[105]

Secure Communities: DHS and FBI

Secure Communities is a deportation program that uses an already existing federal information-sharing partnership between ICE (the immigration enforcement component of the DHS) and the FBI. This partnership helps to identify criminal immigrants without imposing new burdens on law enforcement.[106] Secure Communities was started in 2008 in 14 jurisdictions and is now in more than 1,700. As of January 22, 2013, the Secure Communities strategy has been implemented by ICE in all 3,181 jurisdictions in the United States, U.S. territories, and Washington, D.C.[107]

The process of identifying an individual from the arrest to removal begins at the local level. When a local or state law enforcement officer makes an arrest, the fingerprints of that individual are submitted electronically to the FBI. The FBI checks its database, and if the individual is identified as an illegal immigrant who has previously made contact with ICE, the FBI coordinates with ICE to hold the individual on an ICE detainer or immigration hold. The ICE hold will allow the person to be held in custody for an additional 48 hours to allow ICE time to conduct an interview and determine if the individual should be held for deportation proceedings.[108]

Meanwhile, the FBI has further extended its identification capabilities through a project called Next Generation Identification (NGI) that matches not only fingerprints but also iris scans and facial recognition technology. The project integrates all three methods of identification in an effort to speed identification of wanted individuals. This is another step toward biometric identification of people.[109]

The Secure Communities program is not without controversy. Although it was originally intended to target "serious convicted felons," it has caused others who are only here illegally to be deported as well.[110] Several states are trying to withdraw from the program, most notably Illinois, and the California legislature is considering legislation to allow participation in the program by local law enforcement to be voluntary.[111]

In response to the Secure Communities program, Georgia, Alabama, and most notably Arizona (with the passage of SB 1070) have attempted to implement laws that will allow their law enforcement personnel to enforce immigration laws in their states. In Georgia, the federal courts have stayed the provisions of the laws pending further hearings.[112] The U.S. Supreme Court in *Arizona et al. v. United States* (2012), upheld part of Arizona SB1070, which required the police to determine the immigration status of anyone arrested or detained where there is reasonable suspicion they are not in the United States legally.[113]

In August 2011, the Department of Homeland Security (DHS) notified 39 governors that the fingerprint-sharing program of Secure Communities did not need the approval of their state to operate in it and that the DHS had voided previous signed agreements authorizing their participation.[114]

Office of the Director of National Intelligence (ODNI)

The Office of the Director of National Intelligence (ODNI) was created in 2005 to unite America's national security intelligence under one umbrella. It was based on the 9/11 Commission report, which recommended the creation of a single intelligence director for the United States. The ODNI coordinates information from national security and military intelligence agencies, as well as law enforcement agencies. These agencies include the CIA; the National Security Agency; the Defense Intelligence Agency; the National Geo-Space Intelligence Agency; the National Reconnaissance Office; the FBI's National Security Branch; the Department of Energy's Office of Intelligence and Counterintelligence; the Department of Homeland Security's Office of Intelligence and Analysis; the Department of the Treasury's Office of Intelligence and Analysis; and the Drug Enforcement Administration's Office of National Security Intelligence.[115]

Other Federal Agencies

In addition to the DHS, the FBI, and the U.S. military, several other federal agencies are involved with crisis activities involving terrorism. One example is the Bureau of Alcohol, Tobacco, Firearms and Explosives (ATF), which has special responsibilities in cases of arson and explosives.

In February 2008, the federal Amtrak police announced that it would begin random screening of passengers' carry-on bags and that its officers would patrol trains and platforms with automatic weapons and bomb-sniffing dogs. Amtrak security teams show up unannounced at stations and set up baggage screening areas in front of boarding gates. Officers randomly pull people out of line and wipe their bags with a special swab that is then put through a machine that detects explosives. If the machine detects anything, officers open the bag for visual inspection. Anyone who is selected for screening and refuses it is

Enormous Responsibilities for U.S. Border Protection

- The United States has 5,525 miles of border with Canada and 1,989 miles with Mexico.
- The U.S. maritime border includes 95,000 miles of shoreline and a 3.4 million-mile exclusive economic zone with 329 official ports of entry.
- Each year, more than 500 million people cross the borders into the United States, some 330 million of whom are noncitizens.
- More than 730 million people travel on commercial aircraft each year, and more than 700 million pieces of baggage are screened for explosives each year.
- Approximately 11.2 million trucks and 2.2 million rail cars cross into the United States each year.
- 7,500 foreign flagships make 51,000 calls in U.S. ports annually.

Source: U.S. Department of Homeland Security, retrieved August 18, 2006, from www.dhs.gov.

FBI Priorities Post-9/11

- Protect the United States from terrorist attack
- Protect the United States against foreign intelligence operations and espionage
- Protect the United States against cyber-based attacks and high-technology crimes
- Combat public corruption at all levels
- Protect civil rights
- Combat transnational and national criminal organizations and enterprises
- Combat major white-collar crime
- Combat significant violent crime
- Support federal, state, local, and international partners
- Upgrade technology to successfully perform the FBI's mission

Source: Federal Bureau of Investigation, retrieved August 21, 2006, from www.fbi.gov.

not allowed to board. This screening was a significant change for Amtrak, which, unlike the airlines, had relatively little security even since the 2001 terrorist attacks. Concern about Amtrak security mounted after the 2004 bombings of commuter trains in Madrid, the 2005 train bombings in London, and the 2006 commuter train bombings in Mumbai, India.[116]

Many argue that the federal government has still not done enough for homeland security. In 2005, it was reported that the government had missed dozens of deadlines set by Congress after 9/11 for developing ways to protect planes, ships, and railways from terrorists. A member of the House Homeland Security Committee stated, "The incompetence we recently saw with FEMA's leadership [during Hurricane Katrina] appears to exist throughout the Homeland Security Department. Our nation is still vulnerable." He said that the government has yet to develop a comprehensive plan to protect roads, bridges, tunnels, power plants, pipelines, and dams.

YOU ARE THERE

They Stopped the Terrorists before They Could Attack

The police officers who patrol New York City, the NYPD, are called New York's Finest—an accolade they deserve every day. The finest of the Finest has to be NYPD's elite emergency service unit (ESU). These are the men and women who risk life and limb to climb to the tops of the city's myriad bridges and skyscrapers to rescue potential "jumpers" from themselves, enter blazing buildings, and breathe life back into cardiac victims and others who are near death. The NYPD's ESU is also the city's special weapons and tactical (SWAT) team. They are the Marine Corps of the city, available 24/7 with their automatic weapons to combat armed terrorists and maniacs. Their action on July 31, 1997, was just one of the heroic things cops in New York did that day, but it saved the city from certain disaster.

The events began when a Long Island Railroad police officer, on patrol in his radio car in Brooklyn, observed a man acting irrationally at 10:45 p.m. on July 30, 1997. The man was repeatedly screaming in Arabic, "Bomba," and cupping his hands and moving them apart to mimic an explosion. The officer took the man to the 88th Precinct station house in Fort Greene, Brooklyn, where an interpreter determined that bombs and plans to blow up New York City subways were at a house at 248 Fourth Avenue in the Park Slope neighborhood.

Just before dawn on July 31, the police closed off scores of blocks in Park Slope and called on the ESU to enter the building. The officers entered the cramped apartment, led by hero cops Joseph Dolan, age 34, and David Martinez, age 38, shouting, "Police! Don't move!" whereupon one man reached for one of the officers' weapons and another reached for one of four toggle switches on a pipe bomb. Officers Dolan and Martinez shot both suspects before any actions against them could be taken. A nine-inch pipe packed with gunpowder and nails and a device in which four pipes had been wrapped together and equipped with toggle-switch detonators were among the explosives removed by the police. Further investigation revealed that the men were Middle Eastern terrorists who had planned to carry out a suicide bombing of the New York City subways on that very day.

The police action came a day after a suicide bombing in a Jerusalem market had killed and injured scores. The lives of more than a million New York City commuters and residents were disrupted by the police action and investigation, but no injuries or deaths ensued. Officer Martinez said, "I felt a little sick when I woke up the next day. I started to realize I almost wasn't here. I started to think of the magnitude of what these people were going to do. They would have killed hundreds of people, little children, mothers, people they don't even know. It's a great feeling to know in some way you helped alter the future." Mayor Rudolph Giuliani said, "They [the NYPD] prevented a major terrorist attack from taking place."

Sources: "Heroes of Bomb Scare: Courageous Cops of Emergency Unit Honored," *Daily News*, August 3, 1997, p. 3; Rocco Parascandola, "Hail Storm for City's Finest of Heroes," *New York Post*, August 3, 1997, p. 1; William K. Rashbaum and Patrice O'Shaughnessy, "Raiders Knew Lethal Risk: With Seconds to Spare, Cops Nearly 'Naked' vs. Bomb," *Daily News*, August 3, 1997, p. 2; "They Saved the City: New York Would Be Counting Its Dead If These Hero Cops Had Not Acted," *New York Post*, August 3, 1997, p. 1.

David R. Frazier Photolibrary, Inc./Alamy

U.S. Immigration and Customs Enforcement officers work at the Tijuana, Mexico–San Diego, California, border crossing.

He also said that a broad plan to protect levies and dams might have helped prevent the New Orleans levies from being breached.[117]

State and Local Law Enforcement Efforts for Homeland Security

Although the previous section emphasized the role of our national government in responding to and combating terrorism and homeland defense, we must remember that each act of terrorism is essentially a local problem that must be addressed by local authorities.

D. Douglas Bodrero, former commissioner of public safety for the state of Utah and a senior research associate with the Institute for Intergovernmental Research, writing in 1999, stated, "Every act of terrorism occurring within the United States remains local in nature."[118] Bodrero, writing again in 2002, reiterated his emphasis that terrorism is primarily a concern for local governments:

> The planning or execution of terrorist acts on U.S. soil [is] the concern of every law enforcement agency, regardless of size or area of responsibility. Every terrorist event, every act

of planning and preparation for that event occurs in some local law enforcement agency's jurisdiction. No agency is closer to the activities within its community than the law enforcement agency that has responsibility and jurisdiction for protecting that community.[119]

Expressing similar concerns in 2002, William B. Burger, chief of the North Miami Beach, Florida, Police Department and president of the International Association of Chiefs of Police (IACP), stated,

> State and local law enforcement agencies in the United States—and the 700,000 officers they employ—patrol the streets of our cities and towns daily and, as a result, have an intimate knowledge of those communities they serve. This unique relationship provides these agencies with a tremendous edge in effectively tracking down information related to terrorists.[120]

In a special edition of the *FBI Law Enforcement Bulletin* in December 2007, Willie T. Hulon, executive assistant director of the National Security Branch of the FBI, wrote,

> Local police officers, who are out on the streets, are the frontline of the war on terrorism. They often may be the first to detect potential terrorists. The vast jurisdiction of state, local, and tribal officers brings invaluable access to millions of people and resources, which can help protect the nation and its citizens. The information gathered on the street and in our communities is one of the most powerful tools we have.[121]

In 2008, Los Angeles Police Department (LAPD) chief William Bratton stated,

> The potential threat of terrorism is much more real now than it was in the 20th century. What is necessary is to actually police terrorism. That's where local police come in. There are 700,000 of us in local cities.[122]

Even after the 1993 World Trade Center bombing, most state and local law enforcement administrators continued to view terrorism primarily as an international threat. Many administrators believed that metropolitan centers such as New York, Miami, and Chicago remained the most likely targets. A 1995 National Institute of Justice (NIJ) study confirmed that state and local law enforcement agencies viewed the threat of terrorism as real, but their response varied widely according to the size and resources of the agency and the nature of the threat in the particular community. Major cities developed prevention and preparation programs, often in cooperation with the FBI and its JTTF; in contrast, smaller cities and counties usually operated on their own. Antiterrorism resources varied based on the existing threat potential. Some smaller jurisdictions developed regional alliances to address specific extremist groups and organizations operating locally.[123]

These perceptions changed after the 1995 Oklahoma City explosion. Bodrero wrote that since then most jurisdictions have realized the threat presented by extremist individuals and groups and now assess the threat that such groups pose to their respective communities and to related operational planning and readiness issues.[124]

Although the FBI maintains the lead federal role in the investigation and prevention of domestic terrorism, every terrorist act, as Bodrero and Burger wrote, is essentially local. Local law enforcement officers respond first to a terrorist threat or incident and are the closest to sense the discontent among terrorist movements; they can monitor the activity of extremist causes, respond to hate crimes, and serve as the foundation for an effective assessment of threatening activities in their own communities.

In 2002, a four-day conference was held on the effect of community policing and homeland security. Conference speakers agreed that the community should be involved in countering any chronic crime problem facing the community, including terrorism. In the keynote address, former U.S. Attorney General John Ashcroft noted that the terrorists who committed the atrocities of 9/11 lived in local communities for many months, moving unnoticed in neighborhoods and public places. He emphasized that citizens must become active stakeholders in securing their own safety by being trained by police agencies to become alert observers of dangerous signals, which can result in the supplying of valuable information to law enforcement agencies in their preventive efforts.[125]

In the aftermath of 9/11, state and local agencies are being asked to play a bigger part as first responders to terrorist incidents and in gathering intelligence. Federal funding is available to state and local law enforcement for the development and enhancement of law enforcement information systems relating to terrorism with an emphasis on information sharing.[126]

Some have even suggested changing our traditional concept of policing because of terrorism. Melchor C. De Guzman of Indiana University, South Bend, in a speech at a symposium on the changing role of criminal justice agencies in a time of terror, stated that the attacks of September 11 clearly brought to the limelight not only the false sense of security of the United States but also its vulnerability to the violence of terrorism on its domestic soil. He said that our society must reexamine and revise our strategic thinking and paradigms about the way domestic security is maintained and that public policing has to make the necessary adjustments to contribute to the immediate security requirements of the nation. He concluded by stating,

> The roles and strategies of the police are shaped by the need of the times. In this time of terror, police are required to be more vigilant and perhaps more suspicious. They are required to be more proactive both in detecting and investigating acts of terrorism. The community policing roles that they have embraced for the last decade should be examined in the light of its opposing tenets to the demands of providing police service in time of terror. The police should lean toward a more legalistic style and begin to apply their innate talent for sensing danger. This is the philosophical shift that circumstances demand. This is probably the role that the American people demand from their law enforcement officers.[127]

Subsequent to the 2005 London bombings, many stress the importance of the local police in the war on terrorism. As Los Angeles Police Chief William Bratton noted,

> Terrorist cells seem cut off from al-Qaeda's headquarters. Now, rather than the well-financed groups of highly trained "professional"

terrorists right out of bin Laden's camps, we are dealing with a new breed of young, educated men who are living among us in the United States and Europe. They are following al-Qaeda–influenced websites or heeding the calls to action by radical Imams. Without financing or logistical support from al-Qaeda, their attack plan may be whatever plan they can cobble together with imagination and Internet research. Because of that, now more than ever, it is more likely that the terrorist plot is going to be uncovered by the cop on the beat than a foreign intelligence source.[128]

Commenting on the 2007 attempted bombings in London and Glasgow and the bombings of the Madrid and London transit systems, Sheri H. Mecklenburg, assistant U.S. attorney for the Northern District of Illinois, wrote that the threat of terrorism now comes from local cells, thrusting local police into the role of antiterrorism combatants once thought of as the purview of international and federal agencies. She stated that local law enforcement agencies will have to adapt their traditional policies and training to address new dangers when confronting suicide bombers.[129]

As an example of local efforts to address the problems of terrorism, the NYPD created two new deputy commissioner positions in 2002, a deputy commissioner for intelligence and a deputy commissioner for counterterrorism. It filled these positions with former high-ranking officials from the Central Intelligence Agency and the Marine Corps. The NYPD also created the Counter-Terrorism Bureau (CTB) of 1,000 officers. The CTB consists of the Counter-Terrorism Division as its intelligence and research arm and the JTTF as its investigative arm. New equipment, such as radiation-detection gear and biohazard suits, is now standard issue for all NYPD officers.

Although the actual numbers of the NYPD counterterrorism unit are not readily available, it is believed about 1,000 NYPD employees are working directly on terrorism-related issues every day, including active investigations.[130] The NYPD has its own liaison officers working full time in Britain, France, Israel, Canada, Singapore, Amman, the United Arab Emirates, Jordan, the Dominican Republic, and Australia, filing daily reports on developments there, as well as a group of 80 highly trained civilians working on terrorism. They build profiles of possible terrorists by drawing on confidential informants, surveillance, and links with other law enforcement agencies around the world. The civilians educate the department about terrorist tactics and help search for threats in the city. The NYPD's CTB has Arabic and Farsi linguists and dozens of detectives and liaison officers from other city and state agencies. The department's telephone terrorist tip line receives about 150 calls a day.[131] The LAPD also has a counterterrorism unit with an estimated 300 members.[132]

The following 2003 media description gives a sense of the security changes in the New York City area a year and a half after 9/11:

As the United States wages war on Iraq, New Yorkers and others across the region are witnessing an extraordinary state of heightened security. Police officers are armed like assault troops outside prominent buildings, police boats are combing the waterfronts and trucks are being inspected at bridges and tunnels.... No one can live or work in the region without having noticed the proliferation of armed security guards, surveillance cameras, handbag searches, metal detectors, electronic access cards and bomb-sniffing dogs, all of which have multiplied from Pennsylvania Station to the Metropolitan Museum of Art. Layered atop those are changes hidden from most eyes, like the detectives paying visits to chemical companies that terrorists might contact, the immigration agents demanding credit card numbers from foreign visitors, or the hospital emergency room stockpiles of nerve gas antidotes.[133]

After September 11, 2001, other local governments and local police agencies created new systems to protect their localities against terrorism. Some of these were the following:

- The Pasadena, California, Police Department created its own threat matrix system to prioritize the continual stream of alerts from federal agencies, with the highest level reserved for those that specifically target Southern California.

- Des Moines, Iowa, police developed an intelligence-sharing system called Cop-Link, which has an artificial intelligence component allowing it to combine data so that municipal and county law enforcement do not have to call each other to find out what information the other might have.

• Stafford County, Virginia, developed a Homeland Security Neighborhood Watch to train participants living near railroads, airports, and other key areas to note license plate numbers, directions of travel, and descriptions.[134]

Local police have continued to pay increased attention to terrorism. In 2005, the Palm Beach County, Florida, Sheriff's Office formed its own homeland security department and has instituted around-the-clock marine patrols, created an intelligence operations center, and added strategic intelligence agents. In 2006, it announced officers would be riding trains and buses in plainclothes, blending in with riders in an attempt to stop terrorist or any other threats to or from other passengers. Other Florida law enforcement agencies, including the Broward County Sheriff's Office and Miami-Dade police, have uniformed and plainclothes officers riding the transit systems.[135]

Miami police adopted the Miami Shield program in 2005 to attempt to thwart terrorists by staging random "in-your-face" security operations at so-called soft targets, such as city buses and sports arenas. For example, a group of officers might surround a downtown bank building and check the identification of each person going in and out.[136]

In 2008, the NYPD, using federal funding, continued their counterterrorism strategy by assigning roving teams of NYPD officers armed with automatic weapons and accompanied by bomb-sniffing dogs to the NYC subway system, which carries nearly 5 million people a day along 656 miles of tracks. The subways have long been considered a potential target for terrorists. These teams, under a tactical plan known as Operation Torch, consist of officers from the Emergency Service Unit who are outfitted in heavy bullet-resistant vests and Kevlar helmets and carry automatic weapons, including M-4 rifles or MP5 submachine guns. After the July 2005 London bombings, NYPD officers began doing random inspections of train riders' backpacks and packages. Since 9/11, the NYPD has used similar heavily armed officers patrolling NYC's streets, particularly around Wall Street and landmarks such as the Empire State Building.[137] As many as 100 police officers in squad cars from every precinct converge twice daily at randomly selected times and at randomly selected sites, like Times Square or the financial district, to rehearse their response to a terrorist attack. NYPD

officials say that these operations are believed to be a crucial tactic to keep extremists guessing as to when and where a large police presence may materialize at any hour.[138]

In March 2008, the LAPD opened its National Counter-Terrorism Academy to teach local law enforcement about the roots of terrorism and how to combat it nationally. The five-month course takes mid-level managers from 30 local agencies, including Los Angeles fire and Long Beach police departments and the FBI, through the historical roots of terrorism to culturally sensitive interviewing techniques. Courses include lessons on religious extremism, homegrown terrorist groups, and the evolution of al-Qaeda. The goal of the academy is to shift police officers away from the idea that they are only first responders and train them on prevention techniques.[139]

State and local law enforcement agencies are also participating in increasing their own awareness and training. The Federal Law Enforcement Training Center (FLETC) mission is, "We train those who protect our homeland." Over one million state and local law enforcement officers have been trained through FLETC since its 1970 inception; 70,000 students were trained during the fiscal year 2012. The DHS initiative of "If You See Something, Say Something™" asks citizens and law enforcement to report behavior that is reasonably indicative of criminal activity related to terrorism. This activity will be shared with the federal government.[140]

This training is enhanced by a number of websites that provide awareness training (the lowest level) up to and including very specific training (Law Enforcement Training Network) on various homeland security subjects. Also available to law enforcement is the FEMA training website, which provides free training in NIMS and Incident Command.

Since September 11, 2001, the California Highway Patrol (CHP) has spent more than a million hours in homeland security-related activities. Among CHP efforts are aggressive traffic enforcement, visible patrol, and investigations.[141] In a 2006 article, Dennis M. Rees wrote that patrol officers have become more aware of and alert to possible terrorist targets and signs of terrorist planning in the communities they serve.[142]

Terrorism also affects officer safety. Michael E. Buerger and Bernard H. Levin wrote that because

Photo courtesy of Rosie Machado

JIM NIELSEN

Jim Nielsen is a lieutenant with the Moorhead, Minnesota, Police Department. He has been a police officer for more than 27 years and is a graduate of the Southern Police Administrative Officers Course.

HOMELAND SECURITY

I am a lieutenant employed by the Moorhead Police Department in Moorhead, Minnesota. The 50 sworn officers in our department serve a population of 33,000 residents within a larger metropolitan area of 175,000 along the borders of Minnesota and North Dakota. Our department is highly service oriented, and we do not experience a large amount of serious crime.

Our experiences with homeland security have been positive. New initiatives have allowed us to purchase a great deal of needed equipment and to improve communications among our regional emergency service providers. We also receive much more intelligence information than we did prior to 9/11, via two fusion centers. One of these is the Minnesota Department of Homeland Security, which sends us regular e-mail bulletins containing statewide, regional, and national intelligence information related to homeland security, including information from federal law enforcement agencies. We also receive e-mail intelligence bulletins from a regional center encompassing Minnesota, North Dakota, and Manitoba, Canada, that are focused on our immediate region. They contain information specific to the nearby border crossings into Canada, some of it provided by the Royal Canadian Mounted Police (RCMP).

In a broader sense, our officers now realize they cannot take any suspicious activity for granted. Five years ago I did not believe that our city's water supply was a high-security issue, but today it obviously is. Our city does not have any installations that have required an increase in our staffing or a significant increase in our calls for service, but we do place an increased emphasis on planning our involvement in major community events since 9/11.

However, the greatest benefit our department has obtained as a result of homeland security efforts is the purchase of radio equipment that allows all emergency personnel in our region to instantly communicate with each other. Through a combination of three grants, the Fargo Metropolitan Statistical Area has received over $8 million of funding for radio equipment. Our region includes all emergency services provided in Clay County, Minnesota, and Cass County, North Dakota. This includes the cities of Moorhead, Minnesota, and Fargo, North Dakota.

Prior to receiving the grant, some of the area's law enforcement agencies were using VHF radio frequencies, while others were using UHF radio frequencies. VHF radios could not communicate with UHF radios. The region's two full-time fire departments also used radios operating on different radio bands. These grants allowed us to purchase mobile radios, portable radios, and voting repeaters, which allow all of the region's law enforcement agencies, EMS providers, and fire departments to communicate instantly with each other.

The channels on all mobile and portable radios in our region are now uniformly labeled, allowing officers to easily find the channel they are directed to use in an emergency. The radio system is digital and operates on VHF frequencies. Law enforcement agencies can also send encrypted communications from both their mobile and portable radios. Formerly, there were some small areas of our city where the portable radios we used did not always transmit reliably. We now have clear communication on portable radios throughout the city, because the grants allowed us to replace our existing voting repeaters with new digital voting repeaters, and to add two additional voting repeaters.

Prior to receiving this funding, the Red River Valley SWAT team, the regional tactical team to which our department belongs, had to purchase portable radios just for their team's use. The different agencies' radios were not compatible because of their different frequencies, and they could not send encrypted transmissions. Now the team can not only send such transmissions, but also use the same portable radios their members use as part of their routine law enforcement functions. In addition, they can use any agency's repeaters to speak directly to any assisting agency.

Our region already had a joint dispatch center called the Red River Valley Regional Dispatch Center, a shared law enforcement records system, and a joint mobile data computer system. Obtaining the funding for a regional radio system was another step in making our regional providers of emergency services better able to routinely work together. In the event of a disaster, this new radio system will dramatically improve our ability to serve the citizens of our region.

Source: Reprinted by permission of Jim Nielsen.

of the potential scope and deadliness of a terrorist attack, particularly one that involves biological or chemical weapons, concerns for officer safety should focus on prevention and extensive preplanning for officer protection against the effects of extraordinary weaponry. Buerger and Levin also stated that law enforcement can prevent terrorist attacks by their intelligence gathering. Using their community liaisons, cultural awareness, and close relationships with immigrant communities, police can develop channels for information sharing that can help them detect terrorists' planning activities.[143]

Buttressing Bodrero's emphasis on the importance of local police in the fight against terrorism, Earl M. Sweeney wrote that terrorists are already in this country and likely moving about on our roads and highways, putting patrol officers in a unique position to observe and interdict suspicious vehicles and their occupants during traffic stops. Sweeney stresses that there must be research-based standardized training for all patrol officers in terrorists' tactics.[144]

Smaller and mid-sized agencies have attempted to become more involved in terrorism training and equipping their agencies for possible terrorist activities in their communities. Timothy McVeigh, the Alfred P. Murrah bombing terrorist, was caught by a local police officer making a traffic stop on McVeigh's' vehicle. With terrorism activity occurring at the local level, agencies are turning to the federal government for assistance with training and equipment. The Federal Excess Property Programs, known as 1033 programs, allows law enforcement agencies to obtain extra military equipment from the Department of Defense at no cost to assist with their limited budgets. In this way, agencies have been able to obtain weapons, vehicles, night-vision equipment, boats, safety equipment, and more. The programs are administered through state point of contact officers (SPOC) who review all applications for the equipment to ensure they meet the necessary qualifications. This equipment allows smaller

and mid-sized agencies to participate in terrorist training at a comparable level as their larger agency counterparts.

Major police professional organizations, such as the International Association of Chiefs of Police (IACP), the National Sheriff's Association (NSA), the National Organization of Black Law Enforcement Officials (NOBLE), the Major Cities Chief's Association, and the Police Foundation, with the cooperation of the U.S. Department of Justice, have cooperated to form the *Post-9/11 Policing Project* to help bring domestic preparedness to the top of the law enforcement agenda.[145]

The terrorist attacks of September 11 highlighted the inadequacy of information sharing among many law enforcement and intelligence agencies. Since 2004, state, local, and regional fusion centers have been formally established across the United States. The philosophy behind the **fusion center** concept is that by integrating various forms of information and intelligence, including intelligence from the federal government, governmental entities will be better able to assess the risk of terrorist attack and to respond to both terrorist attacks and natural disasters. A fusion center is defined as a collaborative effort of two or more agencies that provide resources, expertise, and information to the center with the goal of maximizing its ability to detect, prevent, investigate, and respond to criminal and terrorist activity.[146]

The original idea of the fusion centers was embraced by the 9/11 Commission. Most centers are run by state police or other law enforcement agencies. Many also have representatives from a range of other agencies, as well as analysts from the FBI, the Department of Homeland Security, and local fire and public works departments. The centers potentially can tap into state, local, and federal databases containing files on investigations, reports on suspicious incidents, and research material on terrorist weapons and tactics.

Because fusion centers also look at information from local-level criminal activity, they can analyze it to determine whether any connection exists between low-level crime and terrorist activity. One such center, the Joint Regional Intelligence Center in Norwalk, California, has more than 80 full-time staff analyzing this type of information in over 166 law enforcement agencies in southern California.[147] This information has led to further investigations by the LAPD's counterterrorism bureau.[148]

---

fusion center An organization composed of individuals from various federal, state, county, and municipal law enforcement agencies in an area. These individuals facilitate the gathering and sharing of intelligence information and the evaluation of this information. The primary goal of these organizations is in the area of homeland security.

A 2005 report from the Rand Corporation, based on a survey of law enforcement preparedness after 9/11, revealed that most state and local law enforcement agencies had conducted terrorism threat assessments; about one-third of local law enforcement agencies had collaborated with the FBI's JTTFs; and about 16 percent of local law enforcement agencies and 75 percent of states had specialized terrorism units.[149] Counterterrorism is now a part of most law enforcement agencies nationwide, in addition to their other law enforcement duties. This shift in responsibility has cost billions of dollars and changed not only the equipment used by officers, but also the methods used in law enforcement.[150]

In 2008, a leading law enforcement official, Chief John Batiste of the Washington State Patrol, reported that he sees a problem with maintaining an appropriate alert level in regard to potential terrorist threats. Batiste said,

We are entering the seventh year since the Twin Towers fell. As time goes on, without another significant terrorist attack, it becomes increasingly challenging to convince the public and even our own personnel that risk still exists.[151]

On the other hand, some believe that the police are spending too many resources on terrorism and that it soaks up both police attention and resources. Some police executives have deemed it "the new normal," and others talk about "terror-oriented policing."[152] In 2008, Ronald Ruecker, president of the International Association of Chiefs of Police (IACP), in a report calling on the president of the United States to shift money back to crime fighting, said, "The simple truth is that average Americans are much more likely to find themselves victims of crime than of terrorist attack.... In terms of day-to-day crime fighting, we're far worse off than we were before 9/11."[153]

YOU ARE THERE

New York City's Counterterrorism Initiative: Operation Atlas

Since September 11, 2001, the NYPD has instituted numerous counterterrorism initiatives, including Operation Atlas. Core elements of Operation Atlas are increased personnel deployment, transit system security, patrol operations, intelligence, and airspace security.

Increased Personnel Deployment

- Increased deployments of Harbor, Aviation, and Emergency Service Units
- COBRA (Chemical, Biological or Radiological Actions) team deployments
- SAMPSON team deployments
- Harbor units providing increased protection of commuter ferries
- Bomb-sniffing dogs assigned to the Staten Island Ferry
- ARCHANGEL teams, composed of emergency services personnel, bomb experts, and investigators, staged strategically in the city

- HAMMER teams, police, and fire department experts in hazardous materials deployed jointly
- Heavily armed HERCULES teams deployed randomly through the city
- Counterassault teams in unmarked armored vehicles with heavily armed officers deployed
- Counterterrorism inspectors coordinating mobilization drills

Transit System Security

- Transportation Bureau working closely with the Metropolitan Transit Authority and the Port Authority to ensure war-related precautions are in place
- National Guard assisting in patrolling the subway system
- Train Order Maintenance Sweeps (TOMS) deployed to arrest fare evaders and others whose initial low-level offenses are often

(continued)

YOU ARE THERE

New York City's Counterterrorism Initiative: Operation Atlas (*continued*)

precursors of more serious crimes in the subway system, and to discourage or even intercept a terrorist attack

- Mobile Arrest Processing Centers (MAPC) buses on standby
- Additional police officers patrolling high-density transit locations such as Times Square, Grand Central, and Penn Station
- Undercover teams riding the subways
- Radiation detection being used in the subways
- "Surge responses" being conducted in which large numbers of officers saturate a given subway station
- Highway patrol officers on 12-hour tours
- Checkpoints in place along 96th Street and at all bridges and tunnels into the city, with checkpoint locations subject to unannounced change
- Vehicles parked in front of sensitive locations being towed

Patrol Operations

- Counterterrorism inspectors working 12-hour shifts, guaranteeing round-the-clock coverage by executive staff
- Critical response vans deployed to events or simply stopped at certain locations such as hotels, restaurants, landmarks, or tourist attractions
- Financial District under intense 24-hour coverage
- Counter-Terrorism Bureau supplying terrorist-related updates to APPLE, an association of New York City Corporate and Institutional Security Directors
- Ensuring each patrol borough commander has stand-alone plans in place to act as an autonomous police department should police headquarters command and control become disabled

- Systematic citywide search for any radioactive material or devices
- Prepared to use up to 4,000 school safety officers in event of an emergency to evacuate children and adults from schools, transport police resources throughout the city, and staff emergency shelters

Intelligence

- Daily assessments to determine which synagogues and other houses of worship may merit additional protection
- Daily assessments to determine which hotels, museums, landmarks, and other attractions merit additional protection
- Use of greater surveillance at fuel depots in the greater metropolitan area
- Intelligence personnel briefing garage owners and attendants about suspect vehicles that might be left at parking lots in Manhattan
- In cooperation with New Jersey authorities, inspecting sites in New Jersey where radioactive material could be stored clandestinely in close proximity to NYC
- Daily assessment regarding which foreign missions merit additional protection and which dignitaries may need added security
- Review of security at smaller airports in the metropolitan area to make sure general aviation is not used as a weapon against New York City

Airspace Security

- FAA-imposed restrictions on air traffic over Manhattan
- Department of Defense assignment of combat aircraft to protect NYC airspace

Source: New York City Police Department, "Operation Atlas," retrieved August 12, 2006, from www.nyc.gov.

Since my retirement from the New York City Police Department, I have continued to live in the metropolitan New York City area, about 25 miles from midtown Manhattan. I travel about the country often to attend conferences and visit colleagues and relatives. I have seen major changes in security since 9/11 and truly appreciate the efforts of our law enforcement agencies and private security professionals. Improved security is extremely important. I have heard some people complain about the many layers of security they now have to endure and the delays it causes them. I don't agree with these people and believe that if we are to prevent another terrorist attack and ensure our safety, we have to cooperate with these improved security measures and appreciate the efforts of the professionals who are there to protect our security. It might take a few more moments out of one's daily routine to comply with these measures, but they are entirely necessary.

One particular improvement I have noticed is security at the airports. It is completely different than it was before September 11. I see uniformed police and security employees everywhere throughout the airports I travel to and much more professionalism and effectiveness in security and screening processes. Having to go through several layers of security screening may help to prevent the opportunity to commit crimes. I also have noticed that the behavior of passengers has improved greatly since the terrorist acts of 9/11. Before then, I used to hear many passengers making silly comments about security measures and causing inconvenience to other travelers. Since 9/11, I think most people have matured a great deal.

I use local mass transit often in New York and truly appreciate the presence of military, police, and security personnel on these systems. I always go out of my way to say hello and "Thanks for being here" to these people when I pass them. They have a tough but necessary job to do, and a smile and a hello might make their day a little more bearable.

As a former police officer, I am continually amazed at the current operations of my former department, the NYPD. I sense that the very obvious surge responses and HERCULES and Atlas operations involving the massive presence of uniformed officers truly emphasize the importance of local police in our homeland security operations and keep the public aware of the constant possibility of terrorism. Most New Yorkers are used to them by now, but the tourists always seemed awed by them. I think the NYPD is very good for tourism in the city.

Private security is also extremely obvious in the city. I am a big sports fan and often go to ballparks in New York City with my grandchildren from Virginia when they come to visit us. On the way into Madison Square Garden in the city to attend WNBA, NBA, college games, and other events, all patrons are screened and packages they are carrying are searched. Several years ago my 13-year-old granddaughter, Nikki, was subjected to a search of her bag as she was coming into the Garden with me to attend a WNBA New York Liberty game. After the search was completed, I asked her how she felt about the security officer going through her bag. She said, "I feel safe." That is the whole point of security screening, for people like Nikki to be safe.

—John S. Dempsey

Security Versus Civil Liberties

Although no one questions the importance of fighting terrorism, there has been a continuing debate since September 11, 2001, over the tools being used by law enforcement to fight this evil. Many believe that since 9/11 the government has been given too much ability to affect citizens' constitutional rights and civil liberties while combating terrorism.

Recall from Chapter 13, "Police and the Law," that the former colonists wrote the U.S. Constitution to govern themselves as newly freed people after the American Revolution. They then wrote the first 10 amendments to the Constitution, the Bill of Rights, which form the basis of our criminal justice system—the rights and freedoms we possess that can be used against government tyranny. Our Constitution was based on a fear of unreasonable government power, and our criminal justice system evolved based upon this fear. Americans have a long tradition of attempting to strike a balance between security and individual liberty.

According to Thomas Rossler, a paradigm shift has occurred within the American justice system as a result of the terrorist attacks of 2001, and the ensuing legislation has expanded police and governmental powers. This paradigm shift, according to Rossler, involves a change in perspective from post facto responses to criminal activity to an aggressive stance on preventing criminal activities before they are carried out.[154]

As indicated earlier in this chapter, the USA Patriot Act was enacted in the immediate aftermath of the 9/11 attacks. The act has 10 sections or titles outlining new powers for government operations. Titles I, II, III, IV, and VII specifically affect law enforcement's role in antiterrorist activities.[155] (See Table 15.2.)

One of the main objectives of the Patriot Act was to remedy a lack of communication between the federal law enforcement agencies and intelligence agencies that were individually trying to fight terrorism. The 9/11 terrorist attacks demonstrated how critical inter- and intra-agency communications are to prevent and respond to such attacks. The Patriot Act attempts to establish a coordinating mechanism to combat terrorism by employing the combined efforts of all U.S. law enforcement and intelligence agencies.

According to Professor Jim Ruiz, a professor at the Pennsylvania State University at Harrisburg, and Kathleen H. Winters, a Ph.D. student at Ohio State University, the lack of interagency communication was a by-product of multiple federal law enforcement and intelligence agencies gathering information on terrorism but failing to share the intelligence gathered with other departments and even within their respective agencies. The CIA often compartmentalized its information to lessen the likelihood of interception, and the National Security Agency (NSA) exhibited an "almost obsessive protection of sources and methods," thus forcing other agencies to possibly duplicate investigations to obtain information that had already been collected by other federal agencies. Also, "pressure from the Office of Intelligence Policy Review, FBI leadership, and the [*Foreign Intelligence Surveillance Act of 1978*] FISA Court built barriers between agents—even agents serving on the same squads."[156]

TABLE 15.2   Overview of the USA Patriot Act

Title I Designed to Enhance Domestic Security. Creates a counterterrorism fund, increases technical support for the FBI, allows law enforcement to request military assistance in certain emergencies, expands the National Electronic Task Force, and forbids discrimination against Muslims and Arabs.

Title II Designed to Improve Surveillance. Grants authority to federal law enforcement agencies to intercept communication about terrorism, allows searches of computers, allows intelligence agencies to share information with criminal justice agencies, explains procedures for warrants, creates new definitions of intelligence, allows for roving wiretaps, and provides for expanding intelligence gathering.

Title III Designed to Stop Terrorism Finances. Grants expanded powers to law enforcement agencies to seize financial records, provides access to financial records, forces transactions to be disclosed, and expands investigative power in money laundering.

Title IV Designed to Protect U.S. Borders. Outlines measures to protect the borders, tightens immigration procedures, allows foreigners to be photographed and fingerprinted, and gives benefits to victims of terrorism.

Title V Designed to Enhance Investigative Powers. Provides a reward program, calls for sharing of investigative findings among law enforcement agencies, extends Secret Service jurisdiction, and forces educational institutions to release records of foreign students.

Title VI Designed to Compensate the Families of Public Safety Officers Killed during a Terrorist Attack.

Title VII Designed to Expand the Information Sharing Network. Provides for the expansion of law enforcement's nationwide information exchange, the Regional Information Sharing System (RISS).

Title VIII Designed to Strengthen Criminal Laws. Defines terrorist attacks, defines domestic terrorism, provides the basis for charging terrorists overseas, criminalizes support for terrorism, criminalizes cyber-terrorism, allows investigation of terrorism as racketeering, and expands bioterrorism laws.

Titles IX and X contain miscellaneous addenda.

Source: Jonathan R. White, *Terrorism and Homeland Security*, 5th ed. (Belmont, Calif.: Thomson/Wadsworth, 2006).

Ruiz and Winters also reported that the national security strategy upon which the United States had been operating was created in the late 1940s, and because the national and international scene had changed dramatically since the end of the Cold War, the nation was in need of a new national security policy, mostly due to the new climate of terrorism.

Since the Patriot Act was signed into law, civil liberties groups have been in an uproar over violations of privacy, and debates have raged concerning whether the act goes too far and allows the capture of too much information on people. Although the jury is still out, some are sounding the alarm. Nicholas Merrill went to court and got a court order allowing him to talk about the Patriot Act. In 2004, Merrill was visited by the FBI, and in 2010, he was partially released from a gag order prohibiting him from talking about the incident.[157]

FBI Special Agent and legal instructor at the FBI Academy Michael J. Bulzomi writes that the Patriot Act changed the way foreign intelligence gathering is conducted, allowing intelligence officials to work with law enforcement officials to investigate possible threats to national security. Bulzomi writes, "The government must use its new tools in a way that preserves the rights and freedoms guaranteed by America's democracy, but at the same time, ensure that the fight against terrorism is vigorous and effective. No American should be forced to seek safety over liberty."[158] Bulzomi concludes that although it has now become easier to protect the nation with the Patriot Act, care must be taken to ensure any actions against terrorism are employed within the constraints of the Constitution.[159]

Ruiz and Winters, however, have questioned the necessity of the Patriot Act:

One of the main issues underlying the Act involves balancing individual rights with governmental power. Proponents assert that the Act is necessary to combat terrorism, and that certain rights may be conceded to the government during a time of war. In 1944, the Supreme Court ruled that in times of war Congress has the authority to compromise certain rights if the circumstances warrant it (*Korematsu v. United States*, 323 U.S. 214, 1944). Conversely, opponents claim that it gives too much weight to the government's side of the balance. Furthermore, the Act is not limited solely to times of war. In fact, the "war on terrorism" is an ongoing war;

whether or not it will ever end remains to be seen. A balance must be struck between the pursuit of justice and protection of the innocent.[160]

Melanie Scarborough, in a briefing paper for the Cato Institute, seemed to agree with Ruiz and Winters:

Radical Islamic terrorists are not the first enemy that America has faced. British troops burned the White House in 1814, the Japanese navy launched a surprise attack on Pearl Harbor, and the Soviet Union deployed hundreds of nuclear missiles that targeted American cities. If policy makers are serious about defending our freedom and our way of life, they must wage this war without discarding our traditional constitutional framework of limited government.[161]

Jonathan R. White has summarized each view of the Patriot Act as follows. Supporters of the Patriot Act believe it increases federal law enforcement's ability to respond to terrorism and creates an intelligence conduit among local, state, and federal law enforcement agencies. They believe counterterrorism is strengthened by combining law enforcement and national defense intelligence. Opponents of the law argue that it goes too far in threatening civil liberties while expanding police powers and are concerned about sharing noncriminal intelligence during criminal investigations and the increased power of the government to monitor the activities of its own citizens.[162]

According to the ACLU, President George W. Bush and the Congress, in the aftermath of the 9/11 attacks, acted to amass an overabundance of new laws, executive orders, and regulations that expanded government powers, with little thought to their impact on traditional civil liberties or an assessment of whether the actual threat warranted such drastic measures. The ACLU believes that there is no evidence that statutory gaps in the powers of federal and state law enforcement and investigative agencies contributed to the failure to detect and prevent the attacks of 9/11.[163]

Anna R. Oller of the University of Central Missouri has asserted that the Patriot Act and the Bioterrorism Preparedness Act have curtailed academic freedoms, as teaching and research have been impacted by restrictions set forth in these laws that forbid teachers to provide to students from the restricted nations list information that could possibly be used in any terrorist manner.[164] Former FBI

Special Agent James Burnett, a professor of criminal justice at Rockland County Community College, also has expressed concern about curtailment of freedoms by the act, as well as the ultimate effect on our democracy:

> The concern over our government's responses to the very real threat of terrorism goes far beyond the Patriot Act to NSA data mining, detentions of immigrants, material witnesses, and enemy combatants, and the use of coercive interrogation techniques. In these and other policies our government's post-9/11 actions and the justifications for them have raised fundamental concerns as to whether our deliberately inefficient system of checks and balances and limitations on government power can get the job done in this new environment. Will the system itself become a casualty of this so-called war on terror and thus allow the enemy yet another powerful blow against our institutions and values?[165]

Many critics of the Patriot Act question the constitutionality of national security letters. **National security letters** can be issued if a local FBI official certifies that the information sought is relevant to an international terrorism or foreign intelligence investigation. In 2011, the FBI sent 16,511 national security letters concerning 7,201 individuals to finance, telephone, and Internet companies asking for records.[166] National security letters can be used to retrieve the following:

- Internet and telephone data, including names, addresses, log-on times, toll records, e-mail addresses, and service providers

- Financial records, including bank accounts and money transfers, provided the FBI says that they are needed to "protect against international terrorism or clandestine intelligence activities"

- Credit information from individuals' banks, loan companies, mortgage holders, or other financial institutions

---

national security letters Information requests issued by a local FBI official who certifies that the information is relevant to an international terrorism or foreign intelligence investigation.

Foreign Intelligence Surveillance Act (FISA Court) Bill passed in 1978 requiring the NSA and the FBI to seek a special court's (the FISA Court's) permission to conduct searches and electronic surveillance in terrorism and spying cases.

- Consumer, financial, and foreign travel records held by "any commercial entity," if the investigation's target is an executive branch employee with a security clearance[167]

In 2010, the Department of Justice's Office of the Inspector General (OIG) reported that the FBI illegally collected more than 2,000 U.S. telephone call records between 2002 and 2006 by invoking terrorism emergencies that did not exist or simply persuading phone companies to provide records. FBI officials issued approvals after the fact to justify their actions.[168]

The court created under the **Foreign Intelligence Surveillance Act (FISA Court)**, which authorizes search warrants and electronic surveillance in terrorism and spying cases, approved 2,072 warrants and wiretaps and 155 applications for business records in 2005.[169] From 1995 through 2004, FISA received 10,617 such applications and approved all but 4 of them.[170] In 2007, the FISA Court approved 2,370 requests to search or eavesdrop on people in the United States believed to be linked to international terror organizations. This represented a 9 percent increase over 2006. The court denied three warrant applications in full and partly denied one.[171]

In 2005, it was disclosed that the National Security Agency (NSA) had been secretly keeping track of phone calls that millions of ordinary Americans made every day. This information had been collected since 2001 from the nation's three largest phone companies and had produced what was reported to be the largest such database ever. The reasoning behind this huge database was that the NSA could sift through all that data, using a process called link analysis, searching for patterns that indicated terrorism threats. Intelligence experts said figuring out the patterns of communication would help in understanding al-Qaeda. If the NSA came across a call pattern that warranted further investigation, it could take other investigatory actions. When asked about this newly revealed data-mining program, President Bush stated, "We're not mining or trolling through the personal lives of millions of innocent Americans. Our efforts are focused on links to al-Qaeda terrorists and its affiliates." The day after the NSA story broke, a *Washington Post*–ABC News poll found that 63 percent of persons polled said they found the NSA program to be an acceptable way to fight terrorism, and 44 percent said they strongly approved of it.[172]

In March 2010, a federal judge ruled that the NSA's program of surveillance without warrants was illegal. The judge ruled that the government had violated the 1978 federal statute requiring court approval for domestic surveillance when it intercepted phone calls of a now-defunct Islamic charity. He ruled that the expansive use of the so-called state-secrets privilege was amounting to unfettered executive-branch discretion that had obvious potential for governmental abuse and was overreaching. In 2008, Congress had overhauled the Foreign Intelligence Surveillance Act to bring federal statutes into closer alignment with what the government had been secretly doing. The legislation essentially legalized certain aspects of the program. The overhauled law, however, still required the government to obtain a warrant if it was focusing on an American citizen or an organization inside the United States. Therefore, the surveillance of the Islamic charity was still unlawful if no court had approved it.[173]

On March 9, 2006, President Bush signed the USA Patriot Reauthorization Act of 2005, making all sections of the 2001 act permanent. Some sections were amended slightly, but none were deleted. Ruiz and Winters wrote that the bill was passed with little evidence to demonstrate the need for these measures and that evidence had begun to bubble up of abuses of these wide-ranging powers. They related that on the day the bill was signed, the U.S. Department of Justice reported that the FBI had "found apparent violations of its own wiretapping and other intelligence-gathering procedures more than 100 times in the last two years, and problems appear to have grown more frequent."[174]

In a July 2006 Harris Interactive poll, a majority of Americans reported that they were in favor of increasing surveillance of suspected terrorists through cameras, banking records, and cell phones. Seventy percent of those polled stated that they favored expanded camera surveillance on streets and in public places, an increase from 59 percent in June 2005 and from 63 percent shortly after September 11, 2001. Also, 62 percent of respondents said they supported police monitoring of chat rooms and other online forums, an increase from 50 percent in February 2004. In addition, 52 percent of those polled favored police monitoring of cell phones and e-mail, but nearly 6 in 10 respondents said these techniques should be used only with authorization by Congress.[175]

The debate over security versus individual rights is sure to continue.

SUMMARY

- During the terrorist attacks of September 11, 2001, there were 3,047 people murdered: 2,823 at the World Trade Center in New York City, 184 at the Pentagon in Northern Virginia, and 40 in Stony Creek Township, Pennsylvania.

- Terrorism has a long tradition in world history. Terrorist tactics have been used frequently by radical and criminal groups to influence public opinion and to attempt to force authorities to do their will. Terrorists have criminal, political, and other nefarious motives.

- Many Americans as well as many major U.S. firms have been targeted by terrorists in some way. Political extremists and terrorists use the violence and suspense of terrorist acts such as bombing, kidnapping, and hostage situations to put pressure on those in authority to comply with their demands and cause the authorities and public to recognize their power. They use their activities to obtain money for their causes, to alter business or government policies, or to change public opinion.

- Two major definitions of *terrorism* are "the use of violence or threatened violence against innocent people to achieve a social or political goal" and "premeditated politically motivated violence perpetrated against noncombatant targets." Terrorists target civilian populations—noncombatants.

- The major forms of terrorism affecting the United States and its citizens are international terrorism and domestic terrorism.

- The USA Patriot Act (Uniting and Strengthening America by Providing Appropriate Tools Required to Intercept and Obstruct Terrorism), signed into law in October 2001, gives law enforcement new ability to search, seize, detain, or eavesdrop in pursuit of possible terrorists.

- The Transportation Security Administration (TSA) was established after the 9/11 attacks to protect the nation's transportation systems and infrastructure.

- In 2004, the *9/11 Commission Report: The Final Report of the National Commission on Terrorist*

Attacks upon the United States made 41 major recommendations to improve homeland security and prevent future acts of terrorism against our nation. Only some of their recommendations have been implemented by the government.

- The cabinet-level U.S. Department of Homeland Security (DHS) was established in March 2003 and merged 22 previously disparate domestic agencies. The first DHS priority is to protect the nation against further terrorist attacks. The department's agencies analyze threats and intelligence, guard our borders and airports, protect our critical infrastructure, and coordinate the responses of our nation for future emergencies.

- The DHS controls immigration into the United States through its US-VISIT Program. US-VISIT is part of a continuum of security measures that begins outside U.S. borders and continues through a visitor's arrival in and departure from the United States. It applies to all visitors entering the United States.

- The FBI is the lead federal agency in the response to and investigation of terrorism.

- Although the federal government's role in responding to and combating terrorism and promoting homeland security is extremely crucial, each act of terrorism is essentially a local problem and must be addressed by local authorities. State and local law enforcement agencies have significantly increased their homeland security efforts since 9/11.

- Since 9/11, there has been a continuing debate about the tools being used by law enforcement to fight terrorism, particularly the Patriot Act.

KEY TERMS

biological weapons
counterterrorism
Department of Homeland Security (DHS)
domestic terrorism
Foreign Intelligence Surveillance Act (FISA Court)

fusion center
homeland security
Joint Terrorism Task Forces (JTTF) concept
National Counterterrorism Center (NCTC)
national security letters

terrorism
terrorist watchlist
USA Patriot Act

REVIEW EXERCISES

1. List 10 significant changes in U.S. federal, state, and local law enforcement as a result of the 9/11 terrorist attacks on U.S. soil and discuss them.

2. Create a timeline reflecting the emergence of terrorist activities against the United States and its interests.

3. Your professor has arranged for a class debate regarding the war on terrorism and its threats to the civil liberties of American citizens. She asks you to select a position on this issue: (a) the war on terrorism poses no threat to the civil liberties of American citizens, or (b) the war on terrorism poses a significant threat to the civil liberties of American citizens. Prepare a set of talking points to defend your position.

WEB EXERCISES

1. Use the Internet to obtain the latest personnel statistics for the Department of Homeland Security.

2. Use the Internet to prepare a list of five major terrorist groups. Under each entry, include the group's name, its base of operation, its founding philosophy, and its current goals.

3. Search the Internet for a large police department or sheriff's office in your area and review their website to determine what efforts they are making on behalf of homeland security.

END NOTES

1. Jonathan R. White, *Terrorism and Homeland Security*, 5th ed. (Belmont, Calif.: Thomson/Wadsworth, 2006), p. 354.

2. Office of the President, Office of Homeland Security, *National Strategy for Homeland Security* (Washington, D.C.: Office of the President, 2002).

3. White, *Terrorism and Homeland Security*, p. 269.

4. Ibid.

5. Ibid., p. 6.

6. Ibid., p. 7.

7. National Counterterrorism Center, *NCTC Report on Incidents of Terrorism, 2005*, retrieved August 16, 2006, from www.nctc.gov.

8. Louis J. Freeh, "Responding to Terrorism," *FBI Law Enforcement Bulletin* (March 1999): 1–2.

9. National Counterterrorism Center, retrieved April 18, 2010, from www.nctc.gov.

10. 2011 National Counterterrorism Center Report on Terrorism, retrieved March 12, 2012, from http://www.fas.org/irp/threat/nctc2011.pdf

11. John F. Lewis, Jr., "Fighting Terrorism in the 21st Century," *FBI Law Enforcement Bulletin* (March 1999): 3–10.

12. For coverage on Hizballah, see Christopher Allbritton and Nicolas Blanford, "Hizballah Nation," *Time*, July 31, 2006, pp. 44–45; J. F. O. McAllister, "Why Hizballah Can't Be Disarmed," *Time*, August 2, 2006, pp. 32–34; Lisa Beyer, "What Was He Thinking," *Time*, July 31, 2006, pp. 38–43 and "Hate Thy Neighbor," *Time*, July 24, 2006, pp. 24–30. For coverage on Hamas, see "Hamas in a Bind," *Economist*, June 17, 2006, pp. 51–52.

13. Lewis, "Fighting Terrorism in the 21st Century," pp. 3–10.

14. Eric Lipton, "Homeland Report Says Threat from Terrorist-List Nations Is Declining," *New York Times*, March 31, 2005, p. A5.

15. Irwan Firdaus, "Suicide Bombers Kill 25 in Bali Attacks," *Washington Post*, October 2, 2005.

16. Anna Kuchment and Frank Brown, "Stalin Lite Has Its Limits," *Newsweek*, September 20, 2004, p. 37.

17. Michael Elliott, "Rush Hour Terror," *Time*, July 18, 2005, pp. 26–49.

18. J. F. O. McAllister, "Unraveling the Plot," *Time*, July 25, 2005, pp. 42–46.

19. "London's Second Wave," *Time*, August 1, 2005, p. 5.

20. "Terrorism in Egypt," *Time*, August 1, 2005, p. 5.

21. "Punishing the West, All Things Secular and Egyptians Too," *Economist*, April 29, 2006, pp. 49–50.

22. "The Plan to Behead the Prime Minister," *Economist*, June 10, 2006, p. 33.

23. "FBI Says Suspects Sought to Form Own Army," *Associated Press*, June 24, 2006; "Homegrown Terrorists Seen as Dangerous as al-Qaeda," *Christian Science Monitor*, June 26, 2006.

24. Saritha Rai and Somini Sengupta, "Series of Bombs Explode on 7 Trains in India, Killing Scores," *New York Times*, July 12, 2006. Also see "India's Horror," *Economist*, July 15, 2006, p. 10.

25. See "Courting Trouble," *Economist*, July 15, 2006, p. 11; "The Rising Fear of a War of Proxies," *Economist*, July 15, 2006, p. 47.

26. Alan Cowell and Dexter Filkins, "Terror Plot Foiled: Airports Quickly Clamp Down," *New York Times*, August 11, 2006, pp. A1 and A7.

27. Raymond Bonner, Jane Perlez, and Eric Schmitt, "British Inquiry of Failed Plots Points to Iraq's Qaeda Group," *New York Times*, December 14, 2007.

28. Katrin Bennhold and Craig S. Smith, "Twin Bombs Kill Dozens in Algiers," *New York Times*, December 12, 2007.

29. Salman Masood and Carlotta Gall, "Bhutto Assassination Ignites Disarray," *New York Times*, December 28, 2007; Jane Perlez, "New Questions Arise in Killing of Ex-Premier," *New York Times*, December 31, 2007.

30. Carlotta Gall, "Pakistani Police Accuse Militant in Bhutto Death," *New York Times*, March 3, 2008.

31. "Pakistan's Election: The Posthumous Poll," *Economist*, February 16, 2008, pp. 47–48; Ismail Khan, "Bomb Kills 42 as Pakistani Tribal Leaders Discuss Forming Force Against Militants," *New York Times*, March 3, 2008; Jane Perlez, "Suicide Bomber Kills 37 at Pakistan Rally," *New York Times*, February 17, 2008, p. A4.

32. Associated Press, "Afghanistan: Kandahar Hit by 3rd Bomb Attack in 3 Days," *New York Times*, February 20, 2008; Taimoor Shah and Carlotta Gall, "At Least 80 Are Killed in Afghan Suicide Bombing," *New York Times*, February 18, 2008, p. A3.

33. Somini Sengupta, "At Least 100 Dead in India Terror Attacks," *New York Times*, November 27, 2008, p. 1; Somini Sengupta and Keith Bradsher, "Mumbai Terrorist Siege Over, India Says," *New York Times*, November 29, 2008, p. 1.

34. Rama Lakshimi, "Indians Rail at Government after Mumbai Blasts," July 14, 2011, retrieved July 15, 2011, from www.washingtonpost.com/world/rain-hampers-mumbai-blasts-probe/2011/07/14.

35. A. G. Sulzberger and William K. Rashbaum, "Guilty Pleas Made in Plot to Bomb New York Subway," *New York Times*, February 22, 2010, retrieved February 23, 2010, from www.nytimes.com; William K. Rashbaum, "Terror Suspect Is Charged with Plot to Use Bombs," *New York Times*, September 25, 2009, retrieved September 26, 2009, from www.nytimes.com.

36. Scott Shane and Eric Lipton, "Passengers' Quick Action Halted Attack," *New York Times*, December 27, 2009, retrieved December 28, 2009, from www.nytimes.com; Peter Baker and Carl Hulse, "U.S. Had Early Signals of a Terror Plot, Obama Says," *New York Times*, December 30, 2009, retrieved December 30, 2009, from www.nytimes.com.

37. Jeff Zeleny and Helene Cooper, "Obama Details New Policies in Response to Terror Threat," *New York Times*, January 8, 2010, retrieved January 8, 2010, from www.nytimes.com.

38. Clifford J. Levy, "Subway Blasts Kill Dozens in Moscow," *New York Times*, March 29, 2010, retrieved from www.nytimes.com.

39. Elisa Mala and J. David Goodman, "At Least 80 Dead in Norway Shooting," July 22, 2011, retrieved July 23, 2011, from www.nytimes.com/2011/07/23/workd/europe/23.oslo.html.

40. Michael T. Osterholm and John Schwartz, *Living Terrors* (New York: Delta, 2000), pp. 14–23; White, *Terrorism and Homeland Security*, p. 91. Another deadly toxin is ricin. For information about ricin, see Jamie Reno, "Understanding Ricin," *Newsweek*, March 6, 2008.

41. "Bioterror," *Security Management* (January 2004): 18.

42. Department of Homeland Security, *Remarks by the President at the Signing of S.15-Project BioShield Act of 2004*, retrieved September 23, 2006, from www.dhs.gov.

43. White, *Terrorism and Homeland Security*, pp. 94, 350–351.

44. Lewis, "Fighting Terrorism in the 21st Century," p. 3.

45. US DOJ, OJP, Justice Resource Update, "Safeguarding America Together: Suspicious Activity Reporting," December 2010, retrieved December 20, 2010, from www.ojp.gov/justiceresourceupdate/december2010/index.htm.

46. Robert D. McFadden, "Army Doctor Held in Ft. Hood Rampage," *New York Times*, November 6, 2009, retrieved November 6, 2009, from www.nytimes.com; James C. McKinley Jr., "She Ran to Gunfire and Ended It," *New York Times*, November 7, 2009, retrieved November 7, 2009, from www.nytimes.com.

47. UPI, "U.S. Soldier Charged for Planned Attack," August 1, 2011, retrieved August 9, 2011, from www.upi.com/TopNews/Special/2011/08/01/US-soldier-charged-for-planned-attack/.

48. Mark Mazzetti, Eric Schmitt, and Robert F. Worth, "Two-Year Manhunt Led to Killing Awlaki in Yemen," September 30, 2011, retrieved October 1, 2011, from www.nytimes.com/2011/10/01/world/middleeast/anwar-al-awlaki-is-killed-in-yemen.

49. Kevin Sack, "U.S. Says FBI Erred in Using Deception in Olympic Bomb Inquiry," *New York Times*, April 9, 1997, p. A47; Kevin Sack, "Officials Link Atlanta Bombings and Ask for Help," *New York Times*, June 10, 1997, pp. A1, D24.

50. Mark Pitcavage, "Domestic Extremism: Still a Potent Threat" *Police Chief* (August 2003): 32–35.

51. James E. Duffy and Alan C. Brantley, "Militias: Initiating Contact," *FBI Law Enforcement Bulletin* (July 1997): 22–26.

52. Devlin Barrett, "Militia Members Charged in Police-Killing Plot," *Associated Press*, March 29, 2010, retrieved March 29, 2010, from www.officer.com; Nick Bunkley, "U.S. Agent Infiltrated Militia, Lawyer Says," *New York Times*, March 31, 2010, retrieved April 1, 2010, from www.nytimes.com.

53. Lois Romano, "Domestic Extremist Groups Weaker but Still Worrisome," *Washington Post*, April 19, 2005, p. A3. Also see Richard A. Serrano, "Domestic Terror Groups in Disarray After Sept. 11," *Los Angeles Times*, March 11, 2008.

54. Federal Bureau of Investigation, "Domestic Terrorism: The Sovereign Citizen Movement," April 13, 2010, retrieved April 19, 2010, from www.fbi.gov.

55. Paul Clifton, *Sovereigns Arrested for Plot to Kidnap, Kill Officers*, Police, August 23, 2013, retrieved August 23, 2013, from http://www.policemag.com/channel/patrol/news/2013/08/23/nev-sove…n=BreakingNews-20130823&utm_source=Email&utm_medium=Enewsletter

56. Elizabeth M. Gillespie, "Ecoterror Link Eyed in Wash. Fires," *Associated Press*, March 4, 2008.

57. Associated Press, "$1 Million in Luxury SUVs Destroyed in California Arson," *Everett Herald*, August 23, 2003, p. A4.

58. Bryan Denson and Mark Larabee, "U.S. Accuses 7 of Eco-Sabotage," *Oregonian*, December 9, 2005.

59. Gillespie, "Ecoterror Link Eyed in Wash. Fires"; William Yardley, "Ecoterrorism Suspected in House Fires in Seattle Suburb," *New York Times*, March 4, 2008. Also see Federal Bureau of Investigation, "Seattle Eco-Terrorism Investigation," March 4, 2008, retrieved March 9, 2008, from www.fbi.gov.

60. Randolph E. Schmid, "Researchers: Damage Threat from U.S. Extremists May Be Greater than from Foreign Terrorists," *San Diego Union-Tribune*, February 17, 2008.

61. "Ruby Ridge," *Newsweek*, August 28, 1995, pp. 25–33.

62. Ibid.

63. Marc Lacey and David M. Herszenhorn, "In Attack's Wake, Political Repercussions," January 8, 2011, retrieved January 10, 2011, from www.nytimes.com/2011/01/09/us/politics/09giffords.html.

64. Marc Lacy, "Evidence Points to Methodical Planning," January 9, 2011, retrieved January 10, 2011, from www.nytimes.com/2011/01/10/us/10giffords.html.

65. Willie T. Hulon, "Focus on Terrorism," *FBI Law Enforcement Bulletin* (December 2007): 1. For more on homegrown terrorists, see Nancy Gibbs, "Terrified… Or Terrorist?" *Time*, November 23, 2009, pp. 27–31; George Hunter, "Feds Fear Surge of Homegrown Extremism," *Detroit News*, April 13, 2010, retrieved April 13, 2010, from www.detnews.com; Sebastian Rotella, "U.S. Sees Homegrown Muslim Extremism as Rising Threat," *Los Angeles Times*, December 7, 2009, retrieved December 7, 2009, from www.latimes.com; Pierre Thomas, Jason Ryan, and Theresa Cook, "Holder: Homegrown Terror Threat Increasing," *ABC News*, July 29, 2009, retrieved July 30, 2009, from www.abcnews.go.com.

66. Carol Dyer, Ryan E. McCoy, Joel Rodriguez, and Donald N. Van Duyn, "Countering Violent Islamic Extremism: A Community Responsibility," *FBI Law Enforcement Bulletin* (December 2007): 3–8.

67. John S. Dempsey, *Introduction to Investigations*, 2nd ed. (Belmont, Calif.: Thomson/Wadsworth, 2003), pp. 363–365.

68. Richard Bernstein, "Behind Arrest of Bomb Fugitive, Informer's Tip, Then Fast Action," *New York Times*, February 10, 1995, p. 1.

69. Samantha Gross, "Mayor Defends NYPD Surveillance," September 8, 2011, retrieved September 8, 2011, from www.officer.com/news/10344903/mayor-defends-nypd-surveillance.

70. "Ashcroft Announces Plan for DOJ 'Wartime Reorganization,'" *Criminal Justice Newsletter*, November 14, 2001, pp. 1–2.

71. For example, see John Miller and Michael Stone with Chris Mitchell, *The Cell: Inside the 9/11 Plot, Why the FBI and CIA Failed to Stop It* (New York: Hyperion, 2002); Evan Thomas et al., "The Road to September 11th," *Newsweek*, October 1, 2001, pp. 38–49.

72. "President Signs Homeland Security EO and Ridge Sworn In as Its Director," *NCIA Justice Bulletin* (October 2001): 8–10.

73. Office of Homeland Security, www.whitehouse.gov/response/faq-homeland.html.

74. Laura Rozen, *Introducing the National Security Staff*, Politico, January 4, 2010, retrieved June 5, 2014

75. White House Press Release, Executive Order, retrieved June 5, 2014, from: http://www.whitehouse.gov/the-press-office/2014/02/10/executive-order-changing-name-national-security-staff-national-security-

76. Public Law No. 107-56, October 26, 2001, 115 Stat. 272.

77. Ibid.

78. Transportation Security Administration, www.tsa.gov; Office of Homeland Security, www.whitehouse.gov.

79. "Polls: Trade Some Freedom for Security," *Law Enforcement News*, September 15, 2001, p. 1.

80. Brian Bennett, "States Can't Opt Out of Secure Communities Program," August 6, 2011, retrieved August 8, 2011, from www.latimes.com/news/nationworld/nation/la-na-secure-communities.

81. Office of Homeland Security, www.whitehouse.gov/homeland/six_month_update.html.

82. National Commission on Terrorist Attacks upon the United States, *9/11 Commission Report*.

83. Dan Eggen, "U.S. Is Given Failing Grades by 9/11 Panel," *Washington Post*, December 6, 2005, p. A1; Hope Yen, "Ex-Sept. 11 Commissioners: U.S. at Risk," *Associated Press*, December 5, 2005, retrieved December 5, 2005, from www.washingtonpost.com.

84. Eggen, "U.S. Is Given Failing Grades by 9/11 Panel," p. A1.

85. Yen, "Ex-Sept. 11 Commissioners."

86. Officer of Homeland Security, www.whitehouse.gov/deptofhomeland/

87. Department of Homeland Security, "About DHS," retrieved April 30, 2014, from www.dhs.gov.

88. FEMA, "NIMS and the Incident Command System," retrieved April 7, 2012, from www.fema.gov/txt/nims/nims_ics_position_paper.txt.

89. Department of Homeland Security, *Protecting Travelers and Commerce*, retrieved April 22, 2010, from www.dhs.gov.

90. GAO Report to Congressional Requesters, *Combating Terrorism, DHS Should Take Action to Better Ensure Resources Abroad Align with Priorities*, GAO-13-681, September 2013.

91. Ibid.

92. Department of Homeland Security, "US-VISIT," retrieved April 22, 2010, from www.dhs.gov. Also see Department of Homeland Security, *US-VISIT Begins Testing Radio Frequency Identification Technology to Improve Border Security and Travel; Fact Sheet: Radio Frequency Identification Technology*, retrieved

December 15, 2005, from www.dhs.gov; Jonathan Krim, "U.S. Passports to Receive Electronic Identification Chips," *Washington Post*, October 26, 2005.

93. Transportation Security Administration, "Our Workforce," retrieved April 30, 2014, from www.tsa.gov.

94. Thomas Frank, Mimi Hall, and Alan Levin, "Air Marshals Thrust into Spotlight," *USA Today*, December 8, 2005.

95. GAO Report to Congressional Requesters, *Terrorist Watchlist: Routinely Assessing Impacts of Agency Actions since the December 25, 2009, Attempted Attack Could Help Inform Future Efforts*, GAO-12-476, May 2012; James Gordon Meek, Rich Schapiro, *Alleged Nigeria Terrorist Umar Farouk Abdulmutall Tries to Explode Northwest Airlines 253 to Detroit*, Daily News, December 25, 2009, retrieved April 20, 2014, from http://www.nydailynews.com/news/national/alleged-nigeria-terrorist-umar-farouk-abdulmutall-explode-northwest-airlines-253-detroit-article-1.434304

96. U.S. Customs and Border Protection, retrieved May 4, 2014, from www.cbp.gov.

97. U.S. Customs and Border Protection, "Summary of Performance and Financial Information," retrieved May 4, 2014, from www.cbp.gov.

98. U.S. Immigration and Customs Enforcement, "Overview," retrieved May 4, 2014, from www.ice.gov.

99. U.S. Coast Guard, "About Us," retrieved April 22, 2010, from www.uscg.mil; Cole Maxwell and Tony Blanda, "Terror by Sea: The Unique Challenges of Port Security," *FBI Law Enforcement Bulletin* (September 2005): 22–26.

100. Keith Johnson, "Attempts Suggest Shift to Small-Scale Strikes," May 3, 2010, retrieved May 3, 2010, from online, http://wsj.com/article/SB10001424052748703969204572204738755597084.html.

101. Federal Bureau of Investigation, www.fbi.gov/pressrel/speeches/speech052902.htm; from www.fbi.gov.

102. Federal Bureau of Investigation, "National Security Branch," retrieved February 22, 2008, from www.fbi.gov/hq/nsb/nsb.htm.

103. Robert A. Martin, "The Joint Terrorism Task Force: A Concept That Works," *FBI Law Enforcement Bulletin* (March 1999): 23–27.

104. Ibid.

105. James Casey, "Managing Joint Terrorism Task Force Resources," *FBI Law Enforcement Bulletin* (November 2004): 1–6.

106. ICE, "Secure Communities," retrieved April 8, 2012, from www.ice.gov/secure_communities.

107. Activated Jurisdictions, retrieved May 1, 2014, from http://www.ice.gov/doclib/secure-communities/pdf/sc-activated.pdf

108. Ibid.

109. Alfonso Chardy, "FBI Joins Effort to Identify Undocumented Aliens," July 7, 2010, retrieved July 8, 2011, from www.miamiherald.com/2011/07/06/v-print/2304400/fbi-joins-effort-to-identify-udocumented-aliens.

110. Lee Romney, "U.S. to Investigate Secure Communities Deportation Program," May 18, 2011, retrieved May 19, 2011, from www.latimes.com/news/nationworld/natioin/la-na-secure-communities.

111. Julia Preston, "States Resisting Program Central to Obama's Immigration Strategy," May 5, 2011, retrieved May 6, 2011, from www.nytimes.com/2011/05/06/us/06immigration.html.

112. Brian Lyman, "Law Enforcement Unsure about Funding in Enforcing New Immigration Law," June 28, 2011, retrieved July 2, 2011, from www.montomeryadvertiser.com/fdcp.

113. *Arizona, et al., v United States* 567 U.S._____ (2012).

114. Brian Bennett, "States Can't Opt Out of Secure Communities Program," August 6, 2011, retrieved August 8, 2011, from www.latimes.com/news/nationworld/nation/la-na-secure-communities.

115. Jonathan R. White, *Terrorism and Homeland Security*, 6th ed. (Belmont, Calif.: Wadsworth/Cengage Learning, 2009), p. 399.

116. Associated Press, "Amtrak to Screen Carry-On Bags at Random," *New York Times*, February 19, 2008, p. A19.

117. Leslie Miller, "Government Misses Dozens of Security Deadlines Since Sept. 11," *Associated Press*, October 30, 2005, retrieved November 2, 2005, from www.startribune.com.

118. D. Douglas Bodrero, "Confronting Terrorism on the State and Local Level," *FBI Law Enforcement Bulletin* (March 1999): 11–18.

119. D. Douglas Bodrero, "Law Enforcement's New Challenge to Investigate, Interdict and Prevent Terrorism," *Police Chief* (February 2002): 41–48.

120. Gene Voegtlin, "IACP Testifies on Local Law Enforcement Role in Homeland Defense," *Police Chief* (February 2002): 8.

121. Willie T. Hulon, "Focus on Terrorism," pp. 1–2.

122. Rachel Uranga, "LAPD Academy Fights Terror," *Daily Breeze*, March 10, 2008, retrieved March 11, 2008, from www.dailybreeze.com.

123. Kevin Riley and Bruce Hoffman, *Domestic Terrorism: A National Assessment of State and Local Law Enforcement Preparedness* (Santa Monica, Calif.: Rand Corporation, National Institute of Justice, 1995).

124. Bodrero, "Confronting Terrorism on the State and Local Level."

125. Mike Terault, "Community Policing: Essential to Homeland Security," *Sheriff* (September/October 2002): 36–37.

126. Mathew J. Hickman and Brian A. Reaves, "Local Police and Homeland Security: Some Baseline Data," *Police Chief* (October 2002): 83–88.

127. Melchor C. De Guzman, "The Changing Roles and Strategies of the Police in Time of Terror," *Academy of Criminal Justice Sciences Today* (September/October 2002): 8–13.

128. William Bratton, "Responding to Terror," *Subject to Debate* (newsletter of the Police Executive Research Forum) 7 (2005): 2.

129. Sheri H. Mecklenburg, "Suicide Bombers: Are You Ready?" *Police Chief* (September 2007): 24–31.

130. Mark Toor, "Bratton: Adding Cops Would Help to Drive Down Crime Further," March 31, 2014, retrieved May 4, 2014, from https://www.nycpba.org/news/ch/ch-140331-morecops.html

131. Erika Martinez, "NYPD's Global Eyes and Ears: Cops Abroad on Terror Beat," *New York Post*, November 28, 2005,

p. 20; Robert F. Worth, "In a Quiet Office Somewhere, Watching Terrorists," *New York Times*, February 23, 2005, pp. B1, B6.

132. Uranga, "LAPD Academy Fights Terror."

133. Richard Perez-Pena, "A Security Blanket, but with No Guarantees," *New York Times*, March 23, 2003, pp. A1, B14, B15.

134. "Domestic Security Demands More of Local PDs," *Law Enforcement News*, December 15/31, 2002, p. 9.

135. Leon Fooksman, "Deputies to Ride Palm Beach County Trains, Buses in Search of Suspicious Activity," *South Florida Sun-Sentinel*, May 11, 2006.

136. Curt Anderson, "Police Go 'In-Your-Face' to Deter Would-Be Terrorists in Miami," *Associated Press*, November 28, 2005.

137. Al Baker, "New Operation to Put Heavily Armed Officers in Subways," *New York Times*, February 2, 2008; Verena Dobnik, "NYPD Plans to Step Up Subway Patrols," *Associated Press*, February 4, 2008, retrieved February 4, 2008, from www.officer.com.

138. Eric Schmitt and Thom Shanker, "U.S. Adapts Cold-War Idea to Fight Terrorists," *New York Times*, March 18, 2008. Uranga, "LAPD Academy Fights Terror."

139. Uranga, "LAPD Academy Fights Terror."

140. Welcome to FLETC, www.fletc.gov.

141. M. L. Brown and L. D. Maples, "No Time for Complacency: Leadership and Partnerships Are Key in Homeland Security Efforts," *Police Chief* 3 (2006): 18–20.

142. Dennis M. Rees, "Post-September 11 Policing in Suburban America," *Police Chief* 2 (2006): 72–77.

143. Michael E. Buerger and Bernard H. Levin, "Future of Officer Safety in an Age of Terrorism," *FBI Law Enforcement Bulletin* (September 2005): 2–8.

144. Earl M. Sweeney, "Patrol Officer: America's Intelligence on the Ground," *FBI Law Enforcement Bulletin* (September 2005): 14–21.

145. U.S. Department of Justice, National Institute of Justice, *Assessing and Managing the Terrorism Threat* (Washington, D.C.: National Institute of Justice, 2005).

146. IACP State and Provincial Police Division Homeland Security Committee and Rick Fuentes, "The Demands and Capacities of Protecting and Policing the Homeland," *Police Chief* (February 2008): 20–33; Bart R. Johnson, "A Look at Fusion Centers: Working Together to Protect America," *FBI Law Enforcement Bulletin* (December 2007): 28–32; Bart R. Johnson and Shelagh Dorn, "Fusion Centers: New York State Intelligence Strategy Unifies Law Enforcement," *Police Chief* (February 2008): 34–38; Todd Masse, Siobhan O'Neil, and John Rollins, *Fusion Centers: Issues and Options for Congress* (Washington, D.C.: United States Congress, 2007); Robert O'Harrow, Jr., "Centers Tap into Personal Databases," *Washington Post*, April 2, 2008, p. A1; Eileen Sullivan, "Intel Centers Losing Anti-Terror Focus," *Seattle Post-Intelligencer*, November 29, 2007; U.S. Department of Justice, *Fusion Center Guidelines: Developing and Sharing Information and Intelligence in a New Era* (Washington, D.C.: U.S.

Department of Justice, 2007); Shaun Waterman, "Fusion Centers," *Homeland Defense Journal* 1 (2007): 60–61.

147. Ken Dilanian, Brian Bennett, "Anti-Terror Data Centers Criticized," October 3, 2012, *Los Angeles Times*, retrieved May 4, 2014, from http://articles.latimes.com/2012/oct/03/nation/la-na-fusion-centers-20121003

148. Ibid.

149. K. Jack Riley, Gregory F. Treverton, Jeremy M. Wilson, and Lois M. Davis, *State and Local Intelligence in the War on Terrorism* (Santa Monica, Calif.: Rand Corporation, 2005).

150. Jessica Garrison, "Counter-Terrorism Becomes Part of Law Enforcement," September 6, 2011, retrieved September 7, 2011, from www.latimes.com/news/nationworld/nation/september11/la-na-911-homeland-security.

151. John Batiste, "Police Executives Look to 2008," *Law and Order* (December 2007): 39–40.

152. Marie Simonetti Rosen, "Terror-Oriented Policing's Big Shadow," *Law Enforcement News*, December 2004, pp. 1, 4.

153. Ronald Ruecker, quoted in Mimi Hall, "Rethink Spending on Anti-Terrorism, Report Says," *USA Today*, October 2, 2008.

154. Thomas Rossler, "New Mission and New Challenges: Law Enforcement and Intelligence after the U.S.A. Patriot Act," *Journal of the Institute of Justice and International Studies* 3 (2003): 70–79.

155. White, *Terrorism and Homeland Security*, 5th ed., pp. 293–297.

156. Jim Ruiz and Kathleen H. Winters, "The USA Patriot Act: A Review of the Major Components," in Craig Hemmons, ed., *Legal Issues in Criminal Justice* (Los Angeles: Roxbury, 2007), pp. 29–44. Ruiz and Winters cite the National Commission on Terrorist Attacks upon the United States, *9/11 Commission Report*, pp. 79, 87, 88.

157. Ellen Nakashima, "Plaintiff Who Challenged FBI's National Security Letters Reveals Concerns," August 10, 2010, *The Washington Post*, retrieved May 4, 2014, http://www.washingtonpost.com/wp-dyn/content/article/2010/08/09/AR2010080906252.html

158. Michael J. Bulzomi, "Foreign Intelligence Surveillance Act: Before and After the USA Patriot Act," *FBI Law Enforcement Bulletin* 6 (2003): 25.

159. Ibid., pp. 25–32.

160. Ruiz and Winters, "The USA Patriot Act," p. 41.

161. Melanie Scarborough, *The Security Pretext: An Examination of the Growth of Federal Police Agencies* (Washington, D.C.: Cato Institute, 2005), retrieved August 17, 2006, from www.cato.com.

162. White, *Terrorism and Homeland Security*, 5th ed., pp. 295–297.

163. American Civil Liberties Union, "Insatiable Appetite: The Government's Demand for New and Unnecessary Powers after September 11," in William C. Nicholson, ed., *Homeland Security Law and Policy* (Springfield, Ill.: Charles C. Thomas, 2005), pp. 179–196.

164. Anna R. Oller, "Impact of Counter-Terrorism Legislation on Civil Liberties in the Sciences," *Journal of the Institute of Justice and International Studies* 3 (2003): 80–87.

165. Personal communication with James Burnett, August 27, 2006.

166. Fox News, "Judge Rules Secret FBI National Security Letters Unconstitutional, March 16, 2013, retrieved May 13, 2014, from http://www.foxnews.com/politics/2013/03/16/judge-rules-secret-fbi-letters-unconstitutional/

167. Richard Willing, "With Only a Letter, FBI Can Gather Private Data," *USA Today*, July 6, 2006.

168. John Solomon and Carrie Johnson, "FBI Broke Law for Years in Phone Record Searches," *Washington Post*, January 19, 2010, p. A01; Carrie Johnson, "Inspector General Cites 'Egregious Breakdown' in FBI Oversight," *Washington Post*, January 21, 2010, p. A19.

169. Richard Willing, "With Only a Letter, FBI Can Gather Private Data." Also see Michael J. Bulzomi, "Foreign Intelligence Surveillance Act," pp. 25–32. The Foreign Intelligence Surveillance Act of 1978 (FISA) was passed in 1978 and established a requirement of judicial approval for the use of electronic surveillance for foreign intelligence gathering. FISA also established the FISA Court, consisting of U.S. district judges, whose purpose is to review government applications for national security electronic monitoring and searches. FISA requires a showing of probable cause to use electronic monitoring techniques.

170. Karen Tumulty, "Inside Bush's Secret Spy Net," *Time*, May 22, 2006, pp. 33–36.

171. Associated Press, "Record on Warrants for Spying Court," retrieved May 1, 2008, from www.nytimes.com.

172. Karen Tumulty, "Inside Bush's Secret Spy Net," pp. 33–36. For further information on the NSA data-sifting program, see Siobhan Gorman, "NSA's Domestic Spying Grows as Agency Sweeps Up Data," *Wall Street Journal*, March 10, 2008, p. A1.

173. Charlie Savage and James Risen, "Federal Judge Finds N Wiretaps Were Illegal," *New York Times*, March 31, 2010, retrieved April 1, 2010, from www.nytimes.com.

174. Ruiz and Winters, "The USA Patriot Act," p. 43. Ruiz and Winters cite E. Lichtblau, "Justice Depart. Report Cites FBI Violations," *New York Times*, March 9, 2006.

175. "Majority of Americans Support Increased Surveillance, Poll Shows," *Wall Street Journal Online*, August 17, 2006.

A

adverse impact A form of de facto discrimination resulting from a testing element that discriminates against a particular group, essentially keeping members of that group out of the applicant pool.

affirmative action An active effort to improve employment or educational opportunities for minorities that includes ensuring equal opportunity as well as redressing past discrimination.

age-progression photos Photo systems that show changes that will naturally occur to the face with age; also called age-enhanced photos.

AIDS Acquired immune deficiency syndrome.

ambiguous The concept that the police role is very diverse and dynamic.

Americans with Disabilities Act Signed into law in 1990, the world's first comprehensive civil rights law for people with disabilities. The act prohibits discrimination against people with disabilities in employment, public services, public accommodations, and telecommunications.

arrest The initial taking into custody of a person by law enforcement authorities to answer for a criminal offense or violation of a code or ordinance.

automated crime analysis The automated collection and analysis of data regarding crime (when, where, who, what, how, and why) to discern criminal patterns and assist in the effective assignment of personnel to combat crime.

automated fingerprint identification system (AFIS) Fingerprinting innovation begun in the 1980s in which a print technician can enter unidentified latent fingerprints into a computer. The computer automatically searches its files and presents a list of likely matches.

B

background investigation The complete and thorough investigation of an applicant's past life, including education, employment, military, driving, and criminal history, as well as relationships and character. It includes verification of all statements made by the applicant on the background form and the evaluation of both detected and undetected behavior to determine whether the candidate is the type of person suited to a career in law enforcement.

ballistics Scientific analysis of guns and bullets.

beat The smallest geographic area an individual officer can patrol.

beat system System of policing created by Sir Robert Peel for the London Metropolitan Police in 1829 in which officers were assigned to relatively small permanent post.

biased-based policing Any police-initiated activity that relies on a person's race or ethnic background rather than on behavior as a basis for identifying that individual as being involved in criminal activity.

bike patrol Officers patrol an assigned area on bicycle rather than in a patrol car.

biological weapons Weapons made from live bacterial, viral, and other microorganisms.

biometric identification Automated identification systems that use particular physical characteristics to distinguish one person from another; can identify criminals or provide authentication.

blending Plainclothes officers' efforts to blend into an area and attempt to catch a criminal.

blue curtain A concept developed by William Westley that claims police officers only trust other police officers and do not aid in the investigation of wrongdoing by other officers.

blue flu Informal job actions by officers in which they call in sick and/or refuse to perform certain job functions in an attempt to win labor concessions from their employees.

blue wall of silence A figurative protective barrier erected by the police in which officers protect one another from outsiders, often even refusing to aid police superiors or other law enforcement officials in investigating wrongdoing of other officers.

bribe Payment of money or other contribution to a police officer with the intent to subvert the aim of the criminal justice system.

broken windows model Theory that unrepaired broken windows indicate to others that members of the community do not care about the quality of life in the neighborhood and are unlikely to get involved; consequently, disorder and crime will thrive.

bureaucracy An organizational model marked by hierarchy, promotion on professional merit and skill, the development of a career service, reliance on and use of rules and regulations, and impersonality of relationships among career professionals in the bureaucracy and with their clientele.

C

***Carroll* doctrine** Based on the landmark 1925 U.S. Supreme Court case *Carroll v. United States*, the legal doctrine that automobiles have less Fourth Amendment protection than other places.

castle doctrine Reflects the English common law practice that a person's home is his or her castle; codified in the Fourth Amendment to the U.S. Constitution.

centralized model of state law enforcement Combines the duties of major criminal investigations with the patrol of state highways.

chain of command Managerial concept stating that each individual in an organization is supervised by and reports to only one immediate supervisor.

citizen oversight Also referred to as civilian review or external review. A method that allows for the independent citizen review of complaints filed against the police through a board or committee that independently reviews allegations of misconduct.

citizen patrols A program that involves citizens patrolling on foot or in private cars and alerting the police to possible crimes or criminals in the area.

citizen police academies Academies provided by the police department for the citizens of the community to enhance their understanding of the workings of their police department.

civil liability Potential liability for payment of damages as a result of a ruling in a lawsuit.

Civil Rights Act of 1964 Prohibits job discrimination based on race, color, religion, sex, or national origin.

civil service system A method of hiring and managing government employees that is designed to eliminate political influence, favoritism, nepotism, and bias.

civilianization The process of removing sworn officers from noncritical or nonenforcement tasks and replacing them with civilians or nonsworn employees.

cold-case squads Investigative units that reexamine old cases that have remained unsolved. They use the passage of time coupled with a fresh set of eyes to help solve cases that have been stagnant for years and often decades.

cold hit A DNA sample collected from a crime scene that ties an unknown suspect to the DNA profile of someone in the national or a state's database.

Combined DNA Index System (CODIS) Database that contains DNA profiles obtained from subjects convicted of homicide, sexual assault, and other serious felonies.

Community Emergency Reponse Team (CERT) A program in which civilians are trained in basic emergency response, first aid, and search and rescue.

community policing Philosophy of empowering citizens and developing a partnership between the police and the community to work together to solve problems.

community service officers (CSOs) Entry-level police employees without general law enforcement powers, as suggested by the President's Commission on Law Enforcement and Administration of Justice.

composite sketches Sketches prepared by forensic artists or by automated means of people wanted by the police for a crime.

CompStat Weekly crime strategy meetings, featuring the latest computerized crime statistics and high-stress brainstorming; developed by the New York City Police Department in the mid-1990s.

computer-aided dispatch (CAD) System that allows almost immediate communication between the police dispatcher and police units in the field.

computer-aided investigation/computer-aided case management The use of computers to perform case management and other functions in investigations.

computer/digital forensics The science of identifying, collecting, preserving, documenting, examining, analyzing, and presenting evidence from computers, computer networks, and other electronic devices.

consent decree An agreement binding an agency to a particular course of action for hiring and promoting women and minorities.

constable An official assigned to keep the peace in the mutual pledge system in England.

corruption Acts involving misuse of authority by a police officer in a manner designed to produce personal gain for the officer or others.

counterterrorism Enforcement efforts made against terrorist organizations.

crackdown An enforcement effort targeting a specific violation of the law.

crime Any act that the government has declared to be contrary to the public good, that is declared by statute to be a crime, and that is prosecuted in a criminal proceeding. In some jurisdictions, crimes only include felonies and/or misdemeanors.

crime analysis The use of analytical methods to obtain pertinent information on crime patterns and trends that can then be disseminated to officers on the street.

Crime Bill The Violent Crime Control and Law Enforcement Act, signed by President Clinton in 1994.

crime fighting A major view of the role of the police that emphasizes crime fighting or law enforcement.

crime scene The location where a crime occurred.

Crime Stoppers A program in which a cash reward is offered for information that results in the conviction of an offender.

criminalistics A branch of forensic science that deals with the study of physical evidence related to crime.

criminal liability Subject to punishment for a crime.

CSI effect The phenomenon in which the popularity of the television series *CSI: Crime Scene Investigation*, as well as its spin-offs *CSI: Miami* and *CSI: New York*, and other television shows and movies makes the public and jurors believe that the police can do what their television counterparts can.

custodial interrogation The questioning of a person in police custody regarding his or her participation in a crime.

cybercrime Criminal activity involving computers and networks, ranging from fraud to viruses to infiltrating networks or sites to obtain personal information for identity theft or to shut systems down.

D

deadly force Force that can cause death.

decentralized model of state law enforcement Makes a clear distinction between traffic enforcement on state highways and other state-level law enforcement functions.

decoy operations Operations in which officers dress as and play the role of potential victims in the hope of attracting and catching a criminal.

de facto discrimination The indirect result of policies or practices that are not intended to discriminate, but which do, in fact, discriminate.

defense of life standard Doctrine allowing police officers to use deadly force against individuals using deadly force against an officer or others.

deoxyribonucleic acid (DNA) The basic building code for all of the human body's chromosomes.

Department of Homeland Security (DHS) Federal cabinet department established in the aftermath of the terrorist attacks of September 11, 2001.

detective mystique The idea that detective work is glamorous, exciting, and dangerous, as it is depicted in the movies and on television.

differential response to calls for service The police response to calls for service varies according to the type and severity of the call.

directed patrol Officers patrol strategically to address a specific crime problem.

Dirty Harry problem A moral dilemma faced by police officers in which they may feel forced to take certain illegal actions to achieve a greater good.

discretion Freedom to act or decide a matter on one's own.

discrimination Unequal treatment of persons in personnel decisions on the basis of their race, religion, national origin, gender, or sexual orientation.

DNA profiling/genetic fingerprinting/DNA typing The examination of DNA samples from a body fluid to determine whether they came from a particular subject.

domestic terrorism Terrorism committed by citizens of the United States in the United States.

double marginality The simultaneous expectation by white officers that African American officers will give members of their own race better treatment and hostility from members of the African American community who consider black officers to be traitors to their race.

***Dred Scott* decision** Infamous U.S. Supreme Court decision of 1857 ruling that slaves had no rights as citizens because they were considered to be property.

drone/unmanned aerial vehicle (UAV) Unmanned aircraft piloted remotely, used for surveillance and reconnaissance.

Drug Abuse Resistance Education (DARE) The most popular antidrug program in which police officers teach students in schools about the dangers of drug use.

E

emotional intelligence (EI) The ability to interpret, understand, and manage one's own and others' emotions, which encompasses the competencies valued in law enforcement such as self-awareness, self-control, conflict management, and leadership.

entrapment A legal defense that holds that police originated the criminal idea or initiated the criminal action.

Equal Employment Opportunity Act of 1972 (EEOA) Extended the 1964 Civil Rights Act and made it applicable to state and local governments.

ethics The study of what constitutes good or bad conduct.

evidence-based policing Using available scientific research on policing to implement crime-fighting strategies and department policies.

exclusionary rule An interpretation of the U.S. Constitution by the U.S. Supreme Court that holds that evidence seized in violation of the Constitution cannot be used in court against a defendant.

exigent circumstances One of the major exceptions to the warrant requirement of the Fourth Amendment. Exigency may be defined as "emergency."

F

familial DNA analysis A technique whereby a crime scene profile is deliberately run through the offender databank in the hopes of getting a list of profiles that are genetically similar to the DNA evidence and using this information as an investigative lead to interview family members of the near matches.

field interrogation Unplanned questioning of an individual who has aroused the suspicions of an officer.

field notes The brief written record made by an officer from the time of arrival on a scene until completion of the assignment.

field training An on-the-job training program that occurs after the police academy under the direction of an FTO.

field training officers (FTOs) An experienced officer who mentors and trains a new police officer.

fleeing felon doctrine Doctrine widely followed prior to the 1960s that allowed police officers to use deadly force to apprehend a fleeing felon.

flight-or-fight response The body's reaction to highly stressful situations in which it is getting prepared for extraordinary physical exertion.

foot patrol Police officers walk a beat or assigned area rather than patrolling in a motor vehicle.

Foreign Intelligence Surveillance Act (FISA Court) Bill passed in 1978 requiring the NSA and the FBI to seek a special court's (the FISA Court's) permission to conduct searches and electronic surveillance in terrorism and spying cases.

forensic science That part of science applied to answering legal questions.

Fourteenth Amendment Amendment to the U.S. Constitution passed in 1868 that guarantees "equal protection of the law" to all citizens of the United States; frequently used to govern employment equality in the United States.

***Frye* test** Standard to admitting new scientific evidence into U.S. courts; based on the U.S. Supreme Court case *Frye v. United States* (1923).

fusion center An organization composed of individuals from various federal, state, county, and municipal law enforcement agencies in an area. These individuals facilitate the gathering and sharing of intelligence information and the evaluation of this information. The primary goal of these organizations is in the area of homeland security.

G

Gang Resistance Education and Training (GREAT) An educational program designed after DARE that addresses the issue of gangs.

global positioning system (GPS) A satellite system used to locate any position on the map.

grass-eaters Police officers who participate in the more passive type of police corruption by accepting opportunities of corruption that present themselves.

gratuities Items of value received by someone because of his or her role or job rather than because of a personal relationship.

Guardians Association of New York City Police Department v. Civil Service Commission of New York A landmark appellate court decision on the issue of job analysis.

H

habeas corpus A writ requiring that an arrested person be brought before a court to determine whether he or she has been legally detained.

Hogan's Alley A shooting course in which simulated "good guys" and "bad guys" pop up, requiring police officers to make split-second decisions.

homeland security Efforts made since the terrorist acts of September 11, 2001, to protect the United States against terrorist acts.

hot spot An area receiving a high volume of calls for service.

hue and cry A method developed in early England for citizens to summon assistance from fellow members of the community.

human relations Everything done with each other as human beings in all kinds of relationships.

I

imminent danger standard The standard that allows the use of deadly force if the officer feels in immediate danger of great bodily harm or death.

incident report The first written investigative report of a crime, usually compiled by the officer conducting the preliminary investigation.

inked prints (ten-prints) Result of the process of rolling each finger onto a ten-print card.

Innocence Project A national litigation and public policy organization dedicated to exonerating wrongfully convicted people through DNA testing and reforming the criminal justice system to prevent future injustice.

in-service training Training that occurs during a police officer's career, usually on a regular basis and usually within the department; often required by department policy or state mandate.

Integrated Automated Fingerprint Identification System (IAFIS) A system for searching an individual's fingerprints against a computerized database of fingerprints.

integrity tests Proactive investigation of corruption in which investigators provide opportunities for officers to commit illegal acts.

intelligence-led policing Using data analysis and other intelligence to focus police efforts on incidents and offenders causing the most harm to the community.

internal affairs divisions The unit of a police agency that is charged with investigating police corruption or misconduct.

Internet Protocol (IP) telephony A collection of communication technologies, products, and services that can facilitate communication across diverse systems.

investigative task forces A group of investigators working together to investigate one or more crimes. These investigators are often from different law enforcement agencies.

J

job analysis Identifies the important skills that must be performed by police officers, and then identifies the knowledge, skills, and abilities necessary to perform those tasks.

job relatedness Concept that job requirements must be necessary for the performance of the job a person is applying for.

joint federal and local task forces Use of federal, state, and local law enforcement agents in a focused task force to address particular crime problems.

Joint Terrorism Task Forces (JTTF) concept Use of single-focused investigative units that meld personnel and talent from various law enforcement agencies.

judicial review Process by which the actions of the police in areas such as arrests, search and seizure, and custodial interrogation are reviewed by the court system to ensure their constitutionality.

jury nullification A vote by jurors to either ignore the evidence in a trial or disregard the instructions of a judge to reach a verdict based on their own consciences.

K

Kansas City patrol study The first study conducted to test the effectiveness of random routine patrol.

Knapp Commission Commission created in 1970 to investigate allegations of widespread, organized corruption in the New York City Police Department.

knowledge, skills, and abilities (KSAs) Talents or attributes necessary to do a particular job.

L

latent prints Fingerprint impressions left at a crime scene.

lateral transfers The ability and opportunity to transfer from one police department to another.

Law Enforcement Education Program (LEEP) A federal scholarship and loan program operated by the DOJ between 1968 and 1976. LEEP put money into developing criminal justice programs in colleges and provided tuition and expenses for in-service police officers to go to college.

leadership An influence relationship among leaders and followers who intend real changes that reflect their mutual purposes.

LEMAS Statistical reports on law enforcement personnel data issued by the National Institute of Justice under its Law Enforcement Management and Administrative Statistics program.

less-than-lethal weapons Innovative alternatives to traditional firearms, such as batons, bodily force techniques, chemical irritant sprays, and Tasers or stun guns.

license plate recognition (LPR) technology Employs cameras and computer software to discern the letters and numbers of vehicle license plates and then compares them with records contained in state and federal databases, including department of motor vehicles and NCIC records.

lineup Police identification procedure involving the placing of a suspect with a group of other people of similar physical characteristics so that a witness or victim of a crime can have the opportunity to identify the perpetrator of the crime.

Live Scan The electronic taking and transmission of fingerprints as opposed to traditional ink methods.

local control The formal and informal use of local or neighborhood forms of government and measures to deter abhorrent behaviors.

M

malum in se An act that is "wrong in itself"—that is, illegal in its very nature based on English common law and because it violates the natural, moral, or public principles of a civilized society.

malum prohibitum A "wrong due to being prohibited"—an act that is made a crime by statute.

management The process of running an organization so that the organization can accomplish its goals.

Managing Criminal Investigations (MCI) Proposal recommended by the Rand study (research funded by the LEAA) regarding a more effective way of investigating crimes, including allowing patrol officers to follow up on cases and using solvability factors in determining which cases to follow up.

meat-eaters Officers who participate in a more aggressive type of corruption by seeking out and taking advantage of opportunities of corruption.

mentoring Filling a role as teacher, model, motivator, coach, or advisor in someone else's professional growth.

Minneapolis Domestic Violence Experiment An experiment conducted in Minneapolis, Minnesota, to determine the deterrent effect of various methods of handling domestic violence, including mandatory arrest.

Miranda **rule (or** *Miranda* **warnings)** Rule established by the U.S. Supreme Court in the landmark case *Miranda v. United States* (1966) that requires the police to advise suspects confronting custodial interrogation of their constitutional rights.

mitochondrial DNA (MtDNA) analysis DNA analysis applied to evidence containing very small or degraded quantities from hair, bones, teeth, and body fluids.

mobile digital terminal (MDT) A device put into a police vehicle that allows the electronic transmission of messages between the police dispatcher and the officer in the field.

Mollen Commission A commission created in the 1990s to investigate corruption allegations in the New York City Police Department.

mug shot imaging A system of digitizing a mug shot picture and storing its image on a computer so that it can be retrieved later.

mutual pledge A form of community self-protection developed by King Alfred the Great in the latter part of the ninth century in England.

N

National Advisory Commission on Civil Disorders (Kerner Commission) Commission created in 1968 to address the reasons for the riots of the 1960s.

National Advisory Commission on Criminal Justice Standards and Goals Presidential commission formed to study the criminal justice system and recommend standards for police agencies to adhere to in order to reduce discrimination.

National Counterterrorism Center (NCTC) The National Counterterrorism Center was created in 2004, under the Intelligence Reform and Terrorism Prevention Act (IRTPA), to serve as the primary organization in the U.S. government for integrating and analyzing all intelligence pertaining to terrorism and counterterrorism and for conducting strategic operational planning by integrating all instruments of national power.

National Crime Information Center (NCIC) Computerized database of criminal information maintained by the FBI.

National Crime Victimization Survey (NCVS) National Institute of Justice survey of a random sample of U.S. households, asking them if a crime was committed against anyone in the household during the prior six months.

National Criminal Justice Reference Service (NCJRS) A national clearinghouse of criminal justice information maintained by the National Institute of Justice.

National DNA Index System (NDIS) The final level of CODIS that supports the sharing of DNA profiles from convicted offenders and crime scene evidence submitted by state and local forensic laboratories across the United States.

National Institute of Justice (NIJ) The research arm of the U.S. Justice Department.

National Law Enforcement Officers Memorial (NLEOM) A memorial in Washington, D.C., established to recognize the ultimate sacrifice of police officers killed in the line of duty.

national security letters Information requests issued by a local FBI official who certifies that the information is relevant to an international terrorism or foreign intelligence investigation.

Neighborhood Watch A specific crime prevention program, and also a generic term for crime prevention programs in which community members participate and engage in a wide range of specific crime prevention activities, as well as community-oriented activities.

Newark foot patrol study A study conducted to determine the effectiveness of foot patrol officers in preventing crime.

night vision devices Photographic and viewing devices that allow visibility in darkness.

noble cause corruption Stems from ends-oriented policing and involves police officers bending the rules to achieve the "right" goal of putting a criminal in jail.

nonsworn (civilian) members Police employees without traditional police powers generally assigned to noncritical or nonenforcement tasks.

O

Office of Community Oriented Policing Services (COPS) Established to administer the grant money provided by the 1994 Crime Bill and to promote community policing.

Officer Next Door (OND) A plan initiated in 1997 allowing police officers to receive 50 percent discounts and low-cost loans to purchase homes in "distressed" areas nationwide. It is now under the umbrella Good Neighbor Next Door program, which also includes teachers, firefighters, and emergency medical technicians.

Omnibus Crime Control and Safe Streets Act of 1968 Enacted to aid communities in reducing the crime problem, it created the Law Enforcement Assistance Administration (LEAA), which provided grants for recruitment, training, and education.

omnipresence The impression of always being there.

Operation Identification Engraving identification numbers onto property that is most likely to be stolen.

order maintenance A major view of the role of the police that emphasizes keeping the peace and providing social services.

organization A deliberate arrangement of people doing specific jobs, following particular procedures to accomplish a set of goals determined by some authority.

P

Peel's Nine Principles Basic guidelines created by Sir Robert Peel for the London Metropolitan Police in 1829.

Pendleton Act A federal law passed in 1883 to establish a civil service system to test, appoint, and promote officers on a merit system.

phishing Fraudulently acquiring private or sensitive information using computer program expertise and techniques.

photo array Police identification procedure similar to a lineup, except that photos of the suspect (who is not in custody) and others are shown to a witness or victim of a crime.

physical agility testing A test of physical fitness to determine if a candidate has the needed strength and endurance to perform the job of police officer.

plain view evidence Evidence seized by police without a warrant who have the right to be in a position to observe it.

platoon All of the people working on a particular tour or shift.

PODSCORB Acronym for the basic functions of management: planning, organizing, directing, staffing, coordinating, reporting, and budgeting.

police academy The initial formal training that a new police officer receives to learn police procedures, state laws, and objectives of law enforcement. The academy gives police officers the KSAs to accomplish the police job.

Police Athletic League (PAL) A large sports program involving police officers and youth.

police cadet A nonsworn law enforcement position for young adults over 18. Generally, these positions are part-time, paid, education-oriented positions in police departments, and the targeted candidates are college students interested in moving into a law enforcement career.

police–community relations The relationships involved in both human relations and public relations between the police and the community.

police–community relations (PCR) movement Beginning in the 1950s and 1960s, a few officers in a department were assigned as community affairs or community relations specialists to interact with the public and reduce tension between the public and the department.

police culture or police subculture A combination of shared norms, values, goals, career patterns, lifestyles, and occupational structures that is somewhat different from the combination held by the rest of society.

police cynicism An attitude that there is no hope for the world and a view of humanity at its worst.

police deception Form of misconduct that includes perjury and falsifying police reports.

Police Explorers A program for young adults between the ages of 14 and 20 in which they work closely with law enforcement and explore the police career.

police operational styles Styles adopted by police officers as a way of thinking about the role of the police and law in society.

police paramilitary unit (PPU) A term popularized in the late 1990s to refer to police units organized in a more militaristic manner (such as SWAT teams), with their primary function to threaten or use force collectively.

police personality Traits common to most police officers. Scholars have reported that this personality is thought to include such traits as authoritarianism, suspicion, hostility, insecurity, conservatism, and cynicism.

police public relations Activities performed by police agencies designed to create a favorable image of themselves.

police pursuit policies Policies regulating the circumstances and conditions under which the police should pursue or chase motorists driving at high speeds in a dangerous manner.

police pursuits The attempt by law enforcement to apprehend alleged criminals in a moving motor vehicle when the driver is trying to elude capture and increases speed or takes evasive action.

police role The concept of "what do the police do."

police storefront station or ministation A small satellite police station designed to serve a local part of the community and facilitate the community's access to its police officers.

police suicide The intentional taking of one's own life by a police officer.

polygraph Also called a lie detector; a mechanical device designed to ascertain whether a person is telling the truth.

polymerase chain reaction-short tandem repeat (PCR-STR) One of the latest DNA technology systems; requires only pinhead-size samples rather than the dime-size samples needed for RFLP.

posse comitatus Common law descendent of the old hue and cry. If a crime spree occurred or a dangerous criminal was in the area, the U.S. frontier sheriff would call upon the *posse comitatus*, a Latin term meaning "the power of the county."

Praetorian Guard Select group of highly qualified members of the military established by the Roman emperor Augustus to protect him and his palace.

precinct/district/station The entire collection of beats in a given geographic area; the organizational headquarters of a police department.

predictive policing The application of crime analysis, data analysis, and statistical predictions to identify targets for police attention, also called forecasting.

President's Commission on Law Enforcement and Administration of Justice Commission that issued a report in 1967 entitled *The Challenge of Crime in a Free Society*. The commission was created in the wake of the problems of the 1960s, particularly the problems between police and citizens.

probable cause Evidence that may lead a reasonable person to believe that a crime has been committed and that a certain person committed it.

probationary period The period in the early part of an officer's career in which the officer can be dismissed if not performing to the department's standards.

problem-solving policing Analyzing crime issues to determine the underlying problems and addressing those problems.

Q

quasi-military organizations An organization similar to the military along structures of strict authority and reporting relations.

quotas Numbers put into place as part of goals and objectives in affirmative action plans.

R

random routine patrol Officers driving around a designated geographic area.

rapid response to citizens' calls to 911 Officers being dispatched to calls immediately, regardless of the type of call.

reasonable force The amount of force an officer can use when making an arrest.

reasonable suspicion The standard of proof that is necessary for police officers to conduct stops and frisks.

recruitment process The effort to attract the best people to apply for the police position.

red light cameras Automated cameras mounted on poles at intersections. The cameras are triggered when a vehicle enters the intersection after the light has turned red. The camera records the violation and the license plate number. A citation and the photos are sent to the owner of the vehicle along with instructions on how to pay the fine or contest the ticket.

Regional Community Policing Institutes (RCPIs) Part of the COPS program, the more than 30 RCPIs provide regional training and technical assistance to law enforcement around the country regarding community policing.

Regional Crime Analysis Geographic Information Systems (RCAGIS) spatial analysis Computer programs to help police locate crime hot spots, spatially relate a list of potential suspects to actual crimes, profile crime geographically to identify where a serial criminal most likely lives, and forecast where the next crime in a series might occur.

repeat offender programs (ROPs) Enforcement efforts directed at known repeat offenders through surveillance or case enhancement.

reserve officer Either part-time compensated or noncompensated sworn police employees who serve when needed.

resident officer programs Programs through which officers live in particular communities to strengthen relations between the police and the community.

restricted fragment length polymorphism (RFLP) Traditional method of DNA technology analysis.

retroactive investigation of past crimes by detectives The follow-up investigation of crimes by detectives that occurs after a crime has been reported.

reverse discrimination The label used by those who believe quotas discriminate against whites and males to describe the preferential treatment received by minority groups and women under affirmative action.

robotics The science of using robots to perform operations formerly done by human beings.

Rodney King Incident The 1991 videotaped beating of an African American citizen by members of the Los Angeles Police Department.

"rotten apple" theory Theory of corruption in which it is believed that individual officers within the agency are bad, rather than the organization as a whole.

S

SARA Acronym for the four parts of the problem-oriented policing strategy: scanning, analysis, response, and assessment.

saturation patrol Assigning a larger number of uniformed officers than normal to an area to deal with a particular crime problem.

search and seizure Legal concept relating to the search for and confiscation of evidence by the police.

search warrant A written order, based on probable cause and signed by a judge, authorizing police to search a specific person, place, or property to obtain evidence.

selection process The steps or tests an individual must progress through before being hired as a police officer.

serology Scientific analysis of blood, semen, and other body fluids.

shared leadership Power-sharing arrangement in which workplace influence is shared among individuals who are otherwise hierarchical unequals.

shire-reeve Early English official placed in charge of shires (counties) as part of the system of mutual pledge; evolved into the modern concept of the sheriff.

showup Police identification process involving bringing a suspect back to the scene of the crime or another place (for example, a hospital where an injured victim is) where the suspect can be seen and possibly identified by a victim or witness of a crime.

silver platter doctrine Legal tactic that allowed federal prosecutors to use evidence obtained by state police officers through unreasonable searches and seizures.

slave patrols Police-type organizations created in the American South during colonial times to control slaves and support the southern economic system of slavery.

smart policing A funding initiative from the Bureau of Justice Administration that partners local law enforcement agencies with academics to develop and evaluate solutions to chronic crime problems.

solvability factors Factors considered in determining whether or not a case should be assigned for follow-up investigation.

span of control The number of officers or subordinates a superior can supervise effectively.

Specialized Policing Responses (SPRs) A tailored law enforcement response to individuals with mental illness that involves trained first responders and prioritizes crisis de-escalation and treatment over arrest and incarceration.

split-force patrol A method in which the patrol force is split; half responds to calls for service and the other half performs directed patrol activities.

spyware Computer software that collects personal information, changes computer settings, or generates advertising.

squad A group of officers who generally work together all the time under the supervision of a particular sergeant.

stakeout The hidden surveillance of a location or person.

sting operations Undercover police operations in which police pose as criminals to arrest law violators.

stop and frisk The detaining of a person by law enforcement officers for the purpose of investigation, accompanied by a superficial examination of the person's body surface or clothing to discover weapons, contraband, or other objects relating to criminal activity.

strategic policing Involves a continued reliance on traditional policing operations.

straw buyers People with no criminal record who purchase guns for criminals or illegal immigrants who cannot legally buy them.

suicide by cop The phenomenon in which a person wishing to die deliberately places an officer in a life-threatening situation, causing the officer to use deadly force against that person.

swatting A growing and dangerous trend of making a hoax call to incite SWAT deployment or other law enforcement response.

sworn law enforcement employee average Number of sworn law enforcement employees for each 1,000 residents.

sworn members Police employees given traditional police powers by state and local laws, including penal or criminal laws and criminal procedure laws.

T

Tennessee v. Garner U.S. Supreme Court case that ended the use of the fleeing felon rule.

terrorism Premeditated, politically motivated violence perpetrated against noncombatant targets.

terrorist attacks against the United States of America on September 11, 2001 The terrorist attacks committed by al Qaeda.

terrorist watchlist A list maintained by the federal government of individuals who are not allowed to fly on airlines.

***Terry* stop** Based on the U.S. Supreme Court decision in *Terry v. Ohio*, the standard for allowing police officers to perform a stop and frisk (pat down) of a suspect.

thief-takers Private English citizens with no official status who were paid by the king for every criminal they arrested. They were similar to the bounty hunter of the American West.

third degree The pattern of brutality and violence used by the police to obtain confessions by suspects.

Triad A joint partnership between the police and senior citizens to address specific problems seniors encounter with safety and quality-of-life issues.

Trojan horse A computer virus acting or disguising itself as a legitimate program that when opened infects the target computer(s) and then searches for sensitive data.

tuition reimbursement Money a police department will pay officers to reimburse them for tuition expenses while they are employed by the police department and are pursuing a college degree.

U

undercover investigation A covert investigation involving plainclothes officers.

Uniform Crime Reports (UCR) Yearly collection of aggregate crime statistics prepared by the FBI based upon citizens' reports of crimes to the police.

unity of command A managerial concept that specifies that each individual in an organization is directly accountable to only one supervisor.

USA Patriot Act Public Law No. 107-56, passed in 2001, giving law enforcement new ability to search, seize, detain, or eavesdrop in their pursuit of possible terrorists; full title of the law is USA Patriot Act—Uniting and Strengthening America by Providing Appropriate Tools Required to Intercept and Obstruct Terrorism.

V

vehicle tracking systems Transmitters that enable investigators to track a vehicle during a surveillance; also called transponders, bumper beepers, or homing devices.

Vigiles Early Roman firefighters who also patrolled Rome's streets to protect citizens.

Voiceover IP (VoIP) A subset of IP telephony that is a set of software, hardware, and standards designed to enable voice transmissions over packet-switched networks, which can be either an internal local area network or the Internet. VoIP is not associated with a physical telephone number line, but rather with an IP address that is linked to a phone number.

Volstead Act (National Prohibition, Eighteenth Amendment) Became law in 1920 and forbad the sale and manufacture of alcohol.

W

walking The practice of having weapons move across the border illegally.

watch and ward A rudimentary form of policing, designed to protect against crime, disturbances, and fire. All men were required to serve on it.

Wickersham Commission Published the first national study of the U.S. criminal justice system, in 1931.

A

AARP, 342, 343
abandoned property searches, 428–429
Abel, Rudolph, 428
Abel v. United States, 427, 428
Academy of Criminal Justice Sciences, 240
Achieving Community Together (ACT), 372–373
acquired immune deficiency syndrome (AIDS), 183–185
Act for Improving Police in and near the Metropolis (Metropolitan Police Act (1829)), 6–8
Adkins, Jonathan, 288
administrative license revocation (ALR), 287
administrative units, 98–99
advanced photographic techniques, 488–490
Advisory Council of the Mental Health Association of Portland, 172
aerial dispersion shotgun round, 481
aerial photography, 488
Aerko (Punch), 479
aerosol subject restraints (ASRs), 479
affirmative action, 26, 202
affirmative action programs, 200–201
African Americans, 335
  animosity toward police, 243–244
  attitudinal beliefs, 205–206
  black community and, 208
  challenges in policing, 220
  detectives, 196
  disciplinary actions against, 197
  discrimination, 196–197, 335
  double marginality, 196
  experiences of executives, 207–208
  friendly fire or fraternal fire shooting, 220
  loyalty, 207–208
  Northern states, 196
  performance, 205
  police commissioners or chiefs, 210
  police culture, 207–208
  preferential treatment to African Americans, 196
  professionalism, 207–208
  racist behavior from white officers, 196
  recruiting qualified, 220
  representation in policing today, 210–211
  social acceptance by white officers, 207–208
  Southern States, 196
  stopped by police, 244–245
  tokenism, 220
  unfair treatment by law enforcement, 335
  white community and, 208
  women associated with command positions, 209
Agema Thermovision 210, 416
age-progression photographs, 489

aggressive driving, 288–289
aggressive patrol tactics, 277–278, 384
aging population, 342–343
Aguilar v. Texas, 419, 421
Ahmad A. v. Superior Court, 445
Air Force Office of Special Investigation (OSI), 63
Alabama Department of Public Safety, 200
Alaska's Villiage Public Safety Officer (VPSO) program, 46
alcohol, federal laws relating to, 60
alcohol-monitoring ankle bracelets, 287
alcohol testing unit, 99
ALERT (Advanced Law Enforcement Response Technology), 488
Alfred the Great, King of England, 4, 12
al-Gama's Islamiyya, 528
Ali, Mohammed, 347
All Hands on Deck saturation patrol, 278
Allison, William Thomas, 78
allocation of resources, 275–277
all-terrain vehicles (ATVs), 373
al-Qaeda, 528, 536, 540
alternative light sources (ALSs), 475
alternative organizational models and structures of police departments, 82–84
alternative patrol work strategies
  alternative vehicle deployment, 282–284
  decoy vehicles, 281–282
  Specialized Policing Responses (SPRs) to individuals with mental illness, 279, 281
  tactical operations, 277–279
alternative vehicle deployment, 282–284
Alzheimers, 343
AMBER Alerts, 306, 315, 346, 356
ambiguity of police role, 136–137
American Academy of Forensic Sciences (AAFS), 492
American Association for the Advancement of Science, 536
American Bar Association (ABA), 109
American Board of Criminalists (ABC), 498
American Civil Liberties Union (ACLU), 485, 507, 509, 511, 559
American College of Pathologists, 156
American Federation of Labor (AFL), 18, 92
American Federation of State, County and Municipal Employees (AFSCME), 93
American Indians, policing, 48–49
American Institute of Stress, 169
American Law Institute, 153, 154
  Model Penal Code, 324
American Police Systems (Fosdick), 19
American policing
  civil law enforcement system, 9

colonial experience, 9–10
early police departments, 10–11
eighteenth and nineteenth centuries, 10–17
firearms, 14
frontier experience, 15–17
jobs in 19th century, 12–13
1960s and 1970s, 20–26
1980s and 1990s, 26–29
nineteenth century problems, 11–12
1900 to 1960, 17–20
northern colonies, 9
police corruption, 25
politics and, 11–14
slave patrols, 9–10
southern colonies, 9–10
southern experience, 15
twentieth and twenty-first century, 17–34
2000s, 29–34
vigilantism, 9
American Psychological Association's Psychologists in Public Service Division, 176
American Society of Crime Laboratory Directors (ASCLD), 497–498
Americans with Disabilities Act (ADA), 105, 107, 121
America's Most Wanted, 316, 355
Amnesty International, 156
Amtrak, 64, 547–548
Anderson, Margaret, 219
Animal Liberation Front (ALF), 535–536
Annals of Emergency Medicine, 173
antibullying programs, 345
anti-child abduction programs, 346–347
anticipatory search warrant, 421
Anti-Defamation League (ADL), 338
antiterrorism units, 32–33
anti-Vietnam War demonstrations, 22–23
AOL, 471, 472
appellate courts, 395
applied ethics, 227
Arab Americans, 337–338
arches, 474
Ares, 472
Aristotle, 227
Arizona and illegal immigration, 51
Arizona et al. v. United States, 546
Arizona Rangers, 16
Arizona v. Evans, 427, 431
Arizona v. Fulminate, 441, 446
Arizona v. Gant, 427, 430
Arizona v. Hicks, 427
Arizona v. Roberson, 435
Arlington Police Department, 117
arm's reach doctrine, 421–422, 430

arraignment, 447
arrests, 135, 407–414
    custodial, 407
    deadly force, 410–411
    disorderly conduct, 135
    driving under the influence (DUI), 135
    driving while intoxicated (DWI), 135
    Fifth Amendment, 407
    Fourth Amendment, 407
    legality, 409
    liquor law violations, 135
    loitering, 135
    misdemeanor assaults, 135
    probable cause, 408–409, 422
    reasonable force, 410–411
    reasonable suspicion, 409
    requirements for, 409
    surreptitious recording of suspects'
        conversations, 445
    traffic offenses, 135
    traffic stops, 411–414
    vagrancy, 135
    violent crimes, 135
    warrantless, 407–408
arrest warrants, 408
Ashcroft, John, 459, 550
Asians, 336
    representation in policing today, 212–213
assessment centers, 117
Assistance in Disaster (AID) program, 388
Association of Firearms and Tool Mark
        Examiners (AFTE), 496
Association of White Male Peace Officers, 202
Atlanta Police Department, 15, 209
Atwater, Gail, 407–408
Atwater v. City of Lago Vista, 407
Austin, Stephen, 16
Austin Police Department, 209
authentication and biometric systems, 509
authoritarianism, 165, 166
automated clerical processing systems, 468
automated crime analysis, 464–465
automated databases, 463–464
Automated Fingerprint Identification System
        (AFIS), 463–464, 475–478
automated palm print technology, 478
Automated Regional Justice Information System
        (ARJIS), 306–307
automatic vehicle location (AVL) systems, 461,
        484
automobile exception, 429–430
automobiles, searching, 429–430
auxiliary services units, 99
Aviation and Transportation Security Act, 541

B

background interview, 120
background investigation, 120
backups, 163
backup teams, 323
ballistics, 494–496
ballistics recovery tank, 495
Baltimore County Police Department, 43
    CrimeStat, 465
Baltimore Police Department, 144, 200
Band-It electronic restraint, 481
Batiste, John, 210, 555
baton launcher, 481
batons, 155, 156, 481
beadles, 5

beanbag gun, 479, 481
Bearshare, 472
beat officer, 93
beats, 7, 93
Beers, Anne, 209
Behind the Shield: The Police in Urban Society
        (Niederhoff), 167
Belmar v. Commonwealth, 445
Beltway Sniper Case, 30, 459
Bennett, Michelle, 124–125
be on the lookout (BOLO) alarms, 290
Berghuis v. Thompkins, 444, 446
Berkeley Police Department, 118
bias-based policing, 243–246, 335
    Muslims, 244
    racial profiling, 243–245
bicycles, 282, 284, 373
bike patrol, 283–284
Bill of Rights, 228, 399, 402–403
biological weapons, 530–531
biometric identification, 509–511
biometric systems, 509
Bioterrorism Preparedness Act, 559
Birmingham Police Department, 209
BitTorrent, 472
BlackBerry, 469
Black in Blue: A Study of the Negro Policeman
        (Alex), 196
Black Liberation Army, 25, 536
Black Panther Party, 23, 25, 536
Black Police, White Society (Leinen), 196
blending, 317
Block Watch, 352
Bloomingdale Police Department, 419
Bloomington Police Department, 88
Blue Campaign, 308
blue curtain, 165, 233–234
blue flu, 92
Blue Moon, 218
blue veil, 233–234
blue wall of silence, 164–165
bobbies, 7
Boca Raton Police Department, 219, 281
Bodrero, D. Douglas, 549, 550
body armor, 181, 183
Bollingbrook Police Department, 243
bomb disposal, 511
Bond v. United States, 415–416, 418, 427
Booker, Cory, 209
Bopp, W.J., 92
border search, 430
Boston Marathon bombing, 314, 357
Boston Police Department, 209, 316, 357
    criticisms, 31
    Real Time Crime Center (RTCC), 467
Boston police strike (1919), 18
Boston Social Club, 18
Bowers v. Hardwick, 214
Bowman, Theron, 210
Bow Street Runners, 6
Boyd, Lorenzo M., 12–13, 145
Boy Scouts of America (BSA), 346, 347
Brady cops, 239
Brady v. Maryland, 239
Branch Davidians, 154, 536
Brantley, Alan C., 534
Bratton, William J., 27, 30–31, 41–42, 278, 382,
        386, 387, 549, 550–551
breath-test interlock devices, 287–288
Brendlin v. California, 412–413
Brewer v. Williams, 436, 437, 446
bribes, 234–235

Brigham City v. Stuart, 425, 427
Brinegar v. United States, 409
British Journal of Criminology, 8
Broken Arrow Police Department (BAPD),
        83–84
"Broken Windows: The Police and
        Neighborhood Safety," 366
"Broken Windows" and Police Discretion
        (Wilson and Kelling), 368
broken windows model, 366, 382, 384, 385–386
Brookings Institute, 334
Brown, Lee P., 210
Brown, Michael K., 163
Brown, Robert A., 146
Brown v. Board of Education of Topeka, 21, 243,
        335
Brown v. Mississippi, 403, 432, 433, 446
Brucia, Carlie, 314–315
Bruno v. Cadd, 349
brutality, 30, 229
brutal police officers, 227
budget and finance unit, 99
Buffalo Police Department, 171
Bulger, James "Whitey," 316
Bullcoming v. New Mexico, 498
Bully-Cummings, Ella, 209, 216
bullying, 345
Bulzomi, Michael J., 416, 422, 558–559
Bumper v. North Carolina, 426, 427
Burbeck, Elizabeth, 166
Burdeau v. McDowell, 432
bureaucracies, 73–74
Bureau of Alcohol, Tobacco, Firearms, and
        Explosives (ATF), 60, 307, 311, 321
    Integrated Ballistics Information System
        (IBIS), 495
    National Tracing Center (NTC), 495
Bureau of Diplomatic Security, 64
Bureau of Emergency Communication (BEOC),
        462
Bureau of Engraving and Printing, 64
Bureau of Export Enforcement, 63
Bureau of Indian Affairs (BIA), 48, 62, 336
Bureau of Investigation, 57
Bureau of Justice Assistance, 106, 182
Bureau of Justice Statistics (BJS), 40–41, 108
    campus law enforcement report, 49
    Citizen Complaints about Police Use of Force
        (2006), 150
    Contacts between Police and the Public (2008),
        146, 150
    Law Enforcement Management and
        Administrative Statistics (LEMAS),
        40–41
    screening procedures, 114
    victimization and offender rates for Native
        Americans, 336
    women in policing today, 208
Bureau of Land Management, 62–63
Bureau of Reclamation, 63
Burger, Warren E., 435
Burger, William B., 549
burglaries
    decreasing number of, 6
    English policing, 5
    police corruption, 234–235
Burke, Tod W., 90
Burlington Police Department, 116
businesses cooperating with police departments,
        358–359
Butler, Smedley, 78
Bykerek, Terry, 175

C

cadets, 86
cainine sniffs by trained dogs, 416–417
Caldero, Michael A., 235, 236
Caldwell, Rex, 331–332
California Association of Criminalists, 491
California Department of Parks and Recreation, 44
California Highway Patrol (CHP), 33, 55, 180, 240–241, 552
    discrimination against women, 202
    enhancing safety of farm laborers, 372
    police pursuits, 289–290
California v. Carney, 427, 430
California v. Ciraola, 429, 488, 511
California v. Greenwood, 427, 428–429, 500
California v. Hodari, D., 427, 429
California v. Riley, 427
campus disorders, 23–24
campus law enforcement, 49–50
Canadian Charter of Rights and Freedoms, 206
Canton v. Harris, 254
captains, 88
carbon-14 dating, 497
carbon dusting powders, 475
carotid holds, 155
Carraway, Mel, 210
Carroll doctrine, 430
Carroll v. United States, 427, 430
case law, 407
castle doctrine, 414–415
Catholic Emancipation, 8
cayenne pepper, 479
cell phones, 501
    monitoring, 487–488
    911 calls, 462–463
cell phone technology, 462–463
cellular tracking systems, 483
Center for Constitutional Rights, 423
Center for Crime Prevention and Control, 42
Center for Public Safety, 129
Centers for Disease Control and Prevention (CDC), 156, 178, 183, 530–531
Central Intelligence Agency (CIA), 29
centralized model of state law enforcement, 55
chain of command, 78–82
The Challenge of Crime in a Free Society report (1967), 25
chaplain programs, 357
character traits, 227
Charlotte-Mecklenburg Police Department, 373, 480
Chavez v. Martinez, 443, 446
chemical irritant sprays, 155, 478–480
Chemical Mace, 479
chemistry, 497
Chertoff, Michael, 545
Chicago Alternative Policing Strategy (CAPS), 375
Chicago Eight trial, 23
Chicago Law Enforcement Study Group, 151
Chicago Seven trial, 23
chief of police, 88–89
child pornography, 324, 470–473
child predators sting operations, 319
Child Protection Act of 1984, 324
Child Protection and Sexual Predator Punishment Act (1998), 471
Children and Teens Service (CATS), 377
Chilton, Richard, 423
Chimel, Ted, 422
Chimel v. California, 421–422, 427
choke holds, 155

"Christian Burial Speech," 437
Christopher Commission, 204, 247
cities, 10
    social problems, 366
    urban riots, 24–25
Citizen Complaints about Police Use of Force (2006), 150
Citizen Corps, 354
Citizen Corps Council, 388
citizen-initiated situations and discretion, 145
citizen oversight, 250–251
citizen patrols, 353, 374
citizen police academies, 357–358
citizens
    arresting for offenses committed in presence, 85
    complaints about police deadly force, 150
    complaints about police officer, 249
    equal protection under the law, 198
    number shot by police, 151
Citizens Academy, 374
citizen volunteer programs, 353–354
City of Indianapolis v. Edmond, 412, 418
City of Maple Valley Police Department, 124
City of Miami Police Department police pursuits, 290
civic duties, 140
civil authority, 3
civil disobedience, 22
civilian complaint review board, 246
civilianization, 89, 105, 113, 275
civilian review, 250–251
Civil Liabilities in American Policing: A Text for Law Enforcement Personnel (del Carmen), 253
civil liability, 251–255
civil liberties
    versus security, 557–561
    technology and, 511
Civil Rights Act of 1964, 21, 26, 195, 198, 201, 203, 217, 335
Civil Rights Act of 1991, 198, 199
civil rights movement, 21–22
civil rights violations, 199
civil service system, 84–85
Clark, M. Wesley, 48, 462
Clark, Tom C., 406
Clearwater Police Department, 383
clerical/secretarial unit, 99
Cleveland Police Department, 423
Click It or Ticket campaign, 286
Clinton, Bill, 379
closed-circuit television (CCTV) systems, 485–487
cloud storage, 473
CN tear gas, 479
code of silence, 233–234
Code of Silence Antidote (COSA), 165
codes of ethics, 228
Coffal, Elizabeth, 195
Coffey, Alan, 137
Cold Bath Fields riot (1833), 8
cold-case squads, 315–316
cold hits, 507–508
Coley, Sheilah, 209
collective bargaining, 91–92
college campuses, 24, 112
college education, 108–110
college job fairs, 106
Collins, John M., 88–89
Colorado Springs Police Department, 373
Colorado v. Bertine, 427
Columbian Society, 93

Combined DNA Index System (CODIS), 464, 503–504, 505
Combs, Lincoln, 61
commanders, 88
Commission on Accreditation for Law Enforcement Agencies (CALEA), 148–149, 229
    college education for police, 109
    undercover and decoy operations guidelines, 321
Commission on Campus Unrest, 25
Commission to Combat Police Corruption (CCPC), 248
communications unit, 99
communities
    animosity toward police, 243–245
    crime prevention and public safety, 198, 270
    defining, 383–384
    dividing into parcels, 384
    human disorder, 366
    improving relations, 198
    low esteem for police, 111
    partnering in policing process, 372
    pepper spray, 23
    physical disorder, 366
    police corruption, 236, 384
    Police Training Program (PTO), 126
Community Alert, 352
community crime prevention programs, 352
    chaplain programs, 357
    citizen patrols, 353
    citizen police academies, 357–358
    citizen volunteer programs, 353–354
    Community Emergency Response Teams (CERTs), 358
    Crime Stoppers, 355
    home security surveys, 355
    mass media campaigns, 355–357
    ministations, 355
    National Night Out, 353
    Neighborhood Watch, 352–353
    Operation Identification, 355
    police storefront stations, 355
    ride-along programs, 358
    tours of precincts and police facilities, 358
Community Emergency Response Team (CERT) programs, 343, 358, 374
    youth programs, 374
community-oriented policing
    crime analysis, 305
    examples, 372–373
    training police officers, 381
Community Patrol Police Officer Program (CPOP), 367
community police officers and discretion, 368
community policing, 7, 26, 83, 119, 221, 333, 365, 367–370, 377–378
    accomplishments, 382–383
    addressing causes of crime and social disorder, 370
    beginnings, 366
    broken windows model, 366
    Chicago Alternative Policing Strategy (CAPS), 375
    Community Emergency Response Team (CERT), 374
    cooperation, 385
    crime reduction, 27, 382
    crisis intervention team (CIT) officers, 376
    customer-based approach, 384
    cutting back on, 387
    debate on, 383–387

community policing (*continued*)
  decentralized neighborhood-based precincts, 367
  defining community, 383–384
  displacing crime, 385
  dividing community into parcels, 384
  expanding work with communities, 368
  federal government, 379–382
  feeling part of community, 374
  future of, 388–389
  how police function in, 206–207
  keeping police departments fully staffed, 387
  long-term problem solving, 377
  ministations, 373
  multiagency effort, 381–382
  negative effects, 384
  Neighborhood Watch programs, 374
  Office of Community Oriented Policing Services (COPS), 379–382
  perception of officers about, 385
  policemen and activities, 384
  police working with community, 368
  prevention of terrorist acts, 388–389
  problem solving, 382
  reducing crime and fear, 367
  reducing violence, 367
  relationship between police and community, 372, 382
  resident officer programs, 376, 378–379
  responsibility of all officers, 385
  small towns and mid-sized suburbs, 375
  supporting throughout department, 368–369
  training, 370
  universities, 376
  various modes of transportation, 373–374
"Community Policing: Now More Than Ever," 388
community policing officer, 367
community preservation, 366
community relationships, 329–330
community relations programs, 374
community relations unit, 98, 366
community service officers (CSOs), 89
community services unit, 98
Comparative Statistics file, 28
composite sketches, 489–490
CompStat program, 27–28, 30, 84, 307, 382, 465
computer-aided case management, 465–467
computer-aided dispatch (CAD), 460–463
computer-aided dispatch (CAD) systems, 469
computer-aided investigation, 465–467
computer-assisted instruction (CAI), 467
Computer-Assisted Terminal Criminal Hunt (CATCH), 465–466
computer-controlled visual simulations, 128
Computer Crime Research Center (CCRC), 500
computer crime units, 499
computer forensics, 498–501
computer networks, 469
computers, 459–478
  administrative uses, 467–468
  automated clerical processing systems, 468
  automated crime analysis, 464–465
  automated databases, 463–464
  cell phone technology, 462–463
  composite sketches, 489–490
  computer-aided case management, 465–467
  computer-aided dispatch (CAD), 460–463
  computer-aided investigation, 465–467
  computer-assisted instruction (CAI), 467
  identity theft, 500–501
  jail and prison management, 468

  management information systems, 468
  911 emergency system, 460
  patrol allocation design, 468
  revolution in policing, 26
Concerns of Police Survivors Inc. (COPS), 182
conducted energy devices (CEDs), 156, 478
conflict management training, 155
Connecticut State Police Department, 311
consent decrees, 209
consent once removed, 426
consent searches, 425–426
conservatism, 165
constables, 4, 6, 10
Contacts between Police and the Public, 2008, 146, 150
contagious diseases, 183–185
Container Security Initiative (CSI), 53
content wiretaps, 489
contraband, 418
Contracts between Police and the Public report (2011), 136
Contreras, Robert, 253
controversial police shootings, 31
Coolidge, Calvin, 18, 20, 92
Coolidge v. New Hampshire, 427
cops, origin of, 11
Cops on Donut Shops, 331
Cordner, Gary W., 111, 143, 164
co-responder team, 279
corporal or master patrol officer, 87
corporate strategies for policing, 364–365
corruption, 227, 229
  See also police corruption
  grass-eaters, 230
  internal, 235
  meat-eaters, 230
Cosa Nostra, 20
Cosby, Bill, 347
Council on Alcohol and Drug Abuse, 169
counter-terrorism, 53, 545
county law enforcement, 45–46
County of Riverside v. McLaughlin, 409
county sheriffs, 9
county sheriff's departments, 12–13
Courcelle, Charles, 196
courts
  creation, 395
  history of DNA in, 504–505
Cox Commission, 24
crackdown, 279
Crank, John P., 235, 236
Crawford, Kimberly A., 432
credit check, 120
crime, 395
  act and intent, 398
  amount occurring, 397–398
  arrests in United States, 398
  characteristics, 145
  collection and analysis of data, 464–465
  defenses, 399
  detailed information about, 58
  eighteenth century America, 10
  involving juveniles, 343
  measuring, 396–397
  National Crime Victimization Survey (NCVS), 397, 398
  national statistics on, 58
  patterns, 371
  plea bargains, 399
  prevention, 140
  prohibited by statute (malum prohibitum), 398
  punishment, 398–399

  retroactive investigation of past crimes, 299–300
  strong relationship with disorder, 386
  surveillance cameras, 314–315
  Uniform Crime Reports (UCR), 397
  wrong in itself (malum in se), 398
Crime Act (1994), 48
crime analysis, 305–307
Crime and Punishment: A History of the Criminal Justice System (Roth), 9
Crime Bill (1994), 379–380
crime fighters, 141
crime-fighting role, 134–136
Crime-Free Housing Unit, 374–375
Crime in the United States report, 58, 397
Crime Laboratory Accreditation Program, 498
crime labs, 493
  accreditation, 497–498
  ballistics, 494–496
  criminalistics, 496–497
  private, 494
  problems with, 491–492
  serology, 496
crime mapping, 464–465
crime prevention programs, 374
crime prevention specialists, 354
crime prevention unit, 98
crime rates, decrease in, 30, 299
crime reduction, 26–28
crime reports, 6
crimes
  victims, 347–348
crime scene exception, 427
crime scene search, 428
CrimeStat, 465
Crime Stoppers, 355
Crime Watch, 352
criminal enterprises and forfeiture laws, 61–62
criminal histories, 58, 120
Criminal Intelligence Coordinating Council (CICC), 381
"Criminal Intelligence Sharing: A National Plan for Intelligence-Led Policing at the Local, State and Federal Levels," 381
The Criminal Investigation, 299
Criminal Investigation Division (CID), 63
The Criminal Investigation Process, 303
criminal investigations
  DNA profiling, 502
  patrol officers, 304
  solvability factors, 304
criminal investigations unit, 98
criminalistics, 490–493, 496–497
Criminalistics: An Introduction to Forensic Science (Saferstein), 490
criminalists, 494
Criminal Justice Institute at University of Arkansas National Center for Rural Law Enforcement (NCRLE), 48
criminal justice planning agencies, 26
criminal justice programs, 107, 110
Criminal Justice Review, 507
criminal justice system
  discretion, 143
  effectiveness, fairness, and coordination, 198
  freedoms and rights, 402
  reports on, 25
criminal liability, 251–255
criminal record restrictions, 111
criminals
  body armor, 181
  registering, 312–313

relationship with police, 145
relationship with victim, 145
repeat offender programs (ROPs), 309, 312
Criminal Victimization in the United States, 397
Crisis Intervention Team (CIT), 279
critical incident stress debriefing (CISD), 175
Critical Issues in Police Civil Liability
(Kappeler), 253
CS gas (tear gas), 479, 481
CSI effect, 492–493
cultural diversity instruction training, 155, 334
culture, 162
Cumming, Elaine, 136
custodial arrests, 407
custodial interrogations
end of third degree, 432–434
entry of lawyers into station house, 434
erosion of *Miranda* rule, 435–444
Miranda rule, 434–435
path to *Miranda*, 432–434
prompt arrangement rule, 434
third degree, 432
cyber-based attacks, 59
cyberbullying, 320, 345
cybercrimes, 320, 500–501
CyberTipline, 471, 473
cynicism, 165

D

Daley, Richard J., 23
DalNets, 471
Dane County Chiefs of Police, 400
dangerous offenders, 312
dangerous work zones, 285
Daniels, Deborah J., 212
Danziger Bridge case, 232
Dark Blue, 231
databases of criminal information, 58
Dateline, 319
Daubert v. Merrell Down Pharmaceuticals, Inc., 505
David, James, 204
Davis, Edward F., 173
Davis, Jefferson, 15
Davis, Kenneth Culp, 143
Davis v. United States, 441, 446
Day, William R., 404
Days of Rage (Chicago), 23
dazzler, 482
deadly force, 149–156, 410–411
Branch Davidian compound, 154
fleeing felon doctrine, 152–154
imminent danger standard, 154
jurisdictional variations in, 151
police, 150
second guessing, 149
unarmed fleeing felon, 153
deaf community, 341–342
decentralized model of state law enforcement, 55
decentralized neighborhood-based precincts, 367
decoy operations, 316–317, 318
decoy vehicles, 281–282, 317
de-escalation, 280
de facto discrimination, 199
Defense Advanced Research Projects Agency
(DARPA), 511
defense of life standard, 154
Def-Tee (Pepper Mace), 479
DeKalb Police Department, 379
Delaware v. Prouse, 411, 418
Dempsey, John S., 121, 347, 369, 407, 557

Denver Post, 49
Deorle v. Rutherford, 479
department policies and discretion, 145
deputies, 42
Dershowitz, Alan M., 435, 511
DeSalvo, Albert, 316
desegregating schools, 21
desk officer, 94
desks, 94
Des Moines Police Department, 551
detective mystique, 302–303
detectives, 14, 87
alternatives to retroactive investigation of past
crimes, 303–305
canvasses, 301
cold-case squads, 315–316
effectiveness, 300
follow-up reports, 301
information management, 306–307
investigative process, 300–301
jobs, 301–302
mentoring, 305
multiagency investigative task forces, 307–309
nonproductive work, 299
overseeing processing of crime scene, 301
as person with promotional rank, 302–303
as plainclothes police officer, 302–303
reinterviewing victims or witnesses, 301
relationships with prosecutors, 302
repeat offender programs (ROPs), 309, 312
retroactive investigation of past crimes,
299–300
solving crimes, 301, 303
specialized, 301–302
training, 305
detective units, 301–302
detention unit, 99
Detroit Mini-Station Program, 367
Detroit Police Department, 116, 209, 216, 491–492
Detroit Police Officers Association, 202
Detroit riot, 24
Devine, Elizabeth, 502
diabetics, 342
Dickerson, Timothy, 423
Dickerson v. United States, 441–444, 446
differential response to calls for service, 273–274
digital fingerprints, 473
digital forensics, 498
alteration of evidence, 499
cell phones, 501
evidence, 499
identity theft, 500–501
media, 499
searching, seizing, and preserving evidence,
499
digital photography, 488
DiPetro, Louis, 432
directed patrol, 272–273
Dirty Harry problem, 167–168
Dirty Harry syndrome, 235–236
disabilities, 341–342
discipline, 82
discoverpolicing.org website, 106, 208
discretion, 142–149
characteristics of crime, 145
citizen-initiated situations, 145
Commission on Accreditation for Law
Enforcement Agencies (CALEA), 148–149
community police officers, 368
controlling, 147–148
criminal justice system, 143
dealing with similar issues in same way, 147

defining, 143
department policies, 145
domestic violence, 146
employee early warning systems, 147
exercising, 144
factors influencing, 144–147
formal set of policies or guidelines, 147–148
gender, 146
internal control mechanisms, 147
lessons learned training, 147
race, 145–146
relationship between alleged criminal and
victim, 145
relationship between police and criminal or
victim, 145
self-initiated situations, 145
stop-and-frisk policies, 144
suspect's behavior, 145
discretionary authority, 83
discrimination, 56–57, 194
affirmative action programs, 200–201
African Americans, 196–197, 335
candidates not meeting standards, 200
Civil Rights Act of 1964, 198
Civil Rights Act of 1991, 198, 199
de facto discrimination, 199
equal employment opportunities, 201
Equal Employment Opportunity Act of 1972
(EEOA), 198, 199
federal courts, 199–200
Fourteenth Amendment, 198
height requirement, 200
Hispanics, 335
job analysis, 200
job requirements must be job related, 199
minorities, 203
national commissions to study, 197
Omnibus Crime Control and Safe Streets Act
of 1968, 198
personnel tests, 200
physical ability testing, 200
police departments, 194–197
police shootings, 151
quotas, 201
redressing past, 201
striving for equality, 197–201
in testing, 199
tests and examinations job related, 199–200
white male backlash, 201–203
women, 194–196, 203
*Disorder and Decline: Crime and the Spiral of
Decay in American Neighborhoods* (Skogan),
385
disorderly conduct arrests, 135
disorder relationship with crime, 386
distracted drivers challenge, 286–287
district courts, 395
districts, 93–95
DNA databases, 503, 506–507
DNA (deoxyribonucleic acid), 502–504
backlog of cases, 507, 509
cold hits, 507–508
current issues, 507–509
dragnets, 508
exonerations, 509
familial DNA analysis, 508–509
history in U.S. courts, 504–505
reliability, 505
storage, 508
uniqueness, 502
warrants, 508
DNA evidence, 491, 494

DNA profiling, 501–509
    criminal investigations, 502
    cross-country, 504
    current technology, 506
    endorsements, 505
    mitochondrial DNA (MtDNA) analysis, 502
    polymerase chain reaction-short tandem
        repeat (PCR-STR), 502
    property crimes, 509
    restricted fragment length polymorphism
        (RFLP), 502
DNA technology, 315–316
DNA typing, 501–509
document analysis, 497
domestic terrorism, 59
    anarchists, 536
    animal rights groups, 534
    Atlanta Olympic Games, 537
    Centennial Olympic Park bombing, 533
    extremist groups, 536
    far-left environmentalists, 534
    gun control laws, 532
    hate groups, 536
    left-wing extremist groups, 535
    lone-wolf extremists, 534, 536
    Major Nidal Malik Hasan, 533
    militia movement, 533–534
    New World Order, 532
    Oklahoma City Federal Building, 537
    reflecting violent Islamic extremism, 536–537
    right-wing extremism, 533–534
    sovereign citizens movement, 534–535
    special-interest terrorist groups, 535–536
    Unabomber, 538–539
    violence, 536
    white supremacy, 532
domestic violence, 338
    discretion, 146
    mandatory arrest, 349
    police families, 241–243
domestic violence victims, 348–349
Dothard v. Rawlinson, 107
double marginality, 196
Douglas, Robert, 178, 180
Dover Police Department, 59
Downs, Gerard F., 58
Draper v. United States, 409
Dred Scott v. Sandford, 9
driving record, 120
driving under the influence (DUI), 135, 497
driving while black (DWB), 243, 335
driving while intoxicated (DWI), 135, 497
Drone Act, 485
drones, 484–485
DropBox, 473
dropsy, 239
drug abuse arrests, 135
Drug Abuse Resistance Education (DARE)
    programs, 345, 374
drug-detection dogs, 416–417
Drug Endangered Children Program (DEC), 381
Drug Enforcement Administration (DEA), 60
drugged drivers, 285
drug investigations, 322
drug recognition experts (DREs), 285
drug-related misconduct, 238
drug-related police corruption, 238
drugs, 181
    cases involving, 53
    dropsy, 239
    in Florida, 65
    prior use by police candidates, 110–111

small-town law enforcement, 46
    war on, 60
drug-trafficking locations, 278
drug undercover operations
    buy-bust operation, 322–323
    infiltrating criminal organizations, 322
    staking out locations, 322
drunk drivers, 287–288
drunkenness
    arrests, 135
    eighteenth century America, 10
dual policing careers, 218
due process clause, 402
Duffy, James E., 534
Duluth Police Department's Safety and
    Accountability Audit of the Response
    to Native Women Who Report Sexual
    Assault, 383
Durham Police Department, 47
Durk, David, 25, 230, 231
DWI (driving while intoxicated) checkpoint, 287

E

E911, 461, 487
early intervention systems, 249
early police, 3–4
early police departments, 10–11
Earth Liberation Front (ELF), 535–536
economic sanctions, 62
education
    importance of, 344
    law enforcement, 55
    rural and small-town law enforcement, 48
educational records, 120
education requirements, 108–110
Eighteenth Amendment, 18
Eisenberg, Alice, 502
electric bikes, 282
Electric Rifle, 479
electrolaser, 482
Electronic Crime Scene Investigation: A Guide
    for First Responders, 499
electronic custody control belt, 481
electronic devices, 155
electronic video surveillance, 485–487
Elgin Police Department
    community policing, 374–375
    ROPE, 376, 378–379
Ellensburg Police Department, 209
Emerald Society, 93
emotional intelligence (EI), 116
Employee Polygraph Protection Act (EPPA), 118
employment records, 120
enforcers, 141–142
English policing, 4–8
    Act for Improving Police in and near the
        Metropolis (Metropolitan Police Act
        (1828)), 6–7
    beat system, 7
    Bow Street Runners, 6
    civil administration, 3
    constables, 4, 6, 11
    crime reports, 6
    first police department, 4
    horse patrol, 6
    hue and cry, 4, 5
    magistrates, 5
    metropolitan police, 6–8
    modern-style police departments, 3
    pawnbrokers, 6

Peel's Nine Principles, 7
    seventeenth-century, 5
    shire-reeve, 4
enhanced 911, 461
enhanced CAD, 461
entrapment, 323–324
Environmental Protection Agency (EPA), 64
equal employment opportunities, 201
Equal Employment Opportunity Act of 1972
    (EEOA), 26, 198, 199
Equal Employment Opportunity Commission
    (EEOC), 199, 217
equal protection under the law, 198, 201
equipment unit, 99
Escobedo v. Illinois, 21, 432, 434, 446
Ethical Dilemmas in Criminal Justice (Pollock), 228
ethical leadership, 75, 76–77
ethics, 227–229
European Police Systems (Fosdick), 19
Evanoff, Mike, 315
evidence, 491
    describing, 428
    digital forensics, 499
    illegally seized, 404–405
    plain view evidence, 426–428
    probable cause, 409
    violation of U.S. Constitution, 403–407
evidence-based policing, 270
Evolving Strategy of Policing: Case Studies of
    Strategic Change (Kelling and Wycoff), 265
excessive force, 246
exclusionary rule, 403–407
Executive Office for Asset Forfeiture (EOAF),
    61–62
Executive Office for Terrorist Financing and
    Financial Crime (EOTF/FC), 62
Executive Office of the President of the United
    States, 506
Executive Order 11246, 200
Executive Sessions on Policing, 364
exigent circumstances, 418, 424–425
explosive ordinance disposal (EOD), 511
explosives, federal laws relating to, 60
external stress, 169–170
eyewitness identification, 446–447, 449–450

F

Facebook, 306, 356, 472, 473
Face2Face, 345
"Faces, the Ultimate Composite Picture"
    CD-ROM, 489
facial recognition, 510–511
facilities unit, 99
fact pattern, 395
Fairfax County Police Department, 117
false alarms, 274
Famega, Christine N., 144
familial DNA analysis, 508–509
Family Finder program, 375
Fantino, Julian, 493
Fargo, William G., 17
Farrar, Emile, 196
fasces, 4
fatalities
    alcohol-impaired drivers, 287
    police pursuits, 289–291
fatigued or distracted drivers, 285
FBI Academy, 20, 57, 129
    Leadership Development Institute (LDI), 57
FBI Child Exploitation Task Force, 138

FBI Crime Laboratory, 58
FBI Laboratory, 493
  DNA Analysis Unit, 502
FBI Law Enforcement Bulletin, 47, 90, 416, 425, 462, 499, 545, 549
FBI Virtual Academy, 228
Federal Aviation Administration (FAA), 485
Federal Building in Oklahoma City, Oklahoma bombing (1995), 26, 162
Federal Bureau of Investigation (FBI), 20, 29, 40, 57–60, 307, 311, 471, 546–548
  analyzing gunshot residue (GSR), 495
  assisting state and local law enforcement agencies, 57
  Behavioral Science Unit (BSU), 173
  citizens' constitutional rights violations, 57
  cold-case serial homicides, 58
  comparative lead analysis, 495
  corruption convictions, 58
  counterrorism, 545
  Counterterrorism Division, 536
  Crime in the United States, 397
  Criminal Justice Services Division, 173–174
  Critical Incident Response Group, 58
  drug standards, 111
  facial recognition system, 489
  federal crimes, 58
  federal laws enforcement, 57
  Field Intelligence Groups (FIGs), 60
  handling evidence and contagious diseases, 185
  homeland security, 545–546
  Identification Division, 58
  Integrated Automated Fingerprint Identification System (IAFIS), 477–478
  investigatory activities, 57–60
  Joint Terrorism Task Forces (JTTF), 59, 545–546, 551
  Law Enforcement Online (LEO) Program, 59
  matching bullet and shell casings, 495
  National Alert System (NAS), 59
  National Center for the Analysis of Violent Crime (NCAVC), 58–59
  National Crime Information Center (NCIC), 58, 463–464
  National Incident-Based Reporting System (NIBRS), 58
  National Instant Criminal Background Check (NICS), 464
  National Security Branch (NSB), 545
  National Security Division, 528
  nationwide searches and capture of notorious criminals, 57
  Next Generation Identification (NGI), 489, 510, 546
  nonenforcement personnel, 57
  officers killed by friendly fire, 220
  officers killed in line of duty, 181
  organized crime, 58, 59
  police corruption, 248
  political corruption, 58
  Practical Pistol Course, 128
  priorities post-9/11, 547
  reorganization, 59
  stalking cases, 59
  Ten Most Wanted Criminals Program, 20
  terrorism, 59, 527
  Training Division Research and Development Unit, 177
  Uniform Crime Reports, 20
  Uniform Crime Reports (UCR) Program, 58
  Violent Criminal Apprehension Program (ViCAP), 464, 477

virtual command center (VCC), 59
  white-collar crime, 58
Federal Communications Commission (FCC), 501
federal courts
  college education for police, 109
  discrimination, 199–200
  security, 60
federal Courts of Appeals, 395
Federal Emergency Management Agency (FEMA), 542
Federal Excess Property Programs, 554
federal government and community policing, 379–382
Federal Judiciary Act of 1789, 16
federal law enforcement, 56–66
  agents and corruption, 233
  homeland security, 543–546
  Operation Fast and Furious, 60–61
  women, 56
Federal Law Enforcement Training Center (FLETC), 129, 209, 308, 542, 552
federal liability, 252–253
federal marshals, 16
federal prisoners, transporting, 60
Federal Trade Commission (FTC), 63
federal undercover operations, 321
Fernandez v. California, 426, 427
Field Intelligence Groups (FIGs), 60
field interrogations, 277, 422–424
field notes, 301
field training, 123, 126–127
field training officers (FTOs), 123
Fifth Amendment, 407
Financial Crimes Enforcement Network (FinCEN), 62
fingernail scrapings, 496–497
fingerprints, 509
  automated fingerprint identification system (AFIS), 475–478
  Henry System of classification, 476
  Identification Based Information System (IBIS), 478
  inked prints, 473
  lasers in fingerprint lifting, 474
  latent prints, 473–474
  mobile fingerprint-reading devices, 474
  plastic prints, 474
  scanning, 476–477
  ten-prints, 473
  visible prints, 474
fingerprint technology, 472
Finn, Mary, 204
firearms
  federal laws relating to, 60
  tracing, 495
  training, 128, 154–155
Firearms Training System (FATS), 467
Firman, John, 110
first-line supervisors ethical behavior, 250
Fish and Wildlife Service, 62, 63
"Fixing Broken Windows: A Collaborative Approach to Housing Remediation," 382
Flame of Hope torch, 331, 332
fleeing felon doctrine, 152–154
flight-or fight response, 169
Florida Criminal Justice Standards and Training Commission (CJSTC), 109
Florida Department of Law Enforcement, 170, 307–308
Florida Fish and Wildlife Conservation Commission, 44

Florida v. Bostick, 426, 427
Florida v. Harris, 417, 418
Florida v. J.L., 424, 427
Florida v. Riley, 429, 488
follow-up reports, 301
Fong, Heather, 209, 213
Food and Drug Administration (FDA), 63
footpad (street robber), 5
foot patrols, 261, 266–267, 269–270, 284
forecasting, 270
foreign intelligence operations and espionage, 59
Foreign Intelligence Surveillance Act (FISA Court), 560
Forensic Examination of Digital Evidence: A Guide for Law Enforcement, 499
forensic science, 490–493
  crime labs, 493–497
  CSI effect, 492–493
  evidence, 491
  problems with crime laboratories, 491–492
  turn around for evidence, 493–494
Forst, Linda, 27, 65, 90, 119, 149, 150, 179, 219, 237, 267, 318, 340–341, 377–378, 413, 476, 531
Fourteenth Amendment, 198, 201, 214, 399, 402–403
Fourth Amendment, 407, 410, 411, 415–416, 416
France, 3–4
  Container Security Initiative (CSI), 53
  patrols of Paris police, 7
Frankfurter, Felix, 405, 406, 407
Franklin County Sheriff's Office, 511
Fraternal Order of Police (FOP), 92
Freedom Riders, 21
Freeh, Louis J., 527
Freitag, 460
frontier experience in American policing, 15–17
Frye test, 505
Frye v. United States, 505
function or purpose organization, 97–99
Furnham, Adrian, 166
fusion centers, 388, 554
Fyfe, James J., 151

G

Gaithersburg Police Department, 209
gang investigations, 282–283
Gang Resistance Education and Training (GREAT), 345, 374
gangs, 46–47
  global positioning systems (GPSs) monitoring, 313
Garfield, James, 84
Garrett, Andy, 170
Gary Police Department, 165
Gates, Henry Louis, Jr., 244
gay bashing, 339
Gay Officers Action League (GOAL), 93, 214–215
gays and lesbians, 213–215, 339
gender
  discretion, 146
  police stress, 172
General Accountability Office (GAO), 238
General Electric Co. v. Joiner, 505
Generation Next, 112
genetic fingerprinting, 501–509
geographic area organization, 93–95
geographic information systems (GISs), 461, 484
Georgia Bureau of Indentification (GBI), 477
Georgia v. Randolph, 426, 427
Germany and professional police, 4

ghost officer, 323
Giuliani, Rudolph, 232, 382, 548
glass, 496
global positioning systems (GPSs), 313–314, 461, 483, 484
Gold, Marian, 218
golden apples, 235, 236
Golden Mean, 227
Golden State Peace Officers Association (GSPOA), 214
Goldsboro Police Department, 479
Goldstein, Herman, 134, 370
Gonzales, Adolfo, 386–387
good faith exception, 430–431
Good Neighbor Next Door program, 379
GoogleDrive, 473
Gordon v. Warren Consolidated Board of Education, 320
Governors Highway Safety Association, 288
Grady, Paul, 284
Grand Rapids Police Department, 175
grass-eaters, 230, 234
gratuities, 234–235
Great Britain
    Home Office Large Major Enquiry System (HOLMES), 466
    surveillance cameras, 485
Greenwood, Billy, 428
Grennan, Sean, 204
Griggs v. Duke Power Company, 199
Groh v. Ramirez, 427, 431
Gross Hearings, 25
Grubbs, Jeffrey, 421
Guardian Angels, 353
Guardian Personal Security Products (Bodyguard), 479
guardians, 127
Guardians Association, 93, 196, 197
Guardians Association of New York City Police Department v. Civil Service Commission of New York, 113–114, 200
Guidelines on Cell Phones Forensics, 501
gun control laws, 532
gun dealers sting operations, 319
gun run, 168
guns, 60–61

H

habeas corpus, 441
hairs and fibers, 496
Hamas, 528
Hampton v. United States, 324
hand-geometry systems, 509–510
Harding, Warren G., 20
Harlem riot (1964), 24
Harris, Victor, 410–411
Harris County Sheriff's Office, 51
Harris v. New York, 427, 435–436
Harris v. United States, 427
Hart, William, 210
Harvard, Beverly, 209
Harvard University, 364
Hate Crime Statistics Act, 58
height and weight requirements, 107
Henry v. United States, 409
hepatitis B and C, 183
Hernandez, Bobby, 215
Herndon Police Department, 376
Herschel, John, 483
Herschel, William, 483

Hester v. United States, 427, 429
Hezbollah, 528
Hibel v. Sixth Judicial District Court of Nevada, Sixth District, 427
high-rate offenders, 312
high-technology crimes, 59
highwaymen, 5
Hiibel v. Sixth District Court of Nevada, Humbolt County, 423
Hillsborough County Sheriff's Department, 116
Hiring and Keeping Police Officers report (2004), 111
Hiring in the Spirit of Service strategy, 116, 119
Hispanic American Police Command Officers Association (HAPCOA), 212
Hispanics, 335–336
    challenges in policing, 221
    cultural differences, 211
    disproportionately stopped by police, 244
    representation in policing today, 211–212
Hogan's Alley courses, 128
Holder, Eric C., Jr., 49, 61, 368
Holmes, Oliver Wendell, Jr., 407, 429
Homant, Robert, 204
home invasion robbery, 65
homeland defense, post-9/11 response to, 540–542
Homeland Defense Initiative, 526
homeland security, 388–389, 526
    border protection, 547
    Federal Bureau of Investigation (FBI), 545–546
    federal law enforcement, 543–546
    state and local law enforcement, 549–556
Homeland Security Investigations (HSI), 53
Homeless Outreach Team (HOT), 373
homeless people, 350–351
Home Office Large Major Enquiry System (HOLMES), 466
home security surveys, 355
Homestead Riots, 16
Homework Assistance Program, 376
Homicide Investigation and Tracking System/ Supervision Management and Recidivist Tracking (HITS/SMART), 466
homicide rate, 151
Hoover, Herbert, 18
Hoover, J. (John) Edgar, 19–20, 57
horses, 373
hot-spot policing, 271, 273
Houston Police Department (HPD), 50–51, 208, 491
    Crisis Intervention Response Team (CIRT), 279
    neighborhood-oriented policing (NOP), 384–385
Hudson, Booker T., 420
Hudson v. Michigan, 420–421
hue and cry, 4–5
Huff, Henry, 511
Hughes, Charle E., 433–434
Hulon, Willie T., 536, 549
human immunodeficiency virus (HIV), 183–185
human relations, 330, 332–333
human trafficking, 138, 308
Hurricane Katrina, 33–34, 170, 232

I

IACP website, 228
iCloud, 473
idealists, 141
Idea of Police (Klockars), 136
identification, 448–450, 509

Identification Based Information System (IBIS), 478
identification unit, 99
identity theft, 58, 500–501
Ignitus Worldwide, 345
illegal immigrants, 386–387
illegal immigration, 50–51, 341
Illinois v. Caballes, 416–417, 418
Illinois v. Gates, 419, 421
Illinois v. Krull, 427, 431
Illinois v. Lidster, 412, 418
Illinois v. McArthur, 421, 424
Illinois v. Perkins, 439–440
Illinois v. Rodriquez, 426, 427
Illinois v. Wardlow, 423–424, 427
immigrants problems with police, 366
Immigration and Customs Enforcement (ICE), 50, 53, 62
    287(g) program, 50–51
Immigration and Naturalization Service, 62
imminent danger standard, 154
impaired drivers, 287–288
Incident Command System (ICS), 400
incident-driven policing, 370–371
Incident Management System (IMS), 313
incident report, 301
incident to lawful arrest, 421–422
Indianapolis Police Department, 195
Indiana State Police, 106, 210
Indian country and tribal law enforcement, 48–49
indictment, 447
inducement, 323
"inevitability of discovery" rule, 436
informants
    search warrants, 418–419
    terrorism, 539
information, 447
information management, 306–307
infrared technology, 483–484
inked prints, 473
Innocence Project, 509
in-service training, 128–129
inspections unit, 99
inspectors, 87, 88
Institute for Law Enforcement Administration, 129
Institute of Public Administration, 19
Integrated Automated Fingerprint Identification System (IAFIS), 477–478
Integrated Ballistics Information System (IBIS), 495
integrity tests, 247
intelligence analysis, 307
intelligence-led policing, 307
intelligence-oriented policing, 305
Intelligence Reform and Terrorism Prevention Act (IRTPA), 527
intelligence unit, 99
internal affairs divisions, 99, 247–248
internal corruption, 235
Internal Revenue Service (IRS), 61
International Association for Identification (IAI), 478
International Association of Chiefs of Police (IACP), 17, 93, 106, 110, 156, 165, 205, 208–209, 213, 331, 375, 549, 554
    awards for community policing, 382–383
    closed-circuit television (CCTV) systems survey, 485
    computer network, 469
    Crime Prevention Committee, 352

"Ethical Standards in Police Service, Force Management, and Integrity Issues," 228
foot patrols, 267
Highway Safety Committee, 285
HIV/AIDS, 184–185
homeland security awards, 388
"Improving Safety in Indian Country" summit, 336
Law Enforcement Code of Ethics, 228
police-involved domestic violence, 242
pregnancy policy, 217
public relations, 333
sex-related misconduct study, 240
Tasers and electronic devices, 155
Triad, 343
"Value-Centered Leadership: A Workshop on Ethics and Quality Leadership," 228
Victim Services Committee, 347
Women's Leadership Institute, 215
International Association of Women Police (IAWP), 218
International Brotherhood of Police Officers (IBPO), 91, 93
International City Management Association, 19
International Conference of Police Associations (ICPA), 92–93
International High Technology Crime Investigation Association (HTCIA), 500
International Law Enforcement Academy (ILEA), 53
International Police, 66
international terrorism, 528
    arrests, 529–530
    foreign sponsors threats, 528
    formalized terrorist groups threats, 528
    international radical extremist threats, 528
    London bombings, 529
    millenium bomb plot, 532
    suicide bombers, 529–530
    United States, 528–529
    U.S. Embassy bombings, 528, 532
    U.S.S. *Cole* bombing, 532
    World Trade Center Attack (1993), 532
    world-wide, 529–530
International Training Center, Sensitive Investigations Unit, 47
International Union of Police Associations (IUPA), 92, 183
Internet, 469
    child pornography, 470–473
    cyberbullying, 320
    law enforcement job opportunites, 106
    pepper spray outrage, 23
    registries, 312–313
    safety brochures and programs, 347
Internet Crimes Against Children (ICAC) Task Force, 471–473
Internet Protocol (IP) telephony, 463
Internet Relay Chats (IRCs), 471
Interpol (International Criminal Police Organization), 66
interrogation
    police deception, 238–239
    right to counsel, 432
Interstate Commerce Commission (ICC), 63
inventory searches, 429
investigations
    police corruption, 247–248
    police deception, 238–239
    visual information to aid, 485–486
investigative process, 300–301
investigative task forces, 307–309

investigators, 87
    training, 305
    undercover operations, 320–321
InVEST Services (Intimate Violence Enhanced Services Team), 349
iodine fuming, 475
iPhone, 472
Ireland, 8
iris-based systems, 509
Irish National Police, 209
isolation, 166

J

Jacobson v. United States, 323, 324
jail and prison management, 468
J.D.B. v. North Carolina, 443, 446
Jews, 338
job analysis, 113–114, 200
job related skills, 113
jobs in policing, 106–107
"John Doe Indictment Project," 508
"John Doe" warrant, 508
John F. Kennedy School of Government, 364
John Jay College of Criminal Justice, 114, 181
Johnson, Charles L., 240–241
Johnson, Lyndon B., 198, 200–201
joint federal and local task forces, 66
Joint Regional Intelligence Center, 554
Joint Terrorism Task Forces (JTTF), 59, 545–546
Jones, Arthur, 203
judicial process, 395–396
judicial review, 230, 403
jury nullification, 29
Justice Department, 535
Justice for All Act of 2004, 506
juvenile investigation guidelines, 302
juveniles, 343–347
juvenile services unit, 98

K

Kansas City patrol study, 263–264
Kansas City Police Department, 263, 267, 272
Kansas City Preventive Patrol Experiment, 26
Kappeler, Victor E., 28, 98, 253
Katz v. United States, 415, 416, 418
Kaupp v. Texas, 443, 446
Kefauver, Estes, 20
Kefauver Committee, 20
Kehoe, Michael K., 310–312
Kelling, George L., 352, 364, 386
Kelly, Clarence, 263
Kelly, Raymond W., 422, 485
Kennedy, Daniel, 204
Kennedy, John F., 21
Kent Police Department, 138
Kerik, Bernard, 232–233
Key West Police Department, 214
kinetic energy rounds, 155
King, Donald, 405, 407
King, Rodney, 22, 28–29, 227, 236, 246, 335, 410
King County Sheriff's Department, 116
King County Sheriff's Office, 124, 126, 209
    RADAR (Risk Awareness, De-escalation, and Referral) program, 279–281
Kirby v. Illinois, 447–448, 450
Kirk, Kennedy, 415
Kirkham, George L., 134–135, 163
Kirkpatrick, Anne, 209

Kirk v. Illinois, 421
Kirk v. Louisiana, 415
Klinger, David, 172, 175
Knapp Commission, 25, 229–230, 231, 247
knock-and-announce rule, 420–421
knowledge, skills, and abilities (KSAs), 114
Knowles, Patrick, 422
Knowles v. Iowa, 422, 427
Koon, Stacey C., 29
Kuhlman v. Wilson, 445
Ku Klux Klan, 536
Ku Klux Klan Act, 252
K-9 units, 156, 293
Kyllo, Danny, 416
Kyllo v. United States, 416, 418

L

laboratory unit, 99
Lalezary, Shervin, 354
Lambda Legal Defense and Education Fund, 339
Landslide, Inc. website, 471
Lanier, Cathy L., 209, 278
Largo Police Department, 105
lasers in fingerprint lifting, 474–475
Las Vegas-Clark County Police Department, 43
Las Vegas Metro Police Department (LVMPD), 534–535
latent prints, 473–475, 477–478
lateral transfers, 91
Lau, Fred, 213
Lautenberg Act, 242
law, 407
law enforcement
    antiterrorism focus, 32–33
    civilianization, 54
    cost of providing, 40
    diversity, 208, 334
    education, 55
    effectiveness, fairness, and coordination, 198
    layoffs, 51, 54
    local, 40, 42–51
    military, 63
    multiagency task forces, 64
    Muslims, 337
    reduced budgets era, 51, 54–55
    sharing information, 307–309
    Special Olympics and, 331–332
    sworn employees, 41–42
    volunteers, 54
    women, 338
    working together, 307–309
law enforcement agencies
    career opportunities for college educated, 110
    investigative and analysis services for, 58
    traffic unit, 285
Law Enforcement and Emergency Services Video Association, 485
Law Enforcement Assistance Administration (LEAA), 25–26, 198, 203
    Managing Criminal Investigations (MCI), 304
    Women on Patrol: A Pilot Study of Police Performance in New York City, 203
Law Enforcement Code of Ethics, 228
Law Enforcement Education Program (LEEP), 26, 109
Law Enforcement Exploring program, 347
Law Enforcement for Gays and Lesbians, 214
Law Enforcement Gays and Lesbians International (LEGAL), 215
Law Enforcement Leadership Institute, 129

Law Enforcement Management and
    Administrative Statistics (LEMAS)
    program, 40–42
Law Enforcement News, 32
Law Enforcement Online (LEO) Program, 59
Law Enforcement Training Network, 552
law enforcers, 141
Lawrence v. Texas, 214
lawsuits, 251–255
law *versus* order dilemma, 229
leadership, 74–75
Leadership Development Institute (LDI), 57
LED incapacitator, 482
Lee, Donald J., Jr., 214
legal assistance unit, 99
legalistic style, 142
legal liability, 252
Leinen, Stephen, 196–197
lesbians, 339
less-than-lethal weapons (LTLW), 155–156,
    478–482
Lewis, John F., Jr., 528
Leyva, Claudia, 282–283
liason officer, 374
Library of Congress, 64
license plate recognition (LPR) technology,
    469, 472
license plate scanners, 314
lictors, 4
lie detectors, 118
lieutenants, 88
Lifecodes, 504–505
Limewire, 472
Lincoln, Abraham, 16
Lindsey, John V., 25, 229
line functions, 97–98
lineups and right to counsel, 447–448
liquor law violations, 135
Live Scan, 476–477
local control, 40
local law enforcement
    campus law enforcement, 49–50
    county law enforcement, 45–46
    deputized as immigration agents, 50
    federal immigration officials and, 50–51
    homeland security, 549–556
    illegal immigration, 50–51
    Indian country and tribal law enforcement,
        48–49
    metropolitan police departments, 42–44
    police protection, 42
    racial and ethnic minorities, 42
    rural and small-town law enforcement, 46–48
    sheriff's departments, 42
loitering arrests, 135
LoJack, 313
London Metropolitan Police, 7–8, 75
long range acoustic device (LRAD), 482
loops, 474
Los Angeles, California
    first officially designated policewoman, 194
    riots, 29
    sworn law enforcement employees, 41–42
Los Angeles County, California v. Rettele, 420, 421
Los Angeles County Sheriff's Department, 45,
    202, 488
    Scientific Services Bureau, 502
    suicide by cop, 173
Los Angeles Police Department (LAPD), 204,
    386, 466, 549, 550
    Academy Training Program, 216
    baton procedures, 29

Candidate Assistance Program, 216
    Christopher Commission investigation (1991),
        165
    corruption, 31
    excessive force, 205
    gays and lesbians, 213
    gross incompetence, 29
    indictment of, 29
    lawsuits, 253
    National Counter-Terrorism Academy, 552
    police-involved domestic violence, 242
    Rampart scandal, 232
    Women's Coordinator, 216
Los Angeles' Strategic Extraction and
    Restoration (LASER) program, 272
Louisiana State Police - Criminal Patrol Unit, 245
Louisiana State Police - Traffic Patrol, 245
Louisville Division of Police, 376
Lovick, John, 344
Low Copy Number (LCN) DNA, 504
Low Life: Lures and Snares of Old New York
    (Sante), 11
loyalty and police corruption, 236
Luckie, Timothy M., 470–473
luminol, 496
Lundman, Richard J., 231
Lunneborg, Patricia, 218
Lunsford, Jennifer, 313
Luttman, Jennifer, 504
lynching, 9

M

Madison, Wisconsin policing protests, 400–401
Madison Police Department, 115, 216
Mafia, 20
Magers, Jeffrey S., 76–77
magistrates (judges), 3
mail fraud, 63
maintenance unit, 99
Major Cities Chiefs Association, 50, 554
Mallory v. United States, 433, 434, 446
malum in se, 398
malum prohibitum, 398
management, 74
management information systems, 468
management training, 129
managerial definitions, 72–74
managers, 74
Managing Criminal Investigations (MCI), 304
Mapp, Dollree (Dolly), 405, 407
Mapp v. Ohio, 21, 230, 239, 403, 405, 406
Marden, Leo W., 194
marijuana, 110, 288
Marine Police, 3, 6
Martin, Robert A., 545
Maryland State Police, 202, 244
Maryland v. Buie, 424, 427
Maryland v. Garrison, 427, 431
Maryland v. King, 507
Maryland v. Pringle, 409
Maryland v. Shatzer, 444
Maryland v. Wilson, 412, 418
Massachusetts, 12
Massachusetts Law Enforcement Technology
    and Training Center, 389
Massachusetts v. Sheppard, 427, 431
mass media campaigns, 355–357
McCutcheon, Charles, 219
McFadden, Martin, 423
McGruff, 356

McLaren, Roy Clinton, 262
McNabb-Mallory rule, 432, 433
McNabb v. United States, 433, 434, 446
McNeil v. Wisconsin, 441
Meara, Paula, 209
meat-eaters, 230, 234
Mecklenburg, Sheri H., 551
media
    AMBER Alerts, 356
    attention for complaints against the police, 255
    civil disobedience, 22
    fighting crime, 356
    letting public know crime is occurring, 356
    pepper spray outrage, 23
    police portrayals, 333
    suicide by cop, 173
    surveillance videos, 356
mediation training, 155
medical marijuana laws, 322
Memphis Police Department, 209
    Blue CRUSH (criminal reduction utilitizing
        statistical history), 464
Mena, Iris, 420
mental illness and Specialized Policing Responses
    (SPRs) to individuals with, 279, 281
mentoring, 305
Mesa Police Department's Cellular Digital
    Packet Data (CDPD), 463
methamphetamine
    preventing use and production, 381
    registering users, 313
    small towns, 46
Metro-Data Police Department, 290
metropolitan police departments, 42–44
metropolitan police for London, 6–8
Mezquia, Jesus, 316
Miami Beach Police Department, 215, 552
Miami-Dade County Police Department, 43
Miami Police Department, 202
Miami Shield program, 552
Michenfelder v. Sumner, 480
Michigan Department of State Police v. Sitz,
    412, 418
Michigan State Police, 491–492
Michigan v. Mosley, 436
Michigan v. Summers, 420, 421
Microsoft, 471
Microsoft OneDrive, 473
mid-sized suburbs crime and disorder problems,
    375
Mieth v. Dothard, 200
military, 3, 16, 63
military history, 120
millenium bomb plot, 532
Millennials, 112
Miller, Mike, 284
Milwaukee Police Department, 180, 203, 209, 242
Mincey v. Arizona, 424, 427–428
ministations, 355, 373
Minneapolis Domestic Violence Experiment, 349
Minnesota Homeland Security Department, 553
Minnesota Multiphasic Personality Inventory
    (MMPI), 166
Minnesota State Patrol, 209
Minnesota v. Carter, 415
Minnesota v. Dickerson, 423, 427
Minnesota v. Olson, 421
Minnick v. Mississippi, 441
minorities
    academic studies, 203–208
    college education, 109
    discrimination, 203

marches for equality, 21
police departments, 26
populations, 334
preferential treatment, 201
promoting with lower scores, 202–203
proving themselves on the job, 203–208
race-based police discretion, 146
recruitment, 112
stereotypes, 221
striving for equality, 197–201
supervisory ranks, 197
minorities challenges in policing, 215–221
African Americans, 220
Hispanics, 221
women, 215–220
minorities in policing today
African American representation, 210–211
Asian representation, 212–213
female representation, 208–210
gay and lesbian representation, 213–215
Hispanic representation, 211–212
Muslim representation, 213
minority communities
African Americans, 335
Arabs, 337–338
Asians, 336
gays and lesbians, 339
Hispanics, 335–336
Jews, 338
multiculturalism, 334–335
Muslims, 337–338
Native Americans, 336–337
new immigrants, 339–341
police and, 334–341
women, 338–339
Miranda, Ernesto, 407
Miranda rule, 434–435
erosion of, 435–445
Miranda v. Arizona, 21, 230, 403, 432, 434–435, 436, 446
Miranda warnings, 435
misdemeanor assaults, 135
Missouri v. McNeely, 448, 450
Missouri v. Seibert, 443–444, 446, 447
Mitchell, Brian David, 348
mitochondrial DNA (MtDNA) analysis, 502
mobile crime labs, 493–494
mobile data terminals (MDTs), 469
mobile digital terminals (MDTs), 461
mobile fingerprint-reading devices, 474
Mobile Police Department, 15
mobile substations or precincts, 283
mobile technology, 469, 472
mobile wireless report entry (MRE), 469
Model Penal Code, 153
modus operandi (MO), 306, 465–466
Mollen Commission to Investigate Police Corruption (1990s), 165, 247–248
Molly Maguires, 16
money laundering, 62
Monroe, Rodney, 480
Montejo v. Louisiana, 444
Moore, David Lee, 414
Moorehead Police Department, 553
morals, 227
Moran v. Burbine, 439, 440, 446
Morgan, J.P., 479
Morris, Earl K., 344
Mothers Against Drunk Driving (MADD), 287–288, 511
motorcycles, 18, 282
motorcycle swarms, 289

The Move to Community Policing: Making Change Happen (Morash and Ford), 384
Muehler v. Mena, 420, 421
Mueller, Robert S., 59, 545
mug shot imaging, 488
multiagency investigative task forces, 307–309
human trafficking, 308
Sandy Hook Elementary School shooting investigation and response, 310–313
Washington, D.C. sniper investigation, 308–309
multiculturalism, 334–335
multiterrain vehicles, 283
Municipal Police, 11–12
Municipal Police Administration, 19
Murphy, Patrick V., 231
Muslims, 337–338
bias-based policing, 244
representation in policing today, 213
MySpace, 472

N

Namath, Joe, 74
Nassau County Police Department, 43, 95, 494
National Academies of Emergency Dispatch, 460
National Academy of Science, 492, 505
National Action Network's Brooklyn East Chapter, 146
National Advisory Commission on Civil Disorders (Kerner Commission), 25, 197, 229
National Advisory Commission on Criminal Justice Standards and Goals, 197, 229, 264, 304
National Advisory Commission on Higher Education, 110
National Alert System (NAS), 59
National Association of Field Training Officers (NAFTO), 126
National Association of Medical Examiners, 156
National Association of Women in Law Enforcement Executives (NAWLEE), 206, 217
National Black Police Officers Association, 206
National Center for Community Policing, 367
National Center for Forensic Science, 499
National Center for Missing and Exploited Children (NCMEC), 471, 489
National Center for Rural Law Enforcement (NCRLE), 48
National Center for the Analysis of Violent Crime (NCAVC), 58–59
National Center for Women and Policing, 205, 218
National City Police Department, 386–387
National Coalition Against Domestic Violence (NCADV), 348
National Commission on Law Observance and Enforcement (Wickersham Commission), 18, 108–109, 229
National Commission on Terrorist Attacks upon the United States, 541
National Commission on the Future of DNA Evidence, 505–506
national commissions
creation, 25
overseeing police, 229
National Conference on Preventing the Conviction of Innocent Persons, 509
National Counterterrorism Center (NCTC), 527–528

National Crime Information Center (NCIC), 20, 58, 463–464
National Crime Prevention Council (NCPC), 356
National Crime Victimization Survey (NCVS), 57, 341, 348, 397, 398
National Criminal Justice Reference Service (NCJRS), 57
National Democratic Convention (1968), 22–23
National DNA Index System, 316, 506
National DNA Index System (NDIS), 503–504
National Emergency Number Association, 461
National Forensic Laboratory Information System (SFLIS), 497
National Gallery of Art, 64
National Guard, 33
National Highway Traffic Safety Administration (NHTSA), 285
National Human Trafficking Resouce Center (NHTRC), 308
National Incident-Based Reporting System (NIBRS), 58
National Incident Management System (NIMS), 313, 400, 543
National Instant Criminal Background Check (NICS), 464
National Institute of Ethics, 165
National Institute of Justice (NIJ), 30, 57
Corrections and Law Enforcement Family Support program, 177
deaths by stun guns or electronic devices, 156
Electronic Crime Scene Investigation: A Guide for First Responders, 499
Forensic Examination of Digital Evidence: A Guide for Law Enforcement, 499
Hiring and Keeping Police Officers report (2004), 111
job-related stress report, 174
monographs on policing, 364
National Crime Victimization Survey (NCVS), 397
pepper spray study, 479
policing American Indians, 48
possibly infected evidence, 185
"Solving Cold Cases with DNA" program, 316
state and local law enforcement and terrorism, 550
Study of Deaths Following Electro Muscular Disruption, 156
The 2007 Survey of Law Enforcement Forensic Evidence Processing, 492
Technical Working Group on Crime Scene Investigation (TWGCSI), 498
national landmarks, 63
National Latino Peace Officers Association, 212
National Law Enforcement Officers Memorial (NLEOM), 182, 219
National Marine Fisheries Administration, 63
National Night Out, 353
National Organization of Black Law Enforcement Executives (NOBLE), 93, 220, 554
National Park Service, 58, 62, 63
National P.O.L.I.C.E. Suicide Foundation, 180
national police force, 40
National Police Services of Canada's National DNA Data Bank, 507
National P.O.L.I.C.E Suicide Foundation, 178–179
National Railroad Passenger Corporation, 64
National Security Agency (NSA), 487
National Security Council Staff, 541
national security letters, 560

National Security Staff, 540–541
National Sex Offender website, 313
National Sheriff's Association (NSA), 343, 352, 554
National Strategy for Homeland Security, 526
National Survey of Police Practices Regarding the Criminal Investigations Process: Twenty-Five Years After Rand, 300
National White Collar Crime Center, 499
National Youth Gang Center, 46
Nationwide Suspicious Activity Reporting (SAR) Initiative (NSI), 533
Native Americans, 336–337, 383
Naval Criminal Investigative Service (NCIS), 63
Naval Investigative Service (NIS), 441
Naval Special Warfare Development Group (DEVGRU), 52
neck restraints, 155
Neighborhood Improvement Programs, 377
Neighborhood Office Program of Elgin (NOPE), 374
Neighborhood Watch, 352–353, 374, 388, 389
Newark Foot Patrol Experiment, 26
Newark foot patrol study, 269
Newark Police Department, 209
Newark riot, 25
Newby, Alan, 214
New Jersey State Police, 42, 202, 490
New Mexico Mounted Patrol, 16
New Orleans Police Department (NOPD), 33–34, 170
New Orleans Tribune, 196
New Rochelle Police Department, 382–383
Newtown Police Department, 310, 311
New Westminster Police Service, 7
New World Order, 532
New York City, 9
    crime rate (mid-1990s), 278
    decreasing crime rate, 382
    early police department, 10–11
    Municipal Police, 11–12
    sworn law enforcement employee average, 41–42
    World Trade Center, 31–32
New York City Department of Personnel, 114, 200
New York City Police Department (NYPD), 31–32, 42–43, 114, 167, 200
    African American police officers, 196
    age requirements, 108
    aggressive police tactics, 27–28
    Asian policemen, 213
    badges, 11
    ballistics lab, 495
    bars, 230
    changes in policies and operations, 229–230
    Community Patrol Police Officer Program (CPOP), 367
    CompStat program, 27–28, 84, 465
    Computer-Assisted Terminal Criminal Hunt (CATCH), 465–466
    construction, 230
    coppers, 11
    corruption, 11–12, 25, 230, 247–248
    Counter-Terrorism Bureau (CTB), 551
    counterterrorism units, 32
    elite emergency service unit (ESU), 548
    "Firearms Discharge Report," 154
    First Precinct, 14
    gambling, 230
    Gay Officers Action League (GOAL), 214–215
    height requirements, 202
    homeless people, 352
    improved security, 557
    institutionalized discrimination, 196–197
    intradepartmental payments, 230
    mental health counseling to deal with 9/11, 177
    narcotics, 230
    officers and bomb-sniffing dogs in subways, 552
    Operation Atlas, 32, 555
    parking and traffic, 230
    pedestrian stops, 245
    Police Organization Providing Peer Assistance (POPPA), 176–177
    police shootings, 151
    police stress, 176
    police suicides, 176–177
    politics, 11–12
    prostitution, 230
    race and discretion, 145–146
    Real Time Crime Center (RTCC), 466–467
    retrieving seized automobiles, 230
    Sabbath law, 230
    sale of information, 230
    shared leadership, 84
    stop-and-frisk policy, 146, 422–423
    surveillance cameras, 485
    wildcat strike, 92
New York City Police Museum, 14
New York Civil Liberties Union, 423, 469, 472, 485–486
New York Cops Talk Back (Alex), 196
New York Fire Department, 31–32
New York State Police (NYSP), 55, 113, 179
New York Supreme Court, 505
New York Times, 25, 230, 231, 239
New York v. Belton, 427, 430
New York v. Quarles, 436–437, 439, 446
Next Generation Identification (NGI), 489, 510, 546
Nicomachean ethics, 227
Nielsen, Jim, 553
night vision devices, 483–484
night watchmen, 9, 10
9/11, 526, 540
    police role in aftermath, 137
    World Trade Center, 162
9/11 and aftermath, 31–33
9/11 Commission, 541–542
9/11 Commission Report: The Final Report of the National Commission on Terrorist Attacks upon the United States, 541–542
911 emergency system, 274, 460
    cell phones, 462–463
1983 suits, 252
1960s and 1970s policing, 20–26
1980s and 1990s policing, 26–29
1900 to 1960 policing, 17–20
ninhydrin, 475
Ninth Circuit Court of Appeals, 420, 421
Nix v. Williams, 436, 437, 446
noble cause corruption, 149, 235–236
non-Hispanic whites, 335
nonlethal weapons, 155–156, 478–482
nonsworn (civilian) members, 86, 89, 115
norms, 162
North Dakota Highway Patrol, 55
North Miami Beach Police Department, 549
NOVARIS (Northern Virginia Regional Identification System), 475
Nunn, Annetta, 209

O
oath of office, 228
Occupy movement, 246
O'Connor, Sandra Day, 439
offender-based policing, 271
offenders and surveillance, 313–314
Office of Community Oriented Policing Services (COPS), 105, 116, 228, 370, 379–382, 388
    retaining officers hired with grants, 386–387
Office of Foreign Assets Control (OFAC), 62
Office of Homeland Security, 540
Office of Investigation, 63
Office of Justice Programs (OJP), 57
    Bureau of Justice Assistance (BJA), 533
Office of Juvenile Justice and Delinquency Prevention (OJJDP), 470
Office of Labor Racketeering, 63
Office of National Drug Control Policy, 57
Office of the Director of National Intelligence (ODNI), 547
Office of Victims of Crime, 342
Officer Friendly programs, 346
Officer Next Door (OND) program, 379
officers assaulted in line of duty, 183
officers killed in line of duty, 181–183, 184–185
Ohio Defense Force, 534
Ohio Department of Natural Resources, 44
Ohio State Patrol, 177
O.J. Simpson criminal trial, 29, 491
Oklahoma City Police Department, 491
Oklahoma Federal Building bombing, 526
oleoresin capsicum (OC), 156, 479
Oliver v. United States, 427, 429
Omnibus Crime Control and Safe Streets Act of 1968, 26, 198
omnipresence, 140, 262, 316–317
one-officer patrol cars, 19, 267, 268–269
one-way radio, 18
online education, 109
online training, 129
OnStar, 314
Ontario Provincial Police, 493
open field searches, 429
operational stress, 170–171
operational styles, 140–142
operational units, 98, 292–293
Operation Atlas, 555–556
Operation Avalanche, 471
Operation Fast and Furious, 60–61
Operation Gatekeeper, 387
Operation Graduate, 383
Operation Identification, 355
optimists, 141
oral interview, 118–120
order maintenance, 134, 136, 366
Oregon v. Elstad, 437–439, 443, 444, 446
Oregon v. Mathiason, 441
organizational stress, 170
organizational value systems, 228
organization of police departments
    bureaucracies, 73–74
    chain of command, 78–82
    delegation of responsibility and authority, 82
    division of labor, 72
    ethical leadership, 75
    leadership, 74–75
    management, 74
    managerial definitions, 72–74
    by personnel, 84–93

PODSCORB (planning, organizing, directing, staffing, coordinating, reporting, and budgeting), 74
  rules, regulations and discipline, 82
  span of control, 82
  traditional organizational model and structure, 75, 78
  unity of command, 82
organizations, 72–73
organized crime, 58
  child pornography, 470–473
  Cosa Nostra, 20
  intelligence analysis, 307
  Mafia, 20
  search warrants, 418
organized crime unit, 98
Orlando Police Department, 209, 349
O'Toole, Kathleen, 209
outstanding warrants, 58
"Overcoming Language Barriers: Solutions for Law Enforcement," 334

P

Palm Beach County Sheriff's Office, 181, 552
Palm Beach County Violent Crime Task Force, 307–308
Palmiotto, Michael J., 231
palm prints, 509
park rangers, 63
Pasadena Police Department, 379, 551
pat-down search, 423
Patrick, Connie, 209
patrol allocation design, 468
Patrolmen's Benevolent Associations (PBAs), 92, 176
patrol officers, 98, 262, 304
  Managing Criminal Investigations (MCI) program, 304
  random routine patrol, 263–264
  traffic stops, 284
patrol unit, 98
patrol work
  academic studies of, 265–266
  activity studies, 265–266
  allocation models, 266–268
  allocation of resources, 275–277
  alternative strategies, 277–284
  differential response to calls for service, 273–274
  directed patrol, 272–273
  evidence-based policing, 270
  goals, 265
  hot-spot policing, 273
  innovations, 270–272
  911 system, 274
  one-officer patrol cars, 267, 268–269
  personnel deployment, 272–275
  predictive policing, 270–271
  random routine patrol, 263–264
  rapid response to citizens' 911 calls, 261, 264–270
  return to foot patrol, 269–270
  smart policing, 271–272
  split-force patrol, 272–273
  311 system, 274
  two-officer patrol cars, 267–269
pawnbrokers, 6
Payton, Theodore, 408
Payton v. New York, 408, 415, 421
Peel, Robert, 4, 6–8, 12, 75, 109, 137, 261–262, 367
Peel's Nine Principles, 7
peer support officers (PSOs), 176

Peirson, Julia, 209
Pendleton Act (1883), 17, 84
Pennington, Richard, 210
Pennsylvania State Police, 55
Pennsylvania v. Mimms, 411–412, 418
Pennsylvania v. Muniz, 441
people with disabilities, 105
pepper ball system, 481
pepper spray, 23, 156, 481
persistent offenders, 312
personal digital assistants (PDAs), 469
personal electronics seizure, 422
personal identification, stealing, 500–501
personal stress, 170
personnel
  allocation of resources, 275–276
  civilianization, 89, 275
  civil service system, 84–85
  community service officers (CSOs), 89
  disparity between sworn and nonsworn personnel, 90
  merit employment, 85
  nonsworn (civilian) members, 86, 89
  organizing by, 84–93
  police reserves/auxiliaries, 90–91
  rank structure, 86–89
  scheduling officers, 275–276
  sworn members, 85–86
personnel deployment, 272–275
personnel unit, 98
pervasive and organized corruption, 235
pervasive and unorganized corruption, 235
Philadelphia Police Department, 78, 292
phishing, 500
Phoenix Neighborhood Patrol (PNP), 381
Phoenix Police Department, 50, 147, 381
photo array, 447
PhotoDNA, 473
photos and fingerprints, 120
physical agility test, 117–118
physical evidence examination, 490–493
physically challenged, 341–342
pimps, 139
Pinellas County Sheriff's Office, 494
Pinkerton Agency, 16
place-based policing, 271
plain view evidence, 426–428
planning and analysis unit, 98–99
plastic prints, 474
platoons, 88
plea bargains, 399
Pleasant Prairie Police Department (PPPD), 477
Plessy v. Ferguson, 243
PODSCORB (planning, organizing, directing, staffing, coordinating, reporting, and budgeting), 74
Polar Plunge, 331
police
  arrests, 407–414
  broken windows model, 366
  as civil authority, 3
  civil liability, 251–255
  criminal liability, 251–255
  custodial interrogations, 432–446
  deadly force, 150
  discretion, 142–149
  early, 3–4
  employment, 41
  evidence in violation of U.S. Constitution, 403–407
  exclusionary rule impact, 406–407
  federal liability, 252–253

history of, 3–34
  legal liability, 252
  lost-and-found department, 140
  marches for equality, 21
  versus military, 3
  minority communities and, 334–341
  negative press, 21
  omnipresence, 140
  public opinion and, 333
  radical groups, 20
  relationship between criminal or victim, 145
  research into policing, 25–26
  response to civil disobedience, 22
  responsibility to public, 7
  review of, 229–231
  social media, 22
  special populations and, 341–343, 345–352
  state liability, 252
  unconstitutional actions, 20
  urban riots, 24–25
  U.S. Constitution and, 399, 402–407
Police: Streetcorner Philosophers (Muir), 142
police academy, 86, 122–123
Police Administration (Wilson), 19, 195, 262
Police and Citizens Together Initiative (PACT), 375
Police Athletic Leagues (PALs), 347, 374
police blotter, 94–95
police brutality, 229, 246
Police Cadet programs, 54
police candidates
  advice to, 121
  knowledge, skills, and abilities (KSAs), 114
  screening procedures, 114
  selection process, 114–121
police cars, 18
police chiefs, 208
Police Chiefs Guide to Immigration Issues, 51
police commissioner, 88–89
police-committed time, 143–144
police-community partnerships, 367
police-community relationships (PCR) movement, 329–330, 332, 366
police corruption, 25, 30, 229, 231
  See also corruption
  adequate supervision, 249–250
  bending rules to attain right result, 235–236
  bribes, 234, 235
  citizen complaints about, 249
  citizen oversight, 250–251
  community relationships, 236
  decertification, 248
  discipline, 248
  drug-related, 238
  early intervention systems, 249
  effects of, 236–238
  exposure to wrongdoing, 233
  federal law enforcement agents, 233
  grass-eaters, 234
  gratuities, 234, 235
  high-liability policies, 249
  hiring and screening process, 248
  integrity tests, 247
  internal affairs divisions, 247–248
  internal corruption, 235
  investigations, 247–248
  looting, 232
  loyalty, 236
  Mama Rosa's test, 236
  meat-eaters, 234
  morale of officers, 236
  neighborhoods with social disorganization, 233
  noble cause corruption, 235–236

police corruption (*continued*)
   organizational culture, 250
   pervasive and organized, 235
   pervasive and unorganized, 235
   police organization, 233
   police subculture, 233
   policy and procedure manual, 249
   preventative administrative actions, 248–250
   proactive attacks on, 247
   questionable shootings, 232
   relative attacks on, 247
   rotten apples, 233, 235
   ruining police reputation, 237–238
   rumors and lack of official information, 236
   social structures, 233
   termination, 248
   theft or burglary, 234–235
   training, 249
   uniform cams, 250
   work or personal lives more difficult, 237
police culture, 149
police culture or police subculture, 162–165
   women, 216
police cynicism, 166
police dangers, 181–185
police deception, 238–239
police departments, 72
   African Americans, 196–197
   alternative organizational models and
      structures, 82–84
   antiterrorism units, 32–33
   beats, 93
   candidates, 200
   civilianization, 105, 113
   collective bargaining, 91–92
   community relations units, 366
   consent decrees, 209
   cooperation with businesses, 358–359
   corruption and mismanagement, 14, 84–85
   crime statistics, 239
   customer-based approach, 384
   dealing with stress, 176–178
   decentralizing operations, 83
   detectives, 14, 72
   discretionary authority, 83
   discrimination, 194–197
   disparity between sworn and nonsworn
      personnel, 90
   domestic violence in police families, 242
   early American, 10–11
   early technological advances, 15
   effects of lawsuits, 254
   function or purpose organization, 97–99
   geographic area organization, 93–95
   health and fitness programs, 177
   homosexuals, 339
   internal affairs divisions, 247–248
   job analysis, 113–114
   lateral transfers, 91
   minorities, 22, 26, 197
   modern-style, 3
   organizing, 72–82
   patrol functions, 72
   people with disabilities, 105
   personnel, 84–93
   police pursuit policies, 291
   police unions, 91–93
   policies or guidelines, 147–148
   politics, 12–13, 84–85
   qualities wanted in officers, 385
   quasi-military organizations, 75, 78

   shared leadership, 83–84
   social science, 30
   special investigative units, 348
   time organization, 95–97
   traditional employment inequities, 26
   tuition reimbursement, 108
   victims services units, 348
   volunteers, 353–354
   websites, 106
   women, 26, 194–196
police department units, 98–99
Police Ethics: The Corruption of Noble Cause
      (Caldero and Crank), 235
Police Executive Research Forum (PERF), 30,
      54, 93, 123, 300, 377, 380, 388
   *Managing a Multijurisdictional Case:
      Identifying Lessons Learned from the Sniper
      Investigation* report, 309
Police Explorer programs, 54, 346, 347
police families and police stress, 176
Police Foundation, 30, 153, 154, 263, 554
   Police Women on Patrol: Final Report, 203
   *Role of Local Police: Striking a Balance
      Between Immigration Enforcement and Civil
      Liberties* report, 51
   team policing study, 26
Police Foundation Standard, 153
Police in a Time of Change (Broderick), 141
police misconduct, 30
   domestic violence in police families, 241–243
   drug-related misconduct, 238
   organizational culture, 250
   police deception, 238–239
   sex-related misconduct, 239–241
   sleeping on duty, 238
police officers, 42, 86–87, 87
   abusive or derogatory behavior, 237
   advanced training, 19
   blending, 317
   brutality, 14
   college education funds, 26
   decoys, 317
   effects of lawsuits, 254–255
   effects of stress on, 174–175
   eighteenth and nineteenth century, 14–15
   emotional intelligence (EI), 116
   ethics, 228
   exercising discretion, 143
   felonious attacks on, 269
   fraternal organizations, 93
   good characteristics, 115–116
   informal code of conduct, 228
   job analysis, 113–114
   knowledge, skills, and abilities (KSAs), 114
   maturity, 115–116
   moral decline, 235
   online education, 109
   perceiving and coping with working
      environments, 164
   physical fitness, 117–118
   Praetorian Guard, 3
   professional organizations, 93
   training, 27
   use of force, 246
police operational styles, 140–142
Police Organization Providing Peer Assistance
      (POPPA), 176–177
police paramilitary units (PPUs), 28, 98,
      292–293, 333
police patrols, 266
   alternative vehicle deployment, 282–284

   community preservation, 366
   holistic approach, 367
   operations, 261–262
   order maintenance, 366
   public safety, 366
"Police Patrol Work Load Studies: A Review
      and Critique," 143
police personality, 165–168
police powers, 85
Police Practices Survey, 268
police public relations, 330
police pursuits, 289–291
police recruits
   maturity, 115–116
   work values, 105
Police Reserve Officers, 54
police reserves/auxiliaries, 90–91
police role, 134–137, 149
police selection standards, 107–111
Police Services Study (PSS), 136
police shootings, 149–156
police storefront stations, 355
police stress, 162
   alcohol problems, 174
   community expectations and demands, 176
   confrontation with tragedies of urban life,
      170–171
   critical incidents, 174–175
   defining, 169
   divorce, 169
   drug problems, 174
   on duty 24 hours a day, 171
   effects on police officers, 174–175
   employee assistance programs (EAPs),
      177–178
   external, 169–170
   factors causing, 171–174
   family relationships, 176
   fatigue, 171
   gender, 172
   health problems, 174
   intrusion into family life, 176
   job-related personal change, 176
   marital problems, 174
   nature of, 169–171
   operational stress, 170–171
   organizational stress, 170
   personal stress, 170
   physical enforcement activities, 170
   physical fitness, 172
   police departments, 176–178
   police families, 176
   police suicides, 178–180
   post-traumatic stress disorder (PTSD), 175
   psycho-social stress, 170
   quasi-military character of police service,
      170
   race, 172
   rotating work environment, 176
   rotation shift work, 176
   stress management programs and services,
      176
   suicide by cop, 172–174
   suicides, 169
   unhealthy diets, 174
   wives dissatisfied with job, 176
   working hours, 174
   workplace conditions, 170
police suicides, 176–177, 178–181
Police Systems in the United States (Smith), 19
police trading cards, 346

police traffic operations
  dangerous work zones, 285
  distracted drivers challenge, 286–287
  drugged drivers, 285
  drunk drivers, 287–288
  DWI (driving while intoxicated) checkpoint, 287
  fatigued or distracted drivers, 285
  fighting aggressive driving, 288–289
  impaired drivers, 287–288
  incident clearance, 285
  motorcycle swarms, 289
  new laws and tactics, 285
  new types of vehicles, 285
  police pursuits, 289–291
  safer traffic stops, 285
  seat belt law, 285–286
  sleep-deprived officers, 285
  speed enforcement, 285
  traffic officers and homeland security, 285
  traffic stops, 284
  video camera traffic enforcement, 286
police training process
  field training, 123, 126–127
  firearms training, 128
  in-service training, 128–129
  management training, 129
  police academy, 122–123
  probationary period, 127–128
  recruit training, 122
  specialized training, 129
Police Training Program (PTO), 123, 126–127
police undercover investigations, 321
police unions, 91–93
police wagon, 18
police-woman-as social-worker, 194
Policewoman's Endowment Society, 93
policewomen, 194–196, 203–205
  See also women
Police Women on Patrol: Final Report, 203
police work, 261–263
policies, formal set of, 147–148
policing
  American Indians, 48–49
  community policing, 26
  finding information on jobs, 106–107
  illegal immigration, 386–387
  modern management and administrative techniques, 19
  police research into, 25–26
  primary goals and objectives, 140
  private citizens, 3
  problem-solving policing, 26
  professionalizing, 19
  protests at Madison, Wisconsin, 400–401
  secondary goals and objectives, 140
  traditional, 26
polis, 3
politia, 3
political corruption, 58
politics
  American policing, 11–14
  New York Police Department (NYPD), 11–12
  police departments, 12–13, 84–85
  police unions, 91
Pollock, Joycelyn, 228
polygraph examination, 118
polymerase chain reaction-short tandem repeat (PCR-STR), 502
Port Authority of New York and New Jersey police and rescue operations, 31

Port Authority of New York and New Jersy Police Department (PAPD), 44
Port of Seattle Police Department, 209
posse comitatus, 16
Posse Comitatus Act of 1879, 16
Post-9/11 Policing Project, 554
post-9/11 response, 540–542
post-traumatic stress disorder (PTSD), 175
Powell, Colin, 74
Powell, Lewis F., 429
power to arrest, 85
Poynter Institute, 356
Praefectus Urbi (Urban Cohort), 3
Praetorian Guard, 3
precincts, 93–95
predictive policing, 270–271
Pregnancy Discrimination Act (PDA), 217
preliminary investigation, 300
Premise Alert program, 374
prescription drug fraud, 322
President's Commission on Law Enforcement and Administration of Justice, 25, 89, 109, 122–123, 197, 229
  The Challenge of Crime in a Free Society, 330
  police relations with minority groups, 330
  Task Force Report, 268
  Task Force Report: Science and Technology, 264
Presumed Guilty: The Tragedy of the Rodney King Affair (Koon), 29
pretextual traffic stops, 412
preventive patrol, 263–264
prima facie, 200
Prince George County Police Department, 176, 468
Pringle, Joseph, 409
Priority Prosecutors of High-Rate Dangerous Offenders report, 312
private crime labs, 494
private police, 16–17
private security companies, 8, 389
proactive tactics
  cybercrime investigations, 320
  decoy operations, 316–317
  stakeout operations, 317–318
  sting operations, 318–319
probable cause, 85, 408–409
  arrests, 422
  search warrants, 418, 419–421, 428
probationary period, 127–128
problem analysis, 371–372
problem-oriented policing
  crime analysis, 305
  solving problems, 372
problem-solving policing, 26, 365, 370–372
  crime reduction, 27
professionalizing policing, 19
professional police department, 6
progressive era of government, 75, 78
prohibition, 18
Project BioShield, 531
Project Global Shield, 54
Project on Policing Neighborhoods (POPN), 206
prompt arrangement rule, 434
property crimes
  arrests, 398
  DNA profiling, 509
property unit, 99
prosecutors and detectives relationships, 302
prostitution, 138–139

Protect Act, 346
"Protecting Your Community from Terrorism: Strategies for Local Law Enforcement," 388
protective sweep, 424
Prouse, William, 411
psychological appraisal, 120–121
Public Administration and Public Affairs (Henry), 72
Public Enemies, 20
public information unit, 99
Public Law 107-56, 32
Public Law 83-280 (PL 280), 48
public opinion and police, 333
public perception of police, 150
public safety, 366
Public Safety Answering Point (PSAP), 275
public safety curriculum, 112
Public Safety Testing, 117
punishment, 398–399
Purcellville Police Department, 376

Q

"Quality of Life Task Force," 383
quasi-military organizations, 75
questors, 3
quotas, 201

R

R911, 463
race
  discretion, 145–146
  discrimination in police shootings, 151
  police stress, 172
racial and ethnic minorities, 56
racial profiling, 243–244, 335
racism, report on (1968), 25
radio frequency (RF) tracking systems, 483
Rampart scandal, 232
Ramsey, Charles, 338
Rand Corporation, 245, 299, 555
  criminal investigative process study, 26
random routine patrol, 261, 263–264
rank structure, 86–89
rapid response to citizens' 911 calls, 261, 264–270, 273
Real Time Crime Center (RTCC), 466–467
reasonable force, 410–411
reasonable suspicion, 409
reciprocators, 142
records management systems (RMSs), 469
records unit, 99
recreational marijuana laws, 322
recreation and tutoring programs, 374
recruitment process, 111–113
recruit training, 122
Redlands Police Department, 485
red light cameras, 286
Redmond Police Department, 209
referral, 281
Regional Community Policing Institutes (RCPIs), 381
Regional Crime Analysis Geographic Information Systems (RCAGIS) spatial analysis, 465
Rehabilitation Act of 1973, 121
release of information form (waiver), 120
Reno, Janet, 250, 380, 509

Reno model, 380
Reno Police Department, 123, 380
repeat offender programs (ROPs), 309, 312
Reppetto, Thomas, 8
"A Requiem for the Exclusionary Rule," 435
Reserve Police Officers, 354
reserver officers, 90–91
Resident Officer Program of Elgin (ROPE), 374–375
resident officer programs, 376, 378–379
restricted fragment length polymorphism (RFLP), 502
Rethinking Police Culture: Officers' Occupational Attitudes (Paoline), 164
retroactive investigation of past crimes, 261, 299–300
reverse 911, 463
reverse discrimination, 201, 202–203
reverse-sting operation, 323
reverse 911 systems, 274–275
review of police, 229–231
Rhode Island State Police, 55
Rhode Island v. Innis, 436, 438
Ricci v. DeStefano, 203
Richmond Police Department, 15
ride-along programs, 358, 374
Ridgway, Gary, 138
right against self-incrimination, 432
right to counsel during interrogation, 432
Riley, Warren, 33–34
Riley v. California, 488
riots, 29, 31
Riseling, Susan, 400–401
risk awareness, 280
road rage, 288–289
robotics, 511–512
robots, 504, 511–512
Rochester Institute of Technology, 179
Rochin v. California, 404, 405–406, 448
Rocky Mountain Detective Agency, 17
Rokeach study (1971), 166
Role of Local Police: Striking a Balance Between Immigration Enforcement and Civil Liberties report, 51
Romans, 3–4, 22
Roosevelt, Theodore, 17, 57
rotten apples, 235
rotten apples and rotten pockets theory, 235
routine traffic stops, 411
Roy, Ruth, 206–207
Royal Canadian Mounted Police (RCMP), 206, 553
Royal Irish Constabulary (RIC), 8
rubber projectiles, pellets, 481
Rugala, Eugene, 58
Run from the Cops, 331, 332
rural law enforcement, 46–48

S

Sacramento Police Department, 116, 273
Saferstein, Richard, 474, 490, 502
Safety and Accountability Audit of the Response to Native Women Who Report Sexual Assault, 383
Salt Lake City Police Department, 388
Samson v. California, 427, 431
Sandberg, Annette, 209
Sanders, Darrell, 506

Sandy Hook Elementary School shooting investigation and response, 310–313
San Francisco Police Department (SFPD), 202, 209, 213, 469, 492
San Franciso Sheriff's Department, 213
San Jose Police Department, 123
San Marcos Police Department, 372–373
saturation patrol, 277, 278–279
Scalia, Antoinin, 420–421
scanning, analysis, response, assessment (SARA), 371–372
Schmerber v. California, 448, 450
Schmitt, Glenn, 156
Schneckloth v. Bustamonte, 425, 427
Schomrin Society, 93
school resource officers, 346
schools public safety curriculum, 112
schouts, 9
Scientific Working Group for Forensic Document Examination (SWGDOC), 497
Scientific Working Group on Digital Evidence (SWGDE), 499
scooters, 283, 373
Scott, Yolanda M., 170–171
Scott v. Harris, 291, 410, 418
Scott v. Hart, 349
SDS, 24
Seabury Hearings, 25
search and seizure, 414–417
searches
  abandoned property, 428–429
  arm's reach doctrine, 421–422
  automobiles, 429–430
  border search, 430
  consent searches, 425–426
  crime scenes, 428
  exigent circumstances, 424–425
  field interrogations, 422–424
  good faith exception, 430–431
  incident to lawful arrest, 421–422
  inventory, 429
  open fields, 429
  pat-down search, 423
  plain view evidence, 426–428
  by private persons, 432
  suspicionless search of parolee, 431
search warrants, 417–432
  anticipatory, 421
  automobile exception, 429–430
  consent once removed, 426
  conspiracy-type investigations, 418
  crime scene exception, 427
  detaining occupants, 420
  exceptions, 421–432
  gang investigations, 283
  informants, 418–419
  knock-and-announce rule, 420–421
  lengthy investigations, 418
  obtaining, 417–418
  organized crime, 418
  probable cause, 418, 419–421, 428
  totality of circumstances test, 419
  two-pronged test, 419
seat belt law, 285–286
Seattle Internet Crimes Against Children (ICAC) Task Force, 470
Seattle Police Department, 209, 470
Section 1983 of Title 42 of the U.S. Code, 252
Secure Communities, 546–548
Securities and Exchange Commission (SEC), 63
security cameras, 485–487

security *versus* civil liberties, 557–561
selection process
  adverse impact, 115
  assessment centers, 117
  background investigation, 120
  emotional intelligence (EI), 116
  emphasizing person, 115
  good police officers characteristics, 115–116
  mature recruits, 115–116
  medical examination, 121
  nonsworn (civilian) members, 115
  oral interview, 118–120
  physical agility test, 117–118
  polygraph examination, 118
  psychological appraisal, 120–121
  steps defensible in court, 115
  validity to job performance of police officer, 115
  voice stress analyzer, 118
  written examination, 116–117
self-defense training, 155
self-incrimination, 432
self-initiated situations, 145
senior citizens, 342–343
Senior Management Institute for Police, 129
sensitivity training, 332
separate but equal doctrine, 335
Seremeth v. Frederick County et al., 444
sergeants, 87–88
serology, 496
Serpico, Frank, 25, 230, 231
Sewell, James D., 170
sex offenders, 312–314
sex-related misconduct, 239–241
sex trafficking, 138–139
sexual assault, 383
Shareaza, 472
shared leadership, 83–84
sharing information, 307–309
Sheindlin, Gerald, 505
Shepard, Matthew, 339
sheriffs, 4, 45
  early American policing, 9
  frontier experience in American policing, 15–16
  role of, 12
  women, 208
sheriffs departments
  deputies, 86
sheriff's departments, 42, 45–46
  county and rural areas, 12
  deputies, 13, 42
  duties, 45
  full-time sworn employees, 45
  origins, 12
  responsibilities, 12–13
  Sheriff's Emergency Response Teams (SERT), 12
Sherman, Lawrence W., 270
Sherman Report, 110
shifts, 95
shire-reeve, 4
showups, 447, 448
silver nitrate, 475
silver platter doctrine, 404
Silverthorne Lumber Company v. United States, 404
Simoncelli, Tania, 509, 511
Sinaloa drug cartel, 60–61
Skolnick, Jerome H., 41, 165–166
slave patrols, 9–10, 15

Slave Patrols: Law and Violence in Virginia and the Carolinas (Hadden), 9–10
sleep-deprived officers, 285
sleeping on duty, 238
slippery slope model, 236
Sliwa, Curtis, 353
small-town law enforcement, 46–48
   police stress, 170–171
Smart911, 275
smartphones, 286, 313–314, 320
smart policing, 271–272
Smart Policing Initiatives (SPI), 271–272
Smith and Wesson, 479
smoking, 107–108
Sniper Task Force, 30
Snohomish County sheriff, 344
social agents, 141
socialization process, 216
social media, 313–314
   cyberbullying, 320
   fighting crime, 356–357
   informing residents about crime, 357
   police activity, 22
social science, 30
social service functions, 136
social services coordinator, 374
Soderstrom, Erik, 280
Solano, Greg, 510
solvability factors, 304
South Carolina Law Enforcement Assistance Program (SCLEAP), 177
South Dakota Highway Patrol, 55
southern experience in American policing, 15
Southern Police Institute, 129
Southern Poverty Law Center, 341
special investigative units, 348
specialized detectives, 301–302
specialized investigative units, 3
Specialized Policing Responses (SPRs), 279, 281
specialized training, 129
special jurisdiction police agencies, 44
Special Olympics Law Enforcement Torch Run (LETR), 331–332
special populations
   aging population, 342–343
   crime victims, 347–348
   domestic violence victims, 348–349
   homeless people, 350–351
   physically challenged, 341–342
   young children, 343, 345–347
special response teams (SRTs), 292
speed enforcement, 285
Spinelli v. United States, 419, 421
split-force patrol, 272–273
Springfield Police Department, 209
spyware, 500
squads, 88
St. Charles County Sheriff, 173
St. Louis Police Department, 109
St. Martin Parish sheriff's deputies, 245
Stafford County Police Department, 552
staff (support) functions, 97–98
stakeout operations, 317–318
Stalans, Loretta, 204
stand-your-ground laws and castle doctrine, 414
Stanek, Rich, 181
Stanley v. Wainright, 445
Stansbury v. California, 441
state courts, 395, 396

state law enforcement, 55
   homeland security, 549–556
   troopers, 86
state liability, 252
state point of contact officers (SPOC), 554
state police agencies, 16
state police departments, 55
State Police Officer Standards and Training (POST), 122
states
   appeals court level, 396
   criminalizing homosexual acts, 214
   criminal justice planning agencies, 26
   primary law enforcement agencies, 55
   reserve officers, 90
   sodomy laws, 214
   supreme court level, 396
   trial court level, 396
state troopers, 46
station house, 93–94
stations, 93–95
Statute of Winchester (1285), 4, 5
steady (fixed) tours, 97
Steffens, Lincoln, 14
Steinheider, Brigitte, 78, 83
Step Up to Law Enforcement, 216
Stewart, Potter, 415
sticky foam gun, 482
sting ball grenade, 481
sting operations, 318–319
Stingrays/IMSI Catchers, 487
Stockton Police Department, 184–185
stop-and-frisk policies, 144, 146, 422–424
Stormo, Vicky, 217
Stoval v. Denno, 448, 450
strategic policing, 365
Strathy, Scott D., 280–281
straw buyers, 60–61
Street, John F., 149
street riots, 10
Strengthening Forensic Science in the United States: A Path Forward, 492
stress, 169
strikes and police unions, 92
Stuccio, Donna, 218
Student Nonviolent Coordinating Committee (SNCC), 24
student protests, 23–24
Students Against Drunk Driving (SADD), 287
Students for a Democratic Society (SDS), 23
Study of Deaths Following Electro Muscular Disruption, 156
stun belt, 481
stun devices, 479
stun guns, 155, 156
subject-specific de-escalation, 280
Suffolk County Police Department, 43, 217
Suhr, Greg, 213
suicide by cop, 172–174
suing police officers, 253
Sullivan, Mary, 316
Sumner Police Department, 209
super glue fuming, 475
supervisors, 74, 323
supply unit, 99
surreptitious recording of suspects' conversations, 445
surveillance aircraft, 484–485
surveillance cameras, 314–315, 485–487
surveillance technology
   cell phone monitoring, 487–488

   electronic video surveillance, 485–487
   global positioning systems (GPSs), 484
   IP-based surveillance, 485
   night vision devices, 483–484
   surveillance aircraft, 484–485
   surveillance vans, 482–483
   vehicle tracking systems, 483
surveillance vans, 482–483
suspicion, 165
suspicionless search of parolee, 431
suveillance technology, 482–488
Suwanee Police Department, 375
SWAT teams, 28, 292–293
swatting, 293
Swift, Thomas A., 479
Swim, David H., 184–185
sworn law enforcement employee
   average, 41–42
   police powers, 85
sworn members, 85–86
   rank structure, 86–89

T

tactical operations, 277–279, 284
tactics training, 310
"Take a Bite Out of Crime," 355–356
Taking Liberties: A Decade of Hard Cases, Bad Laws, and Bum Raps, 511
Target, 359
Target and Blue program, 359
target-hardening programs, 355
Tasers, 155–156, 478–481
Taser X-26, 480
tax law violators, 57
team-building workshops (TBW), 84
team policing, 377–378
technology, 476
   Agema Thermovision 210, 416
   automated crime analysis, 464–465
   automated databases, 463–464
   automated fingerprint identification system (AFIS), 475–478
   Automated Fingerprint Identification System (AFIS) technology, 463–464
   automated palm print technology, 478
   automatic vehicle location (AVL) systems, 461
   cell phone technology, 462–463
   child pornography, 470–473
   civil liberties, 511
   cloud storage, 473
   computer-aided case management, 465–467
   computer-aided investigation, 465–467
   computer-assisted instruction (CAI), 467
   computers, 26, 459–478
   cost-saving for police agencies, 54–55
   geographic information systems (GISs), 461
   global positioning systems (GPSs), 313–314, 461
   information management, 306–307
   Internet Protocol (IP) telephony, 463
   license plate recognition (LPR) technology, 469, 472
   LoJack, 313
   mobile technology, 469, 472
   motorcycles, 18
   1900 to 1960 policing, 18
   one-way radio, 18
   OnStar, 314
   police cars, 18

technology (*continued*)
  police wagon, 18
  reverse 911, 463
  Smart911, 275
  smartphones, 286, 313–314
  Smart Policing Initiatives (SPI), 271–272
  social media, 22, 313–314
  surveillance cameras, 314–315
  texting, 286
  text message alerts on crime, 353
  two-way radio, 18
  Voiceover IP (VoIP), 463
Ten Most Wanted Criminals Program, 20
Tennessee v. Garner, 147, 152, 153, 410
Tennessee Valley Authority (TVA), 63–64
ten-prints, 473
Terrill, William, 145
terrorism, 526, 527–528
  biological weapons, 530–531
  combatting financing, 62
  crime scene processing and analysis, 538–539
  Department of Homeland Security, 32
  domestic, 532–537
  Federal Building in Oklahoma City bombing
    (1995), 26
  following up on leads and tips, 539
  informants, 539
  international, 528–532
  methods of investigating, 537–540
  metropolitan police departments, 44
  New York City's World Trade Center
    bombing (1993), 26
  9/11 and aftermath, 31–33
  officer safety, 552, 554
  police as front line against, 137
  post-9/11 response to, 540–542
  preventing, 388–389
  proactive methods, 537
  protecting United States against, 62
  reactive methods, 537–540
  response to incident, 537–538
  surveillance, 539–540
terrorist watchlist, 543, 544
Terry stop, 424
Terry v. Ohio, 422, 423, 424, 427
testimonial, 448–449
Texas Department of Public Safety, 55, 498
Texas Education Agency Law Enforcement
    Course, 411
Texas Negro Peace Officers Association, 196
Texas Parks and Wildlife Department, 44
Texas Rangers, 16
Texas v. Cobb, 442, 446
texting, 286
theft
  decreasing number of, 6
  police corruption, 234–235
thermal imaging (TI), 416, 484
thief-takers, 5
third degree, 432
  end of, 432–434
311 system, 274
three-tour system, 95
Time magazine, 30, 491
time organization, 95–97
Tip-a-Cop, 331
*Tired Cops: The Importance of Managing Police
    Fatigue* (Vila), 171
tobacco, federal laws relating to, 60
Top Cops: Profiles of Women in Command
    (Gold), 218

torts, 252
totality of circumstances test, 419
tours, 95
  conditions, 96–97
  length, 95–96
tours of precincts and police facilities, 358
town marshal, 9, 15–16
trade sanctions, 62
traditional law enforcement, 367, 370–371
traditional methods of police work, 261
traditional organizational model and structure,
    75, 78
traditional policing, 26
traffic fatalities, 285
traffic offenses, 135
traffic officers and homeland security, 285
traffic police operations, 284–291
traffic stops, 284, 411–414
traffic unit, 98, 285
trainees, 86
training
  basic strategies, 155
  community policing, 370
  conflict management, 155
  cultural diversity instruction, 155
  detectives, 305
  firearms training, 154–155
  human relations, 332–333
  in-service training, 128–129
  investigators, 305
  management training, 129
  mediation, 155
  nonlethal weapons training, 155
  online, 129
  police corruption, 249
  police officers, 27
  police paramilitary units (PPUs), 292
  rural law enforcement, 48
  self-defense training, 155
  sensitivity training, 332
  small-town law enforcement, 48
  specialized training, 129
  SWAT teams, 292
  use-of-force training, 155
Training Day, 231
training unit, 98
Transportation Security Administration, 62
Triad, 343
Tribal Census (2008), 49
Trojan horses, 500
Truman, Harry S., 62
tuition reimbursement, 108
Turley, Lisa, 462
twentieth and twenty-first century American
    policing, 17–34
Twenty-First Amendment, 18
Twitter, 356
two-officer patrol cars, 267, 268–269
two-pronged test, 419
2000s policing, 29–34
*The 2007 Survey of Law Enforcement Forensic
    Evidence Processing*, 492

U

ultraviolet light, 475
Ultron II Contact Stun Device, 481
unarmed fleeing felon and deadly force, 153
undercover officer (U/C), 323
undercover operations, 320–323

UnderNets, 471
uniform cams, 250
Uniform Crime Reports (UCR), 20, 58, 239,
    299, 397
  Crime in the United States 2010, 151
United States
  crime, 395
  history of civil disobedience, 22
  international terrorism, 528–529
  policing, 3
  racial and ethnic minorities, 334
  racism report (1968), 25
United States Department of Labor,
    Occupational Safety and Health
    Administration, 175
United States v. Ash, 448, 450
United States v. Banks, 420, 421
United States v. Dionisio, 449
United States v. Grubbs, 421
United States v. Jones, 483
United States v. Karo, 462
United States v. Knotts, 462
United States v. Leon, 427, 430–431
United States v. Mara, 449
United States v. Martinez-Fuerte, 427, 430
United States v. Matlock, 425–426, 427
United States v. Murphy, 500
United States v. Patane, 443, 446
United States v. Place, 416, 418
United States v. Pollard, 426, 427
United States v. Robinson, 422, 427
United States v. Villamonte-Marquez, 427, 430
United States v. Wade, 447, 449, 450
United States v. Wurie, 488
United Way, 383
Uniting and Strengthening America By
    Providing Tools Required to Intercept and
    Obstruct Terrorism, 541
unity of command, 82
universities and community policing, 376
University of California at Berkeley School of
    Criminology, 19
University of California at Davis, 23
University of Mississippi, 21
University of Vermont Department of Public
    Safety, 376
University of Wisconsin-Madison Police
    Department, 400–401
unmanned aerial vehicles (UAV), 484–485
unreasonable search and seizure, 414–415
Unsolved Mysteries, 490
urban experience in American policing
  early police departments, 10–11
  early police officer's job, 14–15
  politics, 11–14
Urbanovsky, Ron, 498
urban riots, 24–25
U.S. Army, 48
U.S. Attorney, 311, 471
U.S. Attorney General, 56
U.S. Attorney's Office fo the Western District of
    Washington, 308
U.S. Bankruptcy Court, 395
U.S. Border Patrol, 387
U.S. Bureau of Alcohol, Tobacco, Firearms, and
    Explosives (ATF), 60
U.S. Capitol Police, 64
U.S. Census, 213, 334
U.S. Census Bureau, 196, 212, 335
U.S. Citizenship and Immigration Services
    (USCIS), 542

U.S. Coast Guard, 33, 62, 542–544
U.S. Commission on Civil Rights, 176
U.S. Constitution, 228
  Bill of Rights, 399, 402–403
  evidence seized in violation of, 403–407
  Fourteenth Amendment, 198, 399
  police and, 399, 402–407
U.S. Court of Appeals for the Second Circuit, 505
U.S. Court of Claims, 395
U.S. Court of International Trade, 395
U.S. Criminal Code, 56
U.S. Customs and Border Protection (CBP), 53, 62, 387, 471, 542, 544
U.S. Customs Service, 62, 543
  Marine Enforcement Officer (MEO) program, 52
U.S. Department of Agriculture, 63
U.S. Department of Commerce, 63
U.S. Department of Defense (DoD), 63
  Defense Advanced Research Projects Agency (DARPA), 511
  terrorism, 527
U.S. Department of Health and Human Services (DHHS), 63
U.S. Department of Homeland Security, 308
U.S. Department of Homeland Security (DHS), 32, 53, 62, 232, 526, 541, 543–545
  career opportunities, 542
  combatting terrorism overseas, 543–544
  controlling immigration, 544
  illegal immigration, 51
  Office of Intelligence and Analysis, 388
  protection against further terrorist attacks, 543
  thermal imaging, 484
U.S. Department of Housing and Urban Development (HUD), 379
U.S. Department of Justice (DOJ), 20, 30, 56–61, 156, 201, 202, 211, 313, 354, 368, 470
  Bureau of Alcohol, Tobacco, Firearms, and Explosives (ATF), 60
  Bureau of Justice Administration (BJA), 271
  Bureau of Justice Statistics (BJS), 40–41
  Civil Rights Division, 56–57
  civil rights issues and police departments, 252–253
  Community Relations Service, 337
  Criminal Division, 57
  DNA evidence, 501
  Drug Enforcement Administration (DEA), 60
  drunk driving guide, 288
  excessive brutality, 246
  Federal Bureau of Investigation (FBI), 57–60
  integrity report, 250
  Law Enforcement Assistance Administration (LEAA), 25–26
  Law Enforcement Education Program (LEEP), 109
  less-than-lethal weapons, 480
  National Institute of Justice (NIJ), 57
  nonlethal force, 155
  Office of Community Oriented Policing Services (COPS), 116, 334, 388
  Office of Justice Programs (OJP) bureaus, 57
  Office of Juvenile Justice and Delinquency Prevention (OJJDP), 470
  Office of National Drug Control Policy, 57
  Operation Fast and Furious, 60–61
  policing American Indians, 49
  public safety in tribal communities, 337

  suing state and local governments for violations of Title VII, 199
  Survey of Local Police Departments, 244
  Tax Division, 57
  traffic stops, 243–244
  U.S. Marshals Service, 60
U.S. Department of Labor, 63, 216
U.S. Department of State, 64
U.S. Department of the Interior, 48, 58, 62–63
U.S. Department of the Treasury, 61–62
U.S. Department of Transportation, 286
U.S. Department of War, 48
U.S. District Courts, 395
U.S. Drug Enforcement Administration (DEA), 60, 321, 419
  International Training Center, Sensitive Investigations Unit, 47
  National Clandestine Laboratory Registry, 313
  policing American Indians, 48
U.S. Embassy bombings, 528, 532
U.S. Environmental Protection Agency (EPA), 64
U.S. Equal Opportunity Commission (EEOC), 115
U.S. Food and Drug Administration (FDA), 63
U.S. Forest Service, 63
U.S. General Accounting Office (GAO), 531
U.S. Holocaust Memorial Museum (USHMM), 338
U.S. House of Representatives, 238
U.S. Immigration and Customs Enforcement (ICE), 542, 544, 546–548
U.S. Immigration and Naturalization Services (INS), 340, 543
U.S. Marshal, 16
U.S. Marshals Service, 60, 307, 311
U.S. Mint, 64
U.S. Patriot Act-Uniting and Strengthening America by Providing Appropriate Tools Required to Intercept and Obstruct Terrorism, 32, 558–559
U.S. Pentagon, 32
U.S. Postal Inspection Service, 421
U.S. Postal Inspectors, 471
U.S. Postal Service, 63, 324
U.S. public security industry, 40–42
U.S. Secret Service, 62, 209, 542, 543
  Forensic Services Division, 474
U.S. Senate
  Crime Committee, 20
U.S. Sentencing Commission, 398
U.S. Sentencing Guidelines (USSG), 398
U.S. State Department, 64
U.S. Supreme Court, 64, 395–396, 410–411, 413, 420–421
  affirmative action, 201
  consensual sex, 214
  decisions in 1960s and 1970s, 20–21
  Dred Scott decision, 9
  exclusionary rule, 20–21
  judicial review, 403
  reasonableness in using force to terminate police pursuit, 291
  rights of individual and rights of society, 403
  role in regulating police, 399, 403
  use of deadly force, 152
  Warren Court, 20
U.S. Trafficking Victims Protection Act, 308
U.S. Transportation Security Administration (TSA), 541, 542, 543, 544

U.S. Treasury Department, 66
USA Freedom Corps, 354
USA Patriot Act, 541
USA Patriot Reauthorization Act, 561
use-of-force training, 155
U.S.S. Cole bombing, 532
US-VISIT (United States Visitor and Immigrant Status Indicator Technology), 544

V

vagrancy arrests, 135
Vanguard Society v. Hughes, 200
Van Maanen, John, 166
Varieties of Police Behavior: The Management of Law and Order in Eight Communities (Wilson), 142, 265
Varieties of Police Behavior (Wilson), 145
vehicles
  allocation of resources, 276–277
  breath-test interlock devices, 287–288
vehicle tracking systems, 483
Vera Institute of Justice, 334, 337
Vermont Department of Labor, 216
Vermont's Step Up to Law Enforcement, 216
Vermont Works for Women (VWW), 216
Veterans Health Administration (VHA), 64
Vice President's Task Force on Drugs, 65
vice unit, 98
victims, 145
victims services units, 348
video camera traffic enforcement, 286
videotaping, 511
Vietnam War demonstrations, 22–23
vigilance, 4
vigilante, 4
vigilantism, 9
Vigiles, 3–4
Villiage Public Safety Officer (VPSO) program, 46
Violanti, John M., 47, 163, 179, 180
violence after sporting events, 31
Violent Crime Control and Law Enforcement Act (1994), 379–380
Violent Crime Impact Teams (VCIT), 312
violent crimes, 135, 398
Violent Criminal Apprehension Program (ViCAP), 464
VIPS (Volunteers in Police Services), 54
VirTra Systems 300 LE, 467
visible prints, 474
vision requirements, 107
Viverette, Mary Ann, 209
Voiceover IP (VoIP), 463
voice recognition, 510
voice stress analyzer, 118
Vollmer, August, 19
Volstead Act (National Prohibition), 18
Volunteers in Police Service (VIPS), 354
Vulcan Society v. Civil Service Commission, 200

W

Wade, Henry, 508
Walker, Sam, 9, 13, 14
Walker Report, 23
walking a beat, 261
Wallace, Mike, 181
Walsh, John, 355

Ward, Benjamin, 210
Warden v. Hayden, 424
war on drugs, 60, 293
warrantless arrests, 407–408
warrants, 408
 DNA, 508
Warren, Vincent, 423
Warren Court, 20
Warren v. Hayden, 427
Washington Advisory Committee on
 Trafficking (WashACT), 308
Washington Anti-Trafficking Response
 Network (WARN), 308
Washington Association of Sheriffs and Police
 Chiefs, 126, 331
Washington D.C. Metropolitan Police
 Department, 209, 339
Washington D.C. Metropolitan Police Force,
 338
Washington D.C. Police Department, 239
Washington State Criminal Justice Training
 Academy, 124
Washington State Criminal Justice Training
 Commission, 126
Washington State Department of Corrections,
 466
Washington State Patrol, 209, 210, 288, 555
Washington State Troopers, 33
watch and ward, 4–5
watches, 95
watchmen, 5, 141–142
Watson, Elizabeth, 208–209
Watts riot, 24–25
Wearing, Melvin H., 210
Weathermen, 23
Weeks, Fremont, 404
Weeks v. United States, 403–404, 406
Weitzel, Thomas Q., 82
Wells, Alice Stebbins, 194, 195, 216
Wells, Henry, 17
Wells Fargo and Company, 17
Westley, William, 164–165
Wexler, Chuck, 30
"What's Wrong at the FBI: The Fiasco at the
 Crime Lab," 491
White, Byron R., 429, 430–431
white-collar crime, 58
white male backlash, 201–203
white supremacy, 532

whorls, 474
Whren v. United States, 412, 418
"Why Law Enforcement Organizations Fail:
 Mapping the Organizational Fault Lines in
 Policing," 73
Wickersham, George W., 18
Wickersham Commission, 18–19, 246
Wickersham Commission Report (1931), 18–19
Wickersham Commission Report (1931), 109
Wickett, Jeffrey, 52–55
Wieigman, Matthew, 293
wilderness programs for at-risk youth, 374
wildlife enforcement agents, 63
Williams, Willie, 210
Wilmington Police Department, 266
Wilson, James Q., 20
Wilson, O. W., 19, 195, 262, 265, 268
Wilson v. Arkansas, 424, 427
Wilton Police Department, 375
Winston v. Lee, 448–449, 450
Winters, Frank, 347
Wisconsin Chiefs of Police Association, 400
Withrow v. Williams, 441
Wolf v. Colorado, 404–405, 406
women, 338–339
 See also policewomen
 academic studies, 203–208
 advancement in law enforcement careers, 218
 arrested for crimes, 338
 challenges in policing, 215–220
 discrimination, 194–196, 203
 domestic violence cases, 338
 excluding from performing basic police
  duties, 195
 experience associated with command
  positions, 208–209
 height requirement, 200
 incapable of performing same duties as men,
  195
 jealousy of police officers' wives, 195
 killed in line of duty, 219
 law enforcement, 338
 physical ability testing, 200, 216
 police chiefs, 208
 police culture, 216
 police departments, 26
 police-woman-as social-worker, 194
 pregnancy, 216–217
 rape, 338

 recruitment and hiring issues, 216
 representation in policing today,
  208–210
 sexual assaults, 338
 sheriffs, 208
 social forces against, 195
 socialization process, 216
 striving for equality, 197–201
 victims of crimes, 338
 workplace harassment, 216
 workplace romances, 216, 217–218
*Women on Patrol: A Pilot Study of Police
 Performance in New York City*, 203
Women Police: Portraits of Success (Lunneborg),
 218
Women's Leadership Institute, 215
women's rights movement, 195
Wood, Fernando, 11
Worcester Police Department, 177
word-of-mouth advertising, 106–107
Working the Street (Brown), 163
working together, 307–309
World Customs Organization, 54
World's Fair EXPO 2000, 332
World Trade Center, 31–32
World Trade Center Attack (1993), 532
Wray, Noble, 210
Wuestewald, Todd, 78, 83
Wyoming Law Enforcement Academy, 46

Y

Yahoo!, 471
young children, 343, 345–347
Youth Crime Watch of America, 345
Youth International Party (Yippies), 22–23
youth programs, 374
youth services bureau, 374
YouTube, 315, 356
Yuma Police Department, 282

Z

Zapata, Mia, 316
Zarc (Cap-Stun), 479
zero-tolerance policing, 27, 384
Zimring, Franklin E., 42